A Companion to Wittgenstein

Blackwell Companions to Philosophy

This outstanding student reference series offers a comprehensive and authoritative survey of philosophy as a whole. Written by today's leading philosophers, each volume provides lucid and engaging coverage of the key figures, terms, topics, and problems of the field. Taken together, the volumes provide the ideal basis for course use, representing an unparalleled work of reference for students and specialists alike.

Already published in the series:

1. The Blackwell Companion to Philosophy, Second Edition
   Edited by Nicholas Bunnin and Eric Tsui-James
2. A Companion to Ethics
   Edited by Peter Singer
3. A Companion to Aesthetics, Second Edition
   Edited by Stephen Davies, Kathleen Marie Higgins, Robert Hopkins, Robert Stecker, and David E. Cooper
4. A Companion to Epistemology, Second Edition
   Edited by Jonathan Dancy, Ernest Sosa and Matthias Steup
5. A Companion to Contemporary Political Philosophy (two-volume set), Second Edition
   Edited by Robert E. Goodin and Philip Pettit
6. A Companion to Philosophy of Mind
   Edited by Samuel Guttenplan
7. A Companion to Metaphysics, Second Edition
   Edited by Jaegwon Kim, Ernest Sosa and Gary S. Rosenkrantz
8. A Companion to Philosophy of Law and Legal Theory, Second Edition
   Edited by Dennis Patterson
9. A Companion to Philosophy of Religion, Second Edition
   Edited by Charles Taliaferro, Paul Draper, and Philip L. Quinn
10. A Companion to the Philosophy of Language
    Edited by Bob Hale and Crispin Wright
11. A Companion to World Philosophies
    Edited by Eliot Deutsch and Ron Bontekoe
12. A Companion to Continental Philosophy
    Edited by Simon Critchley and William Schroeder
13. A Companion to Feminist Philosophy
    Edited by Alison M. Jaggar and Iris Marion Young
14. A Companion to Cognitive Science
    Edited by William Bechtel and George Graham
15. A Companion to Bioethics, Second Edition
    Edited by Helga Kuhse and Peter Singer
16. A Companion to the Philosophers
    Edited by Robert L. Arrington
17. A Companion to Business Ethics
    Edited by Robert E. Frederick
18. A Companion to the Philosophy of Science
    Edited by W. H. Newton-Smith
19. A Companion to Environmental Philosophy
    Edited by Dale Jamieson
20. A Companion to Analytic Philosophy
    Edited by A. P. Martinich and David Sosa
21. A Companion to Genethics
    Edited by Justine Burley and John Harris
22. A Companion to Philosophical Logic
    Edited by Dale Jacquette
23. A Companion to Early Modern Philosophy
    Edited by Steven Nadler
24. A Companion to Philosophy in the Middle Ages
    Edited by Jorge J. E. Gracia and Timothy B. Noone
25. A Companion to African-American Philosophy
    Edited by Tommy L. Lott and John P. Pittman
26. A Companion to Applied Ethics
    Edited by R. G. Frey and Christopher Heath Wellman
27. A Companion to the Philosophy of Education
    Edited by Randall Curren
28. A Companion to African Philosophy
    Edited by Kwasi Wiredu
29. A Companion to Heidegger
    Edited by Hubert L. Dreyfus and Mark A. Wrathall
30. A Companion to Rationalism
    Edited by Alan Nelson
31. A Companion to Pragmatism
    Edited by John R. Shook and Joseph Margolis
32. A Companion to Ancient Philosophy
    Edited by Mary Louise Gill and Pierre Pellegrin
33. A Companion to Nietzsche
    Edited by Keith Ansell Pearson
34. A Companion to Socrates
    Edited by Sara Ahbel-Rappe and Rachana Kamtekar
35. A Companion to Phenomenology and Existentialism
    Edited by Hubert L. Dreyfus and Mark A. Wrathall
36. A Companion to Kant
    Edited by Graham Bird
37. A Companion to Plato
    Edited by Hugh H. Benson
38. A Companion to Descartes
    Edited by Janet Broughton and John Carriero
39. A Companion to the Philosophy of Biology
    Edited by Sahotra Sarkar and Anya Plutynski
40. A Companion to Hume
    Edited by Elizabeth S. Radcliffe
41. A Companion to the Philosophy of History and Historiography
    Edited by Aviezer Tucker
42. A Companion to Aristotle
    Edited by Georgios Anagnostopoulos
43. A Companion to the Philosophy of Technology
    Edited by Jan-Kyrre Berg Olsen, Stig Andur Pedersen, and Vincent F. Hendricks
44. A Companion to Latin American Philosophy
    Edited by Susana Nuccetelli, Ofelia Schutte, and Otávio Bueno
45. A Companion to the Philosophy of Literature
    Edited by Garry L. Hagberg and Walter Jost
46. A Companion to the Philosophy of Action
    Edited by Timothy O'Connor and Constantine Sandis
47. A Companion to Relativism
    Edited by Steven D. Hales
48. A Companion to Hegel
    Edited by Stephen Houlgate and Michael Baur
49. A Companion to Schopenhauer
    Edited by Bart Vandenabeele
50. A Companion to Buddhist Philosophy
    Edited by Steven M. Emmanuel
51. A Companion to Foucault
    Edited by Christopher Falzon, Timothy O'Leary, and Jana Sawicki
52. A Companion to the Philosophy of Time
    Edited by Heather Dyke and Adrian Bardon
53. A Companion to Donald Davidson
    Edited by Ernest Lepore and Kirk Ludwig
54. A Companion to Rawls
    Edited by Jon Mandle and David Reidy
55. A Companion to W.V.O Quine
    Edited by Gilbert Harman and Ernest Lepore
56. A Companion to Derrida
    Edited by Zeynep Direk and Leonard Lawlor
57. A Companion to David Lewis
    Edited by Barry Loewer and Jonathan Schaffer
58. A Companion to Kierkegaard
    Edited by Jon Stewart
59. A Companion to Locke
    Edited by Matthew Stuart
60. The Blackwell Companion to Hermeneutics
    Edited by Niall Keane and Chris Lawn
61. A Companion to Ayn Rand
    Edited by Allan Gotthelf and Gregory Salmieri
62. The Blackwell Companion to Naturalism
    Edited by Kelly James Clark
63. A Companion to Wittgenstein
    Edited by Hans-Johann Glock and John Hyman

A Companion to Wittgenstein

Edited by
Hans-Johann Glock and John Hyman

WILEY Blackwell

This edition first published 2017
© 2017 by John Wiley & Sons, Ltd

Registered Office
John Wiley & Sons, Ltd, The Atrium, Southern Gate, Chichester, West Sussex, PO19 8SQ, UK

Editorial Offices
350 Main Street, Malden, MA 02148-5020, USA
9600 Garsington Road, Oxford, OX4 2DQ, UK
The Atrium, Southern Gate, Chichester, West Sussex, PO19 8SQ, UK

For details of our global editorial offices, for customer services, and for information about how to apply for permission to reuse the copyright material in this book please see our website at www.wiley.com/wiley-blackwell.

The right of Hans-Johann Glock and John Hyman to be identified as the authors of the editorial material in this work has been asserted in accordance with the UK Copyright, Designs and Patents Act 1988.

All rights reserved. No part of this publication may be reproduced, stored in a retrieval system, or transmitted, in any form or by any means, electronic, mechanical, photocopying, recording or otherwise, except as permitted by the UK Copyright, Designs and Patents Act 1988, without the prior permission of the publisher.

Wiley also publishes its books in a variety of electronic formats. Some content that appears in print may not be available in electronic books.

Designations used by companies to distinguish their products are often claimed as trademarks. All brand names and product names used in this book are trade names, service marks, trademarks or registered trademarks of their respective owners. The publisher is not associated with any product or vendor mentioned in this book.

Limit of Liability/Disclaimer of Warranty: While the publisher and authors have used their best efforts in preparing this book, they make no representations or warranties with respect to the accuracy or completeness of the contents of this book and specifically disclaim any implied warranties of merchantability or fitness for a particular purpose. It is sold on the understanding that the publisher is not engaged in rendering professional services and neither the publisher nor the author shall be liable for damages arising herefrom. If professional advice or other expert assistance is required, the services of a competent professional should be sought.

Library of Congress Cataloging-in-Publication Data

Names: Glock, Hans-Johann, 1960– editor. | Hyman, John, editor.
Title: A companion to Wittgenstein / edited by Hans-Johann Glock and John Hyman.
Description: Hoboken : Wiley, 2017. | Includes bibliographical references and index.
Identifiers: LCCN 2016034790 | ISBN 9781118641163 (cloth) | ISBN 9781118641477 (epub) | ISBN 9781118641460 (PDF) | ISBN 9781119307945 (paper)
Subjects: LCSH: Wittgenstein, Ludwig, 1889–1951.
Classification: LCC B3376.W564 C633 2017 | DDC 192–dc23
LC record available at https://lccn.loc.gov/2016034790

A catalogue record for this book is available from the British Library.

Cover image: Ludwig Wittgenstein, 1930. © The Wittgenstein Archive

Set in 10/12pt Photina by SPi Global, Pondicherry, India

Contents

List of Contributors — ix
Acknowledgments — xiii
Wittgenstein's Published Works in Order of Composition — xiv

    Introduction — 1
    John Hyman and Hans-Johann Glock

    Ludwig Wittgenstein: A Sketch of His Life — 5
    Ray Monk

Part I   Introductory — 21

1. Wittgenstein's Philosophical Development — 23
   Wolfgang Kienzler

2. Wittgenstein's Texts and Style — 41
   David G. Stern

Part II   Influences — 57

3. Wittgenstein and Schopenhauer — 59
   Dale Jacquette

4. Wittgenstein and Frege — 74
   Michael Beaney

5. Wittgenstein and Russell — 92
   Graham Stevens

6. Wittgenstein, Hertz, and Boltzmann — 110
   John M. Preston

Part III   Early Philosophy — 125

7. Logical Atomism — 127
   Leo K.C. Cheung

8. The Picture Theory — 141
   Colin Johnston

CONTENTS

9.	Wittgenstein on Solipsism *Ernst Michael Lange*	159
10.	Resolute Readings of the *Tractatus* *James Conant and Silver Bronzo*	175
11.	Ineffability and Nonsense in the *Tractatus* *Leo K.C. Cheung*	195
12.	Metaphysics: From Ineffability to Normativity *P.M.S. Hacker*	209

Part IV   Philosophy and Grammar   229

13.	Philosophy and Philosophical Method *Hans-Johann Glock*	231
14.	Grammar and Grammatical Statements *Severin Schroeder*	252
15.	The Autonomy of Grammar *Michael N. Forster*	269
16.	Surveyability *Joachim Schulte*	278

Part V   Logic and Mathematics   291

17.	Logic and the *Tractatus* *Roger M. White*	293
18.	Wittgenstein's Early Philosophy of Mathematics *Pasquale Frascolla*	305
19.	Wittgenstein's Later Philosophy of Mathematics *A.W. Moore*	319
20.	Wittgenstein and Antirealism *Mathieu Marion*	332
21.	Necessity and Apriority *Eric Loomis*	346

Part VI   Language   359

22.	Names and Ostensive Definitions *Kai Büttner*	361
23.	Meaning and Understanding *Jason Bridges*	375
24.	Rules and Rule-Following *Gary Ebbs*	390

25. Vagueness and Family Resemblance 407
   Hanoch Ben-Yami

26. Languages, Language-Games, and Forms of Life 420
   Daniel Whiting

27. Wittgenstein on Truth 433
   David Dolby

Part VII   Mind and Action **443**

28. Privacy and Private Language 445
   Edward Kanterian

29. The Inner and the Outer 465
   William Child

30. Wittgenstein on "I" and the Self 478
   Maximilian de Gaynesford

31. Wittgenstein on Action and the Will 491
   Maria Alvarez

32. Wittgenstein on Intentionality 502
   Stefan Brandt

33. Wittgenstein on Seeing Aspects 517
   Arif Ahmed

34. Wittgenstein on Color 533
   Jonathan Westphal

Part VIII   Epistemology **545**

35. Wittgenstein on Knowledge and Certainty 547
   Danièle Moyal-Sharrock

36. Wittgenstein on Skepticism 563
   Duncan Pritchard

37. Wittgenstein on Causation and Induction 576
   Constantine Sandis and Chon Tejedor

38. Wittgenstein and Philosophy of Science 587
   Vasso Kindi

Part IX   Ethics, Aesthetics, and Religion **603**

39. Wittgenstein and Ethics 605
   Robert L. Arrington

40. Wittgenstein and Aesthetics 612
   Severin Schroeder

41.	Wittgenstein and Anthropology *Brian R. Clack*	627
42.	Wittgenstein and Philosophy of Religion *John Cottingham*	639
43.	Wittgenstein and Psychoanalysis *Edward Harcourt*	651

Part X Philosophical Schools and Traditions — 667

44.	Wittgenstein and the Aristotelian Tradition *Roger Pouivet*	669
45.	Wittgenstein and Kantianism *Robert Hanna*	682
46.	Wittgenstein and the Vienna Circle *Thomas Uebel*	699
47.	Wittgenstein and Ordinary Language Philosophy *Anita Avramides*	718
48.	Wittgenstein and Pragmatism *David Bakhurst and Cheryl Misak*	731
49.	Wittgenstein and Naturalism *Christopher Hookway*	746
50.	Wittgenstein and Continental Philosophy *Stephen Mulhall*	757

Index	771

List of Contributors

Arif Ahmed
University of Cambridge

Maria Alvarez
King's College London

Robert L. Arrington[‡]
Georgia State University

Anita Avramides
St Hilda's College, Oxford

David Bakhurst
Queen's University, Kingston

Michael Beaney
King's College London and Humboldt University, Berlin

Hanoch Ben-Yami
Central European University, Budapest

Stefan Brandt
Friedrich-Alexander University, Erlangen-Nürnberg

Jason Bridges
University of Chicago

Silver Bronzo
Higher School of Economics, Moscow

Kai Büttner
Independent Scholar

Leo K.C. Cheung
Chinese University of Hong Kong

William Child
University College, Oxford

[‡]Deceased

LIST OF CONTRIBUTORS

Brian R. Clack
University of San Diego

James Conant
University of Chicago

John Cottingham
University of Reading

Maximilian de Gaynesford
University of Reading

David Dolby
Independent Scholar

Gary Ebbs
Indiana University, Bloomington

Michael N. Forster
University of Bonn and University of Chicago

Pasquale Frascolla
University of Basilicata

Hans-Johann Glock
University of Zurich

P.M.S. Hacker
University of Kent at Canterbury and St John's College, Oxford

Robert Hanna
Independent Scholar

Edward Harcourt
Keble College, Oxford

Christopher Hookway
University of Sheffield

John Hyman
The Queen's College, Oxford

Dale Jacquette[‡]
University of Bern

Colin Johnston
University of Stirling

[‡]Deceased

Edward Kanterian
University of Kent

Wolfgang Kienzler
University of Jena

Vasso Kindi
University of Athens

Ernst Michael Lange
Free University, Berlin

Eric Loomis
University of South Alabama

Mathieu Marion
University of Quebec at Montreal

Cheryl Misak
University of Toronto

Ray Monk
University of Southampton

A.W. Moore
St Hugh's College, Oxford

Danièle Moyal-Sharrock
University of Hertfordshire

Stephen Mulhall
New College, Oxford

Roger Pouivet
University of Lorraine

John M. Preston
University of Reading

Duncan Pritchard
University of Edinburgh

Constantine Sandis
University of Hertfordshire

Severin Schroeder
University of Reading

LIST OF CONTRIBUTORS

Joachim Schulte
University of Zurich

David G. Stern
University of Iowa

Graham Stevens
University of Manchester

Chon Tejedor
University of Hertfordshire

Thomas Uebel
University of Manchester

Jonathan Westphal
Independent Scholar

Roger M. White
University of Leeds

Daniel Whiting
University of Southampton

Acknowledgments

We have incurred several debts of gratitude during the long process of assembling and editing this *Companion to Wittgenstein*. First and foremost, we are grateful to the contributors, not only for their excellent work, but also for their patience while the volume was in preparation. We are also deeply indebted to Sebastian Grève. His work on the typescript was superb, not only regarding style and format, but especially regarding the content of each chapter. We are also very grateful to Javier Kalhat. As a copy-editor for Wiley-Blackwell he did an excellent job on a challenging typescript. We note with sadness that Robert Arrington, Frank Cioffi and Dale Jacquette passed away while the *Companion* was in preparation. Frank Cioffi accepted the commission to write a chapter, but was not able to complete it before he died. Robert Arrington and Dale Jacquette did complete their chapters, on "Wittgenstein and Ethics" and "Wittgenstein and Schopenhauer" respectively, and we are especially glad and privileged to have been able to include their work. Finally, we wish to thank the Faculty of Philosophy in the University of Oxford, the University of Zurich, and the Alexander von Humboldt Foundation for their generous support.

Wittgenstein's Published Works in Order of Composition

The date of composition is specified in square brackets where appropriate.

RCL   Review of Coffey, *The Science of Logic*. 1913. *Cambridge Review*, 34, 351. Reprinted in PO.

NL   *Notes on Logic*. [1913]. Edited in NB (pp. 93–107).

NM   *Notes Dictated to Moore in Norway*. [1914]. Edited in NB (pp. 108–119).

NB   *Notebooks 1914–16*. (1961/1979). Ed. G.E.M. Anscombe and G.H. von Wright. Trans. G.E.M. Anscombe. Second edition. Oxford: Blackwell. [German–English parallel text.] References are to dates of entries. *Tagebücher 1914–16*. (1960). Edited in *Schriften* (Vol. 1). Frankfurt: Suhrkamp. References are to dates of entries.

GT   *Geheime Tagebücher, 1914–1916*. [Secret Notebooks, 1914–1916.] (1991). Ed. W. Baum. Wien: Turia+Kant. [Contains transcriptions of coded remarks which have been omitted from NB, and which are of mainly biographical relevance.]

PT   *Proto-Tractatus*. [1917]. (1971). Ed. B.F. McGuinness, T. Nyberg, G.H. von Wright. Trans. D.F. Pears and B.F. McGuinness. London: Routledge and Kegan Paul. [German–English parallel text.]

TLP   *Tractatus Logico-Philosophicus*. (1922). Trans. C.K. Ogden. London: Kegan Paul. [German–English parallel text.] References are to numbered sections. *Tractatus Logico-Philosophicus*. ([1922] 1961). Trans. D.F. Pears and B.F. McGuinness. London: Routledge and Kegan Paul. (Original work published 1922.) References are to numbered sections. *Logisch-Philosophische Abhandlung, Kritische Edition*. [*Tractatus Logico-Philosophicus*, Critical Edition]. ([1922] 1989). Ed. B. McGuinness and J. Schulte. Frankfurt: Suhrkamp.

WV   *Wörterbuch für Volksschulen*. [Dictionary for Primary Schools.] (1926/1977). Facsimile reproduction with an introduction by A. Hübner. Wien: Hölder-Pichler-Tempsky.

RLF   *Some Remarks on Logical Form*. (1929). *Proceedings of the Aristotelian Society* (Supplementary Volume), 9, 162–171.

CV   *Culture and Value: A Selection from the Posthumous Remains*. (1977/1998). Ed. G.H. von Wright in collaboration with H. Nyman. Revised edition of the text by A. Pichler. Trans. P. Winch. Oxford: Blackwell. [German–English parallel text.] *Vermischte Bemerkungen*. (1984). Edited in *Werkausgabe* (Vol. 8). Frankfurt: Suhrkamp.

PR   *Philosophical Remarks*. [1929–1930]. (1975). Ed. R. Rhees. Trans. R. Hargreaves and R. White. Oxford: Blackwell. *Philosophische Bemerkungen*. (1964). Edited in *Schriften* (Vol. 2). Frankfurt: Suhrkamp.

DB   *Denkbewegungen: Tagebücher 1930–1932, 1936–1937*. [Movements of Thought: Notebooks 1930–1932, 1936–1937.] (1999). Ed. I. Somavilla. Frankfurt: Fischer. Translated in PPO.

GB   *Remarks on Frazer's Golden Bough*. [1931, 1936]. (1967). Ed. R. Rhees. *Synthese*, 17, 233–253. Complete version edited in PO.

PG   *Philosophical Grammar*. [1932–1934]. (1974). Ed. R. Rhees. Trans. A.J.P. Kenny. Oxford: Blackwell. *Philosophische Grammatik*. (1969). Edited in *Schriften* (Vol. 4). Frankfurt: Suhrkamp.

BT   *The Big Typescript: TS 213*. [1933]. (2005). Ed. and trans. C.G. Luckhardt and M.A.E. Aue. Chichester: Wiley-Blackwell. [German–English parallel text.] References are to the original pagination of TS 213, which is given in the margins.

BB   *The Blue and Brown Books*. [1933–1935]. (1958/1969). Ed. R. Rhees. Second edition. Oxford: Blackwell.

EPB   *Eine philosophische Betrachtung*. [1936]. [A philosophical Reflection.] (1970). Ed. R. Rhees. In *Schriften* (Vol. 5). Frankfurt: Suhrkamp.

CE   *Cause and Effect: Intuitive Awareness*. [1937]. (1976). Ed. R. Rhees. Trans. P. Winch. *Philosophia*, 6, 392–430. Reprinted in PO.

RFM   *Remarks on the Foundations of Mathematics*. [1937–1944]. (1956/1978). Ed. G.H. von Wright, R. Rhees and G.E.M. Anscombe. Trans. G.E.M. Anscombe. Third, revised, and reset edition. Oxford: Blackwell. References are to numbered parts followed by numbered sections. *Bemerkungen über die Grundlagen der Mathematik*. (1973). Edited in *Schriften* (Vol. 6). Frankfurt: Suhrkamp. References are to numbered parts followed by numbered sections.

PI   *Philosophical Investigations*. [1938–1945]. (1953/1958). Ed. G.E.M. Anscombe and R. Rhees. Trans. G.E.M. Anscombe. Second edition. Oxford: Blackwell. References are to numbered sections of Part I (except for footnotes), and to pages of Part II. *Philosophical Investigations*. (1953/2009). Ed. G.E.M. Anscombe and R. Rhees. Fourth, revised edition by P.M.S. Hacker and J. Schulte. Trans. G.E.M. Anscombe, P.M.S. Hacker and J. Schulte. Oxford: Wiley-Blackwell. [German–English parallel text.] References are to numbered sections; references to what was formerly known as "Part II" are now to

	PPF. *Philosophische Untersuchungen, Kritisch-genetische Edition*. [*Philosophical Investigations*, Critical Genetic Edition.] (2001). Ed. J. Schulte. Frankfurt: Suhrkamp.
PPF	*Philosophy of Psychology – A Fragment*. [1946–1949]. In PI (1953/2009, pp. 183–243). Ed. P.M.S. Hacker and J. Schulte. Trans. G.E.M. Anscombe, P.M.S. Hacker and J. Schulte. [German–English parallel text.] References are to numbered sections. [Previously known as PI "Part II."]
RPP I	*Remarks on the Philosophy of Psychology* (Vol. 1). [1945–1947]. (1980). Ed. G.E.M. Anscombe and G.H. von Wright. Trans. G.E.M. Anscombe. Oxford: Blackwell. [German–English parallel text.] References are to numbered sections. *Bemerkungen über die Philosophie der Psychologie*. (1982). Edited in *Schriften* (Vol. 7). Frankfurt: Suhrkamp. References are to numbered sections.
RPP II	*Remarks on the Philosophy of Psychology* (Vol. 2). [1948]. (1980). Ed. G.H. von Wright and H. Nyman. Trans. C.G. Luckhardt and M.A.E. Aue. Oxford: Blackwell. [German–English parallel text.] References are to numbered sections. *Bemerkungen über die Philosophie der Psychologie*. (1982). Edited in *Schriften* (Vol. 7). Frankfurt: Suhrkamp. References are to numbered sections.
Z	*Zettel*. [1945–1948]. (1967). Ed. G.E.M. Anscombe and G.H. von Wright. Trans. G.E.M. Anscombe. Oxford: Blackwell. [German–English parallel text.] References are to numbered sections. *Zettel*. (1984). Edited in *Werkausgabe* (Vol. 8). Frankfurt: Suhrkamp. References are to numbered sections.
LW I	*Last Writings on the Philosophy of Psychology* (Vol 1). [1948–1949]. (1982). Ed. G.H. von Wright and H. Nyman. Trans. C.G. Luckhardt and M.A.E. Aue. Oxford: Blackwell. [German–English parallel text.] References are to numbered sections. *Letzte Schriften über die Philosophie der Psychologie*. (1984). Edited in *Werkausgabe* (Vol. 7). Frankfurt: Suhrkamp. References are to numbered sections.
LW II	*Last Writings on the Philosophy of Psychology* (Vol. 2). [1949–1951]. (1992). Ed. G.H. von Wright and H. Nyman. Trans. C.G. Luckhardt and M.A.E. Aue. Oxford: Blackwell. [German–English parallel text.]
OC	*On Certainty*. [1951]. (1969/1974). Ed. G.E.M. Anscombe and G.H. von Wright. Trans. D. Paul and G.E.M. Anscombe. Oxford: Blackwell. [German–English parallel text.] References are to numbered sections. *Über Gewißheit*. (1984). Edited in *Werkausgabe* (Vol. 8). Frankfurt: Suhrkamp. References are to numbered sections.
ROC	*Remarks on Colour*. [1951]. (1977/1980). Ed. G.E.M. Anscombe. Trans. L.L. McAlister and M. Schättle. Oxford: Blackwell. [German–English parallel text.] References are to numbered parts followed by numbered sections. *Bemerkungen über die Farben*. (1984). Edited in *Werkausgabe* (Vol. 8). Frankfurt: Suhrkamp. References are to numbered parts followed by numbered sections.
PO	*Philosophical Occasions: 1912–1951*. (1993). Ed. J. Klagge and A. Nordmann. Indianapolis: Hackett. [German–English parallel texts where appropriate.] Unless otherwise specified, writings in this anthology are cited after the original paginations, which are given in brackets.
PPO	*Public and Private Occasions*. (2003). Ed. J. Klagge and A. Nordmann. Lanham: Rowman and Littlefield. [German–English parallel texts where appropriate.] Unless otherwise specified, writings in this anthology are cited after the original paginations, which are given in brackets.

Lectures and Conversations

WVC	*Wittgenstein and the Vienna Circle: Conversations recorded by Friedrich Waismann*. [1929–1932]. (1979). Ed. and trans. B.F. McGuinness. Oxford: Blackwell. *Ludwig Wittgenstein und der Wiener Kreis*. (1967). Edited in *Schriften* (Vol. 3). Frankfurt: Suhrkamp.
LE	A Lecture on Ethics. [1929]. (1965). *Philosophical Review*, 74, 3–12.
M	Wittgenstein's Lectures in 1930–33. (1954–55). *Mind*, 63, 1–15 and 289–316; 64, 1–27 and 264. Reprinted in PO.
MWL	*Wittgenstein: Lectures, Cambridge 1930–1933, From the Notes of G.E. Moore*. (2016). Ed. D. Stern, B. Rogers, and G. Citron. Cambridge: Cambridge University Press. References are to the pagination of the notebooks reproduced in this edition.
LWL	*Wittgenstein's Lectures, Cambridge 1930–32, From the Notes of J. King and D. Lee*. (1980). Ed. D. Lee. Oxford: Blackwell.
AWL	*Wittgenstein's Lectures, Cambridge 1932–35, From the Notes of A. Ambrose and M. MacDonald*. (1979). Ed. A. Ambrose. Oxford: Blackwell.
LSD	The Language of Sense Data and Private Experience, Notes taken by R. Rhees of Wittgenstein's lectures, 1936. (1984). *Philosophical Investigations*, 7, 1–45.
LPE	Wittgenstein's Notes for Lectures on "Private Experience" and "Sense Data." [1936]. (1968). Ed. R. Rhees. *Philosophical Review*, 77, 275–320.
LC	*Lectures and Conversations on Aesthetics, Psychology and Religious Belief*. [1938–1946]. (1966). Ed. C. Barrett. Oxford: Blackwell.

LFM   Wittgenstein's Lectures on the Foundations of Mathematics, Cambridge 1939, From the Notes of R.G. Bosanquet, N. Malcolm, R. Rhees and Y. Smythies. Ed. C. Diamond. Sussex: Harvester.
LFW   Lectures on Freedom of the Will, From the Notes of Y. Smithies. [1939]. Edited in PO.
NPL   Notes for the Philosophical Lecture. [1941]. Ed. D. Stern. In PO.
LPP   Wittgenstein's Lectures on Philosophical Psychology 1946–47, Notes by P.T. Geach, K.J. Shah, and A.C. Jackson. (1988). Ed. P.T. Geach. Sussex: Harvester.

Anthologies and Collections

Schriften. [Writings.] (1960–1982). Frankfurt: Suhrkamp. Vol. 1 (1960): TLP, NB, PI; Vol. 2 (1964): PR; Vol. 3 (1967): WVC; Vol. 4 (1969): PG; Vol. 5 (1970): "The Blue Book," EPB, Z; Vol. 6 (1973): RFM; Vol. 7 (1978): LFM; Vol. 8 (1982): RPP I, RPP II. [German text.]

Werkausgabe. [Works.] (1984). Frankfurt: Suhrkamp. Vol. 1: NB, TLP, PI; Vol. 2: PR; Vol. 3: WVC; Vol. 4: PG; Vol. 5: "The Blue Book," EPB; Vol. 6: RFM; Vol.7: RPP I, RPP II, LPP; Vol. 8: ROC, OC, Z, CV. [German text.]

The Wittgenstein Reader. (1994). Ed. A.J.P. Kenny. Oxford: Blackwell. [Selections from TLP, PG, BT, BB, RFM, PI, RPP, Z, OC, LPE, LC.]

Works Derived from Dictations by, or Conversations with, Wittgenstein

WAM   *Wittgenstein – A Memoir.* (1958/1984). N. Malcolm. Second edition. Oxford: Oxford University Press.
PLP   *The Principles of Linguistic Philosophy.* (1965). F. Waismann. Ed. R. Harré. London: Macmillan.
SDE   Some Developments in Wittgenstein's View of Ethics. (1965). R. Rhees. *Philosophical Review*, 74, 17–26.
RR   On Continuity: Wittgenstein's Ideas 1938. R. Rhees. In R. Rhees. (1970). *Discussions of Wittgenstein* (pp. 104–157). London: Routledge and Kegan Paul.
LSP   *Logik, Sprache, Philosophie.* [Logic, Language, Philosophy.] (1976). Ed. G.P. Baker and B.F. McGuinness. Stuttgart: Reclam.
RW   *Recollections of Wittgenstein.* (1984). Ed. R. Rhees. Oxford: Oxford University Press.
WC   *Wittgenstein: Conversations 1949–1951.* (1986). O.K. Bouwsma. Ed. J.L. Craft and R.E. Hustwit. Indianapolis: Hackett.
VW   *The Voices of Wittgenstein – The Vienna Circle, Ludwig Wittgenstein and Friedrich Waismann.* (2003). Ed. G.P. Baker. Trans. G.P. Baker *et al.* London: Routledge.
CRR   Wittgenstein's Philosophical Conversations with Rush Rhees: From the Notes of Rush Rhees. (2015). Ed. G. Citron. *Mind*, 124, 1–71.
WMC   A Discussion Between Wittgenstein and Moore on Certainty: From the Notes of Norman Malcolm. Ed. G. Citron. *Mind*, 124, 73–84.

Correspondence

Letters are quoted by *date*, as specifically as possible. They are collected in the following editions:

Letters from Wittgenstein, with a Memoir. (1967). Ed. B.F. McGuinness. Trans. L. Furtmüller. Oxford: Blackwell. [Letters to P. Engelmann.]

Letters to L. von Ficker. (1969). Ed. G.H. von Wright and W. Methlagl. Salzburg: Müller. Translation in *Wittgenstein: Sources and Perspectives.* (1979). Ed. C.G. Luckhardt. Trans. B. Gillette. Hassocks: Harvester.

Letters to C. K. Ogden. (1973). Ed. G.H. von Wright. Oxford: Blackwell. [With an appendix containing letters by F.P. Ramsey.]

Letters to Russell, Keynes and Moore. (1974). Ed. G.H. von Wright. Trans. B.F. McGuinness. Oxford: Blackwell.

Briefe. [Letters.] (1980). Ed. B.F. McGuinness and G.H. von Wright. Trans. J. Schulte. Frankfurt: Suhrkamp. [Correspondence with B. Russell, G.E. Moore, J.M. Keynes, F.P. Ramsey, W. Eccles, P. Engelmann, and L. von Ficker; in German, with appended original versions of Wittgenstein's own letters when in English.]

Ludwig Hänsel – Ludwig Wittgenstein: Eine Freundschaft. Briefe. Aufsätze. Kommentare. [Ludwig Hänsel – Ludwig Wittgenstein: A Friendship. Letters. Essays. Commentaries.] (1994). Ed. I. Somavilla, A. Unterkircher, and C.P. Berger. Innsbruck: Haymon.

Wittgenstein in Cambridge: Letters and Documents 1911–1951. (1995/2008). Ed. B. McGuinness. Fourth edition. Oxford: Blackwell.

Ludwig Wittgenstein: Familienbriefe. [Ludwig Wittgenstein: Family Letters.] (1996). Ed. B. McGuinness, M.C. Ascher, and O. Pfersmann. Vienna: Hölder-Pichler-Tempsky.

Wittgenstein und die Musik: Briefwechsel Ludwig Wittgenstein – Rudolf Koder. [Wittgenstein and Music: Correspondence Ludwig Wittgenstein – Rudolf Koder.] (2000). Ed. M. Alber, B. McGuinness, and M. Seekircher. Innsbruck: Haymon.

Wittgenstein: Gesamtbriefwechsel/Complete Correspondence: Innsbrucker Electronic Edition. (2004/2011). Ed. A. Coda, G. Citron, B. Halder, A. Janik, U. Lobis, K. Mayr, B. McGuinness, M. Schorner, M. Seekircher, A. Unterkircher, and J. Wang. Charlottesville: Intelex. http://www.nlx.com/collections/166 [Original letters in German, English, Norwegian, and Russian.]

Wittgenstein – Engelmann: Briefe, Begegnungen, Erinnerungen. [Wittgenstein – Engelmann: Letters, Encounters, Memories.] (2006). Ed. I. Somavilla. Innsbruck: Haymon.

Er "ist eine Künstlernatur von hinreissender Genialität": Die Korrespondenz zwischen Ludwig Wittgenstein und Moritz Schlick sowie ausgewählte Briefe von und an Friedrich Waismann, Rudolf Carnap, Frank P. Ramsey, Ludwig Hänsel und Margaret Stonborough. [He "is a natural artist of mesmerizing ingenuity": Correspondence between Ludwig Wittgenstein and Moritz Schlick, and selected letters exchanged with Friedrich Waismann, Rudolf Carnap, Frank P. Ramsey, Ludwig Hänsel, and Margaret Stonborough.] (2015). Ed. M. Iven. *Wittgenstein-Studien*, 6, 83–174.

Nachlass

References to Wittgenstein's manuscripts and typescripts are by MS or TS number, following G.H. von Wright's catalogue. (See von Wright, *Wittgenstein* (1982). Oxford: Blackwell, pp. 35 ff; reprinted with an addendum in PO.) Most of the *Nachlass* is kept in the Library of Trinity College, Cambridge. It is also available on a microfilm produced by Cornell University, the so-called *Cornell Copy*. The *Nachlass* has been collected in the following editions:

Wiener Ausgabe/Vienna Edition. (1994–). Ed. M. Nedo. New York: Springer. [This is presently incomplete. The volumes so far published contain early parts of the *Nachlass*, with the original paginations. In addition to an *Introduction* and *Concordance*, it is projected to comprise 15 volumes.]

Wittgenstein's Nachlass: The Bergen Electronic Edition. (2000). Ed. the Wittgenstein Archives at the University of Bergen. Oxford: Oxford University Press. [This is the most comprehensive published edition of the *Nachlass* to date. It comprises six CDs, one containing edited *Nachlass* texts and software, and five containing facsimiles.]

Wittgenstein Source Bergen Nachlass Edition. (2015–). Ed. the Wittgenstein Archives at the University of Bergen under the direction of Alois Pichler. In *Wittgenstein Source*. (2009–). Bergen: The Wittgenstein Archives at the University of Bergen. http://www.wittgensteinsource.org/ [This provides open access to *Nachlass* items in the form of facsimiles and text editions in both normalized and diplomatic versions.]

Introduction

JOHN HYMAN AND HANS-JOHANN GLOCK

Wittgenstein crossed the second Styx, from living memory to history, during the years since the present century began. He is recognized today as one of the most original and powerful thinkers of the twentieth century, and his work belongs to the body of literature philosophers will read and interpret afresh in each generation, for as long as the European intellectual tradition survives. The scope of his writings is much smaller than that of, say, Locke, Hume, or Kant. He wrote nothing in political philosophy or jurisprudence, very little in ethics, and the only sustained record of his philosophical ideas about religion and art consists in notes taken by students at his lectures. Wittgenstein's intellectual focus was narrow and intense. But the influence of his thought about logic, language, mathematics, and the mind, and about philosophical enquiry itself, has been immense. Indeed, one of the deepest divisions among analytic philosophers today is between those who see a close affinity between the goals and methods of philosophy and of natural science, and those who follow Wittgenstein, and see philosophy as a discipline *sui generis*, "which stands above or below, but not beside the natural sciences" (TLP 4.111). Another is between those on the one hand whose intellectual genealogy leads to Wittgenstein's early philosophy, to the work in which it was crystallized, the *Tractatus Logico-Philosophicus*, and to the Vienna Circle, who were inspired by it; and those on the other hand whose ideas owe more to Wittgenstein's later philosophy, and to the book in which it received its fullest expression, the *Philosophical Investigations*.

But although Wittgenstein's influence on twentieth-century philosophy was second to none, philosophy developed during the half century after his death, in 1951, in ways inimical to his ideas. The philosophy of mind and language was transformed, successively, by the impact of linguistics, artificial intelligence and cognitive science; metaphysics was invigorated by developments in modal logic; epistemology was dominated for 40 years by a research program quite alien to his thought; and the conception of philosophy itself that became increasingly predominant conformed to Russell's belief that philosophy is bound to be a fruitless exercise if it is divorced from science and Quine's view that philosophy is "continuous with" science, as opposed to Wittgenstein's conviction that the desire to imitate science "leads philosophers into complete darkness" (BB 18).

A Companion to Wittgenstein, First Edition. Edited by Hans-Johann Glock and John Hyman.
© 2017 John Wiley & Sons, Ltd. Published 2017 by John Wiley & Sons, Ltd.

Wittgenstein's conception of philosophy changed in the course of his career, but it always involved a sharp distinction between philosophy and science, and it was always coordinated with his conception of language.

In the "Notes on Logic," a typescript he produced with Russell's help in 1913, Wittgenstein argued that while natural science provides us with pictures of reality, philosophy does not. Philosophy cannot contribute to any part of science; it is "the doctrine of the logical form of scientific propositions." By logical form Wittgenstein means the form which a proposition, i.e., a meaningful sentence, must have in common with the situation that it represents, in order to be capable of representing it at all. For example, a musical score is a spatial arrangement of marks, whereas the corresponding piece of music is a temporal arrangement of sounds. Hence they do not share a spatial or a temporal form. What they must share, if one represents the other, is their logical form. Thus Wittgenstein initially believed that philosophy has its own field of enquiry: not the natural world itself, which is the province of natural science, but the structure that a fact in the world and a logical picture of it must have in common. But the conception of language he developed while writing the *Tractatus* soon forced him to abandon this idea of philosophy.

The *Tractatus* was completed in 1918 and published in 1921. In this book, Wittgenstein argues that the logical form of a proposition is utterly different from its superficial grammatical form. Words are combined in sentences to form pictures or models of possible states of affairs in the world. All of the meaningful sentences we use in our daily lives or in scientific work are truth-functional combinations of logically independent elementary propositions, whose only constituents are simple, unanalyzable names. Each of these names corresponds to an object, whose name it is. The syntax of a name, i.e., the ways in which it can and cannot be combined with other names to form a sentence, reflects the essential nature of the object which it names, i.e., the ways in which it can and cannot be combined with other objects to form a state of affairs. Hence, a meaningful combination of words corresponds to a possible combination of objects. If the arrangement of the simple names concealed in a sentence represents the actual arrangement of the objects that they name, then the sentence is true; if not, it is false.

It follows from these doctrines that the only meaningful use of words is to state (or mis-state) the facts. For a fact is the existence of a state of affairs, and a state of affairs is a combination of objects. Any attempt to describe the essential nature of an object or the syntax of a name, and any attempt to expound a theory of representation – such as the attempt we made in the last paragraph to explain the doctrines presented in the *Tractatus* – is bound to result in nonsense. Nevertheless, what the propositions of the *Tractatus* attempt to say is made evident without transgressing the rules of logical syntax by the well-formed sentences of a language. For a meaningful combination of names cannot fail to show that these names can be combined in this way. But "what expresses itself in language, we cannot express by means of language" (TLP 4.121). Hence, the *Tractatus* itself consists in a series of nonsensical sentences. For the same reason, the traditional aim of metaphysics, namely, to set down the essential nature of the world in a body of necessary propositions, is unattainable. For the only statement of a necessary truth that the syntax of a language will permit is a tautology: for example, "Either it is raining or it is not raining." But a tautology says nothing, and it shows that it says nothing (TLP 4.461).

INTRODUCTION

Thus, Wittgenstein was forced to abandon the idea that philosophy can explain the logical form of scientific propositions, and he adopted instead a novel conception of philosophy, which he formulated at the end of the *Tractatus* as follows:

> The correct method in philosophy would really be to say nothing except what can be said, i.e. what belongs to natural science, i.e. something that has nothing to do with philosophy, and then whenever someone else tried to say something metaphysical to show him [NB: not "tell him"] that he had not given any reference to certain signs in his sentences. (TLP 6.53)

The philosophical method that Wittgenstein recommends here, like the conception of language that underlies it, is extremely austere, and he concedes that someone who "tries to say something metaphysical" is unlikely to find it satisfying. But several remarks in the *Tractatus* present a more expansive picture of what he believes the purpose of philosophy must be, if it cannot expound "the doctrine of the logical form of scientific propositions." The aim of philosophy, he claims, is "the logical clarification of thoughts":

> Philosophy is not a theory but an activity. A philosophical work consists essentially of elucidations. The result of philosophy is not a number of 'philosophical propositions', but to make propositions clear. (TLP 4.112)

In broad terms, Wittgenstein adhered to this conception of philosophy for the rest of his life, but what it meant in detail changed profoundly in the 1930s, because his conception of language changed. He abandoned the doctrines that a sentence is a logical picture composed of names, that the meaning of a name is the object it stands for, and that the intelligible use of language always serves the same purpose, to describe the facts. He came to believe, on the contrary, that sentences do not have a uniform logical structure, that the meaning of a word is its use in a language, and that language in general consists in a vast and heterogeneous variety of "language-games," which serve an indefinitely heterogeneous range of human purposes. (Language-games are simply human activities involving speech or writing in which distinctive ranges of concepts are employed. The word "game" is there to remind us that the use of language is constrained by rules, and occurs both in the context of a specific human culture and in the larger context of human life in general.)

In spite of this transformation in his views about the nature of language, Wittgenstein continued to believe that the purpose of philosophy is to clarify the use of language, and he continued to regard philosophy as a critical activity rather than a body of doctrine. But he now argued that the clarification philosophy aims at cannot be achieved either by logical analysis or, as suggested in section 6.53 of the *Tractatus*, by policing the misuse of language in metaphysics. It can only be achieved by describing various language-games – especially ones that involve mathematical, logical, linguistic, and psychological concepts – which the author of the *Tractatus*, and Russell, and earlier philosophers, had misunderstood. Hence, beginning in the early 1930s, a large part of Wittgenstein's philosophy consists in exploring language that does *not*, he believes, conform to the model expounded in the *Tractatus*, i.e., language in which words are *not* names, and sentences are *not* descriptions. The aim is not simply "to make propositions clear," but to reveal and dissipate the confusion that results when the Tractarian model of linguistic meaning is mistakenly assumed to apply – e.g., to the language we use to describe our thoughts and feelings, or to express our values. We need, he wrote, to make a "radical break with the idea that language always functions in one way, always serves the same purpose: to convey thoughts – which may be about houses, pains, good and evil, or anything else you please" (PI §304). The enduring value of Wittgenstein's philosophy of mind and his philosophy of mathematics is due in large part to the original and fruitful ideas this strategy produced.

The greatest obstacles to understanding Wittgenstein's philosophy are not any inherent obscurity in his ideas, but the aphoristic style in which he wrote and the introverted character of his thought. For the most part, Wittgenstein composed philosophical remarks and fragments, selecting some and discarding others, arranging and rearranging the ones he thought worth keeping, so that the more polished texts are a kind of collage. "Forcing my thoughts into an ordered sequence is a torment for me," he wrote. "I squander an unspeakable amount of effort making an arrangement of my thoughts which may have no value at all" (CV 28). And while his early philosophy was principally motivated by his reaction to Frege's and Russell's philosophies of logic, his later philosophy, at least in the critical years between 1929 and 1945, is above all a response to his own earlier work, and a dialogue with himself. His "new thoughts," he says in the preface to the *Philosophical Investigations*, can only be properly understood "by contrast with and against the background of my old way of thinking." And in 1948, he remarks that most of his writings are private conversations with himself, "things that I say to myself *tête-à-tête*" (CV 88).

This *Companion* was planned with this difficulty in mind. Following a biographical sketch, it contains an introductory section containing essays that outline Wittgenstein's philosophical development, and discuss the corpus of his writings and his style; a section covering the main influences on his thought, including Schopenhauer, Frege, Russell, Hertz, and Boltzmann; a section on his early philosophy, which is focused on the *Tractatus*; six sections covering the main topics in which he made important contributions, entitled "Philosophy and Grammar," "Logic and Mathematics," "Language," "Mind and Action," "Epistemology," and "Ethics, Aesthetics, and Religion"; and a concluding section, which examines Wittgenstein's relationship with the Aristotelian tradition, Kantianism, the Vienna Circle, Ordinary Language Philosophy, Pragmatism, Naturalism, and Continental Philosophy. The *Companion to Wittgenstein* as a whole is designed to help Wittgenstein's readers to navigate his writings and respond to them critically; to understand the sources of Wittgenstein's thought, and its relationships with the thought of philosophers working in various schools and traditions that flourished in the twentieth century; and to understand a conception of philosophy, and a powerful and coherent set of philosophical ideas, which challenge some of the positions that dominate philosophy syllabuses today. The lively interest in Wittgenstein's work among philosophers today, and the recent revival of approaches in philosophy that reflect his influence, give reason to hope that this challenge will bear fruit.

Ludwig Wittgenstein: A Sketch of His Life

RAY MONK

Ludwig Wittgenstein was born on 26 April 1889, the eighth and youngest child of one of the wealthiest and most remarkable families of Habsburg Vienna. The Wittgensteins owned several grand residences, but the one Ludwig, his four brothers, and three sisters regarded as their chief home was the magnificent Palais Wittgenstein in the Alleegasse (now Argentinerstraße). The house no longer stands. It was demolished in the 1950s, by which time it had become a relic of a way of life that had become unsustainable ("Who can nowadays live in and upkeep a palais of such extravagance of space and grandiosity?," Ludwig's brother Paul remarked when he heard his erstwhile family home was to be razed to the ground (Waugh, 2008, p. 296)). Surviving photographs, however, attest to its *haute bourgeoisie* grandeur: its stately marble staircase, its lavishly decorated "red salon," and its music salon, in which Johannes Brahms and the famous violinist Joseph Joachim played regularly for the family and their guests. Wittgenstein was once overheard by F.R. Leavis telling someone at Cambridge that in the house in which he grew up there had been seven grand pianos. And this was just one of the family's homes. In addition, there was another large house on the Neuwaldeggergasse on the outskirts of Vienna and a large estate in the country, the Hochreit, to which they retired during the summer.

This wealth had not been inherited; it had been amassed by Wittgenstein's father, Karl, an industrialist of extraordinary talent and energy, who rose to become the leading figure in the Austrian iron and steel industry. Because he had himself earned the money that paid for his family's opulent lifestyle, Karl regarded himself as a self-made man, and was, in a sense, right to do so. It should, however, be noted that he came from a family which for generations before him had been one of the wealthiest and most notable in Austria.

Though Karl Wittgenstein was brought up in the Protestant faith, and though, by the time Ludwig was born, the family had long ceased to identify themselves as members of the Jewish community, the family was originally Jewish. The founder of the family fortunes was Moses Maier, Karl's grandfather and Ludwig's great-grandfather, who was a land agent for the aristocratic Wittgenstein family. After the Napoleonic decree of 1808, which demanded that Jews adopt a surname, Moses Maier took the name of his employer. His son, Hermann, took a further step to separate himself

---

A Companion to Wittgenstein, First Edition. Edited by Hans-Johann Glock and John Hyman.
© 2017 John Wiley & Sons, Ltd. Published 2017 by John Wiley & Sons, Ltd.

from the family's Jewish ancestry by taking the middle name "Christian." Hermann Christian Wittgenstein and his wife, Franziska ("Fanny"), had 11 children, 8 daughters and 3 sons, whom they brought up in the elegant Palais Kaunitz in Laxenburg, just outside Vienna. Built in the early eighteenth century, this beautiful and stately palace had previously housed the Ambassador of Piedmont and then Prince Esterhazy. Ludwig Wittgenstein knew it as the home of his Aunt Clara, who lived there until her death in 1935.

Mozart probably performed in the Palais Kaunitz, which was possibly one reason why Hermann and Fanny, who were great music lovers, were drawn to it. Mainly through Fanny, the Wittgensteins had close ties to the leading figures in the cultural life of Austria. They acquired an impressive collection of paintings, they were friends of the poet Franz Grillparzer, and they counted among their acquaintances Johannes Brahms (who gave piano lessons to their daughters) and Felix Mendelssohn. The children of Hermann and Fanny were brought up as Protestants and when they grew up, they took their place as established members of the Habsburg bourgeoisie. Thus was established a network of judges, lawyers, professors, and clergymen that the Wittgensteins could rely on if they needed the services of any of the traditional professions. So complete was the family's assimilation that one of Hermann's daughters had to ask her brother Louis if the rumors she had heard about their Jewish origins were true. "*Pur sang*, Milly," he replied, "*pur sang*" (Monk, 1990, p. 5).

Against the background of this wealth, privilege, and social acceptance, it seems strange and perverse of Karl Wittgenstein to regard himself as a self-made man, and yet that is what he was. He was fiercely independent and determined to succeed on his own. So much so that, turning his back on the advantages of his family background, he ran away to New York, where he made a living as a waiter, a saloon musician, a bartender, and a teacher. When he returned, he did so on his own terms, forsaking the family business of estate management in favor of engineering. Within a few years he was head of a cartel that held a virtual monopoly of the iron and steel industry in the Habsburg Empire and one of the wealthiest men in Europe. By the time he retired from business in 1898, Karl's personal fortune was on a scale that dwarfed that of his father.

In the meantime, he had married Leopoldine ("Poldy") Kalmus, who, though also from a partly Jewish family, had been raised as a Catholic (all Hermann's other offspring had followed their father's instruction to marry a Protestant). With Poldy, Karl had eight children, the youngest of which was Ludwig. To a greater extent even than the home of Hermann and Fanny, the Palais Wittgenstein became a center for the musical and artistic life of Habsburg Vienna. Musical evenings there were attended by, among others, Brahms, Mahler, Bruno Walter, and the blind organist and composer Josef Labor, who owed his career largely to the patronage of the Wittgenstein family. After he retired from the iron and steel trade, Karl Wittgenstein became widely known as a great patron also of the visual arts. The painter Gustav Klimt called him his "Minister of Fine Art" in recognition of the important role Karl played in the *Jugendstil* movement through, for example, his financing of the Secession Building, in which the works of Klimt, Schiele, and Kokoschka were shown. When Wittgenstein's sister Margarete got married in 1905, Klimt was commissioned to paint her wedding portrait. Margarete ("Gretl") was the youngest of Wittgenstein's sisters and the one closest to him. She was regarded as the intellectual of the family, and it was through her that Wittgenstein was introduced to some of the thinkers who were to exert a lifetime's influence on him, including Sigmund Freud, Karl Kraus, Otto Weininger, and Arthur Schopenhauer.

Unlike that in which he and his siblings had grown up, however, the home Karl created with Poldy was marked by emotional tension and trauma as well as by comfort and high culture. Ludwig's two oldest brothers, Hans and Rudi, both committed suicide during his childhood. When Ludwig was 13, Hans, who had, like his father, fled to America, disappeared from a boat in Chesapeake Bay and was assumed to have taken his own life. Hans was a musical prodigy on a Mozartian scale, a genius. He mastered both the violin and the piano as an infant and was composing orchestral music at the age of four. With encouragement and support he might have become a great composer. Karl, however, was determined that he pursue a career in industry, which is no doubt why he ran away to the United States. His younger brother Rudi also rebelled against Karl and also ran away from home, in his case to Berlin where he hoped to pursue a career in the theatre. In 1904, two years after Hans went missing, Rudi's much more public and melodramatic suicide was reported in sensational fashion by the *Berliner Tageszeitung*, which related how Rudi had gone into a bar and ordered two drinks. After sitting by himself for a while, he asked the piano player to play a love song called "I am Lost" and, as the music played, took cyanide and died.

After Rudi's suicide, Karl relented and took a softer line with his remaining sons, Kurt, Paul, and Ludwig, allowing them to pursue whatever path in life they chose. Kurt chose a military career, while Paul became a musician. Such were the standards of musicality in the Wittgenstein family that Paul's playing, even after he became a successful concert pianist, was not greatly admired by them. His older sister Helene was regarded as having better technique and superior taste.

Ludwig was regarded as one of the least gifted of the family; a nice, polite boy, but not possessed of either great intellect or exceptional talent. When it came to his education, it was decided that he would not be taught by private tutors, as Hans, Rudi, and Kurt had been, nor would he be sent to the Viennese *Gymnasium* that Paul attended. Instead, he was sent to the rather second-rate *Realschule* in Linz, a school famous only for having among its alumni Adolf Hitler, who later recalled that it was the history teacher at the school who first converted him to the *Völkisch* nationalism of the pan-German movement. I have yet to see a really satisfying explanation of why Karl and Poldy thought it was a good idea to send their youngest son away to Linz to attend this rather undistinguished school. It was apparently feared that Ludwig would not pass the rigorous entrance requirements of a top *Gymnasium* and also felt that a more technical and less academic education would suit him (since he had always shown an interest in engineering), but, still, why Linz? Could they not have found a suitable school in Vienna? In any case, the three years that Wittgenstein spent at the school, 1903 to 1906, were, on the whole, fairly miserable. He failed to make friends among his predominantly working-class classmates, to whom he seemed like a being from another world, and neither did he find at the school anything to spark his intellectual enthusiasm. His grades were mediocre and his teachers seem to have left no lasting impression on him.

His greatest intellectual influence during his school years was Gretl. Under her encouragement, he read Karl Kraus's satirical journal *Die Fackel* ("The Torch"), Schopenhauer's *The World as Will and Representation*, and Otto Weininger's *Sex and Character*. From this last, Wittgenstein seems to have acquired a particular conception of genius as consisting in a twofold set of duties, the first to think clearly and the second to behave decently, these two, logic and ethics, being fundamentally the same, two aspects of the single "duty to oneself."

As well as Kraus, Schopenhauer, and Weininger, Wittgenstein read the work of two scientists during these years that was to have a lasting influence on his philosophical outlook, namely Heinrich Hertz and Ludwig Boltzmann. From Hertz's *Principles of Mechanics* Wittgenstein learned a lesson that would inform all his philosophical thinking, namely that sometimes the difficulties one faces in understanding a concept can be overcome, not by *solving* the problems raised by that concept but rather by *dissolving* them. In Hertz's case, the concept in question was "force," the problems with which, he suggests, can be dealt with by restating Newtonian physics without using "force" as a basic concept. Thus, Hertz writes in the introduction to the book:

> When these painful contradictions are removed, the question as to the nature of force will not have been answered; but our minds, no longer vexed, will cease to ask illegitimate questions. (Hertz, [1894] 1956, p. 8)

Wittgenstein may well have been led to read Hertz by reading Boltzmann's *Populäre Schriften*, a collection of his more popular lectures that was published in 1905. Boltzmann was a professor at the University of Vienna and there was talk of Wittgenstein studying with him after he left school. In 1906, however, the year Wittgenstein left the *Realschule* in Linz, Boltzmann committed suicide. Instead of studying physics at Vienna therefore, Wittgenstein went to Berlin to study mechanical engineering at the *Technische Hochschule*, after which, in the summer of 1908, he went to England to study aeronautics at the University of Manchester.

At Manchester, Wittgenstein's status was that of a research student in the Engineering Department. He was not working toward a degree, but pursuing his own line of research, which centered on his attempts to design and build an aircraft engine. His design was novel but impractical. It envisaged driving a propeller by means of high-speed gases rushing out of a combustion chamber. After a year of conducting experiments with his combustion chamber, Wittgenstein's interests shifted from the engine to the propeller, his design for which he patented in the autumn of 1910. His work in engineering was taken sufficiently seriously by the University of Manchester for them to award him a research studentship for the year 1910–1911, which was renewed the following year, but by this time the problems of aeronautical engineering had taken second place in his mind to the philosophical problems raised by logic and mathematics.

Wittgenstein's interest in the philosophy of mathematics seems to have been aroused soon after his arrival in Manchester, when, while attending lectures on mathematics by the famous mathematician J.E. Littlewood, he began attending weekly discussions with other research students, discussions which came to focus on the problems of providing mathematics with logical foundations. This led Wittgenstein, first to Russell's *The Principles of Mathematics* and then to Frege's *Grundgesetze der Arithmetik*. He evidently hoped to find a solution to the problems raised by Russell's paradox. As early as April 1909, Russell's friend Philip Jourdain was writing in his correspondence book about an attempted solution to the paradox that Wittgenstein had evidently sent him. The only trace of this "solution" that survives is Jourdain's dismissal of it. After receiving Jourdain's response to this early foray into philosophy, Wittgenstein tried to concentrate on his aeronautical researches. According to his sister Hermine, however, Wittgenstein suffered terribly during this time from the feeling of being torn between conflicting vocations, his researches into engineering fighting a losing battle with his obsession with the philosophy of mathematics. Finally, in the summer of 1911, "in a constant, indescribable, almost pathological state of agitation" (in Hermine's words, see RW 2), Wittgenstein, having drawn up a plan for a proposed book on philosophy, traveled to Jena to discuss it with Frege. (Russell, Elizabeth Anscombe, and Rush Rhees all believed that Wittgenstein went to see Russell before going to Jena, but I am following Hermine's recollections here, which are supported by the account given by G.H. von Wright in his "Biographical Sketch" of Wittgenstein's recollections of meeting Frege before he went to Cambridge to see Russell.) Wittgenstein later told friends that Frege "wiped the floor with him" on this occasion, but he was sufficiently encouraged by the meeting to go to Cambridge to discuss his ideas with Russell.

Thus it was that on 18 October 1911, two weeks into the Michaelmas Term, Russell was having tea with his friend C.K. Ogden, when "an unknown German appeared, speaking very little English but refusing to speak German. He turned out to be a man who [...] had acquired by himself a passion for the philosophy of mathematics & has now come to Cambridge on purpose to hear me" (Monk, 1990, pp. 38–9). Actually, as Russell learned in the following weeks, Wittgenstein could speak English perfectly well and had not come to hear Russell so much as to compel Russell to hear him. At the end of the term, Wittgenstein told Russell that he was hesitating between philosophy and aeronautics and asked for advice on whether or not he was "utterly hopeless at philosophy." Russell advised him to write something on philosophy during the Christmas vacation so that he (Russell) might make an informed judgment.

When Wittgenstein brought his manuscript (which has not survived) to Russell in the New Year, Russell pronounced it "very good, much better than my English pupils do" and the decision was made. Wittgenstein later told his friend David Pinsent that, in encouraging him to pursue philosophy, Russell had ended a nine-year period of loneliness and suffering during which he had often thought of suicide. Free to pursue what *really* interested him, Wittgenstein blossomed, so much so that, by the end of his first year at Cambridge, when he was visited there by Hermine, she was surprised to hear Russell say: "We expect the next big step in philosophy to be taken by your brother" (Monk, 1990, p. 55).

Frustratingly, however, there is no way of knowing what, exactly, Wittgenstein had done to prompt such an extravagant prediction. During this period, Russell wrote almost daily (and sometimes several times a day) to his lover, Lady Ottoline Morrell, but, though there is much in these letters about how impressed Russell was with his new student, there are almost no details of what philosophical questions Wittgenstein was concerned with. The letters Wittgenstein wrote to Russell in the summer of 1912 establish that he was thinking about the nature of logic, but again they provide few details.

In the summer of 1912 Wittgenstein took a horse-riding holiday in Iceland with his closest friend at Cambridge, the mathematics undergraduate David Pinsent. When he returned to Cambridge for the start of the new academic year, any lingering doubts about his ability in philosophy seem to have disappeared entirely and to have been replaced with a strident assertiveness. He felt no hesitation in expressing to Russell his fierce dislike of Russell's newly published article on "The Essence of Religion," nor in telling G.E. Moore that his lectures on the philosophy of psychology were "very bad." He seemed to be in a state of constant agitation. Once, when he was pacing up and down Russell's room, silent but deep in thought, Russell asked him if he was thinking of logic or of his sins. "Both," replied Wittgenstein and continued his pacing.

For the academic year 1912–1913 we have, at last, some record of what Wittgenstein was doing in philosophy, albeit nothing very precise or detailed. Pinsent's diary for

25 October 1912 records Wittgenstein announcing a new solution to a problem "in the most fundamental Symbolic Logic," a solution that Russell thought was sound and which, if correct, will "solve a problem which has puzzled Russell and Frege for some years" (von Wright, 1990, p. 37). The following month Wittgenstein gave a paper to the Moral Sciences Club which, in four minutes ("thus cutting the previous record [...] by nearly two minutes," the minutes record), addressed itself to the question "What is Philosophy?" The answer he gave is that philosophy consists in "all those primitive propositions which are assumed to be true without proof by the various sciences" (Monk, 1990, p. 70).

More significant – and more obviously a breakthrough – is Wittgenstein's announcement in a letter to Russell written during the Christmas vacation of 1912 that he had come to think that "there cannot be different Types of things! [...] every theory of types must be rendered superfluous by a proper theory of symbolism" (16 January 1913). What he had in mind, he made clear later in the letter, was that the difference between, e.g., individuals and universals (Socrates and mortality, say) must show itself in different kinds of *symbol* rather than in the assertion of different types of *thing*: "what seem to be *different kinds of things* are symbolised by different kinds of symbols which *cannot* possibly be substituted in one another's places."

As Pinsent noted in his diary, by this time Russell was inclined to acquiesce in almost every pronouncement Wittgenstein made with regard to logic, a field he was now inclined to bequeath to Wittgenstein, while he pursued problems in epistemology. As the wearer of Russell's mantle in logic, Wittgenstein was in 1913 asked by the *Cambridge Review* to review a textbook on logic, *The Science of Logic*, written by a traditional Catholic logician called Peter Coffey. Wittgenstein's review was extraordinarily vitriolic, self-confident, and didactic, announcing himself as a belligerent and partisan champion of the logic of Frege and Russell against the Aristotelian kind of logic espoused by Coffey. The advance of the former over the latter, Wittgenstein claims, is "comparable only to that which made Astronomy out of Astrology and Chemistry out of Alchemy."

At the very time that Wittgenstein was presenting himself as such an evangelist for the work of Frege and Russell, however, he was himself taking large strides *away* from their work. In the summer of 1913, Wittgenstein told Pinsent about his "latest discoveries," which, Pinsent wrote in his diary, constituted a system that "has upset a lot of Russell's work" (von Wright, 1990, p. 59). Still, however, there is no surviving written record of the work, a fact explained in a letter Wittgenstein wrote to Russell at about the same time in which he told him that there were still unsolved problems and that he would not begin to write until he had solved them.

That summer Wittgenstein took Pinsent on a holiday to Norway, but, compared to the previous year's adventures in Iceland, it was, for Pinsent, rather dull. Wittgenstein spent large amounts of time working on logic, feeling that he was on the brink of complete success and growing increasingly anxious that he might die before he was able to finish his work. In the face of this anxiety, Wittgenstein made two momentous decisions: first, that he would leave Cambridge and live alone in a remote part of Norway until he had finished his work on logic, and second, that, before he did so, he would dictate his ideas to Russell.

Russell tried to dissuade Wittgenstein from going to Norway:

> I said it would be dark & he said he hated daylight. I said it would be lonely & he said he prostituted his mind talking to intelligent people. I said he was mad & he said God preserve him from sanity. (God certainly will.) (Monk, 1990, p. 91)

But, when he found Wittgenstein to be immovable on the subject, he arranged for him to dictate his thoughts on logic to a secretary. These notes were then supplemented by a typescript that Wittgenstein had prepared in Birmingham, when he said his goodbyes to Pinsent, to make up the earliest piece of philosophical writing by Wittgenstein to survive: the "Notes on Logic." Much that is distinctive about the views that Wittgenstein would later publish as *Tractatus Logico-Philosophicus* is already present in these notes. This includes, not only his views on logic, but also his conception of philosophy, which he says here "consists of logic and metaphysics" though "logic is its basis." The "first prerequisite for philosophizing," he announces, is "distrust of grammar." What he means by this is that, in order to understand the true nature of logic, the philosopher must see beyond the grammar of our ordinary and formal languages, which, again and again, seem to suggest that there are "things" where there are not. "Symbols are not what they seem to be," Wittgenstein warns. Thus, the R in "aRb" appears to be a substantive, but it is not one. Nothing corresponds to it. This is true also for the so-called "logical constants" – $\sim$, $\vee$, $\supset$, etc. – which do not *refer* to anything, either. Similarly, the meanings of propositions are not "things." Indeed, in every case, the temptation to believe in "logical objects" has its origin in a misunderstanding of the logic of language (i.e., in not distrusting grammar enough) and is to be resisted. There are no logical objects. Logic is not the study of a special kind of object, nor (as he had earlier insisted in a letter to Russell) of *types* of objects; it is the study of language. The nature of logic will be clear when, and only when, the nature of a proposition is clear.

Wittgenstein left for Norway in October 1913 and moved into a remote cottage by the side of the Sognefjord in the village of Skjolden. There he lived alone and worked intensely on a book he at this time referred to as "Logik." After spending the Christmas of 1913 in Vienna, he returned to Norway in a state of almost frenzied anxiety. "Deep inside there's a perpetual seething, like the bottom of a geyser," he wrote to Russell, "and I keep hoping that things will come to an eruption once and for all, so that I can turn into a different person." "Perhaps you regard this thinking about myself as a waste of time," he added, "but how can I be a logician before I'm a human being" (Letter to Russell, December 1913). Partly because he felt that Russell did not understand this earnest and deeply felt desire to "turn into a different person," and partly as a step in the direction of turning into a different person, Wittgenstein, in February 1914, decided to break off relations with Russell. After, however, receiving from Russell a letter "*so* full of kindness and friendship that I don't think I have the *right* to leave it unanswered," Wittgenstein relented, at least to the extent of resuming his correspondence. He insisted, though, that they should restrict their relationship "to the communication of facts capable of being established objectively" while avoiding "any kind of value-judgment" (Letter to Russell, 3 March 1914).

In the meantime, Wittgenstein turned his attention to G.E. Moore, to whom he now began to write urging him to come to Norway. Toward the end of March 1914, Moore succumbed to this pressure and spent two weeks with Wittgenstein in his remote cottage, during which Wittgenstein dictated to him a second series of notes on logic that Wittgenstein took to be a great advance on the notes he had left with Russell a few months earlier. At the center of this advance was a distinction between what can be *said* and what has to be *shown*. In this distinction, Wittgenstein believed, he had found the solution to the problems about logic that had bothered him and Russell. "Logical so-called propositions," the notes begin, "*show* the logical properties of language and therefore of the Universe, but *say* nothing" (NB 108). What Russell had tried to say in the Theory of Types, for example, cannot be said; it is, rather, shown by the different types of symbols used in propositions.

When Moore left Norway to return to Cambridge, Wittgenstein, as he wrote to Russell, "relapsed into a state of exhaustion," unable to do any more work. In dictating his notes to Moore, however, Wittgenstein believed himself to have achieved what he had sought to achieve: a written account of the thoughts on logic he had been developing since he first came to Cambridge in 1911. While he urged Russell to read those notes carefully and to discuss them with Moore, he asked Moore to investigate whether they might be accepted as a BA thesis. The answer to this last question was "no": however important the ideas they contained, the notes did not fulfill the formal requirements of a Cambridge BA thesis. There was no preface, for example, nor a bibliography. When Moore communicated this to Wittgenstein he received in reply an outburst so violent, so unfair, and so petulant that it put an end to their friendship for 15 years. "If I am not worth your making an exception for me *even in some STUPID details* then I may as well go to HELL directly," Wittgenstein thundered, "and if I *am* worth it and you don't do it – by God – *you* might go there" (Letter to Moore, 7 May 1914).

Though enraged that they did not merit the award of a BA, Wittgenstein did not regard the notes he had dictated to Moore as the final and definitive statement of his ideas on logic, and, after a break of a few months, he intended to resume his work. In July 1914, he returned to Vienna intending to spend some time with his family before taking another holiday with Pinsent, possibly in Spain. In fact, he would never see Pinsent again. On 28 June 1914, the Archduke Ferdinand was assassinated and by the 4 August the whole of Europe was at war. In the weeks in between, Wittgenstein took a step closer to integrating himself into the intellectual and literary avant-garde of the Habsburg Empire when he arranged to distribute 100 000 crowns (then equivalent to about £4000, and so about £350 000 in today's money) "among Austrian artists who are without means." His chosen method of distributing the money was to give it to Ludwig von Ficker, the editor of a journal published in Innsbruck called *Der Brenner*. Ficker in turn disbursed the money to various writers. The three main beneficiaries were Rainer Maria Rilke, Georg Trakl, and Carl Dallago, but several other writers and artists also received a share.

By the time Wittgenstein and Ficker had finalized the arrangements for this bequest, the war had begun. On 7 August, Wittgenstein enlisted into the Austrian army and was assigned to an artillery regiment serving on the Eastern Front. For the first two years of the war, he served behind the lines. For the most part, he hated it. He found it impossible to befriend the people he served alongside ("unbelievably crude, stupid and malicious" (Monk, 1990, p. 114)) and was certain that he was fighting on the losing side. His diary notes of the time show that he thought often of suicide. What saved him from that was the gospel, or, more precisely, Leo Tolstoy's *Gospel in Brief*, which he bought in his first month in Poland and read and reread until he knew it by heart.

In March 1916, Wittgenstein was granted his oft-repeated wish to transfer from being an engineer serving behind the lines to being an ordinary soldier fighting on the front line. He was ordered to man the observation post, one of the most dangerous assignments he could have been given. "Thought of God," he wrote in his diary. "Thy will be done. God be with me" (Monk, 1990, p. 138). Remarkably, during this time, Wittgenstein was able to do what he had been unable to do in his last month in Norway: write on logic. He wrote about propositions and functions and facts. And then on

11 June 1916, his reflections on these subjects are interrupted with the question: "What do I know about God and the purpose of life?" He answers with a list that includes:

> I know that this world exists
> That I am placed in it like my eye in its visual field
> That something about it is problematic, which we call its meaning.
> That this meaning does not lie in it but outside it.
>
> (NB 11.6.16)

"The meaning of life," he says later in the same journal entry, "i.e. the meaning of the world, we can call God."

Until this point, Wittgenstein was in the habit of writing personal remarks alongside his philosophical reflections, which he distinguished from the latter by writing them in a simple code he had learned as a child (a = z, b = y, etc.). The remarks quoted above about God and the meaning of life, however, are not written in code but presented as if they somehow belonged to the work on logic that preceded them. The connection between the two lies in the distinction he had earlier made central to his thoughts in the notes dictated to Moore: the distinction between saying and showing. Just as logic was ineffable, so, he now believed, is ethics. Both are "transcendental." As Wittgenstein was to put it in the *Tractatus*: "There are, indeed, things that cannot be put into words. They *make themselves manifest*. They are what is mystical" (6.522).

While Wittgenstein's thoughts were extending from logic to the meaning of life, he was engaged in some of the most brutal fighting of the war. He showed himself to be an extremely good and brave soldier, and was rewarded by being mentioned in dispatches and in being promoted to corporal and then being sent to his regiment's headquarters in Olmütz, Moravia, to be trained as an officer.

Wittgenstein was at Olmütz for the last three months of 1916. There he met the man who was to be his closest friend and confidant for the next 10 years or more: Paul Engelmann, a cultured man with a training in architecture who, having been invalided out of the Austrian army, was now helping Karl Kraus in his campaign against the war. Engelmann proved to be a sympathetic discussion partner, one who was predisposed to take a similar view to Wittgenstein's about the importance of, and ineffability of, "the mystical."

Soon after Wittgenstein returned to the Russian Front, the Tsarist government collapsed. To begin with, however, this led to a heightening of activity on the front, the Kerensky Offensive being followed by a counteroffensive in which the Austro-Hungarian forces made significant advances. For his part in this fighting, Wittgenstein was awarded the Silver Medal for Valor. Though the fighting ended soon after the October Revolution, Wittgenstein remained stationed in the Ukraine while the peace negotiations were taking place and it was not until March 1917 that he was transferred to the Italian Front.

In Italy, Wittgenstein again distinguished himself in battle and was again awarded a medal for bravery. In July 1918 he was given a long period of leave that lasted until September. He chose to spend it, not in Vienna, but at his uncle's house in Hallein. It was there that what we now know as *Tractatus Logico-Philosophicus* was finally finished. It was also there that he received a letter from Pinsent's mother giving him the news he had been dreading since the war began: Pinsent was dead, killed in an airplane while conducting research on aerodynamics. The book was, naturally, dedicated to Pinsent's memory.

In his preface to the book, Wittgenstein, with characteristic immodesty, announced himself to have found "on all essential points" the solution to "the problems of philosophy." The book is unusual in many ways, not least in the way that it is structured. It is arranged, not in paragraphs and chapters, but in numbered propositions. The seven main propositions are assigned the numbers 1 to 7. The other remarks are given numbers that reflect their place in the hierarchy of thought, so that, e.g., remark 2.151 is a comment on 2.15, which in turn elaborates the point made in 2.1, and so on. Most of the book is taken up with a statement of the theory of meaning that Wittgenstein had been developing since he arrived in Cambridge, a consequence of which is that the truths of logic, ethics, and philosophy lie outside meaningful discourse, as do the propositions of the book itself, which are described as like the rungs of a ladder which one must throw away when one has used it to gain a position from which one can see language, logic, and the world aright.

As soon as the book was finished, Wittgenstein sent it to Karl Kraus's publisher, Jahoda, who, however, rejected it. Meanwhile, Wittgenstein returned to Italy, where he was taken prisoner, one of about half a million prisoners that the Italians kept to use as bargaining material in the peace negotiations. For nearly a year, Wittgenstein remained in captivity. Remarkably, he was able to exchange cards with Bertrand Russell, to whom he announced that he had written a book that had "solved all our problems finally." Through John Maynard Keynes, Wittgenstein managed to send Russell his manuscript. When Russell read it, he wrote to Wittgenstein to say that he admired it greatly and that he was convinced by what he regarded as Wittgenstein's "main contention," namely that the propositions of logic were not true in the same sort of way that other propositions were true. This, Wittgenstein told him, was *not* his main point. The main point, rather, was the distinction between what can be said and what can only be shown, "which, I believe, is the cardinal problem of philosophy" (Letter to Russell, 19 August 1919).

In August 1919, Wittgenstein was finally able to return to Vienna. On arrival, the first thing he did was to rid himself of the immense fortune he had inherited from his father, to, as the family accountant put it, "commit financial suicide." He then enrolled at the teacher-training college in Vienna and moved out of his family home into humble lodgings in Vienna's Third District. Having survived the war and solved all the problems of philosophy, he evidently wanted to start life anew, as, so to speak, a different person.

Even after it had been rejected by Jahoda, Wittgenstein was confident that his book would find a publisher in Vienna, but this turned out to be mistaken. After receiving two more rejections, Wittgenstein approached von Ficker to see whether it might be published in *Der Brenner*. As a "key" to understanding this strange book, Wittgenstein told Ficker that the book consists of two parts: "of the one which is here, and of everything which I have *not* written. And precisely this second part is the important one" (Monk, 1990, p. 178). Understandably, perhaps, Ficker's response was cool. He was advised not to accept it, he told Wittgenstein, but was prepared to publish it *as a favor to Wittgenstein*. This obviously would not do.

The book found a publisher only after Russell, who was by this time one of the most famous intellectuals in the world, offered to write an introduction to it. To facilitate this, Wittgenstein and Russell met in Holland in December 1919, where they went through the book line by line, after which Russell wrote a fairly lengthy introduction which emphasized the book's importance, attempted to summarize its views, and expressed some misgivings about the book's "mysticism." Because of Russell's introduction the book was finally accepted by the German publishers Reclam. However, when

Wittgenstein received Russell's manuscript, he could not bring himself to agree to its publication alongside his book, and so Reclam withdrew their offer. Wittgenstein comforted himself with the following argument:

> Either my piece is a work of the highest rank, or it is not a work of the highest rank. In the latter (and more probable) case I myself am in favour of it not being printed. And in the former case it's a matter of indifference whether it's printed twenty or a hundred years sooner or later. (Letter to Russell, 6 May 1920)

The book was still not published when, in the autumn of 1920, Wittgenstein began his new career as a primary schoolteacher. The school was in the tiny lower Austrian village of Trattenbach and his pupils mostly the sons and daughters of farmers, to whom Wittgenstein appeared, as he had to the schoolchildren in Linz and his fellow soldiers during the war, as an alien and incomprehensible being. Wittgenstein's career as a teacher was brief and, for the most part, unsuccessful. There were a few students with whom he got on well and on whom he had an inspirational effect, but most of the students he taught were unable to achieve the very high standards he expected. He reacted with exasperation, sometimes hitting his students or pulling their hair, thereby alienating both them and their parents.

The one bright spot during his time at Trattenbach was the news that his book was, finally, going to be published. Russell's friend, C.K. Ogden, representing the publishers Kegan Paul, had agreed to publish it in English in a series called "The International Library of Psychology, Philosophy and Scientific Method." Meanwhile, another friend of Russell's, Dorothy Wrinch, had arranged for it to be published in German in the journal *Annalen der Naturphilosophie*. A condition of both agreements was the inclusion of Russell's introduction. Wittgenstein had nothing to do with the publication of the German edition, which he always regarded as a "pirate edition." For the English edition, on the other hand, he participated fully in the preparations for publication, corresponding with both Ogden and Frank Ramsey, the translator, who was then only 18 years old, but already recognized at Cambridge as a student of exceptional intelligence and ability. The English edition was published in the summer of 1922, which was in other ways a difficult time for Wittgenstein. His relations with the villagers and even his fellow teachers at Trattenbach had become so bad that he felt compelled to leave, and a meeting with Russell in Innsbruck turned out to be so disappointing on both sides that the two had very little to do with one another for the rest of their lives.

Wittgenstein was to spend another four years as a teacher, and a further two-and-a-half years living in Vienna, before returning to Cambridge, but the publication in England of *Tractatus Logico-Philosophicus* started a chain of events and associations that, in retrospect, seems to have made his return inevitable. From Trattenbach, Wittgenstein moved to the more attractive and pleasant village of Puchberg, where, though the villagers were still fairly hostile, he made at least one good friend. This was the music teacher Rudolf Koder, who was both a talented pianist and a very cultured man.

Meanwhile, the *Tractatus* was attracting the admiring attention of philosophers in both Vienna and Cambridge. Frank Ramsey wrote a lengthy, perceptive, and fulsome review for *Mind*, and, when he visited Vienna in the summer of 1923, took the opportunity to meet Wittgenstein in Puchberg. Wittgenstein, in turn, took the opportunity to forge a renewed link with Cambridge and asked Ramsey to inquire whether it might be possible to submit the *Tractatus* as a BA thesis. The answer was "no" (the regulations had changed since 1914), but, as Ramsey told Wittgenstein, it *would* be possible to obtain a PhD for it, so long as Wittgenstein were willing to come back to Cambridge for a year. In the years that followed, this became an increasingly attractive option. The following spring, Ramsey returned to Vienna and to Puchberg and became increasingly convinced that, if Wittgenstein could get away from his surroundings, then, as he put it to Keynes, if he "had me to stimulate him, he might do some more very good work."

For reasons that are not entirely clear, Wittgenstein left Puchberg in the summer of 1924 and went to a village near Trattenbach called Otterthal. The reason for this move is perhaps that the head of school, Josef Putre, had been Wittgenstein's only friend during his time at Trattenbach. In any case, he was no happier there than he had been at the other two village schools and during his second year at Otterthal his ill-fated career as a primary schoolteacher came to what was by then a welcome end.

From 1926 to 1928 Wittgenstein lived in Vienna and worked, astonishingly, as an architect. Paul Engelmann, his friend from Olmütz, had by this time an established architectural practice and had been hired by Wittgenstein's sister Gretl to design a new house. Wittgenstein became interested in the project and the final plan, dated 13 November 1926, is stamped "P. Engelmann & L. Wittgenstein, Architects." The building is starkly modernist – "house-embodied logic," Hermine Wittgenstein called it – but has a certain unadorned elegance, owing principally to the proportions of its doors and windows. While the house was being built, Wittgenstein got drawn back into philosophy, first through his contacts with the philosophers based at Vienna led by Moritz Schlick, and then through correspondence with Frank Ramsey, who had managed to persuade him that the *Tractatus* did not, after all, provide a definitive solution to all the problems of philosophy. And so, in January 1929, Wittgenstein returned to Cambridge, officially as a postgraduate student with Ramsey as his supervisor. "God has arrived," as Keynes put it in a letter to his wife, "I met him on the 5.15 train."

From the time of his return to Cambridge until his death in 1951, Wittgenstein developed a new style of philosophy that has no precedent in the history of the subject and is, in the opinion of many of his admirers, his greatest achievement. For the first few years of being back in academic life, his pattern was to spend the three eight-week terms in Cambridge and the rest of the year in Vienna. In Cambridge his thinking was stimulated by discussions with Frank Ramsey and the economist Piero Sraffa, while in Vienna he met regularly with a few members of the group of philosophers led by Moritz Schlick that called themselves "Logical Positivists."

Wittgenstein spent his first year back in academic life trying to repair the holes in his theory of logic that Ramsey's criticisms had exposed. Fairly soon, however, he came to the conclusion that his earlier theory could not be repaired, it had, rather, to be abandoned altogether. A pivotal moment, according to Wittgenstein's later recollections to his friends, was when, in a conversation with Sraffa about logical form, Sraffa made a Neapolitan gesture of brushing his chin with his fingertips and asking: "What is the logical form of *that?*" His earlier view, that a proposition was a picture of a possible fact with which it shares a logical form, now struck him not only as mistaken but as a perfect illustration of the kind of mistakes that philosophers are prone to make. That is, driven by the "craving for generality" philosophers are inclined to impose upon a messy, irregular reality a smooth uniformity that distorts the truth and leads to confusion.

Just a year after Wittgenstein's return to Cambridge, Frank Ramsey died after an abdominal operation. He was only 26 years old, but had, in his short life, made significant contributions to a wide range of intellectual disciplines including mathematics, economics, and philosophy. Ramsey's death was a great loss to Wittgenstein, though, by the New Year of 1930, it was already clear that the two were heading in different philosophical directions, with Wittgenstein criticizing Ramsey for being too conservative, too "bourgeois" in his thinking. Formally, Ramsey's role as Wittgenstein's supervisor came to an end in the summer of 1929, when Wittgenstein was awarded a PhD for the *Tractatus*, the examiners being Moore and Russell. After that, Wittgenstein was awarded a series of grants by Trinity College before, at the end of 1930, being made a Fellow.

In the meantime, starting in the New Year of 1930, just a few days after Ramsey's death, Wittgenstein gave lectures under the uniquely general title of "Philosophy." Wittgenstein's lecturing style was like no one else's. He had no notes and appeared to be simply standing in front of his audience, thinking aloud. Indeed, his lectures were one of the ways in which he sought to develop his new style of philosophical thinking. Others were his regular discussions with Sraffa and the notes he made in journals. Sometimes, he would take a selection of these notes and have them typed. Then, he would cut up the typescript, rearrange the remarks and have it typed again. From the early 1930s onwards, he hoped that, by this means, he would be able to produce a satisfactory book of his later thought. Despite several attempts, however, he was never able to accomplish this and the task of publishing his work has fallen to his literary executors, who have had the unenviable responsibility of deciding which journals and typescripts to print and in what form.

The nearest Wittgenstein came during his lifetime to publishing his later work was during the academic year 1933–1934, when he canceled his lectures and, instead of lecturing, dictated his ideas to a small group of his favorite students, who then distributed them to the much larger group that had registered for the class. These notes were bound in blue paper covers and came to be known as the "Blue Book," the circulation of which was by no means restricted to Wittgenstein's Cambridge students. Against Wittgenstein's will, copies of the book found their way to Oxford and even to philosophy departments in the United States. The following year, Wittgenstein dictated another set of notes to his two very favorite students, Francis Skinner and Alice Ambrose, which became known as the "Brown Book" and is recognizably an early attempt at something like the typescript that was published after Wittgenstein's death as *Philosophical Investigations*.

Occasionally, in his preparations for publication, Wittgenstein would write a preface to his intended book, which, invariably, would express his sense that his thinking was at odds, not just with the philosophy of his time, but with the entire *Zeitgeist*. In one such preface, he writes of the spirit "which informs the vast stream of European and American civilization in which all of us stand" as something to which his own thinking stands opposed. In an earlier preface, he had said: "It is all one to me whether or not the typical western scientist understands or appreciates my work, since he will not in any case understand the spirit in which I write."

In 1935, Wittgenstein's sense of being out of place in Western culture led him to investigate the possibility of moving to the Soviet Union. He visited Leningrad and Moscow, meeting with Soviet officials of various kinds, as a result of which he was offered a university lectureship. He had hoped, it seems, to be offered work in a collective farm. In any case, he returned somewhat disillusioned with what he had seen, and took no further steps to become a Soviet citizen.

When his five-year fellowship came to an end in the summer of 1936, Wittgenstein did what he had done in 1913 and relocated to his hut in Norway, where he hoped to be able to finish his book. As in 1913, too, Wittgenstein considered thinking about logic and thinking about his "sins" to be two sides of the same coin. Or, as he now put it: "If anyone is unwilling to descend into himself, because this is too painful, he will remain superficial in his writing." In the light of remarks like this, Wittgenstein's decision to make a series of confessions at this time seems likely to have been part of his preparations for finishing his book. At the end of 1936 and the beginning of 1937, he met separately with several friends, in both Vienna and Cambridge, in order to tell them of the times in his life when he had been dishonest or had behaved in a way he considered unworthy. One of these confessions was that he had allowed people to believe falsely that he was just one-quarter Jewish, whereas in truth he was three-quarters Jewish. Another was that, as a teacher, he had struck a pupil and then denied it. These confessions, Wittgenstein thought, "brought me into more settled waters, into a better relation with people, and to a greater seriousness." Perhaps not coincidentally, the piece of writing with which he was most satisfied during his later period – that which has been published posthumously under the title *Philosophical Investigations* ("Part I" of earlier editions) – was written immediately after these confessions.

Wittgenstein stayed in Norway until the end of 1937, by which time living alone had become unendurable to him. He moved to Dublin, where his old student, Maurice Drury, was training to be a psychiatrist. He was there when, on 12 March 1938, he heard the dreadful news that Austria had become part of Hitler's Third Reich. Overnight, Wittgenstein had ceased to be an Austrian citizen and was now in the intolerable situation of being, officially, a German Jew. A few days later, he went to Cambridge to discuss the situation with Piero Sraffa, who advised him, first, to seek an academic job at Cambridge and then to apply for British citizenship. Chiefly through the influence of Keynes, both applications were successful and by the early summer of 1939 he was able to travel to Austria with a British passport. In Austria, together with his sister Gretl and his brother Paul (who, by this time, were both American citizens), Wittgenstein negotiated a deal with the Nazis whereby, in return for a vast amount of gold, the sisters who had decided to remain in Austria, Hermine and Helena, were accepted as being of mixed race rather than Jewish. They were thus able to survive the war.

Wittgenstein, meanwhile, returned to Cambridge, where he lived for a year with his former student and now lover, Francis Skinner. In the summer of 1938, he submitted the typescript he had prepared in Norway to Cambridge University Press, who were only too pleased to accept it. Soon afterwards, however, Wittgenstein had second thoughts and withdrew it. In February 1939, he was chosen to be Moore's successor as Cambridge's Professor of Philosophy, which, he wrote to an old friend from Manchester, "is very flattering & all that, but it might have been very much better for me to have got a job opening and closing gates" (Monk, 1990, p. 415).

During the war, Wittgenstein worked first as a porter at Guy's Hospital in London and then as a technician for a medical research unit based in Newcastle. Soon after starting at Guy's, he lost the person he cared most about, when Francis Skinner died of polio. Though he was glad to be given the opportunity to do work related to the war, Wittgenstein continued to think about the publication of his book. In 1943, he approached Cambridge University Press again, this time with the suggestion that they publish his new work alongside the *Tractatus*. In January 1944, the Press agreed to this plan, and the following month Wittgenstein left Newcastle for Swansea, where his student and disciple Rush Rhees lived and where Wittgenstein hoped to finish his book before resuming his professorial duties at Cambridge.

When, however, in October 1944, the time came to return, the book was still not finished. A few months later, Wittgenstein wrote the final version of the book's preface, but he still did not deliver it to the Press.

At Cambridge, Wittgenstein found himself in a strange position. On the one hand (as Bertrand Russell discovered to his dismay on his own return to Cambridge in 1944), he was by far the most influential and admired philosopher among the younger generation of academic philosophers. On the other hand, he himself had grown increasingly contemptuous of academic philosophy. He did not even think of publishing his work in academic journals and avoided academic conferences. In the years immediately after the war, the tension between holding these attitudes and being a professor of philosophy at Cambridge became harder and harder to bear, and by 1947 he could bear it no longer and resigned his chair.

For two years after that, Wittgenstein lived in Ireland, first in County Wicklow, then in Connemara, where he was looked after by employees of the Drury family, and finally in Dublin, where he could be looked after by Drury himself. Though not particularly old (he was 60 in 1949), Wittgenstein was by this time beginning to feel old and becoming noticeably frail. He had abandoned any plan of seeing his book published in his lifetime. He continued to write philosophical remarks – about color, about the concept of certainty – but these were not directly related to the book that, one way or another, he had been working on since 1930. He named three friends as his literary executors – Elizabeth Anscombe, Rush Rhees, and Georg von Wright – and left to them the task of deciding which parts of his *Nachlass* should be published.

Toward the end of 1949, Wittgenstein was diagnosed with cancer of the prostate. Earlier that year, he had accepted an invitation from his friend and ex-student Norman Malcolm to visit Cornell University in upstate New York. When he fell ill, he was desperately worried that he might die on the wrong side of the Atlantic. "I don't want to die in America," he told Malcolm, "I am a European – I want to die in Europe" (WAM 77). When, back in England, he received the diagnosis of cancer, he immediately made plans to return to the city of his birth. "In Vienna," he told his sister Helene, "I hope to find peace" (Monk, 1990, p. 559). After a few months in Vienna, staying in his old room in the family home in the Alleegasse, he came back to England, where he lived as a guest, first of von Wright in Cambridge and then of Anscombe in Oxford. During this time, he prepared himself for death. In Oxford, Anscombe introduced him to the Dominican friar Father Conrad Pepler, with whom he discussed God and the soul. By the New Year of 1951, he needed constant medical attention. Horrified at the thought of dying in an English hospital, he moved into the Cambridge home of his doctor, Edward Bevan. It was there that, on 29 April 1951, Wittgenstein died. His last words were: "Tell them I've had a wonderful life" (WAM 81).

References

Hertz, H.R. ([1894] 1956). *The Principles of Mechanics presented in a new Form*. Trans. D.E. Jones and J.T. Walley. New York: Dover. (Original work published 1894.)

Monk, R. (1990). *Ludwig Wittgenstein: The Duty of Genius*. London: Jonathan Cape.

Waugh, A. (2008). *The House of Wittgenstein: A Family at War*. London: Bloomsbury.

von Wright, G.H. (ed.). (1990). *A Portrait of Wittgenstein as a Young Man. From the Diary of David Hume Pinsent*. Oxford: Basil Blackwell.

Further Reading

McGuinness, B. (1988). *Wittgenstein: A Life (Vol. 1): Young Ludwig 1889–1921*. London: Duckworth.

McGuinness, B. (Ed.) (1995/2008). *Wittgenstein in Cambridge: Letters and Documents 1911–1951*. Fourth edition. Oxford: Blackwell.

Redpath, T. (1990). *Ludwig Wittgenstein: A Student's Memoir*. London: Duckworth.

Wittgenstein, L. (1961/1979). *Notebooks 1914–16*. Ed. G.E.M. Anscombe and G.H. von Wright. Trans. G.E.M. Anscombe. Second edition. Oxford: Blackwell.

Wittgenstein, L. (1977/1998). *Culture and Value: A Selection from the Posthumous Remains*. Ed. G.H. von Wright in collaboration with H. Nyman. Revised edition of the text by A. Pichler. Trans. P. Winch. Oxford: Blackwell.

Part I

Introductory

1

Wittgenstein's Philosophical Development

WOLFGANG KIENZLER

There are two good reasons why Wittgenstein's development is a philosophically intriguing problem as well as a complex and intricate matter.

The first reason is that Wittgenstein wrote the *Tractatus* and the *Philosophical Investigations*, two philosophical classics and two very different books. Ever since the publication of the *Investigations* their mutual relation has been a matter of debate.

The second reason is that during the decades since Wittgenstein's death a wealth of material has been published from his papers, including several books as well as nearly complete electronic editions of his manuscripts and his correspondence. These books do not constitute independent treatises on various topics or questions; to a large degree they contain variations, preparatory material, or continuations of things Wittgenstein expounded in his *Investigations* or in the *Tractatus*.

The question about Wittgenstein's development could therefore be phrased thus: how does all this material connect and make sense, and how can we best understand "Wittgenstein's progress?" (assuming that he was indeed progressing).

Early introductions to his philosophy established a simple two-part scheme, still in widespread use today, sometimes labeled "Wittgenstein I" and "Wittgenstein II" (Pitcher, 1964; Fann, 1969; Pears, 1971; Biletzky and Matar, 2014). The first more detailed presentation, proceeding publication by publication, can be found in Kenny (1973). On the whole this abundance of material has deterred scholars from attempting manuscript-based interpretations of Wittgenstein's philosophy in its entirety. In the meantime, the topic of the early and the later Wittgenstein surfaces even in quite popular treatments of his philosophy (e.g., Hankinson, 1999).

Many authors writing on him have focused either on the early or on the later Wittgenstein. It is fairly easy to dismiss the *Tractatus* as less important if one believes the *Investigations* to be his one true masterwork (see for instance Hacker, 1996), and one can also find the *Investigations* of less interest if one believes that symbolic logic is the modern philosopher's indispensable tool (Russell). There exists, however, a tradition of "hardcore Wittgensteinians" opposing the division into Wittgenstein I and Wittgenstein II on account of strong underlying continuities. This line started with Anscombe (1959), Rhees (1970), Winch (1969), and Mounce (1981), with more recent contributions

---

A Companion to Wittgenstein, First Edition. Edited by Hans-Johann Glock and John Hyman.
© 2017 John Wiley & Sons, Ltd. Published 2017 by John Wiley & Sons, Ltd.

from Diamond (1991), who took her start into Wittgenstein through editing his 1939 *Lectures on the Foundations of Mathematics*, and Conant (2012). Reading the *Tractatus* with the later developments in mind, one can easily fall into the trap of reading too much of the later Wittgenstein into his early work – yet doing so can also sharpen one's understanding of the ways in which those later ideas developed from his earlier ones.

This first chapter discusses some general features of Wittgenstein's work, then gives an overview of his early writings, and finally surveys his philosophical activities after 1929 (his "development" in the more specific sense of the term).

The evidence collected will suggest that there is quite substantial continuity, but also one major turning point in Wittgenstein's way of handling philosophical questions. This turning point took place around 1931–1932, as will be explained in Section 4 below.

1 Some Basic Features of Wittgenstein's Work

Some of the features of Wittgenstein's way of doing philosophy hardly changed over time. These include:

(1) Wittgenstein did not write philosophical books – he wanted to write *the* philosophical book. His ambition was to settle the matter of philosophy once and for all. In his view, the proper study of philosophy was mainly philosophy itself. His first paper on record was a four-minute piece entitled "What is Philosophy?" It was delivered in late 1912 to the Moral Sciences Club in Cambridge, defining philosophy as "all those primitive propositions which are assumed without proof by the various sciences." His last lecture, given to the same club in 1946, was again simply on "Philosophy" (McGuinness, 2008, pp. 35, 404; PPO 332, 338–9).

Once we have gained clarity about the nature of philosophy we will have the key to treat all particular questions – and Wittgenstein was only interested in giving the master key: most of the remaining work he would happily leave for others to do. It was only during his later career that he decided that there could not be one single key after all, but that all he could do was to give examples of his way of treating philosophical questions. He thus found it worthwhile to conduct some extended investigations into the nature of meaning and understanding, the foundations of mathematics, and the maze of psychological concepts. About some of his unwanted followers he remarked in 1949: "They show you a bunch of stolen keys, but they can't use them to open any door" (MS 138, p. 17a).

Therefore, excepting the first two years, when he asked: "What is logic?," his prime question and topic was "What is philosophy?" For this reason, the titles of his books and book projects all sound very general and quite similar: *Philosophical Remarks*, *Philosophical Grammar*, and the like. Wittgenstein was convinced that nobody had given an adequate answer to this question, and that it was his job to work one out. This overarching aim gives his work a high degree of unity – but also sometimes an appearance of amorphousness, as everything is very much intertwined and cannot be separated neatly into different topics discussed or questions raised and answered (as already Frege complained about in a letter to Wittgenstein dated 28 June 1919).

(2) The second feature is closely related to the first: the basic unit of Wittgenstein's work is not the book, nor the scholarly article, but rather what he called a "remark." This is usually a self-standing, compressed paragraph intended to illuminate one aspect

of a philosophical problem. It may take on the form of a short aphorism but it can also extend up to a page and a half. This has been compared to the work of an artist or a poet, and again and again Wittgenstein tried to sum up highly complex matters into one short paragraph. He liked to speak of the liberating, "spell-breaking word" (*das erlösende Wort*) and kept on searching for it (BT 409; PO 164).

(3) When writing philosophy, Wittgenstein would first write down a large number of such remarks, and then he would try to arrange these remarks into a larger whole, eventually into a book. He intended his book to be the best possible *arrangement* of all his good remarks. He did, for a while at least, regard the *Tractatus* as such a book, but he was never completely satisfied with the *Investigations* and did not publish them himself.

(4) Wittgenstein was a perfectionist. On every issue he aimed at just the right way of expressing it – and here his style makes it at the same time easy and hard for academic, as well as nonacademic, readers. Both of Wittgenstein's books are written in a concise, terse style, with many striking metaphors and comparisons, and this has made them appealing to a wide range of readers. However, academic interpreters have wildly disagreed about why he says what he says. In the course of composition he pruned away so much that to most readers the result seemed quite hermetic. Many have admired his style but have at the same time complained that they cannot make out what he is "really driving at" (see Chapter 2, WITTGENSTEIN'S TEXTS AND STYLE).

This way of writing philosophy resulted in many different versions of the same, or almost the same material, and many of the books posthumously published under his name are very similar in subject matter, and even contain a large amount of verbatim repetitions.

(5) Wittgenstein took great care of his manuscripts. He knew that they were valuable and he cared about what became of them. In 1917, and again in 1938, he had the most important ones stored in safe places (McGuinness, 2008, p. 266). Although, or because, he never had a permanent residence, he repeatedly reread and sifted his manuscripts. His care about his manuscript volumes shows some similarity to Heidegger, whose *Nachlass* has become the source of an even greater output of publications. To Wittgenstein, the process of developing his philosophical thoughts mattered almost as much as the final result. The overall structure of his *Nachlass* is, by comparison, very orderly and the most striking overall feature of his work is the ongoing *transformation* of his thought. His later thought is thoroughly shaped by responding to his earlier thought. Wittgenstein may not have cared much for the history of philosophy as others have written it, and he is not known to have read any contemporary philosopher, but he continuously read, rewrote, commented on, and copied his own manuscripts. This also makes for a high degree of continuity in his work.

(6) Wittgenstein's views about the general nature and aim of philosophy hardly changed (see Chapter 13, PHILOSOPHY AND PHILOSOPHICAL METHOD). To him philosophy was definitely not one of the sciences, but neither was it to consist of "transcendental twaddle" (Letter to Engelmann, 18 January 1918). Philosophy had to start from considerations of language, and especially the language it was to be expressed in, otherwise it would be quite hopeless. In this sense, Wittgenstein always practiced the linguistic turn and advocated the liberation from the entanglement of our thinking within the loops of language. Already when he wrote the *Tractatus* he referred to Hertz and his clarificatory work on the concept of "force" as a paradigm of philosophical work.

In 1933–1934 (BT 421; BB 26), 1939, and late 1946 he still referred to Hertz when explaining his own notion of philosophy (PPO 379, 399). The 1945 typescript of the *Investigations*' preface carries a motto from Hertz:

> When these painful contradictions are removed, the question as to the nature of force will still not have been answered, but the mind, no longer tortured, will cease to ask the illegitimate question. (See Chapter 6, WITTGENSTEIN, HERTZ, AND BOLTZMANN)

This was eventually replaced by the motto from Nestroy about progress always looking much larger than it really is. This too, emphasizes the continuity in Wittgenstein's work. In addition, the Nestroy motto can be seen to echo the Kürnberger motto to the *Tractatus* (both are from Austrian nineteenth-century writers). Although he mostly lived in an English-speaking philosophical environment, Wittgenstein remained an author writing in his own style of German. These features set Wittgenstein aside from all other philosophical writers.

In 1941 Wittgenstein said the following in conversation:

> It's like this. If you find your way out of a wood you may think that it is the only way out. Then you find another way out. But you might never have found it unless you had gone along the other way first. I should not be where I am now if I had not passed through what is expressed in the *Tractatus*. (PPO 387)

2 The Early Work

Coming from an engineering background, Wittgenstein entered philosophy through reading and meeting Frege and Russell around 1911. Frege had invented modern symbolic logic in 1879; Russell had just co-authored and published the first volume of his monumental *Principia Mathematica*, and was becoming widely regarded as the leading proponent of modern logic-based philosophy. (Without Russell's intervention the *Tractatus* might never have been published.) While Frege had invented modern logic in order to prove "logicism," i.e., the claim that arithmetic is a branch of logic, Russell had intended to set up a logic-based system that would put all our knowledge on a secure (preferably *absolutely* secure) foundation. In pursuit of these extra-logical objectives both had written rather voluminous books. Wittgenstein was impressed by both, but quite from the start his interest took another turn. He wanted to know: what is the *nature of logic itself*? If logic was to be the foundation: what kind of foundation was it? Wittgenstein had moved to Cambridge to study with Russell and wanted to clarify this in a short book.

In 1913 he composed his first few pages of philosophical text (from notebooks now lost), written down in collaboration with Russell and a typist, later called *Notes on Logic*. The *Notes* start from the idea that the logical connectives, like negation in "~p," or conjunction in "p.q," can only be applied to propositions that are already complete. He thus separated the propositions and their content from all specifically logical vocabulary. This means that the connectives, the "logical constants" could not contribute to the content or meaning of propositions. There cannot be "logical objects" corresponding to the logical vocabulary. Therefore logic is not *about* anything; it is not informative and it is no science (NL 107; see Chapter 17, LOGIC AND THE *TRACTATUS*).

The *Notes* conclude that purely logical propositions must be of an altogether *different* nature from ordinary, informative propositions. This at once put the projects of Frege and Russell in severe doubt, since both wanted to start from logic and advance as far as they could. But this could only work if the propositions used were all of basically the same kind – they should express and secure *knowledge*. Only then could they serve as the foundation of other knowledge.

After this discovery, Wittgenstein was convinced that neither Russell nor Frege had understood the "nature of the proposition." Propositions are essentially bipolar, they can be true or false, and they must *retain* this bipolarity. Only that which could conceivably be false could possibly be true.

This also means that a proposition and its negation must have the same content. Negation simply *reverses* the sense of the original proposition, but it does not alter it. Neither negation nor other logical vocabulary can therefore be part of the sense of a proposition.

Logic could thus not generate any sense but must presuppose it. This put the notion of *sense*, as it had been introduced by Frege, at the center of Wittgenstein's inquiries.

Wittgenstein also found that Frege had, in order to make his logical system more versatile, re-assimilated propositions to names by introducing "truth values," now regarding propositions as "names of truth values." This had distorted Frege's original conception of the sense of a proposition as it committed him to the claim that a proposition and its negation would designate different objects, and hence that they could not have the same sense. Frege had downplayed this because he was only interested in the true propositions of his system.

Wittgenstein also found that Russell had no clear conception of sense at all and could not distinguish between a false and a nonsensical proposition. Russell believed that every proposition claims that at least two items stand in some relation to each other, thus forming a complex of items ("A stands to B in the relation L: 'A loves B'"). If such a complex really exists, the proposition will be true; if it does not exist, it will be false. But it may just as well be nonsensical. Russell showed the same attitude in his analysis of "The present king of France is bald." According to Russell this sentence *must* be either true or false, and he analyzed it as false.

In 1914 Wittgenstein dictated some new results to G.E. Moore. These *Notes Dictated to Moore* introduce Wittgenstein's fundamental distinction between saying and showing. Wittgenstein believed that now he could explain the difference between ordinary and logical propositions. The notes commence: "Logical so-called propositions *show* [the] logical properties of language and therefore of [the] Universe, but *say* nothing" (NM 109). Ordinary propositions *say* something and they claim that what they say is true. We then have to check if what they say (the *sense* of the proposition) is actually true. With logical propositions, however, "by merely looking at them you can *see* these properties" (NM 109). This means that for ordinary propositions we must distinguish their sense from their being true or false – we understand them *without* knowing whether they are true or false. With logical propositions it is different. From looking at the structure of the proposition itself we can determine whether it is logically true (tautological) or false (contradictory). Therefore logical propositions are "true" and "false" in a different sense of these terms. Wittgenstein would go on to find that everything essential – and this amounts to everything philosophical – can at best be shown, but never said.

During World War I, Wittgenstein served in the Austrian Army, all the while continuing his philosophical work. Some of his wartime notebooks have been preserved.

They show how he tried to elaborate his basic ideas into a systematic whole. In particular, he came upon the idea that ordinary propositions are like models or pictures. In a picture one can transmit claims about how things look like, but no picture can prove its own truthfulness (see Chapter 8, THE PICTURE THEORY). This finally gave him an explanation of ordinary propositions.

Wittgenstein then tried to find the systematic unity of all propositions, the "general form of the proposition." He was convinced that this must exist and that it should be capable of fairly easy expression. In 1916 he wrote: "It must be possible to set up the general form of the proposition because the possible forms of propositions must be a priori" (NB 21.11.16). He also concluded that his results were close to encompassing not just logic but quite literally everything.

In late 1915 Wittgenstein started a large volume containing the "Prototractatus," an early version of his book (MS 104). In it he introduces his seven main propositions, including the "general form of the proposition." Wittgenstein wrote down the bulk of his remarks, taken from other sources, and only then arranged them by giving them numbers, partially changing and rearranging them in the process. The volume shows that (and how) Wittgenstein did not write but rather *arranged* his first book, and the facsimile reproduction shows how hard he worked on every detail of it. The volume contained an introductory note that "all the good propositions from my other manuscripts" should be assembled between the major propositions of his work (PT 41). He would work in a similar spirit again after 1929.

In 1918 Wittgenstein was able to complete his investigations and to arrange all of his material into his *Logisch-Philosophische Abhandlung*, as he preferred to call it. It was first published as a book in an English–German parallel edition in 1922. On this occasion Moore suggested the title *Tractatus Logico-Philosophicus* and Wittgenstein accepted it, after rejecting the first suggestion "Philosophical Logic." The book consists of 526 individually numbered remarks, ordered around seven main propositions. In this book Wittgenstein expanded his logical investigations into a general view on the "logic of language." He believed that, at bottom, philosophy and logic were very simple and crystal clear. He underlined this conviction by selecting a motto stating that "everything can be said in three words." While everyday language seems very complicated, the basic "logic of language" ought to be very simple. This, however, is only possible if we apply logical analysis and reduce the apparent surface complexity to the underlying simplicity of fundamental elements. After analysis every proposition would be self-explaining. Every meaningful proposition would be a picture of some simple state of affairs, claiming it to be the case. All meaningful propositions could then be described as made up from such elementary propositions, and each of the latter would be a "logical picture" of something that "is the case." The set of all meaningful propositions (true or false) can then be described through a general scheme of operations: the "general form of the proposition." Apart from the propositions describing states of affairs, the book explains how logical propositions are tautologies or contradictions ("senseless"), while philosophical propositions are elucidations rather than pictures of anything ("nonsensical"). Ethics and aesthetics deal with values, which cannot be expressed in meaningful propositions, but only in an attitude toward the world. The systematic structure of the book seems to climax in the general form of the proposition, encompassing in one formula "everything that can be said." Putting it in more concrete terms, the book explains some basic differences between various types of propositions or proposition-like structures. Besides those already mentioned, Wittgenstein discusses identity statements, definitions, belief sentences, mathematical equations, laws of nature, and statements of probability. Taken together this constitutes a series of (extremely short) chapters on logical syntax, or grammar, as Wittgenstein would say later. Philosophy thus comes out as the activity of making the differences between these types of propositions as clear as possible. In the end, we will be able to find our way about language and thus will "see the world aright," as the penultimate remark of the book says.

While the wartime notebooks, especially those from 1916, contain quite extensive passages on ethical matters, the *Tractatus* is very brief in this regard. Wittgenstein once remarked that for ethical reasons one should be silent about ethics. He also said that his book had an "ethical point," and that it had two parts, of which he had left the more important ethical part unwritten. In 1929, on the occasion of his sole "popular" lecture, "A Lecture on Ethics," he explained his views on ethics in more detail. No amount of facts can have any ethical import, he claimed, because value is something extra, not an additional fact. This extra cannot be expressed in meaningful propositions and therefore we have to use comparisons that are, strictly speaking, nonsensical – e.g., "I feel perfectly safe," "I wonder at the existence of the world." "A Lecture on Ethics" seems very much inspired by Kierkegaard's writings about the "paradox": "It is the paradox that an experience, a fact, should have supernatural value" (LE 10; PO 43). In the end, it is the attitude toward the world and life that counts, independently of all facts. The lecture still has the early Wittgenstein speaking.

From 1919 until 1928 Wittgenstein retired from philosophical research. All he did was explain his *Tractatus* to his friend, Russell (in 1919), to the editor of his book, Ogden (in 1921), and to his translator, Ramsey (in 1923; with an extra note in 1927). Professionally, he worked first as a primary schoolteacher, during which time he edited a *Dictionary for Elementary Schools* (1926). The entries of the *Dictionary* were arranged alphabetically, but in some cases Wittgenstein permitted exceptions when he believed that this would help his schoolchildren find a word more easily. From 1926 to 1928 he worked as an architect, collaborating with Paul Engelmann, who had worked with Loos, building a house for his sister. This presented Wittgenstein with the opportunity to combine his aesthetic sensibility and his perfectionism. (On the related question of Wittgenstein's later acknowledgment of Loos's influence on his philosophy, see Hyman, 2016.) The stamp they used for the documents reads: "Paul Engelmann – Ludwig Wittgenstein. Architects" (Wijdeveld, 1993, p. 36). Beginning in 1927, Wittgenstein spoke to members of the Vienna Circle about the *Tractatus*. Eventually, this drew him back into philosophy.

3   Thinking about Wittgenstein's Development

There has been some debate about when to date the change from the early to the later Wittgenstein. In chronological order, the following choices have been offered. (1) Early 1929, the return to philosophical work, the new start. (2) Late 1929, when he abandoned the search for a "phenomenological language" and decided that all he had to investigate was the grammar of ordinary language. (3) Somewhere between 1929 and 1932, when he wrote the first 10 philosophical manuscript volumes; or in 1933, when he prepared the *Big Typescript*, which almost looks like a book and contains much material later used in the *Investigations*. (4) In 1934, when he introduced language-games in the "Blue Book." (5) In 1936–1937, when he wrote the first portion of the

Investigations, which is quite close to its eventual form. (6) There also have been proposals for just one Wittgenstein who never changed all that much, as well as for several Wittgensteins, such as the early (TLP), the middle (PR and BT), and the late (PI) – sometimes complemented by a very late Wittgenstein after 1945 (OC), or an early middle (PR) and a late middle Wittgenstein (BT). It appears, however, that these several Wittgensteins have been introduced mainly in order to mark off research fields more conveniently.

Very often the criteria for drawing these distinctions are not stated very clearly. When they are, the picture becomes much clearer and the motivations for controversy diminish. Below are the different results concerning the development of Wittgenstein's work according to the different criteria applied (where (0) and (4*) indicate ways of refusing the introduction of clear distinctions):

(0) The *One-Wittgenstein View* insists that actually there is too much continuity in his thought and work to divide Wittgenstein into two distinct portions, early and late. As already explained, there is a lot to be said in favor of this view, especially when Wittgenstein is compared to other philosophers, contemporaries or not. He stands out and it is hard to find anybody working in a similar way. It is also true that the particular features of his earlier *and* later work can be appreciated much better if taken together and if held against the backdrop of his philosophical personality and his general character. Regarding the wealth of material and information that has come to light it seems equally indisputable, however, that Wittgenstein underwent some substantial developments during his career. Thus, a "moderate" One-Wittgenstein View that doesn't ignore such changes may well agree with the varieties of distinctions to be explained shortly. It may be mentioned that a "not so moderate" One-Wittgenstein View, advocating some sort of stable unity in his work, seems to be especially popular with readers who emphasize Wittgenstein's personality and his ethical, aesthetical, and religious views. Yes, he always remained a severe person, contemplating his sins and shortcomings, taking religious matters very seriously, and he also remained a perfectionist in every detail of his writings, as well as a person whose tastes had been shaped for good by nineteenth-century Central European literature and music in particular; and he was always highly suspicious of modernity and of almost any form of progress. But from all this it does *not* follow that he did not develop philosophically.

(1) From his *biography* it seems obvious to attribute to the later Wittgenstein the time span from 1929 to 1951. However, this period might still be subdivided into the earlier period until 1935, when Wittgenstein, after his attempts at writing a book had seemingly failed, traveled to Russia with the firm intention to find a nonphilosophical job and stay there. The time after his second return to philosophy would then coincide with the actual work toward the *Investigations*.

(2) On *bibliographical* grounds concerning *manuscripts*, it seems reasonable to consider all the material starting with MS 105 in February 1929 as belonging to the later Wittgenstein, especially when considering the numerous interconnections and rewritings.

(3) On other *bibliographical* grounds, the different *books* since published under Wittgenstein's name have made it seem natural to introduce a middle Wittgenstein who "wrote" *Philosophical Remarks* and the *Big Typescript* as well as *Philosophical Grammar*, and a very late Wittgenstein who wrote *Remarks on the Philosophy of Psychology*, *Remarks On Colour*, and *On Certainty*, not to mention the very early Wittgenstein up to the

Prototractatus. There are scholars specializing in just one or two of the four to six Wittgensteins thus distinguished. Middle Wittgenstein has even been honored with his own *Vienna Edition*. (One could call this the "Wittgenstein-Industry View.")

(4) From a more *philosophical* perspective it is tempting to look for differences of *doctrine*. In this way we can distinguish, e.g., Wittgenstein's early logical atomism, his middle theoretical holism, and his late practical holism (Stern, 1995). In another way, Wittgenstein can be viewed as moving from an essentialist to an anti-essentialist position. While the early Wittgenstein tried to define the essence of language by finding the crystalline logical form of *any* possible language, the later Wittgenstein contented himself with describing "family resemblances" within the varieties of *our* language (see Chapter 25, VAGUENESS AND FAMILY RESEMBLANCE).

These differences can also be framed in various other ways. However, all can be contested. For Wittgenstein strongly emphasized that he found philosophy primarily not a matter of doctrine but rather a matter of method and approach. But then again it is not so easy to separate "doctrine" from "method" in Wittgenstein's work – as can be seen in the debate concerning the question "Did Wittgenstein follow his own pronouncement that in philosophy there 'can be no theses'?" (see e.g., PI §128; cf. Glock, 2007).

(4*) Some interpreters who argue that Wittgenstein (early and late) considered it a mistake to have *any* doctrine in philosophy but who still want to bring out the difference between both, have claimed that the early Wittgenstein held some metaphysical views *without meaning to* (e.g., about philosophy necessarily having to be simple) while only the later Wittgenstein resolutely abstained from any doctrine. Such a suggestion brings in the difference between Wittgenstein claiming to have certain views in theory and his actually practicing a certain approach. Wittgenstein himself supported such a view by repeatedly stating that he really should have done philosophy as "pure description" and "without putting forward any claim," but fell short of his own standard (WVC 183). He also liked to repeat certain slogans with only slight modifications: for instance, "Logic/ Language/ Grammar – must take care of itself" (TLP 5.473/PG 40), or "Process and result are equivalent'" (TLP 6.1262/RFM I §82).

Things get even more complicated if readings attribute to him the idea that the apparent claims of the early Wittgenstein are really to be understood as targets of his later criticisms. Such an ironic, two-layered reading of the *Tractatus* seems, however, hardly compatible with his motto about "saying everything in three words" (Kienzler, 2012).

(5) Another criterion could be a distinction regarding Wittgenstein's *method*. Thus we could have the early Wittgenstein advocating logical analysis, the middle Wittgenstein using the method of tabulating rules of philosophical grammar, and the late Wittgenstein developing his views mainly by the method of describing language-games. A variant of this idea contrasts the early Wittgenstein, who believed in one method (methodological monism), with the later Wittgenstein who advocated the use of several methods in philosophy (methodological pluralism). Sometimes this pluralism is extended into a form of Pyrrhonism where all methods (sometimes called "voices") are balanced out so that no answer to any question is reached and philosophy can end peacefully (Fogelin, 1987; Stern, 2006). It is, however, by no means obvious that Wittgenstein believed that he followed a method, or applied two (or more) methods. His use of the word "method" remains quite informal throughout (see BT 414–21, 431–2; PI §§48, 133).

(6) From a philosophical point of view, the most "Wittgensteinian" way to distinguish periods in his work would be to check when he changed his overall *style* of doing philosophy, of handling philosophical problems. To him, doctrine, if considered important at all, *followed* from the general approach. As will be seen, it is quite obvious and well documented that there is just one such major change of general style in his career, and that this change occurred gradually but definitely around 1931–1932. This is his move away from a variety of "dogmatisms." As the way Wittgenstein wrote down his remarks changed little between 1930 and 1950, questions concerning the particular style of his projected book are, by comparison, of lesser importance.

(7) There is another important element in Wittgenstein's writing, namely his quest to find the perfect *expression* for his way of doing philosophy. From 1932 until 1937 he worked especially intensely on this problem, and he rejected several versions of a reworking of the *Big Typescript* before he found the form of what was later to become the *Investigations*. Considering the importance of style for Wittgenstein, some commentators have argued that everything intermediate is just "unfinished business" and that the later Wittgenstein can only be the author of a finished work, such as the *Investigations* (Schulte, 1987). To many readers this book almost palpably stands out, not just from other philosophical books, but also from everything else Wittgenstein wrote.

If we follow this line of reasoning all the way, however, we find that, strictly speaking, there *never* was a later Wittgenstein. For he continued to introduce changes into the *Investigations* until the very end of his life, including a change of motto. Not only did he not publish his second book in his lifetime, he did not finish it either.

(8) Finally one might try to admit Wittgenstein's own testimony on this issue. In 1931 he drew up a list of people who influenced him (CV 41). This list names Hertz, Frege, Russell, and Spengler and it ends with Ramsey and Sraffa, both of whom are mentioned in the preface to the *Investigations*. There is no obvious later addition to this list. In the same year, he voiced his critique of dogmatism, to be discussed below. In addition, many of the best-known remarks about the nature of philosophy were first written down in 1931–1932. He even seems to have compared himself to Copernicus and Darwin during this time (MS 112, p. 233/CV 55). It is also around this time that Wittgenstein, who earlier had simply dismissed the history of philosophy as meaningless, starts to consider the way philosophical misconceptions, including his own, arise from pre-theoretical, seemingly everyday platitudes. He uses passages from Plato, Augustine, and his own *Tractatus* to illustrate and trace these sources. Around this time he even considers beginning his projected book with some material from Frazer's *Golden Bough* (PO 116-19; on Wittgenstein on Frazer see Chapter 41, WITTGENSTEIN AND ANTHROPOLOGY). He becomes interested in retracing the steps that lead into dead alleys that are then mistaken for "philosophical problems." The most famous of these retracings deals with the genesis of the kind of super-skepticism Kripke later located in the *Investigations* and attributed to Wittgenstein.

Wittgenstein's commentaries on later stages of his work mostly concern his problems in finding the right way to fit all of these aspects and the best of his remarks into one book. In April 1932, even before he started to assemble the *Big Typescript*, he wrote: "I'm growing more and more doubtful as to the publication of my own work, that is, of what I've been writing in the last 3 or 4 years" (Letter to Watson, 8 April 1932).

These problems of finding the right expression for his thoughts within the scope of a book also led to the plan that Friedrich Waismann should write a book that would explain Wittgenstein's philosophy. This book was first announced in 1929, and the letter just quoted also mentions the project. Wittgenstein abandoned his part in it only around 1936, and for nonphilosophical reasons. Such a project would not have made sense with somebody like Russell, who was liable to change his philosophical views at short intervals.

None of Wittgenstein's commentaries on his own development mention more than one major change in his philosophical outlook. Wittgenstein changed his book-plans several times, and he often despaired over them, but after 1931 he remained very single-minded about his way of thinking.

There are, of course, many features in Wittgenstein's work that changed over time, such as changes between language, mathematics, or psychology as the main surface topic. There also are some late manuscripts, those published as *On Colour* and most famously *On Certainty*, which can be regarded as belonging to a very late Wittgenstein. There he investigates particular language-games concerning color and certainty along the lines of his basic approach to doing philosophy and they will therefore not be considered here.

4   The Transformation

When Wittgenstein returned to philosophy he mainly worked on two projects. First, he tried to explain his *Tractatus* to members of the Vienna Circle. Second, he slowly began to return to active philosophical work. At first he considered the need to expand on some of the issues he had thought to be irrelevant while writing the *Tractatus*.

Looking back on his path in late 1931, Wittgenstein explained that the worst fault in his *Tractatus* had been some sort of "dogmatism" (WVC 182). This was the notion that it was philosophy's task to lay down that which is necessarily so, to put down the requirements for signs to be used as language. The second aspect of this "dogmatism" was the idea that all that cannot be decided in advance can be left to others to worry about. Wittgenstein had stated in the preface to the *Tractatus* that all problems had, "in essentials," been solved. In 1929, Wittgenstein returned to a question he had put aside in the *Tractatus*, namely what are the elementary propositions? His first try was a language that would immediately describe visual experience. It would have to be a "phenomenological language" that was modeled on the logical form of experience itself. This project, however, did not proceed very far, as Wittgenstein soon came to realize that in trying to get closer to the visual phenomena themselves he would have to abandon all use of ordinary language. In the end he would not be able to say more than: "This!" He concluded that the phenomena would not speak for themselves, but that he had to learn how our everyday language works when we are describing visual and other phenomena. This opens the study of grammar, i.e., the grammar of our language, not grammar as deduced from logical syntax. This 1929 change to the study of ordinary language has been taken to be the decisive turn towards the later Wittgenstein (Hintikka and Hintikka, 1986). The first typescript collecting his results in 1930 starts with the observation:

> A proposition is completely logically analyzed if its grammar is laid out completely clearly. It might be written down or spoken in any number of ways.
>
>   The phenomenological or 'primary' language, as I called it, is no longer my aim; I don't hold it to be necessary. All that is possible and necessary is to separate the essential of *our* language from its inessential elements. (PR §1; see also BT 417/PO 177)

Another problem arose from the idea that elementary propositions are like semantic atoms (see Chapter 7, LOGICAL ATOMISM). In 1929 Wittgenstein still believed that our analysis *must* come to the point where we find such propositions, or else we would be "destroying the propositional form as such" (RLF 162/PO 29). The paradigm for this is the way we use variables p, q, r, and the like in elementary logic to stand for propositions that can take on truth values independently of each other. This leads to the much-discussed "color exclusion problem". If "a is red" is an elementary proposition, it must not exclude any other elementary proposition such as "a is green." In the *Tractatus*, and even his earlier *Notebooks*, Wittgenstein had already discussed this problem and decided that because we feel that there *is* a contradiction, "a is red" cannot be an elementary proposition (TLP 6.3751). But if "a is red" is not an elementary proposition, what else could possibly be one? In discussing the exclusion problem, he had at first argued: "Two elementary propositions *indeed* cannot contradict each other!" (MS 105, p. 26). The investigation of the "logic of color" led him to consider *systems* of propositions: if A is red, then it cannot be green, blue, brown, and so on (see PR §§76–85). In the end, Wittgenstein concluded: "The notion of an elementary proposition loses its earlier importance" (PR §83). In 1931 he reworked his remark about color exclusion and also found that the statement "There can be only *one* colour in *one* place at the same time" has nothing to do with a logical contradiction in the technical sense; rather, "It is a proposition of our grammar. Negating it yields no contradiction, but it contradicts a rule of the grammar we have adopted" (MS 112, p. 251/BT 477). We don't have to *infer* how anything *must* be; we just have to describe grammar as it *is* now before our eyes (see Chapter 34, WITTGENSTEIN ON COLOR).

Wittgenstein slowly found that he had been asking the wrong kind of question. His aim changed from deducing logical syntax to a description of the *grammar* of our language. Grammar describes the forms of language we use. In this sense, grammar will be *shown* in the way language is used, while language is used to *say* things about the world. For a while he called this "the limit of the world" (see the late allusions to this idea in PI §133). In describing grammar we have to describe what we are presupposing as soon as we speak – we cannot separate ourselves from this "object." While earlier Wittgenstein had found the first-person singular, the ego, to be the limit of the world, now he finds that grammar shapes everything we can express.

In 1930 Wittgenstein assembled his first typescript from his notes, but there are no indications that he considered it for publication.

Wittgenstein went on to transform his entire work. The hardest change was to shake off the urge to be "dogmatic". It had always seemed natural that philosophy was to describe the "essence of the world," or at least "the essence of language," but now he needed to prepare himself to take language (and grammar) as it is.

In 1931–1932 Wittgenstein illustrated this change of direction in a series of examples. He took his own 1929–1930 remarks and went over them. For example, one of them reads: "In a certain sense an object cannot be described, i.e. the description must not attribute any properties to it, the lack of which would annihilate its existence" (MS 105, p. 13). Wittgenstein now quotes the first half and adds: "Here 'object' means 'reference of a non-definable word' and 'description' or 'explanation' really: definition" (MS 111, p. 31/TS 214, p.14/PG 208). He collects the criticisms of his earlier ways of speaking of "complex" and "fact" as well as "object" in an extra typescript (TS 214), appended to the *Big Typescript*.

Wittgenstein concludes that he had been misled by his own analysis of logical forms into believing that there must be simple objects, which cannot, because of their simplicity, be described. He also notices that he could have taken this step away from atomism already in the *Tractatus*; there he had remarked that "a coloured body is in a colour-space" (PR §83; see TLP 2.0251). In his first book, however, he had disregarded this insight, as he wanted to have it purely analytic and logical all the way. Now he returns to his initial observation.

In a similar way he moves away from his picture theory, and contemplates how propositions can be compared to pictures. Now he is also more careful to describe the use of sentences – items that can be written on a board – while the word "propositions" is liable to oscillate between "thoughts," "logical pictures," and plain sentences.

Thus, Wittgenstein moves away from transcendental arguments like this one: "Because language works, and because language can only work on the condition S, therefore condition S *must* be fulfilled." Thus, he moves from a Kantian toward a Humean attitude, that is toward *describing* what we find people doing and saying. In another sense, however, he moves closer to Kant, as he recognizes something that might be called "synthetic a priori"– except that he feels it would be wrong to speak of "knowledge" in this connection (see Chapter 21, NECESSITY AND APRIORITY and Chapter 14, GRAMMAR AND GRAMMATICAL STATEMENTS). Grammar is not built on the principle of contradiction and this attitude can also be seen in his investigations into mathematics. There Wittgenstein points out again and again that mathematics does not simply proceed according to the principle of contradiction. But mathematics uses synthetic methods and part of it consists in inventing new conceptual connections ("The mathematician is an inventor, not a discoverer," RFM I §168).

There are some features that gained prominence in Wittgenstein's work only after 1932. This is especially true of the method to describe language-games and, closely connected, his "anthropological view," often attributed to the influence of Sraffa. While Wittgenstein worked out this way of presentation only later, the initial discussions with Sraffa had taken place earlier. This can be seen from some passages mentioning Sraffa from 1931–1932 (e.g., BT 242), and also from their correspondence (Letter to Sraffa, 31 January 1934). Although the famous incident when Sraffa asked Wittgenstein about the grammar (or possibly the logical form) of a Neapolitan gesture cannot be dated exactly (Engelmann, 2013, pp. 152–4), there is a response to Sraffa's point at BT 10 (handwritten addition). Furthermore, Wittgenstein had already in late 1931 accepted the possibility that there might not always be a definite grammar and definite rules: "Let's say: we investigate language for its rules. If here and there it does not have any, then *this* is the result of our enquiry" (MS 112, p. 190/BT 254).

Language-games, too, can already be found this early (BT 202), and even a list showing their wide variety (BT 162, handwritten addition; see also PI §23), although their extended use comes only later. On the other hand, Wittgenstein keeps speaking of "grammar" and he calls his investigations "grammatical remarks." The same holds for the notion of family resemblance as opposed to a precise definition of concepts (PG 75). The quotation from and reference to Augustine at the beginning of the *Investigations* can also be traced back to 1931 (MS 111, p. 15/BT 25–7/PG 56). The fact that this example acquired such prominent use only gradually marks no substantial change in Wittgenstein's philosophy. Remarks about the importance of a "perspicuous representation" also occur in 1931 (MS 110, p. 257/BT 417; see PI §122 and Chapter 16, SURVEYABILITY). Wittgenstein links this idea to Spengler (also mentioned on the 1931 list of influences; see above).

All these features first appear between 1930 and 1932, but just having them was not enough. Wittgenstein worked very hard to form a coherent and unified book from the mass of his resources, and this took him years to achieve. This work is mainly centered on the adequate *presentation* of his philosophy, not on its transformation. In his 1933 letter to *Mind* he states quite plainly:

> That which is retarding the publication of my work, the difficulty of presenting it in a clear and coherent form, a fortiori prevents me from stating my views within the space of a letter. (PO 167)

While the *Investigations* has become a classic, it is hard to imagine that any of the earlier versions might have reached quite the same status. When it comes to doing something with Wittgenstein, however, many readers are happier to deal with some of his earlier writings – unless they just tear some remarks out of context. Thus, especially the "Blue Book" has been very popular (more so than the "Brown Book"), and quite a few readers have found the more discursive and spread-out writings of the middle Wittgenstein more accessible and sometimes even more convincing than the pruned-down later versions. The earlier versions also help to identify the persons or positions Wittgenstein refers to, since he deleted most of these names in the process of revision. To some it seemed almost as if he wanted to cover up his traces. This situation has made it appear natural to explain the *Investigations* by adducing large amounts of earlier material through "passage-hunting" where his opinions seem easier to discern (Glock, 1990). Wittgenstein had considered this possibility himself: "I waste an inordinate amount of toil arranging my thoughts – and quite possibly to no avail" (CV 46).

Wittgenstein's major change can also briefly be described as follows. In the *Tractatus* his favorite words were "it is clear" and interjectives like "indeed" (*ja*), forcefully expressing the idea that anyone not blind *must* positively and clearly see things this way. In the *Investigations*, on the other hand, his favorite words are particles like "well" (*nun*), often followed by a long dash (a "thought-stroke," *Gedankenstrich*). They help to express hesitation in answering a question on the terms suggested by the question itself – often the hesitation before rejecting the question. Wittgenstein wants us to *slow down* – then we will all by ourselves refrain from advancing theses about how things must be – so that we can be more open to seeing things as they *are*. "Don't think [how it must be] – but look [how it is]" (PI §66) might be taken as his motto.

5   The Typescripts and Revisions

From 1929 to 1932 Wittgenstein wrote, with the help of many notebooks, 10 large manuscript volumes, numbered I to X (MSS 105–14). In 1930 he had a selection from volumes I–IV typed up in chronological order as TS 208. (A somewhat revised version, TS 209, was posthumously published as *Philosophical Remarks*.) In late 1930 he assembled TS 210 from the rest of volume IV. In 1931–1932 he dictated the bulk of material from volumes V–X into the 771 pages of TS 211. Again Wittgenstein planned to collect "all his good remarks" in one typescript. In order to achieve this he had earlier mined the first part of TS 208 and copied all that he still found useful into volumes V–X, usually revising the remarks – sometimes quite heavily, more often only slightly.

Then he took material from the second half of TS 208, from TS 210, and most of the remarks from TS 211 to form one big collection, TS 212. This collection consists of almost 2000 items, entire pages as well as cuttings of various sizes. Wittgenstein first sorted the material roughly according to catchwords that he arranged in alphabetical order, as Josef Rothhaupt (2010) has discovered. In the next step he wrote small slips with headings for 19 chapters and 140 sections and thus tried to organize all this material. From this he went on to dictate TS 213, the so-called *Big Typescript*, as well as five short appendices (TS 214–18). Because of its surface organization, it has sometimes been mistaken for a book, and has even been called Wittgenstein's third *Hauptwerk*. But the chapter headings were only intended to help him find his way around the huge amount of material and he would never have considered publishing it. While Wittgenstein was generous in giving titles, even to his manuscript volumes, he did not give a title to his "large typescript" (thence its name) – and there is neither a motto nor a preface nor a title page. The German–English version published in 2005 increases this bulkiness by including the handwritten changes and revisions along with the typewritten material. This is truly a "scholars' edition" of material still farther removed from an actual book.

In his 1938 preface Wittgenstein remarked that "four years ago" he had made a first attempt at writing his book in a fashion where "the thoughts should proceed from one subject to another in a natural, smooth sequence" (MS 225, p. 1/PI, Preface). This does not refer to the *Big Typescript*, but rather to his next step. In 1933–1934 he tried to rewrite the *Big Typescript* into one long continuous manuscript (MS 114–15), later published as *Philosophical Grammar*, but he eventually abandoned this attempt. (On the flyleaf of MS 115 he wrote in despair: "This book can be shortened – but it would be *very* difficult to do this in the right way.") In late 1933, while he was still working on this new version, Wittgenstein started to dictate to some of his students what would become his "Blue Book." This was done in English, and it was, by comparison, a very simple text explaining some of the basic features of his way of doing philosophy. It was *not* a serious alternative to his original book project. Rather, he intended to have some copies of these "lecture notes" made for the use of his students and friends to convey some preliminary idea of what he was doing. "I explain things to my pupils and then dictate to them short formulations of what we've been discussing and of the results" (Letter to Watson, 12 November 1933). The students had the idea that Wittgenstein felt some connection to his book project: "I understand Wittgenstein is in a snag with his book. It's thought these sessions with us are also by way of clarifying his own difficulties" (Ambrose to Stevenson, 1 January 1934, quoted in McGuinness, 2008, p. 219). In 1934–1935 he dictated his "Brown Book," which was not intended for any circulation but rather as a fresh start toward writing his book. Here he tried to arrange his thoughts in an orderly fashion by developing everything from the description of simple language-games that became increasingly more complex. Some more general comments were added in parenthesis. This already starts from the Augustine quotation and it shows many similarities with the arrangement of the *Investigations*. In October 1935 he expressed the intention to have "something publishable ready by the end of this academic year" (Letter to Watson, 19 October 1935). In August 1936 Wittgenstein tried to carry out this plan by producing a German version of the "Brown Book" (see MS 115, pp. 118–73; published in German as "*Eine Philosophische Betrachtung*," but not published in English). However, he abandoned this attempt fairly close to the end, expressing his dissatisfaction with the result. Later he explained that trying to follow his own text had made his thought "cramped" and that his new attempt seemed to be turning out "a little better."

Soon afterward Wittgenstein started anew. This time he wrote freely but he also used his older material from TS 213 and MSS 114–15. This resulted in MS 142, the first version of the *Investigations* up to §188. In 1937 he wrote a continuation on the philosophy of mathematics, and by August 1938 the typescript of the early version of the *Investigations*, including a preface and two parts, was finished (TSS 225, 220, 221; TS 221 is a close predecessor of RFM I). The preface explains that "four years ago" he had made a first attempt to organize his thoughts into one orderly book, but that the results were unsatisfactory, and that "several years later" he had become convinced that he had to abandon these attempts, in favor of just writing remarks (TS 225, p. 1). There is no hint that he had in the process changed much of the content that he wanted to express.

Wittgenstein also tried to produce an English translation of the first part, and he even approached a publisher. These plans came to nothing, and from 1938 until 1944 Wittgenstein wrote much new material on the philosophy of mathematics (much of it now published in RFM II–VII) and also worked to make Part I more complete. In several layers he prepared a revised early version (TS 239), an intermediate version of 300 remarks (using TS 243 in the process), and finally the late version of 693 remarks (TS 227). (All these versions are described and meticulously edited in Schulte's *Kritisch-genetische Edition* of Wittgenstein's later masterpiece (Schulte, 2001).)

In order to prepare this final version, Wittgenstein first collected the best of all his leftover remarks from 1929 to 1945, many of them from TS 213, in a new extra typescript (TS 228). These make up the majority of remarks in the final version of the *Investigations*. Thus in a certain sense the *Investigations* are a slimmed-down and more refined version of the *Big Typescript* material.

In early 1946 the typescript of the late version was finished. Wittgenstein felt that he had worked on the *Investigations*, at least from 1931, as part of one continuous process of giving his philosophical ideas a shape that he could be content with. In his 1945 preface he calls the book "the precipitate of [...] the last 16 years." However, he even then still added some clippings to his TS, and he changed the motto, probably in 1947. A few weeks before he died he wrote some final notes that he intended to insert into the preface (Nedo, 2012, p. 403).

While he did a lot of polishing on Part I of his main work, Wittgenstein did not try to do further work on his material on mathematics. In 1949–1951 he composed instead new material on the philosophy of psychology, even preparing two voluminous typescripts. Wittgenstein found much of this material unsatisfying but he produced a selection of it (MS 144). This was posthumously published as "Part II" of the *Investigations*. (This has been rectified in the recent edition by Hacker and Schulte, which labels it "Philosophical Psychology – A Fragment.") Wittgenstein also kept a box of cuttings containing "leftovers" from the preparation of TS 227, mostly from TS 228, which was later published as *Zettel*.

Still later, in 1950–1951, he wrote connected notes on problems regarding language-games about color (*Remarks on Colour*), and in his very last months and weeks, on questions concerning the language-games of knowing and being certain. These have become very well known as *On Certainty* (see Chapter 35, WITTGENSTEIN ON KNOWLEDGE AND CERTAINTY and Chapter 36, WITTGENSTEIN ON SKEPTICISM). It seems that Wittgenstein considered all these writings as applications of his way of doing philosophy as laid down in his *Investigations*.

A coherent and comprehensive history of "Wittgenstein's progress" has yet to be written.

References

Anscombe, G.E.M. (1959). *An Introduction to Wittgenstein's Tractatus*. London: Hutchinson.
Biletzky, A. and Matar, A. (2014). Ludwig Wittgenstein. In E.N. Zalta (ed.). *The Stanford Encyclopedia of Philosophy*. http://plato.stanford.edu/archives/spr2014/entries/wittgenstein/ (last accessed 31 May 2016).
Conant, J. (2012). Wittgenstein's Methods. In O. Kuusela and M. McGinn (eds). *The Oxford Handbook of Wittgenstein* (pp. 620–45). Oxford: Oxford University Press.
Diamond, C. (1991). *The Realistic Spirit: Wittgenstein, Philosophy, and the Mind*. Cambridge, MA: MIT Press.
Engelmann, M. (2013). *Wittgenstein's Philosophical Development*. Basingstroke: Palgrave Macmillan.
Fann, K.T. (1969). *Wittgenstein's Conception of Philosophy*. Oxford: Blackwell.
Fogelin, R.J. (1987). *Wittgenstein*. London: Routledge and Kegan Paul.
Glock, H.-J. (1990). *Philosophical Investigations*: Principles of Interpretation. In J. Brandl and R. Haller (eds). *Wittgenstein: Towards a Re-Evaluation* (pp. 152–162). Vienna: Hölder-Pichler-Tempsky.
Glock, H.-J. (2007). Perspectives on Wittgenstein: An Intermittently Opinionated Survey. In G. Kahane, E. Kanterian, and O. Kuusela (eds). *Wittgenstein and his Interpreters: Essays in Memory of Gordon Baker* (pp. 37–65). Oxford: Blackwell.
Hacker, P.M.S. (1996). *Wittgenstein's Place in Twentieth-Century Analytic Philosophy*. Oxford: Blackwell.
Hankinson, J. (1999). *The Bluffer's Guide to Philosophy*. London: Oval.
Hintikka, M. and Hintikka, J. (1986). *Investigating Wittgenstein*. Oxford: Basil Blackwell.
Hyman, J. (2016). The Urn and the Chamber Pot. In S.S. Grève and J. Mácha (eds). *Wittgenstein and the Creativity of Language* (pp. 198–217). Basingstoke: Palgrave Macmillan.
Kenny, A. (1973). *Wittgenstein*. Harmondsworth: Penguin.
Kienzler, W. (2012). Reading the *Tractatus* from the Beginning: How to Say Everything Clearly in Three Words. In P. Stekeler-Weithofer (ed.). *Wittgenstein: Zu Philosophie und Wissenschaft* (pp. 70–102). Hamburg: Meiner.
McGuinness, B. (ed.). (2008). *Wittgenstein in Cambridge: Letters and Documents, 1911–1951*. Oxford: Wiley-Blackwell.
Mounce, H.O. (1981). *Wittgenstein's Tractatus: An Introduction*. Oxford: Blackwell.
Nedo, M. (ed.). (2012). *Ludwig Wittgenstein: Ein Album*. [Ludwig Wittgenstein: An Album.] Munich: Beck.
Pears, D. (1971). *Wittgenstein*. London: Fontana.
Pitcher, G. (1964). *The Philosophy of Wittgenstein*. Englewood Cliffs: Prentice-Hall.
Rhees, R. (1970). *Discussions of Wittgenstein*. London: Routledge and Kegan Paul.
Rothhaupt, J. (2010). Wittgenstein at Work: Creation, Selection and Composition of "Remarks." In N. Venturinha (ed.). *Wittgenstein after his Nachlass* (pp. 51–63). Basingstoke: Palgrave Macmillan.
Schulte, J. (1987). *Wittgenstein: An Introduction*. Albany: SUNY Press.
Schulte, J. (ed.). (2001). *Ludwig Wittgenstein: Philosophische Untersuchungen, Kritisch-genetische Edition*. [Ludwig Wittgenstein: *Philosophical Investigations*, critical-genetic Edition.] Frankfurt: Suhrkamp.
Stern, D.G. (1995). *Wittgenstein on Mind and Language*. Oxford: Oxford University Press.
Stern, D.G. (2006). How Many Wittgensteins? In A. Pichler and S. Säätelä (Eds). *Wittgenstein: The Philosopher and his Works* (pp. 205–229). Frankfurt: Ontos.
Wijdeveld, P. (1993). *Ludwig Wittgenstein: Architect*. Amsterdam: Pepin Press.
Winch. P. (1969). The Unity of Wittgenstein's Philosophy. In P. Winch (ed.). *Studies in the Philosophy of Wittgenstein* (pp. 1–19). London: Routledge and Kegan Paul.

Further Reading

Diamond, C. (2006). Peter Winch on the *Tractatus* and the Unity of Wittgenstein's Philosophy. In A. Pichler and S. Säätelä (eds). *Wittgenstein: The Philosopher and his Works* (pp. 141–71). Frankfurt: Ontos. [Traces a tradition of continuity readings, starting with Anscombe, Rhees and Winch.]

Engelmann, M. (2013). *Wittgenstein's Development*. Basingstroke: Palgrave Macmillan. [The only book in English explicitly devoted to the topic of this chapter, describing the rise of the "genetic method" and the "anthropological view."]

Kienzler, W. (1997). *Wittgensteins Wende zu seiner Spätphilosophie 1930–1932*. [Wittgenstein's Turning-Point toward his Later Philosophy, 1930–1932.]. Frankfurt: Suhrkamp. [A close study of Wittgenstein's doings and writings from 1930 to 1932.]

Kuusela, O. (2012). The Development of Wittgenstein's Philosophy. In O. Kuusela and M. McGinn (eds). *The Oxford Handbook of Wittgenstein* (pp. 597–619). Oxford: Oxford University Press. [Advocating a perspective of basic continuity regarding Wittgenstein's aims with some important discontinuity regarding the means employed toward achieving those aims.]

Pichler, A. (2007). The Interpretation of the *Philosophical Investigations*: Style, Therapy, *Nachlass*. In G. Kahane, E. Kanterian, and O. Kuusela (eds). *Wittgenstein and his Interpreters: Essays in Memory of Gordon Baker*. Oxford: Blackwell. [Emphasizes the importance of stylistic changes during the years 1933–1937.]

Rothhaupt, J. (1995). *Farbthemen in Wittgensteins Gesamtnachlass*. [Color Themes Within Wittgenstein's Entire *Nachlass*.] Weinheim: Beltz Athenäum. [The most comprehensive study of the succession of Wittgenstein's writings and their mutual connections.]

Stern, D.G. (2006). How many Wittgensteins? In A. Pichler and S. Säätelä (Eds). *Wittgenstein: The Philosopher and his Works* (pp. 205–229). Frankfurt: Ontos. [Raises objections against all clear-cut divisions, but considers the years 1936–1937 as of special importance.]

von Wright, G.H. (1982). *Wittgenstein*. Oxford: Blackwell. [Contains groundbreaking first-hand research reports relating to the origin and composition of both the *Tractatus* and *Philosophical Investigations*.]

2
Wittgenstein's Texts and Style

DAVID G. STERN

1   Internalism and Externalism about Style and Method

What did Wittgenstein write, and how did he write it? At first sight, such questions about texts and style will strike many readers as peripheral, if not simply irrelevant to an appreciation of his contribution to philosophy. Philosophers usually take it for granted that concerns about the way in which philosophy is written, and the nature of the texts in question, while perhaps of interest from a philological, aesthetic, or literary standpoint, are of little or no consequence once one turns to assessing the arguments and conclusions that a philosopher advances. However, Wittgenstein's principal works, the *Tractatus Logico-Philosophicus* and *Philosophical Investigations*, are each written in such strikingly unconventional ways that it takes considerable effort to translate them into conventional philosophical writing. Neither book contains any chapter or section headings. Neither book has a clear narrative, or straightforwardly states the author's intentions. Neither book has a table of contents.

Each remark in the *Tractatus* is numbered in an elaborate decimal system, which supposedly indicates "the logical importance of the propositions" (TLP 1, footnote). However, while this arrangement certainly looks extremely systematic, the intricate structure of the text raises many more questions than it answers. Frank Ramsey, one of the first reviewers of the book, began his review by noting that it is "very difficult to understand," at least in part because it is not written in "consecutive prose, but short propositions numbered so as to show the emphasis laid upon them in his exposition" (Ramsey, 1923, p. 465). Ramsey, like many subsequent readers, considered that while this way of writing gave the work "an attractive epigrammatic flavour […] it seems to have prevented him from giving adequate explanations of many of his terms and theories" (1923, p. 465). Indeed, the *Tractatus* is so concise that it looks much more like an analytical table of contents than a conventional philosophical text. In a conversation with a friend, Wittgenstein said that every sentence "should be seen as the heading of a chapter, needing further exposition" (RW 159–60).

Each remark in *Philosophical Investigations* is numbered sequentially, from 1 to 693. Despite the linear arrangement, the topics discussed are intricately connected; many

---

A Companion to Wittgenstein, First Edition. Edited by Hans-Johann Glock and John Hyman.
© 2017 John Wiley & Sons, Ltd. Published 2017 by John Wiley & Sons, Ltd.

readers have approached it as a book in need of an analytical table of contents. Peter Strawson, one of the first reviewers of that book, began his review by saying that it is a treatment of

> a number of intricate problems, intricately connected. It also presents in itself an intricate problem: that of seeing clearly what the author's views are on the topics he discusses, and how these views are connected. The difficulty of doing this arises partly from the structure and style of the book. (Strawson, 1954, p. 70)

Strawson connects this with the part of Wittgenstein's preface to *Philosophical Investigations*, where Wittgenstein says: "The best I could write could never be more than philosophical remarks [...]. Thus this book is really only an album."

In their brief opening remarks about Wittgenstein's way of writing, and their subsequent interpretive practice, Ramsey and Strawson anticipated the predominant philosophical approach to its style and structure. They each regard it as an impressive authorial achievement, but one that significantly adds to the interpretive challenges in tracing and connecting the main lines of his thought. In a recent survey of the main approaches to Wittgenstein interpretation, Kahane, Kanterian, and Kuusela characterize this view of his method as an "externalist" one, on which "his style is external to method and content, and the latter can be extracted from his writings without any loss of substance" (Kahane *et al.*, 2007, p. 20). In addition to Strawson, they list "Hintikka, Hilmy, Fogelin, Rundle, von Savigny and Glock" (p. 21) as examples of those who explicitly endorse externalism. They all hold that the style is "characteristic of the *man* Wittgenstein" (p. 20) but independent of his philosophical method and content, which can be stated without loss in the explicit argumentative exposition ordinarily found in a journal article or scholarly book. Kahane, Kanterian, and Kuusela contrast this with "internalist" readings, on which Wittgenstein's style of writing is an essential part of his philosophical method, and his method and style are internally related. They further distinguish a variety of "internalist" approaches, including a "moderate" version on which the style serves argumentative ends, and a "strong" internalism on which the aim of the book is not ultimately argumentative at all, but is rather therapeutic, a matter of persuading readers to "give up their craving for a metaphysical point of view" (p. 23). They consider "Malcolm, Kenny, the 'second' Baker, Hacker, Kienzler and Schulte" (p. 21) to be examples of moderate internalists, and the "later" Baker, Cavell, Pichler, and myself as proponents of strong internalism.

In other words, the externalist holds that Wittgenstein's style is independent of his method and his arguments; the moderate internalist holds that his style serves methodological ends, but the method can be independently expressed and justified; the strong internalist holds that the style is more or less the method. While this way of dividing the field may seem clear-cut at first, it soon turns out that the range of possible views is considerably more complex than this classification suggests. This is largely because there is little agreement about just how to understand the crucial term, namely "style." Externalists tend to use it as a catch-all term for all those aspects of Wittgenstein's writing which they regard as not germane to the expository project of explicitly stating his problems, or laying out his arguments. If they do have an explicit understanding of the term, it is usually akin to Frege's conception of "tone": whatever aspects of a piece of writing that do not affect its sense or reference, aspects that could be removed by rephrasing that text without changing its semantic significance, and so are only of interest from a literary, poetic, or aesthetic perspective. While internalists naturally pay much closer attention to the way Wittgenstein wrote and his mode of composition, they tend to disagree about which aspects of his style are essential to his philosophical methods. Some strong internalists, such as O.K. Bouwsma and the later Baker, seem to hold the view that every aspect of Wittgenstein's writing is an integral part of his method. However, for the most part, there is a range of varying internalist readings, each turning on different aspects of Wittgenstein's style. These include not only the disparity between the highly structured decimal numbering system of the *Tractatus* and the apparent lack of structure of the sequentially numbered *Philosophical Investigations*, and the related contrast between the condensed and oracular pronouncements of the *Tractatus* and the extended conversations typical of much of the later work, but also his use of such devices as multiple voices, thought experiments, provocative examples, striking similes, rhetorical questions, irony, and parody.

My own view is that the most important aspect of Wittgenstein's style for an understanding of his philosophy is his use of multiple voices, and the way he forces his reader to engage with those voices in order to understand him, and it is this aspect that I emphasize here. Cavell's reading of *Philosophical Investigations* along these lines is the best-known and most influential example of this approach to interpreting Wittgenstein (Cavell, 1979 is the *locus classicus*, but see also Cavell, 1966 and 1996). Perhaps this is why it is often taken for granted that questions about style and voice, and their relationship to the debate between externalists and internalists, are primarily an issue that arises for interpreters of the later Wittgenstein. Nevertheless, closely related concerns also arise for readers of the *Tractatus*. Externalists regard the last two paragraphs of the preface as making a very strong case on their behalf, as Wittgenstein clearly distinguishes there between what is said in the book, and how it is said. He says that the value of the work consists in the expression of thoughts "and this value will be greater the better the thoughts are expressed." After acknowledging that others may well be able to do better in expressing those thoughts, Wittgenstein goes on to insist that "the *truth* of the thoughts communicated here seems to me unassailable and definitive." However Wittgenstein ends his preface by saying that the value of the book also consists "in the fact that it shows how little has been done when these problems have been solved." Internalist readers of the *Tractatus* take this as an anticipation of the very different approach to what is said there that is provided in the penultimate remark:

> My propositions serve as elucidations in the following way: anyone who understands me eventually recognizes them as nonsensical, when he has used them as steps – to climb up beyond them. (He must, so to speak, throw away the ladder after he has climbed up it.)
> He must overcome these propositions, and then he will see the world aright. (TLP 6.54)

From this perspective, the ultimate aim of the book is not to prove certain results, results which could equally well be formulated in other words, but to bring about a change in self-understanding that is not primarily of a cognitive nature (see Diamond, 1991, ch. 6).

At this point, it may seem as though Wittgenstein's style of writing, and the question of the significance of his way of writing, only really matters to the internalist. After all, the core of the externalist position is that the style of the author is philosophically inessential: the same points could equally well be presented in other ways, and indeed that is the task of the philosophical interpreter. Thus it is natural for the externalist to paint the internalist as holding that there are "good reasons why no attempt at all should be made to present his views in a more conventional form" and to exasperatedly respond that "this could be true only on a very specialised view of the nature of philosophical understanding" (Strawson, 1954, p. 70). In a similar spirit, Hans-Johann Glock, a leading advocate of externalism, has argued that internalist interpreters "owe us a clear and well-argued account of what *philosophical* substance (concerning problems, arguments or insights) is lost by rephrasing Wittgenstein's thought in a more conventional manner" (Glock, 2007, p. 63; his preferred term is "stylistic," not "internalist"; see also Chapter 13, PHILOSOPHY AND PHILOSOPHICAL METHOD). Indeed, one might think, insofar as the moderate internalist is able to state the philosophical substance that has supposedly been lost in the conventional rephrasing, it should not be too difficult to take those points and use them to supplement or complete the conventional account. Moreover, insofar as the strong internalist maintains that the philosophical substance is inseparable from his style, and so cannot be independently restated, the externalist will respond that we are left with an irrationalist conception of philosophy as unargued persuasion.

The question whether there are aspects of Wittgenstein's views which are lost when restated in a more conventional manner is indeed an important one for the debate over the relationship between Wittgenstein's way of writing and his philosophical method. However, the most important difficulty for the externalist, and one that is obscured by this focus on what, if anything, is lost in a conventional exposition, has to do with the relationship between Wittgenstein's way of writing and the externalist's philosophical method. For *any* interpretation of Wittgenstein's philosophy, *any* expository restatement of his problems, arguments, or views, has to begin from a reading of the relevant texts. That, in turn, will presuppose, either explicitly or implicitly, views about what sort of text he wrote or was aspiring to write, and how to approach his way of writing.

In other words, the externalist and the internalist are in the same boat: there is no way out of the hermeneutical circle, no way of reading Wittgenstein's writing without taking a position on his way of writing. This is not simply the platitude that every reading of a text involves presuppositions about how to interpret that text. Rather, it is the point that the implications of that very general principle in the quite particular case of Wittgenstein's writing are considerably more far-reaching in comparison to the conventional monograph or journal article. For any interpretation of an author who published very little of his writing, and who wrote in a highly unusual way, will require the interpreter to take a position on a number of questions about those texts, and the way in which they were written, questions that are usually peripheral, if not entirely unproblematic. These include not only questions about the role of the author's style, and the genre to which the work belongs, but also what counts as a work by that author, and how to identify the author's projects, views and arguments. Furthermore, precisely because the answers to these questions can usually be taken for granted in reading conventional philosophical writing, externalists are often unaware of the extent to which their expository reconstructions of Wittgenstein's philosophy depend on their interpretation of his way of writing. Indeed, the Achilles heel of most externalist readings of Wittgenstein is that they turn on controversial assumptions about Wittgenstein's writing that are either presented as obvious, or simply taken for granted. Perhaps the most important of these is the assumption that the only alternative to rational argument is irrational persuasion.

2 Identifying Texts and Works

The *Tractatus* is the only major work by Wittgenstein published during his lifetime. The many posthumous books and articles that followed all involved, often to a remarkable extent, decisions by his editors as to what to publish, and how to present it. Even in the case of *Philosophical Investigations*, which Wittgenstein clearly authorized for publication and regarded as the best statement of his later work, there is a significant disagreement between on the one hand, G.E.M. Anscombe and Rush Rhees, the editors of the first three editions, who published a typescript from the late 1940s under the title of "Part II," and on the other, P.M.S. Hacker and Joachim Schulte, the editors of the fourth edition, who renamed it "Philosophy of Psychology – A Fragment." As a result, we face a number of serious and difficult questions about what to count as a work of Wittgenstein's. For the vast majority of authors, the answer is very simple: one can start from the body of writing the author saw to the press, perhaps subtracting those publications that are not sufficiently significant to count as a work, and then adding those projects that were more or less complete but remained unpublished at the time of the author's death. The first part of this calculation is straightforward: the only other piece of philosophical writing that Wittgenstein published is a short conference paper that he disowned before he was due to present it; the only other book he published was a spelling dictionary for children in Austrian schools. It is the second part of the calculation that is problematic, precisely because he published so little, and left us so little more that he was close to being ready to publish.

One problem that any interpreter of Wittgenstein's philosophy has to address at the outset is the issue of which text, or texts, to take as a starting point. Which of Wittgenstein's writings set out his philosophy, and which set out views he rejected? There are a number of related but distinct questions here. One way of approaching this issue is at the "macro-level," namely as a question about his writing as a whole. In that case, it becomes a matter of asking which parts of Wittgenstein's writings to count as a "work" of Wittgenstein's. In other words, which of the many publications created by his editors on the basis of his *Nachlass*, the approximately 20 000 pages of manuscripts and typescripts he left to his literary executors, is best considered as a piece of preparatory, transitional, or rejected writing, and which is actually a work. "Work" is used as a semi-technical term for those writings that are of primary importance, or major interest, writings that have a certain unity and "finishedness."

Furthermore, the *Nachlass* itself is only a fraction of what Wittgenstein wrote, and is itself a selection from a larger body of philosophical work. In addition to Wittgenstein's own writing, he was also the author, or co-author, of a great deal of work written down by others, principally in the 1930s, which is not part of the collection of papers that Wittgenstein entrusted to his literary executors. These include Moore's 1930–1933 lecture notes and many other notes by others who attended Wittgenstein's lectures and took part in conversations with him, Waismann's dictations and expository writing from the first half of that decade, and the recently discovered Skinner archive, dating from the mid-1930s. This chapter concerns the stylistic and textual issues raised by the body of writing Wittgenstein left to his literary executors. (For some further discussion of this greater body of philosophical writing, see M; MWL; PPO; VW; Gibson, 2010; Schulte, 2011; and Stern, Citron, and Rogers, 2013.)

There are two "default" approaches to answering this question about what to count as a work. One is to hold with Hacker, von Savigny, and Cavell, that only the *Tractatus* and *Philosophical Investigations* are works of Wittgenstein's; the other, probably taken for granted by most interpreters, is to add in all or most of the posthumous publications as works, in effect deferring to the judgment of his editors (see e.g., Hintikka, 1991; Kenny, 1976; 2005 on the history of Wittgenstein editing). On another, more systematic, approach one would only include those writings that reached some level of sufficiently polished revision, or that Wittgenstein once considered to be prepared for publication (see Schulte, [1989] 1992, ch.1.3; 2005; Glock, 2007). Some *Nachlass* interpreters would contend that this is still much too restrictive, and that in view of the extent to which a trail of revised and rearranged remarks connects every stage of Wittgenstein's writing, the *Nachlass* as a whole should really be regarded as a single work (Hrachovec, 2000; 2005). Other *Nachlass* interpreters, including Baker and Hacker (1980–2000/2014; 1980/2009; 1985/2014) and Glock (1990; 1996), while repudiating this revisionary view, nevertheless draw extensively on the *Nachlass* sources of the *Tractatus* and *Philosophical Investigations* for guidance in understanding those works.

In view of the far-reaching implications of any answer to this question about what counts as a work of Wittgenstein's, it is surprisingly rare for commentators to explicitly discuss and defend criteria for identifying a work. Even when interpreters do discuss the issue of which writings qualify as works, the meaning of the term, or its application in the case in question, is usually taken for granted. (Exceptions to this rule include Schulte, [1989] 1992; 1999; 2005; and Stern, 1996; 2005.) For instance, as mentioned earlier, Hacker maintains that only the *Tractatus* and *Philosophical Investigations* are works of Wittgenstein's, holding that "all the other books published under his name are unfinished or discarded writings" (Hacker, 2012, p. 2). Danièle Moyal-Sharrock has replied that the criterion for a text's qualifying as a work by Wittgenstein, or as part of his philosophy, "is not whether Wittgenstein intended to form books from his notes, but whether or not those notes do form what can be considered a genuine and original contribution to philosophy" (Moyal-Sharrock, 2013, p. 358). Authorial intent and philosophical originality are both relevant considerations, but neither one considered in isolation is sufficient to settle the question of what counts as a work. Part of the difficulty one faces in adjudicating the disagreement between Hacker and Moyal-Sharrock is that there are a number of different factors that are *prima facie* relevant in assessing whether or not a piece of Wittgenstein's writing qualifies as a work, and the relationship between his works and other writings. Indeed, Hacker is one of the leading exponents of a genetic approach to the *Tractatus* and *Philosophical Investigations*, on which Wittgenstein's "unfinished or discarded writings" provide essential evidence as to what he meant to say in his masterpieces. Insofar as they play this role, Hacker in fact holds that they are a significant philosophical contribution, and his four-volume *Commentary on Philosophical Investigations* is devoted to making use, not only of the other books published under Wittgenstein's name, but also his extensive *Nachlass*.

Alternatively, one can take the question about which texts to start from to be a question about authorship, rather than one about what counts as a work. In other words, one can ask whether all of Wittgenstein's works are part of a unitary philosophical project, or whether they should be divided into two or more, each with its own distinctive character. Here, once again, there are two widely accepted views. "Two Wittgensteins"-interpreters – among them Malcolm, Cavell, Hacker, Hintikka and Hintikka, Fogelin, Kienzler, and Glock – draw a sharp distinction between an "early Wittgenstein" or "Wittgenstein I," the author of the *Tractatus* and the pre-*Tractatus* writings, and a "later Wittgenstein" or "Wittgenstein II," the author of *Philosophical*

Investigations and most, if not all, of Wittgenstein's post-*Tractatus* writings. Some, such as Cavell and Fogelin, take this to be essentially a distinction between the philosophy of the *Tractatus* and *Philosophical Investigations*. Others, including Hacker, Hilmy (1987), Hintikka and Hintikka (1986), Glock, and Kienzler (1997; 2001; Chapter 1, WITTGENSTEIN'S PHILOSOPHICAL DEVELOPMENT), who make extensive use not only of Wittgenstein's other publications, but also his *Nachlass*, are equally concerned with identifying the point at which there is a break between the early and the later work. These interpreters maintain that much of his later philosophy had already been formulated by the early 1930s, and that we can find clear formulations of many central commitments of the later Wittgenstein in his "middle period" writings. On the other hand, Moyal-Sharrock has argued that Wittgenstein's work underwent a further turn after the completion of *Philosophical Investigations*. In particular, she holds that the "third Wittgenstein" of *On Certainty* solves epistemological and methodological problems that were not resolved by the "second Wittgenstein" of *Philosophical Investigations*.

"One Wittgenstein"-interpreters hold that there is more unity than discontinuity between the early and later work. While this might, at first sight, seem to be the most plausible strategy, in view of the strangeness of speaking of one person's writing as though it were the work of multiple authors, it has proven remarkably difficult to get away from the assumptions that frame the "multiple Wittgensteins"-approach. Early exponents of this view, among them Feyerabend and Kenny, tend to make the later philosophy look like a relatively modest revision of the earlier; more recently, Diamond, Goldfarb, Conant, Kuusela, and other "resolute" readers, have argued that the methods usually attributed to the later Wittgenstein also animate his earlier work. At first, their insistence on the unitary character of Wittgenstein's thought appeared to commit them to denying that there were any major changes in his philosophical outlook during the 1930s (see Hacker, 2001, sec. 4). This seemed particularly hard to reconcile with his writings from 1929–1930, which are the work of a philosopher criticizing and changing his earlier views (see Stern, 1995; but also 2010a). However, since then "resolute" readers have developed a variety of accounts of the continuities and discontinuities in Wittgenstein's work during these years, including work by Diamond (2004), Conant (2007; 2011), Kuusela (2008; 2011), and Cahill (2011). (See also Chapter 10, RESOLUTE READINGS OF THE *TRACTATUS*.)

The idea of a "middle Wittgenstein" has also played a significant role in this debate, although the precise boundaries of this period and its distinguishing characteristics are disputed. It even has an entry of its own in the *Oxford Bibliographies Online* series, under the title "Ludwig Wittgenstein: Middle Works" (Biletzki, 2011), alongside entries on the "Early Works" (McManus, 2010) and the "Later Works" (Coliva and Moyal-Sharrock, 2010). Proponents of a "two Wittgensteins"-view usually see this as a relatively short period of transition from the earlier to the later philosophy in the late 1920s or early 1930s, followed by several years during which the later views were fully articulated (Hacker, 1972/1986; Hilmy, 1987; Glock, 1990; 1996; 2001; 2007). "Resolute" readers construe this period as a matter of an evolution from a unitary conception of philosophical method toward a plurality of philosophical methods. On both of these approaches, the "middle period" is a time of transition to be understood in terms of what comes earlier and later. However, others have argued that it is best understood as a distinctive phase in Wittgenstein's work from the first half of the 1930s that cannot be accounted for in terms of the dissolution of the Tractarian approach to philosophy and the emergence of the later Wittgenstein. Wittgenstein's thought was rapidly changing during the first half of the 1930s, and his writing from this period should not be taken as a blueprint for his later work. During these years, Wittgenstein began to set out a conception of philosophy as aiming at systematic clarification of the rules of our language in a philosophical grammar. However, by the time he composed the first draft of *Philosophical Investigations* in 1936–1937 he had given up this conception of philosophical grammar in favor of piecemeal criticism of specific philosophical problems. This approach challenges the assumption that the only available alternative to the standard account, on which there is a definitive rift between the early and the later Wittgenstein, is a "resolute" reading on which Wittgenstein's philosophy is unitary (Stern, 2005). Versions of this reading can be found in work by Stern (1991; 2004, ch.5.2; 2005), Schulte (2002; 2011), Pichler (2004), and Engelmann (2011; 2013).

3   Identifying Voices in the Text

The previous section provided a brief outline of the leading "macro-level" or (what one might call) "big picture" answers to the question which of Wittgenstein's writings set out his philosophy, and which set out views he rejected. There is no quick or simple way of choosing between these positions about the identity of Wittgenstein's works, each of which has its erudite and expert advocates. An informed judgment not only calls for an evaluation of the competing views about which pieces of writing qualify as a work of Wittgenstein's, and why, but also turns on identifying the particular views set out in those pieces of writing. In other words, the macro-level is dependent on the micro-level. Furthermore, the question as to which of Wittgenstein's writings set out his philosophy, and which set out views he rejected, often arises again at the micro-level, and particularly when identifying different voices and their respective positions in his most polished dialogical writing.

Indeed, there is a strong case to be made that the micro-level, working on the scale of the paragraph or the page, not the book or the typescript, is the best place to look for answers to questions about the way Wittgenstein wrote, his mode of composition, and the role of these stylistic considerations in his philosophical writing. On such a finer-grained approach, the principal frame of reference is not the work, but those relatively short sequences of sentences that he repeatedly revised and rearranged. For the basic unit in almost all of Wittgenstein's writing, from *Notebooks 1914–16* to the manuscripts written during the last year of his life, including the posthumously edited selection published as *On Certainty*, is the remark (*Bemerkung*). A remark is a passage that may be as short as a single sentence, or as long as a series of paragraphs stretching over several pages. A blank line usually separates remarks from one another. First drafts were often composed in notebooks; revised and topically arranged selections were copied into larger manuscript volumes, and repeatedly reorganized.

Delving further into the microstructure of the author's writing, one can also distinguish between a number of different representations of any given paragraph in a particular manuscript, such as a normalized version, showing the result of implementing earlier revisions and choosing from undecided alternatives, and a diplomatic version, which provides detailed information about each stage of revision. For instance, *The Big Typescript* (2005, BT) is a diplomatic edition of a heavily revised typescript, which was probably dictated to a typist in the summer of 1933; later manuscript additions, deletions, and alternatives are shown in footnotes. Part One of *Philosophical Grammar* (1974, PG) can be regarded as a normalized version of the opening chapters of the same typescript, with the proviso that it also follows two separate sets of plans for revisions. The German-language edition of Wittgenstein's 1930–1932 and 1936–1937 diaries (1997, DB) provides both normalized and diplomatic editions of those texts in a pair of parallel volumes; the diplomatic edition is reprinted, with a translation on facing pages, in *Public and Private Occasions* (PPO). In principle, the same approach could also be applied to successive stages of revision of a given remark across different manuscripts and typescripts. The Bergen edition of the Wittgenstein *Nachlass* (2000) provides both normalized and diplomatic transcriptions, plus images of each page of the source text. The online Wittgenstein Source edition also offers a user-customizable view in which the viewer can control how much editing information is provided. (See Stern 2010c for details.)

Wittgenstein's method of composition, revision, and rearrangement, leads from the remarks written down in his wartime notebooks, to a manuscript containing several stages of construction of the *Prototractatus*, and from there to the polished typescript of the *Tractatus*. In the case of *Philosophical Investigations*, there remains a much longer and more intricate trail of revision and rewriting available, including at least three successive drafts of the book (for details, see Schulte's preface to the *Kritisch-genetische Edition*, 2001). Remarks are often numbered sequentially in the more polished typescripts – each numbered section in the *Tractatus* and *Philosophical Investigations* is a remark.

The preface to *Philosophical Investigations*, dated January 1945, begins by highlighting the role of the remark in the composition – in the sense of both the genesis and the arrangement – of the book. Indeed, Wittgenstein underlined the word "remark" in the text, although the current English translation, provided below, does not:

> The thoughts which I publish in what follows are the precipitate of philosophical investigations which have occupied me for the last sixteen years [...]. I have written down all these thoughts as remarks, short paragraphs, sometimes in longer chains about the same subject, sometimes jumping, in a sudden change, from one area to another. – Originally it was my intention to bring all this together in a book whose form I thought of differently at different times. But it seemed to me essential that in the book the thoughts should proceed from one subject to another in a natural, smooth sequence.
>
> After several unsuccessful attempts to weld my results together into such a whole, I realized that I should never succeed. The best that I could write would never be more than philosophical remarks. (PI, preface)

Wittgenstein goes on to describe the remarks as "sketches of landscapes [...] which then had to be arranged and often cut down, in order to give the viewer an idea of the landscape. So this book is really just an album."

Because so much of Wittgenstein's post-*Tractatus* writing takes the form of a conversation between multiple voices – voices that are rarely clearly identified or demarcated – the mere fact that a given passage sets out a view, or argues for it, is at most a *prima facie* reason to attribute that position to Wittgenstein. Indeed, even if a position is not put in inverted commas, and does chime with a number of other passages, that does not by itself show that it is a view that Wittgenstein endorsed. For a substantial fraction of what is said there consists of attempts to express "what we are 'tempted to say'" about philosophical problems, which is "of course, not philosophy; but is its raw material" (PI §254). If the dissenting voice usually known as "Wittgenstein's interlocutor" speaks, often indicated by putting those words in quotation marks, or placing a double dash before or after them, the very fact that the passage in question sets out the views that it does is actually excellent evidence that Wittgenstein did not accept them. In the case of a full-voiced statement of such a temptation, with an immediate response in the text, the interlocutory character of the words is unmistakable. Such cases include the following examples:

> "Surely I can (inwardly) undertake to call THIS 'pain' in the future." (PI §263)

> "Once you know *what* the word signifies, you understand it, you know its whole application." (PI §264)

However, in most cases, it is not so easy to tell the many voices in Wittgenstein's writing from his "philosophical *treatment*" (§254) of them. Many readers take it for granted that it is Wittgenstein who replies to "the interlocutor." But the interlocutory voices, and the narrator's responses show no such unity – they defend a variety of disparate views at different points in the conversation. Instead of defending polished or systematic philosophical positions, they explore intuitions and convictions – starting points for philosophical discussion, not its sophisticated results. In doing so, both voices articulate a wide variety of philosophical theories. In addition to these voices, we also encounter a voice that provides an ironic commentary on their exchanges. This consists partly of objections to assumptions the debaters take for granted, and partly of commonplace observations about language and everyday life they have both overlooked. The commentator is a much more plausible candidate for an authorial representative than the disputing voices that dominate the conversation, though none of them can be unproblematically identified as Wittgenstein's spokesperson. The closest the author of *Philosophical Investigations* comes to expressing his own views is when he steps back from this debate and offers us a striking simile, such as the proposal that "the philosopher treats a question; like an illness" (§255) or draws our attention to "what we are 'tempted to say'" (§254). (For further discussion, see Stern, 2004, sec.1.3.)

However, matters are often not so clear-cut. Consider the following example of a passage that Hacker construes as evidence that Wittgenstein held that it is conceivable that a solitary individual could invent a language (Hacker, 1990/1993a, ch.3; 1990/1993b, ch.1). At a crucial stage in the discussion of a private language, we are asked to explore the imaginary scenario, raised at the very end of §256, in which I didn't have "any natural expression of sensation, but only had sensations [...]. And now I simply *associate* names with sensations, and use these names in descriptions." The next section, §257, opens with a question and reply, all enclosed in quotation marks, making the point that "if human beings did not manifest their pain [...] it would be impossible to teach a child the use of the word 'toothache.'" It is not entirely clear who speaks each of the next six sentences, mostly interspersed with single dashes, which make up the middle of this remark; they are more like a series of reflections on the issues raised by the opening material, than a clear back-and-forth dialogue. They begin with the following exclamation:

> – Well, let's assume the child is a genius and invents a name for the sensation by himself! (PI §257)

It is possible to construe this exclamation as the narrator's way of moving the discussion along, or as the interlocutor's impatient reply, or as part of an indecisive soliloquy. Nevertheless, regardless of who speaks these words, the mere fact that they give voice to the view that a solitary individual could invent a language does nothing to settle the question whether Wittgenstein actually endorsed it. However, the rest of the remark does raise a number of pointed questions about the imagined act of inventing a name for a sensation that cannot be named in a public language, among them:

– But what does it mean to say that he has 'named his pain'? – How has he managed this naming of pain? And whatever he did, what was its purpose? (PI §257)

The answer that follows is not a direct answer to this series of questions, but rather a reminder of what we overlook when we imagine that a super-child could invent a super-private word for a pain all by herself, or when we say that such a thing is logically possible, and thus conceivable, albeit not practically possible:

– When one says "He gave a name to his sensation" one forgets that a great deal of stage-setting in the language is presupposed if the mere act of naming is to make sense. And when we speak of someone's having given a name to pain, what is presupposed is the existence of the grammar of the word "pain"; it shows the post where the new word is stationed. (PI §257)

On an orthodox reading of this passage, of which Hacker is a leading representative, this is a grammatical claim about the meaning of the words in question, and our use of them. As I read them, they are rather one of the commentator's "remarks on the natural history of human beings; not curiosities, however, but facts that no one has doubted, which have escaped notice only because they are always before our eyes" (PI §415). To be more specific, it is a point about what must already be in place before we can give any ostensive definition that Wittgenstein has already insisted on in the discussion of that topic in §§28–38. Looking back at the history of this remark's composition, we can see how Wittgenstein's reflections on the stage-setting that an act of ostension presupposes antedate his first explicit discussion of a "private language." (For further discussion of PI §§256–8 along these lines, see Stern, 2004, sec. 7.2; 2010b; and 2011.) However, for present purposes, it also provides an excellent example of why one cannot take an idea presented in the course of Wittgenstein's polished discussion of a topic, such as the idea of the language-inventing child genius, at face value. Wittgenstein discusses any number of scenarios that he ultimately aims to convince us are nonsensical; we cannot infer from the fact that he discusses a given scenario that he regards it as philosophically unobjectionable.

Philosophical Investigations §372, a very short remark about language and necessity, is an excellent example of the hazards involved in recognizing the various voices in that book, and how large a role such considerations can play in any interpretation of the author's views. In the first edition of Baker and Hacker's analytical commentary, a section on "Arbitrariness and the autonomy of grammar" (1985/2014, vol. 2, p. 329) starts by quoting that remark in full:

Consider: "The only correlate in language to an intrinsic necessity is an arbitrary rule. It is the only thing which one can milk out of this intrinsic necessity into a proposition." (PI §372)

Baker and Hacker tell us that while other philosophers who have considered this suggestion have been baffled by it, it sets out a point that Wittgenstein insisted on, namely that "rules of grammar, and hence 'necessary propositions,' are arbitrary" (Baker and Hacker, 1985/2014, vol. 2, p. 329; see also Chapter 15, THE AUTONOMY OF GRAMMAR). Their extensive exploration of this idea starts by appealing to the manuscript sources of §372 in *Philosophical Grammar* and the "Big Typescript," where the point is discussed in much greater detail. Indeed, surely one reason why they begin by quoting §372 is that it is one of the few places in *Philosophical Investigations* where the very idea that grammar is arbitrary is explicitly discussed. The vast majority of quotations in this part of their exegetical essay are from other sources, and almost entirely from material dating from the 1930s. Baker and Hacker do make a strong case that Wittgenstein develops and articulates this view of grammar and necessity in some detail in the early 1930s. Like a number of other middle-period views about the nature of philosophy and philosophical method which play a leading role in Baker and Hacker's overall approach to *Philosophical Investigations*, they seem to regard the fact that there is very little direct discussion of them in *Philosophical Investigations* as evidence that it is taken for granted there (see Stern, 2004, sec.5.2 for further discussion).

By the time Hacker wrote the third volume of the first edition, he had a change of mind. He now held that the pair of quoted sentences does not set out Wittgenstein's later view, but a Tractarian one. Instead of construing §372 as a statement of Wittgenstein's later conception of necessity, he proposed that "we are being invited to consider the quoted remark by way of *contrast* with the conception of necessity or essence that characterizes Wittgenstein's later philosophy" (Hacker, 1990/1993b, p. 238). Hacker now construed them as alluding to the position set out in the *Tractatus* on which "there *are* intrinsic necessities" (1990/1993b, p. 237), and so one diametrically opposed to the view he attributes to the later Wittgenstein. Instead of reading them as an invitation to consider what he and Baker once regarded as the narrator's view, he now construes them as voiced by a Tractarian interlocutor.

Hacker originally read the quoted passage as a compact statement of the conception of the "arbitrariness of grammar" that he attributed to the *later* Wittgenstein; he subsequently came to think of it as summarizing Wittgenstein's *early* position on intrinsic necessities. Hacker does note that the quoted sentences were originally "typed into the 'Big Typescript' without prefix or quotes, [which] were added in pencil" (Hacker, 1990/1993b, p. 238). However, Hacker never considers the possibility that the view the author of the *Investigations* is quoting for our consideration is the view of the *middle* Wittgenstein who dictated the "Big Typescript." For that is the place where it is stated, without quotation marks, as part of a section of that book with the heading: "Grammar is not Accountable to any Reality. The Rules of Grammar Determine Meaning (Constitute it), and Therefore they are not Answerable to any Meaning and in this Respect are Arbitrary" (BT 233). In short, as Engelmann (2011; 2013) puts it in his insightful discussion of Hacker on "grammar," to which I am indebted here, Hacker assumes that there was a single crucial change in Wittgenstein's philosophy with the emergence of his "later" conception of grammar around 1930, and so his writings on grammar from the early 1930s can be taken as a guide to the interpretation of *Philosophical Investigations*.

The preceding discussion of Hacker's reading of Wittgenstein on whether a solitary individual could invent a language, and on the arbitrariness of grammar, is only the briefest outline of his approach and some of the problems it faces. My aim in this final section here has not been to resolve these issues, but rather to illustrate how one cannot even begin to interpret Wittgenstein's remarks without taking a position on questions about texts and style, voice and authorship.

References

Baker, G.P. and Hacker, P.M.S. (1980–2000/2014). *An Analytical Commentary on the Philosophical Investigations*. 4 Vols. Oxford: Wiley-Blackwell.

Baker, G.P. and Hacker, P.M.S. (1980/2009). *Wittgenstein: Understanding and Meaning. Volume 1 of an Analytical Commentary on the Philosophical Investigations. Part 1. Essays*. Second edition. Extensively revised by P.M.S. Hacker. Oxford: Wiley-Blackwell.

Baker, G.P. and Hacker, P.M.S. (1985/2014). *Wittgenstein: Rules, Grammar and Necessity. Volume 2 of an Analytical Commentary on the Philosophical Investigations. Essays and Exegesis of §§185–242*. Second edition. Extensively revised by P.M.S. Hacker. Oxford: Wiley-Blackwell.

Biletzki, A. (2011). Ludwig Wittgenstein: Middle Works. In *Oxford Bibliographies Online*. Oxford: Oxford University Press.

Cahill, K. (2011). *The Fate of Wonder*. New York: Columbia University Press.

Cavell, S. (1966). The Availability of Wittgenstein's Later Philosophy. In G. Pitcher. *Wittgenstein: The Philosophical Investigations* (pp.151–186). London: Macmillan.

Cavell, S. (1979). *The Claim of Reason: Wittgenstein, Skepticism, Morality, and Tragedy*. Oxford: Oxford University Press.

Cavell, S. (1996). The *Investigations*' Everyday Aesthetics of Itself. In S. Mulhall (Ed). *The Cavell Reader* (pp.369–389). Oxford: Blackwell.

Coliva, A. and Moyal-Sharrock, D. (2010). Ludwig Wittgenstein: Later Works. In *Oxford Bibliographies Online*. Oxford: Oxford University Press.

Conant, J. (2007). Mild Mono-Wittgensteinianism. In A. Crary (Ed.). *Wittgenstein and the Moral Life: Essays in Honor of Cora Diamond* (pp.29–142). Cambridge, MA: MIT Press.

Conant, J. (2011). Wittgenstein's Methods. In O. Kuusela and M. McGinn (Eds). *The Oxford Handbook of Wittgenstein* (pp.620–645). Oxford: Oxford University Press.

Diamond, C. (1991). *The Realistic Spirit: Wittgenstein, Philosophy and the Mind*. Cambridge, MA: MIT Press.

Diamond, C. (2004). Criss-cross Philosophy. In E. Ammereller and E. Fischer (Eds). *Wittgenstein at Work: Method in the Philosophical Investigations* (pp.201–220). London: Routledge.

Engelmann, M. (2011). What Wittgenstein's "Grammar" is *Not*: On Garver, Baker and Hacker, and Hacker on Wittgenstein on "Grammar." *Wittgenstein Studien*, 2, 71–102.

Engelmann, M. (2013). *Wittgenstein's Philosophical Development: Phenomenology, Grammar, Method and the Anthropological View*. Basingstoke: Palgrave Macmillan.

Gibson, A. (2010). The Wittgenstein Archive of Francis Skinner. In N. Venturinha (Ed.). *Wittgenstein after his Nachlass* (pp.64–77). Basingstoke: Palgrave Macmillan.

Glock, H.-J. (1990). *Philosophical Investigations:* Principles of Interpretation. In R. Haller and J. Brandl (Eds). *Wittgenstein: Towards a Re-Evaluation* (pp.152–62). Vienna: Hölder-Pichler-Tempsky.

Glock, H.-J. (1996). *A Wittgenstein Dictionary*. Oxford: Blackwell.

Glock, H.-J. (2001). The Development of Wittgenstein's Philosophy. In H.-J. Glock (Ed.). *Wittgenstein: A Critical Reader* (pp.1–25). Oxford: Blackwell.

Glock, H.-J. (2007). Perspectives on Wittgenstein: An Intermittently Opinionated Survey. In G. Kahane, E. Kanterian, and O. Kuusela (Eds). *Wittgenstein and his Interpreters: Essays in Memory of Gordon Baker* (pp.37–65). Oxford: Blackwell.

Hacker, P.M.S. (1972/1986). *Insight and Illusion: Themes in the Philosophy of Wittgenstein*. Revised edition. Oxford: Clarendon Press.

Hacker, P.M.S. (1990/1993a). *Wittgenstein: Meaning and Mind. Volume 3 of an Analytical Commentary on the Philosophical Investigations. Part I. Essays*. Oxford: Blackwell.

Hacker, P.M.S. (1990/1993b). *Wittgenstein: Meaning and Mind. Volume 3 of an Analytical Commentary on the Philosophical Investigations. Part II. Exegesis §§243–427*. Oxford: Blackwell.

Hacker, P.M.S. (2001). Was he Trying to Whistle it? In P.M.S. Hacker. *Wittgenstein: Connections and Controversies* (pp.98–140). Oxford: Clarendon Press.

Hacker, P.M.S. (2012). Wittgenstein on Grammar, Theses and Dogmatism. *Philosophical Investigations*, 35, 1–17.

Hilmy, S. (1987). *The Later Wittgenstein: The Emergence of a New Philosophical Method*. Oxford: Blackwell.

Hintikka, J. (1991). An Impatient Man and his Papers. *Synthese*, 87, 183–201.

Hintikka, M.B. and Hintikka, J. (1986). *Investigating Wittgenstein*. Oxford: Blackwell.

Hrachovec, H. (2000). *Wittgenstein on Line/on the Line. In Fragments*. Bergen: The Wittgenstein Archives at the University of Bergen. http://wab.aksis.uib.no/wab_contrib-hh.page (last accessed 1 June 2016).

Hrachovec, H. (2005). Evaluating the Bergen Electronic Edition. In A. Pichler and S. Säätelä (Eds). *Wittgenstein: The Philosopher and his Works* (pp.364–376). Frankfurt: Ontos.

Kahane, G., Kanterian, E., and Kuusela, O. (Eds). (2007). *Wittgenstein and his Interpreters: Essays in Memory of Gordon Baker*. Oxford: Wiley-Blackwell.

Kenny, A. (1976). From the Big Typescript to the *Philosophical Grammar*. *Acta Philosophica Fennica*, 28, 41–53.

Kenny, A. (2005). A Brief History of Wittgenstein Editing. In A. Pichler and S. Säätelä (Eds). *Wittgenstein: The Philosopher and his Works* (pp.341–355). Frankfurt: Ontos.

Kienzler, W. (1997). *Wittgensteins Wende zu seiner Spätphilosophie 1930–1932. Eine historische und systematische Darstellung*. [Wittgenstein's Turn to his Late Philosophy, 1930–1932: A Historical and Systematic Presentation.] Frankfurt: Suhrkamp.

Kienzler, W. (2001). About the Dividing Line between Early and Late Wittgenstein. In G. Oliveri (Ed.). *From the Tractatus to the Tractatus and other Essays* (pp.125–130). Frankfurt: Peter Lang.

Kuusela, O. (2008). *The Struggle against Dogmatism: Wittgenstein and the Concept of Philosophy*. Cambridge, MA: Harvard University Press.

Kuusela, O. (2011). The Development of Wittgenstein's Philosophy. In O. Kuusela and M. McGinn (Eds). *The Oxford Handbook of Wittgenstein* (pp.597–619). Oxford: Oxford University Press.

McManus, D. (2010). Ludwig Wittgenstein: Early Works. In *Oxford Bibliographies Online*. Oxford: Oxford University Press.

Moyal-Sharrock, D. (2013). Beyond Hacker's Wittgenstein. *Philosophical Investigations*, 36, 355–380.

Pichler, A. (2004). *Wittgensteins Philosophische Untersuchungen: Vom Buch zum Album*. [Wittgenstein's *Philosophical Investigations:* From Book to Album.] New York: Rodopi.

Ramsey, F.P. (1923). Critical Notice of *Tractatus Logico-Philosophicus*. *Mind*, 32, 465–478.

Schulte, J. ([1989] 1992). *Wittgenstein: An Introduction*. Trans. W.H. Brenner and J.F. Holley. Albany: SUNY Press. (Original work published 1989.)

Schulte, J. (1999). What Wittgenstein Wrote. In M.R. Egidi (Ed.). *In Search of a New Humanism: The Philosophy of Georg Henrik von Wright* (pp.79–91). London: Synthese Library.

Schulte, J. (2001). *Ludwig Wittgenstein: Philosophische Untersuchungen, Kritisch-genetische Edition*. [Ludwig Wittgenstein: Philosophical Investigations, a Critico-Genetic Edition.] Frankfurt: Suhrkamp.

Schulte, J. (2002). Wittgenstein's Method. In R. Haller and K. Puhl (Eds). *Wittgenstein and the Future of Philosophy: A Reassessment after 50 Years* (pp.399–410). Vienna: Hölder-Pichler-Tempsky.

Schulte, J. (2005). What is a Work by Wittgenstein? In A. Pichler and S. Säätelä (Eds). *Wittgenstein: The Philosopher and his Works* (pp.356–363). Frankfurt: Ontos.

Schulte, J. (2011). Waismann as Spokesman for Wittgenstein. In B. McGuinness (Ed.). *Friedrich Waismann: Causality and Logical Positivism* (pp.225–242). Dordrecht: Springer.

Stern, D.G. (1991). The "Middle Wittgenstein": From Logical Atomism to Practical Holism. *Synthese*, 87, 203–226.

Stern, D.G. (1995). *Wittgenstein on Mind and Language*. Oxford: Oxford University Press.

Stern, D.G. (1996). The Availability of Wittgenstein's Philosophy. In H. Sluga and D.G. Stern (Eds). *The Cambridge Companion to Wittgenstein* (pp.442–476). Cambridge: Cambridge University Press.

Stern, D.G. (2004). *Wittgenstein's Philosophical Investigations: An Introduction.* Cambridge: Cambridge University Press.

Stern, D.G. (2005). How Many Wittgensteins? In A. Pichler and S. Säätelä (Eds). *Wittgenstein: The Philosopher and his Works* (pp.205–229). Frankfurt: Ontos.

Stern, D.G. (2010a). Another Strand in the Private Language Argument. In A. Ahmed (Ed.). *Wittgenstein's Philosophical Investigations: A Critical Guide* (pp.178–196). Cambridge: Cambridge University Press.

Stern, D.G. (2010b). Tracing the Development of Wittgenstein's Writing on Private Language. In N. Venturinha (Ed.). *Wittgenstein after his Nachlass* (pp.110–127). Basingstoke: Palgrave Macmillan.

Stern, D.G. (2010c). The Bergen Electronic Edition of Wittgenstein's *Nachlass*. *European Journal of Philosophy*, 18, 455–467.

Stern, D.G. (2011). Private Language. In O. Kuusela and M. McGinn (Eds). *The Oxford Handbook of Wittgenstein* (pp.333–350). Oxford: Oxford University Press.

Stern, D.G., Citron, G. and Rogers, B. (2013). Moore's Notes on Wittgenstein's Lectures, Cambridge 1930–1933: Text, Context, and Content. *Nordic Wittgenstein Review*, 2, 161–179.

Strawson, P. (1954). Critical Notice of Wittgenstein's *Philosophical Investigations*. *Mind*, 63, 70–99.

Further Reading

Anscombe, G.E.M. (1969). On the Form of Wittgenstein's Writing. In R. Klibansky (Ed.). *Contemporary Philosophy: A Survey* (Vol. 3, pp.373–378). Florence: La Nuova Italia.

Bazzocchi, L. (2014). User Instructions. In L. Bazzochi (Ed.). *Wittgenstein: The Tractatus according to its own Form* (pp.i–xiv). Raleigh: Lulu.

Fogelin, R. (2009). *Taking Wittgenstein at his Word*. Princeton: Princeton University Press.

Hacker, P.M.S. (2015). How the *Tractatus* was Meant to be Read. *The Philosophical Quarterly*, 65, 648–668.

Kuusela, O. (2015). The Tree and the Net: Reading the *Tractatus* Two-Dimensionally. *Rivista di storia della filosofia*, 1, 229–232.

Perloff, M. (2011). Writing Philosophy as Poetry: Literary Form in Wittgenstein. In O. Kuusela and M. McGinn (Eds). *The Oxford Handbook of Wittgenstein* (pp.714–728). Oxford: Oxford University Press.

Pichler, A. (2015). Wittgenstein and us 'typical Western Scientists'. In S.S. Grève and J. Mácha (Eds). *Wittgenstein and the Creativity of Language* (pp.55–75). Basingstoke: Palgrave Macmillan.

Stern, D.G. (2017). Wittgenstein in the 1930s. Forthcoming in H. Sluga and D.G. Stern (Eds). *The Cambridge Companion to Wittgenstein*, second edition. Cambridge: Cambridge University Press.

Wallgren, T. (2013). The Genius, the Businessman, the Sceptic: Three Phases in Wittgenstein's Views on Publishing and on Philosophy. In J. Rothhaupt and W. Vossenkuhl (Eds). *Kulturen und Werte: Wittgensteins "Kringel-Buch" als Initialtext* (pp.113–139). Berlin: de Gruyter.

Part II

Influences

3

Wittgenstein and Schopenhauer

DALE JACQUETTE

1 Early and Later Wittgenstein

Wittgenstein's thought, in diametrically opposed ways, was profoundly shaped in both *Tractatus* and post-*Tractatus* periods by Schopenhauer's transcendental idealism. Schopenhauer's philosophy in highly modified form undergirds many of the most important early distinctions and conclusions in Wittgenstein's 1922 *Tractatus Logico-Philosophicus*. In the later *Philosophical Investigations*, posthumously published in 1953, Wittgenstein identifies rules of philosophical grammar for language-games in relation to their pragmatic point and purpose, practically grounded in forms of life. The later Wittgensteinian understanding of meaning is anti-Schopenhauerian in its adamant anti-transcendentalism.

Sometime during 1929–1930 Wittgenstein came to see the *Tractatus* as having ultimately failed in its primary purpose of undermining traditional philosophy. Wittgenstein wanted to show that discursive philosophy is exposed as literally meaningless by its own self-defeating discursive meaning conditions, when called upon to make sense of philosophical discourse. The *Tractatus* offers the best and perhaps the only possible solution to the problem of discursively explaining the conditions for meaningful linguistic expression. When the *Tractatus* theory of meaning disappoints its own conditions, it is supposed to take down with it the possibility of any meaningful discursive philosophical language, and thereby the possibility in particular of any meaningful semantic philosophy. Whereupon we can responsibly set aside all pretend propositions, questions, answers, and solutions to the presumed but fictitious problems of traditional philosophy (cf. Chapter 12, METAPHYSICS: FROM INEFFABILITY TO NORMATIVITY).

To play this role, the hypothetical discursive theory of meaning developed in the *Tractatus* needs to maintain its own initial plausibility until it is finally rejected as meaningless by its own criteria of meaningfulness (cf. Chapter 11, INEFFABILITY AND NONSENSE IN THE *TRACTATUS* and Chapter 10, RESOLUTE READINGS OF THE *TRACTATUS*). Later Wittgenstein realizes in the crisis year that the *Tractatus* explanation of the necessary and sufficient conditions for meaning is logically inconsistent and in related ways inadequate, considered on its own terms and regardless of whether or not it should be thought to imply its own

---

A Companion to Wittgenstein, First Edition. Edited by Hans-Johann Glock and John Hyman.
© 2017 John Wiley & Sons, Ltd. Published 2017 by John Wiley & Sons, Ltd.

meaninglessness. As a result, Wittgenstein abandons the *Tractatus* anti-philosophical project. He accumulates several philosophical debts in mounting the putative discursive explanation of the conditions for discursive meaning in the *Tractatus*, and might have blamed the argument's failure on a variety of contributing factors. He seems however to attribute the problem to the Schopenhauerian transcendentalism latent in the indispensable *Tractatus* distinction between perceptible sign and perception-transcending symbol.

The primary evidence for Wittgenstein's implicitly holding Schopenhauerian assumptions responsible for the *Tractatus* unraveling is the fact that, whereas the *Tractatus* depends on and revels in Schopenhauerian transcendentalism, in the post-*Tractatus* period Wittgenstein renounces transcendentalism in explaining the conditions for meaningful expression in a language (cf. Chapter 45, WITTGENSTEIN AND KANTIANISM). After 1930, he makes no further mention of the Schopenhauerian transcendence of logical form and pictorial relations, the metaphysical subject, the sense of the mystical, or ethical and aesthetic value, that had featured prominently in the *Tractatus*, or in his 1929 "Lecture on Ethics." These transcendentalist braveries are all banished after 1930, and Wittgenstein shifts instead toward a pragmatic account of meaning in which there is no need to invoke a distinction between the perceptible sign and perception-transcending aspects of a linguistic expression (see Chapter 26, LANGUAGES, LANGUAGE-GAMES, AND FORMS OF LIFE).

Understanding the transition in Wittgenstein's (anti-) philosophy requires an appreciation for both the largely unspoken importance of Schopenhauerian transcendentalism in the sign–symbol distinction and other *transcendentalia* in the *Tractatus*, and of Wittgenstein's decisive pragmatic turn away from Schopenhauer and transcendentalism in explaining the conditions for meaningful linguistic expression in the post-*Tractatus* period.

2   Schopenhauer's Influence on the Early Wittgenstein

There is anecdotal evidence that Wittgenstein, like many other young Austrian intellectuals near the end of the nineteenth century, discovered Schopenhauer and found in his moral pessimism a touchstone for a sense of adolescent *Weltschmerz*. Wittgenstein, with his more specialized technical interests in philosophical logic and semantics, apparently found something more.

G.H. von Wright, a student of the later Wittgenstein at Cambridge in the 1930s, writes:

> If I remember rightly, Wittgenstein told me that he had read Schopenhauer's *Die Welt als Wille und Vorstellung* in his youth and that his first philosophy was a Schopenhauerian epistemological idealism. (von Wright, 1982, p.18)

A.J. Ayer, another acquaintance of Wittgenstein's, though not a member of the inner circle of his students, similarly recounts:

> Wittgenstein was not entirely dismissive of the philosophers of the past, but his reading of them was markedly eclectic. As a boy he was strongly influenced by Schopenhauer's principal work, *The World as Will and Representation*, and we shall see that this influence persists in the *Tractatus*, though the only philosophers to whom he acknowledges a debt in the *Tractatus* are Frege and Russell. The book contains a passing reference to Kant and has

been thought by some critics to display a Kantian approach, but there is no evidence that Wittgenstein made any serious study of Kant's writings and his knowledge of Kant was probably filtered through Schopenhauer. (Ayer, 1985, p.13; concerning Wittgenstein's familiarity with Kant's writings see Chapter 45, WITTGENSTEIN AND KANTIANISM; cf. also Monk, 1990, p.158; and McGuinness, 1988, p.39)

The *Tractatus* embodies a revisionary Schopenhauerian transcendentalism in several ways. The overall structure of Wittgenstein's reasoning in the first place is best understood as that of a Kantian transcendental inference. It exhibits precisely the style of thinking that Schopenhauer unconditionally accepts in the Transcendental Aesthetic of Kant's *Critique of Pure Reason* (1781/1787). Just as Kant begins a train of transcendental reasoning with something given, a *datum*, and asks what must be true in order for the given to be possible, so similarly, albeit less methodologically self-consciously, Wittgenstein in effect begins with the given fact that we can use language to express determinate meaning, or that genuine uses of language are determinately meaningful, and asks transcendentally what must be true in order for such a thing to be possible.

What Wittgenstein discovers in the process are *Tractatus* conditions for meaningful expression in a language. He concludes, with all the assurance of any of Kant's or Schopenhauer's synthetic a priori pronouncements, that in order for the determinate meaningfulness of language to be possible, it must be the case that sentences can be analyzed as concatenations of simple names. Names for simple objects in turn stand in one-one representing relations with the logically basic corresponding components of truthmaking states of affairs that signs as meaningful sentences symbolically picture. At the most fundamental level of analysis, the logically simple atomic facts pictured by elementary propositions are correspondingly decomposable into juxtapositions of simple objects denoted by simple names, each possessing one of the forms of space, time, and color (TLP 2.0251), and fastened together like the links in a chain (TLP 2.03) (see Chapter 7, LOGICAL ATOMISM and Chapter 8, THE PICTURE THEORY).

As Stenius (1960, pp.214–26), Janik (1966), Janik and Toulmin (1973, pp.74, 164), and other commentators have maintained, there is perhaps no more insightful way to understand the argument of the *Tractatus* in presenting its presumed discursive theory of meaning than in these Kantian–Schopenhauerian transcendental reasoning terms.

3 Schopenhauerian Perceptible Sign and Transcendent Symbol

In the *Tractatus* period, Wittgenstein believes that he has pulled the rug out from under all discursive philosophy. The theory of discursive meaning that finally excludes without exception the meaningfulness of any discursive theory of meaning depends for its plausibility and interest on a selection of conceptual debts, prominently including a version of Schopenhauerian transcendentalism applied to the problem of understanding the objects of expressive content in language.

The *Tractatus* explanation of meaning presupposes a modified but easily recognizable Schopenhauerian distinction between the phenomenal appearance of meaningful signs in a language and their perceptually transcendent structures under Wittgenstein's sign–symbol distinction (TLP 3.32–3.324). Signs conventionally express meaning in a perceptually transcendent symbolic semantic order where symbols upon analysis are in direct one-one contact with corresponding parts of their truth conditions, construed as existent or nonexistent truthmaking states of affairs. Wittgenstein distinguishes between phenomenal sign and transcendent symbol when he writes: "The sign is the part of the symbol perceptible to the senses" (TLP 3.32). He thereby implies that there is also an imperceptible part of a symbol that transcends the perceptible written or spoken sign, which is all we need mean in speaking of Wittgenstein's early logical and semantic Schopenhauerian transcendentalism. If the picture theory of meaning is to be plausible, then it must have to do with meaning-related factors that go beyond what is perceivable in linguistic signs. No one would suppose that the sign "It is raining" is itself a conjunction of concatenations of simple names for all the simple objects that must be correlatively juxtaposed in order for "It is raining" to picture a state of affairs in which it is raining, as the picture theory otherwise seems to require.

Symbols have meaning first and foremost above their perceptible expression in sentence signs in the *Tractatus*, where the picturing relation is supposed to transcend the perceivable world of facts. Meaning is only secondarily expressed by a symbol's perceptible sign aspect, conventionally mapped from a convenient repeatable concrete medium onto the possibilities of describing the contingent state of the world, and nothing more. Thought projects meaning from sign to symbol in using language, making a pictorially meaningful expression by thinking the sense of a proposition, appointing a physical mark to symbolically represent the meaning that a philosophically innocent user might otherwise attach only to the sign (TLP 3.11). The possibilities of meaning for the *Tractatus* are then a purely combinatorial matter. The domain of meaningful expressions is comprehended in its entirety by the generous general form of proposition, from a starter subdomain of contingently true or false elementary propositions. An operation of joint propositional negation is applied to every set and subset taken from the stock of elementary propositions of the Red-here-now type. The *Elementarsätze* provide the semantic raw material of all expressible meaning in the logically contingently true or false description of every logically possible situation (cf. Chapter 17, LOGIC AND THE *TRACTATUS*).

It is only by distinguishing between two aspects of language, the perceptible sign part of a symbol and its transcendent imperceptible part, that Wittgenstein is able to explain the logic and picture theory semantics of all genuine languages despite their superficial confusions, ambiguities, and equivocations. Whereas colloquial language disguises the meanings of thoughts (TLP 4.011), its sign-transcending symbolism expresses a definite meaning by virtue of picturing an existent or nonexistent state of affairs. The symbolic picturing of the world is supposed to be accomplished by means of a one-one correspondence between the fully analyzed elements of a sentence in the linguistic order and the fully reduced logical atomistic elements of a state of affairs in the ontic or metaphysical order. The colloquial sentence "It is raining" does not picture precipitation in its sign aspect at the superficial level of appearance in conventional English. It does so, according to Wittgenstein, only at the imperceptible symbolic level as a truth function of elementary propositions corresponding to the co-presence of the relevant atomic states of affairs, and in the one-one alignment of the simple names concatenated in each elementary proposition with the simple objects correspondingly juxtaposed in each pictured atomic state of affairs.

Tautology and contradiction tag along for the ride as genuine propositions by Wittgenstein in a general syntactical amnesty, despite their inability to picture facts. They are ham-fistedly third-tracked by Wittgenstein as having neither *Sinn* nor being *unsinnig* (nonsensical), but rather as *sinnlos* (senseless), in what looks to be a makeshift category. Tautology and contradiction are included as genuine propositions for further unexplained reasons of simplicity in syntactical preference, on the unanswerable grounds that they are "part of the symbolism" by analogy with 0 (zero) in arithmetic (4.46–4.463).

The three pillars of the *Tractatus*, logical atomism, the picture theory of meaning, and general form of proposition, are thus predicated on a uniquely Wittgensteinian application of Schopenhauerian transcendentalism in the best and only possible discursive explanation of the meanings of names and sentences. We begin with the possibility of expressing determinate meaning in a language, which implies the making of an artifact, a picture of a fact (TLP 2.1). Wittgenstein, reasoning transcendentally, as we suppose, wants to know what must be true in order for the picturing of facts to be logically possible. The question can only be answered philosophically by explaining the general conditions for meaningful expression in any language. The meanings of pictures, which are themselves facts, whereby we picture other facts, do not attach merely to those fact-picturing signs, but to similar uses of signs, and in principle to any set of superficially dissimilar but transcendentally logically isomorphic signs in different colloquial and technical languages. This is young Wittgenstein giving discursive philosophical "prosifying" its best chance of making sense, and watching it fail as literally meaningless on the basis of its own requirements.

A critic unsympathetic to Wittgenstein's early enthusiasms may question classifying the best and only possible discursive theory of meaning as nonsensical. If tautologies are tolerated as genuine propositions in a correct logical notation by virtue of being part of the symbolism, then why should there not be logically necessarily true propositions in a discursive philosophical explanation of the general conditions for meaningful linguistic expression? The general form of proposition as Wittgenstein simplifies its successive operations of joint negation on a given domain of elementary propositions is powerless to exclude tautologies, despite not picturing any particular logically contingent world-constituting states of affairs. They are additionally useful for many purposes in logical methods and reasoning, such as proceeding in argument from *tertium non datur* dilemma assumptions. The *Tractatus* theory of meaning might equally reasonably be tolerated as useful and necessarily true, possibly in the sense of being tautological itself or logically reducible to a tautology from a conjunction of logically necessary truths. Wittgenstein does not seem to have conducted the sort of inquiry needed to know whether or not the three pillars of the mock-discursive *Tractatus* explanation of meaning are really tautologies. Why should they be nonsense, *unsinnig*, like "Socrates is identical" and worse, gibberish, as 6.54 still brazenly attempts to declare, rather than senseless, *sinnlos*, like tautologies and contradictions?

4 Transcendent *Tractatus* Logic and Semantics

The sign–symbol distinction is crucial to Wittgenstein's efforts to provide a general semantics for the possibility of determinate meaning in any logically possible language. Unlike Frege and Russell, Wittgenstein is unwilling to take refuge from the semantic defects of colloquial language in an ideal language or *Begriffsschrift*.

Wittgenstein recognizes that, from a historical point of view, formal-technical and mathematical languages derive from preexistent natural languages in which it is already possible to express determinate meaning. He knows that it does not contribute to the purpose of understanding the meaning conditions of languages generally to turn one's back especially on colloquial languages (TLP 4.002).

If we think of Wittgenstein's sign-aspect of language as a semantic version of Schopenhauer's concept of the world as representation, perceptible to intuition and represented in thought, and of Wittgenstein's transcendent symbol-aspect of language as a semantic version of Schopenhauer's concept of thing-in-itself understood as the transcendent reality underlying the world of appearances or representations, then the application is unmistakable. Wittgenstein does not need to posit the existence of an ideal language if there is already an ideal transcendent aspect of every language by virtue of which it expresses meaning, and similarly, therefore, he has no need to abandon all conventional colloquial language for the sake of limiting semantic theory exclusively to an ideal language.

Within the German logic and semantic tradition, to which Wittgenstein's early thought also belongs, Bolzano in his *Wissenschaftslehre* ([1837] 1972, esp. pp.20–31, 171–80) had previously distinguished in similar fashion between sentences (*Sätze*) and sentences-in-themselves (*Sätze an sich*). Bolzano's propositions are sometimes taken to be the linguistic counterpart of Kant's or Schopenhauer's perception-transcending reality. It is an evident even if only coincidental terminological echoing of Kant's *Ding an sich*, by an otherwise staunchly anti-Kantian nineteenth-century philosopher. The Kantian thing-in-itself is further interpreted by Schopenhauer as will (*der Wille*), transcending the principle of identity and individuation. This means effectively that the world as will transcends space and time, although Schopenhauer prefers to arrive at metaphysics only secondarily through epistemology, as something we can know at least about the limits of knowledge, rather than the other way around. He locates *Wille* as Kantian thing-in-itself beyond the explanatory reach of the fourfold root of the principle of sufficient reason (see Schopenhauer, [1818/59] 1966, vol.1, pp.127–8). Wittgenstein appears to endorse much the same division of factual world and transcendental logic and arithmetical form, in maintaining that the cardinality of simple names, simple objects, and logical forms is anumerical (TLP 4.1272–4.128). The simple names, simple objects, and logical forms collectively – because they cannot be numbered, univocally counted as individual entities – are situated as much beyond any Schopenhauerian *principium individuationis* as the noumenal Kantian *Ding an sich*. Schopenhauerian *Wille* is nevertheless a *will*, and Schopenhauer chooses his terminology carefully in this regard, something at least metaphorically psychological. Wittgenstein invokes a similar Schopenhauerian concept again when he describes the transcendent thinking metaphysical subject or philosophical I as constituting a will to represent, establishing the picturing lines of projection from symbol to fact, rather than logically isomorphic fact to symbol in the opposite direction, to make meaningful expression possible in the fact-transcending symbolic aspect of language (cf. Chapter 30, WITTGENSTEIN ON "I" AND THE SELF and Chapter 9, WITTGENSTEIN ON SOLIPSISM).

Wittgenstein accordingly writes: "Logic is not a theory but a reflexion of the world. Logic is transcendental" (TLP 6.13). The perceptible part of language and the states of affairs in logical space that constitute a world for early Wittgenstein are the equivalent of Schopenhauer's world as representation. Logical form, pictorial and representational form, among other items of interest, in turn transcend the world of facts, where they cannot be described, but only show themselves in the identical structures of pictured and picturing facts. They do not exist as objects or states of affairs, but stand outside of

WITTGENSTEIN AND SCHOPENHAUER

all facts and objects by virtue of which there is a transcendent logical structure of the world through which pictorial meaning functions. It is possible in this light to understand Wittgenstein's early (picture) theory of meaning in the *Tractatus* as a Schopenhauerian semantics in which the distinction between the world as representation and as thing-in-itself is applied on a limited scale to the linguistic order, for the sake of interpreting the meanings expressed by sentences in their similarly dual perceptible sign and transcendent symbolic attributes (see especially TLP 2.151, 2.172, 2.18, 4.12–4.1212, 4.461, 5.541–5.5422, 5.631–5.641, 6.22, 6.432–6.45, 6.522).

5   Transcendence of Convergent Ethical-Aesthetic Value

It is not only logical, pictorial, and representational form that transcends the empirical world of facts according to the *Tractatus*. Wittgenstein places value, ethics, and aesthetics identified as one outside the world, by which all attempts to express value are relegated extra-semantically to the category of literal nonsense. Value thereby joins representational form, logical form, the metaphysical subject, and whatever cannot be said but only shown.

Moral and aesthetic value transcends the world. The elimination of value from the world implies that ethics, including attempts at ethical judgment in theory and practice, is nonsensical. According to the general form of proposition in the *Tractatus*, only logically contingent statements of fact convey meaning. Wittgenstein maintains:

> 6.41 The sense of the world must lie outside the world. In the world everything is as it is and happens as it does happen. *In* it there is no value – and if there were, it would be of no value.
>
> If there is a value which is of value, it must lie outside all happening and being-so. For all happening and being-so is accidental.
>
> What makes it non-accidental cannot lie *in* the world, for otherwise this would again be accidental.
>
> It must lie outside the world.
> [...]
> 6.421 It is clear that ethics cannot be expressed.
> Ethics is transcendental.
> (Ethics and aesthetics are one.) (TLP 6.41–6.421)

Wittgenstein locates undifferentiated value outside the world. He explains the semantic implications of transcendence for the ineffability of ethics and the pseudo-propositional status of efforts to express ethical value. Finally, he concludes with the intriguing identification of ethics and aesthetics as one. The semantic dimensions of transcendent value are implicit in the *Notebooks 1914–16*, but clearly spelled out in the *Tractatus* transcendence passages (see e.g., NB 24.7.16 and 21.10.16; cf. Barrett, 1991, pp. 30, 60–3). Wittgenstein elaborates on the insight in a Spinozistic entry that complements his Schopenhauerian transcendentalism in the *Notebooks*: "The work of art is the object seen *sub specie aeternitatis*; and the good life is the world seen *sub specie aeternitatis*. This is the connexion between art and ethics" (NB 7.10.16).

The *Tractatus* discussion of transcendence, on the other hand, does not draw directly on the transcendence of the metaphysical subject as conferring transcendence on value by constituting the transcendental ground of subjective valuation, as in the second of two *Notebooks* arguments on the same topic where Wittgenstein in distinctively Schopenhauerian terms writes:

> Good and evil only enter through the *subject*. And the subject is not part of the world, but a boundary of the world.
>
> It would be possible to say (à la Schopenhauer): It is not the world of Idea that is either good or evil; but the willing subject. (NB 2.8.16)

The *Tractatus* develops Wittgenstein's concept of the subject's transcendence even more fully than the *Notebooks*, but leaves the connection between the subject's transcendence and the transcendence of value unstated. It is the world seen in a certain way, but not literally describable as such in a factual predication of properties to objects (see Jacquette, 1997).

Wittgenstein discerns no meaningful difference between ethics and aesthetics, because they are merely different ways of emphasizing what persons choose to do or not to do. We are good or bad artists in every action we undertake. In some cases, the actions for which ethics and aesthetics are one involve the making of art and artifacts as narrowly conceived, in painting, sculpting, writing or reciting poetry, drafting a novel, or designing a work of architecture or composing or whistling a song. In other cases, the actions are diapering a baby, having a conversation with a friend, negotiating a treaty, serving in the military, or deciding whether or not violently to avenge a perceived wrong. The ethical terms we use in judging the merits of such behavior are equally aesthetic, and the aesthetic vocabulary by which we assess the merits of artistic endeavors is equally a pronouncement of the artist's morality. To be a good or bad conductor of an orchestra is no different in principle, although the applicable criteria are specialized, than to be a good or bad soldier, husband, mother, or prime minister (see Chapter 39, WITTGENSTEIN AND ETHICS).

The *Tractatus* reaches its denouement when Wittgenstein denies the previously unquestioned intelligibility of the preceding discursive explanation of the conditions for meaning:

> My propositions are elucidatory in this way: he who understands me finally recognizes them as [nonsensical (*unsinnig*)], when he has climbed out through them, on them, over them. (He must so to speak throw away the ladder, after he has climbed up on it.) (TLP 6.54)

Schopenhauer expresses similar ideas in the second volume of the third edition of *The World as Will and Representation*, in the course of contrasting shallow discursive learning with a more searching philosophical inquiry that uses discursive texts as a means to the higher end of attaining transcendental understanding:

> However, for the man who studies to gain *insight*, books and studies are mere rungs of the ladder on which he climbs to the summit of knowledge. As soon as a rung has raised him one step, he leaves it behind. (Schopenhauer, [1818/59] 1966, vol.2, p.80)

The strands of Wittgenstein's 1929–1930 rejection of Schopenhauerian transcendentalism are as tightly interwoven with the failure of the *Tractatus* as the success of the *Tractatus* was expected to depend on the book's Kantian–Schopenhauerian transcendental reasoning, and on the Kantian–Schopenhauerian duality of perceivable and transcendental aspects of all meaningful expression. To explain Schopenhauer's influence on Wittgenstein's philosophy, we must accordingly look from the pro-Schopenhauerian transcendentalism of the *Tractatus* period to the later anti-Schopenhauerianism and more generally anti-transcendentalism of the post-*Tractatus* period.

6 Later Anti-Schopenhauerian Anti-Transcendental Antipode

The chronology of Wittgenstein's early distinctive pro-Schopenhauerian transcendentalism and later anti-Schopenhauerian anti-transcendentalism marks exactly the main division in the two major periods of Wittgenstein's thought, from the time including the *Tractatus* and related documents, leading up to his writing and then disowning the 1929 paper, "Some Remarks on Logical Form" (see Jacquette, 1998a, especially pp.160–92; 1998b; 2002).

Wittgenstein makes a valiant but ultimately ineffectual effort to rescue the *Tractatus* logic from the color incompatibility problem. This is the difficulty Ramsey emphasized in his 1923 *Mind* review of the *Tractatus*. TLP 6.375–6.3751 commits the three pillars of the *Tractatus*, its logic, semantics, and ontology, to the necessity of reducing presumably impossible predications of the form "*RPT* and *BPT*" ("Red here now and blue here now, at the same place *P* and time *T*") to an explicit *logical* inconsistency of the form "*RPT* and not-*RPT*," or "*BPT* and not-*BPT*." Wittgenstein says that color incompatibility must be reducible to logical inconsistency, but he offers no deductively valid transformation schema from the syntax of supposedly mutually independent predicationally incompatible *Elementarsätze* to the syntax of explicit logical contradictions (Jacquette, 1990; 1998a, pp.172–89; 2010a; 2010b). He attempts but does not produce the needed reduction in TLP 6.371 and NB 16.8.16 and 11.9.16.

The *Tractatus* presents an account of meaning for purposes of *reductio ad absurdum* as philosophy's best hope of discursively explaining discursive meaning. The language of such an explanation must itself be incapable of having discursive meaning according to its own theory of meaningfulness. For the strategy to succeed, Wittgenstein's at first hypothetically meaningful *Tractatus* account of meaning must hold together well enough not only to be taken as an assumption for *reductio* reasoning, but as the only possible discursive explanation of discursive meaning. When Wittgenstein in the final passages of the *Tractatus* rejects all the propositions of the *Tractatus* as nonsensical according to the presumedly meaningful discursive theory of meaning presented in *Tractatus*, he expects thereby to have shown that even the best possible account of meaningfulness makes no adequate provision for the meaningfulness of philosophical discourse. That would be a monumental anti-traditional-discursive-philosophical conclusion. If the theory of meaning in the *Tractatus* turns out on its own terms to be hopelessly incompetent, then it is not even a plausible candidate for advancing a possible discursive explanation of discursive meaning. In developing an orthogonally opposed new pragmatic direction in the explanation of meaning, Wittgenstein in the later period rejects the *Tractatus* presentation of the only possible conditions for the meaningfulness of language, and with them the Schopenhauerian transcendentalism that the *Tractatus* presupposes.

The elementary propositions are supposed to be logically independent (5.134), in the sense that they cannot imply or contradict one another (2.11). To infer *RPT* and not-*RPT* from *RPT* and *BPT*, *BPT* would have to logically imply not-*RPT*, which is to say that

BPT would have to logically contradict *RPT*. If, on the other hand, the inference is disallowed within the *Tractatus*, then there are logically false propositions that are not syntactically reducible to logical contradictions. The embarrassment in that case is not merely that the *Tractatus* has no inferential mechanism by which to negotiate such a syntactical reduction, but that with equal justification it requires both logically incompatible possibilities that the Red-here-now elementary propositions are logically independent of and logically dependent on one another, and that some logically contradict others. These objections with their implications must have dawned on Wittgenstein, and may have played a part in his decision to return to philosophy upon realizing that the *Tractatus* had not accomplished its anti-philosophical purpose.

The *Tractatus* project quickly unravels along these lines in the later part of the intervening seven years. If the elementary propositions Red-here-now and Blue-here-now are both logically independent and not logically independent of one another, then what the *Tractatus* touts as the best and only possible discursive account of meaningfulness is confused. It is internally contradictory for more fundamental reasons than the fact that the theory is required impossibly to validate its own meaningfulness. If the model in its entirety is nonsensical on more pedestrian theory-building grounds anyway by virtue of incorporating a whopping albeit previously unnoticed internal contradiction of the sort Ramsey emphasizes, then there is no anti-philosophical mileage to be gained by revealing as Wittgenstein does with a certain theatrical flourish that the entire model of meaning painstakingly revealed in the previous roughly 70 pages of the *Tractatus* is on its own terms literally *unsinnig* (6.54–7). Equally, then, Wittgenstein offers no adequate justification for setting aside traditional discursive philosophy on the grounds that discursive meaning, logical form, the self or subject, and with them conflated ethical and aesthetic value, transcend the sensible world of logically contingent facts.

Wittgenstein's empathy for Schopenhauer undergoes a similar reversal from his early- to later-period (anti-) philosophy. As a consequence, we can only hope to understand Wittgenstein's intellectual development spanning both major periods of his thought by bringing Schopenhauer prominently into the story – first, pro-Schopenhauerian, as Wittgenstein transforms Schopenhauerian transcendental idealism in the service of a different set of purposes in the *Tractatus*, and second, as anti-Schopenhauerian, when he forcefully rejects transcendentalism after judging the *Tractatus* to have failed. He does so when he decisively lays down the conceptual framework for a relatively transparent pragmatism to explain the meaning conditions of language use that seek again from a very different direction to discredit the meaningfulness of conventional philosophy. There are many possible pragmatically justified language-games for the later Wittgenstein, but traditional philosophy, in any of its content or methods, is not one of them (cf. however Chapter 13, PHILOSOPHY AND PHILOSOPHICAL METHOD; see also Chapter 47, WITTGENSTEIN AND ORDINARY LANGUAGE PHILOSOPHY). Schopenhauer in contrast is far more old-fashioned, following in his own estimation the great thinkers of Western philosophy from Plato through Kant, as their next heir apparent.

After seven years of taking comfort in the *Tractatus* denunciation of discursive philosophy, with the support of its unquestioned semantic Schopenhauerian transcendentalism, Wittgenstein makes a dramatic volte-face. Sometime during 1929–1930, Wittgenstein begins to reject the three tightly interwoven *Tractatus* pseudo-theories, and with them the transcendence of logical and pictorial representational form, the thinking metaphysical subject, mystical awe at the world grasped as a unity, and combined ethical-aesthetic value. When it becomes clear that the *Tractatus* must be discarded, Wittgenstein significantly does not seek to develop an alternative revisionary Schopenhauerian concept of transcendence by which to explain the conditions for the meaningfulness of language. Instead, he goes back to his engineering drawing board and retrenches with an entirely different strategy. He sets up his anti-philosophy shop again under new management. He charts an un-game-like un-rule-governed inquiry into the philosophical grammars of pragmatically warranted language-games integrated into a form of life. Once again, though now for very different reasons, philosophy is excluded as meaningful discourse. Philosophy lacks meaning in Wittgenstein's later philosophy, not because it fails to picture facts, but because it lacks the external pragmatic point and purpose of a genuine language-game whose rule-governed moves are rooted in human practice, rather than in an infinite regress of interpretive rules. Language-games for the later Wittgenstein involve linguistic tokens whose legitimate uses are established by pragmatically determined point-and-purpose-driven rules. These Wittgenstein considers to be transparent rather than transcendent. There is no distinction invoked between the transcendent symbolic meaning of signs, or perception-transcending logical or picturing relations (see also Chapter 14, GRAMMAR AND GRAMMATICAL STATEMENTS). Schopenhauer, in contrast with the *Tractatus*, is conspicuously absent from Wittgenstein's later pragmatic explanation of meaning. As such, Schopenhauer provides an interesting pivot of reversal for the transition in Wittgenstein's thought, given the complex internal structure of the *Tractatus* and the many opportunities that its variety of commitments seems to afford.

Post-*Tractatus* Wittgenstein finds a desired release from philosophical concerns and dispelling of philosophical confusions in the self-satisfying activity of working out the philosophical grammars of key words in what passes for philosophical discourse. These are terms that seem to present both philosophical problems and possibilities when they are lifted from their native genuine language-game habitats and made to play an entirely non-game-like role in the essentially different applications of traditional discursive philosophy. Such language-related activity ironically has no philosophical grammar, because there are no point-and-purpose-driven rules for philosophical discourse as moves in a legitimate, pragmatically motivated language-game. By definition, there can be no philosophically grammatical or ungrammatical philosophical language-game. There is no genuine pragmatic form of life underwriting the doing of conventional philosophy. The therapeutic effort of working out the philosophical grammars of rule-governed language-games belongs to a family of therapies targeted to assuage specific philosophical anxieties (PI §133). Unfortunately, the few examples Wittgenstein offers do not comfortably generalize (see Jacquette, 2014). Philosophy in Wittgenstein's later period is not controverted by its meaninglessness under picture theory requirements, but as a consequence of an anti-transcendental pragmatism that excludes philosophy on entirely different grounds as grammatical investigations that of necessity stand outside of any practically grounded language-game (cf. Chapter 48, WITTGENSTEIN AND PRAGMATISM). Since only practically grounded language-games contain meaningful rule-governed expressions and exchanges, philosophy in Wittgenstein's later thought is again rendered literally meaningless. Philosophical discourse is uniquely beyond the pale of rule-regulated linguistic activities, lacking in the rules of a philosophical grammar pragmatically determined for genuine language-games in each case by a particular practical point and purpose (PI §§62, 108, 562–8). What sense would it make, Wittgenstein hints but does not explicitly ask, for an investigation into the rules of philosophical grammar to follow the rules of philosophical grammar? The relevant rules would then need to be presupposed rather than discovered in the course of inquiry.

Wittgenstein thereby achieves a precisely parallel anti-philosophical conclusion when compared with that attempted in the *Tractatus*. There we could not speak philosophy because we could only meaningfully express the contingent descriptive propositions truth-functionally built out of "Red-here-now"-type elementary propositions available within a language, all else being literal nonsense. In *Philosophical Investigations* and later writings, Wittgenstein holds that we cannot speak philosophy because there are no pragmatically supported philosophy language-games, because there are no point-and-purpose-determined rules to provide a philosophical grammar applicable to philosophical discourse. For the later Wittgenstein, this is to say that there is no pragmatic justification for anything that traditional philosophy tries to say. The difference extensionally is that from the early to the later philosophy, Wittgenstein enormously enlarges the domain of meaningful expression, from whatever we can build out of Red-here-now to unlimitedly many continuously evolving different kinds of uses for different parts of language.

The early passages of the *Investigations* attack all three *Tractatus* pillars. The general form of proposition is defeated by candid appeal to the multiple uses of language by analogy with the variegated tools in a toolbox and the variety of handles in a locomotive cabin (PI §§11–15, 23–4). Description of contingent facts is not all that language can and needs to do for the roles it plays in our practical lives. There are many things to be done with language-game tokens. We generally communicate when we need or want something like five red apples or a slab or beam to be brought to a worksite (PI §§1–2, 8–10, 19–21). Logical atomism is refuted by the commonsense consideration that there is no single way in which things like chessboards or the broom in the corner can be univocally analyzed into their ultimately simple components, offering little encouragement to suppose that there could be a single univocally correct analysis of a proposition's logical structure (PI §§47–50, 59–63). The propositions to be analyzed are supposed to be transcendent in logical structure, and in that sense unavailable for scrutiny as to their actual form. The picture theory of meaning, finally, presupposes precise isomorphisms between transcendent aspects of elementary language use and the atomic facts of the world. With the failure of logical atomism, the required isomorphisms cannot be established when they are called into challenge by the problem of reducing color incompatibility to logical contradiction.

Wittgenstein's *Philosophical Investigations* and other post-*Tractatus* writings undermine the meaningfulness of philosophical problems, questions, and answers in a different way than the *Tractatus*. After 1929, Wittgenstein knows that whatever is salvageable from the objectives of the original project must proceed without the benefit of the three *Tractatus* pillars. In the later period, references to language-games emphasize the forms of life that pragmatically explain how it is possible for language to function in lieu of insupportable infinite regresses of discursive rules for following other discursive rules. If we want to know how all of language works, then we cannot make exceptions for discursive rules themselves. The regress can only be avoided by breaking out of the circle of rules through the appeal to something extra-semantic, something that is external to all particular rules, that enables us to play any particular game, involving the way we live and what Wittgenstein calls our form of life as it has evolved. Arrows mean what they mean because as a species we have needed to be successful bow hunters and we know without appeal to a system of rules that the pointy end is supposed to indicate a forward direction. We do not need a book of instructions to explain this, and another book to explain each of the explanations in previous books in an endless sequence, which would be incompatible anyway with our manifest rapid-fire, real-time language use (PI §§217–19). (See Chapter 24, RULES AND RULE-FOLLOWING.)

The watershed dividing the early from the later period is marked by Wittgenstein's return to Cambridge University beginning in 1930. There he dictated a series of remarks on language and mind that became the locally circulated, posthumously published *Blue and Brown Books*, the material of which evolved into the much-rethought revolutionary *Philosophical Investigations*. From this time forward, Wittgenstein's later philosophical anti-Schopenhauerianism is severe and unequivocal. A relevant historical analogy involving early magnetic attraction for Schopenhauer's ideas and later equally forceful diametrically reactive repulsion is seen in the polar development of Nietzsche's ethics and aesthetics, from the markedly Schopenhauerian *Birth of Tragedy* (*Die Geburt der Tragödie aus dem Geiste der Musik*, 1872) to his diametrically anti-Schopenhauerian *On the Genealogy of Morals* (*Zur Genealogie der Moral*, 1887). The latter work Nietzsche self-consciously describes in its subtitle as *A Polemic* (*Eine Streitschrift*); which, indeed, it is, directed specifically against what Nietzsche denounces as Schopenhauer's life-denying "European Buddhism" ([1887] 1998, p.4). As for Nietzsche beginning with *Genealogie*, Schopenhauer becomes Wittgenstein's unloved antipode in the post-*Tractatus* period.

Wittgenstein later denies any strong impact of Schopenhauer on his own early thinking. In conversation with M.O'C. Drury, Wittgenstein reportedly said the following:

> WITTGENSTEIN: My fundamental ideas came to me very early in life. DRURY: Schopenhauer? WITTGENSTEIN: No; I think I see quite clearly what Schopenhauer got out of his philosophy – but when I read Schopenhauer I seem to see to the bottom very easily. He is not deep in the sense that Kant and Berkeley are deep. (WAM 158)

The passage quoted further above from Wittgenstein's *Notebooks* is the only place in the surviving early writings where he mentions Schopenhauer by name. In the preface to the *Tractatus*, Wittgenstein offers effusive praise to Frege, extended with somewhat less enthusiasm to Russell. Schopenhauer is not mentioned. If the proposed reading of the *Tractatus* is correct, then Wittgenstein's early philosophy is nevertheless run through with Schopenhauer's influence, an almost palpable presence in the semantic theory that depends on the distinction between sign and symbol, the theory of aesthetics and ethics as one, transcendence of logic, mathematics, and all semantic form, *Form der Darstellung*, *Form der Abbildung*, and in the theory of the metaphysical subject or philosophical I. Limited and idiosyncratic as all of Wittgenstein's Schopenhauerianism seems to be in the early philosophy of logic and semantics, in their implications for philosophy generally, the parallel concept in Wittgenstein is not quite Schopenhauer's "*der Wille*," but what might be characterized instead as the individual psychology transcending metaphysical subject's will to represent.

Wittgenstein in the later philosophy denies and distances himself from any Schopenhauerian transcendentalism in the theory of meaning. In the *Investigations*, he declares that meaning can be understood in terms of the imminently observable features of language-games with grammatical rules determined in each case by their pragmatic point and purpose. As contrasted with the *Tractatus* commitment to a kind of

Schopenhauerian semantic transcendentalism, Wittgenstein in the post-*Tractatus* period roundly insists that nothing is hidden in the workings of language. In explaining meaning we need to offer a perspicuous articulation of the way the rules for language-games are praxeologically grounded in a complex network of linguistic and extra-linguistic activities that constitute a form of life. Wittgenstein explains:

> If it is asked: "How do sentences manage to represent?" – the answer might be: "Don't you know? You certainly see it, when you use them. For nothing is concealed."
> How do sentences do it? – Don't you know? For nothing is hidden.
> But given this answer: "But you know how sentences do it, for nothing is concealed" one would like to retort, "Yes, but it all goes by so quick, and I should like to see it as it were laid open to view." (PI §435)

With the firm conviction that in understanding sentential meaning nothing is hidden, the later Wittgenstein turns away from Schopenhauerian semantic transcendentalism. Whether and to what extent, if any, Wittgenstein remains influenced in more subtle ways by his early immersion in Schopenhauer's idealism is as interesting and important a question in coming to terms with Wittgenstein's valuable contributions to philosophy as it is in trying to understand Nietzsche's early devotion to and later rejection of Schopenhauerianism.

The movement constitutes a philosophical reversal that in some ways, in a very different sphere of application and with very different results, anticipates Wittgenstein's similar experience almost a century later. Wittgenstein's second philosophy, like Nietzsche's, after losing affection for Schopenhauer's transcendental idealism, would not have been what it became if it had not first been seasoned in a system of thought that emphasized a transcendental reality, of thing-in-itself characterized as pure willing. The *Tractatus* hypothesis of the best possible explanation of meaning comes apart at the seams during the transitional period over the color incompatibility problem in Wittgenstein's post-*Tractatus* deliberations. Wittgenstein attributes the failure of the *Tractatus* to its Schopenhauerian semantic transcendentalism, and in rejecting it he renounces as well anything that the model might be understood as implying for the transcendence of logic and theory of meaning, of the self or subject, and of judgments and attitudes reflected in the language of ethics and aesthetics, no longer considered as transcendentally one.

References

Ayer, A.J. (1985). *Wittgenstein*. Chicago: University of Chicago Press.
Barrett, C. (1991). *Wittgenstein on Ethics and Religious Belief*. Oxford: Blackwell.
Bolzano, B. ([1837] 1972). *Theory of Science: Attempt at a Detailed and in the Main Novel Exposition of Logic with Constant Attention to Earlier Authors*. Ed. and trans. R. George. Berkeley: University of California Press. (Original work published 1837.)
Jacquette, D. (1990). Wittgenstein and the Color Incompatibility Problem. *History of Philosophy Quarterly*, 7, 353–365.
Jacquette, D. (1997). Wittgenstein on the Transcendence of Ethics. *Australasian Journal of Philosophy*, 75, 304–324.
Jacquette, D. (1998a). *Wittgenstein's Thought in Transition*. West Lafayette: Purdue University Press.

Jacquette, D. (1998b). Wittgenstein's Manometer and the Private Language Argument. *History of Philosophy Quarterly*, 15, 99–126.

Jacquette, D. (2002). Wittgenstein on Thoughts as Pictures of Facts and the Transcendence of the Metaphysical Subject. In R. Haller and K. Puhl (Eds). *Wittgenstein and the Future of Philosophy: A Reassessment after 50 Years* (pp.160–70). Vienna: Öbv and Hölder-Pichler-Tempsky.

Jacquette, D. (2010a). Measure for Measure? Wittgenstein on Language-game Criteria and the Paris Standard Metre Bar. In A. Ahmed (Ed.). *Wittgenstein's Philosophical Investigations: A Critical Guide* (pp.49–65). Cambridge: Cambridge University Press.

Jacquette, D. (2010b). Wittgenstein as Trans-Analytic-Continental Philosopher. In J. Williams, J. Reynolds, J. Chase, and E. Mares (Eds). *Postanalytic and Metacontinental: Crossing Philosophical Divides* (pp.157–72). London: Continuum.

Jacquette, D. (2014). Later Wittgenstein's Anti-Philosophical Therapy. *Philosophy*, 89, 251–272.

Janik, A.S. (1966). Schopenhauer and the Early Wittgenstein. *Philosophical Studies*, 15, 76–95.

Janik, A.S. and Toulmin, S. (1973). *Wittgenstein's Vienna*. New York: Simon and Schuster.

McGuinness, B. (1988). *Wittgenstein: A Life (Vol. 1): Young Ludwig 1889–1921*. London: Duckworth.

Monk, R. (1990). *Wittgenstein: The Duty of Genius*. Harmondsworth: Penguin.

Nietzsche, F. ([1872] 1956). *The Birth of Tragedy and the Genealogy of Morals*. Trans. F. Golffing. Garden City: Doubleday. (Original work published 1872.)

Nietzsche, F. ([1887] 1998). *On the Genealogy of Morality*. Trans. M. Clark and A.J. Swenson. Indianapolis: Hackett. (Original work published 1887.)

Ramsey, F.P. (1923). Critical Notice of *Tractatus Logico-Philosophicus*. *Mind*, 32, 465–478.

Schopenhauer, A. ([1818/59] 1966). *The World as Will and Representation*. 2 Vols. Trans. E.F.J. Payne. New York: Dover.

Stenius, E. (1960). *Wittgenstein's Tractatus: A Critical Exposition of its Main Lines of Thought*. Oxford: Blackwell.

von Wright, G.H. (1982). *Wittgenstein*. Minneapolis: University of Minnesota Press.

Further Reading

Churchill, J. (1983). Wittgenstein's Adaption of Schopenhauer. *Southern Journal of Philosophy*, 21, 489–501.

Engel, M. (1969). Schopenhauer's Impact upon Wittgenstein. *The Journal of the History of Philosophy*, 7, 285–302.

Glock, H.-J. (1999). Schopenhauer and Wittgenstein: Representation as Language and Will. In C. Janaway (Ed.). *The Cambridge Companion to Schopenhauer* (pp.422–458). Cambridge: Cambridge University Press.

Goodman, R.B. (1979). Schopenhauer and Wittgenstein on Ethics. *Journal of the History of Philosophy*, 17, 437–447.

Griffiths, A.P. (1974). Wittgenstein, Schopenhauer, and Ethics. *Royal Institute of Philosophy Lectures*, 7, 96–116.

Lange, E.M. (1989). *Wittgenstein und Schopenhauer: Logisch-philosophische Abhandlung und Kritik des Solipsismus*. [Wittgenstein and Schopenhauer: *Tractatus Logico-Philosophicus* and Critique of Solipsism.] Cuxhaven: Junghaus.

Young, J. (1984). Wittgenstein, Kant, Schopenhauer and Critical Philosophy. *Theoria*, 50, 73–105.

4

Wittgenstein and Frege

MICHAEL BEANEY

1 Introduction

Of all philosophers, it is Frege whom Wittgenstein held in greatest esteem. In the preface to the *Tractatus*, in commenting on the influences on him, he remarked that "I will only mention that I am indebted to the magnificent writings of Frege and the work of my friend Mr Bertrand Russell for a large part of the stimulation of my thoughts." Wittgenstein soon became disappointed by the reception of the *Tractatus* by both Frege and Russell, but whereas his relationship to Russell became more and more strained as the years went by, he retained his respect for Frege's writings to the very end of his life. At Cornell in August 1949, for example, he was still reading and struggling with Frege's most famous essay, "Über Sinn und Bedeutung" ([1892a] 1997; WC 18, 25–7; WAM 70). When J.L. Austin's translation of Frege's *Foundations of Arithmetic* was published in 1950, Wittgenstein discussed it with Ben Richards on a trip to Norway (Kienzler, 2011, p.81, n.7). Just two weeks before his death on 29 April 1951, in the last of the notes published in *Culture and Value*, he remarked that "Frege's style of writing is sometimes *great*" (CV 87).

That Wittgenstein admired Frege's writing style is perhaps unsurprising. The aim of philosophy, Wittgenstein wrote in the *Tractatus*, "is the logical clarification of thoughts" (TLP 4.112), a characterization that might well be taken to be true of Frege's philosophy. The clarity that Wittgenstein saw as an important philosophical virtue is arguably nowhere better illustrated than in Frege's writings, even if one disagrees with the substantive philosophical claims that Frege makes. Peter Geach reports a remark that Wittgenstein made to him when they were discussing Frege's essay "On Concept and Object": "How I envy Frege! I wish I could have written like that" (LPP xiv). That this remark should be made about this particular essay is significant. It counts as the most "elucidatory" of all of Frege's writings, and the notion of elucidation (*Erläuterung*) was of crucial importance to both Frege and Wittgenstein. If Wittgenstein is right that "A philosophical work consists essentially of elucidations" (TLP 4.112), then "On Concept and Object" is a paradigm.

Wittgenstein may have envied Frege's style, but he nevertheless felt it had a strong effect on his own writing. In a remark published in *Zettel*, again dating from the last years of his life, he wrote: "The style of my sentences is extraordinarily strongly influenced by Frege. And if I so wanted, I could most likely establish this influence where no one at first sight would see it" (Z 123). Wittgenstein does not elaborate on this, but someone's first impression might well be that the aphoristic style of his own writing shows no obvious trace of Frege's influence. On deeper comparison, though, the clarity and elucidatory quality of Frege's writings does indeed come through, and maybe this is what Wittgenstein meant (see also Chapter 2, WITTGENSTEIN'S TEXTS AND STYLE).

Whatever speculations might be offered about this, however, Frege's influence on Wittgenstein is far more profound than matters of style, even allowing for the inclusion of elucidatory qualities. Most importantly, Wittgenstein found in reading Frege's work a continual source of philosophical problems with which he grappled obsessively from the moment when he was first trapped in the fly-bottle. It was the paradox that Russell discovered in Frege's logicist project that drew Wittgenstein seriously into philosophy; and another remark that Geach reports illustrates how fascinated Wittgenstein became with Frege's views:

> The last time I saw Frege, as we were waiting at the station for my train, I said to him "Don't you ever find *any* difficulty in your theory that numbers are objects?" He replied "Sometimes I *seem* to see a difficulty – but then again I *don't* see it". (Geach, 1961, p.130)

Wittgenstein never held that numbers are objects, but he was intrigued as to what led someone as sharp as Frege to take that view.

Frege is explicitly cited as an influence on the *Tractatus*, but although he is rarely mentioned by name in his later writings, his views continued to be a major source of inspiration to the very end of Wittgenstein's life. O.K. Bouwsma reports on what Wittgenstein told him in talks they had about Frege in August 1949: "Frege is so good. But one must try to figure out what was bothering him, and then see how the problems arise. There are so many of them" (WC 27). To identify these problems and understand how Wittgenstein tried to diagnose them is virtually to provide a complete account of the development of Wittgenstein's philosophy. All I can do here is indicate some of those problems and some of his responses, in both his early and his later work. First, however, I will say more about the relationship between Wittgenstein and Frege from Wittgenstein's first encounter with Frege's ideas.

2   Wittgenstein's Relationship with Frege

Wittgenstein probably first became acquainted with Frege's work in late 1908 or early 1909, when he was a student of aeronautical engineering at Manchester. The standard story is that he attended J.E. Littlewood's lectures on mathematical analysis, and joined a group of fellow students interested in the foundations of mathematics, which led him to Russell's book *The Principles of Mathematics* (1903; Monk, 1990, pp.28–35; Reck, 2002, pp.4–6). That book has two appendices, the first on "The Logical and Arithmetical Doctrines of Frege" – this was the first reasonably substantial exposition of Frege's philosophy to appear in English – and the second on "The Doctrine of Types," Russell's first attempt to solve the paradox that he had discovered in Frege's work. Wittgenstein was hooked by the paradox, and in April 1909 he wrote to Philip Jourdain in Cambridge offering his own solution. Although Jourdain – with Russell's endorsement – rejected that solution, Wittgenstein continued to work on his philosophical ideas. He read some of Frege's writings, at the very least parts of *Grundgesetze der Arithmetik* (1893/1903), and according to his own account, made some criticisms, which he sent to Frege himself, asking if he could visit him (Geach, 1961, p.129; cf. RW 2).

Wittgenstein's visit to Frege in Jena in summer 1911 was of decisive importance to his philosophical career. In their discussions, as Wittgenstein reported on more than one occasion (Geach, 1961, p.130; RW 110, 214), Frege "wiped the floor" with him but nevertheless invited him to come again. More importantly, bearing in mind that Frege was by then in his sixties and suffering from ill health, Frege recommended that Wittgenstein go to Cambridge to study with Russell. Thus it was that Wittgenstein turned up, unannounced, at Russell's rooms in Cambridge on 18 October 1911, and began attending Russell's lectures and discussing philosophy with him. He officially registered as a student at Cambridge in February 1912. Wittgenstein worked with Russell until October 1913, when, having left some "Notes on Logic," he went off to Norway to live by himself. He was back in Vienna the following summer, and when World War I broke out, enrolled in the Austrian army. During this period, he visited Frege at least twice more, in December 1912 and December 1913, in Brunshaupten on the Mecklenburg coast, where Frege frequently spent his vacations. They went for walks together and discussed philosophy over several days. Throughout this time, and especially during the war, they corresponded regularly, and some of this correspondence (from Frege to Wittgenstein) has survived, shedding light on their relationship and their different philosophical views.

While on leave from the war, Wittgenstein twice invited Frege to visit him in Vienna, but Frege never made the trip, for health reasons. On 25 March 1918 Wittgenstein wrote a letter to Frege (now lost) expressing a great debt of thanks and making him a gift of money. As his reply of 9 April shows, Frege was taken aback by this but accepted it gratefully: it helped him to buy a house in Bad Kleinen in Mecklenburg, where he lived after retiring from Jena in December 1918 (for further details, see Kreiser, 2001, pp.504–5). Wittgenstein finished a complete draft of the *Tractatus* during his leave in summer 1918, and Frege received a copy in early 1919. It took Frege several months to reply, and when he did, he confessed that he found it difficult to understand.

> You place your propositions next to one another without justifying them or at least without justifying them in enough detail. So I often don't know whether I should agree, since the sense is not distinct enough to me. A thorough justification would make the sense much clearer. The everyday use of language is in general too vacillating to be readily useable for difficult logical and epistemological purposes. Elucidations are necessary, it seems to me, to make the sense sharper. Right from the beginning you use rather a lot of words on whose sense much obviously depends. (Letter from Frege, 28 June 1919)

Frege goes on to give examples of such words: "der Fall sein" ("to be the case"), "Tatsache" ("fact"), and "das Bestehen von Sachverhalten" ("the existence of states of affairs"). As he notes at one point, he struggled from the very opening propositions and found it impossible to go further.

Wittgenstein was deeply disappointed with this response. As he reported on 19 August 1919 in a letter to Russell from Cassino, where he was then in a prisoner-of-war camp, "[Frege] wrote to me a week ago and I gather that he doesn't understand a word of it all. So my only hope is to see *you* soon and explain all to you, for it is VERY hard not to be understood by a single soul!" Wittgenstein was to be disappointed by Russell, too, but his main concern at the time was to find a publisher for his work. He approached Frege, one suggestion being the journal in which the first two essays of Frege's "Logical Investigations" had just been published, edited by Frege's colleague at Jena, Bruno Bauch. But as Frege made clear in a letter dated 30 September 1919, this would require rewriting the *Tractatus*, breaking it up into parts, each of which would focus on a single philosophical problem, with Wittgenstein's solution to this problem presented not as bald assertions but with sufficient justification provided (Frege, 1989, p.23). This was not a suggestion likely to have gone down at all well with Wittgenstein.

Frege's last known letter to Wittgenstein was written on 30 June 1920, responding to an earlier letter from Wittgenstein (now lost) in which he had criticized Frege's treatment of idealism in "Der Gedanke," a copy of which Frege had sent him. Frege also raises some further objections to the opening propositions of the *Tractatus*. By this time Wittgenstein had decided to become a schoolteacher, qualifying in July 1920 and taking up his first post in the small Austrian village of Trattenbach in September. So by then, it might be suggested, Wittgenstein's thoughts were elsewhere, and he may no longer have felt any inclination to respond to Frege. However, given that he remained in correspondence with Russell, who did indeed help in getting the *Tractatus* published, I suspect that Frege's reluctance to recommend publication, rooted as it was in his professed inability to get further than the opening page of the *Tractatus*, was the key reason why Wittgenstein broke off the correspondence.

Frege died in 1925, and Wittgenstein did not fully return to philosophy until 1929, although he met and corresponded with, among others, F.P. Ramsey during his time as a schoolteacher. Wittgenstein may have had no more contact with Frege, but he continued to read Frege's writings. Just a month into his job in Trattenbach, he wrote to Paul Engelmann asking him to send "registered and express" the two volumes of Frege's *Grundgesetze* (Engelmann, 1967, p.39). He recommended Frege to Ramsey, as is clear from a letter from Ramsey dated 11 November 1923: "I do agree that Frege is wonderful; I enjoyed his critique of the theory of irrationals in the Grundgesetze enormously." Six weeks later Ramsey writes:

> I think *Frege is more read now*; two great mathematicians *Hilbert and Weyl* have been writing on the *foundations of mathematics* and *pay compliments to Frege*, appear in fact to have appreciated him to some extent. His unpopularity would naturally go as the generation he criticized dies. (Letter from Ramsey, 27 December 1923)

Wittgenstein continued to recommend Frege, and maintained his interest in his writings, on his return to philosophy and throughout his subsequent life. I will say something about Wittgenstein's later engagement with Frege's ideas in due course. Here I will end by noting Wittgenstein's role in the first collection of Frege's papers to be published in English, *Translations from the Philosophical Writings of Gottlob Frege*, edited and translated by Peter Geach and Max Black, which appeared in 1952. This included all three of Frege's seminal essays from 1891–1892 as well as other articles and selections from both the *Begriffsschrift* (1879) and *Grundgesetze*. Wittgenstein had encouraged the project; both Geach and Black had studied with Wittgenstein at Cambridge, and Wittgenstein had advised on the selection. The book does not include excerpts from

The Foundations of Arithmetic, since, as noted above, this had appeared in an English translation by J.L. Austin in 1950. Nor does it, surprisingly to us now, contain the first of the three essays of Frege's "Logical Investigations" but, instead, the second. Here is how Geach later reported this decision:

> [Wittgenstein] advised me to translate 'Die Verneinung', but not 'Der Gedanke': that, he considered, was an inferior work – it attacked idealism on its weak side, whereas a worthwhile criticism of idealism would attack it just where it was strongest. Wittgenstein told me he had made this point to Frege in correspondence: Frege could not understand – for him, idealism was the enemy he had long fought, and of course you attack your enemy on his weak side. (Geach, in Frege, 1977, p.viii)

We catch a glimpse here not only of the dialogue that Frege and Wittgenstein actually engaged in at a crucial point in their relationship but also of one of the main, and perhaps deepest, differences in their philosophical approach.

3   Frege and Wittgenstein's Early Work

As mentioned above, Wittgenstein's first piece of philosophical writing appears to have been an attempt to solve Russell's paradox that he sent to Jourdain in April 1909. We do not know what that attempted solution was, nor do we have Jourdain's actual reply. But we do have an entry in Jourdain's notebook that records the essence of that reply, as well as revealing that he had discussed the matter with Russell:

> Russell said that the views I gave in a reply to Wittgenstein (who had 'solved' Russell's contradiction) agree with his own. These views are: The difficulty seems to me to be as follows. In certain cases (e.g., Burali-Forti's case, Russell's 'class' [...], Epimenides' remark) we get what seems to be meaningless *limiting cases* of statements which are not meaningless. (Grattan-Guinness, 1977, p.114)

If this is the view that was transmitted to Wittgenstein, then it is prescient in its anticipation of one of Wittgenstein's central claims in the *Tractatus* – that (senseless) tautologies and contradictions are limiting cases of (meaningful) empirical propositions (cf. 4.46, 4.466) – as well as of what might be regarded as his central preoccupation throughout his life, that of understanding and delimiting the boundaries between meaningfulness and meaninglessness.

The ideas that Wittgenstein sent to Frege in asking if he could visit him would surely have included further thoughts on the resolution of the paradox, and it was presumably one of the main topics that they discussed on their first meeting. Frege would have been deeply interested in Wittgenstein's thoughts. He had been devastated when Russell had informed him, in June 1902, of the contradiction in his system, which arises in the following way. In his attempt to demonstrate the logicist claim that arithmetic can be reduced to logic, Frege had defined the natural numbers as extensions of (logically definable) concepts, and had treated extensions of concepts – and hence numbers – as objects. He had also made the crucial assumption that all concepts must be defined for all objects, including extensions of concepts. Now if every concept is defined for all objects, then every concept can be thought of as dividing all objects into those that do, and those that do not, fall under it. Furthermore, if extensions of concepts are objects, then extensions themselves can be divided into those that fall under the concept whose extension they are (for example, the extension of the concept "( ) is an extension") and those that do not (for example, the extension of the concept "( ) is a horse"). But now consider the concept "( ) is the extension of a concept under which it does not fall." Does the extension of *this* concept fall under the concept or not? If it does, then it does not, and if it does not, then it does. This contradiction is one version of Russell's paradox.

In a hastily written appendix to the second volume of the *Grundgesetze*, which was in press when Russell wrote to Frege informing him of the contradiction, Frege attempted to respond to the paradox. An obvious way out is to abandon the assumption that extensions of concepts are objects. But this would have been to reject one of Frege's key claims, that numbers are objects. Frege does consider the suggestion that extensions of concepts are "improper objects," for which only some concepts are defined, excluding those engendering the paradox. However, he rejects this on the grounds that the resulting system would be too complex, requiring "an incalculable multiplicity of types," since it would have to be specified for every function what kind of objects are admissible as either argument or value (cf. Frege, 1997, p.282). A theory of types was what Russell was led to develop in response to the paradox; and not only did it indeed prove complex but it also generated problems of its own, not least concerning the status of the additional axioms that Russell felt obliged to introduce in seeking to demonstrate the logicist claim.

Frege's own response was simply to outlaw concepts from applying to their own extensions. However, the resulting restriction of the axiom of his system that had given rise to the paradox has also been found to generate a contradiction, and Frege was in any case unable to provide any principled reason for outlawing this possibility (see Beaney, 2003, sec.5). As noted above, we do not know what Wittgenstein's first "solution" to the paradox was, but it does seem that from very early on, he was skeptical of the existence of any kind of "logical object," whether numbers, extensions of concepts, or the "logical constants" that Russell had been inclined to posit. In his first surviving letter to Russell, he remarks that the consequence of a correct account of logic "*must* be that there are NO *logical* constants" (NB 120). In the *Tractatus* he calls this his "fundamental thought" ("*Grundgedanke*"), viz., that the "logical constants" do not represent (4.0312).

This suggests a fundamental difference in philosophical attitude between Wittgenstein, on the one hand, and Frege and Russell, on the other. This difference is rooted in the claim that Wittgenstein immediately goes on to make in the letter to Russell just cited: "Logic must turn out to be a *totally* different kind than any other science" (NB 120). For both Frege and Russell, logic was a science just like other sciences, except for being maximally general. As a science, it was seen as having a subject matter – for Frege, logical objects and functions; for Russell, the logical constants. Wittgenstein agreed that logic was maximally general, but for just this reason, he noted in October 1913, "logic cannot treat a special set of things" (NB 98; cf. TLP 5.4). For him, what characterized logical propositions was not topic-neutrality but vacuity.

Frege held that logic was maximally general because its laws governed all thought. The laws of logic, as laws of truth, he wrote, are "boundary stones set in an eternal foundation, which our thought can overflow but not dislodge" ([1893] 1997, p.203). This remark is made in the preface to Frege's *Grundgesetze*, in a passage where Frege attacks psychologism. Wittgenstein was reportedly able to quote large parts of this preface by heart, and this passage would almost certainly have been among them. Like Frege, he rejected psychologism (cf. e.g., TLP 4.1121; on the differences between their understanding of "psychologism," however, see Potter, 2009, pp.99–101). But unlike Frege, he did not think that treating the laws of logic as laws of truth answered the question of how logic governed our thinking. If logic is a science treating a special set of things, then how can it apply to everything? The metaphor of "boundary stones set in an eternal foundation" needs unpacking. What Wittgenstein came to believe was that logic is built into the essential nature of propositions (so thought cannot even overflow the eternal foundation that logic provides, since "illogical thought" is not, strictly speaking, thought at all). Precisely how is what he attempted to work out and explain in the *Tractatus*.

One argument that Wittgenstein gives for rejecting Frege's and Russell's view of logic is provided at the very beginning of the "Notes on Logic" that he wrote for Russell before departing for Norway in October 1913:

> One reason for thinking the old notation wrong is that it is very unlikely that from every proposition p an infinite number of other propositions not-not-p, not-not-not-not-p, etc., should follow. (NL 93; cf. TLP 5.43)

Wittgenstein went on to conclude from this that "not-not-p" must be taken as the same symbol as "p." This in turn suggests that what might be regarded as a law of logic, namely, the principle of double negation, stating the equivalence between p and not-not-p, lacks content, in the way that "a = a" lacks content. In the *Tractatus*, after reiterating the reason just noted, he goes on to remark: "All propositions of logic, however, say the same. Namely, nothing" (5.43).

That logical propositions say nothing, in other words, lack sense, is one of the most characteristic and fundamental claims of the *Tractatus*, and is in direct opposition to Frege's views. It also provided a way of articulating another objection that Wittgenstein had to Frege's and Russell's views, concerning their account of logical inference. The best way to explain this is to take a very simple example of a logical inference:

$$P$$
$$P \supset Q$$
$$\overline{}$$
$$Q$$

Here Q follows by modus ponens, which it is tempting to express by formulating the logical proposition "(P & (P ⊃ Q)) ⊃ Q" and saying that the inference is only valid if this proposition is true. However, we must not treat this proposition as a missing premise in the argument, which needs to be "completed" as follows:

$$P$$
$$P \supset Q$$
$$(P \& (P \supset Q)) \supset Q$$
$$\overline{}$$
$$Q$$

If we do this, then an infinite regress threatens. Should we not add as a further premise "(P & (P ⊃ Q) & (P & (P ⊃ Q))) ⊃ Q"? (If the rule has to be formulated as a premise, then we generate the so-called "paradox of inference," first formulated – though not under that name – by Lewis Carroll in 1895.)

Unlike "P," "P ⊃ Q," and "Q," all of which may have content, "(P & (P ⊃ Q)) ⊃ Q" *lacks* content, in the sense that it adds nothing to the inference. All it does is reflect that "Q" can indeed be inferred from "P" and "P ⊃ Q," i.e., it reflects the *rule* licensing the inference. As Wittgenstein put it in notes dictated to Moore in April 1914, "Logical propositions *are forms of proofs*: they shew that one or more propositions *follow* from one (or more)" (NM 109; cf. TLP 6.1264). All logical propositions, he came to believe, are tautologies, and as such, no one set of logical propositions is more privileged than another, implying a rejection of Frege's and Russell's axiomatic conception of logic. (See TLP 6.1, 6.1201, 6.127, 6.1271.) They simply *show* that a certain inference is valid (cf. TLP 6.1264).

Wittgenstein's notes to Moore open with the remark: "Logical so-called propositions *shew* [the] logical properties of language and therefore of [the] Universe, but *say* nothing" (NM 108; cf. TLP 6.12). This distinction between saying and showing is another fundamental idea of the *Tractatus*, but it does not appear in the notes he wrote for Russell in October 1913. Wittgenstein went to Norway immediately after writing these notes to Russell and stayed there until July 1914, with the exception of several weeks over Christmas, when he went home to Vienna via a visit to Frege in Mecklenburg. (Moore visited Wittgenstein in Norway in March, and Wittgenstein dictated the notes to him during the first two weeks of April.) There is nothing in the letters that Wittgenstein wrote during this period to shed any light on exactly when Wittgenstein came to draw the distinction, but an obvious suggestion is that it had something to do with his discussions with Frege.

In an influential paper published in 1976, Peter Geach suggested that Wittgenstein's distinction between saying and showing was already foreshadowed in Frege's philosophy, and indeed can be invoked in making sense of (if not actually resolving) a problem in Frege's philosophy. This is the problem that has come to be known as the paradox of the concept "horse." According to Frege, there is an absolute distinction between objects and concepts (or functions, more generally): the former are "saturated," reflecting the fact that the names for them are "complete," and the latter are "unsaturated," reflecting the fact that the names for them are "incomplete." In "Pegasus is a horse," for example, "Pegasus" is a proper name, referring to an object, while "( ) is a horse" is a concept-word, with the gap indicating where the name goes to complete the expression to form a sentence. But now consider the sentence "The concept *horse* is a concept," which might seem obviously true. On Frege's view, however, the use of the definite article in "the concept *horse*" indicates an object (if anything), not a concept, so that, strictly speaking, the sentence is false. As Frege wrote in "On Concept and Object," in discussing the problem, "By a kind of necessity of language, my expressions, taken literally, sometimes miss my thought; I mention an object, when what I intend is a concept" ([1892b] 1997, p.192). He found no way round the problem, which he thought was "founded on the nature of our language," and he therefore concluded "that we cannot avoid a certain inappropriateness of linguistic expression; and that there is nothing for it but to realize this and always take it into account" ([1892b] 1997, p.193).

If I had to select a single remark or idea that demonstrated the profound effect that Frege had on Wittgenstein, then it would be this. (It is no accident that it is this idea that has inspired so-called "New Wittgenstein" readings of the *Tractatus*, from the work of Cora Diamond onwards; see especially Diamond, 1988.) We see revealed here the central theme that came to obsess Wittgenstein: the way that language can mislead us, especially when doing philosophy, which easily gives rise to the temptation to utter nonsense. Armed with Wittgenstein's distinction between saying and showing, however, we can at least offer a formulation of what Frege wants to convey: namely, that what the sentence "The concept *horse* is a concept" tries to *say* can only be *shown* – shown, that is, by *using* the concept-word "( ) is a horse" to say, truly or falsely, that an object is a horse. (It is but a short step from here to Wittgenstein's later conception of meaning as use: the meaning of "( ) is a horse," for example, is not given by specifying some entity (whether object or function) but is simply revealed by its use.)

The distinction between objects and concepts (functions) is the most fundamental distinction in Frege's philosophy, and yet this distinction cannot actually be stated in Frege's "Begriffsschrift" (literally, "concept-script"), as he called his logical language, which had been specifically designed to capture all legitimate thoughts. Any attempt to formalize "No concepts are objects" would require quantifying over entities of which it could be meaningfully asserted either that they are concepts or that they are objects. But there are no such entities, on Frege's view. (As Wittgenstein was to put it, the concept of an object and the concept of a concept are "formal concepts"; TLP 4.126 ff. For discussion of this, see McGinn 2006, ch.7.) Here, too, though, we might suggest that what Frege is trying to *say* in uttering a sentence such as "No concepts are objects" can only be *shown* in the correct use of his logical language. The idea here generalizes. Any attempt to express the distinctions upon which the logical language itself depends cannot be expressed within that language. If we now recognize that, in his early work, Wittgenstein understood by "logic" precisely the logic that Frege saw himself as formalizing in his Begriffsschrift (not that Wittgenstein thought that Frege had got his *notation* right; see e.g., TLP 3.325, 4.442, 5.42, 5.53 ff.), then we arrive at the result that everything that we might try to say about the conditions of the applicability of this logic cannot actually be said but only shown. In the light of all this, it is perhaps not surprising that Wittgenstein himself was eventually forced to admit that his own attempts in the *Tractatus* to elucidate these conditions resulted in nonsense that had to be "overcome" at the end.

We do not know whether Frege and Wittgenstein discussed the paradox of the concept "horse" when they met in December 1913. But we do know from what Wittgenstein wrote to Russell immediately after his discussions with Frege the previous year, i.e., in December 1912, that Wittgenstein had come to appreciate the basic idea of Frege's distinction between object and concept. At this point Wittgenstein was clearly under the spell of Russell's conception of a proposition as some kind of complex entity composed of simpler entities. But this raised the question of the unity of such a proposition. If the only constituents of a proposition are objects, then how do they combine to generate a meaningful proposition? As Wittgenstein was to put it, what makes "Socrates is mortal" meaningful but "mortality is Socrates" meaningless? Frege's answer was clear: concepts are "unsaturated," reflected in the fact that the concept-word, as properly represented in this example by "( ) is mortal," contains a "gap" indicating where the proper name goes to complete the sentence.

Wittgenstein seems to have recognized what is in effect Frege's solution to the problem of the unity of the proposition. On 26 December 1912 he wrote to Russell: "I had a long discussion with Frege about our theory of symbolism of which, I think, he roughly understood the general outline. [...] The complex-problem is now clearer to me and I hope very much that I may solve it" (NB 121). On 16 January 1913, he then writes to Russell:

> I have changed my views on "atomic" complexes: I now think that qualities, relations (like love) etc. are all copulae! That means I for instance analyse a subject-predicate proposition, say, "Socrates is human" into "Socrates" and "something is human", (which I think is not complex). The reason for this is a very fundamental one. I think that there cannot be different Types of things! In other words whatever can be symbolized by a simple proper name must belong to one type. And further: every theory of types must be rendered superfluous by a proper theory of symbolism: For instance if I analyse the proposition Socrates is mortal into Socrates, mortality and $(\exists x,y) \in_I (x,y)$ I want a theory of types to tell me that "mortality is Socrates" is nonsensical, because if I treat "mortality" as a proper name (as I did) there is nothing to prevent me to make the substitution the wrong way round. *But* if I analyse (as I do now) into Socrates and $(\exists x).x$ is mortal or generally into x and $(\exists x) \varphi x$ it becomes impossible to substitute the wrong way round because the two symbols are now of a different *kind* themselves. What I am *most* certain of is not however the correctness of my present way of analysis, but of the fact that all theory of types must be done away with by a theory of symbolism showing that what seem to be *different kinds of things* are symbolized by different kinds of symbols which *cannot* possibly be substituted in one another's places. I hope I have made this fairly clear! (NB 16.1.13)

Wittgenstein's "analysis" here differs from Frege's, and he did indeed soon come to reject it, but the essential idea that there are different "kinds" of things that can only be shown by a correct symbolism remained. The distinction between saying and showing is not formulated explicitly until April 1914, in the notes he dictated to Moore, but it is clearly implicit in this letter. It provides a good example of an idea that was inspired by Wittgenstein's dialogue with Frege, which he used both in articulating his objections to the views of Frege and Russell and in attempting to resolve the problems raised by their work.

Most of Wittgenstein's objections to Frege's and Russell's views are already made in his "Notes on Logic" of 1913 (for a full discussion, see Potter, 2009). He attempts to resolve the problems raised by their work in the years that follow, developing a positive account of logic and language rooted in his so-called picture theory of the proposition. The idea of treating propositions as "pictures" first emerged in September 1914 (NB 7), and his positive account found its definitive articulation in the *Tractatus* (see Beaney, 2006; McGinn, 2006, chs1–5; Diamond, 2013). As far as Frege is concerned, he is mentioned by name in 17 of the numbered propositions of the *Tractatus* (for further discussion, see Kienzler, 2011). He cites Frege favorably in four of these propositions (3.318, 3.325, 4.431, 5.451), although with some qualification in two of them (3.325, 4.431). In most of them, however, he criticizes Frege. Some of these criticisms have already been mentioned: his repudiation of Frege's conceptions of logic (6.1271), logical inference (5.132), and logical objects (5.4, 5.42). Space prohibits discussion of the other criticisms, but for the record they can be noted here. Wittgenstein also raises objections to Frege's views on sense (*Sinn*) and reference (*Bedeutung*), and especially his treatment of propositions as names of truth values (3.143, 4.063, 5.02, 5.4733, 6.232), and he criticizes Frege's introduction of an assertion-sign into logic (4.442; cf. BT 160–1; PI §22) and his conception of generality, where he takes issue with Frege for failing to appreciate the role of "formal concepts" (4.1272, 4.1273, 5.521; cf. BT 247–8). (See the end of this chapter for suggested further reading on these topics.)

4   Frege and Wittgenstein's Later Work

The *Tractatus* was essentially complete in 1918. In that same year Frege published "Der Gedanke" ("Thought"), the first of his "Logical Investigations," and sent a copy to Wittgenstein. The second essay, "Die Verneinung" ("Negation"), was published in 1919 and "Gedankengefüge" ("Compound Thoughts") followed in 1923. None of these influenced the *Tractatus* directly, although ideas that Frege expressed in these works may have been discussed in Frege's earlier conversations with Wittgenstein. But their influence can certainly be traced in Wittgenstein's later work, and Wittgenstein re-engaged with Frege's thinking on his return to philosophy in 1929.

As mentioned above, Frege and Wittgenstein corresponded during and immediately after World War I, and the letters from Frege to Wittgenstein in 1919 and 1920, in which Frege comments on the draft of the *Tractatus* that had been sent to him and responds to Wittgenstein's own comments on "Der Gedanke," are especially revealing. I will note just two issues here, one raised by Frege's comments on the *Tractatus* and the other by Wittgenstein's comments on "Der Gedanke." The first issue concerns the opening propositions of the *Tractatus*. In 1.1 Wittgenstein states that "The world is the totality of facts, not of things." A few propositions later he claims both that a fact (*Tatsache*) is the obtaining of states of affairs (*das Bestehen von Sachverhalten*) and that a state of affairs is a combination of objects (2, 2.01). This would seem to imply that objects are constituents of facts, so that the world, after all, is a totality of things and not just of facts; and it is this implication that Frege draws out and criticizes in the letter he wrote to Wittgenstein on 28 June 1919 (Frege, 1989, pp.19–20). On Frege's own view, "facts" are simply true thoughts, and the constituents of thoughts are the *senses* of the expressions that constitute the sentences that express the thoughts; the constituents of thoughts are not the references (*Bedeutungen*) of those expressions.

We do not have Wittgenstein's reply to this, although one might argue that, properly interpreted, facts are not *identified* with (existing) states of affairs; it is *that* a state of affairs obtains that is the fact. (On the difficulties in interpreting Wittgenstein here, see the entry under "fact" in Glock, 1996.) In remarks on "Complex and Fact" written in June 1931, however, Wittgenstein says the following:

> To say that a red circle is *composed* of redness and circularity, or is a complex with these component parts, is a misuse of these words and is misleading. (Frege was aware of this and told me.)
> It is just as misleading to say the fact that this circle is red (that I am tired) is a complex whose component parts are a circle and redness (myself and tiredness). (PR 302)

Wittgenstein does not indicate whether he took himself to have failed to distinguish adequately between fact and complex in the *Tractatus*; but it is clear that he now recognizes how important this distinction is, parenthetically suggesting that it was Frege who taught him this.

The second issue concerns Wittgenstein's comments on Frege's treatment of idealism in "Der Gedanke." As reported above, Wittgenstein thought that Frege had attacked idealism on its weak side, whereas the most effective critique needed to uncover its deepest, strongest roots. Wittgenstein must have raised this objection in a letter (now lost) to Frege himself, as on 3 April 1920 Frege wrote back to him:

> Many thanks for your letter of 19 March! Of course I don't mind your frankness. But I would very much like to know what deep grounds of idealism you think I have not grasped. I understood that you yourself do not take epistemological idealism to be true. You thus recognize, I think, that there are no deeper grounds at all for this idealism. The grounds for it can then only be apparent grounds, not logical grounds. One is indeed misled at times by language, since language does not always satisfy logical demands. In the formation of language, as well as the logical abilities of human beings, much that is psychological has had an effect. Logical errors do not originate from logic, but arise from the contaminations or disruptions to which the logical activity of human beings is exposed. It was not my intention to track down all such disruptions of psychological-linguistic origin. Please just go through my essay on thought until you come to the first sentence with which you disagree and let me know which this is and the reasons for your disagreement. This may well be the best way for me to see what you have in mind. I might not have wanted to combat idealism at all in the sense you meant. I may well not have used the expression 'idealism' at all. Take my sentences just as they are, without imputing an intention that might have been foreign to me. (Letter from Frege, 3 April 1920)

We do not have Wittgenstein's reply, nor do we have any subsequent letters from Frege. But Frege was right that he does not use the term "idealism" in his essay; and it is equally clear that Wittgenstein thought he saw a deep truth in idealism – or at least in solipsism – that he attempted to articulate in the notoriously difficult sections of the *Tractatus* that discuss "the limits of my language" (5.6–5.641). What Wittgenstein presumably had in mind in criticizing Frege, though, was the passage in "Der Gedanke" where Frege discusses the thesis that only what is my idea can be the object of my awareness ([1918] 1997, pp. 337–41). Frege argues that since ideas require an owner, my ideas must have an owner, which must then be recognized as an object of my awareness that is not itself an idea. This frees the way, he suggests, for acknowledging other people as independent owners of ideas, which in turn makes the probability "very great, so great that it is in my opinion no longer distinguishable from certainty" that such people, and hence an external world, exist ([1918] 1997, p. 341). This argument from "probability" is presumably what Wittgenstein was alluding to in his talk of Frege's attacking idealism on its weak side. A far more effective attack is to identify a fundamental assumption on which one might well be tempted to agree (like Frege) with the idealist and show how that assumption needs repudiating or qualifying (e.g., by reinterpreting or disambiguating) in order to resist the idealist's conclusion.

Just such an assumption is Frege's claim in "Der Gedanke" that "Nobody else has my idea," which might seem to be as incontrovertible as "Nobody else has my pain," which Frege also asserts ([1918] 1997, p. 335). But this is precisely the assertion that Wittgenstein interrogates in §253 of his later *Philosophical Investigations*, as part of his so-called private language argument. (For further discussion of one source of the private language argument lying in Wittgenstein's reading of "Der Gedanke," see Künne, 2009, pp. 36–40.) This later argument, we might say, does indeed attack idealism on its strong side. Frege's and Wittgenstein's approaches to idealism thus reveal very different philosophical methodologies. Frege criticizes a doctrine by taking its formulation literally (as he urges Wittgenstein to do of his own sentences in the letter just cited) and drawing out its consequences in an attempt to refute it by *reductio ad absurdum*. Wittgenstein's approach, by contrast, seeks to identify the underlying assumption that might be accepted on both sides of a dispute in order to show how the dispute itself is fundamentally misguided.

In this respect §308 of the *Investigations* is particularly revealing of Wittgenstein's methodology. Wittgenstein here talks about the "first step" in a philosophical dispute being "the one that altogether escapes notice" and "that's just what commits us to a particular way of looking at the matter," adding in parentheses: "The decisive movement in the conjuring trick has been made, and it was the very one that seemed to us quite innocent." Frege's work, I would say, provides excellent examples of precisely the kind of "first steps" or "decisive movements" that generate the philosophical disputes that Wittgenstein aimed to dissolve; and this is one of the main reasons why Wittgenstein found in Frege's writings a continual source of inspiration. It is significant that it is after this passage that Wittgenstein makes his famous remark about the aim of philosophy being to show the fly the way out of the fly-bottle (PI §309).

In his early thinking, Wittgenstein had himself been trapped in a fly-bottle of Frege's making. As noted above, he had accepted Frege's view that logic is essentially what Frege had attempted to formalize in his Begriffsschrift. For Frege, this was rooted in his use of function–argument analysis and his consequent emphasis on the distinction between concept and object. Frege's assumption that concepts are functions was a "first step" that did indeed commit him to a particular way of looking at things. (I discuss how Frege's use of function–argument analysis led to all his characteristic doctrines in Beaney, 2007; 2011.) In his later critique of Fregean logic, the concept/object distinction was one of the first doctrines that Wittgenstein attacked. In the *Philosophical Remarks*, for example, Wittgenstein treats this distinction as just a version of the subject/predicate distinction, which reflects not just one logical form but "countless fundamentally different logical forms" (PR 119). Such forms, he writes, are norms of representation, "moulds into which we have squeezed the proposition" (PR 137).

One feature of Frege's way of looking at things was his assumption that concepts are – or should be – sharp, in other words, that it must be determined for any (genuine) concept whether any given object falls under it or not (see e.g., Frege, [1903] 1997, p.259). This, too, was something that Wittgenstein later criticized. In §71 of the *Investigations*, for example, where Frege is explicitly mentioned, his imagined interlocutor asks "But is a blurred concept a *concept* at all?," and Wittgenstein goes on to reply that a blurred concept such as that of a game may actually have advantages over sharper concepts (cf. BT 68–9). Wittgenstein writes:

> We want to say that there can't be any vagueness in logic. The idea now absorbs us that the ideal '*must*' occur in reality. (PI §101)

> The ideal, as we conceive it, is unshakable. You can't step outside it. [...] The idea is like a pair of glasses on our nose through which we see whatever we look at. It never occurs to us to take them off. (PI §103)

These remarks can be seen as addressed to Frege just as much as to his own earlier self. (On Wittgenstein's account of vagueness, see also Chapter 25, VAGUENESS AND FAMILY RESEMBLANCE.)

Wittgenstein also had Frege in mind in his discussion of rule-following, which is central to both *Philosophical Investigations* and *Remarks on the Foundations of Mathematics*. Frege, he thought, was someone who held the view that he was concerned to criticize – that the applications of a rule are already somehow predetermined, in the way that a line between two points is already there before it has been drawn or a series of numbers is already there once the rule has been given (see e.g., RFM I §21; BT 343, 570). Especially in the *Philosophical Investigations*, Frege's name may rarely be mentioned, but his ideas are certainly among the targets in many of Wittgenstein's discussions.

5 Conclusion

I have concentrated in the previous two sections on Wittgenstein's criticisms of Frege's ideas, suggesting that Wittgenstein came to see in Frege's philosophy a source of "first steps" that he sought to identify in order to dissolve philosophical disputes. But there are also ideas and attitudes that Wittgenstein endorsed. Wittgenstein shared Frege's anti-psychologism and admired his critique of formalism, for example. (Anti-psychologism permeates Wittgenstein's work, but for particularly clear statements, see e.g., TLP 4.1121; BB 6; PPF §xiv. For Wittgenstein's attitude to Frege's critique of formalism, see e.g., BB 4; BT 3.) But where he does endorse aspects of Frege's philosophy, he nearly always does so in a qualified form. In the *Tractatus*, for example, he writes: "Only the proposition has sense [*Sinn*]; only in the context of a proposition has a name reference [*Bedeutung*]" (3.3). Although Frege is not mentioned by name, this is a clear reference to Frege's famous context principle. But Frege formulated this principle at a time (1884) when he had not yet distinguished between sense and reference, and once he had done so, this complicated issues sufficiently for him to quietly drop the principle. For the early Wittgenstein, propositions have sense but not reference, and names have reference but not sense. So the context principle means something different for Wittgenstein than it did for Frege.

In §49 of the *Investigations*, Wittgenstein again endorses the context principle, in arguing that mere naming is not yet to make a move in a language-game. He then explicitly mentions Frege in claiming that "This is what Frege meant too when he said that a word has a meaning only in the context of a sentence." Given the different context in which Frege formulated this principle, this is highly contentious; but it is significant that Wittgenstein should want to endorse Frege on this point. The context principle was clearly influential. Indeed, one might argue that Wittgenstein generalized the principle in his later philosophy: only in the context of a language-game – or more broadly still, in the context of a "form of life" – does a linguistic expression have a meaning. The context principle thus provides a further example of how exploring the relationship between Frege and Wittgenstein takes us to the heart of both philosophers' work. Seeing how Wittgenstein criticized and transformed Frege's ideas also sheds light on some of the deepest issues in analytic philosophy.

Let us leave the last word with Frege, in a letter to Wittgenstein that he wrote on 16 September 1919:

> In long conversations with you I have come to know a man who, like me, has searched for the truth, partly along different paths. But it is precisely this that allows me to hope to find something in you that can complete, perhaps even correct, what was found by me.

References

Translations from Wittgenstein's *Tractatus* and Frege's letters to Wittgenstein are my own.

Beaney, M. (2003). Russell and Frege. In N. Griffin (Ed.). *The Cambridge Companion to Bertrand Russell* (pp.128–170). Cambridge: Cambridge University Press.

Beaney, M. (2006). Wittgenstein on Language: From Simples to Samples. In E. Lepore and B. Smith (Eds). *The Oxford Handbook of Philosophy of Language* (pp.40–59). Oxford: Oxford University Press.

Beaney, M. (2007). Frege's Use of Function-Argument Analysis and his Introduction of Truth-values as Objects. *Grazer Philosophische Studien*, 75, 93–123.

Beaney, M. (2011). Frege. In B. Lee (Ed.). *Key Thinkers: Philosophy of Language* (pp.33–55). London: Continuum.

Carroll, L. (1895). What the Tortoise said to Achilles. *Mind*, 4, 278–280.

Diamond, C. (1988). Throwing away the Ladder: How to Read the *Tractatus*. *Philosophy*, 63, 5–27.

Diamond, C. (2013). Reading the *Tractatus* with G.E.M. Anscombe. In M. Beaney (Ed.). *The Oxford Handbook of the History of Analytic Philosophy* (pp.870–905). Oxford: Oxford University Press.

Engelmann, P. (1967). *Letters from Wittgenstein, with a Memoir*. Ed. B.F. McGuinness. Trans. L. Furtmüller. Oxford: Blackwell.

Frege, G. (1879). *Begriffsschrift*. [Concept-script.] Halle: L. Nebert.

Frege, G. ([1884] 1950). *The Foundations of Arithmetic*. Trans. J.L. Austin. Oxford: Blackwell. (Original work published 1884.)

Frege, G. ([1891] 1997). Function and Concept. Translation in G. Frege. (1997). *The Frege Reader* (pp.130–148). Ed. M. Beaney. Oxford: Blackwell. (Original work published 1891.)

Frege, G. ([1892a] 1997). On *Sinn* and *Bedeutung*. Translation in G. Frege. (1997). *The Frege Reader* (pp.151–171). Ed. M. Beaney. Oxford: Blackwell. (Original work published 1892.)

Frege, G. ([1892b] 1997). On Concept and Object. Translation in G. Frege. (1997). *The Frege Reader* (pp.181–193). Ed. M. Beaney. Oxford: Blackwell. (Original work published.)

Frege, G. ([1893] 1997). *Grundgesetze der Arithmetik* (Vol. 1). Translation of selections in G. Frege. (1997). *The Frege Reader* (pp.194–223). Ed. M. Beaney. Oxford: Blackwell. (Original work published 1893.)

Frege, G. ([1903] 1997). *Grundgesetze der Arithmetik* (Vol. 2). Translation of selections in G. Frege. (1997). *The Frege Reader* (pp.258–289). Ed. M. Beaney. Oxford: Blackwell. (Original work published 1903.)

Frege, G. ([1918] 1997). Der Gedanke. Eine logische Untersuchung. Translation in G. Frege. (1997). *The Frege Reader* (pp.325–345). Ed. M. Beaney. Oxford: Blackwell. (Original work published 1918.)

Frege, G. ([1919] 1997). Die Verneinung. Eine logische Untersuchung. Translation in G. Frege. (1997). *The Frege Reader* (pp.345–361). Ed. M. Beaney. Oxford: Blackwell. (Original work published 1919.)

Frege, G. (1923). Logische Untersuchungen. Dritter Teil: Gedankengefüge. [Logical Investigations: Third Part: Compound Thoughts.] *Beiträge zur Philosophie des deutschen Idealismus*, 3, 36–51; trans. in G. Frege. (1977). *Logical Investigations* (pp.55–78). Ed. P.T. Geach, trans. P.T. Geach and R.H. Stoothoff. Oxford: Blackwell.

Frege, G. (1952). *Translations from the Philosophical Writings of Gottlob Frege*. Ed. and trans. P.T. Geach and M. Black. Oxford: Blackwell.

Frege, G. (1977). *Logical Investigations*. Ed. P.T. Geach, trans. P.T. Geach and R.H. Stoothoff. Oxford: Blackwell.

Frege, G. (1989). Briefe an Ludwig Wittgenstein. [Letters to Ludwig Wittgenstein.] Ed. A. Janik. In B. McGuinness and R. Haller (Eds). *Wittgenstein in Focus/Im Brennpunkt: Wittgenstein* (pp.5–33). Amsterdam: Rodopi.

Frege, G. (1997). *The Frege Reader*. Ed. M. Beaney. Oxford: Blackwell.
Geach, P.T. (1961). Frege. In G.E.M. Anscombe and P.T. Geach. *Three Philosophers* (pp.129–162). Oxford: Blackwell.
Geach, P.T. (1976). Saying and Showing in Frege and Wittgenstein. *Acta Philosophica Fennica*, 28, 54–70.
Glock, H.-J. (1996). *A Wittgenstein Dictionary*. Oxford: Blackwell.
Grattan-Guinness, I. (1977). *Dear Russell, Dear Jourdain: A Commentary on Russell's Logic, Based on his Correspondence with Philip Jourdain*. New York: Columbia University Press.
Kienzler, W. (2011). Wittgenstein and Frege. In O. Kuusela and M. McGinn (Eds). *The Oxford Handbook of Wittgenstein* (pp.79–104). Oxford: Oxford University Press.
Kreiser, L. (2001). *Gottlob Frege: Leben – Werk – Zeit*. [Gottlob Frege: Life, Work, Times.] Hamburg: Felix Meiner.
Künne, W. (2009). Wittgenstein and Frege's *Logical Investigations*. In H.-J. Glock and J. Hyman (Eds). *Wittgenstein and Analytic Philosophy: Essays for P.M.S. Hacker* (pp.26–62). Oxford: Oxford University Press.
McGinn, M. (2006). *Elucidating the Tractatus: Wittgenstein's Early Philosophy of Logic and Language*. Oxford: Clarendon Press.
Monk, R. (1990). *Ludwig Wittgenstein: The Duty of Genius*. London: Jonathan Cape.
Potter, M. (2009). *Wittgenstein's Notes on Logic*. Oxford: Oxford University Press.
Reck, E.H. (2002). Wittgenstein's "Great Debt" to Frege: Biographical Traces and Philosophical Themes. In E.H. Reck (Ed.). *From Frege to Wittgenstein: Perspectives on Early Analytic Philosophy* (pp.3–38). New York: Oxford University Press.
Russell, B. (1903). *The Principles of Mathematics*. Cambridge: Cambridge University Press.

Further Reading

For further discussion of the relationship between Frege and Wittgenstein (some of which has been cited above), see:

Baker, G.P. (1988). *Wittgenstein, Frege and the Vienna Circle*. Oxford: Blackwell.
Beaney, M. (2012). Logic and Metaphysics in Early Analytic Philosophy. In L. Haaparanta and H. Koskinen (Eds). *Categories of Being: Essays on Metaphysics and Logic* (pp.257–292). Oxford: Oxford University Press.
Conant, J. (2002). The Method of the *Tractatus*. In E.H. Reck (Ed.). *From Frege to Wittgenstein: Perspectives on Early Analytic Philosophy* (pp.374–462). New York: Oxford University Press.
Diamond, C. (2010). Inheriting from Frege: The Work of Reception, as Wittgenstein Did It. In M. Potter and T. Ricketts (Eds). *The Cambridge Companion to Frege* (pp.550–601). Cambridge: Cambridge University Press.
Diamond, C. (2013). Reading the *Tractatus* with G.E.M. Anscombe. In M. Beaney (Ed.). *The Oxford Handbook of the History of Analytic Philosophy* (pp.870–905). Oxford: Oxford University Press.
Dummett, M.A.E. (1981). Frege and Wittgenstein. In I. Block (Ed.). *Perspectives on the Philosophy of Wittgenstein* (pp. 31–42). Oxford: Blackwell. Reprinted in M.A.E. Dummett (1991). *Frege and Other Philosophers* (pp.237–248). Oxford: Oxford University Press.
Floyd, J. (2011). The Frege–Wittgenstein Correspondence: Interpretive Themes. In E. de Pellegrin (Ed.). *Interactive Wittgenstein: Essays in Memory of Georg Henrik von Wright* (pp.75–107). Dordrecht: Springer.
Geach, P.T. (1976). Saying and Showing in Frege and Wittgenstein. In J. Hintikka (Ed.). *Essays on Wittgenstein in Honour of G.H. von Wright* (pp. 54–70). *Acta Philosophica Fennica*, 28, Amsterdam.
Goldfarb, W. (2002). Wittgenstein's Understanding of Frege: The Pre-Tractarian Evidence. In E.H. Reck (Ed). *From Frege to Wittgenstein: Perspectives on Early Analytic Philosophy* (pp.185–200). New York: Oxford University Press.

Hacker, P.M.S. (1986). *Insight and Illusion: Themes in the Philosophy of Wittgenstein*. Oxford: Clarendon, ch.2.
Hacker, P.M.S. (2001a). Frege and the Early Wittgenstein. In P.M.S. Hacker, *Wittgenstein: Connections and Controversies* (pp.191–218). Oxford: Clarendon Press.
Hacker, P.M.S. (2001b). Frege and the Later Wittgenstein. In P.M.S. Hacker, *Wittgenstein: Connections and Controversies* (pp.219–241). Oxford: Clarendon Press.
Kienzler, W. (2011). Wittgenstein and Frege. In O. Kuusela and M. McGinn (Eds). *The Oxford Handbook of Wittgenstein* (pp. 79–104). Oxford: Oxford University Press.
Künne, W. (2009). Wittgenstein and Frege's *Logical Investigations*. In H.-J. Glock and J. Hyman (Eds). *Wittgenstein and Analytic Philosophy* (pp. 26–62). Oxford: Oxford University Press.
McGinn, M. (2006). *Elucidating the Tractatus*. Oxford: Clarendon Press, chs 2–3.
Potter, M. (2009). *Wittgenstein's Notes on Logic*. Oxford: Oxford University Press.
Reck, E.H. (1997). Frege's Influence on Wittgenstein: Reversing Metaphysics via the Context Principle. In W.W. Tait (Ed.). *Early Analytic Philosophy: Frege, Russell, Wittgenstein* (pp. 123–185). Chicago: Open Court.
Reck, E.H. (2002). Wittgenstein's "Great Debt" to Frege: Biographical Traces and Philosophical Themes. In E.H. Reck (Ed). *From Frege to Wittgenstein: Perspectives on Early Analytic Philosophy* (pp.3–38). New York: Oxford University Press.
Ricketts, T. (2002). Wittgenstein against Frege and Russell. In E.H. Reck (Ed). *From Frege to Wittgenstein: Perspectives on Early Analytic Philosophy* (pp.227–251). New York: Oxford University Press.
Travis, C. (2006). *Thought's Footing: A Theme in Wittgenstein's Philosophical Investigations*. Oxford: Oxford University Press.

More specifically, on Wittgenstein's objections to Frege's treatment of propositions as names of truth values, see:
Diamond, C. (2010). Inheriting from Frege: The Work of Reception, as Wittgenstein Did It. In M. Potter and T. Ricketts (Eds). *The Cambridge Companion to Frege* (pp.550–601). Cambridge: Cambridge University Press, secs 4–7.
Goldfarb, W. (2002). Wittgenstein's Understanding of Frege: The Pre-Tractarian Evidence. In E.H. Reck (Ed). *From Frege to Wittgenstein: Perspectives on Early Analytic Philosophy* (pp.185–200). New York: Oxford University Press.
Ricketts, T. (2002). Wittgenstein against Frege and Russell. In E.H. Reck (Ed). *From Frege to Wittgenstein: Perspectives on Early Analytic Philosophy* (pp.227–251). New York: Oxford University Press, sec. 4.

On Wittgenstein's criticism of Frege's introduction of an assertion-sign into logic, see:
Künne, W. (2009). Wittgenstein and Frege's *Logical Investigations*. In H.-J. Glock and J. Hyman (Eds). *Wittgenstein and Analytic Philosophy* (pp. 26–62). Oxford: Oxford University Press, pp.54–57.
Potter, M. (2009). *Wittgenstein's Notes on Logic*. Oxford: Oxford University Press, ch.10.

On Wittgenstein's repudiation of Frege's conception of generality and his related claim that Frege fails to appreciate the role of "formal concepts," see:
Fogelin, R.J. (1987). *Wittgenstein*, 2nd edn. London: Routledge, ch.5.
McGinn, M. (2006). *Elucidating the Tractatus*. Oxford: Clarendon Press, ch.7.

On "New Wittgenstein" readings of the *Tractatus*, which take seriously Frege's influence on Wittgenstein, see especially the papers collected in:
Crary, A. and Read, R. (Eds) (2000). *The New Wittgenstein*. London: Routledge.

For a recent account, see:
Kremer, M. (2013). The Whole Meaning of a Book of Nonsense: Reading Wittgenstein's *Tractatus*. In M. Beaney (Ed.). *The Oxford Handbook of the History of Analytic Philosophy* (pp.451–485). Oxford: Oxford University Press.

For discussion of Wittgenstein's anti-psychologism, see:

Travis, C. (2006a). *Thought's Footing: A Theme in Wittgenstein's Philosophical Investigations*. Oxford: Oxford University Press, ch.1.

Travis, C. (2006b). Psychologism. In E. Lepore and B. Smith (Eds). *The Oxford Handbook of Philosophy of Language* (pp.103–126). Oxford: Oxford University Press.

Finally, on the controversial question of Frege's later adherence to the context principle, see:

Beaney, M. (1996). *Frege: Making Sense*, London: Duckworth, §8.2.

Ricketts, T. (2010). Concepts, Objects and the Context Principle. In M. Potter and T. Ricketts (Eds). *The Cambridge Companion to Frege*. Cambridge: Cambridge University Press, pp.149–219.

and on the role of the context principle in the work of both Frege and Wittgenstein, see:

Reck, E.H. (1997). Frege's Influence on Wittgenstein: Reversing Metaphysics via the Context Principle. In W.W. Tait (Ed.). *Early Analytic Philosophy: Frege, Russell, Wittgenstein* (pp. 123–185). Chicago: Open Court.

5

Wittgenstein and Russell

GRAHAM STEVENS

1 Introduction

Bertrand Russell's influence on Wittgenstein, personally and philosophically, was profound. Russell's work on the foundations of mathematics apparently played a decisive role in persuading Wittgenstein to abandon his aeronautical engineering studies in favor of philosophy. In 1909, while still studying engineering at Manchester, Wittgenstein wrote to Philip Jourdain, suggesting a solution to Russell's paradox. Jourdain, with Russell's approval, dismissed the solution (Monk, 1990, p.33; cf. LUDWIG WITTGENSTEIN: A SKETCH OF HIS LIFE). But Wittgenstein appears to have been hooked by the subject Russell's writings had introduced him to and, two years later, he arrived in Cambridge and commenced his philosophical studies with Russell. Russell perhaps did not realize the tremendous personal significance of his positive appraisal of Wittgenstein's intellectual promise. According to Monk:

> Wittgenstein later told David Pinsent that Russell's encouragement had proved his salvation, and had ended nine years of loneliness and suffering, during which he had continually thought of suicide [...]. The implication is that, in encouraging him to pursue philosophy and in justifying his inclination to abandon engineering, Russell had, quite literally, saved Wittgenstein's life. (Monk, 1990, p.41)

Wittgenstein's influence on Russell turned out to be profound as well: two years after they first met, Wittgenstein had delivered an objection to Russell's theory of judgment that was so devastating that it led to the abandonment of a major philosophical project of Russell's, leaving him reportedly "paralysed" (Wittgenstein, letter to Russell, 22 July 1913). Wittgenstein's own work during this period culminated in his *Tractatus Logico-Philosophicus*, a book which was published largely thanks to Russell's support, and which is so deeply indebted to Russellian themes (either as sources of agreement or disagreement) as to be incomprehensible to anyone unfamiliar with Russell's work.

Wittgenstein's later philosophical work was far less influential on Russell. We can get a clear measure of Russell's relative evaluations of the "early" and "later" Wittgenstein from what he has to say in *My Philosophical Development* (1959), an intellectual autobiography to which an entire chapter was devoted to discussing Wittgenstein's influence on him (cf. also Chapter 1, WITTGENSTEIN'S PHILOSOPHICAL DEVELOPMENT). "Wittgenstein's doctrines influenced me profoundly," Russell writes, explaining that the impact of Wittgenstein came in "two waves" – one shortly before World War I, and one shortly after. However: "His later doctrines, as they appear in his *Philosophical Investigations*, have not influenced me at all" (Russell, 1959, p.83). Wittgenstein held much of Russell's later philosophy in similar disdain. No doubt personal issues between the two men, whose once close friendship deteriorated in later years, go some way toward explaining their attitudes toward each other. Certainly it explains the petty, sniping, quality of some of the comments each made regarding the other. Here is Russell on Wittgenstein:

> I have not found in Wittgenstein's *Philosophical Investigations* anything that seemed to me interesting and I do not understand why a whole school finds important wisdom in its pages [...]. [T]he later Wittgenstein [...] seems to have grown tired of serious thinking and to have invented a doctrine which would make such an activity unnecessary. (Russell, 1959, p.161)

And Wittgenstein on Russell:

> Russell's books should be bound in two colours [...] those dealing with mathematical logic in red – and all students of philosophy should read them; those dealing with ethics and politics in blue – and no one should be allowed to read them. (Letter to Drury, cited RW 112)

But there is a genuine philosophical point of division that explains this mutual hostility, revealed perhaps most explicitly by Wittgenstein's comment that "'Mathematical logic' has completely deformed the thinking of mathematicians and philosophers" (RFM V §48). What this comment reveals is that the later Wittgenstein rejects the entire methodology of Russell's philosophy. The rejection is so fundamental as to leave no real room for philosophical interaction between the two. In what follows, I will be exclusively interested in the *early interaction* between Wittgenstein and Russell. In particular, I will seek to uncover just what it was that Wittgenstein objected to in Russell's philosophy of 1913 and why this objection had the devastating impact on Russell that it did.

2   Russellian Background

To fully appreciate the underlying concerns of the *Tractatus* it is important to understand the extent to which Wittgenstein is responding to themes in Russell's philosophical logic. Two fundamental elements are pivotal to the logicism of Russell's *Principles of Mathematics* (1903): his conception of a proposition, and his commitment to the doctrine of the unrestricted variable.

When Russell first advanced the logicist thesis that mathematical truth is a species of logical truth in his *Principles of Mathematics*, he adhered to a very simple and elegant ontology. At this time, Russell insisted that there was only one fundamental ontological category, the category of what he called *terms*. Russellian terms, it should be noted, are not (generally) linguistic items but the *meanings* of linguistic items:

> Whatever may be an object of thought, or may occur in any true or false proposition, or can be counted as *one*, I call a *term*. This, then, is the widest word in the philosophical vocabulary [...] and to deny that such and such a thing is a term must always be false. (Russell, 1903, sec.47)

Russellian propositions are also nonlinguistic. They are the meanings of declarative sentences, and are composed of the terms that are the meanings of the words of those sentences.

In Russell's technical development of the logicist thesis, this ontological principle finds its formal counterpart in what has come to be called "the doctrine of the unrestricted variable." This doctrine maintains that any term may be the value of a variable of pure logic. Having adopted the doctrine that whatever can be an object of thought must be a term, Russell maintained that it is self-contradictory to deny that a term could fail to be a suitable logical subject for any proposition (see 1903, sec.52). But to deny the doctrine of the unrestricted variable is, in effect, to deny this. For if we maintain that only entities of a certain restricted sort may be values of the variable "x" in a monadic propositional function "ϕx," we are effectively committing ourselves to denying that every entity is a value of the variable in the propositional function "x is a term"; but as we saw above, Russell thinks that such a denial must "always be false" (sec.47). The doctrine of the unrestricted variable, then, is a key commitment of Russell's metaphysics in 1903.

Let us now examine Russell's notion of a proposition. Russellian propositions, as we now call them, are abstract entities that contain the objects that they are about (rather than, e.g., *modes of presentation* of those things, as Frege proposed). So, for example, the proposition that Socrates is mortal is a complex composed of the individual Socrates and the property of mortality. There are numerous reasons why this notion of a proposition was appealing to Russell, many of which anticipated important contemporary work on direct reference semantics. However, it also raised some seemingly intractable difficulties regarding belief reports, informative identity statements, and the semantics of empty names. Russell (mistakenly) thought that a combination of his famous theory of descriptions, along with his infamous theory that names are disguised definite descriptions, would resolve such difficulties.

But a further problem remains: what is the difference between a true proposition and a false proposition? Russell identified true propositions with facts. But false propositions are just as real as true ones. So Russell's ontology now must be extended to include fact-like falsehoods. These non-facts differ from facts only by virtue of lacking the property of truth. Why they lack this property while truths have it, Russell claimed, is "incapable of analysis"; it is simply the case that "some propositions are true and some false, just as some roses are red and some white" (Russell, 1901, pp.75–6).

In addition to these ontological problems facing his theory of propositions, Russell also became convinced that his ontology of propositions contained fundamental logical problems, as he encountered recurring contradictions in his attempts to formalize a propositional logic that would comport with his philosophical theory. Under such pressures, he abandoned his ontology of propositions shortly prior to the completion of the first volume of *Principia Mathematica* in 1910. In place of his theory of propositions,

Russell now developed a new theory of propositional content that has come to be called the Multiple-Relation Theory of Judgment (MRTJ). When committed to propositions as the objects of propositional attitudes, Russell naturally construed judgment as a dyadic relation between an agent and a proposition. On the MRTJ, this is replaced by a radical new analysis.

3 The Multiple-Relation Theory of Judgment

On the MRTJ, truth ceases to be a matter of identity between propositions and facts, evolving instead into a relation of correspondence between *judgments* and their truthmakers. Judgment is now analyzed as a *many-placed* relation (n-placed where the number of constituents of the judgment's truthmaker is $n-1$). So, for example, a subject s's judgment that aRb will be analyzed as:

$$J(s, a, R, b).$$

Russell was no doubt struck by the many advantages of this new analysis of belief. Perhaps most importantly, the MRTJ has a role to play in the justification of the order-part of the ramified hierarchy of types in *Principia* by shifting at least that part of the hierarchy onto Russell's epistemology rather than his ontology. Previous incarnations of that theory applied the hierarchy to propositions, thus resulting in an infinite number of different orders of proposition, a position that Russell struggled to make sense of as a metaphysical doctrine. But with propositions rejected, Russell thought that the imposition of this hierarchy onto judgments was less problematic, for the simple reason that judgments were not mind-independent elements of his ontology. Hence, Russell thought, the logical doctrine of orders (explained later in this chapter) did not have to extend into his metaphysics. Furthermore, as many have noted, the shift to a correspondence theory of truth relieved Russell of some outstanding ontological debts incurred by his earlier identity theory of truth, such as the problem of explaining what the ontological status of false propositions was.

The theory was not without problems of its own, however. In fact these problems are not really new problems, they are new forms of an old problem: the problem of the *unity of the proposition*. Central to the project of analysis endorsed by Russell and Moore at the turn of the nineteenth to the twentieth century was the idea that propositions are to be analyzed by breaking them down into their constituent parts. But this conception of analysis immediately invites the problem of the unity of the proposition, for there is a clear difference between the *proposition* that Socrates is mortal and the *collection* {Socrates, mortality}. No amount of listing or aggregation of the constituents of a proposition is going to be the same as that proposition which has a unity lacking from lists or aggregates. The problem of the unity of the proposition is just the problem of explaining what this difference consists in.

This problem, explicitly recognized by Plato and occasionally surfacing without solution in discussions of propositional content ever since, is notoriously hard to solve. For whenever a candidate is suggested as guarantor of propositional unity, the question arises whether this candidate is itself a constituent of the proposition. If it is not, then it can hardly provide the unity; if it is, we face the question of what relates this new entity to the other constituents so as to make them all cohere into a unity.

If the answer to that question is "nothing," then the new constituent can hardly provide the unity, if the answer is that another relation does the relating, we can ask the same question of this new relation and, obviously, find ourselves propelled onto an infinite regress.

The problem re-emerges in the context of the MRTJ in two new forms, often referred to as the "Direction Problems."

4   The Narrow Direction Problem (ND)

Consider Othello's belief that Desdemona loves Cassio:

$$B(o, d, L, c)$$

B is a many-placed relation over o,d,L,c. But in that case what is the difference between Othello's belief that Desdemona loves Cassio and his belief that Cassio loves Desdemona? At first Russell thought the order needed to distinguish the two beliefs could be provided by the subordinate relation (L), but this won't do as L has to be one of the objects related by B – it cannot be what Russell calls a "relating relation": "The relation 'loving,' as it occurs in the act of believing, is one of the objects – it is a brick in the structure, not the cement" (Russell, 1912, p.74). In *The Problems of Philosophy* (1912) Russell instead suggested that the order is provided by the primary relation (B). But, as he soon came to see, simply bestowing that property on B leaves the property wholly mysterious. To say that belief – i.e., believing – somehow orders its objects is not an *explanation* of the ordering of beliefs, of what is believed: it is a labeling of a problem, not a solution. Eventually Russell (1913/84) settled on invoking "logical forms" to provide the order where necessary. Logical forms act as templates in which elements are assigned a position. Thus, in addition to Othello, Desdemona, love, and Cassio, the belief-complex under discussion will also include (or at least somehow *involve*; see below) a logical form **xRy**:

$$B(o, d, L, c, \mathbf{xRy})$$

We now, however, face a new problem of how to explain the status of **xRy**. If it is a constituent of the judgment, then we will need to know what relates this to the other constituents in such a way that it can furnish the complex with the correct order. But this question will just lead us headlong onto a regress much the same as that considered previously with regard to the original problem of the unity of the proposition. Russell's (1913/84, p.118) diagram of the structure of judgment makes it clear that the logical form is a constituent of the judgment, though he does not think that they are constituents of the facts they correspond to.

5   The Wide Direction Problem (WD)

Wittgenstein's criticisms were clearly focused on this problem, viz., WD. WD can be seen as an extension of ND. ND shows that the subordinate relation is not a relating relation. But, if it is just another term of the primary relation, why should its relational status survive *at all*? If the subordinate relation is really just another "brick," not "cement," in other words, we will be unable to distinguish a judgment-complex as being of the form

$$J(s,a,R,b)$$

rather than being of the form

$$J(s,a,b,c).$$

As Wittgenstein puts it (albeit with use of an example having a slightly different logical form), there is nothing in the MRTJ to show that there is anything wrong with the "judgement" that "this table penholders the book" (NL 96). Thus Russell's theory is unable to account for the difference between sense and nonsense. Wittgenstein's point, and with it the distinction between ND and WD, can be summarized very clearly:

> ND shows MRTJ cannot account for the difference between Othello's belief that Desdemona loves Cassio and Othello's belief that Cassio loves Desdemona.

> WD shows MRTJ cannot distinguish between those possible beliefs of Othello's and his nonsensical pseudo-belief that Love desdemonas Cassio.

6 Wittgenstein's Objection and Russell's Paralysis

As mentioned above, Russell was reportedly "paralysed" by Wittgenstein's objection to the MRTJ (Wittgenstein, letter to Russell, 22 July 1913). In the absence of sufficient surviving correspondence between Russell and Wittgenstein from the relevant period to explain Russell's response, the challenge of determining what led Russell to react this way has proved difficult to resist for many Russell scholars. It is hardly satisfactory to rest content with the objection as phrased by Wittgenstein in the *Tractatus* as providing illumination on the issue. "The correct explanation of the form of the proposition, '*A* makes the judgement *p*,'" Wittgenstein announces, "must show that it is impossible for a judgement to be a piece of nonsense." And, he adds in parentheses: "Russell's theory does not meet this requirement" (TLP 5.5422). However, it is far from clear from this *why* a theory of judgment should meet this condition. Wittgenstein himself, it might be thought, ought to recognize that at least some of the propositions he holds to be nonsensical in the *Tractatus* at least *appear* to be believed by at least some people who don't recognize them as nonsensical (Griffin, 1985, p.240; 1986, p.144 – it should be noted, of course, that Wittgenstein himself consistently maintained that nonsense cannot be believed). At least on the face of it, then, a correct *descriptive* theory of judgment *should* make it possible for a judgment to be a piece of nonsense. Otherwise it will have failed to adequately describe the actual forms that judgments can take. The objection, and how it led to Russell's paralysis, clearly needs some further unpacking.

Attempts to decipher the exact nature of Wittgenstein's objections and the precise reason why Russell abandoned the MRTJ have diverged from one another dramatically, as is unsurprising given the poverty of evidence available to support any interpretation. However, following the influential interpretation offered by Stephen Sommerville and Nicholas Griffin, it has become fairly well accepted that the fatal blow to the MRTJ hinged on an incompatibility between the MRTJ and the theory of types (notable dissenters to this view are Landini, 1991; and Pincock, 2008). According to Sommerville (1981) and Griffin (1985; 1986), Russell has no choice but to accept the "no nonsense" criterion forwarded by Wittgenstein because this criterion is demanded of the MRTJ if it is to remain consistent with the theory of types. As mentioned above, the MRTJ is intended to play a central role in the justification of the hierarchy of orders required by ramified type-theory. Detailed consideration of type-theory is found below but, at this point, it suffices to remind ourselves that the theory is commonly thought of as an attempt to outlaw certain "nonsensical" formations. If the MRTJ is going to lend support to such a theory then, evidently, Wittgenstein's criterion must have at least some relevance: judgments must be well formed by the strictures of type-theory if the theory of types is not to be doomed from the outset, hence WD will need to be solved if the MRTJ is to churn out judgments that do not run into direct conflict with type-theory. But, in that case, Sommerville and Griffin think, further reflection on Wittgenstein's criterion reveals a horrendous problem for Russell.

The only solution to WD (according to Sommerville and Griffin) seems to be to appeal to a distinction in type between the subordinate relation – L and R in our examples – and the other objects of the primary relation of a judgment-complex. That Wittgenstein drew this moral is strongly suggested in the following letter to Russell:

> If I analyse the prop[osition] Socrates is mortal into Socrates, Mortality and $(\exists x,y)\varepsilon_1(x,y)$ I want a theory of types to tell me that 'Mortality is Socrates' is nonsensical, because if I treat 'Mortality' as a proper name (as I did) there is nothing to prevent me to make the substitution the wrong way round. (Letter to Russell, 16 January 1913)

The problem as Griffin and Sommerville see it, however, is that although one wants a theory of types to preserve the theory of judgment, one first needs the theory of judgment to *generate* the theory of types. In short, this "solution" to WD puts things hopelessly back to front. If the MRTJ generates and provides the philosophical justification for the theory of types, we cannot presuppose type-theory when setting out the MRTJ.

Viewed in this way, Russell's paralysis is unsurprising: Wittgenstein's criticisms go right to the foundations of *Principia*, leaving the philosophical justification of ramified type-theory in tatters. Sommerville and Griffin's interpretation has firmly established the view that the collapse of the MRTJ is, at least in part, determined by its connections with the theory of types. However, even if one agrees with them about this, the interpretation of Wittgenstein's criticisms does not end there. Consider the form in which their interpretation of the situation is given in the following passage from Griffin:

> Why won't Wittgenstein allow us to make these stipulations [regarding the type of the constituents of judgment-complexes]? Because to make them would require further judgements. We are trying to analyze what is supposed to be the simplest type of elementary judgement. But to do so would seem to involve us in yet further judgements. Moreover the further judgements required are of an extremely problematic character. For to judge that *a* and *b* are suitable arguments for a first-order relation is to make a judgement of higher than first-order. Yet, as Russell makes quite clear in *Principia* (pp.44–6), higher-order judgements are to be defined cumulatively on lower-order ones. Thus we cannot presuppose second-order judgements in order to analyze elementary judgements. (Griffin, 1986, p.144)

There is, I think, both something right and something wrong about this interpretation. It is right to recognize the connection between MRTJ and type-theory as the source of the former theory's difficulty. It is wrong, however, to see this problem as involving a regress of judgments or as an *epistemological* problem. As the MRTJ is clearly the centerpiece of Russell's epistemology, it is easy to be led astray into thinking that the conflict with type-theory must also occur at the epistemological level. I will call this interpretation the *epistemological interpretation* (EI). I think there are two fundamental problems with EI that show it to be false. After illustrating these, I will go on to suggest my own *ontological interpretation* (OI) as a solution to these two problems. (EI) and (OI), more precisely defined, are as follows:

> (EI) is the view that Wittgenstein's criticisms exposed an incompatibility between Russell's epistemology and his theory of types in the sense that the theory of types is justified by Russell's epistemology (in particular the epistemic relation of judgment as analyzed by the MRTJ), yet the MRTJ relies on a theory of types. Thus the theory of types and the MRTJ cannot be rendered compatible with one another without circularity.

> (OI) is the view that Wittgenstein's criticisms exposed an incompatibility between Russell's ontology and his theory of types in the sense that the theory of types is justified by the MRTJ and the MRTJ relies on treating all *elements* of a judgment as being of the same ontological type, while imposing order distinctions within the *epistemic* domain of judgments. Yet it is impossible to answer Wittgenstein's objection without imposing *ontological* type distinctions on judgments.

I will explain OI in detail shortly. First, the two problems with EI are:

(1) EI conflates the roles of the MRTJ and the so-called *direct inspection argument* (explained below) in *Principia*.
(2) EI overlooks the importance of the role played by the logical status of the subordinate relation in a judgment-complex in WD.

Let us look at each problem in turn.

7 Direct Inspection and the MRTJ (First Problem with EI)

If EI is correct, then the incompatibility of type-theory and the MRTJ arises because, in order to avoid nonsensical judgments, we must first *judge* that the constituents of our judgments are of the requisite types. But, as Griffin says in the passage quoted above, we cannot presuppose such judgments when making elementary judgments, if we are to appeal to a hierarchy of judgments that places elementary judgments at the most fundamental level. If the lowest level of the hierarchy depends on judgments that can only be reached at a higher level of the hierarchy, then such judgments cannot be available after all and the entire project seems doomed. This story, central to EI, rests on a misconception about type-theory, however. For the kinds of distinctions needed to guard against WD are not distinctions that require us to traverse the hierarchy of judgments in order to secure them.

The formal language contained in *Principia* is stratified with respect to two distinct hierarchies: the hierarchy of *types* and the hierarchy of *orders*. The type hierarchy yields "simple type-theory"; when combined with the order hierarchy, it yields "ramified type-theory." Simplifying matters somewhat, the type hierarchy assigns a type to a function determined by the type of the arguments it can meaningfully apply to, while the order hierarchy assigns an order to a function determined by the range of any quantifier used to define it, as summed up by the *vicious circle principle*: "Whatever involves *all* of a collection must not be one of the collection" (Whitehead and Russell, 1910, p.37).

Historically, the relationship between the two hierarchies has been shrouded in mystery. Russell himself did not distinguish the two hierarchies in a clear way, often appearing to be appealing to the vicious circle principle as the justification of both hierarchies. Ramsey first urged the separation of the two, which he suggested had only been unified in *Principia* by virtue of "being both deduced in a rather sloppy way from the 'vicious circle principle'" (Ramsey, 1925, p.24). Gödel agreed that the simple theory of types "is entirely independent of [the hierarchy of orders] and has nothing to do with the vicious circle principle" (Gödel, 1944, pp.134–5).

Let us briefly clarify the workings of ramified type-theory so as to be as clear as possible about the alleged impact of WD on that theory that is proposed by EI. The simplest way to understand the theory of types is to momentarily overlook Russell's doubts (explained in the next paragraph) about the reality of classes and begin by recognizing a hierarchy dictating membership restrictions on classes. A class can only be a member of a class of higher type. So the class of philosophers can be a member of a class of classes but not of a class of people. This is not an observation about the truth conditions of such claims, but a restriction on the very admissibility of those claims. The claim that the class of philosophers is a member of the class of people is not *false* in the formal language of type-theory; it is *inexpressible* within the grammar of the language. Type-restrictions, in other words, add to the formation-rules of the language to restrict what counts as a well-formed formula.

Now, Russell and Whitehead insist that the formal language of *Principia Mathematica* is a "no-classes" theory, so the above sketch needs revision when applied to their version of type-theory. The items subject to type-restrictions in their system are propositional functions. So we will say that propositional functions are stratified into a hierarchy determining which functions can be functions of which arguments. The easiest way to (very roughly) grasp this is by analogy with predication – the predicate "is a person" cannot be predicated of the predicate "is a philosopher," for example. We can make this clearer by symbolizing type-indices as subscripts on function variables as follows:

$$F_1, F_2, F_3, \ldots, F_n.$$

We then specify that a function of type n may only be argument to a function of type $n+1$. This will be sufficient to ensure that the propositional-function version of Russell's paradox is banished from the formal system. But the above hierarchy is only half of the story of *Principia*'s type-theory. Russell was convinced that the full defense of logicism should solve all of the paradoxes (including those we now recognize as semantic rather than merely logical). But consider the Epimenides paradox, otherwise known as the Cretan Liar Paradox, which we assume to be uttered by the Cretan, Epimenides:

(CL) All Cretans are Liars.

(CL) is contradictory if we assume that all utterances made by Cretans prior to Epimenides' utterance of (CL) were indeed lies. Yet (CL) does not violate the above hierarchy in any way. An additional diagnosis is needed here, and Russell's proposal is that we recognize a second hierarchy which is the outcome of the "vicious circle principle," according to which no statement made about a given totality can itself be a member of that totality. Epimenides violates this principle when he seeks to make a claim about the totality of utterances made by Cretans using a statement which itself adds to that totality. To avoid such violations, we must now impose a second hierarchy on top of the previous hierarchy of functions. To distinguish the two (a distinction which Russell only imperfectly respected in his own formulation), we will call the first hierarchy the hierarchy of *types*. This hierarchy by itself is the hierarchy of *simple type-theory*. If we add a hierarchy restricting statements concerning totalities as just outlined, we will call this the hierarchy of *orders*. The addition of this hierarchy to simple type-theory, yields *ramified type-theory*. In ramified type-theory, every level of the type hierarchy further divides into a hierarchy of orders (thus every level of types branches, or *ramifies*, into orders). We can add superscripts to our already subscripted (for type) expressions to display their orders. The expression "F_n^m," for example can only be argument to an expression of the right type and order, such as "G_{n+1}^{m+1}."

Without going too far into the formal details of this baroque edifice, we can note that the two hierarchies have quite independent justifications, and that only the hierarchy of orders is justified by appeal to the vicious circle principle. This in turn is unquestionably linked to the MRTJ as Russell and Whitehead explicitly argue that the hierarchy of orders has its origins in the recognition that the MRTJ leads to a hierarchy of orders of truth (Whitehead and Russell, 1910, p.42). Justification for the hierarchy of *types* (as opposed to *orders*), however, must come from elsewhere. Russell and Whitehead offer the "direct inspection" argument as justification for the imposition of this hierarchy: direct inspection of the nature of a propositional function is supposed to reveal that

> not only is it impossible for a function $\phi\hat{u}$ to have itself or anything derived from it as argument, but that, if $\psi\hat{u}$ is another function such that there are arguments a with which both 'ϕa' and 'ψa' are significant, then $\psi\hat{u}$ and anything derived from it cannot significantly be argument to $\phi\hat{u}$. (Whitehead and Russell, 1910, p.47)

The direct inspection argument, puzzling to interpret though it is, clearly has nothing whatsoever to do with acts of judgment. It is an argument to the effect that direct inspection of a propositional function will reveal it to have a logical type. The argument concerns the significance of propositional functions, and is intended to justify the hierarchy of types by showing how consideration of the range of significance of a function naturally leads to a division in logical types among functions. It is not our making a judgment that introduces the type – the type is presumably already there for us to discover on inspection. Types, in short, can be fixed prior to, and wholly independently of, judgments and the fixing of their orders. But, in that case, EI offers no explanation for the severity of Wittgenstein's objection after all: we can simply help ourselves to a theory of *types* in order to solve WD without embroiling ourselves in any circularity so long as we do not appeal to the hierarchy of *orders*. We would thereby ensure that the MRTJ meets Wittgenstein's criterion of excluding nonsense without any further problem. Thus EI fails to explain what was wrong with the MRTJ.

8 The Logical Status of the Subordinate Relation (Second Problem with EI)

The importance of the subordinate relation in understanding where the MRTJ goes wrong can be illustrated by briefly considering a set of distinctions drawn by Miller (2006) in his diagnosis of the MRTJ's demise. Miller suggests that Russell's favored solution to the direction problem (he does not specify whether wide or narrow) involved distinguishing the "object-terms" from the "object-relation" of a judgment-complex. Let $j = B(o,d,L,c)$; then d and c are object-terms, and L is an object-relation (as they are the terms and relation of Othello's belief). The main problem with Miller's account of the MRTJ is its failure to take seriously the following question: if B is simply a 4-place relation, what gives L any special status? Miller does not address this problem. But no account of why Russell abandoned the theory can afford to ignore it. To do so is to miss the whole force of WD. Indeed we can see this if we consider what would happen were Miller's analysis given in response to WD. It would clearly beg the question against the objection by presupposing a solution to WD in the analysis of j: we cannot help ourselves to the distinctions posited in Miller's analysis until we have a solution to the direction problems. If L is a brick in the structure of j, rather than the cement of j, there can be no way of determining if L is an object-term or object-relation. In short: Miller's analysis fails to account for WD.

What is the relevance of this fault in Miller's analysis to EI? What it shows is that there is a feature unique to MRTJ, missing from Miller's account, which is intrinsically tied up with the status of the subordinate verb. This is clear enough when we consider that there is no equivalent to WD in the early case of the problem of the unity of the proposition. Desdemona cannot be a relation on Russell's (1903) theory of propositions, as Russell there draws a (perhaps questionable) distinction between things that can only be the relata of properties and relations, and "concepts" (embracing properties and relations) which have a "two-fold status" enabling them to occur as both *relata* of relations and as *relating*-relations. But, such a distinction cannot be drawn in the MRTJ: when relations are occurring as *terms of other relations* (as they are when they are subordinate relations in judgment-complexes) they are logically on a par with all the other terms and, therefore, a distinction between individuals and relations will be no help. Even if relations do retain a twofold status, occurring either as relating relations or as subordinate relations, they are not relating-relations when they occur as subordinate ones. Thus, whatever holds for the subordinate relation in j, holds for *everything* related by the primary relation of j.

Now notice that, most importantly for the present discussion, this has nothing whatsoever to do with epistemology. Again, we should not be misled by the fact that we are discussing the analysis of judgments into thinking that the problem we have located is an epistemological one. The important point is simply that, in the above example, L is a *term* of a relation, not a *relating*-relation – and that is an ontological (or perhaps logical) distinction, not an epistemological one. EI has nothing to say about it.

These two problems leave EI looking deeply unconvincing as an account of the downfall of the MRTJ. Another answer is needed if we are to determine exactly what was wrong with the theory. I will now propose an answer.

9 Solution to these two Problems: OI

What the above objections to EI reveal is that the clash between the MRTJ and the theory of types cannot have occurred at the level of Russell's epistemology if it was really responsible for his rejection of the MRTJ. Where then did it occur? The answer is, I suggest, clearly given in Wittgenstein's letters to Russell discussing the MRTJ. Perhaps the most explicit is the following comment: "I think that there cannot be different types of things! In other words whatever can be symbolized by a simple proper name must belong to one type" (16.1.13, NL, p.121). This is not an objection to Russell's epistemology, but to his ontology. It is Russell's ontology that is drawn into conflict with the theory of types by the MRTJ. The MRTJ makes two mutually exclusive demands on judgments. On the one hand, all *relata* of the primary relation must be terms of the same logical type (bricks, not cement) if they are to be related by the primary relation. But, in order to capture the difference between well-formed judgments and nonsense like "Love desdemonas Cassio," a special status must be bestowed on the subordinate relation. Only the theory of types can salvage the MRTJ. But to do that, it must apply directly to the entities in the world that are the constituents of judgments: only an ontological theory of types will do the trick.

Why would the imposition of an ontological theory of types be problematic for Russell? After all, we have seen that there is no circularity involved in appealing to the theory of types in order to solve WD. Why would Russell be so concerned by the problem? To answer this question, we need to consider one final elusive aspect of Russell's philosophy, namely the ontology he envisaged for *Principia*'s ramified type-theory.

10 Propositional Functions

Principia's type-theory applies to what Whitehead and Russell call "propositional functions," stratifying them into a hierarchy whereby a propositional function can only be applied to a function below it in the hierarchy. But much discussion has centered on what Whitehead and Russell took the precise nature of propositional functions to be. Traditionally the theory has been assumed to operate at the level of Russell's ontology, arranging the constituents of mathematical reality into types (Quine, 1953; 1966). However, as several commentators have pointed out, this interpretation does not sit comfortably with the philosophical introduction to *Principia*. There, as in later works, Russell is insistent that the things subject to type-distinctions, namely propositional functions, are *linguistic* items. Thus it often seems that Russell envisages type-theory as operating merely at the level of the linguistic expression of mathematical truths, not at the level of whatever entities those truths are about and, furthermore, it seems that he holds this to be central to the philosophical justification of the theory of types. For example, he is adamant in correspondence with Wittgenstein after reading the *Tractatus* that "the theory of types is [...] a theory of correct symbolism" (see Wittgenstein, Letter to Russell, 19 August 1919).

In the informal exposition of the intended interpretation of the formal system of *Principia*, as just noted, Whitehead and Russell speak as if predicate variables stand for things called "propositional functions." If propositional functions are understood along the same lines as they feature in the *Principles of Mathematics*, the traditional interpretation seems to be right. There, propositional functions are as much a part of Russell's ontology as propositions are. Taking propositional functions to be of this sort guarantees that the theory of types is an ontological theory, despite Whitehead and Russell's apparent statements to the contrary.

A number of problems face this traditional way of interpreting *Principia*. For one thing, the interpretation is in the unfortunate position of being openly contradicted by one of the authors of the work it is intended to interpret. Russell, in *My Philosophical Development*, explicitly states that propositional functions are linguistic entities only: "A propositional function is nothing but an expression. It does not, by itself, represent anything. But it can form part of a sentence which does say something, true or false" (Russell, 1959, p.69). Admittedly, this passage cannot be taken as conclusive evidence of Russell's position, as he contradicts himself awkwardly on this issue (and others) in *My Philosophical Development* (1959, p.68). But more reliable sources contain similar claims. For example, in "The Philosophy of Logical Atomism" (1918), Russell is explicit in his denial of the existence of propositional functions as entities: "A propositional function is nothing, but, like most of the things one wants to talk about in logic, it does not lose its importance through that fact" (Russell, 1918, p.202). However, it should be noted that even this source is written after *Principia* and so cannot be deemed decisive. Secondly, and more importantly, however, *Principia* (officially, at least) lacks the ontological resources to support an ontological hierarchy of types. Propositions are rejected in *Principia* in line with the adoption of the MRTJ. But this now poses a serious problem for the interpretation we have been considering, as we can see if we look at how Whitehead and Russell describe functions in *Principia*:

> Let ϕx be a statement containing a variable x and such that it becomes a proposition when x is given any fixed determined meaning. Then ϕx is called a 'propositional function'; it is not a proposition, since owing to the ambiguity of x it really makes no assertion at all. (Whitehead and Russell, 1910, p.14)

> By a 'propositional function' we mean something which contains a variable x, and expresses a proposition as soon as a value is assigned to x. That is to say, it differs from a proposition solely by the fact that it is ambiguous: it contains a variable of which the value is unassigned. (Whitehead and Russell, 1910, p.38)

The problem with this talk of propositional functions "becoming" or "expressing" a proposition upon the assignment of a value to x is that this means, according to the official ontology of *Principia*, there is nothing for a propositional function *to* become under such circumstances. Propositions just don't exist.

Perhaps there is no conclusive evidence for either interpretation of *Principia*. The authors of that work, it seems, were simply not clear enough in what they said on the matter. However, I propose that reflection on Wittgenstein's criticisms of Russell's MRTJ helps to resolve this debate, since it provides compelling evidence that Russell was anxious to avoid the very ontological type-distinctions that the traditional interpretation of *Principia* attributes to him.

The traditional interpretation of propositional functions gives entirely the wrong prediction regarding Russell's response to Wittgenstein's objection. In fact, it predicts that Russell would not be at all troubled, let alone paralyzed, by the objection. If the traditional interpretation were correct, then Russell's paralysis would be no more explicable by OI than it was by EI. For it would arm Russell with the mechanism to block the formation of nonsensical judgments with ease. All that is needed to block the objection is an ontological theory of types, which assigns a special status to the subordinate relation. Why Russell should respond in the way that he did to Wittgenstein's objection is therefore utterly inexplicable if OI is coupled with a traditional interpretation of the theory of types.

When on the other hand, the linguistic interpretation of the theory of types is coupled with OI, Russell's paralysis becomes fully explicable: OI demonstrates that the solution to WD is incompatible with a linguistic interpretation of the predicate expressions of *Principia*. Unless universals divide into types (i.e., unless propositional functions and universals are identified), the theory of types cannot help with WD. It is not *expressions* that are the terms of the primary relation in a judgment-complex; it is the individuals and relations that the judgment is about. Hence, no theory of types will be able to play a role in solving WD until it applies to those individuals and relations also. The linguistic interpretation holds that the primary motivation for the version of type-theory it attributes to *Principia* was the authors' desire to avoid imposing type restrictions onto the ontology of the work. A demonstration from Wittgenstein that Russell's attempt to avoid ontological type-restrictions could only succeed if it were to presuppose the very restrictions it is designed to avoid, makes Russell's reaction unsurprising. Thus the linguistic interpretation, unlike the traditional interpretation, of propositional functions explains Russell's paralysis.

11 Wittgenstein on Logical Form

The above discussion is intended to provide an explanation of Russell's paralysis, i.e., his response to Wittgenstein's objections. But it would be a mistake to assume that what paralyzed Russell was also the main concern of Wittgenstein. Wittgenstein was not concerned to mount a defense of ramified type-theory, nor was he particularly interested in the details of the theory as manifested in *Principia*. That much is clear from the brief and characteristically cryptic "disposal" of Russell's paradox offered at TLP 3.333 (cf. Chapter 17, LOGIC AND THE *TRACTATUS*). Whatever interpretation one might want to offer of this passage, it is certainly obvious that Wittgenstein did not think a theory of types was required for the solution of the paradox. And, of course, by implication this means that the theory is wholly redundant; for it has no other purpose beyond the solution of this and related paradoxes. Indeed, Wittgenstein thinks that "the whole of the 'theory of types'" (TLP 3.331) can be summarized by the observation that "No proposition can make a statement about itself because a propositional sign cannot be contained in itself" (TLP 3.332).

If Russell's paralysis was caused by the impact of Wittgenstein's objection on the theory of types, then that is likely to have been collateral damage and not the main target of Wittgenstein's own thoughts. While there is of course no reason to think that Wittgenstein would not have raised an objection to Russell's theory just as an end in itself, examination of the correspondence between the two from the period in question strongly suggests that Wittgenstein's objection arose as an upshot of the development of his own ideas, and these were certainly not aimed at type-theory. It is true that Wittgenstein was devoting some sort of attention to the theory of types in 1913. He reported to Russell that he was "thinking about the beastly theory of types" in September of 1913 (NL 122). This may tempt us to think that he was more interested in the details of type-theory in 1913 than he was when he completed the *Tractatus* five years later. However, the following discussion of types between Russell and Wittgenstein shows that Wittgenstein had already arrived at the view expressed in TLP 3.332 by mid-January of 1913:

> All theories of types must be done away with by a theory of symbolism showing that what seem to be different kinds of things are symbolized by different kinds of symbols which cannot possibly be substituted in one another's places. (NL 121)

When one scrutinizes the discussions of the theory of types in the correspondence between the two, there is scant evidence that Russell and Wittgenstein ever really managed to talk about the same thing. Wittgenstein showed no real interest in the formal aspects of the theory, and Russell never seemed to fully understand Wittgenstein's view on types, much to the latter's frustration. Even by the time Russell had read the finished manuscript of the *Tractatus*, his response to Wittgenstein's criticisms of the theory of types clearly missed Wittgenstein's intended point. Russell defended the theory by explaining that it was "a theory of correct symbolism: a simple symbol must not be used to express anything complex: more generally, a symbol must have the same structure as its meaning," to which a seemingly exasperated Wittgenstein retorted:

> That's exactly what one can't say. You cannot prescribe to a symbol what it *may* be used to express. All that a symbol *can* express it *may* express. This is a short answer but it is true! (Letter to Russell, 19 August 1919)

If Wittgenstein's attack on type-theory was not understood by Russell by 1919, it clearly cannot have been the cause of his paralysis in 1913. Thus it seems clear that the impact on types that Russell took the theory to have was not the intended target of Wittgenstein's objection.

To understand Wittgenstein's intention we have to see how these kinds of ideas fit into the overall account of logic and propositional structure on offer in the *Tractatus*. While it is true that much of that book is inspired (either as a source of agreement or disagreement) by Russell, we cannot overlook the other of Wittgenstein's great influences, namely Frege (see Chapter 4, WITTGENSTEIN AND FREGE). Frege's distinction between concept and object and his hierarchy of concepts (which Russell acknowledged as a forerunner of his own theory of types) are obviously relevant to the discussion of types in the *Tractatus*. Most importantly, I think, this proto-"type theory" of Frege's is offered as a solution to a very different problem to the one Russell's theory addresses. Frege's hierarchy is his proposed solution to the problem of the *unity of the proposition* rather than to set-theoretic or semantic paradoxes. This concern is inherited by Wittgenstein in the *Tractatus* and provides the link between Wittgenstein's discussion of types and his objection to the MRTJ.

For Frege, the explanation of how the parts of an atomic proposition combine to form a unity is to be found in his distinction between concept and object. There is a fundamental difference between two different types of entity in the realm of reference: the complete entities (objects) and the incomplete entities (concepts). The incompleteness of the latter can only be resolved by their combination with the former, and only when these two kinds combine (or when a similar combination is effected between concepts of different levels in the hierarchy in the case of non-atomic propositions) can a proposition be produced. Propositions (Fregean thoughts) reside in the realm of sense, not reference, but their combination reflects and depends on this mode of combination between elements in the realm of reference, as Fregean thoughts are modes of presentation of truth values. These values occur in the realm of reference as the values of concepts, which are construed as functions whose values are always truth values. The distinctions at play are, according to Frege, fundamental features of reality, "deep in the nature of things" (Frege, [1891] 1952/80, p.41).

Wittgenstein sees a deep insight in Frege's distinction but rightly rejects the appeal to brute metaphysical facts as a ground for the distinction. If one is seeking a solution to the unity of the proposition, it is not enough to state that propositions are unities because of distinctions deep in the nature of things. The problem is a serious objection to the claim that propositions exist on the grounds that how their constituents combine to form something propositional is mysterious. Embracing this mystery as inexplicable is hardly a satisfactory response to that objection.

Wittgenstein's proposal in the *Tractatus* is to relocate Frege's distinction within a new theory of propositional content, namely the picture theory of the proposition (cf. Chapter 8, THE PICTURE THEORY, and Chapter 32, WITTGENSTEIN ON INTENTIONALITY). According to this theory, what distinguishes propositions from mere collections of their constituents is that in a proposition the elements are arranged in a *pictorial* form. An often-overlooked feature of the picture theory is the appeal made to the *use* that elements of the picture are put to in explaining this pictorial form:

> In order to recognize a symbol by its sign we must observe how it is used with a sense. A sign does not determine a logical form unless it is taken together with its logico-syntactic employment. (TLP 3.326–3.327)

A proposition, for Wittgenstein, is a logical picture of facts (TLP 3). But to picture a fact simply is to *use* the elements of the picture in the right kind of way (see also Chapter 23, MEANING AND UNDERSTANDING). This is the fundamental insight Wittgenstein sees in the picture theory, revealed by his first thoughts on the subject in his reflections on the use of models to represent facts (see e.g., NB 29.9.14). Accordingly, what makes a sentence nonsensical is not something we can prescribe against independently of the use of the sentence (as for example, the theory of types attempts to do), but simply that we have failed to use the sentence to picture something. This claim was fundamental to the picture theory from its earliest inception:

> Let us remember the explanation why "Socrates is Plato" is nonsense. That is, because we have not made an arbitrary specification, NOT because a sign is, shall we say, illegitimate in itself! (NB 22.8.14)

This view remains central to the theory in the *Tractatus* (5.473) and lies behind Wittgenstein's insistence that the theory of types is dispensable. Wittgenstein's brief "disposal" of Russell's paradox in the *Tractatus* is based on the following passage:

> The reason why a function cannot be its own argument is that the sign for a function already contains the prototype of its argument, and it cannot contain itself.
>
> For let us suppose that the function $F(fx)$ could be its own argument: in that case there would be a proposition '$F(F(fx))$', in which the outer function F and the inner function F must have different meanings, since the inner one has the form $\phi(fx)$ and the outer one has the form $\psi(\phi(fx))$. Only the letter 'F' is common to the two functions, but the letter by itself signifies nothing. (TLP 3.333)

The letter "F" by itself signifies nothing because it signifies only when it is used in a proposition. In other words, it signifies only when it is used as an element in a picture. But to attempt to use the letter in a proposition picturing the application of a function to itself is impossible, because any such attempt must use the letter in two different ways. But once the way in which it is used differs, the logical form thereby automatically differs because that logical form is *determined by* the use (TLP 3.327).

We can see quite clearly how the "theory of types" is being made redundant on the above theory of propositions as pictures. But the theory of types in question is more recognizable as Frege's hierarchy of concepts than Russell's ramified type-theory of *Principia Mathematica*. What Wittgenstein offers us is an account of the sorts of distinctions that Frege appeals to in order to explain the unity of the proposition but one that attempts to give a full explanation for why such distinctions exist, rather than resting content with positing them as metaphysical limitations on propositional structure. This was what interested Wittgenstein about the theory of types, not the details of the theory as it fitted into the formal apparatus of *Principia Mathematica*.

12   Conclusion

I have attempted to explain some of the complex philosophical interactions between Russell and the early Wittgenstein in a way that respects the insights of each and the different projects each were embarked on. There is no doubt that, at one stage, the two saw themselves as working together on a common project. But it is equally obvious that their two projects diverged quite dramatically in the end. Great philosophers respond to those who inspire them in original ways, developing new and exciting views of their own that often pursue very different concerns to those of the work that influenced them. Such was the case here. As time passed their projects drifted further and further apart. But there can be no question that their mutual influence on each other during the period of Wittgenstein's first philosophy was of profound importance to the development of the work of each. Understanding the work of either during this period requires careful study of the other.

References

Frege, G. ([1891] 1952/80). Function and Concept. Translation in G. Frege. *Translations from the Philosophical Writings of Gottlob Frege*. Ed. P. Geach and M. Black. Third edition. Oxford: Blackwell. (Original work published 1891).

Gödel, K. (1944). Russell's Mathematical Logic. In P.A. Schilpp (Ed.). *The Philosophy of Bertrand Russell* (pp.123–153). London: Harper and Row.
Griffin, N. (1985). Russell's Multiple Relation Theory of Judgement. *Philosophical Studies*, 47, 213–241.
Griffin, N. (1986). Wittgenstein's Criticisms of Russell's Theory of Judgement. *Russell*, 4, 132–145.
Landini, G. (1991). A New Interpretation of Russell's Multiple-Relation Theory of Judgement. *History and Philosophy of Logic*, 12, 37–69.
Miller, A. (2006). Russell, Multiple Relations, and the Correspondence Theory of Truth. *The Monist*, 89, 85–101.
Monk, R. (1990). *Ludwig Wittgenstein: The Duty of Genius*. London: Jonathan Cape.
Pincock, C. (2008). Russell's Last (and Best) Multiple-Relation Theory of Judgement. *Mind*, 117, 107–139.
Quine, W. (1953). Logic and the Reification of Universals. In W. Quine. *From a Logical Point of View* (pp.102–129). Cambridge, MA: Harvard University Press.
Quine, W. (1966). Russell's Ontological Development. *Journal of Philosophy*, 63, 657–667.
Ramsey, F.P. (1925). The Foundations of Mathematics. Reprinted in F.P. Ramsey. (1931). *The Foundations of Mathematics and other Logical Essays* (pp.1–61). Ed. R.B. Braithwaite. London: Routledge.
Russell, B. (1901). Part I of the *Principles*, Draft of 1901. Edited in G.H. Moore (Ed.). (1994). *The Collected Papers of Bertrand Russell (Vol. 3): Toward the Principles of Mathematics, 1900–1902*. London: Routledge.
Russell, B. (1903). *The Principles of Mathematics*. Cambridge: Cambridge University Press.
Russell, B. (1912). *The Problems of Philosophy*. Oxford: Oxford University Press.
Russell, B. (1913/84). *Theory of Knowledge: The 1913 Manuscript*. Ed. E.R. Eames. London: George Allen and Unwin.
Russell, B. (1918). The Philosophy of Logical Atomism. Reprinted in R.C. Marsh (Ed.). (1956). *Logic and Knowledge: Essays 1910–1950* (pp.177–281). London: George Allen and Unwin.
Russell, B. (1959). *My Philosophical Development*. London: Routledge.
Sommerville, S. (1981). Wittgenstein to Russell (July, 1913): "I am very sorry to hear ... my objection paralyses you." In R. Haller and W. Grassl (Eds). *Language, Logic and Philosophy* (pp.182–188). Vienna: Hölder-Pichler-Tempsky.
Whitehead, A.N. and Russell, B. (1910). *Principia Mathematica* (Vol. 1). Cambridge: Cambridge University Press.

Further Reading

Copi, I.M. (1971). *The Theory of Logical Types*. London: Routledge.
Glock, H.-J. (2013). Judgement and Truth in the Early Wittgenstein. In M. Textor (Ed.). *Judgement and Truth in Early Analytic Philosophy and Phenomenology* (pp.242–270). Basingstoke: Palgrave Macmillan.
Klement, K. (2004). Putting Form before Function: Logical Grammar in Frege, Russell and Wittgenstein. *Philosopher's Imprint*, 4, 1–47.
Landini, G. (2007). *Wittgenstein's Apprenticeship with Russell*. Cambridge: Cambridge University Press.
Levine, J. (2013). *Principia Mathematica*, the Multiple-Relation Theory of Judgement and Molecular Facts. In N. Griffin and B. Linsky (Eds). *The Palgrave Centenary Companion to Principia Mathematica* (pp.247–304). Basingstoke: Palgrave Macmillan.
Linsky, B. (1999). *Russell's Metaphysical Logic*. Stanford: CSLI Publications.
Stevens, G. (2005). *The Russellian Origins of Analytical Philosophy*. London: Routledge.

6

Wittgenstein, Hertz, and Boltzmann

JOHN M. PRESTON

1 Introduction

In 1931, during a moment in which he took himself never to have invented an original line of thinking, Wittgenstein listed those whose work he considered himself to have been influenced by (CV 16). The list starts with the names of two figures who made very significant contributions to the development of physical science in the late nineteenth century, Ludwig Boltzmann and Heinrich Hertz.

2 Boltzmann and Hertz

Boltzmann (1844–1906), the great Viennese theoretical physicist, was the founder of statistical thermodynamics, the modern theory of heat. He defended traditional classical mechanics and atomism in the face of figures such as Gustav Kirchhoff and Ernst Mach, who had argued against the idea that physics explains natural phenomena by developing and testing visualizable hypotheses that constitute "models" of physical reality. Considering these too metaphysical, in going too far beyond experience, these quite extreme antirealists instead strove to understand science as a labor-saving descriptive catalogue of observable phenomena. Boltzmann's defense was heroic, since we now have no doubts about the reality of submicroscopic phenomena, but he died by his own hand before realizing that his approach had truly been vindicated (by Perrin, Einstein, and others).

Hertz (1857–1894) was that rare combination, a brilliant theoretical *and* experimental physicist. In his most famous series of experiments, he generated electric waves, proved that they were transmitted through the air, were reflected and refracted like light waves, and that they traveled at the speed of light. These waves, originally called Hertzian waves, we now know as radio waves, and their existence confirmed Maxwell's theory of electromagnetism. In the final years of his short life, Hertz turned his attention to another area of physics, criticizing two existing systems of mechanics

(Newtonian–Lagrangian and "energeticist"), developing a new system of his own, and comparing the three in a fascinating philosophical introduction to his last work, which was posthumously published as *The Principles of Mechanics Presented in a New Form* (orig. in German 1894, trans. 1956).

Commentators on Wittgenstein used to treat Hertz as the more important and more seminal influence upon Wittgenstein, and used to treat Boltzmann himself as a Hertzian. These views have been challenged, though, by more recent scholarship (see, especially, Wilson, 1989 and 1993, two of the most important essays on this subject).

3   Wittgenstein's Knowledge of Boltzmann and Hertz

We do not know exactly how or when Wittgenstein came across the work of these two great physicist-philosophers. He is known to have read works by Schopenhauer, the third figure on his list of influences, during his youth (Anscombe reported that this was when he was 16; see Chapter 3, WITTGENSTEIN AND SCHOPENHAUER). The (plausible and as-yet-unrefuted) conjecture that this list was chronologically ordered suggests that he must have encountered Boltzmann's and Hertz's work shortly after his three years at the *Oberrealschule* in Linz (1903–1906). On leaving this school, Wittgenstein had specified his intention to study physics, and apparently to do so in Vienna under Boltzmann himself (von Wright, 1958, p.3; Spelt and McGuinness, 2001, p.131; Waugh, 2008, p.48). He would certainly have known the 1894 address "On Aeronautics" (reproduced in Sterrett, 2006) in which Boltzmann argued for the superiority of heavier-than-air craft over dirigibles. This may even have stimulated his interest in aeronautics (at school), his later choice to study engineering at the University of Manchester (1908–1911), and his work there on jet-reaction aircraft engines and a new kind of aircraft propeller. Any such plan to study under Boltzmann, though, would have been frustrated by Boltzmann's suicide in 1906.

Brian McGuinness conjectures that Wittgenstein came to know Hertz's work before leaving school (based on his mentioning Hertz immediately after Boltzmann, and the fact that Hertz and Maxwell were "the sort of authors read in the *Alleegasse* [the Viennese family mansion]," McGuinness, 1990, p.39). Ray Monk speculates that it may have been reading Boltzmann's *Populäre Schriften* that led Wittgenstein to read Hertz's *Principles of Mechanics*, during his teenage years (Monk, 1990, p.26; see also von Wright, 1958, p.7, n.3; and Wilson, 1989). During his time as a student of mechanical engineering at the *Technische Hochschule* in Charlottenburg, Berlin (October 1906–May 1908), Wittgenstein may also have encountered their works. Certainly by the time he was thinking of studying philosophy he would already have known about Hertz, since while still studying engineering in Manchester one of his fellow students had recommended to him Russell's 1903 book *The Principles of Mathematics*, which includes a sketch of Hertz's mechanics (Russell, 1903, secs. 470–1).

But *how* might Wittgenstein have been influenced by Hertz and Boltzmann? Although neither certainty nor completeness is possible here, we can fairly safely identify *some* respects in which there was a positive influence. In doing so, it makes sense to consider Hertz before Boltzmann, even if Wittgenstein did not encounter them in this order, since most of the works of Boltzmann that Wittgenstein knew had certainly taken the relevant and preexisting ideas of Hertz into account.

JOHN M. PRESTON

4 Hertz and His Mechanics

The context within which Hertz and Boltzmann worked was one in which many prominent theoretical physicists accepted the Kantian restriction that our thought cannot access "things in themselves," but works only with *representations* (phenomena). These physicists applied this idea to science, conceiving of their *theories* as representations, and conceiving of these representations in pictorial terms, as *Bilder*, pictures or models. In this respect they may also have been influenced by contemporary psychology.

In *The Principles of Mechanics*, Hertz, although conceiving of all physical theories in this way, applied the idea in detail only to mechanics. There, his aim is a foundational one of stripping "the last remnant of obscurity" from the fundamental concepts of mechanics, notably that of *force* (Hertz, [1894] 1956, preface). Like Boltzmann, one of his chief concerns is the extent to which existing scientific representations (of mechanics, for example) are *unclear*, and this very prominent ideal of clarity is one thing that Wittgenstein may have taken from the two of them (albeit transposed, as it were, into a distinctively philosophical key).

Wittgenstein commentators have often remarked on Hertz's aim, but few have really considered the way he proposed to accomplish it in his entire book (not merely in its more famous and often-read Introduction). The way in which Hertz does this involves a somewhat austere, formal version of what is now known as a *Bildtheorie*, that is, the above-mentioned conception of physical theories as pictures or "images." The *method* by which physicists proceed, according to Hertz, is "always" to

> form for ourselves images or symbols of external objects; and the form which we give them is such that the necessary consequents of the images in thought are always the images of the necessary consequents in nature of the things pictured. (Hertz, [1894] 1956, p.1)

Hertz famously lays down three requirements, or *desiderata*, which our "images" must have in order to be acceptable. The first is that they should be *logically permissible*, meaning that they must not contradict "the laws of our thought." The second is that the "essential relations" of our images must not contradict "the relations of external things," they must be *correct*. However, even two permissible and correct images of the same external objects may yet differ in respect of the third feature, *appropriateness* (as Hertz calls it). This feature has two ingredients. The first (*distinctness*) is a matter of how many of the object's essential relations the image pictures. The second (*simplicity*) is a matter of how few "superfluous or empty relations" the image contains, "in addition to the essential characteristics" (p.2). These three *desiderata* marry up with a familiar Kantian triumvirate with which Hertz operates: some features of our "images" are given by the nature of our minds, some are given in experience, and some are "permissibly and yet arbitrarily" added by us (p.11).

These are the features in terms of which Hertz then goes on to consider three different representations of the principles of mechanics. By varying the choice of the propositions we take as fundamental in such a representation, we can obtain different "images" of things, each of which we can then "test and compare with each other in respect of permissibility, correctness, and appropriateness" ([1894] 1956, p.4).

Having then effected this comparison, and having convinced himself that the two existing representations of mechanics are problematic, Hertz proposes a new one of his own. Because he suspects that the problems attending the familiar Newtonian–Lagrangian representation derive from its taking force as a fundamental concept, that concept does not appear as a fundamental one in his own representation. Instead, its place is taken by the idea that masses are *connected* with one another (in invisible ways), and that in addition to the masses that we can perceive there are "hidden" or "concealed" masses, which we cannot perceive.

Finally, Hertz replaces the laws of Newtonian mechanics with a single "fundamental law" of his own, which he expresses informally as "Every natural motion of an independent material system consists herein, that the system follows with uniform velocity one of its straightest paths" (p.27). Of this new law he says:

> The law condenses into one single statement the usual law of inertia and Gauss's Principle of Least Constraint. [...] In our image this fundamental law is the first proposition derived from experience in mechanics proper: it is also the last. From it, together with the admitted hypothesis of concealed masses and the normal connections, we can derive all the rest of mechanics by purely deductive reasoning. (Hertz, [1894] 1956, pp.27–8)

This fundamental law, then, is supposed to encapsulate the entire empirical content of Hertz's system of mechanics. (For the first, best-informed, most sustained, and detailed reading of Hertz's mechanics as a whole, see Jesper Lützen's magisterial book *Mechanistic Images in Geometric Form: Heinrich Hertz's Principles of Mechanics*, 2005.)

Hertz is one of the very few people mentioned by name in *Tractatus Logico-Philosophicus*, where his discussion of dynamical models in sections 418ff of *The Principles of Mechanics* is invoked to elucidate the idea of a proposition's logical multiplicity (TLP 4.04), and his notion of uniform or *law-like* connections (between "concealed masses," in Hertz's system) is used to explain Wittgenstein's take on the "law of causality" (TLP 6.3, 6.36–6.361; see Hertz, [1894] 1956, p.28 and sec.119). The different "systems for describing the world" and "systems of mechanics" discussed in propositions 6.341–6.35, whose properties can be given a priori, may well also include the three systems of mechanics which Hertz's text investigated, and the idea of *"materielle Punkte"* (material points) therein seems to have been taken from that text, too.

5 The Picture Conception of Language

Many commentators agree that Wittgenstein took the idea that propositions are *Bilder* (models), or at least the *terminology* of *Bilder*, from Hertz, or from Hertz and Boltzmann (e.g., Barker, 1980). When for the first time in the *Tractatus* he connects propositions with their users by saying "*Wir machen uns Bilder der Tatsachen*" ("We picture facts to ourselves," TLP 2.1), he is surely echoing Hertz's dictum, "*Wir machen uns innere Scheinbilder oder Symbole der äusseren Gegenstände*" ("We form for ourselves images or symbols of external objects," Hertz, [1894] 1956, p.1). But whether Hertz has a stronger claim than Boltzmann here is controversial.

Across several decades, various commentators have gone on to claim either that the account of representation in the *Tractatus* derives from Hertz, or that Wittgenstein took over from Hertz a picture theory of meaning. (See, for example, Griffin, 1964; McGuinness, 1969; Goddard and Judge, 1982; McDonough, 1994; Grasshoff, 1998; Harré, 2001; Pârvu, 2001.) Attempts to establish anything like a detailed and genuine *identity* between their views in either of these respects are problematic, though. I doubt, for example, that Hertz would have understood his own work as containing any theory of meaning, since his concern was limited to representation in *science* (see Preston, 2006a). Wittgenstein may have found what Hertz said attractive, but even if he did develop a theory of representation or a picture theory of meaning, neither was something that he just took over from Hertz, fully formed, and his main concerns were puzzles about intentionality, not science (see Chapter 8, THE PICTURE THEORY and Chapter 32, WITTGENSTEIN ON INTENTIONALITY).

6 Wittgenstein's Way of Reading Hertz's Mechanics

From what I've already said it is clear that I don't doubt that Hertz influenced Wittgenstein. However, I suspect that the way Wittgenstein understood Hertz's *mechanics* (by which I mean Hertz's system, not merely his book's Introduction) involves a good deal of misappropriation. I would suggest, though, that this misappropriation was *creative*, in that Wittgenstein understood Hertz's mechanics in a way which drew upon an approach to high-level laws and theories into the philosophy of science which neither Hertz nor Boltzmann had explored.

Writing in the mid-1930s, Wittgenstein's close associate Friedrich Waismann contrasted two ways of taking the "fundamental law" of Hertz's system of mechanics:

> If we are *always* free to add such supplements [Hertz's "concealed masses" and their "concealed motions"], the fundamental law becomes a mere form of representation. It would then be best expressed as a prescription saying: "Supplement the system with hidden masses and their hidden movements in such a way that the law of motion for the whole assumes such-and-such a form", which is like saying in the case of a geometrical problem: "Construct a circle corresponding to this ellipse which..."
>
> But the fundamental law can also be interpreted in another way. We only need to determine when the introduction of hidden masses is permissible and when not, by appealing to certain experiences; the fundamental law, combined with the assumption of hidden masses, then acquires a clear physical sense. (Waismann, 1977, p.55)

Waismann then says of this second way of taking Hertz's fundamental law that "this is at least the sense in which Hertz himself wanted it to be understood." I believe he was right (see Preston, 2008). Wittgenstein, though, read Hertz's mechanics in the *first* way.

Wittgenstein wrote nothing about Hertz's "fundamental law," and his writings mention Hertz's "concealed masses" only very occasionally, but he seems to have taken a very definite view of the latter. Immediately after the first occurrence, in *Notebooks 1914–16*, of what was later to become proposition 6.343 of the *Tractatus*, he remarked that:

> Mechanics is *one* attempt to construct all the propositions that we need for the description of the world according to a *single* plan. (Hertz's invisible masses). Hertz's invisible masses are admittedly pseudo-objects [*Scheingegenstände*]. (NB 6.12.14)

Here "admittedly" might mean "admitted by Hertz" – in other words, that Wittgenstein thought that Hertz himself treated his concealed masses as "pseudo-objects," fictions. That would be wrong, I think. But it might instead just mean "in fact," i.e., that Hertz's concealed masses *are* pseudo-objects, whatever Hertz might have thought.

To interpret Wittgenstein's remark in the first way is to think of him as seeing Hertz's concealed masses as something other than physically real, space-occupying individuals. Concealed masses become fictions which are introduced *by postulation* where and only where they are necessary to preserve the "fundamental law" from falsification. The fundamental law then becomes a *norm of expression*, rather than an empirical claim (for conclusive evidence of this from later on, viz., 1932–1933, and another mention of Hertz's concealed masses, see LWL, p.16). In terms Wittgenstein will later use, that law comes to be seen as part of our "form of representation," rather than as something therein represented (it will be "about the net, and not about what the net describes," TLP 6.35).

Among Wittgenstein commentators, this has become one standard way of understanding something that Wittgenstein took from Hertz. For Glock, for example, Wittgenstein's remarks on natural laws and induction in the *Tractatus* contain the idea that "the principles which underlie particular scientific theories are conventions," and Wittgenstein's picture of science "is *conventionalist*, in the vein of Hertz and Boltzmann" (1996, pp.342, 343, emphasis added). The attribution of conventionalism to Wittgenstein's remarks on networks in the *Tractatus* may be correct, but its attribution to Hertz and Boltzmann is dubious. What encourages this idea is Hertz's declaration that the images physicists construct have to conform with things in only *one* respect, namely that "the form which we give them is such that the necessary consequents of the images in thought are always the images of the necessary consequents in nature of the things pictured" (Hertz, [1894] 1956, p.1). But Hertz's "fundamental law," after all, is supposed to embody the entire empirical content of his system, and thus is a poor candidate for being a convention. Boltzmann's thought, however, lies even further from conventionalism, since he is always clear that the images he has in mind, although they feature some arbitrary aspects, are genuine hypotheses.

Finally, many commentators claim that Hertz *showed* how one could eliminate force from mechanics. Hertz showed no such thing. This was indeed the *program* of his own mechanics, but no one (physicist or philosopher) has ever shown that Hertz's own system is the equal of, let alone preferable to, the Newtonian–Lagrangian one, and there are considerations which suggest that it could never really supplant the latter (see Preston, 2008).

7   Hertz's Influence on Wittgenstein's Conception of Philosophy

Although Hertz's book is unambiguously a work of theoretical physics, he clearly conceived of its aim as *philosophical*. For example, he concludes its preface as follows:

> What I hope is new, and the only thing to which I attach value, is the arrangement and putting together of the whole – the logical or philosophical aspect of the matter. My work has reached or failed to reach its aim, depending on whether it marks an advance in this direction or not. (Hertz, [1894] 1956, preface, translation revised)

It is this philosophical aspect of his work, I think, which had the greatest impact upon Wittgenstein.

The most definite manifestation of Hertz's philosophical attitude comes when he complains of "statements which one hears with wearisome frequency, that the nature of force is still a mystery, that one of the chief problems of physics is the investigation of the nature of force" (p. 7). He notes the same about questions as to the "nature" of electricity, and asks why no one would ask such questions about velocity, or gold. His answer is this:

> With the terms 'velocity' and 'gold' we connect a large number of relations to other terms; and between all these relations we find no contradictions which offend us. We are therefore satisfied and ask no further questions. But we have accumulated around the terms 'force' and 'electricity' more relations than can be completely reconciled amongst themselves. We have an obscure feeling of this and want to have things cleared up. Our confused wish finds expression in the confused question as to the nature of force and electricity. But the answer which we want is not really an answer to this question. It is not by finding out more and fresh relations and connections that it can be answered; but by removing the contradictions existing between those already known, and thus perhaps by reducing their number. When these painful contradictions are removed, the question as to the nature of force will not have been answered; but our minds, no longer vexed, will cease to ask illegitimate questions. (Hertz, [1894] 1956, pp. 7–8)

Of all the things in *The Principles of Mechanics*, this passage seems to have been what stuck most firmly in Wittgenstein's mind. He refers to or echoes its idea of confused questions and their disappearance in several places. Indeed, until April 1947 he used its final sentence to serve as the motto for his *Philosophical Investigations* (see Baker and Hacker, 1980/2009, p. 30; see also Chapter 1, WITTGENSTEIN'S PHILOSOPHICAL DEVELOPMENT).

In the "Blue Book," for example, he mentions Hertz when discussing the question "What is time?," conceiving of that question not as the demand for a cause or reason, but as "an expression of mental discomfort," and diagnosing this discomfort as a matter of there being apparent contradictions in the grammar of the word "time" (BB 26). (For another example, where he discusses the question "What does seeing a two-dimensional figure three-dimensionally consist in?," see BB 169.)

The flavor of Hertz's approach also figures explicitly in one of Wittgenstein's more general pronouncements about his method, when he says in *The Big Typescript* that "As I do philosophy, its entire task is to shape expression in such a way that certain worries disappear ((Hertz))" (BT 421).

A further, related and important feature of Hertz's method pertains to his third *desideratum*, "appropriateness." Its second aspect is that a *Bild* should be *simple*, that is, "sparing in unessential characteristics – ones added by ourselves, permissibly and yet arbitrarily, to the essential and yet natural ones" (Hertz, [1894] 1956, p. 11). When we consider the idea of force in *this* light, says Hertz, we cannot deny "that in very many cases the forces which are used in mechanics for treating physical problems are simply *idling side-wheels*, which keep out of the business altogether when actual facts have to be represented" (pp. 11–12, translation improved). Wittgenstein seized upon this phrase "idle wheels," using it to stand for aspects of our thought that appear to have a function, but in fact have none. One important example of its use occurs in *Philosophical Remarks* (PR 51), where he uses it to refer to aspects of our language that are not essential to its ability to represent. Other echoes occur in *Philosophical Investigations*, in remarks to the effect that philosophical problems arise "when language *goes on holiday*," or "when language is like an engine idling, not when it is doing work" (PI §§38, 132), as well as in the private language argument's "beetle in the box" metaphor (§293).

Moments like these in Wittgenstein's later philosophy often bring together, in an interesting way, the very idea of thinking as involving "pictures" (that is, models) and the idea that the methodology of philosophy consists in providing clarifications. In such moments, where Wittgenstein shows up some confusion or mental cramp that is to be massaged away, the idea in question is often characterized as a *picture* which, for example, "is before our minds" (PI §59), or "held us captive" (PI §115; see also §§191, 251, 295, 352, 374, 402, 422–7, 573, and p.184). Where in the *Tractatus* the notion of a *Bild* had been conceived linguistically and deployed emphatically, here it has migrated closer to that of a metaphor, simile, or comparison, and is often (but not always) portrayed not as part of the solution to some problem, but as itself a problem.

Claims that Hertz (*and* Boltzmann) influenced various related conceptions of the aims and methods of philosophy exhibited and practiced in Wittgenstein's work are important and well founded, I believe. However, this does not mean that we should think that Wittgenstein simply took over a single method, from Hertz, and made it his (one and) own method (see, e.g., Janik, 2001; Kjærgaard, 2002). If *The Principles of Mechanics*, in particular, can be said to feature the serious use (not merely the mention) of a method in its attempt to show the superiority of Hertz's representation of mechanics, this is not a method that Wittgenstein used (see Preston, 2006a, 2006b, and 2008).

8 Boltzmann

As a student, Boltzmann took several philosophy courses, although by the time he was making his major contributions to science he had apparently come to despise traditional philosophy. In his later life, though, he threw himself into the subject, writing several important philosophical papers and giving courses in philosophy. Insofar as the philosophical thoughts he expressed in these later years could be said to form a single position, it is complex and qualified. (Feyerabend, 1967 is a good early summary; but see also Blackmore, 1982, 1999; de Regt, 1999, 2005; and Wilson, 1993.) Here we can consider only those aspects of his work which may have been known to Wittgenstein, that is, Boltzmann's two-volume treatise on mechanics (see Blackmore, 1983, p.536), and the papers collected together in his *Populäre Schriften* (1905), a copy of which Wittgenstein is known to have owned and read. (Many, but not all of these papers are collected and translated in Boltzmann, 1974, together with the most salient parts of his treatise on mechanics.)

One aspect of Boltzmann's scientific work that has often been thought to leave its mark on the *Tractatus* is his development of the idea of *phase-space*. A phase-space is a multidimensional geometrical representation of a given system, each axis of which represents a degree of freedom of that system. The resulting "space" charts every possible state of the system, each such state corresponding to a single point in the phase-space, and each change of state corresponding to a trajectory there. Stephen Toulmin was the first person to suggest that this idea, developed in Boltzmann's thermodynamics, is echoed in the Tractarian conception of logical space (Toulmin, 1969, p.66; Janik and Toulmin, 1973, pp.143–5).

Whether logical space is really a kind of phase-space is not so evident, though. Phase-spaces are used to represent systems with multiple parameters, but it has not yet been shown convincingly how *logical* relationships between propositions (or between facts), like "p if and only if q," can be represented in a phase-space. The relationship between logical space and phase-space may be no more than a loose analogy (see Preston, 2015).

Another aspect of Boltzmann's scientific work that more clearly and convincingly has an impact on the *Tractatus* is his *Bildtheorie*, that is, his version of the claim that scientific theories are pictures or models (see D'Agostino, 1990; Wilson, 1993; de Regt, 1999; Visser, 1999; and van Fraassen, 2008). Boltzmann cites Hertz as his authority for the common post-Kantian idea that "no theory can be objective, actually coinciding with nature," drawing from this the conclusion that "each theory is only a mental picture of phenomena, related to them as sign is to *designatum*" (Boltzmann, [1905] 1974, pp.90–1). His own examples of scientific *Bilder* include atomism, Maxwell's electrodynamics, Hertz's representation of mechanics, and Boltzmann's own such representation. Unlike Hertz, though, whose *Bildtheorie* is more restricted (in applying only to science), Boltzmann explicitly suggested that the *whole* of our thought has this character (e.g., pp.33, 36, 59, 69, 104, 105, 161, 225). But where Boltzmann himself had merely declared that "all our ideas and concepts are only internal mental pictures" (p.104), Wittgenstein worked out a linguistic version of this idea in detail in his account of representation and intentionality in the *Tractatus*.

As for Boltzmann's philosophical thought, around 1904 his antipathy to what he called "metaphysics" – by which he meant traditional philosophy, not mere quasi-scientific speculation – came to the fore. He was extremely scathing about this, condemning the systems of Kant, Hegel, and Schopenhauer. His important lecture from that year "On Statistical Mechanics" begins as a defense of hypotheses in physics, arguing that physical theories are bold hypotheses. It then takes a different turn, identifying questions on the borderline between physics and philosophy, such as the question concerning the continuity or noncontinuity of matter. With respect to these questions, Boltzmann argues that they should be tackled by scientists *and* philosophers together. He disapproves of the traditional assumption that such questions are to be left entirely to philosophers, indeed he takes the fact that Kant had proven that *antinomies* arise if one tackles such questions on a purely philosophical basis to show that "philosophical thought becomes enmeshed in contradictions" ([1905] 1974, p.164). The "logic" of the purely philosophical reasoning involved he finds inadequate, and he traces its inadequacy to the "laws of thought," which he himself treats as having developed over time in an evolutionary way, and thus (in contrast to Hertz here) as in no way inviolable (see also pp.104, 251). Boltzmann then diagnoses the inadequacy of these laws of thought as the source of our inappropriate tendency to "overshoot the mark," generating "apparent contradictions between the laws of thought and the world, and between those laws themselves" (p.166). (Compare these contradictions with those which Hertz supposed to lie among the relations that we have accumulated around the terms "force" and "electricity.") Asking, for example, about the value of life itself, or trying to explain the simplest and most fundamental physical laws, are examples of such mark-overshootings. Boltzmann's comments on these issues are especially worth comparing with Wittgenstein's remarks on the same subjects in propositions 6.371–2 and 6.521 of the *Tractatus*. In the former, moderns who imagine that science might explain *everything* are compared unfavorably to the ancients, who realized that explanation must come to an end in a "clear and acknowledged terminus." In the latter remark, the "problem of life," which seems to be identified with the issue of the meaning of life as a whole, is deemed solvable only in that it vanishes. In addition, though, the idea of going beyond explanations of what happens *in* the world, to the point where one sees or feels the entire world "as a limited whole" (6.45) might well be another example of overshooting the mark.

At this point in his article, Boltzmann announces:

My present theory is totally different from the view that certain questions fall outside the boundaries of human cognition. For according to that latter theory this is a defect or imperfection of man's cognitive capacity, whereas I regard the existence of these questions and problems themselves as an illusion. (Boltzmann, [1905] 1974, p.167)

He compares these philosophical illusions to perceptual illusions, in their hold on us and in our inability to free ourselves from them, even when we are aware of their existence, and makes clear the centrality of these illusions to his conception of philosophy:

Only very slowly and gradually will all these illusions recede and I regard it as a central task of philosophy to give a clear account of the inappropriateness of this overshooting the mark on the part of our thinking habits; and further, in choosing and linking concepts and words, to aim only at the most appropriate expression of the given, irrespective of our inherited habits. Then, gradually, these tangles and contradictions must disappear. (Boltzmann, [1905] 1974, p.167)

He continues:

If therefore philosophy were to succeed in creating a system such that in all cases mentioned it stood out clearly when a question is not justified so that the drive towards asking it would gradually die away, we should at one stroke have resolved the most obscure riddles and philosophy would become worthy of the name of queen of the sciences. (Boltzmann, [1905] 1974, p.167)

Boltzmann goes on to clarify that on his conception, the "old" philosophical questions do not really get *answered*. Rather, "we are cured of the urge to want to decide [them] along a path that is devoid of sense and hope" (p.169). There is here a clear parallel with Wittgenstein's idea that we should *dissolve* philosophical problems, rather than merely making further futile efforts to solve them.

Those writings of Boltzmann's to which Wittgenstein was exposed feature several somewhat different conceptions of philosophy and its method (see also Boltzmann, [1905] 1974, pp.137, 157, 196). They are mere remarks, too, in that Boltzmann did little to put them into practice in these works. Where Boltzmann called for an end to meaningless questions, Wittgenstein attempted to identify the limit of the meaningful, and rejected the idea that anything discussable lies beyond it. To say merely that Boltzmann's remarks made an impact upon Wittgenstein's conception of philosophy may well be an understatement: there can be little doubt that they, and others like them (pp.88, 90, 104, 109–110), are strikingly suggestive of the ways in which Wittgenstein conceived of philosophy (cf. Chapter 13, PHILOSOPHY AND PHILOSOPHICAL METHOD).

However, in one respect at least Wittgenstein did cleave closer to Kant and Hertz: he never accepted the naturalistic or, more specifically, *evolutionary* aspect of Boltzmann's epistemology. His remark that "Darwin's theory has no more to do with philosophy than any other hypothesis in natural science" (TLP 4.1122) may well have been directed at both Mach and Boltzmann, not merely because they were both early "evolutionary epistemologists," but because, in another article from this same collection of Boltzmann's writings, the latter expressed the view that "all salvation for philosophy may be expected to come from Darwin's theory" ([1905] 1974, p.193).

Boltzmann would not have accepted one major conclusion of the *Tractatus*, that of the philosophical *irrelevance* of natural science. However, if the *Tractatus* tells us that philosophy is the logic of representation, and that the only *bona fide* representations are the potential claims of natural science, Boltzmann's view that philosophy of science should be the only kind of philosophy might be seen to coincide with Wittgenstein's conception. Boltzmann would certainly agree with the *Tractatus* that natural science is a genuine subject, whereas traditional philosophy is not. *Tractatus* 6.52 presents this theme most forcefully: "We feel that when all *possible* scientific questions have been answered, the problems of life remain completely untouched. Of course there are then no questions left, and this itself is the answer." The appearance that there are philosophical "problems" or "riddles" that science absolutely cannot address can *only* be an appearance, since proposition 6.5 tells us plainly that "*the riddle* does not exist. If a question can be framed at all, it is also *possible* to answer it." Philosophical "problems" are not of the sort for which one can state solutions. Rather, when correctly treated, they *disappear*. This is the attitude that Boltzmann took toward traditional philosophical questions, and which, as we saw, Hertz also took toward some questions about fundamental physical concepts.

Finally, one other aspect of Boltzmann's philosophical thought that may have exerted an influence on Wittgenstein is his emphasis on the importance of *surveys* and of scientific representations being *surveyable*, or *perspicuous* (*Übersichten* and *übersichtlich*; see Chapter 16, SURVEYABILITY). By and large (and with the *caveat* about "laws of thought" above) Boltzmann accepted Hertz's three *desiderata* for scientific representations. Sometimes, though, he seems to add the extra requirement that such representations be perspicuous. While he did not deploy this concept in a systematic way, there are several important uses of it in his writings. He was concerned, for example, that the adherents of "energetics" had given no survey of all the phenomena that his own favored atomic hypothesis accounted for (Boltzmann, [1905] 1974, pp.38, 46). Those who favor "phenomenological" approaches (such as Kirchhoff and Mach), too, are berated for needing equations that fail to meet this same requirement (pp.44–5, 46). One of the main reasons Boltzmann continues to place his bets with atomism is that the atomistic picture *is* perspicuous in the sense he has in mind (pp.46, 49).

Although Boltzmann never explained in any detail what he meant by *Übersicht* and *Übersichtlichkeit*, and although he applied the notion mainly to scientific representations, this is surely one of the things that Wittgenstein could have taken over from him, transposing it along the way from a scientific into a philosophical key, in requiring that grammatical representations and mathematical proofs be surveyable.

9 Concluding Remarks

Hertz and Boltzmann did influence various aspects of the *Tractatus*. Their greatest and most lasting influence on Wittgenstein, though, was on his conception of philosophy itself: its aim (conceptual clarity or perspicuity), and its method (the removal of conceptual confusions). This influence made itself felt throughout his philosophical career.

Very shortly after presenting that famous list of his influences, Wittgenstein remarked: "It is typical for a Jewish mind to understand someone else's work better than he understands it himself" (CV 17). Leaving aside racial stereotypes, I suspect that Wittgenstein may have known that he was not understanding Hertz's mechanics, for example, in the way Hertz had intended. Like the work of the others on his list, what Wittgenstein did was, as he himself puts it in that same place, to "passionately take it up for my work of clarification" (CV 17). That he was influenced by Hertz's *Mechanics* (the book) is clear, but that he was influenced by Hertz's *mechanics* (the system) doesn't mean that what he took from it was what Hertz had put into it.

The moment in which Wittgenstein wrote this list of influences, feeling that he had never initiated a line of thinking, was a moment of depression, for that feeling was derogatory. We can have little certainty about the ways in which he was influenced by Hertz and Boltzmann, but his relationship to their ideas was probably one of creative appropriation.

References

Baker, G.P. and Hacker, P.M.S. (1980/2009). *Wittgenstein: Understanding and Meaning. Volume 1 of an Analytical Commentary on the Philosophical Investigations. Part 1. Essays.* Second edition. Extensively revised by P.M.S. Hacker. Oxford: Wiley-Blackwell.

Barker, P. (1980). Hertz and Wittgenstein. *Studies in History and Philosophy of Science*, 11, 243–256.

Blackmore, J.T. (1982). Boltzmann's Concessions to Mach's Philosophy of Science. In R. Sexl and J.T. Blackmore (Eds). *Ludwig Boltzmann: Gesamtausgabe (Vol 8): Ausgewählte Abhandlungen* (pp.155–190). Wiesbaden: Vieweg.

Blackmore, J.T. (1983). Boltzmann and Wittgenstein. In P. Weingartner and J. Czermak (Eds). *Epistemology and Philosophy of Science* (pp.534–537). Vienna: Hölder-Pichler-Tempsky.

Blackmore, J.T. (1999). Boltzmann and Epistemology. *Synthese*, 119, 157–189.

Boltzmann, L. ([1905]1974). *Theoretical Physics and Philosophical Problems: Selected Writings.* Ed. B.F. McGuinness. Dordrecht: Reidel.

D'Agostino, S. (1990). Boltzmann and Hertz on the *Bild*-Conception of Physical Theory. *History of Science*, 28, 380–398.

de Regt, H.W. (1999). Ludwig Boltzmann's *Bildtheorie* and scientific Understanding. *Synthese*, 119, 113–134.

de Regt, H.W. (2005). Scientific Realism in Action: Molecular Models and Boltzmann's *Bildtheorie*. *Erkenntnis*, 63, 205–230.

Feyerabend, P.K. (1967). Boltzmann, Ludwig (1844–1906). In P. Edwards (Ed.). *The Encyclopedia of Philosophy* (Vol. 1, pp.334–337). New York: Macmillan.

Glock, H-J. (1996). *A Wittgenstein Dictionary*. Oxford: Blackwell.

Goddard, L. and Judge, B. (1982). *The Metaphysics of Wittgenstein's Tractatus*. Australasian Journal of Philosophy Monograph, no.1.

Grasshoff, G. (1998). Hertz's Philosophy of Nature in Wittgenstein's *Tractatus*. In D. Baird, R.I.G. Hughes and A. Nordmann (Eds). (1998). *Heinrich Hertz: Classical Physicist, modern Philosopher* (pp.243–268). Dordrecht: Kluwer.

Griffin, J. (1964). *Wittgenstein's logical Atomism*. Oxford: Oxford University Press.

Harré, R. (2001). Wittgenstein: Science and Religion. *Philosophy*, 76, 211–237.

Hertz, H.R. ([1894] 1956). *The Principles of Mechanics Presented in a New Form*. Trans. D.E. Jones and J.T. Walley. New York: Dover Publications. (Original work published 1894.)

Janik, A.S. (2001). *Wittgenstein's Vienna revisited*. Brunswick: Transaction Publishers.

Janik, A.S. and Toulmin, S.E. (1973). *Wittgenstein's Vienna*. New York: Simon and Schuster.

Kjærgaard, P.C. (2002). Hertz and Wittgenstein's Philosophy of Science. *Journal for General Philosophy of Science*, 33, 121–149.

Lützen, J. (2005). *Mechanistic Images in Geometric Form: Heinrich Hertz's Principles of Mechanics*. Oxford: Oxford University Press.

McDonough, R.M. (1994). Wittgenstein's Clarification of Hertzian Mechanistic Cognitive Science. *History of Philosophy Quarterly*, 11, 219–235.

McGuinness, B.F. (1969). Philosophy of Science in the *Tractatus*. *Revue Internationale de Philosophie*, 23, 1969, 155–164.

McGuinness, B.F. (1990). *Wittgenstein: A Life (Vol. 1): Young Ludwig 1889–1921*. London: Penguin.

Monk, R. (1990). *Ludwig Wittgenstein: The Duty of Genius*. London: Jonathan Cape.

Pârvu, I. (2001). "*Mein Grundgedanke ist...*": The structural Theory of Representation as the Metaphysics of Wittgenstein's *Tractatus Logico-Philosophicus*. *Synthese*, 129, 259–274.

Preston, J.M. (2006a). Harré on Hertz and the *Tractatus*. *Philosophy*, 81, 357–364.

Preston, J.M. (2006b). Janik on Hertz and the Early Wittgenstein. *Grazer Philosophische Studien*, 73, 83–95.

Preston, J.M. (2008). Hertz, Wittgenstein, and Philosophical Method. *Philosophical Investigations*, 31, 48–67.

Preston, J.M. (2015). Logical Space and Phase-Space. In D. Moyal-Sharrock, V. Munz, and A. Coliva (Eds). *Mind, Language and Action* (pp. 35–44). Berlin: de Gruyter.

Russell, B. (1903). *The Principles of Mathematics*. Cambridge: Cambridge University Press.

Spelt, P.D.M. and McGuinness, B.F. (2001). Marginalia in Wittgenstein's Copy of Lamb's Hydrodynamics. In G. Oliveri (Ed.). *Wittgenstein Studien (Vol. 2): From the Tractatus to the Tractatus and Other Essays* (pp. 131–148). Frankfurt: Peter Lang.

Sterrett, S.G. (2006). *Wittgenstein Flies a Kite: A Story of Models of Wings and Models of the World*. New York: Pi Press.

Toulmin, S.E. (1969). Ludwig Wittgenstein. *Encounter*, 32, 58–71.

van Fraassen, B.C. (2008). *Scientific Representation: Paradoxes of Perspective*. Oxford: Oxford University Press.

Visser, H. (1999). Boltzmann and Wittgenstein or How Pictures Became Linguistic. *Synthese*, 119, 135–156.

von Wright, G.H. (1958). Biographical Sketch. In N. Malcolm (Ed.). *Ludwig Wittgenstein: A Memoir* (pp. 1–22). Oxford: Oxford University Press.

Waismann, F. (1977). Hypotheses. In B.F. McGuinness (Ed.). *Friedrich Waismann: Philosophical Papers* (pp. 38–59). Dordrecht: Reidel.

Waugh, A. (2008). *The House of Wittgenstein: A Family at War*. London: Bloomsbury.

Wilson, A.D. (1989). Hertz, Boltzmann and Wittgenstein Reconsidered. *Studies in History and Philosophy of Science*, 20, 245–263.

Wilson, A.D. (1993). Boltzmann's Philosophical Education and its Bearing on his Mature Scientific Epistemology. In G. Battimelli, M.G. Ianniello, and O. Kresten (Eds). *Proceedings of the International Symposium on Ludwig Boltzmann* (pp. 57–69). Vienna: Verlag der Österreichischen Akademie der Wissenschaften.

Further Reading

Baird, D., Hughes, R.I.G. and Nordmann, A. (Eds). (1998). *Heinrich Hertz: Classical Physicist, Modern Philosopher*. Dordrecht: Kluwer.

Blackmore, J.T. (Ed.). (1995a). *Ludwig Boltzmann: His Later Life and Philosophy, 1900–1906: Book 1: A Documentary History*. Dordrecht: Kluwer.

Blackmore, J.T. (Ed.). (1995b). *Ludwig Boltzmann: His Later Life and Philosophy, 1900–1906: Book 2: The Philosopher*. Dordrecht: Kluwer.

Brockhaus, R.R. (1991). *Pulling up the Ladder: The Metaphysical Roots of Wittgenstein's Tractatus Logico-Philosophicus*. La Salle: Open Court.

Cercignani, C. (1998). *Ludwig Boltzmann: The Man who trusted Atoms*. Oxford: Oxford University Press.

Hamilton, K. (2002). *Darstellungen* in *The Principles of Mechanics* and the *Tractatus*: The Representation of Objects in Relation in Hertz and Wittgenstein. *Perspectives on Science*, 10, 28–68.

Hyder, D. (2002). *The Mechanics of Meaning: Propositional Content and the Logical Space of Wittgenstein's Tractatus*. Berlin: de Gruyter.

McGuinness, B.F. (2002). *Approaches to Wittgenstein: Collected Papers*. London: Routledge.

Mulligan, J.F. (Ed.). (1994). *Heinrich Rudolf Hertz (1857–1894): A Collection of Articles and Addresses*. New York and London: Garland.

Nordmann, A. (2002). Another New Wittgenstein: The Scientific and Engineering Background of the *Tractatus*. *Perspectives on Science*, 10, 356–384.

Part III

Early Philosophy

7

Logical Atomism

LEO K.C. CHEUNG

1 The Tractarian Logical Atomism

Logical atomism – a term first coined by Bertrand Russell in 1911 (see Russell, [1911] 2003, p.94) – in general consists of a methodological part and a metaphysical part. In the methodological part, there is a process of logical analysis of propositions. In the metaphysical part, there is the view that logical analysis reveals the metaphysics of reality. More precisely, logical analysis discloses that what correspond to true propositions are atomic facts, or facts as the obtaining of determinate combinations of logical atoms, of which the world is constituted (see Russell, 1918; 1924). In the *Tractatus*, Wittgenstein adopts a version of logical atomism (although he does not use the term "logical atomism"). In the course of the present chapter, I shall offer an exposition of the Tractarian version of logical atomism.

According to the *Tractatus*, "a proposition has one and only one complete analysis" (TLP 3.25). By this, Wittgenstein means that every proposition is completely and uniquely analyzable into a truth function, or a truth-functional combination, of elementary propositions (TLP 5). An elementary proposition is an immediate combination of what he calls "simple signs" or "names" (TLP 3.202, 4.221). Names in propositions denote objects, and those objects are their meanings (TLP 3.202–3.203). A state of affairs is a determinate combination of objects (TLP 2.01). The obtaining of a state of affairs is a fact (TLP 2). The obtaining and non-obtaining of states of affairs is reality (TLP 2.06). The sum total of reality, or the totality of the obtaining of states of affairs, or facts, is the world (TLP 2, 2.04, 2.063).

Objects are simple, or not composite (TLP 2.02, 2.021). They are devoid of internal complexity. So an object only possesses its combinatorial possibility, that is, its logical form (TLP 2.032–2.033), and its being a different object from all other objects (TLP 2.02, 2.0233–2.02331), that is, its individuality. Moreover, objects subsist, or necessarily exist (TLP 2.027–2.0271). The forms and contents of objects constitute the substance, including the unalterable form, of the world, which is also the substance of reality (TLP 2.021, 2.024–2.025, 2.05–2.06). Therefore, substance also subsists and is unalterable (TLP 2.024). Objects must be necessarily existent simple objects. Since

A Companion to Wittgenstein, First Edition. Edited by Hans-Johann Glock and John Hyman.
© 2017 John Wiley & Sons, Ltd. Published 2017 by John Wiley & Sons, Ltd.

objects are the end products (or, more precisely, the meanings of the constituents of the end products) of logical analysis, they are the logical atoms of the Tractarian world. In this way, logical analysis reveals the metaphysics of reality.

Wittgenstein argues for the possibility of complete analysis. By doing this, he also argues for the claims that the constituents of the end products of complete analysis are simple signs, and that there are necessarily existent objects. Their conjunction is the thesis that the world has substance, or that there are necessarily existent simple objects. His main argument is that if there are necessarily existent simple objects, then a proposition has a complete analysis (the first premise); and there are necessarily existent simple objects or, equivalently, the world has substance (the second premise); hence, a proposition has a complete analysis. What may be called "the substance argument" in TLP 2.0211–2.0212 is actually a sub-argument for the second premise, that is, the thesis that the world has substance.

In the remaining three sections, I shall first explain Wittgenstein's main argument for the possibility of complete analysis, assuming that its second premise is true. Then I shall comment on three recent interpretations of the substance argument; finally, I shall offer an exposition of the substance argument.

2   The Possibility of Complete Analysis

Wittgenstein holds that thinking is making to us a logical picture of facts, and that a logical picture of facts is a thought (TLP 2.1, 3–3.001, 4.021). A proposition is a perceptible expression, or symbol (TLP 3.31), of a thought, and is also a picture of reality (TLP 3.1, 4.01). A symbol, or an expression (TLP 3.31), is a sign used in accordance with a logical form (TLP 3.326–3.328), that is, a combinatorial possibility (TLP 2.01, 2.0123, 2.014–2.0141) or a possibility of structure (TLP 2.033). The sign is its sign, and the logical form its form. A sign is what is perceptible of a symbol (TLP 3.32). The perceptible sign of a proposition, as a symbol, is its propositional sign, and its logical form its propositional form (TLP 3.12, 4.5). A proposition is a propositional sign used, or applied, in accordance with its propositional form, via thinking, to represent a possible situation, that is, its sense (TLP 3.11, 3.5, 4.031). More precisely, when a propositional sign is used or applied, the objects of which its constituent signs are their representatives are thought to be connecting with one another in accordance with its propositional form such that a possible situation is represented (TLP 3.221, 4.031–4.0312). In this way, a thought, whose perceptible expression is a proposition, is a propositional sign applied and thought out (TLP 3.1, 3.5). It is also in this way that a proposition is a picture of reality. The fact that a proposition is a picture of reality is to be accounted for by the picture theory, which will be explained by means of the example of the proposition "fa" later.

The notions "completely analyzed proposition," "simple sign," and "name" are introduced as follows:

> 3.2   In a proposition a thought can be expressed in such a way that elements of the propositional sign correspond to the objects of the thought.
> 3.201 I call such elements 'simple signs', and such a proposition 'completely analyzed'.
> 3.202 The simple signs employed in propositions are called names.
> 3.203 A name means an object. The object is its meaning. (TLP 3.2–3.203)

Since the propositional elements denote objects, the objects of the thought mentioned here are not the constituents of the thought, but the objects to which the constituents correspond. Moreover, reality and its sum total – the world – are always thinkable (TLP 3.001–3.01). If there were unthinkable reality or world, we could not think about it, nor could we talk about it (TLP 5.61). If the world has objects, they must be the objects of thought. The constituents of thought correspond to objects of the world in the same way as the constituent names of a relevant propositional sign.

The notion "completely analyzed proposition" can be characterized as follows:

A proposition is completely analyzed if and only if it has a propositional sign with simple signs (names) as its constituent elements.

However, Wittgenstein also seems to hold a different characterization of the notion: a proposition is completely analyzed if and only if it is analyzable into a truth function of immediate combinations of names, or elementary propositions (TLP 4.22–4.221, 5, 5.5). The truth function is produced by applying logical operations to elementary propositions. Logical operations are symbolized by logical constants (TLP 5.5, 5.51s, 5.52s). So, amongst the end products of logical analysis, there are also logical constants.

Logical operations are always definable in terms of a single fundamental operation (TLP 6–6.001). The fundamental operation in the Tractarian system is symbolized by the logical constant N (TLP 5.502; see also Geach, 1981; 1982; and Cheung, 2000). But the sign "N" is inessential here. In a completely analyzed proposition, in which N occurs, no sign is needed to symbolize N, although brackets indicating the applications of N may be needed (TLP 5.46–5.4611). There are no primitive signs of logical operations. For Wittgenstein, this entails the *Grundgedanke* that logical constants do not denote (TLP 4.0312; see also Cheung, 1999). Therefore, logical constants should not be seen as the constituent elements of propositions. This explains why, in TLP 3.2–3.203, none of the constituents of the completely analyzed propositional sign is the sign of a logical constant, even though the proposition still contains logical constants.

Logical analysis proceeds via the dissection of signs by means of definitions, and arrives at signs, which are not further dissectible – primitive signs (TLP 3.24–3.25). Yet, in TLP 3.2–3.203, Wittgenstein calls the constituents of a completely analyzed proposition "simple signs" or "names." Thus, primitive signs are also simple signs. Moreover, he also says in TLP 3.26 that "a name cannot be dissected any further by means of a definition; it is a primitive sign." Simple signs are then also primitive signs. Any acceptable interpretation of the Tractarian notion of logical analysis must explain why primitive signs are simple signs (or names), and vice versa.

To investigate in detail the idea of analysis via the dissection of signs by means of definitions, consider this:

3.24   A proposition about a complex stands in an internal relation to a proposition about a constituent of the complex.

A complex can be given only by its description, which will be right or wrong. A proposition that mentions a complex will not be nonsensical, if the complex does not exist, but simply false.

When a propositional element signifies a complex, this can be seen from an indeterminateness in the propositions in which it occurs. In such cases we *know* that the proposition leaves something undetermined. (TLP 3.24)

Let us call a sign that is further dissectible by means of definitions "a nonprimitive sign." TLP 3.24 concerns, amongst other things, a special type of nonprimitive sign, namely, propositional elements signifying complexes. I shall employ the proposition "The broom is in the corner" – taken from section 60 of *Philosophical Investigations* – as an example to illustrate some of the points here. Let "a" be a symbol for the broom, and "f—" short for "—is in the corner." The proposition "The broom is in the corner" can be expressed as "fa." Since the broom is composite, it would be called "a complex" in the *Tractatus*. For the sake of illustration, let us take the property, or the attribute, signified by "—is in the corner" to be a complex, though admittedly this may sound odd. The proposition "fa" is then about the complexes f and a.

How does the proposition "fa" say anything about the world? The answer is to be given by the so-called "picture theory (of proposition)." The picture theory consists of the introduction of the notion of a picture and the explanation of how a picture depicts reality, mainly in TLP 2.1–2.225 and 4.011–4.016, and the theses in TLP 3–3.001 that a thought is a logical picture of facts, and in TLP 4.01 that a proposition is a picture of reality. The latter thesis may be called "the picture thesis (of proposition)."

According to the picture theory, a proposition expresses a sense, or says something about the world, because it is a picture of reality (TLP 4.03). A picture is an already obtained determinate combination of things (physical signs, in the case of a proposition), and thus is a fact (TLP 2.14–2.141). The form of the fact, or the possibility of structure constituted by the forms of its constituents, is the pictorial form (TLP 2.0141, 2.032–2.034, 2.15). A fact becomes a picture, when its constituent elements are correlated with, or denote, objects in a way subject to this constraint:

2.1511	*That* is how a picture is attached to reality; it reaches right out to it.
2.1512	It is laid against reality like a measure.
2.15121	Only the end-points of the graduating lines actually touch the object that is to be measured.
2.1513	So a picture, conceived in this way, also includes the pictorial relationship, which makes it into a picture. (TLP 2.1511–2.1513)

That is, only objects of the same forms (combinatorial possibilities) of the constituent elements can be correlated with the constituent elements. This guarantees that the picture and the situation it represents have the same form. In this way, the fact becomes a picture by representing a situation – the obtaining and non-obtaining of states of affairs (TLP 2.11).

The picture theory, especially the account in the 2.15s, is applicable to the case of a proposition in this way: the constituent signs of a proposition denote objects of the same forms, respectively, such that its propositional sign represents a situation whose objects are connected to one another in the same determinate way as the constituent signs. This is described vividly in TLP 4.031:

> In a proposition a situation is, as it were, constructed by way of experiment.
> Instead of, 'This proposition has such and such a sense', we can simply say, 'This proposition represents such and such a situation'. (TLP 4.031)

The account in TLP 2.15 s, which is part of the picture theory, appears to be applicable to elementary propositional signs only, because the constituent elements of the picture appear to be simple, that is, not further analyzable. But, as suggested by David Pears (1987, p.78), it can also be taken to be applicable to the case of nonelementary propositional signs, as if "a short cut" is taken. So let us apply the picture theory to the case of the propositional sign "fa," and let us answer the question how "fa" says anything about the world. In this case, the following holds:

(1) If the complexes f and a exist, then "fa" makes sense, or represents a situation.

That is, the constituent signs "f" and "a" of "fa" can be symbolized to denote the complexes f and a, respectively, such that "fa" represents the situation that fa, provided the complexes f and a exist.

However, "fa" may still make sense, even if, say, the complex a does not exist. Recall that TLP 3.24 says, amongst other things, that "a complex can be given only by its description, which will be right or wrong." With respect to the present example, the broom is given by one of its descriptions, say, "The broomstick is fixed in the brush." Let "b" and "c" be the propositional elements signifying the broomstick and the brush, respectively, and "—R—" be short for "—is fixed in—." The broomstick and the brush are, of course, complexes, and the relation —is fixed in—, or R, may be regarded as a complex. The complex a, or the broom, is then given by the description "bRc." The complex a exists if and only if the description "bRc" is true.

If "bRc" is false, then the complex a does not exist; and yet the proposition "fa" may still make sense. For Wittgenstein would hold this:

(2) If the complexes f, b, c, and R exist, then "fb.fc.bRc" makes sense, and is equivalent to the proposition "fa."

(Here, "fa.fb.fc" means the conjunction of the propositions "fb", "fc" and "bRc".) In other words, if —is in the corner, the brush, the broomstick, and —is fixed in—— exist, then the proposition "The broomstick is in the corner, the brush is in the corner, and the broomstick is fixed in the brush" (i.e., "fb.fc.bRc") makes sense, and is equivalent to "The broom is in the corner." This is indeed suggested by an entry dated 5 September 1914 in the *Notebooks*, where there is the sentence, or formula, "ϕ(a).ϕ(b). aRb = *Def*ϕ[aRb]" (NB 4; see also Kenny, 1973, pp.79–80). Moreover, according to TLP 5.14–5.141, Wittgenstein accepts uncritically the view that two logically equivalent propositions are actually "one and the same proposition." Thus, he would regard "fa" and "fb.fc.bRc" as one and the same proposition, provided the complexes f, b, c, and R exist. Hence, "fa" may still make sense, even if the complex a does not exist. For instance, when f, b, c, and R exist, but a doesn't (or "bRc" is false), "fb.fc.bRc," and thus "fa," still makes sense.

Actually, (2) illustrates a step in the analysis of the proposition "fa." The logical equivalence fa ≡ (fb.fc.bRc), under the assumption that those complexes exist, can be seen as involving a contextual definition of the sign "a" in terms of the signs "b", "c," and "R." In this case, "a" is a nonprimitive sign. Thus, the process of analysis is one of the dissection of nonprimitive signs by means of definitions. This is why "a proposition about a complex stands in an internal relation to a proposition about a constituent of the complex" (TLP 3.24) – for example, if the relevant complexes exist, "fa" entails "bRc."

However, the description "bRc" is *not* an instance of those complete descriptions mentioned in TLP 2.0201:

> Every statement about complexes can be resolved into a statement about their constituents and into the propositions that describe the complexes completely. (TLP 2.0201)

This is because the complexes b, c, and R have internal complexities, which are also that of the complex a, and thus "bRc" cannot describe a *completely*. Nevertheless, this explains why TLP 3.24 says, amongst other things, this:

> When a propositional element signifies a complex, this can be seen from an indeterminateness in the propositions in which it occurs. In such cases we *know* that the proposition leaves something undetermined. (TLP 3.24)

For example, the propositional sign "fa" has at least the constituent element "a" signifying the complex a. It does not reflect any internal complexities of the complex a, including the internal complexities shown by the description "bRc," structurally. Therefore, the propositional sign "fa" has an indeterminateness, or has left something undetermined.

When Wittgenstein claims in TLP 2.0201 that "every statement about complexes can be resolved into a statement about their constituents and into the propositions that describe the complexes completely," he is assuming the conclusion of the substance argument and its implication that complexes are constituted solely by necessarily existent simple objects. It is only when complexes are constituted solely by objects that there are *complete* descriptions of complexes. If there are objects, then every proposition (about complexes) can be expressed as a truth function of propositions about the constituent objects of the complexes it is about. Since *objects exist necessarily*, there is the logical equivalence between the proposition and the truth function, *under no condition of existence*. (Note that both the simplicity *and* necessary existence of objects are crucial here.) Let me explain this by considering the proposition "fa" again.

Suppose that the complexes f and a are constituted by necessarily existent simple objects, and, without loss of generality, that f, b, c, and R are objects (and thus "f", "b", "c," and "R" are simple signs or names). Then Wittgenstein would hold this:

> (3) The propositional sign "fb.fc.bRc" expresses a sense, and produces a proposition logically equivalent to the proposition "fa."

Here, the biconditional fa ≡ (fb.fc.bRc) is a logical equivalence, *under no condition of existence*. For, as objects exist necessarily, there is no chance of reference failure with respect to the propositional sign "fb.fc.bRc"; and thus the possibility of the biconditional's not being a logical equivalence is ruled out. In this case, "bRc" is a complete description of the complex a. (The object f is also completely, but trivially, described by the sign "f" in the propositional signs "fa" and "fb.fc.bRc.") Hence, it is only under the assumption that the world has substance that "every statement about complexes can be resolved into a statement about their constituents and into the propositions that describe the complexes completely" (TLP 2.0201), and that "a proposition that mentions a complex will not be nonsensical, if the complex does not exist, but simply false" (TLP 3.24).

Wittgenstein never gives any example of completely analyzed propositions. But he would accept that, given the assumption that f, b, c, and R are objects, fa ≡ (fb.fc.bRc) is a logical equivalence, indicating the final step of the complete analysis of "fa." The signs "f", "b", "c," and "R" in the relevant propositional sign cannot be further dissected by means of definitions. (Notational variants are, of course, possible.) They are primitive signs, as well as simple signs (TLP 3.26). This answers the previous question why primitive signs are simple signs, and vice versa.

The proposition "fa" therefore can be completely and uniquely – disregarding notational variants – analyzed into the proposition "fb.fc.bRc," with "fb," "fc," and "bRc" being elementary propositions. The consideration here is supposed to be applicable to any proposition about the world. This shows that if there are necessarily existent simple objects, which Wittgenstein certainly thinks he has already proven in TLP 2.0211–2.0212, every proposition has a complete unique analysis.

3 Some Recent Interpretations of the Substance Argument

To complete the exposition of the Tractarian logical atomism, it remains for me to explicate the substance argument in the following entries:

> 2.0211   If the world had no substance, then whether a proposition had sense would depend on whether another proposition was true.
> 2.0212   In that case we could not sketch any picture of the world (true or false).

However, before offering my interpretation, I shall first comment on three recent interpretations of the substance argument by Ian Proops (2004), Michael Morris (2008), and José Zalabardo (2012), respectively.

Proops (2004) thinks that when the substance argument is put forward in TLP 2.0211–2.0212, both the possibility of complete analysis and the rejection of the possibility of the contingent existence of objects are assumed. The aim of the substance argument is then only to argue that there are objects, which exist necessarily. The simplicity of objects, however, is not assumed, but follows from the conclusion that there are necessarily existent objects.

Proops's reconstruction of the substance argument starts with the first inference in TLP 2.0211. Suppose, *for reductio*, that the world has no substance, or that everything exists contingently. Then everything is complex, because contingently existent simples were ruled out already. Thus, since the possibility of complete analysis is assumed here, there must be names in fully analyzed propositions referring to complexes. Hence, the sense of a proposition about a complex depends on the truth of another proposition, whose truth constitutes the complex as existing. This is applicable to any proposition about any number of complexes. Therefore, in general, whether a proposition has sense depends on whether another proposition is true. Since Proops construes "having sense" as a matter of having truth value, this means that "every interpreted sentence lacks a truth-value with respect to at least one possible world" (2004, p.116).

To see the second inference in TLP 2.0212, suppose that whether any sentence "has sense," that is, is truth-valued, depends on whether another is true. Then every sentence will have an "indeterminate sense" such that it will lack a truth value with respect to at least one possible world. But an indeterminate sense is no sense at all, because, according to TLP 3.42, a proposition is truth-valued with respect to every possible world. Hence, no sentence has a determinate sense; and so no sentence has sense. In this case, we cannot frame propositions (viz., sentences that have a sense), or "draw up pictures of the world (true or false)." This is an unacceptable consequence, as we can frame propositions. The final conclusion is then that the world has substance.

Proops's interpretation has at least the following two difficulties, however. First, the view that both the possibility of complete analysis and the rejection of the contingent existence of objects are assumed in the substance argument does not seem to be right. In fact, as I have already argued in the previous discussion, the presence of necessarily existent simple objects guarantees that every proposition has a complete analysis. Therefore, they should not only be assumed there, but they are entailed by the conclusion of the substance argument.

Second, Proops's interpretation fails to explain the employment of the picture theory in the substance argument. He explains that the reason why "we could not sketch any picture of the world (true or false)" is that it would follow that every proposition had an indeterminate sense, and thus that we would be unable to frame any propositions at all. But this kind of reasoning fails to employ the picture theory. This failure is probably due to Proops's construing "having sense" as a matter of having a truth value, which leaves out the formal, or structural, aspects of sense. But it is exactly the formal aspects of sense that identify sense with a possible situation, and thus support the picture theory.

Morris (2008, pp. 39–50) holds that the claim that the world has substance is equivalent to the claim that there must be a fixed form which is common to all possible worlds, and that the latter, in turn, is equivalent to the claim that whatever is possible is necessarily possible. Thus, the substance argument aims to argue for the claim that every possibility is a necessary possibility. Morris's reconstruction of the substance argument is as follows. For any combination of names, say, "abcde," since we can sketch pictures of the world, "abcde" has sense if and only if "abcde" is a possible combination (that is, the corresponding objects can be combined in the same way). So the picture theory supports the following claim:

(A) The sentence "abcde" has sense if and only if "It is possible that abcde" is true.

Thus, whether the sentence "abcde" has sense depends on whether "It is possible that abcde" is true. The proposition "It is possible that abcde" is the "other proposition" mentioned in TLP 2.0211, with respect to the case of the arbitrarily chosen sentence "abcde." Moreover, Wittgenstein would hold this:

(B) The sentence "abcde" has sense if and only if "It is possible that abcde" has sense.

It follows from (A) and (B) that:

(C) "It is possible that abcde" has sense if and only if "It is possible that abcde" is true.

But (C) implies that "It is possible that abcde" is necessarily true. Thus, what is asserted by "abcde" is necessarily possible. Since "abcde" is arbitrarily chosen, the conclusion that every possibility is a necessary possibility, that is, that the world has substance, is derived. Finally, Morris seems to think that one can see that his interpretation explains the text, if one sees that the argument he presents is basically the reverse of what Morris takes to be the *reductio ad absurdum* in TLP 2.0211–2.0212.

Morris's interpretation apparently has the merits that the "another proposition" in TLP 2.0211 is specified, and that the picture theory is employed in the argument. But, like Proops's, Morrris's interpretation has some serious difficulties. First, in his reconstruction, the picture theory entails the statement that whether a proposition has sense depends on whether another proposition is true. So, according to him, Wittgenstein would hold this statement in the *Tractatus*. This cannot be right. In TLP 2.0211–2.0212, the statement, or, rather, the proposition that "whether a proposition had sense would depend on whether another proposition was true," is only a step in a *reductio ad absurdum*. Moreover, the fact that this step is leading to the unacceptable conclusion that we could not sketch any picture of the world (true or false) proves that Wittgenstein would not hold the statement.

Second, the preceding point also shows that Morris's reconstructed argument cannot be the substance argument. For, if his reconstructed argument were the reverse of the *reductio ad absurdum* in TLP 2.0211–2.0212, then the picture theory should entail the denial of the statement that whether a proposition has sense depends on whether another proposition is true, and not, as Morris mistakenly thinks, the statement itself.

Third, according to the *Tractatus*, propositions show the logical form of reality, which is constituted by the logical forms of states of affairs (TLP 2.031–2.033, 2.06, 4.121). The logical forms of states of affairs cannot be said; that is, cannot be represented by propositions (TLP 4.121, 4.1212). Hence, Wittgenstein would never hold that "It is possible that abcde" is a proposition, not to mention its having a truth value. What is supposed, by Morris, to be said by "It is possible that abcde" is actually unsayable, but is shown by the relevant proposition's having sense. That is, that "abcde" makes sense shows that it is possible that abcde. (Of course, Wittgenstein would say that, strictly speaking, the "it is possible that abcde" in the preceding sentence is nonsensical.)

In order to explain the substance argument, Zalabardo (2012) appeals to an entry dated 21 October 1914 in the *Notebooks*:

> I thought that the possibility of the truth of the proposition ϕa was tied up with the fact $(\exists x,\phi).\phi x$. But it is impossible to see why ϕa should only be possible if there is another proposition of the same form. ϕa surely does not need any precedent. (For suppose there existed only the two elementary propositions 'ϕa' and 'ψa' and that 'ϕa' were false: Why should this proposition make sense only if 'ψa' is true?) (NB 17)

According to Zalabardo, Wittgenstein takes $(\exists x,\phi).\phi x$ to be a logical form, which is also a constituent (complex) of the understanding complex $U[S, P, a, (\exists x,\phi).\phi x]$ which was introduced by Russell in order to account for the possibility of false representations in his 1913 manuscript *Theory of Knowledge* (Russell, 1913/84, pp.115–17; Zalabardo, 2012, p.139). Moreover, a Russellian logical form, like $(\exists x,\phi).\phi x$, exists only if one of its substitution instances obtains.

Zalabardo's interpretation of the substance argument goes as follows. First, substance consists in possibilities of combination. The claim that the world has substance means that "the way in which certain objects are combined in an actually obtaining state of affairs can be a possible mode of combination for other objects" (2012, p.141). Second, if the world had no substance, then, in order for a false representation to be possible, there would have to be a Russellian logical form, which was a constituent of a representational state. But the logical form would not exist, unless one of its substitution instances obtains. Thus, the meaningfulness of a false representation would depend on the truth of a proposition expressing a substitution instance of the existentially generalized proposition representing the Russellian logical form. The latter is the "another proposition" in TLP 2.0211. Third, it follows that an infinite regress would be generated in this way: "the particular fact that would make the logical form exist would have to be understood, and for this another logical form would be required and so on" (2012, p.143). The unacceptable consequence is then the impossibility of false representations.

Zalabardo's interpretation has the merits that the "another proposition" in TLP 2.0211 is specified as well as that an elegant *reductio ad absurdum* is reconstructed for the substance argument. But, like Proops's and Morris's, Zalabardo's interpretation also suffers from serious difficulties. The first is this. The substance argument belongs to the group of comments on the simplicity of objects (TLP 2.02). The simplicity of objects, however, plays no role in Zalabardo's reconstructed argument. The second difficulty is that the picture theory is not employed in the reconstructed argument at all. Instead, Zalabardo makes use of Russell's accounts of understanding complex and false representations. But these are very different from the picture theory. The third difficulty is that whereas Wittgenstein says in TLP 2.0212 that we could not sketch *any* picture of the world (true or false), the unacceptable conclusion drawn by Zalabardo's reconstructed argument only states that *false* representations are impossible.

4   The Substance Argument

I am now going to offer my own interpretation of the substance argument. In my reconstructed argument, both the possibility of complete analysis and the necessary existence of objects are not assumed, but derived; the "another proposition" mentioned in TLP 2.0211 is specified, and the picture theory is employed in a nontrivial, crucial manner.

Before proceeding further, a remark should be made here. Probably, because the antecedent of the counterfactual in TLP 2.0211, or the first premise of the substance argument, refers to the world, Wittgenstein uses the term "any picture of the world (true or false)" in TLP 2.0212, or the second premise of the substance argument. Actually, "any picture of the world (true or false)" means the same as "any picture of reality." To see this, first, note that the totality of existing states of affairs is the world (TLP 2.04), and that the existence and nonexistence of states of affairs is reality (TLP 2.06). "A proposition shows how things stand *if* it is true. And it *says that* they do so stand" (TLP 4.022). Moreover, "a proposition can be true or false only in virtue of being a picture of reality" (TLP 4.06). It follows that, in general, a picture of the world (true or false) is actually a picture of reality. For if a picture of the world is true, it depicts the existence of states of affairs and thus is a picture of reality; and if it is false, it depicts the nonexistence of states of affairs and is still a picture of reality.

The substance argument is a *reductio ad absurdum*. The *reductio* is the premise that the world had no substance, which is equivalent to the claim that there were no necessarily existent simple objects. It also implies that all complexes are constituted by complexes only, or that complexes are gunky. The unacceptable conclusion to be deduced is that we could not sketch any picture of the world (true or false) (true or false). It is unacceptable, because Wittgenstein takes it to be a plain truth that we can sketch any picture of the world (true or false).

To produce a thought, or a proposition, is to sketch a picture of the world (true or false), that is, a picture of reality. That a proposition is a picture of reality can be seen from the fact that "we understand the sense of a propositional sign without its having been explained to us" (TLP 4.02; see also 4.01, 4.021). Wittgenstein even thinks it follows that we "can actually see from the proposition how everything stands logically if it is true" (TLP 4.023). For we understand the sense of a proposition when we understand how, as depicted by the proposition, things stand, if it is true (TLP 4.022). The reason why we can see the sense of a proposition is that a proposition shows or displays its sense (TLP 4.022, 4.121). This leads to what may be called "the doctrine of showing," which includes at least the thesis that a proposition "*shows* its sense," or "how things stand *if* it is true" (TLP 4.022).

Sense, as the content of a proposition, is determinate (TLP 3.23). Because a proposition, as a picture, shows its sense, it can always be expressed in a determinate manner that its sense can be "set out" clearly:

> What a proposition expresses it expresses in a determinate manner, which can be set out clearly: a proposition is articulate. (TLP 3.251)

Remember that a proposition is a picture of reality, *because* it shows its sense. Therefore, "it is only in so far as a proposition is logically articulated that it is a picture of a situation" (TLP 4.032).

TLP 3.251 is the immediate comment on the thesis that "a proposition has one and only one complete analysis" (TLP 3.25). Thus, the possibility of unique complete analysis is guaranteed by the fact that a proposition shows its determinate sense. Moreover, Wittgenstein also says in TLP 3.23 that "the requirement that simple signs be possible is the requirement that sense be determinate." This, together with TLP 3.25–3.251, also suggests that the thesis that there are simple objects (or that the world has substance) is supported by the thesis that a proposition shows its determinate sense. It is precisely because of the thesis that a proposition shows its determinate sense that the substance argument provides support for both the possibility of complete analysis and the existence of necessarily existent simple objects.

Owing to factors like "the outward form of clothing" and "the tacit conventions" of language (TLP 4.002), there may be expressions of the proposition from which one cannot see its sense. Thus, not all propositional signs show its sense. Nevertheless, the thesis that a proposition shows its sense can be formulated as follows:

> (i) A proposition must have a propositional sign showing its sense.

What plays a crucial role in the substance argument is actually this conditional:

> (ii) If we can produce a proposition as a picture of reality (that is, if we can sketch a picture of the world (true or false)), then it must have a propositional sign showing its determinate sense.

The substance argument would deduce from the *reductio* that the world had no substance the proposition that a proposition could not have any propositional sign showing its sense. Form this, and employing (ii), the unacceptable conclusion that we could not sketch any picture of reality would be derived.

Let me now turn to the substance argument, and begin by considering the first step:

> If the world had no substance, then whether a proposition had sense would depend on whether another proposition was true. (TLP 2.0211)

The *reductio* is that the world had no substance, or that there were no necessarily existent simple objects. It follows that there would only be complexes, and that:

> A complex must be constituted by complexes, and those constituent complexes are constituted by other complexes, and so on and so forth.

If there were no objects, complexes had to be *gunky*. Moreover, since, of course, there are propositions about the world, they could only be propositions about complexes.

Wittgenstein would hold that, if there were no objects, a proposition (say) "gb", viz. about the complexes g and b, had sense if and only if one of the following would hold:

(a) The complexes g and b existed;
(b) g and some constituent complexes of b existed;
(c) b and some constituent complexes of g existed;
(d) Some constituent complexes of g existed or some constituent complexes of b existed.

If the convention of regarding a complex as a constituent complex of itself is adopted, the general point here can be expressed as follows:

(iii) *If there were no objects*, then a proposition (about the world) had sense if and only if some relevant constituent complexes of the complexes the proposition was about existed (and there were true descriptions of those complexes).

Thus, if there were no objects, then a proposition had sense if and only if the descriptions of some relevant constituent complexes of the complexes the proposition was about were true. It might not be known which descriptions were true, but there had to be those true descriptions.

This also leads to another general point, which, if the aforementioned convention is adopted, can be expressed as follows:

(iv) If there were no objects, then whether a proposition (about the world) had sense would depend on whether some descriptions of the constituent complexes of the complexes it was about were *true*.

The answer to the controversial exegetical question "What is the 'another proposition' mentioned in TLP 2.0211?" is then this: *the conjunction of some descriptions of the constituent complexes of the complexes the proposition was about*. With this, TLP 2.0211 is explained.

Let me now turn to the second, and final, step of the substance argument:

> In that case we could not sketch any picture of the world (true or false). (TLP 2.012)

To begin, note that (iv), together with the adoption of the aforementioned convention, implies this:

(vi) Under the assumption that there were no objects, if a proposition (about the world) had sense, then there had to be a *true* description of a constituent complex of one of the complexes it was about.

But then whenever a proposition had sense, its propositional sign in that case could not have a propositional part that was a propositional sign of the relevant true description of the relevant complex. For, otherwise, the propositional sign might still express a sense, even if the description were false. This, in turn, entails that:

(vii) Under the assumption that there were no objects, for any propositional sign of a proposition (about the world), there had to be a true description of a constituent complex of the complexes it was about such that the propositional sign did not have a propositional part that was a propositional sign of the description.

It follows from (vi) that no propositional sign of a proposition (about the world) could reflect the internal complexities of the complexes it was about *completely*. Thus, every propositional sign of the proposition had an indeterminateness. Hence, a proposition could not be articulate, and also could not have a propositional sign showing its sense completely. But a picture must show its sense. Therefore, if there were no objects, the proposition could not be a picture of the world (true or false). This applies to any proposition about the world. In this case, every proposition about the world had intrinsic indeterminateness, and thus could not show its sense. Consequently, if there were no objects, one could not sketch any picture of the world (true or false). Since we can sketch any picture of the world (true or false) by producing propositions or thoughts, those complexes must be constituted by necessarily existent simple objects solely; and, thus, there must be objects. The final conclusion is then that the world has substance constituted by necessarily existent simple objects.

References

Cheung, L.K.C. (1999). The Proofs of the *Grundgedanke* in Wittgenstein"s *Tractatus*. *Synthese*, 120, 395–410.

Cheung, L.K.C. (2000). The Tractarian Operation N and expressive Completeness. *Synthese*, 123, 247–261.

Geach, P. (1981). Wittgenstein"s Operator N. *Analysis*, 41, 168–171.

Geach, P. (1982). More on Wittgenstein"s Operator N. *Analysis*, 42, 127–129.

Kenny, A. (1973). *Wittgenstein*. London: Penguin.

Morris, M. (2008). *Wittgenstein and the Tractatus*. London: Routledge.

Pears, D. (1987). *The False Prison* (Vol. 1). Oxford: Oxford University Press.

Proops, I. (2004). Wittgenstein on the Substance of the World. *European Journal of Philosophy*, 12, 106–126.

Russell, B. ([1911] 2003). Analytic Realism. Translation in S. Mumfold (Ed.). *Russell on Metaphysics* (pp.91–96). London: Routledge. (Original work published 1911.)

Russell, B. (1913/84). *Theory of Knowledge: The 1913 Manuscript*. Ed. E.R. Eames. London: George Allen and Unwin.

Russell, B. (1918). The Philosophy of Logical Atomism. Reprinted in R.C. Marsh (Ed.). (1956). *Logic and Knowledge: Essays 1910–1950* (pp.177–281). London: George Allen and Unwin.

Russell, B. (1924). Logical Atomism. Reprinted in R.C. Marsh (Ed.). (1956). *Logic and Knowledge: Essays 1910–1950* (pp.323–343). London: George Allen and Unwin.

Zalabardo, J. (2012). Reference, Simplicity, and Necessary Existence in the *Tractatus*. In J. Zalabardo (Ed.). *Wittgenstein"s Early Philosophy* (pp.119–150). Oxford: Oxford University Press.

Further Reading

Allaire, E.B. (1966). The "Tractatus": Nominalistic or Realistic? In I.M. Copi and R.W. Beard (Eds). *Essays on Wittgenstein"s Tractatus* (pp.325–341). London: Routledge and Kegan Paul.

Hacker, P.M.S. (1972/86). *Insight and Illusion: Themes in the Philosophy of Wittgenstein*. Revised edition. Oxford: Clarendon Press. Chapter 3.

Kenny, A. (1973/2006). *Wittgenstein*. Revised edition. Oxford: Blackwell. Chapters 5 and 6.

Pears, D. (1987). *The False Prison* (Vol. 1). Oxford: Oxford University Press. Chapters 4 and 5.

White, R. (2006). *Wittgenstein"s Tractatus Logico-Philosophicus*. London: Continuum.

8

The Picture Theory

COLIN JOHNSTON

1 Introduction

What is Wittgenstein's picture theory a theory of? An easy answer to this question is that it is a theory of representation, but insofar as this answer is indeed easy, so too is it uninformative. If I roll my eyes thereby communicating to an intended audience that the person I'm telephoning is being unreasonable, this will not be an instance of the kind of representing Wittgenstein wants to understand. So what *does* he want to understand?

The picture theory is sometimes spoken of as a theory *of the proposition*, and for two reasons this seems a good start. First, it indicates that we have a theory of representing not *by means of* propositions but *by propositions themselves* – a theory of how the proposition determines what it represents, its sense. And second, a proposition is complex, and so we have the suggestion that the species of representing in view essentially involves complexity in the representation. Putting these two together, the idea appears of a proposition as something that determines its sense by means of its internal structure.

This idea is of course familiar from Frege. In Frege, however, the matter goes a step further. A Fregean proposition does not merely determine its sense by means of internal structure: it determines its sense by means of *a match in* internal structure. As Frege puts it, a proposition involves a "correspondence between the way words are concatenated and the structure of the concepts" (Frege, 1979, pp. 12–13). And this too we find in the *Tractatus*. By a proposition, Wittgenstein like Frege means something that determines its sense by means of a correlation between the mode of combination of its constituent symbols and the structure of its sense.

Such a structural correlation between a proposition and its sense implies, of course, a correlation between the elements of the correlated structures: correlating the structures means correlating their elements. A proposition's component symbols can therefore be said to *mean* the elements of the sense, to have the sense elements as their meanings:

The name means the object, the object is its meaning. (TLP 3.203)

A Companion to Wittgenstein, First Edition. Edited by Hans-Johann Glock and John Hyman.
© 2017 John Wiley & Sons, Ltd. Published 2017 by John Wiley & Sons, Ltd.

And here we have the beginnings of an idea that, as Wittgenstein says, a proposition *puts its sense into words* (TLP 4.116, 6.5): in a proposition, the constituent symbols mean the sense elements, and the way those symbols combine mirrors the combination of the meanings in the sense. Or as both Frege and Wittgenstein put it, a proposition *expresses* its sense:

> I call any sentence a sentence proper if it expresses a thought. (Frege, 1984, p.392)
>
> The proposition is the expression of its truth conditions. (TLP 4.431)

A first-pass answer to the question of what Wittgenstein's picture theory is a theory of, then, is that it is a theory of the expression of sense.

Having *some* idea of what the picture theory is a theory of, we can ask what it maintains. And a central answer to this question will be that Wittgenstein holds the correlation between the way words are combined in a proposition and the way their meanings combine in the represented fact to be a species of *identity*:

> That the elements of the picture are combined with one another in a definite way, represents that the things are so combined with one another. (TLP 2.15)

What an elementary proposition represents is that the objects its constituent names stand for are *so* combined, that they are combined as their names are combined in the proposition. Much of what follows will serve, in the end, to understand this identity. Our route here will include, however, considerable further elaboration of the notion of expression. In particular, we shall need to see that this notion involves for Wittgenstein more than the bare idea of a correspondence (or identity) between the mode of combination of a proposition and that of the fact it represents. As the idea has so far been indicated, Russell could hold that the propositions of his concept script express facts: the Russellian sentences "*Fa*" and "*aRb*" could be held to identify the Russellian facts *Fa* and *aRb* by means of a match in their internal structures. But for (Frege and) Wittgenstein the idea of expressing a sense, of putting a fact into words, runs deeper than anything Russell would, or could, subscribe to. In the expression of a sense, the fact is not merely identified by means of its internal structure but *fully laid out to view*. As Peter Sullivan puts it:

> To express a sense is to *give* the sense in a much fuller or more immediate way than merely identifying that sense. [...] Someone who understands the *expression* of a sense *is thereby possessed of* that sense. (Sullivan, 2001, p.90)

Understanding this notion of expression and understanding Wittgenstein's "in the same way" condition will be two aspects of the same project; the phenomenon is clearly grasped only simultaneously with its account.

These remarks leave unanswered the question of why Frege and Wittgenstein are interested in the expression of sense. Why do they ignore the possibility, indeed actuality, of alternative modes of communication? One central response to this will be that their notion of a fact itself involves that of its possible expression. A Tractarian fact, I shall suggest, is precisely an expressible: where other possible forms of fact communication are incidental to, or a consequence of, the nature of facts, a Tractarian fact is in its conception the kind of thing to be expressed. Before considering this, however, and indeed before taking on the picture theory, I want to set the notion of expression to one side. So far I have used the terms "fact" and "sense" interchangeably, and this is obviously unproblematic in connection to Frege, for whom a fact just is an obtaining propositional sense, a true thought (Frege, 1984, p.368). With Wittgenstein, by contrast, commentators have often wanted to distinguish facts – or at least atomic facts – from senses. Senses are held to be *truth conditions*, and this is of course quite correct (consider for example TLP 4.431 above, and also Frege, [1893/1903] 2013, §32). Tractarian facts, it is however added, are not truth conditions but items whose existence explains the obtaining of truth conditions: a Tractarian atomic fact is not a truth *condition* but a truth*maker*. The first task of this chapter will be to reject this position and affirm the identity of fact and sense. Subsequently, we shall take a lead from Frege in drawing certain lessons from this affirmation, lessons regarding how both the constituents of senses and their modes of combination are to be understood. Only then will we return to the matter of fact expression and the picture theory.

2   The Identity of Fact and Sense

It has been an orthodoxy amongst *Tractatus* interpreters, and continues to be such in the wider philosophical community, that Wittgenstein follows the 1910 Russell in offering a correspondence theory of truth (See Chapter 27, WITTGENSTEIN ON TRUTH). Russell writes that "when we judge truly some entity 'corresponding' in some way to our judgment is to be found outside our judgment, while when we judge falsely there is no such 'corresponding' entity" (Russell, 1910, p.119). He gives the example:

> If A loves B, there is such a complex object as 'A's love for B', and vice versa; thus the existence of this complex object [which Russell identifies as a fact] gives the condition for the truth of the judgment 'A loves B'. (Russell, 1910, p.123)

And comparably, one might think, Wittgenstein writes:

> If an elementary proposition is true, the atomic fact exists: if an elementary proposition is false, the atomic fact does not exist. (TLP 4.25)

Like Russell, Wittgenstein maintains that the obtaining of a truth condition, and so the truth of a judgment with that truth condition, consists in the existence of a corresponding fact. My belief that Jack loves Jill and the sentence "Jack loves Jill" both have as their truth condition that Jack loves Jill. And the obtaining of this truth condition – its being the case that Jack loves Jill – consists in the existence of the fact of Jack loving Jill.

Such theorizing involves a conception of facts as truth*makers*. But that conception is of course not compulsory. Following Frege, one might choose not to indulge the idea of truthmaking, using the word "fact" to speak simply of truth *conditions* (or if one prefers, of obtaining truth conditions). Where the Russellian distinguishes facts and truth conditions, taking facts to be what make truth conditions obtain, the Fregean makes no such distinction: the fact that Jack loves Jill is precisely the truth condition of my belief that Jack loves Jill. But what, the Russellian may then press, for the obtaining of such conditions? Here the Fregean position is simple: such obtaining is *brute*. Some truth conditions obtain and some fail to obtain, but no account of this is to be offered by reference to some further "element of reality." (Rather, if you like, the obtaining fact is itself already "reality.") As, further, for the correspondence theorist's emphasized talk of fact *existence*, this may be dismissed by, as it were, identifying a fact's existence with the fact itself. To recognize, affirm, deny, or hypothesize the existence of a certain fact will simply be to recognize, affirm, deny, or hypothesize that fact. As Ramsey wrote in rejection of Russell's correspondence idea, "'The fact that *a* has *R* to *b* exists' is no different from '*a* has *R* to *b*'" (1927, p.159).

Ramsey attributes his repudiation of Russell to Wittgenstein (Ramsey, 1927, p.170). So which interpretation, we may ask, is correct, Ramsey's or the correspondence view? I shall argue that whilst a quick reading of the *Tractatus* readily suggests an idea of atomic facts as existing or nonexisting truthmakers, attending more closely to, thinking slightly harder about, Wittgenstein's theorizing reveals that the Tractarian system simply doesn't support, *simply doesn't provide for*, thinking of the obtaining of a truth condition in terms of distinct fact-items (cf. Chapter 7, LOGICAL ATOMISM).

To set the scene, let's ask how Russell's system provides content to his correspondence idea. Russell writes:

> The judgment that two terms have a certain relation *R* is a relation of the mind to the two terms and the relation *R* with the appropriate sense: the "corresponding" complex consists of the two terms related by the relation *R* with the same sense. The judgment is true when there is such a complex, and false when there is not. (Russell, 1910, p.124)

But a definition of truth might equally well have been made as follows. The judgment is a relation of the mind to the two terms and the relation *R* with the appropriate sense; it is true when those two terms are related by the relation *R* with the same sense, and false when they are not. So what is the cash value of the talk about corresponding complexes? My alternative definition inflates into Russell's just when we add that for *a* to stand in relation *R* to *b* is for the complex *a*-in-relation-*R*-to-*b* to exist. But what is the cash value of *this* claim – how is *this* claim not a mere tautology? Well, the claim draws for Russell on a wider theoretical context in which complexes are themselves constituents as objects of further complexes, a structuring which explains certain relations of necessitation amongst truth conditions. For example, the complex knife-to-the-left-of-book – the complex whose existence constitutes the knife's being to the left of the book – is for Russell a constituent, along with Jack and the relation of perceiving, of the further complex Jack-perceiving-(knife-to-the-left-of-book), this latter complex again existing just in case Jack enjoys the relevant perception. And as the existence of a whole requires the existence of its parts, Russell has an explanation of why Jack's perception is possible only if the knife is indeed to the left of the book. Such explanations to one side, however, the key thought here is that it is Russell's general theory of *complexes*, and not in itself his theory of *judgment* – not in itself, that is, his theory of a judgment's possession of a truth condition – that provides content to his correspondence idea.

Turning with this to Wittgenstein, we can straightaway note that he emphatically rules out any such context for thinking of facts other than as truth conditions. He both vigorously disassociates facts from objects and insists that objects are simple (see, e.g., TLP 1.1, 2.02, 3.144). A fact is not a possible constituent, as an object, of further facts. As for perception, Wittgenstein writes:

> To perceive a complex means to perceive *that* its constituents are related to one another in such and such a way. (TLP 5.5423)

Perceiving *a*-in-relation-*R*-to-*b* is to be understood as perceiving *that a* stands in relation *R* to *b*. And perceiving that *aRb*, Wittgenstein further implies, is a matter of having a true perceptual representation that *aRb*. We shall, it seems, need to look elsewhere if we want to think of Tractarian facts other than as truth conditions.

But where? Well, the obvious place is where for Russell we didn't find the relevant provision, namely the theory of judgment. The thought here is this: perhaps one's theory of the *possession* of a truth condition will carry implications for what it is for a truth condition to obtain. Russell has a judgment connect to a fact by virtue of having a truth condition. His theory of judgment explains a proposition's having a truth condition, whose obtaining is then, for reasons external to the theory of judgment, identified with the existence of a particular fact. Alternatively, though, one could suggest that a proposition has a truth condition by virtue of connecting to a fact. A proposition first picks out a fact; subsequently it does something like "affirm the fact (or the fact's existence)," coming thereby to have the relevant truth condition. If a theory of this shape of the functioning of a proposition could be ascribed to Wittgenstein then all would be set for thinking of Tractarian facts other than as truth conditions. An atomic fact would be the object of a "picking out" relation, and – depending on how the affirmation part of the theory is understood – the door would be open for thinking of the obtaining of an atomic truth condition in terms of the existence (or something similar) of such an item.

Certain commentators have understood the *Tractatus* as proposing just such a two-step theory of elementary propositions. First, the proposition picks out a fact: it depicts or images a (non-truth condition) fact in a way that does not presume that fact's existence. Subsequently, the proposition affirms (or something similar) the picked-out fact, thereby coming to have a truth condition. There is, however, ample reason to reject any such understanding of Wittgenstein's picture theory. For a start, the attribution is seriously undermined by criticisms Wittgenstein makes of Frege:

> The verb of a proposition is not 'is true' or 'is false', as Frege thought: rather, that which 'is true' must already contain the verb [i.e., already have a truth condition].
> Every proposition must *already* have a sense [truth condition]: it cannot be given a sense by affirmation. (TLP 4.063–4.064)

Rightly or wrongly (I take it wrongly), Wittgenstein here *accuses* Frege of explaining the possession of a truth condition by reference to an affirmation, or asserting as true, of some prior item. What most severely undermines the attribution to Wittgenstein of a two-step picture of elementary judgment, however, is its complete and conspicuous absence from Wittgenstein's central statement of his account:

> In the picture the elements of the picture are the representatives of objects. (TLP 2.131)

> A picture is a fact.
> That the elements of the picture are combined with one another in a definite way, represents that the things are so combined with one another. (TLP 2.141–2.15)

A proposition's having a certain truth condition – its representing that *p* – is explained *directly* in terms of its elements referring to objects; it is not explained via the proposition as a whole imaging some non-truth-condition fact.

Nothing in Wittgenstein's theorizing, it would thus seem, provides for interpreting those points at which he talks of fact existence as the expression of a Russellian correspondence theory, or indeed of any theory in which facts are distinguished from truth conditions. A Tractarian fact is nothing other than a truth condition.

3 The Priority of Sense (i)

We asserted in the introduction that a Tractarian fact is in its conception an expressible, and some progress has now been made toward this. A fact, we have argued, is a truth condition, and the idea of a truth condition is immediately that of a truth condition of a possible representation, and so the idea of a representable. From here it needs to be added only that the going notion of representation in the *Tractatus* is that of *expression* and we shall have that a Tractarian fact is precisely an expressible. Before considering the idea of expression, however, I want in the next two sections to draw out some consequences of our identification of fact and truth condition.

To begin, we can consider the following passage from Frege:

> What is distinctive about my conception of logic is that I begin by giving pride of place to the content of the word 'true', and then immediately go on to introduce a thought as that to which the question 'Is it true?' is in principle applicable. So I do not begin with concepts and put them together to form a thought or judgement; I come by the parts of a thought by analyzing the thought. (Frege, 1979, p.253)

This distinctive Fregean conception of logic, I want to press, is also that of the *Tractatus* (see also Chapter 4, WITTGENSTEIN AND FREGE). Following Frege, Wittgenstein too gives pride of place to truth and introduces facts as truth conditions. And so Wittgenstein too does not begin with objects and put them together to form facts but comes by objects as elements of facts.

There is a good deal here to unpack; let's start with Frege's first sentence. Thoughts, Frege says, are the kind of things to be true or false. One might read this introduction simply as a singling out by Frege of a class of items in which he is interested: he is interested in thoughts, and one way to identify a thought is as something that is either true or false. This obviously mistaken reading ignores, however, the role signaled for truth in the first half of the sentence. Keeping the first half of the sentence in view, it is clear that Frege is introducing his *notion* of a thought as the *notion of something true or false*, as the notion of a truth or falsehood. And Wittgenstein's identification of facts and truth conditions, we can underline, is an introduction of this same kind. It would be a serious misunderstanding of the argument of the last section to read its conclusion as a claim that facts, on some prior understanding of that notion, "play the role of truth conditions." The point is not that the *Tractatus* has a notion of fact separate from that of truth condition but then commits to the identification of facts, so conceived, with truth conditions. What was argued was rather that Wittgenstein does not conceive of facts other than as truth conditions, that the Tractarian idea of a fact is, from the start, that of a truth condition.

One useful way to drive this home is to draw the consequence that Wittgenstein's identification does not stand only against a particular, Russellian version of the correspondence theory but against the correspondence theory in all its versions. The basic idea of the correspondence theory is of truth as a match of some kind between representations on the one hand and reality on the other. And the content of talking of two hands here includes that reality is "constitutively separate" from representation. In giving one's account of "the intrinsic character of reality," one's account of the intrinsic nature of what is found on the reality side of the representational affair, one does not deploy notions which are bound to that of representation. In itself, in the shapes it takes, the world is ignorant of any possibility of being represented. This is Russell's stance in 1910, and it is here that the correspondence theory involves a certain metaphysical realism. But this point of realism is rejected by Frege's and Wittgenstein's beginning with truth. Tractarian facts have no account separate from the notion of truth, no more basic understanding to which their status as truth conditions is external. And this means they have no account separate from the notion of representation, for a truth condition is precisely a truth condition of possible representations: it is precisely a representable.

But Frege's and Wittgenstein's beginning with truth goes deeper still than this. Consider the "So" of Frege's second sentence. It is a consequence, Frege asserts, of his beginning with truth that he comes by the parts of a thought only by analyzing the thought. How so? One can imagine a position in which certain items are in their conception the kinds of things to be true or false, but nonetheless have parts arrived at other than by analyzing the wholes. More specifically, an item could *in its mode of combination* be essentially a truth or falsehood and yet have parts given independently of the whole. (This is the position of the early, pre-correspondence theory Russell.) So what supports Frege's inference? Well, Frege's idea here is that a thought would have an understanding other than as, simply, a truth or falsehood if its parts were understood other than as possible parts of truths and falsehoods. Even if a thought has a mode of combination connected essentially with the notion of truth, if the parts arrive from elsewhere, then there will be substance to the whole other than that of a truth. And just this is what Frege is set against. What is distinctive of Frege's conception of logic is that it gives *sole* pride of place to the content of the word "true," where this means that no substance arrives into his theorizing separately from that content. His theorizing is in this sense nothing other than an *unpacking* of the notion of truth. So in particular no elaboration of his notion of a thought can be in view other than its unpacking as the notion of a truth or falsehood. And this means that the parts of a thought cannot be understood other than as such. What a thought part is, essentially and from the start, is a part of thoughts.

Wittgenstein takes exactly the same line. Directly after introducing his notion of an object with the remark:

An atomic fact is a combination of objects (entities, things). (TLP 2.01)

Wittgenstein writes:

It is essential to things that they should be possible constituents of atomic facts. (TLP 2.011)

In itself this sentence could be taken in two ways. One could read Wittgenstein as saying that objects have essential natures that *suit* them to be possible constituents of facts. Or one could find the claim that an object's essential nature *consists* in its being a possible constituent of facts. As the passage continues, Wittgenstein makes clear many times over that he is affirming the second of these and rejecting the first:

> In logic nothing is accidental: if a thing can occur in an atomic fact, the possibility of the atomic fact must be written into the thing itself.
> It would seem to be a sort of accident, if it turned out that a situation would fit a thing that could already exist entirely on its own.
> If things can occur in atomic facts, this possibility must be in them from the beginning. [...]
> Just as we are quite unable to imagine spatial objects outside space or temporal objects outside time, so too there is *no* object that we can imagine apart from the possibility of combining with others. (TLP 2.012–2.0121)
>
> If I know an object I also know all its possible occurrences in atomic facts.
> (Every one of these possibilities must be part of the nature of the object.)
> A new possibility cannot be discovered later. (TLP 2.0123)

If a thing can occur in an atomic fact, this possibility must be written into the thing itself, into its basic nature, from the beginning. One cannot be given the object apart from its possibilities for occurring in facts, and then later consider (discover) that the nature of what one has grounds certain such possibilities. This cannot be so for the object's basic nature doesn't *ground* its possibilities for occurring in facts: it *is* its possibilities for occurring in facts. What a Tractarian object essentially is, is a possible part of facts.

As Frege, then, Wittgenstein gives sole pride of place to truth. Tractarian facts are not only essentially truth conditions but *exhaustively* truth conditions, their constituents having no account separate from the notion of truth.

4   The Priority of Sense (ii)

The Tractarian conception of an object as a possible part of facts carries a conception also of object combination. Tractarian objects have their possibilities of occurrence in atomic facts written into them; object combination, it follows, is simply the realization of such inscribed possibilities. And this means that if certain objects combine to form an atomic fact, this will involve no go-between or copula additional to the objects. For to suppose that an object combination involves such an additional item is to suppose that the constituent objects' possibility for so combining is not written into them "from the beginning," but is grounded instead in their suitability to this "something more": the copula defines a mode of combination, and the objects will be combinable in this mode by virtue of their suitability to the copula. In hand with his repudiation of any such grounding, then, Wittgenstein writes:

> In the atomic fact objects hang one in another, like the links of a chain. (TLP 2.03)

Wittgenstein's translator C.K. Ogden had initially rendered the German here as "In the atomic fact objects hang one *on* another, like the links of a chain." But Wittgenstein made the correction:

> Here instead of "hang one on another" it should be "hang one in another" as the links of a chain *do*! The meaning is *that there isn't anything third* that connects the links but that the links *themselves* make connexion with one another. (Letter to Ogden, 23 April 1922)

There is no copula beyond the objects themselves in or by which they are combined: rather, the objects *concatenate*, holding themselves together.

The idea of concatenation implicated by Wittgenstein's conception of objects runs deeper, however, than the mere rejection of "non-object copulae." Objects come, Wittgenstein envisages, in a variety of different types or forms, with two objects being of the same form if they can combine in the same ways with the same other objects:

The possibility of occurrence in atomic facts is the form of the object. (TLP 2.0141)

And what I want to draw out of Wittgenstein's conception of objects is that a Tractarian concatenative mode has no content, no internal understanding, other than as a mode of the unique forms which may so combine. If entities of forms f and g can combine in mode M, then there is nothing to mode M beyond its being a mode in which forms f and g may combine. Or to put the matter in terms of roles rather than modes, the role an entity of form f plays in an f-g combination has no internal characterization other than as that of combining, as an entity of form f, with an entity of form g.

To see this, suppose for *reductio* that Tractarian modes of combination and so Tractarian combinatorial roles were given independently of unique Tractarian entity types suited to those modes or roles. Then the entity types would equally be given independently of the combinatorial modes. Why? Well, because without such an independent understanding of the types no sense could be made of an entity – with a nature – playing a combinatorial role. To think of some *thing* playing such a role is to think of something of a certain basic kind playing that role, and so if having the role in view does not mean having in view also a unique entity kind, then the entity's kind must arrive from elsewhere, from the entity itself in separation from the role it is there playing. But this is precisely what Wittgenstein is set against: a Tractarian entity has no nature other than that of a role player in facts. Now one might complain that this reasoning is a little quick. Specifically, one might suggest that when making sense of the idea of an entity playing some role, an appeal to the entity type in separation from the role in view does not (immediately) amount to an appeal to the entity's nature in separation from its role-playing profile, for that profile may involve a variety of different roles. But this complaint is readily deflected, for if, as is being supposed, roles are given independently of types, then the idea of a single entity playing different roles itself depends upon an idea of the entity in separation from its nature as a role player. If roles are independent of types, then identifying the same entity across different roles – this entity here is the same as that entity there – means deploying an idea of the entity in itself, an idea distinct from that simply of a role player. If there is no nature and so no entity to hold on to independently of the roles in view, then sense can be made of one and the same entity playing different roles only if it is internal to those roles that they are roles of the same type, and so only if roles are not given independently of types.

This argument is somewhat abstract, but its force and conclusion should not be unfamiliar. The pride of place Frege gives to truth renders it incoherent at the level of reference to suppose that something other than a Fregean object might fall under a Fregean concept, that something other than a Fregean concept might have a Fregean object falling under it, and so on. At the level of sense, it renders it incoherent to suppose that the sense of a proper name might be substitutable in a thought for the sense of a concept expression. And what I am pressing is that the same theoretical vision renders the idea incoherent for Wittgenstein that objects of different forms might play the same role in facts. A fact's being exhaustively a truth condition, its constituents being precisely possible constituents of truth conditions, means that to give the fact's mode is to give its constituent types, and *vice versa*.

5 The Expression of a Sense (i)

The last three sections have sought to provide a substantial understanding of Tractarian facts as truth conditions. To progress further in this same project we need now to consider the notion of expression. Somewhat vaguely, this notion was said above to be one of a fact's being *fully laid out to view*: a proposition expressing a fact *gives that fact without remainder*, where this giving is a kind of *displaying*.

Perhaps the easiest approach to the idea here of "giving without remainder" is to contrast it with the first and most basic idea of fact expression we considered in the introduction, namely that of a proposition's singling out a fact by means of a match in their internal structures. We noted that with only this idea in view, a Russellian sentence "*Fa*" could be held to "express" the Russellian fact *Fa*: a Russellian sentence "*Fa*" can be thought to indicate the Russellian fact *Fa* by means of a match in their internal structures. Unlike a Tractarian proposition, we however continued, there is an important sense in which a Russellian sentence does not *fully give* the fact it singles out. And this is something on which we can now take a substantial grip. The Russellian sentence provides, by its subject–predicate syntax, the mode of combination of the fact's elements: this is a mode of combination as term and property. But in doing this the syntax does not thereby give us the "full ontology," as one might put it, of the fact *Fa*, for it does not thereby provide the ontological kinds of the fact's constituents. The most obvious way to digest this point is to note Russell's position that entities of different kinds can appear in facts as term, and to infer that the syntax of "*Fa*" does not tell us the ontological kind of *a*. For all the syntax tells us, *a* could be a particular, a property, a dual relating relation, or whatever. To be clear, though, the syntax of "*Fa*" would not by itself give us the full ontology of the fact *Fa* even if Russell held – as he indeed does in 1918 (Russell, 1918, p.206) – that only particulars can appear in facts as term, that universals can appear only as relating relations. For the question for Russell of whether universals can appear as term is a matter independent of his notion of combination as term and property. It is not *incoherent* for Russell, even in 1918, to suppose that entities of different basic types can appear in facts as term. If only one kind of entity can play the Russellian term role, this does not belong to the role itself but is a further thesis on the part of Russell, one he sometimes holds and sometimes rejects. For Wittgenstein, by contrast, it precisely is incoherent to suppose that entities of different forms might play the same role in facts. And so where the expression of a fact gives us, through its structure, the fact's mode of combination, it *thereby* gives us – without the need for any additional premise – the full ontology of that fact. The expression of a Tractarian fact provides that fact's mode of combination, and from here there can be no further question as to the ontological types of its constituents.

This view on the provision by a proposition of a Tractarian fact's "full ontology" underplays, however, its directness, making it look as if the provision happens only via an indication of the fact's combinatorial mode. But in fact an object's ontological type is already indicated by the syntactic type of its name, no matter the wider propositional context. The contrast with Russell can thus be put as follows: whilst it does not immediately follow from the fact that two Russellian symbols are of the same syntactic type that their referents are of the same ontological type, one is committed merely in identifying the syntax of two Tractarian names to identifying the form of their referents. To arrive at this version of the contrast, however, more work needs to be done. One thing we shall need to do is to take a short look at the Tractarian notion of a "symbol," considering in particular that just as Wittgenstein understands objects as essentially possible parts of facts, so too he understands names, and indeed symbols more generally, as essentially possible parts of propositions. On top of this though, we shall need also to affirm that the relation between syntax and ontology is in an important sense internal.

So what is a Tractarian symbol? Well, perhaps the first thing to say, something we have already implied, is that it is an essentially syntactic element, and so something distinct from its associated mark or sound, what Wittgenstein calls its "sign":

> A sign is what can be perceived of a symbol. (TLP 3.32)

As for the relation between symbols and their perceptible aspects, their signs, Wittgenstein then writes:

> In order to recognise the symbol in the sign we must consider the significant use. (TLP 3.326)

And in a comment on Ogden's translation, Wittgenstein explains this remark as follows:

> I think "significant" is alright here. The meaning of the prop is: that in order to recognise the symbol in a sign we must look at how this sign is *used* significantly in propositions. I.e. we must observe how the sign is used in accordance with the laws of logical syntax. Thus "significant" here means as much as "syntactically correct". (Letter to Ogden 4 August 1922)

A symbol is a sign in what Wittgenstein calls "logico-syntactic use," use in accordance with the laws of logical syntax. In such a use, the sign has a syntactic character, it is the sign of a symbol, a syntactic element of a particular kind (see also Chapter 23, MEANING AND UNDERSTANDING). In his comment to Ogden, however, Wittgenstein does more than imply that a symbol is a sign in syntactic use: he further characterizes such use as a use *essentially in propositions*. In order to find the symbol we *must* look at how it is used *in propositions*: the logico-syntactic use of a sign, the use of a sign as the sign of a symbol, is essentially a use of the sign as an element of propositions. This position that "the proposition is the unit of language" (LWL 119) parallels in its structure the stance we have examined regarding facts and their constituents. As what an object essentially is, is a possible part of facts, so what a symbol essentially is, is a possible part of propositions. And parallel consequences may be drawn for propositional modes of combination. The syntactic use of a sign is not a use by which the symbol is suited to some copula; rather, it is essentially a use *together with other signs in such use*. The combination of names – the "simple symbols" (TLP 4.24) – in elementary propositions is thus a species of concatenation:

> The elementary proposition consists of names. It is a connexion, a concatenation, of names. (TLP 4.22)

And mirroring the consequences drawn above for objects and facts, it follows with this that a symbolic mode of combination is exhaustively given by the unique syntactic types which may so combine. To give the types of a proposition's constituents is to give its mode of combination, and *vice versa*.

Here with symbols rather than objects, this last result should be completely familiar. To say that an atomic proposition is composed of a singular term and a predicate is to say that it has a subject–predicate mode of combination, and to say that such a proposition has such a mode is to say that it is composed of a predicate and a singular term. More generally, to find the syntactic mode is to find the syntactic types, and *vice versa*. Familiar or not, it is in any case this result that moves us toward our claim above that the ontological type of an object is given by the syntactic type of its name. It belongs to the most basic notion of expression that a proposition's syntactic mode provides the ontological mode of the fact it expresses. But if syntactic and ontological modes have no substance beyond the syntactic and ontological types that may so combine, then this correlation of modes is just as such a correlation of types. To correlate a syntactic mode with an ontological mode is to correlate the types of the syntactic mode with the types of the ontological mode. And with this, it may seem, we have our projected result that an object's ontological type is given by the syntactic type of its name.

We need, however, to be slightly careful. Whilst it is true that the correlation of modes is a correlation of types, nothing so far said rules out that the type correlations might vary depending upon the mode. It has not been ruled out, that is to say, that a name's syntactic type might indicate different ontological types depending on the wider syntactic context. Now this is of course not something the *Tractatus* envisages; it would imply, amongst other things, that different occurrences of the same name might be barred from bearing the same meaning. Equally, it is not hard to sense what it is we need in order to rule the possibility out: what we need further to bring into play here is that as Wittgenstein conceives of the provision by syntax of ontology, this is in some sense *internal*. A proposition's syntax is not correlated merely externally with the ontology of the fact it represents; rather, it tells us that ontology "in or by itself." Such a claim is, as we shall see, certainly present in the *Tractatus*. And with such a claim in play it is certainly ruled out that a syntactic type might indicate different forms in different contexts: because the modes' substance is that of the types, a propositional mode can be correlated "in or by itself" with an ontological mode only if its types are correlated "in or by themselves" with those of the ontological mode. What we now need to do, it seems, is investigate this claim of internality.

6 The Expression of a Sense (ii)

One might think that in understanding a proposition there is a substantial move from syntax to ontology. Given a proposition, one notes its syntax, the syntactic character of its constituents, and from this one infers the form of the fact, the ontological character of its constituents. But for Wittgenstein the expression of a fact is not merely the *provision* of that fact: it is *a laying out* of that fact, where this rules out there being any such inference, any kind of question, given the syntax, of what ontology it signalizes. Indeed, that there is no such inference is a central point of Wittgenstein's analogy with pictures:

> The proposition must enable us to see the logical structure of the situation that makes it true or false. (As a picture must shew the spatial relation in which the things represented in it must stand if the picture is correct (true).) (NB 20.10.14)

We do not recognize the structure of the proposition and from there move, somehow, to that of its sense; rather, we *see* the latter *in* the former.

Let's consider for such "seeing in" a traditionally painted picture of a grouping of people. If one were to come across such a picture in a gallery, one might well find next to the picture a key telling us who the various figures in the picture represent. Think here of David's *Coronation of Napoleon*. We will not, however, find a further key telling us how the represented people are to be spatially interrelated if the picture is correct: so much is shown by the picture itself. That a certain represented person is to be to the left of another and in front of a third is something we can see in the picture itself. David's painting *shows* us, *displays* to us, how the people represented by the various figures within it are to stand with each other if the picture is to be correct. In the same way, Wittgenstein presses:

> A proposition *shows* how things stand, *if* it is true. (TLP 4.022)
>
> One can actually see from the proposition how everything stands logically if it is true. (TLP 4.023)

As we can see in a picture how the things represented within it are to stand with each other spatially if the picture is correct, so a proposition enables us to see how things stand logically if it is true. We may need a key to determine what is represented by the various representatives (names) in the proposition, but we do *not* need a further key to tell us how the represented objects are to stand with each other if the proposition is to be true – *that* is given in the proposition-picture itself.

Wittgenstein insists, then, that there is no substantial move from the proposition's syntax to the mode of combination of its sense. And this means, as we have argued, that there is no move from the proposition's syntax to the sense's "full ontology"; rather, *one can see in the proposition all there is to the fact*. The fact is *fully on display, set out without remainder*, in the proposition. Here we are finally, I think, approaching the full depth of Wittgenstein's notion of expression. But we do not yet have a clear understanding of what it is we are reaching: how is it that in "seeing" the syntax of the proposition one thereby "sees" the ontology of the fact?

A tempting but in the end unhelpful answer to this question considers again the picture analogy. An obvious, naive construal of the operation of a simple picture of two people next to each other would run as follows. The picture represents the two people as next to each other first by containing two figures that stand for the two people, and second by having those two figures located next to each other in the picture. More generally, one might suggest, a picture represents people as related spatially by having figures standing for those people related in that same spatial way in the picture. The reason, the thought will go, that one can see in the picture how the represented people are to be spatially interrelated if the picture is true, the reason why no key is necessary for telling us this, is that it is *there* in the picture to be seen: the spatial interrelations are one and the same. This naive idea will not of course carry us terribly far in understanding the general operation of pictures of groupings of people – one person is not (standardly) represented as behind another by having its figure located behind that of the other – but Wittgenstein's thought, one might suggest, is nevertheless that it is through such a combinatorial identity that propositions represent objects as combined. So Wittgenstein writes:

> In order for a proposition to present a situation it is only necessary for its component parts to represent those of the situation and for the former to stand in a connexion which is possible for the latter. (NB 15.11.14)

> How does the picture present a situation? [...]
>   One name is representative of one thing, another of another thing, and they themselves are connected. [...]
>   The logical connexion must, of course, be one that is possible as between the things that the names are representatives of. [...]
>   In this way the proposition represents the situation – as it were off its own bat. (NB 4.11.14)

Off its own bat, a Tractarian proposition represents that objects are combined together in a certain way by containing representatives of the objects which are themselves connected together in that same way.

This thought, I said, is unhelpful. One way of querying it is to note that it provides no way of deflecting the apparent but bizarre consequence that a name and its meaning will be intersubstitutable. As we have seen, a propositional or fact mode of combination determines the unique types that may so combine, and so if a proposition and its sense have the very same mode, then their constituent types must also be identical. A name will be identical in type to the object for which it stands. But this in turn entails that just as a figure in a picture could be next to a person just as well as it could be next to another such figure, so in general one could substitute in a proposition a name's meaning for the name itself, or substitute in a fact a name of an object for the object itself. But it is unclear at best what such substitutions could amount to. A symbol is a sign in use together with other signs in a proposition. So what could it possibly mean to have something nonlinguistic in place of a symbol in a proposition? What could it possibly mean to take a sign in use together with other signs, extract it from those other signs in use, and put it in place of a nonlinguistic object in a nonlinguistic fact?

Second, we can usefully step back and wonder what sort of an account is supposed to be on offer here. Insofar as the story has any naive appeal, it is surely as a *reductive* account of situation representation. The representation of a sense is being given a straightforward explanation in terms of two more basic notions: that of reference, standing for, and that of two combinations being of the same kind. On reflection, however, this can't be what is going on. For one, the Tractarian notion of reference is transparently not prior to the notion of sense expression (see e.g., TLP 3.2). More than this, though, the "in the same way" condition is equally not so prior. The modes of combination in play here are modes of facts, and facts, we have argued, are precisely representables and so understood only in hand with the notion of representation. Absorbing this point must leave us, I think, off balance. The "in the same way" condition seemed to be presented here as a simple type identity given in advance of the notion of representation and in terms of which representation is to be understood; if this priority is taken away, it becomes unclear what to make of the identity claim, unclear what place it could have in an account – of whatever sort – of representation.

Third, and perhaps most worrying, one can doubt whether the story on offer here captures – in any manner – the phenomenon we were after. The internality of the provision of ontology by syntax was supposed to rule out there being any question, given the syntax, what ontology it signalizes. But here it seems there *is* such a question, indeed a question we have answered: the ontology is the same as the syntax. The "in the same way" claim threatens to appear here, that is to say, as something external to syntax: one has the syntax; separate from this one has the "in the same way" claim; putting the two together one infers the ontology. To repeat the point, we suggested above that one is committed merely in identifying the syntax of two Tractarian names to identifying the form of their referents, but this now appears incorrect: one has this commitment only when one is given also the identity claim. From this perspective, identity is just as external as any other substantial correlation. This complaint might prompt one, of course, to retrace and revise one's understanding of what it is one is after, but enough has been said to move on.

7 The Expression of a Sense (iii)

We need a rather different route to understanding how for Wittgenstein a fact is fully on display in the proposition, a different route to understanding how "seeing the syntax" is "seeing the ontology." We are already equipped, I however think, for finding such a route. First we need to redeploy Wittgenstein's basic Fregean tenet of giving (sole) pride of place to truth in order to arrive at a deeper understanding of Tractarian symbols. And second we shall need to recall and place that Tractarian facts are in their conception the kinds of things to be expressed.

We talked somewhat blandly above of propositions as having "syntactic" structure, of symbols as "syntactic" elements. And then we found Wittgenstein asserting that the proposition is the unit of syntax: as what an object is, is a possible part of atomic facts, so what a name is, is a possible part of elementary propositions. Where the worldly priority was explained by Wittgenstein's giving pride of place to truth, however, the priority in language was left unexplained. But the two have, of course, the very same source. As Wittgenstein's giving pride of place to the notion of truth dictates that facts are not understood other than as truth conditions, so too it dictates that propositions are not understood other than as expressions of truth conditions. What a proposition is, essentially and from the start, is the expression of a truth condition. And on both sides the Fregean tenet austerely demands that propositional or fact elements are not understood other than as such. A separate understanding of propositional elements would be an understanding of them independent of truth, and so, for Wittgenstein, a *nonlogical* understanding. To repeat: the syntactic use in which a sign is a sign of a symbol is not a use in some system comprehensible without reference to truth; rather it is a *logico*-syntactic use, a use essentially in the expression of sense. So immediately after "The proposition is the expression of its truth-conditions" we find: "Frege has therefore quite rightly put them [truth conditions] at the beginning, as explaining the signs of his logical symbolism" (TLP 4.431).

Wittgenstein considers no phenomenon of language, no phenomenon of sentences or syntax, given separately from the notion of truth for which he then asks how *these* kinds of things, being what they are, come to represent the world and so to be truth-bearers. There is no theory of *that* kind in the *Tractatus*. Rather, Wittgenstein's notion of a proposition is from the start one of something "world-involving" (TLP 3.12): it is that of the expression of a sense. It is, therefore, in terms of sense expression that a proposition's structure, its syntax, is to be understood. If what a proposition essentially is, is the expression of a truth condition, then propositional structure is precisely structure in the expressing of such a condition. There is no understanding a proposition as dividing in a certain way and then asking whether (or substantially asserting that) it is by this division that its sense is expressed. Rather, to say that the proposition divides in a certain way *is already to say* that it is in this way that its sense is expressed. *Structure in a proposition means structure through which its sense is expressed.* (Compare here a slightly different case in Frege. To say that the Fregean singular term "The capital of Denmark" divides into the Fregean symbols "The capital of ..." and "Denmark" just is to say that it is in this division that its referent is determined: structure in the Fregean expression means structure in the determination of its referent.)

Propositional structure, we thus have, is expressing structure. More than this, though, Wittgenstein writes:

> I call any part of a proposition that characterizes its sense an expression (or a symbol).
> (A proposition is itself an expression.)
> Everything essential to their sense that propositions can have in common with one another is an expression. (TLP 3.31)

Propositional structure, Wittgenstein here asserts, is structure in its sense. A symbol or propositional part – "the common characteristic mark of a class of propositions" (TLP 3.311) – is at the same time something that characterizes the proposition's sense. A commonality amongst propositions is a commonality in their senses. A move is made, it thus seems, from propositional structure as expressing structure to propositional structure as structure in what is expressed. What underwrites this move?

Well, here we need simply to bring to center stage something that has been running through our discussion: representable means *expressible*. We are not dealing here in the *Tractatus* with some undifferentiated notion of representation, a notion of "fact indication by means of signs" which could take a variety of different forms; rather, our concern is with *expression*, and with that our idea of a truth condition is that of an expressible. And it is this that takes us from propositional structure as expressing structure to propositional structure as structure in the sense expressed. Expressing a fact is not a matter of latching on in a certain way to something given separately from the possibility of so latching on. If it were, then a distinction and comparison would indeed be possible between the way one is latching on and the nature of the item being latched on to, between the structure of the act of latching, as it were, and the structure of its object. With a fact understood as an expressible, however, no such distinction can be made, and this means no contrast is possible between the structure of the expressing and that of what is expressed. To repeat: if, given the expression of a fact, one doesn't take the structure of the expression to provide *in itself* that of the fact, then one is taking the fact to have an expression-independent structure, and so to be something other than an expressible.

This thought that propositional structure is structure in its sense is Wittgenstein's position that what an elementary proposition represents is that its objects are *so* combined (TLP 2.15). We arrive here by holding at once that a proposition is the expression of a sense and that a sense is an expressible. The thought at which we arrive is not, however, the thought above of a simple identity of combinatorial modes between a proposition and its sense, the thought that there is no more distinction between the combinatorial modes of the proposition "Jack loves Jill" and the fact that Jack loves Jill than there is between those of the fact that Jack loves Jill and the fact that

Mike loves Jane. Rather, the view is one in which the logico-syntactic mode of a proposition and the logical mode of the fact it expresses arrive together but are differentiated in that one is the mode of a representation and the other the mode of what such a representation represents. This exhausts, however, their differentiation. Indeed, the modes form an internally related pair such that the one is the mode of a representation and the other the mode of a representable such a representation can represent. Identifying an elementary proposition's composition, then, identifying it as the type of combination it is, will mean identifying how it represents its objects as combined. Or again, given what has been said above, identifying a name, identifying it as the logico-syntactic element it is, will mean identifying the logical form of its referent. One *sees* the form of the fact or object – one *has* that form – *in* that of its representing name or proposition.

8   Truth as the Given

One may have a sense here of groundlessness or circularity, and of course there *is* a certain circularity. To close it may be helpful briefly to place this point. The general structure in Wittgenstein's thinking being found in this chapter involves the rejection of a realism that starts from facts and their constituent objects and then seeks to deploy such ideas in coming to an understanding of the operation of language and the nature of truth. Our proposal is rather that for Wittgenstein language and the world are comprehensible only together: a proposition is precisely the expression of a fact, and a fact is precisely an expressible. This is of course circular in a sense, but the circle should raise no obvious point of concern: the lesson is merely that proposition and fact are coeval notions for Wittgenstein. If one wants something to speak of as basic in the *Tractatus*, something to call a given, then what one should reach for is neither "the world," nor indeed "our language game of propositions," but *truth*. For Wittgenstein, language and the world are to be understood together as aspects of the unfolding of the single notion of truth. In this way the *Tractatus* is profoundly Fregean.

References

Frege, G. ([1893/1903] 2013). *Basic Laws of Arithmetic*. Ed. and trans. P.A. Ebert and M. Rossberg. Oxford: Oxford University Press. (Original work published 1893/1903.)

Frege, G. (1979). *Posthumous Writings*. Ed. H. Hermes, F. Kambartel, and F. Kaulbach. Trans. P. Long and R. White. Oxford: Blackwell.

Frege, G. (1984). *Collected Papers on Mathematics, Logic and Philosophy*. Ed. B. McGuinness. Trans. M. Black, V.H. Dudman, P. Geach, H. Kaal, E.-H.W. Kluge, B. McGuinness, and R.H. Stoothoff. Oxford: Blackwell.

Ramsey, F.P. (1927). Facts and Propositions. *Proceedings of the Aristotelian Society* (Supplementary Volume), 7, 153–170.

Russell, B. (1910). On the Nature of Truth and Falsehood. Reprinted in J. Slater (Ed.). (1992). *The Collected Papers of Bertrand Russell* (Vol. 6, pp.116–124). London: Routledge.

Russell, B. (1918). Philosophy of Logical Atomism. Reprinted in R.C. Marsh (Ed.). (1956). *Logic and Knowledge: Essays 1910–1950* (pp.177–281). London: George Allen and Unwin.

Sullivan, P. (2001). A Version of the Picture Theory. In W. Vossenkuhl (Ed.). *Wittgenstein: Tractatus – Klassiker Auslegen* (pp.89–110). Berlin: Akademie Verlag.

Further Reading

Glock, H.-J. (2006). Truth in the *Tractatus*. *Synthese*, 148, 345–368.
Ramsey, F.P. (1923). Critical Notice of *Tractatus Logico-Philosophicus*. *Mind*, 32, 465–478.
Sullivan, P. (2004). Frege's Logic. In D. Gabbay and J. Woods (Eds). *Handbook of the History of Logic* (Vol. 3, pp.671–762). Amsterdam: North-Holland.
Sullivan, P. (2005). Identity Theories of Truth and the *Tractatus*. *Philosophical Investigations*, 28, 43–62.

9

Wittgenstein on Solipsism

ERNST MICHAEL LANGE

Solipsism is an extreme position. It starts out from an epistemological claim, namely that only my experiences can be known; from there it moves on to ontological claims, notably "only my experience is real experience" or "my consciousness is all the consciousness there is." Wittgenstein addressed this position several times over more than 20 years.

The earliest mention of solipsism in Wittgenstein's *Nachlass* is in a notebook entry of 12 August 1914 (NB). There he asks, after reading Nietzsche, how certain possibilities of leading a life are compatible with a strict solipsistic standpoint. Wittgenstein's latest known treatment is in his *Notes for Lectures on "Private Experience" and "Sense Data"* from 1936 (LPE), where he declares himself to be in search of a philosophy "that would be the diametrical opposite of solipsism" (LPE 282; PO 225). Two later references to solipsism, dated 1941–1944, are only marginal: in one Wittgenstein declares himself not to be entering into a discussion of solipsism (MS 165, p.101); in the other, he says he is concerned with the "half solipsism" of the argument from analogy in the philosophy of mind (MS 165, p.150). On the basis of this small amount of data, it would seem that Wittgenstein moved from espousing solipsism to giving a critique of solipsism and seeking to replace it with its "diametrical opposite." But this simple interpretation of his development is not really successful. Moreover, interpretations holding that Wittgenstein embraced solipsism in his early notebooks and in the *Tractatus* "not as an intellectual exercise, but a moral and mystical attitude" (McGuinness, 1988, p.228) tend to conflate biographical information and textual evidence. This seems particularly inappropriate in the interpretation of a work as systematic as the *Tractatus*. A systematic written work, as I am using the term here, is one that claims to be self-contained and demands to be understood as such, i.e., primarily on the basis of its text.

Wittgenstein first became familiar with solipsism under the title of "theoretical egoism" when reading Schopenhauer at the tender age of 16. Elizabeth Anscombe related a personal conversation in which Wittgenstein said that Schopenhauer's theory of the world "as idea" struck him as fundamentally right, if in need of a few clarifications and adjustments, but that he opposed the theory of the world "as will" (see Anscombe, 1959/63, pp.11–12). Wittgenstein's first philosophy was that of Schopenhauer and he

---

A Companion to Wittgenstein, First Edition. Edited by Hans-Johann Glock and John Hyman.
© 2017 John Wiley & Sons, Ltd. Published 2017 by John Wiley & Sons, Ltd.

was only liberated from it by Frege's conceptual realism (cf. WAM 6). Since it was so significant to Wittgenstein, it is clearly important to determine whether Schopenhauer's position was solipsistic.

There is an important difference between the two designations "solipsism" and "theoretical egoism." "Solipsism" is a one-word descriptive term combining the Latin words "*solus*" (alone, unique) and "*ipse*" (self) and therefore meaning "that there is only one self" or "that *the* self is alone and unique." "Theoretical egoism," which contrasts with "practical egoism," is a two-word description. It denotes the view that in each case of representing the world what is represented exists only for a theoretical ego – the subject of representation. But this seems to leave open the possibility that the theoretical ego has multiple instantiations, i.e., that there is more than one subject of representation (just as the idea of practical egoism leaves open the possibility that there is more than one egoistic subject). Citing the later Wittgenstein here (anachronistically), one could say that "theoretical egoism" (in contrast to "solipsism") is "spreading the use of the word 'I' over all human bodies as opposed to [...] [the solipsist's body] alone" (LPE 281; PO 225). Theoretical egoism certainly is egocentric, but it does not seem to be necessarily solipsistic.

I shall argue that Wittgenstein held a kind of theoretical egocentrism early in his philosophical career, but that he never held solipsism proper – thus agreeing with his disciple Rush Rhees, who arrived at a similar assessment as early as 1947 (see Rhees, 1947, p. 388). Insofar as Wittgenstein restricted "solipsism" to what it has in common with "theoretical egoism" from the start, he may be seen as having intended a critique of solipsism throughout.

The first two parts of the following exposition deal with Schopenhauer's influence on the early Wittgenstein and his treatment of solipsism in the *Tractatus*. Since it is primarily Wittgenstein's later dismissal of solipsism which is of enduring interest, the third section deals with the successful critique of solipsism in the "Blue Book," which is part of his all-embracing self-critique of the Tractarian system. The fourth, and final, section presents a proposal as to how a certain lacuna in the later self-critique concerning the notion of the "metaphysical self" can be closed by means that are essentially Wittgenstein's own.

1   The Impact of Schopenhauer

To believe that the "conceptions of philosophy Wittgenstein was familiar with as a young man were primarily those of Frege and Russell" (Hacker, 2001, p. 324) is simply wrong. It was the Kantianism of Schopenhauer that Wittgenstein first came to embrace wholeheartedly (see also Chapter 3, WITTGENSTEIN AND SCHOPENHAUER). And, since Frege too was a Kantian philosopher of sorts, the division between idealism and realism as pertaining to these two most important philosophical influences on Wittgenstein (viz., Schopenhauer and Frege) set one of the central themes of Wittgenstein's philosophy – not only in his Tractarian period but until at least the early 1930s. Early on, he described this theme as "THE problem of philosophy" and over the years he gave various other names to it, such as "what can be said in language and what can only be shown," "the limits of language," and "the relation of language and the world," until he claimed finally to have found a "Kantian solution" (NB 3.9.14, 1.11.14, 6.3.15; MS 109, p. 16; MS 110, p. 61). Schopenhauer had an influence on many metaphors in the *Tractatus* – the three most important ones being: first, "the ladder" which the reader has to throw away after having climbed it in order to see the world aright (TLP 6.54; cf. Schopenhauer, [1818/59] 1966, vol.2, ch.7); second, "the riddle" that does not exist, because where one can ask a question one can find an answer as well (TLP 6.5; cf. [1818/59] 1966, vol.1, sec.18, and appendix); and third, the characterization of the metaphysical self as an "extensionless point" in the context of the discussion of solipsism (TLP 5.64; cf. Schopenhauer, [1818/59] 1966, vol.2, ch.22).

But Schopenhauer also influenced the very conception of the *Tractatus* in two respects:

(1) Wittgenstein followed a program for the exposition of philosophy that was familiar to him from the preface to Schopenhauer's *magnum opus The World as Will and Representation* (*Die Welt als Wille und Vorstellung*, 1818/59);
(2) Wittgenstein's discussion of solipsism in the *Notebooks 1914–16* and the *Tractatus* was not only externally motivated by Schopenhauer's theory but also internally, as is revealed on a close textual reading of *Tractatus* 5.631 (see discussion below).

There is an obvious need for an explanation of why, in a book that could have been given the descriptive title *The Proposition* (Wuchterl and Hübner, 1979, p. 79), there is a discussion of the epistemological and somewhat *recherché* topic of solipsism at all. A discussion of Schopenhauer is therefore necessary in this connection. It was Russell's theory of knowledge by acquaintance that preceded Wittgenstein in framing the discussion of solipsism in linguistic terms. But Russell could not have motivated Wittgenstein's discussion, because Russell gave no explicit treatment of the idea of the subject (see Pears, 1972, pp.58–9), which is central to Wittgenstein's first discussion of solipsism in the *Tractatus*.

Once the relation between Schopenhauer's philosophy and the theoretical conceptions developed in the *Tractatus* are given their appropriate weight, the *Tractatus* conception of the relation between language, world, and the metaphysical subject can be seen as attempting a realist transformation of Schopenhauer's conception of the relation between ideas, the world, and the subject of cognition. Of course, the adjustments to and clarifications of Schopenhauer's theory, which Wittgenstein considered necessary (as he told Anscombe), are fairly drastic in the *Tractatus*. (See also Lange, 1989, especially ch.5.)

Ad (1). According to Schopenhauer, an "organic" philosophy needs an organic exposition. An organic philosophy is one that develops one single thought only, and in which every part supports every other part and is therefore itself supported by all the other parts. It stands in contrast to systematic philosophy, which argues sequentially "in the form of a chain" of propositions (*kettenartig*) starting from one fundamental principle. That this program was important to Wittgenstein can only be seen from later evidence at the beginning of the "Yellow Book" (see the beginning of AWL). (Evidence from the Tractarian period is unfortunately missing, because Wittgenstein burnt his later pre-Tractarian notebooks in Vienna in March 1950; cf. NB, Editors' preface.) Schopenhauer did not formulate his single thought concisely, but arguably it can be rendered as: "the will is the thing-in-itself." Wittgenstein stated his single thought in the preface and as TLP 7: "whereof one cannot speak, thereof one must remain silent." Both sought an "organic" way of expressing that thought. Schopenhauer thought that his program could not be carried out in a literal sense, because a book inevitably has a first and a last line and therefore remains utterly dissimilar to an organism. Wittgenstein dissolved this contradiction by tying the first and the last proposition of the *Tractatus* together in reciprocal presupposition, leaving nothing philosophical to say after the last sentence. The argument of the book thus forms a circle and it does no harm that the book has a first and a last line.

The reasoning for this reading is as follows. What one has to be silent about in TLP 6.522 is "the Mystical" and TLP 6.44 says what the Mystical is in the first place: namely, that the world is (or exists). (Wittgenstein here, with Schopenhauer – [1818/59] 1966, vol.1, sec.15 – is referring to Leibniz's fundamental question of metaphysics: why is there anything at all and not nothing?) The restriction of TLP 7 is respected in the formulation of TLP 1, which does not say *that* the world exists, but only says what it *consists of*: namely, everything that is the case. This formulation tacitly presupposes, however, *that* the world exists. This presupposition is *shown* by the fact, which logic presupposes, that elementary propositions have sense and that names have reference (TLP 6.124; cf. 5.552). What is shown thereby is the internal relation that holds between language and the world (see 4.014). Thus TLP 1 and 7 relate to one another in reciprocal presupposition, and Wittgenstein has dissolved the contradiction on which Schopenhauer thought his program for the exposition of an organic philosophy foundered. The further execution of the program for the exposition of the organic philosophy in the *Tractatus* turns on formal relations in its numbering system (see Lange, 1989, ch.1).

Ad (2). I have said that one part of the internal motivation for the discussion of solipsism in the *Tractatus* can be gathered from a close reading of the first proposition in TLP 5.631, which says that "the thinking, representing, subject does not exist." According to conventional punctuation in German, the comma after "representing" would be redundant if the expression had *only* an elucidatory meaning. The "way of ideas" of traditional epistemology and of Schopenhauer conceived of representing predominantly as imagining. On this understanding, representing and thinking form a contrasting pair. Wittgenstein builds on a superior conception of representing which is part of the Kantian tradition (alongside with the inferior one just mentioned). He conceived of representing as thinking and of thinking as a "kind of language" (NB 12.09.16). On this understanding, thinking does not contrast with representing but elucidates it.

Accordingly, I propose to read 5.631 thus: there exists neither a *thinking* subject, which could be thought to be implied by the *Tractatus*-conception of the use of language (to be explained below), nor a *representing* subject, as advocated by early modern epistemology and Schopenhauer. Wittgenstein's discussion of solipsism is meant to treat of both conceptions of the subject, the epistemological one being of relevance, for Wittgenstein, only in relation to Schopenhauer.

There is another salient point concerning punctuation at the end of TLP 5.631. It is the long hyphen at the end of that remark, which is the sixth of 12 separately numbered remarks. The hyphen therefore marks the middle of that passage. This hyphen is a unique occurrence in the *Tractatus*, being placed at the end of a remark and before the next numbered remark begins. (Other hyphens occur within numbered remarks only; see e.g., 3.031, 3.141, 4.002, 4.441, 5.4731, 5.553, 5.5563, 6.31.) The hyphen after 5.631 is designed to indicate that the subject as "a limit," which Wittgenstein deals with in the second part of the 12 numbered remarks under 5.6, is different from the one said not to exist in 5.631. That Wittgenstein was very conscious of formal features such as punctuation in his polished texts can be seen from several remarks on style published in

Culture and Value (see especially his remark from 1947, according to which he tried to induce slow reading by making extensive use of punctuation signs; cf. Chapter 2, WITTGENSTEIN'S TEXTS AND STYLE). The division of the passage by the long hyphen after 5.631 into two parts, each containing six separately numbered remarks, is a first insight into the structure of the text of the *Tractatus* 5.6 s, to which I shall now turn.

2   Wittgenstein on Solipsism in the *Tractatus*

Wittgenstein's overarching aim in the *Tractatus* is to delimit sense by expounding the limits for the expression of thoughts in language (preface). In the passages that come before TLP 5.6, Wittgenstein identifies limits to the expression of thoughts in language set by logic – he calls tautology the "inner" and contradiction the "outer" limit (5.143) – and by the empirical meaning of all propositions proper. To continue Wittgenstein's use of spatial metaphors, empirical meaning is the "lower" limit of sense, given by the totality of objects and showing itself in the totality of elementary propositions. To this limit of empirical reality (5.5561) there corresponds an "upper" limit of sense, which is the subject as a limit of the world (5.632), the "metaphysical subject" (5.633) or "philosophical I" (5.641) that survives the Tractarian critique of solipsism.

There is a more specific reason for the discussion of solipsism than the reference to Schopenhauer discussed above. It is necessitated by the implicit mental dimension of the *Tractatus* account of language. Although deeply influenced by Frege's anti-psychologism, Wittgenstein's conception of the use of language in the *Tractatus* is nonetheless mentalistic (cf. Chapter 32, WITTGENSTEIN ON INTENTIONALITY). He tacitly postulates a language of thought in which the complete logical analysis of propositions necessary for their sense to be determinate (the demand of determinateness of sense – 3.23) already operates in each case in which the sense of a proposition is thought. According to TLP 3.11, thinking the sense of the proposition is the method of its projection. Who does the projecting, who thinks, if a thinking subject does not exist? Wittgenstein's answer is: no one! Rather, there is a sequence of sentences in the language of thought, and these sentences are intrinsically representative. This raises the question of why we are not aware of thinking such a sequence of sentences. And here Wittgenstein was the first to take refuge in the beloved resort of later proponents of language-of-thought hypotheses: tacit knowledge (cf. TLP 5.5562). At this point, he already thought that propositions in the language of thought cannot be taken to consist of words, but rather of unknown elements (see Letter to Russell, 19 August 1919) whose concatenations must be taken "to have the structure of sentences under analysis" (Harman, 1973, p.67). Wittgenstein's later self-critique at one point intimates that he thought of the "inner process of analysis" (Malcolm, 1986, pp.74–5; also chs VI–VII) as an "unconscious process," in analogy to Freud's psychoanalysis (Z §444; cf. BB 42, and PI §81).

There is plenty of evidence for Wittgenstein's postulation of a language of thought hypothesis in his writings immediately before and after the *Tractatus* (NB 12.9.16; Letter to Russell, 19 August 1919) as well as in his later self-critique (MS 108, p.277; BB 42; PG 152; PI §§81, 98, 102; Z §444). However, that hypothesis is not as evident in the text of the *Tractatus*: there it is mainly a structural implication of the order of exposition in the text. The notion of a thought is treated in the 3 s, that of a proposition from 4 onward. But the concept of an elementary proposition is given a sustained treatment both in the 3.2 s and in the 4.2 s. As Wittgenstein's text is remarkable for its ambition to avoid any redundancy, this calls for explanation; all the more so, given that the concept of an elementary proposition is the only operative concept of systematic relevance treated twice in the text. (Of course, "logic" and "philosophy" are also treated more than once; but this is due not to the demands of construction for the philosophical system, but to the reflexive character of the text as philosophical.) In the sections following 3.2 (3.201 to 3.263), elementary propositions are treated as elements of a language of thought. This is clear from the fact that they are placed under the general theme begun in 3, viz., "the thought." In the sections following 4.2 (4.21 to 4.28), they are treated as elements of an analytical notation to be developed for spoken and written language. (This argument for reading the idea of a language of thought into the *Tractatus* is premised on the supposition that Wittgenstein not only stated the difference between what can be said and what can only be shown or shows itself – the "cardinal problem of philosophy" (Letter to Russell, 19 August 1919) – but also made use of it in his exposition, despite many violations of the principle. That there is a language of thought in the *Tractatus* is primarily shown, not said.)

But in one place the hypothesis of a language of thought is more clearly implied; namely, in Wittgenstein's sketch of an analysis of propositions attributing propositional attitudes (5.541 to 5.5422), which is presented in order to deal with a counterexample to the thesis of extensionality (5–5.01). The form of propositional-attitude ascriptions is said to imply not a coordination of a fact ("p") and an "object" (the subject "A" in "A judges p"), but a coordination of facts by means of the coordination of their objects (5.5421). The immediate consequence is that, because thoughts are facts, there is a language of thought (pictures in general being facts, 2.141). The implication of the form of thoughts is said to show that there is no soul or subject as it is conceived in superficial psychology (5.5421), because the analysis shows the subject to be no unitary entity.

The main negative thesis of the discussion of solipsism underlines this consequence of the propositional form for philosophical conceptions of the subject (5.631). Consequently, it is meant to forestall the misunderstanding that, because a language of thought is operated in thinking the sense of a proposition, there must also be a thinking subject. This contrasts with the active conception of the subject in Kant, for example, whose central contention had been that synthesis is always a performance (*Verrichtung*) of the subject but never given in the (perception of an) object (Kant, 1781/87, B135). Schopenhauer had criticized the Kantian conception, thinking of the subject, which is the bearer of the "world as idea," as a perspective associated with a process of thinking. In the last analysis, this was thought to be a physiological process in the brain ([1818/59] 1966, vol.2, ch.18). In the *Tractatus*, the process of thinking is the process of operating the mental calculus of analysis (see PI §81; BB 71; and Malcolm 1986, ch. VII: "The inner process of analysis.").

Schopenhauer's conception of the subject is an intricate one. Schopenhauer thought that the subject is necessarily incarnated in the body and somehow identical with the will – this identity being the unexplainable "world-knot" (*Weltknoten*) and the philosophical truth κατ' εξοχήν (*par excellence*) (especially [1818/59] 1966, vol.1, sec.18). In the "immediate experience" of willing and acting this could be known to be the thing-in-itself for every thinking being. Wittgenstein's critique of this unfathomable unity of theoretical ego and will was to deny that there is a logical relation between will and world even though there is a logical relation between "a limit" of the world and the world (TLP 6.373–4). In Schopenhauer's metaphysics there is a logical relation between will and world, because the will should be the "thing-it itself," necessarily appearing in everything, although as a metaphysical principle it is designated in a "denominatio a potiori." Even though inanimate objects do not have a will strictly speaking, Schopenhauer metaphysically applies that term to them because of the analogy to the human will. For Wittgenstein, subject and will are distinct. Even the ethical will is distinct from the subject. For, while the subject merely correlates to the world as a perspective, the ethical will is thought of as active, because it should change the world's limits (TLP 6.423–6.43; cf. Finch, 1971, p.151).

Even if we assume that the issue of a thinking subject in relation to the language of thought provides the internal rationale for the discussion of solipsism, the contentious question remains: does the *Tractatus* defend a kind of solipsism?

There is a consensus about this: Wittgenstein's position in the book is not straightforwardly solipsistic, as the term "solipsism" first occurs in 5.62, where Wittgenstein asks "to what extent" there is truth in solipsism and not whether solipsism is true.

There are two external hermeneutic reasons for reading the text from an anti-solipsistic perspective. The first relates to Schopenhauer, from whom Wittgenstein took not only the theme of solipsism but also a critical perspective on it. Schopenhauer saw theoretical egoism as an extreme version of skepticism and compared it to a fortress whose garrison cannot be conquered, but which cannot leave its abode either ([1818/59] 1966, vol.1, sec.19). In this picture the pragmatic refutation of solipsism is hidden: to an avowal of solipsism in conversation one could retort "why do you tell us, if we can't hear, let alone understand you?" This retort is correct insofar as it points out the pragmatic contradiction in which a solipsist's avowal is caught. But it is the kind of "common-sense answer" (cf. BB 58) that does not solve the problem; it can only silence the solipsist, not cure her. Schopenhauer, though, saw the solipsist as being in need of therapy, not of refutation. Wittgenstein may have drawn from this the natural motivation to look for a problem-solving answer to the solipsist. Indeed, he had reasons to understand Schopenhauer himself as a solipsist *malgré lui*. Schopenhauer was quite candid about the fact that there was only one assumption that saved him from solipsism: the assumption that there is at least one perceived object that is something in itself and not only for others. If this were not so, all perceived objects would be mere ideas and this would lead to theoretical egoism, in which all reality vanishes and the world becomes a mere subjective phantasm ([1818/59] 1966, vol.1, sec.19; vol.2, ch.18). And Schopenhauer's assumption turned on the singular position of the body in which the cognizing subject is located and in whose willing and action the will as the thing-in-itself should be manifest to every subject. It was precisely this assumption, however, that seemed untenable to Wittgenstein. At the same time, he tried to avoid solipsism in a different manner. The subject of representation to which the world reduces is a mere point of reference and solipsism collapses into realism. In this fashion, his criticism of Schopenhauer led him from solipsism to realism (cf. NB 2.9.16, 15.10.16; TLP 5.64; see also below).

The other semi-external hermeneutic reason for giving an anti-solipsistic reading of the treatment of solipsism in the *Tractatus* relates to Wittgenstein's own development (for a general account of this, see Chapter 1, WITTGENSTEIN'S PHILOSOPHICAL DEVELOPMENT). His solution in the *Tractatus* makes use of a comparison between the relation of the eye to the visual field and the relation of the metaphysical subject to the world (5.633–1). But exactly the same comparison shows up in the later treatment of solipsism, which is universally regarded as conclusively critical. The simplest hermeneutic proposal is arguably to take the occurrence of the picture in the *Tractatus* as indicating a critical stance as well.

However, the case for a qualified solipsistic interpretation has been found *prima facie* overwhelming (Glock, 1996, p.349) for the following reasons: Wittgenstein not only seems to find some kernel of truth in solipsism, but also states that what solipsism "means is quite correct" (5.62) and seems to say "in propria persona" that "world and life are one" (5.621) and that "I am my world. (The microcosm.)" (5.63). And in the *Notebooks* this interpretation finds "purple passages which identify the world with life, life with consciousness in general, and consciousness with the metaphysical self" (Glock, 1996, p.349).

This reading can be found compelling, however, only if one fails to take into account the development in Wittgenstein's views on solipsism in the *Notebooks*. When the theme is mentioned there for the first time (23.5.15), the question asked is not whether, but to what extent, solipsism is true. Whether or not he started as a solipsist, however, by 1916 he declared himself to have made the journey from idealism via solipsism to strict realism (NB 15.10.16) because idealism and solipsism "strictly thought out" lead to pure realism. The reason for this change is that Wittgenstein had come to dismiss the singular position of the body of the cognizing subject in Schopenhauer's thought – the thesis that my body is given to me not as part of the world, but in the immediate "experience" of willing (NB 2.9.16, 12.10.16, 4.11.16). Wittgenstein came to opt for the givenness of my body only as part of the world; and this, he said, led him to realism. The first solipsistic-sounding remark in the *Tractatus* (5.621) for Wittgenstein "in propria persona" no longer appears to be rationally warranted, as soon as the Schopenhauerian reasoning from the special position of the subject's body as the *locus* of manifestation of the thing-in-itself is given up. For "my body" then belongs with the rest of reality as one part of it; a part which has no privileged position (NB 12.9.16, 12.10.16). In TLP 5.621 Wittgenstein should be read as citing the position he criticizes. This is "shown" by the numbering of the remark, which makes it a comment to 5.62 with lower "logical weight." The proposed interpretation as an implicit quote claims to make explicit what the text only "shows" by subordinating 5.621 as a comment on 5.62 as a formulation of the position. (For a fuller defense of this reading of TLP 5.621, see Lange, 1989, pp.81–3.) The second solipsistic-sounding remark ("5.63 I am my world") can be given a reading consonant with his novel position.

Looking at the text from an anti-solipsistic perspective, then, Wittgenstein can be seen to find four faults with solipsism. First, in formulating its own position in epistemological terms, solipsism does not say what, according to Wittgenstein, it should say. The following must be charitably attributed to the solipsist: "that the world is *my* world" (5.62). (Here I take "I mean to say" as equivalent to "I want to say," and "he means to say" as equivalent to "he should say.") Prior to the *Tractatus*, no solipsist had given her view this formulation. To say that what she "means" is quite right is therefore a criticism. Second, the solipsist tries to say what cannot be said but only shown – that the world is *my* world, because the limits of language (*der Sprache*, that is, with definite article) (the only language I understand) indicate the limits of my world (5.62). Thirdly, the subject, whose uniqueness the epistemological solipsist must assert, simply does not exist (5.631). What exists is the theme of the second part of the text after the salient hyphen. It is the extensionless point as a limit to the world (the "upper" bound of sense), a mere perspective of experience and judgment associated with the microcosm (5.63) that, as a mosaic of thoughts (and therefore no "soul," no subject as a unitary entity; cf. 5.5421), corresponds to the macrocosm of the world, that is a mosaic, namely the totality of facts. (The picture of a "mosaic" was invented by Black, 1964, p.37; and with good reason, because the totality of thoughts/facts is said to show "a picture of the world", 3.01.) And, fourthly, solipsism, in its corrected formulation concerning the relation of language and the world, coincides with pure realism. This gives a reason from philosophical methodology for the anti-solipsistic reading: in philosophical dialectic the demonstration that a position cannot be distinguished from its diametrical opposite should certainly be understood as a critique of the position.

These four faults found in solipsism are so many reasons for an anti-solipsistic reading of the 5.6s. A fifth reason is a coherentist one: solipsism, as a radicalization of idealism, has skeptical implications (idealism denying the independence of the "outer world"; solipsism denying the existence of other conscious beings as well). But skepticism – being not irrefutable (as both Schopenhauer and Russell said about solipsism), but outright meaningless (6.51) – is given short shrift, even in the *Tractatus*. Wittgenstein treated skepticism exactly as Schopenhauer treated solipsism: he dismissed it as meaningless and in need of therapy, not refutation. Would it not be contradictory if he treated solipsism otherwise? (That he did not treat it in a single remark is due to the internal rationale explained above.)

Is the solipsistic reading interpretatively charitable? Not if a superior alternative is available. David Pears has proposed such an alternative: one that marks the difference mentioned in the introduction between "solipsism" and "theoretical egoism" in an explanation of meaning that remains faithful to the etymology of "solipsism." Wittgenstein's subject as *a*, not *the*, "limit of the world," although called the "metaphysical self" or the "philosophical I" for dialectical reasons, is simply not an "ipse" (self) and is not "solus" (alone, unique). Pears therefore called Wittgenstein's position "sliding-peg egocentrism" (Pears, 1988/9). That there is a difference between this view, which allows for the existence of several a-personal subjects of representation, and solipsism proper can only be denied if one equates "solipsistic" with "egocentristic" (which Wittgenstein himself unfortunately did at one point; see MS 147, p.18r). But in the later contexts he also said that solipsism is on the way to destroying the illusion that the focus on words in language and linguistic representation neglects the world behind the words – an illusion which is behind the desperate move to identify "idea" (representation) and "world" and therefore embrace solipsism (LPE 297; PO 255).

Even if he intended to give a critique of solipsism in the *Tractatus*, intention does not, of course, imply success. And although Wittgenstein did not present a version of solipsism (such as the "egoless transcendental solipsism" combined, as in Kant, with empirical realism attributed to him by Hacker, 1972/86, ch.4), his position is too closely related to the solipsism that has haunted modern epistemology since Descartes.

3 Wittgenstein on Solipsism in the "Blue Book"

In his second critique of solipsism, which is found in the "Blue Book," Wittgenstein follows a three-step-strategy. First, he provides four distinct explicit formulations of epistemological solipsism, showing how each one transgresses the bounds of sense. Secondly, he offers a telling redescription of what the solipsist is really doing in trying to convey her conviction. And thirdly, he offers an explanation of how one may be tempted by solipsism – an illness of the understanding though it is – namely as a result of misunderstanding the use of the first-person pronoun. As Wittgenstein was fond of comparing his philosophical therapies to psychoanalysis (cf. BT 410; see Chapter 43, WITTGENSTEIN AND PSYCHOANALYSIS), the three steps (which in the text are taken in a different order) can be compared to anamnesis, the interpretation of symptoms, and the presentation of the whole case given by analysts to their colleagues.

The four formulations of solipsism are as follows:

(a) "When anything is seen (really *seen*), it is always I who see it" (BB 61).
(b) "Always when anything is seen, something is seen" (BB 63).
(c) "'whenever anything is seen, it is *this* which is seen', accompanying the word 'this' by a gesture embracing my visual field (but not meaning by 'this' the particular objects which I happen to see at the moment)" (BB 64).
(d) "'Only what I see (or: see now) is really seen' for which the variant is 'I am the vessel of life'" (BB 64–5).

I cannot follow Wittgenstein's dialectic in minute detail here (see, however, Lange, 1989, pp.124–8). In summary, one can say: the movement from (a) to (d) is, as it were, a movement from subject to object, in spite of the reappearance of "I" in (d). And it is a movement from senselessness to speechlessness. (a) is discarded in favor of (b) on account of a discussion of the normal criteria of personal identity in which it is shown that the solipsist's use of "I" does not serve to indicate an individual person, "but the experience of seeing itself" (BB 63). This also accounts for the insufficiency of (b), which is not *per se* solipsistic, but is a step in the dialectic with the solipsist interlocutor. It is insufficient for the solipsist's purposes, because the expression "something" is liable to be understood as meaning a particular object or situation. (c) seems to express the "experience of seeing itself," but it has to be admitted that pointing to the visual field is meaningless, because it is deprived of its normal contexts. In normal contexts, pointing, like the use of personal and other pronouns, has "neighbors" for what is pointed to or indicated. The visual field has no neighbors: it is not something individual, but a formal trait in the seeing of everyone capable of seeing (perceiving) at all. This leads to (d). There the "I" reappears, yet it cannot mean a specific person but only a metaphysical entity. And Wittgenstein comments that, for logical reasons, nobody is able to understand this utterance: "It should be meaningless, not false, to say that he [sc. the hearer] understands me" (BB 65). Intending not to be understood amounts to saying nothing, and hence the solipsist is condemned to silence: "Thus my expression is one of the many which is used on various occasions by philosophers and supposed to convey something to the person who says it, though essentially incapable of conveying anything to anyone else" (BB 65). (d) would belong to a "private" language and it is merely assumed in the "Blue Book" that a "private" language understandable to its user alone is not possible. This was later demonstrated in the private language argument (PI §§243ff; cf., LPE 287, 292; PO 234, 241–3; see Chapter 28, PRIVACY AND PRIVATE LANGUAGE). But the idea of a "private" language is already touched upon in the form of the possibility that the solipsist might express herself by using drawings of a perceived situation made by several perceivers and saying of the one she produced herself that it alone was derived from reality (BB 72; cf. PI §292).

In Wittgenstein's diagnosis of what the solipsist is really doing in formulating her conviction, the autonomy of grammar is presupposed (see Chapter 15, THE AUTONOMY OF GRAMMAR). This was the central semantic insight of his self-critical transformation of the metaphysical system of the *Tractatus* into the descriptive clarification of sense of the later work. Among other things, this conception implies that there are justifications *within* language-games only, and not *for* language-games. This insight plays a double role. It is used to make a concession to the solipsist, but also used to point out her mistake. On the one hand, Wittgenstein has to concede that the changes of grammar which the solipsist proposes to make are, although perhaps very uncomfortable, nevertheless possible. The solipsist claims a singular position for her experience. If I, as a solipsist, claimed that "only my pain is real pain," then others could say of me that "There is real pain" and that other people "behave as Ernst Michael Lange behaves, when there is real pain." Furthermore, they would have to adjust their language to an account for simulated pain. This would be awkward, but it is a possible notation. The solipsist's mistake, on the other hand, is to look for and to try to give justifications for the notation accommodating her singular position. For this is not possible on account of the aforementioned implication of the autonomy of grammar that no system of description can be justified on the basis that it is more suitable to represent the facts (cf. BB 59–60, 66). The solipsist fights the operative conventions for the use of certain expressions, but with reasons that are not really available:

> The man who says 'only my pain is real' doesn't mean to say that he has found out by the common criteria [...] that the others who said they had pain were cheating. But what he rebels against is the use of *this* expression with *these* criteria. That is, he objects to using this word in the particular way in which it is commonly used. On the other hand, he is not aware that he is objecting to a convention. He sees a way of dividing the country different from the one used on the ordinary map. He feels tempted, say, to use the name "Devonshire" not for the county with its conventional boundary, but for a region differently bounded. He could express this by saying: "Isn't it absurd to make *this* a county, to draw the boundaries *here?*" But what he says is: "The *real* Devonshire is this". We could answer: "What you want is only a new notation, and by a new notation no facts of geography are changed". (BB 57)

The diagnosis of the solipsist's illness of the understanding says that she looks for justifications where none are to be had and therefore objects to conventions of expression that, on account of the autonomy of grammar, cannot and need not be justified.

The third step is to explain how solipsism is possible. Wittgenstein finds the explanation in the use of psychological predicates without criteria in the first-person present-tense – more specifically, in the use of the first-person pronoun to mean "I as subject" as opposed to "I as object" (see also Chapter 30, WITTGENSTEIN ON "I" AND THE SELF, and Chapter 29, THE INNER AND THE OUTER). The objective use of "I" occurs in propositions such as "I am 1.80 m tall," while the subjective use occurs in propositions such as "I see so-and-so." The putative difference is given a scintillating formulation: "The man who cries out with pain, or says that he has pain, *doesn't choose the mouth which says it*" (BB 68; cf. LPE 310–11; PO 274). To this, one only can retort: the man who says "I am 1.80 m tall" *does not do this either*.

Technically, the peculiarity of the use of "I" with psychological predicates in the first-person present-tense – the usage that Wittgenstein singles out as the subjective use – has been called immunity against referential failure through misidentification. But this diagnostic description presupposes that "I" should be understood as a referring expression in the first place. In fact, "I" is better understood as an *indicator*. By using this expression I do not want to commit myself to any technical explication of the concept, but merely to take up Wittgenstein's own comparison of using "I" to raising one's hand before giving an answer in a classroom. Just as by raising one's hand one shows that one wants to answer a question and so enables the teacher to call one out; so the use of "I" enables others to refer to the person who uses it by means of objective referring expressions (names or definite descriptions) by which the first-person pronoun must be replaced to form third-person ascriptions according to the prevailing conventions of use. By the use of "I" alone the person does not *refer* to himself: he only indicates to whom one should refer. The man who says "I am 1.80 m tall" cannot be in error about whom he is speaking about, but at best about his height (the only difference being that the man who sincerely utters "I am in pain" can not only not be in error about whom he means, but cannot be in error about being in pain either). The alleged difference between a subjective and an objective use of "I" boils down to a difference between the verification conditions of predicates and the fact that first-person, present-tense uses of psychological predicates have no verification conditions because here the truthfulness of the utterer guarantees the truth of the corresponding third-person ascriptions (PPF §319). Peter Hacker has proposed the following picture for distinguishing between objectively referring expressions and the indicator "I": while names and definite descriptions aim at and often hit a target, the use of "I" merely marks the target that can be hit by a referring expression that is to be substituted for the indicator in third-person and other objective uses (Hacker, 1972/86, p.236).

Since I criticize Wittgenstein in this respect, I owe an explanation as to how he could go wrong, if I accept the third step of his critique. I think the reason is to be found in the very demand for an explanation of how solipsism is possible. Wittgenstein believed that in treating philosophical errors one cannot proceed cautiously enough because they contain so much truth (Z §460). In his second treatment of solipsism, by singling out the use of "I" as subject and denying that it designates a person at all, Wittgenstein therefore proceeded *too* cautiously in order to capture the truth in the illusory philosophical conception he alluded to in the following remark:

> We feel that in the cases in which "I" is used as subject, we don't use it, because we recognize a particular person by his bodily characteristics; and this creates the illusion that we use this word to refer to something bodiless, which, however, has its seat in our body. In fact this seems to be the real ego, the one of which it was said, "Cogito, ergo sum". (BB 69)

But if the indicator-conception as glossed by Hacker's picture of the target is correct, then, *pace* Wittgenstein, a person is *indicated* in the use of "I" with psychological predicates in the present-tense after all because of the rules for the substitution of the indicator by names and definite descriptions. Wittgenstein sometimes mentions these substitution relations (PI §410; cf. LSD 32–3) but never investigates them, let alone describe them in full. Yet his own later context principle, with its holistic scope ("the meaning of a word is its use *in the language*," PI §43, emphasis added; or "in the run of thoughts and life," Z §173), should have motivated him to do so. His second critique of solipsism is nevertheless successful, as long as all the points made in the first two steps can be upheld. The misfiring how-possible explanation can be replaced by the explanatory aspect of the redescription given in the second step. The solipsist is right in thinking that other conventions of description are possible (and this explains how her position can seem possible), but wrong in attempting to justify her proposals as "more true to the facts" (and this shows that her position is impossible after all).

4 Critique of Solipsism and the Self that Takes Responsibility for a Judgment

The solipsist who is driven to silence in the "Blue Book" is of the epistemological kind. He is not a version of Kant's "I think" or of the metaphysical self of the *Tractatus*. The allusion to Descartes's *Cogito* near the end of Wittgenstein's second critique of solipsism (BB 69) shows that Wittgenstein intended to criticize the metaphysical variant too. But his critique remains undeveloped.

There are two main reasons why Wittgenstein didn't even feel the need to retract his own construction of the metaphysical self as a limit to the world. The first is that the metaphysical self as limit was itself the result of a critique of the more full-blooded conceptions of Descartes, Kant, and Schopenhauer. For that critique reduced the actively thinking theoretical subject of the idealist tradition to an extensionless point, a mere perspective necessarily associated with the mental calculus, in which the sense of propositions is thought by being made determinate in sense through logical analysis. This explains how Wittgenstein could think that it sufficed, in order to reaffirm that a thinking subject doesn't exist (in analogy to the ("geometrical") eye in relation to the field of vision), to extend this explicitly to the metaphysical self in relation to language of his own former theory (MS 109, p.31; cf. TLP 5.633–1), and then to start from scratch with a new critique of solipsism. The second reason is this: in his self-critique, Wittgenstein separated the language-of-thought hypothesis, which provides the internal motivation for the discussion of solipsism in the *Tractatus*, from his later discussion of solipsism. The hypothesis is discarded on the grounds that it is not explanatory. A language of thought stands just as much in need of interpretation as a public language (see PG 152; BB 42). The Tractarian motivation for discussing the metaphysical subject thus disappears.

But it can easily be seen that the metaphysical subject, or theoretical ego, was in need of a separate treatment: unlike the solipsism discussed in the "Blue Book," the solipsism of the metaphysical subject does not simply propose a new convention of description (and try, fallaciously, to justify it as being true to the facts): it is also supposed to play a foundational role in the justification of knowledge. Kant's "I think," for instance, was the highest point of such attempts to give justification (on which even logic was thought to depend; Kant, 1781/87, B134, note). The "Blue Book" critique of solipsism, with its allusion to the *Cogito*, captures, at best, the function of a theoretical ego as the most explicit form of consciousness, but not its justificatory role for claims to knowledge. If the *Cogito* or "I think" were to be understood as illusory, this would have to be shown independently.

Wittgenstein's later philosophy only needs supplementation on one point in order to provide all the elements required for such an independent argument. Wittgenstein repeatedly pointed out that the use of a word tends to become metaphysical when removed from its normal contexts of utterance and when not considered in contrast to alternative words (cf. BB 46). In the metaphysical use of "I," the word is considered in isolation from the other personal pronouns and from its substitution relations to names and definite descriptions. And the word "think" in "I think" is isolated from the connections and contrasts to other cognitive verbs (cf. PI §§95–7). Moreover, the metaphysical use of "think" runs up against a fact of grammar (see Chapter 14, GRAMMAR AND GRAMMATICAL STATEMENTS), namely that the verb "to think" has no expressive first-person, present-tense use like, for instance, "being in pain" (cf. RPP II §§12, 231; also

Chapter 29, THE INNER AND THE OUTER). By contrast to the avowal "I am in pain," the avowal "I think that so-and-so" should be taken as withholding the endorsement of a claim. That is the reason why the "I" in the "I think" of epistemology cannot indicate an individual person. But then why call it the "subject thinking in us" (Kant, 1781/87, B770), the ego inhabiting a body, that Wittgenstein thought to be abolished (LPE 282; PO 225)? Why at all call it "I"?

What is needed, according to the second step of Wittgenstein's critical method vis-à-vis the solipsist in the "Blue Book," is a redescription of what is really being done in ascribing a foundational role to the "I think." Paradoxically, Wittgenstein was prevented from giving such a redescription because he also tended to deflate the singular role of "I." As he wrote (MS 109, p. 31; LPE 307), his strategy in dealing with solipsism was to reduce everything to the misunderstanding of the role of "I" (see also Chapter 30, WITTGENSTEIN ON "I" AND THE SELF). And this strategy, he thought, implied that there is no difference between "I" and "this" or "that." According to him, none of them are "signals" used to call attention to a place or a person (PI §410). As I have shown for the elusive subjective use of "I," this is wrong. "I" indicates a person in this use. And of course the alternative "place or person" is far from being exhaustive. For a critique of the theoretical ego, the possibility could be investigated that "I" calls attention to different roles, functions, or statuses of the utterer when used in connection with different cognitive predicates. Every use of "I" calls attention to the speaker and presents him as language-user. As the understanding is the faculty of judgment, the "I think" in Kant and early modern epistemology should be understood in relation to the language-game of judging or making truth claims. The one who says "I think that...," "I judge that...," "I assert that..." is making a truth claim and thereby implies that he is following the rules of this game. What are these rules? I think that Kant made an attractive proposal that can be used to state the rules of the judgment-game when he stated the maxims of enlightened thinking in section 40 of his *Critique of Judgment* (1790/2008). These maxims are: thinking oneself, thinking in place of everyone else capable of judgment, and thinking consistently. The one who judges is expected to stand up for her claims, to defend them, and to retract them if they are refuted. That is what thinking oneself consists in, within the game of making truth claims. Furthermore, the one who judges is expected to adjust her claims to what everyone who is capable of judgment, and is good-willed and well informed, could uphold under comparable conditions. That is what thinking in place of everyone else consists in within the game of making truth claims. And not to contradict oneself, finally, is a general condition of sense – not merely in the game of making truth claims.

If this is even remotely correct, then the following redescription of what is really being done in assigning a foundational role to the "I think" in epistemology can be given. The epistemologist mistakenly interprets the claims that a speaker necessarily makes according to the rules of the game of judging as structural conditions of the faculty of understanding. The theoretical ego is therefore no empirical "I," but, as it were, the fusion of the "I" of the empirical subject of judging and the "she" of a ratification of the judgment by other empirical subjects. But no one and no theoretical construction can preempt the ratification of truth claims by simply fulfilling the function of the theoretical ego. That is why the theoretical ego is spurious, an illegitimate projection that is apt to mislead us about the normative character of our games of judgment.

The "I think" of epistemology in its foundational role was already the "sliding-peg" ego-center that Pears identified as the metaphysical subject of the *Tractatus*. As a philosophical error or illusion, Wittgenstein would have wanted to treat it cautiously because of the truth contained in it. What is this kernel of truth? I think the truth is this. The distortion of the use of "I," which constitutes the construction of the foundational "I think," reflects a limit for every empirical subject of judgment: the empirical subject cannot make his claim and at the same time observe himself making it from a third-person perspective (cf. TS 228, pp. 560–2). The very condition of the impossibility of a theoretical ego – i.e., that it cannot preempt the rational reaction of other subjects; that there is no view from nowhere – is at the same time an exoneration of the empirical subject of judgment. He must do his best in making his claim, but must not aspire to a view from nowhere. When his claim is stated as conscientiously as possible, he can leave everything else to the ongoing rational debate.

Wittgenstein himself could have said so, but did not. He could have, because he ultimately criticized as meaningless the theoretical self-consciousness of epistemology, which is a reflexive enhancement of the "I think": "It is right to say 'I know what you think,' and wrong: 'I know what I think.' (A whole cloud of philosophy condensed in a drop of grammar.)" (PPF § 315) (This idea does not depend on accepting Wittgenstein's noncognitive account of avowals, but only on his observation that "to think" has no present-tense, first-person expressive use in connection with a critique of iterated reflexivities.) He did not say so, because of contingencies in the ways he went about deconstructing the metaphysical system of the *Tractatus* (see Chapter 12, METAPHYSICS: FROM INEFFABILITY TO NORMATIVITY). But these cannot detract from the impressive example of intellectual truthfulness that Wittgenstein set in his thorough critique of his magnificent first book.

References

Anscombe, G.E.M. (1959/63). *An Introduction to Wittgenstein's Tractatus*. Second edition. London: Hutchinson. (Cited from Hutchinson edition, 1971.)
Finch, H.L. (1971). *Wittgenstein: The Early Philosophy*. New York: Humanities Press.
Glock, H.-J. (1996). *A Wittgenstein Dictionary*. Oxford: Blackwell.
Hacker, P.M.S. (1972/86). *Insight and Illusion: Themes in the Philosophy of Wittgenstein*. Revised edition. Oxford: Clarendon Press.
Hacker, P.M.S. (2001). Philosophy. In H.-J. Glock. *Wittgenstein: A Critical Reader* (pp. 322–347). Oxford: Blackwell.
Harman, G. (1973). *Thought*. Princeton: Princeton University Press.
Kant, I. (1781/87). *Kritik der reinen Vernunft*. Riga: J.F. Hartknoch.
Kant, I. (1790/2008) *Critique of Judgment*. Ed. N. Walker. Trans. J.C. Meredith. Oxford: Oxford University Press.
Lange, E.M. (1989). *Wittgenstein und Schopenhauer*. [Wittgenstein and Schopenhauer.] Cuxhaven: Junghans.
Malcolm, N. (1986). *Nothing is Hidden: Wittgenstein's Criticism of His Early Thought*. Oxford: Oxford University Press.
McGuinness, B. (1988). *Wittgenstein: A Life. Young Ludwig 1889–1921*. Berkeley: University of California Press.
Pears, D. (1972). Wittgenstein's Treatment of Solipsism in the *Tractatus*. *Critica*, 6, 57–80.
Pears, D. (1988/9). *The False Prison*. Two volumes. Oxford: Oxford University Press.
Rhees, R. (1947). Critical Notice of Maurice Cornforth, *Science versus Idealism*. *Mind*, 56, 374–392.
Schopenhauer, A. ([1818/59] 1966). *The World as Will and Representation*. Trans. E.F.J. Payne. New York: Dover. (Original work published 1818/59.)
Wuchterl, K. and Hübner, A. (1979). *Wittgenstein*. Hamburg: Rowohlt.

Further Reading

Brandom, R.B. (2015). *Wiedererinnerter Idealismus.* [Re-remembered Idealism.] Frankfurt: Suhrkamp.

Glock, H.-J. (1999). Schopenhauer and Wittgenstein: Representation as Language and Will. In C. Janaway (Ed.). *The Cambridge Companion to Schopenhauer* (pp.422–458). Cambridge: Cambridge University Press.

Moore, A. (2013). Was the Author of the *Tractatus* a Transcendental Idealist?. In M. Potter and P. Sullivan (Eds). *Wittgenstein's Tractatus: History and Interpretation* (pp.239–255). Oxford: Oxford University Press.

Schneider, H.J. (2013). *Wittgenstein's Later Theory of Meaning: Imagination and Calculation.* Oxford: Wiley-Blackwell.

Sullivan, P. (2013). Idealism in Wittgenstein: A Further Reply to Moore. In M. Potter and P. Sullivan (Eds). *Wittgenstein's Tractatus: History and Interpretation* (pp.256–270). Oxford: Oxford University Press.

von Wright, G.H. (1969). The Wittgenstein Papers. Reprinted in G.H. von Wright. (1982). *Wittgenstein.* Oxford: Blackwell.

10

Resolute Readings of the *Tractatus*

JAMES CONANT AND SILVER BRONZO

1 Introduction

A spectator of the passing philosophical scene, recently encountering the current controversy about "resolute readings" of the *Tractatus*, might be forgiven for finding it difficult to figure out what the debate is supposed to be about and who exactly is on which side and why. A superficial glance at the debate, if viewed from a considerable distance, might yield the impression that it involves two major parties: those who represent some sort of new movement in which they advocate a (so-called) "resolute reading" of the book (whatever that is), and those who represent an old guard and take themselves to oppose any such reading. If the spectator moves only slightly further in and takes a closer look, the debate will begin to seem to involve at least three kinds of protagonist: the old sort of reader, the allegedly newfangled sort, and those who take themselves to occupy an alleged middle ground between "traditional" and "resolute" readers of the book. A yet closer look, however, ought to begin to cast doubt on the assumption that the parties to this debate can properly be sorted along a single spectrum – say, a spectrum of those who are comparatively traditional, those who are comparatively revolutionary, and those who are simply somewhere in the middle between those two extremes.

Our aim, in this chapter, is not to attempt to strengthen the case for any particular approach to the *Tractatus*, but to demonstrate, through a reconstruction of some relevant features of "the" debate, that at this point there are in fact several orthogonal debates taking place, confusedly cast as contributions to a single debate. In so doing, we will indicate some of the respects in which the term "resolute reading" has come to acquire different meanings – and sometimes even (what one might term) a different logic. By thus tracing the shifts in the meaning of the term "resolute reading" and the related family of cognate and contrastive expressions, and thereby also tracing correlative shifts in the contours of the ongoing debate, we hope to remove certain obstacles to genuine progress and mutual understanding and to discriminate and pinpoint some of the existing *loci* of genuine disagreement.

A Companion to Wittgenstein, First Edition. Edited by Hans-Johann Glock and John Hyman.
© 2017 John Wiley & Sons, Ltd. Published 2017 by John Wiley & Sons, Ltd.

2 The Original Concept of a Resolute Reading

Cora Diamond and James Conant are often presented as the main proponents of a "resolute reading" of the *Tractatus*. We will begin, in this section, by characterizing the sense in which they employed the term "resolute reading" when they first adopted it. Before we do that, it is worth pausing for a moment to note how the term "resolute" was introduced into the debate and why it was considered, fairly or unfairly, by those who introduced it to be an apt term for marking a certain sort of difference among commentators of the *Tractatus*. The term was coined by Thomas Ricketts (1992). Warren Goldfarb is the person who officially introduced it into the secondary literature to characterize an approach to the interpretation of the *Tractatus* that at that time had been advocated by Diamond and Conant, among others (Goldfarb 1997, p.64). It is a hallmark of this approach that it seeks to take the penultimate remark of the book (TLP 6.54) as seriously as possible. In that remark, the author tells us that his sentences (*Sätze*) are meant to serve as elucidations and that the reader understands *him* only when he comes to recognize those sentences as *nonsensical*, throwing away the ladder of elucidatory sentences of which the book (largely) consists after he has climbed up it. What it meant to be resolute had to do with avoiding a certain sort of irresolution in one's interpretation of this remark. On the originally proposed employment of the antonym of the term, to be *irresolute* in one's understanding of that remark is to pay lip-service to the idea that the elucidatory sentences of the *Tractatus* are to be recognized as nonsensical, while continuing to treat those sentences as nonetheless managing to do something very much like what non-nonsensical sentences do – namely, convey propositional or quasi-propositional contents or insights from speaker to hearer: contents or insights about which it is then claimed that, though they cannot be "said," they can be "shown." (The Tractarian distinction between saying and showing is thus wheeled in as the key to understanding 6.54.) According to this original terminology, a reading is irresolute when it claims that some or all of the sentences of the *Tractatus* are nonsense, while at the same time taking back the apparent implications of any straightforward construal of what that claim might have been thought to mean. This is usually marked by commentators by their flagging in one way or another that, according to their interpretation, the relevant sentences of the work are actually only "strictly speaking" nonsensical. Only "strictly speaking": for they are to come into view for the reader as trying but failing to say something – something that cannot be said – where the "something" in question (though never fully said) turns out to be nonetheless intelligible and conveyable by other means (than that of saying) by that very same bit of nonsense. By contrast, to be *resolute* in one's reading of 6.54 – and in one's reading of the book as a whole – is to claim that the elucidatory sentences of the *Tractatus* must ultimately be recognized as *simply* nonsensical, i.e., as forms of words that neither say nor quasi-say anything.

When Diamond and Conant took over the term "resolute" from Ricketts and Goldfarb as a fitting description of their own approach to the *Tractatus*, they were careful to specify what they meant by it. They emphasized, in particular, that the commitments that make a reading resolute, in the sense in which they wished to use the term, "say something about how the book ought *not* to be read, thereby still leaving much undetermined about how the book ought to be read" (Conant and Diamond, 2004, p.43). Moreover, they were explicit about the fact that a resolute reading, as they conceived of it, "is better thought of as a *program* for reading the book, [...] because conformity to the basic features of such a reading leaves undetermined exactly how a great deal of the book works in detail" (p.43). One could reformulate these two points in the following way: the logical grammar of the term "resolute reading" should be understood to be both *logically posterior* and *highly generic*. Logically posterior, in as much as the contours of the concept of such a reading are taken to be defined in relation to those of the sort of reading that Conant and Diamond then sought to reject. (An understanding of what it is to be resolute in this sense presupposes some prior understanding of the specific character of the sort of irresolution here under indictment.) And highly generic, insofar as the bare concept of such a reading is a highly determinable one, admitting of a wide variety of specifications. (The concept of a resolute reading thereby denotes a family of programmatically overlapping but in other respects possibly highly divergent readings.)

In addition to its logically posterior and highly generic character, there is a third logical feature that belongs to the concept of a resolute reading originally employed by Diamond and Conant. It is a feature which may seem to be so obvious as not to be worth mentioning – namely, that the concept in question is a concept of how best to read the *Tractatus*. That is to say, it is the concept of an *exegetical* proposal for how to make the best possible sense of *one particular work* of philosophy – and, in the first instance, only this one work. In particular, it is not the concept of a possible philosophical position or a conception of how philosophy as such ought to proceed. Thus one can endorse the proposal in question without thereby endorsing the conception of the practice of philosophy that one thereby ascribes to the author of that book. (Indeed, Conant and Diamond were originally motivated to put forward such a proposal in order to understand better wherein the later Wittgenstein's critique of the *Tractatus* should be properly understood to lie – a critique that they themselves endorse; see for example Conant, 2007.)

As we are going to show in the subsequent sections, what happens in the later stages of "the" debate is that the term "resolute reading" comes to be used in ways that gradually shed each of these three features of its original grammar. It goes from being the logically posterior member to being the logically primary member of a pair of related terms. It goes from being a fairly generic concept to being one that involves a whole raft of further commitments. And it goes from being a concept that concerns the exegesis of a particular book to being one that applies to other books; and eventually to being a concept whose primary meaning, as far as we can see, has nothing to do with matters of exegesis at all. In a way, this is all fine, of course. No one owns these words and everyone has a right to use them in whatever way they like. But tremendous unclarity is bound to result when someone thinks she is using the term in the same way as someone else, but is not.

Let's proceed for the moment with our elucidation of the concept of a resolute reading as it figures in the work of Diamond and Conant. For this purpose, some terminological stipulations will prove helpful. We shall refer to the concept of a resolute reading that is to be found in their work – that is, one that exhibits the three aforementioned logical features – as the *logically posterior concept of a resolute reading*. A reading is "resolute" in this sense if it *rejects* certain positive tenets of what Diamond and Conant called "standard readings," which they saw, at the time they began writing about this issue, as dominant. On their original understanding of how this pair of terms ("resolute"/"standard") relate to one another, the concept of a standard reading is logically prior and the concept of a resolute reading is logically parasitic upon that prior notion: the latter is simply defined as involving the rejection of certain commitments that characterize the former. We shall henceforth refer to *that* concept of a standard reading – that is, the one upon which the logically posterior concept of a resolute reading is constructed – as the *logically prior concept of a standard reading*.

It is worth noting that the term "standard reading" has become an awkward one since the time it was originally employed by Conant and Diamond to refer to the readings they were reacting against. While those readings had in fact been dominant during roughly the previous two decades of *Tractatus* scholarship, from the mid-1960s to the mid-1980s, they no longer clearly represent a prevailing scholarly orthodoxy, and thus are no longer "standard" in the originally intended sense of the term. Our use of the term "standard" in this chapter should not be taken at any point to involve a claim on our part as to what sort of reading, if any, constitutes a currently prevailing orthodoxy among contemporary scholars of the *Tractatus*. (What is the currently dominant view among *Tractatus* scholars is a sociological issue about which we take no view.) When we talk about the "logically prior concept of a standard reading," we simply want to refer to the concept of a reading identified by certain commitments (namely, the commitments in terms of which Conant and Diamond originally defined the concept of a resolute reading), without suggesting that readings with such commitments continue to enjoy their former ascendancy. A reason for our retaining the term "standard" is that in much of the tertiary literature on the *Tractatus* this term has come to be employed simply as the complement of the term "resolute" (whatever that is taken to mean) and so, as the debate itself has shifted focus, the intertwined senses of these two terms have undergone parallel shifts in meaning – an evolution that we will discuss later in this chapter.

We said a moment ago that the logically posterior concept of a resolute reading is defined as involving the rejection of certain commitments that characterize the logically prior concept of a standard reading. Which commitments? We may distinguish four positive commitments that Diamond and Conant considered to qualify a reading as "standard" in their originally intended sense. These in turn correspond to four negative commitments that Diamond and Conant originally understood as jointly characterizing the sort of reading that they termed "resolute." These four negative commitments are closely interconnected. More specifically, the last three are commitments that one incurs when one tries to think through the consequences of the first. We shall henceforth refer to these four negative commitments as the *core commitments of the logically posterior concept of a resolute reading*.

Since the various commitments at issue here are closely interrelated, there is a certain arbitrariness to what one counts as constituting a separate commitment and what one counts as constituting an internal aspect of a particular commitment. In their co-authored paper (2004), Conant and Diamond individuated and counted "the core commitments" in a slightly different way. For the purposes of this chapter, we have found it helpful to organize the issue in slightly different terms; but we do not take this to represent anything more than a difference in mode of presentation.

(i) The first core commitment of the logically posterior concept of a resolute reading has a general methodological character. It involves a rejection of the once widely held interpretative assumption that the *Tractatus* aims to put forward a particular sort of philosophical theory or doctrine. As an exegetical proposal, it suggests that various aspects of the text can come into view in a new and illuminating way for the reader, if she takes seriously the *Tractatus*' insistence that "philosophy is not a theory but an activity," and specifically a form of activity whose object is not to think philosophical thoughts but rather to offer a logical clarification of thought – and whose result is not "a number of 'philosophical propositions,'" but rather simply "*das Klarwerden von Sätzen*" (TLP 4.112). This first exegetical proposal arises from dissatisfaction with the manner in which interpretations falling under the logically prior concept of a standard reading dealt with these and similar remarks in the *Tractatus*. Actually there are two sorts of standard readings at issue here – a less interesting sort and a more interesting one. The less interesting sort simply tried to solve the problem by *fiat*, by stipulating that in rejecting philosophical theories the *Tractatus* is not rejecting most of what most people would understand as cases of such theories. On the contrary, according to this first sort of standard reading, the *Tractatus* does indeed aim to argue for a number of substantive philosophical positions (about ontology, language, thought, ethics, etc.) and to take a theoretical stand on a whole host of recognizably classic philosophical issues. Then there is the second and more common sort of standard reading. These commentators simply bite the bullet and claim that there is a gross inconsistency between the *Tractatus*' official account of what is going on in the book and what is actually going on in the book. Peter Hacker is helpfully explicit on this point:

> To understand Wittgenstein's brief remarks about philosophy in the *Tractatus*, it is essential to realize that its practice and its theory are at odds with each other. The official *de jure* account of philosophy is wholly different from the *de facto* practice in the book. (Hacker, 1972/86, p.12)

It is this idea, above all, that Diamond and Conant originally sought to disagree with as a matter of exegesis. The proposal was to see how far one could get in making sense of the book if one assumes the negation of what Hacker here claims is the case. The logically posterior concept of a resolute reading therefore takes its point of departure from the idea that one ought to first see if it is possible to construe the *de facto* practice of philosophy in the book in such a way that it can come into view as an attempt to realize the official *de jure* account of philosophy it espouses. The subsequent three core commitments of the logically posterior concept of a resolute reading simply involve a further working out of this idea: that the *Tractatus* does *not* aim to put forth any form of philosophical theory or doctrine. (This commitment, as we shall see in the last section, is compatible with the claim that the *Tractatus* in fact *failed*, in various ways, to do philosophy in a way that lives up to its own aspiration.)

(ii) The second core commitment of the logically posterior concept of a resolute reading is the rejection of the idea that the *Tractatus* seeks to convey an *ineffable* theory or doctrine. By an "ineffable doctrine" we mean a body of propositional or quasi-propositional contents – a set of contents that be conveyed from speaker to listener by having the listener work out what the sentences of the book *would* say if they were meaningful. More specifically, according to the logically prior concept of a standard reading, the *Tractatus* puts forth a philosophical theory which entails its own inexpressibility: the very sentences that are used to formulate the theory, in light of the standards of meaningfulness laid down by the theory, must be regarded as nonsensical. This is what some standard readers have called the "paradox" of the *Tractatus* (see e.g., Williams, 2004). A central commitment of the logically posterior concept of a resolute reading is therefore the following: whatever else it might be right or wrong to say about 6.54, that passage should *not* be understood as saying that the propositions of the book convey, or are used to convey, a body of doctrines that are "ineffable" in this sense.

(iii) The third core commitment of the logically posterior concept of a resolute reading is that the *Tractatus* rejects (what has come to be called) the "substantial" conception of nonsense and endorses (what has come to be called) the "austere" conception of nonsense. This commitment follows from the first, in as much as it refuses to see the *Tractatus*' entitlement to deploy "nonsense" as a term of philosophical criticism as resting upon anything like a prior philosophical theory of meaningfulness. The capacity to distinguish sense from nonsense is one that must come together with the reader's capacity to think and speak. These are interrelated capacities that the reader must bring to an encounter with the book and which are then refined over the course of the activity of reading the book and climbing its ladder. These are not capacities that are in any sense first conferred upon the reader only upon her having been persuaded of the truth of a particular theory of some sort. This is rather obviously true of the reader's capacity to understand and speak – and thus to grasp and traffic in the expression of thought. But a central point here is that this is no less true, for the early Wittgenstein, of the reader's capacity to detect cases of only *apparently* grasping and trafficking in the expression of thought. We are able to recognize some things as nonsense even before we learn from the *Tractatus*. The office of the book is not to confer this capacity upon us but to deepen and sharpen it. More specifically, the austere conception of nonsense holds that a sentence is nonsensical, on a particular occasion of use, if and *only* if we have failed, on that occasion, to give a meaning to its constituent words (cf. TLP 5.4733). There is no such thing as substantial nonsense, i.e., nonsense that arises when meaningful words are combined in a way that transgresses the bounds of significant discourse, as those bounds have been demarcated in accordance with the terms of a particular theory of what can and cannot be said. Indeed, it is essential to the logically posterior concept of a resolute reading that the *Tractatus* itself involves an attack on the very idea of a theory of meaningfulness of such a sort – on the very idea that it is possible to codify, in advance of the exercise of our capacity of thought and speech, some putatively prior set of rules that off their own bat determine when units of thought or speech are meaningfully combined in legitimate (i.e., fully significant) or in illegitimate (i.e., substantially nonsensical) ways. Nonsense, according to the austere conception, always arises from a failure of determination of sense (a failure to put words to logical use), rather than from putting words to a fully determinate, but nonetheless illegitimate use (a *logically wrong* kind of use; cf. TLP 5.473–5.4732). From this it follows that the *Tractatus*, when it states that the reader must recognize the author's elucidatory sentences as nonsensical, does *not* mean (as the logically prior concept of a standard reading maintains) that the reader must apply to those sentences a theory of meaningfulness – one which is to license the inference that what those sentences are trying to say, in virtue of the meanings that *have* been assigned to each of their constituent parts, is nonsensical. Instead, according to the logically posterior concept of a resolute reading, the reader is meant to be brought to the point at which she realizes, contrary to her impression that she has conferred a fully determinate method of symbolizing upon the elucidatory sentences of the *Tractatus*, that in fact she has done no such thing – that there is only an illusion of understanding here. This realization, this dissipation of the illusion of understanding, is what is involved in climbing up and throwing away the individual rungs of the ladder of sentences of which the book is largely composed. The reader, in other words, is not meant to come to realize that she has been wandering beyond the limits of significant discourse, but rather that she has been subject to *illusions* of meaning – including the illusion that what lies beyond significant discourse can be characterized in logically positive terms. The austere conception of nonsense that underlies the logically posterior concept of a resolute reading therefore is not a self-standing theory of nonsense, but merely a way of expressing a rejection of an apparently tenable form of philosophical theory that the *Tractatus* seeks to show rests upon an illusion.

(iv) The fourth core commitment of the logically posterior concept of a resolute reading is that the role of a proper logical notation or *Begriffsschrift* in the activity of the logical clarification of thoughts is *not* to serve as a test for determining whether the sentences of ordinary language comply with the proscriptions of some theory of meaningfulness putatively laid down in the book. According to the logically prior concept of a standard reading, the *Tractatus* understands a logical notation as a codification of the requirements of such a theory, so that translatability into permissible formulae of the notation is the ultimate arbiter of meaningfulness. The test is supposed to proceed in the following way: we first identify the logical units that compose the sentence under interrogation, as well as the logically relevant ways in which those units are put together; we then translate those units into symbols of the *Begriffsschrift* and combine them in the same way in which the units of the original sentence are supposedly put together; finally, we establish whether the resulting formula of the *Begriffsschrift* is well-formed or ill-formed. In the former case, the sentence has passed the test and is significant; in the latter case, it has failed the test and is *therefore* nonsensical. This account of the role of the notation in the logical clarification of thought turns on the idea that a sentence can be nonsensical *because* the logical units of which it is composed are combined in an illegitimate way. It presupposes, in order words, the possibility of substantial nonsense. The logically posterior concept of a resolute reading must hold that the role of the notation is not to be understood along these lines.

Individual resolute readers, in their writings on the *Tractatus*, have of course gone well beyond merely offering a defense of these four negative exegetical claims that constitute their core commitments. The point of these four commitments is simply to articulate a framework within which one can try to go on and make sense of the whole of the book. Hence the highly generic nature of the logically posterior concept of a resolute reading. Each individual resolute reader has gone on to offer more determinate answers to any number of pressing exegetical questions, such as: How does the *Tractatus* conceive in detail of the activity of philosophical clarification? What is the overall point of the *Tractatus*, if it is not to put forth effable or ineffable doctrines? How is the manner in which the book is composed supposed to lead the reader to realize that she has in fact failed to assign a determinate meaning to the words of some of the sentences of the *Tractatus* that she initially takes herself to understand? How in detail should we understand the role of a *Begriffsschrift* in the context of the logical clarification of thoughts? What is the role of the specific forms of notation that Wittgenstein introduces for this purpose, such as the truth-table notation, the N-operator notation, the bracket notation in TLP 6.1203, etc.? If the *Tractatus* did not *aim* to put forth any doctrine, how should we understand the evolution of Wittgenstein's thought and his later criticisms of the *Tractatus*? If the *Tractatus* rejects the idea of ineffable (propositional or quasi-propositional) contents, how should we understand the saying/showing distinction?

The four core commitments surveyed above introduce significant constraints on how such questions are to be answered, but they do not dictate any specific answer to these questions or to any of a great many other intimately related exegetical questions. In fact, such questions have been taken up and answered in remarkably different ways by different resolute readers.

3 Two Sorts of Criticism of "Resolute Readings"

A first significant shift in the meaning of the term "resolute reading" is already to be detected if we survey the criticisms that have come to be mounted against interpretations that the critics in question have thus classified. (For an overview of the relevant literature, see Bronzo, 2012.) These criticisms divide in fact into two very different kinds. On the one hand, there are criticisms that are meant to involve a rejection of the negative commitments of the logically posterior concept of a resolute reading, and thus a defense of some version or other of the logically prior concept of a standard reading. Using the term "standard" in the above-explained sense, we could refer to criticisms of this first sort as *standard criticisms*. On the other hand, there are criticisms that are not meant to involve a rejection of any of those negative commitments. Criticisms of this second sort we might call *nonstandard*. They involve no defense of any of the four constitutive commitments of the logically prior concept of a standard reading. They are directed instead against further particular positive commitments which are alleged to be held by some or all "resolute readers," where what now allows for the subsumption of some commentator under the concept of a resolute reader goes well beyond any understanding of the term "resolute" that can be funded by the logically posterior concept elucidated above. When these criticisms are understood as criticisms of resolute readings *qua* resolute readings, the term "resolute" has shifted its sense: the concept of a resolute reading is no longer understood to have a logically posterior grammar and its content has become considerably more determinate.

In the next section, we will look at a criticism of so-called "resolute readings" that illustrates this sort of shift in meaning. It is a particularly interesting case, because it has been put forth by some commentators as a standard criticism, and by others as a nonstandard criticism. Thus, where there appears to be a single criticism, corresponding to a single form of words, there are in fact two different criticisms. By examining this case we will explore an example of a phenomenon to be encountered in a number of different forms in the secondary literature about resolute readings: we come to see not only how the term "resolute reading" undergoes a shift in its meaning, but also how self-described critics of such readings who take themselves to be on the same side of some supposed single battlefield are sometimes merely in apparent agreement with one another.

4 Shedding the First Two Logical Features

There is a widespread tendency among critics of resolute readings to characterize their target as someone who claims that the *Tractatus* does not aim to convey any insight or understanding, but only to engage in an exercise of "therapy," where this is taken to mean, to put it crudely, that the only point of the book is to lead us to throw away the book. Roger White, for example, has written that in the *Tractatus*, for resolute readers, "nothing is shown, no insights are vouchsafed, other than that we have been led on a wild goose chase," which leads him to conclude that the resolute approach is an "immensely trivializing account of Wittgenstein's work" (White, 2011, p.46). In a similar vein, some critics have characterized the resolute approach as "nihilistic" (Emiliani, 2003; Stern, 2004, p.45) or "post-modernist" (Hacker, 2000, pp.356–60) or "purely therapeutic" (McGinn, 1999, 2006; Hutto, 2003), where each of these epithets is supposed to be justified by the fact that the *Tractatus*, according to resolute readers, does not aim to communicate any insight.

This sort of criticism – call it *the no-insight objection* – has been put forth by commentators who differ greatly from one another in their interpretations of the *Tractatus* and in their stances toward resolute readings. There are in fact two rather different forms of objection here entered – where much confusion is caused by the fact that each is entered by calling upon exactly the same form of words to make the objection in question. On the one hand, there are commentators who have put forth the no-insight objection as a way of defending some version of the logically prior concept of a standard reading of the *Tractatus* (and thus as a *standard criticism* of resolute readings, in the sense defined above), assuming that the *only* way in which the reader can be meant to gain insight or understanding from the *Tractatus* is by grasping a body of propositional or quasi-propositional truths. On the other hand, there are commentators who have put forth the no-insight objection without wishing to disagree with any of the core commitments of the logically posterior concept of a resolute reading (thereby entering the objection as a form of *nonstandard criticism* of resolute readings).

Commentators belonging to the first camp, such as Peter Hacker (2000, pp. 356–60), in effect argue that the logically posterior concept of a resolute reading in the very moment that it embraces its core commitments thereby deprives itself of the resources required to make sense of the idea that the *Tractatus* seeks to confer some sort of insight or understanding upon its reader. This is not obviously true. All that such a resolute reading deprives itself of is the right to make sense of that idea *in the way someone like Hacker does* – namely, by claiming that the *Tractatus* aims to convey a body of propositional or quasi-propositional contents (see the list of the putative Tractarian insights in Hacker, 2000, pp. 353–6). This does not show that such resolute readers cannot make sense of the very idea that in reading the book we make a form of genuine and valuable intellectual and existential progress. Most resolute readers, after all, do emphasize throughout their writings that the *Tractatus* is interested in the achievement and conferral of forms of *clarity*. Depending upon what one means in speaking of "insight" or "understanding," the claim that this is what we achieve may remain more or less consistent with something that resolute readers are happy to say about what happens to us as we read the book and make progress with it. The question therefore is not well posed in the following terms: do resolute readers oppose the very idea that the *Tractatus* seeks to confer "insight" or "understanding" on any possible specification of what the words "insight" or "understanding" might be taken to mean? The question rather is: what sort of "insight" or "understanding" can the *Tractatus* be said to confer? If expressions such as "insight" or "understanding" are spelled out in terms of grasping bits of propositional or quasi-propositional knowledge, then, yes, in *that* sense, resolute readers are indeed committed to denying that the *Tractatus*, through its elucidatory sentences, seeks to "convey insights" or "impart understanding." But there are, of course, other no less natural and intelligible things to mean by those terms. According to most resolute readers, to understand the book requires, among other things, "understanding its aim," "understanding its author" (following 6.54), "understanding and mastering its logical notation," "understanding the logical differences in the modes of symbolizing expressed through different sorts of signs in the notation" (to mention just four of the forms of "understanding" that resolute readers make much of). Depending upon what is meant by terms such as "understanding" and "insight," resolute readers may or may not wish to allow for additional forms of insight and understanding.

It is worth emphasizing that we do not see these remarks as involving any sort of repudiation of what was originally maintained by Diamond and Conant. Consider for example this passage from the conclusion of a relatively old paper of Conant's, in which he summarizes his understanding of the method of the *Tractatus*:

> The *Tractatus* seeks to bring its reader to the point where he can *recognize* sentences within the body of the work as nonsensical, not by means of a theory that legislates certain sentences out of the realm of sense but rather by *bringing more clearly into view* for the reader the life with language he already leads – by *harnessing the capacities* for distinguishing sense from nonsense [...] implicit in the everyday practical mastery of language that the reader already possesses. [...] The work seeks to do this, not by instructing us in how to identify determinate cases of nonsense, but by enabling us to *see more clearly* what it is we do with language when we succeed in achieving determinate forms of sense [...] and what it is we fall short of doing when we fail to achieve such forms of sense [...]. (Conant, 2002, pp.423–4, emphases added)

This passage speaks of what the reader is brought to recognize by the book, what is brought clearly into view for the reader by the book, the forms of mastery which the reader achieves through reading the book, and so on. Metaphors of "sight," "improvement," and "mastery," and references to the forms of clarity and recognition that come with such forms of vision and mastery, pervade this whole passage and much of the rest of the essay from which it is drawn. It hardly seems a stretch to paraphrase what is at issue here in terms of the idea that the *Tractatus* seeks to enable its reader to attain certain forms of *insight*. Everything depends simply upon what is meant by that last word. (It is true that at many points in that paper the author denies that the *Tractatus* seeks to convey "insights," but in those contexts the author is using the term "insight" for the specific form of grasping inexpressible truths that belongs to the logically prior concept of a standard reading. He is taking over the term as employed by such standard readers and simply using it as they do.)

The core commitments of the original, logically posterior concept of a resolute reading in no way *demand* an account of "Tractarian insights" along the lines that Conant allows in the previous passage. That passage is part of an early effort on his part to fill in the schema of a resolute reading in a particular way. Other commentators have retained the aforementioned core commitments but have attempted to fill in the schema in sometimes subtly differing ways, in sometimes radically different ways. What matters for our present point is simply that those core commitments, taken by themselves, in no way force one to conclude anything remotely resembling the following: "There are *no* insights to be gained from reading the *Tractatus*," or "The only point of the book is to lead us to throw away the book." It is true that nothing in the four commitments taken by themselves necessarily precludes that conclusion either. In that sense, a no-insights thesis is an exegetical extra that a resolute reader *qua* resolute reader may, but need not, endorse. But that is true of a great many other things that must go into any textually satisfying account of the *Tractatus*.

The commentators who form the second camp mentioned above (namely those who take the no-insight objection to be a criticism of resolute readers, but do not wish to disagree with any of their core commitments) have come to regard the supposed no-insight thesis to be constitutive of what it means to be a resolute reader. They then often go on to ascribe further commitments to resolute readers to make sense of their initial supposed commitment to the no-insight thesis. They thereby introduce a great deal of additional content into the concept of a resolute reading. Some of these commentators then turn around and represent themselves as far more moderate or measured than the other parties to the debate in seeking to occupy a *middle ground* between standard and resolute readers. Such commentators claim to agree with resolute readers and disagree with standard readers when it comes to the core commitments of resolute readings, but to agree with standard readers as against resolute readers when it comes to the question of whether the *Tractatus* is concerned to confer forms of insight and understanding. However, the latter idea, so specified, does not necessarily suffice to identify a ground of disagreement with a given resolute reader. This does not mean that in such cases there is no ground of disagreement. What some of these middle-way commentators go on to say about the logical character of the insights conveyed, as well as about the means by which they are to be conveyed, may well strike a resolute reader as either exegetically implausible or philosophically confused and sometimes both. Readers such as Conant, Diamond, Goldfarb, and Ricketts, insofar as they continue to employ the term "resolute" in its original sense, do generally take themselves to be disagreeing with such middle-way readers about how best to fill in the exegetical schema specified by the logically posterior concept of a resolute reading. On this understanding of the disagreement, the question is not one of *whether* to be a resolute reader, but rather one of *how* to be a resolute reader. But, in the revised use of the term "resolute" that self-avowed middle-way readers tend to prefer, the nature of that disagreement frequently is described in the following terms: as a disagreement between a resolute reader and a non-resolute reader. Their deployment of the terminology depends on their having conferred a self-standing grammar on the concept of a resolute reading – one that allows one to classify a reader in this way on grounds that are no longer logically posterior to the concept of any other sort of reading. The logically prior concept is now that of a resolute reading (defined by the supposed commitment to the no-insight thesis), and the logically posterior one is that of a non-resolute reading (defined by the rejection of the no-insight thesis). Moreover, an interpretative approach thus classifiable as a "non-resolute" reading may come in either of two flavors: "standard" or "middle-way." When such commentators employ the term "resolute reading" they mean something significantly different by it than what it was supposed to denote on its original employment: the first two logical features of the original concept of a resolute reading (i.e., its logically posterior and highly generic character) have been shed. It is now the highly generic concept of a "non-resolute reader" that is the logically posterior one, and the concept of a "resolute reader" has become far more determinate – in some cases building into the very idea of such a reading some form of commitment to a self-evidently implausible ("nihilistic," "postmodernist," etc.) exegetical thesis.

These considerations apply, for example, to the "middle-way" interpretation proposed by Marie McGinn (1999, 2001, and 2006, especially preface, ch.1, and pp. 251–4). She wants to agree with resolute readers about the fact that the *Tractatus* does not seek to convey any metaphysical doctrine, and in particular does not seek to communicate any *ineffable* metaphysical truth about a language-independent reality. But she takes herself to disagree with resolute readers because she holds that the *Tractatus* does seek to give us insights into what is involved in a full mastery of our language. At this point, McGinn has her own story about how such forms of insight should be construed. The elucidatory propositions of the *Tractatus*, McGinn argues, do not purport to give us any sort of genuine information or metaphysical insight, but do serve to *remind* us of what we already know in virtue of our being competent language-users, in analogy with the "grammatical remarks" to be found in the works of the later Wittgenstein (see McGinn, 1999, pp.499, 512; 2001, pp.26–7, 33–4; 2006, e.g., p.33).

It is not immediately clear whether McGinn's positive proposal about how to understand the character of the insights that the *Tractatus* seeks to convey is or is not compatible with all four of the negative commitments of the logically posterior concept of a resolute reading. (For different views on the matter, cf. Read and Hutchinson, 2006 and Kuusela, 2007.) It is not our aim, here, to try to resolve this issue, but only to make the following conditional point: *if* McGinn's proposal is compatible with those negative commitments, then it will simply appear to resolute readers who employed the term "resolution" in its original sense as an attempt to develop *a* particular form of resolute reading of the *Tractatus*, rather than as an attempt to trace a third way between standard and resolute readings, as she herself would describe the situation. This is not to deny that Conant, or Diamond, or Goldfarb, or Ricketts could still find much to disagree with McGinn's positive proposal; but this disagreement would represent a new front in the debate about resolute readings – one which is not concerned at all with the question of whether the *Tractatus* should be read "resolutely" in the original sense of this term, but rather with how to fill in the interpretative schema such a reading proposes.

Proponents of middle-way interpretations do not exhaust the second camp of commentators mentioned above – namely, the camp of those who put forth the no-insight objection as a *nonstandard* criticism. There are in fact commentators who resemble the proponents of middle-way interpretations in taking the no-insight thesis to be constitutive of what it is to be a resolute reader, but who do not describe themselves as occupying a middle position between resolute readers and standard readers. This is because for them the term "resolute reader" has simply come to name someone who thinks that there is no way to make sense of the idea that the *Tractatus*, through its artful employment of nonsense, is aiming to lead its reader to a state of greater insight. Moreover, for them the term "standard reader" has now simply become the logical complement of "resolute reader," on this new understanding of the term. So to think that there is some way to make sense of the idea that the *Tractatus* through its artful employment of nonsense is aiming to lead its reader to a state of greater insight just *is* for them what it is to be a standard reader. We now have reached the point where a complete reversal has been effected in the logical dependence of the two complementary terms. In the parlance of such commentators, the concept of a resolute reading is the logically prior concept and the concept of a standard reader is the logically posterior one. To be a standard reader is to reject the supposedly essential and defining feature of all resolute readings – the no-insight thesis. At this point, we have shed the first two logical features of the original concept of a resolute reading, as well as the correlative logical features of the original complementary concept of a standard reading.

One example of a commentator many of whose remarks suggest that he schematizes the controversy in these terms is Roger White (2006, 2011). Like McGinn, White rejects the no-insight thesis and understands such a rejection as the repudiation of any resolute reading. For White, as for McGinn, the no-insight thesis is a constitutive feature of resolute readings. However, unlike McGinn, White does not purport to occupy a "middle ground" between "standard" and "resolute" readings; he purports instead to be defending a version of the "standard" or "orthodox" reading. Indeed, White claims to be in substantial agreement with "orthodox" readers such as Hacker (White, 2011, p.47). This serves to obscure the extent to which White is in fact in considerable disagreement with commentators such as Hacker on at least some of the issues that were originally deemed to be essential to the debate between standard and resolute readers. White himself tends to relegate his discussion of these points of disagreement with commentators such as Hacker to footnotes and asides, as they do not represent for him the essential front of what he takes to be his own disagreement with resolute readers. This, however, in no way alters the fact that the concept of a "standard" or "orthodox" reading that White employs is actually quite different from the one canvassed at the outset of this chapter. This does not make White's terminology correct or incorrect. He has the right to classify commentators in any way he likes. But it does make for considerable confusion if one takes the terminology itself to already indicate the manner in which his disagreement with resolute readers aligns with those of other recent commentators (such as McGinn) with such readers.

In some of the aforementioned footnotes and asides, White appears to reject at least some of the core positive commitments of the logically prior concept of a standard reading, and thus to endorse at least some of the core negative commitments of the logically posterior concept of a resolute reading. This applies, in particular, to the second and third commitments of the respective sorts of reading. White, in explicit disagreement with Hacker, claims the following:

> We cannot present Wittgenstein as holding that [for example] the sentence 'Objects form the substance of the world' is nonsense, and hence that one could not say 'Objects form the substance of the world', but that nevertheless *that* was what he thought. (White 2011, p.53)

For White, the resulting philosophical position would not only be inconsistent, as Hacker concedes, but would also be "so absurd that it is not credible that it should have ever been Wittgenstein's actual position" (White, 2011, p.65, n.71). This was one of the main points of the original resolute criticism of standard readings. Moreover, White explicitly denies that the insights that the *Tractatus* wishes to communicate are propositional in nature (2011, pp.44–5), and the way in which he describes what Wittgenstein is doing in the *Tractatus* – an "exercise in Socratic midwifery" which consists in "drawing attention to something he believes is already implicit in our mastery of language" (p.44) – suggests that he wants to deny that the "insights" communicated by the *Tractatus* should even be *modeled* on propositional contents. (Indeed, his account of what is shown by the *Tractatus* here is very close to Conant's and Diamond's account of what is shown; as evidenced, for example, in the long passage from Conant quoted several pages above.) If one focuses just on these moments in White, one might be inclined to think that he would be happy to accept the second negative commitment of the logically posterior concept of a resolute reading. There are also passages that suggest that White would be equally happy to accept the third negative commitment of such a reading – namely, the attribution to the *Tractatus* of the austere conception of nonsense (see, e.g., 2011, pp.33–5). However, if one focuses instead on various details of his own positive account of what the *Tractatus* seeks to accomplish by specifying the general form of the proposition – for example, his contention that the nonsensicality of certain linguistic constructions, including the propositions of the *Tractatus*, *follows* from the specification of the general form of the propositions (White, 2006, pp.83, 125) – it is difficult not to be left with the impression that White's positive account of these matters in fact commits him to a rejection of both the first and the third commitment of the logically posterior concept of a resolute reading.

It is therefore a delicate task to determine whether White's overall interpretation does or does not fall under the logically prior concept of a standard reading. Moreover, it is at least equally difficult to determine whether White's positive account of the character of the insights that the *Tractatus* seeks to convey is or is not compatible with the four negative commitments of the logically posterior concept of a resolute reading. Like McGinn, White has a very particular and idiosyncratic take on the issues involved here. For White, the first step in seeing how nonsensical utterances can convey that special sort of insight while lacking sense is to come to appreciate how metaphorical utterances work – which, for White, also may be said to convey insight while lacking sense (White, 2011, pp. 35–45). The question is what the idea of "lacking sense" comes to here. White has his own very particular way of making this out. According to White's extremely inclusive way of employing the term "nonsense," metaphorical utterances are to be counted as species of the genus *nonsense*. White's proposal is to model the nonsensical but insight-conveying propositions of the *Tractatus* – not on the platitudinous grammatical remarks that occur in the works of the later Wittgenstein, as McGinn suggests, but rather – on the complicated form of marshaling linguistic resources involved in the making of a metaphorical utterance.

This is not the place to attempt to lay out the details and assess the merits of White's own fascinating and original positive account of how Tractarian nonsense conveys insight. (For a more extensive discussion, see Conant and Dain, 2011.) Our aim, here, is simply to emphasize the following two conditional points: (1) *If* White's interpretation is consistent with the four negative commitments of the logically posterior concept of a resolute reading, then he is not disagreeing with commentators such as Conant and Diamond about whether the *Tractatus* should be read "resolutely." Merely insisting that the *Tractatus* seeks to communicate "insights" does not amount to the rejection of "resolute readings," as this term was originally understood; it all depends on how the nature of the form of insight here in question is to be construed. (2) *If* White rejects (or if his reading is implicitly committed to rejecting) some of the core negative commitments of the logically posterior concept of a resolute reading, then he and Conant and Diamond may well be able to agree that he should be classified as a "standard" rather than a "resolute" reader in the original sense of the expression, but the ground of that classification would rest on features of White's reading that have nothing to do with anyone's supposed commitment or rejection of a no-insight thesis.

If the first alternative obtains, resolute readers such as Conant, or Diamond, or Goldfarb, or Ricketts could still find much to disagree with in White's positive account of how the elucidatory sentences of the *Tractatus* seek to convey insights. But this would be, once again, a completely new front of the debate. It would coincide neither with the original disagreement between "standard" and "resolute" readers, nor with the disagreement that obtains between some self-described resolute readers and self-avowed middle-way commentators (such as McGinn) even if their proposal for how to read the book turns out to be consistent with the four negative commitments of the logically posterior concept of a resolute reading.

Once we put aside White's and McGinn's respective forms of misleading rhetoric about "no insights," the genuine differences between their respective interpretative proposals and the various readings that fall under the logically posterior concept of a resolute reading may come more sharply into relief. It is here that there are a number of genuinely interesting exegetical questions to be further debated and resolved. But these differences will generally be obscured if we employ, following White and McGinn, a logically prior concept of a resolute reading defined by a commitment to the no-insight thesis – a thesis that is not part of the original concept of resolution, that has remained largely unclarified, and that many self-avowed resolute readers (such as Conant or Diamond or Goldfarb or Ricketts) do not endorse.

5 Shedding the Third Logical Feature

So far we have discussed ways in which the original use of the term "resolute" has shed its first two logical features. Now we come to the third logical feature, which one might have thought to be the most stable of all: the idea that a "resolute reading" is an exegetical proposal about how best to read the *Tractatus*.

There has been a tendency in the secondary literature to extend the term "resolute" in a variety of ways, including to other texts and to other matters. The term is sometimes applied to exegetical questions extending far beyond the interpretation of the *Tractatus* (so that some now speak, for example, of a resolute reading of the *later* Wittgenstein), or to matters altogether beyond the merely exegetical (so that some now speak, for example, of certain philosophical positions *qua* forms of philosophy as being more or less weakly or strongly resolute). We will conclude by mentioning some examples of each of these developments and the further forms of confusion they have helped to introduce.

We now have to do with entirely new fronts of controversy that have recently opened up in the secondary literature. While the focus of the debate has thus shifted, the terminology has remained confusingly uniform, with each new front being characterized as a dispute between a supposedly "resolute" and "anti-resolute" point of view on the topic in question. For example, there are some who wish to defend and others who wish to criticize what some parties to the dispute in question now term "a resolute reading of the later Wittgenstein." Thus Stephen Mulhall (2007) has defended a "resolute reading" of the private language argument, and Genia Schönbaumsfeld (2008) has criticized it. Now, there may be some justification for calling certain readings of the later Wittgenstein "resolute" – for instance, in order to highlight significant forms of continuity between the views that those readings attribute to the later Wittgenstein and those that resolute readers (in the original sense of the term) attribute to the *Tractatus*. What is essential, in this case, is that one makes clear what one means by a "resolute reading of the later Wittgenstein." This is not usually done. Not surprisingly, people on either side of the resulting debate can be found to be talking past one another. For instance, Schönbaumsfeld objects to Mulhall that there is no *prima facie* rationale for a "resolute reading" of the *Investigations*, because "the *Investigations* does not declare itself, like the *Tractatus*, to be nonsensical" (2008, p.1109). But it is hard to believe that Mulhall wishes to disagree with Schönbaumsfeld on this point. How could he have failed to notice that in the *Investigations* there is nothing strictly analogous to 6.54? Much more plausibly, the attempt to read 6.54 resolutely is not among those features of the original concept of a resolute reading that Mulhall wishes to retain as part of his newly introduced concept of a resolute reading of the *Investigations*. Similarly, according to Schönbaumsfeld, Mulhall regards as non-resolute "*any* reading [...] that regards Wittgenstein as advancing a non-empty view, or some form of argument" (2008, p.1110). The concept of a resolute reading that Schönbaumsfeld here attributes to Mulhall is analogous to the logically prior concept of a resolute reading (of the *Tractatus*)

189

that we discussed in the previous section, insofar as it is essentially characterized by a commitment to something analogous to the no-insight thesis: a reading of the *Investigations* is resolute, according to Schönbaumsfeld, if it maintains that the book does not aim to put forth any argument or any nonempty view, on any possible construal of these notions. But Mulhall might in fact be working with a different concept of a resolute reading of the later Wittgenstein – for example, one which denies, more limitedly, that the book aims to put forth a body of propositional or quasi-propositional theses or arguments aiming to establish the truth of such theses (e.g., arguments aiming to establish the truth of the putative philosophical claim that "a private language is logically impossible"). Be that as it may, misunderstandings could be avoided if one were to make clear what exactly is meant by a "resolute reading of the later Wittgenstein," rather than assuming that there is some single way of projecting the term "resolute" into this further context of controversy.

Perhaps more surprising still is what has become of such terminology at the hands of Rupert Read and his co-authors. Their employment of the terminology takes its point of departure from a very particular moment in an intramural exegetical disagreement among self-declared resolute readers of the *Tractatus*. The intramural dispute at issue is focused on the question of whether the *Tractatus* is committed to the idea of a canon of analysis (and thus to the correlative idea of a perfect *Begriffsschrift* – one which makes absolutely perspicuous what we are saying whenever we succeed in saying anything at all). This issue, in turn, is seen as having implications for how we should understand the evolution of Wittgenstein's thought and, in particular, his later criticisms of the *Tractatus*. In this dispute, there are commentators such as Conant and Diamond, on the one hand, arguing that the *Tractatus* is indeed genuinely committed to the idea in question. They see it as playing an essential role in the early Wittgenstein's conception of philosophical clarification. For these commentators, the early Wittgenstein's conception of the role of a logically perspicuous notation in philosophical clarification brings with it a host of substantive metaphysical views which the author of the *Tractatus* was unable to recognize as such at the time of writing that book, but which the later Wittgenstein gradually came to target as the philosophically most suspect aspects of his early conception of philosophy. (See e.g., Diamond, 1991, especially pp.18–22 and ch.6; Conant and Diamond, 2004, pp.80–7; Conant, 2007.) The dispute also involves commentators such as Juliet Floyd, on the other hand, who argue, *pace* Conant and Diamond, that the *Tractatus*' conception of clarification does not bring any such commitments with it – indeed, that it is already self-consciously concerned to criticize such ideas. Thus, on Floyd's reconstruction of Wittgenstein's thought, the discontinuities between the early and later Wittgenstein must be construed otherwise than along the lines suggested by Conant and Diamond (see Floyd 2001, especially pp.176–80; Floyd, 2007; cf. also Ostrow, 2002, especially pp.9, 71–2). We have here, yet again, a case of a further front in the family of controversies surrounding resolute readings – with the important difference that in the case of this disagreement all parties to the dispute take themselves to be one or another kind of resolute reader.

Warren Goldfarb has introduced some nomenclature that has proved influential in schematizing the landscape of this dispute. He refers to commentators of the former sort (such as Conant and Diamond) as "Girondists" and to commentators of the latter sort (such as Floyd) as "Jacobins" (2011, p.19; an earlier version of that paper has been in circulation since 2000). While issues may be raised about the exact nature of this dispute, this much about it seems to be clear: (a) it is an *exegetical* dispute about how to read the *Tractatus*, and (b) it is not – as characterized thus far – a dispute between commentators committed to two different "degrees" of resolution. While Goldfarb's terminology does suggest the idea of different degrees of radicalism in one's reading of the *Tractatus*, the forms of radicalism in question do not concern a reader's degree of "resolution." On the contrary, in accordance with the logically posterior concept of a resolute reading elucidated above, resolution is here understood to be an all-or-nothing affair: either one claims that the aim of the *Tractatus* is to convey, through its elucidations, a body of propositional or quasi-propositional contents (in which case one's reading is irresolute), or one doesn't (in which case one's reading is resolute).

When Rupert Read and Rob Deans first step into the dispute between Girondists and Jacobins, they purport to side with Floyd and dub the approach they favor "strong resolutism," in contrast to "weak resolutism" (Read and Deans, 2003). This distinction was originally meant to be basically equivalent to Goldfarb's (Read and Deans 2003, p.267, n.27). But the newly introduced terminology, with its insinuation of grades of strength of "resolutism," already signals the beginning of a shift from the original intramural debate between Girondin and Jacobin resolute readers. The term "resolutism" (which is modeled on terms such as "idealism," "realism," "quietism," etc.) appears to designate a philosophical position, rather than an exegetical proposal; and the modifiers "weak" and "strong" appear to indicate that there is a spectrum of ways of developing or inhabiting such a position or orientation, from the less optimal to the more optimal.

As the dispute evolves, these appearances turn out to be more than mere appearances. Thus, in a subsequent contribution, Read characterizes the disagreement or "struggle" between "resolutists" such as Floyd and himself on the one hand, and "resolutists" such as Conant and Diamond on the other, as being about "the *kind* or *degree* of 'therapeutic' philosophy to ascribe to Wittgenstein, and to practice" (Read, 2006, p.81). According to Read, "resolutism" is, in the first instance, something that comes in degrees, and in the second instance, something only *accidentally* tied to an exegetical proposal for how to read some particular philosophical work or other. Resolutism is something that one may practice, to a greater or lesser degree, and that one may then also (but not necessarily) go on to ascribe to the particular conception of philosophical practice to be found in the *Tractatus* or some other philosophical work. These logically novel features that differentiate the concept of "resolutism" from the prior concept of "resolution" are even more evident in a yet more recent publication by Read and Deans, where they try to demonstrate, in their response to various criticisms, that "strong resolutism" is *also* viable "*as a reading* of the *Tractatus*" (Read and Deans, 2011, p.149). Indeed, even though Read and Deans argue in this essay for a certain way of reading the *Tractatus*, they openly declare that the exegetical matter is only of secondary importance for them. What really matters, for them, is that "strong resolutism" (or, as they now sometimes prefer to call it, "resolute resolutism") is "what philosophy *needs*" (Read and Deans, 2011, p.165):

> If our reading turns out to be wrong [...] then in the end this is not that important. For what is more important is: to be on the path to doing philosophy aright. And that path is what [...] the resolute (as opposed to irresolute) application of 'the resolute reading' [...] does for us. [...] In the end, whether or *not* this was Wittgenstein in the *Tractatus* – whether or not he was a resolute resolutist – it is where philosophy needs to go. And that is where we want to be. (Read and Deans, 2011, p.166)

"Strong resolutism" indicates here a certain way of doing philosophy (and perhaps of leading one's life), occupying one end of a spectrum of forms of resolutism that differ from one another in relative strength or resolution. Whatever the issues are that have now been placed at the center of the discussion, they have come to have remarkably little to do with the original controversy discussed in the earlier parts of this chapter.

6 Conclusion

At this point in the history of Wittgenstein scholarship, if someone tells you that they or someone else is a "resolute" reader of Wittgenstein, or asks you if you yourself are, our advice is to get that person first to tell you what they mean by the term. To give one example of how one will sort matters differently depending upon whose terminology one is using, the authors of this chapter would say of themselves, if they are using the term as Ricketts or Goldfarb or Diamond does, that they *are* resolute readers; using the term as McGinn or White does, that they are *not*; and using it as Read and his co-authors sometimes do, that they have simply *lost track of what the topic is* and thus that they do not know, but they strongly suspect that it is not a topic on which they ever previously meant to take a position.

References

Bronzo, S. (2012). The Resolute Reading and its Critics: An Introduction to the Literature. *Wittgenstein Studien*, 3, 45–80.

Conant, J. (2002). The Method of the *Tractatus*. In E.H. Reck (Ed.). *From Frege to Wittgenstein: Perspectives on Early Analytic Philosophy* (pp.374–462). Oxford: Oxford University Press.

Conant, J. (2007). *Mild Mono-Wittgensteinianism*. In A. Crary (Ed.). *Wittgenstein and the Moral Life: Essays in Honor of Cora Diamond* (pp.29–142). Cambridge, MA: MIT Press.

Conant, J. and Dain, E. (2011). Throwing the Baby out: A Reply to Roger White. In R. Read and M. Lavery (Eds). *Beyond the Tractatus Wars: The New Wittgenstein Debate* (pp.66–83). London: Routledge.

Conant, J. and Diamond, C. (2004). On Reading the *Tractatus* Resolutely: Reply to Meredith Williams and Peter Sullivan. In M. Kölbel and B. Weiss (Eds). *Wittgenstein's Lasting Significance* (pp.44–99). London: Routledge.

Diamond, C. (1991). *The Realistic Spirit: Wittgenstein, Philosophy, and the Mind*. Cambridge, MA: MIT Press.

Emiliani, A. (2003). What Nonsense Might Do: The Metaphysical Eye Opens. *Philosophical Investigations*, 26, 205–229.

Floyd, J. (2001). Number and Ascriptions of Number in Wittgenstein's *Tractatus*. In J. Floyd and S. Shieh (Eds). *Future Pasts: The Analytic Tradition in Twentieth-Century Philosophy* (pp.145–191). Oxford: Oxford University Press.

Floyd, J. (2007). Wittgenstein and the Inexpressible. In A. Crary (Ed.). *Wittgenstein and the Moral Life: Essays in Honor of Cora Diamond* (pp.177–234). Cambridge, MA: MIT Press.

Goldfarb, W. (1997). Metaphysics and Nonsense: On Cora Diamond's *The Realistic Spirit*. *Journal of Philosophical Research*, 22, 57–73.

Goldfarb, W. (2011). *Das Überwinden*: Non-Realist Readings of Wittgenstein's *Tractatus*. In R. Read and M. Lavery (Eds). *Beyond the Tractatus Wars: The New Wittgenstein Debate* (pp.6–21). London: Routledge.

Hacker, P.M.S. (1972/86). *Insight and Illusion: Themes in the Philosophy of Wittgenstein*. Revised edition. Oxford: Clarendon Press.

Hacker, P.M.S. (2000). Was He Trying to Whistle It? In A. Crary and R. Read (Eds). *The New Wittgenstein* (pp.353–388). London: Routledge.

Hutto, D.D. (2003). *Wittgenstein and the End of Philosophy: Neither Theory nor Therapy*. Basingstoke: Palgrave Macmillan.

Kuusela, O. (2007). Review of M. McGinn: *Elucidating the Tractatus*. *Notre Dame Philosophical Reviews*, 21 July 2015 http://ndpr.nd.edu/review.cfm?id=10524.(last accessed 4 June 2016).

McGinn, M. (1999). Between Metaphysics and Nonsense: Elucidation in Wittgenstein's *Tractatus*. *The Philosophical Quarterly*, 49, 491–513.

McGinn, M. (2001). Saying and Showing and the Continuity of Wittgenstein's Thought. *The Harvard Review of Philosophy*, 9, 24–36.

McGinn, M. (2006). *Elucidating the Tractatus: Wittgenstein's Early Philosophy of Logic and Language*. Oxford: Oxford University Press.

Mulhall, S. (2007). *Wittgenstein's Private Language: Grammar, Nonsense and Imagination in Philosophical Investigations, §§243–315*. Oxford: Oxford University Press.

Ostrow, M. (2002). *Wittgenstein's Tractatus: A Dialectical Interpretation*. Cambridge: Cambridge University Press.

Read, R. (2006). A No-Theory? Against Hutto on Wittgenstein. *Philosophical Investigations*, 29, 73–81.

Read, R. and Deans, R. (2003). Nothing is Shown: A "Resolute" Response to Mounce, Emiliani, Koethe and Vilhauer. *Philosophical Investigations*, 26, 239–268.

Read, R. and Deans, R. (2011). The Possibility of a Resolutely Resolute Reading of the *Tractatus*. In R. Read and M. Lavery (Eds). *Beyond the Tractatus Wars: The New Wittgenstein Debate* (pp.149–170). London: Routledge.

Read, R. and Hutchinson, P. (2006). The Elucidatory Reading of Wittgenstein's *Tractatus*: A Critique of Daniel Hutto's and Marie McGinn's Reading of *Tractatus* 6.54. *International Journal of Philosophical Studies*, 14, 1–29.

Ricketts, T. (1992). The Theory of Types and the Limits of Sense. Unpublished manuscript.

Schönbaumsfeld, G. (2008). Review of S. Mulhall: *Wittgenstein's Private Language*. *Mind*, 117, 1108–1112.

Stern, D.G. (2004) *Wittgenstein's Philosophical Investigations: An Introduction*. Cambridge: Cambridge University Press.

Williams, M. (2004). Nonsense and the Cosmic Exile: The Austere Reading of the *Tractatus*. In M. Kölbel and B. Weiss (Eds). *Wittgenstein's Lasting Significance* (pp.6–31). London: Routledge.

White, R. (2006). *Wittgenstein's Tractatus Logico-Philosophicus*. London: Continuum.

White, R. (2011). Throwing the Baby out with the Ladder: On "Therapeutic" Readings of Wittgenstein's *Tractatus*. In R. Read and M. Lavery (Eds). *Beyond the Tractatus Wars: The New Wittgenstein Debate* (pp.22–65). London: Routledge.

Further Reading

Crary, A. and Read, R. (Eds). (2000). *The New Wittgenstein*. London: Routledge.

Kremer, M. (2001). The Purpose of Tractarian Nonsense. *Noûs*, 35, 39–73.

Kremer, M. (2002). Mathematics and Meaning in the *Tractatus*. *Philosophical Investigations*, 25, 272–303.

McCarthy, T. and Stidd, S.C. (Eds). (2001). *Wittgenstein in America*. Oxford: Oxford University Press.

Read, R. and Lavery, M. (Eds). (2011). *Beyond the Tractatus Wars. The New Wittgenstein Debate*. London: Routledge.

Reck, E.H. (Ed.). (2002). *From Frege to Wittgenstein: Perspectives on Early Analytic Philosophy*. Oxford: Oxford University Press.

Ricketts, T. (1996). Pictures, Logic and the Limits of Sense in Wittgenstein's *Tractatus*. In H. Sluga and D.G. Stern (Eds). *The Cambridge Companion to Wittgenstein* (pp.59–99). Cambridge: Cambridge University Press.

Sullivan, P. (2002). On Trying to be Resolute: A Response to Kremer on the *Tractatus*. *European Journal of Philosophy*, 10, 43–78.

11

Ineffability and Nonsense in the *Tractatus*

LEO K.C. CHEUNG

1 The Orthodox Reading of the *Tractatus*

A substantial part of the *Tractatus* appears to put forward various philosophical and metaphysical theses concerning reality, language, and logic. It is therefore rather surprising that the author also writes the following:

> My propositions serve as elucidations in the following way: anyone who understands me eventually recognizes them as nonsensical, when he has used them – as steps – to climb up beyond them. (He must, so to speak, throw away the ladder after he has climbed up it.)
> He must transcend these propositions, and then he will see the world aright. (TLP 6.54)

How can the elucidatory sentences of the book, which obviously include ones that appear to be talking about various philosophical theses, be nonsensical? How can these nonsensical sentences be elucidations? How can they help one see the world aright by recognizing their nonsensicality? Understanding the Tractarian notions of nonsense and elucidation is not only crucial to answering these questions, but is also necessary in order to read the *Tractatus* correctly.

Early commentaries on the *Tractatus*, such as Russell's introduction and Ramsey's review in *Mind* (1923) already noted and commented on Wittgenstein's peculiar views concerning nonsense and elucidation. Russell says, "what causes hesitation is the fact that, after all, Mr Wittgenstein manages to say a good deal about what cannot be said" (TLP xxi). Ramsey also complains that "sentences apparently asserting such properties of objects are held by Mr Wittgenstein to be nonsense, but to stand in some obscure relation to something inexpressible" (1923, p.474).

However, there would not be "the orthodox reading" of the *Tractatus* exemplified by these remarks, were it not for the emergence of the "resolute reading" (Goldfarb, 1997, pp.64; 73, n.10), the "New Wittgensteinian" (Crary and Read, 2000, p.1), the "therapeutic reading" (McGinn, 1999), or the "post-modernist interpretation" (Hacker, 2000), which challenge it. The so-called resolute reading was initially put forward by Cora Diamond (1988) and further developed by James Conant (1989), as well as

---

A Companion to Wittgenstein, First Edition. Edited by Hans-Johann Glock and John Hyman.
© 2017 John Wiley & Sons, Ltd. Published 2017 by John Wiley & Sons, Ltd.

Thomas Ricketts (1996), Warren Goldfarb (1997, 2011), Michael Kremer (2001, 2002, 2007), and others. The resolute readers attack what they variously call the "standard readings" (Conant, 2002, p.392), the "irresolute readings" (Goldfarb, 1997, p.64; Conant, 2004, p.171), the "traditional reading" (Crary and Read, 2000, p.5), and the "ineffability interpretations" (Conant, 2000). The major proponents of the standard readings include Ramsey (1923), G.E.M. Anscombe (1959), Howard Mounce (1981), Peter Hacker (1972/86), David Pears (1987), and Hans-Johann Glock (1996). Anscombe and Hacker are the two principal targets of the resolute readers. The interpretations of the *Tractatus* proposed by members of the latter group can be seen as comprising a unity. I shall refer to them as the "orthodox reading" (White, 2011). Consequently, the resolute reading can be regarded as an "unorthodox" reading. I shall introduce it and examine it in detail later.

First, I shall give a summary of the main points that constitute the orthodox reading. Each of the points presented below is shared by some of the orthodox readers, and does not appear to be criticized by any of them. The cluster of those points constitutes the general content of the interpretation held by the orthodox readers.

According to the orthodox reading, Wittgenstein takes the elucidatory sentences in the *Tractatus* to be intended as attempts to say what cannot be said about, for example, the metaphysics of reality and the nature of language and logic (see, for example, Ramsey, 1923, p.474; Anscombe, 1959, pp.85–6, 161–73; Hacker, 1972/86, pp.15–27). One who understands the author of the *Tractatus* should be able to recognize the nonsensicality of the elucidatory sentences. They are nonsensical because their constituent signs are combined in ways that contravene the relevant rules of logical syntax (Hacker, 1972/86, pp.25–6; Glock, 1996, pp.258–62). Being nonsensical, they cannot say, show, or convey anything (Hacker, 1972/86, pp.25–7). However, what the nonsensical elucidatory sentences are intended to say can be shown by the features of significant sentences (propositions) saying something else, or by the senseless (*sinnlos*) propositions of logic. The nonsensical elucidatory sentences elucidate by drawing our attention to the significant sentences (or senseless propositions of logic), which show what they (the nonsensical sentences) are intended to say (Ramsey, 1923, p.474; Hacker, 1972/86, pp.18–19). They can do this because their constituent signs are familiar words in ordinary language, and their nonsensicality is a result of contravening the rules of logical syntax of familiar signs. Through the recognition of their nonsensicality, one can be directed to see that those significant sentences (propositions), in which the same signs symbolize, show what they (the nonsensical sentences) are intended to say (Mounce, 1981, pp.101–9; 2001, pp.187–9).

2   The First Criticism and Responses

The resolute readers have been the most prominent, and perhaps most consistent, critics of the orthodox reading. In what follows, I shall introduce four of the resolute readers' strongest criticisms, and explain how orthodox readers have responded, or can respond, to them. These criticisms are as follows. (1) The orthodox readers hold that the nonsensical elucidatory sentences mentioned in TLP 6.54 can "show," "gesture at," "convey," or "communicate" ineffable "insights" or "truths." But there is no such view in the *Tractatus*. (2) The orthodox readers hold that there are two different types of nonsense – mere nonsense and substantial nonsense. In particular, Hacker also holds that substantial nonsense is a result of the violation of logical syntax. But these views are mistaken, because the *Tractatus* holds the austere conception of nonsense, according to which there is only one type of nonsense, mere nonsense. (3) According to the orthodox reading, the *Tractatus* proposes a theory of meaning specifying sense conditions, the application of which is required for the recognition of substantial nonsense. But the *Tractatus* would not accept such a view. (4) The resolute readers hold that the nonsensical Tractarian sentences are just gibberish, and that they are not intended to convey anything. The orthodox readers are therefore wrong to hold that nonsensical Tractarian sentences are "attempts," or "are intended," to say, show, or convey what cannot be said.

The first criticism is that, according to the orthodox reading, the nonsensical elucidatory sentences mentioned in TLP 6.54 can "show," "gesture at," "convey," or "communicate" ineffable "insights" or "truths" (Diamond, 1988, pp.7, 10; 2001, p.153; 2004, p.66; 2011, p.348; Conant, 2000, pp.177, 199; 2002, pp.376, 425; 2004, pp.170–1; 2007, p.44; Goldfarb, 1997, pp.61, 64; 2011, pp.7, 12–14). But, resolute readers hold, there is no such view in the *Tractatus*. The orthodox readers do not take what TLP 6.54 says about nonsense seriously. Despite 6.54, they see Wittgenstein as attempting "to represent to ourselves something in reality, the possibility of what a sentence says being so, as not sayable but shown by the sentence" (Diamond, 1988, p.10). Diamond calls this "chickening out": "To chicken out is to pretend to throw away the ladder while standing firmly, or as firmly as one can, on it" (1988, p.20; see also p.7).

This criticism indicates a grave misunderstanding of the orthodox reading by the resolute readers (see Cheung, 2008). It is important to note that the orthodox reading also holds that nonsensical sentences cannot say, show, or convey anything. The *Tractatus* does hold that what the nonsensical elucidatory sentences are intended to say cannot be said, but can be shown; however, those ineffable truths are not shown by the nonsensical sentences, but by the features of significant sentences saying something else (or by the senseless propositions of logic). Resolute readers seem to mistakenly think that, since according to the orthodox reading what the nonsensical Tractarian sentences are intended to say can be shown, they must be shown or conveyed by those nonsensical sentences themselves. Let me offer textual evidence to support these points. Anscombe writes:

> An important part is played in the *Tractatus* by the things which, though they cannot be 'said', are yet 'shewn' or 'displayed'. That is to say: it would be right to call them 'true' if, *per impossible*, they could be said; in fact they cannot be called true, since they cannot be said, but 'can be shewn', or 'are exhibited', in the propositions saying the various things that can be said. (Anscombe, 1959, p.162)

Here, Anscombe says clearly that what cannot be said is not shown by any nonsensical sentences, but by "the propositions saying the various things that can be said," that is, by significant sentences saying something else. Hacker says similar things on many occasions, e.g., in the following passage:

> Wittgenstein's own propositions [...] are, by the light of the *Tractatus*, nonsensical pseudo-propositions. They show nothing at all. The propositions that *are* held to show the ineffable truths which the *Tractatus* seems to be trying to say are not the pseudo-propositions of the book but well-formed propositions (including the senseless propositions of logic). (Hacker, 2000, p.356; see also Hacker, 1972/86, p.18; 2001, p.326)

Hacker says very clearly here that the nonsensical Tractarian sentences do not show anything, and that what they are intended to say, which cannot be said, is shown by well-formed propositions.

What is more, one can easily find textual evidence supporting the orthodox readers' views concerning nonsense and showing. For instance:

> Thus one proposition '*fa*' shows that the object *a* occurs in its sense, two propositions '*fa*' and '*ga*' show that the same object is mentioned in both of them. (TLP 4.1211)

The sentence "*a* occurs in the sense of '*fa*'" is intended to say something, but that something cannot actually be said (see TLP 4.1211). The sentence "*a* occurs in the sense of '*fa*'" is nonsensical. Although it is intended to say something, it cannot say, show, or convey anything. But the significant sentence (proposition) "*fa*" shows that *a* occurs in the sense of "*fa*." What the nonsensical sentence "*a* occurs in the sense of '*fa*'" is intended to say cannot be said, but is shown by the significant proposition "*fa*." In other words, what shows something is not the nonsensical sentence "*a* occurs in the sense of '*fa*,'" nor the equally nonsensical sentence "'*fa*' shows that *a* occurs in the sense of '*fa*,'" but the significant sentence "*fa*."

There are indeed earlier prominent commentators who think Wittgenstein takes his own nonsensical sentences to be able to show ineffable truths. For example, Max Black suggests that the nonsensical elucidatory Tractarian sentences are "formal statements, 'showing' something that *can be* shown" (Black, 1964, p.381). But Hacker points out the incorrectness of Black's suggestion (Hacker, 1972/86, pp.25–6). Similar mistakes are also made by recent commentators, who are sympathetic to the orthodox reading. One example is Roger White, who knows that, for the *Tractatus*, nonsense cannot say or show anything, and that what the nonsensical Tractarian sentences are intended to say cannot be said, but is shown by "our meaningful use of language" (White, 2011, p.44). Yet he still tries to argue that, and explain how, the nonsensical sentences can direct us to what is shown by the meaningful use of language, and holds that a kind of indirect communication is involved here (White, 2011, pp.52–9). This doesn't seem to be right. For the orthodox reading, and for the *Tractatus*, nonsensical sentences cannot "communicate" anything, directly or indirectly. How can the nonsensical Tractarian sentences "direct" one, in a way different from conveying or "communicating," to significant sentences showing what cannot be said? This question was already answered briefly in the summary above, and will be further explained when we consider the responses to the fourth criticism below.

3   The Second Criticism and Responses

According to the second criticism made by resolute readers, the orthodox reading implies that there are two different types of nonsense – mere nonsense and substantial nonsense – and that ineffable insights can be shown, "gestured at," or conveyed by nonsensical elucidatory Tractarian sentences, whose nonsensicality is substantial (Diamond, 2001, pp.150–4). Moreover, it is alleged that Hacker – a leading representative of the orthodox reading – holds that substantial nonsense is a result of the violation of logical syntax (Conant, 2000, p.177). For the resolute readers, these views are mistaken, because the *Tractatus* holds the austere conception of nonsense, according to which there is only one type of nonsense, mere nonsense, and there is no such thing as a violation of logical syntax (Conant, 1989, pp.247–8; 2000, pp.190–1). Their major textual evidence is TLP 5.4733:

> Frege says that any legitimately constructed [*rechtmäßig gebildeter*] proposition [*Satz*; sentence] must have a sense. And I say that any possible proposition is legitimately constructed [*rechtmäßig gebildet*], and, if it has no sense, that can only be because we have failed to give a *meaning* to some of its constituents. (Even if we think that we have done so.)
>
> Thus the reason why 'Socrates is identical' says nothing is that we have not given *any adjectival* meaning to the word 'identical' [*wir dem Wort 'identisch' als Eigenschaftswort keine Bedeutung gegeben haben*]. For when it appears as a sign for identity, it symbolizes in an entirely different way – the signifying relation is a different one – therefore the symbols also are entirely different in the two cases: the two symbols have only the sign in common, and that is an accident.

According to Diamond (1988, pp.22–3; 2005, pp.88–9), one of the main points of TLP 5.4733 is that "no sentence-construction is illegitimately put together," and this entails that "there is no such thing as a sentence which is nonsensical in virtue of use of the signs in it in ways which are excluded" (2005, p.89), and thus there is no such thing as violation of logical syntax. According to Conant (2002, pp.411–12; 2004, p.184), the word "only" in TLP 5.4733 proves that, for the *Tractatus*, there is only nonsense caused by the failure to make a determination of meaning, and thus, again, there is no such thing as violation of logical syntax.

The resolute readers seem to have provided two different ways of distinguishing between mere nonsense and substantial nonsense. On the one hand, Diamond characterizes the distinction as being between mere nonsense, or gibberish like "piggly wiggle tiggle," and "sentences that are nonsense but would mean these things if they could count as sense," or "sentences count as nonsense but do manage to gesture towards those things that cannot be put into plain words" (2001, p.150). Conant also holds that "according to the substantial conception, the task of elucidation is to 'show' something which cannot be said" (2000, p.177), and that "[the elucidatory propositions of the *Tractatus*] are a form of deep nonsense by means of which a special sort of insight can be conveyed" (2004, p.171).

On the other hand, Conant also characterizes mere nonsense as gibberish, while substantial nonsense is intelligible nonsense whose forms are "ways of transgressing the syntax of our language" (1989, p.248). He also characterizes mere nonsense as simply unintelligible (Conant, 2000, p.176) or "a string composed of signs in which no symbol can be perceived, and which hence has no discernible logical syntax" (p.191), and substantial nonsense as what is "composed of intelligible ingredients combined in an illegitimate way – it expresses a logically incoherent thought" (p.176) or "a proposition composed of signs which symbolize, but which has a logically flawed syntax due to a clash in the logical category of its symbols" (p.191). Roughly, the distinction here is between mere nonsense like gibberish and nonsense resulting from the violation of logical syntax.

Let me now turn to the responses to the second criticism. As already pointed out, the orthodox reading insists that nonsense cannot say, show, or convey anything, and that what cannot be said is not shown by nonsensical sentences, but by significant sentences (or senseless propositions of logic). The claim that the orthodox readers think that some nonsense is capable of showing or conveying something is quite wrong.

Now the claim that orthodox readers like Hacker hold that substantial nonsense is the result of the violation of logical syntax cannot be right either, because the orthodox readers simply do not hold that there *is* substantial nonsense. However, the orthodox reading does hold that there are nonsensical combinations of signs that are results of the violation, or contravention, of logical syntax, and that they are exactly the kind of nonsensical sentences mentioned by TLP 6.54. It is therefore also important for orthodox readers to refute the resolute readers' claim that there is no such thing as violation of logical syntax.

Hacker points out that Conant's view that "logical syntax does not treat of (mere) *signs*; it treats of symbols" (Conant, 2001, pp.41–2) is incorrect. According to Hacker, Conant's view "is a confused statement of the correct point that, according to the *Tractatus*, there can be nonsensical signs, but not nonsensical symbols, since a symbol just is a sign used according to the rules for its correct use" (Hacker, 2003, p.13). Actually, it is easy to find textual evidence supporting the view that the rules of logical syntax govern the use of signs; for example, TLP 3.325 ("a sign-language that is governed by [...] logical syntax"), TLP 3.33–3.331, TLP 6.124 ("If we know the logical syntax of any sign-language, then we have already been given all the propositions of logic"), and TLP 6.126.

Hacker concedes that the term "violation of logical syntax" does not occur in the *Tractatus*; but then he says, "obviously there can be no such thing as using a sign in accordance with logical syntax if there is no such thing as using it in contravention of logical syntax" (Hacker, 2003, p.13). Having pointed out that logical syntax concerns signs and not symbols, Hacker seems to think it is rather obvious that signs can be used in contravention of logical syntax.

But this is still not enough to counter the attack from the resolute readers, because of their appeal to TLP 5.4733, which appears to be saying that there cannot be nonsense produced by the contravention of logical syntax, and that there is no such thing as using signs in contravention of logical syntax. The orthodox readers need to show that the resolute readers' interpretation of TLP 5.4733 is incorrect. This, as I shall argue, can be done in a way such that TLP 5.4733 is proved to be contrary to the resolute reading's understanding of the notion of nonsense.

Although the sign "identical" is not used as the sign of an adjective in English, it is supposed to have been assigned the logical form of an adjective, that is, symbolized as an adjective, in the context of TLP 5.4733. This explains why it is said to be an adjective (*Eigenschaftswort*) there. In this case, the sign "identical" is used innovatively as the sign of an adjective in "Socrates is identical." It is used in accordance with the rules of logical syntax of an adjective. The sentence "Socrates is identical" is then legitimately constructed (*rechtmäßig gebildete*) or well formed, and thus is a possible sentence. The sentence "Socrates is identical," as a possible sign, must be capable of signifying a sense (see also TLP 5.473). But, according to TLP 5.4733, it still does not have a sense because a meaning, an adjectival meaning, has not been assigned to the constituent sign "identical." So what Wittgenstein is saying in TLP 5.4733 is mainly that if a possible sentence, which must be legitimately constructed, has no sense, that can only be because no meaning has been given to some of its constituents. Wittgenstein is talking about legitimately constructed sentences there. One cannot gather from this that there is no such thing as illegitimately constructed sentences or using signs in contravention of logical syntax.

What is more, TLP 5.4733 actually allows for the possibility of using signs in contravention of logical syntax. Wittgenstein says in the last part of TLP 5.4733 that when "identical" is taken to be the sign of the identity symbol, it is used as the sign of a symbol different from an adjective. He seems to be suggesting that if "identity" is intended to be used as the sign of the identity symbol in the sentence "Socrates is identical," then it is used in contravention of the rules of logical syntax of the identity symbol, and thus the sentence "Socrates is identical" is nonsensical. It seems that TLP 5.4733 allows for the possibility of using signs in contravention of logical syntax. The resolute readers' major textual evidence actually goes against their view that there is no such thing as the contravention of logical syntax (see also Cheung, 2008, pp.205–10).

4   The Third Criticism and a Simple Response

The third criticism from the resolute readers is that the orthodox reading holds that the *Tractatus* advances a theory of meaning specifying sense conditions, the application of which is required for the recognition of substantial nonsense, and that the *Tractatus* would not accept such a view (Diamond, 2005, pp.78–9; Conant, 2001, p.39; 2002, pp.393–4; 2007, p.44).

Hacker (2003, pp.11–13) has a simple response to this criticism. The *Tractatus* need not, and does not, hold that the recognition of nonsense needs a theory of meaning, nor does the *Tractatus* advance any theory of meaning. For one can recognize nonsense if one knows the rules of logical syntax, without employing any theory of meaning at all.

5   The Fourth Criticism and Responses

The fourth criticism by resolute readers is that, according to the resolute reading, the nonsensical Tractarian sentences are just gibberish. They are not intended to convey anything. The orthodox readers are therefore wrong to hold that the nonsensical Tractarian sentences are "attempts," or "are intended," to say, show, or convey what cannot be said (Diamond, 1988, p.7; 2011, pp.335–7; Conant, 1989, p.247; 2004, p.171). It is not entirely clear what the argument for this is supposed to be, but perhaps it is something like this: the *Tractatus* adopts the austere conception of nonsense, according to which there is only one kind of nonsense – mere nonsense – and holds that mere nonsense cannot say, show, or convey anything. Wittgenstein does of course not think that mere nonsense *can be intended to* say, or convey, ineffable "insights," any more than gibberish can.

In fact the orthodox reading does hold that the nonsensical Tractarian sentences *are intended to* say something ineffable. But the *Tractatus* does not hold the austere conception of nonsense. The nonsensical Tractarian sentences are not gibberish, and, according to the *Tractatus*, they can direct one to see that what they are intended to say can be shown by significant sentences (or senseless propositions of logic). But having said that, it is incumbent on the orthodox readers to show that, in the *Tractatus*, some nonsensical sentences *are intended to* say something, which actually cannot be said, and that the recognition of their nonsensicality helps one see that what they are intended to say is shown by significant sentences. And it is also incumbent on them to explain how, according to the *Tractatus*, these nonsensical sentences can *direct* readers, in a way different from saying, showing, conveying, or "communicating," to the significant sentences showing ineffable "truths."

It is not difficult to find textual evidence for the claim that the nonsensical sentences of the *Tractatus*, including sentences found in philosophical works, can be intended to say something ineffable. Here is one example:

> What the axiom of infinity *is intended* to say [*sagen soll*] would express itself in language through the existence of infinitely many names with different meanings. (TLP 5.535, emphasis added)

According to Wittgenstein, the axiom of infinity is nonsensical, and yet it can be intended to say something profound. He also thinks, as he says in TLP 6.54, that one can be directed to see the world aright by recognizing its nonsensicality, and this presumably means that one can see that what is intended to be said by the nonsensical axiom of infinity is shown by our use of symbols and names in language. But what is this "directing" if it is not saying, showing, conveying, or communicating?

Many orthodox readers, including Anscombe and Hacker, do not try to answer this question, perhaps because they think the *Tractatus* is mistaken at this point, and thus there is no need to find out how the "directing" is possible and how it can be something different from saying, showing, and conveying. Nevertheless, Mounce (1981) has tried to explain Wittgenstein's idea. As we know, Wittgenstein takes metaphysical confusions to be the result of misunderstanding the logic of our language. Mounce writes:

> In metaphysical confusion, we do not notice this because the words we use are familiar ones. It is this which distinguishes them from mere gibberish, which gives them their appearance of sense. (Mounce, 1981, p.105)

For example, the fact that familiar words are used, but not used significantly, in the metaphysical sentence "A is an object" gives it the appearance of sense. But it is still nonsensical. It still cannot say, show, or convey what it is intended to say. Yet, according to the *Tractatus*, it can direct us to what shows itself in the propositional context in which the familiar words (signs) symbolize, as explained by Mounce (2001) in the following passage:

> The propositions of the *Tractatus* are not intended to indicate what eludes the medium of language but to direct our attention to what shows itself in that medium. That is how they are elucidatory. For example, should Wittgenstein say 'A is an object', we direct our attention, if we understand him, to what shows itself in *the use of the sign 'A'*. (Mounce, 2001, p.188; see also 2003)

Let me explain this using the example "*a* occurs in the sense of '*fa*'" (again). According to the *Tractatus*, this sentence is nonsensical, because its constituent signs are combined in contravention of the relevant rules of logical syntax. To see this, note that the sign "*a*" symbolizes in the proposition "*fa*," but not in the sentence "*a* occurs in the sense of '*fa*.'" The constituent sign "*fa*" of the sentence also does not symbolize a proposition. What is intended by the utterer of the sentence cannot be said by any proposition, nor can it be shown or conveyed by the nonsensical sentence itself; but it can be *shown* by the significant sentence "*fa*." Hence, the nonsensical sentence "*a* occurs in the sense of '*fa*'" is elucidatory, because, through the recognition of its nonsensicality, and thus grasping the rules of logical syntax of the familiar signs, familiar signs like "*a*" and "*fa*" in it direct our attention to the significant sentence "*fa*," in which "*a*" and "*fa*" symbolize, and thus to what is shown by "*fa*."

However, it is reasonable to doubt if the "directing" explained above really can direct, in a way different from saying, showing, and conveying, our attention to the significant use of familiar words (signs) in ordinary language. In fact, orthodox readers like Ramsey (1923, p.474), Anscombe (1959, pp.85–6), Hacker (1972/86, pp.26–7), Mounce (1981, pp.107–9; 2003, pp.187–9), and Glock (2004, pp.237–8) all think that Wittgenstein is mistaken at this point. This is a problem for the author of the *Tractatus*.

6   The Resolute Reading as an Unorthodox Reading of the *Tractatus*

The resolute reading proposes a new way of reading the *Tractatus*, and tries to give prominence to its distinctness and correctness by attacking the orthodox reading. It should then be seen as an unorthodox reading. In what follows, I shall introduce and examine it as such.

Proponents of the resolute reading urge us to take seriously what Wittgenstein says in TLP 6.54 about the nonsensicality of the elucidatory sentences. To take TLP 6.54 seriously, they claim, requires holding what Conant and Diamond (2004, pp.47–9) regard as the two basic features of the resolute reading, which are sufficient to characterize the resolute reading. The first basic feature is that nonsense, including the nonsensical elucidatory sentences, cannot convey any ineffable truths. The second basic feature is that the *Tractatus* does not advance any theory of meaning specifying the conditions of sense, the application of which is required for the recognition of the nonsensicality of the elucidatory Tractarian sentences (see also Diamond, 2005, pp.78–9; Conant, 2001, p.39; 2002, pp.393–4; 2007, p.44).

Conant and Diamond maintain that these two basic features are sufficient to characterize a resolute reading, and they also take these as strong objections to the orthodox reading. In this way, the two basic features account for the novelty and distinctness of the resolute reading. Moreover, the negative nature of the two basic features allows a large number of different versions of the resolute reading. It is then important to see the resolute reading as a program, rather than as a specific interpretation of the *Tractatus* (Conant and Diamond, 2004, p.47).

Besides the two basic features, there are also two main ideas of the resolute reading. The first main idea is that all the sentences of the *Tractatus*, except those few serving as "the frame" that instructs how the book should be read, are nonsensical. This idea is related to the resolute readers' urge to take seriously what TLP 6.54 says about the nonsensicality of the elucidatory sentences. However, while Wittgenstein clearly holds that the elucidatory Tractarian sentences are nonsensical, there are reasons to doubt whether he takes all the non-elucidatory sentences to be reading instructions. First, neither TLP 6.54 nor any other entry of the *Tractatus* says that all those non-elucidatory sentences are reading instructions. Second, one can easily find examples in the *Tractatus* of significant sentences that are certainly not reading instructions; for example: "Philosophy is not one of the natural sciences" (TLP 4.111). Third, Diamond and

Conant also employ non-frame entries to argue for their claims. For example, as we have seen before, they use TLP 5.4733 to argue for the claim that Wittgenstein holds that there is no such thing as violation of logical syntax (Conant, 2002, pp.411–2; Diamond, 2005, p.89). TLP 5.4733 is clearly not a reading instruction, but it is also seen by them as significant. This is an inconsistency in their positions (see also Cheung, 2008, pp.211–12).

Conant (2002, 2007) has modified their position concerning the frame sentences, including many more frame sentences than he and Diamond did in their earlier works (viz., TLP 3.32–3.326, 4–4.003, 4.111–4.112, 6.53–6.54). He still thinks there are significant sentences of the *Tractatus* serving as reading instructions, that is, the frame sentences. But he will not *list* the frame sentences, because whether a sentence belongs to the frame depends on "its role within the work." The distinction between "what is part of the frame and what is part of the body of the work is [...] a function of how it occurs" (Conant, 2002, pp.457–8, n.135).

The second main idea of the resolute reading is that the aim of the *Tractatus* is *merely* to liberate nonsense-utterers from nonsense, and that this is to be achieved by the non-frame sentences serving as elucidations. The elucidatory sentences are not attempts to convey anything; they merely liberate those nonsense-utterers who were misled by the nonsensical sentences (into having illusions of sense) from the illusions of sense (Diamond, 2001, pp.156–62; Conant 2000, p.196; 2001, p.59). The process of liberation is done on a "case-by-case" basis (Diamond, 2004, pp.153–4).

The notion of liberation from nonsense in the second main idea should be further explained. Diamond and Conant have made at least two attempts to explain it. In one attempt, Diamond appeals to the notion of imagination, and draws our attention to the word "me" in TLP 6.54, which refers to a person who talks nonsense. To understand one who utters nonsense is "to enter imaginatively the taking of that nonsense for sense" (Diamond, 2001, p.157). The nonsensical sentences of the *Tractatus* elucidate by invoking the imagination of taking nonsense for sense by a nonsense-utterer "who is in the grip of the illusion that there is philosophy in the traditional sense" (p.160); by doing this, the nonsense-utterer can be led out of the illusion.

In another attempt, Diamond and Conant argue that the *Tractatus* employs logical analysis and a logical notation to serve the purpose of elucidation or clarification. Endorsing some of Kremer's (2001, 2002) views, Diamond (2004, pp.154, 157) argues that the *Tractatus* takes a piecemeal approach to philosophical clarification, and that the clarification process involves making clear the inferential behavior of the utterance concerned by adding a tautology to it. Conant (2007, pp.44–7) also emphasizes that, for the *Tractatus*, the forms of logical notation employed must be elucidatory instruments, and that their employment does not require commitment to any particular philosophical theses.

However, according to Diamond and Conant, the adoption of the notions of logical analysis and a logical notation requires a commitment to philosophical theses about the nature of language, and, in this case, about the general propositional form. Diamond and Conant do think that, in laying down the requirement of logical analysis, there are moments of "metaphysical insistence" (2004, pp.80–4). In other words, the *Tractatus* has unwittingly committed itself to philosophical and metaphysical theses. Hermeneutically, such a move has the merit of being able to explain the fact that there are severe criticisms of those philosophical and metaphysical theses in Wittgenstein's later works.

7 The Strong and Weak Resolute Readings

Resolute readings can be divided into "strong" and "weak" readings (Read and Deans, 2003, p.251) or, more or less equivalently, "Jacobin" and "Girondin" readings (so called by Goldfarb; see Lavery, 2011, p.118). The major representatives of the weak, or Girondin, resolute reading include Diamond, Conant, and Kremer, while the major representatives of the strong, or Jacobin, resolute reading include Juliet Floyd (2002, 2007) and Rupert Read and Rob Deans (2003, 2011). One distinction between the two readings is that, in the weak resolute reading, the "frame" is held onto; while, in the strong resolute reading, the "frame" "is seen as yet another expression of the impulse towards metaphysics, and is to be surmounted as well" (Read and Deans, 2003, p.251). For example, although as already mentioned, Conant has modified his position concerning the frame sentences, he still regards them as reading instructions, or at least not something to be thrown away. But the strong resolute readers prefer the claim that "the *Tractatus* might be read as consisting entirely of elucidations" (Read and Deans, 2011, p.154).

Another, more important, distinction is that, as already mentioned in the above discussion of Diamond and Conant's views concerning analysis and logical notation, the weak resolute reading accepts that the *Tractatus* employs logical analysis and a logical notation for philosophical elucidation or clarification. The strong resolute readers, on the other hand, accept the continuing clarifying or therapeutic role for logical analysis, but think the attempt to completely reduce a sentence to something fully expressed by a logical notation must result in nonsense (Read and Deans, 2003, p.251). Floyd, as a strong resolute reader, holds that the notions of logical analysis and a logical notation (a *Begriffsschrift*) in the *Tractatus*, as well as "*the* inferential order," "*the* logical grammar of language," "*the* logical form of a proposition," are all chimeras (Floyd, 2002, pp.339–40). However, she is not saying that the *Tractatus* sees logical analysis as something useless. Although the *Tractatus* does not seek *the* logically correct notation, Floyd writes,

> we can take the *Tractatus* to be recasting our understanding of the formal use of the notion of analysis itself [...] and [moving] toward a more complicated, piecemeal conception of the role that translation into formalized languages may play in the activity of philosophical clarification. (Floyd, 2007, p.206)

The second distinction, however, points to serious difficulties of the weak and strong resolute readings, respectively. The weak resolute readers, as proponents of the resolute reading, must hold that the nonsensical Tractarian sentences are not attempts to say any ineffable truths, even when such sentences are translated into a perspicuous notation. If the weak resolute readers are really taking TLP 6.54 seriously, they should agree that the *Tractatus* takes the notions of logical analysis and a logical notation, in the end, to be chimeras. For it is unreasonable to think Wittgenstein failed to notice that holding on to the notions means being committed to certain philosophical and metaphysical theses.

The strong resolute readers, on the other hand, face the difficulty of explaining Wittgenstein's later criticisms of the *Tractatus* (see Kuusela, 2011, p.143; Proops, 2001). For example, Wittgenstein criticizes the *Tractatus* in texts like *Philosophical Investigations* §§60–4 and 134–42, which contain critical remarks on the notions of logical analysis and the general propositional form in the *Tractatus*, respectively. The difficulty for the strong resolute readers is to explain what Wittgenstein is actually doing in those later texts, if the notions of logical analysis and a logical notation were already considered meaningless in the *Tractatus*. Strong resolute readers like Read and Deans try to show that it is possible to respond to this challenge by sketching an argument for the claim that the later Wittgenstein is often not a charitable and reliable interpreter of his own early thought (Read and Deans, 2011, pp.163–4). However, until they have defended this idea persuasively, the difficulty remains.

8   Criticisms and Comments

It was already argued in previous sections that the orthodox reading also holds that the nonsensical sentences of the *Tractatus* cannot say, show, or convey anything, that the *Tractatus* does not advance any theory of meaning signifying sense conditions, and that contraventions of logical syntax do not produce substantial nonsense (see Chapter 8, THE PICTURE THEORY). Therefore, the two basic features do not distinguish the resolute reading from the orthodox reading, and therefore also do not characterize the resolute reading.

What really characterizes the resolute reading, I think, are the two main ideas mentioned above, especially the second main idea. As I already pointed out, according to the orthodox reading, the nonsensical elucidatory sentences are attempts to say ineffable truths, which cannot be said, but can be shown by significant sentences (or senseless propositions of logic). The nonsensical sentences cannot convey anything, yet they can direct, in a way different from saying, showing, and conveying, one's attention to the significant sentences showing what they are intended to say. Such a view actually fits the text of the *Tractatus* much better than the resolute readers' second main idea that the nonsensical sentences merely serve to liberate nonsense-utterers from nonsense. What is more, one can find no textual evidence in the *Tractatus* to support the resolute readers' claim that mere nonsense, which is of the same nature as gibberish, is capable of liberating one from nonsense.

The above criticisms are, of course, applicable to both strong and weak versions of the resolute reading. Together with the further difficulties mentioned above, the fact that the weak resolute reading does not seem resolute enough, and the fact that the strong resolute reading fails to explain the later Wittgenstein's criticisms of the *Tractatus*, show that the resolute reading, in both versions, has serious difficulties.

References

Anscombe, G.E.M. (1959). *An Introduction to Wittgenstein's Tractatus*. London: Hutchinson.
Black, M. (1964). *A Companion to Wittgenstein's Tractatus*. Ithaca: Cornell University Press.
Cheung, L.K.C. (2008). The Disenchantment of Nonsense: Understanding Wittgenstein's *Tractatus*. *Philosophical Investigations*, 31, 197–226.
Conant, J. (1989). Must We Show What We Cannot Say? In R. Fleming and M. Payne (Eds). *The Senses of Stanley Cavell* (pp.242–83). Lewisburg: Bucknell University Press.
Conant, J. (2000). Elucidation and Nonsense in Frege and Early Wittgenstein. In A. Crary and R. Read (Eds). *The New Wittgenstein* (pp.149–73). London: Routledge.

Conant, J. (2001). Two Conceptions of *die Überwindung der Metaphysik:* Carnap and Early Wittgenstein. In T. McCarthy and S.C. Stidd (Eds). *Wittgenstein in America* (pp.13–61). Oxford: Clarendon Press.
Conant, J. (2002). The Method of the *Tractatus*. In E.H. Reck (Ed.). *From Frege to Wittgenstein* (pp.374–462). Oxford: Oxford University Press.
Conant, J. (2004). Why Worry about the *Tractatus?* In B. Stocker (Ed.). *Post-analytic Tractatus* (pp.167–192). Aldershot: Ashgate.
Conant, J. (2007). Mild Mono-Wittgensteinianism. In A. Crary (Ed.). *Wittgenstein and the Moral Life: Essays in Honor of Cora Diamond* (pp.31–142). Cambridge, MA: MIT Press.
Conant, J. and Diamond, C. (2004). On Reading the *Tractatus* Resolutely: Reply to Meredith Williams and Peter Sullivan. In M. Kölbel and B. Weiss (Eds). *Wittgenstein's Lasting Significance* (pp.46–99). London: Routledge.
Crary, A. and Read, R. (Eds). (2000). *The New Wittgenstein*. London: Routledge.
Diamond, C. (1988). Throwing Away the Ladder: How to Read the *Tractatus. Philosophy*, 63, 5–27.
Diamond, C. (2001). Ethics, Imagination and the Method of Wittgenstein's *Tractatus*. In A. Crary and R. Read (Eds). *The New Wittgenstein* (pp.149–173). London: Routledge.
Diamond, C. (2004). Saying and Showing: An Example from Anscombe. In B. Stocker (Ed). *Post-analytic Tractatus* (pp.151–166). Aldershot: Ashgate.
Diamond, C. (2005). Logical Syntax in Wittgenstein's *Tractatus. Philosophical Quarterly*, 55, 78–89.
Diamond, C. (2011). We Can't Whistle It Either: Legend and Reality. *European Journal of Philosophy*, 19, 335–356.
Floyd, J. (2002). Number and Ascription of Number in Wittgenstein's *Tractatus*. In E.H. Reck (Ed.). *From Frege to Wittgenstein* (pp.308–352). Oxford: Oxford University Press.
Floyd, J. (2007). Wittgenstein and the Inexpressible. In A. Crary and R. Read (Eds). *The New Wittgenstein* (pp.177–234). London: Routledge.
Glock, H.-J. (1996). *A Wittgenstein Dictionary*. Oxford: Blackwell.
Glock, H.-J. (2004). All Kinds of Nonsense. In E. Ammereller and E. Fischer (Eds). *Wittgenstein at Work: Method in the Philosophical Investigations* (pp.221–245). London: Routledge.
Goldfarb, W. (1997). Metaphysics and Nonsense: On Cora Diamond's *The Realistic Spirit. Journal of Philosophical Research*, 22, 57–73.
Goldfarb, W. (2011). *Das Überwinden:* Anti-Metaphysical Readings of the *Tractatus*. In R. Read and M. Lavery (Eds). *Beyond the Tractatus Wars* (pp.6–21). New York: Routledge.
Hacker, P.M.S. (1972/86). *Insight and Illusion: Themes in the Philosophy of Wittgenstein*. Revised edition. Oxford: Clarendon Press.
Hacker, P.M.S. (2000). Was He Trying to Whistle It? In A. Crary and R. Read (Eds). *The New Wittgenstein* (pp.253–288). London: Routledge.
Hacker, P.M.S. (2001). Philosophy. In H.J. Glock (Ed.). *Wittgenstein: A Critical Reader* (pp.322–347). Oxford: Blackwell.
Hacker, P.M.S. (2003). Wittgenstein, Carnap and the New American Wittgensteinian, *The Philosophical Quarterly*, 53, 1–23.
Kremer, M. (2001). The Purpose of Tractarian Nonsense. *Noûs*, 35, 39–73.
Kremer, M. (2002). Mathematics and Meaning in the *Tractatus. Philosophical Investigations*, 25, 272–302.
Kremer, M. (2007). The Cardinal Problem of Philosophy. In A. Crary (Ed.). *Wittgenstein and the Moral Life: Essays in Honor of Cora Diamond* (pp.143–176). Cambridge, MA: MIT Press.
Kuusela, O. (2011). The Dialectic of Interpretations: Reading Wittgenstein's *Tractatus*. In R. Read and M. Lavery (Eds). *Beyond the Tractatus Wars* (pp.121–148). New York: Routledge.
Lavery, M. (2011). Toward a Useful Jacobinism: A Response to Bronzo. In R. Read and M. Lavery (Eds). *Beyond the Tractatus Wars* (pp.112–120). New York: Routledge.
McGinn, M. (1999). Between Metaphysics and Nonsense: Elucidation in Wittgenstein's *Tractatus. The Philosophical Quarterly*, 49, 491–513.

Mounce, H.O. (1981). *Wittgenstein's Tractatus: An Introduction.* Oxford: Blackwell.
Mounce, H.O. (2003). Reply to Read and Deans. *Philosophical Investigations,* 26, 269–270.
Pears, D. (1987). *The False Prison* (Vol. 1). Oxford: Oxford University Press.
Proops, I. (2001). The new Wittgenstein: A Critique. *European Journal of Philosophy,* 9, 375–404.
Ramsey, F.P. (1923). Review of *Tractatus Logico-Philosophicus.* Mind, 32, 465–478.
Read, R. and Deans, R. (2003). "Nothing is shown": A "Resolute" Response to Mounce, Emiliani, Koethe and Vilhauer. *Philosophical Investigations,* 26, 239–268.
Read, R. and Deans, R. (2011). The Possibility of a Resolutely Resolute Reading of the *Tractatus.* In R. Read and M. Lavery (Eds). *Beyond the Tractatus Wars* (pp.149–171). New York: Routledge.
Ricketts, T. (1996). Picture, Logic, and the Limits of Sense in the *Tractatus.* In H. Sluga and D.G. Stern (Eds). *The Cambridge Companion to Wittgenstein* (pp.59–99). Cambridge: Cambridge University Press.
White, R. (2011). Throwing the Baby out with the Ladder: On "Therapeutic" Readings of Wittgenstein's *Tractatus.* In R. Read and M. Lavery (Eds). *Beyond the Tractatus Wars* (pp.22–65). New York: Routledge.

Further Reading

Bronzo, S. (2012). The Resolute Reading and its Critics: An Introduction to the Literature. *Wittgenstein Studien,* 3, 45–80.
Cheung, L. K. C. (2008). The Disenchantment of Nonsense: Understanding Wittgenstein's *Tractatus. Philosophical Investigations,* 31(3): 197–226.
Crary, A. (Ed.). (2007). *Wittgenstein and the Moral Life: Essays in Honor of Cora Diamond.* Cambridge, MA: MIT Press.
Diamond, C. (1991). *The Realistic Spirit: Wittgenstein, Philosophy, and the Mind.* Cambridge, MA: MIT Press.
Hacker, P.M.S. (2001). When the Whistling Had to Stop. In D.O.M. Charles and T.W. Child (Eds). *Wittgensteinian Themes: Essays in Honour of David Pears* (pp.13–48). Oxford: Clarendon Press.
Mounce, H. O. (2001). Critical Notice: *The New Wittgenstein.* In A. Crary and R. Read (Eds). *Philosophical Investigations,* 24(2), 185–192.
Read, R. and Lavery M. (Eds.). (2011). *Beyond the Tractatus Wars.* New York: Routledge.

12

Metaphysics: From Ineffability to Normativity

P.M.S. HACKER

1 Metaphysics

Throughout its long history metaphysics has been variously conceived. At its most sublime, it has been taken to be the study of the super-sensible, in particular of the existence of a god, the nature of the soul, and the possibility of an afterlife. Hardly less sublimely, it has been thought to concern itself with the essence of all things and the ultimate categories of being (*ontology*). It is not surprising that once physics had started to trespass on this terrain, metaphysics had to be differentiated from the natural sciences that were successfully investigating the nature of things. So metaphysics was held to be the *most general* investigation into the nature of reality – the conclusions of which are *presupposed* by all the particular sciences. This conception was duly sharpened and refined. Meta-physicists laid claim to investigate not the empirical nature of things, but rather the necessary nature of the world – as it were, its scaffolding. So, it was held, the natural sciences investigate empirical questions, study the contingencies of the world, its inessential, quasi-accidental features, whereas metaphysics investigates the essential, great, and universal features of reality.

When the young Wittgenstein entered the lists, it was entirely reasonable to conceive of metaphysics in this manner. Its subject matter was held to be the language-independent and thought-independent *de re* necessities of the world. Moreover, the truths it strives to attain are synthetic a priori. They are not analytic: the predicate is not contained in the concept of the subject (as Kant put it) nor are they true in virtue of explicit definitions and the laws of logic (as Frege put it). They are synthetic – substantive truths concerning the world. But they are a priori – can be known independently of experience. They are established by rational argument, not by empirical observation, hypothesis-formation, and experimental confirmation. Kant had decried transcendent metaphysics. The question he posed was "How is metaphysics as a science possible?" His answer was that its synthetic a priori truths are presupposed for the possibility of conceptualized experience and hence for empirical knowledge of nature. Metaphysics is limited to the domain of possible experience. The young Wittgenstein's route was different.

A Companion to Wittgenstein, First Edition. Edited by Hans-Johann Glock and John Hyman.
© 2017 John Wiley & Sons, Ltd. Published 2017 by John Wiley & Sons, Ltd.

He moved not from the conditions of the possibility of empirical knowledge to their transcendental idealist roots, but rather from logic and the necessary truths of logic to their metaphysical presuppositions. His concern was with the presuppositions of the possibility of representation in general, and with the presuppositions of logic in particular.

In his first surviving writing on philosophy, the "Notes on Logic" of September 1913, he wrote, "Philosophy gives us no pictures of reality, and can neither confirm nor confute scientific investigations," so "the word 'philosophy' ought always to designate something over or under, but not beside, the natural sciences" (NL 93; cf. TLP 4.111). "Philosophy," he added, "consists of logic and metaphysics, the former its basis" (NL 93). This was a fundamental commitment while writing the *Tractatus*.

By the time he wrote his second surviving piece six months later, the "Notes Dictated to G.E. Moore in Norway," Wittgenstein had arrived at the deepest commitment of his first masterwork, namely the distinction between what can be said, and what can only be shown, by language (NM 107). It is of this that he wrote to Russell in August 1919:

> Now I'm afraid that you haven't really got hold of my main contention, to which the whole business of logical prop[osition]s is only a corollary. The main point is the theory of what can be expressed (gesagt) by prop[osition]s – i.e. by language – (and, which comes to the same, what can be *thought*) and what cannot be expressed by prop[osition]s, but only shown (gezeigt); which, I believe, is the cardinal problem of philosophy. (Letter to Russell, 19 August 1919)

A consequence of this "main contention" was that the truths of metaphysics, which concern the essential forms of the world, cannot be stated or described by *any* proposition, but only shown – by *every* proposition. The reason for this lies in the nature of any system of representation. As he explained to Moore:

> Logical so-called propositions *show* [the] logical properties of language and therefore of [the] Universe, but *say* nothing. [Cf. TLP 6.12]
> This means that merely by looking at them you can *see* these properties; whereas, in a proposition proper, you cannot see what is true by looking at it. [Cf. TLP 6.113]
> It is impossible to say what these properties are, because in order to do so, you would need a language, which hadn't got the properties in question, and it is impossible that this should be a *proper* language. Impossible to construct [an] illogical language.
> In order that you should have a language which can express or *say* everything that *can* be said, this language must have certain properties; and when this is the case, *that* it has them can no longer be said in that language or in *any* language. (NM 107)

So the truths of metaphysics, as well as the metaphysical truths about the essence of language, can become apparent by careful logical analysis of language, but they cannot be stated.

> Every *real* proposition *shows* something, besides what it says, about the Universe: *for*, if it has no sense, it can't be used; and if it has a sense, it mirrors some logical property of the Universe. (NM 107)

Metaphysical truths, therefore, are shown by the logical properties of language.

By January 1915, Wittgenstein had come to the following conclusion:

> My *whole* task consists in explaining the nature of the proposition.
>   That is to say, in giving the nature of all facts, whose picture the proposition *is*.
>   In giving the nature of all being. (NB 22.1.15)

From the essential nature of the proposition, he thought to derive the essential nature of logic, of logical propositions, and of logical necessity. This would *show* the essential nature of the world. For the "all-embracing world-mirroring logic" forms "the great mirror" (NB 22.1.15; cf. TLP 5.511). A year and a half later, he noted with satisfaction, "Indeed, my work has extended from the foundations of logic to the essence of the world" ("*Ja, meine Arbeit hat sich ausgedehnt von den Grundlagen der Logik zum Wesen der Welt,*" NB 2.8.16).

2 The Master-Problems of the *Tractatus*

The *Tractatus* is dominated by three problems: first, the nature of logic and logical necessity (cf. Chapter 21, NECESSITY AND APRIORITY); secondly, the essence of the proposition and hence the characterization of the general propositional form (cf. Chapter 17, LOGIC AND THE *TRACTATUS*); and thirdly, the intentionality (pictoriality) of the proposition (and of thought) (cf. Chapter 32, WITTGENSTEIN ON INTENTIONALITY and Chapter 8, THE PICTURE THEORY). The latter is presented as "the mystery of negation," that is: how can a proposition be false yet meaningful? – a problem that needs considerable clarification before it can even be apprehended, let alone associated with intentionality.

These three problems are interwoven. To grasp the nature and necessity of the propositions of logic, one must grasp the essence of the proposition, of propositional representation, and of truth-functional propositional combination. To grasp the essence of the proposition, one must resolve the mystery of negation. In the course of resolving these great problems, the metaphysical presuppositions of logic and of representation in general are brought to light. Once the nature of representation is laid bare, the limits of language are revealed and the theory of what cannot be said but only shown is evident. Metaphysics, mathematics, ethics, aesthetics, and religion all belong beyond the bounds of possible description. Hence, in a final, but appealing, paradox, the very sentences of the *Tractatus* are manifestly attempts to say what cannot be said but can only be shown. Once one has apprehended the intentions of their author in writing these meticulously crafted and intentionally ill-formed sentences, one will be able to apprehend *in* language – in the forms of well-formed, fully analyzed propositions of language – the essence and nature of all that is there mirrored. One will have attained a correct logical point of view. Thenceforth, the sole task of philosophy will be analysis of propositions and the curbing of the metaphysical impulse to transgress the limits of language.

Although the order of presentation in the *Tractatus* moves from ontology to representation, from representation in general to propositional representation, and from propositional representation to the nature of the propositions of logic, the *ordo cognoscendi* is from reflection on the nature of logic to its ontological presuppositions. It should be no surprise that the initially proposed title for the book was *Der Satz* (*The Proposition*). It was by examining the nature of representation, in particular representation by means of propositions (sentences with a sense) that Wittgenstein came to construct an ontology – a metaphysical account of the essential constituents and forms of the world, and a corresponding metaphysics of symbolism, as presuppositions of the possibility of representation and of logic. Later, in June 1916, he added an obscure metaphysics of subjectivity, advancing what seems to be a form of transcendental solipsism conjoined with empirical realism.

Unlike his predecessors, Frege and Russell, Wittgenstein did not think that logic was the most general of the sciences. Nor did he think that the mark of a proposition of logic is complete generality. Frege had thought that logic is the science of thoughts, that its laws are descriptions of the topic-neutral relationships between thoughts, and that all the laws of logic are generalizations. Russell had thought that logic is the science of the most general facts in the universe, and its task is to catalog their logical forms. Wittgenstein denied these claims. *Essential generality* is not a mark of the propositions of logic at all. Rather it is *essential validity*, i.e., necessity, that characterizes them. The proposition "Either it is raining or it is not raining" *is* a logical truth, and not, as Frege and Russell thought, merely an instantiation of the essentially general logical truth that every proposition is either true or false. (Indeed, he argued, "Every proposition is either true or false" is not even a proposition.) What precisely *is* a proposition of logic? If it does not describe relationships between thoughts, or the most general facts of the universe, what does it describe? If a mark of the propositions of logic is necessity, what explains this necessity and how can we recognize it? What is presupposed by logic? Frege and Russell would have said that logic presupposes the truth of its self-evident axioms. Wittgenstein did not think that logic rests on self-evidence, or that it presupposes axioms. But that does not mean that it does not have presuppositions.

3 Ontology, Metaphysics of Symbolism, and the Truths of Logic

The conclusions at which Wittgenstein arrives are bold. All propositions are truth-functional combinations of elementary propositions (the principle of extensionality). Elementary propositions (propositions containing only simple names, and no logical connectives or quantifiers) are logically independent of each other. They consist of logically proper names, combined in accordance with logical syntax. Such logically simple names have both form and content. Their form consists in their logico-syntactical combinatorial possibilities. Their content consists in their meaning, which is the simple object (thing, entity) in reality for which they stand. The objects for which these names stand must be beyond existence and inexistence – otherwise sense, which is presupposed by any statement, would depend upon the facts, and analysis would have no *terminus*. What simple objects there are is for analysis to disclose. But *pro tempore*, we might imagine these objects as *minima sensibilia*, such as shades of color and such like, and perhaps also spatiotemporal points (since space and time are the forms of all objects, TLP 2.0251). Such entities (things, objects) are obviously *prima facie* candidates for *sempiternalia* and for concatenation without the glue of a relation to connect them (as in Fa and aRb). So the question that exercised Bradley and Russell of how an object that stands in a relation to another object is related to the relation cannot arise.

The form of a name is represented in a logically perspicuous notation by a variable, the values of which are the various objects that share the same form. So, for example, the words "color" and "sound" signify forms of visual and auditory objects respectively.

If presented explicitly as variables, e.g., "( )$_c$" and "( )$_s$," it is obvious that what appears to be a necessary metaphysical proposition, e.g., "red is a color," is not a well-formed proposition at all, since it contains an unbound variable: "red ( )$_c$." So it is a mere nonsense. But that red is a color is shown by the form of the word "red," i.e., by the combinatorial possibilities it shares with all other names of the same ontological category, i.e., color names. All names that are intersubstitutable in a well-formed sentence *salva significatione* belong to the same ontological category. It is this that *shows* that red, green, orange, etc., are colors.

Elementary propositions have a sense. They describe, or depict, a possibility (a state of affairs) in reality, namely that the meanings of their constituent names are combined in reality as the names are combined in the proposition, given the conventions of representation. If "*a*" is the name of *a*, and "*x*R*y*" is the name of the relation "larger than," and "*b*" the name of *b*, then "*a*R*b*" describes the state of affairs that *a* is larger than *b*, whereas "*b*R*a*" describes the state of affairs that *b* is larger than *a*. With different conventions, "R*ab*" might describe the former, and "R*ba*" the latter. So simple names have the same logical form as the simple objects in reality that are their meanings. A proposition, which is *essentially* a description of a state of affairs, is an abstract, logical, picture or model of what it depicts. Simple names are representatives of simple objects. *Relations represent relations* (it is not simply "R" that represents standing-in-the-R-relation, but rather *that* 'R' is flanked by two simple names). And *facts represent facts*. For what represents in a proposition such as "*a*R*b*," what makes it possible for the sequence of signs to represent what it represents, is *the fact* that they are arranged as they are, given the conventions of this method of representation.

Names are *connected* to reality by lines of projection. The method of projection is: thinking the sense of the sentence. To think the sense of the sentence is to *mean*, by the sentence, the state of affairs it depicts (TLP 3.11), and hence too, to mean by the names conjoined in the sentence the objects the concatenation of which is a possibility in reality. It is of the nature of possibilities that they may obtain, i.e., be actualized, or fail to obtain, i.e., not be actualized. The actualization of a possibility is a positive fact. Its non-actualization is a negative fact. What an elementary proposition *describes* is a possibility. What it *says*, is that it obtains (is actualized). If things are in fact as the proposition depicts them as being, then the proposition is true. If they are not, then it is false.

Truth and falsity are not objects, and propositions are not names of anything, let alone of a pair of logical objects (the True and the False, as Frege held). They are not, as both Frege and Russell had supposed, on the same level, like black and white, but are more akin to a shape and a space into which it fits (truth has priority). For a proposition to be true is for things to be as the proposition describes them as being. For a proposition to be false is for things *not* to be as the proposition describes them as being. So a deflationary (disquotational) account of truth ("'*p*' is true" = "*p*") is taken for granted. A true proposition *agrees* with the possibility that obtains, and *disagrees* with the non-obtaining of that possibility. Conversely, a false proposition disagrees with what is actually the case, and agrees with what is not the case. The sense of a proposition is its agreement and disagreement with the possibility of the obtaining and non-obtaining of states of affairs (TLP 4.2).

With this apparatus, the "mystery" of negation dissolves, and the intentionality of thought and proposition becomes perspicuous. The problem is produced by the following compelling consideration. If a proposition is true, then what it depicts is what is the case. If a proposition is false, then what it depicts is not what is the case. But what a proposition depicts is the same, no matter whether it is true or false. How can this be? Or to put the problem slightly differently: how can a proposition be false but meaningful? For if it is true then what it depicts is what is the case. But if it is false, what it depicts is not what is the case. But what-is-not-the-case is nothing. Yet the false proposition depicts something, not nothing. How can this be? The picture theory of the proposition, together with the attendant ontology resolves the predicament. For the proposition depicts a *possibility*, and *says* that it obtains. If what it says is true then the possibility is actualized and what it says is indeed what is the case. If what it says is false, it is not. But the proposition says the same, no matter whether it is true or false. It describes reality "give or take a Yes or No." The *Tractatus*' metaphysics, its *modal realism*, provides (or seemed to provide) the key with which to unlock the mystery of negation and the puzzle of the intentionality of proposition (and thought).

It is the essence of a proposition not merely to be bivalent (either true or false) but to be bipolar (to be capable of being true and capable of being false). This follows from the proposition's having a sense, i.e., being essentially a picture of a possibility that may or may not obtain. It also gives a further reason why metaphysical propositions, such as "One is a number" or "Red is a color" are nonsense. They are not bipolar, and they are not pictures of reality. (One cannot picture red's being a color, but this is shown by the proposition "A is red.") The bipolar nature of the proposition mirrors the nature of states of affairs, since it is of their nature to obtain or not to obtain. The world consists of facts, not of things. It is everything that is the case, i.e., the totality of facts. This is shown by a complete statement of the facts being a complete world-description. A complete list of objects, by contrast, would not be a world-description at all, but a catalogue of the substance of all possible worlds. Simple objects are the substance of the world – that which persists through all change. Change consists in the combination and separation of objects. Destruction consists in decomposition of complexes. What objects actually furnish the universe is a matter for experience to disclose. What the facts are is an empirical matter. But *what logic presupposes*, is this: namely, that there are simple objects and that the world consists of the obtaining and non-obtaining of states of affairs. No elementary proposition can be a logical truth, since it is of the essence of the elementary proposition to be bipolar. But it is of the essence of a logical proposition to be necessary, so it must be unipolar. So all the propositions of logic result from combining elementary propositions. (For the sake of brevity and simplicity, I bypass Wittgenstein's account of quantified propositions.) So logic presupposes that names have meaning and that elementary propositions have sense (TLP 6.124). So it presupposes that objects are the substance of the world, that they are constituents of states of affairs, and that the world consists of facts.

Logical propositions are combinations of elementary propositions by means of truth-functional logical connectives. Contrary to what Frege thought, these are not names of properties (e.g., negation is not a property of a proposition) or of relations (alternation, conjunction, and conditionality are not relations between propositions). There *are* no such logical entities or "logical constants." This Wittgenstein announces, is his *Grundgedanke* (TLP 5.4). The whole of logic flows from the essential nature of the elementary proposition. With its bipolarity, negation is given. From the possibility of successive assertion, conjunction is given. If negation and conjunction are given, then all forms of logical combination are given. The logical connectives are not function names, as Frege had thought, rather they signify combinatorial operations by means of which we generate various nonelementary propositions out of a given stock of elementary ones. If we are given two elementary propositions "*p*" and "*q*," for example, we can generate four truth-possibilities (TT, TF, FT, FF), and 16 different truth functions. Of all the possible truth functions, there are two limiting cases, namely, when the combination is true no matter what the distribution of truth values, and when it is false no matter what the distribution of truth values. These are limiting cases in as much as they say nothing: they are true come what may (tautologies), or false come what may (contradictions). So they give us no information about how things stand. So they are senseless (not nonsense, since they are well formed). They are necessarily true, or necessarily false. *The former* are the propositions of logic. The price that tautologies pay for their necessity, so to say, is their vacuity. They say nothing. They delimit reality in no way: for a tautology is compatible with any state of affairs whatsoever – it makes no difference. "*p* & (*q* v ~ *q*)" = "*p*." But any tautology can be transformed into the form of a *modus ponens*, and so is correlative to an inference rule. All the propositions of logic say the same, to wit – nothing. So logic does not describe sempiternal relations between thoughts (propositions), as Frege supposed. Nor does it describe the most general truths in the universe, as Russell supposed. The propositions of logic describe nothing whatsoever. So there is no logical knowledge. So there can be no science of logic (there cannot be a science all the propositions of which say nothing). Logic is a calculus, and logical truths are not descriptions of anything. But they show the logical properties of the world.

4 Ineffability and Expressibility

The *Tractatus* advances a bold, elegant, and schematic logical atomist ontology of facts, sempiternal objects, and *de re* possibilities. It is schematic in as much as the book is a treatise *on logic*. So only so much is laid bare as is necessary to clarify the essential nature of logical combinatorics and to explain the nature of logical necessity and of the propositions of logic. What belongs to the analysis of elementary propositions themselves is of no concern to logic (all logic presupposes, as we have seen, is that names have meanings and elementary propositions have sense). For all logical propositions are consequences of truth-functional combination, irrespective of the content of the elementary propositions thus combined. The analysis of the inner forms of elementary propositions belongs to *the application of logic*, which is not the concern of the book. It is striking that it was precisely to this that Wittgenstein turned when he resumed work in philosophy in 1929. It was then that he wrote "Some Remarks on Logical Form," which gives us some idea of what he meant by analysis of elementary propositions. Notoriously, it was this paper that led to the collapse of the whole system of the *Tractatus*, and to a profound anti-metaphysical turn.

The metaphysics adumbrated in the *Tractatus*, Wittgenstein thought, was *required* for the possibility of representation *and* for the possibility of logic. Things *must be so*, otherwise we could not represent things by means of language, and there could be no truths of logic. Side by side with this ontology, we have a metaphysics of symbolism, according to which only simple names *can* represent simple objects, only relations *can* represent relations, and only facts *can* represent facts. Conjoined with the metaphysics of symbolism, we have an array of metalogical principles linking language to reality. Language *must* be connected to reality – otherwise propositions could not "reach right up" to it. Propositions *must* agree and disagree with how things stand – otherwise they would lack sense. So propositions *must* be bipolar – otherwise they would not be able to do what they do, describe truly or falsely how things are. All these "musts" and "cans" Wittgenstein would later characterize as "dogmatism."

On top of the ontology, the metaphysics of symbolism, and the metalogical principles Wittgenstein added, late in 1916, a bizarre form of transcendental solipsism conjoined with empirical realism (TLP 5.6–5.621). Space does not permit its description here (but cf. Chapter 30, WITTGENSTEIN ON "I" AND THE SELF; also Hacker, 1986, ch.IV). This was to evolve into the methodological solipsism of *Philosophical Remarks*, and thence to the brilliant demolition of solipsism and idealism in the "*Blue Book*" and the *Investigations*.

Two broad features distinguish the metaphysics of the *Tractatus* from previous metaphysical systems. First, Wittgenstein derived his metaphysical system from the (apparent) requirements of logic and representation by means of language, rather than from epistemological considerations. Secondly, these metaphysical sentences, *by reference to the very doctrines propounded in the book*, transgress the bounds of sense – for three interconnected reasons:

(i) They all employ formal concepts (such as color, number, fact, object, proposition) as if they were material concepts. So the sentences of metaphysics, such as "The world consists of facts," "Red is a color," and of the metaphysics of language, such as "Propositions with a sense are bipolar," are actually ill formed. They in effect contain a formal concept, i.e., an unbound variable, in the role of a material one. So they are, technically speaking, *nonsense* (as are all sentences of mathematics, ethics, aesthetics, and religion). They are nonsense *in the same sense and to the same degree* as any other ill-formed sentence of the language. But these pseudo-sentences are not of the same *kind* as mere gibberish. There are, indeed, no degrees of nonsense, but that does not mean that there are not many different kinds of nonsense (for an excellent discussion, see Glock, 2004). For

(a) they are formed out of expressions which, in other combinations, yield perfectly sensible sentences (the formal concepts *can* occur as bound variables);
(b) unlike traditional metaphysics, they involve no misunderstanding of the logical syntax of language. On the contrary, they are put together with acute awareness of it. They violate logical syntax, but deliberately, not on the basis of a misunderstanding;
(c) they are crafted for a specific philosophical purpose, namely to get one to realize, for example, the nature of the propositions of logic (that they are tautologies, and that tautologies say nothing), the nature of logical connectives (that they are not names of logical properties or relations, but signify operations), that truth tables not only provide a decision procedure for the propositional calculus, but can be used in a new notation (the T/F notation) to symbolize the propositions themselves in such a manner that whether a combination of propositions is a tautology or contradiction can literally be seen. So unlike gibberish, they elucidate (TLP 6.54) matters of the first importance.
(d) They are deliberate attempts to say what can only be shown, and they are advanced with the intention that the reader realize that what they are trying to say *is* shown by appropriate propositions, either by empirical propositions with a sense or by tautologies with "zero-sense."

(ii) None of the metaphysical or metalogical sentences of the *Tractatus* are bipolar. But bipolarity has been argued to be a condition of sense. Unlike senseless tautologies and contradictions, these sentences are not well formed, since they contain unbound variables (formal concepts). So they are not senseless either. So they are nonsense, albeit nonsense of a special kind, nonsense which is written with the intention of getting the reader to realize ineffable truths concerning the essence of the world, the essential nature of representation, and the essence of logical truth, *and* to apprehend why they are ineffable. They also constitute a propaedeutic to the application of logic, i.e., to the critical activity of logical analysis.

(iii) They are not pictures of reality. But pictoriality is of the essence of representation. It is of the nature of a picture, and so too of a sentence with a sense, to represent a possibility, which may and may not obtain, and to say that it *does* obtain. So the metaphysical sentences of the *Tractatus* are not representations at all. And not being well formed, they show nothing.

Consequently, as the paradoxical penultimate remark of the book explains, the sentences of the book serve as *elucidations*, i.e., clarifications (the expression "elucidation" is not a term of art, but the common or garden notion of making something clear). For anyone who understands their author will recognize them as deliberate nonsense. The nonsensical sentences of the book are, of course, not intelligible nonsense (that is an oxymoron). Rather it has been made intelligible that and *why* they are nonsense. The comprehending reader will have come to understand the limits of language and to apprehend *what is shown by language* but *cannot be said*. He will then see the world from a correct logical point of view.

Wittgenstein, as he wrote in the preface, believed himself "to have found, on all essential points, the final solution of the problems." He viewed his work as the culmination, correction, and the perfection of the great tradition of Western philosophy. He had indeed made room for high metaphysics, but had demonstrated that its truths cannot be described in putatively metaphysical sentences. In that sense, they are ineffable. On the other hand they not only *can* be expressed or made manifest, they are *inevitably* expressed or made manifest, since they are *shown* by the forms of fully analyzed sentences of natural language.

5 A Digression into Postmodernist Austerity and Resoluteness

The *Tractatus* ends with paradox. As Ramsey remarked, it is like the small child who, when instructed to say "breakfast," replies "Can't say 'breakfast.'" Russell too found the doctrine of the ineffability of essences implausible: "after all, Mr Wittgenstein manages to say a good deal about what cannot be said" (TLP, Introduction). Carnap thought that Tarski's methods of metalinguistic ascent showed how to circumvent it. In fact, none of them understood clearly *why* the propositions of the *Tractatus* are, *according to the Tractatus itself*, nonsense. But Wittgenstein, after 1929, patiently dismantled the *Tractatus*, showing what was right and what was wrong about it. It was not, he later remarked to Anscombe, just a pile of old junk, but a clock that didn't work. As we shall see, in the 1930s he assigned a wholly different role to apparent metaphysical truths, namely as grammatical propositions that are actually *norms of representation*, i.e., *rules for the use of words,* in the guise of descriptions. And he gave a completely different account of the drive to construct metaphysical systems and of the consequent metaphysical confusions, namely as implicitly hankering after alternative forms of representation, as being mesmerized by the model of the natural sciences and their method of inference to the best explanation, and as illicitly crossing different forms of representation. We shall examine this below.

In recent decades, a new interpretation of the *Tractatus* has been vigorously propounded in the United States by a group of philosophers, led by Cora Diamond and James Conant. They became known as the New Wittgensteinians or American Wittgensteinians, and amusingly described themselves as "austere" and "resolute" in their puritanical interpretation of the nonsense of the *Tractatus*. Actually, their interpretation was not austere New England puritanism, but merely a postmodernist malaise of the time. Alas, when America sneezes, Britain catches cold, and the New Wittgensteinian interpretation severely infected some university departments in Britain too. Other British philosophers, in the traditional spirit of the British foreign office, tried to find a compromise between right and wrong by splitting the difference (cf. Chapter 10, RESOLUTE READINGS OF THE *TRACTATUS* and Chapter 11, INEFFABILITY AND NONSENSE IN THE *TRACTATUS*).

According to the New Wittgensteinian interpretation, one must *resolutely* embrace the penultimate sentence of the book, and not pretend that some nonsense (the nonsense of the *Tractatus*) makes more sense than any other nonsense. The simple fact, they insisted, which no reader of the *Tractatus* had yet been *bold* and *resolute* enough to confront, is that the book is simply gibberish, albeit written with the wit of a Zen master or a Kierkegaardian pseudonymist, in order to curb our natural desire to advance metaphysical pronouncements. Nonsense is nonsense, they *austerely* insisted. There can be no illuminating nonsense or elucidatory nonsense that deliberately tries to say what can only be shown.

But all *this* is mere *postmodernist nonsense*. It is an internally inconsistent interpretation. It violates every exegetical principle known to philosophical hermeneutics. It pays no attention to Wittgenstein's remarks about what he was doing when composing the book. It pays no attention to everything Wittgenstein later wrote about the book. It pays no attention to what Wittgenstein later said to friends and pupils about the book. We shall deal with it briefly (for more detailed discussion, see Hacker, 2000, 2001b).

First, it is internally inconsistent in as much as the only reasons for thinking that metaphysical propositions are nonsense is given by metaphysical propositions concerning the essential nature of all possible methods of representation. If these are *simply* gibberish, then there is no reason at all for considering non-tautologous necessary truths like "The world is everything that is the case" or "Red is a color" to be nonsense.

Secondly, the author's preface to the *Tractatus* asserts that the book will be *understood* by some readers, namely by those who have had similar thoughts (which cannot be said about Edward Lear's nonsense poems). It also presages the final sentence of the book in saying in advance that "what we cannot talk about we must pass over in silence" (TLP, preface). So *there are things that cannot be said* (which, as he later said to Russell, is the cardinal point of the book). The preface concludes with the bold assertion that the truth of the thoughts set forth in the book seems to the author "unassailable and definitive" and that he believes himself to have found, "on all essential points, the final solution to the problems." Indeed, he wrote to both Russell and Keynes, that he believed that he had solved the problems *they* had been working on (and he did not mean either that their problems or that his solutions were gibberish).

Thirdly, in the body of the book, quite apart from the metaphysics, metalogic, and metaphysics of symbolism, Wittgenstein advanced a large number of highly compressed but immensely powerful criticisms of Frege and Russell, that are unquestionably meaningful (on the early Wittgenstein on Frege, see Hacker, 2001a; also Chapter 4, WITTGENSTEIN AND FREGE; on Russell, see Hacker, 1986, ch.II; also Chapter 5, WITTGENSTEIN AND RUSSELL). But, according to the New Wittgensteinians, Wittgenstein thought that these criticisms are just more gibberish.

Fourthly, while composing the book in 1916, as we noted, Wittgenstein remarked that his researches had led him from the foundations of logic to the essence of the world. So he cannot *then* have realized that he was writing carefully composed gibberish – that must have come later!! But, as we have seen, the distinction between what can be said and what cannot be said but only shown had already occurred to him back in 1914, when it became clear to him that internal relations cannot be expressed in propositions, but are shown by the symbols themselves (NM 115).

Fifthly, among the permanent achievements of the book, are deep insights into the nature of logic, supported by extensive argument, such as

> that the propositions of logic are not descriptions of anything;
> that they are not essentially characterized by generality, but by necessity;
> that the tautologies of logic say nothing, but are correlative to rules of inference;
> that the logical connectives are not names of logical functions (i.e., logical properties and relations), but are operators;
> that all the logical connectives can be reduced to the single operation of joint negation, and all the truth functions can be generated by that operation;
> that the truth tables provide a decision procedure for the propositional calculus;
> that the T/F notation eliminates the need for *any* connectives in the propositional calculus, thus demonstrating their status.

All these insights are perfectly true and immensely important. They transformed our understanding of logic. But, according to the New Wittgensteinians, Wittgenstein held that all this is mere gibberish, supported only by pseudo-argument (which it took six years to produce!).

Sixthly, in a very large number of later writings about the *Tractatus* and about what he wrote in it, Wittgenstein speaks of what he *used to think*, what *mistakes he made* and why, and of what he *should have said*. But, according to the New Wittgensteinians, he never did think that what he said in the book was true; he thought it was just plain nonsense (not mistake).

The *Tractatus*, as its author came to realize in 1929–1930, is not a consistent book. For the New American Wittgensteinians to try (unsuccessfully, as we have seen) to save its consistency by reducing it to intentional gibberish is not a licit hermeneutical method. It is merely a postmodernist one, which is neither austere nor resolute. What needs to be done is what the author of the *Tractatus* did between 1929 and 1945: to recognize the "grave mistakes" in his first book (as he confessed in the preface to the *Investigations*), to explain what they are and why he was tempted to make them, to strive to see clearly what he had seen only through a glass darkly, and to salvage from the wreck what was still valuable, even if it had to be cleaned up and repaired.

6 From Metalogic to Grammar

The tapestry of the *Tractatus* began to unravel in 1929 because of the color exclusion problem (cf. Chapter 1, WITTGENSTEIN'S PHILOSOPHICAL DEVELOPMENT). What this showed was that not all logical relations are consequences of truth-functional composition. "A is red," for example, entails that "A is not green (yellow, blue, etc.)." But this logical relation is not a consequence of any inner complexity or truth-functional compositionality of "A is red." This undermined the idea that the whole of logic is given with the mere idea of the essence of the elementary proposition as such. Once Wittgenstein pulled at this little dangling thread of determinate exclusion, the whole fabric came apart. Over the next two years, he came to realize that there are, and can be, no simple objects, as he had conceived of them. Whatever legitimate needs called simple objects into apparent existence are fully met by

(i) the use of samples in ostensive definitions;
(ii) the fact that such samples are tools or instruments of language, and so *belong to the means of representation*, not to *what is represented*;
(iii) abandoning the ultimately incoherent demand for determinacy of sense (cf. TLP 3.23), and accepting the legitimacy and irreducibility of vague propositions;
(iv) abandoning the conception of logic as providing the hidden depth-grammar of any possible language and as specifying the depth-structure of any possible sentence.

Logic is indeed a calculus, but it is not a calculus that *underlies* every possible language. It is rather a grid that we can place *over* certain patterns of sentence-sequences and derivations in natural language to determine formal validity. The world does not *consist of* facts, Wittgenstein now realized. (Rather, a description of (any part of) the world consists in a statement of facts.) Facts are not spatiotemporal denizens – they have no spatiotemporal location. Facts do not consist of objects in concatenation – they don't *consist* of anything. So the ontology of the *Tractatus* was both incoherent and, as we shall see, unnecessary.

There are no elementary propositions, as he had conceived them. There are no simple names standing for simple objects. The meaning of a name is not an object it stands for. Sentences are not concatenations of names. They are not composed of names alone. Propositions are not facts, and a proposition does not say what it says in virtue of being a fact. So the metaphysics of symbolism had to be jettisoned. So the picture theory of representation had to be rejected. Names are not *connected* to reality by lines of projection, and *meaning something* by a sentence and by its constituent names is not the method of projection. There are no sense-endowing or meaning-endowing connections between language and reality. The sense of a sentence is not its agreement and disagreement with possibilities of the existence and nonexistence of states of affairs. The meaning of an expression is, in most cases, its use, and its use is given by an explanation of meaning. An explanation of meaning is a rule for the use of the expression explained. So there are no metalogical connections between language and reality, and there are no metalogical truths presupposed by any form of representation.

The calculus conception of language that characterized the *Tractatus* was swept away. As the spell was broken, the illusory metaphysical foundations disappeared. What had appeared to be wondrous jewels set in a golden crown was just a pile of old stones and rusty iron. Language is a human institution, a practice of communicative interaction in the stream of human life. It is indeed rule-governed, but not in the manner of a calculus (cf. Chapter 24, RULES AND RULE-FOLLOWING). The meaning-determining rules for the use of words constitute the *grammar* of a language (cf. Chapter 14, GRAMMAR AND GRAMMATICAL STATEMENTS). Grammatical rules, unlike the previously envisaged rules of logical syntax, are not hidden – awaiting discovery by means of depth-analysis. Rather they are visible to all in the practices of explaining the meanings of expressions, in correcting mistakes and in the practice of going by the rules. They are often open-ended, dealing with cases that actually arise, not (impossibly) with all possible cases. The concept of a proposition is a family-resemblance one, and propositions have no essence. In particular, a proposition is not essentially a logical picture, nor is it essentially a description of a possibility. Indeed, it is not even essentially a description. What had seemed to be the general propositional form, "This is how things are," is merely a device for anaphoric reference to something already said, no different in principle from "That is how the cookie crumbles" (which plumbs no metaphysical depths). Bipolarity is indeed an important feature of many kinds of proposition, but not of all. Propositions of arithmetic and geometry, of ethics, aesthetics, and religion are indeed not bipolar, but they are perfectly well-formed propositions for all that, and they belong to the family of propositions. So too, as we shall see in a moment, are "grammatical propositions," which bring out into the light what good metaphysics saw only in the dark.

There are no metalogical concepts, and there are no metalogical connections between language and reality. So the problem of the intentionality of thought and language has to be confronted afresh. And so it is. In the *Tractatus* the problem was solved by means of the picture theory of meaning and a metalogical relation between word and world. Now Wittgenstein resolves it in terms of intra-grammatical relationships between alternative descriptions without recourse to isomorphism between language and reality. The proposition does indeed "reach right up to reality," for if it is true, what it says or describes is indeed what is the case. It is perfectly correct to say that if it is false then what it says is *not* what is the case. And it is also true that what it says is the same, no matter whether it is true or false. But although what it says when it is true is what is the case, it is not *the same* as what is the case, insofar as this means that one is dealing with one and the same entity. We must not confuse the relative Wh-pronoun with the interrogative Wh-pronoun. The question "What does the true proposition say?" and "What is the case?" *have the same answer*. Shared logical form does not enter the tale. The expression "the proposition that *p*" and the expression "the proposition made true by the fact that *p*" are simply two different ways of referring to the same proposition. The same goes for the two expressions "the proposition that *p*" and "the proposition made false by the fact that not-*p*." So, of course, it is one and the same proposition that is made true by the fact that *p* and is made false by the fact that not-*p*. The harmony between language and reality is orchestrated *in language*, not *between language and reality* (cf. Chapter 15, THE AUTONOMY OF GRAMMAR). So what seemed like a metalogical relation between language and reality is no more than the grammatical coordination of two different ways of speaking of the same proposition.

7   From Metaphysics to Grammar

So what is the fate of metaphysics? To be sure, we think of metaphysical propositions as necessary. However, the questions to confront are not "What is the source of their necessity?" and "How do we recognize it?," but rather "Why do we conceive of them as necessary?" and "What is their role – how are they used, and to what purpose?" What appear to be necessary truths describing *de re* necessities, such as "Red is a color," "One is a number," "Nothing can be red and green all over," "Red is more like orange than it is like yellow," are in fact *expressions of rules*. Wittgenstein called them "grammatical propositions." They are rules for the use of their constituent expressions *in the guise of descriptions of reality*. Of course, for anyone who actually knows what the constituent words of a grammatical proposition mean, such sentences convey nothing new. For those who do not, such sentences give partial explanations of the meaning, the use, of these words. Some are, in effect, inference rules. If you have three cushions, one red, one orange, and one yellow, then you may infer, without more ado, and without looking, that color-wise the first cushion is more like the second than it is like the third. If you know that something is red all over, you may infer, without more ado, that it is not green all over. And so forth. Such propositions are rules of grammar, not descriptions of necessities in nature and, so too, not synthetic a priori metaphysical truths.

Such propositions are humdrum affairs. But their truth has long puzzled philosophers, since they are obviously "necessary truths" and, equally obviously, they are not true in virtue of the laws of logic and explicit definitions. So they seemed to be "synthetic a priori propositions." The supposition that they describe *de re* necessities seemed irresistible – until Wittgenstein showed that they are *expressions of norms*, not statements of metaphysical fact. Of course, rules are not true or false. But there is nothing unusual about saying of the statement of a rule that *it* is true (e.g., that it is true that the chess king moves one square at a time). To say of a grammatical proposition that it is true is simply to say that a rule of grammar runs thus. But what of more general and august examples that have captured the attention of meta-physicists throughout the ages, such as the principle of causality, "Every event has a cause"? This principle, insofar as we do actually accept it, is the expression of commitment to a very general norm of representation to the effect that it always makes sense to ask of any event what caused it, and that it never makes sense to say that nothing caused it. It is doubtful, despite Kant, whether we are committed to this rule of representation. However, one might argue, as Collingwood did, that it was a commitment of Newtonian physics.

The "must" of such apparently metaphysical propositions is indicative not of a *de re* necessity, but of a commitment to a rule of use. The rule, of course, is not necessary – there are no necessary or contingent rules (cf. Chapter 21, NECESSITY AND APRIORITY and Chapter 15, THE AUTONOMY OF GRAMMAR). But the appearance of an objective necessity in nature is the shadow which the rule of grammar casts upon the world. What *follows*, according to a rule that is partly constitutive of the meaning of its constituent expressions, appears to be an objective necessity in nature. If something is red, then it *must* be colored; if something is red all over, it *cannot* also be green all over; if something is red, then it *must* be darker than anything pink; and so on through the geometry of color that determines its internal relations. But the "must" adds nothing to the "follows" of "If A is red all over, it follows that it is not green all over." And this "follows" is indicative of a rule: in *this* system of representation, *this* may be inferred from *that*.

Most grammatical propositions, once stripped of their metaphysical finery, are obvious to any speaker of the language. After all, they are partly constitutive of the meanings of words familiar to us all. They express inference patterns and combinatorial possibilities we employ daily. They are news from nowhere, and if they were really news, they would be nonsense (e.g., that colors are merely ideas in the mind; that no material object is really colored). Nevertheless, it is false that grammatical propositions are *always* immediately obvious. For the mastery of the use of ordinary (i.e., nontechnical) words, which is possessed by all competent speakers, does not imply mastery of their comparative uses or awareness of all analogies and disanalogies with the uses of other words. In the *Investigations*, Wittgenstein shows us that there cannot be a private ostensive definition, i.e., an analogue of a public ostensive definition, but which uses a recollection of a sense-impression as a sample (see Chapter 28, PRIVACY AND PRIVATE LANGUAGE). He then goes on to show that there cannot be a private language, that is, a language the names of which refer to experiences that only the subject has and that only he knows. These claims look as if they are making metaphysical statements about what *cannot* be the case, i.e., disclosing hitherto unknown impossibilities in nature. But these kinds of proposition are grammatical propositions. "There cannot be" amounts to "there is no such thing as" (not: "Try as you may, you will not...," but rather "There is nothing to try!"). And "there is no such thing as a private ostensive definition (or private language)" amounts to this: the word sequence "private ostensive definition" (or "private language") makes no sense, has no use, and is excluded from the language. It is correct that these propositions are anything but obvious. They are the upshot of *reductio ad absurdum* arguments, each step of which, when properly laid forth, is indeed obvious. In this respect they are similar to the *reductio ad contradictionem* arguments characteristic of impossibility proofs in mathematics. The conclusion of such *reductio ad absurdum* arguments may well be an *unobvious* grammatical proposition (e.g., there can be no transparent white glass = there is no such thing as transparent white glass = the string of words "transparent white glass" is excluded from our language).

What is left of metaphysics, what can be salvaged from its castles in the air, are merely rules for the use of expressions in our language. Does metaphysics not deal with the objective, language-independent natures and essences of all things? No, the a priori nature of things is *determined* by grammar (PI §§371–3), and grammar itself is autonomous. Grammar is not answerable to reality in the currency of truth. It is not a mirror of the scaffolding of the world, but the scaffolding from which we describe the world. The world has no scaffolding, and what looks like scaffolding is merely the shadow of grammar. Is metaphysics not concerned with the essential, great, and universal features of reality? No, there are no such features – only the illusion of such features (BT 407). What is left of the majesty of metaphysics are merely rules for the use of very general or very important expressions in our language, such as "substance" and "property," "cause" and "effect," "space" and "time," "mind" and "body," and "I" (cf. Chapter 29, THE INNER AND THE OUTER; Chapter 30, WITTGENSTEIN ON "I" AND THE SELF; and Chapter 37, WITTGENSTEIN ON CAUSATION AND INDUCTION). *Descriptive metaphysics*, as Peter Strawson used this expression, is just more linguistic (grammatical) analysis, at a high level of generality.

8 High Metaphysics Brought Low

Does this mean that the great metaphysical systems of the past are all mere nonsense? – That the whole endeavor was worthless? No. Wittgenstein remarked to Drury:

> Don't think I despise metaphysics. I regard some of the great philosophical systems of the past as among the noblest productions of the human mind. For some people it would require a heroic effort to give up this sort of writing. (Drury, 1973/96, p.105)

Philosophical systems of the past often contain great conceptual insights, seen through a glass darkly. They raise deep problems that need to be confronted. Their mistakes are great mistakes from which there is much to be learnt. But "this sort of writing" must indeed be given up. For it is now clear that metaphysics, conceived as an investigation into *de re* necessities and impossibilities, is an illusion. To be sure, to those who are accustomed to pursuing this holy grail, renouncing it may be as difficult as holding back one's tears, or as giving up an addiction.

At one stage, when he was contemplating the second book that he wanted to write in repudiation of his earlier vision, Wittgenstein remarked that it seemed to him that it would be right to begin his book with remarks on metaphysics as a kind of magic. Of course, he added, the *depth* of this magic must be preserved. After all, is it not *deep* magic that gets us to believe that nothing is *really* colored, that material objects are not *really* solid, that one cannot *really* know whether the sun will rise tomorrow, and that a person is *really* his brain? (And, of course, when a meta-physicist says that things are *really* thus-and-so, that means that they *really* aren't.) Breaking the spell of metaphysics is a major task of philosophy, and this too involves a kind of magic (MS 110, p.177).

So it was that Wittgenstein, in the early 1930s came to think that one of his major tasks was to hunt metaphysics down in all its hidden lairs. What then is the mark of metaphysical propositions? The essential thing about metaphysics, he thought, is that it obscures the distinction between factual and conceptual investigations. Metaphysics characteristically gives the appearance of being concerned with factual problems: What are the fundamental constituents of reality? What is the nature of substance? Are colors real? – whereas in fact all the problems are conceptual (see Z §458). The pseudo-empirical air is deceptive, for it is not as if the results of metaphysics are amenable to empirical confirmation or refutation. No experiment could prove that there are universals; or that falling trees on uninhabited desert islands make no sound; or that there is something ("inexpressible") that it is like to be a bat. Equally deceptively, the meta-physicist presents the results of his super-physics as necessary: their negation is, he insists, impossible. Things *must* be so, for the contrary is *unimaginable* or *inconceivable*. So metaphysical propositions seem to be substantial truths about the world, but nevertheless a priori. Of course they do, Wittgenstein explained:

> The avowal of adherence to a form of expression, if it is formulated in the guise of a proposition dealing with *objects* (instead of signs) must be '*a priori*'. For its opposite will really be unthinkable, inasmuch as there corresponds to it a form of thought, a form of expression, that we have excluded. (Z §78)

This requires clarification.

When Berkeley declares that there are no material objects, that reality consists only of ideas and spirits, he does not mean that the chair on which he is about to sit will not hold his weight. When Hume declares that people are but bundles of perceptions, he does not mean that one cannot talk to them, fall in love with them, merrily dine and wine together with them. The great metaphysical systems of the past purport to tell for the first time what the world is *really* like, but in fact, nothing changes (a solipsist still calls for a doctor when his wife is ill). For what looks like an insight into the essential nature of the world, is actually the expression of an inchoate dissatisfaction with our existing grammar or form of representation, and a confused recommendation of an alternative grammar. Meta-physicists purport to make geographical discoveries, whereas all they are *actually* doing, at best, is redrawing the administrative boundaries in the landscape (BB 57). Nevertheless, it would be misleading to say that alternative forms of representation make *no* difference. They make no difference to the facts, but they make a difference to the way in which we view the facts. The difference between two distinctly tailored suits makes no difference to the form of the body they clothe. But they make a great deal of difference to the way it looks.

Now, there is nothing amiss in wanting to draw new boundaries: it amounts to recommending different concepts and inference patterns in a given domain of thought. What is amiss is to think that one is rejecting *false* boundaries, and discerning the *real* boundaries (the *real* Devonshire, the meta-physicist proclaims, is not where you think it is at all, it is over here, where I say it is (BB 57)). What is even more misguided is to proclaim that *real* boundaries are not administrative conventions at all – they are adamantine herms "set in an eternal foundation, which our thought can overflow, but never displace" (Frege, 1893, p.xvi). Worst of all is to suppose that our existing concepts that are part of our present conceptual scheme, *really* signify the new boundaries that the meta-physicist purports to have discovered. For then one crosses two different grammars, and produces news from the *Metaphysical Times*: nothing is *really* solid; colors are *really* ideas in the mind; only *I* really exist; the past does not *really* exist.

What explains this intellectual malaise? The dissatisfaction with our existing grammar typically rests upon the *distorted* apprehension of a *genuine* feature of grammar. It is perfectly true that the first-person pronoun is not used in the same way as the other personal pronouns: there is here no such thing as reference-failure or misidentification. So the meta-physicist (e.g., Descartes) concludes that it is a *super-referring* expression that never fails to hit its target, namely: *one's self*. On rebound from this, unable to find anything in experience to which "I" refers (no "self" to be encountered in introspection), another meta-physicist (Hume) concludes correctly that we are not selves, and incorrectly that we are no more than a bundle of perceptions. Whereas the simple fact is that "I" is not a referring expression at all; or, if you prefer, it is a limiting, degenerate, case of a referring expression (as a point is a limiting case of a conic section). The meta-physicist (e.g., Descartes) correctly notes that perceptual statements are not incorrigible, and that when we are unsure of what we perceive, we can always withdraw to "It sensibly seems to me just as if…" He then jumps to the conclusion that the latter kinds of statement (Cartesian "thoughts," Lockean ideas, or sense-datum statements) are *certain*, *infallible*, and *incorrigible* and that they constitute the foundations of empirical knowledge; that they are the causal effects of objects; that they are the grounds for inferences to the best explanation (the causal theory of perception). On rebound from this unverifiable principle, other meta-physicists (idealists) conclude that what we take ourselves to perceive (e.g., material objects) are really mere collections of seemings, of ideas in the mind. Yet others (phenomenalists) conclude that material things are logical constructions out of sense-data. The solipsist observes correctly that self-ascription of experience is wholly unlike other-ascription, notes that in one sense he cannot have another's experience, and concludes that all experience is *his* experience. He fails to see that in the sense in which it is correct that I can't have *your* experience, I can't have *my* experience either. (For "my experience" = "the experience I have"; so "I have my experience" = "I have the experience I have" – which, far from expressing a deep metaphysical insight, says nothing at all.)

Dissatisfied with the existing grammar of some segment of our language, typically misconstrued, the meta-physicist presents us with the "ultimate hidden truth" about reality. But his revelations are, in effect, no more than recommendations, typically mangled and incoherent, to adopt a new system of representation. So the phenomenalist tells us that the world consists of nothing but sense-data; but what this actually amounts to is that we should abandon a material object language in favor of a sense-datum language. But this is incoherent, because a sense-datum language is essentially a fragment of our existing grammar, and is unintelligible when severed from it (like chess without the king). The solipsist, impressed by the use of the first-person pronoun, asserts "Only *I* really exist!," "I am the center of the world," or "Only *my* experience exists." But "I" belongs to the same grammatical system as "you," "he," and "she." If it makes no sense to ascribe experience to others, then it makes no sense to ascribe it to oneself. We *can* imagine a language in which "I" has no privileged role. It would be a language without any personal pronouns at all. Instead of Jack saying "I have a pain," he would say "There is pain," and instead of "Jill has a pain," one would say "Jill is behaving as Jack behaves when there is pain." In such a language, no one could be said to have a pain. But doctors would not go out of business, and people would still need analgesics.

A feature of metaphysics is the tendency to idealize ordinary expressions, and to give them a "special metaphysical sense," which is typically no more than a special philosophical confusion. So, in the *true* sense of "certainty," we are informed, only the propositions of mathematics are really certain; in the *proper* sense of "know," one cannot know the future; in the *real* meaning of "name," what are ordinarily called "names" are not really names at all – the only *real* names are "this" and "now." So too, the meta-physicist *discovers*, as Frege announced he had, that truth and falsehood are really a pair of coordinate logical objects that are values of functions for arguments. Or he *discovers* that there really are no vague propositions: that apparent vagueness disappears on analysis; or that it is merely an epistemic defect; or that what seem to be vague concepts (e.g., the concept of a Christian) are not really concepts at all. And he *discovers* that "exists" is not *really* a predicate: it *really* is a second-level function name – and that is why one cannot meaningfully say things we all say, e.g., that God does (or does not) exist, that Moses really did (or did not) exist.

So a further task for philosophy, Wittgenstein suggested, is to bring ordinary words back from their metaphysical use to their normal, everyday use (PI §116). We need to be reminded that it is no part of our ordinary use of "knowledge" that something counts as knowledge only if all *possible* doubts have been excluded – all we need do, before we claim to know something, is to ensure that all *actual* doubt has been excluded. We should remind ourselves that "I" is much more like "now" than it is like "he" – and that "now" does not *refer to*, but *signals* a time. We must bear in mind the fact that the simultaneous occurrence of an eclipse of the moon and a court case is not, *pace* Frege, an object, just as knowing something is not what we call "being in a certain mental state" (*pace* Williamson), and understanding something is not a process. If it is said that these are special philosophical uses of "know," "name," "object," "mental state," and that the philosopher has as much right to introduce new technical terms for the purpose of a philosophical theory as scientists do, then we must show that this is a muddle. For scientists construct verifiable or falsifiable theories that are tested against experience, experiment, and observation. But metaphysics produces no testable hypotheses. The propositions of metaphysics are not confirmable or refutable by experience or experiment. Its putative theories are pseudo-theories. There are no theories in philosophy in the sense in which there are theories in science. The purported "special technical terms" are no more than misconstruals of ordinary terms. This is a consequence of misunderstanding the workings of our conceptual scheme, and projecting our own misunderstanding onto the grammatical forms that we misconstrue. Of course, none of this means that philosophers may not introduce special technical terms for purposes of philosophical classifications and typologies.

The main inspiration for metaphysics typically lies in the culture of the day. It is therefore unsurprising to find Wittgenstein observing that the main seedbed for metaphysics in our times is science. Our culture is, overwhelmingly, a scientific, technological culture. If there is a serious problem, then, we are prone to think, it must have or will have, a scientific answer. So we turn to science to tell us whether the world is really multicolored or whether colors are mere illusion. And it tells us that nothing is actually colored. We are baffled at the nature of the mind. So we turn to science, and are told that the mind is really the brain. We wonder whether our will is free, and neuroscientists tell us that the motor centers of the brain are active 350 milliseconds before we even felt a decision or an intention to act. We are puzzled by the nature of morality and its dictates. So we turn to evolutionary sociobiologists, who advise us to study the morality of chimpanzees. Science is ill equipped to combat such scientism. The task of showing that it is nonsense, and to explain why it is nonsense, falls to the philosopher who has understood how to break the spells of intellectual illusion. That task is of capital importance.

Metaphysics, Wittgenstein showed, is not a science. It is not even a legitimate part of philosophy. The criticism of metaphysics is a part of the *dialectic* of philosophy, of the logic of illusion. The task of good philosophy is to curb the metaphysical impulse, to dispel its beguiling magic, and to expose its legerdemain.

References

Drury, M.O'C. (1973/96). *The Danger of Words*. Bristol: Thoemmes Press.
Frege, G. (1893). *Grundgesetze der Arithmetik (Bd. I)*. [Basic Laws of Arithmetic (Vol. 1).] Jena: Hermann Pohle.
Glock, H.-J. (2004). All Kinds of Nonsense. In E. Ammereller and E. Fischer (Eds). *Wittgenstein at Work: Method in the Philosophical Investigations* (pp.221–245). London: Routledge.
Hacker, P.M.S. (1986). *Insight and Illusion: Themes in the Philosophy of Wittgenstein*. Revised edition. Oxford: Clarendon Press.
Hacker, P.M.S. (2000). Was He Trying to Whistle It? In A. Crary and R. Read (Eds). *The New Wittgenstein* (pp.253–288). London: Routledge.
Hacker, P.M.S. (2001a). *Wittgenstein: Connections and Controversies*. Oxford: Clarendon Press.
Hacker, P.M.S. (2001b). When the Whistling Had to Stop. In D.O.M. Charles and T.W. Child (Eds). *Wittgensteinian Themes: Essays in Honour of David Pears* (pp.13–48). Oxford: Clarendon Press.

Further Reading

Baker, G.P. and Hacker, P.M.S. (1980 and 1986). *An Analytical Commentary on the Philosophical Investigations*, 1 and 2 Vols. Oxford: Blackwell. Second revised editions, P.M.S. Hacker (2005, 2009), Oxford: Wiley-Blackwell.
Glock, H.-J. (1996). *A Wittgenstein Dictionary*. Oxford: Blackwell.
Glock, H.-J. (Ed.). (2001). *Wittgenstein: A Critical Reader*. Oxford: Blackwell.
Hacker, P.M.S. (1996). *Wittgenstein's Place in Twentieth-Century Analytic Philosophy*. Oxford: Blackwell.
Hacker, P.M.S. (1990 and 1996). *An Analytical Commentary on the Philosophical Investigations*, 3 and 4 Vols. Oxford: Blackwell.
Schroeder, S. (2006). *Wittgenstein: The Way out of the Fly-bottle*. Cambridge: Polity.

Part IV

Philosophy and Grammar

13

Philosophy and Philosophical Method

HANS-JOHANN GLOCK

This chapter canvasses the main features of Wittgenstein's conception of philosophy, both early and late. It also assesses these features for their merits, partly with a view to current debates. I shall argue that his radical position is more than a whimsical manifestation of an anti-scientific ideology: it is supported by arguments deriving from astute observations about the peculiar character of philosophical problems on the one hand, and logico-semantic ideas on the other. In particular, I shall defend Wittgenstein's claim that the distinctive task of theoretical philosophy is a priori and hence conceptual. The chapter also diagnoses three tensions in Wittgenstein's account of conceptual elucidation: (i) treating it as a kind of (psycho-) therapy or propaganda for a particular point of view vs. regarding it as a type of dialectic argument; (ii) insisting on it having a purely critical purpose in dissolving philosophical puzzles vs. allowing for a more positive project of conceptual self-understanding; (iii) rejecting systematic theories vs. envisaging systematic surveys of our conceptual scheme. It urges, moreover, that these tensions should be resolved in favor of the second members of these pairs of alternatives. Finally, in line with my contention that Wittgenstein's metaphilosophical views are both supported by and in turn support certain of his philosophical views, the chapter casts aspersions on an ambition that Wittgenstein and many of his followers share with other metaphilosophers (notably Descartes, phenomenologists, and logical positivists). According to the "myth of mere method," one can metaphilosophically reform philosophy by devising procedures for the resolution of philosophical problems that do not in turn depend on contestable philosophical views derived by way of equally contestable methods. Abandoning the myth leads to a more sober and modest conception of philosophy's "metaphilosophical" reflection on its own nature.

1   Wittgenstein's Conception of Philosophy and the Cognitivist Mainstream

Wittgenstein's interest goes back to 1912, when he gave a paper "What is Philosophy?" to the Moral Sciences Club at Cambridge. In the preface of the *Tractatus* he boasted of having provided a "definitive solution" to "the problems of philosophy." In 1930 he maintained that his "new method" of philosophizing constituted a "kink" in the "development of human thought" comparable to the Galilean revolution in science. To the end of his career he insisted that what mattered most about his work was not its specific results but its new *way of philosophizing*, a method or skill which would enable us to fend for ourselves (M 322; MWL 5.2; AWL 97; MS 155, pp.73ff; Letter to Moore, 17 June 1941; PPF §202).

Wittgenstein was right to regard his methodological views as novel and radical. They run up not just against the scientific spirit of the twentieth century (CV 6–7), but against a predominant tendency within Western philosophy. Ever since its inception, philosophy has been regarded as a *cognitive* discipline, one that aspires to knowledge about reality. For Platonists philosophy is an a priori endeavor that scrutinizes not empirical reality, but a world of abstract "ideas," and grounds our knowledge by deducing all truths from ultimate principles about these entities. For Aristotelians it is continuous with the special sciences because it describes more general and fundamental features of reality – it is the "queen" of the sciences. And according to Locke it is continuous with the sciences because it is their "underlaborer," removing obstacles in their path. Finally, radical empiricists contend that all disciplines, including philosophy, mathematics, and logic, describe reality on the basis of empirical evidence.

By contrast, Kant conceived his transcendental philosophy as a *second-order* discipline. While science describes reality, philosophy is not directly concerned with objects of any kind, whether physical, mental, or abstract. Instead, it reflects on the preconditions of our knowing or experiencing the objects of the material world. In spite of this *reflective turn*, however, Kant remained within the cognitivist orthodoxy. He insisted that philosophy can deliver "synthetic a priori" truths which express necessary preconditions of experience, e.g., that any experience must be a potential object of self-consciousness, that substances persist through qualitative change, and that every event has a cause.

2   The Early Work

Wittgenstein's conception of philosophy stands in the tradition of Kant. First, for both philosophy is primarily a critical activity which curbs the excesses of metaphysics and clarifies nonphilosophical thoughts (TLP 4.112, 6.53; Kant, [1781/1787] 1998, A 11/B 24–5, A 735/B 763, A 851/B 879). Secondly, inspired by Schopenhauer and Hertz, Wittgenstein draws a Kantian contrast between science, which pictures or represents the world through a posteriori propositions, and philosophy, which reflects on the nature and preconditions of this representation (TLP 4.11ff). This diverges from Frege and Russell, to whom his deliberations are indebted in other respects. Frege never propounded a general conception of philosophy. But he intimated a hierarchy of disciplines in which logic grounds metaphysics and psychology (1893/1966, p.XIX). Russell, throughout his numerous evolutions, held fast to a "scientific conception of philosophy," according to which it shares the tasks of science and should emulate its methods. And during his middle period he identified philosophy with logic (1914/1993, pp.216–17; 1918, pp.75, 95–119).

In his earliest recorded reflections, Wittgenstein (echoing Frege) claimed that philosophy consists of logic – its basis – and metaphysics, and (echoing Russell) that it differs from science in being the "doctrine of the logical form of scientific propositions"

(NL 106). Later he reserves the label "metaphysics" for the illegitimate philosophy of the past. Legitimate philosophy is a "critique of language." "Most of the propositions and questions to be found in philosophical works are not false but nonsensical" (TLP 4.003; see preface; 3.323–5, 6.51; NB 22.8.14, 1.5.15). They stem from failure to understand the logic of language, a failure that results in asking pseudo-questions that admit of no answer. The task of philosophy is not to answer these questions, but to show that they violate the bounds of sense.

The *Tractatus* takes over Frege's anti-psychologistic separation of logic from psychology (4.1121, 6.3631, 6.423) and accepts Russell's identification of philosophy with logic (4.003–1) (see also Chapter 4, WITTGENSTEIN AND FREGE and Chapter 5, WITTGENSTEIN AND RUSSELL). But Wittgenstein's philosophy of logic departs radically from his predecessors. With considerable chutzpah, he included their avant-garde formal systems under the label "the old logic," and castigated them for having failed to clarify the *nature* of logic (4.003f, 4.1121, 4.126).

At the turn of the century, there were four positions concerning this topic. According to Mill's radical empiricism, logic consists of well-corroborated inductive generalizations. According to psychologism, logical truths or "laws of thought" describe how human beings (by and large) think, their basic mental operations, and are determined by the makeup of the human mind. Against both positions Platonists like Frege protested that logical truths are both necessary and objective, and that this special status can only be secured by assuming that their subject matter – logical objects, concepts, thoughts – are abstract entities inhabiting a "third realm" beyond space and time, rather than material objects or private ideas in the minds of individuals. Finally, Russell held that the propositions of logic are supremely general truths about the most pervasive traits of reality.

Wittgenstein eschews all four alternatives (see Chapter 17, LOGIC AND THE *TRACTATUS*). Necessary propositions are neither inductive generalizations about the world nor statements about the way people actually think. Nor are they about a Platonist *hinterworld* or the most pervasive features of reality. Philosophy *qua* logic is a second-order discipline. "Logic is transcendental" (6.13). Unlike science, it does not itself represent any kind of reality. Instead, it concerns the preconditions of representing reality, just as Kant's philosophy reflects on the "transcendental" preconditions of experiencing reality. Philosophy is the "logical clarification of thought." It investigates the nature and limits of thought, because it is in thought that we represent reality. Echoing Kant's critical philosophy, the *Tractatus* aims to draw the bounds between legitimate discourse, which represents reality, and illegitimate speculation – notably metaphysics (4.11ff). At the same time, it gives a linguistic twist to the Kantian tale.

> Thus the aim of the book is to draw a limit to thought, or rather – not to thought but to the expression of thoughts: for in order to be able to draw the limits of thought, we should have to find both sides of the limit thinkable (i.e. we should have to be able to think what cannot be thought). It will therefore only be in language that the limit can be drawn, and what lies on the other side of the limit will simply be nonsense. (TLP, preface)

Language is more than a secondary manifestation of something pre- or nonlinguistic. For a thought is neither a mental process nor an abstract entity, but itself a proposition (*Satz*), a sentential sign (*Satzzeichen*) that has been projected onto reality (3.5f). Thoughts can be completely expressed in language, and philosophy can establish the limits and preconditions of thought by establishing the limits and preconditions of the *linguistic expression of thought*.

Indeed, these limits *must* be drawn in language. They cannot be drawn by propositions talking about both sides of the limit. By definition, such propositions would have to be about things that cannot be thought about and thereby transcend the bounds of sense. The limits of thought can only be drawn *from the inside*, namely by delineating the "rules of logical grammar" or "logical syntax" (3.32–3.325). These rules determine whether a combination of signs is meaningful, that is, capable of representing reality *either* truly *or* falsely. What lies beyond these limits is not unknowable things in themselves, as in Kant, but only nonsensical combinations of signs, e.g., "The concert-tone A is red." The special status of necessary propositions is due not to the fact that they describe a peculiar reality, but to the fact that they reflect "rules of symbolism" (6.12ff). These cannot be overturned by empirical propositions, since nothing contravening them counts as a meaningful proposition. Logical syntax *antecedes* questions of truth and falsity, and thereby matters of fact.

Wittgenstein's "logic of representation" (4.015) comprises the most general preconditions for the possibility of symbolic representation. Consequently, there is no such thing as a logically defective language. Any language, any sign-system capable of representing reality, must conform to the rules of logical syntax. Natural languages are capable of "expressing every sense." Therefore their propositions must be "in perfect logical order" just as they are.

> They are not in any way logically *less correct* or less exact or *more confused* than propositions written down [...] in Russell's symbolism or any other "Begriffsschrift" (Only it is easier for us to gather their logical form when they are expressed in an appropriate symbolism.). (Letter to Ogden, 10 May 1922; see TLP 4.002, 5.5563)

Ordinary language allows the formulation of nonsensical pseudo-propositions because it conceals the logical form of propositions: quantifiers look like proper names ("nobody") or predicates ("exists"), ambiguities lead to philosophical confusions ("is" functions as copula, sign of identity, and existential quantifier), and "formal concepts" like *object* look like genuine concepts employed in empirical classification, such as *apple*. To guard against such deception, however, we require not an *ideal language* capable of expressing things natural languages cannot express, but an *ideal notation* (*Zeichensprache*). Such a notation is "governed by *logical* grammar – by logical syntax" (3.325); it displays the hidden logical form that ordinary propositions possessed all along.

> The idea is to express in an appropriate symbolism what in ordinary language leads to endless misunderstandings [...] where ordinary language disguises logical structure, where it allows the formation of pseudo-propositions, where it uses one term in an infinity of different meanings, we must replace it by a symbolism which gives a clear picture of the logical structure, excludes pseudo-propositions, and uses its terms unambiguously. (RLF 163)

Persistent misinterpretations notwithstanding, therefore, the *Tractatus* is not a contribution to an ideal language philosophy in the vein of Frege, Russell, Carnap, and Quine; instead, it is a precursor of the project of a formal theory of meaning for natural languages launched by Davidson.

Wittgenstein's account of the logico-semantic system that makes representation possible, his "theory of symbolism," revolves around his picture theory (see Chapter 8, THE PICTURE THEORY, and Chapter 32, WITTGENSTEIN ON INTENTIONALITY). It distinguishes three types of sentential sign-combinations. The only strictly meaningful propositions are empirical statements of the kind advanced by science. They have a "sense" by virtue of depicting possible states of affairs. This implies that they are bipolar, capable of being true (if the depicted state of affairs obtains), yet equally capable of being false (if it does not).

The propositions of logic are "tautologies" and "contradictions." Their necessity simply reflects the fact that through truth-functional operations they combine bipolar elementary propositions in such a way that all information cancels out. They exclude and hence *say nothing*, which means (in Wittgenstein's terminology) that they are "senseless," i.e., have *zero* sense (factual content). "It is raining" says something true or false, and so does "It is not raining." By contrast, "Either it is raining or it is not raining" says nothing about the weather, nor about anything else.

Finally, the pronouncements of metaphysics are nonsensical "pseudo-propositions." They try to say what could not be otherwise, e.g., that red is a color, or 1 a number. What they seem to exclude – e.g., red being a sound – contravenes logic, and is hence nonsensical. More importantly still, the attempt to *refer* to something nonsensical, if only to exclude it (as in Russell's theory of types), is itself nonsensical. For we cannot refer to something illogical like the class of lions being a lion by means of a meaningful expression. What such philosophical pseudo-propositions try to *say* is *shown* by the structure of genuine propositions – e.g., that in bipolar propositions "red" can combine only with names of points in the visual field, not with names of musical tones.

The distinction between what can be said by meaningful propositions and what can only be shown pervades the *Tractatus* from the preface to the famous final admonition "Whereof one cannot speak, thereof one must remain silent." The *Tractatus* pronouncements themselves are in the end condemned as nonsensical, because they try to articulate metaphysical truths about the essence of language. Such truths, by Wittgenstein's own lights, cannot be expressed in philosophical propositions, yet they manifest themselves in *nonphilosophical propositions properly analyzed*.

> My propositions serve as elucidations in the following way: anyone who understands me eventually recognizes them as nonsensical, when he has used them – as steps – to climb up beyond them. (He must, so to speak, throw away the ladder after he has climbed up it.) He must transcend these propositions, and then he will see the world aright. (TLP 6.54)

Readers as diverse as Russell, Ramsey, Carnap, and Neurath have shrunk back from this paradoxical conclusion. Some recent commentators retort that the *auto-da-fé* at the end must be taken literally (see Chapter 10, RESOLUTE READINGS OF THE *TRACTATUS*). The *Tractatus* does not consist of "illuminating nonsense," nonsense that vainly tries to hint at ineffable truths, but of "plain nonsense," nonsense in the same drastic sense as gibberish like "ab sur ah" or "piggly tiggle wiggle." The purpose of the exercise is *therapeutic*. By producing such sheer nonsense, Wittgenstein tries to unmask the idea of metaphysical truths (effable or ineffable) as absurd and to wean us off the temptation to engage in philosophy.

These "resolute" readings are susceptible to both exegetical and substantive criticism (see Chapter 11, INEFFABILITY AND NONSENSE IN THE *TRACTATUS*). At the same time, we need not rest content with lumbering the *Tractatus* with the idea of ineffable truths. It is crucial to take seriously its *propadeutic* aim, explicit in 6.53. The book *is* self-defeating, because, in delineating the essential preconditions of representation it violates its own restrictions on what it makes sense to say – the principle of bipolarity. This is a pitfall for any a priori attempt to draw the bounds of knowledge or sense in such a way as to exclude nonempirical knowledge or propositions – witness Kant and the logical positivists. Wittgenstein heroically tried to brave it by violating his self-imposed prohibitions solely to attain a "correct logical point of view" (4.1213), an insight into the essence and structure of language that would allow one to engage in critical logical analysis, *without* committing further violations. Once we have devised an ideal notation that displays the logical structure of meaningful propositions, we can throw away the ladder on which we have climbed up, namely the pronouncements on the essence of meaningful propositions that we needed to construct the notation.

From this perspective, Russell's aspiration to introduce scientific method into philosophy is misguided. Proper philosophy cannot be a doctrine, since there are no philosophical propositions. It is an *activity*, not of deliberately uttering nonsense with the therapeutic aim of debunking philosophy, mind you, but of *logical analysis*. Without propounding any propositions of its own, analysis clarifies the logical form of meaningful propositions – i.e., of bipolar empirical propositions – by translating them into the ideal notation. This *positive* task is complemented by the *negative* task of demonstrating that the would-be propositions of metaphysics violate the rules of logical syntax since they resist such translation.

3   The Later Work

Wittgenstein later took this linguistic turn in a different direction. The core of his method remained the "transition from the question of truth to the question of meaning" (MS 106, p.46). The connection between philosophy and language is twofold. First, philosophy is interested in language because of the latter's "paramount role in human life" (BT 194–5, 413). There is an internal connection between thought and its linguistic expression. *Qua* rational beings, humans are therefore at the same time essentially language-using animals. The second connection is that the a priori nature of philosophical problems and the necessary status of philosophical propositions are rooted in linguistic rules: "Philosophy is the grammar of the words 'must' and 'can', for that is how it shows what is a priori and what a posteriori" (CE 411). Philosophy is an activity striving for clarity rather than a cognitive discipline (LWL 1; AWL 225; RPP I §115). At the same time Wittgenstein drops the ineffable metaphysics, and he replaces the mere promise of critical analysis by a dialectic practice: philosophy dissolves the conceptual confusions to which philosophical problems are alleged to owe their existence.

This noncognitivist picture chimes to varying degrees with other analytic critiques of metaphysics, notably those of *some* logical positivists (Schlick, Waismann, Carnap) and of some conceptual analysts (Wisdom, Ryle) (see Chapter 46, WITTGENSTEIN AND THE VIENNA CIRCLE and Chapter 47, WITTGENSTEIN AND ORDINARY LANGUAGE PHILOSOPHY). But it appears to impoverish philosophy, and is generally considered to be the weakest part of Wittgenstein's later work – slogans unsupported by argument and belied by his own positive "theory construction" which can be isolated from the rest (e.g., Dummett, 1978, p.434). Wittgenstein's methodological views must ultimately be judged by their results – the proof of the pudding is in the eating. But the impression that they are unsupported by argument arises from failure to recognize the connections which hold, firstly, between various aspects of his conception and, secondly, between his conception of philosophy as a whole and other parts of his later philosophy, notably his account of logical necessity and his understanding of language or grammar. Indeed, they arise from a coherent line of thought that can be reconstructed along the following steps:

(A) Philosophy differs in principle from the sciences because of the a priori character of its problems.
(B) A priori propositions do not depict necessary states of affairs; they are "grammatical propositions" that determine our concepts by expressing linguistic rules. As a result, philosophy is a second-order enterprise: instead of describing and explaining reality, it is concerned with the "grammatical rules" that constitute our conceptual scheme.
(C) These rules are not responsible to an "essence of reality"; therefore philosophy has no license to justify or reform our conceptual scheme on metaphysical grounds. Philosophy can only explicate that scheme by describing our linguistic practices.
(D) These descriptions cannot take the form of discoveries, theory-construction, or decompositional analysis. They remind us of how we actually speak when we are not in the grip of philosophical puzzlement, of grammatical rules we are already familiar with as competent speakers.
(E) Consequently the main (though not necessarily sole) purpose of grammatical investigations and thereby of philosophy is critical and to that extent negative.
(F) This critique is neither systematic nor does it make progress in the way science does.

In what follows, I shall examine these specific aspects of Wittgenstein's conception of philosophy (sections 3.1–3.6). The final sections (3.7–3.8) are devoted to two wider issues.

3.1 Philosophy and the A Priori

What links Wittgenstein's philosophizing with the metaphysical tradition is that both aim to resolve the *problems* that constitute the subject matter of philosophy (PG 193; BT 416, 431; Z §447; PLP 6). Wittgenstein suggests his "new method" as a new way of *dealing with* these problems. That method is superior because it is based on Wittgenstein's phenomenology of philosophical puzzlement, which furnishes a better understanding of the character of philosophical problems (see LWL 1; PG 193; AWL 27–8; M 113–14). In the main, the problems concerned are those of *theoretical* philosophy – logic, metaphysics, epistemology, philosophy of mind (BB 62; RW 160; M 314–5; CV 25). Wittgenstein illustrates their peculiar nature by reference to Augustine's question "What is time?." Such problems concern not arcane phenomena but notions we are familiar with in nonphilosophical (everyday and specialized) discourse. Nonetheless they have proven intractable, as is evident from philosophy's dismal failure to make progress in its ambition to fathom the nature of reality (see BT 424 and below).

Wittgenstein explains this enigmatic combination by insisting, against empiricism and naturalism, that philosophy is *a priori* (LWL 79–80; AWL 3; see 97, 205).

Philosophical problems cannot be solved by empirical observation or scientific experiment, since they concern concepts mastery of which is a precondition of establishing new empirical facts; at the same time such mastery does not guarantee the kind of comprehension required to avoid philosophical puzzlement (PI §89; see §§95, 428; BB 30–1; BT 435; RPP II §289; Z §452; CV 4).

One might retort with Russell (1912/1967, p.90; 1956, p.281) that philosophy is a *proto-science*, dealing with questions not yet amenable to empirical methods. "Kicking upstairs" (Austin, 1961/1970, pp.231–2) topics like infinity, matter in motion, types of learning, forms of theoretical and practical reasoning, or linguistic universals by passing them on to specialized disciplines is a role that philosophy as an academic discipline has fulfilled admirably. Whether or not it is their queen, philosophy is the mother of all (non-applied) sciences, even though its children are rarely grateful to their parent. Nevertheless, the fact that the special sciences developed out of philosophy does not entail that the questions that exercise philosophy are after all invariably empirical. For while the *topics* may be shared, they can give rise to distinct *kinds of problems*.

Some problems have remained within the purview of philosophy ever since its inception. Among them are problems that concern topics investigated by independent academic disciplines. Accordingly, disciplinary secession from philosophy is no panacea for philosophical perplexities (see Hacker, 2009, pp.131–3). Finally, at present philosophy as a distinctive intellectual pursuit is constituted at least in large part by such problems. These include questions such as "What is truth?," "Is knowledge possible?," "How is the mind related to the body?," and "Are there universally binding moral principles?." These puzzles are of a *peculiar* kind. They continue to defy the otherwise highly successful methods of empirical science. What is more, in many cases at least there are principled reasons for this failure. For instance, there is a difference between the questions "What is true?" about a particular topic and "What is truth?," i.e., how is that notion to be explained; one cannot without circularity allay skeptical doubts about the possibility of empirical knowledge by appeal to empirical scientific findings; one cannot on pain of a naturalistic fallacy deduce the (non)existence of normative principles from the (non)existence of a moral consensus among human beings; and so on.

Such considerations provide at least a *prima facie* case for regarding philosophy as a priori in a minimal sense: the philosophical questions and disputes concern not the empirical findings themselves, but at most the *relevance* the latter have for such problems. Thus the discoveries of the neurosciences, impressive though they are, have not simply solved either the mind–body problem or the problem of free will. Instead, they have provoked fresh disputes about the relation between mental and neurophysiological phenomena and about notions like decision, liberty, responsibility, and rationality.

Finally, Wittgenstein argues powerfully against attempts to reduce the necessary propositions of logic, mathematics, and metaphysics to empirical generalizations; in the course of doing so he even managed to anticipate weaknesses in Quine's renowned attacks on analyticity, apriority, and necessity (see Glock, 1996, pp.129–35). Wittgenstein has been accused of indulging in *armchair science*, yet he would respond that it is scientistic philosophers who engage in an incoherent discipline – *empirical metaphysics*, the attempt to invoke empirical data to resolve conceptual issues that are prior to experience.

3.2 Philosophy and Science

Wittgenstein was hostile to the scientific spirit of the twentieth century, which he deplored in Russell and the logical positivists. He rejected the belief in progress, and abhorred the "idol worship" of science as both a symptom and a cause of cultural decline (CV 6–7, 49, 56, 63; RW 112).

However, it is imperative to distinguish between Wittgenstein's *personal ideology* and his *philosophical methodology*. The latter rejects not science but *scientism*, the imperialist tendencies of scientific thinking that result from the idea that science is the measure of all things. Wittgenstein insists that *philosophy* cannot adopt the tasks and methods of science. There should be a division of labor between science and philosophy's reflection on our conceptual apparatus (CV 16), a division that is difficult to uphold given the twentieth-century obsession with science (PR 7; BB 17–18). Accordingly, Wittgenstein's notorious prohibition of theories, hypotheses, and explanations in philosophy (PI §§109, 126, 496; RFM VI §31) does not evince a general irrationalism.

Causal explanations of empirical phenomena are of course legitimate, yet their place is in the nomological sciences (see Chapter 37, WITTGENSTEIN ON CAUSATION AND INDUCTION). They are banned from philosophy, on the grounds that they are irrelevant to the solution of problems that are *conceptual* rather than factual (Z §458; CV 79). Furthermore, Wittgenstein's animadversions against explanation in philosophy must be interpreted with care, since his own philosophizing features two types of non-nomological explanations. First, it provides etiological explanations that pinpoint the sources of philosophical confusions (see below). More importantly, it revolves around *explanations of meaning*. These are not explanations of *why* we use a certain term, or of what the (perlocutionary) effects of using it are on particular hearers, but of *how* we use it correctly, i.e., they specify "grammatical" rules for its established use (PI §§120, 491–8). Such explanations are not, therefore, incompatible with the idea that philosophy is descriptive, in the sense of articulating the rules that guide our linguistic practice.

But why should philosophical investigations be conceptual to begin with? Wittgenstein's general answer derives from his conventionalist account of apriority and necessity. The a priori and necessary status of the propositions sought by metaphysics is due to the fact that they reflect concepts and conceptual connections. Furthermore, our conceptual scheme is embodied in our language. What Wittgenstein (misleadingly) calls the "grammar" of a language is not confined to morphology and syntax; it is the overall system of logico-semantic rules, of the constitutive rules that determine what it makes sense to say in that language (PR 51; LWL 46–59; PG 60, 133, 143; PI §496). Therefore, explicating our concepts and thereby our "form of representation" takes the form of articulating linguistic rules through "grammatical propositions" (see Chapter 14, GRAMMAR AND GRAMMATICAL STATEMENTS).

Grammatical propositions *antecede experience* in an innocuous sense (PR 143; LWL 12; AWL 90). They can neither be confirmed nor confuted by experience. "Black is darker than white," for instance, cannot be overthrown by the putative statement "This white object is darker than that black object," since in established usage nothing counts as being both white and darker than black. This antecedence to experience renders intelligible the apparently mysterious "hardness" of necessary propositions (PI §437; RFM I §121; PG 126–7). To say that it is logically impossible for a white object to be darker than a black one is to say that given our semantic rules, it makes no sense to apply "white" and "darker than black" to one and the same object.

Defending this position is beyond the remit of this chapter (see Chapter 21, NECESSITY AND APRIORITY; cf. Kalhat, 2008). In any event, the idea that philosophy seeks to analyze or define concepts rather than to decide what they actually apply to on the basis of experience has a venerable pedigree. Ever since Socrates, philosophers have been concerned with "What is X?" and "What are Xs?" questions, e.g., "What is justice?," "What is knowledge?," "What is truth?." In response to these questions, they have traditionally sought *analytic definitions* of X(s). Such definitions specify conditions or features which are individually necessary and jointly sufficient for being X. Furthermore, these features should not just *in fact* be possessed by all and only things that are X; rather, only things possessing all of the defining features *can be X*, and anything possessing them all is *ipso facto* X.

Admittedly, questions of the "What is (are) X(s)?" form can be requests for empirical information about contingent features of X(s). But as posed in philosophical reflection they are not directed at contingent features of X(s), features that X(s) may or may not possess and that need to be established empirically by looking at these instances. They are directed instead at the *nature* or *essence* of X, at *what makes something an X* in the first place. That kind of question is properly answered by an explanation of *what "X" means*. For such an explanation specifies what counts as X, or what it is to be an X, independently of features that X(s) may or may not possess. Similarly for questions of the form "What makes something (an) X?": these can be requests for a *causal* explanation that specifies how come that certain objects are X. But they can also be requests for a *semantic* explanation that specifies what *constitutes* being an X, i.e., conditions *by virtue of which something qualifies as X* in the first place. As regards their explanatory role in actual practice, there is no difference between what Carnap called, respectively, the "material" and the "formal mode." It matters little, for instance, whether we answer the question "What is a drake?" by saying that a drake is a male duck or by saying that "drake" means *male duck*. (The essentialism of Kripke and Putnam creates a gap between nature and meaning; but it is subject to Wittgensteinian objections, e.g., Hanfling, 2000, ch.12; Glock, 2003, ch.3.)

At the same time, the Witttgersteinian idea that philosophy is simply "grammatical investigation," i.e., conceptual analysis, stands in need of qualification and modification. First, many questions that are of supreme philosophical relevance are *not* simply of the definitional "What is X?" type. Consider the question of whether nonhuman animals possess mental powers. In tackling it we must pay heed to the *conditions for the applicability* of mental terms. And our knowledge of what these conditions are is a priori in that it is independent of empirical knowledge whether these conditions are fulfilled in particular cases. At the same time, it is obvious that the question to which creatures these terms *actually apply* also hinges on contingent facts about these creatures to be established empirically.

But couldn't one extract exclusively conceptual questions? For instance: Does it make linguistic sense to apply mental expressions to animals? Would anything count as an animal thinking that something is the case? Such an approach might be feasible in principle. Yet it remains difficult to see how one might make progress with these questions without at least considering ethological findings as a *heuristic device*. The complexity and flexibility of some animal behavior alerts us to the possibility that relatively advanced mental phenomena can be manifested without linguistic expression, contrary to the convictions of many Wittgensteinians. Furthermore, a purist isolation of conceptual issues is barren in at least one respect. Even philosophers are interested in the question of what mental capacities animals actually have. Unsurprisingly, since it is *that issue* which has so many important implications inside and outside of philosophy.

Finally, we must avoid the Socratic mistake of thinking that a cast-iron definition of "*X*" is needed in advance of building empirical theories about *X*. What is required is a preliminary understanding of "*X*"; and this understanding is subject to critical elucidation in philosophical reflection and modification in the course of scientific theory-building. Wittgenstein was fully aware of the pitfalls of the Socratic stance (TS 302, p.14; PG 121–2; see Chapter 25, VAGUENESS AND FAMILY RESEMBLANCE). But he was reluctant to acknowledge that philosophical reflection can and must be sensitive to scientific claims, provided that it is to contribute to a full understanding of topics that raise both scientific and philosophical problems. The interaction of conceptual and factual aspects implies that the division of labor between the conceptual clarification of philosophy on the one hand and the factual discoveries and theory formation in science on the other requires *dynamic interaction* rather than *splendid isolation*.

3.3 "Grammar" and Reality

According to the *Tractatus* there are metaphysical truths, albeit ineffable, about the logical structures shared between language and reality. By contrast, the later Wittgenstein demythologizes metaphysics (LWL 21; MS 157b, p.4; see Chapter 12, METAPHYICS: FROM INEFFABILITY TO NORMATIVITY). It is constitutive of metaphysics that it conflates factual (*sachliche*) and conceptual issues, as well as scientific theories (or hypotheses) and norms of representation (Z §458). Metaphysics claims to establish true propositions about the essence of reality. Its propositions have the *form* of statements of fact. Science teaches us that no human can run faster than 40 kilometers per hour, or that there is no intra-mercurial planet; metaphysics that no human can have the pains of another, or that there is no uncaused event. According to Strawson (1959), such pronouncements belong to "descriptive metaphysics," since they explicate our conceptual framework. According to Wittgenstein, they are grammatical rules – often distorted – in propositional disguise (BB 18, 35; AWL 18, 65–9; WVC 67). By these lights, "Every event has a cause" is a rule that partly determines what counts as an "event." But such a diagnosis is inaccurate. Our conceptual scheme does not simply rule out as nonsensical the expression "uncaused event." Let's assume that one morning we find dinosaur footprints on the ceiling. Let's further assume that we have a reason to abandon the search for an explanation of the footprints, such as that the laws of nature not only fail to provide one but also suggest that none is to be had (the example of quantum mechanics shows that this is at any rate a possibility). Even in that case, we would not cease to call the appearance of the footprints an event. A *physical change* would be an event, even if a causal explanation of it could be ruled out *ab initio*. Consequently, being caused is not part of our explanation of the term "event," or of the linguistic rules governing its use.

Kant was right, therefore, to deny that the law of causality simply explicates the concept of an event. Insofar as it is less susceptible to falsification than common-or-garden empirical generalizations it is by virtue of being a regulative principle. A *qualified* version of it may also possess a constitutive role in our conceptual scheme (see Glock, 2012). First, we need to acknowledge – contra Kant and Wittgenstein – that not all loosely speaking conceptual truths are trivial. Next, some conceptual truths are nontrivial because they are not definitional. The connection between the constituent concepts of such propositions is provided by their complex interplay with other concepts that do not themselves occur in the proposition. Thus Strawson has argued powerfully that *most* events must be caused, not because random changes do not qualify as events, but because persistently chaotic events are not possible objects of self-conscious experience.

What about "revisionary metaphysics"? A specimen Wittgenstein considers is the solipsist who insists "Only my present experiences are real!" (see Chapter 9, WITTGENSTEIN ON SOLIPSISM). Sentences of this kind are not disguised grammar, but either nonsense or "expressions of discontent with our grammar" (BB 55–7). Yet the attempt to improve our conceptual scheme by aligning it to reality is misguided. Grammar is "autonomous," not responsible to putative essences (see Chapter 15, THE AUTONOMY OF GRAMMAR). Consequently, there are *no metaphysical grounds* for either defending or reforming our conceptual scheme.

Empirical science operates with concepts. It decides whether they *in fact apply* to certain phenomena; it also provides causal explanations of *how phenomena come* to satisfy these concepts. By contrast, philosophy clarifies concepts, if and when the need arises, notably by investigating their *conditions of application*, the conditions that something must fulfill to satisfy these concepts.

In addition to the application and the elucidation of concepts, there is also conceptual construction or *concept formation*, the devising of novel conceptual structures. This activity is one of the hallmarks of mathematics, which invents novel formal tools for describing and explaining empirical phenomena. Of course, there is concept formation outside mathematics as well. It plays an indispensable role in the empirical sciences, notably when these develop new paradigms during scientific revolutions. Concept formation also features in other forms of discourse, ranging from religion through morality to the historical and social sciences. It occurs whenever new ways of classifying or explaining phenomena, of thinking about or making sense of them are introduced. Philosophy is no exception. The concepts of family resemblance and language-game, for instance, are no less philosophical innovations than analyticity and apriority. The moot question is whether concept formation has the same purpose and importance in philosophy as in empirical science, namely of furnishing novel tools for classifying and explaining phenomena in the world.

3.4 *Discoveries, Reminders, and Analysis*

The *Tractatus* insisted that language must be governed by a complex system of exact rules if it is to represent reality. After his return to philosophy Wittgenstein came to reject this imputation as "dogmatic" (PI §§81, 92–7, 108–9, 131). Speaking a language is not operating a calculus of arcane rules (WVC 77; LWL 16–17; PG 114–15; PI §§126–9). By this token, both the *Tractatus* and contemporary formal semantics go wrong in seeking "deep" or "unheard of" discoveries through logical analysis. There are no "surprises" in grammar (WVC 77; LWL 16–17; BT 418–19, 435–6; PG 114–15, 210; PI §133; MS 109, p.212 MS 116, pp.80–2). "What is hidden, is of no interest to us" (PI §126). As competent speakers we are already familiar with the grammar of our language. Alas, we can be tempted into ignoring or distorting grammar. One cause of such lapses is misleading analogies and pictures suggested by the surface-grammar of language; a whole "mythology" is laid down in our language (GB 133; BT 433–5; PI

§§422–6; OC §90; MS 110, p.184). Another cause is general intellectual tendencies such as a science-induced "craving for generality" (BB 17–18) or an urge to seek further explanations and justifications when "we ought to look at what happens as a 'proto-phenomenon'" and simply to note "this language-game is played" (PI §§654–5). The antidote, however, consists neither in replacing ordinary language by an ideal one nor in uncovering the logical syntax disguised by the school-grammatical surface with the aid of logical analysis. Instead, what is needed is grammatical reminders of how we use words outside philosophy "It makes sense to say 'I know that she has toothache'" or "A dog cannot be said to believe that its master will return in a week." These are articulations of rules that we have been following all along. Their point is to draw attention to the violation of grammar by philosophers. They are part of a dialectical critique of sense, an "undogmatic procedure" that contrasts with the dogmatic insistence of the *Tractatus* that only certain combinations of signs can make sense because of the constraints imposed by the picture theory (WVC 183–6; see PR 54–5; PI §§89–90, 127; BT 419, 424–5 and below). Wittgenstein tries to show that his interlocutors use words according to conflicting rules, without relying on contentious views of his own.

Wittgenstein and his followers have provoked the complaint of setting themselves up as "guardians of semantic inertia" (Gregory, 1987, pp.242–3) who criticize philosophical and scientific theories as confused simply because they diverge from ordinary use. These complaints ignore that by "ordinary use" they do not necessarily mean *everyday use*; instead, they mean *established use*, whether it be in common parlance or in technical forms of discourse with a tightly regimented vocabulary (see Ryle, 1971b, ch.23). Thus, Wittgenstein does not extol the virtues of everyday over technical language, or of the mundane everyday over the sophisticated specialized employment of a term. Nor does he prohibit the introduction of technical terminology in either science or philosophy. He refrains explicitly from criticizing philosophical positions merely for violating "common sense" (BB 48–9, 58–9) or for employing novel terms or familiar words in ways that differ from the established patterns of use (see PI §254; RPP I §548; RPP II §289; LPP 270).

Rather, Wittgenstein insists that such novel terms or uses need to be adequately explained by laying down clear rules. He further alleges that metaphysical questions and theories – no matter whether propounded inside or outside of the academic discipline of philosophy – get off the ground only because they employ terms in a way which is at odds with their official explanations, and that they trade on deviant rules along with the ordinary ones. In effect, Wittgenstein tries to confront metaphysicians with a *trilemma*: either their novel uses of terms remain unexplained (unintelligibility), or it is revealed that they use expressions according to incompatible rules (inconsistency), or their consistent employment of new concepts simply passes by the ordinary use – including the standard use of technical terms – and hence the concepts in terms of which the philosophical problems were phrased (*ignoratio elenchi*).

On his return to philosophy Wittgenstein castigated as "hellish" Moore's idea that logical analysis is required to establish what, if anything, we mean by our propositions (WVC 129–30). A "correct logical point of view" is achieved not through a quasi-*geological* excavation, but through a quasi-*geographical* "overview" (*Übersicht*; see Chapter 16, SURVEYABILITY). Such an overview displays, in a synoptic fashion, features of our linguistic practice that lie open to view. It is vain to hope for a decomposition of propositions into ultimate components, or even for detecting a single definite structure in them. Insofar as analysis is legitimate, it either amounts to the description of grammar, or to the substitution of one kind of notation by another, less misleading one (PR 51; WVC 45–7; BT 418; PI §§90–2). But Wittgenstein's only example of the latter method is a notation which paraphrases "is" by either "=" or "∈" (TS 220, §§98–9). And the former method is a version of "connective analysis" in Strawson's sense (1992, ch.2): the explanation of concepts and the description of conceptual connections by way of implication, presupposition, and exclusion.

Wittgenstein's case for connective analysis and against philosophical discoveries and surprises in grammar rests on his critique of the "calculus model" of linguistic meaning and understanding. He attacks the view – widespread within contemporary theories of language – that normal speakers follow complex logical and semantic rules of which they have tacit knowledge even though they can never become aware of these rules (see also Baker and Hacker, 1984, chs 8–9; Searle, 1997). Its central shortcoming is that it ignores the difference between *following a rule* and *merely acting in accordance* with it. The former presupposes that the rule provides the agent's reason for acting as she does. But while the physiological causes of speech and understanding may be completely unknown to speakers, this cannot hold of their reasons.

Wittgenstein knew from personal experience that the dissolution of conceptual confusions can be as complex as the knots it unties (Z §452). He sometimes maintains, however, that the articulations of grammatical rules that play a decisive role in this process are *platitudes* and *trivialities* (see below). Yet he himself, not to mention Ryle, taught us that people often follow rules without explicitly consulting them, as in the case of proficient chess players. In most cases, they will be able to specify these rules when prompted. There are exceptions, however. For example, competent speakers may be incapable of explaining the difference between pairs like "automatically" and "inadvertently," "bottle" and "jar," "almost" and "nearly" (Rundle, 1990, ch.4). More to the philosophical point, they may be at a loss to explain their use of the definite article, and of the subjunctive, or the sequence of tenses in conditionals. Wittgenstein would accept examples as adequate explanations. But in some cases even they may not be forthcoming. What he would rightly insist on is that speakers must nevertheless be *capable of recognizing* the correct formulations of the relevant rules, if only with a little help from their friends. Even this potentiality is absent in the case of many of the rules featuring in formal theories of syntax and semantics. Indeed, many speakers of natural languages are incapable of as much as *learning* the *recherché* rules thereby imputed to them, even when these are expressed in a less formal way. This means that there is not even a minimal sense in which such rules guide their linguistic behavior (Glock, 2003, pp.244–9).

The bottom line is this: insofar as language is governed by grammatical rules, these are not simply open to view. As Wittgenstein himself remarked: "The aspects of things that are most important to us are hidden because of their simplicity and familiarity" (PI §129). Grammatical rules need to be made explicit. This is not a matter of gathering new information about reality – as competent speakers we have all the information we need. But it is a matter of spelling out the "participatory knowledge" we have by virtue of having mastered a natural language (see Hare, 1960; Hanfling, 2000, pp.52–5). It requires elicitation, reflection, and articulation; and it may involve trial and error, as the history of conceptual analysis amply demonstrates.

3.5 Quietism, Critique, and Conceptual Survey

According to step (C) (section 3.3), philosophy is concerned with grammatical rules that it can neither justify nor reform but only *describe*; according to step (D) (section 3.4), these descriptions are reminders and may be downright trivial. This raises the question: what are grammatical reminders good for? One disparaging suspicion is: very little!

> Philosophy may in no way interfere with the actual use of language; it can in the end only describe it. For it cannot give it any foundation either. It leaves everything as it is. (PI §124)

This dictum has been read as licensing a type of intellectual *quietism* (Blackburn, 1984, p.146). However, Wittgenstein does not deny that language changes (PI §18). And there are *nonphilosophical* grounds for conceptual change, e.g., in science. His point is that it is not philosophy's business to bring about such reform by introducing an ideal language. More importantly, Wittgenstein does not purport to leave *philosophy* as it is. Instead, he tries to reveal it as "plain nonsense" and "houses of cards" (PI §§ 118–19; BT 413, 425). This leaves the possibility that philosophy exclusively serves a *critical* purpose, the unmasking of conceptual confusions. And sure enough, Wittgenstein often states the aim of philosophy in purely *negative* terms, namely "to show the fly the way out of the fly-bottle" by making philosophical problems "*completely* disappear" (PI §§309, 133; see AWL 21; BT 425; CV 43). But why should one engage in philosophy at all, if it only gets rid of errors it itself has created? One answer is that philosophy is of value to "the philosopher in us" (TS 219, p.11): the temptation to conceptual confusion is not confined to professional philosophers. Yet that still leaves unanswered Ryle's astute question of what a fly *would* miss that never got into the fly-bottle (1971a, p.114). Here we must appreciate that philosophy should not dissolve our urge to ask philosophical questions by any old means, e.g., a knock on the head, but through an understanding of their nature and sources. A fly which never got into the bottle will not only lack the ability to extricate itself, a kind of know-how, but also the conceptual clarity which Wittgenstein regarded as an end in itself (PR, preface; CV 7).

What is more, Wittgenstein attached "fundamental significance" to the concept of a perspicuous representation (*übersichtliche Darstellung*) since it affords "an understanding which consists in 'seeing connections'" between different parts of grammar (PI §122; see GB 133; BT 417).

Whether one regards a successful overview merely as a tool of philosophical critique or as interesting in its own right (as Strawson does on behalf of descriptive metaphysics) is a matter of intellectual temperament. One way of putting this point is that philosophy contributes to human understanding though not to human knowledge (Glock, 1996, p.283; Hacker, 2009). Even this undersells the positive side of philosophy, however. After all, it makes perfectly good sense to *know* the meaning of expressions, or to "know one's way around" (RPP I §§303, 1054) the conceptual landscape, e.g., by knowing that "A knows that p" entails "p."

3.6 Systematicity and Progress

Even confining oneself to philosophy's critical task, one may hold – with Kant – that it can be systematic and make progress. Rejecting such aspirations appears to be a hallmark of Wittgenstein's later conception. The hostility to systematic investigations seems to be borne out by Wittgenstein's notorious prohibition of hypotheses and theories. This appearance is partly deceptive, however. Wittgenstein had an overly restrictive conception of theory, confining it either to the hypothetico-deductive theories of empirical science (PI §109; see Hanfling, 2004) or to the attempt to provide analytic definitions of what he regarded as family-resemblance concepts (e.g. PG 119–20; RPP I §633). Neither proscription rules out dealing with philosophical questions in a sustained and orderly fashion.

It is two other claims that militate against systematic aspirations. One is Wittgenstein's stress on the motley of "language-games" and the disorderly and dynamic character of natural languages, as opposed to the artificial formal calculi (BB 16–17; PI §§18, 23, 108). The other is his acknowledgment that an overview of grammar establishes "an order" in our understanding of language which is *purpose-relative* – namely to the resolution of specific problems – not "*the* order" (PI §132; TS 220, §107). There are different potentially helpful articulations of the same grammatical rules.

Nevertheless, the very notion of an overview suggests that there is a sense in which Wittgensteinian philosophy can be systematic. Indeed, Wittgenstein provided two different "classifications of psychological concepts" (RPP I §895; RPP II §§63, 148; Z §472). He also envisaged a "genealogical tree" (*Stammbaum*) for them, as for number concepts, presumably a way of showing how e.g., the system of natural numbers can be extended into that of signed integers (RPP I §722). These overviews do not aspire to "precision." But Wittgenstein envisaged a "complete overview of everything which can create unclarity" (Z §§273, 464). This need not mean that there is a "totality" or "complete list of rules" for our language: the notion of "*all* rules" is dubious even for a single term, since clear criteria of identity exist only for codified rules, e.g., those of chess (MS 157a, p.108; TS 220, p.92). But it suggests that overviews of particular segments of grammar can be as comprehensive as one pleases.

Accordingly, there can be *progress* in mapping conceptual landscapes and resolving particular problems. But this is compatible with Wittgenstein's claim that philosophy is *open-ended* (Z §447; BB 44). Like the expansion of π, philosophy can get better, without ever getting nearer to completion. The reason is that even a global overview of grammar cannot provide a once-and-for-all panacea for philosophical puzzles. First, the language in which they are rooted changes, thereby creating new problems, as happened with the development of the new physics, of formal logic, or of computers; secondly, there is no definite number of ways of getting confused. By a similar token, "there is not *a* philosophical method, though there are indeed methods, like different therapies" (PI §133). Philosophy cannot terminate if, as Kant and Wittgenstein suggest, the fascination with philosophical problems is part of the human condition (BT 422–4). Some passages intimate that this tendency might be eradicated by cultural change (RFM II §23; CV 68–9). Yet unlike postmodern prophets of the demise of philosophy such as Rorty, Wittgenstein provides no clues as to what such a change would amount to.

3.7 Irrationalism vs. Rationalism

There have always been "irrationalist" interpretations, which distance both Wittgenstein's philosophical practice and his metaphilosophical views from the ideal of rational argument (for a critical survey see Glock, 2007; cp. Chapter 2, WITTGENSTEIN'S TEXTS AND STYLE). One of them is Pyrrhonian. Wittgenstein does not just aim to overcome traditional, metaphysical philosophizing by a better "critical" variety, the story goes;

he seeks to bring philosophy as such to an end. Just as the Pyrrhonian skeptic studiously eschews taking a stance even on the possibility of knowledge, Wittgenstein decries the very notion of having a philosophical view, while also avoiding having a metaphilosophical view about having philosophical views (see Rorty, 1979, p.371; Fogelin, 1987, ch.15; Stern, 2004).

There is no gainsaying that some passages lend succor to this interpretation.

> If one tried to advance theses in philosophy, it would never be possible to debate them, because everyone would agree to them. (PI §128; see §599)

Philosophical remarks are "homely," "stale truisms" (TS 213, p.412; MS 109, p.212; TS 220, §§89–90; TS 219, p.6). Indeed, Wittgenstein professes not to rely on "opinions" anybody could dispute (AWL 97; LFM 22; RFM 160; LC 72). But as argued above, this is part of a dialectic procedure. Philosophy provides "reminders" (PI §127) of patterns of linguistic use that competent speakers are perfectly familiar with.

To be sure, Wittgenstein opines that philosophy is "flat" (PI §§126, 599). Unlike the deductive-nomological sciences and formal disciplines like mathematics or logic it does not revolve around deductive reasoning (even though the latter can feature in its exposition). Deduction establishes the consequences of premises, but a dialectical critique of sense scrutinizes the meaning of those premises and the intelligibility of the questions.

Accordingly, Wittgenstein's style of argument is *elenctic* rather than demonstrative, yet this is no bar to it being perfectly rational. Furthermore, the Pyrhonnian insistence that Wittgenstein refuses to advance claims *of any kind* is blatantly incompatible with the descriptions of the "actual use of language" and "the quiet weighing of linguistic facts" he explicitly propagates (e.g., PI §124; Z §447). Finally, if, textual evidence notwithstanding, Wittgenstein had indeed adopted a Pyrrhonian "no position"-position, he would confront a fatal dilemma. Either his remarks conform to his "no position"-methodology, in which case they cannot amount to a genuine contribution to philosophical or metaphilosophical debate. Or they do not, in which case his practice belies his stated methodological views. Furthermore, he would be propounding the (non-obvious) thesis that there are no (non-obvious) philosophical theses. In either case – incommensurability and inconsistency – his attacks on traditional philosophy would be self-contradictory and his conception of philosophy incoherent.

It is true that the *Investigations* feature few explicit answers to Wittgenstein's numerous self-posed questions (Kenny, 2004, p.78). But many of the questions are *rhetorical*. Again, Wittgenstein did not take sides in traditional philosophical disputes like realism vs. idealism, monism vs. dualism, nominalism vs. Platonism, etc.; instead, he tried to undermine the dubious assumptions common to the participants. But once again this is a perfectly rational strategy pioneered by Kant's transcendental dialectic and embraced by Ramsey (1990, pp.11–12). Wittgenstein also tried to *dissolve* questions that lead to such misguided alternatives. But the strategy of questioning vexing questions is once again prudent and was recommended by the supremely sober G.E. Moore (1903, preface). Moreover, in questioning a question Wittgenstein sought the "right question" (see PI §§133, 189, 321; RPP I §600; MS 130, p.107; WAM 27–8). And he did provide answers to Socratic questions like "What is understanding?," since doing so is a prerequisite of dissolving misguided questions and theories. What he rejects with respect to such Socratic questions is merely the insistence that they can only be answered by *analytic definitions* (BB 17–20; PI §64).

Even where Wittgenstein rejects a traditional question as phrased, his remarks must nevertheless address an *underlying problem*. Otherwise he simply would not have anything to say on the topics at issue and his rejection would be no more than an expression of lack of interest, something those pursuing the question can ignore. Thus, when Wittgenstein dismisses questions like "What is the ground of necessary truth?" he still addresses the philosophical problem of necessity by other questions like "What is it for a proposition to be necessary?." Questioning a question in a philosophically relevant sense must involve taking up an underlying common problem in a more adequate way.

Wittgenstein suggested that philosophical illumination may arise from a book featuring nothing but jokes and questions and that we should respond to *all* philosophical questions not by giving an answer, but by asking a new question (RFM III §5; WAM 27–8). In that very remark, however, he willy-nilly provides an *answer* to the question of what role questions play in philosophy. This rejoinder sounds bloody-minded only because it has to match the obstinacy of seriously adopting a "no position"-position.

As these occasional remarks show, Wittgenstein was not entirely immune to Pyrrhonian urges. He was also fond of comparing his philosophical critique to a kind of psychotherapy that disabuses us of the inclination to raise philosophical questions (PI §§133, 254–5; BT 407–10; Z §382; see Chapter 43, WITTGENSTEIN ON PSYCHOANALYSIS). Moreover, in a lecture he confessed to "making propaganda for one style of thinking as opposed to another" (LC 28). Unfortunately, both procedures are philosophically immaterial. For their only criterion of success appears to be the suppression of a certain intellectual urge. They cannot distinguish between achieving this goal by *extrinsic* means, such as hypnosis, drugs, or a knock on the head, and achieving it in the only way that can be philosophically pertinent, namely through showing that something goes wrong in a philosophical question or view.

It is fortunate, therefore, that Wittgenstein himself acknowledged that philosophical critique ought to be a rational rather than medical or rhetorical enterprise. He insisted that philosophy should provide arguments that are "absolutely conclusive," and he described his own thought as the "rejection of wrong arguments," an avenue open to those feeling a need for "transparency of their own argumentation" (MS 161, p.3; BT 408, 421). Wittgenstein's work contains or at least intimates plenty of powerful and profound arguments of an elenctic type. It is just that, because of his idiosyncratic style, these arguments need to be spelled out by painstaking exegesis. The rational line for *interpreters* is to acknowledge that Wittgenstein's work combines rationalist and irrationalist elements. The rational line for *philosophers* is to explore the arguments, insights, and instructive errors it has to offer. This exhortation presupposes, of course, that philosophy is a rational enterprise based on arguments. But one cannot argue against this presupposition without engaging in precisely such an enterprise. And in the absence of such arguments there is no reason to abandon the ideal of rational philosophizing. Therefore it is a presupposition to which we should commit.

3.8 The Myth of Mere Method

At the same time, let us be mindful of the limits of rational argument. Wittgenstein himself insisted on this point, e.g., in his discussion of the autonomy of grammar and of the foundations of certainty and knowledge. As regards the nature of philosophy, however, he failed to draw one important lesson. In his early work, at least, he succumbed to what one might call the *myth of mere method*. This is the illusion that one can fashion philosophical methods in a presuppositionless manner, one which does not in turn draw on philosophical views, e.g., about logical necessity, linguistic meaning, or the nature of philosophical problems. In the *Tractatus* the method, in particular an ideal notation for the analysis of propositions, is supposed to be put in place by propaedeutic claims about the essence of representation that are then disowned as nonsensical. In the *Investigations* it seems that the method and the metaphilosophical remarks describing it are supposed to emerge automatically as a spin-off from reflections on specific philosophical problems. But the *Tractatus* procedure is self-refuting; and the philosophical problems discussed in the *Investigations* only cry out for Wittgenstein's treatment on a certain understanding of their nature, an understanding which itself is philosophically contentious. Consider just one looming circularity. Wittgenstein entreats us to address philosophical problems by looking at nonphilosophical linguistic use. That recommendation depends on two ideas: the content of these problems (their constitutive concepts) is determined by the linguistic meaning of the expressions involved; the meaning of those expressions is a function of their use. These ideas are in turn supported by observations concerning the nonphilosophical use of "meaning," its cognates and related notions like that of what is said or asked. We have reason to condone this particular circle, since it is difficult to envisage a better starting point for clarifying or even modifying a notion like meaning than its established use. Nevertheless, in urging that point one cannot bootstrap oneself onto a privileged methodological plane.

The nature of philosophy is itself a contested philosophical issue, and views about this issue are philosophically controversial. The label "metaphilosophy" notwithstanding it is not a distinct higher-order discipline, but an integral part of philosophy itself. By contrast to therapeutic followers like Lazerowitz (1964/2004), who theorized about philosophy from the external vantage point of psychoanalysis, Wittgenstein himself was aware of this point (PI §121). Once it is acknowledged that one cannot engage in metaphilosophy without doing philosophy, however, the myth of mere method collapses. One cannot swim without venturing into the water. And one cannot address philosophical problems, the nature of philosophy included, without doing philosophy, and hence without philosophical arguments and commitments of one's own. What one can do is to ensure consistency between philosophical methods, metaphilosophical and substantive views, and to argue for all of them in as plausible and unassuming a way as possible. Such a modest procedure must treat the actual character of philosophical investigations as *one* starting point. In that respect, normative metaphilosophy *refers back* to descriptive methodology. And here Wittgenstein's phenomenology of philosophical puzzlement can make a lasting contribution, even to those who disagree vehemently with his overall conception of our subject.

References

Austin, J.L. (1961/1970). *Philosophical Papers*. Ed. J.O. Urmson and G.J. Warnock. Second edition. Oxford: Oxford University Press.
Baker, G.P. and Hacker, P.M.S. (1984). *Language, Sense and Nonsense*. Oxford: Blackwell.
Blackburn, S. (1984). *Spreading the Word*. Oxford: Oxford University Press.
Dummett, M.A.E. (1978). *Truth and other Enigmas*. London: Duckworth.
Fogelin, R.F. (1987). *Wittgenstein*. London: Routledge.

Frege, G. (1893/1966). *Grundgesetze der Arithemtik*. [The Foundations of Arithmetic.] Hildesheim: Olms.
Glock, H.-J. (1996). *A Wittgenstein Dictionary*. Oxford: Blackwell.
Glock, H.-J. (2003). *Quine and Davidson on Language, Thought and Reality*. Cambridge: Cambridge University Press.
Glock, H.-J. (2007). Perspectives on Wittgenstein: An Intermittently Opinionated Survey. In G. Kahane, E. Kanterian, and O. Kuusela (Eds). *Wittgenstein and his Interpreters: Essays in Memory of Gordon Baker* (pp.37–65). Oxford: Blackwell.
Glock, H.-J. (2012). Strawson's Descriptive Metaphysics. In L. Haaparanta and H. Koskinnen (Eds). *Categories of Being* (pp.391–419). New York: Oxford University Press.
Gregory, R.L. (1987). In Defense of Artificial Intelligence – A Reply to John Searle. In C. Blakemore and S. Greenfield (Eds). *Mindwaves* (pp.234–244). Oxford: Blackwell.
Hacker, P.M.S. (2009). Philosophy: A Contribution, not to Human Knowledge, but to Human Understanding. *Royal Institute of Philosophy Supplement*, 65, 129–153.
Hanfling, O. (2000). *Philosophy and Ordinary Language*. London: Routledge.
Hanfling, O. (2004). The Use of "Theory" in Philosophy. In E. Ammereller and E. Fischer (Eds). *Wittgenstein at Work: Method in the Philosophical Investigations* (pp.183–200). London: Routledge.
Hare, R.M. (1960). Philosophical Discoveries. *Mind*, 69, 145–162.
Kalhat, J. (2008). Has the Later Wittgenstein Accounted for Necessity?. *Philosophical Investigations*, 31, 1–23.
Kant, I. ([1781/1787] 1998). *Critique of Pure Reason*. Trans. P. Guyer and A. Woods. Cambridge: Cambridge University Press. (Original work published 1781/87.)
Kenny, A. (2004). Philosophy States Only What Everyone Admits. In E. Ammereller and E. Fischer (Eds). *Wittgenstein at Work: Method in the Philosophical Investigations* (pp.173–182). London: Routledge.
Lazerowitz, M. (1964/2004). *Studies in Metaphilosophy*. London: Routledge.
Moore, G.E. (1903). *Principia Ethica*. Cambridge: Cambridge University Press.
Ramsey, F.P. (1990). *Philosophical Papers*. Ed. D.H. Mellor. Cambridge: Cambridge University Press.
Rorty, R. (1979). *Philosophy and the Mirror of Nature*. Princeton: Princeton University Press.
Rundle, B. (1990). *Wittgenstein and Contemporary Philosophy of Language*. Oxford: Blackwell.
Russell, B. (1912/1967). *The Problems of Philosophy*. Oxford: Oxford University Press.
Russell, B. (1914/1993). *Our Knowledge of the External World*. London: Routledge.
Russell, B. (1918). *Mysticism and Logic*. London: Longmans, Green.
Russell, B. (1956). *Logic and Knowledge: Essays 1901–1950*. Ed. R.C. Marsh. London: Allen and Unwin.
Ryle, G. (1971a). *Collected Papers* (Vol. 1). London: Hutchinson.
Ryle, G. (1971b). *Collected Essays* (Vol. 2). London: Hutchinson.
Searle, J. (1997). The Explanation of Cognition. In J.M. Preston (Ed.). *Thought and Language* (pp.103–126). Cambridge: Cambridge University Press.
Stern, D.G. (2004). *Wittgenstein's Philosophical Investigations: An Introduction*. Cambridge: Cambridge University Press.
Strawson, P.F. (1959). *Individuals*. London: Methuen.
Strawson, P.F. (1992). *Analysis and Metaphysics*. Oxford: Oxford University Press.

Further Reading

Ammereller, E. and Fischer, E. (Eds). *Wittgenstein at Work: Method in the Philosophical Investigations*. London: Routledge.
Baker, G.P. (2004). *Wittgenstein's Method: Neglected Aspects*. Ed. K.J. Morris. Oxford: Blackwell.

Baker, G.P. and Hacker, P.M.S. (1980/2009). *Wittgenstein: Understanding and Meaning. Volume 1 of an Analytical Commentary on the Philosophical Investigations. Part 1. Essays*. Second edition. Extensively revised by P.M.S. Hacker. Oxford: Wiley-Blackwell.

Hacker, P.M.S. (2001). Philosophy. In H.-J. Glock (Ed.). *Wittgenstein: A Critical Reader* (pp. 322–347). Oxford: Blackwell.

Horwich, P. (2012). *Wittgenstein's Metaphilosophy*. Oxford: Clarendon Press.

Kuusela, O. (2008). *The Struggle against Dogmatism: Wittgenstein and the Concept of Philosophy*. Cambridge, MA: Harvard University Press.

Pihlström, S. (Ed.) (2006). *Wittgenstein and the Method of Philosophy*. Special issue of *Acta Philosophica Fennica*, 80.

von Savigny, E. (1991). No Chapter "On Philosophy" in Wittgenstein's *Philosophical Investigations*. *Metaphilosophy*, 22, 309–317.

Wyss, S. (2015). Does Wittgenstein have a Method? The Challenges of Conant and Schulte. *Nordic Wittgenstein Review*, 4, 167–193.

14

Grammar and Grammatical Statements

SEVERIN SCHROEDER

1 Grammar: The Rules of Language

"Grammar" is Wittgenstein's preferred term for the workings of a language: the system of rules that determine linguistic meaning. A philosophical study of language is a study of "grammar," in this sense, and insofar as any philosophical investigation is concerned with conceptual details, which manifest themselves in language, it is a grammatical investigation.

In the *Tractatus Logico-Philosophicus* Wittgenstein offered a mathematical picture of language: presenting language as a calculus. The essence of language, the general form of the proposition was given by a simple formula (TLP 6). Like a calculus, language was claimed to be governed by syntactic rules: (i) formation rules about the licit combination of names to form elementary propositions; (ii) formation rules about the licit combination of elementary propositions to make complex propositions; and finally (iii), truth-table rules, which enable us to identify logical truths and entailments. Notoriously, the existence of the first type of rule remained a postulate. As no examples of actual names were given, the rules governing their use could of course not be presented either. Moreover, Wittgenstein insisted rather perversely that no syntactic rule could be meaningfully stated.

When Wittgenstein grew dissatisfied with this view of language, it was not the idea that language was essentially rule-governed that he found fault with. On the contrary, *that* idea he held on to emphatically at least until about 1936, only correcting his account of what those rules were and how they functioned. In fact, it would not be much of an exaggeration to say that Wittgenstein's break with his early philosophy was largely due to a careful reconsideration of the role of rules in language. Roughly speaking, while the author of the *Tractatus* thought that rules could work in secret and that their workings had to be discovered and analyzed (just as one has to discover and analyze invisible chemical processes), the Wittgenstein of the 1930s realized that language is an artifact and to the extent to which it is governed by rules, those rules must be made and applied by us (BB 27 f.; BT 268). Hence the idea that those rules could to a large extent be unknown to competent speakers and awaiting to be unearthed by future

---

A Companion to Wittgenstein, First Edition. Edited by Hans-Johann Glock and John Hyman.
© 2017 John Wiley & Sons, Ltd. Published 2017 by John Wiley & Sons, Ltd.

logicians (cf. TLP 4.002) must be absurd — "a hellish idea," as Wittgenstein now called it in conversation with Friedrich Waismann (WVC 129 f.) – just as absurd as the idea that nobody yet knows exactly what the rules of football are. Indeed, the comparison between language and a game becomes one of the leitmotivs of Wittgenstein's later philosophy, as suggested by his concept of a language-game. The title of Chapter 45 of the so-called *Big Typescript* makes his new view explicit:

> Language functions as language only by virtue of the rules we follow in using it, just as a game is a game only by virtue of its rules. (BT 196)

Rejecting the idea of postulated "subterranean" rules, not known to those who follow them, and focusing instead on rules that are actually manifest in our ordinary language use Wittgenstein became aware of the contingency of some of those rules: the fact that different languages with significantly different rules are at least conceivable. By contrast, in the *Tractatus* Wittgenstein had presented logical syntax as the essence of any possible language (see Hacker, 1972/86, p.181).

Moreover, attention to actual linguistic detail made Wittgenstein realize that ordinary language is a good deal less tidy, less precisely regulated than a calculus. While the author of the *Tractatus* had insisted on the determinacy of sense and on perfect linguistic precision, appearances to the contrary notwithstanding, the later Wittgenstein rejected this ideal as a prejudice and declared that our grammatical rules are often vague. He now states explicitly that there is no logical calculus underpinning our language, although we may conveniently use such a calculus as an object of comparison:

> remember that in general we don't use language according to strict rules – it hasn't been taught us by means of strict rules, either. *We*, in our discussions on the other hand, constantly compare language with a calculus proceeding according to exact rules. (BB 25; cf. PI §81)

Indeed, the rules that could be written out to reflect the meanings of our words are not only vague, our lists of such rules would also remain incomplete: the game which we play with words "is not everywhere circumscribed by rules" (PI §68). For example, we have no rules by which to decide how the word "chair" is to be applied to chair-like objects that keep disappearing like hallucinations (PI §80).

Finally, it is noteworthy that in the *Tractatus* account there is no mention of semantic rules. Logical grammar, for the young Wittgenstein, is only logical syntax (TLP 3.325); and logical syntax can be determined without paying any attention to the meaning of the signs (TLP 3.33). The connection between a name and its meaning, that is, the object named, is not fixed by a rule, but by a mental act of meaning (NB 104, 130; cf. PG 97). (Hence, Wittgenstein will spend a lot of time in his later philosophy exorcising this idea that linguistic meaning depends on mental processes of meaning something.) In the 1930s, by contrast, Wittgenstein's concern with linguistic rules is mainly focused on semantic rules, explanations of the meanings of words, which are now emphatically included in grammar:

> There is not grammar *and* an interpretation of signs. Rather, in so far as one can talk about an interpretation, i.e. an explication of signs, it is grammar itself that has to take care of that. (BT 58)

Even ostensive explanations, such as "This colour → ■ is called 'black,'" are now regarded as rules of grammar (BT 199, 234; PG 88), which is not an entirely felicitous use of the term. An ostensive explanation can perhaps be called a "rule" if it involves a canonical sample (such as the standard meter in Paris). Ordinary ostensive explanations, however, that explain a word by pointing to whatever suitable instance of the concept is at hand, are more plausibly regarded as *explanations by example* than as rules. The difference between these two types of explanation is that statements of rules, unlike instantiations, are not themselves "moves in the game." Thus, to explain the waltz by giving a list or diagram of the correct steps can be called: giving a rule. The explanation is not itself a performance of the dance. But one can also teach the waltz by giving the learner a demonstration of it. This would not be a rule, but an explanation by example. For the instructor's teaching is itself an instance of dancing the waltz, a "move in the game." Similarly, a casual ostensive explanation of the word "purple" by pointing at and naming the color of a violet is simply an instance of a correct application of the word ("This flower is purple"); and as such it is already a move in the language-game (teaching by doing) (cf. Schroeder, 2001).

Wittgenstein admits that the way he uses the term "grammar" differs from common usage (MS 110, 195; AWL 31). Explanations of word meaning, as given in dictionaries, are not normally subsumed under grammar. On the other hand, the usual morphological concerns of grammarians – declination, conjugation of irregular verbs, tense, gender, and word order – the stock in trade of school grammar, is quite irrelevant to philosophical investigations of language. The key difference lies in the aims for which the study of language is pursued by the linguist and the philosopher. The philosopher does (or should) not attempt to give a comprehensive and detailed picture of language for its own sake. Rather, philosophical attention to language is just a means to resolving philosophical problems. Hence philosophical accounts of grammar can ignore most areas of school grammar, but have to focus on the relations between some interesting concepts and their criteria of application. Thus a philosopher's grammatical investigation bears more resemblance with the work of a lexicographer than a grammarian, yet it is extremely selective and often pays attention to aspects of a word's meaning that are not spelled out in a dictionary.

2   The Autonomy of Grammar

"Grammar," writes Wittgenstein in an important passage in the *Big Typescript*, "is not accountable to any reality. The rules of grammar determine meaning (constitute it), and therefore they are not answerable to any meaning and in this respect arbitrary" (BT 233). In the early days of developing his conception of grammar (1929–1933), Wittgenstein suggested the following argument for the arbitrariness, or autonomy of grammar:

> The conventions of grammar can't be justified by a description of what is represented. Any description of that kind already presupposes the rules of grammar. (BT 238)

This is a rather odd way of putting it: if something is a convention then of course it can't be justified as being true to the facts. The idea seems to be that one may mistakenly think that it is not a convention, but a metaphysical truth. Wittgenstein gives the example "There are only four primary colours" (BT 236; Z §331), which however is difficult to assess as there are different concepts of a primary color. But in the same passage he considers the idea that colors must be classified together, because they are similar, "as opposed to, say, shapes or tones"; and he suggests the response that this similarity is only the result of our classification and so cannot be invoked to justify it (BT 237). But that is hardly convincing. The obvious difference between red and green, on the one hand, and C and D, on the other, is that the former can only be seen and the latter can only be heard. Stating it does not presuppose the concept of a color. Of course it would be possible, as Wittgenstein suggests in the following sentence, to have a concept of something being red, green, or circular. But even familiarity with such a classification, instead of that of a color, would not change the fact that there is a difference between red and green, on the one hand, and circular, on the other: if a surface is entirely red (or green), every visible part of it is red (or green); yet if a surface is circular it doesn't follow that a part of it must be circular too. Moreover, red and green are mutually exclusive, while they are both combinable with circularity.

In a related passage it is claimed that:

> If I could describe the purpose of grammatical conventions by saying that I had to create them because, for instance, colours have certain properties, that would make these conventions unnecessary. (PR 53; BT 238)

Here one could object that if a convention was prompted by certain similarities it would not for that matter be superfluous. That colors have something in common that justifies grouping them together doesn't mean that conventionally doing so (classifying them under one label) isn't a useful convention. After all, there are plenty of cases of things having features in common that we do not bother to pick out by a single word (e.g., trees and bushes with serrated leaves).

However, the continuation of the passage quoted suggests that Wittgenstein had a different kind of case in mind, namely that of a convention laying down, or implying, what combinations of words do and don't make sense:

> That would make these conventions unnecessary, because then I could say precisely what it was the conventions were excluding. Conversely, if the conventions were necessary, i.e. if certain combinations of words had to be excluded as being nonsensical, then for that very reason I couldn't name a single feature of the colours that would make the conventions necessary, for then it would be conceivable that the colours might not have that feature, and that could only be expressed by contravening the conventions. (PR 53; BT 238)

To begin with a different example, it is surely correct that one cannot justify the semantic convention that the word "bachelor" applies to unmarried men by insisting that bachelors really *are* unmarried men. That all bachelors are unmarried men *by definition* can obviously not explain why we chose that definition of the word. However, Wittgenstein's example of the concept of a color is less straightforward, since it is not defined in terms of certain features, but by a list of instances: red, green, blue, yellow, etc., are colors. Now the question may arise as to why, for example, *heavy* or *circular* are not classified as "colors" as well; and one may suggest the answer that colors are perceptible by sight only, which rules out weight or shapes. Arguably, this feature of being perceptible by sight *only* is not a defining feature of color: we do not present it as a criterion when teaching the word. Rather, it is something we realize afterwards when considering the familiar instances of particular colors. Hence it can appropriately be cited to justify the list of particular colors that serves us as a definition. That list is indeed more natural and practical than an alternative list of classification subsuming: red, green, blue, heavy – for these do not all share the feature of being perceptible by sight only.

But to this Wittgenstein might object as follows: we cannot say that colors have the feature of being perceptible only by sight, which makes our classification sensible, "for then it would be conceivable that the colors might not have that feature, and that could only be expressed by contravening the conventions." — However, this objection appears to be based on the *Tractatus* dogma that for a statement to be meaningful its negation must be meaningful too, and that therefore you cannot really express any necessary truths. But that is a dogma we should not accept. Of course you can meaningfully say, for example, that colors are visible. That the negation of such a claim is nonsense doesn't make it unsayable, it only shows it to be a characterization of the concept of a color, rather than an empirical claim. Admittedly, such a characterization of a concept must be a consequence of the way that concept has been defined or fixed; but since it need not be explicit in the concept's definition or explanation, it may well be licit to invoke it in order to justify the concept.

Even if Wittgenstein's argument for the autonomy of grammar fails to convince, there are three other considerations that strongly support the view that grammar is not determined by reality and cannot be faulted by it, even though it may be possible to justify some concepts as more natural and more useful than others (see also Chapter 15, THE AUTONOMY OF GRAMMAR). (That, contrary to some of his earlier remarks, experience can in a certain way be said to justify our grammar is shown by Wittgenstein's account of arithmetical equations as grammatical rules (see section 6 below). If the objects we count were so unstable or evanescent that after adding 7 of them to 5 others we did not regularly count 12 in all, the equation "$7 + 5 = 12$" would be useless as a grammatical norm (RFM 52). Hence, the empirical fact that such counts do almost always yield the result that the corresponding equation makes us expect provides some justification for holding on to the grammar of our arithmetic.)

First, "the rules of grammar determine meaning (constitute it), and therefore they are not answerable to any meaning" (BT 233). Of course, if the meaning of a word is its conventional use in the language (PI §43; cf. Schroeder, 2006, ch.4.4), then a rule suggested to capture that use can be found correct or inaccurate. But taking "the rules of grammar" to be the norms that inform our use, there is no meaning independent of them (BB 28). In particular, where on different occasions or in different contexts a word is used according to different rules, it makes no sense to suggest that some are and some are not in agreement with the word's true meaning. Thus, the meaning of the word "not" does not compel us to take double negation as affirmation; we could also take it as emphatic negation. Each option gives the word "not" a slightly different meaning (BT 234).

Secondly, there is no extralinguistic purpose determining the correct rules of language. One can of course say that language is a means of communication. A system of vocal sounds to be produced according to certain rules, but unsuitable for any communicative purpose, we would probably not call a language (it might be a kind of phonic game). But then, not every use of language is an act of communication (soliloquies are the most obvious counterexample), and communicative success is not by any means the only thing that matters to us about language (various aesthetic considerations are taken very seriously too). Hence suitability for communication may be a minimal requirement for any kind of language, but the concept of communication is immensely wide and compatible with an endless range of different grammatical rules and conceptual schemes. It would certainly not allow us to determine any specific set of concepts as the correct ones.

At one point Wittgenstein contrasted grammatical rules with the rules of cooking, suggesting that "'cookery' is defined by its end, whereas 'speaking' is not":

> You cook badly if you are guided in your cooking by rules other than the right ones; but if you follow other rules than those of chess you are *playing another game*; and if you follow grammatical rules other than such-and-such ones, that does not mean you say something wrong, no, you are speaking of something else. (BT 237; Z §320)

But the contrast is not as neat as this passage suggests. Which are the "right" rules of cooking? There is an endless variety of culinary procedures. Of course where the result of applying a rule is something absolutely unfit for human consumption, we wouldn't call it a rule of cookery. But then, similarly, a rule for producing certain vocal utterances would not count as a grammatical rule if those utterances were just meaningless sounds. In fact, the relation between rules of cookery and nutrition is fairly similar to that between rules of grammar and communication. In both cases, the former are restricted, but not determined by the latter. (The rules of chess are of course not to be compared to the rules of cooking, but, say, to the rules of cooking a Mushroom Stroganoff according to a particular recipe, for instance, Jamie Oliver's *Wild Mushroom and Venison Stroganoff for Two Lucky People* (2008) – and again, the analogy holds: if you don't follow the recipe, you don't necessarily cook badly, you're just preparing a different dish.)

Thirdly, contrary to a widespread philosophical view, our concepts are not determined by the essences of things. This ought to be self-evident, simply a consequence of the trivial fact that language is man-made and conventional (BB 27 f.). We are obviously free to decide that all objects of a certain description are to be called by a label of our invention. Thus I could stipulate that whatever is either red, green, or circular is to be called "*gog*" (cf. BT 237). As a stipulation this may be criticized as impractical or useless, but not as false (BT 236). Unlike propositions or declarative sentences, concepts are not truth-apt. However, the widespread idea of a natural kind concept is an attempt to deny this. To describe a concept as of a natural kind is to make the implicit claim that its classification is scientifically correct. So-called scientific realists believe that on the micro-level (of DNA or atomic structure) nature herself determines how things are to be correctly classified. But that is naive, for apart from the fact that it is still our decision to take anything on the micro-level into account (and for many purposes we don't), down there we are just as much overwhelmed with data and still have to decide which ones (which of an animal's 30 000 genes, for example) are to be relevant to classification. There is no getting away from the fact that words and their meanings are our artifacts and we have to take responsibility for them.

3   From Rules to Norms

It has already been mentioned above that in his later discussions Wittgenstein no longer believes that language is, like a calculus, a *complete* system of *exact* rules. Indeed, he becomes increasingly critical of the idea that language is, like a game, strictly speaking rule-governed, entering some further important reservations:

(i) Linguistic rules are not normally part of the game ("an instrument of the game itself" (PI §54; cf. §82)) in the way they are in some of Wittgenstein's simplified language-games. He imagines, for example, that someone is given a table correlating letters and movements and then a sequence of letters as an order to move in a certain way (EPB 139). To carry out the order one consults the table, that is, the rule. By contrast, if someone directs me in English ("Right. Straight on to the traffic lights, then second left.") I do not consult a rule to derive my movements from his words.

(ii) We have not been taught our mother tongue by rules (cf. PI §54). And this is an important point for Wittgenstein, for he identifies as a typical philosophers' mistake an inclination to describe our learning of language in a way that already presupposes linguistic competence, like the learning of a foreign language (PI §32). Therefore he emphasizes that at the basic stages language teaching cannot be explaining, let alone giving rules, but must be training or drill ("*Abrichtung*") (PI §6; cf. MS 179, 7v: "To follow a rule presupposes a language." ["*Einer Regel folgen setzt eine Sprache voraus.*"]). And even at later stages, language is for the most part learnt by picking up a sufficient number of examples of correct usage, rather than by rules or explicit explanations. "One learns the game by watching how others play" (PI §54).

(iii) Hence linguistic rules for natural languages are not necessary for the actual use of a language; they are only summarizing descriptions of that use (PI §54). As such they can still be called "rules of grammar," but then the latter word is taken in a different sense: referring not to the actual workings of language, but to a systematic account of those workings. "Grammar," Wittgenstein remarks, using the word in this derivative sense, "is a description of language *ex post*" ("*Die Grammatik ist eine nachträgliche Beschreibung der Sprache.*": MS 110, 110). It is of course true that linguists' systematic descriptions of a language, in dictionaries and grammar books, will subsequently have a normative and stabilizing impact on certain aspects (usually fairly subtle aspects) of the use of language by educated speakers; but this is a feature of a highly advanced and sophisticated literary culture. It is clearly not essential to the phenomenon of language and, from a historical point of view, would not have been relevant for most speakers of most languages for most of the time.

(iv) Taking the points made so far into consideration, Wittgenstein withdraws his earlier claim that "language functions as language only by virtue of the rules we follow in using it, just as a game is a game only by virtue of its rules" (BT 196). In a handwritten note he comments:

> That is not correct, in so far as no rules have to have been *laid down* for language; no more than for a game. But one can look at language (and a game) from the standpoint of a process that uses rules. (BT 196)

The rules of a language, he now suggests, are a useful fiction, like that of a social contract:

> "Contrat social" – here too no actual contract was ever concluded; but the situation is more or less similar, analogous, to the one we'd be in if ... And there's much to be gained in viewing it in terms of such a contract. (BT 196v)

It is, after all, a fact that language involves normativity. We do not only use certain expressions, we regard them as correct, and we criticize and reject others, which we regard as incorrect. This important feature of language is rightly emphasized by comparing language to a rule-governed game, even if the comparison does not give an accurate picture of the way linguistic normativity is conveyed and implemented.

(v) Wittgenstein's reservations go further still. Acknowledging that linguistic rules need not actually be consulted, but may be nothing but summary descriptions of people's use of words, he writes (in 1933–1934):

> But what if observation does not enable us clearly to see any rule, and the question [put to a speaker as to what rule he follows] brings none to light? – For he did indeed give me an explanation when I asked him what he understood by 'N', but he was prepared to withdraw and alter it. – So how am I to determine the rule according to which he is playing? He does not know it himself. Or, more accurately: What meaning is the expression 'the rule by which he proceeds' supposed to have left to it here? (PI §82; cf. BB 25)

Wittgenstein seems to envisage two reasons why in many cases no rule can be given. One is illustrated in the following section by an analogy with games:

> Doesn't the analogy between language and games throw light here? We can easily imagine people amusing themselves in a field by playing with a ball so as to start various existing games, but playing many without finishing them and in between throwing the ball aimlessly into the air, chasing one another with the ball and bombarding one another for a joke and so on. [...]
>   And is there not also the case where we play and – make up the rules as we go along? And there is even one where we alter them – as we go along. (PI §83)

The idea seems to be that a variety of different language-games can be played with the same words and that (unlike the builders of §2 of the *Investigations* who always use the same words in the same way) we tend frequently to move between them, mix them up, and introduce new variations (cf. BB 28: "there are words [...] which [...] are used in a thousand different ways which gradually merge into one another"). Picking out one of those uses, we might well be able to produce something like a rule, but then it will not be applicable to what we do with the same expression in another context. So we'd have to "withdraw and alter" our explanation; and will do so again when considering yet other uses. Our grip on linguistic normativity is essentially piecemeal, and the explanations that we can give manifesting our linguistic competence are always just provisional, read off from some language-game which could easily on another occasion shade into, or be developed into, a slightly different one.

The most telling expression of Wittgenstein's claim that linguistic normativity is often piecemeal is of course his introduction of the idea of a family-resemblance concept. He suggests that when we try to formulate a comprehensive rule, that is, a definition, for the use of the word "game," we draw a blank (PI §66). Here, as in many other cases, what is subsumed under a given concept cannot be derived from a general rule, for it has not been decided once and for all, but case by case, according to the way the concept was first introduced with only some applications in mind, and then applied or not applied to new kinds of cases, as people saw fit. Thus, for example, tennis is called a game, whereas judo is not, although they are both competitive rule-governed sports.

Taking stock of Wittgenstein's qualifications of the idea of language as rule-governed, we should, however, be careful not to throw the baby out with the bath water. The essential normativity of grammar is never called into question. It is certainly true that our use of language manifests linguistic norms. Often, though not always, they can be given in the form of rules: general statements summarizing how an expression is to be used (e.g., definitions). But such rules are, for the most part, only *ex-post* abstractions from actual usage (unlike the rules for a calculus, laid down beforehand). In order to acknowledge all the qualifications and reservations Wittgenstein had about speaking of *rules* of language, while holding on to his crucial insight into the normativity of language, it may be better to speak of the *norms* of language, with the proviso that norms can be piecemeal and implicit in a practice, and need not be laid down as general verbal expressions, i.e., as rules.

4   Rules of Grammar and the Discussion of Rule-Following

One may well wonder why, if by the mid-1930s Wittgenstein had so many reservations about regarding language as rule-governed, he should have spent so much time in *Philosophical Investigations* discussing what it is to follow a rule.

Trying to answer this question, we should first of all note an important point about Wittgenstein's use of the word "rule" in the *Investigations*, which is clarified by a passage in "The Brown Book." There he distinguishes between two kinds of (what he calls) rules, namely: semantic rules and instruction rules (BB 96, 98; cf. EPB 140, 143). A semantic rule gives the meanings of signs, e.g., in the form of a table:

(a) move to the right
(b) move to the left
(c) move forward
(d) move backward.

Using those signs to give somebody an order (e.g.: "c a d a") would rely on the previously given rule, but it would not itself be a rule. However, where such an order is meant to be followed again and again, say, in drawing a continuing ornamental pattern, Wittgenstein is happy to call it a "rule," too. It is what may be called an instruction rule:

> In this case I think we should say that "cada" is the rule for drawing the design. Roughly speaking, it characterizes what we call a rule to be applied repeatedly, in an indefinite number of instances. (BB 96)

This, I think, helps us to understand what is going on in the rule-following discussions in the *Investigations*. What I presented above were Wittgenstein's misgivings about the idea of *semantic* rules, but what occupies him in the *Investigations* under the title "following a rule" is something different: it is not semantic rules, but *instruction* rules, that is: orders to continue doing something in a regular manner, e.g., writing down series of numbers. (Note how often he uses the word "order" together with or instead of the word "rule", e.g.: PI §§186–9. 206, 212; cf. MS 165, 40; 84.)

Why then should Wittgenstein be interested in such orders? — Because his main concern in those parts of the book is the concept of *understanding*. And orders and their execution provide the most straightforward and most perspicuous example of semantic understanding (cf. MS 165, p.30). If you make a statement, giving me a piece of information, my understanding may or may not show in my behavior. Telling me that it is snowing may make me go out or not, depending, amongst many other things, on whether I like to be out in the snow or not. In that way, most linguistic understanding has no direct behavioral manifestation. Orders given to somebody assumed to be willing to comply are rather different. Understanding or misunderstanding show immediately in what is done. At this point language comes into direct contact with action. Hence Wittgenstein's preference for language-games of ordering, such as buying apples (PI §1) or directing an assistant to pass building material (PI §2).

Moreover, Wittgenstein had a particular interest in an understanding that goes beyond a particular occasion, such as the understanding of a system (PI §143). For one thing, because such an understanding of complex, possibly even infinite contents seems particularly puzzling, especially as it can happen in a flash. We are inclined to think of understanding as having mental representations; yet how can a highly complex system be represented instantaneously in one's minds? (see Schroeder, 2006, pp.181–97). — For another thing, linguistic understanding is obviously systematic. We do not just understand single utterances (tokens); we understand types of words and expressions, such that we know how to apply them or how to respond to them again and again, on an endless number of occasions.

So, there is no tension between Wittgenstein's reservations about the importance of semantic rules and his intensive discussion of following rules; because the well-known examples of rule-following in the *Investigations* (continuing arithmetical series) are not concerned with semantic rules. They are just cases of carrying out orders with an endless applicability. As such they are just variations of the builders language-game: "Write down the series of even numbers!" is like "Keep bringing me slabs!" (Cf. RFM 341c–f, where "How can I follow a rule?" and "How do I know what to do in response to the order 'slab!'?" are treated as on a par.)

The deviant pupil of §185 could just as well have been presented as a deviant builder's assistant who when given the order "slab" for the fifth time brings a block, etc. — So it's not that all linguistic understanding is a form of rule-following; rather: following rules of instruction is just one simple type of linguistic understanding, one language-game.

There is, however, more to be said about the relation between Wittgenstein's misgivings about semantic rules and his discussion of rule-following. As I said, his concern with understanding how to continue an arithmetical series is that, in this case, one's understanding must cover an infinity of instances. How is that possible? How can an infinity be grasped in an instant? The most natural answer is that such understanding can only be achieved by means of a general rule or formula, which although easily grasped in a moment can determine an infinity of instances.

So, what those discussions in the *Investigations* are meant to investigate is the possibility of an endlessly applicable understanding. That is the *explanandum*, the common phenomenon that needs to be clarified. Rules or formulas are only considered as an *explanans*, as a suggested solution – which is shown not to work: our understanding cannot be *based* on rules. No rule can guarantee understanding: we still have to know how to apply it in any given case. Thus the puzzle about the infinity of instances resurfaces as a puzzle about the infinity of applications of a rule. Of course it *is* possible to learn how to apply a rule to indefinitely many cases. But ultimately, our mastery of rules has to be grounded in an ability to continue in what we regard as a regular manner that is *not* guided by any rule, but can only be taught by examples (MS 136, p.124a; Z §§300–1; see Schroeder, 2006, pp.181–97).

Hence, although Wittgenstein was certainly no skeptic about the possibility of following a rule, it can be said that his reservations about the importance of linguistic rules dovetail neatly with his discussions of continuing an arithmetical series. While earlier he argued that rules are not *necessary* for understanding general notions (cf. Z §295), now he shows that rules are not *sufficient* for such understanding either. Even if there are linguistic rules, ultimately they cannot be the foundation of linguistic normativity. What is held up both as an alternative to and as a basis for rules is the kind of know-how that is acquired through examples and training.

5 Grammatical Statements and Analytic Truths

Wittgenstein speaks not only of "grammatical rules," but also of "grammatical statements" (or propositions) (*grammatische Sätze*). The difference between the two concepts is one of perspective: linguistic meaning can be explained by grammatical rules (or, to take Wittgenstein's own qualifications into account, by expressions of grammatical norms). For example, the meaning of the word "bachelor" can be explained by the grammatical rule:

(1) A bachelor is an unmarried man.

However, when this sentence is not used to teach or to explain, but considered as a statement, Wittgenstein calls it a grammatical statement. After all, we regard it as *true* that a bachelor is an unmarried man, which makes it more natural to speak of a *statement* (or proposition) than a rule. It is a statement, but not an empirical statement, not a "statement of fact" (AWL 18); it is "a statement which no experience will refute" (AWL 16). The nonempirical nature of such a statement can be brought out by a modal verb: "if someone's a bachelor, he *must* be an unmarried man." And yet we ought not to yield to the philosophical temptation of regarding such a nonempirical statement as metaphysical, as a statement of a super-fact, as it were (cf. BB 54 f.). Rather, its necessity is that of a norm of expression (AWL 16).

My hackneyed example (1) is a grammatical statement, yet it can also be regarded as a grammatical rule, even in the light of Wittgenstein's reservations about that concept. It provides a general, but handy description of the use of the word "bachelor," suitable for linguistic instruction. However, many of the grammatical statements Wittgenstein has occasion to consider in the course of his philosophical investigations one would not normally call rules of language, e.g.:

(2) Behind the utterance of a sensation there is nothing [no object]. (MS 124, p.6)
(3) Of course I know what I wish. (BB 30)
(4) My reason for saying that I see is not the observation of my behaviour. (MS 148, p.38r)
(5) We can only conjecture the cause, but we know the motive. (BB 15)
(6) There is no reddish green. (ROC II §16)

None of these sentences would be likely to be employed in a language class. Unlike (1), none of them defines or explains the meaning of a word in a way that would be useful to a learner. Rather, given the ordinary meanings of the words involved, these grammatical statements spell out some implications of the ways in which different concepts relate to each other. They are the results of "conceptual analysis" (ROC II §16); that is to say they are analytic truths.

To be sure, such statements or propositions are not what one might call "Frege-analytic": it is not possible by substituting synonyms for synonyms to transform any of them into a logical truth. But if we follow Wittgenstein in taking the meaning of a word to be its use in the language (PI §43), and if we note further that knowledge of the use of a word cannot be identified with knowledge of a synonymous expression (see Schroeder, 2006, ch.4.4) – we should not expect analyticity to boil down to Frege-analyticity. In other words, if meaning comprises more than can be captured by paraphrase, we should not expect truth in virtue of meaning always to be susceptible of a formal proof by paraphrase.

Indeed, Wittgenstein's examples of philosophically interesting grammatical statements can be described as analytic with even more propriety than a standard example of an analytic truth, such as (1). For they are obtained as a result of conceptual analysis, of a consideration of the meaning of words as manifest in their use, whereas (1) is not. That is because (1) serves as a grammatical rule. We actually *learn* that the word "bachelor" means "unmarried man." This meaning must be clear to anyone understanding the word, hence – psychologically speaking – it is not something to be discovered by conceptual analysis.

Some of Wittgenstein's remarks might be taken to contradict the idea that grammatical (or analytic) statements are true in virtue of the meanings of their ingredient words. Should we not rather say that grammatical statements are rules that *constitute* the meanings of the words in question? For instance, the rule "∼ ∼ $p = p$ does not follow from the meaning of 'not' but constitutes it" (AWL 4; cf. PG 52). — Here, again, it is important to distinguish carefully between the relevant concepts. To recapitulate:

(i) *Grammatical norms* govern the correct use, and hence the meanings of words. That a word is to be used in a certain way, that it is to be applied in this kind of case but not in that, is a grammatical norm. Yet for a grammatical norm to be operative, it need not be made explicit. It is possible that certain uses of a word are commonly accepted while others are rejected as false, a practice that is observed and emulated by learners, without any need for those norms ever to be formulated. Moreover, even where the meaning of a word is explained and not just picked up, the explanation may consist only in giving miscellaneous examples of correct applications as opposed to a rule.

(ii) *Grammatical rules* are general formulations of grammatical norms. Wittgenstein suggested that some grammatical norms (e.g., the meaning of the word "game") can only be taught by examples, not by a general formulation (i.e., a definition). That may be disputed, but it is uncontroversial that most grammatical norms *are*, as a matter of fact, only taught by examples, not by general rules.

(iii) There are also formulations of *implications of grammatical norms*. From games we are familiar with the distinction between a rule and the implications of a rule. For example, it is not a rule of chess that in the position *White: Ka1, Nb7; Black: Kh4* neither side can checkmate the other; but it follows from the rules. Although a logical implication of rules, it does not itself count as a rule because, first, it is too specific; secondly, somebody familiar with all the rules of chess need not be aware of it; and so thirdly, it cannot be invoked to settle a dispute (in the way in which you could cite a rule to explain why in a given position a certain move is impossible). Similarly, there is a distinction between grammatical norms (which may or may not be formulated as rules) and their implications, which we should not themselves regard as grammatical norms. For instance, if Wittgenstein is right, it is an implication of the grammatical norms that govern our use of sensation words that sensations are not inner objects (cf. (2) above). That that is not itself a grammatical norm is shown by the fact that it needs to be supported by philosophical argument and cannot be established simply by appeal to a competent speaker's linguistic intuitions. A competent speaker, as someone who has mastered the grammatical norms of his language, should be able to recognize any infringement of a grammatical norm; but he need not therefore be aware of all the non-trivial implications of grammatical norms. Therefore he is not likely to discern immediately whether a philosophical thesis (such as Cartesian dualism) is indirectly in conflict with the norms of our grammar.

(vi) Both grammatical rules and the formulations of implications of grammatical norms are *grammatical statements*.

Now, grammatical *norms* are indeed constitutive of meaning, not derived from it. For meaning doesn't exist independently of those norms. To say that a word has a certain meaning *is* to say that it is used according to certain semantic norms. However, the same is not true of a grammatical *rule*, a generalizing formulation of a norm. For the norm (and hence the meaning) could exist without being formulated as a rule.

For another reason, *implications of norms* cannot be said to constitute those norms. Of course there is no logical independence between the two (without that implication it would be a different norm), but there is a telling asymmetry: the norms were fixed and understood regardless of those implications, whereas those implications are derived from the norms. The norms can be invoked to justify the implications, but not vice versa, because the implications are not themselves recognized as norms.

Now regarding Wittgenstein's claim that "$\sim \sim p = p$ does not follow from the meaning of 'not' but constitutes it" (AWL 4), we should, first of all, take him to mean the *norm* that is inherent in our use of the word "not," rather than a formulation of that norm. Then we can agree that given our use of the word "not" to express simple negation, it does indeed not follow that double negation must be equivalent to a positive assertion (as was pointed out earlier, it could also be used to express emphatic negation). In other words, our use of double negation is not an implication of the norm that governs the straightforward uses of negation. Rather, it is something that needs to be specially determined, by a further norm.

6 Mathematics as Grammar

The key idea in Wittgenstein's philosophy of mathematics is that mathematical propositions are not descriptions of timeless abstract entities, but norms of representation: rules of grammar. That explains their peculiar dignity: their certainty and necessity. The mathematical reliability and inexorability is ultimately our own reliability and inexorability in insisting on those rules and not allowing any exceptions to them.

There is a fairly uncontroversial sense in which some mathematical propositions can be called "rules". For example, simple equations, such as in the times tables, which we memorize at an early age and apply when doing longer calculations. Thus, "$3 \times 9 = 27$"

is applied as a rule when working out the long multiplication: 399 × 39 (cf. PLP 53). Or, at a slightly more advanced level there are algebraic formulae that are both proven true and, afterward, memorized or consulted for repeated application, e.g., the cosine rule or the quadratic formula. — However, such cases are *not* what Wittgenstein has in mind when he calls mathematical propositions rules. "If one says the mathematical proposition is a rule," he writes, "then of course not a rule in mathematics" (*"Wenn man sagt, der mathematische Satz ist eine Regel, so natürlich nicht eine Regel in der Mathematik."*: MS 127, 236; post 4.3.44). Rather, on his view, mathematical propositions are rules of grammar, and, what is more, not the grammar of mathematical language, but the grammar of nonmathematical language. Thus, the equation "2 + 3 = 5" is a grammatical rule for the use of number words in a natural language, licensing, for instance, the inference from "I have two coins in my left pocket and three coins in my right pocket" to "I have five coins in my pockets" (cf. TLP 6.211).

Wittgenstein lays particular stress on the dependence of mathematics on its having applications *outside* mathematics (BT 566; RFM 257). That is what turns a mere calculus, a game of manipulating signs according to certain rules, into mathematics:

> mathematical propositions containing a certain symbol are rules for the use of that symbol, and [...] these symbols can then be used in non-mathematical statements. (LFM 33)

However, if we now compare elementary mathematical propositions with ordinary grammatical rules – such as:

(1) A bachelor is an unmarried man.

— we find that they are significantly different. (1) expresses a norm that is constitutive of the meaning of its subject term: it explains what the word "bachelor" means. "Bachelor" and "unmarried man" are just two labels for the same concept. Hence, if you understand the expressions, you cannot ever know that one of them applies without knowing that the other one applies as well. By contrast, (as famously pointed out by Kant: *Critique of Pure Reason*, B 15) *7 + 5* and *12* are different concepts: they have different criteria of application (counting to 7 and counting to 5 versus counting to 12) (cf. RFM 357). Hence it is *possible* to count on a given occasion 7 objects and then 5 objects, but only 11 altogether (or, to use Wittgenstein's example, 25 × 25, but not 625) (RFM 358e). In this case we have, initially, two distinct concepts, independently comprehensible – "Only through our arithmetic do they *become one*" (RFM 358; cf. 412, 432). Note the emphasis on "become": if mathematical propositions are grammatical rules they are essentially *additional* ones: *further* rules for terms that are already understandable without them. Mathematical propositions are *enriching existing meanings*. The norm expressed by a grammatical proposition like (1), by contrast, does not *change* or *enrich* the meaning of the word "bachelor," it gives it its meaning in the first place.

Hence, mathematical propositions would be more like the grammatical rule cited in the previous section, according to which double negation is equivalent to positive assertion, formalized as "$\sim\sim p \equiv p$." This rule does not determine the meaning of the negation sign from scratch. Rather, assuming an understanding of the meaning of the sign in single negation, it adds to it by giving a meaning to double negation.

Mathematical propositions can also be compared to a type of grammatical rule that is fairly common in scientific discourse. Sometimes what used to be an empirical discovery is later made part of a definition, for example, the velocity of light or the key properties of an acid. Thus, Wittgenstein writes with reference to mathematical propositions:

> Every empirical proposition may serve as a rule if it is fixed, like a machine part, made immovable, so that now the whole representation turns around it and it becomes part of the coordinate system, independent of facts. (RFM 437)

For example, after first finding the concepts of *2 and 3* and of *5 empirically* correlated, we come to introduce "2 + 3 = 5" as a *mathematical* proposition, that is: a norm of representation (RFM 51, 62, 324). If now the original experiment leads to a different result, we shan't accept it: we shall insist that we must have made a mistake or that something strange must have happened to account for this deviation from our norm. And not only are elementary mathematical propositions based, genetically, upon corresponding empirical propositions, or experiences, they also require that our experiences continue to be, by and large, in agreement with our calculations. Although no individual experience can disprove an arithmetical equation, used as a norm of representation, a regular discrepancy between rule and experience would undermine the rule's usefulness and eventually make us abandon or change it (RFM 51–2).

This is a central aspect of Wittgenstein's account of mathematics that is well worth emphasizing. An equation, such as "2 + 2 = 4," is not an empirical generalization, and hence no contrary experience can disprove it. On the other hand, it is not entirely independent of experience either. It is essentially a norm for describing countable things, like beans and sticks, and hence dependent on its suitability for the purpose (cf. RFM 357).

Elementary mathematical propositions have been grafted onto corresponding empirical observations. By contrast, it could never have been empirically discovered that a bachelor is an unmarried man. If elementary mathematical propositions are essentially additional rules for combining existing concepts, the question is whether these rules become fully integrated in our language, as Wittgenstein seems to suggest when he calls them "grammatical" or "instruments of language" (RFM 99, 162, 164–6, 358d, 359a). There are, I believe, reasons to return a negative answer: reasons not to regard mathematics – except perhaps for its very rudiments – as part of the grammar *of our ordinary language*.

First, what characterizes a grammatical norm is that, as it determines what makes sense, its negation, or a sentence that violates the norm it expresses, is nonsense. Yet that is not generally true of mathematical propositions. It may be so at the most elementary level. The sentence "I had two coffees in the morning and two in the afternoon, so I had only three overall today" is patently inconsistent. It might well be dismissed as not only false, but nonsensical. But suppose someone said:

> (7) The pitch of the roof of my lean-to garage is 15° to the horizontal and the roof extends 5.36 meter horizontally from the wall, and one side of the roof is 1.32 meter higher than the other.

We would hardly be inclined to dismiss that as nonsense, and yet a trigonometric calculation shows that:

> (8) If a right-angled triangle has an angle of 15° and the adjacent side is 5.36 then the opposite must be 1.44.

So (7) cannot be correct after all. And yet one can *believe* it to be correct – which speaks against regarding it as nonsense. For where there is no sense, there is nothing to believe.

Secondly, remember that according to Wittgenstein (at least in the realm of straightforwardly applicable mathematics) "the rule doesn't express an empirical connection but we make it because there is an empirical connection" (LFM 292). The rule's usefulness depends on its continued empirical appropriateness. It is not only that we reject (7) in the light of (8): that we insist that some of the measurements of the roof must have been inaccurate. It is also that when, in such a case, we measure or count again with greater care we shall almost certainly find our empirical observations in agreement with the rule (within the limits of accuracy achievable with our methods of measurement). In this case: if the other measurements prove reasonably accurate, we shall find that

(9) One side of the roof is indeed about 1.44 meter higher than the other side.

That is to say, according to Wittgenstein, we can take an empirical proposition, such as this, (9), as confirmation of a mathematical proposition, such as (8); confirmation not of the *truth* of (8) – for (8) is a rule, not a generalization – but confirmation of its suitability and usefulness in the light of experience. But to take (9) as an *empirical* proposition means to envisage the possibility of its being true *or false*; which means to envisage that something like (7) might have been true. So (7), although ruled out by a mathematical proposition (8), cannot be nonsense (as it would have to be if a mathematical proposition were not only a rule, but a *grammatical* rule: a norm for what makes sense in our language).

Still, in a broader sense of the word "grammatical," we may accept mathematical propositions as grammatical rules, namely if we take the word to refer not to the grammar of our language, but only to a specific form of discourse, or, more generally, to a certain set of activities or of some institutionalized form of life. In a laconic remark in *Philosophical Investigations* Wittgenstein suggests that theology can be regarded as grammar (PI §373), providing rules for what can be said meaningfully about God. But these rules are binding only within a certain religious community. Thus, for a believer God is by definition omnipotent and benevolent. (And: "'You can't hear God speak to someone else, you can hear him only if you are being addressed'. – That is a grammatical remark." [Z §717]) To question these attributes doesn't make any sense within religious discourse: it would be "ridiculous or blasphemous" (AWL 32). And yet an agnostic or atheist may well do so. You can step outside religious language, flouting its grammatical norms, while remaining within language.

If we follow Wittgenstein in regarding mathematical propositions as grammatical rules, we need to understand the word "grammatical" in a similar way: not as determining what makes sense in a natural language, but rather fixing sense and nonsense in a specific kind of discourse or activity. That is, roughly speaking, an activity and discourse in which we try to develop and apply a system of *calculating* quantities, rather than simply counting or measuring them (cf. MS 117, p.138f.).

References

Hacker, P.M.S. (1972/86). *Insight and Illusion: Themes in the Philosophy of Wittgenstein.* Revised edition. Oxford: Clarendon Press.
Schroeder, S. (2001). Elucidation and Ostensive Explanation. In G. Oliveri (Ed.). *Wittgenstein Studies (Special Issue): From the "Tractatus" to the "Tractatus,"* 69–79. Frankfurt: Peter Lang.
Schroeder, S. (2006). *Wittgenstein: The Way out of the Fly-bottle.* Cambridge: Polity.

Further Reading

For more detailed criticisms of scientific realism see:
Hacker, P.M.S. (1996). *Wittgenstein's Place in Twentieth-Century Analytic Philosophy*. Oxford: Blackwell, pp.250–253.
Hanfling, O. (2000). *Philosophy and Ordinary Language*. London: Routledge. Chapter 12.

For a defense of the traditional account of analyticity as truth due to meaning see:
Schroeder, S. (2009). Analytic Truths and Grammatical Propositions. In H.-J. Glock and J. Hyman (Eds). *Wittgenstein and Analytic Philosophy* (pp.83–108). Oxford: Oxford University Press.

For more detailed discussion of Wittgenstein's conception of mathematics as grammar see:
Schroeder, S. (2012). Conjecture, Proof, and Sense in Wittgenstein's Philosophy of Mathematics. In C. Jäger and W. Löffler (Eds). *Epistemology: Contexts, Values, Disagreement* (pp.461–475). Frankfurt: Ontos.
Schroeder, S. (2014). Mathematical Propositions as Rules of Grammar. *Grazer Philosophische Studien*, 89, 21–36.

15

The Autonomy of Grammar

MICHAEL N. FORSTER

Wittgenstein in his later works often implies commitment to a doctrine of the autonomy – or arbitrariness – of grammar (e.g., LWL 49, 58; M 70; PG §§27, 55, 68, 133; Z §§320, 331; PI §497). The present chapter will begin by briefly discussing the conception of grammar that is presupposed in this doctrine; it will then explain the doctrine itself; next, it will explain a sense in which grammar is *not* autonomous or arbitrary for Wittgenstein; finally, it will briefly discuss some possible criticisms of the doctrine. It should be noted here at the outset that this whole area of exegetical concern is one in which the fairly widespread conception in the secondary literature that the later Wittgenstein is a complete "quietist" in philosophy – i.e., someone who advances no positive doctrines of his own – although encouraged by some of his own statements, seems impossible to sustain.

1 Grammar

Wittgenstein's doctrine of the autonomy or arbitrariness of grammar presupposes a highly distinctive conception of grammar, one which at least *prima facie* has little to do with our everyday conception of grammar. This distinctive conception can be found scattered throughout a wide range of his later works. It constitutes in itself a solution to a number of fundamental traditional philosophical problems, including the problems of the nature of necessity and of the nature of meaning. It also forms the foundation of Wittgenstein's various specific diagnoses of traditional philosophical doctrines as consequences of misunderstandings about language, or more precisely about language's grammar. In order to interpret the doctrine of the autonomy or arbitrariness of grammar, it is important to have at least a general overview of this distinctive conception of grammar.

(1) "Grammar" includes all *necessary* principles, and may perhaps for Wittgenstein also be exhausted by them (see e.g., PG §133; PI §§371–2). More specifically, it includes all of the openly necessary principles of formal logic and pure mathematics

(e.g., the law of contradiction, ¬(p&¬p), and the arithmetical law "2 + 2 = 4"), other openly necessary principles that have traditionally been classified as either analytic a priori (e.g., "All bachelors are unmarried") or synthetic a priori (e.g., "An object cannot simultaneously be both red and green all over"), ostensive definitions, behavioral criteria for psychological states, and a class of seemingly empirical but according to Wittgenstein in fact grammatical principles on which he focuses in *On Certainty* (e.g., "The earth existed long before my birth").

(2) Grammatical principles have the character of rules or (categorical) imperatives that govern our use of language (see e.g., PG §§23, 133; RFM V §§13, 17; VI §30; VII §72). This is what constitutes their necessity.

(3) Consequently, they are not true or false. Instead, they are antecedent to – and a precondition of – truth and falsehood. (See e.g., BT 166; AWL 139–40; RFM I §§135, 156; OC §§94, 205.)

(4) They stand in sharp contrast to "empirical" or "factual" propositions, which *are* true or false (see e.g., OC §§96–9). (Notice here that Wittgenstein, notwithstanding his usual tendency to draw more rather than fewer distinctions, operates with just a *twofold* distinction between fundamental types of principles or propositions, namely grammatical vs. empirical, whereas some other major philosophers had distinguished between three or more fundamental types – e.g., Kant with his distinction between analytic a priori, synthetic a priori, and synthetic a posteriori judgments.)

(5) They *regulate* empirical propositions (see e.g., OC §§96–9). For example, if I count two apples in my right hand, then two more in my left, then put them together and count five of them, the mathematical principle "2 + 2 = 4" forbids me from simply judging that in this case two apples plus two apples were five apples; instead, it forces me to adjust my empirical claims, for instance to hypothesize a miscount or the introduction of a new apple by an unnoticed agency at some point in the process.

(6) They also *constitute concepts* or meanings, including those that are used in empirical propositions (see e.g., PG §133; RFM VII §§18, 67). For example, the mathematical principle "2 + 2 = 4" is part of what constitutes the very meanings of the terms "2" and "4," which meanings also occur in empirical propositions such as "Here are two apples" and "Here are four apples." (Stanley Cavell's influential claim (Cavell, 1962) that Wittgenstein rejects the idea that rules constitute meanings is therefore mistaken.)

2   The Autonomy or Arbitrariness of Grammar

As has been mentioned, Wittgenstein often implies that grammar is in an important sense autonomous (*autonom*), or arbitrary (*willkürlich*). These seem to be more or less alternative formulations of a single doctrine for Wittgenstein. The former formulation is prominent in *Philosophical Grammar*, but the latter formulation is co-present with it there, precedes it in earlier works, and predominates over it in subsequent works.

It is perhaps worth pausing briefly here over the etymology of the two terms involved, which points both back to certain facets of the very conception of grammar just discussed and forward to some aspects of the doctrine of grammar's autonomy or arbitrariness. The German word "*autonom*" and its English equivalent "*autonomous*" derive from the

Greek word "*nomos*," meaning a *law* or *custom*, together with the Greek prefix *auto-*, meaning *self-*. The former half of this etymology, the idea of law or custom, points back to aspects (2) and (5) of the very conception of grammar: grammar's consisting of rules or imperatives, in particular ones that regulate other propositions. The latter half of the etymology, the idea of *self-*, in part again points back to those aspects, insofar as it implies a source in human beings' own commitments, and in part also points forward to certain aspects of the doctrine of autonomy or arbitrariness which we shall consider below, in particular to the freedom of grammar from the constraints of justification or refutation.

The German word "*willkürlich*" derives from the German words "*Wille*," meaning the *will*, and "*küren*," meaning *to elect*. The former half of this etymology again points back to aspects (2) and (5) of the very conception of grammar. The latter half, the idea of electing, in part again does so, and in part also points forward to a specific component of the doctrine of autonomy or arbitrariness, namely the idea of electing *from among a range of alternatives*.

Those etymological clues noted, let us now consider what exactly the doctrine of grammar's autonomy or arbitrariness means. Essentially, it amounts to a claim that grammar *cannot be justified or refuted (discredited)*. Wittgenstein has a number of reasons for holding this view. Some of his reasons follow more or less directly from the basic conception of grammar that has already been explained, but others follow from it only indirectly. Let me therefore sketch his main reasons, beginning with the former ones, those that follow more or less directly from the basic conception of grammar.

(a) Since grammatical principles are rules or imperatives and are therefore neither true nor false (see (2) and (3) above), clearly justification in the specific sense of *proving true* and refutation in the specific sense of *proving false* are conceptions that cannot be applied to grammatical principles. (See e.g., M 73; BT 166; PG §133; AWL 69; OC §§94, 205.)

(b) Since grammatical principles, as rules or imperatives governing language, *constitute* all necessities (see (1) and (2) above), and therefore also all essences, clearly they cannot be justified or refuted in terms of their reflecting or failing to reflect the necessities or essences that there really are. (See e.g., Z §357.)

(c) Likewise, since grammatical principles *constitute* concepts or meanings (see (6) above), clearly they cannot be justified in terms of their following from concepts or meanings (as, in particular, the traditional conception that analytic principles are true in virtue of meaning implies), or refuted in terms of their conflicting with them (e.g., in cases such as "Bachelors are married"). To suppose that they could be would be to invert the real nature of the relationship between such principles and the concepts or meanings that pertain to them. (See e.g., PG §133; AWL 4; PI §147, note (b).)

Wittgenstein also has major reasons for holding this view that follow only indirectly from the basic conception of grammar, namely the following.

(d) Nor can grammatical principles be either justified or refuted by reference to corresponding empirical facts (e.g., "2 + 2 = 4" by reference to the empirical fact that whenever we have two things together with another two things it always turns out that we have four things). This is because specifications of empirical facts always *presuppose* corresponding grammatical principles, namely in the two ways that are implied by Wittgenstein's basic conception of grammar: they are already regulated by them (see (5) above) and they already owe their very concepts to them (see (6) above). Consequently, any attempt to *justify* a grammatical principle by reference to corresponding empirical facts will fail: either it will be viciously circular because the statements of the empirical facts that are involved already implicitly presuppose the grammatical principle in question or, if they do *not*, it will be vitiated by a conceptual incommensurability between the statements of the empirical facts and the principle (they will "talk past each other," as it were, even if *verbally* they appear not to do so; e.g., "2" in the empirical statement "Here we have a case of 2 things together with another 2 things yielding 4 things" will not mean the same as "2" in the grammatical principle "$2 + 2 = 4$"). Similarly, any attempt to *refute* a grammatical principle by reference to corresponding empirical facts will fail: either it will be implicitly inconsistent because the statements of the empirical facts that are involved already presuppose the grammatical principle that they are being adduced to refute or, if they do *not*, it will be vitiated by a conceptual incommensurability between the statements of the empirical facts and the principle (they will again "talk past each other"). Nor can this problem be avoided by simply pointing (or directing one's attention) to relevant empirical facts. For without any involvement of grammar and concepts such an act of pointing (or attending) would lack the definiteness of content that is required for any justification or refutation, and if the act *is* made definite by being implicitly articulated in terms of grammar and concepts then the same dilemmas of vicious circularity or incommensurability (in the case of justification), and inconsistency or incommensurability (in the case of refutation), will arise as before. (See e.g., LWL 47–9, 86; PR §7; M 70–1; PG §§133–4; AWL 4, 67; Z §331.)

(e) Nor can grammatical principles be either justified or refuted (discredited) by reference to *purposes* that they do or should serve. Wittgenstein thinks that this *can* be done for certain other types of rules, for example rules of cookery, because in such cases there is a generally accepted independent purpose served by the rules that can be used as a criterion for judging them (say, the purpose of producing tasty and nourishing food). But he thinks that where grammatical principles or rules are concerned there *is no* generally accepted purpose, only multiple and variable purposes. Moreover, he holds that the multiple and variable purposes involved are not independent of such rules, since human purposes are of their very nature implicitly constituted by language and hence by grammatical principles, at least in most cases. This leads to the following problem: any purpose that is appealed to in an attempt to justify or refute (discredit) a grammatical principle will either implicitly presuppose the specific grammatical principle that is supposed to be justified or refuted (discredited) in terms of it, thereby leading to versions of the aforementioned problems of vicious circularity or inconsistency; or it will *not* presuppose that specific principle, in which case using this particular purpose as a criterion for the success of the principle will be merely arbitrary. For example, attempting to justify the grammatical principle "$2 + 2 = 4$" in terms of the purpose of counting accurately turns out to be viciously circular, since that principle is implicitly part of what *constitutes* the relevant notion of counting accurately; whereas attempting to justify it in terms of its contribution to the purpose of constructing stable buildings will be arbitrary, since not everyone need have such a purpose (indeed, some people might even *want* their buildings to collapse). (See e.g., PG §§133, 140; BT 166; Z §§320–2; PI §497.)

(f) Wittgenstein's philosophy of logic and mathematics also contains an argument against the natural suggestion that grammatical principles can sometimes be justified or refuted by means of *other* grammatical principles – for example, when we conduct proofs in formal logic or pure mathematics that lead us from one set of necessary principles as premises to another necessary principle as conclusion. Here Wittgenstein in effect holds that what actually happens when such a proof first becomes accepted is not that previously held grammatical principles themselves dictate or require the acceptance of a new one, but rather that the acceptance of the new one in light of them is a sort of "decision" on our part (see e.g., RFM III §27), a decision that implicitly modifies the character of the grammatical principles in question in such a way that only *now* is the conclusion internal to them (see e.g., RFM I §§82–6; III §§31, 41; IV §47; VI §§7–8).

In addition, Wittgenstein's overall doctrine that grammatical principles can never be justified or refuted is strongly inflected by an insistence that grammatical principles always have *alternatives* – and this not only in the general sense that one could always dispense with them and still be left with other grammatical principles, but also in the more specific sense that one could always do so and still be left with others that are *similar* (see e.g., Z §§373–88). For example, in connection with formal logic, he envisages the possibility of people for whom a double negation would count either as meaningless or else as a repetition of the simple negation, so that their logic would not recognize the law of double-negation elimination, and they would only have "something corresponding to our [concept of] negation" (PI §§554, 147, note (a)). And concerning mathematics, he gives examples such as the following: our mathematics versus that of people who can only count up to five, and whose numerical concepts therefore differ from our counterparts (RPP II §295); people who, unlike us, have a practice of "calculation" in which "everybody believed that twice two was five" so that their numerical concepts differ from ours (PI §226; cf. LFM 97); people who, unlike us, employ elastic rulers, so that "what is here called 'measuring' and 'length' and 'equal length,' is something different from what we call those things" and "the use of these words is different from ours, but it is *akin* to it" (RFM I §5); and people who, unlike us, use as the criterion for setting the price of a quantity of wood not its volume or weight but only the area of the surface it happens to cover, so that "they [...] do not mean the same by 'a lot of wood' and 'a little wood' as we do" (RFM I §150; cf. LFM 202). Consequently, when Wittgenstein's doctrine of the autonomy or arbitrariness of grammar maintains that grammatical principles can never be justified or refuted, an important part of its force is that they can never be justified or refuted *to the disadvantage or advantage of alternative grammatical principles*. (Bernard Williams (1973), Jonathan Lear (1982, 1984), and others have argued that Wittgenstein's strange examples of alternative grammatical principles are ultimately meant to show that such alternatives are implicitly *incoherent*. But this is a misinterpretation of his intentions.)

3 A Sense in which Grammar is NOT Autonomous or Arbitrary

However, Wittgenstein also holds that there is a sense in which grammar is *not* autonomous or arbitrary. As he puts it in *Zettel*, in the course of discussing a specific area of grammar, namely our color system: "It is akin both to what is arbitrary and to what is non-arbitrary" (Z §358; cf. LWL 49; M 70).

This part of his position is an attempt to resist the idea, which talk of grammar being "autonomous" and especially of it being "arbitrary" (*willkürlich*) might easily encourage, that individuals can simply choose which among the various grammatical principles that are possible they will accept, or that they can simply choose to convert any old empirical proposition into a grammatical principle by as it were hardening it into a fundamental rule. In Wittgenstein's view, it is indeed the case that alternative grammatical principles are always possible and that they are always immune to justification and refutation, but they are not for that reason subject to individual volitions in this way. Certain interpretations of Wittgenstein, for example Michael Dummett's (1959), have nonetheless attributed to him just such a view. Admittedly, Wittgenstein does on occasion say things that seem to suggest it. However, he is more usually concerned to *reject* it. I shall return to this tension in the textual evidence later.

Wittgenstein identifies several different sorts of constraints that limit the freedom of individual volition in this area, saliently including the following:

(A) *General human nature.* For example, in *Philosophical Grammar* he writes: "So is the calculus something we adopt arbitrarily? No more so than the fear of fire, or the fear of a raging man coming at us" (PG §68; cf. PI §185).

(B) *Culture and tradition.* For example, in *Philosophical Investigations* he writes: "Compare a concept with a style of painting. For is even our style of painting arbitrary? Can we choose one at pleasure? (The Egyptian for instance.)" (PI 230).

(C) *Empirical regularities.* Thus in *Remarks on the Foundations of Mathematics* he implies that our mathematical laws rest on certain corresponding empirical regularities. For example, the arithmetical law that $25 \times 25 = 625$ rests on the empirical regularities that it rarely occurs in practice that by counting a group of objects by two different methods we arrive by one method at the result that there are 25×25 of them but by the other method at the result that there are 624 of them; that when such discrepancies *do* arise they can almost always be eliminated by recounting; and that when they do so we can almost always discover, or at least plausibly hypothesize, an independently verifiable explanation for their occurrence (such as a counting error or the disintegration or theft of one of the objects). (See e.g., RFM VII §§1, 18.)

Wittgenstein does not, of course, suppose that these constraints amount to *justifications* or *refutations* of grammatical principles. Instead, he evidently understands them to be merely causal and/or normative in character, that is, normative roughly in the manner of a social taboo.

However, he sometimes also implies that they constitute conditions on the very *meaningfulness* of grammatical principles for people. This position is clearest in the case of constraint (C), empirical regularities, where it draws on Wittgenstein's standard thesis that meaning is linguistic *use* (see e.g., PI §43), in a sense of this term that among other things implies *usefulness*. This, I take it, is his implicit thought in *Zettel* when, after making the case that grammatical principles cannot be justified or refuted by reference to facts, he enters the following significant qualification:

> Yes, but has nature nothing to say here? Indeed she has – but she makes herself audible in another way. 'You'll surely run up against existence and non-existence somewhere!' But that means against *facts*, not concepts. (Z §364)

For his point here seems to be that while nature cannot constrain grammar by providing facts that justify or refute it, nature *can* constrain grammar by imposing limits on the concepts or meanings that grammar has available. Hence he writes at one point in *Philosophical Investigations*:

> 'So does it depend wholly on our grammar what will be called (logically) possible and what not, – i.e. what that grammar permits?' – But surely that is arbitrary! – Is it arbitrary? It is not every sentence-like formation that we know how to do something with, not every technique has an employment in our life; and when we are tempted in philosophy to count some quite useless thing as a proposition, that is often because we have not considered its application sufficiently. (PI §520; translation modified)

Accordingly, in *Remarks on the Foundations of Mathematics* he argues in connection with some specific examples:

> Calculating would lose its point, if *confusion* supervened. Just as the use of the words 'green' and 'blue' would lose its point. And yet it seems to be nonsense to say – that a proposition of arithmetic *asserts* that there will not be confusion. – Is the solution simply that the arithmetical proposition would not be *false* but useless, if confusion supervened? Just as the proposition that this room is 16 feet long would not become *false*, if rulers and measuring fell into confusion. Its sense, not its truth, is founded on the regular working of measurements. (RFM III §75)

Wittgenstein may very well also believe that constraints (A) and (B) – that is, general human nature, and culture and tradition – are constraints on the very meaningfulness of grammatical principles. This would in part again be because use, and hence usefulness, is a necessary condition of meaning. But it would also in part be because the support of a grammatical principle by both general human nature and culture and tradition (as opposed to its frustration by them) is indispensable for the sort of *social rule-following* that Wittgenstein takes to be a further necessary condition of meaning and which he accordingly includes as another implicit component of the sense of the word "use" in his doctrine of meaning as use (for Wittgenstein "use" [*Gebrauch*] implies "custom" [*Brauch*]). Accordingly, he writes:

> Is what we call 'obeying a rule' something that it would be possible for only *one* man to do, and to do only *once* in his life? – This is of course a note on the grammar of the expression 'to obey a rule.' It is not possible that there should have been only one occasion on which only one person obeyed a rule [...]. To obey a rule, to make a report [...] are customs (uses, institutions). (PI §199)

The degree of restrictiveness that Wittgenstein means to ascribe to these various sorts of constraints should not be exaggerated, however. He clearly does not believe that the constraints on the very meaningfulness of grammatical principles just discussed are so restrictive that they undermine his thesis that there are always possible alternative grammatical principles in any given area of grammar. Indeed, he may well not even believe that either they or the merely causal and/or normative constraints involved always limit an individual to a single grammar among the many that are possible in a given area. (In other words, although he does not hold the sort of voluntarist position that Dummett (1959) ascribes to him as a *general* position, he may nonetheless hold a version of it concerning a *subset* of cases. This would help to explain the atypical passages in which he seems attracted to such a position.)

4 Concluding Remarks

As can be seen from the above account, Wittgenstein's doctrine of the autonomy or arbitrariness of grammar is deeply rooted in, and indeed to a considerable extent directly derived from, his complex conception of grammar, and is itself complex in additional respects. The doctrine could therefore be challenged in many different ways. For example, the general conception of grammar that the doctrine presupposes might be challenged – say, by rejecting its account of necessity in favor of a theory that postulates language-independent necessities, or by rejecting its account of meaning in favor of a form of Platonism. And other aspects of the doctrine might be challenged as well – for instance, the claim in component (e) that any attempt to justify a grammatical principle in terms of a purpose to which the principle is not internal must be merely arbitrary, or the counterintuitive theory of the nature of logical and mathematical proof that Wittgenstein appeals to in component (f).

I shall not attempt here to consider the full range of challenges that could be leveled against the doctrine any further than this. Instead, I would just like to propose one relatively modest challenge that still seems attractive even if one in the end accepts the bulk of Wittgenstein's position – a sort of "friendly amendment" as it were.

As we saw, Wittgenstein believes that certain possible grammatical principles are favored over others by general human nature, culture and tradition, and empirical regularities. In a similar spirit, he sometimes implies that while actual justification and refutation are not possible here, we may nonetheless have certain *reasons* for preferring one grammatical principle over another, including both empirical reasons and reasons that derive from our multiple and variable purposes (see e.g., M 72; LFM 205, 235, 249; PI §499). However, once this much is conceded, it seems attractive to object to his doctrine of autonomy or arbitrariness – the doctrine that grammatical principles can never be justified or refuted – that it depends on a dubiously narrow conception of justification and refutation: roughly, a conception of them as restricted to the deduction of a principle or of its negation from premises that are known to be true. If such a conception is presupposed, then Wittgenstein's central objection that in cases where the premises do not simply "talk past" the grammatical principle to be justified or refuted they must implicitly presuppose it, so that the justification will be viciously circular or the refutation inconsistent, seems plausible. But suppose that instead of making that presupposition one also allowed coherence, in the sense of mutual support, to count as justification, and incoherence, in the sense of mutual tension, to count as refutation (or discrediting). In that case, the sort of coherence of *some* possible grammatical principles with empirical regularities and purposes but incoherence of *others* with them that Wittgenstein himself envisages could well be seen as constituting a type of *justification* of the former principles and a type of *refutation* of the latter ones. In addition, if one does recognize such a field of possible justifications and refutations, then it becomes attractive to say that different *degrees* of justification and refutation are possible. For instance, one possible grammatical principle in an area might cohere with relevant empirical regularities and our purposes optimally well (e.g., "2 + 2 = 4"), while another did so slightly less well (e.g., "2 + 2 = 4, except at 6 a.m. on Christmas Day, when 2 + 2 = 5"), another slightly less well still (e.g., "2 + 2 = 4, except between 6 and 7 a.m. on Christmas Day, when 2 + 2 = 5"), and so on.

References

Cavell, S. (1962). The Availability of Wittgenstein's Later Philosophy. *Philosophical Review*, 71, 67–93.
Dummett, M. (1959). Wittgenstein's Philosophy of Mathematics. *Philosophical Review*, 68, 324–348.
Lear, J. (1982). Leaving the World Alone. *Journal of Philosophy*, 79, 382–403.
Lear, J. (1984). The Disappearing "We." *Proceedings of the Aristotelian Society* (Supplementary Volume), 58, 219–242.
Williams, B. (1973). Wittgenstein and Idealism. *Royal Institute of Philosophy Supplement*, 7, 76–95.

Further Reading

Baker, G.P. and Hacker, P.M.S. (1985/2014). Wittgenstein: Rules, Grammar and Necessity. Volume 2 of an Analytical Commentary on the Philosophical Investigations. Essays and Exegesis of §§185–242. Second edition. Extensively revised by P.M.S. Hacker. Oxford: Wiley-Blackwell. Chapter 6.
Forster, M.N. (2004). *Wittgenstein on the Arbitrariness of Grammar*. Princeton: Princeton University Press.
Glock, H.-J. (1996a). Necessity and Normativity. In H. Sluga and D.G. Stern (Eds). *The Cambridge Companion to Wittgenstein* (pp.198–225). Cambridge: Cambridge University Press.
Glock, H.-J. (1996b). *A Wittgenstein Dictionary*. Oxford: Blackwell. Entry "Autonomy of Language, or Arbitrariness of Grammar."
Hacker, P.M.S. (1972/86). *Insight and Illusion: Themes in the Philosophy of Wittgenstein*. Revised edition. Oxford: Clarendon Press. Chapter 7.
Stroud, B. (1965). Wittgenstein and Logical Necessity. *Philosophical Review*, 74, 504–518.
Wright, C. (1980). *Wittgenstein on the Foundations of Mathematics*. Cambridge, MA: Harvard University Press.

16

Surveyability

JOACHIM SCHULTE

It is often remarked that it is difficult, or almost impossible, to find an adequate, consistent translation of Wittgenstein's word "*übersichtlich*" and that, owing to this fact, English readers are in danger of overlooking the systematic importance of his notion of *Übersichtlichkeit*. This view does not seem quite right to me. True, if the word "*übersichtlich*" is indeed meant to play a terminological role in Wittgenstein's writings, then it will be desirable to have a consistent translation – if one is available. But not only is the word "*übersichtlich*" an extremely ordinary word of the German language; it also comes along with a wide range of slightly diverging shades of meaning. And as far as I can see, Wittgenstein does not hesitate to exploit the full range of nuances of meaning. Accordingly, finding adequate renderings that fit their surrounding words may seem much more important than choosing a consistent translation (which, anyway, tends to jar with many contexts). (Cf. the first section of Schulte, 2012a.)

The best-known and most widely discussed occurrence of the word "übersichtlich" can be found in *Philosophical Investigations* §122. It is practically impossible to survey the enormous number of discussions of §122 (see Baker and Hacker, 1980/2005, pp. 307–34; and Glock, 1996, "Overview" and "Form of Representation"). Nevertheless, in this chapter, my plan is to arrive at a plausible reading of this remark and to make an attempt at seeing it against the background of certain developments in Wittgenstein's thought.

1   A Letter

Most of the sentences that go to make up the remarks that became §122 of *Philosophical Investigations* can be found in manuscript passages written in June 1931. On 20 November of the same year Wittgenstein writes a letter in reply to a request from Schlick and complains, not only about his own sluggishness, but also about Waismann's inclination to misrepresent his own (i.e., Wittgenstein's) ideas. At this time, Friedrich Waismann was a kind of unofficial assistant to Schlick, who supported him in his efforts at collaborating with Wittgenstein in the attempt to write an account of Wittgenstein's

---

A Companion to Wittgenstein, First Edition. Edited by Hans-Johann Glock and John Hyman.
© 2017 John Wiley & Sons, Ltd. Published 2017 by John Wiley & Sons, Ltd.

present views, especially with regard to his changes of heart about ideas expressed, or latent, in the *Tractatus*. This was not the only occasion on which Wittgenstein expressed his dissatisfaction with Waismann's work. In parts of the literature this work is treated as source material on nearly the same level as Wittgenstein's own manuscripts (e.g. Baker in VW; cf. Schulte, 2011). It may therefore be worth reminding readers of Wittgenstein's doubts. This is the context in which Wittgenstein points out that he does not continue to hold a number of views expressed or suggested in his early work and that

> maybe the chief difference between the position held in my book [TLP] and my present view is this: that I have come to see that the analysis of propositions [*die Analyse des Satzes*] doesn't consist in discovering hidden things but in tabulating, in giving a comprehensive overview of, the grammar – i.e. grammatical use – of words. In this way, all the dogmatic things I used to say about 'object', 'elementary proposition' etc. collapse. For example, if you want to understand the word 'object', you will have to look and see how it is actually used. (Letter to Schlick, 20 November 1931)

This passage from a letter to Schlick is worth quoting not just because it contains the expression "*übersichtliche Darstellung*," and thus one of the earliest anticipations of the central notion of §122, but also because in it Wittgenstein proceeds to give a striking list of – in his view more or less equivalent – features distinguishing his present thought from the ideas of the *Tractatus*. He says that, instead of giving a "dogmatic" kind of analysis, his present technique consists in what he calls "tabulation" and equates with giving a comprehensive overview of the grammar of words, where the grammar in its turn is identified with grammatical use. (Here, I suppose, Wittgenstein means "use as analysed by grammar" rather than "grammatically correct use.") Wittgenstein's German word "*tabulieren*" is very peculiar and may well be an Anglicism, chosen also because its Latin sound can be heard as emphasizing the intended objectivity of the procedure. So, like the expression "*übersichtliche Darstellung*" itself, at this time it functions a bit like a signature tune – only that, unlike the phrase "*übersichtliche Darstellung*," it soon ceases to play a role.

2 The Manuscript Version of PI §122

The history of §122 is a complex one, and its traceable origin can be found in a manuscript (MS 110). The relevant part was written in June and July 1931, in Vienna, probably immediately after Wittgenstein's return from England to Austria. At a later stage, probably in 1932, this material was rearranged and transferred to a typescript (TS 211) and, like many other remarks, moved to the so-called "Big Typescript" (TS 213), where, however, it was separated from its original context and inserted in a section entitled "The Method of Philosophy" (BT 414) of the chapter on "Philosophy." In 1937 Wittgenstein used it, together with a surprising number of remarks appearing in the vicinity of the original manuscript entry, to compose what eventually became a section of the final version of the *Investigations* that many commentators are happy to call the "chapter" on philosophy or, surely more controversially, metaphilosophy (§§89–133 or, according to a different dispensation, §§109–33; cf. Hacker, 2004).

Giving a fairly full account of the genesis of §122 would take us too far afield. But as observations on the original context of its antecedents have played a great role in discussions of its meaning, it will be appropriate to have a look at an early version and to draw on its background in giving an account of it. In the manuscript we read:

[1] 'Und so deutet das Chor auf ein geheimes Gesetz' möchte man zu der Frazer'schen Tatsachensammlung sagen. Dieses Gesetz, diese Idee, *kann* ich nun durch eine Entwicklungshypothese darstellen oder auch, analog dem Schema einer Pflanze, durch das Schema einer religiösen Zeremonie oder aber durch die Gruppierung des Tatsachen-Materials allein, in einer '*übersichtlichen*' Darstellung.

[2] Der Begriff der übersichtlichen Darstellung ist für uns von grundlegender Bedeutung. Er bezeichnet unsere Darstellungsform, die Art, wie wir die Dinge sehen. (Eine Art der 'Weltanschauung', wie sie scheinbar für unsere Zeit typisch ist. Spengler.)

[3] Diese übersichtliche Darstellung vermittelt das Verständnis, welches eben darin besteht, daß wir die 'Zusammenhänge sehen'. Daher die Wichtigkeit des Findens von *Zwischengliedern*.

[4a] Ein hypothetisches Zwischenglied aber soll in diesem Falle nichts tun, als die Aufmerksamkeit auf die Ähnlichkeit, den Zusammenhang, der *Tatsachen* lenken. Wie wenn man eine interne Beziehung der Kreisform zur Ellipse dadurch illustrierte, daß man eine Ellipse allmählich in einen Kreis überführt; *aber nicht um zu behaupten daß eine gewisse Ellipse tatsächlich, historisch, aus einem Kreis entanden wäre* (Entwicklungshypothese), sondern nur um unser Auge für einen formalen Zusammenhang zu schärfen.

[b] Aber auch die Entwicklungshypothese kann ich als weiter nichts sehen als eine Einkleidung eines formalen Zusammenhangs.

'And so the chorus points to a secret law' one feels like saying to Frazer's collection of facts. I *can* represent this law, this idea, by means of an evolutionary hypothesis, or also, analogously to the schema of a plant, by means of the schema of a religious ceremony, but also by means of the arrangement of its factual content alone, in a '*perspicuous*' representation.

The concept of perspicuous representation is of fundamental importance for us. It denotes the form of our representation, the way we see things. (A kind of 'World-view' as it is apparently typical our time. Spengler.)

This perspicuous representation brings about the understanding which consists precisely in the fact that we 'see the connections'. Hence the importance of finding *connecting links*.

But an hypothetical connecting link should in this case do nothing but direct the attention to the similarity, the relatedness, of the *facts*. As one might illustrate an internal relation of a circle to an ellipse by gradually converting an ellipse into a circle; *but not in order to assert that a certain ellipse actually, historically, had originated from a circle* (evolutionary hypothesis) but only in order to sharpen our eye for a formal connection.

But I can also see the evolutionary hypothesis as nothing more, as the clothing of a formal connection. (PO 133)

The quotation opening this selection comes from Goethe's poem on the metamorphosis of plants. What is striking, however, is that there are altogether three quotations from Goethe to be found on the two pages from which our selection is taken (these are nos. 24, 25, and 29 on the list of Goethe quotations given by Hans Biesenbach, 2014). The significance of this is no doubt considerable, and we shall come back to the connection with Goethe toward the end of our discussion.

As the reference to Frazer shows, our remarks come from the context of Wittgenstein's reflections on the *Golden Bough*, which apparently are the result of two temporally distant encounters with this work. The first one was Drury's reading aloud passages from the introductory volume of the full edition over a number of weeks in 1931, and hence probably just before Wittgenstein wrote the remarks we are interested in; the second is not unlikely to have taken place soon after Wittgenstein was presented with a one-volume copy of the work by a friend in 1936, and thus shortly before he embarked on writing what became the first third of the *Investigations*, including the material discussed here. (Cf. the editors' introduction to GB as reprinted in PO and Drury's account in RW 119.)

One of the problems raised by Frazer's account is his tendency to incorporate his findings into a story meant to depict the actual development of human beliefs in myths and magic, and of ritual forms of behavior caused by, or otherwise involved in, these beliefs. This story is supposed to help us to grasp how the human mind developed from superstition to science – a notion which in Wittgenstein's view is itself another myth, this time of a vaguely "scientific" kind. Here, we cannot deal with his many critical remarks on Frazer, but these form the background of what he says about evolutionary hypotheses in the passage quoted here (for a detailed discussion of Wittgenstein's critique of Frazer, see Chapter 41, WITTGENSTEIN AND ANTHROPOLOGY). And he does admit that hypotheses about the actual evolution of our attitudes towards the world constitute a possible way of accounting for the development somehow enshrined in the "undisclosed law" about which the quoted line from Goethe claims that its outlines are indicated by the ensemble of collected facts. But Wittgenstein's point is that this sort of hypothesis is not the only way of arranging these facts in a way that can help us understand things better. He mentions two alternative ways, viz., a schematic approach roughly in the sense of Goethe's idea of the primal plant – the idea that a blueprint for a leaf, an ideal gestalt, can be seen as mirroring all possible realizations of the ideal form of a plant – and the technique of arranging things in such a way that they present themselves as instancing the elements of a perspicuous representation, an *übersichtliche Darstellung*. Perhaps there would be a tension here between Wittgenstein's insistence on arranging nothing but the facts as they are given to us and what he says in the PI-version about inventing intermediate links. But note that this is one of the small additions to the original text: the manuscript version only talks about *discovering* such links; so there is nothing in the relevant paragraph about going beyond the facts by *inventing* intermediate links.

But there are more changes in the text that will give us pause. One change, which has often been mentioned by commentators, concerns the second paragraph of the passage quoted. It consists in shortening the full sentence enclosed in brackets, turning what remains into a question, and leaving out Spengler's name. Of course, these modifications may prove significant, but before considering this possibility we need to look at paragraph [2] in its entirety to see what we can make of it as it stands.

One abiding problem of Wittgenstein exegesis is his use of personal pronouns (see Schulte, 2007, pp.153–4). The main problem is this: that readers are inclined to understand these pronouns as referring to particular people or groups of people without allowing for the eventuality that the reference may be unclear or that the intended reference may be a different, namely a more general, one. Now, our short paragraph contains three occurrences of "our" and one of "we." No other personal pronoun is forthcoming, but there is the name of Spengler, with regard to whom we will obviously have to ask why and in which capacity he is mentioned. The only unequivocal use of a pronoun is the last one, that is, Wittgenstein's remark that our way of looking at things is a *Weltanschauung* of the kind that seems typical of *our* time. In other words, this is a very general reference to people living at the relevant time. Presumably, this need not include absolutely everyone living on planet earth around 1930 or so, but it will include most people living in our kind of civilization or culture. The extension of "our time" remains unclear, but maybe we can find a way of clarifying it. So if this construal is roughly right, then the "we" occurring before the opening bracket will have the same reference, and there is no reason why the "our" in "the form of our representation" should be read in a different way (for complications regarding Wittgenstein's wording, see the discussion of §122 in von Savigny, 1989/1994). The same goes for the "our" in the opening sentence: just like the other pronouns, it bears extremely general reference to people living in today's Western civilization.

With hindsight, this may seem pretty obvious. But is it important? As a matter of fact, it is extremely important for the simple reason that most commentators seem to read these pronouns as a species of the royal *we*, referring to Wittgenstein himself or to him and his followers or to some other narrowly circumscribed group of people including him. (Accordingly, they understand the remark in its entirety as a statement of Wittgenstein's program.) However, for the reasons just spelled out this reading is not acceptable. While Wittgenstein would doubtless consider himself a member of the group specified by "we," etc., his membership would be a trivial consequence of the fact of his being a contemporary.

3   Spengler

What about Spengler? Why does Wittgenstein mention him? He cannot be suggesting that our general way of seeing things is Spengler's own or a related kind of *Weltanschauung*. It would be ridiculous to claim that most of our contemporaries hold a *Weltanschauung* of the Spenglerian type. No, what Wittgenstein must be driving at is that we all tend to see the world in a way characterized by Spengler as our *Weltanschauung*. In fact, Spengler says a number of things about *Weltanschauungen*, and it may well be that several passages could be seen to fill the bill. But among the passages I have noticed there seems to be one that fits particularly well. It can be found toward the end of the third section of the third chapter of the second volume of the *Decline of the West* (Spengler, [1922/1923] 1996, p.936), and it is too long to be quoted in full. I shall confine myself to a few lines:

> '*Weltanschauung*' is the characteristic expression for an enlightened waking-consciousness that, under the guidance of the critical understanding, looks about it in a godless light-world [...]. That which was once myth – the actualest of the actual – is now subjected to the methods of what is called Euhemerism. (Spengler, [1923] 1928, p.306)

Well, it does not really matter if we do not read the rest, for the point is clear: "*Weltanschauung*" is a term which, in Spengler's view, is particularly apt in talking about our "enlightened" time – or one of the other enlightened times of earlier ages. These are periods when people, or influential classes of people, are keen on giving discrediting explanations and on debunking ideas held in high esteem by previous generations. The contrast is with those historical periods where certain kinds of myth were more real than anything else – and as Wittgenstein points out, this is something entirely different from superstition: for superstition is also compatible with an enlightened attitude and staunch common sense. (It is no doubt compatible with all kinds of other attitudes as well, but that is not the point. – Cf. GB 128–9, where our Frazer-inspired recoiling from things that "cannot be explained" is explicitly classified as a "foolish superstition of our time.")

4   Intermediate Links

So, while *übersichtliche Darstellungen* are no doubt a good thing – and a thing, moreover, which is typical of our scientifically minded, enlightened age – there is so far nothing in paragraphs [1] and [2] which one would want to count as a specific feature of Wittgenstein's thought. Nor does [3] appear to add anything that would distinguish his enterprise from ideas defended by other intellectuals. Many people would agree that the discovery of intermediate links between given facts is important and likely to contribute to our understanding of the matter at hand by helping us to "see connections." Adding an expression like "invent" or "think up" might drastically change the situation and make the statement much more controversial. But as we have seen, there is no such expression in the text.

Or is there? In a way, nonfactual intermediate links are introduced in paragraph [4a], which begins by mentioning "hypothetical" connecting links and says that they are merely supposed to draw our attention to connections between facts. Wittgenstein's stress on the word "facts" may be found puzzling, as the example adduced in the next sentence is extremely remote from anything one would be prepared to call an "empirical" fact: if it is a fact, it is shown to obtain in the realm of geometry, and it is shown to obtain in a peculiar fashion, viz., by treating geometrical figures as if they were objects in space and time: we demonstrate by exemplification how an *F*-shaped object can by unnoticeably diverging steps, a continuously sliding movement, be transformed into a *G*-shaped object. (Cf. Wittgenstein's generous use of the word "fact" in TLP 2.0121: "Logic deals with every possibility and all possibilities are its facts.") In Wittgenstein's example, however, we do not do this in order to show anything about physical, or empirical, possibilities, "but only in order to sharpen our eye for a formal connection." It remains remarkable, though, that whatever boundaries we may imagine to exist between purely formal (geometrical, mathematical, etc.) realms, on the one hand, and empirical (physical, observational, etc.) realms, on the other, are nonchalantly transgressed in this example.

I do not think that our impression is deceptive. After all, [4b] confirms our feeling by putting things somewhat differently: an evolutionary hypothesis, i.e., an hypothesis about an actual evolutionary process, can be seen as a mere dressing-up of a formal connection. Wittgenstein emphasizes that it is also possible to "explain" empirical, "historical", data by refraining from articulating empirical hypotheses while placing the data in a "general picture", that is, a nonempirical or formal construction (see GB 130–1). Clearly, the possibility of 'seeing this as that" is not mentioned to allude to a relatively immaterial experience of aspect-perception (on which, see Chapter 33, WITTGENSTEIN ON SEEING ASPECTS); no, it is meant to indicate a whole package of practical procedures serving all kinds of theoretical purposes, in particular, the purpose of coming to understand matters by arranging known (as well as conjectured, i.e., "hypothetical") facts in such a fashion that we virtually cannot help seeing the, or a, way in which they are connected.

In sum, the *übersichtliche Darstellung* envisaged here does not respect putative boundaries between empirical and purely formal realms. It proceeds by employing typically "empirical" examples to illustrate typically "formal" connections: processes presented as taking place in space and time are manipulated or displayed in such a way that we are compelled to recognize (a) that certain objects are but stages of a describable development and (b) how these stages are connected in terms of such a development. Of course, this project involves "hypothetical" (in the sense of conjectured) intermediate links, but one may want to insist on an important difference between these hypothetical links and the "invented" ones of §122.

5 Principles of Organization

Before leaving the early manuscript version of our remark and its surrounding context of observations on Frazer and related matters, we must add, however, that in a sequence of remarks written a few days before the quoted entry Wittgenstein does go far beyond "hypothetical" intermediate links. He repeatedly speaks of a "principle" that would allow us to invent the whole range of primitive practices described by Frazer or other anthropologists. Characteristically, Wittgenstein uses the word "*erdichten*," which on the one hand underlines the fictional aspect of the enterprise, but on the other hand suggests that, like poetry, it can be presumed to be in accordance with a certain system, which for its part can be seen as an unfolding of *one* principle governing a great variety of poetic efforts.

Wittgenstein begins by observing that "one sees how misleading Frazer's explanations are [...] by noting that one could very easily invent primitive practices oneself" and that it would be an astonishing accident if in our social reality nothing corresponding to a given invented practice could be discovered.

> That is, the principle according to which these practices are arranged is a much more general one than in Frazer's explanation and it is present in our own minds, so that we ourselves could think up all the possibilities. (GB 127)

This, I think, is an absolutely central passage. But at the same time it is a passage that needs clarification. Why should the felt ease with which we can invent primitive practices help to make us see how misleading Frazer's explanations are?

Now, one characteristic feature of Frazer's account lies in his treating the practices of primitive people and their self-descriptions as if they were on a par, or in competition, with our own instrumental or explanatory descriptions. (There are instructive discussions of Frazer, partly in defense against Wittgenstein's criticisms, in Cioffi, 1998; see also Cioffi, 2012 and Chapter 41, WITTGENSTEIN AND ANTHROPOLOGY). But in Wittgenstein's view, this means getting off on the wrong foot, as it were. Primitive women performing a ritualized birth-ceremony do not *erroneously think* that this is what giving birth is like. Tribesmen dancing a rain-dance do not make a *mistake* about meteorological causality. To be sure, they are possibly quite ignorant about the causal conditions of rainfall, but this is not the point: their performance is in no way meant to symbolize a quasi-scientific account of what happens when it rains or fails to rain. What Wittgenstein suggests is this: without knowing anything about primitive proto-science or about modern metereological science either, we can effortlessly invent practices like the ones we read about in anthropological descriptions; and this fact provides an objection to Frazer-style explanations. It provides an objection for the reason that we would indeed need knowledge of the kind we (*ex hypothesi*) do not possess to come up with descriptions of possible practices unless we had a different way of finding access to the principle behind these practices. As we do not possess knowledge of this kind (or may assume that we do not possess it) but have no difficulty in coming up with countless plausible stories about primitive practices, we may feel justified in thinking that the principle behind our invention of these stories has nothing to do with empirical research but is due to our own powers.

Of course, reasoning of this kind will never yield a knockdown argument, nor will it convince those who do not want to hear the message. But together with the rest of Wittgenstein's story these considerations may contribute to giving a certain shape to his account. According to the translation quoted, the organizing principle behind the countless ways of arranging primitive practices "is present in our own minds, so that we ourselves could think up all the possibilities." But arguably, while this translation shows that the important point is that *we share* the inclinations of the participants in magic rites, it is too timid. A more literal translation might say that the principle is "available in our own soul" ("*in unserer eigenen Seele vorhanden*"). In the context of remarks about soul-imagery and similar matters we may assume that Wittgenstein has chosen this word 'soul' deliberately. But what is the point of choosing it?

No doubt there are several complex answers to this question, which would have to take into account Wittgenstein's ways of using the word 'soul' and related expressions. Here, I shall try to give a very short answer. Wittgenstein uses the word "principle" literally: he means a fundamental standard or rule telling us, so to speak by an inner voice, how to go on in given cases or which ways of going on do or do not count as natural. Of course, this and similar locutions just express attempts at declaring that our forms of reasoning will have to terminate somewhere – otherwise they would not be forms of *reasoning*. But if one wanted to indicate this by speaking e.g., of human nature and its inclinations, one would invite all sorts of further questions and speculations about the ultimate makeup of our nature. The soul, however, is a true terminus: there is no "as if" about it. Up to a point, we all understand the word, even though its more specific uses ramify into all kinds of different directions (and even though understanding it may involve knowing that views about its nature vary). But there is no going beyond our soul – unless you wish to take the additional step of appealing to divine inspiration. And what is more: as a *locus* of the most fundamental human tendencies, forms of activity, and ways of feeling, it nicely connects with notions like "principle" and "style of going on": maybe it would be sufficient for enlightened people to be told that they should not ask questions where no satisfactory answer is likely to be forthcoming. But why should they mind being told that our techniques of naming things or our gestures of "venting our anger" all rest on related principles or "instincts" (GB 136–9) in our soul? Speaking of the soul has one clear advantage over telling people where to stop asking questions: in contrast with the latter, it is itself a way of indicating how to go on when talking about ultimate inclinations and instincts. To mention just a couple of examples: typical Wittgenstein words like "*sich aufdrängen*" ("to force itself on us," "cannot help ..."; see e.g., PI §§178, 304, 397, 425, 607; PPF §§24, 191, 265) and "*geführt werden*" ("[feelings of] being guided"; see e.g., PI §§170–8) and the attending problems require a "soul" context to make sense, and their discussion is continuously interwoven with questions about the right stopping-place (cf. Chapter 24, RULES AND RULE-FOLLOWING).

6 PI §122

Given this information about the genesis of our remark and the specific questions raised by its words in earlier versions, we should now have another look at the version printed in *Philosophical Investigations*. Are there any alterations that could be seen as demanding a change in our reading of these words? §122 runs as follows:

[a] Es ist eine Hauptquelle unseres Unverständnisses, daß wir den Gebrauch unserer Wörter nicht *übersehen*. – Unserer Grammatik fehlt es an Übersichtlichkeit. – Die übersichtliche Darstellung vermittelt das Verständnis, welches eben darin besteht, daß wir die 'Zusammenhänge sehen'. Daher die Wichtigkeit des Findens und des Erfindens von *Zwischengliedern*.

[b] Der Begriff der übersichtlichen Darstellung ist für uns von grundlegender Bedeutung. Er bezeichnet unsere Darstellungsform, die Art, wie wir die Dinge sehen. (Ist dies eine 'Weltanschauung'?)

A main source of our failure to understand is that we don't have *an overview* of the use of our words. – Our grammar is deficient in surveyability. – A surveyable representation produces precisely that kind of understanding which consists in 'seeing connections'. Hence the importance of finding and inventing *intermediate links*.

The concept of a surveyable representation is of fundamental significance for us. It characterizes the way we represent things, how we look at matters. (Is this a '*Weltanschauung*'?)

There are a number of obvious changes if one compares this version with the one quoted above: (i) Paragraphs [1] and [4] and all the rest of the GB-context have dropped out; (ii) former [2] and [3] have been turned around, so we now have, roughly speaking, [2] following [3]; (iii) in [a] two sentences have been added to the two sentences that used to make up [3]; (iv) in the last sentence of what has become [a] the words "and inventing" have been added; (v) in what has become [b] the remark on *Weltanschauungen* has been much shortened and turned into a question; moreover, Spengler's name has disappeared. What is the bearing, if any, of these modifications?

[i] The fact that the whole GB-context has vanished is of evident and enormous importance. Even if we regard it as obvious that the remarks surrounding §122 are about fairly general questions concerning the nature and relevance of philosophy, the interpretation of every single remark of this "chapter" will greatly influence our way of reading and structuring this portion of the text. So, every change in the accepted interpretation of individual remarks will bear on our understanding of the rest and may lead to further modifications.

The second sentence of [a] has simply been taken from the same page of the "Big Typescript" where earlier versions of [a] and [b] can be found. The first sentence, however, was (as far as we know) added in 1937 to the *Urfassung*, i.e., the manuscript version of the first third of the *Investigations*. (For the terminology used here and further information, see Schulte, 2001.) It stands in no clear connection with the remark preceding it in this manuscript – a remark that dropped out at a later stage of revision. But is it connected to its new neighbor in the *Investigations*, that is, §121? I think it is: §121 responds to a worry about the imagined need to introduce a kind of metaphilosophical discourse by pointing out that orthography can deal with the word "orthography" without introducing an orthography of higher order. What would help, §122 suggests, is an arrangement which permits us to survey the use of the relevant words in such a way that, in virtue of our newly gained capacity to "see connections," problems of understanding disappear. Even though step (ii), the turning around of the original [2] and [3], and step (iii), the addition of the first two sentences, were effected before the present ordering of remarks, they greatly contribute to our seeing §§121 and 122 as connected in the way suggested.

The connection between these remarks may be regarded as slight, and it may well be useful to read §122 as having a relevance that goes far beyond its bearing on the remark preceding it, but it is none the less clearly legitimate and plausible to see them as connected by a common worry. At any rate, this clarification raises a question we discussed before: to whom do the personal pronouns ("our," "we") in our paragraph refer? And at least as far as [a] is concerned, the answer seems fairly unproblematic. These pronouns refer to people in general, maybe to people worrying about certain (philosophical) questions. What about [b]? Perhaps the answer is less obvious, but I think it will have to be the same: the idea of surveyable representations is of fundamental importance to all of us; and it characterizes the way we represent things as well as the way we look at them. The exact scope of this observation will to some extent depend on how one understands, and tends to answer, the question about a *Weltanschauung*. As we have seen, step (v) removed the reference to our present Western civilization as well as Spengler's name. So what could the question be about? I think there are basically two possibilities: on the one hand, you may want to know whether our way of looking at things can rightly be called a *Weltanschauung* at all; on the other, you may want to learn whether we are dealing with one kind of *Weltanschauung* – namely the idea of a surveyable representation – rather than another. Either way, it seems that all we are asking about is whether our style of looking at things can be said to amount to a common perspective that is comprehensive and at the same time specific enough to yield something one might be willing to call a *Weltbild*, a world-picture. (Here I am of course chiefly thinking of Wittgenstein's own use of this term in his late reflections published as *On Certainty*. But as it happens, *Weltbild* is also a Spenglerian word. See, for instance *The Decline of the West*, vol.I, pp.127–8; or the title of section 1 of chapter 3: "*Die Symbolik des Weltbildes und das Raumproblem*," and so on.). In other words, the specifically Spenglerian connotation of the term "*Weltanschauung*" has been lost, and no reference to him will be necessary to make sufficient sense of the text of §122. (This does not mean of course that knowledge of the background alluded to before could not come in useful. Cf. the discussion of immanent vs. genetic approaches in Glock, 2007.)

This leaves step (iv), the insertion of "inventing" intermediate links. And this insertion does make a difference: it widens the scope of our considerations by going far beyond factual connecting links and bringing in invented ones. This, however, does not mean that Wittgenstein is prepared to open the doors of his investigations to all kinds of imagined cases or fantasies. It is the notion of a *Zwischenglied* – an intermediate or connecting link – that strictly delimits the set of admissible examples. An intermediate link is something that has to fit into the place between its neighbors; and it is the very fact of its fitting that can tell us something about the whole chain of relevant phenomena and their way or ways of hanging together. This is the point where the Goethe quotations mentioned above come to play a role. (On Wittgenstein and Goethe, see Schulte, 1982; 2003; and 2014.) The allusion is to Goethe's morphological ideas, which center around various models describable in terms of "chains," "ladders," "series," and related structures. By comparing these more or less metaphorical structures with natural objects and occurrences we may come to understand the development of organisms, the history of certain species, the relations between families of plants, or, as in Spengler's adaptation of Goethe's morphological insights, the history of mankind. Of course, here "come to understand" is tantamount to constructing a picture of the phenomena in question. But is there a form of understanding that does without models of one kind or another?

It is the idea of having to fit an object or an occurrence into the space between its neighbors that brings in its wake a certain element of necessity, which in its turn lends "morphological" arrangements of facts and imaginary states of affairs some of their elucidatory power:

> Seeing that in these investigations we keep asking, 'What would one *have* to say if …', we find the diversity of really occurring cases *insufficient*. What we need to take into consideration is a whole gamut [*Stufenleiter*] of possibilities, irrespective of whether they are invented [*erdichtete*] or real ones. That's why it strikes us as funny, almost as an irrelevancy, when we observe a philosopher hunting for out-of-the-way particular cases, e.g. strange mental illnesses. As if the factual aspect of these cases were of any importance! (MS 120, pp.73r–v; a somewhat later version of this remark describes the philosopher as "hunting with the facial expression of a naturalist," MS 116, p.247)

This morphological way of looking at things is very characteristic of Wittgenstein's approach. It tallies with what he says about concepts and concept-formation (cf. Schulte, 2010 and 2012b), about the surveyability of proofs (once we have arrived at a comprehensive overview, we will find it easier to *reproduce* a proof), and rule-following (or ways of going on in general). (The criterion of reproducibility is rightly emphasized in Felix Mühlhölzer's magisterial book of 2010; see e.g., pp.91–7. I am not sure, however, that I can agree to his judgment that there is a great gulf between Wittgenstein's notion of surveyability as employed in PI §122 and the notion of surveyability as applied to mathematical proof; cf. Mühlhölzer, 2010, p.92, n.96.) So far, most commentators are likely to agree. What may be controversial in my discussion is the emphasis on reading §122 not so much as a programmatic remark about the nature of philosophy, but rather as a diagnostic one about a feature of human understanding: as an observation on natural human tendencies and our ways of exploiting them in our attempts at making us see connections.

References

Baker, G.P. and Hacker, P.M.S. (1980/2005). *Wittgenstein: Understanding and Meaning. Volume 1 of an Analytical Commentary on the Philosophical Investigations. Part 1. Essays.* Second edition. Extensively revised by P.M.S. Hacker. Oxford: Wiley-Blackwell.
Biesenbach, H. (2014). *Anspielungen und Zitate im Werk Ludwig Wittgensteins.* [Allusions and Quotations in the Work of Ludwig Wittgenstein.] Extended edition. Sofia: St Kliment Ohridski University Press.
Cioffi, F. (1998). *Wittgenstein on Freud and Frazer.* Cambridge: Cambridge University Press.
Cioffi, F. (2012). Overviews: What Are They and What Are They For?. In W. Day and V.J. Krebs (Eds). *Seeing Wittgenstein Anew* (pp.291–313). Cambridge: Cambridge University Press.
Glock, H.-J. (1996). *A Wittgenstein Dictionary.* Oxford: Blackwell.
Glock, H.-J. (2007). Perspectives on Wittgenstein: An Intermittently Opinionated Survey. In G. Kahane, E. Kanterian, and O. Kuusela (Eds). *Wittgenstein and his Interpreters: Essays in Memory of Gordon Baker* (pp.37–65). Oxford: Blackwell.

Hacker, P.M.S. (2004). Turning the Examination Around: The Recantation of a Metaphysician. In E. Ammereller and E. Fischer (Eds). *Wittgenstein at Work: Method in the Philosophical Investigations* (pp. 3–21). London: Routledge.

Mühlhölzer, F. (2010). *Braucht die Mathematik eine Grundlegung? Ein Kommentar des Teils III von Wittgensteins Bemerkungen über die Grundlagen der Mathematik.* [Does Mathematics need Foundations? A Commentary on Part III of Wittgenstein's *Remarks on the Foundations of Mathematics*.] Frankfurt: Vittorio Klostermann.

Schulte, J. (1982). Chor und Gesetz. [Chorus and Law.] Reprinted in J. Schulte (1990). *Chor und Gesetz* (pp. 11–42). Frankfurt: Suhrkamp.

Schulte, J. (2003). Goethe and Wittgenstein on Morphology. In F. Breithaupt, R. Raatzsch, and B. Kremberg (Eds). *Goethe and Wittgenstein: Seeing the World's Unity in its Variety* (pp. 55–72). Frankfurt: Peter Lang.

Schulte, J. (2007). Ways of Reading Wittgenstein. In G. Kahane, E. Kanterian, and O. Kuusela (Eds). *Wittgenstein and his Interpreters: Essays in Memory of Gordon Baker* (pp. 145–168). Oxford: Blackwell.

Schulte, J. (2010). Concepts and Concept-Formation. In N. Venturinha (Ed.). *Wittgenstein after his Nachlass* (pp. 128–42). Houndmills: Palgrave Macmillan.

Schulte, J. (2011). Waismann as Spokesman for Wittgenstein. In B. McGuinness (Ed.). *Friedrich Waismann: Causality and Logical Positivism* (pp. 225–242). Dordrecht: Springer.

Schulte, J. (2012a). Die Revision der englischen Übersetzung von Wittgensteins Philosophischen Untersuchungen: Ein Erfahrungsbericht. [The Revision of the English Translation of Wittgenstein's *Philosophical Investigations:* A Report.] In M. Kroß and E. Ramharter (Eds). *Wittgenstein übersetzen* (pp. 173–194). Berlin: Parerga.

Schulte, J. (2012b). Philosophy of Psychology: A Criticism of a Young Science?. In P. Stekeler-Weithofer (Ed.). *Wittgenstein: Zu Philosophie und Wissenschaft* (pp. 224–235). Hamburg: Meiner.

Schulte, J. (2014). Ideen mit den Augen sehen: Goethe und Wittgenstein über Morphologie. [Seeing Ideas with One's Eyes: Goethe and Wittgenstein on Morphology.] In J. Maatsch (Ed.). *Morphologie und Moderne: Goethes "anschauliches Denken" in den Geistes- und Kulturwissenschaften seit 1800* (pp. 141–156). Berlin: de Gruyter.

Schulte, J. (Ed.). (2001). Ludwig Wittgenstein: *Philosophische Untersuchungen,* Kritisch-genetische Edition. [Ludwig Wittgenstein: *Philosophical Investigations*, Critical-Genetic Edition] Frankfurt: Suhrkamp.

Spengler, O. ([1918] 1926). *The Decline of the West* (Vol. 1): *Form and Actuality.* Trans. C.F. Atkinson. London: George Allen and Unwin. (Original work published 1918; revised edition 1922.)

Spengler, O. ([1923] 1928). *The Decline of the West* (Vol. 2): *Perspectives of World-History.* Trans. C.F. Atkinson. London: George Allen and Unwin. (Original work published 1923.)

Spengler, O. ([1922/1923] 1996). *Der Untergang des Abendlandes.* München: C.H. Beck.

von Savigny, E. (1989/1994). *Wittgensteins "Philosophische Untersuchungen": Ein Kommentar für Leser* (Vol. 1). [Wittgenstein's *Philosophical Investigations:* A Commentary for Readers.] Second edition. Frankfurt: Vittorio Klostermann.

Further Reading

Andronico, M. (1998). *Antropologia e metodo morfologico.* [Anthropology and the Morphological Method.] Napoli: La città del sole.

Baker, G.P. (1991). *Philosophical Investigations §122: Neglected Aspects.* Reprinted in G.P. Baker. (2004). *Wittgenstein's Method: Neglected Aspects* (pp. 22–52). Ed. K.J. Morris. Oxford: Blackwell.

Baker, G.P. and Hacker, P.M.S. (1980/2009). *Wittgenstein: Understanding and Meaning. Volume 1 of an Analytical Commentary on the Philosophical Investigations. Part 1. Essays.* Second edition. Extensively revised by P.M.S. Hacker. Oxford: Wiley-Blackwell. Chapter 15.

Brusotti, M. (2014). *Wittgenstein, Frazer und die "ethnologische Betrachtungsweise."* [Wittgenstein, Frazer and the "Ethnological Perspective."] Berlin: de Gruyter.

Iven, M. (2015). Er "ist eine Künstlernatur von hinreissender Genialität." *Wittgenstein Studien*, 6, 83–174.

Kuusela, O. (2014). Gordon Baker, Wittgensteinian Philosophical Conceptions and Perspicuous Representation: The Possibility of Multidimensional Logical Descriptions. *Nordic Wittgenstein Review*, 3, 71–98.

Part V

Logic and Mathematics

17

Logic and the *Tractatus*

ROGER M. WHITE

In a footnote to a discussion of the nature of logical truth, in 1919, Russell wrote:

> The importance of 'tautology' for a definition of mathematics was pointed out to me by my former pupil Ludwig Wittgenstein, who was working on the problem. I do not know whether he has solved it, or even whether he is alive or dead. (Russell, 1919, p.205)

For more than one reason, this passage provides us with an appropriate way in to the logic of the *Tractatus*. Not only is it clear from this, as from other sources such as the 1913 *Notes on Logic*, that the conception of truths of logic as tautologies was a guiding idea in Wittgenstein's investigations from the very earliest stages. It is also clear that at that stage Wittgenstein did not have a worked-out theory of the tautologicality of logic – this was a problem he "was working on." Hence no more can be read into this early use of the word "tautology" than its traditional use as a term from rhetoric used pejoratively to refer to a completely vacuous claim. The truth-functional account of tautologies belongs to the final elaboration of this idea (cf. Dreben and Floyd, 1991). The other idea to be derived from this footnote is that it was dissatisfaction with Russell's treatment of the nature of logic and of logical truth that initially led Wittgenstein into the inquiry into the nature of logic that found fruition in the *Tractatus*.

Whitehead and Russell's *Principia Mathematica* was an attempt to vindicate "logicism" – the claim that truths of mathematics were disguised truths of logic. To overcome Russell's paradox, Russell had introduced the "theory of types," stratifying sets, and with that the properties of sets. The resulting system was too weak to generate number theory without the addition of further axioms, including the "Axiom of Reducibility" (for any predicate of any order, there is an equivalent first-order predicate). If the resulting system is to substantiate logicism, Russell needs to give satisfactory answers to such questions as "Was the Axiom of Reducibility true?", "If so, was it a truth of *logic*?" and behind that "What did we mean when we called something a truth of logic?"

A Companion to Wittgenstein, First Edition. Edited by Hans-Johann Glock and John Hyman.
© 2017 John Wiley & Sons, Ltd. Published 2017 by John Wiley & Sons, Ltd.

Russell's initial answer to the last of these questions was to say that a truth of logic was a true completely general proposition – one that could be expressed using only logical constants and variables. It is to this answer that Wittgenstein is reacting in Russell's footnote cited at the outset. The obvious cause of dissatisfaction is that there seems no good reason why there could not be *contingent* completely general propositions. In a letter to Russell, Wittgenstein makes the point laconically:

> A proposition such as "$(\exists x).x=x$", for example, is really a proposition of *physics*. The proposition
> "$(x) : x = x . \supset . (\exists y).y=y$"
>   is a proposition of logic and it is then for *physics* to say *whether anything exists*. (Letter to Russell, November or December 1913)

And both Wittgenstein and Frank Ramsey protest that the Axiom of Reducibility in particular looks to be a contingent proposition (see TLP 6.1232–3, and Ramsey, 1925, p.220).

Against this background, we may see the *Tractatus* as Wittgenstein's reply to Russell, addressing such questions as "What is a truth of logic?," "Why are the truths of logic unproblematically necessary?," and further "What are logical constants such as 'and,' 'or,' and 'not,' and how are they related to one another?"

1 The Truths of Logic as Tautologies

The first question is this: why was Wittgenstein convinced, from the very outset, that the truths of logic were tautologies? Here, we are initially assuming that no more is to be read into the use of the word "tautology" than the idea of a completely vacuous proposition – one that "says nothing."

We may detect three closely interrelated ideas.

Firstly, the conception of logical truths as tautologies is powerfully explanatory. If the truths of logic are tautologies, then that explains their status as necessary, a priori, propositions. If they say nothing then they cannot but be true since nothing is required to make them true. Also if they say nothing then they cannot be a posteriori, since they are invulnerable to every possible experience.

Secondly, if the propositions of logic are necessary, they are true regardless of the way the world is. But if they are true regardless of the way the world is, then they cannot tell us anything about the way the world is, and hence say nothing.

Thirdly, and this is the point that Wittgenstein stresses, describing it as "containing within it the whole philosophy of logic" (TLP 6.113), if the propositions of logic are true regardless of the way the world is, that can only be because the propositions themselves contain all the information necessary to settle their truth value. In the letter to Russell at the end of 1913, Wittgenstein gives "a rough explanation" of what he means by characterizing the truths of logic as tautologies:

> If I say, for example 'Meier is stupid', you cannot tell by looking at this proposition whether it is true or false. But the propositions of logic – and only they – have the property that their truth or falsity, as the case may be, finds its expression in the very sign for the proposition. (Letter to Russell, November or December 1913; cf. TLP 6.113)

But the only way that it will be possible for the proposition to contain all the information necessary to settle its truth value is if its truth conditions implode in the way that is characteristic of tautologies, even in its traditional sense:

> Tautology and contradiction are the limiting cases of the combination of symbols, namely their dissolution. (TLP 4.466)

The propositions of logic are thus degenerate cases of propositions. They are part of the symbolism – limit cases of propositions – vacuous and senseless, but not nonsense.

There is one other feature of Wittgenstein's characterization of tautologies that must be mentioned at the outset, though, because it has so often been seen as the Achilles' heel of his whole account of logic. I shall discuss it at the end of this chapter. Wittgenstein usually writes in such a way as to imply that in the case of tautologies there will be a procedure whereby we will be able, in every case, to *tell* that a tautology is such. However, we now know that there cannot be such a decision procedure for predicate logic. The question is this: how much damage does that do to his whole conception of logic, and what modifications to his account are necessary to accommodate this fact?

But at this stage, we shall see how Wittgenstein builds up his account of logic to do justice to the basic idea that the propositions of logic are indeed tautological.

2   That the Logical Constants Do Not Stand for Anything

We first examine the logical apparatus of language, "the logical constants" ("and," "or," "not," and the quantifiers) – starting with what at one point (TLP 4.0312) Wittgenstein calls his "fundamental thought" – that the logical constants do not stand for anything. At first sight this looks completely platitudinous, but what are of interest are the less obvious consequences that he draws from this idea.

We may contrast elementary propositions and logically complex propositions, where the mark of an elementary proposition is that it may be expressed without the use of logical constants. (There is of course more to Wittgenstein's conception of an elementary proposition than its freedom from logical complexity, but it is that freedom from complexity that is relevant in our present context.) Elementary propositions directly engage with reality by presenting us with a state of affairs, where names in the elementary propositions stand for elements in the state of affairs, and are true or false according as that state of affairs does or does not obtain. For our purposes, I shall treat such propositions as "John married Jane" as if they were elementary propositions. "John married Jane" presents the state of affairs of John-marrying-Jane, with the names in the proposition standing for elements in the state of affairs. The relation of logically complex propositions is, however, indirect. "John married Jane or Peter married Jane," if true, is either made true by John-marrying-Jane or by Peter-marrying-Jane, and not by a "disjunctive state of affairs" – John-or-Peter-marrying-Jane – a state of affairs that would have disjunction as one of its constituents. Equally, "someone married Jane" could not be barely true without some particular person having married Jane. If true, it will be true because "John married Jane" is true or "Peter married Jane" is true or…, and if false, it will be false because no such particular proposition is true.

Thus, there are propositions that are void of logical complexity – "elementary propositions." These engage directly with the concrete, specific, situations that we find in the world, and are made true or false according as the state of affairs that they represent obtains or not. However, associated with a logically complex proposition there will be a range of logically simpler propositions, where the logically complex proposition derives its truth or falsity from the truth or falsity of the members of this underlying set of propositions. It will be made true by some combinations of truth and falsity of the set and false by the rest.

We may therefore think of the logical constants as "operations" – devices for building complex propositions out of simpler propositions. Wittgenstein stresses that operations are quite different from Russellian propositional functions. Propositional functions map names onto propositions, whereas operations map propositions onto propositions. One consequence of this is that, unlike propositional functions, operations can be applied repeatedly, building up ever more complex propositions (TLP 5.251). What is more, they are truth-functional operations, since we specify the truth or falsity of the complex propositions in terms of the truth or falsity of the underlying set of propositions associated with that complex proposition. This gives us the prominent claim of the *Tractatus*, namely, that every proposition is the result of successive application of truth-functional operations to elementary propositions, and hence that every proposition is a truth function of elementary propositions, including the case of an elementary proposition being a truth function of itself (TLP 5).

This provides a remarkably simple solution to Wittgenstein's initial problem "What are tautologies?" A tautology is now interpreted as a degenerate truth function – a proposition that is a truth function of a set of propositions and that is true for all combinations of truth and falsity of the members of that set. Since every proposition is a truth function of elementary propositions, and the only truth functions of elementary propositions that are necessarily true are the tautologies in this sense, we now have an equation of the idea of a truth of logic and a truth-functional tautology. (It is at this point that the independence that Wittgenstein claims for elementary propositions matters: if two elementary propositions can be incompatible, then that creates the possibility of tautologies that cannot be explained truth-functionally.) In order to do justice to Wittgenstein's development of logic using his N-operator, it should be noted here that the general notion of a truth function includes the case of a proposition being a truth function of *infinitely* many propositions. This is vital if the account is to be capable of giving an account of quantification over infinite domains.

We have now arrived at the following idea: *all* logical complexity is *truth-functional* complexity, and all the basic logical constants are to be explained purely as truth-functional operators. Since this is by no means obvious in the case of the quantifiers, the main task confronting Wittgenstein is to show how this is done. But before turning to that we need to look at another aspect of this task. Wittgenstein is insistent that not only is the whole of logic reducible to truth-functional logic, it must also be possible to develop the whole of logic using *only one* logical constant. His arguments for this are presented in a somewhat elusive way, and as a result the topic has been somewhat neglected in discussions of the *Tractatus*. I shall concentrate here on the argument contained in TLP 5.451 and 5.521, since I believe this to be the most significant argument.

3 Why Only One Logical Constant?

In his notebooks preparatory to the *Tractatus*, Wittgenstein had written:

> Does the general form of proposition exist?
>   Yes, if by that is understood the single 'logical constant'. (NB 45)

It is to my mind astonishing how irrelevant the remarks about the general form of proposition in *Philosophical Investigations* are to the point at issue here. A basic idea lying behind all of the early Wittgenstein's discussion of logic is the idea of the "unity" of logic, expressed most explicitly at TLP 5.4541 – that it must be possible to present logic as a single integrated system based upon one underlying principle, and issuing in a "general form of proposition," a single formula that will generate every possible logical form of proposition, and that any development in logic must be capable of being presented as simply an unfolding of what we had already, and not a radically new departure from what had gone before. It is in this sense that "there can *never* be surprises in logic" (TLP 6.1251). We can, I believe, understand Wittgenstein's concern here best by considering it by analogy with a familiar argument in Hobbes. Hobbes's basic concern was the need for a sovereign body in the state, one that had absolute and ultimate authority for all the laws of the land. He argued that for such a body to be genuinely sovereign, it must be "One and Undivided." Suppose there were two branches of government each of which was given sovereignty – autonomous decision-making powers. Then there would always be the possibility of a conflict between the two branches, and hence the need for a higher authority that can adjudicate between them and negotiate a settlement of the point at issue. But if they are both sovereign, there can be no such higher authority. Hence sovereignty must be One and Undivided and "take care of itself." Similar arguments recur in the history of philosophy, such as Kant's reduction of the whole of morality to one basic categorical imperative. We can see the *Tractatus* as applying a similar style of argument to the case of logic: if logic is to be the ultimate and unimpeachable authority in reasoning, logic too must be One and Undivided, and capable of "taking care of itself" (TLP 5.473). There can be no appeal beyond logic, such as to "intuition," to settle the question what is, and what is not, a truth of logic. (cf. TLP 6.1271)

Our task is to understand why this conception of logic is incompatible with there being more than one basic indefinable logical constant. The key to what follows is Wittgenstein's reference to Frege on definition at the end of TLP 5.451. In *Grundgesetze* II, §§56–65, Frege engages in an extended critique of what he calls the "mathematician's favourite procedure": "piecemeal definition," or definition by stages. What he is attacking is the idea that we may first define a term for a limited domain, and then define it again for a new extended domain. We may see what he has in mind if we consider a familiar example. When we introduce the various number systems, it seems inevitable to begin by explaining the natural numbers, then build on that account to use the natural numbers to introduce the positive and negative integers, then build on that to introduce the rational numbers and so on. In the course of this we will define the basic arithmetical operations such as addition. Proceeding along this route it can again seem inevitable first to explain addition for the natural numbers, and only subsequently for the other domains that we are building on the natural numbers. The kind of definition we might produce in so doing, and to which Frege is objecting, is the following definition of "+" for the rational numbers:

$$a/b + c/d =_{\text{Def}} (ad+cb)/bd$$

At first sight this definition looks circular, with the plus sign appearing on both the left-hand side and the right-hand side of the definition, but that is not quite right. The defense of the definition is that the "+" sign on the right-hand side is applied to whole numbers, and that we have already explained, and we are using that to define the use of "+" on the left-hand side of the "=" sign to apply to rational numbers. Frege's objection to this defense finds expression in the following questions: is addition in the two cases the same operation or different? If different, then to avoid introducing ambiguity into our system we should use a different sign for the new use. If the same, is the definition consistent with the previous use of the "+" sign? If it is inconsistent, then the definition should clearly be rejected. If it is consistent, so that the new definition is conservative, then that needs proving as a theorem and cannot be surreptitiously smuggled in by a definition. Therefore the piecemeal definition must in all cases be rejected and instead we should introduce addition once and for all for every possible application.

We may now see Wittgenstein in TLP 5.451 as confronting what happens when Russell develops his logic in volume I of *Principia Mathematica* with Frege's arguments, adapting them to the case of the introduction of the primitive signs of logic. Russell proceeds in what can be seen as a natural and even inevitable way: we first set up propositional logic, and then when that is in place introduce the quantifiers and build predicate logic as a new extension of logic. He therefore begins with "atomic propositions" – propositions that can be expressed without the use of logical constants – and then in ***1** introduces as his two primitive signs of propositional logic "~" and "v," explaining how you may apply them to atomic propositions to form "elementary propositions" – the truth functions of atomic propositions – and from that to form the elementary propositional functions. As Russell stresses, at this stage the use of "~" and "v" has only been explained, and can only be explained, in their role in forming elementary propositions, since so far these are the only ideas that have been introduced at this point. Then in ***9** he introduces the quantifiers. What Russell realizes at this point is something that it is easy to overlook: nothing he has said so far has determined the sense of a proposition in which a quantified proposition is negated – in which we put a "~" in front of a quantifier or a "v" between two quantified propositions. He therefore reintroduces the "~" and "v," in the following way. He first introduces the universal quantifier and the existential quantifier as applicable to elementary propositional functions, and then gives *definitions* to determine the significance of such propositions. So that we have:

Definition of Negation. We have first to define the negations of $(x).\varphi x$ and $(\exists x).\varphi x$. We define the negation of $(x).\varphi x$ as $(\exists x). \sim \varphi x$, i.e. "It is not the case that φx is always true" is to mean "it is the case that not-φx is sometimes true." Similarly that negation of $(\exists x).\varphi x$ is to be defined as $(x). \sim \varphi x$. Thus we put

*9.01. $\sim\{(x).\varphi x\} . = .(\exists x). \sim \varphi x$ Df.
*9.02. $\sim\{(\exists x).\varphi x\} . = .(x). \sim \varphi x$ Df.

(Whitehead and Russell, 1910, p.135)

He offers a similar battery of definitions for "v". Such definitions are supposed to be repeated every time we embed quantified propositions inside the scope of a quantifier. (In *10 of *Principia*, Russell proposes as an alternative possibility that each "new" "~" is a new primitive sign, producing an infinite hierarchy of negations. Here I shall look at what happens in *9, and only note that, *mutatis mutandis*, this alternative "solution" to the difficulty is equally objectionable from the point of view of Wittgenstein's argument that follows.)

For Wittgenstein this cure was worse than the disease. These "definitions" are objectionable for precisely the reasons that Frege spelled out. If the primitive signs of logic had been properly introduced, there would be no room for a definition at this point: the sense of *every* proposition in which, say, "~" occurred would already have been fixed. The only way in which that can be achieved is by introducing *all* the apparatus of logic simultaneously, explaining the sense of every possible combination of signs in which the different logical constants occur (TLP 5.46). This leads Wittgenstein to see the real primitive notion of logic, not as the particular primitive logical signs that Russell had introduced but as "the most general form of their combination" (TLP 5.46). For Wittgenstein, the problem that became acute in *9 when the quantifiers were introduced in *Principia* was already present for the simple case of propositional logic: if "~" and "v" really represented distinct primitive ideas, we would be left with no possible explanation for the fact that when they were combined in a single proposition such as "$p \vee \sim p$" we would obtain a logical truth, other than to appeal to a dubious intuition, so that logic would no longer "take care of itself." He therefore sees his task as that of discovering a single logical constant that can be introduced once and for all and in terms of which all the particular logical constants of Frege and Russell can be defined.

4 The N-Operator and the General Form of Proposition

Wittgenstein's task then is to introduce a single logical constant that is (a) truth-functional and (b) in terms of which the whole of standard Fregean logic can be defined. Russell had first introduced propositional logic, and then built predicate logic upon it: he was therefore forced to introduce the quantifiers into contexts that already involved the apparatus of propositional logic, leading to the difficulties we have just seen, and making "the propositions '(∃x).fx' and '(x).fx' difficult to understand" (TLP 5.521). Wittgenstein's solution to the difficulties Russell had run into is to in effect reverse the order of procedure. We take as our basic operator what may be regarded as a negative universal quantifier (a "None Of" operation), thus starting from the very outset with predicate logic, and then deriving propositional logic as a special case of predicate logic. We must examine how in detail this is to be done.

At TLP 4.31 Wittgenstein had introduced truth tables, and at TLP 4.442 had proposed the use of truth tables as a possible notation for logic. In TLP 5.5 he proposes (-----T) (ξ, ...) as his fundamental operation for generating every proposition and the whole of logic. This notation is however only appropriate where we are dealing with the operation being applied to a finite set of listed propositions. Therefore at TLP 5.502 he replaces this with the N-operator or joint negation: an operation that when applied to a given range of propositions produces a simultaneous rejection of all the propositions in the range. This is a purely truth-functional operator, but unlike the truth-table operator he had introduced earlier, it can now produce truth-functions of infinitely many propositions.

To show how this can cope with standard quantification Wittgenstein takes two steps that we must consider in turn. The first is that "Every variable can be construed as a propositional variable" (TLP 3.314) and the second is that Wittgenstein "separates out the concept *all* and the truth-function" in the notation for generality (TLP 5.521).

Construing every variable as a propositional variable. On the usual understanding, in "(x).fx," the variable is the letter "x" and has as its values all the objects in the domain over which we are quantifying. However, since the N-operator is intended as a truth-functional operator, it has to apply not to a range of objects, but to a range of propositions. We therefore need an alternative reading of "(x).fx," in which the quantifier is applied to a variable whose values are all propositions. To do this, we take the variable in "(x).fx" to be not the letter "x," but the complex sign "fx," a variable whose values are all propositions of the form "fx."

Separating out the concept "all" and the truth function. The reason someone such as Russell needed to first treat propositional logic and only subsequently predicate logic was that it was held to be impossible to reduce quantificational logic to propositional logic, making predicate logic no more than a development of propositional logic. For Wittgenstein the idea that it was impossible to treat the quantifiers truth-functionally stemmed from a failure to recognize that there were two different components that were run together in the standard quantifier notation. We may understand his conception if we think of quantification as a two-stage process. In "(x).fx," we first define the variable "fx," by specifying that it is to have as its values *all* the propositions of the form "fx". This is the role of "the concept *all*" in the construction of a quantified proposition. But now the concept of generality has done its work, and as the second stage we apply a purely truth-functional operator to the propositions in the range of the variable. In the case of universal quantification, this truth-functional operator is to be thought of as an infinitary analogue of "&," i.e., (x).fx = fa & fb & fc & …

It is now relatively straightforward to see how the N-operator, representing Wittgenstein's single logical constant, can be used to explain the whole of standard Fregean logic. The N-operator is an operator that is applied to a propositional variable to produce a proposition that is the simultaneous rejection of the values of that variable – "none of these are true." We define the variable by specifying what its values are. At TLP 5.501, Wittgenstein gives three different ways in which we could do so, but stresses that it is a matter of indifference how the variables are specified, and there is no reason to suppose that his three ways are intended to be exhaustive. We obtain the different elements of Fregean logic by different specifications of the variable.

The simplest case is where we list the values of the variable, as two propositions p and q, say. Then N{p, q} will be one of the two Sheffer strokes: "neither p nor q." As is well known, once we have the Sheffer stroke, we can use it to define the whole of propositional logic.

Quantification at first sight looks equally simple, but requires some comments. Wittgenstein gives his account as follows:

If the values of ξ are the total values of a function fx for all values of x, then $N(\xi) = \sim(\exists x)$. fx. (TLP 5.52)

Because Wittgenstein is treating every variable as a propositional variable, this gives us a form of substitutional quantification. It is not vulnerable to usual criticisms of the adequacy of substitutional quantification, since it is presented on the assumption that in its fully analyzed form we have a language that is expressively complete: that is, that there is an elementary proposition corresponding to every state of affairs, and every object has one and only one name, together with the background assumption that it is not a contingent matter of fact that these are all the (simple) objects that there are.

In a letter to Russell, Wittgenstein wrote: "identity is the very Devil and *immensely important*" (Letter to Russell, 29 October 1913), and how to handle identity propositions is less obvious. To understand Wittgenstein's position, we have to see him as accepting Russell's idea that in every significant identity proposition, "A = B," one at least of "A" and "B" is either a definite description or can be regarded as an abbreviation for one. We therefore have to give an account of "A = the F," say. Applying the theory of descriptions to that, we obtain as an initial analysis "(x).Fx & (x)(y).(Fx & Fy ⊃ x = y) & (x).Fx ⊃ x = A". Because of the logical properties of identity, we may simplify this as

$$FA \& (x)(y).(Fx \& Fy \supset x = y)$$

At first sight, this has not advanced matters, since we are still using the identity sign in the *analysans*. However, what the analysis shows is that we can give an account of the use of the identity sign outside the scope of a quantifier in terms of propositions in which the only use of the identity sign is within the scope of a quantifier flanked by two variables. We can therefore dispense with an identity sign (TLP 5.533), in favor of a convention for reading the quantifiers in which we always substitute different names for different variables, so that our analysis becomes:

$$FA \& (x)(y). \sim (Fx \& Fy)$$

We now simply modify our specification of the variable to produce a modified quantification theory.

Finally, although Wittgenstein doesn't discuss the case, in principle it will be possible to give an account of higher-order quantification using only the N-operator: It is simply a question of finding an appropriate specification of the variable to which the operator is applied.

With this, Wittgenstein has shown how the whole of standard logic is to be presented using only the one operator. But more generally, *every* truth function of elementary propositions can be generated using only the N-operator: this is the infinitary analogue of Sheffer's proof that all propositional logic can be developed using only the Sheffer stroke. We thus arrive at the conclusion, the general form of proposition:

> Every proposition is the result of successive applications of the operation N'($\bar{\xi}$) to elementary propositions. (TLP 6.001)

Wittgenstein has now arrived at his goal: he has given a truth-functional account of the whole of logic, and can give an account of the whole of logic that is One and Undivided.

(a) Every possible logical form of proposition can be generated using one simple formula;
(b) every logical truth is a degenerate truth function, a tautology, generated by the general form of proposition; and
(c) all logical inference is governed by the principle that q is inferable from p iff "p ⊃ q" is a tautology (see TLP 6.1201).

5 The Propositions of Logic as Tautologies and the Decision Problem

In 1935–1936, Alonzo Church proved that there could be no decision procedure for predicate logic (Church, 1936). Many commentators have concluded from this that Wittgenstein's conception of logic had thereby been refuted. Thus Elizabeth Anscombe writes:

> However, the theory of the *Tractatus*, promising though it looked at the time, has been clearly and cogently refuted in another way. If all truths of logic are tautological truth functions of elementary propositions, then there is in principle a decision procedure for them all. But it was proved by Church in the 1930's that multiple quantification theory has no decision procedure. (Anscombe, 1959, p.137)

What this criticism overlooks is that the N-operator is an *infinitary* truth-functional operator. Whereas for the standard truth functions of propositional logic there is indeed a decision procedure, once we consider truth functions of infinitely many arguments, all such decision procedures have no application.

Approaching matters differently, Gregory Landini sees Church's Theorem as vindicating Russell:

> Logic, in Wittgenstein's view, is by its very definition decidable; and this is connoted by his use of the word "tautology". (Landini, 1998, p.296)

And:

> History proved Russell the master. Church showed that no predicate calculus is decidable. (Landini, 1998, p.297)

But this is simplistic. Certainly it is hard to see Church's Theorem as offering support to the alternative Landini ascribes to Russell: the murky idea of logic as a synthetic a priori science of the structure of the world based upon logical intuition. But we concentrate on this question here: does Church's Theorem refute Wittgenstein's whole conception of logic?

There is no doubt that Wittgenstein did hold that there would be a decision procedure for the whole of logic. There are frequent remarks that are naturally taken to imply this, and most unequivocally the sequence from 6.113 to 6.127 beginning:

> It is the specific mark of logical propositions that one can recognize from the symbol alone that they are true ... (TLP 6.113)

This clearly gives us a simple decision procedure: write the proposition in canonical notation and inspect it. It is, however, wrong to say that logic for Wittgenstein is "*by its very definition* decidable." Insofar as Wittgenstein *defines* tautology in the *Tractatus*, he does so at 4.66: "a proposition that is true for all the truth-possibilities of the elementary propositions," and *that* does not entail the decidability of logic, even if Wittgenstein wrongly thought that it did. The questions we need to ask are these: Why was Wittgenstein so convinced that there would be a decision procedure? and

How much damage does it do to his conception of logic that we now know that he was wrong about this?

The answer to the first question is suggested by TLP 6.113, just cited. If a proposition of logic is true regardless of the way the world is, the proposition itself must contain all the information necessary to determine that it is true. Hence once expressed in a perspicuous notation, it will *show* that it is true (see TLP 4.461). Hence, "we can recognize in an adequate notation the formal properties of the propositions by mere inspection" (6.122). The mistake in this train of thought is that it overlooks the fact that once we permit quantification over infinite domains, there may be no adequate notation in which the fact that the proposition itself determines its own truth value will be humanly surveyable. In this context, as in some others, if we are to retain the notion of "what can be shown," *showing* may not be treated as a straightforward *epistemological* concept: what is shown may be shown in such a way that it is impossible for us to see it.

How much damage does this do to Wittgenstein's conception of logic? Despite widespread opinion, the answer is: very little. It does nothing to refute the idea of the logical constants as truth-functional operations, the general form of proposition, or the conception of the truths of logic as tautologies – if by that we mean propositions that say nothing about the world. However, it was undoubtedly important to Wittgenstein that his conception of the truths of logic as tautologies resolved in principle the question of our *knowledge* of logical truth. And for that we have to tell a more complicated story than Wittgenstein would allow.

We can best assess Wittgenstein's position, both positively and negatively, by considering TLP 6.126–7. Wittgenstein rightly insists that on his account of logic what made a truth of logic a truth of logic was not its status as a theorem in an axiomatic system, but the fact that on its own it determined that it was unconditionally true. However, since we now know that there cannot be a notation from which *we* could infallibly read off the logical status of a proposition, he goes wrong in saying "Naturally this way of showing that its propositions are tautologies is quite unessential to logic." To discover the logical status of a proposition, we must resort to indirect methods, including the use of axiomatic systems.

The point to stress is that citing Church's Theorem does nothing to impugn either Wittgenstein's central claim that the whole of logic is truth-functional, or his explanation of the whole of logic using only the N-operator.

References

Anscombe, G.E.M. (1959). *An Introduction to Wittgenstein's Tractatus*. London: Hutchinson.
Church, A. (1936). A Note on the *Entscheidungsproblem*. *Journal of Symbolic Logic*, 1, 40–41.
Dreben, B. and Floyd, J. (1991). Tautology: How Not to Use a Word. *Synthese*, 87, 23–49.
Frege, G. (1903). *Grundgesetze der Arithmetik* (Vol. 2). Jena: Pohle.
Landini, G. (1998). *Russell's Hidden Substitutional Theory*. New York: Oxford University Press.
Ramsey, F.P. (1925). The Foundations of Mathematics. Reprinted in F.P. Ramsey. (1990). *Philosophical Papers* (pp.164–224). Ed. D.H. Mellor. Cambridge: Cambridge University Press.
Russell, B. (1919). *Introduction to Mathematical Philosophy*. London: Allen and Unwin.
Whitehead, A.N. and Russell, B. (1910). *Principia Mathematica* (Vol. 1). Cambridge: Cambridge University Press.

Further Reading

Geach, P.T. (1981). Wittgenstein's Operator N. *Analysis*, 41, 168–170.
Ramsey, F.P. (1923). Critical Notice of *Tractatus Logico-Philosophicus*. *Mind*, 32, 465–478.
Russell, B. (1922). Introduction. In L. Wittgenstein. (1922). *Tractatus Logico-Philosophicus*. Trans. C.K. Ogden. London: Kegan Paul.
White, R.M. (1978). Wittgenstein on Identity. *Proceedings of the Aristotelian Society*, 78, 157–174.
White, R.M. (2006). *Wittgenstein's Tractatus Logico-Philosophicus: A Reader's Guide*. London: Continuum.

18

Wittgenstein's Early Philosophy of Mathematics

PASQUALE FRASCOLLA

1 Introduction

In this chapter I do not aim to provide a detailed examination of certain specific themes either of the philosophy of mathematics of the *Tractatus* or of that of the writings belonging to the so-called intermediate phase (1929–1933), i.e., the phase characterized by a deep revision of some of the principles of the picture theory, mainly conducted in a verificationist spirit. For instance, I do not go deeply into the definition of natural numbers as exponents of an operation (*Tractatus*) and I do not discuss the status of recursive definitions and proofs, the characterization of real numbers as effective laws of generation of rational approximations, etc. (intermediate phase). These are all topics thoroughly scrutinized in the secondary literature (see e.g., Frascolla, 1994, 2001; Glock, 1996; Marion, 1998). Wittgenstein's conceptions will be considered, instead, from a more general point of view, taking into account, not only classic positions in philosophy of mathematics such as formalism, but the controversy between realism and antirealism as well.

In my opinion, the treatment of arithmetic in the *Tractatus* reveals a radically antirealist stance, where by "radical antirealism" I mean a conception that deprives arithmetical propositions, identified with equations, of assertability and truth-aptness, by construing them as expressions of rules of syntax, of rules dealing with signs. (Following standard practice, I will be using "proposition" in order to avoid changes in the current English translation of the original German *"Satz,"* recalling that, in Wittgenstein's terminology, a *Satz* is not a mere syntactic entity but a declarative sentence with sense.) In the framework of the robust view of propositional meaning espoused in the *Tractatus*, which is to say in the framework of the picture theory (see Chapter 8, THE PICTURE THEORY), to attribute assertability and truth-aptness to arithmetical propositions would inevitably lead either to the Scylla of empiricism or to the Charybdis of Platonism. The *Tractatus*' radical antirealism thus results in a conception of mathematics that has remarkable points of contact with Hilbert's formalism, even though important qualifications will have to be added to that statement in order to make it minimally acceptable.

A Companion to Wittgenstein, First Edition. Edited by Hans-Johann Glock and John Hyman.
© 2017 John Wiley & Sons, Ltd. Published 2017 by John Wiley & Sons, Ltd.

From the viewpoint adopted here, the main difference between the *Tractatus* and the intermediate-phase conception is that, contrary to what happens in the former, the latter allows mathematical propositions of a specific kind, and arithmetical identities among them, to be included in the domain of sense. The abandonment of the picture theory, indeed, frees the notion of the sense of a mathematical proposition from any realistic implications. A sense can be ascribed even to those propositional constructions that don't play a descriptive role, but are instead expressions of rules of grammar in disguise. Wittgenstein's overall linguistic approach prompts him to construe the necessary conceptual connections established by mathematical theorems in terms of *rules* of logical syntax or grammar. This *enduring* feature of his conceptions gives to his intermediate-phase considerations on mathematics a typical formalistic flavor as well, overtly shown by the claim of the priority of signs over the sphere of reference.

However, it seems to me that the genuine *peculiarity* of Wittgenstein's 1929–1933 philosophy of mathematics is his attempt to find an area of mathematical discourse whose propositions have a grammar that, to a certain extent, is *analogous* to that of descriptive propositions. This is tantamount to asking whether there are mathematical propositions that have a definite mathematical content *before* their proof is constructed: the actual availability of a proof would be but the warrant to assert them, not the condition for conferring a sense on them, exactly as it happens with the actual availability of evidence supporting descriptive propositions. As we shall see, within the strong verificationist framework of the 1929–1933 writings (approximately, from the *Philosophical Remarks* to the *Blue Book*), the relative autonomy of sense from proof is confined to those propositions belonging to a system of propositions that can be decided by means of a general procedure of calculation, an algorithm of checking. On the other hand, isolated propositions, i.e., propositions that do not belong to a system and do not meet the verificationist requirements, acquire a definite mathematical content only through the construction of a proof: the proof is the means to determine their sense, not to settle the question of their truth value.

2 Mathematics, Thought, Assertoric Content: *Tractatus*

From our perspective, the axis around which the philosophy of mathematics of the *Tractatus* pivots is the thesis clearly stated in section 6.21: "A proposition of mathematics does not express a thought." To convey thoughts is the function of those linguistic constructions that the picture theory qualifies as meaningful propositions; for that reason, if mathematical propositions don't convey thoughts, they are pseudo-propositions (see TLP 6.2). The identification of mathematical propositions with equations in that same section 6.2 could lead someone to believe that their status as pseudo-propositions essentially depends on that identification and on the peculiar way the relation of identity is treated in the *Tractatus*. In my opinion, that would be a gross error: no mathematical proposition can be the conveyor of a thought. As a matter of fact, however, the restriction of Wittgenstein's focus on equations (arithmetical identities) has a double advantage: (a) it enables him to exploit the rejection of the interpretation of identity as a relation between objects for his purposes in the philosophy of mathematics; (b) it enables him to eschew the problem of how his thesis applies to such propositions as, for instance, "17 is prime," whose superficial syntactic form strongly suggests that a property is predicated of an object, a speech act that can be quite naturally described as the assertive expression of a thought. It is possible that Wittgenstein did not have a clear idea about how to extend his approach to areas of mathematics other than the equational fragment of arithmetic, where it seems to work smoothly. Ramsey's attack on the *Tractatus* conception as a "ridiculously narrow view of mathematics" (Ramsey, 1931, p.17), however, was misdirected. For it is reasonable to think that Wittgenstein did not mean the treatment of the equational fragment of arithmetic as an exhaustive exposition but rather as a model for the interpretation of the remaining parts of mathematics.

In virtue of the characterization of the notion of a thought as the logical picture of states of affairs, a mathematical proposition, insofar as it does not express a thought, is not even the logical picture of a state of affairs. So as not to pointlessly complicate things, we consider only the thoughts conveyed by elementary propositions, which are logical pictures of states of affairs (possible combinations of objects), in clothing accessible to the senses. It is easy to show how truth-aptness is a property of thoughts and hence, derivatively, of the propositions that express them. It is only because it is the logical picture of a state of affairs that a thought, or the corresponding elementary proposition, can be endowed with the bipolarity true/false (and truth-aptness is but a corollary of this bipolarity): truth, indeed, consists in the obtaining of the state of affairs that is depicted; falsity in its non-obtaining (see also Chapter 27, WITTGENSTEIN ON TRUTH). Since a proposition asserts the existence of the state of affairs that it represents and, in so doing, puts forward a claim to truth, the very assertability of a proposition, the belonging of its content to the doxastic and epistemic domain, to the sphere of what can be judged, comes to depend on its being truth-apt and thus, ultimately, on its capacity to express a thought.

In short, the *Tractatus* presents a series of interconnected robust notions of assertoric content (thought), truth-aptness, and truth of a proposition, based on the principles of the picture theory. I speak of "robust notions" because they do not rest either upon superficial syntactic features of propositions (what PI §464 calls their "surface grammar", see also TLP 3.325; NL 106) or on the typical modes of their use. Instead, they have their place and their justification within a theory of the greatest generality about the workings of the linguistic representation of reality. An immediate corollary of that theory is the exclusion of whole classes of sentences from the domain of assertability and truth-aptness, and their condemnation as pseudo-propositions. Mathematical propositions are just a particularly significant case of a class ruled out of that domain, together with the class of propositions of ethics, aesthetics, religion, semantics, metalogic, the theoretical apparatus of natural science, and so on. Acknowledging mathematical propositions as genuine would mean conceiving of them either as pictures of the same states of affairs depicted by meaningful propositions (empiricism), or as pictures of states of affairs of a special kind – ethereal states of affairs in a different logical space, necessarily obtaining, if obtaining (Platonism). But for various reasons neither of the two alternatives was acceptable within the theoretical framework of the *Tractatus*.

This is enough, as far as the *pars destruens* of the *Tractatus*' philosophy of mathematics is concerned, the part leading to the negative conclusion that mathematical propositions don't belong to the domain of assertability, and hence are pseudo-propositions. What, then, is their function, their semantic status? As noted earlier, Wittgenstein's answer to that question is confined to arithmetical identities (equations). But, fortunately, it is developed in detail: it actually contains the cornerstones of the *pars construens* of the *Tractatus*' philosophy of mathematics. Preliminarily, we must not underestimate the circumstance that Wittgenstein gives a definition of the infinite series of expressions of the form $\Omega^{0+1+1+...+1'}x$, by induction on the number of occurrences of "+1" (see TLP 6.02). That definition is to be understood as a characterization of the formal concept of a natural number according to which it is identified with the number of applications of a logical operation to the result of its own application. In this peculiar sense, a natural number is conceived of as "the exponent of an operation" (a clear anticipation of the treatment of natural numbers within Church's λ-calculus), a conception which Wittgenstein opposes to the logicist definition of the notion of a cardinal number as the number of elements of a class (as TLP 6.031 declares: "The theory of classes is completely superfluous in mathematics" – a *leitmotiv* in Wittgenstein's whole reflection on mathematics).

Moreover, a definition of the product of two natural numbers is framed as follows: $\Omega^{\nu\times\mu}{}'x = (\Omega^\nu)^\mu{}'x$ (see TLP 6.241). Sections 6.02 and 6.241, taken together, lend significant textual support to the interpretive conjecture that Wittgenstein had in mind a sort of reduction of arithmetic to the formal properties of logical operations. As a result of that reduction, the operational equation $\Omega^t{}'x = \Omega^s{}'x$ is associated to the arithmetical identity **t = s** in such a way that the latter is a theorem of the equational fragment of arithmetic if, and only if, the former is a theorem of a general theory of operations, whose principles are left partially implicit (on this topic see Frascolla, 1994, ch.1; 1997). Nonetheless, in articulating his properly philosophical reflections, Wittgenstein chooses not to explore his sketchy reductionist project and concentrates upon arithmetical identities as such: for this reason, we will present his views without taking into account that project.

Actually, the first comment on section 6.21, viz., 6.221, is concerned with mathematical propositions in general, not exclusively with equations; "in real life" they are used as inferential devices, which allow us to derive a non-mathematical conclusion from equally non-mathematical premises. Here, "in real life" is to be understood as: in applied mathematics, where calculation is used as a *tool* for the *description of the factual world*. As a very simple example, take the case in which the empirical conclusion that there are 12 apples in a basket, if 5 apples and then 7 apples have been put in it (the two empirical premises), is drawn by means of the arithmetical identity "5 + 7 = 12". That the latter works as a rule is shown by the fact that, if a different result had been found by counting the apples in the basket, the conclusion should have been drawn that either an error in counting had been made or that some apple had disappeared or some new apple had been added.

In section 6.22, equations are compared with tautologies insofar as the former do in mathematics what the latter do in logic, i.e., show "the logic of the world." A plausible reading of that passage goes as follows: just as there are no possible worlds in which it rains and it is cold but, at the same time, it doesn't rain (in virtue of the fact that $p.q\,\colon\,\supset\,\colon p$ is a tautology), so there are no possible worlds in which a number of apples different from 12 is found in the basket mentioned above, if the counting is correct and no apple has disappeared and no new apple has been added (because of the correctness of the arithmetical identity "5 + 7 = 12"). The matching of equations with tautologies, however, is to be taken with a pinch of salt, because, to a certain extent, it is misleading. Whereas tautologies are limiting cases of the meaningful propositional nexus – i.e., propositions true for every truth possibility of their elementary constituents – and therefore are *sinnlos* (senseless), equations are not truth functions of elementary propositions, and therefore are *unsinnig* (nonsensical): they are *Scheinsätze*, as all other linguistic expressions resulting from the attempt to say what can only been shown.

In giving his interpretation of equations, Wittgenstein sets out the task of clarifying the status of the propositions belonging to pure mathematics and, accordingly, the role of proofs. The sign of identity "=" occurs in equations: as is well known (see TLP 5.53–5.5352), the conception of identity as a relation between objects is rejected in the *Tractatus* and the sign "=" is explained away in the logically ideal notation by means of the double move consisting in the exclusive interpretation of variables and in the assumption of a one-to-one correspondence between objects and their names (individual constants). Even though there are no elementary propositions of the form "$a=a$" or "$a=b$," and *a fortiori* no truth functions of them, the sign of identity "=" is at home in equations. Nonetheless, it cannot be used there to make genuine assertions, that is, to do something that has been declared illegitimate in general. Identity statements formulate rules of substitution of signs and hence, in particular, "equations express the substitutability of two expressions" (TLP 6.24). Now, the fact that, if $a=b$, then "a" and "b" are interchangeable *salva veritate* (in every extensional context, and the TLP allows no others) is the Principle of Indiscernibility of Identicals, one of the foundations of the logical theory of identity. According to that theory, the substitutability *salva veritate* of "a" and "b" directly follows from the identity of their denotation. But what is the ground of their interchangeability, in the absence of any objective reference of the arithmetical terms flanking the identity sign "="? This is the true key point in Wittgenstein's view, which he seeks to articulate through a comparison with Frege's position.

First of all, it is worth noting that, in agreement with Frege's terminology, he speaks of identity of meaning (*Identität der Bedeutung*) of the two terms occurring in a correct (*richtige*) equation (see TLP 6.2322). But the convergence is merely terminological since the core of these sections is precisely the outright rejection of Frege's mature view espoused in his article "*Über Sinn und Bedeutung*" (1892) and the grounding of the substitutability of the two expressions occurring in a correct equation, not in the identity of their denotations, but in *the formal properties of the expressions themselves*:

> If two expressions are combined by means of the sign of equality, that means that they can be substituted for one another. But it must be manifest in the two expressions themselves whether this is the case or not. (TLP 6.23)

Let us see in detail how Wittgenstein expounds his conception.

The condition for an equation "$A=B$" to be correct is the formal possibility of transforming "A" into "B" and vice versa, i.e., the possibility of obtaining both the expressions through the manipulation of one and the same expression "C." For instance, the correctness of the identity "$3+1=2+2$" is grounded in the possibility of obtaining both the arithmetical terms "$(1+1+1)+1$" and "$(1+1)+(1+1)$" by grouping the string "$1+1+1+1$" in two different ways. This structural relation between the two expressions can be grasped by *visual perception* (a sort of *seeing as*, on which see Chapter 33, WITTGENSTEIN ON SEEING ASPECTS) and is characterized by Wittgenstein as identity of meaning, or equivalence in meaning (*Bedeutungsgleichheit*), of the two expressions. In Wittgenstein's view, as opposed to Frege's, the identity or equivalence of *Bedeutung* of two arithmetical expressions is not an objective relation between their alleged denotations: it is construed instead as a formal property of the expressions themselves. Despite the terminological similarity, nothing could be farther from Frege's interpretation of identity statements. Since, according to the principles of the picture theory, assertion and reference to objects are indissolubly intertwined, a corollary of Wittgenstein's view is that an equation is not used to make an assertion (there is no thought for whose truth a claim is made), but to mark the fact that the two terms flanking the sign of identity are considered as interchangeable (see TLP 6.2323).

The thesis that an equation's being correct is a circumstance utterly independent of the actual configuration of the world and, therefore, ascertainable a priori, just as a logical formula's being a tautology, is justified by the nature of equations, which deal exclusively with structural properties of signs (see TLP 6.2321). In more complicated cases, it is through *calculation*, namely, through the construction of a proof, that the correctness of an equation can be established. Within the equational fragment of arithmetic, calculation is based on the method of substitution (see TLP 6.24): the conclusion that "A" is interchangeable with "B" is drawn, and the correctness of "A = B" is proven, by obtaining "B" from "A" by means of symbolic transitions which are allowed by other equations (rules of substitution) whose correctness has been previously proven. Since equations express rules of substitution, calculation justifies the adoption of derived rules of substitution and has nothing to do with the process of verification of factual statements. It is not by chance that the sort of slogan that condenses Wittgenstein's later reflections on mathematics – "Calculation is not an experiment" – makes its first appearance in the *Tractatus* (TLP 6.2331); for the same reason, intuition (*Anschauung*), if it is directed to the way the world is, is banished from the processes of solving mathematical problems (see TLP 6.233).

Let me make one final observation regarding the position of the *Tractatus*' view of mathematics with respect to other influential tendencies in the philosophy of mathematics. In my opinion, the treatment of equations shows how the radical antirealism of the *Tractatus* inevitably leads to an account of arithmetic close to *formalism*. When I speak of the formalistic flavor of the *Tractatus*' philosophy of mathematics, I mean only to stress the rejection of a realm of ethereal objects, whose properties and relations would be depicted by mathematical sentences. Its spirit is formalistic insofar as the sole reality that mathematics deals with is that of signs (note: not "the sole reality that mathematics *describes*," because mathematics is neither the description of the physical properties of signs nor the description of the calculating behavior of human agents). It is not enough to say that in pure mathematics there is no thought, no truth-aptness, no assertability; it must be added that it deals only with the formulation and derivation of *rules for the use of signs*, ultimately grounded in the recognition of their *formal properties*. To be sure, when equations are applied "in real life" they prove to be indispensable tools to infer factual conclusions from factual premises, and thus they gain a definitely more solid status than that of mere rules of sign manipulation. Nonetheless, the rank assigned to the propositions of pure mathematics by the radically antirealist view of the *Tractatus* is exactly that of rules dealing with signs.

3 Mathematical Propositions: Sense, Proof, Method of Checking

In presenting Wittgenstein's 1929–1933 views, it is useful to start from an illuminating criticism he advances against the strategy he himself pursued in the *Tractatus*, in order to draw that sharp distinction between meaningful propositions and arithmetical equations that deprives the latter of any assertoric content (the writings of the intermediate phase I will be referring to are those published in PR, BT, WVC, AWL). The earlier approach is charged with inconsistency. One cannot maintain that the general form of the proposition is represented by the schema "This and that is the case" and, at the same time, deny the status of propositions to arithmetical identities; indeed, it is quite correct to say: it is the case that $2 + 2 = 4$. Wittgenstein does not call into question the goal of drawing the factual vs. arithmetical propositions distinction in terms of possession, or lack, of assertoric content; rather, the problem is that the *Tractatus* didn't succeed in achieving it. If one wants to rule mathematical propositions out of the field of assertability, out of the epistemic sphere, "additional rules are needed" (BT 78). But what might these new rules be, once the picture theory is no longer in the background to supply the theoretical means that fix the bounds of sense and, with them, those of assertability and truth-aptness?

Before trying to answer this question, a general remark is worth making: Wittgenstein is still engaged in the attempt to draw distinctions, to throw light on differences in grammar, between the propositions that have a descriptive function, on the one hand, and the propositions of pure mathematics, on the other. Even though it is just a rule of grammar, and nothing else, which establishes the connection between the truth of the belief or statement that p and the obtaining of the state of affairs that p (the belief or statement that p is true if and only if p), its indiscriminate extension to the domain of mathematics would be deeply misleading, because it would lead us to misrepresent the modes of use of mathematical sentences and to generate the false picture of an ontology of ethereal entities.

The core of Wittgenstein's view is that theorems are not used to make assertions but to express rules of grammar (see also Chapter 14, GRAMMAR AND GRAMMATICAL STATEMENTS). It is not only geometrical theorems that express grammatical rules of that portion of language whereby relations (metrical and other) between spatial bodies are described. Arithmetical theorems, too, express grammatical rules of the language whereby both numerical properties of sets of empirical objects and manipulations of the arithmetical signs themselves by calculating agents are described (arithmetic as "a more general kind of geometry", PR §109). Let us take a simple arithmetical identity like "$12 \times 13 = 156$"; an apt paraphrase could go as follows (the availability of the general method of multiplication of two numbers in decimal notation being presupposed): if number 12 is correctly multiplied by number 13, the number 156 *must* result. Here the "must" is to be construed as showing that a rule of grammar has been adopted, an effect of which is that to speak of a correct multiplication of those two numbers resulting in a number different from 156 doesn't make sense (see AWL 16, 162). Because of the acceptance of the proof of that arithmetical identity, obtaining 156 as a result has become part of the meaning of the expression "correctly multiplying 12 times 13." In equivalent non-linguistic terms, because of the acceptance of the proof, obtaining 156 as a result has become a distinguishing mark of the concept of *correctly multiplying 12 times 13*. This is the reason why to assert that an individual X has obtained a number different from 156 by correctly multiplying those two numbers *doesn't make sense*. Once the grammar rule has been adopted, a criterion to judge the multiplications effectively worked out on given occasions by calculating agents becomes available and the possibility of charging them with miscalculations is established.

A perfectly analogous conclusion can be drawn regarding arithmetical theorems of subject–predicate form, such as "65.537 is prime." Taking the meaning of the predicate "prime" for granted and, with it, the knowledge of a method of calculation to establish whether any given number n greater than 2 is prime or not, the theorem can be paraphrased as follows: by correctly dividing the number 65.537 by every number in the interval from 2 to $\frac{65.536}{2}$, a remainder different from 0 must result. The necessity of the "must" rests on the rule of grammar adopted as a consequence of the construction of the proof of the theorem: every statement that anyone of those divisions, correctly worked out, results in a remainder equal to 0, is condemned as nonsense. That rule provides us with a *criterion* to judge the behavior of calculating agents and allows us to infer the conclusion that a miscalculation has been made, whenever a remainder equal to 0 has been obtained.

The above-given paraphrase of arithmetical identities such as "$12 \times 13 = 156$" and of subject–predicate theorems like "65.537 is prime" has the value of a general model and facilitates understanding the relation between Wittgenstein's philosophy of mathematics and formalism. First of all, as the case of "65.537 is prime" clearly shows, we should not allow superficial syntactic form to mislead us. That form of words suggests that we are dealing with the attribution of a property to an object, and hence, that we should construe that arithmetical statement as a statement that is about the entity denoted by the numeral occurring as subject. The paraphrase enables us to free ourselves from the tyranny of syntactic form and to acknowledge the role as a court of last appeal that *use* plays in matters of semantic interpretation. The theorem expresses a rule of grammar that the construction of the proof prompts us to adopt, and therefore does not imply any reference to a reality different from that of signs and of the rules of the language whereby the sign-employing behavior of calculating agents is described. The priority of symbols, i.e., of signs that have a rule-governed use, and the rejection of any ontology of ethereal entities whose properties and relations would be described by mathematical statements also make Wittgenstein's intermediate views close to formalism.

Nonetheless, the equally crucial differences between the two conceptions should not be overlooked. According to Wittgenstein, signs are not the entities that mathematical theorems are about. In other words, it is not a question of replacing a Platonic reality with a concrete reality as the object of mathematical investigations, because mathematics does not *talk about* signs, it *operates* with them (see WVC 34; PR §157; BT 582). Accordingly, there is no epistemological priority that the cognitive relation with signs would have over the (purported) cognitive relation we would entertain with the most abstract regions of mathematics, as in Hilbert's conception of finitary mathematics. Both for Wittgenstein and Hilbert, the intuition (*Einsicht*) of the structural, combinatorial properties of signs is at the root of arithmetic, coming long before any logical performances or insights – contrary to the logicism of Frege and Russell. For Wittgenstein, however, it does not provide mathematics with a firm epistemic foundation, but characterizes our agreed-upon practice of employing certain sign configurations as models of what the correct application of given operations consists in. And that holds good of all areas of mathematics, even of those that are very far from the most elementary part of arithmetic and that involve only inferential transitions.

The role of theorems as rules of grammar, which is opposed to the descriptive function performed by other sentential constructions, places theorems in a sphere where speaking of belief and knowledge would not be appropriate. Despite the substantial continuity with the line of thought of the *Tractatus*, however, that very line undergoes notable changes brought about by the collapse of the picture theory. The latter constrains the notion of the sense of a proposition by the principles of a universalistic schema, culminating in the "general propositional form" being stated as "This is how things stand" (see TLP 4.5; cf. Chapter 17, LOGIC AND THE *TRACTATUS*). Once this constraint is abandoned, the attribution of sense to a mathematical proposition is freed from the realistic implications it inevitably had in the early masterpiece. Actually, a large part of Wittgenstein's 1929–1933 reflections on mathematics is concerned with the question of the sense of mathematical propositions and, inextricably intertwined with it, the question of the relation between *sense* and *proof*. His attention focuses on the issue of the sense that should be acknowledged for mathematical propositions that have *not yet been proven*. And it is in discussing this theme that what can be considered the peculiar trait of the intermediate Wittgenstein's view emerges.

The following question can be our starting point: under what conditions is one allowed to speak of mathematical propositions in a sense that is sufficiently akin to that in which we ordinarily speak of propositions when dealing with the descriptive areas of discourse? Obviously, raising that question presupposes that, as far as the descriptive area is concerned, a general characterization of the notion of a proposition can be given, that provides us with a standard, a term of comparison, by means of which the legitimacy of its extension to mathematics can be measured. Though the intermediate Wittgenstein recognizes that several sentential structures, which widely differ in their modes of use, fall within the grammatical category of propositions, he espouses a verificationist conception of those sentences that carry out a descriptive function: the understanding of a genuine proposition is to be identified with the knowledge of an empirical method to ascertain whether it is true or false. I eschew any discussion of the pros and cons of this interpretation of the intermediate Wittgenstein, but what I am going to say about his view of mathematics lends a strong support to that interpretation.

In order to clarify better the terms of the problem, it is worthwhile recalling an aspect of the verificationist conception on which Wittgenstein much insists. In identifying the sense of a statement with the method of its verification or checking, it is required that that sense be *independent* of the result of the application of the method. It is the old story of the independence of the understanding of a proposition from the knowledge of its truth value (see TLP 4.024). In the verificationist setting, this translates into the independence of the knowledge of the general method of checking from the knowledge of the results of its application in each particular case. A proposition must be understandable without our knowing whether it is true or false and, conversely, there is no feedback from the knowledge of the truth value to the understanding of a proposition. (When I verify the sentence "it's raining" by looking out of the window of my room, the sense of the sentence, its grammar, doesn't change.) In mathematics it is the construction of a proof that establishes the truth of a sentence and transforms it into a theorem (while the construction of a refutation establishes its falsity). For that reason, if we want to extend the use of the notion of a proposition from the descriptive areas of discourse to mathematics, we are required to individuate those cases, if any, in which the understanding of a mathematical statement is independent of the actual construction of its proof. In Wittgenstein's words:

> The proposition $26 \times 13 = 338$ is essentially one of a system of propositions (the system given in the formula $a \times b = c$), and the corresponding question one of a system of questions. The question whether 26×13 equals 338 is bound up with one particular *general method* by means of which it is answered [...]. [The fundamental law of algebra] seems to

> get its sense from the proof, while the propositions stating what the product in a multiplication is do not [...]. In the case of the question about the product of 26 and 13, there is something about it which makes it look like an empirical question. Suppose I ask whether there is a man in the garden. I could describe beforehand a complicated way of finding out whether there is or not. There is a resemblance of the multiplication question to this one, in that before you find out I could tell you how to find out. (AWL 197–8)

It is worth noting that the above passage stems from students' notes of a lecture given by Wittgenstein in 1935, which testifies to the persistence of the verificationist conception of propositions even after 1933. Elsewhere, in the same spirit, he declares:

> We come back to the question: In what sense can we assert a mathematical proposition? That is: what would mean nothing would be to say that I can only assert it if it's correct. – No, to be able to make an assertion I must do so with reference to its sense, not its truth. (PR §150)

These are the conditions that need to be satisfied if the extension of the use of the descriptive notion of a proposition to mathematics is to be legitimate. Indeed, there are large portions of mathematics where those conditions are met, namely, wherever a *general method of checking*, a uniform decision procedure is available, which can be applied to every member of a whole system of propositions sharing the same form. Needless to say, that method can be mastered *independently* of knowledge of the results of its application in each particular case. That is precisely the conclusion Wittgenstein draws from his investigations into the possibility of treating mathematical propositions by analogy with the descriptive ones:

> So if I want to ask a question that's independent of the truth of the proposition, I have to speak of *checking* its truth, not of proving or disproving it. The method of checking corresponds to what one can call the sense of the mathematical proposition. The description of this method is a general one and refers to a system of propositions, for instance of propositions of the form $a \times b = c$. [...] If it's impossible to speak of such a check, then the analogy between 'mathematical propositions' and what we otherwise call propositions collapses. (BT 624–5)

Once this step is taken, others follow in a cascade. Actually, a whole constellation of notions, as characterized by the verificationist conception, can aptly be extended to mathematical propositions, as a consequence of that first step. Such notions as that of assertability, of truth-aptness, of discovery, of conjecture, which are at home in those areas of discourse where propositions carry out a descriptive function, find a natural use also with reference to those parts of mathematics where the conditions imposed by the verificationist model are satisfied. For instance, since an effective method of checking the property of being prime is available, speaking of the *conjecture* that 65.537 is prime, of the *question* whether 65.537 is prime, of the *discovery* of the fact that 65.537 is prime, is acknowledged as appropriate:

> We may only put a question in mathematics (or make a conjecture) where the answer runs "I must work it out". [...] What "mathematical questions" share with genuine questions is simply that they can be answered. (PR §151)

A non-negligible consequence of the strong verificationist delimitation of the domain of meaningful mathematical propositions is that the latter is governed by the laws of classical logic and, in particular, by the Principle of Excluded Middle, represented by the formula "$p \vee \sim p$." In virtue of that delimitation, a meaningful mathematical proposition is effectively decidable, in the sense that an algorithm to prove or disprove it, and hence to establish whether it is true or false, is available. In general, "every significant proposition must teach us through its sense how we are to convince ourselves whether it is true or false. 'Every proposition says what is the case if it is true'. And with a mathematical proposition this 'what is the case' must refer to the way in which it is to be proved" (PR §148). According to Wittgenstein's antirealist reading, the Principle of Excluded Middle entails that every proposition must be either provable or refutable; but this is the very condition that holds by definition of *all* meaningful mathematical propositions, as he characterize them (see BT 626–7). This is the reason why Wittgenstein distances himself from the intuitionists' rejection of the Principle of Excluded Middle: "I need hardly say that where the law of excluded middle doesn't apply, no other law of logic applies either, because in that case we are not dealing with propositions of mathematics (Against Weyl and Brouwer)" (PR § 151).

According to Wittgenstein, as soon as one crosses the boundaries of verificationism, the attempt to represent the grammar of mathematical discourse by analogy with the representation of the grammar of the descriptive areas of discourse loses any glimmer of plausibility. The critical point, which clearly shows the collapse of the analogy when the verificationist requirements are not fulfilled, concerns the relation between sense and proof. To aptly illustrate the point, let's take a look at Wittgenstein's treatment of the statements of number in pure mathematics, like the theorems "there are six permutations of a three-element set" or "there are infinitely many prime numbers". First of all, Wittgenstein makes a general distinction between statements of number about *empirical concepts* and statements of number about *formal concepts*, mathematical concepts included:

> What distinguishes a statement of number that refers to a concept from one that refers to a variable? The first is a proposition about the concept, the second a grammatical rule concerning the variable. (BT 600)

It is one of Wittgenstein's major tenets about formal concepts that, in an adequate notation, these should be represented by variables. There is nothing new here. As we know, the specific role of mathematical theorems in linguistic practice is that of expressing rules of grammar. What is new is that, if we assume that the general formula for calculating the number of permutations of an n-element set is not available, the sentence "there are six permutations of a three-element set" does not fall within the range of genuine mathematical propositions. Under that assumption, it is the proof that determines the sense of the statement of number because it shows us how the predicate "permutation of a three-element set" is to be understood by listing all the objects to which we are inclined to apply it, namely, by exhibiting the ratified extension of the predicate. By means of the proof of the statement that there are six permutations of a three-element set, the single permutations are *distinguished*, not *counted* (and a similar point can be made as far as the statement of number "there are two roots of a second-degree equation" is concerned).

But a reasonable objection can be raised to Wittgenstein's contention, a quite natural objection from a mathematician's viewpoint: an intensional definition of the general predicate "permutation of a set" can easily be given (a permutation of a set A is a one-to-one function from A onto A) and then a proof of the statement that there are six permutations of a three-element set can be constructed, in which those permutations are counted. It is the peculiar way in which the intermediate Wittgenstein construes the relation between general and particular in the whole domain of grammar, and hence of mathematics, that justifies his claim: no general intensional characterization of a concept can determine beforehand what we will be inclined to acknowledge as *particular cases falling under the concept*. It is only by showing what we are willing to count as permutations of a three-element set, that the proof provides the statement of number "there are six permutations of a three-element set" with a definite mathematical content.

A comparison with the different scenario in which the verificationist conditions are met is instructive (see BT 601–2). Let us suppose that the general formula for calculating the number of permutations of an n-element set, that is the formula Perm $(n) = n!$, is available. Then the statement "there are six permutations of a three-element set" belongs to the system of statements of the form "there are m permutations of an n-element set," each one decidable by means of the above-mentioned formula. For that reason, it has a definite mathematical sense *before* the calculation is worked out, i.e., before the general formula is applied to the particular case $n = 3$. In the earlier scenario, instead, the statement of number "there are six permutations of a three-element set" behaves as an isolated proposition and hence gets its sense from the proof, which is not the means for establishing the truth of a proposition previously endowed with a definite mathematical content. Things stand likewise in the case of the isolated statement of number "there are infinitely many prime numbers." Before a proof is given (for instance, Euclid's proof), it is the possibility of formulating the question as to the number of prime numbers in word-language that makes us believe that it has a definite mathematical sense. In this case, as in many others, language *deceives* us because it is only by supplying a proof that such a mathematical content is conferred on that statement: prime numbers are not counted by means of the proof (as if they were empirical objects), but a new distinguishing mark of the concept of a prime number is invented, once the proof is ratified as correct (see BT 628–37).

The problems in the search of whose solution professional mathematicians are engaged are not, of course, the genuine, meaningful problems for which a general method of solution is known in advance. It is only the construction of a solution, and its agreed-upon acceptance, that provides those more advanced problems with a definite mathematical sense. Beyond the boundaries of verificationism, the content of a not-yet proven conjecture is formed in the word-language (prose) and is often based on false analogies between the finite and the infinite. This is the case of Goldbach's conjecture, i.e., the conjecture that every even number greater than 2 is the sum of two primes, where the possibility of mechanically checking, given any even number greater than 2, whether it is the sum of two primes or not, together with the positive outcome of the verifications actually carried out up to now, brings about the deceptive appearance of the possession of a mathematical content. On the contrary, universality in mathematics always entails reference to a determinate general law: "the proposition 'It's possible – though not necessary – that p should hold for all numbers' is nonsense. For in mathematics '*necessary*' and '*all*' go together" (PR §154). It is that very law that we don't know in the case of Goldbach's conjecture and it is this lack of knowledge that deprives the unproven conjecture of any mathematical content.

The well-known story of Fermat's last theorem, i.e., the statement that there no natural numbers a, b, c (all different from 0) and n, with n greater than 2, such that $a^n + b^n = c^n$, enables us to better understand Wittgenstein's position. At the time he was writing, the statement of that then-alleged theorem was but "an empirical structure" which served as a signpost for mathematical research, a stimulus for mathematical constructions (see BT 619, 631). It is evident that the sense of the theorem radically changed, after Gerhard Frey put forward his Epsilon Conjecture, according to which if Fermat's last theorem were false, then an elliptic non-modular curve would exist; after Ken Ribet proved the Epsilon Conjecture; and, in the end, after Andrew Wiles brilliantly proved that every elliptic curve is modular (the Taniyama-Shimura Conjecture). The extremely complex network of inferential connections that form the environment of Wiles's proof is not even imaginable by all those who can grasp just the minimal sense of Fermat's last theorem: it is only its placement in that environment that enables all those who are immersed in it to give Fermat's last theorem a definite mathematical content. Wiles's proof has generated a new sense that nobody could anticipate and it is only the agreed-upon acceptance of the proof that transforms Fermat's last theorem from a mere empirical structure into a genuine piece of mathematics.

One last remark: since the rule-following considerations (see Chapter 24, RULES AND RULE-FOLLOWING) began playing a strategic role in Wittgenstein's reflections (approximately, from 1934 onwards), no room was left for the attempt "to save" one area of mathematics from the doom of the isolated propositions of the intermediate phase. Not even the availability of a general method of calculation turns out to be enough to provide not-yet proven propositions with a definite mathematical content, because the formulation of the algorithm is no longer acknowledged as endowed with the normative force needed to establish what counts as a correct application of the rules of calculation in each particular case. What in the intermediate phase held exclusively of isolated propositions, holds henceforth of all mathematics, with no exceptions whatsoever.

References

Frascolla, P. (1994). *Wittgenstein's Philosophy of Mathematics*. London: Routledge.
Frascolla, P. (1997). The *Tractatus* System of Arithmetic. *Synthese*, 112, 353–378.
Frascolla, P. (2001). Philosophy of Mathematics. In H.-J. Glock (Ed.). (2001). *Wittgenstein. A Critical Reader* (pp.268–288). Oxford: Blackwell.
Frege, G. (1892). Über Sinn und Bedeutung. [On Sense and Meaning.] *Zeitschrift für Philosophie und philosophische Kritik*, 25–50.
Glock, H.-J. (1996). *A Wittgenstein Dictionary*. Oxford: Blackwell.
Marion, M. (1998). *Wittgenstein, Finitism and the Foundations of Mathematics*. Oxford: Oxford University Press.
Ramsey, F.P. (1931). *The Foundations of Mathematics and other Logical Essays*. Ed. R.B. Braithwaite. London: Routledge and Kegan Paul.

Further Reading

Ambrose, A. (1982). Wittgenstein on Mathematical Proof. *Mind*, 91, 264–372.
Black, M. (1965). Verificationism and Wittgenstein's Reflections on Mathematics. *Revue Internationale de Philosophie*, 23, 284–294.

Kremer, M. (2002). Mathematics and Meaning in the *Tractatus*. *Philosophical Investigations*, 25, 272–303.
Lampert, T. (2008). Wittgenstein on the Infinity of Primes. *History and Philosophy of Logic*, 29, 272–303.
Marion, M. (2003). Wittgenstein and Brouwer. *Synthese*, 137, 103–127.
Rodych, V. (1997). Wittgenstein on Mathematical Meaningfulness, Decidability, and Application. *Notre Dame Journal of Formal Logic*, 38, 195–224.
Schroeder, S.J. (2012). Conjecture, Proof and Sense in Wittgenstein's Philosophy of Mathematics. In C. Jäger and W. Löffler (Eds). *Epistemology: Contexts, Values, Disagreement* (pp.459–473). Frankfurt: Ontos.

19

Wittgenstein's Later Philosophy of Mathematics

A.W. MOORE

1 Introduction

The philosophy of mathematics was of colossal importance to Wittgenstein. Its problems had a peculiarly strong hold on him; and he seems, at times, to have thought that it was in addressing these problems that he produced his greatest work. Thus Rush Rhees recounts that, in the mid-1940s, when John Wisdom had written a short paragraph on Wittgenstein for inclusion in a biographical dictionary, he (Wisdom) sent the paragraph to Wittgenstein for comments, whereupon Wittgenstein recommended just one change, namely to add at the end: "Wittgenstein's chief contribution has been in the philosophy of mathematics" (see Monk, 1990/91, p.466; and 2007, p.273 and n.2).

Yet Wittgenstein's writings in the philosophy of mathematics stand in a curious relation to this self-assessment. By 1938 he had written an early version of his masterwork *Philosophical Investigations*, the second half of which was on the philosophy of mathematics (see also Chapter 1, WITTGENSTEIN'S PHILOSOPHICAL DEVELOPMENT). This material did not however survive into the version of *Philosophical Investigations* that was eventually published after his death. Instead it appeared, modified in various ways, along with notes that he wrote during World War II, as *Remarks on the Foundations of Mathematics*, another posthumous publication, assembled by his literary executors. Apart from this there are scattered remarks in other material that he had produced earlier, while his ideas were beginning to take shape, and there are notes taken by some of those who attended his lectures on the philosophy of mathematics (see especially PR, PG, and LFM). None of this was submitted for publication by Wittgenstein himself. And, be his own relation to this body of work as it may, its early reception, when it did appear (starting with RFM in 1956), was largely dismissive, if not positively contemptuous. Michael Dummett, in a passage that was not at all unrepresentative, wrote:

> Many of the thoughts [expressed in *Remarks on the Foundations of Mathematics*] are expressed in a manner which the author recognized as inaccurate or obscure; some passages contradict others; some are quite inconclusive; [...] other passages again, particularly those on consistency and on Gödel's theorem, are of poor quality or contain definite errors. (Dummett, 1959, p.166; see also Monk, 2007, sec.IV)

A Companion to Wittgenstein, First Edition. Edited by Hans-Johann Glock and John Hyman.
© 2017 John Wiley & Sons, Ltd. Published 2017 by John Wiley & Sons, Ltd.

My own view is that Wittgenstein's reflections on the philosophy of mathematics, for all the disarray with which they have been passed on to us, can indeed be seen as incorporating some of his greatest insights; and that the opposition that they provoked when they first appeared, and that they have continued to provoke since, is due largely to the combined difficulty and radicalness of these insights. My chief concern in this chapter is not however to substantiate that view. Instead I want to do something more oblique. I want to look at some questions of Wittgensteinian exegesis on which his philosophy of mathematics has a unique and critical bearing. These are questions in the first instance about his philosophy of philosophy (see also Chapter 13, PHILOSOPHY AND PHILOSOPHICAL METHOD).

2   Wittgenstein's Precept that Philosophy Leaves Everything (Including Mathematics) as it is, and his Distinction between Calculus and Prose

Wittgenstein famously says that "philosophy leaves everything as it is" (PI §124). Immediately after saying this he makes the same point specifically in connection with mathematics: "It also leaves mathematics as it is" (§124). He is expressing his well-known conviction that the proper role of philosophy is to save us from the confusions into which we fall when we misconstrue the functioning of our own language. Philosophy should not try to modify our language, still less to take issue with anything that is said in the proper exercise of it. It should just guide us to a clear view of it. In particular, philosophy has no business challenging any of the developments that mathematics has undergone. Its business is to challenge the extra-mathematical deliverances of those who, when they reflect on the nature of these developments, or on the nature of any other part of mathematics, misperceive the workings of the concepts being exercised and then mangle them in their struggle to provide a coherent account of what is going on there. (See PI §§89–133, and PG 369.)

So far, so familiar. So far, one might think, so reasonable. But here is the rub. Wittgenstein himself, in his own reflections on the nature of mathematics, makes claim after claim to outrage the working mathematician. Sometimes the mathematician's complaint would be that Wittgenstein misunderstands what it is to practice mathematics. Sometimes the complaint would be that he misunderstands the mathematics itself. Thus Gödel, in a letter to Abraham Robinson, dismisses Wittgenstein's remarks on his (Gödel's) famous incompleteness theorem on the grounds that they arise from "a completely trivial and uninteresting misinterpretation" (see Dawson, 1989, p.89). I do not myself believe that Wittgenstein misunderstood Gödel's theorem. (For a helpful corrective see Floyd, 2001; and Kienzler and Grève, 2016. See also Moore, 1998, sec. 5, for reflections of my own on this matter.) But even if I am right about that and Gödel is wrong, what about all the rest of what Wittgenstein says to give mathematicians umbrage? Time after time he seems, either through incompetence or by design, to violate his own philosophical precept that philosophy should leave mathematics as it is. But how credible is it that he should really have done so – so often, and so flagrantly? I hope I am not exhibiting undue deference to the master by registering my skepticism on this score. It is a question of how plausible it is that someone should be as steeped in such a distinctive conception of philosophy as this and then not be sensitive to ways in which his own philosophical work, including what may even be some of his greatest philosophical work, flies in the face of it. If Wittgenstein makes claim after claim to outrage the working mathematician, then the explanation had surely better not be either that he is simply oblivious to the fact or that, despite his own philosophical scruples, he is bent on reform of mathematical practice.

In fact, of course, another explanation is available, and one that looks entirely consonant both with his conception of philosophy and with his practice of it. There is mathematics; and there is what people are inclined to say about mathematics. Wittgenstein's target consists of confusions that beset the latter. And it would not be the least surprising if the people most prone to these confusions were mathematicians themselves. They are the people most likely to have opinions about the nature of mathematics, and there is no reason whatsoever why, in arriving at these opinions, they should be any less susceptible to the kinds of confusions that Wittgenstein is concerned to combat than the rest of us. Just the opposite in fact. "A mathematician is bound to be horrified by my mathematical comments," Wittgenstein writes, "since he has always been trained to avoid indulging thoughts and doubts of the kind I develop" (PG, 381–2). Again: "What a mathematician is inclined to say about the objectivity and reality of mathematical facts, is not a philosophy of mathematics, but something for philosophical *treatment*" (PI §254, emphasis in original).

That last comment has a quite specific target. In an article in *Mind* the celebrated mathematician G.H. Hardy wrote that "[the] truth or falsity [of mathematical theorems] is absolute and independent of our knowledge of them," adding that "in *some* sense, mathematical truth is part of objective reality" (Hardy, 1929, p.4, emphasis in original). The same view has been stoutly defended more recently by another celebrated mathematician, Roger Penrose, who describes the way in which, in mathematics, "human thought [seems to be] [...] guided towards some eternal external truth – a truth which has a reality of its own, and which is revealed only partially to any one of us," and who, in the old debate about whether mathematics is invention or discovery, accordingly places himself, with only minor qualifications, in the latter camp (Penrose, 1989, pp.95–6). This view is an anathema to Wittgenstein. "The mathematician is an inventor," Wittgenstein insists, "not a discoverer" (RFM I §168; cf. RFM II §38). Not that Wittgenstein's stance on this issue puts him at odds with *all* mathematicians. There are distinguished mathematicians who have been as keen as he is to reject the picture of mathematics as discovery (see e.g., Cohen, 1967, and Davies, 2003). When mathematicians reflect on the nature of their own discipline, some of them incline one way in this debate, some of them the other. What *can* plausibly be said to put Wittgenstein at odds with all mathematicians, or at least with all but the most atypical of mathematicians, is not his stance on this issue, but the way in which he maintains it.

Eschewing the picture of mathematics as discovery, he denies that the propositions of mathematics have a subject matter in anything like the way in which the propositions of physics or geography have a subject matter. Rather, in establishing the truth of a mathematical proposition, we are forming new concepts, establishing new ways of making sense of things, contributing to "a network of norms" (RFM VII §67). And, in asserting a mathematical proposition, we are not saying how things are, still less saying how things are independently of us; we are enunciating one of our rules of representation (see e.g., M 72). It follows, for Wittgenstein, that we need to look to the proof of a mathematical proposition to find out what was being proved, and hence that, in one sense of "understand," we cannot really be said to understand a mathematical proposition unless we are in command of a proof of it (e.g., RFM V §§42–6, and PG 369–76; cf. PI §578). *That* is certainly at odds with what the typical mathematician thinks. Very few people are in command of the proof of Fermat's last theorem, for instance, but most mathematicians would feel no compunction about crediting anyone who has mastered basic high-school mathematics with an understanding of what the theorem states, in any but an absurdly and unhelpfully demanding sense of "understanding." Or consider Goldbach's conjecture. At the time of my writing this, the conjecture has been neither proved nor disproved. Yet most mathematicians would not think twice about saying that the conjecture is already fully intelligible, again in any but an absurdly and unhelpfully demanding sense of "intelligible." How else, the mathematician is liable to ask, can anyone be engaged in trying to settle it, something that plenty in the profession are, indeed, engaged in trying to do? (Not that Wittgenstein is unaware of this objection, incidentally: see e.g., RFM VI §13; and cf. PI §578. He acknowledges the less demanding senses of "understanding" and has characteristically helpful comments to make about these. Nevertheless, he continues to insist on the significance of the more demanding sense.)

It is plain, then, that there is a crucial role to be played in Wittgenstein's philosophy of mathematics by the distinction between what the mathematician says when strictly engaged in mathematical practice and what the mathematician says, however instinctively, and with however little sense of departure from such practice, when not so engaged. Wittgenstein notes that mathematicians themselves are alive to this sort of distinction. There is a reference in one of his lectures to the way in which mathematicians look upon "interpretations of mathematical symbols [as] [...] some kind of gas which surrounds the real process, the essential mathematical kernel" (LFM 1). Here he is once again echoing Hardy, who, in the article from which I have already quoted, defines "gas" as "rhetorical flourishes designed to affect psychology, pictures on the board in the lecture, devices to stimulate the imagination of pupils" (Hardy, 1929, p.18). Elsewhere, in a similar vein, Wittgenstein distinguishes between what he calls the "calculus" and what he calls the surrounding "prose" (WVC 149). "Prose" is perhaps a more suitable term than "gas," because it is not pejorative (or at any rate, not relevantly pejorative). Wittgenstein never suggests that there is anything wrong with such prose in itself. Nor should he. As the quotation from Hardy testifies, the prose that surrounds the calculus may play an indispensable heuristic role. The point, however, is that it is the prose that will harbor any confusions of the kind that Wittgenstein is concerned to combat. It is the calculus, and the calculus alone, that can be regarded as sacrosanct.

The question that will primarily concern me is how robust this distinction is. It is clear that Wittgenstein would count, say, a proof of the irrationality of $\sqrt{2}$ as part of the calculus and a claim to the effect that there is therefore at least one gap in "the everywhere dense rational points" as part of the prose (e.g., PG 460 and, more generally, PG 460–74). But why? By what criteria?

We had better not say, what the word "calculus" might encourage us to say, that authentic mathematics comprises all and only the formal proofs that belong to some formal system or other. That is both too broad and too narrow. It is too broad because some such proofs, indeed all but an infinitesimal minority of such proofs, while they may be of mathematical interest in their own right and thus apt objects of mathematical study, are too complex to have a place in real mathematical practice. In fact Wittgenstein even balks at dignifying them with the label "proofs" (see RFM III §§1–62 *passim*). Here we see that Wittgenstein is not thinking of authentic mathematics as an idealization of whatever engages the working mathematician; it is itself what engages the working mathematician. It has no features that the working mathematician cannot in practice recognize it as having (cf. RFM III §1, and PI §126). But this also helps to explain why authentic mathematics comprises not only less, but more, than is indicated in the characterization above. It is, as Wittgenstein puts it, "a MOTLEY of techniques of proof" (RFM III §46, capitalization in original). It comprises the many varied procedures whereby mathematicians actually establish their results; and what survives in the formal proofs of any given formal system is liable to abstract from differences between these procedures.

But this last point merely serves to reinforce the concerns we might have about how robust the distinction between the calculus and the surrounding prose is. For the differences in question, between these various proof procedures, might well be thought to include the flourishes, pictures, and other devices to which Hardy alludes. Or if not, why not?

3   Concerns about the Distinction between Calculus and Prose

At one point Wittgenstein says something that may appear to settle the matter in a very simple and neat way:

> Mathematics consists entirely of calculations.
> In mathematics *everything* is algorithm and *nothing* is meaning; even when it doesn't look like that because we seem to be using *words* to talk *about* mathematical things. Even these words are used to construct an algorithm. (PG 468, emphasis in original; cf. TLP 6.2ff, and PR §157)

Here the suggestion is that *anything* that a mathematician says that is not a contribution to the establishment or implementation of an algorithmic procedure for manipulating symbols is a part of the accompanying prose. Moreover, anything that a mathematician says to intimate that there is more to authentic mathematics than that – in particular, that these symbols are related to an independent reality in the way in which the words and phrases in an empirical proposition such as "she walked to the station" are related to an independent reality – is not just a part of the accompanying prose; it is a breeding-ground for all the confusions that beset the philosophy of mathematics and it can legitimately be challenged by the philosopher. This applies to the case considered earlier. Suppose a mathematician says, "We know exactly how things would have to be in mathematical reality for Goldbach's conjecture to be true or false. What we do not know is which of the two it is." This is paradigmatic prose. Wittgenstein is well within his rights, on his own principles, to take issue with it.

This all appears relatively straightforward. But now consider: must even talk of truth and falsity themselves count as part of the prose? Wittgenstein seems to think so. In his discussion of Gödel's theorem, in Appendix III to Part I of *Remarks on the Foundations of Mathematics*, he urges that our ascription of truth or falsity to mathematical propositions rests on nothing more than their superficial grammatical similarity to other propositions, a similarity that we can readily imagine away: it is not an integral part of the mathematics itself (cf. RFM IV §§15–16, and RFM V §13). And he further insists that, if we *are* going to "play the game of truth functions" with mathematical propositions (cf. RFM I III §2, and PI §136), then we had better understand all ascriptions of truth or falsity to them as relative to some formal system. For a mathematical proposition can count as true or false only insofar as something can count as asserting it, and the only

323

thing that can count as asserting a mathematical proposition is producing it as the result of a proof in such a system (RFM I III–§6; cf. PG 366–8). Again the message seems clear: the concepts of truth and falsity have no purchase in mathematics beyond certain analogies that strike us when we compare mathematical practices with practices of other kinds; all that sustains application of the concepts *within* mathematical practice is the obtaining of certain proof-relations between mathematical propositions and formal systems.

Yet what if we shift our attention from Gödel's theorem to Tarski's theorem – that arithmetical truth resists being defined in a certain way? The notion of truth involved here goes beyond provability in any given formal system. So is this not a case in which a fully fledged conception of truth has to be seen as part of the calculus itself, not just as part of the prose? (For related discussion see Steiner, 2001, and Floyd, 2001, sec.III.)

Or consider the law of the excluded middle. We naturally acquiesce in this law when we consider mathematical propositions. To take the stock example: we naturally assume that any given sequence of digits either occurs somewhere in the decimal expansion of π or does not. Wittgenstein expresses reservations about this, which make clear that he sees this and other such assumptions as a contribution, not to any calculus, but to the accompanying prose (e.g., RFM V §§9–28). He again reminds us that asserting a mathematical proposition is not a way of saying how things are; it is a way of stating a rule. This makes the claim that any given sequence must either occur somewhere in the decimal expansion of π or not do so akin to the totally unwarranted claim that either "The opening move shall be a pawn move" or "The opening move shall not be a pawn move" must be a rule of chess. (Of course, one could insist that the law of the excluded middle had application only to propositions whose assertions *were* a way of saying how things are. This would leave one free to say that Wittgenstein's critique leaves the law completely unchallenged. There are times when Wittgenstein himself suggests that we should adopt this stance: see e.g., RFM V §17; and cf. PR §173. But it would be little more than a terminological stance. It would not gainsay the fact that his critique does present a challenge to the law if the law is construed as having application wherever "the game of truth functions is played" – which is how I am construing it.) The problem for Wittgenstein is that, although some mathematicians have themselves had reservations about the law of the excluded middle, most notably Brouwer, it is hard to see why such reservations do not count as reservations about standard mathematical practice. Mathematicians standardly adopt classical logic, including the law of the excluded middle, when they are establishing and implementing their algorithmic procedures. How is this a fact about extra-mathematical prose and not a fact about – precisely – their establishment and implementation of algorithmic procedures?

We can turn to the infinite for a third example. Wittgenstein is very uncomfortable with the way in which set theorists claim to have shown that some infinite sets are bigger than others, as though they were astrophysicists claiming to have shown that some distant galaxies are bigger than others. He writes: "The dangerous, deceptive thing about [such an idea] [...] is that it makes the determination of a concept – concept formation – look like a fact of nature" (RFM II §19; cf. PG 287). Again he would say that he is casting doubt on the prose surrounding the calculus. Again the concern is that he is casting doubt on the calculus itself. That some infinite sets are bigger than others would be accepted by any orthodox set theorist as an unassailable result of set theory.

There is a fourth example, which might appear as compelling as any. In fact I think that Wittgenstein has ways of addressing it – at least in his own terms – that cannot be extended to the other three examples, though it is worth a digression to see why. The example concerns consistency. Like truth, consistency appears to have a substantive role to play in mathematics, a role whereby its ascriptions are answerable to the investigator-independent layout of mathematical reality. If a mathematician asserts that Zermelo–Fraenkel set theory is consistent, for instance, say as a prelude to proving that the continuum hypothesis is independent of it, then his or her assertion seems to be at the mercy of whether Zermelo–Fraenkel set theory *is* consistent; of whether there is in fact, quite independently of what he or she or any of the rest of the mathematical community might be disposed to say about the matter, a set-theoretical proposition that admits of both a proof and a refutation within the theory. For that matter, the very idea that mathematics consists of algorithmic procedures seems to entail that there is an issue for mathematicians, if not about the truth or falsity of their propositions, at least about the consistency or inconsistency of their procedures, where the consistency or inconsistency of a procedure is a mathematically investigable feature of it that is quite independent of mathematicians themselves. There seems, then, to be a notion at work within mathematics – *within mathematics*, not just within the surrounding prose – which embodies the very picture of mathematics, as answerable to an independent reality, that Wittgenstein is concerned to repudiate.

As I said, I think Wittgenstein has ways of addressing this fourth example. What are they? They are largely a matter of his biting various bullets. Among these are bullets that he notoriously does bite and bullets that I think he would be happy to bite. To begin with the latter: I think he would simply accede to the idea that, when consistency features within mathematics, it is no more answerable to an independent mathematical reality than any other mathematical notion. Thus we are at just as much liberty to declare Zermelo–Fraenkel set theory to be consistent as we are to declare the successor function to be one:one. That declaration can serve as a piece of legislation, a contribution to an algorithmic procedure or to a family of algorithmic procedures. Of course it is natural to protest, "But what if Zermelo–Fraenkel set theory is *not* consistent?" Here, however, Wittgenstein can precisely appeal to his distinction between calculus and prose. For there are two corresponding ways of taking this question. If it is taken as a question within mathematics, then there is plenty to be said in response to it, for instance that if Zermelo–Fraenkel set theory is not consistent, then it is finitely axiomatizable. This poses no threat whatsoever to Wittgenstein. Taken in this way, the question is just an invitation to do more mathematics, mathematics that can sit alongside whatever mathematics we might do on the strength of our declaration that Zermelo–Fraenkel set theory is consistent. If the question is taken as a contribution to the prose, on the other hand, then it adverts to the possibility that we shall one day acknowledge both a proof within Zermelo–Fraenkel set theory and a refutation within Zermelo–Fraenkel set theory of one and the same proposition. And this is where we find the bullets that Wittgenstein notoriously does bite. He is prepared to meet what he calls "the superstitious dread and veneration by mathematicians in the face of contradiction" (RFM I III §17) with a studied nonchalance. His stance, roughly, is that, as long as we do not find any such conflict in our procedures, we do not need to worry about the possibility, and, if ever we do find such a conflict in our procedures, *then* we can decide how to proceed (RFM VII §§12ff, and PG 303–5). He is even prepared to countenance our proceeding by simply circumventing the conflict. In one of his lectures he says: "If you can draw any conclusion you like from [a contradiction], [...] I would say, 'Well then, just don't draw any conclusions from a contradiction'" (LFM 220). This may seem literally laughable: it is reminiscent of the Tommy Cooper joke in which a patient tells his doctor that his arm hurts whenever he raises it and the doctor replies, "Well then, don't raise it." But actually, Wittgenstein's nonchalance does not seem untoward once we rid ourselves of the idea that mathematical propositions are related to an independent reality in the way in which empirical propositions are. As long as we think of mathematicians as establishing and implementing algorithmic procedures, then Wittgenstein's nonchalance can simply be seen as his way of sanctioning mathematicians' continued use and periodic revision of any given procedure until such time as it no longer serves their purposes. And lest it seem utterly fanciful to suppose that mathematicians should work with inconsistent procedures even while fully aware of the inconsistencies, worse still that they should do so by simply negotiating the inconsistencies as they see fit, let us not forget that this is precisely what they did in the seventeenth and eighteenth centuries when the notion of an infinitesimal difference, as both equal to zero and not equal to zero, still informed work on the differential calculus. (See Moore, 1990/2001, ch.4, secs.1–2.)

The fourth example seems to me not telling, then. But the other three remain – as no doubt do variants on them.

4   One Way to Meet these Concerns

There is one obvious way for Wittgenstein to rise to this collective challenge. However robust the distinction between the calculus and the surrounding prose, the prose may infect the calculus; or, more strictly, the prose may infect how we couch the calculus. Thus in all three of the troublesome examples considered in the previous section Wittgenstein can say that the trouble lies, not in the calculus itself, but in our choice of certain vocabulary to express it: "true," "false," "either... or...," "bigger." This vocabulary has a use in non-mathematical contexts that resonates loudly from there. And it harbors a certain view of the calculus that is strictly inessential to it. So the very fact that we say that some infinite sets are "bigger" than others, to take that example, is fair game for Wittgenstein's animadversions on what goes beyond the calculus, however securely lodged within the calculus the result itself may be. There is even an issue about whether we should use the word "infinite" in a strictly mathematical context. "Ought the word 'infinite' to be avoided in mathematics?," Wittgenstein's interlocutor asks at one point. "Yes," Wittgenstein replies, "where it appears to confer a meaning upon the calculus; instead of getting one from it" (RFM II §58).

Moreover – this is a separate point – it is Wittgenstein's firm conviction that, if only we were to recast much of the mathematics that most captivates us, by removing the offending vocabulary in favor of some purpose-specific mathematical jargon (cf. PG 468–9), then interest in it would wane. It would lose what Wittgenstein calls its "schoolboy charm" (LFM 16). We feel a certain heady pleasure when we are told that some infinite sets are bigger than others. We feel considerably less pleasure when we are told that certain one:one correlations yield elements that are not in their ranges. Though Wittgenstein's principal concern is to combat philosophical confusions attending mathematics, he does also see it as part of his mission as it were to cut mathematics down to size. (The two things are related. This is for reasons that we have just seen. As Wittgenstein nicely puts it at one point: "Philosophical clarity will have the same effect on the growth of mathematics as sunlight has on the growth of potato shoots. (In a dark cellar they grow yards long.)" (PG 381).)

One might wonder how even this consists with Wittgenstein's non-revisionary insistence that philosophy should leave mathematics as it is. But there is one marvelous remark in which he makes clear how they consist. The remark is proffered in response to Hilbert, who famously said in connection with the work by Cantor in which transfinite set theory was founded, "No one shall be able to drive us from the paradise that Cantor has created for us" (Hilbert, [1926] 1967, p. 376). Wittgenstein replies:

> I wouldn't dream of trying to drive anyone from this paradise... I would do something quite different: I would try to show you that it is not a paradise – so that you'll leave of your own accord. I would say, 'You're welcome to this; just look about you.' (LFM 103)

Elsewhere he puts the point by saying: "What I am doing is, not to show that calculations are wrong, but to subject the *interest* of calculations to test" (RFM II §62, emphasis in original; cf. LFM 141).

5 Renewed Concerns about the Distinction between Calculus and Prose

Wittgenstein may appear vindicated then. Although he is keen to warn mathematicians about the dangers of transferring vocabulary from one context to another, and although he knows, indeed intends, that heeding his warning will make them reconsider the value of some of their work, he does not himself want to issue a direct challenge to any of that work.

There is still a problem for Wittgenstein, though. Mathematical use of the vernacular is never *just* a matter of transferring vocabulary from one context to another – or, if it is, that is not Wittgenstein's concern. (No harm accrues from the fact that the word "exponent" has a quite different use in mathematical contexts from the use it has in non-mathematical contexts.) When set theorists describe some infinite sets as "bigger" than others, they are not just choosing an arbitrary label which happens to have a use elsewhere. They take themselves to be appropriating a concept with which we are already familiar and extending its application. In fact that is precisely what gives Wittgenstein pause (PG 464). But why does it give him pause? Wittgenstein himself urges that mathematics involves the formation of concepts (RFM VII §67). Why should this formation of concepts not include the modification of concepts as well as their creation? And if it does, then the use of the relevant vocabulary will after all be essential to what the mathematicians are doing. To claim that that vocabulary can be peeled off from the underlying calculus *is* to issue a direct challenge to their work.

For a clear example of what I have in mind, consider Wittgenstein's reluctance, which we noted earlier, to dignify all the formal proofs of any given formal system with the label "proofs". That cannot but be heard as a challenge, not only to each of the systems, but also to proof theory, the branch of mathematics in which our informal notion of a proof is at once idealized and codified.

Or consider this:

> Does the relation $m = 2n$ correlate the set of all numbers with one of its subsets? No. It correlates any arbitrary number with another, and in that way we arrive at infinitely many pairs of sets, of which one is correlated with the other, but which are *never* related as set and subset. (PR §141, emphasis in original, "class" replaced by "set")

Here Wittgenstein is balking at the standard way of couching the result that each natural number can be paired with its double. The standard way of couching this result makes reference to a one:one correlation between the complete set of natural numbers and one of its proper subsets, that which contains only the even natural numbers. But Wittgenstein refuses to sanction this use of the word "set," if it is understood as involving application of a single concept to both the finite case and the infinite case: if we do talk of both "finite sets" and "infinite sets," then these two uses of "sets" must be understood as having fundamentally different grammars from each other (PG 463–5). This is certainly a bold stance. But the issue for us is not whether it is bold or not; nor whether it is justified or not; nor even whether it is a stance to which most set theorists would take exception. The issue, for us, is whether it is a direct assault on set theory. And surely it is.

Wittgenstein could of course beg all the relevant questions and insist that the very challengeability of what he is challenging, in his capacity as a philosopher, ensures that it is not an essential part of any authentic mathematics. That would be uninteresting – save in so far as it highlights what may in any case be a circle that afflicts his philosophy. Wittgenstein believes that, *qua* philosopher, he is entitled to take issue with that which perverts or is in danger of perverting either mathematical thinking or our thinking about mathematical thinking, but that he is not entitled to take issue with mathematical thinking itself. He can take issue with the prose, but not with the calculus. The apparent circularity is this: there is no way, in practice, of respecting this distinction without having a grasp of the calculus; and there is no way of acquiring a grasp of the calculus without being suitably sensitive to authentic mathematical practice; and there is no way of being suitably sensitive to authentic mathematical practice without knowing how to screen those parts of mathematical practice that do not constitute proper exercise of the calculus; and there is no way of knowing which parts to screen without already being able to respect the original distinction.

I do not claim that this apparent circularity is vicious. I do not even claim that it is real. Each step in the sequence can be disputed. For example, Wittgenstein might say that we can tell which parts of mathematical practice to screen because there is a distinctive discomfort that eventually manifests itself when the prose gets out of control (cf. PI §§54 and 123). Perhaps there is – though even then, of course, "distinctive" is the operative word, with its own threat of circularity. (Mathematicians can display plenty of discomfort when they are wrestling with *bona fide* mathematical problems.) The point, however, is that whether the circularity is real or not, the distinction between calculus and prose is not just a piece of theory for Wittgenstein. It is a tool that he needs to be able to implement *in practice*, in his attempt to rid the philosophy of mathematics of the confusions that beset it. And the mere threat of such circularity is surely enough to disturb the confidence that proper handling of this tool requires. It is surely enough to call into question the very project of trying to approach the philosophy of mathematics with that self-conscious detachment which his philosophy of philosophy demands. In sum: there is a real practical issue for Wittgenstein about the effectiveness of this distinction that is so crucial to his philosophy of mathematics, the distinction between calculus and prose.

6 An Issue about the Application of Mathematics

Is part of the problem excessive censoriousness on Wittgenstein's part? How would it be if his attitude were much more one of *laissez-faire*, so that, instead of regarding whatever could be seen as incidental to any given algorithmic procedure as part of the prose, he regarded whatever could be seen as a feature of some algorithmic procedure, however incidental, as part of the calculus? This would mean that set theorists could just be left to get on with their business, be the interest of the exercise as it may. The only point at which philosophers would need to get involved would be the point at which someone reflecting on the exercise began to mishandle the conceptual apparatus involved in it and got into a muddle as a result. The threat of circularity just considered would remain, but it would be mitigated by the fact that the distinction between calculus and prose would need to be drawn much less frequently: only when there was a troublesome uncertainty about how to proceed and the issue was whether it was an uncertainty calling for mathematical insight or an uncertainty calling for philosophical clarification. No doubt this would leave Wittgenstein himself feeling uneasy, but would it be contrary to the strict letter of anything in his philosophy of mathematics?

Well, yes, it would. There is an issue about the application of mathematics that I have not mentioned at all so far. When Wittgenstein says that mathematics involves algorithms, he means to specify a necessary condition for something to count as part of mathematics, not a sufficient condition. He would not reckon the mere algorithmic manipulation of symbols a part of mathematics unless those symbols also had a use in non-mathematical contexts. Wittgenstein puts the point as follows:

> I want to say: it is essential to mathematics that its signs are also employed in *mufti*.
> It is the use outside mathematics, and so the *meaning* of the signs, that makes the sign-games into mathematics.
> Just as it is not logical inference either, for me to make a change from one formation to another (say from one arrangement of chairs to another) if these arrangements have not a linguistic function apart from this transformation. (RFM V §2, emphasis in original; cf. RFM V §25)

Let us not pause to consider what tension there might or might not be between this demand that mathematical vocabulary have a use outside mathematics and the worries that we saw Wittgenstein express earlier about the mathematical use of any vocabulary that has a use outside mathematics. Of more immediate concern is the fact that what we have here is essentially an assault on the very idea of pure mathematics. And it immediately furnishes a new complaint for Wittgenstein to level against transfinite set theory. For, to date, there is no serious use of any of set theory's heavy-duty measuring apparatus in non-mathematical contexts.

This assault on the idea of pure mathematics, which is strictly independent of anything that we have considered hitherto, seems to me problematical for a number of reasons. Here are two. First, even if the algorithmic manipulation of symbols needs to have application to count as a proper part of mathematics and not just a game, it is not clear why it needs to have application *outside mathematics* as opposed to elsewhere within it. Second, a branch of mathematics often remains unapplied until well after its development, so that even those who think that the application of mathematics is what gives it its point should acknowledge the importance of allowing unapplied mathematics to have free rein. Both of these points, whatever general force they might have, have specific force in the case of transfinite set theory, which is both vigorous in its application to other branches of mathematics and relatively young. There is far more to be said about both points, obviously. But there is also a third point that needs to be made in this context, of even greater significance, namely that the assault on the idea of pure mathematics is an assault on mathematicians' very self-image. Hardly any mathematician would agree with Wittgenstein that "it is essential to mathematics that its signs are also employed in mufti." This of course brings us back to square one. For yet again Wittgenstein has made a claim in his philosophy of mathematics to which the typical working mathematician would take exception. This in itself need not worry him. What the typical working mathematician is prepared to count as mathematics was always going to be a clear candidate for classification as prose rather than calculus. But it is another stark reminder of how subversive Wittgenstein is prepared to be in his critique of what mathematicians themselves actually think and say; and of how hard he therefore makes it for himself to draw the distinctions that he needs to draw in order to maintain his precept that philosophy leaves mathematics as it is. There is much that lies deep in the territory within and around mathematics that Wittgenstein's philosophy does *not* leave as it is. It has been one of the main burdens of this chapter to show this.

It remains for me to make one very brief but very significant final point. My aim has been to highlight a tension that I claim to have discerned between Wittgenstein's philosophy of mathematics and his philosophy of philosophy. But even if I have succeeded in this aim, it is a further question where the fault lies. Despite the various reservations that I have voiced about Wittgenstein's philosophy of mathematics, there is much in it that seems to me to embody insights of the most profound kind. I think that what we have been witnessing are, in large part, problems with his philosophy of *philosophy*. In particular, I think that we have been seeing manifestations of a continual struggle that his philosophy of philosophy has with its own highly distinctive brand of conservatism. But that, as they so often say, is a topic for another occasion.

References

Cohen, P.J. (1967). Comments on the Foundations of Set Theory. In D. Scott (Ed.). *Axiomatic Set Theory: Proceedings in Symposia in Pure Mathematics*, 13, 9–15.

Davies, E.B. (2003). *Science in the Looking Glass: What do Scientists Really Know?* Oxford: Oxford University Press.

Dawson, J.W., Jr. (1989). The Reception of Gödel's Incompleteness Theorems. Reprinted in S.G. Shanker (Ed.). *Gödel's Theorem in Focus* (pp. 74–95). London: Routledge.

Dummett, M. (1959). Wittgenstein's Philosophy of Mathematics. Reprinted in M. Dummett. (1978). *Truth and Other Enigmas* (pp. 166–185). London: Duckworth.

Floyd, J. (2001). Prose versus Proof: Wittgenstein on Gödel, Tarski and Truth. *Philosophia Mathematica*, 9, 280–307.

Hardy, G.H. (1929). Mathematical Proof. *Mind*, 38, 1–29.

Hilbert, D. ([1926] 1967). On the Infinite. Translation in J. van Heijenoort (Ed.). *From Frege to Gödel: A Source Book in Mathematical Logic, 1879–1931* (pp.367–392). Cambridge, MA: Harvard University Press. (Original work published 1926.)

Kienzler, W. and Grève, S.S. (2016). Wittgenstein on Gödelian "Incompleteness," Proofs and Mathematical Practice: Reading *Remarks on the Foundations of Mathematics*, Part I, Appendix III, Carefully. In S.S. Grève and J. Mácha (Eds). *Wittgenstein and the Creativity of Language* (pp.76–116). Basingstoke: Palgrave Macmillan.

Monk, R. (1990/91). *Ludwig Wittgenstein: The Duty of Genius*. London: Vintage.

Monk, R. (2007). Bourgeois, Bolshevist or Anarchist? The Reception of Wittgenstein's Philosophy of Mathematics. In G. Kahane, E. Kanterian, and O. Kuusela (Eds). *Wittgenstein and his Interpreters: Essays in Memory of Gordon Baker* (pp.269–294). Oxford: Blackwell.

Moore, A.W. (1990/2001). *The Infinite*. Second, revised edition. London: Routledge.

Moore, A.W. (1998). More on "The Philosophical Significance of Gödel's Theorem". In J.L. Brandl and P. Sullivan (Eds). *New Essays on the Philosophy of Michael Dummett* (Special Issue): *Grazer Philosophische Studien*, 55, 103–126.

Penrose, R. (1989). *The Emperor's New Mind: Concerning Computers, Minds, and the Laws of Physics*. Oxford: Oxford University Press.

Steiner, M. (2001). Wittgenstein as his Own Worst Enemy: The Case of Gödel's Theorem. *Philosophia Mathematica*, 9, 257–279.

Further Reading

Baker, G.P. and Hacker, P.M.S. (1985/2014). Grammar and Necessity. In G.P. Baker and P.M.S. Hacker. *Wittgenstein: Rules, Grammar and Necessity. Volume 2 of an Analytical Commentary on the Philosophical Investigations. Essays and Exegesis of §§185–242*. Second edition. Extensively revised by P.M.S. Hacker. Oxford: Wiley-Blackwell.

Floyd, J. (2005). Wittgenstein on Philosophy of Logic and Mathematics. In S. Shapiro (Ed.). *The Oxford Handbook of Philosophy of Mathematics and Logic* (pp.75–128). Oxford: Oxford University Press.

Frascolla, P. (1994).*Wittgenstein's Philosophy of Mathematics*. London: Routledge.

Marion, M. (1998).*Wittgenstein, Finitism, and the Foundations of Mathematics*. Oxford: Oxford University Press.

Mühlhölzer, F. (2010). *Braucht die Mathematik eine Grundlegung? Ein Kommentar des Teils III von Wittgensteins Bemerkungen über die Grundlagen der Mathematik*. [Does Mathematics need Foundations? A Commentary on Part III of Wittgenstein's *Remarks on the Foundations of Mathematics*.] Frankfurt: Vittorio Klostermann.

Potter, M. (2011). Wittgenstein on Mathematics. In O. Kuusela and M. McGinn (Eds). *The Oxford Handbook of Wittgenstein* (pp.122–137). Oxford: Oxford University Press.

Wright, C. (1980). *Wittgenstein on the Foundations of Mathematics*. London: Duckworth.

20

Wittgenstein and Antirealism

MATHIEU MARION

1 Introduction

The term "realism" is often meant to cover the following theses about any given domain: that there exist entities distinctive of that domain and that their existence is objective and mind-independent (Brock and Mares, 2007, p.2). For example, realism about mathematics, also known as "Platonism," is the belief that there are mathematical objects whose existence is objective and independent of the mathematicians' activities. This claim is denied by constructivists, who would, for that reason, reject the method of proof by *reductio ad absurdum* that allows one to infer the existence of an entity, without explicit construction, merely on the ground that the supposition of its nonexistence leads to an absurdity. It relies on the law of excluded middle, according to which for any *A*, either *A* or not-*A*: if not-*A* leads to a contradiction, one can affirm *A*. Constructivists would argue that no direct proof of *A* has been adduced, and thus reject the law of excluded middle. Although it is the main domain discussed here, mathematics is only one of the many domains where the adoption of a form of realism has traditionally been challenged; other domains include ethics, where the adoption of moral realism has been challenged by the various noncognitivist accounts, e.g., expressivism, error theory, or projectivism (see Chapter 39, WITTGENSTEIN AND ETHICS). Behaviorism and phenomenalism, opposed to realism about, respectively, mental entities and the existence of material objects, are other well-known examples.

In the late 1950s, Michael Dummett made an influential proposal to settle these debates that involved *redefining* realism:

> Realism I characterize as the belief that statements of the disputed class possess an objective truth-value, independently of our means of knowing it: they are true or false in virtue of a reality existing independently of us. The anti-realist opposes to this the view that statements of the disputed class are to be understood only by reference to the sort of thing which we count as evidence for a statement of that class [...] The dispute thus concerns the notion of truth appropriate for statements of the disputed class; and this means that it is a dispute concerning the kind of *meaning* which these statements have.
>
> (Dummett, 1978a, p.146)

A Companion to Wittgenstein, First Edition. Edited by Hans-Johann Glock and John Hyman.
© 2017 John Wiley & Sons, Ltd. Published 2017 by John Wiley & Sons, Ltd.

Under this new definition, realism would now be associated with the claim that statements about a given domain possess a definite truth value independently of our capacity, even in principle, to recognize what it is. Thus the realist would be committed to a notion of "evidence-transcendent" or "investigation-independent" truth conditions, which entails that the principle of bivalence, according to which statements are either true or false, holds for them. This implies in turn the adoption of classical logic, since that principle is the semantic counterpart of the law of excluded middle. Invoking this connection, Dummett issued an antirealist challenge in the form of a theory of meaning that was closely tied to the above rejection of the law of excluded middle. He also meant it as a research program for the various "disputed classes" of statements, namely to assess, for each one of them, if the realist is truly entitled to the principle of bivalence (Dummett, 1991, p.463f).

To settle any such dispute in their favor, antirealists needed to provide an alternative theory, replacing the classical concept of truth as its key semantic concept with another more suitable concept, and then try and argue for its superiority over the realist theory. Dummett argued his case from proof-theoretical semantics in logic and mathematics (a field that begins with the implementation of Heyting semantics for intuitionistic logic in Gentzen's natural deduction), and proceeded to advocating the generalization of this approach via the replacement of truth conditions with assertability-conditions as the key semantic concept (see Dummett, 1978a, pp.215–47; Prawitz, 1977). The resulting view is often seen as a species of verificationism, although it differs from the original version of the logical positivists, e.g., with respect to bivalence.

Dummett's challenge elicited a strong critical reaction in the 1970s and the ensuing debate went unabated for decades, with participants on both sides appealing to Wittgenstein's ideas in order to support their claims. Hilary Putnam also devised a related contrast between "metaphysical" and "internal realism" (Putnam, 1978, pt.4), which also played an important role within the realism debate, but it had little impact on Wittgenstein studies. By contrast, Dummett was understood as having provided the outlines of an interpretation of Wittgenstein as an antirealist, which was influential at first, so that the interpretation of Wittgenstein's philosophy became enmeshed during that period in the larger context of the realism debate.

We can distinguish three phases in the realism debate, the first being constituted by the reaction elicited by Dummett's own challenge, through the development of antirealist readings of Wittgenstein. The rise of what will be termed below "left-wing interpretations" of Wittgenstein was to undermine such readings and, along with suggestions that a proper reading of Wittgenstein would result in a defense of a kind of realism, they form the second phase of the debate. A final phase came with a series of modifications to the antirealist side, proposed by Simon Blackburn, Paul Horwich, and Crispin Wright among others, in the early 1990s. Two caveats must be introduced before examining these phases. One should first note the distinction between *uses* of Wittgenstein's ideas within the antirealism debate, and attempts at backing them up with a more or less detailed *interpretation* of Wittgenstein – they should be kept apart. Given that it is not possible to settle any specific point of interpretation within my remit, only brief indications will be provided of the difficulties confronting, respectively, antirealist and realists readings. Secondly, the realism debate raised a slew of issues, most of which will not even be mentioned, and there will be no attempt at settling those that will be. The aim is merely to provide an outline of the realism debate that serves as the backdrop for a survey of the main links forged by its participants with Wittgenstein's philosophy.

2 Dummett's Antirealism and Wittgenstein

Dummett's own semantic antirealism blended ideas taken from Wittgenstein and intuitionism. Of the various schools of constructivism about mathematics, intuitionism specifically denied the applicability of the law of excluded middle to infinite domains. Its founder, L.E.J. Brouwer, had given it, however, a philosophical basis that was perceived as being not only marred by his "mysticism," but also as embodying a form of psychologism already discredited by Frege (for further details about Brouwer, see van Atten, 2004, ch.1 and 6). Wishing to replace Brouwer's philosophy with semantic antirealism, Dummett used some ideas by Wittgenstein. Thus, he argued in *Frege: Philosophy of Language* (1973/81), that, in his critique of psychologism, Frege had anticipated Wittgenstein's "private language argument," inasmuch as it is aimed at the idea of a private ostensive definition (Dummett, 1973/81, pp.637–42; cf. Chapter 28, PRIVACY AND PRIVATE LANGUAGE), and then further argued that this critique does not cohere with Frege's semantic realism (Dummett, 1991, pp.91–2).

Dummett also put at the center of his semantic antirealism the dictum "Don't ask for the meaning: ask for use" – which is reminiscent of section 43 of Wittgenstein's *Philosophical Investigations*, "the meaning of a word is its use in the language" (see Chapter 26, LANGUAGES, LANGUAGE-GAMES, AND FORMS OF LIFE) – and the associated dictum "Meaning cannot transcend use." The latter is at the basis of Dummett's *manifestation argument* against semantic realism: if knowledge of the meaning of a statement is to be fully exhausted in its use, then one cannot make sense of the realist thesis according to which meaning is determined by truth conditions that obtain or not independently of our capacity even in principle to recognize if they do (Dummett, 1978a, p.216–26). One should note the subtle shifts effectuated by these dictums, given that Wittgenstein hesitated between explaining meaning in terms of use and simply equating them (Rundle, 1990, ch.1; Glock, 1996, pp.376–81; Horwich, 2012, ch.4).

That the meaning of a statement is exhausted by its use was thus seen by Dummett as both a lesson from Wittgenstein and as forming the basis of an argument to replace Brouwer's psychologism, given that one had, with its help, also undermined the above-stated justification of the law of excluded middle (Dummett, 1978a, p.226). The hope was thus to develop semantic antirealism by generalizing this approach from logic and mathematics to natural language, so to propose an alternative to realism for any of the disputed classes – Dummett himself focused mainly, apart from mathematics, on conditionals and statements about the past.

Although he often referred to Wittgenstein in his writings, Dummett only reviewed two of his books by the early 1980s, namely *Remarks on the Foundations of Mathematics* (see Dummett, 1959, pp.166–85) and *Wittgenstein's Lectures on the Foundations of Mathematics, Cambridge 1939* (see Dummett, 1978b; this review is the lesser known of the two, but equally interesting). Dummett was nevertheless understood as suggesting the outline of an interpretation of Wittgenstein's philosophy that would explain the latter's development as a move away from semantic realism in the *Tractatus* to the semantic antirealism of his later philosophy; an antirealism that would differ significantly from Dummett's own version (cf. Chapter 1, WITTGENSTEIN'S PHILOSOPHICAL DEVELOPMENT and Chapter 13, PHILOSOPHY AND PHILOSOPHICAL METHOD). Dummett's ideas were developed early on, in the 1970s, most notably by Crispin Wright in *Wittgenstein on the Foundations of Mathematics* (1980). They were also picked up in the first edition of Peter Hacker's *Insight and Illusion* (1972), where the latter wrote enthusiastically that there is "no more fruitful task in Wittgensteinian exegesis" than the elaboration of the view of Wittgenstein's later philosophy as a "generalized intuitionist theory," and of the transition from early to late as being "from realism in semantics to constructivism" (Hacker, 1972, p.104). Gordon Baker (1974), with whom Hacker was to collaborate, concurred, but they soon began to move away in their review of *Philosophical Grammar* (see Baker and Hacker, 1976), and Hacker then also published a second edition of his book to recant his antirealist reading of Wittgenstein (Hacker, 1972/86).

In his interpretation, Dummett focused mainly on Wittgenstein's philosophy of mathematics, which he described as a form of "full-blooded conventionalism" (Dummett, 1959, p.170). Conventionalism, of the "moderate" sort usually associated with logical positivism, opposed realism with the doctrine that all necessity was projected by us on reality by our language, because we would not count anything as refuting certain statements. In mathematics, this meant that some statements would be adopted by convention, as "true in virtue of meaning," and mathematicians would merely draw consequences from them. That, in an axiomatic system, a given theorem follows with necessity from axioms and rules of inference is something that we must nevertheless recognize as imposed on us, and this cannot be in turn the expression of our having adopted a convention. It is to counter this well-known critique of moderate conventionalism that Wittgenstein, on Dummett's construal, opted for a "full-blooded" version, according to which "the logical necessity of any statement is always the *direct* expression of a linguistic convention" (Dummett, 1959, p.170). In a proof every step is meant to be the result of the application of rules of inference, either to an axiom or to some consequence already obtained in this way, and we naturally feel that we merely have a "spectator's role" to play in following these transitions. Not so for Dummett's Wittgenstein, however:

> There is nothing in our formulation of the axioms and of the rules of inference, and nothing in our minds when we accepted these before the proof was given, which of itself shows whether we shall accept the proofs or not; and hence there is nothing which *forces* us to accept the proof.
>
> (Dummett, 1959, p.171)

In other words, if nothing forces us to accept the proof, then it is always a matter of *decision*.

To support this interpretation, Dummett appealed to the "rule-following argument" (PI §§185–242; cf. Chapter 24, RULES AND RULE-FOLLOWING), which he read as indicating that, in training someone to, say, "add 2," who then goes on adding 4 after 1000, there is nothing either in what one said or what went on in one's mind, that actually showed that this is not what one intended (Dummett, 1959, p.171). This is meant to support the claim that for any future, as yet unconsidered application of a rule, there is no determinate answer to the question whether a putative result is the right one or not (this will have to await a decision), raising doubts about the applicability of the law of excluded middle in such cases. This is the basis of antirealist readings of the rule-following considerations, starting with Wright's treatment (see Wright, 1980, chs.II, XI, XX), in which the element of decision plays a key role – it is one of the central planks of the rule-following considerations according Wright (2001, p.182). As Wright put it, the target is "investigation-independence", i.e., the idea that meaning can be so conferred upon at least some of the statements of our language that whether they are correct is something settled in advance and independently of any investigation we might make.

(Wright, 1993, p.148)

Saul Kripke's notorious interpretation, although differently motivated, still falls within the antirealist ambit, inasmuch as he attributes to Wittgenstein the replacement of truth conditions by assertability-conditions, about the correct answer to a new addition problem; only that, while there is no correct answer to it, the following platitude is implied: "If everyone agrees upon a certain answer, then no one will feel justified in calling the answer wrong" (Kripke, 1982, pp.111–12).

Wittgenstein's remarks about the "surveyability" of proofs were also read as giving support to this interpretation. They involve consideration of cases where calculations are not fully surveyable, so that our results conflict and we cannot reach an agreement about the proper result. Dummett reads Wittgenstein as claiming here that "there is no right answer" (Dummett, 1978b, 65). His strongest textual support comes from Wittgenstein's 1939 lectures:

> Actually there is nothing to stop us postulating that your result is right – so that in future all your children will have to copy what is written on that blackboard. [...] There is nothing there for a higher intelligence to know [...]. We know as much as God does in mathematics.
>
> (LFM 103–4)

Therefore, although Wittgenstein had already drawn, alongside intuitionists and verificationists, a link between the meaning of a mathematical proposition with its proof (PR §§148 and 163; PG 369–70; see also Chapter 18, WITTGENSTEIN'S EARLY PHILOSOPHY OF MATHEMATICS), this new idea provided him, according to Dummett, with an "independent reason" (1978b, p.64), so that his antirealist critique would go further than Dummett's: it ends up giving support instead to a "strict finitism" in the foundations of mathematics (Dummett, 1959, p.182), for which there is no definite truth value attached to any generalization over an infinite domain. Much of our mathematics, even ordinary arithmetic would have to be jettisoned. Dummett naturally found this antirealism "extremely hard to swallow," and he objected to it that predicates such as "surveyable" are simply incoherent (Dummett, 1959, p.173; 1978a, p. 265; cf. also Chapter 16, SURVEYABILITY).

Dummett's reading did not remain unchallenged for long. Barry Stroud argued early on that one cannot simply stipulate a convention either way, e.g., "7 + 5" equaling or not equaling "12," and that it is rather, according to Wittgenstein, our "form of life" that compels us to stipulate one way rather than the other, i.e., to accept certain strings of symbols as proofs (Stroud, 1966). Wittgenstein would, however, remain wedded to a form of antirealism under such a reading: as Putnam pointed out, Stroud's reading still locates the source of necessity "in us" (Putnam, 1983, p.117; see also Dummett, 1991, p.448). Thus, neither Dummett nor Stroud deny that Wittgenstein advanced a form of conventionalism; and it would be best to point out instead that it was neither of the above "full-blooded," nor of the moderate sort espoused by the logical positivists. After all, according to Wittgenstein it is not the fact that we decide to call a mathematical sentence "true" that makes it into a convention, but our use of it as a norm of description (Baker and Hacker 1985/2014, pp.356–70; see Chapter 14, GRAMMAR AND GRAMMATICAL

STATEMENTS). By contrast with moderate conventionalism, Wittgenstein argued that it is therefore not an issue about the form of these sentences: it is about their *role*. Whether this view is ultimately defensible is another matter.

Much ink was spilled about the rule-following considerations in the 1980s and this is not the place to summarize those developments. One should merely insist here against the central claim of the antirealist interpretation that, although Wittgenstein claimed that "it would almost be more correct to say [...] that a new decision is needed at every point" (PI §186), he fell short of claiming that it is, claiming instead that "nothing like an act of decision must take place" (BB 143; see also LFM 237). It is also wrong to interpret Wittgenstein as claiming that a rule does not determine what counts as acting in accord with it – a point argued at length by Baker and Hacker (1985/2014). Furthermore, Dummett simply mislocated the target of Wittgenstein's remarks on surveyability, which were aimed at the Frege–Russell definition of natural numbers, so that they were not meant to provide succor to the antirealist claim that nothing forces us to accept a proof that has a very large number of steps (Marion, 2011; Marion and Okada, 2014). Finally, one cannot really read Wittgenstein as having argued for strict finitism (Marion, 1998, ch.8; *pace* e.g., Rodych, 2011).

3   Quietism and Anti-Antirealism

Antirealist readings of Wittgenstein did not, however, founder on such criticisms, important as they might be. Instead, their popularity suffered from the rise of what is now known as "left-wing interpretations" of Wittgenstein, namely those that

> stress the ideas that philosophical problems arise from misconceptions about grammar and meaning, and that these problems should be resolved by a kind of therapy in which the therapist puts forward no theses, explanations, or theories of any kind.
> (Chihara, 1982, p.105n)

Simon Blackburn coined the label "quietism" to describe this sort of stance, and it has been commonly used since as a label for Wittgenstein's views, under such interpretations (Blackburn, 1984, p.146). Quietism implies that philosophy cannot lead to a revision of any practice. By contrast, "right-wing interpretations" attribute substantial theses to Wittgenstein, including revisionary ones. Antirealist interpretations are clearly right wing, and so are those of some of their critics, e.g., Frascolla (1994) or Marion (1998); not so, however for the earlier, extended critique by Shanker (1986). It is fair to say that right-wing interpretations have since become the minority view, although, as we saw with the topic of Wittgenstein's conventionalism, some problems cannot be so easily dismissed.

One obvious difficulty in this respect concerns the *revisionary* nature of Dummett's antirealism and Wittgenstein's version, supposedly leading to strict finitist strictures: they contradict the claim that philosophy "leaves everything," including mathematics, "as it is" (PI §124). According to left-wing interpretations, there could be no discrepancy between remarks such as these, of a very general nature, and remarks on specific topics that have *prima facie* revisionary consequences. Therefore, no interpretation under which Wittgenstein comes out as proposing that we revise any practice, let alone logic or mathematics, could be considered wholly right, even when supported by textual evidence; it is simply to be assumed without further ado that evidence must have been wrongly interpreted. Thus, despite attempts to provide textual analysis to the contrary, as presented by e.g., Fogelin (1992, pp.196–213) and Marion (2003), it has generally been assumed that Wittgenstein could not have so much as raised doubts about the universal applicability of the law of excluded middle.

A further difficulty involves the use of "theses," against their explicit rejection in PI§128. One can thus argue that both the antirealist and the realist are engaged in the kind of substantive philosophizing that Wittgenstein is rejecting for himself, so that one ought not to enlist him on any side of the realism debate. This could be taken, however, as a mere injunction not to make any *use* of his ideas within that debate. But it is also possible to claim that the whole realism debate is, from Wittgenstein's standpoint, in some way defective, and argue that he provided arguments against the very project of a theory of meaning or that of a semantics for natural languages. Attempts of this kind, e.g., by Baker and Hacker (1984) and Rundle (1990), had, however, little echo, but the issue is taken up recently in more circumspect treatments by Stokhof (2013) and Schneider (2014).

Some philosophers took left-wing interpretations as the basis for "anti-antirealist" readings of Wittgenstein, an expression coined by McDowell (1998, p.viii) and Putnam (2001, p.159). The latter argued for the claim that, far from giving support to antirealism, Wittgenstein was arguing for what amounts to "a species of mathematical *realism*" (Putnam, 2001, p.187). Given that Wittgenstein was supposed to resolve philosophical problems without help from philosophical theses, Putnam could simply dismiss textual evidence in favor of an antirealist reading, under the pretext that these passages involve theses – as well as exhibiting a poor understanding of mathematics. (For a clear example of this, see Putnam, 2007, p.239.) He could thus dismiss in a similar manner the distinctively antirealist claim that the meaning of a mathematical statement is given by its proof (Putnam, 2001, p.189). The problem with such moves is that they cannot be said to result in more than a selective reading of Wittgenstein, for the purpose of an agenda that seems rather foreign to his philosophy.

Putnam also interpreted Wittgenstein on rule-following as arguing against "philosophical accounts," prominently antirealist ones, thus allegedly without offering a philosophical alternative (Putnam, 1996, p.252), while nevertheless arguing for "common sense realism" (Putnam, 2001, p.147). The contrast that Putnam, inspired here by Cavell (Putnam, 1996, p.260; see also 2001, p.176), wished to establish is between the "philosophical" and the "ordinary," understood as "nonphilosophical" (Putnam, 2001, p.177). He also used the distinction between "Wittgenstein" and "Wittgensteinian," for example when writing:

> I would urge that a Wittgensteinian attitude towards the use of the law of excluded middle in mathematics should involve not a scepticism about the applications of the law within mathematics, but a 'scepticism' about the very *sense* of the 'positions' in the philosophy of mathematics.
>
> (Putnam, 1996, p.261)

Given that Wittgenstein did express such doubts, e.g., in section 352 of the *Investigations*, Putnam is thus obliged, a few lines below, to preface his defense of classical logic, under the guise of the "ordinary," with the words "What Wittgenstein *should have said*..." Mathematicians, when they learn number theory, assume that the law of excluded middle applies even where intuitionists have qualms. According to Putnam, it is these qualms that are of a philosophical nature and in need of therapy, and this is why he takes himself as expressing a "Wittgensteinian" thought. But with respect to the intuitionist arguments, this amounts to a *petitio principi*, and no evidence that Wittgenstein expressed similar thoughts has been adduced.

Under the influence of McDowell, Sabina Lovibond put forth in *Realism and Imagination in Ethics* (1983) what she described as a "moral realism derived from the later philosophy of Wittgenstein" (Lovibond, 1983, p.25). The kind of realism argued for by Lovibond was meant to be free of any metaphysical mortgage – in Blackburn's words, it is an "unpretentious realism" (Blackburn, 2010, p.200) – and her strategy was based on the claim that "if something has the grammatical form of a proposition, then it *is* a proposition" (Lovibond, 1983, p.26). This crude "syntacticism," as one may call it following Jackson, Oppy, and Smith (1994), also provides support for realism in other domains, including mathematics: given that mathematical sentences are syntactically akin to declarative sentences in the indicative mood, they are said to describe states of affairs that makes them true. Thus, the postulation of mathematical entities allows semantic realists to aim for a unitary account of truth, applying truth-conditional semantics across the board. Independently of the weight one wants to give to Wittgenstein's quietist claims, it cannot be denied, however, that he rejected realism about mathematics, which he compared to "alchemy" (RFM V §16). He also advocated a "radical break with the idea that language always functions in one way, always serves the same purpose" (PI §304) and argued that "we don't notice the enormous variety of all the everyday language-games, because the clothing of our language makes them all alike" (PPF §335). This is the thesis called "functional pluralism" by Huw Price (2004, p.180). It differs, however, from another claim, embodied in Wittgenstein's metaphor of the handles in the cabin of a locomotive, all looking the same but with a variety of functions, namely that to "describe" or "represent" reality is far from being the only function of language. (This is called "non-representationalism" by Price; see 2004, p.180.)

Lovibond nevertheless attributes the above syntacticism to Wittgenstein – she even sees it as an instance of his prohibition to interfere with actual use of language (PI §124). According to her, Wittgenstein offered us "a homogeneous or 'seamless' conception of language" (Lovibond, 1983, p.25), and he denied that "we can draw any intelligible distinction between those parts of assertoric discourse which do, and those which do not, genuinely *describe* reality" (Lovibond, 1983, p.36). Her claim that Wittgenstein recognized only a "descriptive function" for language has been refuted in many places (see for instance Diamond, 1996, pp.226–36; Conant, 1997, pp.198–202; Blackburn, 2010, pp.200–19; Glock, 2015, pp.113–21). Simon Blackburn provided numerous passages, concerning ethics and religious discourse, mathematics, avowals, and "hinge propositions," where Wittgenstein's point appears to have been, on the contrary, that surface grammar is misleading precisely because it hides the variety of functions that these declarative sentences carry out in a variety of contexts (Blackburn, 2010, pp.204–10). To illustrate the point, Wittgenstein was always suspicious of the surface grammar of mathematical propositions, which he called "pseudo-propositions" in the *Tractatus* (6.2). He writes:

> We are used to saying '2 times 2 is 4', and the verb 'is' makes this into a proposition, and apparently establishes a close kinship with everything that we call a 'proposition'. Whereas it is a matter only of a very superficial kinship.
>
> (RFM I, app.III §3)

Wittgenstein certainly argued in a number of places that mathematical propositions are "essentially akin to rules" (RPP I §266), but he also recognized that they may have a function other than normative: "There is no doubt at all that *in certain language-games* mathematical propositions play the part of rules of description, as opposed to descriptive propositions" (RFM VII §6). So Wittgenstein could be read, against Lovibond's interpretation, not so much as denying that some classes of propositions possess a "descriptive function," but as emphasizing the *multiplicity of functions* to which they may be put, i.e., "functional pluralism." James Conant has also argued, along the same lines, that Wittgenstein wanted to provide "a perspicuous overview of the interplay between the various functions of avowals (among which are its expressive and assertoric functions)" (Conant, 1997, p.207) and, further, that his treatment of mathematics "can [...] be seen in its general approach to parallel his treatment of avowals" (Conant, 1997, p.221; see also Chapter 29, THE INNER AND THE OUTER). Thus, the point seems to be that a given proposition can have more than one function, depending on the language-game in which it occurs.

4   Deflationism, Minimalism, and Quasi-Realism

As it turned out, participants on the antirealist side of the debate did not focus at all on the task of developing a distinctive antirealist semantics or even pay attention to germane developments within linguistics (e.g., Ranta, 1994) implementing Martin-Löf's constructive type theory, or work within the tradition of Lambek (1958; see also the review in Lecomte, 2011). They chose instead to argue that the antirealist could somehow take over a ready-made truth-conditional semantics by suitably reinterpreting the notion of truth. Thus, antirealism about meaning would not be restricted to replacing truth conditions with assertability-conditions; it would also involve replacing a "verification-transcendent" with an "immanent," so to speak, notion of truth (see Chapter 27, WITTGENSTEIN ON TRUTH).

Putnam had already offered in the 1970s an informal account of truth as an "idealization of rational acceptability" on a par with frictionless planes in physics, as part of his internal realism (Putnam, 1981, p.55). In the early 1990s, Crispin Wright introduced the notion of "superassertability" also to capture an epistemic account of truth as assertable, at the limit of inquiry (Wright, 1992, ch.2; 1993, pp.403–25), while Horwich suggested that a thin, non-robust concept of truth would service the assertabilist agenda (Horwich, 1990, p.72). On the latter view, called either "deflationism" or "disquotationalism," the truth predicate stands for no substantial, robust property at all; it is merely a device of disquotation according to the schema:

"p" is true if and only if p.

Wright has argued that this schema entails that "true" and "warrantedly assertible" coincide in normative force, but potentially diverge in extension (Wright, 1992, p.22). One way to understand what Wright means by "minimalism" is that this would be a necessary and sufficient condition for something to be a truth predicate (Wright, 1992, p.24).

One may discern two moves. First, one argues that statements of any of the "disputed classes" are after all "truth-apt" because they exhibit some syntactic features and their use is disciplined by some norms, e.g., they can be embedded in negation or conditional contexts, and within propositional attitudes and truth-ascription contexts – a "disciplined syntacticism" (Jackson, Oppy, and Smith, 1994, p.293). Secondly, the very idea of "deflationism" or "minimalism" about truth is to provide a "metaphysically weightless" predicate (Hale, 1997, p.292), with no room for substantial theses and debates; in other words a predicate that would be acceptable to all. Putting the two moves together, we reach the conclusion that sentences of the disputed classes all display truth-aptness for minimal truth.

There are still grounds for disagreement between realists and antirealists at this stage (see Wright, 1992), but one has to ask how Wittgenstein fits in. There are frequent references to Wittgenstein's approval of the above disquotational schema (e.g., to PI §136 and RFM I, app.III §6), with the minor difference that he states it as an identity, not a biconditional. Furthermore, Wittgenstein appears to claim that the truth-bearers are not sentences but interpreted propositions, e.g., when he writes:

What he says is true = Things are as he says

(PG, p.123; see also Horwich, 1990, p.17.)

Horwich went furthest in the attempt to enlist Wittgenstein, proposing in *Wittgenstein's Metaphilosophy* (2012) what he called the "general form of a philosophical issue." It involves eight steps, from the explicit statement of scientistic expectations, the accompanying paradoxical and philosophical tensions, to philosophical theorization and, finally, to therapeutic dissolution. Horwich provided four illustrations of this scheme, involving numbers, time, the good, and truth, with his deflationary perspective as the therapeutic part of the latter (Horwich, 2012, p.59). And Horwich claimed further that these "illustrations" are what he takes to be Wittgenstein's conception of "how the most characteristic problems in philosophy emerge, and how they should, and should not, be handled" (Horwich, 2012, p.60). It is not clear, however, whether this "metaphilosophical" agenda really is Wittgenstein's or whether it is simply Horwich's, given that Horwich's eight-step formula to eliminate philosophical problems is nowhere to be found in Wittgenstein. One would have thought Wittgenstein more likely to believe that philosophical problems are of a level of complexity that makes them impossible to fit into one general scheme. After all, Wittgenstein claimed that "there is not a single philosophical method" (PI §133).

Simon Blackburn (1998) defended against Wright a more complex view of Wittgenstein (cf. Wright, 1998). Blackburn had originally argued in *Spreading the Word* (1984) for the view that, for some disputed classes such as ethical judgments, our statements are not answerable to (moral) facts, although we talk *as if* these are genuine propositions endowed with truth conditions. We simply "project" our predicates, as it were, and "even on antirealist grounds there is nothing improper, nothing 'diseased' in projected predicates." This "quasi-realism," Blackburn adds, "tries to earn [...] the features of moral language (or of other commitments to which a projective theory might apply) which tempt people to realism" (Blackburn, 1984, p.171). So, there would be a route from some expression with a "non-descriptive function" to the "emergence" of a truth-apt proposition (Blackburn, 2010, p.211). Having already inveighed against Lovibond's syntacticism with a raft of quotations from him, Blackburn noted that Wittgenstein is likely to end up claiming that many of the disputed classes are simply *not* truth-apt. Still, Blackburn argues that Wittgenstein could not have been "hostile" to this quasi-realism, although it provides more of an "explanation" than of a "description" (Blackburn, 2010, pp.212–13). This is an implicit recognition that Wittgenstein has little to do with "quasi-realism." It would perhaps have been better merely to argue, as above, that, according to Wittgenstein, a given proposition can carry out different functions in different language-games (functional pluralism).

What is the point of Wittgenstein's appeal to the disquotational schema? In section 136 of *Philosophical Investigations*, Wittgenstein glossed on the schema, saying that "we call something a proposition if *in our language* we apply the calculus of truth functions to it," while in *Remarks on the Foundations of Mathematics*, he writes that "the game of truth-functions is played with them" (RFM I, app.III §2). One may thus grant to minimalists that the appeal to the disquotational schema is meant to minimize the significance of this identification, given that it implies that truth is not a substantive predicate, with no room for specific conceptions. This is the second of the above moves. But the minimalist wishes to argue for the first move, namely that, given such a significantly weakened truth predicate, it is possible to recognize that sentences of the disputed classes are truth-apt, and there is no clear indication, however, that this was also Wittgenstein's agenda. On the one hand, he also claims that the idea that the concept of truth "fits" a proposition is a "bad picture" (PI §136); truth is not something added, but determined both by the rules of sentence formation and "the use of the sign in the language-game." He also writes that "assertion is not something that gets added to the proposition, but an essential feature of the game we play with it" (RFM I, app.III §2). So truth and assertion are features of language-games in which one may employ given propositions. On the other hand, one should note that the appeal to the disquotational schema occurs just prior to the rule-following considerations, and assume that this is an indication of the contrary move, i.e., from truth conditions, now deprived of any metaphysical mortgage, to assertability-conditions (Kripke, 1982, p.86). This might be more to the point, irrespective of the validity of any antirealist reading of the rule-following argument. There are many passages that can give support to this claim. These include Wittgenstein's appeal to the disquotational schema in the midst of remarks on Gödel's incompleteness theorems (RFM I, app.III §6). These are controversial inasmuch as he appears to deny any distinction between truth and assertion in the system of Russell's *Principia Mathematica*, since the disquotational schema is invoked by Wittgenstein precisely to claim that "'p' is true" is equivalent to asserting p (and "'p' is false" to denying p), and that in "Russell's game" p can only be asserted "at the end of one of his proofs" (RFM I, app.III §6). So, Wittgenstein is arguing in fact that truth is coinciding with warranted assertion *within "Russell's game."* (He might have misunderstood Gödel's results, but this is not the issue here; cf. Chapter 19, WITTGENSTEIN'S LATER PHILOSOPHY OF MATHEMATICS.)

One should note instead that the claim is limited to the logical system of *Principia Mathematica*, in which one can derive counterparts of mathematical theorems. But what of mathematical propositions outside of this or any formal system? There is no evidence that Wittgenstein ever denied that a truth predicate applying to mathematical propositions would coincide with warranted assertability. Although he gestures at times at the idea that in some language-games mathematical propositions can serve a descriptive function (e.g., in RFM VII §6, quoted above), he does not exploit that point. Instead, he nearly always emphasizes that it is their *normative* use that gives them their peculiar status, so that we are back to the above point about conventionalism. The key claim of antirealist interpreters, namely that mathematical propositions have assertability-conditions rather than verification-transcendent truth conditions has not yet been dealt a decisive blow (Frascolla, 2014).

One may conclude that Wittgenstein held this antirealist view about *meaning*, while concurrently holding a minimalist stance about *truth*. How exactly these are fully to fit together, given that the latter commits Wittgenstein to alethic realism, is a task that falls outside my remit (see Glock, 2004).

5 Conclusion

The realism debate, as initiated by Dummett's challenge, appears to have run its course, at least on its original terms, and difficulties have been raised with respect to both anti-realist and anti-antirealist readings of Wittgenstein within that debate. Realism about meaning did not remain unchallenged, however, as successor debates took its place, surrounding Robert Brandom's "inferentialism" (Brandom, 1994) or Price's generalized form of quasi-realism, called "pragmatism" (Macarthur and Price, 2007, p.93). Brandom also espouses "non-representationalism" and predictably made use of Wittgenstein, with a reading akin to Kripke's of the rule-following argument (Brandom, 1994, ch.1; and pp.64–6). He was criticized by McDowell, however, largely for failing to account for Wittgenstein's quietism (McDowell, 2009, pp.96–111). Still, more recent attempts at enlisting Wittgenstein on the side of "pragmatism" (see e.g., Price, 2004), given his adherence to "non-representationalism" and "functional pluralism," show the abiding relevance of the original discussion of his thought within that debate.

References

van Atten, M. (2004). *On Brouwer*. Belmont: Wadsworth.
Baker, G.P. (1974). Criteria: A new Foundation for Semantics. *Ratio*, 16, 156–189.
Baker, G.P. and Hacker, P.M.S. (1976). Critical Notice: *Philosophical Grammar*, by Ludwig Wittgenstein. *Mind*, 85, 269–294.
Baker, G.P. and Hacker, P.M.S. (1984). *Language, Sense and Nonsense*. Oxford: Blackwell.
Baker, G.P. and Hacker, P.M.S. (1985/2014). *Wittgenstein: Rules, Grammar and Necessity. Volume 2 of an Analytical Commentary on the Philosophical Investigations. Essays and Exegesis of §§185–242*. Second edition. Extensively revised by P.M.S. Hacker. Oxford: Wiley-Blackwell.
Blackburn, S. (1984). *Spreading the Word*. Oxford: Clarendon Press.
Blackburn, S. (1998). Wittgenstein, Wright, Rorty and Minimalism. *Mind*, 107, 157–181.
Blackburn, S. (2010). *Practical Tortoise Raising and other Philosophical Essays*. Oxford: Clarendon Press.
Brandom, R. (1994). *Making it explicit*. Cambridge, MA: Harvard University Press.
Brock, S. and Mares, E. (2007). *Realism and Anti-Realism*. Montreal and Kingston: McGill-Queen's University Press.
Chihara, C. (1982). The Wright-Wing Defence of Wittgenstein's Philosophy of Logic. *Philosophical Review*, 91, 99–108.
Conant, J. (1997). On Wittgenstein's Philosophy of Mathematics. *Proceedings of the Aristotelian Society*, 97, 195–222.
Diamond, C. (1996). Wittgenstein, Mathematics, and Ethics: Resisting the Attractions of Realism. In H. Sluga and D. Stern (Eds). *The Cambridge Companion to Wittgenstein* (pp.226–260). Cambridge: Cambridge University Press.

Dummett, M.A.E. (1959) Wittgenstein's Philosophy of Mathematics. Reprinted in M.A.E. Dummett. (1978). *Truth and Other Enigmas* (pp.166–185). London: Duckworth.
Dummett, M.A.E. (1973/1981). *Frege: Philosophy of Language*. Second edition. London: Duckworth.
Dummett, M.A.E. (1978a). *Truth and Other Enigmas*. London: Duckworth.
Dummett, M.A.E. (1978b). Reckonings: Wittgenstein on Mathematics. *Encounter*, 50, 63–68.
Dummett, M.A.E. (1991). *The Seas of Language*. Oxford: Clarendon Press.
Fogelin, R. (1992). *Philosophical Interpretations*. New York: Oxford University Press.
Frascolla, P. (1994). *Wittgenstein's Philosophy of Mathematics*. London: Routledge.
Frascolla, P. (2014). Realism, Anti-Realism, Quietism: Wittgenstein's Stance. *Grazer Philosophische Studien*, 89, 11–21.
Glock, H.-J. (1996). *A Wittgenstein Dictionary*. Oxford: Blackwell.
Glock, H.-J. (2004). Wittgenstein on Truth. In W. Löffler and P. Weingartner (Eds). *Knowledge and Belief: Wissen und Glauben* (pp.13–31). Vienna: Hölder-Pichler-Tempsky.
Glock, H.-J. (2015). Wittgenstein's Anti-Anti-Realism: One "Anti" Too Many?. *Ethical Perspectives*, 22, 99–129.
Hacker, P.M.S. (1972). *Insight and Illusion: Wittgenstein on Philosophy and the Metaphysics of Experience*. Oxford: Clarendon Press.
Hacker, P.M.S. (1972/86). *Insight and Illusion: Themes in the Philosophy of Wittgenstein*. Revised edition. Oxford: Clarendon Press.
Hale, B. (1997). Realism and its Oppositions. In B. Hale and C. Wright (Eds). *A Companion to Philosophy of Language* (pp.271–308). Oxford: Blackwell.
Horwich, P. (1990). *Truth*. Oxford: Blackwell.
Horwich, P. (2012). *Wittgenstein's Metaphilosophy*. Oxford: Clarendon Press.
Jackson, F., Oppy, G., and Smith, M. (1994). Minimalism and Truth Aptness. *Mind*, 103, 287–301.
Kripke, S.A. (1982). *Wittgenstein on Rules and Private Language: An Elementary Exposition*. Oxford: Blackwell.
Lambek, J. (1958). The Mathematics of Sentence Structure. *American Mathematical Monthly*, 65, 154–170.
Lecomte, A. (2011). *Meaning, Logic and Ludics*. London: Imperial College Press.
Lovibond, S. (1983). *Realism and Imagination in Ethics*. Oxford: Blackwell.
Macarthur, D. and Price, H. (2007). Pragmatism, Quasi-Realism, and the Global Challenge. In C. Mysak (Ed.). *New Pragmatists* (pp.91–121). Oxford: Clarendon Press.
Marion, M. (1998). *Wittgenstein, Finitism, and the Foundations of Mathematics*. Oxford: Clarendon Press.
Marion, M. (2003). Wittgenstein and Brouwer. *Synthese*, 137, 103–127.
Marion, M. (2011). Wittgenstein on the Surveyability of Proofs. In O. Kuusela and M. McGinn (Eds). *The Oxford Handbook of Wittgenstein* (pp.138–161). Oxford: Oxford University Press.
Marion, M. and Okada, M. (2014). Wittgenstein on Equinumerosity and Surveyability. *Grazer Philosophische Studien*, 89, 61–78.
McDowell, J. (1998). *Mind, Value and Reality*. Cambridge, MA: Harvard University Press.
McDowell, J. (2009). *The engaged Intellect*. Cambridge, MA: Harvard University Press.
Prawitz, D. (1977). Meaning and Proofs: On the Conflict between Classical and Intuitionistic Logic. *Theoria*, 43, 1–40.
Price, H. (2004). Immodesty without Mirrors: Making Sense of Wittgenstein's Linguistic Pluralism. In M. Kölbel and B. Weiss (Eds). *Wittgenstein's Lasting Significance* (pp.179–206). London: Routledge.
Putnam, H. (1978). *Meaning and the Moral Sciences*. London: Routledge and Kegan Paul.
Putnam, H. (1981). *Reason, Truth and History*. Cambridge: Cambridge University Press.
Putnam, H. (1983). *Realism and Reason: Philosophical Papers Volume 3*. Cambridge: Cambridge University Press.

Putnam, H. (1996). On Wittgenstein's Philosophy of Mathematics. *Proceedings of the Aristotelian Society* (Supplementary Volume), 70, 243–264.
Putnam, H. (2001). Was Wittgenstein *Really* an Anti-Realist about Mathematics?. In T. McCarthy and S.C. Stidd (Eds). *Wittgenstein in America* (pp.140–194). Oxford: Clarendon Press.
Putnam, H. (2007). Wittgenstein and the Real Numbers. In A. Crary (Ed.). *Wittgenstein and the Moral Life: Essays in Honor of Cora Diamond* (pp.235–250). Cambridge, MA: MIT Press.
Ranta, A. (1994). *Type-Theoretical Grammar*. Oxford: Clarendon Press.
Rodych, V. (2011) Wittgenstein's Philosophy of Mathematics. In E. Zalta (Ed.). *The Stanford Encyclopedia of Philosophy*. http://plato.stanford.edu/archives/sum2011/entries/wittgenstein-mathematics/ (last accessed 7 June 2016).
Rundle, B. (1990). *Wittgenstein and Contemporary Philosophy of Language*. Oxford: Blackwell.
Schneider, H.J. (2014). *Wittgenstein's Later Theory of Meaning: Imagination and Calculation*. Oxford: Wiley-Blackwell.
Shanker, S. (1986). *Wittgenstein and the Turning-Point in the Philosophy of Mathematics*. London: Croom Helm.
Stokhof, M. (2013). Formal Semantics and Wittgenstein: An Alternative?. *The Monist*, 96, 205–231.
Stroud, B. (1966). Wittgenstein and Logical Necessity. In G. Pitcher (Ed.). *Wittgenstein: The Philosophical Investigations* (pp.477–496). Garden City: Anchor Books.
Wright, C. (1980). *Wittgenstein on the Foundations of Mathematics*. London: Duckworth.
Wright, C. (1992). *Truth and Objectivity*. Cambridge, MA: Harvard University Press.
Wright, C. (1993). *Realism, Meaning and Truth*. Second edition. Oxford: Blackwell.
Wright, C. (1998). Comrades against Quietism: Reply to Simon Blackburn on Truth and Objectivity. *Mind*, 107, 183–203.
Wright, C. (2001). *Rails to Infinity*. Cambridge, MA: Harvard University Press.

Further Reading

Bouveresse, J. (1992). Wittgenstein, Anti-Realism and Mathematical Propositions. *Grazer Philosophische Studien*, 42, 133–160.
Weiss, B. (2002). *Michael Dummett*. Princeton: Princeton University Press.

21

Necessity and Apriority

ERIC LOOMIS

The nature of necessary truth was a central concern of Wittgenstein's. It was present in his early reflections on logic, a core motif of the *Tractatus*, and a topic he returned to over and again in his reflections on language, logic, and mathematics. A priori knowledge received less direct attention. This was due not to a lack of interest on Wittgenstein's part, but to his belief that an adequate account of logic, which Wittgenstein construed broadly to include all conceptually true statements, would resolve the traditional problems for which apriority had been invoked.

Yet few areas of Wittgenstein's work now appear more at odds with contemporary trends in analytic philosophy than his treatment of necessity and apriority. Where he saw an understanding of the nature of logic as illuminating both, the subsequent tradition has tended to see difference. For many contemporary philosophers, necessity, understood as the metaphysical property of something's being such that it could not possibly be otherwise, is not coextensive with apriority, understood as the epistemological property of being knowable independently of experience. From this perspective, philosophers such as Wittgenstein who assumed them to be coextensive are mistaken.

I will here explore aspects of Wittgenstein's account of necessity and apriority, beginning with the *Tractatus*, where many of his core insights received their first expression. Along the way, I will touch on two more contemporary accounts of these topics: conceptual role semantic theories of the a priori, and the above-mentioned arguments for divorcing apriority from necessity. In both cases, I will claim that Wittgenstein still has much to offer us.

1   Necessity's Dual Source

Necessity in the *Tractatus* appears at two locations. One is at the level of individual elementary propositions. The other is at the level of the inferential connections between propositions. To understand this account of necessity, and how it failed, we must briefly look at the *Tractatus*' theory of the proposition.

A Companion to Wittgenstein, First Edition. Edited by Hans-Johann Glock and John Hyman.
© 2017 John Wiley & Sons, Ltd. Published 2017 by John Wiley & Sons, Ltd.

In the *Tractatus*, Wittgenstein held that a proposition is a fact, that is, an actual arrangement of certain words (TLP 3.14). A proposition represents a possible state of affairs, which may obtain or not, and is itself a fact, if it does. A proposition is therefore a kind of picture, consisting of words concatenated in a certain way (4.22). In a picture, "that the elements of the picture are combined with one another in a definite way, represents that the things are so combined with one another" (2.15). The picture thus shares something, a *logical form*, with the fact that it depicts (2.18). This form is not named by the proposition or any of its parts but is instead mirrored by it by, in elementary propositions, the proposition's names being concatenated in a definite way. Wittgenstein accommodated this by introducing the notion of logical syntax. The logical syntax of a language consists of those rules that allow a configuration of pictorial elements to express a logical form (3.344). For example, in a simple language it might be a rule that when a name "*a*" stands to the left of the name "*b*," the object named by "*a*" is larger than that named by "*b*." Grasping this rule is a condition for understanding that the proposition "*ab*" says that the referent of "*a*" is larger than that of "*b*."

In order to share a form with the possible fact that it pictures, the elementary proposition must be articulate in the same way that the possible fact that it depicts is articulated (cf. 4.04–4.041). A proposition that failed this condition by attempting to depict what is not possible would lack sense; it would not correspond with the existence or nonexistence of any possible fact (3.4, 4.3). Certain combinations of names into meaningful elementary propositions are thereby *necessarily* excluded, such as propositional functions that take themselves as argument (3.333).

A second source of necessity appears at the level of compound propositions. In the *Tractatus*, such propositions are truth functions that have elementary propositions as bases (5.234). They are constructed from the operation of joint-denial, expressed by the operator-sign "N." When applied to a single proposition p, N returns its negation $\sim p$, and when applied to a pair of propositions p, q, N returns their joint denial, $\sim p \bullet \sim q$ (§5.51). The N-operator thus incorporates negation and conjunction, and is truth-functionally complete. What of quantifiers? If we take an elementary proposition and replace one of its names with variables, we form a propositional function. The values of the variable constitute the class of propositions that would result from replacing the variable with an admissible expression, all of which must share a common form (3.311–3.313). For instance, if we imagine that "*ab*" is an elementary proposition that expresses that a is larger than b, "*ax*" is a propositional variable which expresses a form shared by all things that can possibly (truly or falsely) stand in the larger-than relation to a. The universal quantifier is formed from the logical product of all sentences that result from this replacement (5.52). The *Tractatus* thereby treats quantificational logic in truth-functional terms.

By presenting every proposition as a truth function of independent elementary propositions, Wittgenstein made explicit the logical relationships among states of affairs that tie them together into a single logical space (cf. §§5.471–5.4711). Wittgenstein famously observed that propositions allow for two "extreme cases":

> In the one case the proposition is true for all the truth-possibilities of the elementary propositions [...]. In the second case the proposition is false for all the truth-possibilities. In the first case we call the proposition a tautology, in the second case a contradiction. (4.46)

Tautologies and contradictions do not picture facts. Lacking the two truth poles of true and false, they present no state of affairs and consequently are without sense

(4.461–4.462). They are however well formed; they obey the rules of logical syntax and are "part of the symbolism" (4.611). In this respect, they are unlike ill-formed nonsense, for the senselessness of tautologies allows them to express something by showing it:

> The logical propositions describe the scaffolding of the world, or rather they present it. They "treat" of nothing. [...] It is clear that it must show something about the world that certain combinations of symbols – which essentially have a definite character – are tautologies. (6.124)

The scope of the necessary truth, and the "scaffolding" of the world, is thus determined by iteration of the truth-functional N-operator to the base elementary propositions. It alone is sufficient to generate all compound propositions and all tautologies. Logical necessity is thus the only kind of necessity (6.37). Moreover, whether something is a tautology can be calculated, and in this sense determined a priori, from the expression itself, for instance by a truth table (6.126). But since the tautology is senseless, there are no propositions expressive of a priori knowledge (cf. 5.4731). By denying sense to such signs, Wittgenstein displaced talk of a priori knowledge with talk of what can or cannot be meaningfully said (cf. 5.5541–5.5542, 5.4731).

2   Color Exclusion

When we reflect on how the tautological propositions of logic are constructed from the elementary propositions as I have sketched above, we can see both the interconnection and the distinctness of the two *loci* of necessity in the *Tractatus*. Tautologies show the logical scaffolding of the world by presenting the limit cases of propositions formed by the N-operator from the base elementary propositions. Here necessity shows itself as the logical relations among independent base propositions. Yet when we reflect on what constitutes the base propositions, we return to the first *locus* of necessity in the elementary propositions, where the possible substitutions of names determine the class of propositions from which quantifiers are formed. Together, these *loci* fully determine which expressions will be tautologies in a correct symbolism. Thus if, for instance, it is impossible for two primary colors to be jointly asserted of a single point in space, as Wittgenstein claimed (TLP §6.3751), this impossibility must appear on analysis to be a logical contradiction.

Here Wittgenstein's account proved inadequate. Let us express "Red is at point p at time t" as "RPT," and "Blue is at p at t" as "BPT." The conjunction "RPT and BPT" is not a contradiction. The *Tractatus* acknowledged this, but offered no account of how it could be revealed to be one on analysis. Challenged by Ramsey, Wittgenstein sought to revise his account to remove this problem. He initially suggested that the mutual exclusion of RPT and BPT,

> consists in the fact that RPT and BPT are in a certain sense *complete*. That which corresponds in reality to the function "()PT" leaves room for only one entity – in the same sense, in fact, in which we say that there is room for one person only in a chair. Our symbolism, which allows us to form the sign of the logical product of "RPT" and "BPT", gives here no correct picture of reality.
>
> (RLF 169)

This revision was roughly continuous with the *Tractatus* in placing constraints on the permissible values of a variable formed by substituting it for a name. Yet it remained flawed in at least two respects. First, the logical product "RPT and BPT" is obtainable from the N-operator by applying it to the two base propositions. Yet Wittgenstein here conceded that it does not correctly picture reality. As such, the N-operator is not sufficient to fully circumscribe the space of logical possibility. Second, Wittgenstein's explanation of how "()PT" leaves room for only one entity explains the exclusion of colors by way of the spatial exclusion of people in a chair. But it is no clearer how this latter, spatial exclusion might constitute a contradiction than it was with colors (cf. Jacquette, 1998, pp.180–6). The *Tractatus*' commitment to a single form of logical necessity was untenable.

3 Language as Calculus

Wittgenstein's response to this breakdown was to propose that language consists not of a single, overarching logic, but of a variety of systems or calculi, each of which obeys its own set of internal rules (cf. WVC 168–9). Instead of a logically independent picture making contact with reality as a scale (TLP §2.1512), Wittgenstein proposed regarding language as a calculus of such propositions that is laid against it: "I now prefer to say that a *system of propositions* is laid against reality like a ruler" (WVC 64). Color language forms such a system, and the exclusion of one color by another is a consequence of the fact that when we "lay a *system* of propositions against reality, this means that in each case there is only *one* state of affairs that can exist" (WVC 64).

Wittgenstein now regarded logical possibility as what is permissible within a calculus. He claimed that the impossibility of red and green being at the same place involved a "grammatical (logical) concept, not a material one" (WVC 67). Wittgenstein nonetheless preserved his earlier connection of the possible with the meaningful by claiming that what we *count* as a meaningful representation of something, possible or actual, is internally tied to the calculus in which it plays a role:

> I know that a measurement determines only *one* value on a scale and not several values. If you ask me, How do I know that? I shall simply answer, Because I understand the sense of the statement. It is impossible to understand the sense of the statement without knowing the rule.
> (I may know the rule in terms of applying it without having formulated it explicitly.)
> (WVC 78)

As he had in the *Tractatus*, Wittgenstein continued to reject the possibility of substantive a priori knowledge (WVC 67–8). But the internal properties of the *Tractatus*, which there could only be shown, were now reconceived as truths of "grammar."

Wittgenstein understood "grammar" broadly:

> What belongs to grammar are all the conditions (the method) necessary for comparing the [true or false] proposition with reality. That is, all of the conditions necessary for the understanding (of the sense).
> (PG 88)

Grammar specifies the correct use of an expression in terms of rules: to give the meaning of an expression is to give its grammar (PG 62–4). Wittgenstein saw an important difference between the formulations of the rules of grammar and descriptions of states of affairs. He regarded grammatical rules as not being *descriptive* at all, even of the calculus itself (PR 143). As norms of correct use, they are antecedent to the descriptive and inferential functions of language: "I must *begin* with the distinction between sense and nonsense. Nothing is possible prior to that" (PG 126). Rather than describe how things are, grammatical rules specify the linguistic framework in terms of which such descriptions acquire a sense (AWL 16). To violate these rules is to abandon the language that they norm. And by specifying what counts as a true or false description of reality, such norms constitute essential, necessary connections among expressions (AWL 16; RFM I, §8f.). I will return to this below.

Here, I wish to indicate another aspect of grammatical norms: their arbitrariness (see Chapter 15, THE AUTONOMY OF GRAMMAR):

> Grammar is not accountable to any reality. It is grammatical rules that determine meaning (constitute it) and so they themselves are not answerable to any meaning and to that extent are arbitrary.
>
> (PG 184)

This arbitrariness of grammar marked another shift from the *Tractatus*, for which the logic of language was one and "all embracing" (TLP §5.511). Wittgenstein now explicitly granted the possibility of alternative systems of grammar; systems in which measurement, logical operators, or even counting might differ from ours (LFM 202; RFM I, §11f.).

4 Conceptual Roles

Wittgenstein's conception of grammar, and his treatment of a priori knowledge, bear a resemblance to contemporary "conceptual role" theories of a priori knowledge, which I will here briefly consider.

Conceptual role semantics (CRS) refers to a type of theory that treats a person's disposition to engage in certain uses of expressions, such as inferential patterns of reasoning, as forming an at least necessary condition on that person's grasp of the meaning of those expressions. This basic idea, which originates with Wittgenstein, has in recent years been used by some philosophers to provide an explanation of a priori knowledge, such as our knowledge of logical laws (see for instance Peacocke, 2002; Boghossian, 2003; Brandom, 2001; Hale and Wright, 2001). The idea here is roughly that a disposition to engage in the inferences prescribed by certain rule-governed roles is essential to understanding the meaning of certain expressions, such as logical operators. Consequently, to grasp that meaning is to have a kind of a priori justification for accepting the inferences the operator licenses. Thus for instance, grasping the standard meaning of "·" provides some kind of a priori justification for inferring "p," or "q," from "$p \cdot q$" (cf. Boghossian, 2003, p.11; Brandom, 2001, p.70).

Some CRS theorists thus seek to account for a priori justification as being, in part, a product of the meaning of rule-governed conceptual roles. In this respect, there is a parallel with Wittgenstein's use of grammatically-constituted meaning as explaining certain knowledge claims. CRS accounts have nonetheless been subject to criticisms, which might extend to Wittgenstein's account as well. One problem is this: if the meaning of expressions such as logical connectives can be introduced by stipulating inference rules for them, nothing appears to prevent the stipulation of a connective, "tonk," which licenses the following inference: from *p* infer *p tonk q*, and from *p tonk q*, infer *q* (cf. Prior, 1960). The "tonk" rule would allow the inference of any proposition from any other, and so appears flatly defective.

Examples like "tonk" have motivated CRS theorists to impose various constraints on the stipulations that define a conceptual role. One proposed constraint is that rules governing new concepts be truth-preserving. Another is that they be conservative in the sense that one cannot use the new rule-governed expressions to infer any statements about the original expressions of the language that were not derivable from the original language alone (cf. Brandom, 2001, p.74). "Tonk" would be neither truth-preserving nor conservative, since it would allow us to derive contradictions that we cannot derive without it. Yet even truth-preserving or conservative stipulations may nonetheless fail to provide a plausible account of a priori knowledge if, for example, there are truth-preserving inference rules that presuppose extraordinarily complex chains of reasoning that users of the rule cannot be expected to understand (cf. Boghossian, 2003, p.29).

Considerations such as these have led contemporary conceptual role semanticists to impose constraints on possible stipulations of semantical roles. Boghossian (2003) has suggested that for most concepts, the conditions for possessing the concept cannot depend upon the acceptance of contingent, and thus possibly false, claims about the world. This condition can be expressed by framing the rule-stipulations constitutive of an expression's meaning as conditionals ("Carnap conditionals") that impose an existence condition on the acceptance of a conceptual transition. Others have proposed alternative constraints. For example, Peacocke (2002) argues that inferential transitions must be rational in order to provide a priori justification. Transitions are rational only if they are reliable, Peacocke argues, and reliability in turn requires appeal to a notion of the truth at which the judgment aims. This has the consequence that truth cannot be explained in terms of conceptual roles, but must be taken for granted as a condition on them.

Like conceptual role semanticists, Wittgenstein recognized that the stipulation of rules of grammar required qualification. His responses paralleled theirs in one way, but diverged sharply in another.

Wittgenstein saw that grammar's arbitrariness was limited by the broader context in which grammatical rules have a function. This context imposes constraints on what could intelligibly serve as a grammatical rule. For instance, of color exclusion he wrote that simply stipulating that the sentence: "red and green are both at this point at the same time" did not fix a color grammar, since "Further stipulations have yet to be made about how such a sentence is to be used; e.g. how it is to be verified" (PG 127). Wittgenstein also granted that in order to call something reasoning, thinking, or calculating, it must conform to general pragmatic considerations, such as one's aims. For instance, of Frege's remark that a people with a logic that contradicted ours would be "mad," Wittgenstein observed that the madness would stem from the fact that we would be unable to see the *point* of what they are doing (LFM 203).

Wittgenstein eschewed, however, imposing independent notions of truth, reference, or rationality on grammatical stipulations. In this respect his emphasis on the arbitrariness of grammar diverges from most conceptual role semanticists'. From their perspective, it is implausible that an arbitrary stipulation that a sentence be true could *make it the case* that what the sentence expresses is actually true, still less necessarily so.

Boghossian has argued, for instance, that it is implausible to suppose that prior to our stipulating a meaning for the sentence "Either snow is white or it isn't" it wasn't the case that either snow was white or it wasn't (Boghossian, 1996, p.365). Peacocke (2002), Horwich (1998), and others have raised similar objections.

I think Wittgenstein anticipated this general line of objection. Among his responses was an emphasis on the internal connection between meaning-constitutive stipulations and the statements describing those facts that are supposed to justify them or make them true:

> If I could describe the point of grammatical conventions by saying that they are made necessary by certain properties of the colors (say), then that would make the conventions superfluous, since in that case I would be able to say precisely that which the conventions exclude my saying. Conversely, if the conventions were necessary, i.e., if certain combinations of words had to be excluded as nonsensical, then for that very reason I cannot cite a property of colors that makes the conventions necessary, since it would then be conceivable that the colors should not have this property, and I could only express that by violating the conventions.
>
> (PR 53)

Two assumptions of Wittgenstein's need to be borne in mind here. First, a meaningful expression of a descriptive language, such as a color language, is given by the rules of its grammar, and is solely a function of those rules. As such, there is no more expressive latitude in the description than is provided by its grammar (PG 186). Second, there is a fundamental distinction between the expression of a grammatical rule and a descriptive statement. As noted above, Wittgenstein regarded the former as normative and as specifying a course of action (a linguistic use), rather than truly or falsely reporting a fact, as a descriptive statement does.

With these assumptions explicit, I think we can see Wittgenstein's argument as forming a dilemma. On the one hand, if the rules prohibit certain descriptions as nonsensical, then since those descriptions have no more expressive latitude than the rules grant them, they cannot report any possible facts that might contravene the rules. In which case they offer no justification of the rules, but simply reflect them. On the other hand, to assume that the justifying descriptions are meaningful is to accept as a condition on their meaning that they are possibly false, in which case the rules would not be justified as necessary. Yet the possible falsity of the descriptions would presuppose that they possess an expressive latitude that violated the very rules that, *ex hypothesi*, constitute their meaning.

To the extent that this argument is successful, it illustrates one way in which Wittgenstein could have rejected the appeal by conceptual role semanticists to an antecedently available notion of facts or of the truth of descriptions in order to justify linguistic stipulations.

5   Criteria and Symptoms

As Wittgenstein's thought developed, he increasingly avoided speaking of language as a calculus, and by the *Philosophical Investigations* (indeed as early as the time of the *Blue Book* dictations in 1933) was openly critical of the notion that speaking a language is like operating a calculus of definite rules (PI §81). Instead, he brought to the fore his notion of a language-game. His reasons for this transition were multiple. I will briefly address one that is relevant to my discussion of necessity below.

Starting around the time of the so-called *Blue and Brown Books*, Wittgenstein drew ever more attention to the close connection between language and a "form of life" – the particular practices, techniques, and ends – which give language its role. The term "language-*game*," he wrote, "is meant to bring into prominence the fact that the *speaking* of a language is part of an activity, or of a life-form" (PI §23). Language "relates to a way of living. In order to describe the phenomenon of language, one must describe a practice, not something that happens once" (RFM VI, §33). Likewise, in describing possible languages, we must "imagine a form of life" (PI §7), including the interests, techniques, and concerns of the community in which the language is spoken. Wittgenstein suggested that our form of life consists of things we don't typically notice because we take them for granted (RFM I, §142), but which nonetheless form the foundation of language use. One way to see this is to imagine alterations to our practices and concerns, and then to observe how our use of language might change as a result (cf. BB 134–5; RFM I, §5, §§142–50).

Wittgenstein's development of these ideas was accompanied by a further refinement of the distinction between rules of grammar and descriptions into the distinction between criteria and symptoms. It arose against the background of his earlier reflections on grammar, and in particular on the way that certain grammatical explanations could serve to answer questions about knowledge and meaning (BB 23–4):

> To the question "How do you know that so-and-so is the case?", we sometimes answer by giving '*criteria*' and sometimes by giving '*symptoms*'. If medical science calls angina [tonsillitis] an inflammation caused by a particular bacillus, and we ask in a particular case "why do you say this man has got angina?" then the answer "I have found the bacillus so-and-so in his blood" gives us the criterion, [...] of angina. If on the other hand the answer was "his throat is inflamed", this might give us a symptom of angina. I call "symptom" a phenomenon of which experience has taught us that it coincided, in some way or other, with the phenomenon which is our defining criterion.
>
> (BB 24–5)

Criteria connect an expression, such as "angina" or "toothache," with certain evidence, such as the presence of a bacillus, or cheek-holding. They are given by grammatical rules that form part of the explanation of the meaning of an expression (cf. PI §§322, 373–7), and in some contexts can serve as answers to the question of how we know something is the case (cf. PI §182). Symptoms, by contrast, are found in experience, and while they may also serve as answers to how we know something, they do so by appeal to experience, not grammar. Criteria stipulate a connection between an expression and the evidence that licenses its application. Thus for example, we must, if we are said to know what "angina" (tonsillitis) means, say that someone has angina if they have an inflammation caused by *this* kind of bacillus in their blood. By contrast, a symptomatic report is something found, not stipulated, and the expression of that report is descriptive, not normative.

By linking certain expressions with the evidence that licenses their application, criteria are partially constitutive of grammar. Expressions of criterial relations thereby appear to be statements of necessary truth, for Wittgenstein. For example, "if someone has the bacillus so-and-so in his blood, then they have angina" would seem necessary on the above account. Yet when extended to more complex cases, such as many psychological predicates, this poses a problem. For instance, Wittgenstein imagined a language-game in which cheek-holding was a criterion of someone's having a toothache (BB 24). Yet it seems obvious that someone might hold their cheek yet not have a toothache. If so, cheek-holding by itself doesn't seem to entail, or make necessary, the presence of a toothache.

Two main lines of interpretation have appeared in response to this problem. The first argues that in many cases, the meaning-constitutive function of criteria is not an entailment. Rather, criteria are meaning constituting in virtue of providing "grammatically good evidence" – evidence that is conceptually or grammatically tied to the expressions being defined, but whose presence does not entail the truth of any statement containing those expressions (cf. Shoemaker, 1963; Kenny, 1967; Hacker, 1990/93a and b). A second response to the above objection is to argue that there is an entailment from the criterial evidence for a term to the truth of certain statements involving it, but that in particular cases the criterial evidence may be defeated, and so ascription of the criterially-governed expression may be blocked (cf. Canfield, 1981; McDowell, 1982; Loomis, 2007).

Whether Wittgenstein himself would have endorsed such proposals is unclear, for he disavowed any attempt to link his notion of criteria with a search for the "real" meaning of words. Instead, he considered the attempt to decide which phenomenon was the defining criterion and which symptom "arbitrary" (BB 25), and the criteria for certain psychological processes to be "fluctuating" (PI §384). Wittgenstein presented criteria's role not as a theoretical one, but as one of rendering perspicuous certain otherwise misleading uses of language:

> A main source of our failure to understand is that we do not *command a clear view* of the use of our words. – Our grammar is lacking in this sort of perspicuity. A perspicuous representation produces just that understanding which consists in 'seeing connexions'.
> (PI §122)

6 Measures and Language-Games

I want finally to turn to the most significant development in the study of apriority and necessity in recent decades, namely the separation of the notions of apriority and necessity in the writings of Kripke, Putnam, and numerous subsequent philosophers (cf. Kripke, 1980; Putnam, 1975). I will focus here on Kripke's account.

Kripke argued that necessity and apriority are not coextensive. Consider for example the statement that "Hesperus is Phosphorus." Suppose that we stipulate that "Hesperus is identical to some unique star visible in the evening (if any)," and that "Phosphorus is identical to some unique star visible in the morning (if any)." If it turns out that Hesperus is in fact identical to Phosphorus, then that fact, being an instance of the law of identity, is necessary. Yet this identity is known only a posteriori by astronomical investigations. Kripke argued for a similar result for many natural kind terms. Identities involving them, such as "Water is H_2O," might be necessarily true if, as Kripke argued, substances like water have their microstructure essentially, and H_2O is that microstructure. Yet it is only a posteriori that such microstructures are known.

Kripke further argued that other statements, including stipulations, may be a priori yet contingent. As an example, he considered a famous assertion of Wittgenstein's:

There is *one* thing of which one can say neither that it is one meter long, nor that it is not one meter long, and that is the standard meter in Paris. – But this is, of course, not to ascribe any extraordinary property to it, but only to mark its peculiar role in the language-game of measuring with a meter-rule.

(PI §50)

Kripke presented two arguments against Wittgenstein. The first appeals to the fact that the standard meter has a length and, as such, can be measured:

If the stick [serving as the standard meter] is a stick, for example, 39.37 inches long (I assume we have some different standard for inches), why isn't it one meter long?

(Kripke, 1980, p.54)

The second argument began with what Kripke called an "intuitive difference between the phrase 'one meter' and the phrase 'the length of [standard meter stick] S at t_0'" (1980, p.55). "One meter" refers to a certain length, while "stick S at t_0" refers to a particular stick. When someone uses stick S at t_0 in a definition of "one meter," Kripke thought, he is trying to pick out a reference, in this case a certain length, without trying to say anything true about the particular stick he is using at that moment:

There is a certain length which he wants to mark out. He marks it out by an accidental property, namely that there is a stick of that length. Someone else might mark out the same reference by another accidental property. But in any case, even though he uses this to fix the reference of his standard of length, a meter, he can still say, 'if heat had been applied to this S at t_0, then at t_0 stick S would not have been one meter long.'

(1980, p.55)

The referent of the expression "one meter," the length picked out, is self-identical. In all possible worlds, "one meter" picks out that length. It is thus a "rigid designator." But "the length of stick S at t_0" is not a rigid designator. Even though it is used to fix the reference of "one meter" by stipulation, we can imagine possible situations in which S has a different length at t_0. Consequently, the definition of "one meter" as the length of S at t_0, even though stipulated and thus known a priori, is contingent (1980, p.56).

These claims stand at odds with Wittgenstein's accounts of necessity and apriority from the *Tractatus* onward. Wittgenstein's accounts involved an identification of expressions of necessity with tautologies, or conventional rules of syntax or grammar, which were known a priori either through calculation, as in the *Tractatus*, or though stipulation. Wittgenstein was thus committed to the very identifications that Kripke denied.

At the same time, the force of some of Kripke's initial claims has been challenged. One important challenge has been to the identification of the essential properties of substances such as water with their microstructure (cf. Needham, 2010). Such identifications have proven deeply at odds with contemporary biological and chemical theory, as well as with much scientific practice, in which *macroscopic* criteria underlie determinations of whether or not a given quantity of matter is in fact a substance like water. Other philosophers have asserted that even if Kripke's rejection of the identification of necessity with apriority is granted, that rejection is compatible with conventionalism. Sidelle (1989) has argued that if we begin from a richer account of conventions according to which there can exist conventional rules which relate the empirical discovery of certain properties with kinds, and which have necessary truths as their consequences, the necessary a posteriori becomes compatible with conventionalism. Another proposal (Juhl and Loomis, 2010) distinguishes, as "two-dimensional" semantics does, between different semantic contents associated with an utterance; this allows for the contingency of certain statements introduced by stipulation. Yet unlike two-dimensionalism, this account seeks to explain these semantic contents not in terms of possible-world semantics, but in terms of the rules and conventions governing the use of the relevant expressions. Yet another account (Canfield, 1981) disputes the claim that conventional linguistic stipulations could be contingent by arguing that alleged examples to the contrary rest on a subtle equivocation between anthropological statements about how an expression is in fact used and genuine grammatical statements about how it ought to be used.

I wish here to focus on a different issue by looking more closely at the conception of language use that appears to underlie Kripke's standard meter case. It is one that Wittgenstein would have rejected.

Kripke's initial challenge to Wittgenstein's remark about the standard meter was, as quoted above, to suggest that the standard meter might be said to be one meter long if it is 39.37 inches long. This response asserts that a standard in one familiar system of linear measurement can be replaced by a conversion formula that presupposes another familiar system of measurement. Why did Kripke believe this is convincing? I think it is because his argument takes for granted that his readers have mastered the use of basic linear measurements, and he relies upon this shared mastery in order to show how one system can be easily replaced by another, similar one. Within this shared mastery, which particular method or technique of linear measurement we use appears to be external to our grasp of the meaning of expressions such as "one meter long." For Kripke, the meaning of this expression does not rest on a mastery of a system of linear measurement, but rather on a "certain length" that is picked out.

If this is roughly correct, then I think that from Wittgenstein's perspective Kripke has explained the meaning of "one meter" in a conceptually reversed order. Wittgenstein considered the meaning of expressions such as "one meter" to be *products* of the shared mastery of techniques of using things like standards or conversion formulae within systems of measurement (cf. RFM I, §5, §§140–3). It is this mastery that Kripke takes for granted. Here Wittgenstein's remark (PI §50) that the standard meter is a *means* of representation should not be overlooked. Only against a technique of applying the meter bar by, for example, holding it against an object to see if it matches at the end points, can the standard meter measure. There is no way to compare the standard with itself using this technique, and so the condition on saying of something that it is or is not one meter long is not met by the standard bar.

Wittgenstein would likely have regarded Kripke's account of the meaning of "one meter," namely the "certain length" that is picked out, as wholly *irrelevant* to meaning. To see why, imagine a simple language-game in which someone, "the Originator," has a certain length they want to pick out. Suppose for the sake of argument that the Originator can pick out this length with perfect consistency on different occasions, and does so by finding or cutting one or more objects like sticks to fit it. What makes his objects into a *unit of measurement*? By itself, nothing; finding or cutting examples of this length simply produces a collection of same-length objects. To have a unit of measurement, he must *use* the objects in some way. To understand this use, we must describe a form of life in which the object has a role. Perhaps the Originator lays his stick against other materials such as fabric or wood, and cuts them to lengths that match its end points. We now have a technique for using the stick, but still no unit of measurement, only further objects of the same length. Perhaps the Originator is selling the fabric and wood. His customers accept the lengths he measures out with a stick, and, depending upon the material, pay him a uniform amount for each stick-length. Now, his use of the stick is coordinated with others, and serves a *role* within a form of life – that of buying and selling goods, of payments, and of paying the same amount for the same quantity. Over time, other shopkeepers copy the practice to facilitate their exchanges. They copy the length by traveling to the original shopkeeper and cutting a stick to the length of his. To make things easier, a "standard stick" is set up for everyone, shopkeepers and customers alike, to check their objects against. They come to call this object "the standard meter," and one length measured against it is "one meter."

This description of a possible language-game is not intended as armchair anthropology or speculative history. The game could be described in other ways, one of which might describe the actual history of the standard meter in Paris. The point is rather to illustrate, first, that Kripke's "certain length" that someone wanted to pick out is completely irrelevant to the use of "meter" in the context of measurement. Second, what created a system of measurement in which the stick had a role was a *technique of applying it* (laying it against other objects such as fabric and matching them to its end points), which became coordinated within a community (of buyers and sellers) in the *context of an established form of life* (the activity of buying and selling things). Finally, the expression "one meter" acquired a meaning only when it was embedded within some such activity.

Kripke's separation of apriority from necessity in the meter case requires distinguishing between the length picked out, which "one meter" rigidly designates, and the stick used to identify that length. Yet the language-game above illustrates how the meaning of "one meter" as Kripke conceives it may be inessential to the actual use of expressions like "one meter." To the extent that similar conclusions can be drawn with respect to similar examples, a Wittgensteinian might resist Kripke's separation of apriority and necessity.

References

Boghossian, P.A. (1996). Analyticity Reconsidered. *Noûs*, 30, 369–391.
Boghossian, P.A. (2003). Epistemic Analyticity: A Defense. *Grazer Philosophische Studien*, 21, 15–35.
Brandom, R.B. (2001). *Articulating Reasons: An Introduction to Inferentialism*. Cambridge, MA: Harvard University Press.
Canfield, J.V. (1981). *Wittgenstein: Language and World*. Amherst: The University of Massachusetts Press.
Hacker, P.M.S. (1990/93a). *Wittgenstein: Meaning and Mind. Volume 3 of an Analytical Commentary on the Philosophical Investigations. Part I. Essays*. Oxford: Blackwell.
Hacker, P.M.S. (1990/93b). *Wittgenstein: Meaning and Mind. Volume 3 of an Analytical Commentary on the Philosophical Investigations. Part II. Exegesis §§243–427*. Oxford: Blackwell.
Hale, B., and Wright, C. (2001). *The Reason's Proper Study: Essays towards a Neo-Fregean Philosophy of Mathematics*. Oxford: Oxford University Press.
Horwich, P. (1998). *Meaning*. Oxford: Oxford University Press.
Jacquette, D. (1998). *Wittgenstein's Thought in Transition*. Lafayette: Purdue University Press.
Juhl, C., and Loomis, E. (2010). *Analyticity*. New York: Routledge.

Kenny, A. (1967). Criterion. In P. Edwards (Ed.). *Encyclopedia of Philosophy* (pp.258–261). New York: Prentice Hall.

Kripke, S.A. (1980). *Naming and Necessity*. Cambridge, MA: Harvard University Press.

Loomis, E. (2007). Criteria and Defeasibility: When Good Evidence is not Good Enough. In D. Moyal-Sharrock (Ed.). *Perspicuous Presentations: Essays on Wittgenstein's Philosophy of Psychology* (pp.236–257). Basingstoke: Palgrave Macmillan.

McDowell, J. (1982). Criteria, Defeasibility, and Knowledge. *Proceedings of the British Academy*, 68, 455–479.

Needham, P. (2010). Microessentialism: What is the Argument? *Noûs*, 45, 1–21.

Peacocke, C. (2002). Three Principles of Rationalism. *European Journal of Philosophy*, 10, 375–397.

Prior, A. (1960). The Runabout Inference-Ticket. *Analysis*, 21, 38–39.

Putnam, H. (1975). *Mind, Language, and Reality*. Cambridge: Cambridge University Press.

Shoemaker, S. (1963). *Self-Knowledge and Self-Identity*. Ithaca: Cornell University Press.

Sidelle, A. (1989). *Necessity, Essence, and Individuation: A Defense of Conventionalism*. Ithaca: Cornell University Press.

Further Reading

Medina, J. (2002). *The Unity of Wittgenstein's Philosophy: Necessity, Intelligibility, and Normativity*. New York: SUNY Press.

Segerdahl, P. (1996). *Language Use: A Philosophical Investigation into the Basic Notions of Pragmatics*. New York: St Martin's Press.

Soames, S. (2002). *Beyond Rigidity: The Unfinished Semantic Agenda of* Naming and Necessity. Oxford: Oxford University Press.

Stenlund, S. (1990). *Language and Philosophical Problems*. London: Routledge.

Part VI

Language

22

Names and Ostensive Definitions

KAI BÜTTNER

It is well known that the later Wittgenstein finds in a passage from Augustine an intuitive and initially attractive picture of language. According to this picture, every meaningful word refers to a particular object, and this object is the word's meaning (PI §1). The first thesis equates words with names; the second one meaning with reference. Taken together, they imply that a word has a meaning if and only if there is an object to which the word refers, and that two words have the same meaning if and only if they refer to the same object.

Wittgenstein acknowledges that the Augustinian picture also informed his earlier conception of language (PG 56). Although he already observes in his *Tractatus Logico-Philosophicus* that not every word is a name – truth-functional connectives, for example, are not – he nevertheless assumes at this point that those words, which are names, purport to refer to particular objects. The Augustinian identification of the meaning of a word with the word's referent is accepted only with a further restriction. In the *Tractatus*, Wittgenstein distinguishes between *simple* objects and the thereof composed *complex* objects. Whereas the name of a complex object can be verbally defined in terms of the names of the object's simple components, the name of a simple object can only be explained by what he calls *elucidations*. These are propositions, which contain the name and describe external properties of the latter's referent (TLP 3.263). According to the *Tractatus*, a simple object, which – because of its indivisibility – exists necessarily, is indeed the meaning of its name (TLP 3.203). But assuming that whether an expression is meaningful or not is never a contingent matter, complex objects cannot be identified with the meanings of their names. For the existence of a complex object depends on whether its simple constituents are, as matter of fact, configured in the required way. In TLP 3.24 Wittgenstein then seems to suggest that the meaning of the name of a complex object be identified with the meaning of the description by which the name is defined. And this description is meaningful if and only if it describes a possible – but not necessarily actual – configuration of simple objects.

In his later work, Wittgenstein, more naturally, contrasts verbal definitions not with elucidations but with ostensive definitions (PG 60; BB 1). The Augustinian theses about reference and meaning suggest that the object, which is pointed at in the ostensive

---

A Companion to Wittgenstein, First Edition. Edited by Hans-Johann Glock and John Hyman.
© 2017 John Wiley & Sons, Ltd. Published 2017 by John Wiley & Sons, Ltd.

definition of a word, is the word's referent and thus its meaning. And it is one of the essential purposes of the later Wittgenstein's investigation of the mechanism of ostensive definitions to criticize the Augustinian theses from this angle. The following six sections constitute an attempt to provide a systematic reconstruction of Wittgenstein's sometimes opaque remarks on ostensive definitions and his critique of the Augustinian picture of language. The final section will then address the doctrines about names and naming endorsed in the *Tractatus*.

1 Ostensive Definitions of Proper Names

According to the later Wittgenstein the simple ostensive definition of a word, consisting in the utterance of the word accompanied by a pointing gesture, does not unambiguously determine the use of the word. It leaves the *type* of the word – its place in grammar – undetermined (PG 60–1; PI §30). This component, Wittgenstein claims, can be determined by complementing the ostensive definition by certain other terms such as "human being," "color," or "shape," i.e., by terms that in contemporary terminology are called *concrete* or *abstract sortals* (PG 61; PI §29).

Let "*C*" be a *concrete sortal* such as "human being" or "dog." More precisely, "*C*" shall be what Wiggins calls a *substance-concept* and hence not a *phase-sortal* such as "child" or "whelp" (Wiggins, 2001, p. 30). Influenced by discussions with Wittgenstein, Waismann suggested explaining the corresponding notion of *being the same C* by reference to the notion of *spatiotemporal continuity* (PLP 200). Accordingly, an object *x* given on one occasion is *the same C as* an object *y* given on another occasion if and only if "*C*" is applicable to *x* and to *y*, and *x* is connected with *y* by a space-time path on which "*C*" is continuously applicable. This explanation seems basically correct and sufficiently accurate for a discussion of the use of names for *C*s, even though, as Waismann himself acknowledges, further rules would need to be specified in order to decide cases of fusions or fissions in which the continuous applicability of "*C*" does not uniquely determine a space-time path, or cases of dis- and reassembly in which only the spatial parts of a *C* continuously exist (PLP 201ff.; PG 203).

Instead of following them through space and time, we quickly part ways with most of the objects we encounter. Therefore, whether an object given on one occasion is the same *C* as an object given on an earlier occasion is most often decided not by observing the latter's space-time path, but by recognizing that the objects given on both occasions have certain features in common. Such features are called identity criteria. In the case of *human beings* they concern, for example, their visual appearance, their fingerprints, or their DNA.

It should be noted, however, that spatiotemporal continuity remains the *defining criterion* for *being the same C*, whereas the so-called identity criteria are only *empirical criteria* or *symptoms* in Wittgenstein's sense (BB 24–5). Should these criteria clash, it is spatiotemporal continuity that decides the matter. So if, for example, by following a human being on its path through space and time, we were to observe it to have different fingerprints on two different occasions, we should still say that the same human being was present on those occasions. In fact, a feature is accepted as an identity criterion for objects of the kind *C*, only after experience shows it to be generally invariant – or predictably varying – with respect to spatiotemporal continuity. Fingerprints count as identity criteria for human beings only because one can observe that human beings, present on two different occasions, have the same fingerprints if and only if they are spatiotemporally continuous.

Following some of Wittgenstein's observations in *Philosophical Grammar* (203), one may represent the mechanism of an ostensive definition for a name of a C in the following way (see also PLP 200–1). Suppose a word "*a*" is ostensively defined at a space-time point (s_a, t_a) by pointing at a C while uttering "This C is called '*a*.'" Then, at any later point in time,

(C,a)   "*a*" is applicable to a given object *x* if and only if *x* is the same C as the one that at time t_a was located at place s_a.

Thus, the ostensive definition of a C-name determines the name's applicability to be equivalent with *being the same C as the object of the ostension*. This account could be modified in order to allow for the possibility that one and the same name be assigned to different objects. So, if on another occasion (s'_a, t'_a) "*a*" is assigned to a different C, then one could either distinguish these two uses of "*a*," or one could modify (C,a) by determining the applicability of "*a*" as equivalent with being the same C as the one given on (s_a, t_a) or with the one given on (s'_a, t'_a). But, for the sake of simplicity, this complication will be ignored in the following.

The aforementioned points about *being the same C* carry over to the applicability of a so-defined C-name "*a*." Since we do not normally keep track of objects which are pointed at in ostensive definitions, whether "*a*" is applicable to a later given object *x* mostly needs to be decided on the basis of some actual features of *x*. Yet, being spatiotemporally continuous with the C given at (s_a, t_a) remains the *decisive* criterion for the applicability of "*a*," which, should the situation arise, overrules any conflicting evidence.

An applicability rule of the form (C,a) is equivalent to the conjunction of the following two rules:

(I_C)   "*a*" is applicable to an object *x*, given on *one* occasion, and to an object *y*, given on *another* occasion, if and only if
    (1)   "*a*" is applicable to *x*; and
    (2)   *x* is the same C as *y*.

(E_a)   "*a*" is applicable to the C given at (s_a, t_a).

The rule (I_C) determines an *invariance condition* for the applicability of "*a*" on different occasions. Since this invariance rule is common to all C-names, one may actually define the notion of a C-name by determining to call a name a *C-name* if and only if it used according to (I_C). Accordingly, proper names of human beings are those names whose applicability is invariant under *being the same human being*. Dog names, by contrast, are those names whose applicability is invariant under *being the same dog*. And, further generalizing, one may explicate Wittgenstein's notion of a proper name of a spatial object by defining a proper name of a spatial object as a C-name for some concrete sortal "C."

The second rule (E_a) corresponds to the ostensive definition of the particular C-name "*a*." By reference to rules of this kind one can decide whether two C-names "*a*" and "*b*" are names of the same C. Accordingly, "*a*" and "*b*" are names of the same C if and only if the C given at (s_a, t_a) is spatiotemporally continuous with the C given on (s_b, t_b).

2 Reference and Meaning of Proper Names

At the beginning of *Philosophical Investigations* Wittgenstein criticizes the Augustinian thesis according to which *any* meaningful word refers to a particular object by pointing out that words have *different* functions (PI §§10–14). He concedes, however, that proper names of spatial objects can in "the most straightforward sense" be said to refer to (or, designate) particular objects (PI §15). It seems that *this* sense can be explicated by recourse to the kind of invariance rules that were discussed in the first section. That an expression *refers* to a certain object can thus be taken to mean that the expression's applicability on two different occasions is equivalent with its applicability on one occasion and the identity of the objects given on both occasions. And since objects given on two different occasions are identical if and only if they are connected via a corresponding space-time path, one can say that reference – in the straightforward sense – is *applicability invariance under spatiotemporal continuity*.

The co-reference of two referential expressions, then, amounts to their general co-applicability. Accordingly, two C-names "*a*" and "*b*" refer to the same C if and only if on any occasion in which a C is given either both or none of them is applicable. And if "*a*" and "*b*" are nonempty, their co-reference is equivalent with their co-applicability on *one* occasion. For their general co-applicability is then implied by their applicability invariance under *being the same C*.

As was noted in the introduction, the Augustinian identification of the meaning of a word with the object to which the word refers implies firstly that a word has a meaning if and only if there is an object to which the word refers and secondly that two words have the same meaning if and only if they refer to the same object. The problematic character of both principles has long been recognized. The first entails that a singular existential proposition "*a* exists" is not false but meaningless if "*a*" has no referent. And the second seems to imply that identity statements that are formed by two proper names are uninformative.

The later Wittgenstein rejects the identification of meaning and referent by arguing in particular that, as far as proper names are concerned, *having a meaning* is not equivalent to *having a bearer*, since a proper name can also be used in the absence of the bearer (PI §44). Instead he implicitly suggests in PI §79 that one identify the meaning that a speaker attaches to a proper name with the meaning of the descriptive phrase by which the speaker would explain the name. Accordingly, two co-referential names would have different meanings if they are explained by nonequivalent descriptions.

Distinguishing between the referent and the meaning of a proper name is problematic for a simple and by now often noted reason: etymological meaning apart, we usually do not speak of "meaning," but only of "reference" – "application" or "use" – in connection with proper names. Thus what can – and should – be distinguished from the referent of a proper name is not the name's meaning but rather its applicability criterion (cf. Rundle, 1979, p.81). In this way, it seems, one can defend Wittgenstein's correspondingly interpreted claims and clarify the potentially problematic features of singular existential propositions and identity statements.

Thus one can agree with Wittgenstein that most uses of a proper name do not require the name to have a referent. The use of a proper name in a singular existential proposition, in particular, only requires the name to have an applicability criterion, since what such a proposition claims is that there is an object that fulfills this criterion. So if "*a*" is a C-name, which is ostensively defined at (s_a, t_a), then "*a* exists" is true at any later time t

if and only if at t there is a C which is spatiotemporally continuous with the C which at time t_a was located at s_a (cf. Tugendhat, 1992, p.88). And when this C ceases to exist, "a" loses its referent but not its applicability criterion.

By distinguishing between the applicability criteria of proper names and their eventual referents one may also account for the informative character of certain corresponding identity statements in the Fregean manner, i.e., by tracing this character back to different (nonequivalent) applicability criteria of the names involved. Two C-names "a" and "b" with equivalent applicability criteria are generally co-applicable and hence co-referential as the corresponding identity statement "a is the same C as b" claims. And should "a" and "b" have incompatible applicability criteria, then they are on no occasion co-applicable and therefore never co-referential. But if the applicability criteria of "a" and "b" are logically independent, it cannot be deduced from these criteria alone whether or not "a" and "b" are co-applicable on any occasion. In this case the co-reference of "a" and "b" can only be established by the empirical discovery of an occasion in which a given C satisfies the applicability criteria of both names. Suppose, for example, that two corresponding ostensive definitions determine *being the same planet as the one seen on a particular morning* as the applicability criterion of "Phosphorus" and *being the same planet as the one seen on the following evening* as the applicability criterion of "Hesperus." Then "Phosphorus" and "Hesperus" are co-referential if and only if the planet seen in the morning is spatiotemporally continuous with the one seen in the evening. And whether or not this is the case cannot be inferred from the applicability criteria of "Hesperus" and "Phosphorus"; it has to be established by observation.

3 Verbal Explanations of Proper Names

For speakers who did not witness the ostensive definition of a proper name, the name must be re-explained at some later stage. Since the explanation of a proper name explains the name's application rather than its meaning, a re-explanation of a proper name is adequate if and only if it licenses the same applications as the name's initial explanation. So if the C-name "a" is ostensively defined at (s_a, t_a), then any subsequent re-explanation of "a" must determine that "a" is applicable to an object x just in case x is the same C as the one given at (s_a, t_a).

Obviously, an ostensive re-explanation of "a" is adequate if and only if the same C is pointed at. In the absence of its bearer, "a" can only be verbally re-explained. In this case the bearer needs to be described rather than ostended. A trivial option for such a verbal re-explanation of "a" consists in simply specifying the occasion of the initial ostensive definition by explaining: the C that at time t_a was located at s_a is called "a." Quite generally one can say that an utterance of "The C that at time t was located at s is called 'a'" determines "a" to be applicable to x if and only if x is the same C as the one given at (s,t), provided, of course, that there is such a C. Since such an explanation licenses the same applications as the initial ostensive definition of "a" just in case the C given at (s_a, t_a) is identical with the one given at (s,t), "a" can be adequately re-explained by any spatiotemporal description specifying an occasion in which its bearer was present.

Another option for a verbal re-explanation of "a" consists in specifying one of the bearer's uniquely characterizing properties. If at a time t there is one and only one C that is F, then an utterance of "the C that is now F is called 'a'" at time t determines "a" to be applicable to x if and only if x is the same C as the one that at time t was F.

Accordingly, an explanation of the form "the C which is now F is called 'a'" constitutes an adequate re-explanation of "a" just in case the C given at (s_a, t_a) is at the time of the re-explanation the only C that is F.

In the famous section 79 of *Philosophical Investigations*, Wittgenstein claims that a proper name such as "Moses" can be explained by different nonequivalent descriptions. And he concludes that we are using such names "without a fixed meaning." If talk of meaning is again replaced by talk of applicability criteria, both theses are correct. The application of a proper name can indeed be explained by different nonequivalent descriptions, since the applicability criteria specified thereby, though not equivalent, may nevertheless license the same applications. This point can be illustrated by considering the applicability criteria specified by two different spatiotemporal descriptions "the C given at (s_1, t_1)" and "the C given at (s_2, t_2)." The corresponding criteria *being the same C as the one given at (s_1, t_1)* and *being the same C as the one given at (s_2, t_2)* are not equivalent, since the possibility of an object satisfying one and only one of them cannot be excluded a priori. But having on *one* occasion observed that a given object actually satisfies both criteria, we can conclude that on *any* occasion a given object satisfies either both or neither of them.

One might be tempted to conclude that the adequacy of a verbal re-explanation of "a" simply amounts to the co-reference of "a" and the defining description. This, however, is only true if the description is referential in the same sense as a C-name; i.e., if its applicability is invariant under *being the same C*. Since a spatiotemporal description "the C which at time t was located at place s" fulfills this requirement, it indeed explains "a" adequately if and only if it refers to the same C as "a." By contrast, a present-tense description of the form "the C that is now F" is not referential in the required sense, since its applicability is not necessarily invariant under *being the same C*. Although such a description applies at any time to at most one object, it might apply to different objects at different times. Therefore, a present-tense description adequately explains "a" at all and only those times at which both expressions are co-applicable. One may note however that the applicability criterion that "the C that is now F" at time t determines can also be determined by the corresponding temporal description "the C that at time t is F." Since the applicability of such descriptions is invariant under *being the same C*, they provide the possibility of re-explaining "a" by a co-referential expression that identifies the bearer of "a" by specifying one of the latter's uniquely characterizing properties.

Frequently, a proper name is explained by providing *several* descriptions instead of a single one. In any such case the different descriptions need not be equivalent. But, assuming for the sake of simplicity that all of those descriptions are referential, they certainly need to be co-referential. If it turns out that two of them do not refer to the same object, then the explanation needs to be modified (cf. PI §79).

This point has been obscured by Searle's suggestion that if a proper name is explained by a bundle of descriptions, the name's applicability is equivalent with the applicability of the *logical sum* – or a certain *weighted sum* – of the descriptions (cf. Searle, 1958). For if a so-defined name were applicable to an object x if and only if at least one or, in the case of a weighted sum, a sufficient number of the descriptions are applicable to x, then a bundle explanation could count as perfectly adequate, even if the given descriptions are not pairwise co-referential. According to this conception, an empty description, for example, might always be added to any bundle of descriptions, since, provided that sufficiently less weight is put on it, it would not affect the applicability of the corresponding sum. But of course: if a proper name is explained by a bundle of descriptions, it is presupposed that the name is adequately explained by *any* of the individual descriptions. Searle mistakenly conceives of the elements of the bundle as *partial* explanations of the name. In fact, the different descriptions are typically presented as *alternative* explanations, amongst which the addressee of the explanation can choose.

4   Ostensive Definitions of Predicates

The so-called *abstract sortals* such as "color," "length," or "number" do not form a homogenous class, as can be seen from considering contexts of the form "has the same *A* as" (where *A* is an abstract sortal). While *having the same number* can be analyzed as a binary quantifier, insofar as a sentence of the form "The *F* have the same number as the *G*" is equivalent to "There are as many *F* as *G*," *having the same color* and *having the same length* are equivalence relations between spatial objects.

Now it seems that, at least for those cases in which *having the same A* is such an equivalence relation, one may canonically define the corresponding notion of an *A*-name, and represent the mechanism of the ostensive definitions of names of this type in the following way. Firstly it seems adequate to stipulate that a word "*F*" is an *A-name* if and only if its applicability is invariant under *having the same A*, i.e., if it satisfies the following condition:

(I_A)   "*F*" is applicable to an object *x* given on *one* occasion and to an object *y* given on *another* occasion if and only if "*F*" is applicable to *x*, and *x* has the same *A* as *y*.

Accordingly, applicability invariance under *having the same color* is the essential feature of color names, whereas invariance under *having the same length* is necessary and sufficient for being the name of a length.

Secondly, it seems correct to say that the ostensive definition of an *A*-name determines *having the same A as the ostended object* as the name's applicability criterion. So whereas the utterance of "This color is called '*F*'" while pointing at a certain object *x* determines "*F*" to be applicable to all and only those objects that have the same color as *x*, the utterance of "The length of this is called '*F*'" determines "*F*" to be applicable to all and only those objects that have the same length as *x*.

Incidentally, a slightly modified, though basically similar strategy seems available for the case of *number*. The numerically definite quantifiers that are standardly expressed in the form "There are *n*" can be characterized as those monadic quantifiers that are invariant under *having the same number* in the sense that "There are *n F*, and there are *n G*" is equivalent to "There are *n F*, and there are as many *F* as *G*" (cf. Dummett, 1991, p. 107). And the utterance of "This number is called '*n*'" while pointing at a group of objects accordingly determines "There are *n F*" to be true if and only if there are as many *F* as objects in the ostended group (cf. RFM III §10).

It might have been noticed already that the phrase "has the same *A* as the ostended object" can either be read in a *synchronic* sense as "has the same *A* as the ostended object at present," or in a *diachronic* sense as "has the same *A* as the ostended object at the time of the ostension." These two readings have of course to be distinguished for a precise representation of the corresponding mechanisms of ostensive definitions and the applicability criteria determined thereby.

Suppose that "This A is called 'F'" is uttered at place s_F and time t_F while pointing at a given object. The underlying mechanism of this definition is to be codified by the synchronic interpretation if the following applicability criterion is intended:

(A_S) "F" is applicable to an object x given at time t' if and only if at t' x and the object that was located at s_F at time t_F have the same A.

This mechanism can be illustrated by the example of length names that will be of particular interest in the following section. Thus uttering "This length is called '1 meter'" while pointing to a given stick, e.g., the standard meter, determines that "1 meter" is applicable to an object x given at a later time if and only if x and the standard meter have the same length at this time (cf. PG 346).

If (A_S) is intended, then the ostensive definition confers to the ostended object the role of a *sample* for the application of "F," insofar as the applicability of "F" on a later occasion is decided by *comparing* the given object with the object that was pointed at in the ostensive definition. And if, furthermore, "*f*" is the proper name of the ostended object, then "F" might be verbally re-explained by saying: the A of *f* is called "F." Accordingly, the standard meter is the sample of "1 Meter," insofar as the applicability of "1 meter" to x is decided by juxtaposing x to the standard meter. And if the standard meter is called that way, then "1 meter" can be verbally explained by saying: the length of the standard meter is called "1 meter."

The diachronic interpretation of the phrase "having the same A as the ostended object" adequately codifies the ostensive definition of "F," if the following applicability criterion is intended:

(Q_D) "F" is applicable to an object x given at time t' if and only if x has at t' the same A that the object that at time t_F was located at s_F had at time t_F.

If (Q_D) is intended, the ostended object does not become a sample, since whether "F" is applicable to x at a certain time does not depend on how x relates to the ostended object at that time, and is therefore not decided by comparing one with the other. Color names are typically applied without the use of samples. So if "red" is ostensively defined by pointing to an object that, while being pointed at, is red, then the addressee of the explanation is supposed to remember the color that the ostended object had at that time. And should this object change its color, judged on the basis of his memory, then "red" could no longer be explained by pointing to it.

5 Samples Belong to the Symbolism

Samples, Wittgenstein repeatedly tells us, belong to the symbolism. They are not objects to which the symbolism is applied (PI §50; PG 346). According to Wittgenstein, the assignment of the role of a sample to a certain object entails certain restrictions on what can meaningfully be said about that object. So he famously claims in PI §50 that of the standard meter one can neither say that it is 1 meter long, nor that it is not.

The reasoning for this claim can be reconstructed as follows (see PG 346). That *two* objects have the same length means that they cover each other mutually, when they are juxtaposed. As there is no such thing as juxtaposing one object to itself, nothing can be said to *have the same length as itself* or to *have a different length than itself*. Therefore, a proposition of the form "a has the same length as itself" is not a claim about the length of *a*. At best it can be construed as claiming that *a* is a potential object of length comparisons. Now if "is 1 meter long" is short for "has the same length as the standard meter," then the standard meter can indeed neither be said to be 1 meter long, nor not to be 1 meter long. Accordingly, an utterance of "This is 1 meter long" while pointing at the standard meter can only be taken as an ostensive definition, but not as an application of "1 meter." And, similarly, a proposition of the form "The standard meter is 1 meter long" paraphrases either the verbal definition "The length of the standard meter is called '1 meter'" or, if this definition is presupposed, the tautology "The standard meter is as long as itself." But it is in no case a proposition about the length of the standard meter.

As Wittgenstein himself suggests, this line of argument can be generalized. Since there are no self-comparisons, nothing can be said to *have the same A as itself* or to *have a different A than itself*. Therefore the sample of an A-name "F" can neither be said *to be F*, nor *not to be F*. And the fact that the argument can be generalized in this way shows that to say that the standard meter can neither be said to be 1 meter long nor not to be 1 meter long is not to "ascribe any extraordinary property to it, but only to mark its peculiar role in the language-game of measuring with a metre-rule" (PI §50).

At this point one may ask whether the standard meter, then, cannot be said to *have a length* either, a consequence that would contradict Wittgenstein's claim that "Every rod has a length" is a grammatical proposition (PI §251). Though it seems that Wittgenstein nowhere discusses this question, one may argue on his behalf that the answer depends on what is meant by the expression "having a length." The standard meter can of course be said to have a length, insofar as it can be said to have the same length as some other object. And under this interpretation "Every rod has length" can indeed count as a grammatical proposition. If, however, "having a length" is not supposed to mean "being a potential object of length comparisons," but rather "being a potential object for the application of metric length names," then one would have to say that the standard meter has no length. And in this case "Every rod has a length" would have to be supplemented by the clause "apart from the standard meter" in order to be a grammatical proposition.

Wittgenstein's remarks on the standard meter have been contested by Kripke who claims that the standard meter can be said to be 1 meter long (or not to be 1 meter long), because it can also be said to *change its length*. According to Kripke, experience shows that if heat of a given quantity is applied to a stick, then it expands to such and such a length. And this, he claims, is true for any stick, including the standard meter (Kripke, 1980, pp. 54). Kripke thus maintains that by exempting the standard meter from the possibility of metric length ascriptions Wittgenstein does indeed ascribe an extraordinary property to it, presumably the property of being an exception to the expansion law and hence as exemplifying some kind of metaphysical rigidity.

An assessment of this objection requires a discussion of *diachronic* length relations. For this purpose it should first be noted that the synchronic length equality of two objects is equivalent with the synchronic identity of their length ratios with respect to a third object. Therefore, whether two objects have the same length at *one* time can not only be decided by comparing them with each other, but also by comparing each of them with a third object, the standard meter for example. In the case of diachronic length relations, however, this method of *two* comparisons is mandatory, as there is no such thing as a juxtaposition of objects at different times. So, in particular, one can decide whether an object *a* has changed its length by juxtaposing *a* twice with some other object *m*, but not by juxtaposing *a* to its former self. If someone were to protest at this point that one may observe *a* to change its length even without any other object or background of comparison in sight, it would have to be pointed out that the only phenomenon that can be meant is the observation that *a* changes its length ratio with respect to the observer's visual field.

Now it has to be noted that, so far, two length comparisons between *a* and *m* can only show whether their length ratio has changed or not. The comparisons do not, by themselves, provide a reason for saying that the length of *a* has changed, or that the length of *m* has changed. What is needed is a further convention that stipulates that changes of length ratios between *a* and *m* can be asymmetrically described as length changes of *a*. Systematic talk of diachronic length relations presupposes the determination of a length sample. For diachronic length equality consists in the identity of synchronic length ratios with respect to a length sample, and length changes are changes of synchronic length ratios with respect to a length sample. For this reason, the length sample itself can neither be said to have the same length at different times, nor to have different lengths at different times. And contrary to what Kripke claims, the standard meter, if it has that role, can therefore neither be said to change its length, nor can it be said that its length remains constant.

The flaw in Kripke's putative objection is already to be found in its misleadingly formulated premise. What experience shows is that if heat of a given quantity is applied to a given stick, then the length ratio between this stick and an unheated stick changes in a certain way. And the corresponding expansion law is accordingly a law about changes of length ratios to which the standard meter is, of course, no exception. So if heat is applied to the standard meter but not to the objects it is supposed to measure, then the length ratios between any two of those objects remain constant, whereas the length ratios between the standard meter and any one of those objects changes (cf. Carnap, 1966, ch.9). Now, if the standard meter retains its role as the length sample, then we still cannot say that the standard meter has expanded. Instead we would have to say that all of the other objects contracted. And this, of course, would be a good reason to deprive the standard meter of this role (cf. Reichenbach, 1958, pp.20–1). But Wittgenstein's argument still stands: as long as the standard meter serves as the length sample, talk of its length as well as talk of its length changes is senseless, since both length names and diachronic length relations are defined through synchronic length relations with respect to the length sample. What Wittgenstein's argument presupposes is not that the standard meter is metaphysically rigid, but that the notion of absolute – as opposed to relative – rigidity is incoherent. And Kripke's objection simply ignores the point that in order to speak of a change of length – instead of a change of length ratio – some object must be assigned the role of a length sample.

6   Meaning and Reference of Predicates

Just as names of dogs or human beings, names of colors or lengths apply to spatial objects. *A*-names and *C*-names do not apply to different realities; they only differ in the way in which they apply to reality. The applicability of a *C*-name is invariant under *being the same C* and thus under *spatiotemporal continuity*. There is, therefore, at any time at most one object to which a *C*-name is applicable: the name's referent. The applicability of an *A*-name, on the other hand, is invariant under the equivalence relation *having the same A*. Color names apply to equally colored objects; length names to equally long objects. Consequently, an *A*-name might be – and typically is – applicable to different objects at different times and to different objects at the same time.

For this reason an *A*-name does not *refer* to a particular object. Instead one may rather say that it *classifies* objects according to their *A*. Color-names classify objects according to their color; length names according to their length. But neither a color name nor a length name refers to any of the objects to which it is applicable. *A*-names thus constitute counterexamples to the Augustinian thesis that every meaningful word refers.

At this point it might be objected that although an *A*-name does not refer to any of the objects to which it is applicable, it may however be said to refer to an *A*. Accordingly, one might argue that a color name does not refer to any of the equally colored objects to which it is applicable, but to the color which all and only these objects exemplify.

Following Wittgenstein's observations in PI §§10–15, this objection might be countered by pointing out that when the use of expressions that do not refer to particular spatial objects is described in terms of reference, we are no longer using the term "reference" in its primary (or, most straightforward) sense. So it is certainly correct to say that "red," for example, refers to a color, if that means that the applicability of "red" is invariant under *having the same color*. But if, more generally, the expression "refers to an *A*" means the same as "is applicability invariant under *having the same A*," then *A*-names can still not be said to refer in the same sense as *C*-names. For the reference of *A*-names would then consist in their applicability invariance not under spatiotemporal continuity, but under a certain equivalence relation. By uniformly characterizing the use of *C*-names and *A*-names in terms of reference, one does not show that both kinds of names apply in the same way to reality. One only describes in the same terms the very different ways in which they apply to reality (cf. PI §10).

It was noted above that talk of meaning – in contrast to talk of reference – in connection with proper names is problematic. In the case of *A*-names it is rather the other way round. Here it is the talk of reference that needs to be given a precise sense in order to assess the principles about meaningfulness and synonymy that follow from the Augustinian identification of the meaning of a word with its referent. In his discussion of these principles Wittgenstein proposes, for the sake of argument, that one identify the referent of an *A*-name either with its sample or with a corresponding mental image. At least as far as concrete samples are concerned, this step does not seem completely unjustified. The relation of an *A*-name to its sample bears a similarity to the relation of a proper name and its referent, insofar as the occasions in which the sample is given provide the possibility not for the application, but for the ostensive definition of the *A*-name.

Against the idea of equating co-reference with synonymy, Wittgenstein argues that for two words to have the same meaning it is not sufficient that they have the same sample. Since even if "*F*" and "*G*" have the same sample, they are not equivalent – let alone synonymous – if they are names of different types, i.e., if their applicability is invariant under different equivalence relations. So although no color name is equivalent with any shape name, the picture of a red circle might serve as the sample for "red" and for "circle" (PG 61).

Therefore, as Wittgenstein rightly claims, only an ostensive definition that not only correlates the name with a sample, but also makes the name's type explicit by mentioning a corresponding sortal can unambiguously determine the use of the name (PG 61; PI §30). So whereas the utterance of the phrase "This color is called 'red'" while pointing to the red circle does indeed determine "red" to be applicable to all and only those objects that are red, the phrase "This is called 'red'" would also allow for interpreting "red" as applicable to all and only those objects that are circular. And he insists – equally rightly, it seems – that this kind of indeterminacy is not avoided by substituting the concrete sample by a mental image: merely correlating a word with a mental image does not unambiguously determine the word's use, since this image might also be projected onto reality in different ways (PI §140).

Wittgenstein's arguments can be complemented by the observation that having the same sample is not necessary for two terms to be equivalent either. For two *A*-names are not only equivalent if they have the same sample, but also if their respective samples have the same *A*. So in principle, everyone may use his own meterstick as a sample for "1 meter," as long as they all have the same length, namely the length of the standard meter.

In PI §55 Wittgenstein seems to suggest that an *A*-name that is defined by reference to a sample is meaningful just as long as the sample exists. He thereby partially approves the correspondingly interpreted Augustinian principle that equates the meaningfulness of a word with the existence of its referent. But although it is certainly correct that the existence of its sample is sufficient for the meaningfulness of an *A*-name, the converse idea that the name loses its meaning when its sample ceases to exist is not entirely unproblematic.

It is of course true that if we want to continue to use metric length names after the destruction or loss of the standard meter, we would have to choose a new sample. But the decisive question, then, seems to be whether we thereby necessarily give a *new* meaning to those names, or whether we may also so choose a new sample that we keep on using the metric length names in the same sense as before.

And such a continuity of meaning could justifiably be claimed, if the role of the sample can be transferred to an object which was found to have a certain length ratio with respect to the standard meter before the latter's disappearance. The simplest option would consist in choosing another stick that was found to have the same length as the standard meter. Or, if the standard meter was found to be three times as long as the Greenwich foot, the metric length names might be applied on the basis of comparisons with the Greenwich foot and the corresponding conversion rule. So it seems that one can reasonably claim that an *A*-name keeps its meaning after exchanging its disappeared sample for a new one if the latter, before its appointment, had the same *A* as its predecessor.

7   The Tractarian Doctrines about Names and Naming

According to the *Tractatus*, names invariably function as representatives of particular objects. The correlations between names and represented objects are established by corresponding mental acts. And it is in this way – i.e., by naming things – that language gets applied to reality (TLP 3.22, 3.11, 4.0312). The later Wittgenstein "materializes" his earlier mentalistic conception of naming by proposing to conceive of the act of naming something as the attaching of a label to a thing (PI §15). Labeling in this sense corresponds to the ostensive definition of a word rather than to a verbal one, insofar as it is directed to a given object. And the later Wittgenstein's critique of his earlier conception of names and naming can partially be derived from the critique of the Augustinian picture developed in the preceding sections.

The idea that every name is the representative of a corresponding object is extrapolated from the special case of proper names. Such a name can of course be said to be the representative of the object to which alone the name is applicable. But, as was noted in the previous section, names of colors, lengths, or shapes are applicable to different objects and can therefore not be conceived as the representatives of particular objects. And although the relation between such names and their eventual samples might be characterized by the uniqueness that the talk of representing a particular object requires, a color name, for example, does not represent its sample in the same sense as a proper name represents its referent, insofar as the color name does not apply to its sample. So unless the talk of names is restricted to the class of proper names, the thesis that any name is the representative of a particular object must be rejected.

In this connection it should be recalled that the way in which a name applies to reality is not determined by simply correlating it with a particular object. This is also true when the correlation is established by attaching a label to the object rather than by a simple ostensive definition. Since its label accompanies the labeled object on its space-time path, an object given on a certain occasion is spatiotemporally continuous with the object given in the preceding labeling ceremony if and only if it bears the label. Therefore, the name on the label is a proper name – and thus a representative – of the labeled object if and only if *bearing the label* is the intended applicability criterion of the name. The labeled object is the sample of the name, if the name is intended to apply to all and only those objects, which have the same color, length, or shape as the labeled object. Attaching a label to the picture of the red circle, for example, does not determine whether the name on the label is the proper name of that picture, the name of its color, or of its shape, for labels might as well be attached to referents as to samples.

Although the later Wittgenstein still distinguishes between verbal and ostensive definitions, he no longer assumes that the possibilities of verbal and ostensive definition are mutually exclusive. What he takes to be mutually exclusive, though, are the explanation of a word and the word's application (PR 54; PG 88). Verbal and ostensive definitions do not apply the defined words to reality; they determine the rules for such applications. And it is in this sense, it seems, that Wittgenstein's rather provocative claim that even ostensive definitions do not *relate* language to reality – and that language, for this reason, remains self-contained – should be understood: ostensive definitions relate language with reality only in the sense that they provide rules for applying names to reality (cf. PG 97).

The assimilation of explanation and application is particularly tempting in the case of ostensive definitions. Wittgenstein's insistence that the utterance of a word while pointing to an object cannot be both a definition and an application of the word is unproblematic in those cases in which the ostended object is the sample of the word. If it is not, Wittgenstein's claim seems more debatable. So one might argue that the ostensive definition of a sample-less color name, for example, consists precisely in exemplifying the name's application (cf. Schroeder, 2009, pp.105–6).

It seems, however, that even in these cases one may still distinguish the ostensive definition of the name from the name's application by reference to the normative role that the former has for the latter (cf. Glock, 1996, p.276). Accordingly, the utterance of a word accompanied by a pointing gesture can count as an ostensive definition of the word when the utterance is not intended to be justifiable, but rather to set the standard by recourse to which subsequent utterances of the word can be justified. And if the object which is pointed at in the ostensive definition is not intended to serve as a sample, then the subsequent applications of the word are to be justified by reference not to that object but to the definitional utterance.

References

Carnap, R. (1966). *Philosophical Foundations of Physics*. Ed. M. Gardner. New York: Basic Books.
Dummett, M. (1991). *Frege: Philosophy of Mathematics*. London: Duckworth.
Glock, H.-J. (1996). *A Wittgenstein Dictionary*. Oxford: Blackwell.
Kripke, S.A. (1980). *Naming and Necessity*. Cambridge, MA: Harvard University Press.
Reichenbach, H. (1958). *The Philosophy of Space and Time*. New York: Dover.
Rundle, B. (1979). *Grammar in Philosophy*. Oxford: Clarendon Press.
Schroeder, S. (2009). Analytic Truths and Grammatical Propositions. In H.-J. Glock and J. Hyman (Eds). *Wittgenstein and Analytic Philosophy: Essays for P.M.S. Hacker* (pp.83–108). Oxford: Oxford University Press.
Searle, J. (1958). Proper Names. *Mind*, 67, 166–173.
Tugendhat, E. (1992). Existence in Space and Time. In E. Tugendhat. *Philosophische Aufsätze* (pp.67–89). Frankfurt: Suhrkamp.
Wiggins, D. (2001). *Sameness and Substance Renewed*. Cambridge: Cambridge University Press.

Further Reading

Baker, G.P. and Hacker, P.M.S. (1980/2009). *Wittgenstein: Understanding and Meaning. Volume 1 of an Analytical Commentary on the Philosophical Investigations. Part 1. Essays.* Second edition. Extensively revised by P.M.S. Hacker. Oxford: Wiley-Blackwell. Chapters 5, 7.
Hanfling, O. (1989). *Wittgenstein's Later Philosophy*. Albany: State University of New York Press. Chapters 3, 4.
Rundle, B. (1990). *Wittgenstein and Contemporary Philosophy of Language*. Oxford: Blackwell. Chapter 2.

23

Meaning and Understanding

JASON BRIDGES

1 Beyond Normativity

A teacher orders a student, "Add two" (PI §185). The order means that the student is to write down the arithmetic sequence that begins with two and then proceeds by twos. The student understands, and she writes down the correct sequence up to the point at which the teacher indicates she can stop.

Here we see the human capacities for meaning and understanding at work in a natural setting, playing roles familiar to us from our everyday life with language. It is tempting to look to philosophy for deeper insight into the nature of these roles and into how meaning and understanding are able to fulfill them. One of Wittgenstein's primary aims in sections 138–242 of *Philosophical Investigations*, and in related remarks elsewhere in his later writings, is to show how easy it is for us to be led astray as we seek this deeper insight: how prone we are to fall into difficulty and confusion, and to lose our grip on the familiar phenomena whose depths we had sought to plumb.

What roles for meaning and understanding are exemplified by our scene of instruction? Here is one. In writing down 2, 4, 6, 8, and so on, the student responds to the order *correctly*. Had she written down another sequence – beginning, say, with 2, 8, and 16 – her response would have been incorrect. Why is the first response correct and the second not? A natural answer is that it is because the order *means* what it does – namely, that the student is to write down the sequence beginning with two and then proceeding by twos – that the student must produce some initial portion of that very sequence if she is to execute the order aright. As Wittgenstein's interlocutor puts a thought in this vicinity, "The right step is the one that accords with the order – as it was *meant*" (PI §186).

An order to produce an arithmetic sequence provides a particularly sharp example of a phenomenon that obtains more generally: the meaning of an expression or utterance contributes to the determination of correct and incorrect, right and wrong, ways to use or respond to it. A meaningful item's meaning helps to fix a norm, a standard of correctness, in the use of the item. This norm-fixing power of meaning, what we might call meaning's *normativity*, seems to be essential to it. Knowledge of the meaning of an

---

A Companion to Wittgenstein, First Edition. Edited by Hans-Johann Glock and John Hyman.
© 2017 John Wiley & Sons, Ltd. Published 2017 by John Wiley & Sons, Ltd.

assertion, for example, is surely impossible without some knowledge of the circumstances under which it would be right to make it.

There is no doubt that Wittgenstein is concerned with our handling of the thought that meaning is normative. He sees grave problems in what his interlocutor is inclined to say – and so by extension what we all, including Wittgenstein himself, are inclined to say when we are "doing philosophy" (cf. PI §§194, 261) – about how meaning inhabits its normative role. Wittgenstein's treatment of our difficulties in making sense of the normativity of meaning has been the central focus of the post-Kripkean (1982) literature on PI §§138–242. This literature has in turn generated an interest in meaning's normativity as such, quite apart from the question of the interpretation of Wittgenstein. "The normativity of meaning" now labels a subfield in the philosophy of language, whose mandate is to explore the nature and structure of the normative role of meaning in the context of contemporary thinking about semantics and pragmatics.

But if we read PI §§138–242 only through the lens of normativity, we will miss a great deal. One way to see this is to shift our focus from meaning to understanding, to which Wittgenstein pays at least as much explicit attention throughout these passages. Now, understanding, no less than meaning, possesses normative significance. Just as we may speak of the student's response as being in accord (or conflict) with the order's meaning, so we may speak of that response as being in accord (or conflict) with her understanding of the order's meaning. In light of this connection, it might look tempting to organize our reading of Wittgenstein's treatment of understanding around the issue of normativity as well (see, e.g., McDowell, 1992). But in fact it is clear that normative bearing is not the only relationship between understanding and use our grasp of which is under scrutiny in this region of the *Investigations*.

Consider the following remark:

> Perhaps you will say here: to have got the system (or, again, to understand it) can't consist in continuing the series up to *this* or *that* number: *that* is only applying one's understanding. The understanding itself is a state which is the *source* of the correct use. (PI §146)

It is not, or not simply, a thought about normativity that is the focus in this passage. The interlocutor here voices an objection against thinking that understanding the series of natural numbers consists in continuing the series up to some point or other, on the ground that doing so overlooks the distinction between "applying one's understanding" and "the understanding itself." And the idea that understanding is something we might "apply" cannot be analyzed simply in terms of the idea that understanding bears normatively on our use. In particular, applying one's understanding of the series cannot just be a matter of producing a series that is in accord with one's understanding. Consider the distinction between following a rule and merely acting in accordance with a rule (cf. PG 101; BB 13). Following the rule for the Fibonacci series, I write down "1, 1, 2, 3, 5, 8, 13." What I have written is in accord with any number of rules for arithmetical series. But I am following only one: the rule for the Fibonacci series. Analogously, the student's writing down "2, 4, 6, 8" in response to the order accords with any number of possible understandings of the order's meaning. But the student is not thereby "applying" all of these different understandings. The interlocutor's suggestion, brought to bear on this case, is that the student is applying just one understanding: the understanding she in fact has at the time she gives her response.

If applying one's understanding of an order involves something more, or something different, than merely according with that understanding, what does it involve? Whatever else we might want to say about this, it is clear that the new ingredient must have an explanatory aspect. To say that the student is applying a certain understanding of the order in responding to it is to offer an explanation of her response; it is to imply that she responds to the order as she does *because* she understands the order in that particular way. It is just this *explanatory* role that the interlocutor endeavors to account for in speaking of understanding as the "source" of use.

Perhaps owing to its preoccupation with normativity, the secondary literature on PI §§138–242 and related regions of the later work has generally neglected Wittgenstein's concern with the interlocutor's view of the explanatory relationship between understanding and use (though see Haase, 2009, for a noteworthy exception). I will in this chapter press on the scales the other way. I will trace a dialectic between Wittgenstein and his interlocutor centering on the explanatory role of understanding. This dialectic will lead us into the heart of Wittgenstein's complex and subtle treatment of the idea of the mind as a special kind of mechanism.

As I implied above, the proximate cause of the secondary literature's intense focus on normativity is Kripke's influential *Wittgenstein on Rules and Private Language* (1982). But in fact, this circumstance bespeaks an unduly narrow reading of Kripke as well. Kripke's skeptical argument, as with the text that is its inspiration, is as much concerned with the explanatory role of understanding as it is with the normativity of meaning. A further goal of this chapter is therefore to provide the material for a fresh engagement with Kripke's seminal work.

2   The Guidance Conception of Understanding

What is it to apply your understanding of the meaning of an expression or utterance when you use or respond to it? Wittgenstein's interlocutor has a single underlying idea about how to answer this question, which he offers in a variety of guises throughout PI §§138–242. His master thought is that applying one's understanding is a matter of being guided by an image in one's mind. To understand an expression's or utterance's meaning is to have an image in your mind that you can consult when you need to use or respond to the expression or utterance, and that will then show you how to proceed. Let us call this idea the *guidance conception* of understanding (cf. Stroud, 1996).

Consider the proposal that "what really comes before our mind when we *understand* a word" is a "picture" (PI §139). For example, "when you hear the word 'cube,'" a "drawing of a cube" comes "before your mind" (PI §139). Let us say you are participating in an object-identification task: various things are placed before you in succession, and you are told to point at something if and only if it is a "cube." An object is presented that is not a cube – say, a triangular prism – and you refrain from pointing at it. Why? It looks like a perfectly good answer to this question that the word "cube" called to your mind a picture of a cube, and it was evident to you that "this use of the word [i.e., pointing to the prism] doesn't fit the picture" (PI §139). The interlocutor's thought is that it is in such transactions with inner or mental guides that the application of understanding consists.

We noted in the previous section that the idea of applying one's understanding, like the idea of following a rule, is meant to have an explanatory aspect. There is at least this to be said for the guidance conception: the form of explanation to which it connects the application of understanding is one that is familiar and unmysterious. We do often, in everyday life, explain people's performances by citing their consultations with guides, with images or signs that show or tell them what to do. In PI §1, for example, the shopkeeper chooses the right color of apple because he consults a chart of color samples. It is true that the consultation the interlocutor envisions is not with a physical object but with an image "before the mind." But we *can* consult and be guided by such images. If I am asked to determine whether it is appropriate to apply to a given object a word for a shade like "royal blue" or "teal," it can certainly help me to bring to mind images of objects that have been previously presented to me as representatives of the meanings of these words – say, an image of a certain sweater.

In the interlocutor's proposal about "cube," the mental image that one is said to consult is an image of the object or kind of object for which the word stands. The example just mentioned suggests a closely related proposal for color words: that these words call to mind images of objects that are samples of the appropriate shades and colors (see PI §239). But there are less pictorial ways to develop the idea of inner guidance. In the case of the math teacher's order, the interlocutor suggests that the student has an image, not of the sequence of numbers she is supposed to embark upon writing down (after all, the sequence is infinitely long), but of an "algebraic formula," and that she is then able to determine what to write through a "derivation" from that formula (PI §146). Elsewhere he shifts away from visual to auditory imagery, suggesting that one might hear an "inner voice" telling one what to do, which one then "obeys" (PI §213). And no doubt there are other possibilities: what we need to fill out the conception in any given case are images that might plausibly be treated as guides in the use of or response to expressions or utterances of the kind at issue.

But however the conception is spelled out, it is hopeless, and its hopelessness is a central message of this region of the *Investigations*. The problem turns on the following simple point: an item cannot succeed in guiding you a particular way, in showing you to do some particular thing, unless you understand it to show you that. The shopkeeper's color chart, with its juxtaposition of the word "red" and a sample of red, cannot guide the shopkeeper to grab red apples unless he understands it to have that significance. A parallel point goes for any object, be it physical or mental, whose role it is to instruct or direct one to proceed in some particular way: the object can play that role only if you understand it to provide those instructions or directions. As Wittgenstein says of the "inner voice," "if it can guide me right, it can also guide me wrong" (PI §213). And we may add, it can fail to guide me at all. Which of these eventualities obtains will depend upon what, if anything, I understand the inner voice to be telling me to do.

The point can be put this way: if the guidance conception were correct about the connection between use and understanding that obtains when a subject applies her understanding, then that connection would depend upon the subject's having a *second-order* understanding, an understanding of the inner item whose presence constitutes her original understanding. And this circumstance raises an obvious question: how are we to conceive the role of the second-order understanding in bringing about the subject's uses and responses? In particular, does the second-order understanding *guide* the subject's responses to the item constituting her first-order understanding?

Neither a positive nor a negative answer to this question is satisfactory. If the proponent of the guidance conception answers no, then while his conception implies a role for a second-order state of understanding in facilitating the competent use of language, it provides no account of the way in which that state fulfills that role. And yet the point of the guidance conception was to illuminate the role of understanding in facilitating performances. If we see a need for such an account, why should the need not be as pressing with respect to the understanding of mental guides as it is with respect to the understanding of public expressions and utterances? The guidance conception, if applied only to first-order states of understanding, seems just to contrive to push the *locus* of our puzzlement further inward and so out of view.

But on the other hand, if the proponent of the guidance conception answers yes, then he is faced with a regress. The item constituting the subject's second-order understanding can guide her to a particular response to the item constituting her first-order understanding only if she understands it as doing so. Thus a third-order understanding comes into play. And our question simply recurs. (See PI §239 for a concise articulation of the dilemma just traced.)

Faced with this difficulty, there is a temptation to suppose that mental items are different from their external counterparts in just the way needed to prevent a regress. The temptation, in other words, is to think that we can posit mental guides without being saddled by questions about second-order understandings. Mental guides are special. Perhaps we seek to capture their specialness by holding that they are "self-interpreting" (Fogelin, 2009, p.19). Or we say, as does Wittgenstein when confronted with the observation that the same mental picture might be taken to speak either for or against applying "cube" to a triangular prism, "I should have thought that the picture forced a particular use on me," with the elaboration that he had thought the forcing or "compulsion" at stake here to be not "psychological" but "logical" (PI §140). Talk of logical compulsion or self-interpretation attempts to express the idea that a mental guide provides for its own understanding, thereby relieving the subject of the burden of doing the understanding herself.

As Wittgenstein realizes, the "thought" that tempts him is not even false: there is no genuine idea here but only the illusion of one. (PI §140 goes on: "How could I think that? What did I think?," and finds no satisfactory answer to the second of these questions.) If an item is to bear on a person's use of "cube" by showing *her* how to apply it, then *she* must grasp what she is being shown. There is no getting around the fact that her understanding the item in this way will be a state or feature or achievement of her. And so there is no getting around the fact that when we conceive the relationship between the mental item and the subject's performance as one of guidance, we are committed to the presence of a second-order state of understanding on the part of the subject. To insist that the mental item interprets itself, or provides for its own understanding, is in effect an attempt to sidestep this simple point of logic. It is to claim that the subject both understands the item (because she is guided by it) and doesn't understand the item (because the item does the work of understanding itself). However special the mind may be, it cannot be so special as to serve as a *locus* of a logical impossibility.

3   Mind as Mechanism

Why does Wittgenstein spend so much time on the guidance conception? His interlocutor's seemingly inexhaustible penchant for promoting that conception must speak to Wittgenstein's sense of the appeal, even inevitability, that the conception has for us when we reflect philosophically on the role of understanding in explaining performance. But what is supposed to be the source of the appeal? Over the next three sections I sketch an answer to this question.

Wittgenstein tell us that when the interlocutor conceives the relationship between the student's understanding and her performance on the model of a "derivation of a series from its formula" – which we have noted to be a version of the guidance conception – he is supposing that "the understanding is a state which is the *source* of the correct use" (PI §146). The understanding or knowledge that is the source of our use is conceived to be a "state" or "process" of "consciousness" or "thought" (PI §148). Wittgenstein then follows with this remark:

> If one says that knowing the ABC is a state of the mind, one is thinking of a state of a mental apparatus (perhaps of the brain) by means of which we explain the manifestations of that knowledge. (PI §149)

For the interlocutor, one's knowledge or understanding is to be seen as a state of a "mental apparatus" and as explaining one's uses and responses as "manifestations." Wittgenstein does not speak of a mental "apparatus" ("*Apparat*") elsewhere. But the talk of an apparatus is clearly a terminological variant on his frequent ascriptions to the interlocutor of an inclination to posit the existence of mental "mechanisms" (see, in addition to the examples cited below, PI §§157, 613, 689; BB 40, 97; see also the closely related talk of the mind as a "medium" at PI §§102, 109, 308; Z §273; BB 3, 5, 43). As we will see, the interlocutor's attachment to the guidance conception is one manifestation of this inclination.

What is involved in thinking of understanding as a state of a mental apparatus or mechanism (or as persisting in some medium)? The crucial point is that if we are to conceive understanding in this way, then "there ought to be two different criteria for such a state: a knowledge of the construction of the apparatus, quite apart from what it does" (PI §149; see also BB 118; PG 104). That is to say, it belongs to the concept of an apparatus or mechanism that it is possible to characterize a dispositional state of an apparatus in two ways, either in relation to what the apparatus does or in relation to the way in which the apparatus is constructed. To borrow an example from *The Blue Book* (118), we can characterize a player piano's state either in terms of what it is disposed to do (e.g., play "The Entertainer") or in terms of the structure of its parts (the position of the hammers, the location of the hole punches on the roll, etc.). In the first characterization, we relate the state to the player piano's *activity*, and in the second to its *construction*. Wittgenstein's thought is that if we are to make good on our vision of the understanding as a state of a mechanism, we must find both activity-level and construction-level characterizations of that state.

The parenthetical bit in the above quotation – "a state of a mental apparatus (perhaps of the brain)" – might seem to indicate that the interlocutor is open to viewing the mind as a physical mechanism, with construction-level characterizations of its states to be couched in physical (e.g., neurophysiological) terms. But that is not the interlocutor's usual orientation (cf. Goldfarb, 1992). On the contrary, when he is struck by the "curious effects" that the "mechanism of the mind" seems capable of producing, he is inclined rather to suppose "no physical mechanism could behave in this way" (BB 5). He thus seeks to understand the processes of the mind as exercises of a "psychical mechanism" (BB 12).

Now, the idea of a nonphysical mechanism might seem a complete nonstarter, suggesting configurations in some wispy spiritual material. And sometimes Wittgenstein does ascribe such a vision to his interlocutor:

> If one says that thought is a mental activity, or an activity of the mind, one thinks of the mind as a cloudy gaseous medium in which many things can happen which cannot occur in a different sphere, and from which many things can be expected that are otherwise not possible. (PG 100)

This picture is useless: it relies on the idea of material constitution while at the same time denying its application.

But if we interpret the idea of mechanism at a certain degree of abstraction, we can make better sense of what it could be to understand the mind as a nonphysical mechanism, and we can see in particular why Wittgenstein regards the guidance conception as an attempt to understand the mind in this way. We effect this abstraction by hearing the requirement of "knowledge of the construction of the apparatus" (PI §149) as at bottom a demand for *context-independent* characterizations of the apparatus's states and processes.

To elaborate: when we give activity-level characterizations of the states, dispositions, and processes of an object whose activity interests us, our characterizations will very often relate the object to the environment in which it is situated. This will be so, for example, whenever the activity at issue consists in the object's responding to or acting upon things in its surroundings, or in its participating in ongoing practices or institutions. In such cases, the concepts we bring to bear in specifying the object's activity will be such that recognizing those concepts to apply to the object and its doings will involve recognizing the object's interactions and connections with elements in its surroundings. The call for a "construction"-level characterization of a mechanism should be understood as a call for an alternative set of concepts applicable to the object's states and processes, concepts whose suitability for such application we can recognize *without* our needing to bring into view the way in which the object engages with its surroundings. The aim is to find characterizations of these states and processes such that we can abstract from the context in which the object is embedded – such that we can, as it were, blot out the world around the object – and still be in a position to make sense of, and see the applicability of, these characterizations.

When we characterize a person's understanding of the meaning of "cube" as a state that enables her, say, to respond correctly to questions in English of the form "Is this object a cube?", we fail to meet this condition. For we identify the state by relating it to a complex activity on the part of the person, involving both particular social interactions and participation in linguistic practices. What we seek, when we endeavor to conceive understanding as a state of a mental mechanism, is a way of characterizing the relevant state that does not depend upon acknowledgment of such a "wider context" (cf. PI §686).

To construe the mind as a mechanism is thus, as the passage just quoted from *Philosophical Grammar* says, to think of it as a "sphere," as a self-standing realm. But the requirement of self-standing-ness that is ultimately at stake here is not spatial or material: it is conceptual. What is to be self-standing, in the first instance, is our *understanding* of the states and processes of the object when we are conceptualizing them at the level of "construction." The hope is that, if we can find a way of conceiving mental states and processes of meaning and understanding that abstracts from the roles of meaning and understanding in our linguistic acts and interactions, we will thus be able to gain a distinctive kind of insight into the "source" or "spring" (BB 143) of such activity. Nothing in this mission statement rules out the possibility of modes of conceptualizing mental states and processes that do not imply spatiality or materiality, but which nonetheless have the sought-after independence from activity and context.

4   Mechanism and Guidance

What concepts might be suited to this task? One answer, familiar from our philosophical tradition, is concepts of presences in the sensory or perceptual imagination: concepts of what philosophers and psychologists call "mental images." These are, of course, precisely what the interlocutor appeals to in his various attempts to deploy the guidance conception. The conception requires us to find inner items that can be intelligibly understood as showing or telling us things, and the quasi-perceptual character (as philosophers of mind call it) of mental images – the mode of presence that can make it seem appealing to say of an image that "it comes before the mind's eye" (PI §56) – seems to fit them uniquely well for that role.

At the same time, it is the imagistic character of the hypothesized understanding-constituting items that can make the guidance conception seem like an attractive candidate for a mechanistic treatment of the states and processes of the mind that involve understanding. If we think of the student's state of understanding as constituted by the occurrence in her mind of an image – say, of the formula "$x + 2$" – we have access to a way of thinking about that state that does not depend upon our grasp of the context of the teacher's and student's interaction. Furthermore, there is a tempting picture of mental imagery according to which we need essentially *no* context in view in order to make sense of a person as having a certain image. On this picture, concepts of the enjoyment of mental imagery are atomistic: our recognizing them to apply does not depend upon our recognizing the subject to satisfy other concepts (at least outside of a very small circle). One way of arriving at this picture is to suppose that we know what it is to have a certain image immediately from our own case, and that to conceive someone else as having a comparable image then requires nothing more than conceiving her as having what we have. This kind of thought is, of course, equally tempting in the case of sensation. If we allow the concept of sentience to encompass not just sensation and perceptual awareness but exercises of the sensory and perceptual imagination, then we have an attractive way of locating the guidance conception in a long-standing empiricist tradition: that of attempting to explain sapience (as exemplified by, say, the student's competent response to the teacher) in terms of sentience.

The atomistic picture comes under severe criticism later in the *Investigations*, first with respect to sensation and then with respect to images (for the case of images, see the sections beginning around §361). But we do not in fact need to appreciate the untenability of that picture to see that the guidance conception fails in its aim at providing a mechanistic treatment of the application of understanding. For even if we were to grant that the guidance conception satisfies the context-independence requirement in its characterizations of states of understanding, the question would remain how we are to understand its treatment of the explanatory relationship between such states and the subject's performances. And as we have already seen, this treatment is subject to a regress; it presupposes the very nexus for which it is supposed to account.

The guidance conception is just one stab at a mechanistic treatment of the mind. We might take the lesson of its failure to be that we should seek a different mechanistic treatment. But that is not the moral Wittgenstein wants us to draw: he wants us to give up the search for mental mechanisms entirely. Consider the following passage from *Philosophical Grammar*:

> The problem that concerns us could be summed up roughly thus: 'Must one see an image of the colour blue in one's mind whenever one reads the word "blue" with understanding?' People have often asked this question and have commonly answered no; they have concluded from this answer that the characteristic process of understanding is just a different process which we've not yet grasped. [...] Well, 'Understanding' is not the name of a single process accompanying reading or hearing, but of more or less interrelated processes against a background, or in a context, of facts of a particular kind, viz. the actual use of a learnt language or languages. (PG 74)

The realization that understanding a word needn't involve an image coming before one's mind when one hears or reads the word should not prompt us to look for a different "characteristic process of understanding." Rather, it should prompt us to take seriously the observation that understanding takes place against a "background" or "context," comprising such facts as "the actual use of a learnt language." Wittgenstein's exposition implies that acknowledgment of the importance of this "background" stands in opposition to the search for a "characteristic process of understanding." To search for such a process, then, must be to seek a way of conceptualizing understanding that does not depend upon our grasp of the role of the background; it must be to seek concepts capable of providing context-independent characterizations of states and processes of understanding. To give up the search for the "characteristic process" is just to give up the attempt to arrive at a mechanistic account of the operations of understanding.

The same dialectic is traced, if a bit less explicitly, in the more well-known remark PI §154. There Wittgenstein cautions against construing your coming to understand the principle of a series as a process that takes place "behind or side by side" a formula's for the series occurring to you. To construe understanding in this way would be to miss that it is a complex context of "particular circumstances" that makes it intelligible to suppose that you come to understand when the formula occurs to you. Here again, what is at stake in the rhetoric to which the interlocutor is drawn but which Wittgenstein wishes to resist – in this case, talk of a mental process that occurs "behind or side by side" imaginative presences – is the impulse to seek a context-independent, mechanistic account of understanding.

5   Rationality and Guidance

The move that I credited to Wittgenstein at the end of the previous section might strike a contemporary philosopher as unconvincing. Why should the moral of the defeat of the guidance conception be that we should abandon the search for mechanistic accounts of the mind entirely? This can look like a huge leap. In particular, Wittgenstein's disinclination to seriously consider the prospect of treating the mind as a physical mechanism might, with the benefit of hindsight, seem a serious lacuna. Contemporary mainstream philosophy of mind conceives itself as a part of cognitive science, with the project of cognitive science being to explain mental phenomena in terms of computational processes whose implementation in neural activity is in principle possible (if empirically very difficult) to describe. The development of cognitive science is one of the great intellectual achievements of recent decades. In light of this, the idea that the mere untenability of the guidance conception should force us to give up the search for "the characteristic process of understanding" might seem to epitomize the scientific no-nothingism that Burge (2010) argues was endemic in twentieth-century philosophy of mind and epistemology. And indeed, Burge faults the later Wittgenstein in particular as a bad influence on the tradition (2010, p.128). Wittgenstein's excessively "linguistic" orientation is one prominent manifestation of the twentieth-century "hyper-intellectualism" (2010, pp.13, 27) that, in Burge's view, made a clear-eyed appreciation of the true nature of objective thought impossible – with contemporary cognitive science now providing the needed corrective.

In fact the interlocutor's (and Wittgenstein's) relative lack of interest in the potential fruits of the psychological sciences is not a sign of ignorance or antipathy to science, but of insight into the nature of the interlocutor's explanatory project.

The interlocutor's topic is the role of understanding in explaining performance. In particular, he wants to give a mechanistic account of the role ascribed to understanding in our ordinary, everyday appeals to understanding in the explanation of people's uses of and responses to language. Let us now register two related features of that role that we have not yet had occasion to consider explicitly. When we cite a person's understanding of meaning to explain her uses of, or responses to, meaningful items, we typically do so in the service of representing her uses and responses as *rational* and *self-conscious*. Suppose that while we are building an IKEA bookshelf, you ask why I attached a certain board to the base using a certain screw, and I answer that that is what I understand the instructions to say to do at this stage. It will be natural for you to understand me as portraying myself as having a reason, a justification, for doing what I did, and as explaining my action in terms of that reason or justification: I am telling you that I acted as I did *for* the reason that the instructions said to do so. I thus represent my action as an exercise of rationality, of the capacity to respond to reasons. What role does my understanding of the instructions here play? Since the reason my explanation represents me as acting on is a function of what the instructions mean, my appreciation of this reason depends upon my grasp, my understanding, of that meaning. The role of my understanding of the instruction's meaning is to bring the reason into view for me. It is thus necessary for the *self-consciousness* of my exercise of rationality, viz., to my knowing myself to be acting for a reason provided by the meaning of the instructions.

The explanatory nexus into which the interlocutor wishes to achieve insight is one in which the subject does what she does because of her recognition of a justification she has for doing that. The interlocutor wants to find a context-independent way of identifying the states and processes involved in this nexus, but he does not want to thereby lose sight of the elements of self-consciousness and justification. Precisely not: his aim is to capture these elements in the workings of a mechanism.

It is in virtue of this aim that the guidance conception can seem uniquely attractive. First, as we have already noted, concepts of mental imagery can appear to possess a highly atomic character, and hence to enable the framing of context-independent specifications of mental states. But second, the concept of possession of a mental image incorporates the idea of self-knowledge: it is part of the idea of having, e.g., a certain visual image that I know myself to be having it. And third, the concept of guidance, of being shown or told how to do something, introduces an element of justification: when one is shown or told how to do something, one is thereby given a reason for proceeding in a particular way. Of course, our appreciation of this reason depends upon our understanding of what we are being shown or told to do, and it is just this point that ensnares the guidance conception in a regress. But if we have not yet thought through the conception with enough clarity to see the inevitability of regress, then in light of the three points just listed, the conception can seem to provide a satisfying mechanistic analysis of just the explanatory nexus we are trying to understand. It is much less obvious how, starting with naturalistic characterizations of states of the brain, we could work our way up to capturing the elements of self-consciousness and rationality that are definitive of this nexus.

If the appeal of the guidance conception, as an account of acting on an understanding of meaning, lies in its apparent potential to show how self-consciousness and rationality can be incorporated into the workings of a mental mechanism, then we should expect the interlocutor to find it tempting in a wider range of cases – indeed, perhaps, in the case of any exercise of self-conscious rationality. It is in this light that we should view the lengthy set of remarks on reading – glossed as "the activity of rendering out loud what is written or printed" – that Wittgenstein interpolates into his discussion of the student's understanding of the teacher's order. Since Wittgenstein is explicit that understanding the meaning of what one is reading is not essential to reading as he wants to conceive it, the placement of these remarks can seem puzzling, and it is perhaps for that reason that they have received comparatively little attention in the secondary literature (though see Anscombe, 1990). A brief examination of their purport will help to reinforce the interpretation I have offered here of Wittgenstein's concerns in PI §§138–242.

The discussion of reading is largely given over to querying what role the idea of a felt experience of "influence" or "guidance" should play in our reflections on the nature of the activity of reading aloud. The first point to note for our purposes is that Wittgenstein is explicitly concerned with the question of whether such an experience might be connected to the self-conscious rationality of the activity of reading aloud:

> One might [...] say, I feel that the letters are the reason why I read such-and-such. For if someone asks me 'Why do you read such-and-such?' – I justify my reading by the letters which are there.
>   This justification, however, was something that I said, or thought: what does it mean to say that I feel it? I should like to say: when I read I feel a kind of *influence* of the letters working on me. (PI §169)

We can tease apart two thoughts under scrutiny here. One is that the written letters provide my reason for reading aloud what I do, a reason I recognize myself to have and can articulate if asked to do so. My saying what I do is an exercise of self-conscious rationality, in which the written letters provide the justification I have, and know myself to have, for what I say. The second thought is that I *feel* this reason or justification as I read aloud, a feeling that can be characterized as that of "a kind of influence of the letters working on me."

Wittgenstein does not reject the first of these thoughts. To the contrary: he allows that we do say and think that we acted for a reason provided by the letters, and there is no indication that he regards us as mistaken for saying or thinking this. It is rather the second thought that is his target:

> [The thought] that we felt the influence of the letters on us when reading [...] appeals to us especially when we make a point of reading slowly – perhaps in order to see what does happen when we read. When we, so to speak, quite intentionally let ourselves be *guided* by the letters. But this 'letting myself be guided' in turn only consists in my looking carefully at the letters – and perhaps excluding certain other thoughts. (PI §170)

The feeling of being guided or influenced by the letters – which is supposed to constitute our awareness of the letters providing us with a reason – seems most apparent when we intentionally "let ourselves be guided" by what is written. But letting oneself be guided by the letters, Wittgenstein tells us, just consists in looking at the letters carefully and ignoring distractions. The evident implication is that any special "feeling" to be found when we "let ourselves be guided" must just be a matter of what it feels like to look at something carefully, to focus one's attention.

Wittgenstein clearly regards this observation as undermining the point of our initial appeal to the distinctive "feeling" of guidance. Why does it do so? What, indeed, was the point of the appeal? The answer is that we had hoped that the feeling of guidance constituted awareness of a "mechanism" that effects the transition from our seeing the written letters to our speaking them aloud:

> We imagine that a feeling enables us to perceive as it were a connecting mechanism between the look of the word and the sound that we utter. For when I speak of the experiences of being influenced, of causal connexion, of being guided, that is really meant to imply that I as it were feel the movement of the lever which connects seeing the letters with speaking. (PI §170)

Once we realize that the feeling of guidance is just the feeling of paying close attention to something and related phenomena, we are supposed to see that it is not plausibly understood as constituting a peek at the workings of a "connecting mechanism."

Let us draw all these points together. Reading words aloud is an exercise of self-conscious rationality. The words on the page justify my saying what I do, and it is because of my recognition of the justification they provide me that I act. The interlocutor wants to account for this explanatory relationship mechanistically, but he wants to do so in a way that captures the self-conscious rationality in play. So he imagines a "connecting mechanism" his access to which is not third-personal and theoretical, as it would be if we were positing some physical, say computational, process mediating the transition from perception to performance. Rather, the imagined access is first-personal and experiential – a matter of his felt awareness of the letters he sees guiding what he says. The appeal to the experience of being guided by the letters is meant to play a role analogous to the appeal to images in the case of the guidance conception of understanding. In both cases, the aim is to identify items in the realm of sentience that constitute processes of sapience – or as we can now say, of self-conscious rationality. In both cases, finally, Wittgenstein traces the failure of the attempt to an insufficient appreciation of the multiplicity of circumstances that help to constitute the phenomena at issue (see PI §§172–3).

6 Kripke on Rationality and Guidance

Kripke's *Wittgenstein on Rules and Private Language* (1982) has played a decisive role in shaping the literature on Wittgenstein's remarks on meaning and understanding. The skeptical paradox outlined in that book is almost always read as centered on the question of how to account for the normativity of meaning. As I mentioned at the outset, this interpretive assumption is at the root of the great interest in the normativity of meaning in recent decades.

There is no question that Kripke's skeptic has the normativity of meaning in view: he criticizes various candidate accounts of the constitution of meaning, such as dispositionalism, on the ground that they fail to accommodate normativity. But the exposition of the skeptical paradox is complicated and multifaceted. Intertwined with the examination of our various failed attempts to provide for normativity is an additional thread of skeptical thought whose concern at its core is to establish our inability to account for the *explanatory* role that we ordinarily suppose a person's grasp of meaning to play. I have suggested that this role should be understood in terms of the contribution of the subject's understanding of meaning to her exercise of self-conscious rationality in using and responding to expressions and utterances. And I have argued that the interlocutor is attracted to the guidance conception because it seems to provide a way of gaining a distinctive kind of insight into the workings of self-conscious rationality in such cases. In this closing section, I will show that Kripke's skeptic shares just this commitment of Wittgenstein's interlocutor. Indeed, the Kripkean skeptic's commitment to the guidance conception is absolute: he believes the failure of the conception to provide a satisfactory account of the putative rational-explanatory role of understanding implies that understanding cannot in fact play this role.

To see that Kripke, at least some of the time, frames the skeptical paradox as concerned with the rational-explanatory role of our grasp of meaning, consider the following passage:

> Almost all of us unhesitatingly produce the answer '125' when asked for the sum of 68 and 57, without any thought to the theoretical possibility that a quus-like rule might have been appropriate! And we do so without justification. Of course, if asked why we said '125', most of us will say that we added 8 and 7 to get 15, that we put down 5 and carried 1 and so on. But then, what will we say if asked why we 'carried' as we do? Might our past intention not have been that 'carry' meant *quarry*; where to 'quarry' is ...? The entire point of the skeptical argument is that ultimately we reach a level where we act without any reason in terms of which we can justify our action. We act unhesitatingly but *blindly*. (Kripke, 1982, p.87, ellipsis in original)

The question with which the skeptical argument is here said to be concerned is "why we said '125.'" This is an explanatory question about an action of ours; it asks why we responded as we did when presented with a certain problem framed using "+." The import of the skeptical argument, as here represented, is that what we are inclined to say in answer to this question does not have the substance we credit to it. We think we can explain why we said "125" by identifying our reasons for giving that response, reasons we recognize ourselves to possess in virtue of understanding the terms in which the original arithmetical problem was posed to us. But as Kripke sees it, this attempt at explanation does not succeed. For it prompts a further explanatory question, one now targeting our understanding of the terms in which we couched our explanation. Whatever we say in response to this question will raise another question along the same lines, *ad infinitum*. The implication of this regress is that "ultimately we reach a level where we act without any reason in terms of which we can justify our action." At this level, we act "blindly": we do not act for any justifying reasons furnished by our knowledge of the meaning of "+" or other relevant expressions. That our action is blind in this sense is "the entire point of the skeptical argument."

It is in relation to the idea that grasp of meaning can put us in touch with reasons, reasons upon which we may then self-consciously act, that we should hear remarks such as, "The sceptic argues that when I answered '125' to the problem '68 + 57', my answer was an unjustified leap in the dark" (1982, p.15). To take an unjustified leap in the dark is to act while lacking a justification, a reason, for which one thus acts. The skeptic is here represented as arguing that I do not have a reason for answering as I do, and so *a fortiori*, that I do not have an understanding or grasp of the problem's meaning that furnishes me with awareness of such a reason. Of course, our ordinary presumption is that we do have such reasons for using and responding to expressions and utterances as we do. That is why the claim to the contrary amounts to a kind of skepticism.

How does Kripke's skeptic get to the conclusion that linguistic uses and responses are invariably unjustified stabs in the dark? Here is not the place to reconstruct the skeptic's line of thought in detail. What matters for present purposes is one feature of this line of thought: that it rests on an assimilation of acting for a reason provided by one's grasp of meaning to being guided by an item that constitutes one's grasp of the meaning. In the course of his discussion of dispositionalism, for example, Kripke writes the following:

> So it does seem that a dispositional account misconceives the sceptic's problem – to find a past fact that justifies my present response. As a candidate for a 'fact' that determines what I mean, it fails to satisfy the basic condition on such a candidate stressed above [...], that it should tell me what I ought to do in each instance. (Kripke, 1982, p.24)

Here the demand to state the reason for which I give my response gets transmuted, without comment, into the requirement that we identify an item that "tells" me what to do.

This is not an isolated instance, and cannot be dismissed as a rhetorical flourish. The idea that there must be an item in my mind that in some sense or another *shows* me how I am to proceed is everywhere present in the exposition of the skeptical paradox, and our inability to find any regress-proof candidates for this item is precisely what motivates the skeptical conclusion. For example:

> Sometimes when I have contemplated the [skeptical paradox], I have had something of an eerie feeling. Even now as I write, I feel confident that there is something in my mind – the meaning I attach to the 'plus' sign – that instructs me what I ought to do in all future cases [...]. But when I concentrate on what is now in my mind, what instructions can be found there? How can I be said to be acting on the basis of these instructions when I act in the future? [...] To say that there is a general rule in my mind that tells me how to add in the future is only to throw the problem back on to other rules that also seem to be given only in terms of finitely many cases. What can there be in my mind that I make use of when I act in the future? It seems the entire idea of meaning vanishes into thin air. (Kripke, 1982, pp.21–2)

The parallel between Kripke's skeptic and Wittgenstein's interlocutor that emerges here is striking. It suggests that the real source of meaning skepticism lies in a deep commitment to our uncovering a mechanistic basis for any supposed exercise of self-conscious rationality. As a corollary, it suggests that we can defeat the specter of meaning skepticism if we can come to see why such an account does not have to be possible.

References

Anscombe, G.E.M. (1990). Wittgenstein: Whose Philosopher? *Royal Institute of Philosophy Supplement*, 28, 1–10.

Burge, T. (2010). *Origins of Objectivity*. Oxford: Oxford University Press.

Fogelin, R.J. (2009). *Taking Wittgenstein at his Word: A Textual Study*. Princeton: Princeton University Press.

Goldfarb, W. (1992). Wittgenstein on Understanding. *Midwest Studies in Philosophy*, 17, 109–122.

Haase, M. (2009). The Laws of Thought and the Power of Thinking. *Canadian Journal of Philosophy (Supplement)*, 35, 249–297.

Kripke, S.A. (1982). *Wittgenstein on Rules and Private Language: An Elementary Exposition*. Oxford: Blackwell.

McDowell, J. (1992). Meaning and Intentionality in Wittgenstein's Later Philosophy. Reprinted in J. McDowell. (1998). *Mind, Value and Reality* (pp.263–278). Cambridge, MA: Harvard University Press.

Stroud, B. (1996). Mind, Meaning and Practice. In H. Sluga and D.G. Stern (Eds). *The Cambridge Companion to Wittgenstein* (pp.296–319). Cambridge: Cambridge University Press.

Further Reading

Boghossian, P. (1989). The Rule-Following Considerations. *Mind*, 98, 507–549. [Influential survey of the early literature on Kripke, 1982.]

Bridges, J. (2014). Rule-Following Skepticism, Properly So-Called. In J. Conant and A. Kern (Eds). *Skepticism, Meaning, and Justification* (pp.249–288). Berlin: De Gruyter. [A more detailed presentation of the reading of Kripke outlined in this chapter.]

Ginsborg, H. (2011). Review of *Oughts and Thoughts*. *Mind*, 119, 1175–1186. [Illuminating critique of Hattiangadi, 2007.]

Hattiangadi, A. (2007). *Oughts and Thoughts: Rule-Following and the Normativity of Content*. Oxford: Oxford University Press. [Book-length treatment of the normativity of meaning.]

McDowell, J. (1984). Wittgenstein on Following a Rule. *Synthese*, 58, 325–363. [Early touchstone of the post-Kripkean literature on PI §§138–242.]

McDowell, J. (1989). One Strand in the Private Language Argument. Reprinted in J. McDowell. (1998). *Mind, Value and Reality* (pp.279–296). Cambridge: Cambridge University Press. [An interpretation of Wittgenstein's remarks on sensation complementary to the treatment proposed here of mental images.]

Wikforss, A.M. (2001). Semantic Normativity. *Philosophical Studies*, 102, 203–226. [Influential contribution to the "normativity of meaning" literature.]

Wright, C. (1984). Kripke's Account of the Argument against Private Language. *Journal of Philosophy*, 81, 759–778. [Another early touchstone of the post-Kripkean literature on PI §§138–242.]

24

Rules and Rule-Following

GARY EBBS

The concept of a rule that primarily interests Wittgenstein is one that is central to our understanding of "what is possible *before* all new discoveries and inventions" (PI §126). In a practical way, this concept of a rule (which I will from now on just call *the* concept of a rule) is as familiar to us as calling a particular color "blue" (PI §238) or adding 2 (PI §185). When we call a particular color "blue" or add 2, we make new applications of rules "as a *matter of course*" (PI §238), while simultaneously experiencing these new applications of the rules as in some sense rationally guided by our understanding of them. When we try to explain or clarify our idea that the applications of rules that we make "as a matter of course" are rationally guided by our grasp of the rules, however, we soon start to face seemingly intractable difficulties of a sort that I will discuss below. In his great work, *Philosophical Investigations*, Wittgenstein aims both to uncover the sources of these difficulties and to show his readers how to overcome them.

Wittgenstein's investigations of the concept of a rule run "criss-cross in every direction" (PI preface). Although "the same or almost the same points [are] always being approached afresh from different directions" (PI preface), the points about rules are most prominent in PI §§82–7 and §§138–242. What Wittgenstein aims to do in these sections for the concept of a rule is a special case of what he aims to do in all of his later work – to work through, and eventually to see through, or dissolve, philosophical problems that prevent us from "commanding a clear view of the use of our words" (PI §122). In particular, he aims to expose the emptiness of tempting philosophical *explanations* of the notion of grounds for correct continuation of a rule. He does so by contrasting them with contextually apt and satisfying *descriptions* of applications of rules that we make "as a matter of course" (PI §238) – descriptions that help us to articulate an ordinary sense in which such applications are appropriate and correct. "We must do away with all *explanation*," he writes, "and description alone must take its place. And this description gets its light, that is to say its purpose, from the philosophical problems. [...] The problems are solved, not by reporting new experience, but by arranging what we have always known" (PI §109).

As the last several quotations from his work suggest, Wittgenstein developed his own distinctive philosophical method to investigate the philosophical issues that interested him (see also Chapter 16, SURVEYABILITY). His method and his style of presenting and applying it are strikingly different from the methods and styles of other prominent Anglo-American philosophers, and make very different demands on the reader. One can understand Wittgenstein's work only by engaging openly both with his provocative examples and with his questions and comments about them, exploring different ways of looking at the phenomena in question, searching for the best ways of articulating philosophical responses to puzzles or conclusions that for the moment may seem inescapable, and being open to at least trying to question any judgment, especially those judgments that now strike one as beyond question. My aim here is to present an elementary exposition of Wittgenstein's investigation of the concept of a rule, focusing on two of its main episodes in the *Investigations*, and to discuss the prospects for his strategy for dissolving problems we encounter when we try to explain and clarify the concept of a rule.

1 A Mental Picture of a Cube Guides My Application of "Cube"

Wittgenstein's investigations of the concept of a rule are inextricably linked with his investigations of the concept of meaning. He writes:

> This general notion of the meaning of a word surrounds the working of language with a haze which makes clear vision impossible. It disperses the fog to study the phenomena of language in primitive kinds of application in which one can command a clear view of the aim and functioning of the words. (PI §5)

Wittgenstein therefore starts his investigation of the concept of meaning (and hence, also, of the concept of a rule) by describing very primitive languages, in which it is possible to see clearly how the meanings of words are related to the activities associated with them. The simplest of the languages that Wittgenstein describes is that of the builders:

> The language is meant to serve for communication between a builder A and an assistant B. A is building with building-stones: there are blocks, pillars, slabs and beams. B has to pass the stones, and that in the order in which A needs them. For this purpose they use a language consisting of the words "block", "pillar", "slab", "beam". A calls them out; – B brings the stone which he has learned to bring at such-and-such a call. (PI §2)

The aim and functioning of the words in this language are clear to us, according to Wittgenstein – there is no mystery about what they mean. Part of the reason for this clarity is that in a primitive language like that of the builders, the teaching of language "is not explanation, but training" (PI §5). For the assistant builders, for instance, such a training would involve inculcating in a potential assistant builder the disposition to bring a block to a builder when he or she hears the builder call out "Block!"

These remarks are of course just the beginning for Wittgenstein. They require careful further scrutiny. If one reads his text as presenting a theory in response to a problem, one will fail to see what he is up to. He is not offering, for instance, a behavioristic theory of meaning, but is attempting to "disperse the fog" that surrounds our talk of meaning by examining concrete applications of language with which we are familiar. He is fully aware that his remarks about the applications are themselves open to different interpretations, some of which are equally, or even more, problematic than the thoughts they are meant to investigate and clarify.

His awareness that his remarks about the applications are themselves open to different interpretations is clear from the way he examines the relation between meaning and use. At one point he writes, for instance: "For a *large* class of cases – though not all – in which we employ the word 'meaning' it can be defined thus: the meaning of a word is its use in the language" (PI §43). He does not stop there, of course, but expects the reader to ask, "Can this be right? And what exactly does it come to?" Directly following the provocative assertion in PI §43, Wittgenstein explores how it fits our understanding of the meanings of names. I shall skip over these rich, intricate investigations to highlight what I take to be the first of the groups of sections in the *Investigations* that focus most prominently on the concept of a rule, namely sections 138–43.

In section 138, another key topic in the full investigation of the concept of a rule is introduced – that of our *understanding* of the meaning of a word. Here Wittgenstein sympathetically portrays the point of view of an interlocutor who is puzzled by the idea (floated in PI §43) that the meaning of a word is its use:

> But we *understand* the meaning of a word when we hear or say it; we grasp it in a flash, and what we grasp in this way is surely something different from the 'use' which is extended in time! (PI §138)

This puzzlement is articulated further at the start of PI §139:

> When someone says the word "cube" to me, for example, I know what it means. But can the whole *use* of the word come before my mind, when I *understand* it in this way?

Wittgenstein takes this question very seriously. His first response is (indirectly) to concede the commonsense observation that the whole use of a word does not "come before my mind" when I understand it, but to suggest, by posing a number of related but different questions, that this commonsense observation does not have the significance the interlocutor takes it to have:

> Well, but on the other hand isn't the meaning of the word also determined by this use? And can't these ways of determining meaning conflict? Can what we grasp *in a flash* accord with a use, fit or fail to fit it? And how can what is present to us in an instant, what comes before our mind in an instant, fit a *use*? (PI §139)

These are the sorts of questions that I shall highlight in my exposition of Wittgenstein's investigations into the concept of a rule.

The questions are immediately followed by what is generally regarded to be one of the most successful and decisive episodes in Wittgenstein's investigation of the concept of a rule. The episode begins with the following dialogue:

> What really comes before our mind when we *understand* a word? – Isn't it something like a picture? Can't it *be* a picture? (PI §139)

Wittgenstein's response to the interlocutor's suggestion – that what comes before our mind when we understand a word, what constitutes our understanding of the word, is a picture – is to examine it carefully:

Well, suppose that a picture does come before your mind when you hear the word "cube", say the drawing of the cube. In what sense can this picture fit or fail to fit the use of the word "cube"? – Perhaps you say: "It's quite simple; – if that picture occurs to me and I point to a triangular prism for instance, and say it is a cube, then this use of the word doesn't fit the picture.' – But doesn't it fit? I have purposely so chosen the example that it is quite easy to imagine a *method of projection* according to which the picture does fit after all.

The picture of the cube did indeed *suggest* a certain use to us, but it was possible for me to use it differently. (PI §139)

As Wittgenstein immediately notes, a natural reaction to this observation is that "I should have thought that the picture forced a particular use on me." His response is to investigate this reaction:

How could I think that? What *did* I think? Is there such a thing as a picture, or something like a picture, that forces a particular application on us; so that my mistake lay in confusing one picture with another? (PI §140)

He then spells out his point:

What was the effect of my argument? It called our attention to (reminded us of) the fact that there are other processes, besides the one we originally thought of, which we should sometimes be prepared to call "applying the picture of a cube". So our 'belief that the picture forced a particular application upon us' consisted in the fact that only the one case and no other occurred to us. [...]

What is essential is to see that the same thing can come before our minds when we hear the word and the application still be different. Has it the *same* meaning both times? I think we shall say not. (PI §140)

In short, a picture of a cube does not settle the meaning of "cube," since there are different possible applications of it, and on some of these applications, the word "cube" would have a different meaning than it actually does.

It would not help, Wittgenstein adds in PI §141, to say that "not merely the picture of the cube, but also the method of projection comes before our mind." For *any* item that comes before my mind, however complex, I can imagine *different* applications. The thought that my understanding of the meaning of a word consists in a picture that comes before my mind does not survive scrutiny.

Wittgenstein next shifts to an investigation of the relation between understanding of meaning, and rules of language, on the one hand, and the possibility of different applications of an inscription or another sort of item that comes before the mind during language instruction, on the other.

Let us now imagine the following kind of language-game: when A gives an order B has to write down series of signs according to a certain formation rule.

The first of these series is meant to be that of the natural numbers in decimal notation. –How does he get to understand this notation? – First of all series of numbers will be written down for him and he will be required to copy them. (Do not balk at the expression "series of numbers"; it is not being used wrongly here.) And here already there is a normal and an abnormal learner's reaction. – At first perhaps we guide his hand in writing out the series 0 to 9; but then the *possibility of getting him to understand* will depend on his going on to write it down independently. (PI §143)

Wittgenstein notes that there are several different possible cases here: in some cases the pupil will be able to write out the number series flawlessly, or very nearly so; in other cases, the pupil will make a number of random mistakes now and then, and significantly more often than in the first group of cases; in yet other cases the pupil's performance will be systematically mistaken. In the first kinds of cases we will say he understands, in the second we will often, though, not always, say he understands (sometimes the number of random mistakes will be too large, or too salient for attributing understanding), whereas in the last kind "we shall almost be tempted to say that he has understood *wrong*" (PI §143).

These observations lead naturally to the question of whether we can specify criteria for understanding a rule, such as a rule for writing out a series of numbers, in terms of the number of correct applications of the rule that a pupil has produced. And here it is natural to reply, on the contrary:

> to have got the system (or, again, to understand it) can't consist in continuing the series up to *this* or *that* number: *that* is only applying one's understanding. The understanding itself is a state which is the *source* of the correct use. (PI §146)

This reply is closely linked with the assertion that I quoted above about the relationship between understanding and use:

> But we *understand* the meaning of a word when we hear or say it; we grasp it in a flash, and what we grasp in this way is surely something different from the 'use' which is extended in time! (PI §138)

Wittgenstein is revisiting this very natural response to his suggestion that the meaning of a word is its use in a language (PI §43), a suggestion that he thinks is correct in some ways and problematic in others. In the part of PI §146 that I recently quoted, Wittgenstein highlights the closely related but more sophisticated and philosophical idea that understanding is "a state which is the *source* of the correct use."

This idea is especially gripping when we focus on moments when it seems to us that we have suddenly for the first time grasped a rule, as when we say, after some instruction, "Now I can do it!" or "Now I understand!" (PI §151). In such cases, it seems to us that our applications of the rule are guided by our understanding, and that our understanding of the rule is itself present to our consciousness, and therefore is, or is at least partly constituted by, a special kind of experience. We feel like saying, "But being guided is surely a particular experience!" (PI §173). When in the course of writing out the series of natural numbers, I write down the numeral "9" directly after I write "8," it may seem to me that I have the "experience of being influenced" (PI §176). If a person asks me why I wrote "9" directly after I wrote "8," for instance, I might naturally reply, "Because I am writing down the series of natural numbers," and it is natural to think that my writing is *guided* by my understanding of what comes next in the series, and that my understanding must therefore be "a state which is the *source* of the correct use."

Thus Wittgenstein's investigation into the concepts of meaning and understanding lead him to a core question about how understanding is related to correct use – the question how to clarify the idea that one's application of a *rule* is in some sense *guided* by one's understanding of it, while at the same time acknowledging that one and the same *word-form* may be applied in ways that are different enough to lead us to judge that the rules expressed by the applications are different.

2   The Parable of the Wayward Child

In PI §185, Wittgenstein continues his investigation of the idea that one's application of a rule is in some sense *guided* by one's understanding of it by returning to the example of following a series, from PI §143. He imagines a slightly different case, designed to highlight, once more, our puzzlement about the relationship between our understanding of a rule and our applications of it:

> Now – judged by the usual criteria – the pupil has mastered the series of natural numbers. Next we teach him to write down another series of cardinal numbers and get him to the point of writing down series of the form
>
> 0, n, 2n, 3n, etc.
>
> at an order of the form '+n'; so at the order '+1' he writes down the series of natural numbers. – Let us suppose we have done exercises and given him tests up to 1000.
>
> Now we get the pupil to continue a series (say +2) beyond 1000 – and he writes 1000, 1004, 1008, 1012.
>
> We say to him: "Look what you've done!" – He doesn't understand. We say: "You were meant to add *two*: look how you began the series!"—He answers: "Yes, isn't it right? I thought that was how I was *meant* to do it." [...]
>
> Such a case would present similarities with one in which a person naturally reacted to the gesture of pointing with the hand by looking in the direction of the line from finger-tip to wrist, not from wrist to finger-tip. (PI §185)

How shall we characterize the challenge that this Parable of the Wayward Child (as I shall call it) poses for clarifying our concept of a rule?

I want to approach this question indirectly, by examining the interpretation of the Parable that Warren Goldfarb offers in his recent paper "Rule-Following Revisited" (Goldfarb, 2012). By clarifying what I find misleading about Goldfarb's reading of the Parable, I aim both to highlight aspects of the Parable that are otherwise less easy to see, and to illustrate the kind of investigations that I think Wittgenstein's examples and comments are designed to prompt his readers to undertake.

Goldfarb summarizes his interpretation of Wittgenstein's remarks about rules in the *Investigations* as follows:

> Wittgenstein points out that there are many ways of going on; and so we are inclined to conclude that we need something that picks out the correct continuation, but not in the way that our explanations in ordinary life pick it out. We do not want something that gets people to go on in the right way, but something that absolutely picks out for any possible audience the right continuation from all possible continuations.
>
> (Goldfarb, 2012, p.85)

Goldfarb bases each step of this summary on his reading of the dialectic in *Philosophical Investigations*, starting with the Parable of the Wayward Child in PI §185. As I see it there are two crucial steps in Goldfarb's reading of the Parable:

(1)   What the Parable shows is that there is nothing in anything we can say about the rule that mandates the continuation to go one way rather than another, and so there is always a question whether the child understands. (Goldfarb 2012, p.73)

(2)   Given that the examples and the explanations don't seem to force one way on us, how does *anything* count as correct or incorrect? This is a question of the

> *constitution* of correctness. It does not concern our justification in taking ourselves to be right; the example is not meant to shake our *confidence* that we are right when we proceed in a particular way, but rather to get us to ask what it is to *say* that we are right. (Goldfarb, 2012, p.75)

According to this interpretation, after reading the Parable of the Wayward Child the interlocutor feels that to make sense of her confidence that she is right to proceed in a particular way, she must demand that there be some explanation of how to go on "that picks out the correct continuation, but not in the way that our explanations in ordinary life pick it out"; she must demand an explanation of rules that somehow "absolutely picks out *for any possible audience* the right continuation from all possible continuations" (Goldfarb, 2012, p.85, my emphasis). This *super-explanation* would not rely on how particular individuals respond to what we say. In this sense, the demand for such an explanation is "a demand on rules that operates in abstraction from how we *actually* operate with rules" (p.76); a demand for a "self-sufficient item that does all the work in determining the continuation" (p.78), a "demand of operating in a vacuum – of setting up the standard of correctness in and of itself" (p.79). According to Goldfarb, the interlocutor is in the grip of the idea that there must be "a complete story that would serve in all possible circumstances, and that rules out all counter-possibilities, all alternative ways of going on" (p.84). And, again, such a full and ultimate justification would be one that somehow "absolutely picks out *for any possible audience* the right continuation from all possible continuations" (p.85).

This reading of the Parable seems far removed from what Wittgenstein says when he introduces the Parable. What textual basis does Goldfarb have for reading the Parable in this way? One possible answer is that Goldfarb infers his account of the puzzle about rules raised by the Parable from Wittgenstein's strategy for *dissolving* the puzzle, in particular, from Wittgenstein's central suggestion that "there is a way of grasping the rule which is not an interpretation, but which is expressed in what we call 'obeying the rule' and 'going against it' in actual cases" (PI §201). By inviting us, later on in his inquiry, to clarify rules by describing "what we call 'obeying the rule' and 'going against it' in actual cases," Wittgenstein appears to be suggesting that the puzzlement about rules that the Parable evokes for us is due to our implicit demand for "a complete story [about rules] that would serve in all possible circumstances, and that rules out all counter-possibilities, all alternative ways of going on" (Goldfarb, 2012, p.84).

This answer is at least superficially plausible. Wittgenstein's strategy for dissolving the puzzle, when properly understood, surely does shed light on his view of what the puzzle is. The problem with this account of the textual support for Goldfarb's interpretation of the Parable, however, is that we may not be in a position to understand Wittgenstein's strategy if we do not properly understand the problem it is supposed to address. It is therefore worth taking a closer look at Goldfarb's characterization of the point of the Parable.

To begin with, how should we understand Goldfarb's passage (1)? If the rule is "+2," then the Parable does not show that there is more than one possible continuation of it. When the child produces answers that are not in accord with the rule, those answers don't show there is more than one possible continuation of the *rule* + 2, but that the child did not pick up, get, or grasp, that rule, even if the *sign* (linguistic expression) "+2" comes to her mind when she takes herself to be answering our questions. This is not a philosophical response, I think, but just what we would ordinarily say about the case.

In what sense, then does the Parable show that "there is nothing in anything we can say about the rule that mandates the continuation to go one way rather than another"? Only, I think, in the sense that nothing in anything we can say about the *rule + 2* mandates that the Wayward Child, even after all that training, ought to apply the *sign* "+2" in accord with the *rule + 2*, as we of course take ourselves to do. And here it is useful to recall that in his discussion of different ways of applying a picture of the cube, Wittgenstein comments:

> What is essential is to see that the same thing can come before our minds when we hear the word and the application still be different. Has it the *same* meaning both times? I think we shall say not. (PI §140)

The concept of a rule is intimately linked with the concept of meaning. We should conclude that for some contrasting pairs of differing applications of the *sign* "+2," the rules that correspond with and (in a sense yet to be clarified) *guide* those applications are different. In responding to the Parable of the Wayward Child, we should not be tempted to identify the rule + 2 with *signs* that come before our minds. Goldfarb's passage (1) appears to succumb to this temptation, and thereby misses part of the point of the Parable.

Goldfarb's passage (2) seems equally problematic to me. In what sense does the Parable suggest that "the examples and the explanations don't seem to force one way on us"? Here it is helpful to ask: "One way of doing what?" Suppose we say the examples and the explanations don't seem to force on us only one way of adding 2. If "us" refers to those reading the Parable, this seems wrong. As Goldfarb notes, the Parable does not in any way undermine our confidence that we are right about how to add 2. This confidence goes hand-in-hand with what I shall call the *phenomenology of correctness* – our sense, when we make particular applications of a rule, that *these applications are guided by our correct understanding of the rule and are therefore themselves correct*. This phenomenology is closely linked, of course, with the tempting idea, introduced in the previous section above, that our understanding of a rule is "a state which is the *source* of the correct use." We don't lose the phenomenology simply because of the Parable; if anything, the Parable highlights it, makes it seem more vivid to us, and more central to understanding what it is to apply a rule correctly.

In what sense, then, can we accept that "the examples and the explanations don't seem to force one way on us"? Perhaps only in the sense that the examples and the explanations don't seem to force every individual to apply the *sign* "+2" in the same way. But at this stage in the investigation, at least, we are not so confused that we feel we can make sense of their being widely divergent applications of the *rule + 2*. In short, like passage (1), Goldfarb's passage (2) also appears to conflate applications of the *sign* "+2" with applications of the *rule + 2*, and thereby misses part of the point of the Parable.

For these reasons, I think we need a different reading of the Parable. On the reading I favor, the main point of the Parable is to highlight the phenomenology of correctness that goes with our applications of rules. The Parable prompts us to wonder how we can make sense of this phenomenology. In response to it, we are inclined to say things like "I already knew, at the time when I gave the order, that he ought to write 1002 after 1000," which, as I see it, amounts to saying, "I already knew, at the time when I gave the order, that $1000 + 2 = 1002$." This much is okay, according to Wittgenstein, who replies "Certainly, and you can also say you meant it then, only you should not let yourself be misled by the grammar of 'know' and 'mean'" (PI §187).

But *how* are we misled by this grammar, according to Wittgenstein? Do we seek an explanation that somehow "absolutely picks out *for any possible audience* the right continuation from all possible continuations"? I don't find that appealing, and I don't think Wittgenstein does, either. He stresses, instead, our temptation to think that "that act of meaning the order had in its own way already traversed all those steps: that when you meant it your mind as it were flew ahead and took all the steps before you physically arrived at this or that one." Beginning with the phenomenology of correctness, we feel we need to add an *explanation* of that phenomenology, an explanation that somehow gives content to our idea that the steps "were in some unique way predetermined, anticipated – as only the act of meaning can anticipate reality" (PI §188).

In my view, this is the central point of the Parable: it highlights the phenomenology of correctness for us, and illustrates why we are tempted to think that the correct applications of the rule "were in some unique way predetermined, anticipated." Unlike the demand for an explanation that picks out for any possible audience the right continuation from all possible continuations, the idea that the steps are already determined in advance is very tempting and natural. It tempts us to say things like "doesn't our understanding reach beyond all the examples?" Wittgenstein replies that this is "a very queer expression, and quite a natural one" (PI §209). It goes hand-in-hand with this natural way of talking about rules to suppose that each of us has got a deeper or better grasp of rules than we can convey by examples and explanations. And this is puzzling. In what could this deeper or better grasp consist? What I want to stress now, however, is that, as Wittgenstein notes in PI §210, we are inclined to think that if others can understand us, it is because they have *guessed* the meaning that we have given our words. When we are tempted to think that meaning predetermines use, as a reaction to the Parable, therefore, we are inclined to devalue the enterprise of explaining what we mean *to others*, and to resign ourselves to a vulnerability and contingency in communication – to an ever-present possibility, almost inevitability, that we will be misunderstood. Hence as I see it, the Parable tempts us to try to explain the phenomenology of correctness in a way that leads us *away* from a demand for an explanation of rules that picks out for any possible audience the right continuation from all possible continuations.

When Goldfarb says the interlocutor seeks an explanation that "picks out *for* any possible audience the right continuation from all possible continuations" (p.20), he may mean that the interlocutor wants something that picks out *in abstraction from* any particular audience the right continuation from all possible continuations. This way of putting it still involves the phrase "possible continuations," which suggests that a rule (not merely a sign or a mental item) allows for several different continuations – a suggestion that is problematic for reasons I noted above. It is not true to the interlocutor's phenomenology to say that she wants an explanation of how to go on when the *sign* "+2" comes before her mind. She wants an explanation of the phenomenology of correctness for the *rule + 2*. She's *got* the phenomenology, rooted in particular examples and explanations given by particular individuals, and she wonders how to explain the sense in which, for instance, it was *already* the case that $1000 + 2 = 1002$ *before* anyone actually calculated that result. Her problem does not arise in abstraction from any audience, since she takes for granted the explanations and examples from which she learned the rule + 2. But now that she has learned the rule, she sees no reason to think that the explanation of the correctness of a particular new result of adding 2 has anything to do with whether someone has *actually* obtained that result. The crucial point, I think, is not that she seeks an explanation of the phenomenology of correctness *in abstraction* from any audience, but that she seeks an explanation of the phenomenology that somehow vindicates her idea that new steps are predetermined.

3 The Rule-Following Paradox

Almost as soon as we find ourselves gripped by the idea that new applications of our rules are predetermined, however, we start to feel that we don't understand it. This is connected, for instance, with our inclination to say, "It's as if we can grasp the whole use of a word in a flash." The problem, as Wittgenstein points out, is that "we are led to think that the future development must in some way already be present in the act of grasping the use and yet isn't present" (PI §197). Faced with this apparent incoherence, we still try to hang on to the idea that the applications of our rules are predetermined, because we feel that without it, the phenomenology of correctness, and the very idea of correctness itself, are illusory.

In short, we feel there's no way to take the phenomenology of correctness seriously unless new steps are predetermined. This requirement, in turn, leads us to try to explain the phenomenology of correctness by appealing to inner mental acts of *interpreting* the signs we use, of giving them meaning by intending to use them in ways we somehow mentally determine. Without the backing of a predetermined rule, the phenomenology of correctness, we feel, is groundless. It must then be that we somehow select from a number of different ways of meaning signs, and thereby predetermine steps that must be taken if one is to be in accord with the rule we've selected. But we find we don't understand what it means for the steps to be predetermined – the expression suggests itself, but comes to seem to have no more depth than the phenomenology of correctness itself. As Wittgenstein points out, "any interpretation still hangs in the air along with what it interprets, and cannot give it any support" (PI §198). Like our inner mental picture of a cube, what we think of as an interpretation of a rule doesn't by itself predetermine the steps that accord with the rule it supposedly interprets.

This leads us to the puzzling feeling that the phenomenology of correctness is without backing, hence cannot be any guide to what the rule is. *Only now*, in this incoherent, puzzling state of mind, can we wonder whether the Wayward Child of PI §185 is following the same rule as we are. But at this stage we have reached the paradox of PI §201: "No course of action could be determined by a rule, because any course of action can be made out to accord with the rule." We do not see ourselves in this paradoxical position when we first attempt to explain the phenomenology of correctness by talking of predetermined steps. We arrive at this paradox, which apparently undermines even our ordinary understanding of the phenomenology of correctness, only after we find that our initial attempts to explain that phenomenology fall apart, as when "we are led to think that the future development must in some way already be present in the act of grasping the use and yet isn't present" (PI §197).

This characterization of the interlocutor's reaction to the Parable of the Wayward Child fits well with Goldfarb's understanding of the incoherence exposed by the paradox of PI §201. As Goldfarb puts it, "the incoherence arises from the impossibility of distinguishing, from *within*, the correct continuation from any continuation that you wind up making" (Goldfarb, 2012, p.82). Why from *within*? On my reading, the answer is that we each feel we must try to explain our phenomenology of correctness in terms of our own grasp of something that reaches beyond all the examples we've given, or could give, of how it should be applied (PI § 209). In other words, we feel that in some sense our grasp of the rule is "private." But, as Goldfarb says, "the private rule cannot provide a yardstick – beyond the empty assertion that I will do what I will do" (p.82).

4 Guidance Without Mystery?

To take the next step in Wittgenstein's investigation, we must try to see how the paradox of PI §201 reveals that we have an understanding of rules that is not undermined by the incoherence of our attempts to *explain* the phenomenology of correctness. We must try to see what Wittgenstein means when he writes that "there is a way of grasping the rule which is not an interpretation, but which is expressed in what we call 'obeying the rule' and 'going against it' in actual cases" (PI §201).

This is one of the most challenging tasks in Wittgenstein interpretation. In my view, the challenge is to "do away with all *explanation*" of the phenomenology of correctness, and replace it with descriptions of our practices of explaining rules to others, justifying our own applications of rules, correcting misunderstandings of what we have said, and drawing consequences from a rule as "a matter of course" (PI §238). Recall that for Wittgenstein, the description of rule-following practices that we seek "gets its light, that is to say its purpose, from the philosophical problems. [...] The problems are solved, not by reporting new experience, but by arranging what we have always known" (PI §109). It may be helpful to think of Wittgenstein's strategy for finding such descriptions as governed by a sort of *context principle for rules*: don't ask what rules, correctness, agreement, or disagreement are in isolation, but only in the context of our rule-following practices. The most challenging part of this strategy is to make the case that once our understanding of correctness is properly contextualized, we will no longer feel that the phenomenology of correctness is illusory *unless* new steps are predetermined in a special metaphysical way. This is not (or not just) a matter of showing that if we abstract from all our actual linguistic interactions with other speakers, we would have no phenomenology of correctness. That would be too easy, and it would miss the core of the difficulty. For the interlocutor does not see himself as asking for explanations in a vacuum, outside of any interactions with others, but as taking for granted ordinary episodes of learning and teaching, and trying to explain our sense that *new* steps are predetermined by rules. Instead, the most challenging part of the strategy is to make the case that we have no grip on the idea that a new application of a rule can be correct or incorrect apart from our actual practices of *taking* some new applications to be correct and others to be incorrect, and hence that our impression that the correct applications are predetermined in a special way is an illusion.

5 Critical Reception of Wittgenstein's Investigations of the Concept of a Rule

While it is widely accepted that Wittgenstein identifies deep and important problems with our understanding of the concept of a rule, many philosophers find Wittgenstein's strategy for dissolving these problems elusive, at best, and hopeless, at worst. Resistance to his strategy is often linked with confidence that the investigations that lead

Wittgenstein to adopt the strategy of description that I sketched in the previous section overlook *theoretical* options that would enable us to avoid the paradox of PI §201, either by providing a substantive theory of meaning, rules, and guidance, or by simply taking these notions as theoretical primitives that are not in need of elucidation in terms of "what we call 'obeying the rule' and 'going against it' in actual cases" (PI §201).

One early and eloquent expression of resistance to Wittgenstein's strategy can be found in Michael Dummett's article "Wittgenstein's Philosophy of Mathematics" (1959). Dummett takes Wittgenstein's remarks on the Parable of the Wayward Child to show the following:

> Wittgenstein goes in for a full-blooded conventionalism; for him the logical necessity of any statement is always the direct expression of a linguistic convention. That a given statement is necessary consists always in our having expressly decided to treat that very statement as unassailable; it cannot rest on our having adopted certain other conventions which are found to involve our treating it so. This account is applied alike to deep theorems and to elementary computations.
>
> (Dummett, 1959, p.329)

Dummett does not say in detail how he arrives at this interpretation, but I think the main outlines of his reasoning are clear. The key point, I think, is that he is convinced that in the Parable of the Wayward Child, if you instruct the child to follow the rule + 2 beyond 1000, for instance, "[your] act of meaning the order [+2] had in its own way already traversed all those steps: that when you meant it your mind as it were flew ahead and took all the steps before you physically arrived at this or that one" (PI §188). Beginning with the phenomenology of correctness for our own applications of the rule + 2, Dummett demands an *explanation* of that phenomenology, an explanation that somehow gives content to our idea that the steps "were in some unique way predetermined, anticipated – as only the act of meaning can anticipate reality" (PI §188). Wittgenstein explicitly and repeatedly questions the idea that we can *explain* or *ground* new applications of a rule, such as the rule + 2, by finding some fact (a mental state, or an explicit convention about how one is to use a sign, such as "+2") that existed *prior* to the applications, from which the applications follow "of necessity." This convinces Dummett that Wittgenstein rejects the core of the idea that a new application of the rule + 2 is *rationally guided* by our antecedent understanding of that rule. The only option left, according to Dummett, is "a full-blooded conventionalism," according to which "at each step we are free to choose" to accept or reject a new application of a rule (Dummett, 1959, p.330).

Dummett correctly notes that the idea that we are "free to choose" at each new step of applying a rule "is extremely hard to swallow, even though it is not clear what one wishes to oppose to it" (p.332). Dummett does not offer an alternative account and says he does not know what account should be given. Instead, he "give[s] reasons for the natural resistance one feels to Wittgenstein's account, reasons for thinking that it must be wrong" (p.341).

This criticism of Wittgenstein may appear compelling, but I think it rests on a misunderstanding. Wittgenstein writes: "The rule can only seem to me to produce all its consequences in advance if I draw them as a *matter of course*. As much as it is a matter of course for me to call this colour 'blue'" (PI §238). When I draw a consequence of a rule (make a new application of it) "as a matter of course" in the relevant sense I cannot simultaneously regard myself as free to reject that consequence (application). Thus Dummett's interpretation conflicts with Wittgenstein's description in PI §238 of situations in which a rule seems to me to produce all its consequences in advance. Admittedly, to counter the tempting thought that each new application of a rule requires a new intuition about what the rule demands of us, Wittgenstein writes:

> It would *almost* be more correct to say, not that an intuition was needed at every stage, but that a new decision was needed at every stage. (PI §186, my emphasis)

As Goldfarb points out (2012, p.76), however, to understand this remark one must not overlook the word "almost." The remark is clearly *not* a statement of a full-blooded conventionalism about rules, as Dummett thinks, but part of an investigation that is meant to loosen the grip of a certain tempting interpretation of the idea that steps are determined in advance.

Dummett may reply that one cannot loosen this grip without abandoning the concept of rule altogether. He may claim that Wittgenstein fails to see that he has abandoned the core of the concept of a rule, and that he is committed to full-blooded conventionalism, even if some of his remarks appear to deny it.

Saul Kripke agrees with Dummett that Wittgenstein rejects the core of the idea that a new application of the rule + 2 is rationally guided by our antecedent understanding of that rule. He directly confronts the reply that Wittgenstein's descriptions of our rule-following practices reveal that this core idea is based in a *misunderstanding* of the concept of a rule. Kripke compares this reply with Berkeley's "denial of matter, and of any object 'outside the mind.'" According to Kripke, Wittgenstein and Berkeley both "seem to be denying our common beliefs." Kripke sets himself against this strategy, both in Berkeley's philosophy and in Wittgenstein's:

> Berkeley's stance is not uncommon in philosophy. The philosopher advocates a view apparently in patent contradiction to common sense. Rather than repudiating common sense, he asserts that the conflict comes from a philosophical misinterpretation of common language – sometimes he adds that the misinterpretation is encouraged by the 'superficial form' of ordinary speech. He offers his own analysis of the relevant common assertions, one that shows that they do not really say what they seem to say. [...] Personally I think such philosophical claims are almost invariably suspect. What the claimant calls a 'misleading philosophical misconstrual' of the ordinary statement is probably the natural and correct understanding. The real misconstrual comes when the claimant continues, 'All the ordinary man really means is...' And gives a sophisticated analysis compatible with his own philosophy. [...] Wittgenstein makes a Berkeleyan claim of this kind. [...] Personally I can only report that, in spite of Wittgenstein's assurances, the 'primitive' interpretation often sounds rather good to me...
>
> (Kripke, 1982, pp.65–6)

Kripke's explanation of his resistance to Wittgenstein's strategy is one that would appeal, I think, to a majority of the philosophers who resist Wittgenstein's strategy. It is no wonder that such readers balk at Wittgenstein's invitations to describe our rule-following practices without trying to explain our new applications of a rule as in some sense predetermined by our prior understanding of the rule.

This kind of resistance to Wittgenstein's strategy motivates philosophers to search for theoretical accounts of rule-following that vindicate what many take to be our commonsense idea that our grasp of rules "pre-determines" our correct applications of the rules. There are two main theoretical accounts of rule-following currently entrenched in the literature. The first of these is *dispositionalism*, according to which a speaker's grasp of a rule expressed by a given sign, say "+2," is either explained by, or identical with, her *disposition* to apply the sign in new cases. On this sort of view, what a speaker means by a sign, and the rule that her uses of the sign express, are determined by her disposition to apply the sign. Several different versions of dispositionalism have been developed and defended in the literature (see e.g., Ginet, 1992; Horwich, 1984; and Soames, 1998). The second main theoretical account of rule-following is *primitive nonreductionism*, according to which a speaker's grasp of a rule expressed by a given sign is explained by *primitive mental facts* about the speaker – facts expressed by sentences of the form "Speaker A means + 2 by '+2,'" and "A's uses of '+2' are governed by the rule + 2," for instance – where it is taken for granted that such facts "predetermine" correct applications of the rule in a way that simultaneously explains and grounds our experience that our new applications of a rule are rationally guided by our understanding of what the rule requires of us. (For different versions and defenses of *primitive nonreductionism*, see Boghossian, 1989; McDowell, 1984; and McGinn, 1984.)

Despite his strong resistance to Wittgenstein's strategy, Kripke rejects both of these views. The most promising versions of dispositionalism distinguish between a speaker's *competence* in the application of a given rule, and her *performance* in applying the rule. The idea is that a speaker's performance on a given occasion (i.e., a particular one of her applications of a given rule) is *correct* if it is the untrammelled result of a triggering of the dispositions that underlie and explain her *competence* in the application of the rule, and her performance is *incorrect* if it is the result of causes that are additional to, or interfere with the dispositions that underlie and explain her competence in the application of the rule (see e.g., Horwich, 1984; and Goldfarb, 1985). Kripke objects (pp.28–32) that this version of dispositionalism founders on the fact that our specification of the relevant dispositions would have to rely on the very judgments of correctness and incorrectness that we posit those dispositions to explain. This is not a decisive objection, however, since our reliance on those judgments may be only methodological, not explanatory (Goldfarb, 1985, p.477).

Kripke's central objection to dispositionalism applies to all versions of it. The objection is that facts about how a person is *disposed* to behave do not explain the *rational connection* that we experience between our understanding of a rule and our applications of it to new cases. Focusing, in particular, on a case in which you are asked to add 68 and 57, Kripke writes:

> What [the dispositional view] says is: '"125" is the response you are disposed to give, and (perhaps the reply adds) it would also have been your response in the past.' Well and good, I know that '125' is the response I am disposed to give (I am actually giving it!), and may be it is helpful to be told – as a matter of brute fact – that I would have given the same response in the past. How does any of this indicate that – now or in the past – '125' was an answer justified in terms of instructions I gave myself, rather than a mere jack-in-a-box unjustified and arbitrary response? (Kripke, 1982, p.23)

In other words, according to Kripke, when we are presented with a new addition problem, say the problem of calculating the value of 68 + 57, and we arrive at the answer 125, we experience our calculation as guided by our understanding of the rules for addition. We apparently experience the rational "because" when we take a new step. For instance, we apparently experience our step of answering "125" after calculating the value of 68 + 57 as rationally derived from and justified by, and in that sense predetermined by, our prior and independent understanding of the rule for addition.

One might resist this objection on the grounds that an explanation of a given phenomenon need not capture every pre-theoretical assumption we make about the phenomenon. Thus one might say, for instance, that dispositionalism is the *best* explanation of our applications of rules to new cases, even if it does not explain or fully capture our experience that when we make new applications of a rule, our new applications are rationally guided by our understanding of what the rule requires of us. On this view, to explain our new applications of a rule it is enough to posit a causal mechanism that explains the behaviors that occur simultaneously with our experience that these new applications are rationally guided by our understanding of what the rule requires of us.

This reply will not appeal to those philosophers, such as Dummett and Kripke, who resist Wittgenstein's strategy on the grounds that it fails to explain how one's new applications of a rule are *rationally* predetermined by one's understanding of the rule. Dispositionalism does not explain or analyze the relevant notion of rational predetermination, and so fails to provide the sort of account that such philosophers demand. For those who stress the phenomenology of correctness, and demand an explanation of it, in the way I have highlighted above, the most promising of the two standard accounts of rule-following in the literature today is *primitive nonreductionism*.

Kripke takes primitive nonreductionism to amount to the suggestion that, for instance, "meaning addition by 'plus' is [...] simply a primitive state, not to be assimilated to sensations or headaches or any 'qualitative' states, nor to be assimilated to dispositions, but a state of the unique kind of its own" (1982, p.51). If we could make adequate sense of primitive nonreductionism, then it would clearly be a more attractive explanation of the phenomenology of correctness than dispositionalism. Against primitive nonreductionism, however, Kripke writes that it "may in a sense be irrefutable [...]. But it seems desperate: it leaves the nature of this postulated primitive state – the primitive state of 'meaning addition by "plus"' – completely mysterious" (p.51). The problem, according to Kripke, is that to accept primitive nonreductionism, we must posit a primitive mental state that is somehow *fully present* at the times when we mean, for instance, addition by "+," but that also somehow rationally causes our new applications of +. As Kripke says, 'such a state would have to be a finite object, contained in our finite minds" (p.52). The problem is that we have no clear idea of how such an object could rationally guide our new applications of a rule.

Kripke's rejection of primitive nonreductionism is inspired by Wittgenstein's descriptions of our temptation to posit facts that determine what we mean. Consider, for instance, the following two sections:

> 191. 'It is as if we could grasp the whole use of the word in a flash.' Like *what* e.g.? – Can't the use – in a certain sense – be grasped in a flash? And in what sense can it not? – The point is, that it is as if we could 'grasp it in a flash' in yet another and much more direct sense than that. – But have you a model for this? No. It is just that this expression suggests itself to us. As the result of the crossing of different pictures.
> 192. You have no model of this superlative fact, but you are seduced into using a super-expression. (It might be called a philosophical superlative.) (PI §§191–2)

Positing the superlative fact does not help us to understand what we seek to understand – our experience of our new applications of a rule being rationally caused by our prior independent grasp of the rule. The problem is that "we are led to think that the future development must in some way already be present in the act of grasping the use and yet isn't present" (PI §197). We get into a muddle when we try to model the superlative fact. We discover we have no model of it, and in that sense fail to understand it.

Some philosophers who are aware of these problems with clarifying or modeling a supposed superlative fact of the sort posited by primitive nonreductionism nevertheless insist that it is a satisfactory and stable response to the concerns about rule-following that Wittgenstein raises (Boghossian, 1989). This bold claim raises a number of difficult questions, including the following:

> Does primitive nonreductionism make any substantive claims beyond those that can be clarified by Wittgenstein's strategy of describing, in ways we find indisputable, "what we call 'obeying the rule' and 'going against it' in actual cases" (PI §201)?
> If so, what exactly are these claims?
> If not, what do these apparently substantive claims really come to?

We would have to address these questions patiently and carefully in order to move beyond the current impasse in the literature about whether primitive nonreductionism is a satisfactory response to the puzzles about rule-following that Wittgenstein's investigations highlight.

References

Boghossian, P. (1989). The Rule-Following Considerations. *Mind*, 98, 507–549.
Dummett, M. (1959). Wittgenstein's Philosophy of Mathematics. *The Philosophical Review*, 68, 324–348.
Ginet, C. (1992). The Dispositionalist Solution to Wittgenstein's Problem about Understanding a Rule: Answering Kripke's Objections. *Midwest Studies in Philosophy*, 12, 53–73.
Goldfarb, W. (1985). Kripke on Wittgenstein on Rules. *The Journal of Philosophy*, 82, 471–488.
Goldfarb, W. (2012). Rule-Following Revisited. In J. Ellis and D. Guevara (Eds). *Wittgenstein and the Philosophy of Mind* (pp.73–90). Oxford: Oxford University Press.
Horwich, P. (1984). Critical Notice of Kripke's *Wittgenstein on Rules and Private Language*. *Philosophy of Science*, 51, 163–171.
Kripke, S.A. (1982). *Wittgenstein on Rules and Private Language: An Elementary Exposition*. Oxford: Blackwell.
McDowell, J. (1984). Wittgenstein on Following a Rule. *Synthese*, 58, 325–363.
McGinn, C. (1984). *Wittgenstein on Meaning*. Oxford: Blackwell.
Soames, S. (1998). Skepticism about Meaning: Indeterminacy, Normativity, and the Rule-Following Paradox. *Canadian Journal of Philosophy* (Supplementary Volume), 23, 211–249.

Further Reading

Baker, G.P. and Hacker, P.M.S. (1985/2014). *Wittgenstein: Rules, Grammar and Necessity. Volume 2 of an Analytical Commentary on the Philosophical Investigations. Essays and Exegesis of §§185–242*. Second edition. Extensively revised by P.M.S. Hacker. Oxford: Wiley-Blackwell.

Diamond, C. (1991). *The Realistic Spirit: Wittgenstein, Philosophy, and the Mind.* Cambridge, MA: MIT Press.
Ebbs, G. (1997). *Rule-Following and Realism.* Cambridge, MA: Harvard University Press.
Ginsborg, H. (2011). Primitive Normativity and Skepticism about Rules. *The Journal of Philosophy,* 108, 227–254.
Lugg, A. (2004). *Wittgenstein's Investigations 1–33: A Guide and Interpretation.* London: Routledge.
Miller, A. and Wright, C. (Eds). (2002). *Rule-Following and Meaning.* Montreal: McGill-Queen's University Press.
Stroud, B. (2000). *Meaning, Understanding, and Practice.* Oxford: Oxford University Press.
Wright, C. (2001). *Rails to Infinity: Essays on Themes from Wittgenstein's Philosophical Investigations.* Cambridge, MA: Harvard University Press.

25

Vagueness and Family Resemblance

HANOCH BEN-YAMI

Meno: There will be no difficulty, Socrates, in answering your question, what is virtue? Let us take first the virtue of a man: he should know how to administer the state, and in the administration of it to benefit his friends and harm his enemies; and he must also be careful not to suffer harm himself. A woman's virtue, if you wish to know about that, may also be easily described: her duty is to order her house, and keep what is indoors, and obey her husband. Every age, every condition of life, young or old, male or female, bond or free, has a different virtue: there are virtues numberless, and no lack of definitions of them; for virtue is relative to the actions and ages of each of us in all that we do. And the same may be said of vice, Socrates. (Plato, *Meno* 71e–72a)

This is how Meno confidently answers Socrates' request to tell him what virtue is, an answer which is probably derived from Gorgias, as we gather from the dialogue and from Aristotle (*Politics* I 13, 1260a28). And Meno undeniably succeeds in giving us a good idea of what the ancient Greeks understood by virtue.

Socrates, however, is unsatisfied. With characteristic irony, he replies that he is remarkably fortunate, for while he asked for a single virtue Meno presented him with a swarm of them. What he would in fact like Meno to specify is the *common nature* that makes all these different virtues into virtue. Meno has difficulties understanding what Socrates means.

Meno's difficulty, which he shares with several of Socrates' interlocutors in Plato's dialogues, reflects a historical fact. What Socrates is interested in would today be called a *definition*, a specification of something common to all and only the cases to which the concept applies. And the demand for definitions as the correct form of explanation was indeed an innovation of the historical Socrates, who "fixed thought for the first time on definitions" (Aristotle, *Metaphysics* I 6, 987b1). Plato adopted, elaborated, and added his authority to this conception of definition as the only adequate form of the explanation of meaning.

Over the last 24 centuries, the sophisticated philosopher has generally sided with Plato and Socrates, rather than with Gorgias and Meno. Yet it is the latter who

---

A Companion to Wittgenstein, First Edition. Edited by Hans-Johann Glock and John Hyman.
© 2017 John Wiley & Sons, Ltd. Published 2017 by John Wiley & Sons, Ltd.

provide us with a better explanation of what was meant by virtue, as was noted already by Aristotle:

> The temperance of a man and of a woman, or the courage and justice of a man and of a woman, are not, as Socrates maintained, the same; the courage of a man is shown in commanding, of a woman in obeying. And this holds of all other virtues, as will be more clearly seen if we look at them in detail, for those who say generally that virtue consists in a good disposition of the soul, or in doing rightly, or the like, only deceive themselves. Far better than such definitions is the mode of speaking of those who, like Gorgias, enumerate the virtues. (*Politics* I 13, 1260a21–28)

Despite this early observation, to explain a concept has almost invariably meant, from Plato to this day, to define it. If asked, in a philosophical context, what we mean by a word or phrase, we are still generally expected to provide a necessary and sufficient condition for its application, to specify the common nature shared by all its instances.

Wittgenstein set himself against this conception of explanation early in the 1930s. At several places in his writings, he explicitly contrasts his method of explaining concepts with that of the Platonic Socrates. In his "Dictation for Schlick," dating probably from December 1932, we find the following passage:

> I can characterize my standpoint no better than by saying that it is the antithetical standpoint to the one occupied by Socrates in the Platonic dialogues. For if I were asked what knowledge is, I would enumerate instances of knowledge and add the words 'and similar things'. There is no shared constituent to be discovered in them since none exists. (VW 33; cf. BT 67, 70)

Similarly, slightly later, in the "Blue Book," the Platonic Socrates is targeted again, this time in the context of emphasizing the deleterious influence that the quest for definitions has had in philosophy:

> The idea that in order to get clear about the meaning of a general term one had to find the common element in all its applications has shackled philosophical investigation; for it has not only led to no result, but also made the philosopher dismiss as irrelevant the concrete cases, which alone could have helped him to understand the usage of the general term. When Socrates asks the question, 'what is knowledge?' he does not even regard it as a preliminary answer to enumerate cases of knowledge. (BB 19–20; cf. 26–7)

In his later writings, Wittgenstein developed, defended, and used alternative modes of explanation, similar to those Meno and other interlocutors of Socrates provide in the Platonic dialogues.

In this respect, the rejection of the Socratic ideal of explanation is a return to a pre-Socratic and pre-philosophical lost innocence. The words "explanation" and "saying what X is" are brought back from their philosophical to their everyday, pre-philosophical use (PI §116). A picture of what an explanation of meaning must be like held us captive for centuries (PI §115); the realization that explanations of the sort provided by Socrates' interlocutors are legitimate and often the most appropriate ones is at the same time a release from that picture. The latter explanations are also quite often readily available – "I am making it easier and easier for myself in philosophy," Wittgenstein remarks in this context in *The Big Typescript* (56; cf. PG 121). The philosophical project of providing a definition is eliminated, and it is not replaced by any other project of comparable difficulty. The aforementioned realization is in this respect an instance of philosophical therapy, which gives philosophy peace by eliminating its obsessive quest for definitions.

The legitimacy of the pre-Socratic form of concept explanation in philosophy is demonstrated by the use Wittgenstein himself makes of it while introducing new terms in the course of his investigations. "Language-game," for instance, is explained as follows:

> We can also think of the whole process of using words [for communication between a builder and an assistant as described in §2] as one of those games by means of which children learn their native language. I will call these games "*language-games*" and will sometimes speak of a primitive language as a language-game.
>
> And the processes of naming the stones and of repeating words after someone might also be called language-games. Think of certain uses that are made of words in games like ring-a-ring-a-roses.
>
> I shall also call the whole, consisting of language and the activities into which it is woven, a "language-game". (PI §7)

Instead of necessary and sufficient conditions, we are given a few examples, intended to make clear what the new phrase means. Similarly, what is meant by "family resemblance" is explained by means of a specific example, that of a game (PI §§66–7). And later in the work, the explanation of *noticing an aspect* is again by means of an example:

> I observe a face, and then suddenly notice its likeness to another. I *see* that it has not changed; and yet I see it differently. I call this experience "noticing an aspect". (PPF xi § 113)

This mode of explanation is consistent with Wittgenstein's methodology and contrasts with the traditional way of explaining and introducing concepts by means of definitions.

Wittgenstein's neologisms are among the philosophical terms introduced during the twentieth century that have had the widest use, in philosophy as well as in other disciplines. This shows that explanations not by means of definitions are no obstacle to the coining of useful concepts; and if, with Wittgenstein, we identify meaning with use (PI §43), it also shows that such explanations are no obstacle to the coining of meaningful concepts.

Wittgenstein was not the first to either criticize the Socratic demand for definition or to develop and defend alternative ways of explaining concepts. Yet he was the first to do so in such detail and scope and with far-reaching conclusions. We saw that Aristotle preferred Gorgias's explanation of virtue to Plato's; but this preference was limited in scope, and Aristotle generally provides definitions by means of genus and differentia, adopting Plato's method in the *Sophist* and *Statesman*. Other philosophers who described alternative modes of concept formation usually saw these as inferior from a logical or epistemological point of view to definitions. Spinoza, for instance, distinguishes between different ways our concepts or ideas are formed, and suggests a physiological account of the origin of concepts such as "man," "horse," and "dog" through the accumulation of images in our brain. It seems these cannot be defined and should also inevitably exhibit some kind of vagueness. But these "inadequate and confused ideas," which he thinks are the source of endless controversies among philosophers, are involved according to him only in the lowest kind of cognition and are the cause of our mistakes (*Ethics* II 40 Scholia I & II, 41).

A different approach was taken by Dugald Stewart. In his *Philosophical Essays* of 1810, he criticized the preference for definitions by means of genus and differentia, and developed an alternative account of concepts that has points in common with Wittgenstein's ideas of family resemblance (see Baker and Hacker, 1980/2005, pp.207–8). Later in the century, William Whewell, in his *History of Scientific Ideas*, contrasted classification in mathematics with that in natural history and all other "speculations." Unlike mathematical classes, natural ones are determined not by a definition but by a "type":

> The class is steadily fixed, though not precisely limited; it is given, though not circumscribed; it is determined, not by a boundary line without, but by a central point within; not by what it strictly excludes, but by what it eminently includes; by an example, not by a precept; in short, instead of Definition we have a *Type* for our director. (Whewell, 1858, p.121)

This kind of classification inevitably gives rise to vagueness, and with it to indeterminate boundary cases. However, such indeterminacy, Whewell argues,

> would not destroy the reality of the generic groups, any more than the scattered trees of the intervening plain prevent our speaking intelligibly of the distinct forests of two separate hills. (Ibid., p.122)

But these early insights did not have much impact. Mill, although impressed by these passages of Whewell's work, criticized him on various points and claimed that between the kinds that are the object of natural classification "there is an impassable barrier; and what we have to seek is, marks whereby we may determine on which side of the barrier an object takes its place" (Mill, 1882, bk.4, ch.VII, §§3–4). Frege, whose work served as Wittgenstein's point of departure on these issues as on many others, thought that every concept should be sharply defined, and denied the possibility of a vague concept:

> A definition of a concept (of a possible predicate) must be complete; it must unambiguously determine, as regards any object, whether or not it falls under the concept […]. If we represent concepts in extension by regions on a plane, this is admittedly a picture that may be used only with caution, but here it can do us good service. To a concept without sharp boundary there would correspond a region that had not a sharp boundary-line all round, but in places just vaguely faded away into the background. This would not really be a region at all; and likewise a concept that is not sharply defined is wrongly termed a concept. (Frege, 1903, §56; translation based on Frege, 1960, 159)

Similarly, we find the early Wittgenstein brooding over the question, "could it be possible that the sentences in ordinary use have, as it were, only an incomplete sense?" He finds the question of whether the uttered sentence "The book is lying on the table" really has a completely clear sense extremely important, apparently betraying his suspicion that it has not. But after some deliberations he insists: "It seems clear that what we MEAN must always be '*sharp*'" (NB 67–8). The *Tractatus* manifests this position in its claim that "the requirement that simple signs be possible is the requirement that sense be determinate" (3.23). This is the position Wittgenstein will reject in his later work.

The discussion in *Philosophical Investigations* of determinacy of sense, definition, explanation of concepts, and related issues begins with the claim that all the phenomena that we call "language" have no one thing *in common*, no shared *essence*, in virtue of which we use the same word for all, but that there are many different kinds of *affinity* between them on account of which we do that (PI §65). The standard Platonic view of concepts is thus mentioned in order to be rejected. The discussion continues with an examination of a different concept, that of a game (PI §66), which is of course related to that of language-game and thus to that of language. If we examine all that we call "games" we shall find affinities and resemblances, but nothing common to all in virtue of which we call all "games." Not all are entertaining (and there are entertaining activities which are not games); winning and losing are not always part of a game, nor is competition (Solitaire, The Sims, the Israeli Matkot game; and, again, winning and losing exist in war, which is no game); the objective need not be arbitrary or lack significance outside the game (consider the games teachers use in class); and so on. We find nothing in common to all and only games, but rather a complicated network of resemblances, overlapping and crisscrossing.

> I can think of no better expression to characterize these resemblances than 'family resemblances'; for the various resemblances between members of a family – build, features, colour of eyes, gait, temperament, and so on and so forth – overlap and criss-cross in the same way. – And I shall say: 'games' form a family. (PI §67)

Wittgenstein immediately proceeds with an assault on the citadel of crystalline accuracy, mathematics, targeting its most important concept, that of a number. We call something "number," he suggests, because it has a direct affinity with several things that have hitherto been called "number," and thus an indirect affinity with other things that we also call "numbers." Complex numbers have this affinity with the real numbers, the real numbers have it with the rational, the rational with the natural, the transfinite with the finite, and so on. Thus, the kinds of number also form a family. No place is safe from this critique of the Platonic view.

Later in the *Investigations*, Wittgenstein provides a meticulous analysis of our concept of reading and related concepts, showing how hopeless it is to find anything common to all and only cases of reading and how these different cases relate to each other by a complicated network of resemblances (PI §§156–78). He concludes that "we also use the word 'read' for a family of cases. And in different circumstances we apply different criteria for a person's reading" (PI §164). Although subsequent literature on family resemblance has focused on the concept of game, Wittgenstein's analysis of that of reading is the most detailed example in the PI of the failure of the idea that there must be a common essence to all cases in the extension of a concept, as well as of the way in which a complex web of resemblances determines a concept.

One might claim that our failure to find something in common to all and only games does not prove that they have no such thing in common. However, Wittgenstein writes that we do not *see* any such common element and that we use the same name for all instances not *because* they have something in common. This formulation is not committed to the nonexistence of a common essence but rather to the irrelevance of such a commonality to the use of an expression and therefore to its meaning. All the same, the inevitable conclusion from Wittgenstein's examination of specific cases is that such a common essence often does not exist.

The fact that an expression is applied on the basis of a complex web of resemblances does not make it ambiguous or polysemous: the complex web may still yield a unified concept. We extend a concept the way in spinning a thread we twist fiber on fiber, and the thread produced in this way is strong not because some one fiber runs through its whole length but because its many fibers overlap (PI §67). We may of course divide games into board games, card games, ball games, and so on; or into competitive and noncompetitive ones, etc. But this division into sub-concepts does not show that the original concept of game lacks unity any more than the division into even and odd numbers shows that the concept of natural number does.

One might try to criticize the idea that a web of resemblances can determine a concept as follows: if we extended a concept by means of resemblances and affinities then, since war resembles a game (winner and loser, skill, strategies...) it should or at least could be considered a game. However, war is not a game, so a web of resemblances cannot determine a concept. The answer to this criticism is that we typically introduce several mutually exclusive concepts that divide a conceptual field. We introduce game and war, playing and quarreling, as different from each other, and in this way we also determine boundaries between them, albeit *vague* ones.

A concept is vague if it has indeterminate boundary cases, namely cases where its usage and explanation provide reasons for as well as against applying it, without these reasons being sufficient either way. Color concepts, for instance, are vague, for the samples we use to explain or decide which colors are red and which are orange, say, leave some shades hovering between the two. However, color concepts are not family-resemblance ones: they do not have a *plurality* of criteria or of dimensions of resemblance that determine their application. A family-resemblance concept, on the other hand, need not admit of a prototypical sample by means of which its application could be determined. So family-resemblance concepts, although typically vague, are but *one kind* of vague concepts.

However, family-resemblance concepts typically being vague, and philosophers – Frege and Wittgenstein's former self included – having generally been hostile to vagueness, Wittgenstein finds it necessary to defend the legitimacy of vague concepts.

Wittgenstein's treatment of vagueness, although illuminating in several respects, might disappoint some contemporary philosophers interested in the subject. For the last forty odd years, the philosophical discussion of vagueness has focused on the Sorites, the ancient paradox of the heap: if we remove one grain from a heap of grains, the remaining collection of grains is still a heap. It thus seems to follow that never mind how many times we repeat this process, the remaining collection must always be a heap. Yet we shall end up with a single grain, which is no heap. We apparently proved a false conclusion by a sound argument.

Wittgenstein does not mention the Sorites in the *Philosophical Investigations*. He does mention the paradoxical situation in his writings from the early 1930s (BT 34 = PG I, Appendix 8, 236–40; see also PR §§211–13), but even there he does not try to resolve the paradox. In *The Big Typescript* he describes a hypothetical attempt to determine, by a series of questions about the classification of cases around the borderline of a vague concept, a sharp boundary for that concept, and the way the attempt would fail by yielding inconsistent results. Apparently, he subsequently came to realize that such procedures, forcing us to use vague concepts in circumstances in which they are useless, cannot shed much light on the logic of such concepts, and this thought experiment disappeared from his later writings. His dismissal of this hypothetical experiment is in contrast with its painstaking discussion by some contemporary philosophers, who are convinced that this "forced march" could offer us insights into the logic of vague concepts. (See Raffman, 1994 and Shapiro, 2006. For a more detailed and a more sympathetic discussion than mine of these passages from Wittgenstein see Faulkner, 2010.) Yet this is the closest he gets to a discussion of the Sorites. A resolution of the paradox along Wittgensteinian lines is perhaps possible (Ben-Yami, 2010), but none is found in Wittgenstein's own writings.

I quoted Frege's assertion that "a concept that is not sharply defined is wrongly termed a concept." Since Wittgenstein now sees "the concept of a game [as] a concept with blurred edges," Frege's approach should be exposed as misguided. Moreover, vague concepts should be shown not to be a kind of second-best option, acceptable only where sharply defined ones are unavailable. To that end, Wittgenstein first compares vague concepts to a photograph that is not sharp, which may still be a picture of a person. Moreover, he notes that a picture that is not sharp might be just what we need, with no advantage to be gained by replacing it with a sharp one (think of a picture of an approximate triangle, or of a bridge in the mist). Frege's claim that a concept without a sharp boundary corresponds to a region with no sharp boundary line, which is not really a region, is also critically considered: since to have a meaning is, for Wittgenstein, to have a use, Frege's claim comes down to the claim that we couldn't *do* anything with such a concept or with such a region. But the request, "Stay roughly here," where the region is specified not by drawing a boundary but just by a pointing gesture, may work perfectly well. So vagueness is no obstacle to use, nor therefore to meaning (PI §71).

Pushing his criticism further, Wittgenstein investigates what it could mean to replace this apparently inexact explanation by an exact one. Drawing a boundary line around a region with chalk is still "inexact," since the line has breadth. A color edge would be more exact, but we need to lay down what is to count as overstepping it: how and with what instruments it is to be ascertained. And so on. It is clear that such exactness has no function when we say, "Stay roughly here"; it is running idle. And, having no use, it does not contribute to the meaning of what is said (PI §88).

In fact, we have been abusing our concept of exactness in the previous paragraph. We know what it means to set a pocket-watch to the exact time, and the remark, "You should come to dinner more punctually; you know it begins at one o'clock *exactly*" makes perfectly good sense. We call something "inexact" if it attains its goal less perfectly than does the more exact, so whether an explanation or description is exact depends on our goal. If I say, "The ground was quite covered with plants," I might explain what I mean by making a drawing and remarking, "It looked *exactly* like this." So to the extent that talk about exactness makes sense, the use of vague concepts is no obstacle to exactness, for we can use them to attain our goal as perfectly as we need (PI §§70, 88).

Wittgenstein discusses an additional aspect of indeterminacy of sense, which he does not always clearly distinguish from the vagueness discussed above. Many of our concepts are *un*bounded in various ways: for some possible circumstances, nothing is determined by their explanations and use on how to apply them. To use Wittgenstein's example, there are no rules for how high or how hard one may throw the ball in tennis, yet tennis is a game for all that (PI §68). By contrast, if we make a gesture toward a region of roughly one meter in diameter and say "Stay roughly here," then this determines, although not sharply, the boundaries of a region. But the rules of tennis say nothing about how high one may throw the ball. It is not that we know that 1 meter is

413

permissible while 100 meters is not: this height has never been a factor in the game and there are no rules concerning it. In this respect, the concept of a legitimate move in tennis remains unregulated. If this height ever becomes a factor we shall have to *invent* appropriate rules, but these would not sharpen an earlier practice the way a scientific definition of one gram might do. (See also Wittgenstein's chair example, PI §80.)

This is the way, claims Wittgenstein, in which we use the concepts of number and game. When the complex numbers and the transfinite cardinals were invented, what we already counted as numbers did not determine whether these new mathematical entities should also be considered as such. It is not that they were on some vague borderline separating numbers from other mathematical creatures: they constituted a new mathematical dimension, and our use had to be extended toward it. Such new cases might be similar in many respects to old ones, and consequently there may be natural decisions and even obvious ones to make on how to apply our concepts to them; yet even then, these decisions *extend* our concepts.

The boundaries of the concept of number as currently used in mathematics could indeed be made rigid, and we would then not extend it to new cases that might come up. (In that case, we would have some sort of a family-resemblance concept with a determinate sense.) But although the possibility is open to us, this is *not* how we use the concept of number nor is there any *need* to use it in such a way. The fact that the use of a word is not everywhere bounded by rules does not make it unregulated. Moreover, it seems this cannot be done for the concept of game, whose current extension, unlike that of the mathematical concept of number, has vague boundaries (PI §68).

Concepts of this kind, for which the question of applicability in new, unforeseen directions might always arise, can be called, following Friedrich Waismann, *open-textured* (1951; the term was suggested to him by William Kneale). "Most of our empirical concepts are not delimited in all possible directions," writes Waismann. Even for scientific concepts that seem to be defined with absolute precision,

> we can never exclude altogether the possibility of some unforeseen situation arising in which we shall have to modify our definition. Try as we may, no concept is limited in such a way that there is no room for any doubt. [...] We tend to overlook the fact that there are always other directions in which the concept has not been defined. And if we did, we could easily imagine conditions which would necessitate new limitations. [...] That is what is meant by the open texture of a concept. (Waismann, 1951, p.120)

Waismann is careful to distinguish open texture from vagueness. "Heap" and "pink" are vague because they are "actually used in a fluctuating way" – apparently he means that differing classifications of borderline cases can and do occur. An open-textured term, by contrast, need not have this "fluctuating" use. Moreover, "vagueness can be remedied by giving more accurate rules, open texture cannot" (Ibid.). Waismann's "open texture" can thus be used to draw attention to this special, distinct phenomenon of indeterminacy of sense, typical of family-resemblance concepts.

Despite this distinction between vagueness and open texture that exists in Wittgenstein's and Waismann's works, recent literature on vagueness has tended to ignore the distinction and in fact the phenomenon that the term "open texture" is here used to capture. Shapiro, for instance, borrows the phrase "open texture" from Waismann but uses it in order to characterize vagueness and the "fluctuating" use of vague terms like "heap" and color words (2006, §2.2 and p.11, n.5). Although Shapiro is aware that his use of the term departs from Waismann's (Appendix, pp.210ff.), this departure only serves to obscure the fact that open texture characterizes a separate and important variety of indeterminacy of sense.

The Platonic view of meaning as specified by a definition has as a consequence a clear view on knowledge of meaning: to know what a word means is to be able to define it. But this view of knowledge comes at a price. From the Socratic dialogues on, people have failed to provide definitions for most of the words they use; it follows that they do not know the meaning of these words. On the other hand, if one indeed doesn't know the meaning of a word one uses, how could one possibly succeed in defining it? A paradox of analysis seems to lurk behind the Platonic view. As a response, views on knowledge as recollection (Plato), on implicit or latent knowledge (recent philosophy of language and linguistics) and other similar views have been developed.

Having rejected this standard view of the nature of meaning, Wittgenstein has to address the issue of knowledge of meaning. He first remarks on it in §69, while discussing concepts' lack of boundaries:

> How would we explain to someone what a game is? I think that we'd describe *games* to him, and we might add to the description: "This *and similar things* are called 'games'." And do we know any more ourselves? Is it just that we can't tell others exactly what a game is? – But this is not ignorance. We don't know the boundaries because none have been drawn. (PI §69)

The focus of this section is on the lack of boundaries, but it already contains the view that an explanation by means of examples is a legitimate way of expressing knowledge of meaning. "Giving examples is here not an *indirect* way of explaining – in default of a better one" (PI § 71). And such explanations are obviously readily available to anyone who uses the concept of game correctly. They might of course be misunderstood, and some might be clearer than others, but this is also the case with any definition or other general explanation.

Wittgenstein turns again to the nature of knowledge and explanation of meaning in §75. He mentions the view that this knowledge of meaning, which we might not be able to express, is equivalent to an unformulated definition that, once formulated, we would be able to recognize as expressing our knowledge. He is evidently opposed to this view, which he contrasts with his own position, again exemplified by the concept of game:

> Isn't my knowledge, my concept of a game, completely expressed in the explanations that I could give? That is, in my describing examples of various kinds of game, showing how all sorts of other games can be constructed on the analogy of these, saying that I would hardly call this or that a game, and so on. (PI §75)

Our knowledge is *completely* expressed by these explanations; there is nothing latent or implicit in it, nothing unconscious awaiting some kind of Platonic recollection. We again see how philosophical theories have been engendered by a mistaken view of knowledge of meaning and how the need for any such theorizing is eliminated once this view is corrected.

A family-resemblance concept *has to be explained* by means of examples or instances. Some instances of a family-resemblance concept might be more *typical*, in some sense of typicality, than others, but so might be instances of other kinds of concept. And even the typicality of instances of a family-resemblance concept might be not a result of the logical character of the concept but of factors of relative frequency, say, or of some other kind of prominence. A policewoman might not represent a typical grandmother, and 4 might be more typical as an even number than 17 101 962; but these kinds of typicality have *no function in the explanation* of the concept of grandmother or of even number, both concepts being explained by means of a definition. (Although the concept of a mother, on which that of a grandmother depends, might have an open texture: think of the new possibilities of gestational mother versus genetic one.) Having typical instances is thus in itself no indication that a concept is a family-resemblance one. What does show this logical character of a concept is the *role* of instances in explaining its meaning.

Eleanor Rosch, inspired by Wittgenstein's idea of family resemblance, tried to show by means of experiments that this is indeed the structure of some of our concepts. But not having distinguished typicality from role in explanation, she merely asked her subjects to grade "how good an example of a category various instances of the category are" and how well they fit their image of the category, and told them not to worry why they feel so (Rosch and Mervis, 1975, p.588). In this way, what she in fact showed was only that the instances of some concepts might vary in their typicality. As was noted above, this is true of concepts of other kinds as well; and indeed, Armstrong and her colleagues (1983) replicated Rosch's results with other kinds of concept. In order to determine whether a concept is a family-resemblance one we have to examine how it is explained, and not whether some of its instances are more typical than others.

The considerations above on the nature of concepts are among those that lead Wittgenstein to reconsider the nature of logic itself (PI §89). He first describes his former way of thinking, which to a large extent he inherited from the earlier philosophical tradition. Logic, the essence of thought and language, presents the order of possibilities, which must be utterly simple, a purest crystal. Therefore, where there is sense, there must be perfect order. A sentence must have determinate sense, he echoes the *Tractatus* 3.23, for an indeterminate sense would be like a boundary that is not sharply defined, which is not really a boundary (this time echoing Frege). There cannot be any vagueness in logic, for the ideal *must* exist in reality (PI §§96–101).

But all this was misguided. The idea of perfect order was like a pair of glasses fixed on our nose through which we saw whatever we looked at. The perfect order was never in linguistic reality but in our mode of representation of that reality, in our logical constructions. Moreover, since reality failed to comply, we became dissatisfied with what are ordinarily called "sentences," "words," or "signs" and looked in vain for their hypothetical logically pure correlates (as is still so often done in philosophy of language and formal semantics). We should instead take these glasses off and turn the whole inquiry around, by returning to the rough ground. Philosophy of logic should speak of sentences and words in the same sense in which we speak of them in ordinary life. The prejudice of crystalline purity should be dismissed, and we should realize that what we call "sentence" and "language" do not have the formal unity we imagined them to have but are a family of structures more or less akin to one another, with concepts that have indeterminate senses and vague boundaries (PI §§103–8). The rejection of the Platonic view of concepts culminates in a revision of our conception of logic itself.

A tradition of two-and-a-half millennia with its habits of thought cannot be destroyed at one fell swoop, no matter how thorough. And indeed, the Platonic view of concepts and their explanation continues to thrive in philosophy, Wittgenstein's assault notwithstanding. Hordes of philosophers have wasted much time in vain attempts to define the concept of game and show that Wittgenstein was wrong, yet their failures did not help convince them and others that he might have been right.

Some philosophers did of course view Wittgenstein's criticisms and development of alternative paradigms more approvingly. We saw above his influence on Waismann. An attitude toward vagueness that also was probably inspired by Wittgenstein's is apparent throughout Ryle's work as well. For instance, when discussing the intellect, Ryle dismisses the demand for necessary and sufficient conditions for an activity being intellectual:

> But, after all, does it matter if all attempts at giving a hard-edged definition of 'intellectual' and 'thought' break down somewhere or other? We know well enough how to distinguish urban from rustic areas, games from work, and spring from summer, and are unembarrassed by the discovery of undecidable marginal cases. We know that solving a mathematical problem is an intellectual task, hunting the thimble is a non-intellectual task, while looking for an apposite rhyme is a halfway house. [...] Our daily use of the concepts of the intellect and of thought is unembarrassed by the discovery of a moderate number of borderline cases. (Ryle, 1949, pp.258–9)

An interesting instance of what might well be Wittgenstein's influence is provided by one of the important controversies of twentieth-century philosophy, that between Quine and Grice and Strawson on the viability of the analytic–synthetic distinction. Quine tried to clarify this distinction, and with it other semantic concepts such as "meaning the same as," by means of a general definition. Having failed to find a satisfactory definition that does not rely on concepts from the same semantic family, he rejected the analytic–synthetic distinction: "That there is such a distinction to be drawn at all is an unempirical dogma of empiricists, a metaphysical article of faith" (Quine, 1953, p.37). Quine was clearly philosophizing within the Platonic tradition, which considers definition as the only legitimate form of explanation of a concept, and his commitment to it led him to reject the meaningfulness of the concept of synonymy and with it of related concepts, which is absurd. Grice and Strawson, by contrast, rejected that tradition and attempted to clarify one of the relevant semantic concepts, that of logical impossibility, by means of a concrete example that relates it to an epistemic concept, that of understanding. If someone asserted, "My neighbor's three-year-old child is an adult," which is *logically impossible*, and appeared to mean it literally, we would simply not *understand* him (Grice and Strawson, 1956, pp.201–6). This illuminating explanation is, methodologically, clearly Wittgensteinian. As Strawson had closely read the *Investigations* shortly earlier for the critical study of the book he published in *Mind* (1954; cf. especially pp.141–2), it is quite possible that we hear Wittgensteinian echoes in this response to Quine.

But such echoes are seldom heard in more recent philosophy. Many philosophers are as desperate for definitions as ever. Some even deny that any concepts are vague: concepts that are apparently vague are supposed to be sharp, as Wittgenstein insisted while viewing reality through his "ideal" glasses in his twenties, and their apparent vagueness merely reflects our ignorance of their meaning. In addition, one frequently comes across far-fetched cases that are put forward as counterexamples that show a certain explanation of a given concept to be wrong. Wittgenstein, by contrast, would consider more complex cases not as showing that explanations that apply to the basic cases are wrong, but as presupposing such simple explanations while requiring their elaboration:

> When one describes simple language-games in illustration, let's say, of what we call 'motive' of an action, then more involved cases keep on being held up before one, in order to show that our theory doesn't yet correspond to the facts. Whereas more involved cases are just more involved cases. For if what were in question were a theory, it might indeed be said: It's no use looking at these special cases, they offer no explanation of the most important cases. By contrast, the simple language-games play a quite different role. They are poles of a description, not a ground-floor of a theory. (RPP I §633; translation slightly altered)

Wittgenstein's conception of explanation as expressed in this passage, and with it his related ideas on the indeterminacy of sense, on vagueness, and on family resemblance are foreign to most contemporary discussions in analytic philosophy.

References

Aristotle. (1941). *The Basic Works of Aristotle*. Ed. R. McKeon. New York: Random House.
Armstrong, S.L., Gleitman, L.R., and Gleitman, H. (1983). What Some Concepts Might Not Be. *Cognition*, 13, 263–308.
Baker, G.P. and Hacker, P.M.S. (1980/2005). *Wittgenstein: Understanding and Meaning. Volume 1 of an Analytical Commentary on the Philosophical Investigations. Part 1. Essays*. Second edition. Extensively revised by P.M.S. Hacker. Oxford: Wiley-Blackwell.
Ben-Yami, H. (2010). A Wittgensteinian Solution to the Sorites. *Philosophical Investigations*, 33, 229–244.
Faulkner, N. (2010). Wittgenstein's *Philosophical Grammar*: A Neglected Discussion of Vagueness. *Philosophical Investigations*, 33, 159–183.
Frege, G. (1960). *Translations from the Writings of Gottlob Frege*. Ed. and trans. P. Geach and M. Black. Oxford: Blackwell.
Grice, P. and Strawson, P. (1956). In Defense of a Dogma. Reprinted in P. Grice. (1989). *Studies in the Way of Words* (pp.196–212). Cambridge, MA: Harvard University Press.
Mill, J.S. (1882). *A System of Logic, Ratiocinative and Inductive*. Eighth edition. New York: Harper and Brothers.
Plato. (1871). *Meno*. Trans. B. Jowett. Oxford: Clarendon Press.
Quine, W.V.O. (1953). Two Dogmas of Empiricism. Reprinted in W.V.O. Quine. (1961). *From a Logical Point of View* (pp.20–46). Second revised edition. Cambridge, MA: Harvard University Press.
Raffman, D. (1994). Vagueness without Paradox. *Philosophical Review*, 103, 41–74.
Rosch, E. and Mervis, C.B. (1975). Family Resemblances: Studies in the Internal Structure of Categories. *Cognitive Psychology*, 7, 573–605.
Ryle, G. (1949). *The Concept of Mind*. New York: Hutchinson.
Shapiro, S. (2006). *Vagueness in Context*. Oxford: Oxford University Press.
Spinoza, B. (2002). *Complete Works*. Ed. M.L. Morgan. Indianapolis: Hackett.
Stewart, D. (1810). *Philosophical Essays*. Edinburgh: Creech and Constable.
Strawson, P. (1954). Wittgenstein's *Philosophical Investigations*. Reprinted in P. Strawson. (1974). *Freedom and Resentment and other Essays* (pp.133–168). London: Methuen.
Waismann, F. (1951). Verifiability. In A. Flew (Ed.). *Logic and Language* (pp.117–144). Oxford: Blackwell.
Whewell, W. (1858). *History of Scientific Ideas*. Vol 2. Third edition. London: John W. Parker and Son.

Further Reading

Baker, G.P. and Hacker, P.M.S. (1980/2005). *Wittgenstein: Understanding and Meaning. Volume 1 of an Analytical Commentary on the Philosophical Investigations. Part 2. Exegesis §§1–184.* Second edition. Extensively revised by P.M.S. Hacker. Oxford: Wiley-Blackwell. Chapter 3.

Glock, H.-J. (1996). *A Wittgenstein Dictionary.* Oxford: Blackwell.

Puryear, S. (2013). Frege on Vagueness and Ordinary Language. *The Philosophical Quarterly*, 63, 120–140.

Schroeder, S. (2006). *Wittgenstein: The Way out of the Fly-Bottle.* Cambridge: Polity Press. Section 4.2.

Zalta, E.N. (Ed.). *The Stanford Encyclopedia of Philosophy.* http://plato.stanford.edu/. Entries "Sorites Paradox" and "Vagueness."

26

Languages, Language-Games, and Forms of Life

DANIEL WHITING

1 Introduction

A cursory glance at Wittgenstein's work, early and late, reveals a preoccupation with *language*, both as a source of philosophical puzzlement about such concepts as time, knowledge, and causation, and as a phenomenon which is puzzling in various respects itself. One of the key innovations in Wittgenstein's later philosophy is the introduction of *language-games*. As I shall explain, Wittgenstein appeals to language-games in an effort to dispel the kinds of puzzlement just mentioned, as well as to illuminate language itself.

By comparison with talk of language-games, Wittgenstein talks of *forms of life* infrequently. Nonetheless, he is clear that the significance of the former lies in large part in its connection to the latter (PI §23). In what follows, I shall explain this connection. Having done so, I shall comment on the relationship between the view that emerges from Wittgenstein's remarks on language-games and a prominent view in contemporary philosophy of language, namely, contextualism.

2 Objects of Comparison

At first, in *Philosophical Investigations*, Wittgenstein uses the phrase "language-game" to refer to a (fictional) "complete primitive language" (PI §2), which one could also view "as one of those games by means of which children learn their native language" (PI §7). Reflection on language-games, so conceived, is supposed to serve a therapeutic purpose: "It disperses the fog" (PI §5). To appreciate this, consider the so-called "Augustinian picture":

> The words in language name objects – sentences are combinations of such names. – In this picture of language we find the roots of the following idea: Every word has a meaning. This meaning is correlated with the word. It is the object for which the word stands. (PI §1)

A Companion to Wittgenstein, First Edition. Edited by Hans-Johann Glock and John Hyman.
© 2017 John Wiley & Sons, Ltd. Published 2017 by John Wiley & Sons, Ltd.

A picture like this, Wittgenstein suggests, can lead to various forms of philosophical puzzlement. Consider:

(1) Elliot is larger than Stanley.
(2) Seven is larger than five.

(1) contains proper names, "Elliot" and "Stanley," which refer to individuals, in this case persons, which one might bump into, say, if one were in Southampton. It is natural to think that knowing what those words signify in some sense involves knowing those individuals, knowledge one might acquire by meeting them.

(2) is superficially similar in form to (1) – they share a "surface grammar" (cf. PI §664). Accordingly, one might think that "seven" and "five" are also names that refer to individuals, presumably numbers. Might one bump into those individuals? Presumably not. Where, then, are they to be found, if not in Southampton? And how can one know what the names signify, if not by meeting their bearers? One soon finds oneself in deep philosophical waters, and I haven't even touched upon "is larger than."

Needless to say, this is a toy example – there is no suggestion that anyone has fallen into confusion in such a simple-minded fashion – but it suffices for present purposes.

After sketching the Augustinian picture, Wittgenstein introduces an example involving builders:

> A is building with building stones: there are blocks, pillars, slabs and beams. B has to pass him the stones and to do so in the order in which A needs them. For this purpose they make use of a language consisting of the words 'block', 'pillar', 'slab', 'beam'. A calls them out; B brings the stone which he has learnt to bring at such-and-such a call. (PI §2)

This language, Wittgenstein says, could be taught "demonstratively." The teacher directs the pupil's attention to a certain sort of stone, perhaps by pointing, and pronounces a word. Later, the teacher says a word and the pupil is rewarded if she brings one sort of stone, punished otherwise (cf. BB 77).

Wittgenstein invites us to consider "an extension" of the game:

> The builder's man knows by heart the series of words from one to ten. On being given the order, 'Five slabs!', he goes to where the slabs are kept, says the words from one to five, takes up a slab for each word, and carries them to the builder. (BB 79; cf. PI §8)

The builders use the numerals exclusively for counting. Significantly, the teaching of this game would be different. A pupil must memorize "the series of number words" (PI §9). And, where the teaching is demonstrative, "the same word, e.g., 'three', will be taught by pointing either to slabs, or to bricks, or to columns, etc." (BB 79).

These language-games are supposed to help us see how very different the functioning of count nouns like "pillar" is from the functioning of numerals like "five" – differences the Augustinian picture ignores. This might help us steer clear of the waters broached above. In the extended language-game, there is little temptation to speculate about what entities the numerals are correlated with and so where they might be found, or to worry about what kind of contact one would have to have with such entities in order to play the game.

Wittgenstein is *not* denying that numerals signify or stand for numbers: "We see no reason why we shouldn't speak of names of numbers" (BB 82). He asks only: "How is what they signify supposed to come out other than in the kind of use they have?" (PI §10). The point of the language-games is to bring into view, beneath the surface level at which one talks of various words signifying or meaning various things, "how fundamentally different the functions of such words are" (BB 82). What it is for "five" to name a number differs from what it is for "slab" to name a kind of stone – the underlying patterns of use that license the similar semantic descriptions are dissimilar. In Wittgenstein's words, "there is no one relation of name to object, but as many as there are uses of sounds or scribbles which we call names" (BB 173).

Admittedly, the remedy outlined above is as crude as the corresponding confusion. But it serves to illustrate one of the purposes Wittgenstein's descriptions of language-games are supposed to serve.

Clearly, a language like English is quite unlike the builders' "system of communication" (BB 81). For Wittgenstein, language-games serve "as *objects of comparison* which, through similarities and dissimilarities, are meant to throw light on features of our language" (PI §130). Our "everyday language," he says, is "highly complicated" in ways that make it hard to survey and therefore apt to cause confusion. In contrast, language-games are "clear-cut and transparent," though "we recognize in these simple processes forms of language not separated by a break from our more complicated ones" (BB 17; cf. VW 67). Returning to the example:

> By introducing numerals we have introduced an entirely different *kind* of instrument into our language. The difference of kind is so much more obvious when we contemplate such a simple example than when we look at our ordinary language with innumerable kinds of words all looking more or less alike. (BB 79; cf. PI §335)

In a similar fashion, Wittgenstein investigates language-games involving numerous other kinds of expressions, including demonstratives, color words, epistemic terms, and aesthetic vocabulary.

3 Languages as Involving Games

Alongside his use of language-games as objects of comparison, Wittgenstein presents natural languages like English as involving language-games. Recall his talk of "the everyday language-games," quoted above (cf. PI §224), and his claim that "our" language is "not separated by a break" from the primitive activities. Elsewhere, he speaks of "the" (actual) language-games involving terms like "describe" (PI §290), "know" (OC §3), and "looks" (Z §422), and refers to activities like "forming and testing a hypothesis," "reporting an event," and "describing an object by its appearance, or by its measurements" as language-games (PI §23). At one point, he mentions "the human language-game" (OC §554).

These remarks point to a picture of language as involving practices of employing expressions in certain ways, practices governed – following the game analogy – by rules, which determine the correct use of those expressions and by appeal to which participants regulate and evaluate their actions. In Wittgenstein's words: "Following according to the rule is FUNDAMENTAL to our language-game" (RFM VI §28; cf. VW 87). On this picture, expressions mean (and name) what they do in virtue of the rule-governed role they play in the relevant language-game(s) (cf. BB 67; PI §43; RFM VI §41). As

Wittgenstein says: "A meaning of a word is a kind of employment of it [...]. That is why there exists a correspondence between the concepts 'rule' and 'meaning'" (OC §§61–2). Elsewhere: "The meaning of a word is constituted by the rules for its employment" (VW 143). In this respect, a language-game is a "mode of representation" (PI §50).

Wittgenstein insists on viewing language-games as "complete in themselves, as complete systems of communication" (BB 81). This might encourage the following idea, which Crispin Wright captures (without endorsing) thus: "Each is self-regulating and answerable only to standards within it" (1992, p.202). This is faithful to Wittgenstein's position, if it means that the conditions for the correct use of an expression are determined only by the rules of the relevant language-game, which are conventional and arbitrary (PI §§355, 497; PR §4; cf. Chapter 15, THE AUTONOMY OF GRAMMAR). But it is unfaithful to Wittgenstein's position, if it means that *whether* those conditions are satisfied on a given occasion of use is determined only by what is going on in the game, by its rules or by the other linguistic moves its participants make, as opposed to language-(game-)independent reality. The rules of the language-game settle what counts as correctly using "red," for example, by including the principle that "red" be applied only to *this* (pointing to a sample of red) (cf. PI §50). But whether one accords with this principle on a given occasion, and so correctly uses "red," depends on whether one applies it to an object that is, in fact, red. As Wittgenstein remarks: "If I say falsely that something is *red*, then all the same, it is *red* that it isn't" (PI §429).

Above, I indicated how reflection on language-games is supposed to address specific forms of puzzlement. Wittgenstein's presentation of language as a rule-governed activity might address a puzzlement about language itself, which Paul Horwich describes:

> What is meaning? Why are some sounds imbued with it and others not? How, for example, does it come about that the word 'dog' means precisely what it does? How is it possible for those intrinsically inert ink-marks [...] to reach out into the world and latch on to a definite portion of reality: namely, the dogs?
>
> (Horwich, 1998, p.1)

The idea that language is a game, and that uses of expressions are moves in it, might provide the beginnings of an answer to such questions: 'Every sign by itself seems dead. What gives it life? – In use it *lives*' (PI §432; cf. BB 4).

4 (Forms of) Life(-Forms)

Does presenting language as a game address the worries about "dead" signs? After all, there are many games in which tokens are moved subject to rules but in which those tokens do not possess *meaning*, and cannot be used to *say* things (cf. Lycan, 2000, pp.81–2). For example, chess is not a "mode of representation."

Anticipating this, Wittgenstein suggests viewing language-games as embedded in nonlinguistic activities:

> If there were peoples whose troops moved in battle according to the same laws as the pieces on the chessboard, then a position of chess pieces would acquire a meaning at once, and the officers would then bend over the chessboard just as they would now over strategic maps [...]. The movements of the pieces would simply be a representation of events in reality and not a 'mere game'. (VW 149–50)

It is important to stress that Wittgenstein does not mention circumstances of significant activity into which language-games are woven merely to address the "mere game" objection. His remarks highlight a feature of language-games, their embeddedness in larger contexts, which is part of the very idea of a language-game. Such contexts are not *supplementary* to language-games but *integral* to them. From the outset, Wittgenstein presents each language-game as a "whole, consisting of language and the activities into which it is woven" (PI §7). Again: "The word 'language-*game*' is used here to emphasize the fact that the *speaking* of language is part of an activity, or of a form of life" (PI §23). Thus, "to imagine a language is to imagine a form of life" (PI §19).

Following Cavell (1989), one can distinguish "vertical" and "horizontal" senses of "form of life." The vertical, broadly-speaking biological, sense concerns the *life-form* all human beings share, with all its physiological peculiarities. Our use of color terms, for example, is bound up with the distinctive physiology of the human visual system:

> Imagine a *tribe* of colour-blind people, and there could easily be one. They would not have the same colour concepts as we do. For even assuming they speak, e.g. English, and thus have all the English colour words, they would still use them differently than we do and would *learn* their use differently. (ROC I §13)

Similarly, that we play certain language-games is dependent on certain "very general facts of nature" (PI II 241; cf. OC §63; Z §§351–2). To adapt one of Wittgenstein's examples (PI §142), our terms of measurement might not have application were objects to expand and contract randomly.

The horizontal, broadly-speaking social, sense concerns *ways of life*, which humans might or might not share (cf. RFM VI §34). In Wittgenstein's view, "what belongs to a language-game is a whole culture" (LC 8). It is difficult to give uncontroversial examples of terms the use of which is bound up with, and so depends upon, habits and customs that reflect the outlook of a certain group; but consider how the practices involving "chivalrous" are caught up in ways difficult to spell out with certain socio-historical circumstances, which have now passed, and certain values and principles, which are now foreign to us.

In a still more difficult to pin down fashion, language-games reflect their participants' sense for what is or is not important. Wittgenstein writes: "We could say that people's concepts show what matters to them and what doesn't" (ROC III §293; cf. Z §378). For example, that we have a word with which to distinguish unmarried from married adult males but not one with which to distinguish married males with black hair over the age of eleven from anything else might indicate our sense of what needs noting. Someone with no sensitivity whatsoever to the significance of marital status – to the purposes of classifying people in this way – might be unable to participate in language-games involving expressions like "bachelor." As Wittgenstein remarks: "The game, one would like to say, has not only rules but also a *point*" (PI §564; cf. §570).

If language-games – and hence languages – depend upon a form of life's horizontal and vertical dimensions, then where these dimensions vary, the language-games – and hence the languages – might vary. Accordingly, Wittgenstein claims, "an education quite different from ours might also be the foundation of quite different concepts" (Z §387). Elsewhere: "An entirely different game is played in different ages" (LC 8). And, as Wittgenstein explains, "When language-games change, then there is a change in concepts, and with the concepts the meanings of the words change" (OC §65).

Does viewing language-games as embedded in nonlinguistic activities, integrated vertically and horizontally within a form of life, speak to the worry that, on Wittgenstein's view, language might turn out to be a "mere game," not a "mode of representation"? To answer this, one would have to look at actual descriptions of rule-governed patterns of behavior involving signs woven into wider contexts to ascertain whether they warrant semantic descriptions. Some doubt that the calls of Wittgenstein's builders qualify as language use, properly so-called (e.g., Brandom, 2008, p.42); be that as it may, there might be language-games that do so qualify.

5   Context(ualism)

I have outlined several respects in which, for Wittgenstein, language-games are inextricably bound to wider contexts – they are peculiar to environments, natural and social, tied to purposive activities, and play certain roles in the forms of life their participants inhabit. Does Wittgenstein advance any *further* ideas regarding the circumstances surrounding language use?

It is increasingly common to interpret Wittgenstein's remarks on language-games as pointing to an influential position in contemporary philosophy of language: *contextualism*. "Contextualism" is an umbrella term for numerous views – for present purposes, I shall restrict my attention to one. According to it, the use of the very same sentence, with whatever invariant meaning it bears in a language, might in different circumstances of use literally express any of an indefinite range of different propositions or thoughts with different truth conditions. This is *not* due to expressions that are uncontroversially indexical, like "this," "you," or "now." At the level of words, the same word with the same meaning might on different occasions make a different contribution to the proposition expressed by uses of sentences involving it.

To bring this down to earth, consider:

(3) Holly is tall.

Suppose that Holly is 6ft. By uttering (3), the contextualist claims, one might express a falsehood in one context – say, when selecting a basketball team – and a truth in another – say, when deciding what clothes to buy Holly – even though the words (and, in one sense, their meanings) remain the same, as does Holly's height. Insofar as there is nothing special about (3), the lesson generalizes.

James Conant and Charles Travis are among the most influential proponents of a contextualist reading of Wittgenstein, although there are numerous others (see Whiting, 2010 for references). According to Travis, Wittgenstein presents a "new view" of language:

> [Words'] semantics as part of their language, e.g. English, is at most a proper part of their semantics on an occasion of expressing a thought, and underdetermines what thought they would thus express, the latter varying while they mean what they do and have whatever semantics that confers on them. Their fixed, language-contributed semantics must, in general, be supplemented if they are to be properly assessable as to truth, that is, if they are to count either as true or as false [...]. The role of a sentence, on this view, is not to be the

expresser, in its language, of such and such thought, but rather to be usable on many different occasions for expressing any of many thoughts, each with its own condition for truth.

(Travis, 1991, p.242)

In similar terms, Conant writes:

Wittgenstein thinks that it is a misunderstanding of how language works to think [...] that the role of a sentence in our language is to be that which on its own bat allows for the expression of a determinate thought – a determinacy which is achieved simply as a function of (1) the meanings of the individual words and (2) the rules of the language. The role of a sentence is to provide a linguistic instrument which is usable in many different circumstances to express any of many distinct thoughts [...]. Each of these thoughts will be true under different conditions.

(Conant, 1998, p.244)

On the picture developed in previous sections, what an expression means is determined by how it is used according to the rules of the language-games involving it. Insofar as one might play such games on various occasions in various situations, the expression will bear the same meaning on those occasions in those situations. The contextualist claims that the meaning of an expression *in this sense* underdetermines the proposition expressed by the use of a sentence involving it on any given occasion. What is expressed by the use of an expression depends not only on the general principles for its employment, but also on the particular circumstances surrounding its employment. (A more radical contextualist might hold that there are *no* general rules for the use of an expression, only particular uses of that expression in particular situations.)

Those who find contextualism in Wittgenstein often view his talk of language-games as primarily concerning, not rule-governed activities one might participate in on different occasions, but actual, concrete, embedded uses of language on specific occasions. In this manner, Travis writes:

The point of the discussion of language games [...] is that naming, or referring [...] underdetermines conditions for correctness of wholes [i.e., sentences], notably, where relevant, conditions for their truth. Wholes with given referents, embedded in different language games, would be true under any of many very different sets of conditions.

(Travis, 2008, p.254; cf. Conant, 1998, p.233)

Appeal to "context-shifting" examples like that involving (3) above is a common strategy in support of contextualism. But, while it is undeniable that Wittgenstein sees connections between what is expressed in the use of language and circumstances of use, do his writings justify the view that he is a contextualist?

6 This Is Here

In support of their exegetical claims, Conant and Travis cite PI §117:

If, for example, someone says that the sentence 'This is here' (saying which he points to an object in front of him) makes sense to him, then he should ask himself in what special circumstances this sentence is actually used. There it does make sense. (PI §117)

Wittgenstein discusses similar examples in other passages, which Conant and Travis also appeal to:

> A philosopher says that he understands the sentence 'I am here', that he means something by it, thinks something – even though he doesn't call to mind in the least how, on what occasions, this sentence is used. (PI §514)

> I know that a sick man is lying here? Nonsense! I am sitting at his bedside, I am looking attentively into his face. – So I don't know, then, that there is a sick man lying here? Neither the question nor the assertion makes sense. Any more than the assertion 'I am here', which I might yet use at any moment, if suitable occasion presents itself. (OC §10)

> The words 'I am here' have a meaning only in certain contexts, and not when I say them to someone who is sitting in front of me and sees me clearly, – and not because they are superfluous, but because their meaning is not *determined* by the situation, yet stands in need of such a determination. (OC §348)

Note that the relevant sentences contain uncontroversially indexical expressions whose reference varies with context ("I," "here," "this"). While Conant and Travis are right in thinking that Wittgenstein's point is independent of this, they are wrong to suppose that he is advancing contextualism.

The point Wittgenstein explicitly makes is that the relevant sentence "makes sense," i.e., expresses a proposition, only in "special circumstances" or "certain contexts." But there is no suggestion that, in different circumstances in which the sentence makes sense, it would make different sense, i.e., express different propositions. Rather, the idea seems to be that one does not count as playing the language-game with (the English words) "I am here" in just any old situation – for one's use of signs so to count the situation must be "suitable."

What makes a situation suitable? Wittgenstein says little about that here, but recall the idea that language-games have a *point*. Whatever point employing "I am here" might serve – to help others to locate oneself, say – is not served, Wittgenstein seems to suggest, "when I say them to someone who is sitting in front of me and sees me clearly." Hence, whatever is going on in such a situation, it is not recognizable as one in which someone is playing the "I am here" language-game. Contrast the following situation: I'm talking to a friend via the Internet. Aware that I travel, she asks where I am. I hold up a map to the camera, point to it, and say "I am here." This situation, presumably, is recognizable as one in which someone is playing the language-game with "I am here."

So, Wittgenstein is suggesting that context determines *whether* a language-game is being played – and so whether subjects are employing expressions subject to the rules of that game. He is not suggesting that context plays a *further* role, namely, determining which of many propositions the expressions subject to those rules express. Similarly, the fact that not just any context in which subjects move pieces shaped like castles and horses around a chequered board counts as one in which subjects are playing chess does not entail that, in different contexts in which subjects count as playing chess, the pieces have a different significance (cf. PI §200).

One might think that the final passage shows Wittgenstein to be a contextualist, since he claims there that the meaning of a sentence, i.e., the proposition expressed, "is *determined* by the situation," as opposed perhaps to the general rules governing its constituents. In turn, one might think that on this view a different situation might "determine" that the same sentence has a different meaning, i.e., expresses a different proposition.

427

But the passage says nothing whatsoever about different situations determining different meanings; it speaks only of words having "a" meaning "in certain contexts." The point, again, seems to be that "the situation" "determines" that the sentence bears a certain meaning insofar as whether one counts as playing the relevant language-game, and so as using that sentence with that meaning, depends upon the circumstances. If they are not appropriate, one is not playing that language-game, but some other language-game, with similar sign-designs, or none at all.

Note that it is no part of the reading presented here that, for Wittgenstein, a sentence might fail to express a proposition in a given situation because the meaning it has somehow clashes with that situation, "because of an *incompatibility* between the *Satz* and the context of use" (Conant, 1998, p.223). Nor is it part of that reading that the rules governing the expressions the sentence contains somehow determine that they fail to express a proposition or bear a meaning in that context. The proposal is only that, for Wittgenstein, in the absence of a suitable context with suitable purposes being served, the use of a string of signs does not qualify as the use of words bearing certain meanings, and so as governed by certain rules, or, more simply, as the playing of a certain language-game.

7 I Know That That's a Tree

Consider again:

> I know that a sick man is lying here? Nonsense! I am sitting at his bedside, I am looking attentively into his face. – So I don't know, then, that there is a sick man lying here? Neither the question nor the assertion makes sense. (OC §10)

Wittgenstein explores similar examples in the following remarks, which Conant cites as evidence of contextualism:

> 'I know that that's a tree.' Why does it strike me as if I did not understand the sentence? though it is after all an extremely simple sentence of the most ordinary kind? It is as if I could not focus my mind on any meaning. Simply because I don't look for the focus where the meaning is. As soon as I think of an everyday use of the sentence instead of a philosophical one, its meaning becomes clear and ordinary. (OC §347)

> 'I know that that's a tree' is something a philosopher might say to demonstrate to himself or to someone else that he *knows* something that is not a mathematical or logical truth. Similarly, someone who was entertaining the idea that he was no use any more might keep repeating to himself 'I can still do this and this and this'. If such thoughts often possessed him one would not be surprised if he, apparently out of all context, spoke such a sentence out loud. (But here I have already sketched a background, a surrounding, for this remark, that is to say given it a context.) But if someone, in quite heterogeneous circumstances, called out with the most convincing mimicry: 'Down with him!', one might say of these words (and their tone) that they were a pattern that does indeed have familiar applications, but that it was not even clear what *language* the man in question was speaking. I might make with my hand the movement I should make if I were holding a hand-saw and sawing through a plank; but would one have any right to call this movement *sawing*, out of all context? – (It might be something quite different!) (OC §350)

If someone says 'I know that that's a tree' I may answer: 'Yes, that is a sentence. An English sentence. And what is it supposed to be doing?' Suppose he replies: 'I just wanted to remind myself that I *know* things like that?' (OC §352)

In these remarks, Wittgenstein makes a familiar point. If I am to count as playing the relevant language-game with a sentence like "I know that that's a tree,", and so if it is to have the meaning that it does (as determined by the rules governing its parts), the "background" or "situation" must be appropriate, one in which the use of those words can be seen to be serving suitable purposes. Without such a context, the sentence lies "outside its language-game" (OC §393).

Once again, there is no suggestion that context plays an additional role, namely, supplementing whatever meaning the expressions have in virtue of being subject to the general rules of the language-game and, thereby, determining which of many propositions is expressed in their use. For all that Wittgenstein says above, if the circumstances are such that I count in them as playing the ("familiar," "everyday") language-game with "I know that that's a tree," then I count (in that context) as expressing the proposition *that I know that that's a tree*, the proposition I would express by using that sentence in any context in which I count as playing that game.

Conant and Travis might object that I overlooked this overtly contextualist passage:

'I know that that's a tree' – this may mean all sorts of things: I look at a plant that I take for a young beech and that someone else thinks is a black-currant. He says 'that is a shrub'; I say it is a tree. – We see something in the mist which one of us takes for a man, and the other says 'I know that that's a tree'. Someone wants to test my eyes etc. etc. – etc. etc. Each time the 'that' which I declare to be a tree is of a different kind. (OC §349)

Certainly Wittgenstein here recognizes variation of what is expressed with circumstances. But, as the final sentence makes clear, the variation here is of a familiar kind, due to the presence of the indexical "that," which picks out a tree "of a different kind" in each context. This does not support attributing to Wittgenstein contextualism of a more radical sort.

In the midst of the above, Wittgenstein offers the following analogy:

Isn't the question 'Have these words a meaning?' similar to 'Is that a tool?' asked as one produces, say, a hammer? I say 'Yes, it's a hammer'. But what if the thing that any of us would take for a hammer were somewhere else a missile, for example, or a conductor's baton? Now make the application yourself. (OC §351)

If Wittgenstein were arguing for contextualism, one would expect him to develop the analogy as follows: the very same tool, a hammer, could in various contexts be (used as) a missile or a baton. But what he actually says is that something which one would "take for" a hammer might instead be a missile or a baton, depending on "the application." Again, Wittgenstein's point is that whether one counts as using an expression with a certain meaning depends on the situation, including what point one's use of it could there be serving, which is *not* to say that the very same expression with whatever meaning it has in the language might, in different situations, in the service of different points, express any of many propositions.

429

8 A Rose is Red in the Dark

I have suggested that, in attributing contextualism to Wittgenstein, Conant and Travis are going beyond what is to be found in his remarks. Not only is this a misreading – it prevents us from appreciating the point Wittgenstein is actually trying to make. Consider the concluding sentence of PI §514, quoted above:

> And if I say 'A rose is red in the dark too', you virtually see this red in the dark before you. (PI §514)

Wittgenstein continues:

> Two pictures of a rose in the dark. One is quite black; for the rose is not visible. In the other, it is painted in full detail and surrounded by black. Is one of them right, the other wrong? Don't we talk of a white rose in the dark and of a red rose in the dark? And don't we nevertheless say that they can't be distinguished in the dark? (PI §515)

Travis provides the following gloss:

> Is 'The rose is red' true of a rose in the dark? On one picture of a rose's being red, yes; on another, no. Depending on their surroundings, those words, by what they literally say, might present us with either picture as that in terms of which they are to be evaluated.
> (Travis, 1991, p.241)

Travis presents Wittgenstein's "two pictures" as capturing different propositions one might express ("depending on the surroundings") in uttering "The rose is red." But why should either picture, both of which involve black paint, be thought to capture what is expressed by Travis's sentence, which makes no mention of the dark? Note that Travis changes the example from "A rose is red in the dark too" to "The rose is red." Wittgenstein's sentence, unlike Travis's, is one which one can readily imagine being put to what Wittgenstein would call a "philosophical," as opposed to an "everyday," use (OC §347; cf. PI §116). Indeed, the fact that the example immediately follows that of "a philosopher" uttering "I am here" suggests that this is precisely what we are to imagine.

To appreciate what is going on in the passages, consider the context in which they appear (PI §§511–17; also Z §§245–54). Wittgenstein's concern is how someone might "discover that a sentence does not make sense," that "something that at first sight looks like a sentence [...] is not one." She might insist that the relevant string of signs *is* a sentence with a sense, since she "can imagine something in connexion with it" (Z §§247–8). In response, Wittgenstein compares imagining (or "picturing") something with "drawing" something (PI §512) – he commonly employs this strategy of "replacing [a] mental image by some outward object" (BB 5) – and entertains the proposal to "set it up as a criterion of understanding that one [...] be able to represent the sense of a sentence by drawing it" (Z §245).

By way of illustration, Wittgenstein's interlocutor insists that she can "imagine a four-dimensional cube" (Z §249). Various drawings are offered to her as capturing what she imagines, and so what she understands by "four-dimensional cube," but none satisfies ("No; I don't *mean* that!"). Importantly, not only do the drawings fail to provide a sense for the relevant phrase, they seem to unsettle or undermine the interlocutor's conviction that she actually *imagined* something in connection with it: "I have now for a picture only the words and my rejection of anything you can show me."

That forming a mental image is neither necessary nor sufficient for using words with certain meanings is a well-worn point from Wittgenstein (cf. BB 4–5; PI §§139ff). The present point is more radical – Wittgenstein is exploring the possibility "that we *cannot* imagine something which we believed we could imagine," which "might lead us to revise what counts as the domain of the imaginable" (PI §517).

Returning in light of this to PI §§514–15, I suggest that Wittgenstein is concerned with someone who thinks she grasps the sense of the sentence, "A rose is red in the dark too," because she can imagine something in "connexion" with it (she "virtually see[s]" it). The two pictures attempt to capture what she imagines, and so the sense of the sentence. Will the first picture do? Well, the rose seems missing from it. But, while a rose appears in the second, it no longer seems to be in darkness. Neither picture satisfies, and so neither provides a sense for Wittgenstein's sentence as it stands. By the same token, neither reveals what it is that the philosopher takes herself to imagine, which undermines the thought that there is anything that she imagines. Wittgenstein states the lesson as follows (note the scare-quotes):

> Are roses red in the dark? – One can think of the rose in the dark as red. – (That one can 'imagine' something does not mean that it makes sense to say it.) (Z §250)

More positively, Wittgenstein recommends that we "investigate [the sentence's] application in the language-game" (Z §247). Consider: I ask my young son to hide the roses I've bought in the cupboard. He does so. To ensure there's a suitable array, I ask him how many red roses we've got. He replies, "None – the lights are off." Momentarily puzzled, I realize he doesn't quite grasp the logic of color terms yet. By way of instruction, I say, "A rose is red in the dark too." It is in virtue of playing its role in such a context, not in virtue of what one (seems to) imagine, that the string of signs constitutes a sentence expressing a sense.

So, Wittgenstein's point, again, is that a suitable occasion involving suitable purposes is required *if* a sentence is to bear a certain meaning, and hence express a certain proposition, that is, if one is to count as playing a certain language-game. Nothing Wittgenstein says here points toward the idea that the same sentence, with whatever meaning it bears independently of an occasion of use, might express different propositions on different occasions. Moreover, and crucially, these passages are in addition addressing "a lack of clarity about the role of *imaginability* in our investigation. Namely, about the extent to which it ensures that a sentence makes sense" (PI §395). Wittgenstein's remarks are not in the service of promoting contextualism, and thinking that they are prevents us from seeing the work they are supposed to be doing.

9 Conclusion

This chapter outlined the methodological role that appeals to language-games play in Wittgenstein's philosophy, and indicated the picture of language that his discussion of such games and their relations to forms of life suggests. In doing so, it challenged the claim that those remarks point to a kind of contextualism widespread in contemporary philosophy. Of course, this is a limited conclusion. There are other passages that scholars appeal to as evidence of contextualism in Wittgenstein's work, many of which Jason Bridges examines (2010). But perhaps the fact that passages frequently cited as providing such evidence do not do so is reason to re-examine the significance of Wittgenstein's remarks on the use of language and its indissoluble connections to context. For Wittgenstein, the meaningful use of language involves rule-governed practices of employing expressions tied to particular points and purposes, embedded in specific natural and social environments, bound up with, indeed manifesting, distinctive forms of life. Contextualism, of the sort explored here, might be more of a hindrance than a help when it comes to appreciating the importance Wittgenstein sees in this.

References

Brandom. R. (2008). *Between Saying and Doing*. Oxford: Oxford University Press.
Bridges, J. (2010). Wittgenstein vs. Contextualism. In A. Ahmed (Ed.). *Wittgenstein's Philosophical Investigations: A Critical Guide* (pp.109–128). Cambridge: Cambridge University Press.
Cavell, S. (1989). *This New Yet Unapproachable America*. Chicago: University of Chicago Press.
Conant, J. (1998). Wittgenstein on Meaning and Use. *Philosophical Investigations*, 21, 222–250.
Horwich, P. (1998). *Meaning*. Oxford: Oxford University Press.
Lycan, W. (2000). *Philosophy of Language*. London: Routledge.
Travis, C. (1991). Annals of Analysis. *Mind*, 100, 237–264.
Travis, C. (2008). *Occasion-Sensitivity*. Oxford: Oxford University Press.
Whiting, D. (2010). Particular and General: Wittgenstein, Linguistic Rules, and Context. In D. Whiting (Ed.). *The Later Wittgenstein on Language* (pp.114–132). Basingstoke: Palgrave.
Wright, C. (1992). *Truth and Objectivity*. Cambridge, MA: Harvard University Press.

Further Reading

Baker, G.P. and Hacker, P.M.S. (1980/2009). *Wittgenstein: Understanding and Meaning. Volume 1 of an Analytical Commentary on the Philosophical Investigations. Part 1. Essays*. Second edition. Extensively revised by P.M.S. Hacker. Oxford: Wiley-Blackwell.
Goldfarb, W. (1983). I Want You to Bring Me a Slab: Remarks on the Opening Sections of the *Philosophical Investigations*. *Synthese*, 56, 265–282.
Kuusela, O. (Forthcoming). The Method of Language-Games as a Method of Logic. *Philosophical Topics*.
Mulhall, S. (2001). *Inheritance and Originality: Wittgenstein, Heidegger, Kierkegaard*. Oxford: Oxford University Press.
Picardi, E. (2009). Concepts and Primitive Language-Games. In E. Zamuner and D.K. Levy (Eds). *Wittgenstein's Enduring Arguments* (pp.109–134). London: Routledge.
Schulte, J. (2004). The Builders' Language: The Opening Sections. In E. Ammereller and E. Fischer (Eds). *Wittgenstein at Work* (pp.22–41). London: Routledge.
Sellars, W. (1954). Some Reflections on Language Games. Reprinted in K. Scharp and R. Brandom (Eds). (2007). *In the Space of Reasons: Selected Essays of Wilfrid Sellars* (pp.28–56). Cambridge, MA: Harvard University Press.
Travis, C. (2006). *Thought's Footing*. Oxford: Oxford University Press.

27

Wittgenstein on Truth

DAVID DOLBY

In a lecture in 1934–1935 Wittgenstein remarked, "The words 'true' and 'false' are two words on which philosophy has turned, and it is very important to see that philosophy always turns upon nonsensical questions" (AWL 106). He went on to explain that the chief question we face concerning truth is: "Why are false propositions not nonsensical when no fact corresponds to them, as a name would be if nothing corresponded to it?" (AWL 108). Wittgenstein's early and late philosophies of language give very different treatments of this question. Nevertheless, I shall argue, his account of truth remained more or less the same.

1 Truth and the Picture Theory

Inspired by Bertrand Russell's theory of descriptions, Wittgenstein held that the surface grammar of a proposition may be highly misleading as to the underlying structure of a proposition (TLP 4.0031). When fully analyzed, all propositions are revealed to be truth functions of elementary propositions – logically independent propositions that cannot be broken down into more basic propositions. The truth or falsity of a molecular proposition is dependent solely on the truth or falsity of its constituent elementary propositions.

Wittgenstein explains how elementary propositions can have sense by drawing an analogy with a picture or model, such as the model of the scene of an accident (NB 29.09.1914). The elements of a model correspond to the objects at the scene of the accident, while the different possible arrangements of the elements of the model depict different possible arrangements of these objects. For depiction to be possible there must be no licit arrangement of the elements of the model that does not correspond to an arrangement of the objects. The model depicts the objects as being arranged in the way that corresponds to the arrangement of the elements in the model.

Similarly, Wittgenstein argues, elementary propositions must consist of simple signs whose arrangements depict different arrangements of objects in the world. These objects can enter into certain combinations with one another and not into others: each possible

---

A Companion to Wittgenstein, First Edition. Edited by Hans-Johann Glock and John Hyman.
© 2017 John Wiley & Sons, Ltd. Published 2017 by John Wiley & Sons, Ltd.

combination is a state of affairs (TLP 2.01). Just as the possible arrangements of the elements of the model are matched by possible arrangements of the elements in the depicted scene, so must the licit combinatorial possibilities of the names in an elementary proposition match the combinatorial possibilities of the objects in different states of affairs.

The fact that the simple signs are combined in a certain way constitutes an elementary propositional sign (TLP 2.15). A propositional sign, however, cannot say anything on its own. It is necessary for it to be projected onto the world: the structure of possible arrangements of simple signs must be mapped by an isomorphism onto the structure of possible arrangements of objects in the world.

The projection of a propositional sign is a matter of thinking the sense of the proposition (TLP 3.11). The interpretation of this aspect of the picture theory is notoriously difficult. Norman Malcolm has argued that thinking the sense of a proposition involves the occurrence of a sentence in the language of thought (1977); Peter Hacker has argued that thinking the sense of a proposition is an act of the will (2001); but Peter Winch (1987) and Pasquale Frascolla (2007) have argued that the method of projection does not involve a mental aspect.

Employed in a proposition, and thus projected onto the world, the simple signs are names of objects (TLP 3.202). And, in common with Russell and Gottlob Frege, Wittgenstein held that the object for which a name stands is its meaning (TLP 3.203). However, unlike his philosophical forebears, Wittgenstein restricted this referentialist account of meaning to names. Elementary propositions, although "concatenations of names," are not themselves names (TLP 4.22). And the logical constants, which combine with elementary propositions to form molecular propositions, are without reference (TLP 4.0312).

One challenge for referentialist accounts of meaning is to account for the meaningfulness of false propositions. For if a proposition is meaningful in virtue of standing for something in the world, then it is natural to think that the meaning of a true proposition is the fact that makes it true. But then the sentence would not have the same meaning if it were false, since then there would be no fact making it true. We can now see how Wittgenstein addressed the puzzle as to how a false proposition can have sense despite there being no corresponding fact. For in order for a model to represent the world, it is only necessary for the elements of the picture to correspond to objects and for the possible arrangements of the elements of the picture to correspond to possible arrangements of these objects: it is not necessary for the objects in the world actually to be arranged as depicted by the model. The meaning of propositions is thus accounted for in terms of the possibility of the objects named standing to one another in a way that corresponds to the arrangement of the names in the propositions.

One key claim of the picture theory of meaning is that elementary propositions are capable of being true and capable of being false independently of one another. Tautologies and contradictions arise only through the logical combination of elementary propositions and have no sense. All molecular propositions with a sense are also capable of being true and capable of being false: that is, they are bipolar. It follows that what must be the case cannot be meaningfully stated. The logical multiplicity that must be shared by proposition and depicted state of affairs, for example, cannot itself be represented (TLP 4.041). This is because the shared multiplicity of an elementary proposition and the state of affairs it depicts is a precondition of the proposition's depicting that state of affairs and so not a contingent matter of fact. Language cannot represent what it must have in common with reality in order for representation to be possible: the logical form of the world can only be shown in the logical form of the propositions of language.

Having sketched the account of meaning Wittgenstein gave in the *Tractatus*, we are now in a position to address the question as to how he understood truth. It is often claimed that the *Tractatus* gives a correspondence theory of truth (e.g., David, 2009). According to the correspondence theory, truth is a property of a judgment or proposition that consists in standing in a certain relation to something in the world. In standard correspondence theories truth is the property of corresponding to a fact.

If the *Tractatus* does put forward a correspondence theory of truth it is an importantly restricted version of it. According to the standard version of the correspondence theory, it would seem that there must be logically complex facts, such as negative or disjunctive facts, to correspond to logically complex truths, such as negative or disjunctive truths. These facts would include objects such as disjunction and negation, which seem to be out of place in the world. Wittgenstein, as we have seen, rejected the idea that the logical constants represent objects in the world. The truth of molecular propositions is merely a matter of the truth and falsity of the elementary propositions of which they are truth functions. Thus: "Whatever corresponds in reality to compound propositions must not be more than what corresponds to their several atomic propositions" (NL 98).

This treatment of the logical constants was key to Wittgenstein's account of the necessity of logical truths. Russell had interpreted these truths as describing the unchanging relationships that hold between logical objects. Wittgenstein disagreed: logical truths are not truths about logical objects, since there are no logical objects; and their necessity is not a matter of the unchanging nature of their subject matter, but rather of their lacking sense (TLP 4.461). This is not to say that they are nonsense, but that they do not assert the existence of any combination of states of affairs. They are true no matter which states of affairs obtain in the world because they make no assertion about the world.

Thus, if the *Tractatus* gives a standard correspondence theory of truth, it will not apply *directly* to molecular propositions, since the truth of such propositions does not require the existence of a corresponding unitary fact; and it will apply *indirectly* to molecular propositions only if the truth of elementary propositions is explained in terms of correspondence. Moreover, the correspondence account will not apply at all to tautologies and contradictions, since these do not assert the existence of any state of affairs. Any correspondence interpretation of the *Tractatus* will therefore apply directly to elementary propositions at most.

So, does the *Tractatus* give a correspondence account of truth for elementary propositions? At first glance, it might seem that it does. Wittgenstein writes:

> A picture agrees with reality or fails to agree; it is correct or incorrect, true or false. (TLP 2.21)

> If an elementary proposition is true, the state of affairs exists: if an elementary proposition is false, the state of affairs does not exist. (TLP 4.25)

However, the consensus between early commentators that the *Tractatus* offers a correspondence theory has been challenged or rejected in recent years by several others (Beckerman, 1995; Baker and Hacker, 1980/2005; Potter, 2009; Johnston and Sullivan, forthcoming). One reason for thinking that the *Tractatus* account of truth is not a correspondence theory is that Wittgenstein remarks as early as 1914 that "'p' is true says nothing else but p" (NB 06.10.1914). And in the *Tractatus* he states: "A proposition is true, if what we assert by means of it is the case" (TLP 4.062, Ogden–Ramsey translation). These formulations suggest instead a deflationary account of truth, such as that later developed by Frank Ramsey and Arthur Prior, according to which truth is not a property.

2 The Analysis of "'p' is true"

On the terms of the *Tractatus*, it is clearly not possible for "'p' is true" to say anything more than "p." There are several reasons for this. Wittgenstein explains in detail that a proposition asserts the obtaining of a state of affairs. If "'p' is true" is to say something different from "p," then it must assert the obtaining of a different state of affairs. And the claim that "'"p" is true' is true" must assert the obtaining of a further state of affairs. But it is not clear what these states of affairs could be on the *Tractatus* account.

We might suppose that it asserts that the proposition that p has the property of being true. However, as Hacker has pointed out, this interpretation faces difficulties. *Tractatus* properties are objects, and propositions are representing facts in their projective relation to the world; and so for truth to be a property of propositions, they must enter into states of affairs with the property of truth. While the *Tractatus* explains how objects concatenate to form states of affairs, it does not explain how a representing fact in its projective relation to the world can enter into a state of affairs with an object (Baker and Hacker, 1980/2005, p.351).

One possible response to this point would be to argue that truth need not be a *simple* property. According to the correspondence theory, a proposition is true if there is a fact to which it corresponds. Truth may therefore be better understood as a quantified property, and one should not expect a quantified property to be a *Tractatus* object. We might look for a relation of correspondence between the representing fact and the represented fact instead. In his cryptic discussion of judgment, Wittgenstein does mention the possibility of a "correlation of facts by means of the correlation of their objects" (5.542). One possibility would be for the truth of a representing fact to be a matter of the correlation of its objects with the objects from which a fact in the world is composed. There are nevertheless difficulties with this interpretation. One problem is that a proposition is not a mere representing fact, but a representing fact in its projective relation to the world. That is, in order for the correlation of the objects of the representing fact with the objects of the represented fact to amount to truth, the correlating relation would have to involve the naming relation between words and objects. But this is not something that can be spoken of: along with all that is presupposed by depiction, naming cannot be depicted.

The difficulty can be made clearer by considering the following two propositions:

"p" is true
   p & "p" says that p.

The thought that these two propositions are equivalent may be behind Wittgenstein's remark, quoted earlier, in which he says:

"p" is true says nothing else but p.
   "'p' is true" is – by the above – only a pseudo-proposition like all those connexions of signs which apparently say something that can only be shewn. (NB 06.10.1914)

These remarks are strictly speaking inconsistent, since instances of "p" are not pseudo-propositions. However, it is possible to see what might have led Wittgenstein to make these claims: "'p' is true" might seem to say not only that p but also that the proposition "p" means what it does. It would thus be a conjunction of "p" with a pseudo-proposition. It is plausible to think that, by the time of the *Tractatus*, he had abandoned the view that "'p' is true" is a pseudo-proposition and come to regard it as merely equivalent to "p" (see Baker and Hacker, 1980/2005, p.352).

The difficulty in making sense of a truth ascription on *Tractatus* terms is that it is not possible to say what the sense of a proposition is. A proposition shows its sense (TLP 4.022) and what can be shown cannot be said (TLP 4.1212). The most we can do is state both the representing fact and the represented fact. But if we do this, any apparent truth predicate will disappear in the analysis.

This, however, is what we should expect from the *Tractatus*. For the concepts of "proposition" and "fact" are formal concepts and thus it is impossible to say anything about a proposition or a fact (Baker and Hacker, 1980/2005, p.351). A similar point has been made by Colin Johnston and Peter Sullivan (forthcoming), who point out that the words "sense" (*Sinn*) and "meaning" (*Bedeutung*) are, for Wittgenstein, both incomplete symbols. Talk about facts must be analyzed using the symbol for a fact; that is, by using a proposition.

According to the *Tractatus*, then, "'p' is true" does not say anything more than "p" (or, at most, it states in addition merely the representing fact). If a relational analysis of "'p' is true" is essential for a correspondence theory of truth, then the correspondence interpretation of the *Tractatus* is false.

3   The Metaphysics of Truth

It seems clear, then, that the *Tractatus* does not offer an analysis of propositions of the form "'p' is true" by appeal to the notion of correspondence. Perhaps, however, this is merely because of the *Tractatus*' strictures on what can be said. The *Tractatus* notoriously breaks its own rules in the presentation of its account of representation. Could the ineffable metaphysics of logical atomism imply an ineffable correspondence theory of truth? If so, then agreement (*Übereinstimmung*) and depiction (*Darstellung*) seem to be the two candidates for the relation of correspondence. (See Black, 1971, pp.74ff. for a discussion of Wittgenstein's terminology.)

Wittgenstein writes that an elementary proposition is true if its sense agrees with reality (TLP 2.222). In order to assess whether agreement could be understood as a correspondence relation, it is necessary to investigate what it amounts to. The sense of a proposition is the possible existence of a state of affairs, a possible situation in logical space (TLP 2.221, 2.202). According to the *Tractatus*, for this possible situation to agree with reality is simply for it to be actual, for the possible state of affairs to obtain. Now, being actual cannot be regarded as a property of a possibility. The possibility that p meets the actuality that p *in grammar*, as Wittgenstein would later put it. Thus agreement is not a relation between two independent things, but rather a matter of equivalence (Baker and Hacker, 1980/2005, p.350; Glock, 2006, p.359; Johnston and Sullivan, forthcoming). Agreement cannot, therefore, serve as a correspondence relation for a theory of truth. This aspect of the *Tractatus* account invites comparison with contemporary identity theories of truth. It is important to note, however, that the sense of a

Tractatus proposition is not an entity and that the agreement of sense with the world is therefore not a matter of the sense of a proposition being the same entity as a fact.

It seems, then, that the official account of truth in the *Tractatus* proceeds via the notion of obtainment, through the actuality of a depicted possible situation. Since agreement thus understood is no relation, it cannot serve as the relation of correspondence in a correspondence account of truth. Perhaps, however, the notion of depiction can do better. According to the *Tractatus*, a proposition depicts the obtaining of a state of affairs. We are also given an explanation of how this is possible: through the isomorphism that maps a propositional sign onto a state of affairs. The difficulty with ascribing to the *Tractatus* a correspondence account of truth that employs this notion is that isomorphism is a matter of a proposition's having sense and not of it's being true.

Nevertheless, Hans-Johann Glock has argued that "one can accept that the isomorphism between language and reality is a matter of depiction, and yet explain truth by reference to this isomorphism" (2006, p.358). For this to qualify as a correspondence account, however, depiction must be a relation. Hacker has argued that it is not and therefore could not serve as a correspondence relation between proposition and fact (Baker and Hacker, 1980/2005, pp.350–1). For what a proposition depicts is its sense; and the sense of a proposition is not an actuality but a possibility. *Possibilia* cannot be the *relata* of genuine relations. It might be thought that the relation of depiction would hold between two actualities when the state of affairs depicted obtains – that is, when it is a fact. Hacker stresses, however, that what a proposition depicts must be the same whether or not it is true and so a proposition cannot depict a fact (Baker and Hacker, 1980/2005, p.351).

An additional reason for rejecting the idea that depiction could be a relation between a proposition and a fact concerns Wittgenstein's understanding of facts. Johnston and Sullivan (forthcoming) have argued that the *Tractatus* does not contain a "chunk" view of facts, such as would be required to stand in a relation of correspondence. Instead, the *Tractatus* offers a deflationary account of facts whereby there is nothing more to the existence of the fact that aRb than the truth of "aRb."

There are a number of passages in favor of this view. For instance, Wittgenstein wrote to Russell that "there are no such things as facts" and that talk of facts may helpfully be analyzed away (Letter to Russell, November 1913). While it is clear that Wittgenstein later endorsed these views, the ascription of such an account to the *Tractatus* faces difficulties. In remarks posthumously published as *Philosophical Grammar* Wittgenstein argues that we should not understand facts along the lines of complexes. In doing so he criticizes various aspects of the *Tractatus* account of facts. It seems, then, that Wittgenstein later took the concepts of fact and complex to be confused in the *Tractatus*. For instance, he argues that it is misleading to talk of describing a fact and that it is incorrect to think of facts as having parts: "The fact that these links are so concatenated, isn't composed of anything at all" (PG 201).

These criticisms seem to be aimed at the *Tractatus* claims that a state of affairs is a concatenation of objects and the view that facts, such as representing facts, contain elements. The most plausible interpretation, then, is that Wittgenstein had a substantial account of atomic facts as concatenations of objects. His earlier insistence that there are no such things as facts can then be understood as the claim that facts are not objects in the *Tractatus* sense. The words "fact" and "state of affairs" would be eliminated in an ideal notation, since facts and states of affairs cannot be named.

The central difficulty with accounting for truth in terms of a relation of depiction between proposition and fact can be traced to the *Tractatus* notion of a proposition. For a proposition is not a mere fact: it is a fact in its projective relation to the world. The *Tractatus* claims that, in the case of a true proposition, the elements of the representing fact and the objects in the fact must stand in a relation of isomorphism. The difficulty for giving an account of truth in terms of depiction, explained in terms of isomorphism, is that it is the *propositional sign* that is isomorphic to the fact; but it is the *proposition* that is true.

Perhaps, however, these worries can be put aside. Let us instead investigate whether it is possible to interpret the *Tractatus* as giving a correspondence account of truth in terms of depiction. Glock (2006) derives a correspondence account along the following lines:

> A proposition is true if and only if it depicts a state of affairs that obtains.
>> Since an obtaining state of affairs is a fact, it follows that:
>> A proposition is true if and only it depicts a fact.
>> And by glossing "depiction" as "correspondence" we get:
>> A proposition p is true if and only if there is a fact to which p corresponds.

Glock argues that this *Tractatus* account runs parallel to the paradigmatic correspondence account of truth given by G.E. Moore:

> To say that this belief is true is to say that there is in the Universe a fact to which it corresponds; and to say that it is false is to say that there is not in the Universe a fact to which it corresponds. (Moore, 1953, pp.276–7, quoted in Glock, 2006)

The equivalence Glock derives from the *Tractatus* account does indeed have the same form as that account given by Moore. However, the fact that we can derive such an equivalence from the *Tractatus* does not imply that it is the *Tractatus explanation* of truth. The important difference between the correspondence accounts given by Moore and Russell on the one hand and the *Tractatus* account on the other is that Moore and Russell give criteria of identity for truth-bearers and facts independently of their account of the truth relation between them. That is to say, a fact is defined as a complex of objects and relations, and, in Russell's case, a judgment is defined as a complex of the same objects and relations together with the judging subject. The correspondence relation is then *required* in order to explain how a judgment can be true, i.e., how a complex with a certain construction can be true. In the *Tractatus*, however, a proposition is not defined independently of the fact that would make it true: the proposition is already projected onto the world.

The problem with correspondence theories of truth is that the correspondence of truth-bearer and fact is superfluous:

> The proposition that p is true ↔ The fact that p exists & the proposition that p corresponds to this fact.

Here, the first conjunct on the right hand side is sufficient for the truth of the proposition. Talk of correspondence is redundant, since it is guaranteed by the fact being the fact *that p* and the proposition being the proposition *that p*. If the criteria of identity for fact and proposition are given independently, then the relation between them needs to be explained. In the *Tractatus* the criteria of identity for propositions are given in terms of the facts and possible facts they state. Thus, although it is correct to say that the *Tractatus* account implies that a proposition is true if and only if there is a fact to which it corresponds, this is not the *Tractatus* explanation of truth.

4   The Later Wittgenstein

If it is a matter of debate whether or not Wittgenstein adhered to a deflationary account of truth at the time of the *Tractatus*, it is clear that he later espoused deflationary views about truth. In his later work he abandoned the picture theory of meaning and dissolved the problem of false propositions with the help of his account of meaning as use. For, according to the later Wittgenstein, the meaning of a word is not the object it stands for but its use in the language. The meaningfulness of a proposition that happens to be false is therefore a matter of its having a use and does not require the existence of something in the world to which it refers.

In the *Principles of Linguistic Philosophy*, which draws heavily on discussions with Wittgenstein, Friedrich Waismann writes: "'It is true' and 'It is false' are used to express certain operations, viz. those of asserting and of denying, but they do not stand for qualities of propositions" (PLP 31). Waismann claims that "It is true that p" merely asserts what "p" asserts. Similarly, "the proposition that p is true" says no more than "p." And since operators are iterable, the same can be said of "It is true that it is true that p." ("It is false that it is false that p" will also assert the same as "p.") If, however, "It is true that p" were taken to ascribe a property to the proposition "p," then "It is true that it is true that p" would ascribe the same property to the proposition ascribing truth to "p." Since "It is true" is, on Waismann's view, a null operator, it follows that there is no property of truth, and hence no question as to what truth consists in.

It is worth noting that Wittgenstein and Waismann were aware that "It is true that p" and "p" differ slightly in use – and hence in meaning – despite their apparently categorical claims for the eliminability of the word "true." Waismann notes, for instance, that we typically only use formulations with the word "true" in special circumstances, such as when rejecting a doubt or summing up an argument.

It is the occurrence of "is true" that gives the impression that truth is a property. The equivalence between "It is true that p" and "p" suggests that we do not need to understand truth this way. Nevertheless, there are other contexts in which we cannot simply remove the word "true," contexts such as "What the policeman said is true." (The differences in nuance mentioned above would not stand in the way of the elimination of a truth predicate, since the differences in use are not a matter of a proposition possessing the property of being true.)

Wittgenstein remarked that we might give the following paraphrase of a difficult case:

What he says is true = Things are as he says. (PG 123–4)

He also remarked that "This is how things are," an informal version of the general form of the proposition in the *Tractatus*, can be regarded as a sentential variable. This suggests that we can deal with recalcitrant occurrences of the words "is true" by means of quantification into proposition position. (Wittgenstein had a relaxed attitude to propositional, or sentential, quantification – in the *Tractatus* he remarks that all variables could be analyzed in terms of propositional variables (TLP 3.314).) This approach to the analysis of talk of truth has been pursued in great detail by Arthur Prior (1971).

One problem for deflationary accounts of truth along the lines of Prior has been the treatment of propositions in which we seem to be faced with an ascription of truth to a named proposition. "Pythagoras's Theorem is true," for example, seems to present us with an ineliminable occurrence of the truth predicate (see Künne, 2003, pp.72ff.). Wittgenstein does not directly address this problem, but his discussion of truth suggests a couple of possible responses to it. Wittgenstein writes:

> The proposition "'p' is true" can only be understood if one understands the grammar of the sign "p" as a propositional sign; not if "p" is simply the name of the shape of a particular ink mark. In the end one can say that the quotation marks in the sentence "'p' is true" are simply superfluous. (PG 80)

This is clearly not intended as a comment on correct grammar of German or English but rather as a remark on the role quotation marks should be understood as having in such sentences. Wittgenstein's point is that a sentence does not lose its role as a propositional sign simply by being placed in quotation marks.

We can understand "Pythagoras's Theorem" as a propositional sign in two ways. We might regard it as, in effect, shorthand for "The square of the hypotenuse is equal to the sum of the squares of the other two sides." It is plausible that in order to understand sentences containing the name in mathematical discussions, say, one would need to know what the name abbreviates. In this case, "Pythagoras's Theorem is true" could be analyzed as equivalent to a statement of the theorem.

Of course, the natural response to this suggestion is to point out that someone might correctly be said to know that Pythagoras's Theorem is true without knowing that it is an abbreviation for "The square of the hypotenuse is equal to the sum of the squares of the other two sides." This is quite correct. However, it is clear that in such cases knowing that Pythagoras's Theorem is true falls short of knowing the truth of Pythagoras's Theorem. To know that Pythagoras's Theorem is true in this sense, one need only know that for some p, p and saying that p is called "stating Pythagoras's Theorem." Here "Pythagoras's Theorem" is analyzed in terms of a propositional variable. Whichever strategy we use, if we understand names of propositions as having the grammar of a propositional sign, then they no longer provide ineliminable occurrences of the truth predicate.

References

Baker, G.P. and Hacker, P.M.S. (1980/2005). *Wittgenstein: Understanding and Meaning. Volume 1 of an Analytical Commentary on the Philosophical Investigations. Part 1. Essays*. Second edition. Extensively revised by P.M.S. Hacker. Oxford: Wiley-Blackwell.

Beckermann, A. (2005). Wittgenstein, Neurath und Tarski über Wahrheit. *Zeitschrift für Philosophische Forschung*, 49, 529–552.

Black, M. (1971). *A Companion to Wittgenstein's Tractatus*. Cambridge: Cambridge University Press.

David, M. (2009). The Correspondence Theory of Truth. In E.N. Zalta (Ed.). *The Stanford Encyclopedia of Philosophy*. http://plato.stanford.edu/entries/truth-correspondence/ (last accessed 10 June 2016).

Frascolla, P. (2007). *Understanding Wittgenstein's Tractatus*. London: Taylor and Francis.
Glock, H.-J. (2004). Wittgenstein on Truth. In W. Löffler and P. Weingartner (Eds). *Knowledge and Belief* (pp.13–31). Vienna: Östereichischer Bundesverlag & Hölder Pichler Tempsky.
Glock, H.-J. (2006). Truth in the *Tractatus*. *Synthese*, 148, 345–368.
Hacker, P.M.S. (2001). Naming, Thinking and Meaning in the *Tractatus*. In P.M.S. Hacker. *Connections and Controversies* (pp.170–190). Oxford: Oxford University Press.
Johnston, C. and Sullivan, P. (forthcoming). Judgements, Facts and Propositions: Theories of Truth in Russell, Wittgenstein and Ramsey. In M. Glanzberg (Ed.). *The Oxford Handbook of Truth*. Oxford: Oxford University Press.
Künne, W. (2003). *Conceptions of Truth*. Oxford: Oxford University Press.
Malcolm, N. (1977). *Memory and Mind*. Ithaca: Cornell University Press.
Moore, G.E. (1953). *Some Main Problems of Philosophy*. London: Allen and Unwin.
Potter, M. (2009). *Wittgenstein's Notes on Logic*. Oxford: Oxford University Press.
Prior, A. (1971). *Objects of Thought*. Oxford: Oxford University Press.
Winch, P. (1987). Language, Thought and World in Wittgenstein's *Tractatus*. In P. Winch. *Trying to Make Sense* (pp.3–17). Oxford: Blackwell.

Further Reading

Baker, G.P. and Hacker, P.M.S. (1980/2009). *Wittgenstein: Understanding and Meaning. Volume 1 of an Analytical Commentary on the Philosophical Investigations. Part 1. Essays*. Second edition. Extensively revised by P.M.S. Hacker. Oxford: Wiley-Blackwell.
Glock, H.-J. (2013). Judgement and Truth in the Early Wittgenstein. In M. Textor (Ed.). *Judgement and Truth in Early Analytic Philosophy and Phenomenology* (pp.242–270). Basingstoke: Palgrave Macmillan.
Sullivan, P. (2005). Identity Theories of Truth and the *Tractatus*. *Philosophical Investigations*, 28, 43–62.
Textor, M. (Ed.) (2013). *Judgement and Truth in Early Analytic Philosophy and Phenomenology*. Basingstoke: Palgrave Macmillan.
Wright, C. (1992). *Truth and Objectivity*. Cambridge, MA: Harvard University Press.

Part VII

Mind and Action

28

Privacy and Private Language

EDWARD KANTERIAN

1   Preliminary

Wittgenstein's discussion of a private language in *Philosophical Investigations* §§243–315 is of central importance for his later philosophy. It challenges key traditional ideas in the philosophy of mind, epistemology, and philosophy of language. One of these is the idea of a person as a mind or soul, the subject of thought and feeling, interacting with the body, but distinct from it. Another is the idea that knowledge is acquired by two types of observation, internal and external. By introspection we obtain direct and certain knowledge about inner, private objects such as sensations, emotions, and thoughts, and by the senses we obtain indirect, less certain knowledge about external, public objects, including our bodies. A third idea is that we give names to types of inner, private objects, producing the basic vocabulary from which our language is built.

These three mutually supporting ideas suggest that our common language is private, insofar as its psychological vocabulary ("pain," "think," etc.) refers in each person's idiolect to the mental entities they experience. These are unknowable to others, or at best knowable by inference to the best explanation only. In attacking the possibility of a private language, Wittgenstein rejects the conceptions of mind, of knowledge and self-knowledge, and of language, on which the idea of such a language depends. This attack has been labeled "the private language argument" (a phrase Wittgenstein himself never used). The label can be understood in two ways. In a broad sense it covers many arguments in PI §§243–315, concerning the privacy of experience, the relation between the inner and outer, the relation between sensation and its natural and linguistic expression, etc. In a narrow sense it concerns the possibility of inventing a private language, whose words are introduced by private ostensive definitions (PI §258).

I discuss Wittgenstein's private language arguments in both the broad and the narrow sense, focusing on some key sections in PI §§243–315. I begin by introducing the traditional ideas Wittgenstein's arguments can be seen as undermining.

A Companion to Wittgenstein, First Edition. Edited by Hans-Johann Glock and John Hyman.
© 2017 John Wiley & Sons, Ltd. Published 2017 by John Wiley & Sons, Ltd.

2 The Traditional Picture

The idea that each of us enjoys, within the confines of his mind, a radically private form of subjectivity, given to us with complete certainty, but about which others can only conjecture, comes naturally to us. "How can somebody else ever know what I mean by 'pain' and 'love'?," I may ask. The others would need to have *my* experience; but this, it appears, is impossible. Again, I can be in pain and conceal it, and also not be in pain and pretend I am. This seems to make sensations radically private in two ways: nobody else can truly know what I experience (*epistemic privacy*), and nobody else can have the experience I have (*private ownership*). Equally, when I am in pain, I find it impossible to doubt it. This seems to make my sensations indubitably knowable (to myself). We also have general names for sensations, just as we have names for kinds of material objects. This seems to turn sensations into countable objects with criteria of identity similar to those of material objects. Again, in trying to describe to others what we experience when we see something red, don't we come up against the limits of communication? And are not all mental "contents" like this? Don't they all have an indescribable, subjective feel about them, known to the subject alone? Our inner life seems a distinct realm from the outer world, distinct in both epistemological and ontological respects, since it is a world populated by objects known and owned only by the person, ego, or self.

Many philosophers have shared the picture or aspects of the picture underlying these views, and have sublimated them into philosophical theories. Locke argued that no one can err about the simple ideas external objects cause in their mind, for example the idea of blue caused in me when I look at a violet, whether or not the idea corresponds to anything in the violet itself (Locke, 1689, 2.32.14). There is an epistemic gap between me and the external world, and I enjoy a special relation to everything that is in my own mind. This allows for simple ideas caused by the same external object to differ in different people, while each idea remains correct: the "idea that a violet produced in one man's mind by his eyes [could be] the same that a marigold produced in another man's, and vice versa" (Locke, 1689, 2.32.15). But "this could never be known, because one man's mind could not pass into another man's body" (Locke, 1689, 2.32.15). So simple ideas are indubitable and epistemically private, and their owner has privileged and immediate access to them. Since Locke also believes that the meaning of a word is established by its association with an idea, we each speak a private language. "Words, in their primary or immediate signification, stand for nothing but *the ideas in the mind of him that uses them*" (Locke, 1689, 3.3.2, 8).

Similar ideas persisted in the empiricist tradition down to Russell (e.g., Hume, 1739, 1.1.4.2; Russell, 1912, pp.27ff), but were also held by anti-empiricists, for example by Kant and Frege. Kant argued that the "thinking subject is not corporeal," which "is equivalent to saying that thinking beings, as such, can never be found by us among outer appearances, and that their thoughts cannot be outwardly intuited," as "these belong to inner sense" (Kant, [1781/87], A357). Since the only thoughts I can have through my inner sense are mine, I cannot have any experience of other minds. All I can do, on Kant's account, is to project my self onto another outer appearance, a body, "substitute, as it were, my own subject for the object I am seeking to consider" (A353f; for discussion see Hacker, 2013, p.55; cf. Chapter 45, WITTGENSTEIN AND KANTIANISM).

These traditional views reached Wittgenstein indirectly, through the works of Frege and Russell. Even if Wittgenstein was only responding to philosophers he immediately engaged with – Frege, Russell, the participants in his discussions in Vienna and Cambridge (cf. Baker, 1998, p.353; see also Chapter 4, WITTGENSTEIN AND FREGE; Chapter 5, WITTGENSTEIN AND RUSSELL; and Chapter 46, WITTGENSTEIN AND THE VIENNA CIRCLE) – it does not follow that his arguments don't apply to the preceding tradition. The same idea can be developed by different thinkers, in different times, and arguments in favor or against it will be relevant, with some hermeneutic adjustments, to its various historical manifestations.

Frege explicitly argued that each idea (*Vorstellung*) is privately owned and exclusively accessible to one individual, in contrast to the public accessibility of logical and mathematical objects, especially thoughts (*Gedanken*). While "another man's idea is *per se* another idea," the number two is not an idea, or else it would be, absurdly, just mine (Frege, 1884, §27, p.37). He thought that when we both look at the same field, each of us has a numerically distinct sense impression of green. Unlike physical or abstract objects, impressions, ideas, sensations need a bearer. "Nobody else has my pain. Someone may have sympathy with me, but still my pain belongs to me and his sympathy to him" (Frege, 1984, p.361). From the private ownership of ideas, Frege deduces their epistemic privacy. In order for you to know whether you have the same or a similar sense impression as I, it would have to be possible to compare our sense impressions with one another. But my impression is not transferable, he argues.

> [If] one idea disappeared from one mind, and at the same time another idea appeared in another mind, this would not give an answer to the question whether this would be the same idea. (Frege, 1984, p.367)

No one "has another's idea, only his own, and no one even knows how far his idea – e.g. of red – coincides with another's" (Frege, 1984, p.198). What populates the mind is both privately owned and epistemically private. To this inner realm belong not only sensations and ideas, but also intentional states such as "inclinations, wishes and decisions" (1984, p.360), and even thinking, judging, and inferring (1979, p.253). But if the grasping of a thought is private, how can I know I am grasping the same thought or judgment as you? I can only go by your assertions, which are merely the outward expressions of your judgments, which are subjective mental acts (1979, p.2). Since we can find certainty only "in the inner world while doubt never altogether leaves us in our excursions into the outer world" (1984, p.367), I have no means to know what you really think and mean, following Frege. Moreover, Frege admitted the existence of so-called I-thoughts, in which everyone "is presented to himself in a special and primitive way, in which he is presented to no one else" (1979, p.359). This threatens the objectivity of logic as the science of all truth, since true I-thoughts are subjective truths (cf. Kremer, 2010, p.281ff). Given these private foundations of our idiolects, the possibility of our objective scientific language, so important to Frege, remained unexplained by him (see Frege, 1984, pp.182f, 300f; Kanterian, 2012, pp.27ff). Like many philosophers before him, Frege's claim to shared objective knowledge was built on the shifting sands of subjectivity. Let us now see how Wittgenstein challenged this tradition.

3   The Possibility of a Private Language (PI §§239, 243)

In the discussion preceding section 243 Wittgenstein argues that for a language to be a means of communication its speakers must share a common background. This background can't be established by definitions. Definitions, ostensive or otherwise, are not the foundation of a language, but more advanced linguistic phenomena. In order to understand an ostensive definition like "This is called 'blue'" (indicating a sample), one must understand that what is being defined is a color name (PI §30). The stage for the entrance of this name must already be prepared. A variety of things belong to this stage-setting (or, more precisely, to this stage's being set), especially agreement in judgments and forms of life (PI §§241–2; see Chapter 26, LANGUAGES, LANGUAGE-GAMES, AND FORMS OF LIFE). These provide the background against which a speaker can follow linguistic rules (PI §§185–242; see Chapter 24, RULES AND RULE-FOLLOWING) and possess criteria of correctness for meaning, reference, valid inference, etc.

If this is what is presupposed by language's being a means of communication, could there also be an incommunicable language, comprehensible only to one speaker and not learnable by anyone else? The private language hypothesis claims that there could be such a thing. The hypothesis is adumbrated in section 239 of the *Investigations*, which asks how a speaker is supposed to know which color he is to pick out when he hears the word "red." This is to ask for a definition, an explanation of what the word "red" means, a rule for his use of the word. Wittgenstein examines the possibility that here one might invoke a mental process underpinning the definition and offer as a definition of "red" something like "'Red' means the color whose image occurs to me when I hear the word 'red.'" Since this definition is made by reference to a mental, and hence apparently private, image of red, serving as a sample of what "red" means, the possibility opens up of an incommunicable language independent of agreement in forms of life.

Section 243 asks whether such a language is possible, a language "in which a person could write down or give voice to his inner experiences," a language whose words "refer to what only the speaker can know – to his immediate private sensations," "his feelings, moods, and so on," so that another person could not understand this language.

4   The Replacement Model (PI §§244–5)

Wittgenstein focuses next on names for sensations, the supposed basis of a private language. "How do words *refer* to sensations? [...] How does a human being learn the meaning of names of sensations?" (PI §244). One model of what it means to introduce a name for an object is considered earlier in the book: it is to attach a label to the object (PI §15; cf. MS 124, p.222f). But sensations can't be named in this way, because labels cannot literally be attached to them. Another model is to introduce a name by ostensive definition, i.e., by pointing at what is named or at a sample of what is named. This model is considered later, in section 258 (see below). Section 244 indicates a third possibility: neither labeling nor defining, but progressively *replacing* a natural expression or manifestation of a sensation with more sophisticated linguistic expressions. Words like "pain," Wittgenstein writes,

> are connected with the primitive, natural, expressions of sensation and used in their place. A child has hurt itself and cries; adults talk to it comfortingly [*zusprechen*] and teach it exclamations and, later, sentences. They teach the child new pain-behaviour. (PI §244)

In primitive cases pain behavior, such as crying out, is just a manifestation of pain. Later, linguistic expressions of pain are introduced, partly replacing natural pain behavior. They are extensions of that behavior, grafted onto it, but also reflecting the progression of the child from involuntary manifestations of pain to more controlled and discriminate linguistic manifestations.

The ability to control the expression of one's feelings in non-extreme cases opens up the possibility both of concealing and also of describing one's states. Such descriptions cannot be straightforwardly understood as pain behavior (see below). The replacement model, by contrast, is concerned with a more primordial stage. The question whether screams and later expressions like "Ow!" or "It hurts!" refer to anything, as opposed to manifesting something, does not arise in the most primitive case. Screams do not, as a rule, contain an expression that in other cases is used to refer to something. The subject in pain does not observe or look into herself, choose appropriate words and report her feelings by saying "It hurts!," "My leg!," or "I am in pain!" (PI §290). Such exclamations are substitutes for natural groans or cries and, like groaning or crying, *escape* from the speaker (see Kripke, 1982, p.135). In addition, our natural reaction to seeing somebody exhibiting pain behavior is not to postulate a hidden inner state on the basis of observed evidence. "If I see someone writhing in pain with evident cause, I do not think: all the same, his feelings are hidden from me" (PPF §324; see also PI §310; PPF §30). Instead, we pity him, rush to his aid, attempt to comfort him (Kripke, 1982, p.137; Hacker, 1990/93a, p.88). And if we do not do this, it is typically not because we think he is an automaton or made of stone, but perhaps because we are indifferent to his suffering.

Given the close connection Wittgenstein presents between pain and pain behavior, the end of section 244 addresses the charge of behaviorism: "'So you are saying that the word "pain" really means crying?'" Wittgenstein replies: "On the contrary: the verbal expression of pain replaces crying, it does not describe it" (PI §244; see also §§304–315 and LSD 110ff).

Wittgenstein's replacement model undermines the idea of a private language because it denies that the meaning of a sensation name is something private and internal, only contingently related to the natural and linguistic manifestation of the sensation. Language cannot be interposed between pain and the expression of pain (PI §245), i.e., one cannot sever the conceptual connection between the word "pain" and the behavioral manifestations of pain. So the conceptual structure in this domain is quite unlike that in which we label an object or introduce a name for it by definition. Natural expressions of pain, observable by everybody, are part of the phenomenon of pain, and first-person linguistic expressions of pain, while becoming more complex and partly more controllable as a human grows up, remain rooted in these public natural expressions. Wittgenstein concludes in section 256 that since "my words for sensations [are] tied up with my natural expressions of sensation [...] my language is not a 'private' one. Someone else might understand it as well as I" (PI §256).

5   Two Senses of Privacy

In sections 246–54 of the *Investigations*, Wittgenstein addresses the main idea underlying the private language hypothesis, mental privacy. As seen in Locke and Frege, this divides into two ideas, epistemic privacy and private ownership. What is their relation?

My pain is supposed to be epistemically private because only I, the sufferer, can know I am in pain, while others can only make guesses (PI §§246, 303). This is often thought to imply that knowledge of my pain is infallible and immediate. I could not be in pain and fail to feel it, or feel as if I were in pain when I am not. Also, I don't feel it by perceiving something else. So it appears that "I am in pain" is knowable only to me, whereas "He is in pain" is merely a hypothesis. What motivates this view? It could be argued that it is the fact that each of us privately *owns* their pain. If this pain is mine only, nobody else can have it. Therefore, the reason why only I can know I am in pain is the special relation I have to my pain. Private ownership of mental states supports their epistemic privacy. Wittgenstein makes this connection explicit in his lecture notes: the "experience [of pain] is not communicable, but I know it – because I have it" (LPE 277).

Could one also argue from epistemic privacy to private ownership? In section 272 Wittgenstein writes: "The essential thing about private experience is really not that each person possesses his own specimen, but that nobody knows whether other people also have this or something else" (PI §272). Does this suggest that epistemic privacy is independent of whether my pain is privately owned, or rather that epistemic privacy entails private ownership? It could be argued that if my pain is epistemically private, then I must have immediate and complete identifying knowledge about it. Since I can't know your pain in the same way, your pain and my pain must be different. If we shared the same pain, and I didn't know this, there would be an aspect of my pain opaque to me, namely the fact that it is also owned by you. But I am not missing any aspect of my pain. Therefore, the way in which I know my pain determines my pain as a pain only I can have.

If this is correct, then the two notions of privacy are mutually reinforcing. Rejecting one notion undermines the other as well, and vice versa. However, Wittgenstein suggests separate arguments against each notion. Following his lead, I first address private ownership, developing an argument based on a suggestion in section 253 of the *Investigations*, which strengthens Wittgenstein's case against private ownership. Then, I present and defend Wittgenstein's discussion of epistemic privacy.

6   Private Ownership: Numerical and Qualitative Identity (PI §253)

Private ownership is the impossibility of different people having the same sensation. If a pain is mine, it is mine only. But don't we often speak in a way that suggests people can and do have the same sensation? "Take this pill, if you have the same pain as your wife" (said by a doctor to her patient) or "They were both overcome by vertigo" make perfectly good sense. In response, the defender of private ownership can resort to the distinction between numerical and qualitative identity. Yes, two subjects may share the same pain, but only in a qualitative, not a numerical sense. While they cannot have one and the same sensation, they can have similar sensations, that is, distinct sensations possessing the same qualities.

Wittgenstein gives a brief response to this proposal in section 253 of *Philosophical Investigations*. His recommendation is to focus on the criteria of identity involved here. Does the qualitative–numerical distinction apply uniformly to all cases in which we speak of identity or sameness? The paradigmatic application of the qualitative–numerical distinction is the case of physical objects, objects with a spatiotemporal location. So it makes sense to say "This chair is not the one you saw here yesterday, but is exactly the same as it [*ein genau gleicher*]" (PI §253).

Equally, the color of my living room *used to be* the same as the color of your living room, but *now* that I have repainted my living room, it *no longer* is. The value of my house used to be exactly the same as that of your house, but is no longer so. It is more appropriate to speak of identity *simpliciter* in such cases. Prices, addictions, academic degrees, political views, colors, etc., are not objects to which the qualitative–numerical distinction applies. I will now show that the same holds for sensations as well, in spite of the fact that even that we sometimes apply temporal and indeed spatial distinctions to them.

7   Private Ownership and Spatial Specifications of Sensations

Suppose I have a throbbing pain in my left hand and you have a throbbing pain in your left hand. Does this not entitle us to say that these are numerically distinct but qualitatively identical pains, just as we might have numerically distinct but qualitatively identical rings on our fingers? No. To specify the location of a pain is to specify the part of the body that hurts, not the place where an object is to be found, and from which it can be moved. My pain does not move from one room to the other when I do so. It is not in the room in the sense in which the chair is in the room. It is not even in my hand in the sense in which the chair is in the room. There are different senses of "in," of "locality" (cf. BB 8; for a dissenting view see Hyman, 2003). This is why Wittgenstein adds the proviso "In so far as it makes *sense* to say that my pain is the same as his, it is also possible for us both to have the same pain" (PI §253). We cannot share a pain in the sense in which we can share a car, although we may have the same pain in the sense in which we can have the same height or weight. Thus pains are not like, say, material objects, to which the qualitative–numerical distinction applies. The dualistic tendencies of our natural reasoning about ourselves tempt us to treat sensations on a par with material objects, as if having a pain is like having a car.

To avoid philosophical confusion, instead of speaking about "having a pain" it may be preferable to speak of a part of the body aching, hurting, and doing so in a specific manner. Of course, body parts are material objects, unlike pains. But since for me to have a throbbing pain in my big left toe is for my toe to hurt in a specific manner, and since for you to have a throbbing pain in your big left toe is for your toe to hurt in a specific manner, the qualitative–numerical distinction is not applicable here in the way proposed by the defender of private ownership. *What* hurts *is* numerically distinct and qualitatively identical, namely our respective toes, but the specific manner in which they hurt is the same – not just qualitatively, as opposed to numerically the same, but simply the same.

One might object that a certain analogue of the qualitative–numerical distinction can be applied to pains when I have a throbbing pain in my foot and also a throbbing pain in my hand. So – don't I have two distinct, but similar pains? No. Distinct are merely the body parts - which hurt me in exactly the same way.

But what of phantom pain? After all, feeling left-leg-pain when my left leg has been amputated can't mean that my left leg hurts. But phantom pain could not become the rule (Hacker, 1990/93a, p.21). It is an anomaly, which does not sever the conceptual relation between "having a pain" and "a certain body part hurting in a specific way." True, the location of a phantom pain is a kind of illusion – it feels to the amputee just as if he had a pain where his left leg would have been. But the pain is no illusion, and intelligible, as a left-leg-pain, only against the background that I once had a left leg, which has hurt me or could have hurt me in a specific way.

8   Private Ownership and Temporal Specifications of Sensations

Pains have duration. Does this not provide us with a principle of individuation? I may say that I have exactly the same pain in my hand and foot, but since my hand, but not my foot, may stop hurting, this surely shows that I have two numerically distinct pains, which partly overlap in time. — Equally, suppose that Tim and Tom have the same pain in their left feet, and that Tim's pain ceases, while Tom's continues. This seems to prove that Tim has a numerically different pain from Tom, analogously to the case in which the fact that Tim's graduation party ends at 10 p.m., while Tom's graduation party ends at midnight, implies that these are different parties of the same type.

Wittgenstein rejects this line of thought in the "Blue Book" (54f), but does not give an argument (see Glock, 1996, p. 306). He may have had the following in mind. What the example shows is not that the qualitative–numerical distinction applies to pains, but only that Tim's left foot has ceased to hurt him, while Tom's has not, and that, therefore, they don't have the same (*simpliciter*) pain anymore. The suggestion here is that specifications of duration apply primarily to how long the respective *body part* is hurting, and only by extension to pains construed as (countable) entities.

Still, is it not obvious that the pains are numerically distinct, given not only that Tim's pain lasted from the morning to lunchtime, while Tom's from the morning to the evening, but also that Tim's pain was alleviated by an aspirin, while Tom's wasn't, etc.? However, these are not genuine criteria of identity of pains. Tim's pain is not individuated by its termination or what terminates it (aspirin). We don't have to wait to see *whose pain* ends first or what ends *it* in order to distinguish the pains numerically. For otherwise circularity threatens: how would we know which pain has ended first or has been ended by aspirin? If Tim's and Tom's pain never stops and they die at the same time, shall we conclude that Tim and Tom had, after all, the exactly same pain after all? This would make identity a contingent matter.

Overall, the case is parallel to properties of material objects, such as colors. While the qualitative–numerical distinction applies to chairs, it does not apply to their properties as well. Two chairs can have the same color and two people the same pain. We should not confuse the individuating criteria for material objects with those for pains or colors (Rundle, 1979, p. 233).

9   Dependent Particulars?

The proponent of the private ownership thesis may find himself inclined to believe that pains are "dependent particulars," a claim that has also been made with respect to colors of individual objects ("tropes"). As seen, Frege thought this about mental items. The view has also been defended by Strawson and more recently by Wolfgang Künne (Strawson, 1959, p. 57f; Künne, 2009, p. 38f; for a reply to Künne see Schroeder, 2013). In *Philosophical Remarks* Wittgenstein writes:

> What distinguishes *his* toothache from *mine*? If the word "toothache" means the same in "I have toothache" and "He has toothache", what does it then mean to say he can't have the same toothache as I do? How are toothaches to be distinguished from one another? By intensity and similar characteristics, and by location. But suppose these are the same in the

two cases? But if it is objected that the distinction is simply that in the one case I have it, in the other he; then the owner is a defining mark of the toothache itself; but then what does the proposition "I have toothache" (or someone else does) assert? Nothing at all. (PR 91; see also BB 55)

This suggests a *reductio ad absurdum* of the claim that pains are dependent particulars. Particularly intriguing is Wittgenstein's claim that private ownership ultimately entails that the owner is a defining mark of his pain (see also Kenny, 1971, p.215). Consider the parallel case of colors: if what individuates the (alleged) bearer-dependent property *this red* is the fact that it is possessed by this chair, we should be able simply to read off from this property that it is the property of this chair. In fact, nothing about a property tells me to which *specific* object it belongs. This is why it is possible to confuse two objects, because they share a property, e.g., two cats the property of being white. Conversely, we distinguish objects if they differ in their properties. But to infer that this chair is not identical to that chair because they have different bearer-dependent properties (*this red* vs. *that red*), presupposes that their properties are different because their bearers are. This potential circularity undermines the laws of identity, e.g., the Identity of Indiscernibles, which allows us to infer the identity of A and B in a nontrivial manner (by checking their properties without knowing whether A = B). For if we allow a property like *the red of this object* and note the presence of this very bearer-dependent property in an object we call "A" and an object we call "B," we could immediately and trivially infer that A = B, without going through the list of genuine properties. These problems emerge for all so-called dependent particulars, colors as much as properties like *having this toothache*.

Moreover, if the owner is a defining mark of a toothache, *having a toothache* is something entirely different in my case than in yours, since it constitutes a different property range in each case (*having this$_1$ toothache$_{Edward}$, having this$_2$ toothache$_{Edward}$,* etc. versus *having that$_1$ toothache$_{Ludwig}$, having that$_2$ toothache$_{Ludwig}$,* etc.). But without the minimal common ground of the "universal" *having a toothache*, the qualitative–numerical distinction for dependent particulars, including pains, makes little sense, for we can't even say that you and I have (distinct or similar) *toothaches* (see PI §§261, 294, and below). The assumption that toothaches, etc., are dependent particulars implies its refutation.

One could reply that, following this logic, "having a spouse" would mean something different for different subjects, for on the assumption of monogamy, no two people can have the same spouse, which is absurd. But the cases are different. Having a spouse is a relational property, having a pain is not. There are true counterfactual statements for the first case. While my actual spouse is Anna Matzy, my spouse could have been Liv Tyler. The meaning of "spouse" or "my spouse" is stable across these two scenarios. By contrast, none of my toothaches, actual and possible, could have been had by anyone else, *if* they are privately owned by me.

We can conclude, following Wittgenstein's suggestion in section 253 of the *Investigations*, that insofar as it makes sense to say that my pain is the same as yours, it is possible for both of us to have simply the same pain or sensation, and not just qualitatively the same pain or sensation. The idea of private ownership is not coherent and no private language can be built on the basis of it. I will now discuss the notion of epistemic privacy.

10 Epistemic Privacy: Wittgenstein's Main Argument (PI §§246, 248)

Wittgenstein discusses epistemic privacy in sections 246–250. The discussion addresses two related claims: the cognitivist claim that only I can really know I am in pain, and the claim that others can only surmise that I am in pain. (For a defense of cognitivism without privacy see Hyman, 1999; for a reply see Hacker, 2005). Characteristically, Wittgenstein turns these claims on their heads: only others can and often do know I am in pain, while I can't meaningfully be said to know or not to know I am in pain. Where the philosophical tradition had taken propositions like "I am in pain" and "I see something red" as paradigms of indubitable knowledge, Wittgenstein argues that they are not instances of knowledge at all. Where there can be knowledge, there can also be doubt, and vice versa (cf. OC §§10, 115, 121). But I cannot doubt whether I am in pain. That would have to involve some evidence that I am and some evidence that I am not in pain. But neither makes sense. Nothing counts as evidence, for me, that I am in pain or not. We find it odd, indeed unintelligible, to say "From observing myself I know I am in agony" (Glock, 1996, p.308). As Wittgenstein argues in various places (e.g., Z §549), this shows that the impossibility of first-person doubt is connected to other impossibilities, the impossibility of having evidence, of believing, checking, finding out, suspecting, hoping, investigating, thinking but being unsure, being corrected, etc.

Various objections come to mind. One might think that "I can know I am in pain" amounts to "I can recognize what is happening to me" and declare the latter as obviously true when I am in pain (Snowdon, 2011, p.424). But "recognize" is just another cognitive verb, so Wittgenstein's point reapplies, for it does not make sense to say "I had a pain, but I did not recognize it" (see Hacker, 1990/93a, p.28). One could also object to Wittgenstein by pointing out that "I doubt whether I am in pain" might be like "I am dead," a sentence which makes sense even if it can't be true. But the cases are different, which we can see from a grammatical comparison. The opposite of "I am dead" is "I am alive," which is true whenever I say it, unlike "I know I am in pain." "I am dead" makes sense, in part, because it can be embedded in true contexts, e.g., in "When I am dead, you will miss me" or "I am dead, if you can't pay the ransom." This does not work for "I doubt I am in pain." Finally, Wittgenstein's position is also not refuted by pointing out that pain comes in degrees and that somebody experiencing certain levels of discomfort might say they don't know whether they are in pain (cf. Snowdon, 2011, p.425). That is just a matter of semantic doubt, about the boundaries between "pain" and "discomfort," not doubt about whether I am really having this experience, i.e., pain or discomfort (cf. LPE 305).

So Wittgenstein suggests that speaking of knowledge of *one's* pain does not make sense. Pairs of contradictory propositions like "I know/doubt/suspect/am mistaken that I am in pain – I don't know/doubt/suspect/am not mistaken that I am in pain" are excluded by the grammar of "pain" and of the epistemic verbs, i.e., by the rules of the language-games in which these expressions can occur. Conversely, since it is possible to doubt/suspect/be mistaken that *someone else* is in pain, it is also possible to know so (PI §246). To claim otherwise, i.e., that in principle I cannot know, but only believe, suspect, conjecture that you are in pain, is to use these psychological verbs without their customary point and meaning.

> When [...] you granted me that a man can't know whether the other person has pain, you do not wish to say that as a matter of fact people didn't know, but that it made no sense to say they knew (and therefore no sense to say they don't know). If therefore in this case you

use the term "conjecture" or "believe", you don't use it as opposed to "know". That is, you did not state that knowing was a goal which you could not reach, and that you have to be contented with conjecturing; rather, there is no goal in this game. (BB 54)

Wittgenstein's denial that I can know I am in pain may seem obviously false if one takes "I don't know whether I am in pain" to express ignorance, i.e., that I am in pain, but don't know it (cf. Snowdon, 2011, p.424). But this is not what Wittgenstein meant; he was not advancing an ignorance claim, true by necessity. Rather, he argued that if "A knows that P" is to make sense, a certain modal condition has to be fulfilled. This condition is: if it is true that A knows that P, then a genuine possibility is hereby excluded, namely the possibility that A does not know that P (i.e., that it is true that P and A is ignorant about it). In other words, if "A knows that P" makes sense, then its negation must also make sense. If I know I am in Canterbury, the possibility that I don't know whether I am in Canterbury is excluded, but still makes sense. Knowing that P implies that it is possible to know that P and possible to be ignorant that P. Accordingly, "I know I am in pain" would make sense only if "I don't know whether I am in pain" made sense. But it does not.

While, for Wittgenstein, utterances like "I am in pain" don't express knowledge, let alone indubitable knowledge, there is something special about them. My expression of my pain carries special weight. It is a criterion for *others* to judge and know I am in pain. As Glock puts it:

> The kernel of truth in epistemic privacy is first-person authority: I am in a position to say what I feel, experience, think, not because I have infallible access to a private peep-show, but because what I say, unlike what others say about me, is (typically) an avowal, a groundless expression or manifestation of the inner. (Glock, 1996, p.309; see also MS 124, p.228; Hacker, 1990/93a, p.31; and Chapter 29, THE INNER AND THE OUTER)

11   Epistemic Privacy: Meaningful Uses

Wittgenstein's rejection of epistemic privacy rests on the view that sentences like "I know I am in pain" are meaningless. But he actually argues that "I know I am in pain" is either meaningless or redundant, amounting to "I am in pain" (LPE 309; cf. PI §246; BB 55). Obviously, this redundancy claim does not vindicate the thesis that I have (indubitable) self-knowledge about my experiences. There are, however, contexts in which "I know I am in pain," and also corresponding propositions with other psychological verbs, like "think" and "want," are meaningful and not redundant, such as emphatic, decision-based, concessive, and contrastive uses. Do these pose a challenge to Wittgenstein's view?

In the emphatic use, "I know I am in pain" amounts to "I really *am* in pain," countering doubt about the sincerity of one's pain avowal. This does not support cognitivism. The same is true for uses expressing decisions and concessions. If, after deliberating, I exclaim "Now I know what I want," this expresses having made up my mind, not my having discovered what I want. If I don't want to go to the dentist, and you keep repeating that my pain is not going away, I might exclaim "Stop pestering me – I know I am in pain!" This does not express what I already know, but concedes what you say.

What of other contrastive uses? One might argue that to exclude a negation such as "I don't know I am in pain" is not to exclude all possible contrasts to "I know I am in pain." It appears that sometimes "I know I am in pain" can be uttered in contrast to ascriptions of ignorance to others, as in "*I* know I am in pain, but *she* is ignorant of it" (Glock, 1996, p.308). However, by the redundancy thesis this amounts to "I am in pain, but she doesn't know it," and indeed, the pronoun "it" refers here to the fact that I am in pain, not to the fact that I know I am. The cognitive claim concerns somebody else, and is really contrasted with an (emphatic) avowal of my pain. Contrastive uses of this kind don't undermine Wittgenstein's denial that I can know I am in pain.

12 Epistemic Privacy: Lying About Inner Processes, and Logical Transformations

Another objection rests on the assumption that to lie is to utter something one knows (or believes) to be false in order to deceive. So if I can lie about my pain by saying falsely that I am not in pain, I must surely know that I am in pain. A reply on Wittgenstein's behalf might point out that not all cases of lying have to fit this definition. A "lie about inner processes is of a different category from one about outer processes" (MS 169, p.104). It is possible to lie about something of which it makes no sense to say that one knows it to be so. To lie about one's pain is either to be in pain and deny that one is, or not to be in pain and avow that one is, typically with the intent to deceive (see Hacker, 1972/86, p.300; 1990/93b, p.33). (Wittgenstein offers a long and intricate discussion of lying about inner processes at LPE 293 ff.)

It has been claimed, against Wittgenstein, that certain logical transformations show that one can know that one has a sensation. If I feel cold and I know that everyone else in the room feels cold, I can be said to know that everybody in the room feels cold. It seems to follow, by universal instantiation, that I know I feel cold (Williamson, 2000, p.93 and Hacker, 1972, p.267; Hacker, 1972/86, pp.303f recants). But it is a contingent matter whether I am surrounded by other people about whom I know that they feel cold. A contingent matter can't decide a conceptual issue. The testing case still remains the solitary situation, and here the logical transformation loses its bite. If I am alone in the room and feel cold, the primary inference would not be from "I know that everybody in the room feels cold" to "I know I feel cold," but vice versa, and then the question remains what "I know I feel cold" *means*. On Wittgenstein's account it either means nothing, or is an emphatic assertion of "I feel cold."

13 Epistemic Privacy: Reporting that One is in Pain

Another objection to Wittgenstein is that I can provide my doctor with an elaborate *report* about the sort of pain I am experiencing, e.g., by saying "My pain is now more intense than it was in the last five days." Indeed, even "I am in pain" can be used as a report, e.g., when I am asked to describe my state in a daily hospital questionnaire. Does this show that I can have knowledge of my pain? One can grant that we have knowledge in such cases, but still insist on the difference between avowals and descriptions. Thus:

To call the expression of a sensation a statement is misleading because "testing", "justification", "confirmation", "refutation" of the statement are connected with the word "statement" in the language-game. (Z §549; cf. PI §22)

Remarkably, while much of his discussion of privacy and the private language hypothesis indicates differences between descriptions (reports, statements, claims) and avowals/expressions of sensation, in some instances Wittgenstein is more interested in stressing their similarities:

A cry is not a description. But there are intermediate cases. And the words "I am afraid" may approximate more, or less, to being a cry. They may come very close to one, and also be *very* far removed from it. (PPF §83)

These observations leave intact the denial that avowals are descriptions in primitive cases. They also demonstrate that Wittgenstein's aim is not to establish linguistic prohibitions, but direct our attention to the grammatical variety behind the uniform appearance of a form of words that captivates our imagination (cf. Chapter 13, PHILOSOPHY AND PHILOSOPHICAL METHOD). "I know I am in pain" is nonsense (PI §246), if construed on the model of "I know he is in pain" or "I know I am half-Armenian," i.e., if one language-game is crossed with another. In other contexts, it may not be nonsense, although it lends no support to epistemic privacy:

If I say "This statement has no sense", I could just point out statements with which we are inclined to mix it up, and point out the difference. This is all that is meant. – If I say "It seems to convey something and doesn't", this comes to "it seems to be of this kind and isn't". This statement is senseless only if you try to compare it with what you can't compare it with. What is wrong is to overlook the difference. (LSD 130)

14 Epistemic Privacy: Grammatical Uses

This brings us to one more meaningful use of propositions related to "I know I am in pain," namely "Only I know I am in pain" (Glock, 1996, p. 307), "Sensations are private" (PI §248), "Only you can know if you had that intention" (PI §247). These, Wittgenstein maintains, are grammatical propositions, expressing rules of grammar, and can be used to explain how certain words are used: "The sentence 'Sensations are private' is comparable to 'One plays patience by oneself'" (PI §248; see Chapter 14, GRAMMAR AND GRAMMATICAL STATEMENTS). The analogy with rules of games belongs to Wittgenstein's general rejection of metaphysical necessity (see Chapter 21, NECESSITY AND APRIORITY). Just as the fact that patience is played by oneself does not answer to any necessity in the world, but partly determines what we call "patience," so "Sensations are private" expresses a grammatical rule, whether the rule that doubt is excluded in language-games played with psychological terms, that one can hide one's pain, that one can't point at one's own sensation (MS 116, p. 179), or that sincere avowals have a criterial role for others.

In conclusion, neither these grammatical uses nor any of the meaningful contexts discussed above imply that my sensations are epistemically private to me and unknowable to others. (For a discussion of more objections see Hacker, 1972/86, pp. 302 ff.)

15 Knowledge of Other Minds (§§281, 283f, 289f, 293f, 302, 350)

If my inner life is not epistemically private, then others can know it (PI §246). And I can also know what others feel, perceive, or think. Wittgenstein raises various considerations about other minds, e.g., in sections 283, 293f, 302. A familiar thought is to assume that we know what others feel only by analogy to our own case. I attend to my own feelings, learn what "pain" means from my own case and then "transfer the idea to objects outside myself" (PI §§283, 293), as witnessed in Kant above. But that is problematic, for why should it then not be intelligible to transfer my idea of pain onto inanimate objects such as stones or tables or corpses?

In fact, Wittgenstein points out, it is not bodies that have pains (and minds), rather living beings. Only "of a living human being and what resembles (behaves like) a living human being can one say: it has sensations; it sees; is blind; hears; is deaf; is conscious or unconscious" (PI §281). Pain behavior is the natural, criterial, but non-inferential ground for ascribing pain to other living beings (PI §303), while in my own case I don't say "I am in pain" on the basis of any criteria (PI §§289, 290). This undermines the analogy model.

> Look at a stone and imagine it having sensations. – One says to oneself: How could one so much as get the idea of ascribing a *sensation* to a *thing*? One might as well ascribe it to a number! – And now look at a wriggling fly, and at once these difficulties vanish, and pain seems able to get *a foothold* here, where before everything was, so to speak, too *smooth* for it.
> And so, too, a corpse seems to us quite inaccessible to pain. – Our attitude to what is alive and to what is dead is not the same. All our reactions are different. (PI §284)

Wittgenstein questions the very coherence of the analogy model. If I know only from my case what pain is, then in imagining that the other has pain, "I have to imagine pain which I *don't feel* on the model of pain which I *do feel*" (PI §302; see also §350). The best I could do is imagine *my* pain in *his* body, as Kant suggested. This would be not only missing the point, but might be in fact not intelligible, under the premise of ownership privacy. In reality, to imagine him having pain in his body is to imagine his suffering and manifesting it (PI §302; Hacker, 1990/93b, p.124). (For more on this topic see Malcolm, 1971; Strawson, 1974; Kripke, 1982, pp.114ff; and Schroeder, 2001, pp.174–80.)

16 Private Ostensive Definition (PI §§256–8, 261, 265, 270, 293)

As Kenny suggested, one can read sections 243–54 as showing that our public language cannot be a private language, given the intimate connection between sensation terms and natural expressions of sensation. But could this connection be severed? Even if our language is not a private language, could there not be a private language?

Putnam (1963) imagines a race of "super-Spartans" who suppress their nonverbal pain behavior, have never been taught the meaning of "pain" by reference to it, but still know what "pain" means. Kenny (1971, p.281) replies that the only reason to assume that super-Spartans mean by "pain" what we do, is their ability to apply the word correctly to *normal* humans in pain, an ability involving the standard connection between pain and pain behavior. Putnam's scenario does not sever the connection between pain and its expression in behavior.

Wittgenstein explores the possibility of a separate private language in section 256 of the *Investigations*: "Suppose I didn't have any natural expression of sensation, but only had sensations? And now I simply associate names with sensations, and use these names in descriptions." Accordingly, a private linguist could claim to invent a language that only he can understand, whose words refer to his sensations and have no conceptual connection with natural expressive behavior. The words would be introduced by a putatively private analogue of public ostensive definition (see Chapter 22, NAMES AND OSTENSIVE DEFINITIONS). Unlike public ostensive definition, private ostensive definition would employ *private samples*, e.g., mental images, as standards of comparison for the application of the expressions:

> But can't you at least for yourself give an *ostensive* [definition] of toothache? Pointing to the place of your pain and saying "this is ..."? Can't I give a name to the pain I've got? Queer idea to give one's pain a name! [...] what connection is the name to have with the pain? The only connection so far is: that you had a toothache, pointed to your cheek, and pronounced the word "moo". (LPE 296)

"Moo" is not to be understood as a natural or taught expression (or manifestation) of pain here. A private ostensive definition is supposed to be understood independently of any connection to natural expressions of sensations. So what might make "moo" the name of a sensation? Section 257 tells us that giving a name to something (here a sensation) presupposes a complex "stage-setting." But my private ostensive definition is supposed to sidestep this preparation and still introduce a name, what we call a name, with the only difference that it is a name only I understand. This leads to a first rejoinder: if the introduction of any name presupposes a preparation, and a private ostensive "definition" does not have any such preparation, such a "definition" does not introduce a name, hence it is not a definition, merely an empty ritual, mimicking ostensive definition.

Pressing this point further, section 258 introduces a scenario to help decide whether I can introduce a name for a sensation with no reference to natural pain expression and independently of the standard preparation: I keep a diary about a certain sensation by associating the letter "S" with it. Each time I have the sensation, I write "S" in my diary. Wittgenstein's first comment is that such a "definition" of "S" can't actually be expressed (*aussprechen*) – not by words, gestures, or written signs (PI §258; MS 124, p.226). A definition is a rule for the use of a certain word, and one needs to be able to reproduce it, cite it, or look it up. In reproducing an ostensive definition, as opposed to, say, an analytic definition, we often use a sample. For instance, in reproducing the definition for "red" we may utter "Red is *this* color," while indicating a red cloth. Standard samples of ostensive definitions are reproducible and can be pointed at.

But a putative private sensation could not be pointed at "in the ordinary sense" (PI §258). The ostension in a private ostensive definition must therefore be understood thus: I "point" to my sensation inwardly by concentrating my attention on it – this will impress the connection between the sensation and "S" upon my memory. However, this is a mere ceremony and does not give me a definition either, because a definition is normative. To impress upon myself the connection between "S" and the sensation

> can only mean: this process brings it about that I remember the connection *correctly* in the future. But in the present case, I have no criterion of correctness. One would like to say: whatever is going to seem correct to me is correct. And that only means that here we can't talk about "correct". (PI §258)

Where there can be correctness there can also be incorrectness, and apparent correctness. This is inapplicable here: the private ostensive definition has no normative function. To justify the application of a term one must invoke an independent standard of correctness (PI §265). In a public ostensive definition, this is the sample indicated, which can function as a standard of comparison for the application of the name defined. An ostensive sample is a perceptible object, independent of any act of pointing at it, perceiving it, etc. It can be identified as a relevant sample independently of the property defined, thus allowing for reproduction of the definition. A passage in Wittgenstein's *Nachlass* clarifies this:

> But the case of naming the pain is still different from that of naming a body, and that will show in the use of the definition. For when I give, say, this feather the name A, the definition is a means to enable me to get from the name A back to something else, a sample. But when I give the experience a name, how do I reach back from the name to its bearer, to the *this* which I named? For the definition was supposed to *guide me back*, but here there remains, so to speak, only *one* half of the definition. (MS 119, pp.125f, my translation)

"To the *this* which I named": the demonstrative is stressed, because a public ostensive definition includes a sample, the object by means of which a certain name A has been defined. The sample can be invoked to allay doubt – all I need to do is reproduce the definition together with the sample and compare the latter with the object to which A is applied.

If I doubt whether I really saw a nightingale last night, I can try to remember what a nightingale looks like, having seen pictures of nightingales in the past. This may allay my doubt, but if not, I can consult an encyclopedia. I might fail to look in the right encyclopedia or err in some other way. But it is at least conceivable that I could refer my doubt to an independent standard of correctness. In the *de facto* absence of all encyclopedias it would still make sense to say things like "If only I had made a drawing of a nightingale when I was shown one," etc.

None of this is possible when the putative sample is (supposed to be) a private mental item. Section 258 is not about skepticism about memory, as some interpreters claim (e.g., Fogelin, 1987, pp.179ff). The point is not that with a putative private ostensive definition we need to rely on fallible memory alone. For we could object that our senses are also fallible and hence the difficulty arises for public ostensive definitions as well. Saying even *that* – i.e., that our memory is fallible, unreliable, mistaken – presupposes that there *can* be grounds to decide this, and that the veracity of memory could be evaluated, at least in principle. To dispute this is to allow that all memories could be mistaken – but why call them memories then?

> Memory can be compared with a storehouse only so far as it fulfils the same purpose. Where it doesn't, we couldn't say whether the things stored up constantly change their nature and so couldn't be said to be stored at all. (MS 166, p.33)

Standard cases of memory involve criteria for what counts as remembering correctly. This is missing from private ostensive definition; "whatever is going to seem correct to me is correct" (PI §258). "There is no question of my memory's playing me a trick – because (in such a case) there can be no criterion for its playing me a trick" (LSD

8). To have such a criterion, it would be essential "that certain things should be the rule, and that tricks of memory should be exceptions" (LSD 8), which is not possible here.

Section 265 of *Philosophical Investigations* elaborates this. We check the departure time of a train by consulting a timetable. I might memorize the timetable, and then use my memory to check whether I remember correctly that my train departs at 4 p.m. Here one memory ("Train departs at 4 p.m.") appeals to another memory (the memorized timetable). Can't a private ostensive definition be employed in the same way? I think I know what "S" means, but want to be sure – so I revive the memory of the original private ostensive definition, together with a sample of "S." But the cases are not comparable. In the case of the timetable, it makes *sense* to check my memory against something independent, the real timetable. Even if all real timetables were *de facto* destroyed after my initial memorization, my memorized timetable would still count as a memory *of* a real timetable, of something independent of my memory. In the case of the private ostensive definition, all I have, in principle, and not only *de facto*, is my memory. How can I produce a sample of "S" here? Only through my memory of S – which is circular. There is no such thing here as succeeding to remember correctly, and hence to remember at all. The private linguist "is checking whether he remembers what 'S' means against his memory of what 'S' means, and *there is nothing independent* to which to appeal" (Hacker, 1972/86, p.269). It is like buying several issues of today's newspaper to check whether it tells the truth – a fruitless form of "checking" or "testing" (PI §265). If "checking" *only* means here "consulting another copy of today's issue," I have to accept whatever the newspaper says. There will be no difference between the story being correct rather than appearing to be correct, but proving to be false. Of course, this is not what "checking" means with respect to newspapers. But it is what, *ex hypothesi*, "checking," "testing," "justifying" mean with respect to private ostensive definition. "Whatever is going to seem correct to me is correct" (PI §258). But in that case the distinction between being right and seeming right collapses, and with it the very ideas of being right or wrong, which is precisely what is logically necessary for anything to function as a standard of correctness. The normativity of private ostensive definition is a fiction, and so is private ostensive definition itself (Z §134). A private language can't be constructed on its basis (see Schroeder, 2001, pp.183–93, for a different interpretation).

In the case of public ostension I can identify a sample in other ways, consulting a certain page in the encyclopedia, experts who can produce a sample, etc. This makes a public sample an independent standard of correctness. But such a standard is missing in the private ostensive definition. Section 270 continues this point, by attempting to put the private diary to actual use:

> Let us now imagine a use for the entry of the sign "S" in my diary. I find out the following from experience: whenever I have a particular sensation, a manometer shows that my blood pressure is rising. This puts me in a position to report that my blood pressure is rising without using any apparatus. This is a useful result. And now it seems quite indifferent whether I've recognized the sensation *correctly* or not. Suppose that I regularly make a mistake in identifying it, this does not make any difference at all. And this alone shows that the supposition of this mistake was merely sham. (We, as it were, turned a knob which looked as if it could be used to adjust something in the machine; but it was a mere ornament not connected with the mechanism at all.) (PI §270)

The exact interpretation of this passage is controversial (cf. Kenny, 1971, p.220; Candlish, 1980, p.93; Hanfling, 1984, pp.475ff; Hacker, 1990/93b, pp.77ff; Pears, 2008, pp.57ff; Mulhall, 2008, pp.124ff). Following Wittgenstein's slogan "meaning is use" (PI §43), in order for "S" to have a meaning it must have a use; but as soon as we envisage a use for "S," the question of identifying or misidentifying the putative sensation does not arise. All that matters is that whenever I write "S", my blood pressure has increased, regardless of whether I recognize S when I write "S." Its use is to indicate a rise in my blood pressure, not to refer to anything at all. The relation between my blood pressure rising and my writing down "S" is causal, not semantic. Hence, "S" won't be the name for a sensation, but a publicly observable signal or symptom that my blood pressure is rising. The interpretation of "S" as a name for a mental item relying on a private standard of correctness self-destructs. Related points are made in sections 271 and, especially, 293, which introduces the famous scenario of the beetle-in-a-box:

> If I say of myself that it is only from my own case that I know what the word "pain" means – must I not say *that* of other people too? And how can I generalize the *one* case so irresponsibly?
> Well, everyone tells me that he knows what pain is only from his own case! — Suppose that everyone had a box with something in it which we call a "beetle". No one can ever look into anyone else's box, and everyone says he knows what a beetle is only by looking at *his* beetle. – Here it would be quite possible for everyone to have something different in his box. One might even imagine such a thing constantly changing. – But what if these people's word "beetle" had a use nonetheless? – If so, it would not be as the name of a thing. The thing in the box doesn't belong to the language-game at all; not even as a *Something*: for the box might even be empty. – No, one can "divide through" by the thing in the box; it cancels out, whatever it is.
> In conclusion: If we construe the grammar of the expression of sensation on the model of "object and name", the object drops out of consideration as irrelevant. (PI §293)

This can be seen as a reply to Locke (see Schroeder, 2001, pp.176ff) and Frege (see Frege, 1884, §26, pp.33ff for a parallel to PI §293). Both believed that for each of us "pain," "red," etc., refers to a private object, but also that communication takes place nonetheless. If I am to admit that other speakers' use of "pain" is also intelligible, I must generalize from my case to others. But as the beetle analogy shows, if everybody publicly uses a word to refer to what is known only to himself, the private reference becomes irrelevant, "drops out," is not even a "Something." Our concept of pain can't be my private concept of pain. But then the proposition "Each of us speaks a private idiolect" can't mean what it aims to mean. The private language hypothesis is a *general* semantic claim, employing general concepts like "pain" and relying on a general account of meaning stipulated by private ostensive definition. Can it even be formulated coherently? Can *we* even say what S is supposed to be? We can't in fact classify the putatively private object as a sensation, for "sensation" is a word of our common language, not one comprehensible only to the private linguist (PI §261). And it is not that we can do without "sensation" and simply claim that all we can say is that "when he writes 'S' he has *something*," for "has" and "something" also belong to our common language (see also PI §294). From this a dramatic conclusion about radical privacy and the possibility of a private language follow: "So in the end, when one is doing philosophy, one gets to the point where one would like just to emit an inarticulate sound" (PI §261).

References

Baker, G.P. (1998). The Private Language Argument. *Language and Communication*, 18, 325–356.
Candlish, S. (1980). The Real Private Language Argument. *Philosophy*, 55, 85–94.
Fogelin, R.J. (1987). *Wittgenstein*. London: Routledge and Kegan Paul.
Frege, G. (1884). *Die Grundlagen der Arithmetik*. [The Foundations of Arithmetic.] Breslau: Wilhelm Koebner.
Frege, G. (1979). *Posthumous Writings*. Ed. and trans. H. Hermes, F. Kambartel, and F. Kaulbach. Chicago: University of Chicago Press.
Frege, G. (1984). *Collected Papers on Mathematics, Logic, and Philosophy*. Ed. B. McGuinness. Trans. M. Black, V.H. Dudman, P. Geach, H. Kaal, E.-H.W. Kluge, B. McGuinness, and R.H. Stoothoff. Oxford: Blackwell.
Glock, H.-J. (1996). *A Wittgenstein Dictionary*. Oxford: Blackwell.
Hacker, P.M.S. (1972). *Insight and Illusion: Wittgenstein on Philosophy and the Metaphysics of Experience*. Oxford: Clarendon Press.
Hacker, P.M.S. (1972/86). *Insight and Illusion: Themes in the Philosophy of Wittgenstein*. Revised edition. Oxford: Clarendon Press.
Hacker, P.M.S. (1990/93). *Wittgenstein: Meaning and Mind. Volume 3 of an Analytical Commentary on the Philosophical Investigations. Part I. Essays*. Oxford: Blackwell.
Hacker, P.M.S. (1990/93). *Wittgenstein: Meaning and Mind. Volume 3 of an Analytical Commentary on the Philosophical Investigations. Part II. Exegesis §§243–427*. Oxford: Blackwell.
Hacker, P.M.S. (2005). Of Knowledge and of Knowing that Someone is in Pain. In A. Pichler and S. Säätelä (Eds). *Wittgenstein: The Philosopher and his Works* (pp.203–235). Frankfurt: Ontos.
Hacker, P.M.S. (2013). *Wittgenstein: Comparisons and Context*. Oxford: Oxford University Press.
Hanfling, O. (1984). What does the Private Language Argument Prove?. *Philosophical Quarterly*, 34, 468–481.
Hume, D. (1739). *A Treatise on Human Nature*. London: John Noon.
Hyman, J. (1999). How Knowledge Works. *Philosophical Quarterly*, 49, 433–451.
Hyman, J. (2003). Pains and Places. *Philosophy*, 78, 5–24.
Kant, I. (1781/87). *Kritik der reinen Vernunft*. Riga: J.F. Hartknoch.
Kanterian, E. (2012). *Frege: A Guide for the Perplexed*. London: Continuum.
Kenny, A. (1971). The Verification Principle and the Private Language Argument. In O.R. Jones (Ed.). *The Private Language Argument* (pp.204–228). London: Macmillan.
Kremer, M. (2010). Sense and Reference: The Origins and Development of the Distinction. In M. Potter and T. Ricketts (Eds). *The Cambridge Companion to Frege* (pp.220–292). Cambridge: Cambridge University Press.
Kripke, S.A. (1982). *Wittgenstein on Rules and Private Language: An Elementary Exposition*. Oxford: Blackwell.
Künne, W. (2009). Wittgenstein and Frege's *Logical Investigations*. In H.-J. Glock and J. Hyman (Eds). *Wittgenstein and Analytic Philosophy. Essays for P.M.S. Hacker* (pp.26–62). Oxford: Oxford University Press.
Locke, J. (1689). *An Essay Concerning Human Understanding*. London: Thomas Basset.
Malcolm, N. (1971). Exposition and Criticism of Wittgenstein's *Investigations*. In O.R. Jones (Ed.). *The Private Language Argument*. London: Macmillan.
Mulhall, S. (2008). *Wittgenstein's Private Language Argument: Grammar, Nonsense, and Imagination in Philosophical Investigations, §§243–315*. Oxford: Oxford University Press.
Pears, D. (2008). *Paradox and Platitude in Wittgenstein's Philosophy*. Oxford: Oxford University Press.
Putnam, H. (1963). Brains and Behaviour. In R.J. Butler (Ed.). *Analytical Philosophy: Second Series* (pp.1–19). Oxford: Blackwell.

Rundle, B. (1979). *Grammar in Philosophy*. Oxford: Oxford University Press.
Russell, B. (1912). *The Problems of Philosophy*. New York: Henry Holt.
Schroeder, S. (2001). Private Language and Private Experience. In H.-J. Glock (Ed.). *Wittgenstein: A Critical Reader* (pp.174–198). Oxford: Blackwell.
Schroeder, S. (2013). Can I have your Pain?. *Philosophical Investigations*, 36, 201–209.
Snowdon, P. (2011). Private Experience and Sense Data. In O. Kuusela and M. McGinn (Eds). *The Oxford Handbook of Wittgenstein* (pp.402–28). Oxford: Oxford University Press.
Strawson, P.F. (1959). *Individuals: An Essay in Descriptive Metaphysics*. London: Methuen.
Strawson, P.F. (1974). Self, Mind and Body. In P.F. Strawson. *Freedom and Resentment and other Essays* (pp.186–195). London: Methuen.
Williamson. T. (2000). *Knowledge and its Limits*. Oxford: Oxford University Press.

Further Reading

Baker, G.P. and Hacker, P.M.S. (1985/2014). *Wittgenstein: Rules, Grammar and Necessity. Volume 2 of an Analytical Commentary on the Philosophical Investigations. Essays and Exegesis of §§185–242*. Second edition. Extensively revised by P.M.S. Hacker. Oxford: Wiley-Blackwell.
Nielsen, K.S. (2008). *The Evolution of the Private Language Argument*. Aldershot: Ashgate.
Pears, D. (1997/98). *The False Prison*. Oxford: Oxford University Press.
Perkins, M. (1965). Two Arguments Against a Private Language. *Journal of Philosophy*, 62, 443–459.
Rundle, B. (1990). *Wittgenstein and Contemporary Philosophy of Language*. Oxford: Blackwell.
Rundle, B. (2009). The Private Language Argument. In H.-J. Glock and J. Hyman (Eds). *Wittgenstein and Analytic Philosophy. Essays for P.M.S. Hacker* (pp.133–151). Oxford: Oxford University Press.
von Savigny, E. (2004). *Wittgensteins 'Philosophische Untersuchungen': Ein Kommentar für Leser*. [Wittgenstein's *Philosophical Investigations*: A Commentary for Readers.] Frankfurt: Vittorio Klostermann.

29

The Inner and the Outer

WILLIAM CHILD

We can distinguish two uses of the terms "inner" and "outer" in Wittgenstein's writings on philosophy of mind. In one use, the term "inner" – like the term "mental" – is a general label that gathers together a particular class of phenomena: sensations, thoughts, intentions, emotions, and so forth. To say that something is an "inner" phenomenon in this sense is equivalent to classifying it as a mental phenomenon; it carries no particular philosophical commitments about the nature or status of the mental. It is in this vein that Wittgenstein says that "the inner [...] is sensations + thoughts + images + mood + intention, and so on" (LW I §959) or that "the inner differs from the outer in its *logic*" (LW II 62).

In other contexts Wittgenstein uses the terms "inner" and "outer," often in scare quotes, in a different way: to express a particular philosophical picture of the mental, a particular way of conceiving of the mental and its relation to behavior and the non-mental world. It is in this sense that he writes that "the 'inner' is a delusion" (LW II 84). He does not mean it is a delusion that we have sensations, thoughts, and so on. What is a delusion is "the outer–inner picture" (LW II 69): the picture of sensations and thoughts as internal, mental phenomena that are hidden behind the outer surface of people's behavior. He regards this "picture of the inner and the outer" (LW II 28) as a distinctively philosophical way of thinking of the mental. It plays no part in the ordinary practice of applying mental terms to ourselves and others; but it naturally suggests itself – it "forces itself upon us" (PI II iv) – when we step back from the practice and consider it reflectively. But the inner–outer picture, Wittgenstein argues, fundamentally misrepresents the phenomena. "The whole complex of ideas alluded to by [the word "inner"]," he writes, "is like a painted curtain drawn in front of the actual word use" (LW II 84).

The first section of this chapter discusses the inner–outer picture: it explores Wittgenstein's account of the origin and appeal of the picture, his reasons for rejecting it, and his own – very different – way of thinking of common-sense psychology. The second section considers his account of our relation to our own experiences and attitudes, and discusses his suggestion that utterances like "I'm in pain" or "I want an apple" are *avowals* or *expressions* of a person's experiences and attitudes. The third section discusses Wittgenstein's positive view of the relation between "inner" mental states and "outer" behavior.

1 The Inner–Outer Picture

The inner–outer picture, as Wittgenstein describes it, has a metaphysical and an epistemic dimension. The metaphysical dimension is the image of a person's mental and non-mental properties as belonging to separate, ontologically distinct realms. There is an outer realm of behavior, utterances, facial expressions, external circumstances, and so forth. And, lying behind that outer realm, there is an inner realm of sensations, thoughts, intentions, and the rest. There are causal relations between the two realms: a person's outer behavior is produced by the thoughts and intentions in her inner world; and changes in her inner world (sensations, for instance) can be caused by events in the outer world. But there are, as Wittgenstein puts it, no "logical relations" between the two realms; the inner and the outer are "logically independent".

The epistemic dimension of the inner–outer picture involves two ideas. First, each of us is directly acquainted with our own thoughts and sensations. So we all have certain knowledge of what we ourselves are thinking and feeling. Second, no one can be acquainted with another person's thoughts or experiences. So one person can never really know what another person is thinking or feeling; others' thoughts and feelings are hidden behind their outer behavior. As Wittgenstein puts it: "One has to guess at [the mental] in someone else using external clues and is only *acquainted* with it from one's own case" (LW II 61).

What makes the inner–outer picture so natural? We can begin with the obvious fact that there are asymmetries between first-person and third-person uses of mental terms. Our ascriptions of experiences and mental properties to other people are based on observing their circumstances and behavior. But we normally ascribe experiences and mental properties to ourselves without observation and without reference to our own behavior. Wittgenstein illustrates the contrast with an example:

> What is the criterion for the redness of an image? For me, when it is someone else's image: what he says and does. For myself, when it is my image: nothing. (PI §377)

Furthermore, there is normally no room for error about one's own present attitudes or experiences:

> If I ask someone 'whom do you expect?' and after receiving the answer ask again 'Are you sure that you don't expect someone else?' then, in most cases, this question would be regarded as absurd. (BB 21)

The same goes for the questions "What are you feeling?" or "What sensation are you experiencing?" But there is nothing at all absurd about the equivalent questions in the third-person case. For one person can easily be mistaken about another person's attitudes or experiences.

Part of the appeal of the inner–outer picture, Wittgenstein thinks, is the sense that it explains these first-person/third-person asymmetries. Suppose we think that each of us is directly acquainted with the contents of our own inner world, and that no one is acquainted with the contents of anyone else's inner world. That seems to explain how we can have certain knowledge of our own experiences and attitudes without attending to our behavior, and why we are more prone to be wrong about other people's mental states than about our own. As Wittgenstein puts it: "It is obvious what justifies [the] picture" of "something inner [...] which can be inferred only inconclusively from the outer"; it is "the apparent certainty of the first person, the uncertainty of the third" (LW I §951).

According to Wittgenstein, however, the inner–outer picture fundamentally misrepresents our relation to our own and to others' minds. In the first place, he thinks, it is a mistake to think that the appeal to acquaintance does anything to explain a subject's knowledge of her own sensations. He puts the point with characteristic economy:

> 'How do you know that you have pains?' – 'Because I *feel* them'. But 'I feel them' means the same as 'I have them'. Therefore this was no explanation at all. (BB 68)

His thought is this. The inner–outer picture depicts my knowledge of my own sensations as a form of perceptual knowledge: I know that I have a mole on my arm because I see the mole; analogously, it is supposed, I know that I'm in pain because I feel the pain. But the two cases are not analogous at all. When I see a mole on my arm, there are two things involved: the mole, and my perceiving the mole. So we can explain my knowledge of the mole by appeal to the fact that I perceive it. When I feel a pain, on the other hand, there are not two things involved: the pain, and my feeling the pain. On the contrary; feeling pain *just is* being in pain. So "I know I'm in pain because I feel pain" says no more than "I know I'm in pain because I'm in pain." And that does not *explain* how I know that I'm in pain. It simply records the fact that I do.

Wittgenstein is equally dismissive of the idea that our knowledge of our own propositional attitudes – our beliefs, intentions, wishes, and so on – is a kind of observational knowledge. In the first place, he thinks, it is evidently not true that I have to introspect or observe myself in order to tell what I believe, what I intend, and so on. In normal circumstances, I can say what I believe or intend without considering any evidence at all: either "inner evidence" (feelings, images, occurrent thoughts, etc.) or "outer evidence" (my behavior). Furthermore, the observational model misrepresents our relation to our own attitudes, in a way that Wittgenstein brings out in connection with the point – noticed by G.E. Moore – that there is something paradoxical about propositions of the form "I believe it will rain but it won't" or "It will rain but I don't believe it will." Such a proposition may be true. But one cannot coherently judge that it is true. What Moore's paradox highlights is that, when someone judges "I believe it will rain," she does not simply commit herself to a claim about herself and her beliefs; she also commits herself to a claim about the weather. But that would be hard to understand if self-ascribing a belief were simply a matter of observing and reporting on the presence of an inner state. For why should the claim that I am in a certain inner state commit me to any particular claim about the world beyond my beliefs – in the way that the claim that I believe it will rain does commit me to the claim that it will rain? (For Wittgenstein's discussion of this point, see PI II x.)

Wittgenstein, then, rejects the observational conception of our relation to our own minds that comes with the inner–outer picture. He also rejects the associated conception of our relation to others' minds: in particular, the idea that one person can never really know what someone else thinks or feels. Of course, I cannot always tell what other people are thinking or feeling. But facts about one person's mind, he thinks, are not as a class hidden from, and unknowable to, others: "It is only in particular cases that the inner is hidden from me; and in those cases it is not hidden because it is the inner" (LW II 33). Similarly, he insists, "My thoughts are not hidden from him, but are just open to him in a different *way* than they are to me" (LW II 34–5). And again: "If we are using the word 'know' as it is normally used (and how else are we to use it?), then other people very often know if I'm in pain" (PI §246). But Wittgenstein's response to the claim that we cannot know what someone else is thinking or feeling is not simply to insist dogmatically on the opposite claim: that we can know it. He criticizes the reasoning that seems to support the inner–outer picture's skeptical view.

It is tempting, Wittgenstein thinks, to reason in the following way: I cannot know whether S has a gold tooth, say, because I cannot see into her mouth; analogously, I cannot know whether someone else has toothache, because I cannot feel her sensations. (For this analogy, see BB 49.) But, Wittgenstein argues, the two cases are not analogous. In the case of the gold tooth, there is a kind of evidence about another person's teeth that I could have but do not; the evidence I could acquire by looking into her mouth. So my inability to see into S's mouth can make the difference between knowing that she has a gold tooth and not knowing that she does. The case of toothache is different. It is true that I cannot feel S's toothache. But the reason is a conceptual or grammatical one: that any toothache I feel is my toothache, by virtue of the fact that it is me who is feeling it. For that reason, there can be no such thing as feeling someone else's toothache. But in that case, the fact that I cannot feel S's toothache does not mean that there is some deficiency in my evidence that S has toothache; it simply reflects the fact that the person with toothache is S, not me. And, Wittgenstein insists, there is nothing to prevent me from knowing that someone else has toothache. "If I see someone writhing in pain with evident cause, I do not think: all the same, his feelings are hidden from me" (PI II xi 223). And I am obviously right not to think that. In such a case – as in many others – I can know perfectly well what someone else is feeling, on the basis of what he says and does.

At the same time, Wittgenstein recognizes that there is an ineliminable or "constitutional" uncertainty (RPP II §657) in the relation between a person's behavior, on the one hand, and the mental concepts we apply on the basis of that behavior, on the other. "The uncertainty whether someone else" is really in pain, say, or is really irritated, "is an (essential) trait of all these language-games" (LW I §877). There is an "indeterminacy" in "the logic of the concept of pain" (LW II 94) and of other mental concepts. One dimension of this uncertainty or indeterminacy is that there are no "exact rules of evidence" for mental concepts: no exact rules for ascribing mental states to others on the basis of their circumstances and behavior (LW II 94). Similarly, the evidence on the basis of which we ascribe mental states to others includes "imponderable" evidence: evidence that cannot be weighed systematically against competing evidence (PI II xi 228).

This "constitutional uncertainty" in the relation between a person's behavior and her thoughts and feelings, Wittgenstein thinks, is another source of the inner–outer picture. For the conception of mental states as states of an internal, mental mechanism that produces behavior seems to promise an explanation of the uncertainty: for example, that the internal mechanism is too complex for us to be able to infer a person's inner mental states in detail from her behavior; or that the mechanism works indeterministically. But such explanations, according to Wittgenstein, get things back to front.

> It is not the relationship of the inner to the outer that explains the uncertainty of the evidence, but rather the other way around – this relationship is only a picture-like representation of this uncertainty. (LW II 68)

Wittgenstein's idea is that the uncertainty in the relation between mental concepts and behavioral evidence is a primitive feature of the mental scheme. The idea that our behavior is produced by an internal mental mechanism whose operation is either indeterministic or impossible to systematize is just a picture: a reflection of this feature of common-sense psychology. It is not an independent truth about the relations between the states of an inner mental mechanism and the behavior it produces. As before, he thinks, we treat the inner–outer picture as if it explained the central features of our practice. But the explanation it offers is illusory.

If we reject the inner–outer picture, how *should* we conceive of the mental, and of the language-game of ascribing mental states to ourselves and others? Wittgenstein writes: "I look at this language-game as autonomous. I merely want to describe it, or look at it, not justify it" (LW II 40). Common-sense psychology, he thinks, is an autonomous, *sui generis* scheme of description and explanation. It is a scheme that we all use of ourselves and of others. And it does not stand in need of explanation or justification; we should simply accept it at face value, and understand it on its own terms.

But how, exactly, should we understand the common-sense mental scheme? What are we doing when we say that someone is in pain, or is irritated, or intends to do such-and-such, if we are not talking about a system of inner mental states and events that causally produce her behavior? One answer to that question would be the simple and flat-footed one. When we say that someone is in pain, we are saying that she has a sensation of a particular kind; when we say that she is irritated, we are describing her mood; and so on. And if our aim as philosophers really is just to describe the common-sense scheme, the language-game, perhaps there is no more to say than that.

However, Wittgenstein does in places offer a way of thinking of the common-sense mental scheme that is not completely pleonastic: an alternative picture that, he thinks, does not misrepresent the phenomena. In Wittgenstein's picture, life is portrayed as a "weave" or "tapestry" containing patterns that "vary in a multiplicity of ways" and are "interwoven" with each other (see Z §§568-9). When we say that someone is irritated, or that he feels grief or joy, say, we are identifying patterns in the "tapestry of his life" (*Lebensteppich*) or the "weave of his life" (*Band des Lebens*). So, for example, Wittgenstein says that:

> 'Grief' describes a pattern which recurs, with different variations, in the tapestry of life. If a man's bodily expression of sorrow and of joy alternated, say, with the ticking of a clock, here we would not have the characteristic course of the pattern of sorrow or of the pattern of joy. (PI II i 174)

And he describes pretending to be in pain as a "very special pattern in the weave of our lives" (PI II xi 229; cf. LW II 42).

If we see things in this way, we will still say that the way someone behaves is evidence of what she is feeling. But what it is evidence for is not, as in the inner–outer picture, the presence of an inner state that is hidden behind the behavior. It is, rather, the existence of a particular pattern in the person's life.

> Imagine it were really a case of patterns on a long ribbon.
>
> The ribbon moves past me and now I say 'this is the pattern S', now 'This is the pattern V'. Sometimes for a period of time I do not know which it is; sometimes I say at the end 'It was neither'.
>
> How could I be taught to recognize these patterns? I am shown simple examples, and then complicated ones of both kinds. It is almost the way I learn to distinguish the styles of two composers. (LW II 42–3)

We should think of learning to apply mental terms, Wittgenstein thinks, in a similar way: as a matter of pattern-recognition.

2 Avowal, Expression, and Self-Ascription

The inner–outer picture encourages the view that our use of language in self-ascriptions of current experiences and attitudes is analogous to its use in talking about the non-mental world. Someone who says "I've got toothache," "I want an apple," "I believe it will rain," and so on is, on this view, describing inner phenomena that she observes within herself; she is stating or reporting how things are in her inner realm. Wittgenstein rejects that view. He insists, as we have seen, that we do not normally observe our own thoughts and experiences. And in the normal case, he thinks, our first-person, present-tense psychological utterances are not descriptions; they are *expressions* or *avowals* of our experiences and attitudes. That idea has several dimensions and plays a number of roles in Wittgenstein's discussion.

A first point of Wittgenstein's insistence that mental self-ascriptions are typically expressions is to draw a contrast between expressing an experience or attitude on the one hand, and describing or reporting it on the other. He thinks of describing as a definite activity, which involves observation and the assessment of evidence. But utterances like "I've got toothache" or "I hope he'll come" normally require no observation or assessment of evidence at all. So, he thinks, it is wrong to regard them as descriptions. For the same reason, it is misleading to call them "statements."

> To call the expression of a sensation [e.g., the utterance "I've got toothache" or "That tickles"] a *statement* is misleading because 'testing', 'justification', 'confirmation', 'reinforcement' of the statement are connected with the word 'statement' in the language-game. (Z §549)

And it is similarly misleading to treat avowals of sensation or attitudes as reports:

> When someone says 'I hope he'll come', is this a *report* about his state of mind, or a *manifestation* of his hope? – I may, for example, say it to myself. And surely I am not giving myself a report. (PI §585)

Of course there are some cases where first-person, present-tense psychological utterances really do involve a kind of observation and assessment of evidence. For example, we sometimes come to realize what we want or believe only by reflecting on our own behavior. And Wittgenstein describes various other cases in which it is appropriate to regard mental self-ascriptions as descriptions. He says, for example, that in the normal case "the exclamation 'I'm expecting him – I'm longing to see him!' may be called an act of expecting"; it is not a description of oneself or one's attitude.

But I can utter the same words as the result of self-observation, and then they might amount to: 'So, after all that has happened, I'm still expecting him with longing.' (PI §586)

In this latter case I am describing myself. But such cases are the exception. In the normal case, I can say what I am experiencing, what I want, what I believe, etc., without the need for any self-observation. And when I do so, Wittgenstein insists, I am expressing or giving voice to my experiences and attitudes; I am not describing or reporting them.

A second theme in Wittgenstein's discussion of the expression of sensations and mental states concerns our acquisition of mental concepts. He writes:

> How do words *refer* to sensations? – There doesn't seem to be any problem here; don't we talk about sensations every day, and give them names? This question is the same as: how does a human being learn the meaning of the names of sensations? – the word 'pain' for example. Here is one possibility: words are connected with the primitive, the natural, expressions of the sensation and used in their place. A child has hurt himself and he cries; and then adults talk to him and teach him exclamations and, later, sentences. They teach the child new pain-behaviour.
> 'So you are saying that the word "pain" really means crying?' – On the contrary: the verbal expression of pain replaces crying and does not describe it. (PI §244)

Wittgenstein's suggestion is that the word "pain" is learned as an addition to, or replacement of, our natural, pre-linguistic expressions of pain. When we teach a child to utter the words "I'm in pain" in circumstances where she already displays non-linguistic expressions of pain, we are teaching her to apply the word "pain" to herself in circumstances where she feels pain. That establishes a connection between her use of the word "pain" and her own feelings of pain. And crucially, for Wittgenstein, it establishes it in a way that does not depend on the kind of inner ostensive definition that is a central target of the private language sections of *Philosophical Investigations*. Of course, learning to say "I'm in pain" when one is in pain does not suffice for understanding the word "pain"; for that, one must learn the rest of its use, too, including its application to other people. But, Wittgenstein thinks, it is an important first step.

He makes a parallel proposal about our acquisition of the concept of wanting, or desire. There are natural, pre-linguistic expressions of desire: reaching out for an object, for instance, or refusing to let go of it. And, Wittgenstein suggests, we learn the words "I want" in the first instance as an addition to, or replacement of, such natural, pre-linguistic expressions. The child is taught to say "Apple!," and then "I want an apple," in circumstances where she already exhibits natural, pre-linguistic expressions of wanting an apple. (For this idea, see e.g., LPP 23, 25, 141.) That shows how she can learn to apply the words "I want" to herself in appropriate circumstances, without supposing that there is any process of introspectively identifying an inner state of desire. As before, there is more to understanding the word "want" than learning to apply it to oneself in an appropriate way; one must master the third-person use as well. But learning the first-person use is evidently an important part of the whole.

The general idea, then, is that self-ascriptions of experiences and attitudes are developments or replacements of more basic behavior that already expresses the experiences and attitudes in question. In the cases we have discussed so far, the first-person utterances – "I'm in pain," "I want an apple" – supplement or replace *pre-linguistic* expressions of pain or desire. But Wittgenstein does not suggest that the same model can be applied in every case. Accounts of words for other sensations and other attitudes must respect the same principles: they must explain the meanings of mental terms in a way that does not appeal to inner ostensive definitions; they must not represent a subject as an observer of her experiences and attitudes; and so on. But within that framework there is room for significant differences. In particular, the primitive behavior from which the first-person use of mental terms develops may already be linguistic behavior: a judgment, rather than a pre-linguistic expression. Take the case of belief. Here, Wittgenstein thinks, we start with simple judgments like "It will rain." When I judge "It will rain," I make a judgment about the external world. But in making that judgment, I also indicate something about myself: that I believe it will rain. The judgment "It will rain," then, is a verbal expression or manifestation of my belief. And, Wittgenstein suggests, I can learn the first-person use of the word "believe" by learning to move from judgments that express my beliefs, like "It will rain," to judgments that explicitly self-ascribe those beliefs, like "I believe it will rain." As before, that shows how I can learn to apply the word "believe" to myself, and simultaneously start to acquire the concept of belief, without supposing that there is any process of identifying inner states of belief within myself. (For Wittgenstein's discussion of this point, see PI II x. That discussion has inspired a number of influential accounts of self-knowledge; see particularly Evans, 1982, ch.7.4, and Moran, 2001.)

We said above that there is normally no room for error about one's present experiences and attitudes. How should we understand that fact? In rejecting the inner–outer picture, Wittgenstein rejects one traditional explanation of the reliability or authority of a person's judgments about her own experiences and attitudes: the idea that we have a faculty of inner perception that gives each person direct introspective access to the contents of her own mind. His own approach to the question builds on the idea that first-person psychological utterances are expressions of the experiences and attitudes they ascribe.

That idea suggests a straightforward way of understanding the authority of self-ascriptions in certain very simple cases. A natural, pre-linguistic expression of pain – crying or wincing, say – is an automatic, unthinking response to the sensation of pain. When an infant cries in pain, she does not first identify her sensation as a pain and then decide to cry; she simply cries in response to the pain. Correspondingly, there is no possibility of her crying by mistake, because she has misidentified some other sensation as a pain. In a similar way, Wittgenstein suggests, the utterance "That hurts" or "I'm in pain" is in the simplest cases an immediate reaction to one's pain, like flinching or crying out when one pricks one's finger with a needle. These verbal expressions of pain are acquired reactions. But, like the pre-linguistic reactions they supplement or replace, they are in these very simple cases an automatic, involuntary response to the experience. That is why there is no question of their being mistaken.

That is an important point. But even for the case of pain, it applies only in a very limited range of cases. For very few self-ascriptions of pain are involuntary reactions to pain. When I tell the dentist about the character of the toothache I am feeling, my utterance is not an automatic, involuntary response; it is not like wincing when she touches an exposed nerve. So the authoritativeness or reliability of my judgment cannot be traced to the same feature that explains the reliability of the simplest pre-linguistic expressions of pain: the existence of an automatic, involuntary association between the expression and the experience. The same is true for most other avowals of sensations; unlike simple pre-linguistic expressions of sensation, they are not automatic reactions to the experiences they self-ascribe. And similar points apply to self-ascriptions of attitudes and emotions. In a limited range of cases, such utterances really are unthinking, involuntary expressions of the attitudes or emotions they self-ascribe: the words "I don't want you to go!," cried by a small child to a departing parent, are a plausible example. But most self-ascriptions of attitudes are not like that.

Wittgenstein, of course, acknowledges that. But he stresses that our self-ascriptions of sensations and attitudes do quite generally resemble pre-linguistic expressions in another respect; in the normal case, like pre-linguistic expressions of sensation, they do not depend on observation or inference. That means that our mental self-ascriptions are not vulnerable to two sources of error that affect our judgments about the external world and about others' minds: misleading evidence; and mistakes in the inferences we draw from that evidence. Suppose I believe, on the basis of what someone says, that he intends to meet me at the pub in Kidlington. My belief may be false because I am wrong about what he said; he actually said that he would meet me in Kiddington, and that is what he intends to do. Or I may be right about what he said, but wrong to think he meant it; he said he would meet me in Kidlington, but he never intended to do so. But suppose I make the first-person judgment that I intend to meet someone in Kidlington. In the normal case, I do not make that judgment on the basis of what I say, or any other evidence. So my judgment about my own intention cannot be wrong in either of those two ways.

That point reflects a crucial difference between psychological self-ascriptions and other judgments. But it still does not explain the general reliability of our judgments about our own sensations and attitudes. For what the present point tells us is only this: that we have a general capacity to say what we are experiencing, what we want, what we believe, intend, and so on; and that these self-ascriptions are typically made without observation and without reference to our behavior. In order for our self-ascriptions to be true, however, they must cohere with the rest of our behavior. Merely judging that I believe that p, or want x, or intend to Φ, does not make it true that I do; the truth of such self-ascriptions is answerable to my non-linguistic behavior. And it is a striking fact that the self-ascriptions we make without reference to any evidence generally *do* cohere with the rest of our behavior: that they *are* generally true. But it is natural to ask what explains that fact: how is that we are able to produce self-ascriptions that reliably cohere with the rest of our behavior, without needing to rely on any evidence?

That is, indeed, a natural question. But, for Wittgenstein, it is a question that philosophy cannot – and need not – answer. If people could not learn to make groundless self-ascriptions of attitudes that cohered with the rest of their behavior, he thinks, our ordinary mental concepts would have no application to them. For, he suggests, a word that people could not apply to themselves without reference to their behavior would not denote a kind of mental phenomenon at all. For instance:

> One might distinguish between two chimpanzees with respect to the way in which they work, and say of the one that he is thinking and of the other that he is not.
>
> But here of course we wouldn't have the complete employment of 'think'. The word would have reference to a mode of behaviour. *Not until it finds its particular use in the first person does it acquire the meaning of mental activity.* (RPP II §§229–30, emphasis added)

For Wittgenstein, then, the fact that we *can* generally ascribe sensations and attitudes to ourselves without evidence, in a way that coheres with our other behavior, is crucial;

it is one of the "extremely general facts of nature" on which our concepts and our language-games depend. (For the idea of such "extremely general facts of nature," see the boxed comment associated with PI §142, and PI II xii 232.) But from the point of view of philosophy, at least, it is a basic fact: something we must simply accept as given.

3   The Relation between "Inner" Mental States and "Outer" Behavior

What is the relation between our "inner" experiences and mental states and the "outer" behavior on the basis of which we ascribe them to one another? "The inner," according to Wittgenstein, "is tied up with the outer not only empirically, but also logically" (LW II 63). "The connection of the inner and the outer," he says, "is part of those concepts" (LW II 62). Those ideas run through his later philosophy of mind. And they are central to his rejection of the inner–outer picture. But what do they mean? And are they plausible?

On the conventional interpretation, Wittgenstein is making a metaphysical claim: a claim about what must be the case for creatures to have experiences and mental states at all. On this view, Wittgenstein takes it to be essential to pain, for instance, that in normal cases it has the kind of outer behavioral expression it does. He recognizes, of course, that there can be instances of pain without any behavioral manifestation. But such cases, he thinks, are necessarily the exception, not the rule. It is no more possible for there to be a world in which people experience pain but never manifest it in their behavior, or a world in which people have thoughts but never express their thoughts, than it is for there to be a world in which people play games but no one makes anything but false moves in any game. (For this analogy, see LPP 99 and PI §§344–5.)

The evidence for ascribing such a view to Wittgenstein includes passages like these:

> "But doesn't what you say amount to this: that there is no pain, for example, without *pain-behaviour?*' – It amounts to this: that only of a living human being and what resembles (behaves like) a living human being can one say: it has sensations; it sees; is blind; hears; is deaf; is conscious or unconscious. (PI §281)

> Only of what behaves like a human being can one say that it *has* pains. (PI §283)

Wittgenstein talks here about the conditions under which one "can say that" a creature has pains, and so on. On the conventional interpretation, he does not mean merely that we can have no *reason* for saying that a creature is in pain unless it behaves like a living human being. He means that it does not *make sense* to say that something is in pain unless it behaves that way; and relatedly, that it is only *possible* for a thing to be in pain if it behaves like a living human being.

That might seem to rule out as unintelligible various possibilities that we appear to understand perfectly well: for instance, the possibility of someone suffering total paralysis but continuing to feel pain. But Wittgenstein's position is more careful than that. He writes, for example:

> I can perhaps even imagine (though it is not easy) that each of the people whom I see in the street is in frightful pain, but is adroitly concealing it. And it is important that I have to imagine adroit concealment here. That I do not simply say to myself: 'Well, his mind is in pain: but what has that to do with his body?' or 'After all, it need not show in his body.' (PI §391)

His point is that we can make sense of the thought that someone is in frightful pain but doesn't show it; but in order to do so, we have to conceive of something preventing or inhibiting the normal behavioral manifestation of pain. Similarly, Wittgenstein imagines "a tribe" in which people are "brought up from early youth to give no expression of feeling *of any kind*" (RPP II §706), and seems to allow that we can coherently describe a situation in which adults never manifest their pain in any way at all. But it is an important part of this story that people exhibit the usual expressions of pain as infants, and must learn to suppress them as they grow up. So it remains true that the connection between feeling pain and the behavioral expression of pain is part of the nature of pain. Again, Wittgenstein allows that we can make sense of ascriptions of thought and sensation in circumstances where there can be no behavioral expression of thought or sensation, because the subject of our ascription is dying, or anaesthetized, or asleep. (For "dying," see the remarks about Queen Victoria's dying thoughts in RPP I §366 and LPP 32–3, 99, 152, 229, 274. For "anaesthetized" and "asleep," see LW II 57.) But, he insists, such ascriptions make sense only against a background of other cases in which thoughts and sensations are manifest in behavior.

The lesson is that Wittgenstein's view of the connection between thoughts and sensations, on the one hand, and behavior, on the other, is less straightforward and less open to obvious counterexamples than is sometimes supposed. Nonetheless, on the conventional interpretation, Wittgenstein still sees that connection as part of the metaphysics of mind. A world in which there was not, and never had been, any behavioral expression of thought or of pain would be a world in which there was no thought or pain.

But we might read Wittgenstein in a different way. For we could treat the dictum that the inner is "logically tied up with" the outer as a claim, not about the conditions for pain, say, to exist, but rather about the conditions for us to acquire and employ the concept of pain. On this alternative reading, Wittgenstein is not committed to the view that a world in which there was never any behavioral expression of pain would be a world in which there was no pain. His point is simpler and more mundane: that "if there were no characteristic expression of pain" we could not (or, more simply, would not) acquire and employ the concept of pain. In such a world, Wittgenstein says, "our normal language-game" with the word "pain" would "lose its point" (see PI §142). But, on the alternative interpretation, he does not hold that the fact that we could not (or would not) talk or think about pain in such a world entails that pain could not exist in that world. He takes the fact that pain has a characteristic behavioral expression to play an essential role in *fixing the reference* of the term "pain"; but he does not think it is *part of the meaning* of the term that pain has that characteristic behavioral expression, or any characteristic expression at all. Nor does he think that pain is in its nature tied to any kind of behavior or behavioral disposition. (For readings of Wittgenstein along these lines, see the concluding "Postscript" in Albritton, 1968; and Koethe, 1996, ch.5.)

That is a coherent philosophical position. But is it a plausible interpretation of Wittgenstein? A first reason for doubt is this. The interpretation essentially depends on the distinction between the conditions under which it would be *true* that creatures have pain and the conditions under which the concept *pain* would *have a use*. In contemporary philosophy, that is standardly treated as an obvious and crucial distinction. But in Wittgenstein's framework, in which a concept's sense is conceived as being a matter of its use, it is not clear what could be made of the suggestion that an application of the concept *pain* might be true in circumstances where the concept had no use. A defender of the alternative interpretation might respond by calling on another standard contemporary distinction: the distinction between a concept's having a use *in a world* and its having a use *with respect to* a world. It is true, she might say, that people who lived in a world in which there were no behavioral expressions of pain could not acquire, and would have no use for, our concept *pain*. Nonetheless we, who live in a world where there are behavioral expressions of pain, and who have acquired the concept of pain, can intelligibly use our concept with respect to that other world: to speculate, for example, about whether people in that world feel pain despite exhibiting no behavioral expressions of pain. And the thoughts we express when we do so speculate will be straightforwardly true or false. As before, that is in itself a reasonable philosophical view. But it is doubtful whether Wittgenstein would accept the distinction on which it relies: between a concept's having a use in a world and its having a use with respect to that world.

Second, even if this alternative interpretation of Wittgenstein were correct for the particular case of pain, it would be hard to extend it to his treatments of other mental phenomena. Take intention. In Wittgenstein's view, someone's having intentions with definite contents depends on her mastery of, or participation in, relevant techniques, practices, customs, or institutions. And the existence of those practices, customs, and so forth requires the actual existence of repeated patterns of overt behavior. We are prone, he says, to think otherwise: to conceive intention as a wholly inner, mental phenomenon, whose existence does not depend on the existence of anything outer or behavioral. As he puts it:

> "[…] what is remarkable about *intention*, about the mental process, [is] that the existence of a custom, of a technique, is not necessary to it. That, for example, it is imaginable that two people should play a game of chess, in a world in which otherwise no games existed – and then be interrupted." (PI §205)

But, Wittgenstein insists, that is a mistake. For what would make these people's intention an intention to *play a game of chess*? Suppose the people say, "Let's play a game of chess." What makes their words the expression of an intention to play chess? "Chess," says Wittgenstein, "is the game it is in virtue of all its rules (and so on)" (PI §185). So, he asks, "where is the connection effected between the sense of the words 'Let's play a game of chess' and all the rules of the game?" He answers: "Well, in the list of rules of the game, in the teaching of it, in the everyday practice of playing" (PI §185). If there were no such practice, there would be nothing to give these people's intention a content about chess.

> An intention is embedded in a setting, in human customs and institutions. If the technique of the game of chess did not exist, I could not intend to play a game of chess. (PI §337)

And for the technique of playing chess to exist, he thinks, people must actually play chess. On this view, there could not be a world in which people intended to play chess but no one ever did play chess. And more generally, that people regularly act on their intentions is not merely a necessary condition for our acquiring and applying the concept of intention; it is a necessary condition for the existence of intentions. For the case of intention, then, the alternative interpretation of Wittgenstein's dictum that the inner is "logically tied up with" the outer seems untenable. The same goes for other mental states with intentional content: belief, desire, hope, and so on.

It does not follow from what has been said about intention that the alternative interpretation is wrong for every kind of mental phenomenon. The crucial point about intention is that having states with intentional content depends, for Wittgenstein, on mastery of, or participation in, practices. But he does not think the same is true for every mental phenomenon. For example, one need not have mastered a technique in order to have toothache (see PI II xi 208). As we have seen, however, there are other reasons for doubting the alternative interpretation, even in cases where the considerations about practices and techniques do not apply. So even if the alternative interpretation is consistent with some of what he says, and even if it has attractions as a view in its own right, it is implausible to think that it captures Wittgenstein's own understanding of the relation between the inner and the outer. When he says that "the inner is tied up with the outer not only empirically, but also logically," he is advancing a view not only about the conditions for acquiring and employing mental concepts, but also about the nature of the mental: about what it is to be a subject of sensations, thoughts, intentions, and the rest.

References

Albritton, R. (1968). On Wittgenstein's Use of the Term "Criterion." In G. Pitcher (Ed.). *Wittgenstein: The Philosophical Investigations* (pp.231–250). London: Macmillan.

Evans, G. (1982). *The Varieties of Reference*. Oxford: Oxford University Press.

Koethe, J. (1996). *The Continuity of Wittgenstein's Philosophy*. Ithaca: Cornell University Press.

Moran, R. (2001). *Authority and Estrangement: An Essay on Self-knowledge*. Princeton: Princeton University Press.

Further Reading

Budd, M. (1988). *Wittgenstein's Philosophy of Psychology*. London: Routledge.

Finkelstein, D. (2003). *Expression and the Inner*. Cambridge, MA: Harvard University Press.

Hacker, P.M.S. (1972/86). *Insight and Illusion: Themes in the Philosophy of Wittgenstein*. Revised edition. Oxford: Clarendon Press. Chapter 10.

ter Hark, M. (2001). The Inner and the Outer. In H.-J. Glock (Ed.). *Wittgenstein: A Critical Reader* (pp.199–223). Oxford: Blackwell.

Wright, C. (2001). *Rails to Infinity: Essays on Themes from Wittgenstein's Philosophical Investigations*. Cambridge, MA: Harvard University Press. Chapters 5, 9, 10, 11.

30

Wittgenstein on "I" and the Self

MAXIMILIAN DE GAYNESFORD

Consensus identifies an underlying continuity to Wittgenstein's treatment of the self and "I" ("me," "mine," "my"), despite certain obvious surface variations and revisions. As representative here as they are influential are the commentaries of Peter Hacker (1990/93, pp.207–28) and Hans-Johann Glock (1996, pp.160–4). Expressing this consensus view with a certain necessary roughness, four general points come to the fore:

(i) The first person only ever plays second fiddle in Wittgenstein's work. This is so despite the fact that he evidently thought hard about it throughout his working life, and despite the fact that many of the results of his thought have been highly influential in analytic philosophy of mind and language, even if their provenance often goes unnoticed or unremarked.

(ii) What Wittgenstein has to say about the self, its metaphysics and the epistemology associated with it, is directed by and dependent on what he has to say about the first-person pronoun as a linguistic device, a means (putative, at least) of representing the self in language and thought.

(iii) When Wittgenstein attends to the first person, he is usually intent on "denigrating" it in some way; for example, showing that it is redundant or eliminable, or that its role is not so significant as philosophers tend to assume.

(iv) The key feature of the first-person pronoun for Wittgenstein, what seems most salient to him, is the pretension to "ownership" that particularly marks its explicitly possessive forms: expressions like "*my* world," "*my* language," "*my* experience" (in the earlier work); "*my* arm," "*my* body," "*my* sensation" (in the later work).

These four general points can be assembled and condensed in various ways, of course, but this would be a typical form: throughout his philosophical writings, where Wittgenstein is concerned that the primary object of his attention is being distorted by an unwarranted, "exalted" view of the first person or what it represents, it is because he thinks that mistaken views of the possessive forms of the first-person pronoun are in play, cultivating confused or unwarranted ideas about a sense of "ownership."

One way to survey Wittgenstein's treatment of the self and "I," while gaining critical purchase on the relevant arguments and observations, is to test this consensus view for accuracy against the four main occasions on which Wittgenstein paid

---

A Companion to Wittgenstein, First Edition. Edited by Hans-Johann Glock and John Hyman.
© 2017 John Wiley & Sons, Ltd. Published 2017 by John Wiley & Sons, Ltd.

particular and extended attention to the self and "I," viz., *Tractatus Logico-Philosophicus* 5.6–5.641, *Philosophical Remarks* VI. §§57–66, the "Blue Book," pp.61–70, and *Philosophical Investigations* §§398–411. So that is how this chapter will proceed, examining each such occasion in turn and drawing summary conclusions about the consensus view.

1   *Tractatus Logico-Philosophicus* 5.6–5.641

Almost all Wittgenstein's arguments and observations concerning "I" and the self in the *Tractatus* are arranged as attempts to explicate 5.6. Unfortunately, this is one of the obscurest parts of a difficult work. It is necessary to proceed slowly, taking care to use whatever aid is available, particularly the decimal ordering, which indicates which remarks are especially salient, and how they are related to other remarks.

> *The limits of my language* mean the limits of my world. (TLP 5.6)

The first course Wittgenstein takes in explicating 5.6 is to gloss what it is for something to count as the limits of *the* world (5.61). These limits are identified with the limits of logic, which is said to "pervade" (*erfüllen*) the world. And the notion of a limit here is explained in terms of what it is not coherent to exclude. If the limits of the world are the limits of logic, it would not be logically coherent to exclude certain possibilities, namely those that the world does not contain, as one would in saying "the world has this in it, but not that." For this would mean that it is logically coherent to speak of things that the world does not include, and hence that logic is capable of transcending the limits of the world. But this would contradict the notion that the limits of the world are also the limits of logic. And Wittgenstein then expands the point. Logic determines what we can think, so we cannot *think* "the world has this in it, but not that." And "what we cannot think we cannot *say* either" (5.61).

It is particularly worth bearing these remarks in mind, because Wittgenstein describes them as "the key" when he takes a second course to explicating 5.6 (5.62). Here he begins explaining the first-person component of 5.6. Given that he has just provided a gloss on what it is for something to count as the limits of *the* world, we would expect him to set about explaining what it is for something to count as the limits of *my* world. And this is indeed what he goes on to do, though in a way that first leaps ahead and then works its way back:

> This remark provides the key to the problem, how much truth there is in solipsism.
> For what the solipsist *means* is quite correct; only it cannot be *said*, but makes itself manifest.
> The world is *my* world: this is manifest in the fact that the limits of *language* (of that language which alone I understand) mean the limits of *my* world. (TLP 5.62)

The solipsist is someone who would (if he could) state his position as "I alone exist, am real" or, equivalently, "The world has me in it, but nothing else." So 5.62 leaps over what it is for something to count as the limits of *my* world and discusses instead the sense we might make of the claim that the limits of *my* world are the limits of *the* world.

If 5.61 is the "key" here, that is presumably because the puzzle it unlocks is in the second sentence of 5.62, for this is the only sentence on which the earlier remark has a clear, direct bearing. The idea seems to be this. Suppose we add the solipsist's premise: that the limits of *my* world are the limits of *the* world. Then it seems we can move from the point made in 5.61 (that we cannot say "The world has this in it, but not that" because the limits of *the* world are the limits of logic) to the point made in the second sentence of 5.62 (that we cannot say "The world has me in it, but nothing else"). The background idea remains the same: given what it is for anything to be a "limit" in this sense, there are certain possibilities which it would not be logically coherent to exclude.

Wittgenstein says that "what the solipsist *means* is quite correct" (5.62). This is perhaps a loose way of speaking. For if the solipsist cannot state his position and he cannot think it, there is presumably nothing that he could *mean* by it either. It may be safer to put more weight on the first sentence, which goes no further than registering Wittgenstein's interest in asking "how much truth there is in solipsism."

Wittgenstein states that the claim "the world is *my* world" is "manifest" in the fact that "the limits of *language* (of that language which alone I understand) mean the limits of *my* world." This is an ambiguous way of speaking, of course, in the German also (*die Sprache, die allein ich verstehe*). The next remark, tied to 5.62 by the number system, is no great help here: "The world and life are one" (5.621). It may mean the only language I understand, or the language only I understand. (The earlier C.K. Ogden translation favors the latter, but a later note in Wittgenstein's hand favors the former.) It is important to determine which, because the claim that the limits of language mean the limits of my world is almost, but not quite, a straight repetition of the remark being explicated (i.e., 5.6). The one difference is that, here, the ambiguous parenthetical clause replaces the possessive "my" before "language." So this clause appears to take on the burden of explicating the use of "my" here, and the ambiguity complicates things. If what Wittgenstein means is that a language is "my" language in being the one I alone understand, then it would be a private language, and so we are presumably to make sense of this as further explication of the solipsist's position. For 5.62 identifies the limits of my world with the limits of this language, so the world thus limited is presumably to be taken as a private world and one which might fit the solipsist's specifications: in which there is nothing but the referent of this use of the first-person pronoun. If, on the other hand, Wittgenstein means that a language is mine in the sense that it is the only language I understand, then it might be a public language, but one limited by logic, what it is possible to think and understand, and so we are presumably to take 5.62 as an explication of the relationship between logic, language, and the world. The limits of my world are identified with these limits. But if this is what Wittgenstein means, it is difficult to see why he emphasizes "*my* world" (twice) in 5.62. This would serve no purpose, unless what is being said were peculiar to the particular one who is referent of *these* uses of the term. But the point being made is surely to be taken as holding for any who might use the term.

Here it is worth asking how Wittgenstein is able to say and think this, while the solipsist is unable to say or think his position. Evidently "the world is *my* world" is not meant to exclude any possibilities it would be logically incoherent to exclude. To explain how and why this is so is to work back to the question of what it is for something to count as the limits of *my* world. And it is to this issue that Wittgenstein now turns, postponing further discussion of solipsism until he is equipped to answer the "problem" posed in 5.62: namely, how much truth there is in that position.

The possessive pronoun is again central to the next set of remarks, in which Wittgenstein takes a third course toward explicating 5.6. These remarks start out from 5.63:

I am my world. (The microcosm.) (TLP 5.63)

First, Wittgenstein denies that there is such a thing as "the subject that thinks or entertains ideas" (5.631). He links this with the claim that the subject could not be mentioned in a book which set out to describe *The world as I found it*. This point is clarified somewhat in the next remark, which seems to qualify the earlier in another way: if there is no such thing as the subject that thinks or entertains ideas, this is not to deny that the subject exists.

The subject does not belong to the world: rather, it is a limit of the world. (TLP 5.632)

Note that, despite the aim of explicating 5.63 with its "my world," the possessive has now been dropped (though this need not be a deep change; perhaps it is to be assumed). It is because the subject is a limit of the world that it could not appear in a description of the world. Wittgenstein evidently felt this argument needed support, since he moves to an analogy with the eye and the visual field: "But really you do *not* see the eye. And nothing *in the visual field* allows you to infer that it is seen by an eye" (5.633). Similarly, we assume, it is not just that the subject that thinks or entertains ideas (what he now calls the "metaphysical" subject; 5.633) is not to be found within the world, but that it is not to be inferred from what is to be found within the world either. How then are we in a position to say that the subject is even "a limit of the world" (5.632)? The next remark seems to answer this question, though if so, it is stated more vaguely than we might expect: "This is connected with the fact that no part of our experience is at the same time *a priori*" (5.634). If we overlook what is oddly tentative about this, the natural way to interpret 5.634 is as saying that it is a priori that the subject is a limit of the world, and perhaps a priori that the world is *my* world.

In the fourth and final course towards explicating 5.6, Wittgenstein returns to the solipsist:

Here it can be seen that solipsism, when its implications are followed out strictly, coincides [*fällt zusammen*] with pure realism. The self of solipsism shrinks to a point without extension, and there remains the reality co-ordinated with it. (TLP 5.64)

When the solipsist was first mentioned (5.62), it seemed that we were being told his position might be correct, though he was confused in supposing he could express that position. 5.64 could perhaps be interpreted in this way, but if so, that must be because we are also being told that "pure realism" is quite correct. It is a better match with the resources made available at this point to suppose that something more modest is meant: for example, that there is an insight in solipsism which "coincides" with "pure realism" and which is not perhaps apparent to the solipsist himself, since it becomes apparent only when the "implications" of his position "are followed out strictly."

The nature of this "coincidence" is left vague. It may be that solipsism collapses into pure realism, so that they make the same claims. But to make this interpretation work, we have to supply much that Wittgenstein does not overtly supply here. Again, it is a better match to assume something more modest: not that they make the same claims, but that the claims they do make, individually, can be made consistent with each other. More precisely, solipsism may be said to "coincide" with "pure realism" in the sense that the insight that may be forced out of it is consistent with, and can usefully be conjoined with "pure realism." The advantage of this interpretation is that this conjunction is exactly what Wittgenstein takes himself to have shown in the previous set of remarks (thus explaining his "Here it can be seen that..."). The insight is that the self is a point without extension. The "pure realist" claims that there is a reality coordinated with the self. And these two claims are not only consistent but usefully conjoin in a straightforward repeat of 5.632 (transposing from subject to self). As a "limit" of the world, the self does not belong to the world, and is thus an extensionless point, but there is nevertheless a world for it to be the limit of, namely that world with which it is coordinated. This is in keeping with the way Wittgenstein summarizes and concludes:

> Thus there really is a sense in which philosophy can talk about the self in a non-psychological way.
> What brings the self into philosophy is the fact that 'the world is my world'.
> The philosophical self [*das philosophische Ich*] is not the human being, not the human body, or the human soul, with which psychology deals, but rather the metaphysical subject, the limit of the world – not a part of it. (TLP 5.641)

2 The Consensus View and the *Tractatus*

We are now in a position to ask how closely Wittgenstein's one extended treatment of the self and "I" in the *Tractatus* corresponds to the consensus view, with its four general points (i)–(iv).

There seems to be little or no match. The explicitly possessive form of the first-person pronoun does play a salient role in these remarks (*my* world, *my* language), as point (iv) would lead one to expect. But if Wittgenstein identifies a source of confusion here, he finds it in the attempts of solipsists to express their position, together with their failure to "follow out strictly" the implications of their view. Had they done so, they would achieve the insight that the self, as a limit of the world, is an extensionless point. Wittgenstein does not claim that there is anything confused or confusing about the first-personal form itself or its use.

Nor does Wittgenstein make any obvious attempt to "denigrate" "I" or the self in these remarks, as point (iii) requires. Certainly, he makes no attempt to eliminate the self or to treat use of "I" as redundant. It turns out that there is a perfectly appropriate use for the notion of a self: the "philosophical" self, identified with the "metaphysical" subject, that which "thinks or entertains ideas." Equally, it turns out that there are perfectly valid uses of first-person forms, e.g., "my world," "my language." Wittgenstein corrects confusions here precisely so as to make the existence and nature of this self, these uses of the first-person form, stand out clearly.

Pace (ii), the claims Wittgenstein makes about this self follow from his arguments concerning the limits of language quite generally. They do not appear to be either directed by or dependent on any specific claims about the first-person pronoun as a linguistic device. And *pace* (i), there is nothing "second fiddle-ish" about this discussion of "I" and the self. It may well be that Wittgenstein conceived coming to a correct understanding of these features as part of his fundamental aim in the *Tractatus* rather than a mere ancillary task, imposed by other concerns.

This is not, of course, to claim that all uses of "I" or all senses of "self" or "subject" pass muster in the *Tractatus*. Indeed, something very like the consensus view may well match what Wittgenstein has in mind in one particular case: "the subject as it is conceived in the superficial psychology of the present day" (5.5421). "Subject" in this sense arises in relation to the logical analysis of belief sentences of the form "*A* believes that *p*" and "*A* has the thought that *p*." Wittgenstein discusses such sentences in explicating 5.4, noting that "if these are considered superficially, it looks as if the proposition *p* stood in some kind of relation to an object *A*" (5.541). He continues as follows:

> It is clear, however, that '*A* believes that *p*', '*A* has the thought that *p*', and '*A* says *p*' are of the form '"*p*"' says *p*': and this does not involve a correlation of a fact with an object, but rather the correlation of facts by means of the correlation of their objects. (TLP 5.542)

In the remark immediately following, he makes a passing reference to "the soul" and "the subject etc":

> This shows that there is no such thing as the soul – the subject, etc – as it is conceived in the superficial psychology of the present day.
> Indeed a composite soul would no longer be a soul. (TLP 5.5421)

A way to make these two *Tractatus* remarks connect up in analysis of the first-person pronoun is suggested by a remark that Wittgenstein made to G.E. Moore in April 1914:

> The relation of 'I believe p' to 'p' can be compared to the relation of 'p says p' to 'p': it is just as impossible that *I* should be a simple as that 'p' should be. (NM 119)

Here, the project may well be to "denigrate" a particular use of "I" (it is eliminable in the analysis of belief sentences of the relevant form) and a particular sense of "subject" (a composite, as conceived in "superficial" psychology). And it may well be that these notions play second fiddle in the discussion: Wittgenstein only discusses this use of "I" and this sense of "subject" to preserve bipolarity, since it turns out that belief sentences of the relevant sort are *not* such that they can be true and can be false. But the discussion does not match the consensus view at the other two points. Explicitly possessive forms of the first person play no role, and what Wittgenstein has to say about the metaphysics and epistemology associated with the subject is not directed by or dependent on what he has to say about the first-person pronoun. Moreover, we can set the discussion to one side as an exceptional case. As we would expect, given the subsequent explication of 5.6, what Wittgenstein says at 5.5421 leaves us with a perfectly viable subject – a single, simple, enduring but non-encounterable self, one that can be identified as a limit of the world – to whom some uses of "I" may make perfectly ineliminable reference.

3 *Philosophical Remarks* §§57–66

The extended discussion of "I" and the self in Wittgenstein's work of 1929–1930 is closely related to the mode of analysis in phenomenology: the inspection of individual examples of immediate experience in the attempt to uncover the essential character that makes them what they are. The discussion starts out from the observation that there is much uncovering work to be done: "the worst philosophical errors always arise when we try to apply our ordinary – physical – language in the area of the immediately given." Wittgenstein associates these errors with the first person:

> One of the most misleading representational techniques [*irreführenden Darstellungsweisen*] in our language is the use of the word 'I', particularly when it is used in representing immediate experience, as in 'I can see a red patch'. (PR §57)

As his "Foreword" (dated November 1930) indicates, what Wittgenstein seeks is "clarity and perspicuity" about this "technique" in order to "grasp it in its essence" (PR §7). He makes a proposal to that end:

> It would be instructive to replace [*ersetzen*] this way of speaking by another in which immediate experience would be represented without using the personal pronoun; for then we'd be able to see that the previous representation wasn't essential [*wesentlich*] to the facts. Not that the representation would be in any sense more correct [*richtiger*] than the old one, but it would serve to show clearly what was logically essential [*das logisch Wesentliche*] in the representation. (PR §7)

The last sentence is particularly worth bearing in mind. The replacement that will be proposed is methodological only, a scenario that makes something "essential" stand out in "clarity and perspicuity." Wittgenstein's intention is not to eliminate anything. This is in line with the proposals of intent in the "Foreword": not to "add one construction to another, moving on and up, from one stage to the next" but to allow a study to "remain where it is" since "what it tries to grasp is always the same."

The exercise in methodological replacement takes the following form:

> We could adopt the following way of representing matters: if I, L. W., have toothache, then that is expressed by means of the proposition 'There is toothache'. But if that is so, what we now express by the proposition 'A has toothache', is put as follows: 'A is behaving as L. W. does when there is toothache'. Similarly we shall say 'It is thinking' and 'A is behaving as L. W. does when it is thinking'. (You could imagine a despotic oriental state where the language is formed [*so gebildet ist*] with the despot as its centre and his name instead of L. W.) It's evident that this way of speaking is equivalent [*gleichwertig*] to ours when it comes to questions of intelligibility and freedom from ambiguity. But it's equally clear that this language could have anyone at all as its centre. (PR §58)

Evidently we are not to interpret the penultimate sentence in an unrestricted way, as the claim that the replacement formulae of the new language – "Despotic" – are "equivalent" to *all* uses of "I." This is just as well, since Despotic offers no equivalent for sentences like "I am six feet tall" or "I am N. N." Wittgenstein's interest is in a particular use of the term: to report on one's mental goings on at the time of utterance, and not even all one's mental goings on, but just one's "immediate experience." Moreover, we are not to interpret the exercise as an attempt to show that even this particular use of "I" can be replaced *in toto*. Again, this is just as well, since the ascription of immediate experience to others on the basis of what they say would not be equivalent for users of Despotic; it would require observation of the despot's behavior. Wittgenstein's aim is restricted: to seeing whether, from a purely phenomenological standpoint, this particular use of "I" could be replaced. Indeed, it was perhaps misleading to have used the term "equivalent" at all, at least if this implies sameness about the way in which self-ascriptions of immediate experience are made. For no user of "I" is obliged to make such self-ascriptions by observation of the despot's behavior, as is incumbent on all users of Despotic, barring the despot himself.

The relevance of the final point, that "this language [Despotic] could have anyone at all as its centre," becomes clearer when Wittgenstein draws the moral from this exercise in methodological replacement: "Only their application really differentiates languages; but if we disregard this, all languages are equivalent." The bridge between the two is the following:

> Now, among all the languages with different people as their centres, each of which I can understand, the one with me as its centre has a privileged status. This language is particularly adequate. How am I to express that? That is, how can I rightly represent its special advantage in words? This can't be done. For, if I do it in the language with me as its centre, then the exceptional status of the description of this language in its own terms is nothing very remarkable, and in the terms of another language my language occupies no privileged status whatever. – The privileged status lies in the application, and if I describe this application, the privileged status again doesn't find expression, since the description depends on the language in which it's couched. And now, which description gives just that which I have in mind depends again on that application. (PR §58)

The idea seems to be this: as regards self-ascriptions of immediate experience "I" does not represent the self as other kinds of term do (names; pronouns). But this is not necessarily an unalterable or even very deep feature of our language. It comes about because we have chosen to have a center-less language in which everyone is able to use the same form of expression (i.e., the type-term "I") to report their immediate experience. We could equally have chosen a centered-language in which the referring task (to forestall the question "of which one are you speaking?") is carried out by other means.

4   The Consensus View and *Philosophical Remarks*

There is not so great a distance between *Philosophical Remarks* and the consensus view, with its four points (i)–(iv), as there is between the consensus view and the *Tractatus*. But still, it is the dissimilarities that rightly draw the attention.

Pace (iii), Wittgenstein is not attempting to denigrate the first-person term by showing that it is eliminable in our language. He is using a contrast with a centered language to make salient what is the case when we use the term. *Pace* (ii), his points are not general but focus exclusively on the self-ascription of immediate experience. And since analysis of the role played by the first-person term is integral to analysis of this self-ascription, *pace* (i), "I" is not playing second fiddle here. There is a hint of (iv) in these passages, since Wittgenstein does cite pretensions to "ownership" expressed in explicitly possessive forms of the first person as amongst the causes of confusion (e.g., the remarks on "I feel *my* pain" and on the locution "I have [toothache; a pain]" §§61–6.) But they remain hints. The discussion of these matters is hesitant and unordered, more like "notes to self."

5   The "Blue Book," pp. 61–70

Perhaps the most influential of Wittgenstein's remarks on "I" and the self are those in the so-called "Blue Book," where he distinguishes "two different cases in the use of the word *I* (or *My*)," calling one "the use as object" and the other "the use as subject."

> Examples of the first kind are these: 'My arm is broken', 'I have grown six inches'. 'I have a bump on my forehead', 'The wind blows my hair about'. Examples of the second kind are '*I* see so-and-so', '*I* hear so-and-so', '*I* try to lift my arm', '*I* think it will rain', '*I* have toothache'. One can point to the difference between these two categories by saying: The cases of the first category involve the recognition of a person, and there is in these cases the possibility of an error [...] On the other hand, there is no question of recognising a person when I say I have toothache. To ask 'are you sure that it's *you* who have pains?' would be nonsensical. Now, when in this case no error is possible, it is because the move which we might be inclined to think of as an error, a 'bad move', is no move of the game at all [...] To say 'I have pain' is no more a statement *about* a particular person than moaning is. (BB 66–7)

It is not coincidental that this distinction divides neatly between uses of "I" for which Despotic would offer an accurate replacement (uses "as subject") and uses for which it would not (uses "as object"). But the aim has broadened, beyond the attempt to get at the essence of statements that ascribe immediate experience. Hence there is a point to marking off and recognizing what is peculiar to statements whose purpose is not to ascribe such experience.

The argument takes a simple form: (1) there is a certain phenomenon: it would make no sense to ask certain questions; and (2) to explain this phenomenon we need to realize that there is no recognition of a person involved in uses "as subject." This claim holds common ground with another: that such uses of "I" cannot fail to refer. Both have antecedents: there are hints in Hume that one can use "I" to express thoughts about oneself without the need to identify what is being referred to, and it is sometimes said that Kant thought these claims applied to the "I think" of transcendental apperception. But Wittgenstein's version is notably stronger than others have tended to hold, before or after him. In his view, such uses do not even count as being *about* the subject of the ascribed experience, let alone as *referring* to him.

A notable and potentially confusing feature of Wittgenstein's examples is that they seem immune not only to mistakes of identification ("which individual is being spoken of?") but to mistakes of ascription ("what is being said about the individual being spoken of?"). Where I express my immediate experience in saying "I have toothache," it seems equally nonsensical to ask "I know I feel something, but is it *toothache*?" as it is to ask "I know the subject of this experience has toothache, but is it *I* that have it?" The set of examples of uses of "I" as subject ought, presumably, to be extended to include cases in which this double immunity does not hold. But then it becomes difficult to see why the original distinction should hold at all. For if we consider first-personal statements simply in the light of possibilities of misidentification, immunity seems to apply equally to uses "as object." I might well be mistaken in saying "I have grown six inches," for example (I confuse someone else's medical report for my own), but I will not thereby have misidentified myself; I will merely have falsely ascribed certain properties to myself, properties that in truth belong to another. The same applies to the other examples, like "My arm is broken" (numbed by an accident, and seeing an obviously broken arm before me, I may think it is mine when it is in fact yours).

If, as seems to be the case, the difference that Wittgenstein spots has to do with immunity to mis-ascription rather than to misidentification, he was wrong to think of it as marking a distinction between uses of "I." (Wittgenstein's italicization in the quoted passage is itself evidence of a certain confusion, as if what is distinctive about uses "as subject" were audible, something we register if we attend to what bears emphasis in spoken utterance; but sentences using *I* "as object" bear similar emphasis, of course.) It marks instead a distinction in what one may self-ascribe. But the overall effect is to toughen his position. For if there is no such distinction between uses of "I," then what holds for uses "as subject" presumably applies to all. And if there is never a possibility of misidentification for me whenever I use "I," then perhaps "there is no question of recognising a person" whenever I do so, and hence no making "a statement *about* a particular person." It is presumably because he recognized this that Wittgenstein quickly dropped all mention of a distinction in uses of "I."

This does not mean, of course, that there is no possibility of misidentification for others when I use "I." Indeed, it is quite clear that this possibility exists and is often realized. So there is every reason to suppose that recognition of the referent is necessary if an "I"-containing utterance of mine is to be understood by others. Indeed, my uses of "I" fulfill the referring task for others just as any singular term does: by providing a positive answer to the question "which individual is being spoken of?" Hence, for others, my "I"-containing statements refer; they are *about* me. There is no evidence that Wittgenstein ignored the significance of these points, but he does sometimes express himself in a way that may mislead: a remark of 1936 reappears with slight modification in *Philosophical Investigations* as "I does not name [*benennt*] a person" (PI §410). (Context is usually ignored when this remark is quoted; there is a "but" aligned with the "not," and it is the former that receives the stress and to which the point tends: "'I' does not name a person, nor 'here' a place, and 'this' is not a name. But they are connected with names. Names are explained by means of them.") These sayings make sense if we assume what is explicit in the "Blue Book" discussion: that he is here abstracting from what is characteristic of "I" in general, which includes its essential function as a communicative device, so as to focus simply on what is required by the individual who uses the term in expressing their thoughts to themselves.

6 The Consensus View and the "Blue Book"

The consensus view with its four points (i)–(iv) does not adequately represent the "Blue Book" discussion.

Pace (iii), it is not an attempt to denigrate "I," by denying that it is a referring expression. "I" does not fulfill the referring task for the one using it, but it does so for others, and the fact that it is capable of doing so is an essential feature of the term, one that holds even when it is being used without communicative intent. *Pace* (i), the first person does not play second fiddle in Wittgenstein's discussion here.

There is a better match with the other two points. In line with (ii), one reason why the first-person term has prominence here is that Wittgenstein uses his observations concerning it to support his attendant remarks about the metaphysics and epistemology associated with persons. And in line with (iv), Wittgenstein's argument depends on identifying where it is and is not possible to make mistakes in self-ascription, which ensures that confusions about ownership play a key feature in the discussion. This is so, despite the fact that Wittgenstein falls into confusions of his own here (quickly and silently corrected), which led to the false distinction between uses of "I."

7 *Philosophical Investigations* §§398–411

The dominating feature of these passages is that they read like a kind of inner musing. The points made arise out of questions addressed to Wittgenstein by a character who appears to hold very similar views. Moreover, the responses tend to press beyond to a stronger view, but in their own questioning way, so that the underlying sense is of a testing and probing rather than a settled stating of views.

Wittgenstein begins in the familiar, limited context: where one is expressing one's thoughts for no one's benefit but one's own. Here, when I imagine an object or actually see it, and wish to say to myself what distinguishes me from those who do not imagine or see it, the words "At any rate only *I* have got THIS" would serve no purpose:

> Indeed, can't one add: "There is here no question of a 'seeing' – and therefore none of a 'having' – nor of a subject, nor therefore of the I either"? [...] If you logically exclude other people's having something, it loses its sense to say that you have it [...] In so far as it cannot belong to anyone else, it doesn't belong to me either. (PI §398)

It seems likely that the argument here shares a similar form with the "Blue Book" remarks concerning identification and reference, but with two differences. First, Wittgenstein is interested in testing stronger conclusions. The fact that it would make no sense to ask "I know the subject of this experience has got THIS, but is it *I* that do so?" suggests to him not only that there is no recognition of a person here, but that the use of "I" serves no purpose, and is perhaps eliminable. Second, Wittgenstein is interested in extending the argument, from the case of identification and reference to ascription and predication. The fact that, in this context, it would equally make no sense to ask "I know I have got something, but is it THIS?" suggests to him that there is no ascription of properties here either, and that the whole notion of a "having" may serve no purpose, is perhaps eliminable. Similarly, so it appears, with the particular mode of "having," i.e., seeing. The fact that it makes no sense to ask "I know I have got THIS, but am I *seeing* it?" suggests to him that "there is here no question of a 'seeing' either."

Wittgenstein then moves beyond the limited context to consider the role an utterance like "I now have such-and-such a visual image" might play for others (PI § 402). Wittgenstein imagines an interlocutor who treats the words "I have" like "Attention please!," as if they do not serve a referring role for others either. They are "a sign" for them, but the speaker should really express himself differently if he wants to make clear what that sign is. Its purpose is to draw the hearer's attention to the description of the visual image, not to the speaker; hence "Attention please!" rather than "I have..." But Wittgenstein baulks at this stronger view:

> When, as in this case, one disapproves of the expressions of ordinary language (which, after all, do their duty), we have got a picture in our heads which conflicts with the picture of our ordinary way of speaking. (PI §402)

This "picture" is associated with the thought that "our way of speaking does not describe the facts as they really are." And Wittgenstein finds this unappealing, not least because he identifies it with the underlying thought that sustains disputes between idealists, solipsists, and realists (PI §402).

So the interlocutor returns to the limited case, where only the interests of the speaker are invoked, claiming that "I am in pain" does not "point to a person who is in pain, since in a certain sense I don't know *who* is." In case this seems like mere repetition of a now familiar point, Wittgenstein turns it to another use in his response. He claims that it is indeed true that no *person* is being pointed to or named in this case. For although "person" has a great variety of identity criteria, none of them are invoked for one's own benefit when one says "I am in pain." For the same reason, we should not say that one "knows who" (i.e., which person) is in pain. Perhaps for this reason – he gives no other – Wittgenstein is willing to suggest that it may not be to a *person* that one draws attention when one says "I am in pain" for the benefit of others. "No, I just want to draw their attention to *myself*" (PI § 405). Again, he suggests that it is perhaps between *myself* and other people that I distinguish in using the words "I am...," rather than "the person L.W. and the person N.N." (PI §406).

Wittgenstein does describe a peculiar context in which it might make sense to say something like "I know who (which person) is in pain; it's me" (PI §409). If I am amongst a group of people being given electric shocks by a machine, and I know that this machine is so set that it only ever shocks one person at a time, I might observe people's faces to see who is receiving the shock, and then say "I know who is being shocked: it is X," and on the next occasion, "I know who is being shocked: it is Y," and on the next, "I know who is being shocked: it is me." But the point of course is that this is a game with a standard response-formula that the players are to use, no matter who is being shocked. The game would break down if the machine malfunctioned so that more than one person were shocked at the same time. And it is this possibility that indicates what is peculiar and relevant about this particular context: that, when the machine is functioning properly, I do have knowledge of persons to express, knowledge I have gained in an unusual way, by being aware of the sensation of being shocked and by knowing the conditions peculiar to this game. When I say "I know who is being shocked: it is me," what I know, without needing to observe anyone else, is that, in this particular moment, no other person in this group is being shocked.

Change the context sufficiently, therefore, and even the oddest sentences gain practical application. Attending to the changes necessary tells us about those sentences. Wittgenstein goes on to suggest we learn about different uses of the possessive pronoun in this way (PI §411). Thus he compares several uses, where one's imaginings must become progressively energetic if one is to give them practical application: (i) "Are these books *my* books?" (ii) "Is this foot *my* foot?" (iii) "Is this body *my* body? (iv) "Is this sensation *my* sensation?" Practical applications for (i) require little or no imagination. For (ii), one might imagine that one's foot is anaesthetized or paralyzed. For (iii), one might imagine one was pointing to a reflection in a mirror, or that what one meant was "Does my body look like *that*?" The final use (iv), however, goes beyond any imaginative reconstruction that Wittgenstein is willing to fabricate. The problem, as he sees it, centers on the use of "this" rather than the use of "my":

> But which sensation is *this* one? That is, how is one using the demonstrative pronoun here? Certainly otherwise than in, say, the first example [i.e., (i)]. Here, again, one goes astray, because one imagines that by directing one's attention to a sensation, one is pointing at it. (PI §411)

8 The Consensus View and *Philosophical Investigations*

There is little in these passages to support the consensus view and its four points (i)–(iv). Ownership and the use of "my" are salient and much of the discussion is of the first person as a linguistic device, as (iv) specifies. But this issue is not dealt with purely to satisfy the demands of another discussion, as (i) requires, and the first person is not "denigrated" as (iii) requires. Indeed, Wittgenstein goes out of his way to blunt the eliminativist tendencies of his overeager interlocutor, showing how even the oddest uses of "I" and "know" may have practical uses.

The picture that forms around the consensus view is certainly enlightening about Wittgenstein on "I" and the self, but this is so because rather than in spite of the difficulties we face in making it match. Where the picture fits, it is straightforwardly illuminating about Wittgenstein's thought. Where it does not fit, the way in which details are thereby made salient – as exaggerated, or oversimplified, or overlooked – turns out to be at least equally enlightening.

Where the first person does become a subject for Wittgenstein, it is sometimes, but not always, because he thinks a more "exalted" view must distort whatever is then the primary object of his attention. Where he thinks such distortion does occur, it is sometimes, but not always, because he thinks mistaken views of the possessive forms of the first person are in play, cultivating a confused or unwarranted sense of "ownership."

Mismatches can be enlightening about details as well as connections. The regular rejection of more exalted views of the first person certainly gives underlying continuity to the great surface variance in Wittgenstein's developing views of "I" and the self. But finding such continuities is so attractive that differences may be ignored, distinctions lost. Contrary to the consensus view, there is little or no "denigrating" of the first person in his thought, whether of the reductionist or eliminativist kind, and where it may be manifest, it is applied to particular, limited uses only, and by contrast with the general case.

References

Glock, H.-J. (1996). *A Wittgenstein Dictionary*. Oxford: Blackwell.
Hacker, P.M.S. (1990/93). *Wittgenstein: Meaning and Mind. Volume 3 of an Analytical Commentary on the Philosophical Investigations. Part I. Essays*. Oxford: Blackwell.

Further Reading

Anscombe, G.E.M. (1959/63). *An Introduction to Wittgenstein's Tractatus*. Second edition. London: Hutchinson.
de Gaynesford, M. (2006). *I: The Meaning of the First Person Term*. Oxford: Oxford University Press.
Fogelin, R.J. (1976/87). *Wittgenstein*. Second edition. London: Routledge and Kegan Paul.
Hacker, P.M.S. (1972/86). *Insight and Illusion: Themes in the Philosophy of Wittgenstein*. Revised edition. Oxford: Clarendon Press.
Kenny, A. (1973/2006). *Wittgenstein*. Revised edition. Oxford: Blackwell.
Pears, D. (1988). *The False Prison*. Oxford: Oxford University Press.
Schroeder, S. (2006). *Wittgenstein: The Way out of the Fly-Bottle*. Cambridge: Polity Press.

31

Wittgenstein on Action and the Will

MARIA ALVAREZ

Wittgenstein's views on action and the will changed throughout his philosophical writings, although there are common themes to be found within this evolution. His early views on the will and voluntary action were strongly influenced by Schopenhauer but he later abandoned some of the central aspects of that conception of the will. (For accounts of how his views developed see Hacker, 2000 and Hyman, 2011.) This chapter will be concerned mainly with his later views on action and the will, as expressed in remarks on these topics mainly in *Philosophical Investigations* (especially §§611–47) though I shall also refer to *Remarks on the Philosophy of Psychology*, Volume I. I shall identify and explore some core themes in those remarks and examine how some of these were taken up and developed by Wittgenstein's student Elizabeth Anscombe, in her influential monograph *Intention* (1957). Regarded by many as a seminal work in the philosophy of action, *Intention* has recently attracted much renewed attention. As we shall see, the relatively few remarks Wittgenstein made on these topics contain rich insights and raise a variety of important issues; and some of these, partly through the way Anscombe developed and augmented them in *Intention*, are again at the center of contemporary debates about human agency and the will.

Given his conception of philosophy and his (related) writing style, it is not easy to summarize Wittgenstein's views on any topic (see Chapter 2, WITTGENSTEIN'S TEXTS AND STYLE). This is no less true of the topics that concern us. Nonetheless, there are some clear themes that took up his attention, which include the notion of a voluntary movement and the related concepts of willing, trying, intending, and knowledge of one's intentional actions, among others. I shall begin with his discussion of voluntary bodily movements.

One of Wittgenstein's targets in the *Investigations* is the idea, with a long pedigree in the history of philosophy, that a bodily movement is voluntary when it is caused by an act of willing – a "volition." (This idea was explicitly and forcefully attacked also by Ryle in chapter 3 of *The Concept of Mind*, 1949.) Remarks PI §§611–21 challenge this idea, first by depicting the way we are inclined to think about the nature and role of willing in philosophical accounts of voluntary actions, and then by challenging the presuppositions that underpin that picture. So, Wittgenstein points out that we are tempted to think of willing as an extraordinary phenomenon: for it is what makes actions voluntary and yet it is not something within my control, not something that I can bring about, and *a fortiori*, not bring about at will, for I cannot "will willing" (§613). In that sense, it seems to be "an experience" that "comes when it comes, and I cannot bring it about" (§611) and yet it is something at which I cannot fail, as I can fail to move my body or a stone, when I try: "One can say: 'I will, but my body does not obey me' – but not: 'My will does not obey me.' (Augustine.)" (§618). This, we must conclude, makes it very hard to understand how any action can be voluntary in any significant sense, given that what is supposed to make actions voluntary are these elusive, autonomous, and mysterious acts of willing.

Wittgenstein's next move is to examine the presuppositions on which this picture rests in order to dismantle them. First, he draws our attention to the fact that these remarks depend on construing the phrase "bring something about by willing" in a special sense, a sense in which we *can* supposedly bring about, say, the movement of our limbs by willing the relevant movements, but cannot bring about an act of willing by willing it. But (i) we do not bring about the motions of our limbs *by willing them* to happen, indeed it is not clear that there is anything we bring about *by willing it* to happen; and (ii) in the sense in which we can bring about anything, such as the movement of our limbs or stomachache, we can also bring about an act of willing. This is the sense in which we bring about things, more or less directly, in or by acting: I bring about a movement of a chair by moving it, and I can bring about stomachache by overeating. Likewise, I can bring about an act of willing to swim – for instance by jumping into the water (§613). Anscombe makes a related point in *Intention* but considering the matter from the other end, so to speak, when she says:

> People sometimes say that one can get one's arm to move by an act of will but not a matchbox; but if they mean 'Will a matchbox to move and it won't', the answer is 'If I will my arm to move in that way, it won't', and if they mean 'I can move my arm but not the match box' the answer is that I can move the matchbox – nothing easier.
>
> (Anscombe, 1957, p.52: §29)

Thus, the idea that we cannot bring about willing, or the motion of things beyond our bodies "by willing," while we can bring about motions of our limbs in that way, is shown to rest on a confused and ambiguous understanding of the phrase "bring about by willing." When this confusion is dispelled and the phrase disambiguated, it becomes clear that we can either bring about all sorts of things by willing, such as movements of our bodies, as well as acts of will, or nothing at all.

Second, and relatedly, the idea that willing is a special kind of action which is mysterious, like "an extensionless point," a kind of effortless and frictionless doing, is misguided and is encouraged by the thought that, while we can fail at moving our bodies or a table, we cannot fail at willing. Wittgenstein points out that "in the sense in which I cannot fail to will, I cannot try to will either" (§618) and "I can always will only inasmuch as I can never try to will" (§619), because willing is not really an action and so not something I can try, or fail to do. Thus, echoing but overcoming a view of Schopenhauer's that he had once accepted, namely that willing "cannot be allowed to stop anywhere short of the action" (§615), Wittgenstein notes that, if willing is thought of as an action, then it is so in the ordinary sense of the word; so it is speaking, writing, walking, lifting a thing, imagining something. But it is also trying, attempting, making an effort, – to speak, to write, to lift a thing, to imagine something etc.

(PI §615)

But willing is then not a mysterious, infallible, action, "an extensionless point," "separate from all experience" (§620). If it is anything, it is something ordinary that we may be said to do when we speak, walk or lift something, or try to do those things, "at will."

Wittgenstein goes on to make a couple of brief but important remarks about trying, partly intended to illuminate these points about willing but of interest in their own right because of what they say about the notions of trying, intending, and voluntary action. He first says: "When I raise my arm I do not usually *try* to raise it" (§622); and in the next paragraph he says: "'I want to get to that house at all costs.' – But if there is no difficulty about it – *can* I strive at all costs to get to the house?" (§623).

Although the question is rhetorical, Wittgenstein's answer is "No." And the point of these remarks seems to be to suggest that one can try or strive to do something only if there is some difficulty in doing it that opens up the possibility of failure and that, therefore, we don't normally try to do things we can easily do. For example, since I usually have no difficulty in raising my arm, I don't usually try to raise it when I do raise it (see also, RPP I §51). Is Wittgenstein right? And how is this issue related to willing? I take these questions in turn.

Wittgenstein's claim about trying conflicts with a familiar view, often called the "ubiquity thesis," that we try to do everything we intentionally do – a thesis endorsed by Grice (1961 and 1989), O'Shaughnessy (1973 and 1980), Armstrong (1973), McCann (1975), and Hornsby (1980 and 2010), among others. (Some of these philosophers, e.g., O'Shaughnessy, think of the act of trying as playing a role analogous to that played by acts of willing in the traditional view of voluntary action outlined above: so for O'Shaughnessy, tryings are psychological events that cause outer bodily motions.) On the face of it, the ubiquity thesis goes against pre-philosophical intuitions as well as ordinary use, and the onus of proof seems to be with its defenders. I shall assess some of the arguments advanced by the latter, although reasons of space preclude anything like an exhaustive examination.

Brian O'Shaughnessy, for example, gives the following argument. "We speak of trying only when success is in doubt" (1973, p. 365) and this may suggest that trying is not ubiquitous, since very often the success of our actions or those of others doesn't seem to be at all doubtful. However, he adds, this is a mistake because, as a matter of fact, success is *always* in doubt because "no event, including intended act-events, can be foretold as an absolute certainty" (p. 365). "Even if I act with the utmost conviction, say, under the simple heading of moving my arm, I must simultaneously recognize that that arm may fail to budge" (p. 366). He concludes: "It is this special brand of uncertainty hanging like a question mark over everything, that gives trying a permanent foothold in intentional action" (p. 366). The argument is supplemented with the Gricean observation that, though true, it may still be misleading to say that someone tried to A when one knows the person A-ed, because that might suggest that the agent failed to A, which would be false. And that, O'Shaughnessy might add, is why the ubiquity thesis is not reflected in ordinary use.

One might respond to O'Shaughnessy's argument by pointing out that it is right to speak of trying only when grounds for doubt about success go *beyond* the universal possibility of failure that he adverts to – that is, when there is some difficulty that provides such grounds for doubt. That, one might add, is *the point* of the concept "trying." And, since very often there is no difficulty and hence no such grounds, the word "try" does not apply in those cases. If that is right, then O'Shaughnessy's universal possibility of failure only shows that whenever one intends to A, one may encounter a difficulty in A-ing; and when one does, then one will either try to A or give up one's intention to A. What the universal possibility of failure does *not* show is that one always *does* encounter such difficulty, and hence it does not show that one always tries when one does A intentionally.

(The Gricean observation rebuts an objection to the ubiquity thesis, namely, that it is always wrong because misleading to say that someone tried to do something he was able to do; for one can retort that it may always be misleading but it's not *always* wrong, i.e., false. The observation, however, does not provide any evidence in favor of the ubiquity thesis. Moreover, it does not address the different objection that, if the ubiquity thesis were right, then if one says in advance of acting that one is going to try to do something one normally does effortlessly, or say that one tried when one did it without difficulty, the suggestion that one was going to or did encounter a difficulty would be an implicature and so it should be possible to cancel it – but it is not. "I tried to raise my hand – by which I don't mean that I failed, for I succeeded" might be fine but "I tried to raise my hand – by which I don't mean that I had any difficulty in doing so for I did it easily" is decidedly odd. And this suggests that the idea of the possibility of failure because of difficulty is not a mere implicature when one talks about trying to do something.)

In his book *The Will* (1980, vol.2, p.94), O'Shaughnessy gives another argument designed to show that we try even when we encounter no difficulty in A-ing intentionally. He uses the example of an agent who is asked to raise his arm and does so without problem but is persuaded, by means of an elaborate deception, that he has in fact not raised it. In such a case, O'Shaughnessy says, the agent knows that he did something and, he adds, the agent will "properly record" what he did as "I tried." The alleged conclusion is that the man did try to raise his arm, since he can properly record what transpired with that description, even though he raised his arm without difficulty and had no doubt that he would do so prior to raising it.

But is it right that in such a case the agent could "properly record" what he did as "I tried"? It seems uncontroversial that the agent could properly record what he *thinks he did* in that way, given that he knows he did something (say, tighten his muscles) and that he had the intention of raising his arm, and he was then made to believe that he had failed to bring about the intended result (the arm's rising). But whether "I tried" would be a proper record of what the man *actually did* is precisely what is at issue, given that the man raised his arm without difficulty. And O'Shaughnessy says nothing to support his claim that "I tried" is the proper record of what he did.

Jennifer Hornsby has recently reprised an earlier argument for the thesis (from Hornsby, 1980, p.35; a similar point is made in O'Shaughnessy, 1973, p.368), with an example about unlocking a door:

> An onlooker who had not foreseen any problem about unlocking the door could say, when it was revealed that the person had the wrong key, that they had known all along that the person would try to unlock it. And if we change the example, so that the person actually holds the key to the door, but the onlooker supposes that she has taken out a different key, then, when there proves to be no problem about unlocking the door, the onlooker has no

need to withdraw the claim that the person tried to unlock it. It seems, then, that *when an agent is intentionally φ-ing, doubts or difficulties about her succeeding do not bear on the question of whether she is trying to φ.*

(Hornsby, 2010, p.19, italics added)

These examples, however, do not support the italicized claim, in particular the claim that difficulties about someone's succeeding "do not bear on the question whether someone was trying." The reasoning in the passage seems to be as follows. Since in both cases the onlooker could claim to know that the agent tried to unlock the door, it follows that in both cases the agent *did try*. And yet, in the first case the onlooker did not entertain any doubts about the agent's success, while in the second there was no difficulty. Thus, the presence of doubts or difficulties is irrelevant to whether the man tried.

If that is the reasoning, the argument is unconvincing. For one thing, in the first case there were no doubts, but there was difficulty; while in the second case, though there was no difficulty, there was doubt. Thus, even if it were true that the man had tried in both cases, the example would not show that *doubts or difficulties do not bear* on whether someone tried. In any case, Hornsby gives no persuasive reason why we should accept that in the first case the onlooker *knew* that the agent would try, nor why in the second we should accept that the agent *did* try (and that the onlooker could know it). I'll discuss these in reverse order.

Why should we accept that the onlooker could rightly claim to know that the person tried, and hence accept that the person *did* try, in the second case, when there was no difficulty? Surely not because he could claim to know in the first case, when there *was* a difficulty, for that would simply assume the truth of the proposition that the argument is supposed to prove. And Hornsby gives no independent argument for the claim that the man did try in the second case. We may concede that the onlooker was justified in believing that the agent would try to unlock the door, given his belief about the key. But his belief, even if justified, may have been false. And whether the belief was *true* is precisely the point at issue. Hornsby cannot assume that it is and *also* claim that the example itself proves that the agent tried.

What about the first case: what reason is there to accept that the onlooker knew "all along that the person would try to unlock" the door, while not being aware of any possible difficulty? Even though we can agree that the person tried to unlock the door in this case, no reason is given to say that the onlooker knew this all along. It is true that the onlooker knew all along that the person would use a key with the intention of unlocking the door. But, again, whether knowing *that* is the same as knowing that the person would *try* to unlock the door is precisely the moot point, since it depends on whether using a key with the intention of unlocking the door *is*, regardless of difficulty, trying to unlock a door.

Admittedly, once the onlooker learns about the difficulty, he could rightly describe the action that he knew all along the agent would perform, namely put the key in the lock with the intention of unlocking it, as "his trying to unlock the door." That, however, is because he now knows about the difficulty. What we need, but the example does not give, is a reason why the onlooker could be said to know that "trying" was the right description of what the agent was doing *before* coming to know about the wrong key. So this example does not establish the ubiquity thesis either – rather it presupposes it.

Something similar seems true of another pair of cases in that same paper by Hornsby concerning an agent, Adrian, who is walking along with the intention of getting to his office. In the first case, we are told, Adrian turns round because he finds the area where his office is cordoned off due to a bomb scare. In the second, there is no bomb scare: Adrian just changes his mind at the same point on his way and decides to go to the library instead. Hornsby claims that, since in the first case Adrian was trying to get to the office, he was doing so also in the second case even though, she says, in the second case he *did not try* – drawing our attention to the fact that someone may have been doing something and yet not do it, e.g., may "have *been crossing* the street, although they did not *cross* the street, having been knocked over by a bus, as it might be" (2010, p.20). But, again, even if we agreed that Adrian was trying to get to his office in the first case, why should we agree that he was also trying in the second, when he encountered no difficulty in getting there? For the mere fact that in both cases Adrian is "doing the same", i.e., walking with the intention of getting to his office, is not enough to shore up the controversial claim that in both cases he was trying to get to his office.

Moreover, it is doubtful that Adrian tried even in the first case, at least as it is described. For if upon seeing the cordon, Adrian didn't ask to be let through, or try to jump over the cordon, or something of the kind, we may reasonably conclude that he didn't try to get to his office, notwithstanding his having encountered a difficulty: arguably, the presence of a difficulty is necessary but not sufficient for trying. After all, having learnt that others were let through when they asked, Adrian's boss may rightly censure him for his lack of trying. And this seems to be supported by the fact that Adrian could have retorted that he assumed (wrongly, as it turned out) that, in the circumstances, it was futile to try. So, while we may agree that in the first case Adrian was walking with the intention of getting to his office, or that he was walking to his office, we needn't agree that he *tried* to get there if, when he encountered the difficulty, he did nothing to overcome it.

Finally, even if Adrian had tried in the first case, say because he asked to be let through or whatever, it does not follow that he *was trying* all the time he was walking to his office. It is plausible to argue that his trying consisted precisely in what he did when he encountered the difficulty, for instance, in his asking to be allowed to pass, and that the unimpeded office-wise walking he was doing up to that point was *not* trying to get to his office.

Thus these examples do not seem to show or even suggest that the presence of difficulties is irrelevant to whether an agent was trying or did try to do something. Instead, Wittgenstein's remarks that trying involves difficulties seem wholly plausible. As I said above, these remarks are to be understood in the context of his discussion of voluntary movements, willing, intending, meaning, etc., the thrust of which is to dislodge the view that these terms describe "mental activities" (§693) or events, in favor of the view that they describe actions *in their circumstances* (see Hornsby, 2011). In particular, and to paraphrase another remark of Wittgenstein's, the claim that someone tried to do something stands in need of "outward criteria" concerning difficulties in execution: trying is not, *pace* O'Shaughnessy, "the ultimate psychological description" (1973, p.373) of "an inner active chosen event" that "causes or brings about an outer or merely bodily event" (p.375), thus giving rise to a voluntary movement. And the fact that trying requires the presence of difficulty explains why, if one thinks of the willing subject as Schopenhauer did, as "a motor which has no inertia in itself to overcome" (§618), one will be inclined to conclude that the willing subject can never fail to will. But then, Wittgenstein reminds us, neither can he *try* to will. And these are grammatical remarks about the terms "trying" and "willing" (see Chapter 14, GRAMMAR AND GRAMMATICAL

STATEMENTS): they tell us that the phenomena they refer to, if they refer at all, are not inner unobservable mental occurrences but rather things that have public criteria, namely ordinary actions in specific contexts:

> Voluntary movements are certain movements with their normal *surroundings* of intention, learning, trying, acting. Movements, of which it makes sense to say that they are sometimes voluntary, sometimes involuntary, are movements in a special surrounding.
> (RPP I §776)

And this is consistent with the fact that, in some unusual circumstances, an agent's trying to move his body may consist in some internal bodily change that is not manifested in external behavior, such as, for example, the tightening of certain muscles.

As well as the volitionist picture of voluntary action and its "trying" variant, Wittgenstein attacks effectively an alternative: the suggestion, developed by William James (in *The Principles of Psychology*, 1890), that voluntary movements are accompanied by certain "kinaesthetic sensations," which we recognize because we remember experiencing the same sensations in the past when those movements occurred (see also Chapter 48, WITTGENSTEIN AND PRAGMATISM). Voluntary movements, according to James, are not caused by volitions but rather they are produced by the memories of the relevant kinesthetic sensations. Wittgenstein introduces James's suggestion in this familiar passage:

> Let us not forget this: when 'I raise my arm', my arm goes up. And the problem arises: what is left over if I subtract the fact that my arm goes up from the fact that I raise my arm?
> (Are the kinaesthetic sensations my willing?) (PI §621)

James's picture is undermined by two considerations. One is that, even if we assume that I do have such sensations when I move my body, the sensations could not play the role assigned to them. For I have no other criterion for whether the feeling I experience is the right feeling for *this* movement – whether I am "recognizing it right" (§625) – than my knowledge that I have raised my arm. In other words: I don't know that I have raised my arm because I recognize the feelings that accompany my arm raisings; rather, if I do experience such feelings, I know that those are feelings that accompany arm raisings because I *know* that I have raised my arm (I say "even if we assume that I do have such sensations," because Wittgenstein questions whether we always experience them when we move our bodies; see PPF viii 56–63). The other point is that, although I normally know how my limbs are moving when I move them voluntarily, this is not because something, some feelings or kinesthetic sensations advise me of these movements. I don't attend to any feelings or sensations and then infer from their nature what the movements and position of my limbs are. It is true that I may not know my movements other than by looking if I have lost all sensation – but that is because I would have thereby lost the ordinary capacity to make voluntary movements (for further remarks on these issues see RPP I §§390–408).

Both these ideas were taken up and developed by Anscombe in her discussion of things "known without observation" – that is, not by perception, on the basis of sensations, by inference, etc. – because the class of voluntary movements and that of intentional actions, she says, are subclasses of "the class of things known without observation" (p.14: §8).

In the *Investigations*, Wittgenstein wrote: "When people talk about the possibility of foreknowledge of the future they always forget the fact of the prediction of one's own voluntary movements" (§629); and again: "Think of the fact that one can predict one's own future action by an expression of intention" (PPF x §98). And in §631 he draws our attention to these two types of claim: "I'm going to take two powders now" and "in half an hour I shall be sick," arguing that the difference between them is not to be explained by saying

> that in the first case I am the agent, in the second merely the observer. Or that in the first case I see the causal connection from the inside, in the second from the outside.

And he adds:

> It wasn't on the basis of observations of my behaviour that I said I was going to take two powders. The antecedents of this statement were different. I mean the thoughts, actions and so on which led up to it.
>
> (PI §631)

Anscombe develops this point in *Intention*, and the first and last few remarks of the book are devoted to exploring the differences between statements of these two types. She takes up Wittgenstein's point that both are predictions, and suggests that the difference between them is that those of the first type are expressions of intention while those of the second are "estimates of the future." But what is the difference between *those*?

Her own suggestion is that the difference lies in three features: the way each of those statements is "justified"; what counts as a "contradiction" for each type; and the nature of mistakes in each case. These are features also of descriptions of what one is doing intentionally (a concept Anscombe substitutes for Wittgenstein's "voluntary movements" and "voluntary action," roughly on the grounds that the former has greater philosophical and practical significance). I shall say something about the first and third features in that order.

The first feature echoes PI §631, as well as the following passage: "My prediction (in my expression of intention) has not the same foundation as his prediction of what I shall do, and the conclusions to be drawn from these predictions are quite different" (PPF xi §329), for Anscombe's claim is that, while ordinary predictions are justified by giving evidence (and this includes predicting someone else's action on the basis of *their* expressions of intention), one's expressions of intention are justified by giving one's reasons for acting. A substantial part of *Intention* is devoted to examining the notion of a reason for acting, which Anscombe links to the Aristotelian notion of practical reasoning and to the concept of the good (broadly conceived). In essence, her point is that when asked to justify one's action or intention for the future, an agent will refer to some aspect of the action that gives its "desirability characterisation" – but nothing like that would enter a justification of an ordinary prediction. Thus, the thoughts and actions that "lead up" to an expression of intention, Anscombe says, concern the relationship between the proposed action and the good. Moreover, she says that a (true) answer to the question "Why are you doing that?" along the lines "I was not aware I was doing it" would show the action not to be intentional (see p.11: §6). This is because one knows what one is doing intentionally not by observing (and hence discovering) that one is doing it but rather through what she calls the "practical knowledge" we have of our intentional actions. This again echoes Wittgenstein: "So one might say: voluntary movement is marked by the absence of surprise" (PI §628). (But might we not be surprised that we have done what we intended to do, as Davidson's carbon-copy maker who discovers, perhaps with surprise, that he has succeeded in making ten carbon copies as he intended to do? Even so, one would be surprised at the success rather than at the fact that one was doing whatever trying consisted in in the particular case.)

The idea that we have a special kind of knowledge of what we are going to do and of what we are doing intentionally, what Anscombe calls "practical knowledge," is one of the central themes of *Intention*. And by calling it that, she is deliberately extending the ordinary sense of that phrase in two ways. One is that this phrase "is most often used in connexion with specialized skills" but, she says,

> there is no reason to think that this notion has application only in such contexts. 'Intentional action' always presupposes what might be called 'knowing one's way about' the matters described in the description under which an action can be called intentional, and this knowledge is exercised in the action and is practical knowledge.
>
> (Anscombe, 1957, p.88: §48)

The other is something already mentioned: that she includes under "practical knowledge" our knowledge that we are doing something when we do it intentionally, or of what we shall do in the future when we intend to do it.

And this brings us to the third way in which expressions of intention differ from ordinary predictions. Wittgenstein says: "We can often predict a man's actions from his expressions of a decision. An important language-game" (§632). But one way this language-game differs from predictions of the actions of others based on evidence is the ways in which they are each susceptible to error. Anscombe says that, although we have practical knowledge of what we (shall) do intentionally and hence others can predict our actions on the basis of our expressions of intention, we are not infallible: we may sincerely say we're doing A when in fact we are not, or say we are going to do A and yet not do it. This, again, echoes Wittgenstein:

> It is possible to imagine a guessing of intentions like the guessing of thoughts, but also a guessing of what someone is actually *going to do*.
>
> To say "He alone can know what he intends" is nonsense: to say "He alone can know what he will do", wrong. For the prediction contained in my expression of intention (for example "When it strikes five I am going home") need not come true, and someone else may know what will really happen.
>
> (PPF xi §328)

So the predictions that expressions of intention embody are not infallible. However, Anscombe says, a distinctive feature of practical knowledge is that "Theophrastus's principle" applies here: when there is a discrepancy between what the agent says and what he does, then, at least in many cases,

> the mistake is not one of judgement but of performance. That is, we do *not* say: What you *said* was a mistake, because it was supposed to describe what you did and did not describe it, but: What you *did* was a mistake, because it was not in accordance with what you said.
>
> (p.57: §32)

A mismatch between what the agent says and his action need not be a lie (saying what is contrary to one's mind) if, for example, the agent is prevented by someone or something – say, if there is a hole in the pipe when one intends to replenish the water supply of a house. Or again, one may change one's mind. And even when neither is the case, the mismatch need not signify a lie. She gives the example of St Peter's claim that he would not betray Jesus: he was not lying then, nor did he change his mind, and yet he knew that, despite his sincere intention, he would betray Jesus, since Jesus said he would. (Here, the mistake is perhaps also in the performance, although it is what might be called "moral" rather than merely a mistake due to defective materials or a failure of ability or skill.)

Thus, what we are doing, when we express an intention (in a current action as in "I am building a wall," or for the future: "I'm visiting my mother on Tuesday") is not analogous to reporting a mental process going on internally, nor is it a report of a feeling on the basis of which we know about our intentions. Rather, it is describing an action in a particular context of past, present, and future thoughts, feelings, circumstances, further actions, etc. See PI §§634–48, and particularly the following remark:

> "I am not ashamed of what I did then, but of the intention which I had." – And didn't the intention lie *also* in what I did? What justifies the shame? The whole background of the incident.
>
> (PI §644)

Wittgenstein, and Anscombe following him, was concerned with offering a characterization of the concepts of voluntary and intentional action that escaped certain familiar philosophical temptations. A common thread in their discussion is a conviction in "the uselessness of an introspective explanation of intention" (Anscombe, 1957, p. iii), of the idea that an intention is "a particular feeling, an inner experience" (PI §645). Rather, they contend, such a characterization should focus on "what a man actually does" (Anscombe, 1957, p.9: §4): on the action in context, which includes its "normal *surroundings*" of learning and trying, of expressions of intention and attempts at justification, as well as past and future actions. And it is to these, rather than to any feelings or particular mental episodes allegedly accessible through introspection, that we must attend to when seeking to understand what intentions and intentional actions are, and also to understand what someone's intention was on any particular occasion.

References

Anscombe, G.E.M. (1957). *Intention*. Oxford: Blackwell.
Armstrong, D.M. (1973). Acting and Trying. *Philosophical Papers* 2, 1–15.
Grice, H.P. (1961) The Causal Theory of Perception. *Proceedings of the Aristotelian Society* (Supplementary Volume), 35, 121–152.
Grice, H.P. (1989). *Studies in the Way of Words*. Cambridge, MA: Harvard University Press.
Hacker, P.M.S. (2000). *Wittgenstein: Mind and Will. An Analytical Commentary on the Philosophical Investigations* (Vol. 4). Oxford: Blackwell.
Hornsby, J. (1980). *Actions*. London: Routledge and Kegan Paul.
Hornsby, J. (2010). Trying to Act. In T. O"Connor and C. Sandis (Eds). *A Companion to the Philosophy of Action* (pp.18–25). Oxford: Blackwell.

Hornsby, J. (2011). Actions in their Circumstances. In A. Ford, J. Hornsby, and F. Stoutland (Eds). *Essays on Anscombe's Intention* (pp.105–127). Cambridge, MA: Harvard University Press.

Hyman, J. (2011). Action and the Will. In O. Kuusela and M. McGinn (Eds). *The Oxford Handbook of Wittgenstein* (pp.451–471). Oxford: Oxford University Press.

James, W. (1890). *The Principles of Psychology*. New York: Holt and Company. (Cited from Dover edition, 1950.)

McCann, H. J. (1975). Trying, Paralysis, and Volition. *The Review of Metaphysics*, 28, 423–442.

O'Shaughnessy, B. (1973). Trying (as the Mental "Pineal Gland"). *Journal of Philosophy*, 70, 365–386.

O'Shaughnessy, B. (2008). *The Will: A Dual Aspect Theory*. Cambridge: Cambridge University Press.

Ryle, G. (1949). *The Concept of Mind*. London: Hutchinson.

Further Reading

Anscombe, G.E.M. (1983). The Causation of Action. In C. Ginet (Ed.). *Knowledge and Mind: Philosophical Essays* (pp.174–190). New York: Oxford University Press.

Falvey, K. (2000). Knowledge in Intention. *Philosophical Studies*, 99, 21–44.

Ford, A., Hornsby, J., and Stoutland, F. (Eds.). (2011). *Essays on Anscombe's Intention*. Cambridge, MA: Harvard University Press.

Schroeder, S. (2001a). The Concept of Trying. *Philosophical Investigations*, 24, 213–227.

Schroeder, S. (2001b). Are Reasons Causes? A Wittgensteinian Response to Davidson. In S. Schroeder (Ed.). *Wittgenstein and Contemporary Philosophy of Mind* (pp.150–170). Basingstoke: Palgrave.

Scott, M. (1996). Wittgenstein's Philosophy of Action. *The Philosophical Quarterly*, 46, 347–363.

Tanney, J. (2009). Reasons as Non-Causal, Context-Placing Explanations. In C. Sandis (Ed.). *New Essays on the Explanation of Action* (pp.94–111). Basingstoke: Palgrave Macmillan.

32

Wittgenstein on Intentionality

STEFAN BRANDT

In his essay "Being and Being Known" (1963), Wilfrid Sellars attributes to Aquinas and the early Wittgenstein the view that "knowledge involves an isomorphism of the knower with the known" (p.41). He suggests that this view implies that what he calls "intellectual acts" differ in their "intrinsic character as acts" when they differ in content. Sellars claims that this view compares favorably with views according to which intellectual acts do not differ in content by virtue of differences in themselves but "by virtue of being directly related to different relata" (p.41). These relata are traditionally either construed as contents, which have merely "being-for-mind" and are the "immediate and primary objects of knowledge" (p.42), or as objects and states of affairs in the "real order" (p.42). Philosophers holding the first variant of the relational view, which Sellars associates with Descartes, typically have difficulties explaining the relation between the contents of intellectual acts and the genuinely mind-independent objects and states of affairs in the world these acts are supposed to represent, and are therefore naturally tempted by some form of idealism or skepticism. Philosophers committed to the second variant of the relational view, which Sellars associates with early twentieth-century British and American realism, have notorious difficulties accounting for false thoughts. Since, according to them, the contents of true intellectual acts simply are the objects and states of affairs they represent, the content of false intellectual acts must also be the objects and states of affairs *they* represent. But if an intellectual act is false then there are no such objects or states of affairs. Hence, it seems as though false intellectual acts do not have content. But that is absurd. Thinking falsely is not the same as thinking nothing. Realists are therefore typically driven to introduce new and ontologically dubious entities: nonexistent but still subsistent objects and states of affairs that are the content of false representations.

At least as far as the interpretation of Wittgenstein is concerned, Sellars perfectly captures a false dilemma that was very much on Wittgenstein's mind in both his early and his late thinking on intentionality; and he correctly identifies how the early Wittgenstein tried to avoid this dilemma, namely by assuming an "isomorphism of the knower with the known."

A Companion to Wittgenstein, First Edition. Edited by Hans-Johann Glock and John Hyman.
© 2017 John Wiley & Sons, Ltd. Published 2017 by John Wiley & Sons, Ltd.

In this chapter, I shall first discuss Wittgenstein's early account of intentionality in his *Tractatus Logico-Philosophicus* as a sophisticated attempt to avoid Sellars's dilemma for relationist theories of thought. Wittgenstein's later views will then emerge as a fundamental rejection of central assumptions underlying his earlier account.

1 Intentionality in the *Tractatus*

As Sellars suggests, in the *Tractatus* Wittgenstein aims to give an account of intentionality that retains the realist insight that when we represent truly how things are – in thought, language, or by any other means – what we represent is identical with what is the case, while avoiding the mistake of thinking of the contents of false representations as somehow subsistent but not existent objects and states of affairs. And he indeed does so by postulating an isomorphism between our representations and what they represent. All intentional phenomena are *pictures* of states of affairs, i.e., they model how things are and are therefore isomorphic with the reality they represent (see TLP 2.12, 4.01; see also Chapter 7, LOGICAL ATOMISM and Chapter 8, THE PICTURE THEORY). However, before we can properly appreciate how intentional phenomena "picture" or "model" reality we have to understand the nature of the states of affairs that our representations depict. I therefore begin my exposition of the so-called "picture theory" with a few remarks on ontology.

According to the *Tractatus* the world consists of facts (TLP 1.1) and a fact is "the existence of states of affairs" (TLP 2). States of affairs are possible combinations of objects (TLP 2.01). The objects constituting states of affairs are ontologically simple (2.02, 2.021) and exist necessarily (2.021, 2.024, 2.027–2.0271). The combinatorial possibilities of objects determine which states of affairs are possible (2.014). Hence, objects make up "the substance of the world" (2.021). The combinatorial possibilities of an object are its "logical form" (2.0141, 2.0233). Thus, the logical forms of the simple objects determine what can be the case. Their actual combination determines what is the case, i.e., what facts obtain.

The pictures with which we represent states of affairs are themselves facts (TLP 2.141). They are existing combinations of elements, which stand for the elements making up the depicted state of affairs (2.131). Wittgenstein claims that a picture can only depict a state of affairs if it has something in common with it, namely its "pictorial form":

> There must be something identical in a picture and what it depicts, to enable the one to be a picture of the other at all.
> What a picture must have in common with reality, in order to be able to depict it – correctly or incorrectly – in the way it does, is its pictorial form. (TLP 2.161–2.17)

The pictorial form of a picture is a function of the pictorial forms of its elements. It can consist in a multiplicity of commonalities between the elements of the picture and the objects constituting the depicted state of affairs (TLP 2.171) but it at least consists in a shared logical form of the picture and the pictured (2.18). This means that the combinatorial possibilities of the elements of the picture within pictures must exactly match the combinatorial possibilities within states of affairs of the objects they stand for. A picture, which shares a logical form with the states of affairs it depicts, is a "logical picture" (2.181). Since every picture shares at least a logical form with what it depicts "[every] picture is *at the same time* a logical one" (2.182).

Still, a shared logical form is not sufficient to make a specific picture into the picture of a specific state of affairs. Here is why: it is plausible to assume that the logical form of a pictorial element only suffices to specify a determinate object as its referent if there is no more than one object with that form. For otherwise it would be unclear to which one of the several objects sharing its form the pictorial element referred. So, if we wish to say that the pictorial forms of pictorial elements suffice to determine their referent, we must assume that there are never several objects with the same logical form. If we make the further plausible assumption that an object cannot normally occur simultaneously in all the states of affairs it can potentially occur in, then we must conclude that the occurrence of an object in one state of affairs excludes the possibility that certain other states of affairs obtain, in which this object *could* occur. That, however, is incompatible with a fundamental commitment of Wittgenstein's, namely the idea that states of affairs are independent of one another (TLP 2.061–2.062). So, it seems that Wittgenstein assumed that there are normally several objects with the same logical form (2.0233). And this implies that the logical forms of the elements of pictures alone cannot determine their referents (*pace* Winch, 1987).

Wittgenstein therefore concludes that a picture also includes a "pictorial relationship" to what it depicts. This pictorial relationship "consists of the correlations of the picture's elements with things" (TLP 2.1514). These correlations Wittgenstein describes as "feelers [...] with which the picture touches reality." Only once they are set up can the picture "[reach] right out" to reality (2.1511) and depict exactly what is the case if it is true.

In TLP 3, Wittgenstein says: "A logical picture of facts is a thought [*Gedanke*]." The noun "*Gedanke*," just like the English "thought," is commonly used in a *psychological* or a *semantic* sense. In its psychological sense it refers to acts of thinking; in its semantic sense, in which Frege famously uses it, it refers to the content of such an act. Wittgenstein does not appear to use "*Gedanke*" here in its psychological sense. There is no reason to think that he wishes to say that if something is a logical picture then it is an act of thinking. After all, he explicitly says that *all* pictures are logical pictures (2.182). So he must be using "*Gedanke*" in its semantic sense. But unlike Frege, he does not conceive of thoughts as abstract objects in a "third realm" of ideas (Frege [1918]1997b), which are the senses of used sentences. He rather employs "*Gedanke*" to speak about types of pictures. In other words, a picture has a certain thought as its content by instantiating it, and it instantiates a specific thought by having a specific logical form and by standing in a pictorial relationship to a specific state of affairs. It does not have specific content by being related to an abstract Fregean sense.

One form in which a thought in this sense can be instantiated is in a proposition:

In a proposition a thought finds an expression that can be perceived by the senses. (TLP 3.1)

In a proposition a thought can be expressed in such a way that elements of the propositional sign correspond to the objects of the thought. (TLP 3.2)

Wittgenstein is not saying that in a proposition an inner mental act is overtly expressed nor that propositions express abstract inhabitants of Frege's "third realm," but rather that in a proposition a logical picture, i.e., a thought in the semantic sense, can be made visible to the senses. This happens when the proposition is expressed in its fully analyzed form, i.e., when the proposition contains a sign for every element of the thought it expresses. This idea allows Wittgenstein to investigate the nature of intentional phenomena quite generally, i.e., the nature of all those phenomena that have a thought or *Gedanke* as their content, by investigating the nature of propositions. He thereby realizes the strategy that he announces in the preface of the *Tractatus*, namely to investigate the limits of thinking by investigating the limits of language. Hence, I shall now turn to the *Tractarian* account of propositions.

Like all representations, propositions are pictures of states of affairs. Their pictorial form is their logical form; i.e., they are "logical pictures" in the narrow sense that they do not share anything with the states of affairs they depict except their logical form. They are either (so-called) elementary propositions or truth functions of elementary propositions (TLP 4.51, 5). An elementary proposition is a concatenation of names (4.22). The names occurring in elementary propositions are the fundamental units of linguistic representation; they are the "elements" of propositional pictures. They are indefinable "primitive signs" (3.26), which stand for the simple objects that constitute states of affairs. A name shares the logical form of the object it stands for and the object is its meaning or *Bedeutung* (3.203).

Wittgenstein distinguishes between "propositions" and "propositional signs" (3.12). Propositional signs are the acoustical and visual signs we use in speech and writing. The propositional signs we employ in ordinary language are not usually composed of simple names (4.002). Hence, ordinary language often disguises the thoughts it is used to express. However, according to the *Tractatus*, we *can* express every proposition in its true logical form, i.e., as a truth function of elementary propositions containing only simple names (3.2). If we do so, the propositional sign represents via the simple names that are correlated with the simple objects constituting the depicted states of affairs. For it is one of the central thoughts of the *Tractatus* that the only other signs occurring in fully analyzed propositions, i.e., the truth-functional connectives, do not have a representative function: "My fundamental idea is that the 'logical constants' are not representatives" (4.0312).

In order for a propositional sign to become a proposition it has to be used as "a projection of a possible situation" (TLP 3.11). The question is: how do we use a propositional sign in such a way? According to Wittgenstein we have to think its sense: "The method of projection is to think of the sense of the proposition" (TLP 3.11).

But what does it mean to think the sense of a proposition? It can be said to involve usually three, but minimally two, different activities. First, if the propositional sign we employ does not reflect the true form of the thought it expresses, we have to accompany the sign with a thought that has this form. If a proposition is expressed in its fully analyzed form, however, this is not necessary. In that case we only have to do two things. First, we have to give the simple names a specific logical form. This is done by the use of a sign within a language (3.327). Second, like all pictures, linguistic pictures include a pictorial relationship to the states of affairs they depict (2.1513). This means that the simple names making up the proposition have to be correlated with the simple objects that are their meaning.

How are these correlations established? In the *Tractatus* Wittgenstein fails to give an answer. Still, his remark in TLP 3.11 that the method of projecting a propositional sign onto states of affairs consists in "*thinking* of the sense of the proposition" (my emphasis) intimates how he conceives of these correlations. Since even fully analyzed propositions have to be projected onto states of affairs, this remark might suggest that apart from thinking of the analysis of a propositional sign there is a further activity of thinking involved when we project a sign. This may be the mental activity of correlating simple names with the objects that are their meaning. This is also suggested by remarks Wittgenstein made both before and after he wrote the *Tractatus*. In *Notes on Logic*, dating from 1913, Wittgenstein says that the relation between names and their meanings is "psychological" (NB 104) and in a letter to Russell, written after the completion of the *Tractatus*, he writes that investigating this relation is "irrelevant" since it is "a matter of psychology" (NB 130). And psychology, he stresses in the *Tractatus*, is not part of philosophy: "Psychology is no more closely related to philosophy than any other natural science" (TLP 4.1121).

But why does Wittgenstein think that investigating the relation of the constituents of a proposition to the constituents of the depicted fact is not part of philosophy but of psychology? A clue to his answer can again be found in the early *Notes on Logic*:

> Just as little as we are concerned, in logic, with the relation of a name to its meaning, just so little are we concerned with the relation of a proposition to reality, but we want to know the meaning of names and the sense of propositions. (NB 102)

This remark is puzzling. Is not an interest in the senses of propositions and the meanings of names *eo ipso* an interest in the relations of names to their meanings and propositions to reality? How can Wittgenstein say that the former is a concern of logic but the latter is not? His answer seems to be this (see also Ammereller, 2001, pp.119–20): logic and philosophy are concerned with the *role* of names and propositions in language. The role of a name is to stand for an object; that of a proposition is to represent a state of affairs. Propositions and names can only fulfill their respective roles if names are correlated with objects. However, the "psychological mechanism" of *meaning* a specific object by a name or of *understanding* a specific object as the referent of a name by means of which the "correlations" between names and objects are established is not itself part of logic. The correlations of names and objects, and hence the "pictorial relationship" between propositions and pictures they establish, are indeed a part of every picture, since without them the picture would not depict what it depicts, but they are of no concern to the logician or philosopher who merely wishes to understand the different *semantic functions* of propositions and names.

According to this interpretation Wittgenstein makes the very natural assumption that in order to use a proposition with a sense we have to understand it or mean something by it. Additionally, he makes the – as he later came to recognize injudicious – assumption that meaning and understanding consist in some kind of mental activity or process of correlating names with objects, whose exact nature ought to be investigated by the sciences rather than philosophy.

We are now in a position to understand the account of intentionality in the *Tractatus*. Propositions are pictures of states of affairs. They depict states of affairs via the names occurring in elementary propositions, which stand for the necessarily existing simple objects that make up states of affairs. Names stand for objects in virtue of two properties: (a) they share the "logical form" of the object that is their meaning or *Bedeutung*; (b) they are correlated with this object, presumably by means of some mental mechanism of meaning or understanding. By being analyzable into an arrangement of simple names every proposition presents a possible arrangement of simple objects: "In a proposition a situation is, as it were, assembled by way of experiment" (TLP 4.031, my translation). If the objects making up states of affairs are assembled in the way their names are assembled in the propositional picture, the proposition is true; if not, it is false. Since a shared logical form of names and objects is a condition for the possibility of sense, every proposition represents a possible state of affairs but not necessarily an actual one.

The picture theory goes a long way toward avoiding both horns of the dilemma facing relational conceptions of thought. On the one hand, as realists rightly stress, what a true proposition represents is identical with what is the case. Since every name making up a fully analyzed proposition is immediately correlated with an object in reality that is its meaning, every proposition "reaches right out to [reality]" (TLP 2.1511). The *pictorial relationship* between picture and state of affairs is part of the picture (2.1513); it is an "internal relation" (4.014). In other words, it is part of the identity of a picture that its elements are correlated with specific elements of reality and the picture as a whole is thereby correlated with a possible state of affairs. Hence there is no content, which as Sellars puts it, has merely "being-for-mind," is the "primary and immediate object of knowledge" (Sellars, 1963, p.42) and somehow indirectly relates our representations to the facts that make them true.

On the other hand, Wittgenstein stresses that a proposition does not stand in the same relation to reality as a name. Whereas names only have a meaning or *Bedeutung* but no sense or *Sinn*, propositions have a sense but no meaning:

Situations can be described, but not *given names*.
   (Names are like points; propositions like arrows – they have sense.) (TLP 3.144)

Objects can only be *named*. Signs are their representatives. I can only speak *about* them: I cannot *put them into words*. Propositions can only say *how* things are, not *what* they are. (TLP 3.221)

Names merely stand for objects but do not present them as being a certain way. They merely have a referent or Fregean *Bedeutung*, but they do not have a Fregean sense (see also TLP 3.3) or "mode of presentation" (Frege, [1892] 1997a). Propositions, on the other hand, have a sense; they represent things as being thus-and-so. By being an arrangement of names, which share the logical forms of the objects they stand for, a proposition, as it were, *exhibits* a possible situation but does not *refer* to it. Hence, contrary to the "extreme realist" view Sellars criticizes, a proposition can represent a state of affairs although this state of affairs neither exists nor subsists. A false proposition is not directed at some alternate reality of subsisting but not existing objects and states of affairs; it rather represents a possible but not actual combination of actual objects. A false proposition, just like a true proposition, "reaches right out to [reality]" via the names of which it is composed.

Furthermore, with his "fundamental idea" that logical constants do not represent (TLP 4.0312) Wittgenstein does justice to the intuition that a negative proposition denies the very fact that the negated proposition affirms. Since there is no object corresponding to the negation sign a negative proposition represents exactly the same states of affairs as the corresponding positive proposition. It merely says that these states of affairs do not obtain. Wittgenstein puts this as follows: "The propositions 'p' and 'not-p' have opposite sense, but there corresponds to them one and the same reality" (4.0621). Negative propositions are not directed at ontologically dubious negative facts, as "extreme realists" might be tempted to argue; they are directed at exactly the same reality as the propositions they negate.

Finally, since Wittgenstein's account of propositional representation applies to all phenomena that have a Fregean thought as their sense, i.e., to all those mental phenomena that are nowadays subsumed under the label of "propositional attitude," the picture theory of the proposition can be understood as providing a perfectly general account of intentionality.

2   Problems with the Picture Theory

While the picture theory goes a long way towards providing a general account of intentionality in terms of linguistic representation and does so in a way that *prima facie* avoids both horns of Sellars's dilemma for relationist theories of thought, on closer scrutiny, the early Wittgenstein does not seem to be entirely successful at meeting either of these explanatory goals. First, in his explanation of how we use propositions to represent states of affairs he relies on an unexplained mental activity of connecting names with objects. In order to represent a specific state of affairs with a proposition we have to connect the names making up the proposition with objects making up the state of affairs through an underlying activity of meaning or understanding. It seems that the intentionality of propositions derives from this underlying mental activity. This is at odds with Wittgenstein's ambition to provide a completely general account of intentionality in terms of linguistic depiction. Furthermore, since he thinks that thoughts are logical pictures, whose elements, as he points out in a letter to Russell, "have the same sort of relation to reality as words" (NB 131), this view has the odd consequence that we have to project our own thoughts onto the reality they represent through underlying activities of meaning and understanding.

Second, Wittgenstein is not entirely successful at avoiding the problems of the view Sellars calls "extreme realism." Although he does not have to admit subsistent but nonexistent objects and states of affairs, which correspond to false or negative propositions, he is still forced to postulate necessarily existing simple objects, which are the meanings of the names occurring in elementary propositions.

These problems are consequences of Wittgenstein's conception of the "pictorial relationship." The first stems from his assumption that the pictorial relationship between names and objects is established by a psychological mechanism, which does not have to be explained by philosophy. The second is a corollary of the idea that all pictures *include* the pictorial relationship. Since the pictorial relationship between names and objects is part of every proposition with a sense, there has to be an object corresponding to every name occurring in its fully analyzed form. After all, the pictorial *relationship* has to relate the picture to something.

In his later philosophy Wittgenstein sharply criticized both the idea that the use of propositions with a sense requires the accompaniment of mental activities or processes of meaning and understanding, and the idea that a relation to objects in reality is a *part* of every meaningful proposition. I shall begin my discussion of Wittgenstein's later views on intentionality with some of these criticisms.

3   Rejecting the "Pictorial Relationship"

There is great intuitive appeal to the idea that whenever we use language we have to accompany the use of overt signs by inner activities of meaning and understanding. In his later writings Wittgenstein shows a strong interest in this conception of language and a keen awareness of its attractions. He writes:

It seems that there are *certain definite* mental processes bound up with the working of language, processes through which alone language can function. I mean the processes of understanding and meaning. The signs of our language seem dead without these processes; and it might seem that the only function of the signs is to induce such processes [...] Thus, if you are asked what is the relation between a name and the thing it names, you will be inclined to answer that the relation is a psychological one.

(BB 3)

"There is a gap between an order and its execution. It has to be closed by the process of understanding."

"Only in the process of understanding does the order mean that we are to do THIS. The *order* – why, that is nothing but sounds, ink-marks. –" (PI §431)

These remarks capture a very intuitive idea about how meaning is at all possible. It can appear puzzling how mere physical things such as sounds and ink marks can be intentionally directed at other things. How can a name, which is, after all, only a sound or a mark on paper, stand for a specific object? How can an order, which seems to consist merely of "dead signs," determine the action that is its execution? A natural answer is that it is through the mental accompaniments of meaning and understanding that an order determines its execution and a name its referent – just as Wittgenstein thought when writing the *Tractatus*.

However, it is rather unclear how such a mental accompaniment can fix the meanings of signs, as Wittgenstein brings out with a well-known example in PI §185 (see also Chapter 24, RULES AND RULE-FOLLOWING). He asks his reader to imagine a pupil being instructed to develop different series of integers and being given exercises and tests up to 1000. His teacher then tells him to develop the series of even integers. He proceeds correctly up to 1000 and then continues with "1004, 1008, 1012, etc." When asked to continue to add two, he claims to be doing so. What is it about the teacher's order that means that the pupil's continuation of the series after 1000 does not conform to it? It's difficult to give an answer. For even if the teacher thought of the series of even integers, he cannot have thought of all its instances:

So when you gave the order "+2", you meant that he was to write 1002 after 1000 – and did you then also mean that he should write 1868 after 1866, and 100 036 after 100 034, and so on – an infinite number of such sentences? (PI §186)

Obviously, the teacher could not have thought of all these steps. Still he clearly *meant* his pupil to write "1002" after "1000" and "1868" after "1866" (see PI §§187, 693). As Wittgenstein suggests, one would like to say that although the teacher could not have thought of all these steps, he meant his order in a specific way and from this all its applications follow (PI §186). But how can something that is now in my mind achieve this remarkable feat, which cannot be achieved by mere "dead" signs?

Here it is easy to be led into thinking that facts about meaning are just very special, "inordinate" facts (PI §§191–2); that meaning and understanding are special mental phenomena, which in a "strange way" (§195) already contain the correct uses of the words we are employing. But when we think about meaning in this way we replace a puzzle, i.e., the question of how signs come to have meaning, by a mystery, i.e., the idea that they acquire it through underlying mental phenomena that contain all their correct uses. It is like supposing that in meaning the order to add two "your mind, as it were, flew ahead and took all the steps before you physically arrived at this or that one" (§188).

Trying to avoid this assumption might lead us to think that signs are given meaning by an *interpretation*. But this is not so (disregarding a small class of special cases such as the interpretation of poems, say). If signs cannot determine their meaning neither can an interpretation. The teacher and the pupil of PI §185 might agree on an interpretation for the order "+2" – e.g., "Write down the series that is determined by the formula n = 2n" – and still disagree about what to do. The teacher might think that the pupil has to write "1398" after "1396" while the pupil believes he ought to write "1400." Adding further interpretations will not help, as teacher and pupil might again agree on an interpretation while continuing to disagree about what to do, and so on *ad infinitum*. If the meaning of an order or a rule is determined by an interpretation, no order or rule can determine what one has to do to follow it. This may seem paradoxical. Thus Wittgenstein writes:

> This was our paradox: no course of action could be determined by a rule, because every course of action can be brought into accord with the rule. The answer was: if every course of action can be brought into accord with the rule, then it can also be brought into conflict with it. And so there would be neither accord nor conflict here. (PI §201)

It is possible to give many conflicting interpretations for a rule, such as "+2." But that means that the rule ceases to tell us anything. Rules divide the space of possible actions into those that accord with them and those that do not; if they generally fail to do so they do not make sense. Furthermore, the problem Wittgenstein illustrates with the example of the deviant pupil is perfectly general. For any statement we can think of we can think of a variety of conflicting interpretations. Hence, we cannot give signs a specific meaning by means of an interpretation.

Some interpreters, most prominently Kripke (1982), have suggested that this means that there cannot be such a thing as linguistic meaning and that Wittgenstein thought as much. Although Kripke's interpretation is subtle and intriguing, the view he presents is implausible and also mistaken as an interpretation of Wittgenstein. Wittgenstein says explicitly that the "paradox" of PI §201 rests on a "misunderstanding." It is quite clear that the misunderstanding in question is the idea that signs are given meaning by an interpretation. Hence, we should not interpret him as arguing that since interpretations cannot give signs a sense nothing can. He is rather arguing that meaning is not determined by interpretations. Interpretations should be thought of as substitutions of one expression for another (PI §§198, 201) and we can only give an expression meaning through such a substitution if the substituting expression already has a meaning. Hence interpretations cannot initially confer meaning onto signs.

Rather than by an interpretation the connection between a rule and its execution and a sign and its employment is made by the *use* of the rule or sign in a linguistic *practice* (PI §§197–9, 201–2). Quite generally it is the use of signs in "language-games" that gives them their meaning or "life" and not anything accompanying their employment on a particular occasion, such as the mental activity of interpreting signs, i.e., of translating them into different signs: "If we had to name anything which is the life of the sign, we should have to say it was its *use*" (BB 4; see also PI §§43, 432).

It is important not to misunderstand Wittgenstein's invocation of use and linguistic practices at this point. For example, when he says that "the meaning of a word is its use in the language" (PI §43), he does not mean that we can simply give expressions meaning by employing them with certain illocutionary and perlocutionary aims. We can only use expressions that way when they already have a meaning. Nor is he at any point suggesting that the meaning of signs can be *reduced* to their use, e.g., that we can give a description of the use of a sign in non-semantic terms from which a description of its meaning follows. It is part of the point of the scenario of the deviant pupil that this is impossible. The actual applications of "+2" understood in non-semantic terms do not furnish the pupil with a standard of how to proceed after 1000. After all, it is assumed that no applications after 1000 have been made. But if we understand "+2" as being used to express the order or rule to add two these signs do furnish the pupil with such a standard. So when Wittgenstein says that "the meaning of a word is its use in the language," he is not saying that meaning can be reduced to use, but is merely making the "grammatical" observation that we can only attribute semantic properties to expressions if they have an established use in a linguistic practice. Since "+2" has such a use, it determines what one has to do to follow it. Expressions that do not have such a use, on the other hand, cannot be used to mean anything, regardless of what is going through our mind while producing them. We cannot, for example, mean "If it doesn't rain, I shall go for a walk" by saying "bububu" (boxed remark after PI §35), although we can think the thought while making the noise.

Just as the use of signs is not anything "co-existing" with them (BB 5), so understanding signs is not an accompanying mental process either. It is rather a kind of ability:

> [Understanding], the knowledge of the language, isn't a conscious state that accompanies the sentences of the language [...]. It's much more like the understanding or mastery of a calculus, something like the *ability* to multiply. (PG 50)

Understanding is not a mental process. It is a kind of *potentiality* and not an *actuality*. To understand a statement consists in the ability to do certain things with it, just as understanding how to multiply consists in the ability to perform certain mathematical operations. And just as the latter ability is exercised in the multiplications we perform and does not consist in what goes through our minds while performing them, so our understanding is exercised in what we do with, and in response to, statements and not in what goes through our minds while hearing or making them. Occasionally we may exercise our understanding by translating or interpreting some statement but usually we do not. Furthermore this activity of translating will only be an exercise of understanding if we understand the translation. Hence "there is a way of grasping a rule which is not an interpretation, but which [...] is exhibited in what we call 'following the rule' and 'going against it'" (PI §201). The understanding that those who follow a rule thereby display is an ability that is exercised in the very actions they perform and not in what goes through their mind while performing them.

The second mistake informing the Tractarian conception of the pictorial relationship I shall discuss is the idea that this relationship is *included* in the picture. Wittgenstein brings out this mistake by distinguishing between the "method of projection" and "projection lines" (see PG 213). He says that when describing a worker constructing an artifact from a blueprint we may call "the way in which the workman turns such a drawing into an artefact 'the method of projection'" (PG 213). We might think of this method as mediating between the picture, i.e., the blueprint, and the artifact, and compare it to "projection lines which go from one figure to another" (PG 213). This, however, can be misleading:

> This comparison conceals the fact that the picture *plus* the projection lines leaves open various methods of application; it makes it look as if what is depicted, even if it does not exist in fact, is determined by the picture and the projection lines in an ethereal manner; every bit as determined, that is to say, as if it did exist. (It is 'determined give or take a yes or no.') In that case what we may call 'picture' is the blueprint plus the method of its application. And we now imagine the method as something which is attached to the blueprint whether or not it is used. (PG 213)

If we think of the method of projecting a blueprint in terms of projection lines, we might come to think of the blueprint as in some sense *containing* lines, which connect parts of it with corresponding parts of the artifact. The only question then left open by the blueprint is whether the parts of the artifact are assembled as depicted. Hence, the blueprint determines the artifact "give or take a yes or no."

As we have seen, this is the way Wittgenstein thought about the "pictorial relationship" in the *Tractatus*. There he thought that the simple elements of pictures are connected through the pictorial relationship to the simple objects making up the depicted state of affairs. If the picture has a sense, these simple objects exist and the depicted state of affairs is possible. All the picture leaves open is whether the state of affairs obtains. Hence: "A proposition must restrict reality to two alternatives: yes or no" (TLP 4.023).

Later, Wittgenstein came to think that this line of thought is the result of a "confusion" of the method of projection with the projection lines (PG 213). It confuses the representation of the use of a representation, i.e., the projection lines, with the use of a representation, i.e., the method of projection. We may think of the projection lines as part of the picture (PG 213–14), since they are what Wittgenstein on other occasions calls a "means of representation" (e.g. PI §50), i.e., a means of representing how a picture is to be projected. But such a means of representation is itself a representation and like all representations "leaves open various methods of application." It does not connect a representation with what it represents, as the "pictorial relationship" is supposed to do. This would even be true if the projection lines consisted of actual strings connecting blueprint and artifact. In that case the artifact itself becomes part of the representation. It becomes a *sample* (PI §16) of the kind of object that is to be made from the blueprint. The method of projection, on the other hand, does connect the picture and the pictured. After all, it is "the way in which the workman turns [...] a drawing into an artifact." However, it is not *included* in the picture. It does not precede the use of the picture in a concrete situation: "[If] the method of projection is a bridge, it is a bridge which isn't built until the application is made" (PG 213).

Ultimately the confusion at the root of the idea that the pictorial relationship is included in the picture, i.e., the confusion of a representation of the use of a representation with a use of a representation, also underlies the idea that this relationship is established by a mental process or activity. Once we have discarded the idea of meaning and understanding as containing in a "strange way" all the ways in which words are and can be used, the only candidates for mental activities that give signs their "life" are interpretations that users of language have in mind. But interpretations, regardless of whether we merely think of them or produce them in speech or writing, are nothing more than specifications of the meaning, i.e., the *use*, of expressions. An interpretation of what someone said may correctly specify the use she made of the expressions she employed but it cannot replace this use. It must itself have a use before it means anything and this use is given to it by the way it is employed in "language-games" and not attached to it in an "ethereal manner."

4 Thoughts and their Objects

The idea of a pictorial relationship between thought and language on the one hand and states of affairs on the other is an essential element of the Tractarian explanation of how thought and language reach "right out to [reality]." Since all representations are made up of simple elements that are (a) immediately related through the pictorial relationship to simple objects and (b) share the logical form of these objects, what a thought represents is identical with what is the case if it is true. In his later thinking Wittgenstein holds on to the idea that thought and language "reach right out" to reality. He writes:

> "Thinking must be something unique." When we say, *mean*, that such-and-such is the case, then, with what we mean, we do not stop anywhere short of the fact, but mean: *such-and-such – is – thus-and-so*. (PI §95)

> "A thought – what a strange thing!" – But it does not strike us as strange when we are thinking. A thought does not strike us as mysterious while we are thinking, but only when we say, as it were retrospectively, "How was that possible?" How was it possible for a thought to deal with *this very* object? It seems to us as if we had captured reality with the thought. (PI §428)

The idea Wittgenstein expresses by saying that "we do not stop short of the fact" in what we say and that our thoughts seem to "capture" reality is clearly the same idea he expressed in the *Tractatus* by saying that pictures "reach right out" to reality: the ability of thoughts, beliefs, and speech acts to determine exactly at what object, event, or state of affairs they are directed.

Wittgenstein is right about this phenomenon. All intentional acts and states determine exactly what their so-called "intentional objects" are, i.e., they determine exactly what objects, events, or states of affairs they are directed at. There is a necessary relation between our representations and their objects. If I think that Caesar crossed the Rubicon, it is necessarily of Caesar and of the Rubicon that I think that the former crossed the latter. If I were not thinking of Caesar and the Rubicon my thought would not be the same. However, we might wonder how Wittgenstein can account for this after rejecting the pictorial relationship. If it is wrong to assume that our representations *include* a relationship to their intentional objects, how can there be a necessary relation between representations and their objects? Wittgenstein's answer is simple. There is a necessary relation between representations and their objects but it is not a relation *between*, on the one hand, mind and language, and on the other, the world, but it is a relation *within* language. He writes:

> "The proposition determines in advance what will make it true." Certainly, the proposition "p" determines that p must be the case in order to make it true; and that means: (the proposition p) = (the proposition that the fact p makes true). And the statement that the wish for

it to be the case that p is satisfied by the event p, merely enunciates a rule for signs: (the wish for it to be the case that p) = (the wish that is satisfied by the event p). (PG 161–2)

"An order orders its own execution." So it knows its execution before it is even there? – But that was a grammatical proposition, and it says: if an order runs "Do such-and-such", then *doing such-and-such* is called "executing the order". (PI §458)

It is in language that an expectation and its fulfilment make contact. (PI §445)

The necessary relation between our wishes, propositions, and orders and their intentional objects is explained by the "grammatical," and hence necessary, fact that we attribute and express the former with the same words with which we describe and refer to the latter (see Chapter 14, GRAMMAR AND GRAMMATICAL STATEMENTS and Chapter 21, NECESSITY AND APRIORITY; cf. Chapter 15, THE AUTONOMY OF GRAMMAR). For example, if Jack expects Jill to arrive, he can express his expectation with such sentences as "Jill will arrive" or "I expect Jill to arrive," and we can attribute this expectation to him with such statements as "Jack expects Jill to arrive." If Jack's expectation is fulfilled, we can use the same words to speak about the event that fulfills it, namely "Jill arrived," "Jill is arriving," etc.

What is true of expectations is true of intentional phenomena generally. We typically attribute intentional acts and states by combining an expression referring to a person with an expression for the type of act or state attributed and with a clause specifying the content of the act or state – typically a declarative clause (e.g., in "A believes that her car has been stolen"), an interrogative clause (e.g., in "A wonders whether her car has been stolen"), or an infinitival clause (e.g., in "A wants to catch the thief"). What Wittgenstein is suggesting is that we can always use the expressions that we use to specify the content of a person's intentional act or state, and that that person herself might use to express that act or state, to speak about the intentional objects of that act or state.

This grammatical fact not only explains the necessary connection between true thoughts, executed orders, and fulfilled expectations and their objects, it also explains how even false and negative representations can "reach right out to [reality]." If Jack thinks that Caesar did not cross the Volga and Jill thinks that Caesar killed Mark Antony then there are no events at which Jack's and Jill's thoughts are directed. Hence we cannot use the *sentences* occurring in the content-clauses of "Jack thinks that Caesar did not cross the Volga" and "Jill thinks that Caesar killed Mark Antony" to speak about events, whose occurrence is responsible for the truth of Jack's negative thought and the falsity of Jill's positive thought. Still we can use the expressions "Caesar," "the Volga," and "Mark Antony," which occur in these content-clauses, to speak about actual objects, namely two Roman generals and a river in Russia. And it is because we use "Caesar" to refer to Caesar, "Mark Antony" to refer to Mark Antony, and "the Volga" to refer to the Volga that Jack's negative thought and Jill's false thought are still directed at Caesar, Mark Antony, and the Volga. Here is how Wittgenstein puts it:

The agreement, the harmony, between thought and reality consists in this: that if I say falsely that something is *red*, then all the same, it is *red* that it isn't. And in this: that if I want to explain the word "red" to someone, in the sentence "That is not red", I do so pointing to something that *is* red. (PI §429)

5   Conclusion

In *Philosophical Grammar* Wittgenstein says: "Like everything metaphysical the harmony between thought and reality is to be found in the grammar of language" (162). We are now in a position to appreciate this remark. In the *Tractatus* Wittgenstein assumed a complex isomorphism between thought and reality in order to explain how thought can reach "right out to it." All our representations, he held, are pictures of states of affairs consisting of simple elements that stand for necessarily existing simple objects that are their meaning or *Bedeutung*, share their "logical form," and make up the depicted state of affairs. Later, Wittgenstein came to realize that the "internal" pictorial relation that appeared to make this metaphysical harmony necessary is merely a "shadow of grammar." The ability of thought and language to reach "right out" to reality is explained by the grammatical fact that we can use the same expressions we use to specify the contents of our thoughts and utterances to speak about their intentional objects.

Some may find this conclusion disappointing and might object along the following lines: Wittgenstein may have correctly identified confusions underlying his own earlier explanation of intentionality, but he has failed to provide a more adequate explanation in its stead. It may be a grammatical truth that if A believes that p we may use "p" or some expression therein to speak about or refer to the objects of her belief. But here we are invoking such notions as "speaking about" and "referring," which we have to explain if we wish to explain how language and thought can be intentionally directed at a reality outside itself. Wittgenstein simply fails to do this.

An adequate treatment of this objection is beyond the scope of this chapter. But in conclusion I shall briefly draw attention to a reply, which is contained in a passage I have already quoted. In PI §428 Wittgenstein writes:

> "A thought – what a strange thing!" – But it does not strike us as strange when we are thinking. A thought does not strike us as mysterious while we are thinking, but only when we say, as it were retrospectively, "How was that possible?" How was it possible for a thought to deal with *this very* object?

The fact that thoughts do not "strike us as mysterious while we are thinking" shows that we are perfectly familiar with the phenomenon of intentionality. We know perfectly well how to speak and think about objects and we also know how and on what grounds we attribute thoughts, beliefs, and meaningful utterances to others and ourselves. There is no need for a philosophical theory to explain something that we already know (see PI §128: "If someone were to advance *theses* in philosophy, it would never be possible to debate them, because everyone would agree to them"). The task of the philosopher is to disabuse us of the confusions we fall into when we think of the phenomenon of intentionality philosophically, e.g., when we start asking such questions as, "How was it possible for a thought to deal with *this very* object?"

One such confusion is the idea that a necessary relation to their intentional objects is part of all our representations. Wittgenstein himself was subject to this confusion when writing the *Tractatus* but it is not peculiar to his own early thinking. Wittgenstein is not merely treating the "bumps" that his own understanding has got by "running up against the limits of language" (PI §119). He is dispelling a confusion that is widespread in the history of philosophy and lies at the root of Sellars's dilemma for relationist theories of thought. Only if we assume that a relation to what they are about is a part of all our representations will we assume that there always is something our representations are about, even if they are false. This will then typically lead, as Sellars points out, either to the introduction of contents that have merely "being-for-mind" (Sellars, 1963, p.42) and whose relation to genuinely mind-independent objects and states of affairs remains obscure, or to the introduction of subsistent but not existent objects and states of affairs that are the contents of false representations. In the *Tractatus* Wittgenstein avoided these two mistakes, but he still assumed simple, necessarily existing objects that are the meaning of the simple signs of language. In that respect his early work was part of a long and continuing philosophical tradition to which his later criticisms are highly pertinent.

References

Ammereller, E. (2001). Die abbildende Beziehung. Zum Problem der Intentionalität im *Tractatus*. In W. Vossenkuhl (Ed.). *Ludwig Wittgenstein: Tractatus Logico-Philosophicus* (pp.111–140). Berlin: Akademie Verlag.

Frege, G. ([1892] 1997a). On *Sinn* and *Bedeutung*. Translation in M. Beaney (Ed.). *The Frege Reader* (pp.151–171). Oxford: Blackwell. (Original work published 1892.)

Frege, G. ([1918] 1997b). Thought. Translation in M. Beaney (Ed.). *The Frege Reader* (pp.325–345). Oxford: Blackwell. (Original work published 1918.)

Kripke, S.A. (1982). *Wittgenstein on Rules and Private Language: An Elementary Exposition*. Oxford: Blackwell.

Sellars, W. (1963). Being and Being Known. In W. Sellars. *Science, Perception, and Reality* (pp.41–59). London: Routledge.

Winch, P. (1987). Language, Thought and World in Wittgenstein's *Tractatus*. In P. Winch. *Trying to Make Sense* (pp.3–18). Oxford: Blackwell.

Further Reading

Ammereller, E. (2001). Wittgenstein on Intentionality. In H.-J. Glock (Ed.). *Wittgenstein: A Critical Reader* (pp.59–93). Oxford: Blackwell.

Budd, M. (1989). *Wittgenstein's Philosophy of Psychology*. London: Routledge. Chapter 6.

Child, W. (2011). *Wittgenstein*. London: Routledge. Chapter 5.

Crane, T. (2010). Wittgenstein and Intentionality. *Harvard Review of Philosophy*, 17, 88–104.

Hacker, P.M.S. (1996). *Wittgenstein: Mind and Will. An Analytical Commentary on the Philosophical Investigations* (Vol. 4). Oxford: Blackwell. Chapter 1.

33

Wittgenstein on Seeing Aspects

ARIF AHMED

1 Introduction

Seeing the resemblance of one face to another, the analogy of one mathematical form with another, a human form in the lines of a puzzle picture, a three-dimensional shape in a schematic drawing, hearing or pronouncing 'pas' in 'ne... pas' as 'step' – all these phenomena are somehow similar, and yet again very different. (RPP I §316)

In fact what Wittgenstein calls the "lighting up of an aspect" (PPF §118) covers an even greater variety of phenomena. For instance:

(1) I see a jumble of black and white shapes. Then I see the same arrangement as a black cross on a white ground.
(2) I see a figure as a black cross on a white ground. Then I see it as a white cross on a black ground (PPF §212).
(3) I see a pattern of six marks: ...... as two triplets of marks. Then I see the same row as three pairs of marks (Köhler, 1930, p.118; LW I §444).
(4) I hear a 6/8 theme as three pairs of quavers to the bar; then I hear the same theme as two triplets to the bar (cf. PPF §178; LW I §451).
(5) Necker cube: I see a schematic drawing of a cube (a "picture-cube") with its front face pointing downwards. Then I see the same figure as of a cube with its front face pointing upwards (PPF §135).
(6) I see some arbitrary cipher as a strictly correct letter in some alphabet; then as a crudely drawn letter in another alphabet (PPF §234).
(7) I see a jumble of lines. Then I see a human figure in the jumble (PPF §131).
(8) I see Jastrow's figure as a picture-duck. Then I see it as a picture-rabbit (PPF §118).
(9) I see two faces. Then I notice a similarity between them that I had not noticed before, though I see that they have not changed (PPF §111).
(10) I see the formula $\neg(\neg p \land \neg(\neg r \land \neg q)) \land \neg(\neg q \land \neg r)$ as involving two logical constants $\land$ and $\neg$. Then I see it as the repeated application of one operation (joint negation) to its atoms (AWL 181).

A Companion to Wittgenstein, First Edition. Edited by Hans-Johann Glock and John Hyman.
© 2017 John Wiley & Sons, Ltd. Published 2017 by John Wiley & Sons, Ltd.

(11) I think of the proposition that Cato killed Cato as applying the predicate "x killed Cato" to Cato. Then I think of the same proposition as applying the very different predicate "x killed x" to Cato (Frege, 1879, §9).
(12) I see the feeble-minded as degenerate or disordered versions of "normal" people; then as in a more primitive state of order (RPP I §646; Laing, 1990, p.31).

These examples are meant to illustrate the idea that "the lighting up of an aspect" is a family-resemblance concept (PI §65): there is no one thing common to all cases of aspectual lighting up that makes Wittgenstein apply that term to them. On the contrary there are *various* similarities (and differences) relating them, of which five are as follows:

(A) Cases (2) and (3) are both visual phenomena: what one might call the "optical" image does not change, but its "visual organization" can be said to change. Case (4) doesn't have *this* in common with either of them, but in case (3) the two "groupings" of the experience have the same structure as those in case (4) but not those in case (2).
(B) Cases (1) and (7) resemble each other in a different way from (1) and (2): in (1) and (7), but not in (2), the transition is from seeing a figure in no particular way to seeing it in some particular way; whereas in (2) (and also in (3), (5), and (8)) one moves from seeing the figure in *one* way to seeing it in *another* way.
(C) None of the cases (4), (10), (11), and (12) are exclusively visual phenomena; but they are nonvisual in different ways. (4) is exclusively acoustical. (10) is the visual realization of a literally commonsensical fact: you come to see a pattern that you know must figure in *any* perceptible realization of the formula (whether spoken, written, in Braille, or in semaphore). And (11) and (12) have nothing in particular to do with any sense modality at all.
(D) Cases (6) and (12) essentially involve a grouping together of the object that is seen or in mind with objects that are not; and which comparisons I am inclined to make determine how I am seeing (or thinking about) the object. For instance, to see the figure at PPF §234 as a clumsily drawn "H" is to compare it with more correct versions of that Roman letter; to see it as a correct letter in some other script does not involve that comparison (see Figure 1). Similarly, to see the feeble-minded as such is implicitly to compare them with mentally "normal" human beings. In the *Tractatus* Wittgenstein argued that case (11) is also of this type: to see a sign as expressing a thought that instantiates this or that propositional variable is to see it as belonging to a group containing its other instances; in fact he *identifies* the variable with the class of its instances (TLP 3.315). Contrast case (9), in which everything is open to view; also cases (3) and (4), in which the change is in the internal grouping of the complex object of perception – a change in what Wittgenstein called its "organizational aspects" (PPF §221).
(E) Some of these transitions require more intellectual resources than others. Some of them are highly sensual; some require imagination (especially (4), (8), and (12)); some require more conceptual background than others. (I have arranged the examples to reflect a roughly increasing trend in the conceptual demands that they make.)

These and similar phenomena preoccupied Wittgenstein in the period 1946–1949. His main writings on them appear in *Philosophy of Psychology – A Fragment*

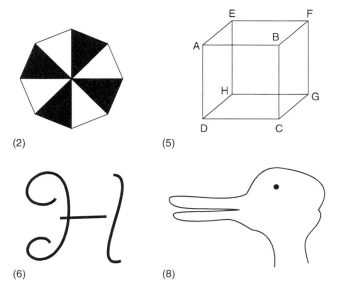

Figure 1 Varieties of aspectual lighting-up. Source for (2), (6) and (8): Ludwig Wittgenstein, Philosophical Investigations (1953/2009). Reproduced with permission of Wiley-Blackwell. Source for (5): https://en.wikipedia.org/wiki/Necker_cube#/media/File:Necker_cube.svg. Used under CC-BY-SA 3.0 http://creativecommons.org/licenses/by-sa/3.0/.

§§111–364; also in *Remarks on the Philosophy of Psychology* (vols I and II), *Last Writings on the Philosophy of Psychology* (vols I and II), and *Zettel*. But these are not his earliest writings on the subject: there are extensive discussions in Part II of *The Brown Book*; briefer comments scattered through *Remarks on the Foundations of Mathematics* (see e.g., III–47), *Wittgenstein's Lectures, Cambridge 1932–35* (see especially 1934–1935 lecture VII), and *The Big Typescript: TS 213* (see esp. BT 177–9); and in the *Tractatus* period there is an allusion to case (5) in connection with the theory of judgment (TLP 5.5423) and to "puzzle pictures" in connection with the theory of probability (NB 28). As this (by no means exhaustive) list suggests – and as you would in any case expect given (a) the diversity that "aspect" covers and (b) Wittgenstein's piecemeal approach to philosophical problems – we cannot extract from his writings any single general doctrine of aspect perception or of aspectual lighting up. On the contrary, his crisscrossing discussions of these topics focus at different times on different points of interest, of which I will mention two at this point and two in conclusion.

First, there are the cases that I have taken as the way in to this area of Wittgenstein's thought, namely the phenomenon of aspectual "lighting up." Wittgenstein's treatment of the more sensory such cases is of particular interest, for as we will see it applies to and also illuminates a number of other doctrines that were central to his later philosophy of language and mind. For this reason I shall focus in this chapter on this cluster of problems. But there are many others.

Of these the one that has occasioned the most scholarly interest is probably his discussion of "continuous" aspect perception. It is natural to say that someone who at first sees (8) as a duck might later *start* to see the rabbit-aspect. But then what about someone who never saw in that figure *anything but* a rabbit? He has never had the experience of that aspect's lighting up for him. Still, it seems plausible to say that the very aspect that *lit up* for you was *always* available to him: that he *continuously* saw that aspect (PPF §118). And then a natural question is: How widespread is this continuous aspect seeing? Is *every* seeing a seeing-as? I shall not enter into these questions here (but see Mulhall, 1990, ch. 1, and Schroeder, 2010).

2   The Paradox

I said that aspectual "lighting up" is a family-resemblance concept. But this doesn't mean that we can't make any generalizations about its instances – only that these generalizations themselves obscure a variety of distinctions. In particular then, in all of cases (1)–(12) there is something that both changes in one respect and simultaneously remains the same in another. What I will call the *paradox* of aspect perception (as identified by Glock (1996), pp. 36 ff.) is the fact that in the more sensory cases (1)–(9), both change and constancy appear to characterize contents of the same sensory modality. That is why we are tempted to say of case (4) that there is an acoustic change – and yet also a constancy that equally seems describable only as acoustic. And of the visual cases, on which I will focus because Wittgenstein does, we are tempted to say just what he says of case (9):

> I observe a face, and then suddenly notice its likeness to another. I *see* that it has not changed; and yet I see it differently. (PPF §113)

This way of putting things, which is as natural in English as it is in German, raises a difficulty. On the one hand you *see* that the face has not changed: you would, for instance, endorse exactly the same image as a copy of it both before and after the aspectual lighting up. On the other hand you somehow *see* it *differently*, or as I shall sometimes say, *in a different way*. But how can you be said to *see* differently in two states that are thus *visually* indistinguishable?

A resolution of this paradox must do two things. First, it must distinguish senses of "seeing that it has not changed" and "seeing it in the same way" such that one can consistently affirm the first and deny the second across an episode of aspectual lighting up, as we do with the paradoxical form of expression. I'll call this requirement the *adequacy condition*. An account of the paradox that fails to meet the adequacy condition cannot be said to resolve the paradox at all, for if "seeing that it has not changed" and "seeing it differently" are understood as antonymous in the paradoxical form of expression ("I see that it has not changed; I see it differently") then the latter really is inconsistent.

It is important to emphasize that this requirement concerns the senses of "seeing that it has not changed" and "seeing it differently" *as they are used in this context*. One might consistently use a similar form of words in other contexts, for instance when one moves closer to or around a static object. But here the sense in which one "sees that it has not changed" is not the visual sense in which one sees e.g., that the Jastrow figure is unchanged both before and after the dawning of the aspect. We should distinguish between (a) seeing that it is the same in the sense of "being informed by the visual faculty that what one now sees is qualitatively unchanged"; and (b) seeing that it is the same in a sense that entails that a perfect copy of what one sees now, and what one saw then, would be identical. Sense (a), which is what is involved in the case where one moves closer to an object, is consistent with the object's changing apparent colour between the times in question, whereas sense (b) is not – one could, for instance, distinguish the shots taken by a camera at your two successive locations. So these are different senses. And the concern is that when an aspect dawns, one sees that the object of vision is the same in sense (b); and yet *still* one wants to say that there is a sense in which one sees it differently.

Second, a resolution must give "seeing it differently" a sense that makes it clear that it is *seeing* that one is doing differently and not something else that is going on at the same time. In a very loose sense one could be said to see differently on occasions A and B if there is some adverb that correctly applies to the seeing on occasion A and not on occasion B. For instance, if I look at the duck–rabbit figure whilst whistling in C minor and then in C major I could be said in this sense to be seeing it differently on the two occasions, because only on the first occasion did the adverb "whilst whistling in C minor" apply to my seeing. But here I am only "seeing" it differently by virtue of doing something *else* differently. With aspectual lighting up one sees it differently by virtue of *seeing* it differently, not by virtue of doing something else differently. I shall refer to this as the *continuity condition*.

The discussion in PPF opens with the paradoxical form of expression and discusses and rejects two responses to it. These are: (i) that at the lighting up of an aspect there is a change in the organization of the visual field, this organization being itself an object of sight; (ii) that there is some difference in the physiological process underlying vision. I'll discuss these in turn.

3 Gestaltism

The Berlin school of gestalt psychology took the view that alongside the colors and shapes traditionally thought to compose the visual field was a similarly perceptible aspect of "organization." For what is given in experience are not only the colors and possibly also shapes of traditional empiricism, but also *structured wholes*. Thus Ernst Mach, an important precursor of the school, wrote: "The tree with its hard, rough grey trunk, its many branches swayed by the wind, its smooth soft shining leaves, appears to us at first a single indivisible whole" ([1886/1903] 1959, p.102). Moreover this whole is itself a further sensory element, as he says in connection with another example:

> If two series of tones be begun at different points on the scale, but be made to maintain throughout the same ratios of vibration, we recognize in both the same melody, by an act of sensation, just as directly as we recognize in two geometrical figures, similarly situated, the same shape. (Mach, [1886/1903] 1959, p.285)

In particular, according to the gestalt psychologists, one holistic feature of the visual field that is given directly in sensation is its organization, that is, which bits of it are grouped together (Köhler, 1930, p.125). And this in turn suggests a resolution of the paradox of aspectual change, at least for cases like (3) and (4) where the change is in the *internal* grouping (though obviously not for case (6) or case (12): see point (D) above).

The attempted "gestalt" resolution of the paradox runs as follows. Something that we see in these cases does *not* change: for the colors and shapes in our visual field do not change. But something else that we see does change, i.e., the visible organization of the visual field. If this is correct then it is easy to see why we say that we see no change and yet *see* it differently. For on this account, we see no change in the colors and shapes in precisely the *same* sense ("by an act of sensation") as we see a change in Köhler's sensory facts of organization. So it is at least clear that the gestaltist account of the paradox meets the continuity condition.

But it clearly does *not* meet the adequacy condition: for, if "seeing it differently" means a change in the content of what one sees (i.e., the organizational content) then the paradoxical form of expression *is* inconsistent after all. For in that case we *do* see a change. To put it another way: if we really do see visual organization just as we see color and shape, then nobody would have felt any attraction toward that form of expression in the first place.

Compare this to the following case. It is plausible that we see both brightness and hue as "sensory elements." So when the brightness of a picture changes (say, on a television screen) whilst the hues remain constant, we can say univocally that we see a change in one respect whilst seeing a constancy in the other respect. But although we do say that we see constancy in one respect, we do *not* report having seen that the picture itself has not changed. On the contrary we see that the picture *has* changed, because we have seen a change *in at least one* of the "sensory elements."

Now contrast what we say when, as the gestaltists would have it, the brightness and hue of a picture (and its shape, and so on) remain constant but the visual organization varies. Here we are tempted to say not only that there is *some* dimension along which what we see remains constant: the paradoxical form of expression is rather that we in some sense see that there is *no change at all* – which is not how one would ever describe a picture that visibly changes in brightness but not hue. So "organization" cannot be an object of sight in the way that colors are: by making it so, the gestaltist does nothing to relieve the tension between the irresistibility of the paradoxical form of expression and its threatened inconsistency.

Wittgenstein's criticisms of gestaltism did not include this one. They were rather more general points that focused on the implausibility of the idea that "visual organization" can be put on the same level as shape and color rather than its specific misapplication to the paradox of PPF §113. Before turning to them, I should mention some evidence that he was broadly sympathetic to the holistic emphasis of gestaltism. For instance, he at least toyed with the idea that amongst the contents of experience are structured wholes irreducible to perceptually local atoms. As early as 1915, he wrote:

> It seems to me perfectly possible that [visually extended] patches in our visual field are simple objects, in that we do not perceive any single point of a patch separately; the visual appearances of stars even seem to be certainly so. (NB 64)

And in *Philosophical Investigations* he draws an analogy between the gestalt nature of experience and the holistic nature of understanding. The point of the analogy is that in each case analysis – atomistic analysis of the visual field or Tractarian analysis of ordinary language – for all that it reveals also misses something essential:

> 63. [...] We may think: someone who has only the unanalyzed form lacks the analysis: but he who knows the analyzed form has got it all. – But can't I say that an aspect of the matter is lost to the latter no less than to the former?

64. Let's imagine language-game (48) [the point of which was to represent combinations of colored squares on a surface] altered so that names signify not monochrome squares but rectangles consisting of two such squares. Let such a rectangle which is half red, half green be called "U", a half green, half white one "V"; and so on. Could we not imagine people who had names for such combinations of colour but not for the individual colours? Think of cases where we say, "This arrangement of colours (say the French tricolor) has a quite special character". (PI §§63–4; cf. RFM VII–64)

But although Wittgenstein accepted that there is a sense in which we see wholes, and hence also in which the organization of an impression belongs to perceptual content, he denied that this was just another sensory fact on the same level as the sensory facts of colors and shapes. On the contrary, he thought that there was good reason to distinguish the sense in which we see organization from the sense in which we see colors and shapes: there is here a categorical difference in the objects of sight (PPF §111).

PPF §§131–6 seem to state the following argument for the distinction. Anyone who, like Köhler, puts the "organization" of a visual impression "on a level with colours and shapes would be taking it for granted that the visual impression is an inner object." But this move fails, because it makes the inner object "chimerical, a strangely vacillating entity. For the similarity to a picture is now impaired" (PPF §134).

To understand this argument we must understand the intellectual pressure that pushes visual organization "inwards." First, the relevant contrast is with "outer" objects, states, and pictures. Inner objects are not commonly observable (i.e., to more than one person) but rather known only to the one that "has" them; whereas an outer picture (a drawing or painting) is in principle open to anyone. Second, if the change in "organization" is in the sensory facts then this must be a change in the picture that the sensory facts present to me. But no *outer* picture, no "copy" of what you see, could exhibit the changes that you notice when an aspect lights up for you.

– My visual impression has changed. – What was it like before; what is it like now? – If I represent it by means of a copy [= drawing] – and isn't that a good representation of it? – no change shows up. (PPF §131; cf. PPF §§135–6)

Therefore the change in the visual organization, if it is a change in the visual impression at all, must be exclusively a change in one's *inner* picture.

But it makes no sense to speak of such a change in the "inner" picture. The reason is that talk of the "inner" *picture*, if it is to illuminate anything, must derive its sense from our acquaintance with *outer* pictures; but now we are appealing to variation of a feature that does *not* appear in outer pictures and so could not be understood on the basis of them. Hence the inner object becomes chimerical: for it is being supposed to have variable features – "visual organization" – that are simply absent from our only model of it.

4 Physiological Account

Wittgenstein also considers the possibility of a physiological explanation of aspect change (again, we are focusing on the more sensory types of case, e.g., (1)–(9)).

> Let it be this. When we look at the figure, our eyes scan it repeatedly, always following a particular path. The path corresponds to a particular pattern of oscillation of the eyeballs in looking. It can happen that one such pattern switches to another, and that the two alternate (A aspects [= switching aspects of the double cross: PPF §215]). (PPF §236)

This explanation at least looks like resolving the paradox. It apparently meets the adequacy condition because it invites a distinction between (a) the optical sequence resulting from any particular saccade or sequence of saccades and (b) the static optical picture that one gets from combining these elements; and these can be thought to specify the senses in which you see no change in something that you see differently. A change in (a) makes for a change in *how* you see something when a new aspect lights up, because then your eyeballs are following a new schedule. But identity in respect (b) means that there is no shift in *what* you see, since there is no change in the overall figure of which the sequence of inputs is a sequence of varying views.

The account *seems* also to meet the continuity condition. After all, both (a) and (b) characterize physiological facts about your *visual* apparatus. So it is natural to describe a change in (a) as a change in how you *see*.

It is clear that whatever the specific merits of this explanation, there is no generalizing from it to aspect changes in nonvisual modalities, let alone to such nonspecific or highly conceptual cases as (10) and (12) – indeed Wittgenstein's own reference to "A aspects" seems to acknowledge that it is only to such conceptually exiguous cases as (1) and (2) that the story has any chance of applying. But this objection does not cut very deep. It may be that there are other facts about the physiology of hearing and touch that explain aspectual changes that are specific to those modalities (and also olfactory facts that explain there not being such things as "aromatic aspects"). And we should hardly be surprised that there is no similar explanation of "conceptual" aspect-shift. In fact given the loose and accommodating character of the target concept, it would be more surprising if a single type of account *were* available to cover all of these cases.

But Wittgenstein's objection to the explanation is fundamental and rules out not only this particular form of physiological account but also any similar treatment of e.g., auditory and haptic cases. He writes: "You have now introduced a new, a physiological, criterion for seeing. And this can conceal the problem, but not solve it" (PPF §236). But this only gestures at an objection that the following passage (from RPP I) really makes explicit:

> 989. Let us suppose that certain aspects could be explained by the movement of the eye. In that case one would like to say that those aspects were of a purely optical character; and so there would have to be a description of them which did not have to make use of analogies from other domains. Then one would have to be able to replace the order "See this as..." by: "Have your gaze shift in such and such a way" or the like.
>
> 990. But it is not true that an experience which is traceably connected with the movement of the eyes, an experience that can be reproduced by such a movement, can for that reason be described by a sequence of optical images. (Any more than someone who imagines a note is imagining a sequence of disturbances in the air.) (RPP I §§989–90)

The trouble with this physiological explanation is that it fails the continuity condition, because it misses the point of the problem itself. That your eyeballs move differently when you see different aspects is an empirical hypothesis, not something that you have always known, or even that you have known for as long as you found the paradoxical form of expression compelling. It is not even a competitor for being what *we* mean by saying "I see it differently; and yet I *see* that it has not changed." Whatever you mean by "see it differently," it cannot be a claim about either the motion of the eyeballs or the optical sequence that arises from it, although it may mean something that is "traceably connected" with these.

Remarks on the Philosophy of Psychology I §873 looks like a different argument against physiological approaches in general. There Wittgenstein writes:

> I am not, however, concerned with an explanation of this understanding [of a painting as of a running horse], say by the assertion that someone who looks at such a picture makes tiny running movements, or feels running innervations. What grounds are there for assumptions of this kind, except *this* one: it 'must' be like that? (RPP I §873)

Here he seems to be questioning whether a physiological basis for aspect perception even exists; this is in line with his more general skepticism about the supervenience of the psychological upon the physiological, or at any rate about the reducibility of the former to the latter (PI §158; Z §§608–14; for criticism see Glock, 1996, pp.178–9).

But this argument is heavily dependent on empirical findings. And Wittgenstein himself thought it plausible in at least some cases to postulate a traceable connection between physiological processes and the experience of aspects (RPP I §997). Perhaps a better way to take this remark would be as an encouragement to question the physiological basis, not because there is none, but because this helps us to see that it is irrelevant to the problem. (RPP I §1012 may be expressing a similar idea.)

So much for the solutions that Wittgenstein rejects. Wittgenstein's own solution to the paradox is a consequence of his account of "seeing it differently." The most important and distinctive feature of that account is the *organic* connection it entails between seeing and thinking. So before turning to it, it is worth looking at Wittgenstein's treatment of the alternative view of that connection, on which seeing – particularly the kind of seeing that figures in aspect shift – may be sharply separated from the thinking or interpreting that accompanies it ("seeing = thinking + looking").

5 Interpretationism

The foundation of the view is a sharp distinction between what we genuinely observe and the judgments, associations, conjectures, and other thoughts that arise in connection with it. We may loosely group these under the umbrella term "interpretation." For instance, when you see the schematic cube at PPF §116 (see figure 2) you may start to think about wire cubes (though you don't in fact form any beliefs or conjectures). This is a fact about your interpretation of the figure.

This understanding of "interpretation" goes beyond RPP I §8, which limits interpretation to conjecture; but this is necessary in any case if we are to understand the range of cases that Wittgenstein considers. And much of what Wittgenstein says – including the key passage PPF §116 – makes sense and is plausible only on this broader interpretation of "interpretation" (see Budd, 1987, pp.11–12).

As for the notion of "perception," and particularly of "seeing," that constitutes the other factor in aspect perception: into that category fall only those things that

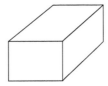

Figure 2 Wire cube. Source: Wittgenstein, 2009. Reproduced with permission of Wiley.

anyone can see, whatever they can think. Its clearest spokesman was not Wittgenstein but Berkeley's Philonous:

> *Phil.* Tell me Hylas, when you behold the picture of Julius Caesar, do you see with your eyes any more than some colours and figures with a certain symmetry and composition of the whole? *Hyl.* Nothing else. *Phil.* And would not a man, who had never known anything of Julius Caesar, see as much? *Hyl.* He would. *Phil.* Consequently he hath his sight, and the use of it, in as perfect a degree as you. *Hyl.* I agree with you. *Phil.* Whence comes it then that your thoughts are directed to the Roman Emperor, and his are not? This cannot proceed from the sensation or ideas of sense by you then perceived; since you acknowledge that you have no advantage over him in that respect. It should seem therefore to proceed from reason and memory: should it not? *Hyl.* It should. (Berkeley, 1734, pp.193–4)

All that we ever really see are shapes and colors: everything else, even (say) the three-dimensional character of a landscape, is the result of some further intellectual operation, i.e., what Philonous calls "reason and memory."

Certainly there is one sense of "see" on which we cannot be brought to see, e.g., Caesar as such: what you might call the purely retinal sense, in which your visual contents supervene on, *inter alia*, your neural stimuli. In *that* sense you and I can't "see" Julius Caesar any more than a newborn child whose retina is being similarly irradiated. It is undeniable that there is such a sense, or at any rate that such a purified notion of vision is attractive to us: that is what accounts for the plausibility of the foregoing passage as well as of Berkeley's argument (1732, §2) that one doesn't see depth because that dimension is orthogonal to the retinal surface.

According to the target position then, "Now I am seeing it as a box" – said, e.g., of the figure at PPF §116 – is a description of a genuinely new experience in the narrowly Berkeleian sense, i.e., one that anyone could have. But it is an *indirect* description of it, i.e., in terms of the interpretation that it provokes and of the thoughts, associations, and conjectures to which it gives rise. Wittgenstein states and criticizes that line as follows:

> Here perhaps one would like to respond: The description of immediate, visual experience by means of an interpretation is an indirect description. "I see the figure [at PPF §116] as a box" amounts to: I have a particular visual experience which is empirically found to accompany interpreting the figure as a box, or looking at a box. But if it amounted to this, I ought to know it. I ought to be able to refer to the experience directly, and not only indirectly. (As I can speak of red without necessarily calling it the colour of blood.) (PPF §117; cf. RPP I §3)

"If I can describe the new experience in these indirect terms then I ought also to be able to describe it in direct terms" – but is that true? After all, there are plenty of things for which I can give indirect descriptions but for which direct descriptions are not available. Suppose that this piano has a peculiar and unique quality of sound. Middle C played on it sounds quite special and you'd recognize it anywhere; but although you can describe that sound *indirectly* (as "Middle C played on this particular piano") you simply do not have the vocabulary to describe that sound in *more direct* terms. Nor can you refer to it by any inner act of ostension, as "*That* sound": for reasons that there is no space to explore here, language is in this case a spinning wheel that engages with nothing (see PI §§258 ff.; see also Chapter 28, privacy and private language). And in any case, if one could refer to that sound directly by ostension, then one could similarly refer directly to experiences of aspects of the schematic cube.

But the disanalogy between this example and Wittgenstein's is that one cannot even *have* the experience of seeing it as a cube, unless one thinks of it in those supposedly indirect terms. On the other hand, one could of course experience that particular timbre (of middle C played on that piano) without having any idea that it was produced by a piano, let alone by this or that particular one. It is *this* point that forces us to abandon the factorization of aspect perception into a purely perceptual factor of *Berkeleian* perception and a purely intellectual factor of "interpretation." As I said, Wittgenstein's account is more organic, and it is to this, and the consequent solution of the paradox, that I now turn.

6   Two Conceptions of Seeing

Before stating the detail of Wittgenstein's account it is worth making three general comments about what explaining a psychological concept involves, according to his later philosophy.

First, there may be no adequate explanation in terms of nontrivial necessary and sufficient conditions for the application of the concept. This may be because there are no nontrivial necessary and sufficient conditions at all; but even if there are, *they* may not be what make us apply the concept to all of its instances. For in many cases psychological concepts are *family-resemblance* concepts (PI §65). In fact the failure to recognize this is one pressure that drives us to postulate an inner realm of psychological facts for which no pattern of behavior could ever be necessary and sufficient (PI §36).

The second point is that introspection is not a way of coming to understand psychological terms. This is for two reasons. First, as I've already mentioned, an inner act of focusing on the quality of a certain kind of experience (in this case, what happens when you see the schematic cube as a box) does nothing to constrain your future use of the concept-word that you are trying to understand (PI §258). Second: that first-personal understanding of the concept, even if it were possible, would be utterly impotent to furnish a third-personal understanding of it. For as Wittgenstein argues elsewhere: it is not a matter of isolating one's own experience and supposing that for another to see it as a box is for him to have "the same experience" as I now have (PI §302; cf. Kripke, 1982, Postscript).

This brings me to the third point, which is that an adequate explanation of a psychological concept demands a statement of its outer *criteria*, these being what Wittgenstein distinguishes from symptoms at PI §354. On the traditional reading of Wittgenstein, the outer criteria of a psychological state constitute evidence for that state that may in any particular situation be defeasible. What is not defeasible is their status *as* evidence of that state; whereas "symptoms" only have contingent evidential bearing on what they are symptomatic of (Canfield, 1974). Thus e.g., crying out is associated with pain, though on any particular occasion there is no ruling out that it is faked. But crying out could not be shown quite generally to be insincere and hence not to have this status. If, for instance, we found that crying out was evidentially irrelevant to C-fiber stimulation, we should conclude, not that crying out isn't after all a sign of pain but rather that C-fiber stimulation is not. (For an alternative reading of PI §354 see McDowell, 1982, p.380.)

In accordance with the second and third points, I will therefore distinguish the relevant senses of *what* one sees and *how* one sees in terms of their behavioral and other outer criteria, rather than by drawing your attention to the introspectible quality of any type of mental state. And in accordance with the first point, I will not attempt to give the totality of relevant criteria by means of a necessary and sufficient condition. Instead, I will specify the central example or examples as a means of getting across concepts that are at least in one case very tangled.

The relevant criterion of *what* the subject sees is what he *acknowledges* as an *exact* copy of it. The object of sight in this *optic* sense is what Wittgenstein calls the "visual impression" (PPF §131). It is important to distinguish this criterion for optic perception from two other *non*-criteria. (a) What one acknowledges as a rough copy of what one sees is not a criterion of what one optically sees. (b) How one would *draw* an exact copy of what one sees is not a criterion of what one optically sees. Note that *how* he would produce a copy is not the same thing as what one would draw if one *were* somehow to draw (what one acknowledged as) an accurate copy. The latter *is* of course criterial of the visual impression, for it does not change when the visual impression does not. (See PPF §112; Budd, 1987, pp.13–14.) As we will see, both (a) and (b) might change although the visual impression remains evidently unchanged.

The optic content of sight is no doubt very close to what Berkeley considered the only content that is available (see Philonous's remarks as quoted above). For in the optic sense you might very well see no more in a picture of Caesar than someone who cannot recognize him as such. Still, I hesitate to identify the optic content of sight with what Philonous claims to see, if only because the latter is ultimately explained in terms of private immaterial objects – ideas – whereas the notion that concerns us carries no such commitment. Nonetheless, it is in my view plausible to say that there is an ordinary sense of "see the same thing" in which one can be said to see the same thing if things are optically the same. There is some evidence for this in the fact that whatever else may be wrong with the passage from Berkeley that I quoted, it is implausible that when Philonous says that the man ignorant of Caesar would "see as much" he is revealing a blank misunderstanding of that English phrase.

At any rate what matters is that we distinguish "what one sees" in this sense from "*how* one sees": what I will call its "*synoptic* content." The criteria of how you see – more generally, of what you synoptically perceive – are relatively complex, consisting in those "fine shades of behaviour" to which Wittgenstein alludes when characterizing the perception of depth (PPF §180) and the understanding of a musical theme (PPF §210). The criteria of your synoptic content are principally as follows:

(i) What you consider to be approximate copies of what you see: for instance, somebody who sees the figure in (6) as a correct letter in one alphabet will not consider acceptable the same approximations to it as somebody who sees it as a badly-executed letter in a different alphabet (PPF §234).

(ii)   *How* you would go about copying it. For instance, it would be easy to copy a bit of cursive script if one sees it as such, hard if ones sees it only as squiggles, or to copy a mirror image of it that one cannot *but* see as squiggles (PPF §151).

(iii) What comparisons you would make when describing what you saw. For instance if asked about (8), someone who saw a (picture)-rabbit might have explained "by pointing to all sorts of pictures of rabbits [i.e., not only to *optical* approximations to this one], would perhaps have pointed to real rabbits, talked about their life, or given an imitation of them" (PPF §120).

(iv)   How he would use it, for instance as a pattern. "For example, somebody who sees the schematic drawing of a cube as a plane figure consisting of a square and two rhombi will perhaps carry out the order 'Bring me something like this!' differently from someone who sees the picture three-dimensionally" (PI §74).

(v)   The forms of expression that would come naturally in your description of it. For instance: the three-dimensional gestures with which one would describe a three-dimensional landscape (PPF §148).

(vi)   Your nondescriptive, expressive reactions, e.g., on seeing a picture of a running horse: "Tally ho!" and an expressive movement of the hand (RPP I §873).

It is principally in these ways that synoptic contents come across. (i)–(vi) are criteria of these contents. Moreover a *change* in these criteria is itself the criterion of a change in these contents. For instance, we should say that a change in how they copy them is a change in *how* children see letters of the alphabet (consider how children "write" Roman script before they have learnt to read it, or how those who cannot read it might copy Arabic script).

It is now easy to see what it means to say that aspect change involves a change in what one sees but not in how one sees. As Wittgenstein repeatedly emphasizes, when a visual aspect lights up there is no change in the contents of one's *optic* perception: for instance, there is no such change in cases (1)–(3) or (5)–(9) (see PPF §131, quoted above). What changes is what one sees *synoptically*. The distinction therefore satisfies the adequacy condition on any solution to the paradox: "I see the figure differently; but I *see* that it doesn't change" means: It is *optically* constant but *synoptically* different.

What about the continuity condition? Is there anything that justifies, or at least explains, our thinking of a change in synoptic content as a change in how one *sees*? The answer is yes, because there *are* similarities between optic and synoptic content, similarities that do not hold between e.g., synoptic content and "interpretation" and which justify the recurrence of "see" in the paradoxical form of expression. First and most obviously, both optic and synoptic content have more to do with one's eyes than with any other perceptual organ: *having* eyes is physically necessary for seeing in either sense, and degradation of the optical system degrades both optic and synoptic vision. Second, both optical and synoptic seeing describe states that have genuine duration (unlike "interpretation," at least on Wittgenstein's narrower interpretation of that term (PPF §248) and plausibly also on the broader construal of it that I recommended above). Third, there is a similarity in the criteria for these states: both involve the attitudes that we take toward drawings, copies, and other forms of visible reproduction.

The most important objection to thinking of them both as ways of characterizing *seeing* derives from a philosophically tempting, but backwards, way of thinking about the concept of seeing. Possibly under the influence of too much traditional empiricism, it's natural to think that the criterion of optic perception is actually just an extrinsic way to pick out something that we can identify by its essence, viz., the *purely* visual contents of one's *inner* visual image. Thus consider the passage from the first *Dialogue* that I quoted above. There it looks as though Berkeley has got hold of the pure or original concept of seeing, in contrast to which our everyday use of the word frequently describes only the leaves of the artichoke and not the vegetable itself: talk of a change in "how we see" describes no real change in *seeing* but only a change in its contemporaneous surrounding ("looking + thinking").

I do not have sufficient space here to examine Wittgenstein's elaborate treatment of that distinctively philosophical delusion. Some of the main points are those that I outlined when I introduced the optic–synoptic distinction. Wittgenstein attacks the central motivation behind this idea: the thought that to see really is to *have* something (PI §398), an inner materialization of the object (PPF §158) that is private to oneself (PPF §214). In his so-called private language argument, Wittgenstein objects that such private objects are semantically inert: nothing about their natures at all constrains one's use of terms denoting them in a multilateral language (PI §293); nor could any "private ostensive definition" turn this trick in a unilateral one (PI §258). So in order to say "what seeing is" we must supply outer criteria (PI §580), as here. It is the private object of "seeing" that is derivative: to notice it is not to discover what seeing really is but rather to invent a *new* concept of "seeing" (PI §401).

So the tangled everyday concept of seeing is not a communal overlay onto a pure and private concept of inner-object-possession that is the native inheritance of every subject. It is not as though there is a private episode, *real* seeing, of which the optical criterion happens to be the outer test and to which synoptic seeing adds extraneous public elements that are foreign to its essence. On the contrary, outer criteria are as essential to *any* concept of seeing as they are to any other psychological concept. And of course *they* do not mark any radical discontinuity between optic and synoptic seeing.

7   Conclusion

That is Wittgenstein's treatment of the paradox. Amongst all of the many things that he says about the variety of phenomena that (1)–(12) illustrate, it is probably this that deserves most prominence, for as I said, it illuminates many Wittgensteinian lines of thought that intersect upon it: the family-resemblance character of psychological concepts, what gestaltism got wrong and what right, the philosophical irrelevance of physiological explanation, the role of criteria in explaining psychological concepts, and the temptation to make "private objects" bear a load that they cannot carry.

But there is a good deal more to say about Wittgenstein's writings on (a) sensory aspects and (b) non-sensory aspects. For instance, some of his most interesting and underappreciated work under both (a) and (b) is of relevance to his philosophy of logic and mathematics, a subject that I have not discussed here at all. Under (a): seeing an array of dots, now as consisting of four altogether, now as two pairs of dots, is the lighting up of a visual aspect; you synoptically see it now as the one, now as the other, whilst optically seeing it as unchanged. But it may also have relevance to the epistemology of at least those simple mathematical equations that one learns in childhood by such methods. Looking at these particular dots tells me more certainly that $2 + 2 = 4$ than could any proof in the style of Russell and Whitehead's *Principia Mathematica*. But how can an intuition of some *particular* array thus convince me of something so general in its application? (See e.g., AWL 180–2.) Kant's proposal was that the intuition is of an a priori manifold; but perhaps what is more plausible is that the objects of synoptic vision are not themselves individuals but *concepts*. If this could be explained convincingly then it might also explain Wittgenstein's remark that "what I perceive in the lighting up of an aspect is not a property of the object, but an internal relation between it and other objects" (PPF §247).

Under (b): the capacity of logic to extend our knowledge depends on there being alternative decompositions of a single thought. Consider the inference from "Mars is smaller than Earth and Earth is smaller than Jupiter" to "something is intermediate in size between Mars and Jupiter" (Dummett, 1991, p.40). The inference is intuitively valid; and yet it is quite possible to understand both premise and conclusion without realizing this. For to understand both premise and conclusion it is not necessary, but to accept the argument as valid it *is* necessary, that you think of the premise as instantiating the pattern "Mars is smaller than x and x is smaller than Jupiter." But equally one must recognize the thought patterned thus to be the *same* thought as before. This capacity, of which (11) is also an instance, plainly has some resemblances to other examples of aspectual lighting up (for further discussion see Ahmed, 2010). I believe that Wittgenstein's discussion of those other cases casts light on this one: if not on the phenomenon itself then at any rate on his own views about the capacity of logic to inform and surprise.

References

Ahmed, A. (2010). Deductive Inference and Aspect Perception. In A. Ahmed (Ed.). *Wittgenstein's Philosophical Investigations: A Critical Guide* (pp.197–217). Cambridge: Cambridge University Press.

Berkeley, G. (1732). *An Essay Towards a New Theory of Vision*. Fourth edition. Reprinted in M. Ayers (Ed.). (1996). *George Berkeley: Philosophical Works* (pp.1–70). London: Everyman.

Berkeley, G. (1734). *Three Dialogues between Hylas and Philonous*. Third edition. Reprinted in M. Ayers (Ed.). (1996). *George Berkeley: Philosophical Works* (pp.155–252). London: Everyman.

Budd, M. (1987). Wittgenstein on Seeing Aspects. *Mind*, 96, 1–17.

Canfield, J. (1974). Criteria and Rules of Language. *Philosophical Review*, 83, 70–87.

Dummett, M.A.E. (1991). *Frege: Philosophy of Mathematics*. London: Duckworth.

Frege, G. (1879). *Begriffsschrift*. Reprinted in J. van Heijenoort (Ed.). (1970). *Frege and Gödel* (pp.1–82). Cambridge, MA: Harvard University Press.

Glock, H.-J. (1996). *A Wittgenstein Dictionary*. Oxford: Blackwell.

Köhler, W. (1930). *Gestalt Psychology*. London: G. Bell. (First published 1929. New York: Liveright.)

Kripke, S.A. (1982). *Wittgenstein on Rules and Private Language: An Elementary Exposition*. Oxford: Blackwell.

Laing, R.D. (1990). *The Divided Self*. London: Penguin.

McDowell, J. (1982). Criteria, Defeasibility and Knowledge. Reprinted in J. McDowell. (1998). *Meaning, Knowledge and Reality* (pp.369–394). Cambridge, MA: Harvard University Press.

Mach, E. ([1886/1903] 1959). *The Analysis of Sensations*. Trans. C.M. Williams. New York: Dover. (Original work published 1886/1903.)

Mulhall, S. (1990). *On Being in the World: Wittgenstein and Heidegger on Seeing Aspects*. London: Routledge.
Schroeder, S. (2010). A Tale of Two Problems: Wittgenstein's Discussion of Aspect Perception. In J. Cottingham and P.M.S. Hacker (Eds). *Mind, Method, and Morality: Essays in Honour of Anthony Kenny* (pp.352–371). Oxford: Oxford University Press.

Further Reading

Day, W. and Krebs, V.J. (Eds). (2010). *Seeing Wittgenstein Anew*. Cambridge: Cambridge University Press.
McGinn, M. (1997/2013). *Wittgenstein's Philosophical Investigations*. Second edition. London: Routledge. Chapter 8.

34

Wittgenstein on Color

JONATHAN WESTPHAL

1 Introduction

In 1949, two years before his death, Wittgenstein wrote the following:

> I may find scientific questions interesting, but they never really grip me. Only *conceptual* and *aesthetic* questions do that. At bottom I am indifferent to the solution of scientific problems. But not the other sort. (CV 79e)

This remarkable confession may not come as a surprise to those who know the trajectory of Wittgenstein's thinking about color, from the *Notebooks on Logic 1914–1916*, and on to the *Remarks on Colour*, which was written over the 18 months before his death in 1951. Wittgenstein's early interest in color was neither in the aesthetics of color nor in the distinctive features of the concept of color, but in the metaphysics of color, which he took, following the empiricists, to be somehow contained in restricted places in the visual field. This narrow interest was transformed into an investigation into the most *recherché* and particular aspects of the language-games that have to do with color, and of related aesthetic matters. How, and why, did this transformation come about? And what exactly was Wittgenstein's final view about color in the *Remarks on Colour* in 1950–1951?

Some of Wittgenstein's readers seem to think that his later observations about color are fragmentary, disorganized, or hard to understand, the late work of a once great mind. I disagree. Their force and direction will become clear once we understand the development of Wittgenstein's thought, and how the *Remarks on Colour* grew out of his earlier work.

2 The Beginning: Before the *Tractatus*

In the very early *Notebooks 1914–1916*, Wittgenstein's principal interests were in logic, but his remarks are scattered through with occasional observations or sequences of observations about epistemology, solipsism, life, God, and other metaphysical subjects.

A Companion to Wittgenstein, First Edition. Edited by Hans-Johann Glock and John Hyman.
© 2017 John Wiley & Sons, Ltd. Published 2017 by John Wiley & Sons, Ltd.

The entry for 6 May 1915 follows an observation about the general form of the proposition, but it concerns logical simples. Wittgenstein says that the pseudo-sentence "Are there simple things?" cannot be expressed in "symbolic notation," "And yet it is clear that I have before me a concept of a thing, of simple correlation, when I think about this matter. He adds:

> As examples of the simple I always think of points of the visual field (just as parts of the visual field always come before my mind as typical composite objects). (NB 6.5.15)

The next day Wittgenstein wants to know what "a uniformly coloured part [*ein gleichförmig gefärbter Teil*] of my visual field [is] composed of" and suggests *minima sensibilia* as a possible answer (NB 7.5.15). But by 24 May Wittgenstein has decided that "we have no acquaintance with simple objects," and he asks, "Is it imaginable that – e.g. – we should *see* that *all the points of a surface are yellow*, without seeing any *single* point of this surface? It almost seems so." This raises the question how we should describe "a surface uniformly covered with blue" (24.5.15). The day after that Wittgenstein continues with this theme, but also discusses the fixed stars as extensionless parts of the visual field, and then "the urge towards the mystical," suggesting that it derives from "the non-satisfaction of our wishes by science" (NB 25.5.15).

Right at the end of the *Notebooks*, on the penultimate day, dated 8 January 1917, and before his final remarks on suicide, Wittgenstein constructs an argument that was to dominate his thinking about color until 1929, and whose effects would be felt long after that.

> It is clear that the logical product of two elementary propositions can never be a tautology.
>
> If the logical product of two propositions is a contradiction, and the propositions appear to be elementary propositions, we can say that in this case the appearance is deceptive. (E.g.: A is red and A is green.) (NB 8.1.17)

Here we have the following ideas:

(1) If propositions cannot be analyzed truth-functionally, then they are elementary.
(2) If propositions are elementary, then they do not contradict one another.
Hence,
(3) if a pair of propositions contradict one another, then they cannot be elementary propositions.

However, propositions attributing incompatible colors to a single place in the visual field *do* contradict each other. In the *Tractatus* Wittgenstein concludes that propositions attributing colors to places in the visual field cannot be elementary propositions, i.e., they must be capable of being analyzed.

3   Tractatus Logico-Philosophicus

The *Tractatus* was published in 1921. Here, as in the *Notebooks*, Wittgenstein is convinced that there must be elementary propositions, propositions that cannot be analyzed, because they are not composed by applying truth functions to other propositions.

Furthermore, since "the only necessity that exists is *logical* necessity," it is logically impossible for two colors to occupy "the same place in the visual field" at the same time. Hence, "the statement that a point in the visual field has two different colours at the same time is a contradiction" (TLP 6.365).

All is in order, with the exception of the fact that the statement asserting the simultaneous presence of the two colors is not as it stands an *explicit* contradiction. "Point *x* is red at *t*" and "Point *x* is green at *t*" is no more a contradiction than "Point *x* is red at *t*" and "Point *x* is round at *t*." For Wittgenstein in the *Tractatus* a contradiction is a *logical* contradiction. It has a form such as, "Point *p* is red at *t* and point *p* is *not* red at *t*." So the two color terms must be analyzed in such a way that to say that a point has one of the colors implies that it does not have the other, which is another way of saying that propositions about the colors of points in the visual field are *not* atomic. Wittgenstein did not give the analysis of these propositions, but he was assuming that it could be given; when it has been given, the contradiction will be explicit.

There is a second color theme in the *Tractatus*. Though objects are simple (2.02), they exist within the logical "spaces" of physical space, time, and being colored (2.0251). Spatial, temporal, and color predicates make sense if they are attached to objects, as other predicates do not, e.g., "prime." These networks or "spaces" that carry the logical complexity of the predicates for the simple objects become, in Wittgenstein's later work, linguistic rather than metaphysical; they become language-games, and they are the bearers of logical structure, though in a sense of "logical" extended to include non-truth-functional relations such as "exclusion."

The two themes work together both in the *Tractatus* and in the later philosophy, and the complexity of their interaction is what produces the intricate logic and epistemology of Wittgenstein's last writings, published in the *Remarks on Colour*.

4   The Middle Period

The metaphysical structure of the *Tractatus* began to disintegrate, however, when Wittgenstein realized, as he reported in "Some Remarks on Logical Form," that he could not analyze propositions about colors as statements of degree. The difficulty hinges on the fact that, as he saw it (RLF 168), statements of degree involve numbers, so numbers must be involved in atomic propositions. If I wish to say that some "entity" in the visual field is colored bright to some degree, say degree 2, Wittgenstein asserts, I will have to express this by saying "E(*b*)&E(*b*)," just as I would from the logical point of view have to assert that some distance is two miles long by saying that it is one mile long and another mile long, and no more. But "E(*b*)&E(*b*)" says the same thing twice. It is in this sense a tautology, and it is equivalent to "E(*b*)," not to "E(2*b*)." It follows, Wittgenstein claims, that attributions of degree cannot be "further analyzed."

Now a further difficulty presents itself. If propositions about colors cannot be further analyzed, then they are atomic. If they are atomic, then there cannot be logical relations between them. For if there are logical relations between propositions *p* and *q*, then these relations will interfere with the "output" column of the truth table. A perfect example is the old problem of color incompatibility.

Let "RPT" represent the proposition that there is a place P in the visual field that is red at time T, and let "BPT" represent the proposition that that place P in the visual field is also blue. We can write the following truth table.

RPT	BPT	RPT & BPT
T	T	T
T	F	F
F	T	F
F	F	F

But according to Wittgenstein this result is wrong on the top-line, because, as he puts it, "'RPT & BPT' is some kind of contradiction" (RLF 168). The output column should read "FFFF." That is the output for a contradiction. Wittgenstein concluded that there is a new relation, "exclusion," which is like contradiction in that the last three outputs in the column are indeed "FFF," but simply lacking an output on the first line, or, it would be better to say, lacking a first line at all. For the two colors "exclude" one another even though the propositions do not explicitly contradict one another. And that is the end of truth-functional logic as the basis of a general account of the proposition that Wittgenstein had offered in the *Tractatus*.

One might wonder why the crux of the argument of "Some Remarks on Logical Form" is not just a straightforward puzzle about "and." We can ask why "E($2b$)" should be analyzed as "E(b)&E(b)." Should it then be written as E($b+b$), where the plus sign takes the place of the ampersand "&"? In this form we find represented both the degree (2) and the addition of the two unit degrees (+). Wittgenstein's view was, however, that there should be no numbers in atomic propositions, as then the atomic propositions would not be simple. "E(b)&E(b)" is not simple, as it is a conjunction.

The remarks posthumously published as *Philosophical Remarks* were written between February 1929 and April 1930, so it is not surprising that there is material common to it and "Some Remarks on Logical Form." The old problems had not been resolved, however, and, where they remained, new ones grew out of them.

Wittgenstein had begun to replace the idea of a logical space with "logical grammar," a conception that was in turn destined to be replaced by "language-games." He wrote, "The colour octahedron is grammar, since it says that you can speak of a reddish blue but not a reddish green, etc." (PR §§39, 75; §§222, 278). But he continued to worry about the basis of the relationships in the octahedron, especially the incompatibility of colors (PR §76, and also §221).

> If $f(r)$ and $f(g)$ contradict one another, it is because r and g completely occupy the f and cannot both be in it. But that doesn't show itself in our signs. But it must show itself if we look, not at the sign, but at the symbol. For since this includes the form of the objects, then the impossibility of '$f(r) \cdot f(g)$' must show itself there, in this form. (PR §78)

The logical form of what is said to be "here now," that is, red and green, or r and g, "here now" being the "function," is what the external sign, the written marks "red" and "green" do not show. "What I said in the *Tractatus* doesn't exhaust the grammatical rules for 'and', 'not', 'or', etc." The logical rules for these words "are *a part* of the grammar of these words, but not *the whole*" (PR §82).

Color incompatibility had shown Wittgenstein the force of a relation that is not logical in the truth-functional sense, yet has all the symbolic power of logic, in that it tells us what is and what is not possible; he called it "grammar." And so Wittgenstein arrived at his later view of color. Some of the *Philosophical Remarks* are carried over intact into the *Remarks on Colour*, for example this methodological one: "What I need is a psychological or rather phenomenological color theory, not a physical and equally not a physiological one" (PR §218). The comment that follows, however, is even more explicit and direct than anything to be found in the *Remarks on Colour*, although it most certainly remained Wittgenstein's view.

> Furthermore, it must be a theory in pure phenomenology in which mention is only made of what is actually perceptible and in which no hypothetical objects – waves, rods, cones and all that – occur. (PR §218)

In the *Remarks on Colour* the point is expressed more broadly: "As I mean it [a proposition about color] it can't be a proposition of physics" (ROC II §3).

5 The Later Period

In *Philosophical Investigations* the discussion of color is more or less subordinated to the main topics in the philosophy of language, metaphysics, and epistemology that Wittgenstein discusses. Throughout *Philosophical Investigations* Wittgenstein used color mainly only as an example, of the meaning of a word, of a universal, of the content of a mental state, and so on. It is almost as though he was saving his thoughts about color in its own right for the remarks composed in the last year of his life.

Among the discussions in *Philosophical Investigations*, however, there are three in which Wittgenstein gives to color more attention than it receives elsewhere in the book, and which give some insight into his thinking: the possibility of meaning without logical simples, the problem of nonbeing, or meaning without a "bearer," and the multiplicity of language-games in which "attention is directed to the colour."

In section 48 Wittgenstein returns yet again to the striking idea that color words are the names of simple objects in a matrix of colored patches, and he illustrates it with a colored diagram, and a "sentence" describing it. The "sentence" is "RRBGGGRWW," and it simply lists in a left-to-right and top-to-bottom order the names of the colors of the nine "elements" as he calls them in a 3×3 matrix of colored square patches (see Figure 1).

The sentence is, and the larger "language" of which it is presumably a part are, completely Augustinian (cf. PI §§1ff), in the sense that every part of it is a name. "Here the sentence is a complex of names, to which a complex of elements corresponds. The primary elements are the coloured squares" (PI §48). Wittgenstein subsequently makes a very important distinction between the functions of the processes of *naming* and

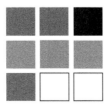

Figure 1 From Wittgenstein, *Philosophical Investigations* §48. Source: Wittgenstein, 2009. Reproduced with permission of Wiley.

describing, attempting to diagnose the idea that the elements can only be named and not described. He makes the point that to say "R" names an element does not imply that it cannot be described. This already tells us that the simplicity of the words in the language does not imply a corresponding simplicity in the objects that its names denote. Whether an element is simple or complex, however, does depend on which language-game it is part of and does not make sense "*outside* a particular language-game." We have here a doctrine that could be called "the relativity of simplicity." What makes an element simple is its role – as the recipient of a name – in the language-game. It is the language-game that tells us whether the squares of color are simple or complex. If the language-game describes universals, there is one red element in three red squares. If it describes particulars, there are three. But nothing forces us to use one rather than the other.

These arguments are followed by one of the odder hangovers of the *Tractatus*: the discussion of the ancient problem from classical philosophy of how it is possible to speak of what is not. What is not must surely *be* in order for us to say, of *it*, that it is not, or else we are speaking of nothing and our assertion that *it* is not is one that is bound to fail. Color or any element must in some sense neither *be* nor *not be*, "for if it did not *exist*, one could not even name it and so one could state nothing at all about it" (PI §50). This might seem a little puzzling, however, for the conclusion that follows the interlocutor's remark in the following passage seems to be that that color *must* be.

> "Something red can be destroyed, but red cannot be destroyed, and that is why the meaning of the word 'red' is independent of the existence of a red thing." – Certainly it makes no sense to say that the colour red is torn up or pounded to bits. (PI §57)

Wittgenstein also imagines us thinking that "sepia" could be defined by "the standard sepia," which would be "hermetically sealed" in Paris, just like the standard meter. He makes the startling claim that we cannot say that the standard sepia either is or is not itself sepia, or that the standard meter either is or is not itself a meter in length (PI §50). And there is some reason to this. If the standard meter bar were accidentally cooled so that it shrank to three feet, one could say, just at that moment at which it stopped being 39.3 inches long, that it was not the standard *meter*. And the same is true with sepia. If the standard sepia sample, say of a laminated chip, turned to a bright fluorescent green, it could hardly remain the standard *sepia*. And there is something wrong with saying, if it *remains* exactly the color it is, that it is the same color as itself: sepia. It cannot be the standard for itself. So it is not the colored sample but the *role* of the sample that produces the standard; and that *role* cannot be destroyed.

And finally, there is a charming passage in PI §33, in which Wittgenstein gives a variety of sentences that could direct our "attention to the colour," a passage that exhibits the imagination born of an affectionate familiarity.

> "Is this blue the same as the blue over there? Do you see any difference?" –
>   You are mixing paints and you say, "It's hard to get the blue of this sky".
> "It's turning fine, you can already see blue sky again."
> "Note how different these two blues look."
> "Do you see the blue book over there? Bring it here."
> "This light blue means..."
> "What's this blue called? – Is it 'indigo'?" (PI §33)

"Just as making a move in chess doesn't consist only in pushing a piece from here to there on the board" – we have the expression, "wood-pusher," a bad or hack chess player – so there are a variety of ways of doing something called "attending to the colour." But Wittgenstein is here attacking the idea that there is a lowest common denominator, a stream of energy called *attention*, which is released by the mind and turned upon the color, just as, in the very last sections of *Philosophical Investigations*, he attacks the idea that *meaning* some thing is a matter of doing a certain thing, directing a stream of "meaning" it onto the thing that one means.

What has been posthumously published as *Remarks on the Philosophy of Psychology* I and II was dictated by Wittgenstein between 1945 and 1948, after the completion of *Philosophical Investigations*. In Volume I, for the first time, Wittgenstein finds his footing with the topic of color; a long section of the book, §§602–45 (34 pages), is devoted to it. He has reached the point of being able to think about color with a complete freedom that allows him to connect it with the psychological "phenomena" that so fascinated him.

In the long extended passage about color (from §§602 to 645) Wittgenstein discusses his usual themes. Among the main points are the following.

(1) Color words cannot be explained by describing colors.
(2) This is not because colors are for some strange reason indescribable, but because the language-game provides for the introduction of color words only by ostension, not by verbal definition.
(3) People equipped and skilled in the use of a system of binary decimal fractions for describing colors would possess an ability that we do not, like perfect pitch.
(4) The idea that an explanation of a color word has to produce an experience of the color in the mind of the person to whom the explanation is offered is as absurd as supposing that defining a triangle has to involve the sudden appearance of a triangle before our eyes.
(5) Even a red sample is an object colored red, and when one attempts to define the term "red" ostensively, by means of the sample, one is pointing not at the color but at the colored object.
(6) "The *employment* of a word is not: to *designate* something."
(7) We can't imagine what someone sees who is red-green color-blind.
(8) Red is not a strangely specific object of experience. What we see is not an indefinable *this*, which we can imagine pointing to but cannot describe.
(9) If a color is a "primary" or "pure" color, this is not a contingent fact about it. The proposition that red is a primary or pure color is not an empirical proposition about human color vision, or physiology, or about optics or physics, but a grammatical proposition.
(10) The equal distances of the primary colors on the color circle are arbitrary.
(11) The impossibility of reddish-green is like an axiom in mathematics.
(12) Our scheme of color concepts could have treated red as a shade of green. There is nothing in the nature of the colors themselves that excludes this. A color scheme of this kind would be simpler than ours, in the sense that it would have fewer primaries, but we can only describe it as *lacking* a primary color if we take our scheme for granted.
(13) We must not believe that we have the concept of color within us because we are looking at a colored object ("any more than you have the concept of a negative number because you are in debt," Z §332).

Volume II of *Remarks on the Philosophy of Psychology* contains two passages, §§293–8 and §§421–33, the second one significantly longer, which lead straight into *Remarks on Colour* I. The passages concern the logical backbone of *Remarks on Colour* I. That backbone is built around the question, what the origin of the logical relationship between colors is, and what its basis. Wittgenstein finishes the line of thought ending at RPP II §297 with an unWittgensteinian conclusion: "The understanding, I say, catches hold of *the one object*; and then we speak of *it* and its qualities according to its nature" that he himself had rejected in the previous paragraph. The remark is unWittgensteinian, because it brings one back to the supposedly unmediated apprehension of the supposedly simple object. What thought had led to this dead end, the Tractarian thing that Wittgenstein himself has just told us he *shouldn't* say?

By §421 Wittgenstein has decided that there is something that works like logic in producing a necessity, but is not part of truth-functional logic. The use of the sentence is in order, and its use determines what the concepts within it mean.

"There is no such thing as a bluish yellow." This is like "There is no such thing as a regular biangle"; this could be called a proposition of colour-geometry, i.e. it is a proposition determining a concept. (RPP II §421)

What does it mean to be "a proposition determining a concept"? We have our two examples: "There is no such thing as a regular biangle" and "There is no such thing as a bluish yellow." Why can't there be a regular biangle, if there can be a regular triangle, a regular quadrangle, and so on? Why is "three" the smallest possible *n* in "There is a regular *n*-angle"? Similarly, we can ask why there can't be a bluish yellow, if there can be a bluish green, and a bluish purple, and a bluish grey, and so on. "Figure *F* is a regular biangle" is not, it seems, a contradiction; nor is it exactly grammar that prevents such a thing. But it is doubtful whether there is more to the idea of a color geometry here than the analogy with geometry proper. At any rate, Wittgenstein does not explain the analogy further, adding only "We have a colour system as we have a number system" (§426).

6 Remarks on Colour

In the last year of Wittgenstein's life, from the autumn of 1950 to the spring of 1951 (he died on 29 April), he wrote three manuscripts that include remarks about color. The 88 "remarks" of *Remarks on Colour* I are a revision of the 350 "remarks" of manuscript III. The exact date of II, which contains only 20 remarks, is uncertain.

It is astonishing and interesting that Wittgenstein should have wanted to write about color as a philosophical problem in its own right. How had color come to assume such importance and interest in his mind? Part of the answer is the aesthetic and conceptual charm of color, perfectly fitted to Wittgenstein's mind. And he was able to show how this interest could be exercised at the expense of and without the scientific understanding of color.

This explains why a number of the *Remarks* are about Goethe. Goethe's phenomenological approach, and his hostility to Newton's dualism of inner sensations and outer stimuli, had led him to try to create a scientific method appropriate to color's simultaneously subjective and objective character. It was a method that made no reference to

Newton's corpuscles, and condemned what Goethe regarded as the narrowness of Newton's laboratory methods and Newton's tortuous inferences. Goethe preferred what is sometimes today called "the natural image situation," the color image as it appears outside the laboratory.

Remarks on Colour I can be divided into five sections, approximately equal in length, whose themes are as follows:

(1) §§1–15 Pure color and the concept of an intermediate color
(2) §§16–32 Transparent white and the expression of norms vs. the expression of experience
(3) §§33–53 The spatial appearances of color
(4) §§54–76 Goethe and the indeterminateness of color
(5) §§77–88 Psychology and blindness

Apart from remarks specifically about color, there are also general observations (and, in one case, a question) that mostly do not mention color and come at the end of each section, like a sort of finale, but also lead forward to the next section. They are as follows:

§15 In every serious philosophical question uncertainty extends to the very roots of the problem.
§32 Sentences are often used on the borderline between logic and the empirical, so that their meaning changes back and forth and they count now as expressions of norms, now as expressions of experience [...]
§53 There is no such thing as phenomenology, but there are phenomenological propositions.
§76 Does describing a game always mean: giving a description through which someone can learn it?
§88 If the psychologist teaches us, "There are people who see", we can ask him: "And what do you call 'people who see'?" The answer to that would have to be: people who behave so-and-so under such-and-such circumstances.

Remarks on Colour I begins with the comparison of a pair of statements about lengths and about the lengths of two sticks with a pair of statements about the lightness of two colors and the lightness of two colored things (§1). Statements about lengths and the lightness of colors are atemporal and internal, and statements about the lengths of sticks and the lightness of colored things are temporal and external. By this comparison Wittgenstein brings to the center of the stage the idea of the pure or abstract concept of color, "pure" in a sense yet to be explicated. This remark is complicated by the fact that in a picture a piece of paper that gets its light from the sky might be *lighter* than the blue sky. For blue is a dark color, and the lightest blue is darker than white. His next remark is about pure white and Lichtenberg's claim that most people have never seen it. Do they not know what "white" means, then? Wittgenstein's next step is toward the idea of a pure or non-intermediate color. Yellow-green is intermediate, but there is no intermediate red-green. And why is green not the intermediate between yellow and blue? Why is green not a yellowish blue?

Section 2 opens with the arresting question why there cannot be a transparent white, though there can be a transparent green (§19). And now Wittgenstein reverts to the idea of a *logic* of color concepts, in the non-truth-functional sense that he had come to after 1929. He gives a "rule of appearance" for transparency, depth, and color.

> Something white behind a coloured transparent medium appears in the colour of the medium, something black appears black. According to this rule, black on a white background would have to be seen through a 'white transparent' medium as through a colourless one. (ROC I §20)

This ingenious a priori deduction shows that we cannot describe what a transparent white piece of glass would be like (§23). Furthermore:

> When dealing with logic, "One cannot imagine that" means: one doesn't know what one should imagine here. (ROC I §27)

We find an unimaginability of this sort when we are dealing with the "logic" involving the concepts of whiteness, transparency, depth, and so on. The logical sentences that result look as though they were empirical. We discover a posteriori that there is no transparent white or reddish green, and we are *surprised* by the discovery. So in logic there are such surprises, but here we have sentences that are the expressions of norms giving us the concept of whiteness or of redness. And these same sorts of sentences ("There is no transparent green in this stained-glass window") have very different functions.

White, then, is tied in a particular way to the spatial background and the dimension of depth. Wittgenstein proceeds to the asymmetries in the way colors are related to what is called the "spatial appearance" of color. His target, as always, is the empiricist view that colors interchangeably occupy distinct places in the visual field. He has already given us the prime example: X cannot be "white" in the phrase "transparent X." There is no brown-hot, there is no grey-hot, grey cannot be luminous (Wittgenstein seems not to have considered a grey winter sky), there are no grey flames, and a color cannot shine unless it is in its surroundings. A blackish color can't shine; presumably Wittgenstein is setting aside glossy black metals, which have an extra transparent coat.

"A painting cut up into small, almost monochromatic bits" (§60) is made into a jigsaw puzzle. Only with the other pieces do we get shine, highlights, transparency, opacity, and the rest. What does this tell us? It tells us that the concept "sameness of colour" is an *indeterminate* one (§56).

> Imagine someone pointing to a place in the iris of a Rembrandt eye and saying: 'The walls in my room should be painted this colour'. (ROC I §58)

What counts as *this* color? Difficulties of this sort, Wittgenstein suggests, are "those which Goethe wanted to get sorted out in his *Theory of Colours*" (§56). This seems to be a narrow interpretation of the purposes of the *Farbenlehre*, including, as Wittgenstein himself acknowledges elsewhere, Goethe's distrust of anything except the "natural image situation," of the methods of laboratory science, and of theoretical entities, all familiar to any educated German-speaker of Wittgenstein's period.

Wittgenstein and Goethe, however, are most certainly in agreement when it comes to their belief that it is not enough to see colors as indefinable blobs of consciousness in an otherwise narrowly understood material world, a world only of physical objects and structures and electromagnetic radiation, to which psychology is an inexplicable addition. "Someone who agrees with Goethe believes that Goethe correctly recognized the *nature* of colour," which results not from experiments, but "lies in the concept of colour" (§71). Here there is some room for disagreement. Was Goethe's distrust of laboratory experiment a distrust of natural image situations and non-intrusive experiment within them? Or was it, as Wittgenstein believed, a distrust of any experiment at all? Certainly Goethe's sequences of experiments are designed to bring out the concept of color, the appearance of the "primary phenomenon," but his own view was that the experiments that recapitulate the elements found in observation *can* reveal the essence of the phenomenon, the idea or concept.

Remarks on Colour I ends with a dramatic passage, ten sections in all, centered on color blindness and blindness. Its relevance to color and color concepts derives from the claim, repeated by Wittgenstein in various places and at *Remarks on Colour* I §§13–14, that the existence of a "tribe of colour-blind people," who had different concepts from the ones "we" have, and who used the expression "reddish-green," would not force us to recognize that there are colors that we do not see. "There is, after all, no *commonly* accepted criterion for what is a colour, unless it is one of our colours." (§14) ("Commonly accepted" does not, I think, mean "practiced by most or even ordinary people," but "possessed in common," in the same usage as "*The Book of Common Prayer*.") If some concept (*reddish-green*) is not one that is common to us and to the other tribe, there is a clear difficulty in calling it a color concept at all; certainly *our* concepts are *color* concepts, in *our* sense of "color." (Could one be unsure whether one's color concepts are color concepts, and not, say, shape concepts?) Here I do not see a latent relativism, but a practical consideration about translation and what is meant in other languages. "Psychology describes the phenomena of seeing," Wittgenstein observes. "For whom does it describe them? What ignorance can this description eliminate?" (§79) Is it for the sighted? But they *already* know what seeing is. They have the concept. Is it for the blind? But no description can be of any assistance to them. They cannot acquire the concept, and for them it is a concept about what people do, added to a mystery. Accordingly the basis of psychology is something other than simple description, and seeing, including seeing colors, is something other than a phenomenon.

The entire arc of Wittgenstein's thought from 1914 to 1951 is from empiricism about colors as phenomenological simples in the visual field, through the logical difficulties that this view generates, to an anti-empiricist and even a near-rationalist conception, in which the understanding of color concepts is the understanding of the logic of the language-games in which the concepts are deployed. The logic of language-games played with color words turns out to be complicated, more complicated than the empiricist could have expected, and the puzzle problems find their resolution in tracing out the structure of these games. The intrinsic interest and subtle logical resources of the games attest to the strength and importance of Wittgenstein's conception of the language-game. But the understanding of color may require that behind it there is something with even greater logical finesse: the geometry of color or the arithmetic of color.

It is certainly a good thing to understand the logic of color concepts with the subtlety of mind that Wittgenstein brought to the topic. The topic by its nature invites it. As Wittgenstein himself observed, almost defining the combination of the simultaneously conceptual and the aesthetic,

Die Farben scheinen uns ein Rätsel aufzugeben, ein Rätsel, das uns anregt – nicht aufregt. (CV 67)

Peter Winch translates this as,

> Colours seem to present us with a riddle, a riddle that stimulates us – not one that disturbs us. (CV 67e)

Winch adds in a footnote to the text, "In the German there is a play on the two cognate verbs *anregt* and *aufregt* which I have not been able to capture."

Further Reading

Brenner, W. (1982). Wittgenstein's Color-Grammar. *Southern Journal of Philosophy*, 20, 289–298.

Ciuni, R. (2004). The Colour Exclusion Problem and "Synthetic a Priori" Propositions between *Tractatus Logico-Philosophicus* and *Some Remarks on Logical Form*. In A. Coliva and E. Picardi (Eds). *Wittgenstein Today* (pp.121–139). Padova: Il Poligrafo.

Gierlinger, F.A. and Riegelnik, Š. (Eds). (2014). *Wittgenstein on Colour*. Berlin: De Gruyter.

Lee, A. (1999). Wittgenstein's *Remarks on Colour*. *Philosophical Investigations*, 23, 215–239.

McGinn, M. (1991). Wittgenstein's *Remarks on Colour*. *Philosophy*, 66, 435–453.

Rowe, M.W. (1991). Goethe and Wittgenstein, *Philosophy*, 66, 283–303.

Vendler, Z. (1995). Wittgenstein, and the Essence of Color. *The Monist*, 78, 391–410.

Westphal, J. (1991). *Colour: A Philosophical Introduction*. Oxford: Blackwell.

Part VIII

Epistemology

35

Wittgenstein on Knowledge and Certainty

DANIÈLE MOYAL-SHARROCK

The *questions* that we raise and our *doubts* depend on the fact that some propositions are exempt from doubt, are as it were like hinges on which those turn. (OC §341)

Wittgenstein's last notes were posthumously entitled *On Certainty*. They constitute his attempt, prompted by G.E. Moore's "Proof of an External World," to understand the nature of our basic assurance – our assurance about such things as "Human beings are born and die," "The earth has existed long before I was born," "I am standing here," "I have a body," "Here is a hand." As he develops his thought, Wittgenstein employs and considers several options besides "certainty," but what he rules out from the outset is that this assurance is a *knowing*: "If you do know that *here is one hand*, we'll grant you all the rest" (OC §1). Of course, he does not leave it there; much of *On Certainty* is devoted to fleshing out the distinction between certainty and knowledge.

1 Certainty vs. Knowledge

For when Moore says 'I know that that's […]' I want to reply 'you don't *know* anything!' (OC §407)

In seeking to describe something certain that he cannot prove and that nevertheless seems to him the most indubitable of all, Moore (1939) refers to it as "knowledge" because that is to him the concept that expresses the greatest degree of conviction on our epistemic continuum. Wittgenstein agrees that the objects of Moore's assurance are those of our most unquestionable beliefs, but disagrees that the certainty in question is of an epistemic nature; he believes this assurance to be of a more foundational breed than knowing:

When I say 'how do I know?' I do not mean that I have the least *doubt* of it. What we have here is a foundation for all my action. But it seems to me that it is wrongly expressed by the words 'I know'. (OC §414)

A Companion to Wittgenstein, First Edition. Edited by Hans-Johann Glock and John Hyman.
© 2017 John Wiley & Sons, Ltd. Published 2017 by John Wiley & Sons, Ltd.

Why does Wittgenstein not take this certainty to be a knowing? Because he adheres to the standard view of knowledge as justified true belief:

> One says 'I know' when one is ready to give compelling grounds. 'I know' relates to a possibility of demonstrating the truth. (OC §243)

> If Moore says he knows the earth existed etc., most of us will grant him that it has existed all that time, and also believe him when he says he is convinced of it. But has he also got the right ground for his conviction? For if not, then after all he doesn't know. (OC §91)

For Wittgenstein, our certainty that the earth existed long before we were born cannot be said to be *justified*, for it was never *verified*: "I did not get my picture of the world by satisfying myself of its correctness; nor do I have it because I am satisfied of its correctness" (OC §94). In fact, unlike the objects of our *knowledge*, we have probably never even thought about many of the objects of our basic certainty:

> I believe that I had great-grandparents, that the people who gave themselves out as my parents really were my parents, etc. This belief may never have been expressed; even the thought that it was so, never thought. (OC §159)

Of course, we can formulate our certainty of these truisms, and this is what Moore does, but he mistakes these formulations for *epistemic claims*. This is where Wittgenstein corrects him. He takes Moore to task for confusing knowledge with the non-epistemic brand of conviction that logically underlies it, and he drives a categorial wedge between them: "'Knowledge' and 'certainty' belong to different *categories*" (OC §308). In doing this, Wittgenstein breaks with the traditional presupposition in epistemology that we *know* our basic beliefs. On his view, beliefs are not necessarily propositional attitudes, and basic belief is described as a non-propositional attitude: a belief *in*, not a belief *that*; a trust or taking-hold (e.g., OC §150; 509–11). As we shall see, this is not incompatible with his taking them to be expressions of rules of grammar.

But in spite of Wittgenstein's categorial distinction, some commentators of *On Certainty* insist on seeing the certainty that underpins knowledge as itself knowledge. As Michael Williams puts it: "Knowledge [...] emerges out of prior knowledge" (2001, p.176). To concede that this does not require that the prior knowledge be individually generated but can be "a shared and socially transmitted accomplishment" (*ibid.*) does not take away from its conceptual link to truth and (ultimate) justification. Moreover, though Williams acknowledges a default background and a pragmatic component of this background, on his view, our "bedrock certainties" are unavoidably propositional. For, he asks, how could our basic beliefs *not* be propositional, if they are to generate our nonbasic beliefs:

> However basic knowledge is understood, it must be capable of standing in logical relations to whatever judgements rest on it. For example, it must be capable of being consistent or inconsistent with them. But this means that even basic knowledge must involve propositional content [...]. (Williams, 2001, p.97)

But the message of *On Certainty* is precisely that knowledge does not have to be at the basis of knowledge. For Wittgenstein, underpinning knowledge are *not* default justified propositions that must be susceptible of justification *on demand* but, as we shall see, non-propositional certainties – certainties "in action" or ways of acting – which can nevertheless be verbally expressed, and whose conceptual analysis uncovers their function as unjustifiable *rules of grammar* (see Chapter 14, GRAMMAR AND GRAMMATICAL STATEMENTS). (Note: the fact that they can be verbally expressed does not imply they would have propositional content, for expressions of rules have no propositional content.) Hence basic certainties stand to nonbasic beliefs, not as propositional beliefs stand to other propositional beliefs, but as rules of grammar stand to propositional beliefs. Knowledge need not emerge from knowledge: "For why should the language-game rest on some kind of knowledge?" (OC §477).

To say that our basic certainties underpin knowledge is not to say that knowledge is all they underpin. As Wittgenstein writes: they "form the foundation of *all* operating with thoughts (with language)" (OC §401, my emphasis), of our language-games (OC §403) –which means that they are as much the basis of our false beliefs as of our true ones. Our basic certainties make up our world picture, which Wittgenstein refers to as a "mythology" (OC §95), not in the sense that it is a mystifying picture, but in the sense that it is a picture that is not *grounded in* – that is, *justified by* – science (knowledge).

The non-epistemic nature of our basic certainties is ascertained by the logical absence of justification and verification as regards our assurance of them. This shall now be fleshed out in an examination of the other features shared by basic certainties that further preclude their being knowledge claims.

2 The Necessary Features of Basic Certainty

Wittgenstein's deliberations in *On Certainty* bring him to see that our basic certainties share the following conceptual features; they are *all*:

(1) non-epistemic: they are not known; not justified
(2) indubitable: doubt and mistake are logically meaningless as regards them
(3) foundational: they are the unfounded foundation of thought
(4) non-empirical: they are not conclusions derived from experience
(5) grammatical: they are rules of grammar
(6) non-propositional: they are not propositions
(7) ineffable: they are, *qua* certainties, ineffable
(8) enacted: they can only show themselves in what we say and do

3 Indubitability: Doubt and Mistake are Logically Meaningless

> There are cases where doubt is unreasonable, but others where it seems logically impossible. (OC §454)

Our basic certainties are not objects of subjective or psychological conviction, but of logical conviction: "I cannot doubt this proposition without giving up all judgment" (OC §494). Doubt here is tantamount to having lost the bounds of sense: "If someone said to me that he doubted whether he had a body I should take him to be a half-wit" (OC §257).

Nor is it possible to be *mistaken* about a basic certainty: if I believed that I am sitting in my room when I am not or that my biological parents are wolves, it isn't my possibly being mistaken that would be under investigation, but my sanity or, at any rate, my knowledge of English. A mistake results from negligence, fatigue, or ignorance, for instance; we cannot say of someone who believes that they were never born that they are "mistaken":

> In certain circumstances a man cannot make a *mistake*. ('Can' is here used logically, and the proposition does not mean that a man cannot say anything false in those circumstances.) If Moore were to pronounce the opposite of those propositions which he declares certain, we should not just not share his opinion: we should regard him as demented. (OC §155)

In thus *logically* closing the door to doubt and mistake as regards our basic certainties, Wittgenstein closes the door to universal skepticism, and thereby also to the *contextualism* Williams attributes to Wittgenstein (1991, p.26). On Williams's neo-Humean reading, Wittgenstein believes skeptical doubt to have no bearing in the pragmatic air of ordinary life, but to be legitimate and serious in the context of philosophical reflection. But this is a misreading: for Wittgenstein, the Cartesian demon is *never* a plausible threat; he has no more grip in the philosophical study than he does in our ordinary life. According to Wittgenstein, there can be *no context* in which our basic certainties can be doubted or justified, for their indubitability is *conceptual*, not *contextual*. A *basic certainty* cannot be doubted in some contexts and not in others; it can *never* be doubted, whereas the *doppelgänger* of a basic certainty – that is, a twin sentence that expresses an empirical or an epistemic proposition – can be, and this misleads Williams into thinking that the certainty itself can, in some contexts, be doubted. An example of an empirical *doppelgänger* of our normally basic certainty of having two hands is the proposition "I have two hands" uttered by someone able to make sure from removing the bandages that were concealing his wounded hands (OC §23).

What may have given Williams the impression that Wittgenstein defends a form of contextualism is the difference he marks in *On Certainty* between the use of "I know" in ordinary life and its use in philosophical discourse:

> What I am aiming at is also found in the difference between the casual observation 'I know that that's a...', as it might be used in ordinary life, and the same utterance when a philosopher makes it. (OC §406)

But Wittgenstein suggests we treat these knowledge claims differently not because he thinks we *know* our basic certainties in ordinary life and not in the philosopher's study, but because Moore's being a philosopher ought to constrain him to use "I know" with technical precision; that is, exclusively in cases of true justified belief; whereas this cannot be demanded of the ordinary person: we cannot and should not expect her to use "I know" only when it is "justified true belief" she means by it. Wittgenstein refuses to admonish or correct our *ordinary* use of language, but the *philosopher* must be made accountable:

> So if I say to someone 'I *know* that that's a tree', it is as if I told him 'that is a tree; you can absolutely rely on it; there is no doubt about it'. And a philosopher could only use this

statement to show that this form of speech is actually used. But if his use of it is not to be merely an observation about English grammar, he must give the circumstances in which this expression functions. (OC §433)

For when Moore says 'I know that that's a...' I want to reply 'you don't *know* anything!' – and yet I would not say that to anyone who was speaking without philosophical intention. (OC §407, original emphasis)

And so, for Wittgenstein, a non-philosopher may say "I know" in cases where a philosopher may not, but this does not imply that the non-philosopher *knows* where the philosopher does not.

It isn't, as Williams claims, that skeptical doubts are *unnatural doubts* (1991, p.2), and therefore sustainable only in the artificial or unnatural conditions of philosophical reflexion, but that they are *not doubts at all*. Williams seems not to have noted that, in *On Certainty*, Wittgenstein elucidates the concept of doubt in two ways: he shows that universal doubt is impossible, and he shows that not everything that has the *appearance* of doubt *is* doubt:

If someone said that he doubted the existence of his hands, kept looking at them from all sides, tried to make sure it wasn't 'all done by mirrors', etc., we should not be sure whether we ought to call that doubting. We might describe his way of behaving as like the behaviour of doubt, but his game would not be ours. (OC §255)

In some cases, what looks like doubt is only *doubt behavior*. Of course, where doubt has no rational motivation or justification, it may have (pathological) *causes* (OC §74), but normal doubt must have *reasons*. It isn't enough to *say* or *imagine* we doubt: genuine doubt, like suspicion, must have *grounds* (OC §§322, 458). If Williams thinks skeptical doubt possible, it is because – like Moore and most philosophers since Descartes – he takes the mere *articulation* of doubt for doubt: "One gives oneself a false picture of *doubt*" (OC §249).

Wittgenstein's recognition that the skeptic's doubt is only doubt behavior is spurred by his realization that it is hinged on the very certainties it dismisses. For, were she not hinged on some certainties, the skeptic could not even formulate her doubt:

If I wanted to doubt whether or not this was my hand, how could I avoid doubting whether the word 'hand' has any meaning? So that is something I seem to *know* after all. (OC §369)

But more correctly: The fact that I use the word 'hand' and all the other words in my sentence without a second thought, indeed that I should stand before the abyss if I wanted so much as to try doubting their meanings – shews that absence of doubt belongs to the essence of the language-game, that the question 'How do I know...' drags out the language-game, or else does away with it. (OC §370)

Its being essential to our making sense means that this certainty underpins all our questions and doubts (OC §341), including the skeptic's (attempted) universal doubt, thereby invalidating it. At "the foundation of all operating with thoughts (with language)" (OC §401) is an essential certainty, a certainty endorsed every time a doubt (towards it) is formulated. What we have here is a knockdown objection to universal skepticism.

Although Hume may be seen to have progressed from Descartes when he admits that skeptical doubt is not sustainable in ordinary life, it takes Wittgenstein to recognize that universal doubt is not sustainable at all, inside the study or out – and this, not for pragmatic but for conceptual reasons: "A doubt that doubted everything would not be a doubt" (OC §450); "If you tried to doubt everything you would not get as far as doubting anything. The game of doubting itself presupposes certainty" (OC §115). Wittgenstein has demystified skeptical doubt; he has shown that the skeptic is only under an *illusion of doubt* (OC §19).

Basic certainty, as depicted by Wittgenstein and as it operates in our life, cannot be subsumed under "knowledge." For it has no truck with truth or justification. To say that basic certainties are logically indubitable is not to say that they are *necessarily true*. There is no question of truth or falsity in the bedrock: "If the true is what is grounded, then the ground is not *true*, nor yet false" (OC §205). The indubitability of our certainties does not result from our having confirmed them, but stems from their not being susceptible of confirmation or falsification at all. Basic certainties are *logically* impervious to doubt. At some point, justification and doubt lose their sense; where the spade turns, there is the ungrounded ground, where "justification comes to an end" (OC §192).

4 Foundational: Basic Certainties are the Unfounded Foundation of Thought

I have arrived at the rock bottom of my convictions. (OC §248)

In spite of the abundance of foundational images and remarks, commentators have denied the presence of foundationalism in *On Certainty* on the grounds that basic certainties, as depicted by Wittgenstein, lack some of the traditional features of foundational beliefs. But, as previously mentioned, Wittgenstein's basic certainties have their place in a foundationalist structure as the grammatical underpinnings of our beliefs. This is a *modification* of foundationalism, not the absence of it.

There can be no mistaking Wittgenstein's foundationalism; it is both explicitly stated – "At the foundation of well-founded belief is belief that is not founded" (OC §253); "What we have here is a foundation for all my action" (OC §414); "the matter-of-course foundation for ... research" (OC §167) – and repeatedly illustrated: our basic certainties are said to be like the "substratum of all [our] enquiring and asserting" (OC §162), "the rock bottom of my convictions" (OC §248). What is also clear is that their ungrounded or unjustified nature is not a pragmatic but a logical feature of basic certainties: "it belongs to the *logic* of our scientific investigations that certain things are *in deed* not doubted" (OC §342; first emphasis mine). In fact Wittgenstein explicitly denies that absence of justification as regards basic beliefs might be due to practical considerations: "But it isn't that the situation is like this: We just *can't* investigate everything, and for that reason we are forced to rest content with assumption" (OC §343). He is unequivocal in declaring that "the end [i.e., our basic belief] is not an ungrounded presupposition" (OC §110) and that he does not want "to regard this certainty [...] as something akin to hastiness or superficiality" (OC §358).

For Wittgenstein, it isn't, as Williams suggests, that the justificatory process need not *actually* occur (though grounds must be produced on demand), or that it need not be self-conscious (2001, p. 35), but that objective certainty is groundless by nature: "I want to conceive it as something that lies beyond being justified or unjustified" (OC §359). If our certainty stems, or could stem, from justification, it is not a *basic* certainty: "I did not get my picture of the world by satisfying myself of its correctness" (OC §94).

Crispin Wright holds a view in substance not very different from that of Williams. He accepts the groundlessness of what he calls "hinge propositions" while at the same time upholding (what he takes to be) their rational nature. He seeks to do this by thinning down the type of rationality at work here. Wright argues that absence of justification does not imply absence of a warrant to believe; there is "a type of rational warrant which one does not have to do any specific evidential work to earn"; this nonevidential or "unearned warrant" or "warrant for nothing," he also calls "entitlement" (2004b, p.174). It is an "entitlement to trust"; and trust, though not as robust as belief proper when it comes to rationality, "is not per se irrational"; Wright still finds enough reason in trust: "Entitlement is rational trust" (2004b, p.194). How rational? The prevailing answer seems to be: that our forming basic beliefs "falls short of the ideals of our reason" does not prevent it from being rational; we accept strategic entitlement in order to avoid *cognitive paralysis* (2004a, p.50), and so there is still rational merit here. By now, however, it has become clear that the rationality in question is pragmatic, and not properly cognitive or epistemic; that the substance of Wright's argument lies in pragmatism, and so the same objections apply to him as to Williams (above). A more recent attempt at adulterating reason without emasculating it completely is Wright's suggestion that "basic judgments" are made "for *no reason that can be captured via the modus ponens model*" rather than "made for *no reason at all*" (2007, p.499). However, having rightly rejected John McDowell's account of reasons furnished by experience as inadequate, Wright does not then offer an account of his own, therefore making no advance on his attempt to dilute Wittgenstein's groundless certainty into a certainty with *some* grounds (reasons) – of the pragmatic kind.

Pace Williams and Wright, for Wittgenstein, basic certainty is where reasons or justifications come to an end, full stop. His is a logical, not a pragmatic, account of some things having to hold fast for us if we are to speak and act with sense.

That basic certainties lack some of the features of foundational beliefs as traditionally conceived should not prevent them from being foundational. In fact it is precisely their differing from the rest of our beliefs in being non-propositional and non-epistemic that makes for the success of Wittgenstein's foundationalism. It is the realization that what we have traditionally taken to be propositional beliefs, rationally posited or arrived at, are in fact ungrounded or logical ways of acting that allows Wittgenstein to put a stop to the regress of justification.

5 Non-Empirical: Basic Certainties are not Conclusions Derived from Experience

> The difficulty is to realize the groundlessness of our believing. (OC §166)

If our basic certainties are not arrived at by reasoning, they are not arrived at by induction either. In *Philosophical Investigations*, Wittgenstein asks:

> 'The certainty that the fire will burn me is based on induction.' Does that mean that I argue to myself: 'Fire has always burned me, so it will happen now too?' Or is the previous experience the *cause* of my certainty, not its ground? (PI §325)

And in *On Certainty*, he replies:

> The squirrel does not infer by induction that it is going to need stores next winter as well. And no more do we need a law of induction to justify our actions or our predictions. (OC §87)

Of course, many natural phenomena are unquestionably predictable – e.g., that human beings are born and die, that mountains don't spring up in a day. On an empirical reading, our basic certainties are rational conclusions that we come to (tacitly or not) from having observed such regularities. Wittgenstein opposes this: "No, experience is not the ground for our game of judging. Nor is its outstanding success" (OC §131). But to say that our certainties are not *grounded* (that is, *justified*) by regularity of experience and recurrent success is not to rule out *all* impact of experience on our certainty. Recurrent experience and success sometimes do contribute to the formation of our certainties, but they do so non-inferentially and non-inductively; that is, through *conditioning*, which includes training and repeated exposure, not reasoning: "Indeed, doesn't it seem obvious that the possibility of a language-game is *conditioned* by certain facts?" (OC §617) This is what Wittgenstein means when he speaks of experience as a *cause* rather than a *ground*: "This game proves its worth. That may be the cause of its being played, but it is not the ground" (OC §474).

We think we come to the basic certainty that "Human beings need nourishment" in the same way we come to a conclusion from reasoning. This confusion is due to our assuming that some reasoning must always take place for certainty to occur: "Normal thought envelops even our basic judgments with a rhetoric of reasons," notes Wright (2007, p.140). But Wittgenstein insists that although we do invariably invoke (an implicit) reasoning to explain our most basic beliefs, in fact no such reasoning takes place: we do not arrive "at the conviction by following a line of thought" (OC §103). Our basic certainty is not rational but a-rational, animal: "I want to conceive it as something that lies beyond being justified or unjustified; as it were, as something animal" (OC §359). Whether it starts out as instinctive (e.g., our certainty of having a body) or is the result of conditioning (e.g., "This is (what we call) a table"), basic certainty is best described as an involuntary reaction, and not as a thought:

> It is just like directly taking hold of something, as I take hold of my towel without having doubts. (OC §510)

> And yet this direct taking-hold corresponds to a *sureness*, not to a knowing. (OC §511)

Basic certainty is not the result of judgment; that is the province of knowledge. Knowledge is *rationally grounded* in reality, in nature, in experience: "Whether *I* know something depends on whether the evidence backs me up or contradicts me. For to say one knows one has a pain means nothing" (OC §504). And in the same way that it is nonsensical to claim "I *know* I have a pain" as if I had discovered it by observation, it is nonsensical to claim that "I *know* I exist" or "I *know* external objects exist" for the same reason.

My certainty that I exist, that I am sitting at my desk, or that human beings need nourishment to exist is as logical and unreasoned as "2+2=4." It is a certainty that is not *justified* by reality (thereby guaranteeing the autonomy of grammar), but *logically* underpins all I can say or doubt about reality. In order for our words and deeds to make sense, we must take as starting points such regularities as "Human beings need nourishment"; what Wittgenstein has understood is that these are not empirical, but *logical* (or grammatical) starting points.

6 Grammatical: Basic Certainties are Rules of Grammar

Passages in *On Certainty* point out a peculiarity of Moore-type certainties, such as "There exists at present a living human body, which is *my* body," "This body was born at a certain time in the past" (1925, p. 33). They look like empirical propositions, but what they express is indubitable, non-hypothetical. In fact, we can say of them what we say of mathematical sentences: "Dispute about other things; *this* is immovable – it is like a hinge on which your dispute can turn" (OC §655).

Wittgenstein asks himself whether Moore-type certainties might be a kind of hybrid, but this possibility does not pass muster. It is not that rule and empirical proposition merge into one another (OC §309), but that what *looks like* an empirical proposition is not always one. Here again, as is so common in our philosophical speculations, we are misled by *form*:

> That is, we are interested in the fact that about certain empirical propositions no doubt can exist if making judgments is to be possible at all. Or again: I am inclined to believe that not everything that has the form of an empirical proposition *is* one. (OC §308)

Wittgenstein's view is that Moore-type propositions, though they have the form of empirical propositions, are in fact rules of grammar:

> So one might grant that Moore was right, if he is interpreted like this: a proposition saying that here is a physical object may have the same logical status as one saying that here is a red patch. (OC §53)

> When Moore says he *knows* such and such, he is really enumerating a lot of empirical propositions which we affirm without special testing; propositions, that is, which have a peculiar logical role in the system of our empirical propositions. (OC §136)

"A peculiar logical role": in other words, a grammatical role. As Wright puts it: "the unwavering – dogmatic – confidence we repose in these propositions [...] attaches to them in their role as in effect rules" (2004a, pp. 35–6). But what Wright does not see is that inasmuch as our basic certainties are rules, they cannot be propositions, empirical or otherwise. This is not a mere technical point: the non-propositionality of basic certainties is one with their being "animal." And if for Wright: "There is no animal in epistemology!" (Kirchberg 2003 Q&A), Wittgenstein has no qualms about saying that he wants to conceive of certainty as "something animal" (OC §358–9).

7 Non-Propositionality: Basic Certainties are not Propositions

It can be argued that for Wittgenstein, for a sentence to be a proposition, it must be susceptible of truth or falsity (see e.g., AWL 101; PLP 288; BT 61 [76]). And inasmuch as basic certainties are neither true nor false – "the ground is not *true* nor yet false" (OC §205) – they cannot, on Wittgenstein's view, be propositions. Indeed, one passage in *On Certainty* leaves no doubt as to the non-propositionality of our fundamental certainties: "the end is not certain propositions striking us immediately as true" (OC §204). So why does Wittgenstein, in other passages, refer to our fundamental beliefs as "propositions"? The inconsistency is partly justified by the fact that the non-propositionality of basic certainties is not immediately clear to Wittgenstein in *On Certainty*, and so out of philosophical habit and in reference to Moore's "propositions," he calls these certainties "propositions." Of all the insights Wittgenstein comes to in *On Certainty*, basic beliefs being ways of acting (and not propositions striking us as true) is the most groundbreaking, and must therefore have been the most difficult to achieve and process. He does, however, make the point here:

> Giving grounds, however, justifying the evidence, comes to an end; – but the end is not certain propositions striking us immediately as true, i.e. it is not a kind of *seeing* on our part; it is our *acting*, which lies at the bottom of the language-game. (OC §204)

While Annalisa Coliva and Duncan Pritchard both agree that basic certainty is non-epistemic, they find my non-propositional reading problematic. This seems to reflect the general resistance of epistemologists in admitting the "animal" into their midst. Here is Coliva:

> I [...] think that Wittgenstein's definitive view on the nature of certainty wasn't that it is of an animal, non-propositional nature. But, of course, there is no denying that, at least at places, he also talked of this kind of certainty. Hence, the question is: how do the propositional and the non-propositional account of certainty go together, if they do? (Coliva, 2010, pp.172–3)

Coliva's way of reconciling the two is to see basic certainties as judgments (and therefore propositions) that have a normative role (and therefore non-propositional; they are, like rules, exempt from doubt) (2010, p.80). This is not the view, explicitly voiced by Wittgenstein, that the same sentence can at one time express a judgment and at another a rule of testing (OC §98), but that a "hinge proposition" is both at once; Coliva writes: "'Here is my hand,' 'The Earth has existed for a very long time,' 'My name is AC' [...] play a normative role, while also being judgements." This, claims Coliva,

> can be evinced from the fact that they constitutively contribute to the determination of what would count as, for instance, normal conditions of perception, evidence for or against historical or geological empirical judgements, normal conditions of human functioning and so on. (Coliva, 2010, p.142)

But I fail to see how this makes them judgments. If I appeal to "2+2=4" or "This is (what we call) red" or "Human beings die" as "evidence" (say to a child, a non-English speaker, or an alien), I am not appealing to a judgment.

Pritchard also finds the non-propositional reading of basic certainties problematic, particularly because of what is known in the literature as "the closure principle." This is how he succinctly puts it:

> The key difficulty facing the non-propositional reading is to see how it ultimately amounts to anything more than simply embracing a mystery. [...] How could one recognise that a certain historical event (e.g., the battle of Austerlitz) took place at such-and-such a date, and that this entails that the universe has been around for more than 5 min, and yet not adopt a positive propositional attitude (e.g., belief, or something similar) to the entailed proposition? (Pritchard, 2012, p.266)

I would reply that "The universe has been around for more than 5 min" is not an "entailed proposition" at all but a formulation of the certainty on which recognizing that the battle of Austerlitz took place in 1805 is hinged. It may look like an entailment, but is only an apparent or otiose entailment. We have not deduced the certainty that the universe has been around for more than five minutes from recognizing that the battle of Austerlitz took place in 1805, for that certainty logically *underpinned* that recognition. The claim that the battle of Austerlitz took place in 1805 could not be meaningfully formulated were it not for the underlying certainty that the universe has existed for more than five minutes. However, rather than the latter, Pritchard chooses to place an *über hinge* as the underlying certainty. What is this, and why do that?

Pritchard agrees that at the basis of our rational practices is an a-rational, non-propositional commitment, but he must reconcile this with what he takes to be the entailment of "hinge *propositions*." He does this by suggesting we think of "hinge propositions" as

> in effect just *exemplifying a general hinge conviction that we are not fundamentally in error in our beliefs about the world*. That general conviction, however, need not take the form of a commitment to any particular proposition, even though it might manifest itself in various commitments to specific propositions which exemplify that general conviction. (Pritchard, 2011, p.282, my emphasis)

So that the general conviction, which he calls an "*über* hinge commitment" (2012, p.267) provides the needed non-propositional basis, while the *specific* hinge commitments take the form of (entailed) propositions. This is how we get the essential non-propositionality as well as the putatively required propositionality. The hinge *proposition* "The universe has been around for more than five minutes" would then be the entailed expression of the non-propositional *über* hinge commitment that one is not radically and fundamentally mistaken in one's beliefs.

My first remark here is that Pritchard's *über* hinge commitment – "We are not fundamentally in error in our beliefs about the world" – seems to be a *reification* of an aspect of hinge certainty or of a hinge certainty. If, as Pritchard writes (above), the general conviction need not take the form of a commitment to any particular proposition, how does an *über* hinge commitment manifest itself before it gets codified? Is it a kind of general trust without an object? Are we hinge-committed to nothing before the general hinge commitment gets individualized? This sounds like a general force distributed amongst occurrences, and smacks of the metaphysical. The kind of picture (e.g., of the will) Wittgenstein tried to wean us away from.

On my reading, basic certainties are non-epistemic, non-propositional, unjustified certainties that can only manifest themselves as ways of acting. These ways of acting in the certainty of *x*, can be philosophically rendered as grammatical rules or as non-propositional beliefs or beliefs-*in*, and this applies to all our basic certainties. Putting these certainties into words for the benefit of philosophical elucidation is a mere heuristic aid; it no more makes our certainties into propositions than the alleged codifications of a general hinge commitment does.

On Pritchard's view, rejecting the closure principle puts the non-propositional reading in a quandary "given that we do seem very able to formulate the propositions expressed in hinge commitments, and recognise their logical relationships to other propositions which we rationally believe and know" (2012, p.269). But the fact that we are able to formulate our hinge commitments should not lure us into thinking that this evinces their propositionality; as to the logical relationship between basic certainties and propositions, it is that between rules and propositions. And it is precisely their being rules that makes basic certainties *logically* ineffable in the language-game.

8   Ineffability: Basic Certainties are Logically Ineffable

> Thus it seems to me that I have known something the whole time, and yet there is no meaning in saying so, in uttering this truth. (OC §466)

Articulating a basic certainty in the language-game does not result in a display of certainty, but in a display of nonsense. It is perceived as queer; incomprehensible; a joke; a sign of madness; or a piece of philosophy (OC §§553, 347, 463, 467). This is because grammatical rules are *nonsense*: they *have* no sense; they *determine* sense. "This rod has a length" is, on Wittgenstein's view, as nonsensical as "This rod has no length"; the latter is nonsense in that it contravenes a rule of grammar, the other in that it *expresses* a rule of grammar (PG 129). This explains why he writes: "'There are physical objects' is nonsense" (OC §35). It is nonsense because it expresses a basic certainty and a basic certainty functions like a grammatical rule.

To utter a basic certainty in the flow of ordinary discourse is to utter a rule where no reminder of the rule was needed. If I were to say to the cloakroom attendant as I hand him my token: "This is a token," he would look at me perplexed. Why am I saying this? "The background is lacking for it to be information" (OC §461); the information the attendant requires in order to retrieve my coat is what the number on the token is. *That this is a token* is the ineffable hinge upon which his looking for the number on the token – and eventually my coat – revolves. Our shared certainty that "this is a token" can only *show* itself in our normal *transaction* with the token; it cannot *qua certainty* be meaningfully *said*. To utter a basic certainty *within* the language-game invariably *arrests* the game. Conversely, think of the fluidity of the game poised on its invisible hinges: I hand the attendant my token, he glances at the number on it and fetches my coat. Our foundational certainty is operative only *in action*, not in words.

We might be tempted to think that the ineffability of basic certainties in the language-game makes them mere Gricean implicatures, those "bizarre things we 'should not say' [but which] would, for all that, be true," as Charles Travis puts it (1997, p.95). But it is precisely this reference to truth – as also the implicatures' conceptual link with intentionality, knowledge, and inference – that preclude any nontrivial rapprochement between them and basic certainties. To say that basic certainties are ineffable is not merely to point out the superfluity of articulating the obvious; it is to stress their logical unsayability. For Wittgenstein, sayability is internally linked to meaning and use:

558

> Just as the words 'I am here' have a meaning only in certain contexts, and not when I say them to someone who is sitting in front of me and sees me clearly, – and not because they are superfluous, but because their meaning is not *determined* by the situation, yet stands in need of such determination. (OC §348)

In certain contexts, the words "I am here" *are* sayable (say, in a game of blind man's buff where a child lets his playmate know: "I am here"); in other contexts, where the same words serve neither to inform, nor to express or describe, they are useless, and therefore meaningless: *they say nothing*. It is important, however, not to confuse the relevance of context here with Williams's *contextualism*. As we saw earlier, for Wittgenstein our basic certainties are *conceptually*, not *contextually*, non-epistemic and indubitable: if something is susceptible to doubt, it is not a basic certainty (though it may look like one).

Basic certainty is a kind of non-propositional, inarticulate, animal trust in certain things: "I want to regard man here as an animal; as a primitive being to which one grants instinct but not ratiocination" (OC §475). Moore and Wittgenstein have given some of our certainties articulation. This is important in that it allows us to individuate and elucidate the objects of our basic certainty, but it can also be misleading: it can give the impression that our basic beliefs are propositional, epistemic, and intellectual. We must remember that formulating and elucidating our animal certainty does *not* make it into an intellectual or propositional certainty. Our basic certainty is animal through and through. We can verbalize it, but the verbalization of a basic certainty is never an *occurrence* of basic certainty. Our basic certainty manifests itself exclusively *in action*. It is, as we shall see, a *logic in action*.

9   Enacted: Basic Certainties Can only Show Themselves in What We Say and Do

> The fragments of a world-picture underlying the uses of language are not originally and strictly *propositions* at all. The pre-knowledge is not propositional knowledge. But if this foundation is not propositional, what then *is* it? It is, one could say, a praxis. (G.H. von Wright, 1982, p.178)

As Wittgenstein writes: "it is our *acting*, which lies at the bottom of the language-game" (OC §204). Indeed Moore's *saying* "I know that 'here is a hand'" conveyed no certainty that was not already *visible* in his speaking *about* his hand, in his ostensibly *showing* it to his audience, or simply in his unselfconsciously *using* it. In the same way, our certainty that "Tables, chairs, pots and pans do not think" shows itself in our *treating* them as unthinking, inanimate objects. Our basic certainty that "There are physical objects" shows itself in our *reaching out* to pick a flower, but not a thought. Basic certainties are grammatical rules whose only manifestation *qua* basic certainty is in action:

> That is to say, it belongs to the logic of our scientific investigations that certain things are *in deed* not doubted. (OC §342)

In deed [*in der Tat*], certain things are not doubted. Logic is embedded in our practices – in our *deeds*: "Children do not learn that books exist, that armchairs, exist, etc., etc., – they learn to *fetch* books, *sit* in armchairs, etc., etc." (OC §476, my emphasis). Our life, *our deeds*, show that we do not, *cannot*, doubt some things if we are to proceed to doubt and knowledge.

With *On Certainty* we come to see that our basic beliefs are not propositional beliefs that lie dormant in some belief box tacitly informing our more sophisticated thoughts. The basic belief verbalized as "I have a body" is a disposition of a living creature that manifests itself in her *acting in the certainty of having a body*. When asleep or unconscious, this belief remains a disposition, but becomes occurrent in any normal use she makes of her body – e.g., in her eating, running, her not attempting to walk through walls as if she were a disembodied ghost. The occurrence of certainty resembles an instinctive reaction, not a tacit belief. My basic certainty that "I have a body" is much the same as a lion's instinctive certainty of having a body. In both cases, the certainty manifests itself in acting embodied; in my case, however, it can also manifest itself *in* what I say; *in* the verbal references I make to my body, as when I say "I lost weight." Similarly:

> Doesn't "I know that that's a hand", in Moore's sense, mean the same, or more or less the same, as: I can make statements like "I have a pain in this hand" or "this hand is weaker than the other" or "I once broke this hand", and countless others, in language-games where a doubt as to the existence of this hand does not come in. (OC §371)

Their being ineffable does not prevent our certainties from showing themselves *in* what we say, but here too, certainty is beyond being justified or unjustified – in every case, something animal (OC §359).

10   Conclusion: Wittgenstein's Enactivism Meets Epistemology

Far from devaluing knowing, Wittgenstein reaffirms its role in our epistemic practices, but he also makes two major adjustments: first, he removes it from its position as the most fundamental of our assurances, and secondly, he points out the erroneous conflation of knowing and claiming to know that results from our impression that the latter, when done in earnest and in the appropriate circumstances, guarantees knowledge (OC §21). In the position traditionally held by knowledge, Wittgenstein places certainty. A certainty that is both animal and logical. By this he means that its indubitability, though essential to our making sense, is not the result of thought and can only manifest itself as a way of acting.

The skeptic may then claim partial victory in Wittgenstein's affirmation that we don't *know* that external objects exist or that we are not brains in vats; but the more radical victory is on the side of certainty: "That is to say, it belongs to the logic of our scientific investigations that certain things are *in deed* not doubted" (OC §342). With this, Wittgenstein recognizes that the real certainty that underpins our investigations – in fact, all that we say and do, our language-games generally – is an enacted, not a propositional certainty:

> But is it wrong to say: 'A child that has mastered a language-game must *know* certain things'?
> If instead of that one said 'must be *able to do* certain things', that would be a pleonasm, yet this is just what I want to counter the first sentence with. (OC §534)

And with this, Wittgenstein's enactivism has an impact on epistemology.

I have attempted in this chapter to elucidate Wittgenstein's account of basic certainty by fleshing out the features that define it. Other commentators have, in their own accounts, left out some of these features: basic certainty has been deemed epistemic but not justified; non-epistemic but not animal; unreasoned but not a-rational; a-rational but propositional; non-propositional but not completely so; and so on. These come down to two main difficulties: it is difficult for epistemologists to give up the idea that knowledge is our fundamental form of conviction. This would mean, as Pritchard puts it, "granting that an awful lot of what we take ourselves to know is in fact unknown" (2012, pp. 268–9). But that it is psychologically repugnant for philosophers to say they don't "know" that the earth exists, etc., is a psychological, not a logical difficulty (for our more fundamental certainty is there to make skepticism logically nonsensical). Once this is crossed, the next real barrier is non-propositionality. Propositionality is difficult for the epistemologist to give up because its absence makes room for the "animal" in epistemology; with non-propositionality, we seem to give up our grip on the rational. But what *On Certainty* shows us is that our distrust of the a-rational (the animal) and our reliance on propositions are excessive. It is only by realizing that putting ways of acting into propositions is an artificial intellectualization designed to harness the animal, that we can take, as Wittgenstein did, the uncompromisingly revolutionary step to stop the regress of justification.

References

Coliva, A. (2010). *Moore and Wittgenstein: Scepticism, Certainty, and Common Sense*. Basingstoke: Palgrave Macmillan.

Moore, G.E. (1925). A Defense of Common Sense. Reprinted in G.E. Moore. (1959). *Philosophical Papers* (pp. 32–59). London: Collier Books.

Moore, G.E. (1939). Proof of an External World. Reprinted in G.E. Moore. (1959). *Philosophical Papers* (pp. 127–150). London: George Unwin.

Pritchard, D. (2011). Epistemic Relativism, Epistemic Incommensurability and Wittgensteinian Epistemology. In S. Hales (Ed.). *The Blackwell Companion to Relativism* (pp. 266–285). Oxford: Wiley-Blackwell.

Pritchard, D. (2012). Wittgenstein and the Groundlessness of our Believing. *Synthese*, 189, 255–272.

Travis, C. (1997). Pragmatics. In B. Hale and C. Wright (Eds). *A Companion to the Philosophy of Language* (pp. 87–108). Oxford: Blackwell.

von Wright, G.H. (1982). *Wittgenstein*. Oxford: Basil Blackwell.

Williams, M. (1991). *Unnatural Doubts: Epistemological Realism and the Basis of Scepticism*. Oxford: Blackwell.

Williams, M. (2001). *Problems of Knowledge: A Critical Introduction to Epistemology*. Oxford: Oxford University Press.

Williams, M. (2004). Wittgenstein's Refutation of Idealism. In D. McManus (Ed.). *Wittgenstein and Scepticism* (pp. 76–95). London: Routledge.

Williams, M. (2007). Why (Wittgensteinian) Contextualism is not Relativism. *Episteme*, 4, 93–114.

Wright, C. (2004a). Wittgensteinian Certainties. In D. McManus (Ed.). *Wittgenstein and Scepticism* (pp. 22–55). London: Routledge.

Wright, C. (2004b). Warrant for Nothing (and Foundations for Free)? *Proceedings of the Aristotelian Society* (Supplementary Volume), 78, 167–212.

Wright, C. (2007). Rule-Following without Reasons: Wittgenstein's Quietism and the Constitutive Question. In J. Preston (Ed.). *Wittgenstein and Reason: Ratio*, 20, 481–502.

Further Reading

Conway, G. (1989). *Wittgenstein on Foundations*. New Jersey: Humanities Press.

Descartes, R. ([1641] 1996). *Meditations on First Philosophy*. Trans. and ed. J. Cottingham. Revised edition. Cambridge: Cambridge University Press. (Original work published 1641.)

Moyal-Sharrock, D. (2007). *Understanding Wittgenstein's On Certainty*. Basingstoke: Palgrave Macmillan.

Moyal-Sharrock, D. and Brenner, W.H. (Eds). (2007). *Readings of Wittgenstein's On Certainty*. Basingstoke: Palgrave Macmillan.

Pritchard, D. (2005). Wittgenstein's *On Certainty* and Contemporary Anti-Scepticism. In D. Moyal-Sharrock and W.H. Brenner (Eds). *Readings of Wittgenstein's On Certainty* (pp.189–224). Basingstoke: Palgrave Macmillan.

Strawson, P.F. (1985). *Skepticism and Naturalism: Some Varieties. The Woodbridge Lectures 1983*. London: Methuen.

Stroll, A. (1994). *Moore and Wittgenstein on Certainty*. Oxford: Oxford University Press.

Williams, M. (1999). Afterword. In M. Williams. *Groundless Belief: An Essay on the Possibility of Epistemology* (pp.183–201). Second edition. Princeton: Princeton University Press.

36

Wittgenstein on Skepticism

DUNCAN PRITCHARD

The difficulty is to realize the groundlessness of our believing. (OC §166)

1 Introductory Remarks

The general topic of skepticism crops up in several places in Wittgenstein's work, from his remarks on solipsism in the *Tractactus*, to the potentially skepticism-inducing claims about rule-following in *Philosophical Investigations*. Our interest here, however, will be in a particularly sustained treatment of issues associated with the topic of radical skepticism that can be found in his final notebooks, parts of which were published as *On Certainty*. These are fragmentary affairs, unedited by the man himself for public consumption and almost certainly concerned in places with distinct (though superficially similar) philosophical issues. There is thus a limit to the extent to which we can reasonably extract an argument from these remarks that we can attribute with full confidence to Wittgenstein (see Chapter 2, WITTGENSTEIN'S TEXTS AND STYLE and Chapter 1, WITTGENSTEIN'S PHILOSOPHICAL DEVELOPMENT). Nonetheless, there is one particular train of thought in *On Certainty* that can be delineated and that we could plausibly claim is a distinctively *Wittgensteinian* proposal, and that is a radically new conception of the structure of rational evaluation, one that has the idea of a "hinge" commitment at its heart. It is this aspect of *On Certainty* that I will focus on here. Many have seen in this proposal a way of dealing with the problem of radical skepticism. As we will see, however, the devil, as is often the case with philosophy, is with the detail. In particular, there are several ways of developing this account of the structure of rational evaluation, all of which are problematic to a greater or lesser extent.

2 Wittgenstein on the Structure of Rational Evaluation

The primary critical target of *On Certainty* is G.E. Moore's famous argument against skepticism in his "A Defence of Common Sense" (1925; cf. Moore, 1939). Moore responded to the skeptical challenge by enumerating some of the many things that he

---

A Companion to Wittgenstein, First Edition. Edited by Hans-Johann Glock and John Hyman.
© 2017 John Wiley & Sons, Ltd. Published 2017 by John Wiley & Sons, Ltd.

took himself to be most certain of, and thus to know. Indeed, these *Moorean certainties* were meant to be such that if Moore knows anything, then he knows these propositions. The most famous Moorean certainty is the claim that he has two hands. Such Moorean certainties are meant to play a kind of foundational epistemic role, in the sense that in virtue of being optimally certain they can be employed as the epistemic basis from which Moore can extract more controversial, and less certain, claims. As Moore points out, if one does know that one has two hands, then it surely follows that one can know that there is an external world (hands being, after all, physical items which occupy such an external world). Wittgenstein would grant Moore this conditional claim, since as he notes in the very opening line of *On Certainty*:

> If you do know that here is one hand, we'll grant you all the rest. (OC §1)

That the structure of rational evaluation should be thought of along foundational lines is of course nothing new in the history of philosophy. Typically, though, the items that served the foundational role (beliefs typically, though not exclusively) tended to be philosophical in nature, in that it took a certain kind of philosophical project, such as the Cartesian project of pure inquiry, to uncover them. What is distinctive about Moore's proposal, in contrast, is that he wanted to treat what he regarded as perfectly "everyday" certainties – i.e., the kinds of claims which folk in normal circumstances are most certain of, such as that one has two hands, that the earth has existed for many years before one was born, and so on – as being able to perform this foundational role.

Despite the intuitive appeal of Moore's proposal, Wittgenstein argues in *On Certainty* that there is something profoundly problematic about it. Moore's idea is that the certainties he cites can play this foundational epistemic role because, due to their optimal certainty, they possess a kind of epistemic groundedness that less certain propositions lack. Wittgenstein contends, in contrast, that it is in the very nature of these Moorean certainties, in virtue of the fact that they are optimally certain, that they cannot be coherently thought of as rationally grounded. That is, Wittgenstein contends that that which we are most certain of must be by its very nature rationally groundless.

Consider the Moorean certainty – for most people, and in normal circumstances – that one has two hands. Wittgenstein writes:

> My having two hands is, in normal circumstances, as certain as anything that I could produce in evidence for it.
> That is why I am not in a position to take the sight of my hand as evidence for it. (OC §250)

That is, Wittgenstein is suggesting that to conceive of this proposition as rationally grounded is to suppose that the rational grounds are more certain than the proposition itself, which of course is *ex hypothesi* impossible since it is held to be optimally certain. Wittgenstein brings this point into sharp relief by highlighting how odd it would be for one to treat one's conviction that one has two hands as being grounded in one's sight of one's hand. Consider this passage:

> If a blind man were to ask me "Have you got two hands?" I should not make sure by looking. If I were to have any doubt of it, then I don't know why I should trust my eyes. For why shouldn't I test my *eyes* by looking to find out whether I see my two hands? *What* is to be tested by *what*? (OC §125)

In normal circumstances, one doesn't need to check by looking that one has two hands, and indeed to check by looking would make no sense anyway. If one doubts that one has two hands, then one ought not to believe what one's eyesight tells one, since this is no more certain than that one has two hands, which is in doubt.

A quite striking claim is emerging here. For not only are these Moorean certainties necessarily groundless, but it also seems they are by that same token immune to rational doubt. For any rational basis for doubting the Moorean certainty would be necessarily less certain than the optimally certain Moorean certainty, and hence one would have more reason to doubt the grounds offered for doubting the Moorean certainty than to doubt the Moorean certainty itself. At the very least, what Wittgenstein seems to be suggesting in this passage is that there could be no rational basis that would *mandate* doubt of a Moorean certainty, since one rational response to the presentation of this ground for doubt could simply be to doubt the ground itself. That claim falls short of the stronger thesis that rational doubt of a Moorean certainty is impossible, but it is even so a dramatic claim to make.

It soon becomes clear, however, that Wittgenstein wants to defend the stronger thesis. That is, not only are Moorean certainties necessarily groundless, but rational doubt of a Moorean certainty is simply impossible, as opposed to being merely rationally unmandated. Wittgenstein claims that the very idea of a rational evaluation, whether positive or negative, presupposes a backdrop of Moorean certainties that are themselves exempt from rational evaluation. To attempt to rationally evaluate a Moorean certainty is thus an attempt to do something impossible. In particular, Wittgenstein repeatedly urges that the very idea of rationally doubting a Moorean certainty is incoherent. Such a doubt, he writes, would "drag everything with it and plunge it into chaos" (OC §613). Doubt of a Moorean certainty is deemed akin to doubting everything, but Wittgenstein cautions:

> If you tried to doubt everything you would not get as far as doubting anything. The game of doubting itself presupposes certainty. (OC §115)

And elsewhere:

> A doubt that doubted everything would not be a doubt. (OC §450; cf. §§370, 490, 613)

The picture that emerges is thus one on which all rational evaluation is essentially local, in that it takes place relative to fundamental commitments which are themselves immune to rational evaluation, but which need to be in place for a rational evaluation to occur. In a memorable passage, Wittgenstein refers to these fundamental commitments – the Moorean certainties – as the "hinges" on which rational evaluations turn:

> The *questions* that we raise and our *doubts* depend upon the fact that some propositions are exempt from doubt, are as it were like hinges on which those turn.
> That is to say, it belongs to the logic of our scientific investigations that certain things are *in deed* not doubted.
> But it isn't that the situation is like this: We just *can't* investigate everything, and for that reason we are forced to rest content with assumption. If I want the door to turn, the hinges must stay put. (OC §§341–3)

Wittgenstein is thus offering a radical new conception of the structure of rational evaluation. In particular, he is arguing that both the skeptical project of offering a wholesale negative rational evaluation of our beliefs and the traditional anti-skeptical (e.g., Moorean) project of offering a wholesale positive rational evaluation of our beliefs are simply incoherent. This is because the very idea of a wholesale rational evaluation is itself incoherent, for it is in the very nature of rational evaluations that they take place relative to hinge commitments that are both groundless and indubitable.

Moreover, notice that Wittgenstein is quite emphatic that it is an *inherent*, and thus nonnegotiable, feature of rational evaluation that it be local in this way. In particular, Wittgenstein isn't merely making the point that our everyday epistemic practices usually involve local rational evaluations. This latter claim has been made by other philosophers – J.L. Austin (1946), for example – but by itself it doesn't gain one much purchase on the radical skeptical problem. After all, as a number of commentators have pointed out – most notably Barry Stroud (1984) – the skeptic isn't claiming that their wholesale doubts are ones that would naturally arise in day-to-day life. Rather, the skeptical thought is that if one steps back from everyday life and employs everyday epistemic principles in a thoroughgoing way, while setting aside the practical limitations of everyday contexts, then one is led to skeptical doubts. It is precisely in this sense that radical skepticism is held to "fall out" of our ordinary epistemic practices even while involving doubts that simply do not arise in quotidian situations.

Wittgenstein's radical new conception of the structure of rational evaluation, if tenable, blocks even this route to radical skepticism, since it excludes even the possibility that the radical skeptic's wholesale rational evaluations could constitute a "purified" version of our everyday local rational evaluations. On the Wittgensteinian picture, the wholesale rational evaluations at the heart of radical skepticism could not be our normal rational evaluations in their purified form, since the very idea of a wholesale rational evaluation is itself incoherent. There is thus an important difference of kind, and not merely degree, when it comes to our everyday practices of rational evaluation and the type of rational evaluation attempted by the radical skeptic (or, for that matter, that attempted by the traditional anti-skeptic, such as Moore).

If this new conception of the structure of rational evaluation could be made defensible, then it would clearly have far-reaching ramifications for epistemology. The difficulty, however, is knowing how to turn Wittgenstein's sketchy remarks on this topic into a concrete proposal. In particular, part of the challenge here is to develop this proposal in such a way that it doesn't end up looking like a form of radical skepticism in disguise. After all, to be told that all rational support takes place relative to a backdrop of ungroundable certainties does sound an awful lot like skepticism. Indeed, it invites the thought that the "rational support" in question, being inherently local in this way, is not really *bona fide* rational support at all, in virtue of being ultimately groundless.

Wittgenstein was certainly alert to this worry, writing that the "difficulty is to realize the groundlessness of our believing" (OC §166). On his view the regress of reasons comes to an end, but it does not come to end with further reasons of a special foundational sort as we were expecting. Instead, when we reach bedrock we discover only a rationally groundless "animal" commitment (OC §359), a kind of "primitive" trust (OC §475). For Wittgenstein, understanding that this is so is meant to be the antidote to radical skepticism, and yet, superficially at least, it looks very much like a version of radical skepticism.

3   A Core Problem for the Wittgensteinian Account of the Structure of Rational Evaluation

We just noted that one general concern with the Wittgensteinian account of the structure of rational evaluation is that it might ultimately collapse into a variant of the very kind of radical skepticism that it was meant to evade. In particular, from a skeptical point of view it is hard to see just what is so *anti*-skeptical about the claim that the structure of rational evaluation is ultimately grounded in a-rational commitments. Isn't that just what the radical skeptic claims? But if so, then how is this view to be distinguished from radical skepticism, exactly?

We can bring this general concern about the Wittgensteinian proposal into sharper relief by considering how one's hinge commitments are related to one's non-hinge commitments. The latter are, presumably, beliefs in the normal way, and for that matter are meant to be (ordinarily) supported by reasons. The former, however, are a more controversial class. They can't be supported by reasons if Wittgenstein is right (reasons for thinking the target proposition true, anyway – the point of this distinction will become clearer below). But now we face a puzzle. For is it not possible, at least in some cases, to reason one's way from rationally held belief in non-hinge propositions to beliefs in the propositions at issue in hinge commitments (i.e., reason one's way to belief in a hinge proposition)? But if that's right, then why can't one's hinge commitments be thought of as rationally held beliefs after all (and thus, potentially anyway, rationally held knowledge)? Conversely, if Wittgenstein is right that such rational support for our hinge commitments is impossible, then doesn't that undermine the idea of even "local" rational support too, such that local rational support is ultimately no rational support at all?

In order to put some flesh onto the bones of the concern in play here, let's take a concrete example, based on one that Wittgenstein himself discusses (see OC §183). One can surely know on a rational basis that Napoleon won the battle of Austerlitz in 1805. But a relevant hinge commitment in the background here on the Wittgensteinian picture is presumably that the world has been in existence for a relatively long time, and didn't just spring into existence in the last five minutes replete with the traces of a distant ancestry. *Qua* hinge commitment, this is not the kind of commitment that could be rationally supported. And that seems right, since what could rationally support such a commitment, given that it is in effect the denial of a radical skeptical scenario? Any reasonably reflective agent could presumably recognize, however, that their knowledge of the historical claim regarding Napoleon's victory entails the denial of the target "historical" radical skeptical hypothesis that the world might have sprung into existence in the last five minutes. But if the former is rationally supported, then what is stopping this agent from inferring, on this rational basis, that the latter anti-skeptical claim must obtain also? Moreover, once such an inference is made, doesn't our agent thereby have a rationally grounded belief in a hinge proposition – something that Wittgenstein claims is impossible? And if they don't, then how can it be that they still have a *bona fide* rational basis for believing the more concrete historical claim that Napoleon won the battle of Austerlitz in 1805?

It is worthwhile making explicit the principle that is being appealed to here, which is a closure principle for rationally supported knowledge:

> *Closure for Rationally Supported Knowledge*: if S has rationally supported knowledge that p, and S competently deduces q from p, thereby forming her belief that q on the basis of this competent deduction while retaining her rationally supported knowledge that p, then S has rationally supported knowledge that q.

That is, if one has rationally grounded knowledge that Napoleon won the battle of Austerlitz in 1805 – knowledge that is rationally grounded in the testimony of reliable historical records – and one competently deduces on this basis that the universe did not come into existence five minutes ago, then via this principle one ought to have rationally grounded knowledge of this hinge proposition. Conversely, according to this principle if one is unable to have rationally grounded knowledge that the universe did not come into existence five minutes ago, then the subject's putative rationally grounded knowledge that Napoleon won the battle of Austerlitz in 1805 is under threat.

The closure principle for rationally supported knowledge looks eminently plausible. In particular, it is hard to see how one would go about denying this principle. Given that competent deduction is itself a rational process, how could it be that a belief gained via competent deduction, and that was derived from rationally supported knowledge, could be any less rationally supported than the belief from which it is derived? What then could possibly prevent the deduced belief from being knowledge, and moreover from being any less rationally supported knowledge than the original belief?

But with this principle in play it ought to be possible for the rationally articulate subject to undertake competent deductions from their rationally supported knowledge of non-hinge propositions and in doing so gain rationally supported knowledge of hinge propositions. Since this would clearly be unacceptable on the Wittgensteinian account of the structure of rational evaluation, the upshot is that either this principle has to go or else one must deny that the non-hinge beliefs in these cases constitute genuine rationally supported knowledge. Neither claim is particularly appealing. Indeed, to take the latter route seems to be to straightforwardly concede that the Wittgensteinian account of the structure of rational evaluation cannot deal with the problem of radical skepticism, since it is tantamount to allowing that "local" rational support is ultimately no rational support at all. We are thus faced with an apparent dilemma between, on the one hand, giving into radical skepticism, and, on the other hand, rejecting a highly intuitive epistemic principle. Call this dilemma the *closure problem* for the Wittgensteinian account of the structure of rational evaluation (Pritchard, 2012).

4 Epistemic Proposals

There are four main ways of developing Wittgenstein's account of the structure of rational evaluation in the contemporary literature, and each of them struggles to answer the closure problem. In this section we will consider two of these proposals, which share as a common theme that while we lack a rational basis for thinking hinge propositions to be true, they nonetheless can constitute knowledge. (It is in this sense that they count as *epistemic proposals*.)

The first proposal is to ally the Wittgensteinian account of the structure of rational evaluation to a form of epistemic externalism – i.e., the view according to which one can have knowledge even in the absence of reflectively accessible supporting reasons. Call this the *externalist proposal*. According to epistemic externalism, knowledge can be sometimes "brute," at least from a rational point of view. The merit of taking this line as regards the Wittgensteinian account of the structure of rational evaluation is that we needn't conclude from the fact that hinges lack rational support that they are thereby unknown (Pritchard, 2005; cf. Williams, 1991).

Part of the attraction of developing the Wittgensteinian account of the structure of rational evaluation along these lines is that it potentially gives one a principled basis for rejecting the closure principle for rationally supported knowledge, and hence avoiding the closure problem just set out. In particular, proponents of this line are in a position to claim that while Wittgenstein's conception of the structure of rational evaluation is incompatible with the closure principle for rationally supported knowledge, it is nonetheless entirely compatible with a related principle, which is the closure principle for knowledge *simpliciter*:

> *Closure for Knowledge*: if S knows that p, and S competently deduces q from p, thereby forming her belief that q on the basis of this competent deduction while retaining her knowledge that p, then S knows that q.

Whereas the closure principle for rationally supported knowledge demands that one's rationally supported knowledge should transfer across competent deductions, the closure principle for knowledge merely demands that one's knowledge should transfer across competent deductions (such that one can extend one's knowledge by employing competent deductions). So, for example, the closure principle for knowledge demands that if one knows that Napoleon won the battle of Austerlitz in 1805, and one competently deduces on this basis that the world did not come into existence five minutes ago, then one also knows the entailed proposition. What the closure principle for knowledge doesn't demand, however – unlike the closure principle for rationally supported knowledge – is that where the subject's knowledge of the antecedent proposition is rationally supported, it follows that the knowledge she gains of the consequent proposition via the competent deduction is rationally supported also.

As such, the closure principle for knowledge is even more compelling than the closure principle for rationally supported knowledge, since it demands less. With that in mind, however, one might be tempted to hold that we can live with the rejection of the closure principle for rationally supported knowledge just so long as we can retain the closure principle for knowledge. In particular, if one can appeal to epistemic externalism in order to make sense of the idea that hinge propositions can be known even despite their lack of rational support, then we can in principle allow agents to use competent deduction to acquire (mere) knowledge of a hinge proposition even while denying, *contra* the closure principle for rationally supported knowledge, that agents can use competent deductions to acquire *rationally supported* knowledge of a hinge proposition. One could then diagnose the appeal of the closure principle for rationally supported knowledge as arising out of a failure to recognize that it is a stronger epistemic principle than the closely related closure principle for knowledge.

Indeed, from an epistemically externalist perspective it is open to one to argue that the closure principle for rationally supported knowledge is independently dubious because it illicitly incorporates epistemic internalist commitments. If, as the epistemic externalist maintains, not all knowledge is rationally grounded, then why should we hold that the process of extending our knowledge via competent deduction should guarantee that where the agent's knowledge of the entailing proposition is rationally supported it follows that her knowledge of the consequent proposition is rationally supported also? The upshot would be that while it would indeed on this view be intellectually disastrous to deny the closure principle for knowledge, so long as one can retain that principle one could live with the rejection of the closure principle for rationally supported knowledge.

There are several problems with the externalist proposal, but I will focus here on three key worries. The first is a general concern about the plausibility of denying the closure principle for rationally supported knowledge. For while I agree that it would be even more problematic to deny the closure principle for knowledge, it remains that rejecting even the closure principle for rationally supported knowledge has large *prima facie* costs. For example, such a denial appears to commit us to (a variant of) what Keith DeRose (1995) has called "abominable conjunctions." That is, rejecting the closure principle for rationally supported knowledge in the way suggested seems to commit us to endorsing conjunctions such as "I have excellent reasons for believing that Napoleon won the battle of Austerlitz in 1805, but have no reason whatsoever for believing that the Universe was in existence at this time." At the very least, in denying the closure principle for rationally supported knowledge one also needs to further show that these conjunctions are not as bizarre as they at first appear.

A related issue in this regard is that the supposed epistemic externalist motivation for denying the closure principle for rationally supported knowledge is not very plausible on closer inspection. Epistemic externalists do not usually deny that there can be *any* rationally supported knowledge, and the thesis motivating the closure principle for rationally supported knowledge is only that when it comes to this specific type of knowledge the rational support should transfer across the relevant competent deduction. There therefore seems no inherent reason why this should be in conflict with epistemic externalism, specifically.

A third concern about this strategy is more specific to the details of the proposal. For notice that while epistemic externalism can open up the theoretical space within which we can make sense of an agent's possessing knowledge even in the absence of supporting reasons, it still remains to be shown that the target beliefs amount to knowledge by externalist lights. The problem, however, is that it is hard to see how such an account would go.

Consider, for example, the prospects of developing this account along process reliabilist lines, whereby one is to essentially understand knowledge in terms of reliably-formed true belief (e.g., Goldman, 1986). The difficulty is that it doesn't seem at all plausible to suppose that we know hinge propositions in virtue of forming the target beliefs via a reliable belief-forming process. Indeed, our hinge commitments do not seem to be the product of *any* specific kind of belief-forming process, but are rather part of the backdrop against which we acquire our beliefs in non-hinge propositions. For example, my hinge commitment to the universe having not come into existence five minutes ago was not acquired via a specific cognitive process, but is rather something that is presupposed in the specific cognitive processes by which I come to acquire particular historical beliefs, such as that Napoleon's victory at Austerlitz was in 1805. If that's the right way to think about hinge commitments, however, then it's going to be hard to tell even an externalist-friendly story about how one might have knowledge of hinge propositions, since whatever externalist epistemology we opt for will inevitably assess this putative knowledge by evaluating the epistemic credentials of the manner in which it was acquired.

A second way of developing Wittgenstein's account of the structure of rational evaluation is cast along broadly epistemic internalist lines (i.e., such that genuine knowledge always has a rational basis). Like the epistemic externalist strategy, this proposal also argues that one can have knowledge of hinge propositions even while lacking a rational basis for thinking that these propositions are true. Accordingly, this stance also rejects the closure principle for rationally supported knowledge while retaining the closure principle for knowledge. What is distinctive about this proposal is that rather than grounding our putative knowledge of hinge propositions in externalist epistemic support it instead appeals to a type of rational – and thus, in principle at least, internalistically respectable – epistemic support, albeit a special kind of rational support that does not consist in reasons for thinking the target propositions *to be true*. This special kind of rational support is known as *entitlement*. Accordingly, call this the *entitlement proposal* (Wright, 2003; 2004a; 2004b; 2004c).

In essence, the idea is that where we are obliged, on pain of cognitive paralysis, to be committed to certain propositions that we have no reason for thinking are true, then, so long there is no reason available for thinking those propositions to be false, one has a default rational basis – an *entitlement* – for these commitments. After all, or so the thinking goes anyway, one is surely rational in avoiding cognitive paralysis, and hence in cases where one has no reason to believe that not-*p*, and where a failure to believe that *p* would result in cognitive paralysis, it is arguably rational to believe that *p* even when one has no rational basis for believing that *p* is true. Thus a lack of rational basis for the truth of a proposition is compatible, on this view, with there being a rational basis for believing it nonetheless. And hence there is an epistemic basis on which one can know this proposition too (even, potentially, by epistemic internalist lights, since the story told here is an entirely *rational* story).

In this way the entitlement proposal can motivate the claim that we can know hinge propositions. We noted above, for example, that one distinctive feature of hinge propositions is that to doubt them would lead to cognitive paralysis. Moreover, one can also plausibly argue that there are no grounds for believing the denials of hinge propositions too. Our beliefs in hinge propositions thus pass the "entitlement" test and hence can count as knowledge, even though we lack rational support for supposing these propositions true. And if we can know hinge propositions, then in principle at least we can retain the closure principle for knowledge. That is, it will no longer follow that agents who undertake competent deductions from their rationally held beliefs in non-hinge propositions to form beliefs in hinge propositions will fall foul of this principle by failing to know the deduced propositions. But the closure principle for rationally supported knowledge does have to go on this view, as it remains the case that one cannot have a rational basis for believing hinge propositions to be true, no matter what competent deductions one has made, and hence *a fortiori* one cannot have rationally supported knowledge in hinge propositions, no matter how this knowledge was acquired.

There are a number of problems with the entitlement proposal, but the overarching concern is that it does not ultimately offer us the kind of epistemic support that could suffice for knowledge of hinge propositions. This is important, since it is only if the entitlement proposal can preserve knowledge of hinge propositions that it is able to retain the closure principle for knowledge, and the retention of the closure principle for knowledge is meant to be something that by the lights of this approach is nonnegotiable (unlike the retention of the closure principle for rationally supported knowledge).

One way of putting this worry is to say that the rational basis for believing hinge propositions provided by this strategy is of a *pragmatic* rather than *epistemic* nature, on the grounds that it is ultimately a rational basis rooted in the prudential value of believing these propositions rather than being a rational basis for thinking these propositions true. But this is too quick. For while it is true that an entitlement to believe does not on this view involve a reason for believing the target proposition to be true, such an entitlement is meant to be rooted in a rational perspective that is purely epistemic. That is, the claim is that given that not believing hinge propositions would result in cognitive paralysis (and given also that there is no reason for thinking these propositions false), then from a *purely epistemic point of view* it is rational to believe hinge propositions (cognitive paralysis is, after all, something that it is *epistemically* rational to avoid). Accordingly, it is not at all clear that the rationality at issue in this proposal is ultimately prudential as opposed to being epistemic.

But the worry about epistemic *versus* prudential rationality in play here is indicative of a deeper problem, which is the very idea of a *belief* being rationally grounded in something like an entitlement. To believe a proposition, after all, is to believe that proposition *to be true*. But if that's right then there is something very puzzling about an entitlement being an epistemic reason to believe a proposition without at the same time being an epistemic reason to believe that proposition to be true.

It is for this reason that proponents of this strategy talk of the propositional commitment in play as being something distinct from belief, such as a *trusting* in or an *acceptance* of a proposition (e.g., Wright, 2004c, p.194). After all, one can make sense of one trusting or accepting a proposition that one is aware that one has no reason for thinking is true because one independently recognizes some epistemic benefit in doing so. This is because trusting in, or acceptance of, a proposition only commits one to acting *as if* the proposition in question is true, and does not commit one to actually regarding it as true (as belief does). But this maneuver just trades in one problem for another, for the obvious worry now is that one needs to believe a proposition if one is to have knowledge of it; mere trust or acceptance of that proposition will not suffice. In particular, it will not suffice precisely because trusting or accepting that p is compatible (unlike believing that p) with agnosticism about the truth of p. If that's right, however, then one who takes this line is forced to grant that the hinge propositions are unknown after all, and hence the strategy is undermined. In particular, the proponent of this strategy is now forced to deny not just the closure principle for rationally supported knowledge, but also the closure principle for knowledge (Pritchard, 2014).

5   Non-Epistemic Proposals

Given the problems facing the externalist and entitlement proposals, one might be tempted to adopt a more radical proposal, one that is arguably closer in spirit to what Wittgenstein himself intended. According to this proposal, we need to take very seriously how Wittgenstein talks of these commitments as being utterly visceral – or "animal" (e.g. OC §359) – in nature, and conclude on this basis that such commitments simply are not in the market for knowledge. With this in mind, we are not to think of them as beliefs at all, or indeed as any other kind of propositional attitude either for that matter. Rather, they represent ways of *acting* rather than a particular propositional attitude. Consider the following passage:

> Giving grounds [...] comes to an end; – but the end is not certain propositions' striking us immediately as true, i.e. it is not a kind of *seeing* on our part; it is our *acting*, which lies at the bottom of the language-game. (OC §204; cf. §§110, 148, 232, 342, 402)

On this view there is a very good reason why we do not have knowledge of hinge propositions – there simply isn't the corresponding propositional attitude that could put us in the market for knowledge of these propositions in the first place. Indeed, as we will see below, on its strongest reading this view maintains that one simply cannot express our hinge commitments as propositions. Call this the *non-propositional proposal* (e.g., Moyal-Sharrock, 2004; cf. Chapter 35, WITTGENSTEIN ON KNOWLEDGE AND CERTAINTY).

Like the epistemic proposals just considered, this proposal also struggles with the closure problem described earlier. For while we can surely make sense of the idea that these hinge commitments are simply ways of acting rather than propositional attitudes, it doesn't seem all that hard to convert such ways of acting into a corresponding propositional attitude in such a way as to generate the closure problem. What happens, on this view, when an agent reasons from her rationally grounded knowledge that Napoleon's victory at Austerlitz was in 1805 to the entailment that the universe must not have come into existence five minutes ago? Is not the result of this competent deduction a propositional attitude toward the entailed proposition, something very much akin (if not identical to) a belief? But insofar as there is a propositional attitude in play here then we can reasonably ask whether it amounts to rationally grounded knowledge or mere knowledge, and on either score a negative answer will lead to the closure problem.

One way around this problem might be to wed the non-propositional proposal to a radically contextual account of meaning, such that the very idea that expressions denying radical skeptical hypotheses are contentful is itself called into question. A radical interpretation of Wittgenstein's conception of the structure of rational evaluation is thus wedded to an arguably even more radical proposal regarding the nature of meaning. Even so, there are grounds for thinking that Wittgenstein might well have a view of this sort in mind, for at several junctures he describes assertions expressing our hinge commitments as meaningless, comparing them, for example, to someone saying "good morning" in the middle of a conversation (OC §464; cf. §§10, 35–7, 461, 463, 500).

Interestingly, there may well be a middle ground available here between the epistemic accounts of the structure of rational evaluation offered in the last section and the non-propositional proposal just considered. For regarding our hinge commitments as visceral in the way that Wittgenstein demands, while no doubt inconsistent with regarding them as akin to normal beliefs, could well be thought compatible with them being, at least sometimes, manifest in corresponding propositional attitudes. That is, given that our hinge commitments are *ex hypothesi* never the result of a rational process and are in their nature unresponsive to rational considerations, then they are not plausible candidates to be beliefs. Beliefs, after all, are propositional attitudes which by their nature are responsive to rational considerations, at least to the extent that it simply makes no sense, for example, for there to be an agent who believes that *p* while taking herself to have no reason whatsoever for thinking *p* to be true (the propositional attitude in question would be better cast as a wishful thinking rather than a believing).

Call this the *non-belief proposal* (e.g., Pritchard, 2012; 2015). Like the non-propositional proposal, it precludes the possibility that we can have knowledge, much less rationally grounded knowledge, when it comes to our hinge commitments, since if we are not even in the market for belief in this regard then we are, *a fortiori*, not in the market for knowledge either, rationally grounded or otherwise. But unlike the non-propositional proposal, this proposal doesn't demand that we should think of our hinge commitments in inherently non-propositional terms. For sure, such commitments can never coherently be thought of as beliefs, but that doesn't prevent them from being expressed via other propositional attitudes.

Now on the surface of things, one might be puzzled as to how this can possibly help matters. For insofar as one can conceive of one's hinge commitments in terms of a propositional attitude, albeit one that can never amount to knowledge, then why doesn't that simply exacerbate the closure problem? Notice, however, how the relevant closure principles are being formulated, in particular the core closure principle regarding rationally supported knowledge:

> *Closure for Rationally Supported Knowledge:* if S has rationally supported knowledge that p, and S competently deduces q from p, thereby forming her belief that q on the basis of this competent deduction while retaining her rationally supported knowledge that p, then S has rationally supported knowledge that q.

It is key to this principle that it is describing the *acquisition* of a belief via the *rational process* of competent deduction. Moreover, these are not incidental features of this principle, since without these elements it would not capture the point that a rational process like competent deduction from rationally supported knowledge cannot lead one to form a belief in the entailed proposition that has weaker epistemic credentials than one's belief in the entailing proposition.

With this point in mind, it follows that the proponent of the non-belief proposal can argue that they do not face the closure problem for the simple reason that one can never, via the kind of competent deduction at issue in the relevant closure principles, come to acquire a belief in a hinge commitment. Of course, the proponent of the non-propositional proposal can make this point too, on the grounds that for them there is no hinge proposition to be believed in the first place, but on their view they face the further mystery of accounting for the apparent propositional attitude that is generated by such competent deductions. In contrast, the non-belief proposal can grant that someone who undertakes the relevant competent deductions could be described as having a propositional attitude toward the entailed hinge commitment, without thereby having to face the question of why this propositional attitude doesn't amount to knowledge.

6 Concluding Remarks

I have here focused on one core element of Wittgenstein's thinking about radical skepticism, as it arises in *On Certainty*. I noted at the outset there is so much more to be said about Wittgenstein's thinking on skepticism, not least regarding how his treatment of this problem altered throughout his philosophical development. But one could equally note that there is also much more to be said even about Wittgenstein's treatment of this problem in *On Certainty*. Still, I hope that the foregoing will at least provide the reader with a sense of one important research program that arises out of this work – viz., how ought we to conceive of Wittgenstein's radical new conception of the structure of rational evaluation.

References

Austin, J.L. (1946). Other Minds. Reprinted in J.L. Austin. (1961). *Philosophical Papers* (pp.44–84). Ed. J.O. Urmson and G.J. Warnock. Oxford: Clarendon Press.
DeRose, K. (1995). Solving the Skeptical Problem. *Philosophical Review*, 104, 1–52.
Goldman, A. (1986). *Epistemology and Cognition*. Cambridge, MA: Harvard University Press.
Moore, G.E. (1925). A Defence of Common Sense. In J.H. Murihead (Ed.). *Contemporary British Philosophy* (pp.193–223). London: Allen and Unwin.
Moore, G.E. (1939). Proof of an External World. *Proceedings of the British Academy*, 25, 273–300.
Moyal-Sharrock, D. (2004). *Understanding Wittgenstein's On Certainty*. London: Palgrave Macmillan.
Pritchard, D.H. (2005). Wittgenstein's *On Certainty* and Contemporary Anti-Scepticism. In D. Moyal-Sharrock and W.H. Brenner (Eds). *Investigating On Certainty: Essays on Wittgenstein's Last Work* (pp.189–224). London: Palgrave Macmillan.
Pritchard, D.H. (2012). Wittgenstein and the Groundlessness of our Believing. *Synthese*, 189, 255–272.
Pritchard, D.H. (2014). Entitlement and the Groundlessness of our Believing. In D. Dodd and E. Zardini (Eds). *Contemporary Perspectives on Scepticism and Perceptual Justification* (pp.190–213). Oxford: Oxford University Press.
Pritchard, D.H. (2015). *Epistemic Angst: Radical Skepticism and the Groundlessness of our Believing*. Princeton: Princeton University Press.
Stroud, B. (1984). *The Significance of Philosophical Scepticism*. Oxford: Clarendon Press.
Williams, M. (1991). *Unnatural Doubts: Epistemological Realism and the Basis of Scepticism*. Oxford: Blackwell.
Wright, C. (2003). Wittgensteinian Certainties. In D. McManus (Ed.). *Wittgenstein and Scepticism* (pp.19–48). London: Routledge.
Wright, C. (2004a). Hinge Propositions and the Serenity Prayer. In W. Löffler and P. Weingartner (Eds). *Knowledge and Belief* (pp.287–306). Vienna: Hölder-Pichler-Tempsky.
Wright, C. (2004b). Scepticism, Certainty, Moore and Wittgenstein. In M. Kölbel and B. Weiss (Eds). *Wittgenstein's Lasting Significance* (pp.228–248). London: Routledge.
Wright, C. (2004c). Warrant for Nothing (and Foundations for Free)? *Proceedings of the Aristotelian Society* (Supplementary Volume), 78, 167–212.

Further Reading

Coliva, A. (2010). *Moore and Wittgenstein: Scepticism, Certainty, and Common Sense*. London: Palgrave Macmillan. [A survey of different treatments of the Wittgensteinian response to radical skepticism.]
Coliva, A. (2015). *Extended Rationality: A Hinge Epistemology*. London: Palgrave Macmillan. [A discussion of Wittgensteinian epistemology, which offers a novel way of thinking about Wittgenstein's notion of a hinge commitment.]
McGinn, M. (1989). *Sense and Certainty: A Dissolution of Scepticism*. Oxford: Blackwell. [A treatment of Wittgenstein's response to skepticism, which set the scene for many of the discussions that followed.]
Moyal-Sharrock, D. and Brenner, W.H. (Eds). (2005). *Investigating On Certainty: Essays on Wittgenstein's Last Work*. London: Palgrave Macmillan. [A collection of papers exploring the epistemological issues raised by *On Certainty*.]
Pritchard, D.H. (2002). Recent Work on Radical Skepticism. *American Philosophical Quarterly*, 39, 215–257. [A survey of recent work on radical skepticism, which also includes treatments of the problem inspired by *On Certainty*.]
Schönbaumsfeld, G. (2016). *The Illusion of Doubt*. Oxford: Oxford University Press. [Explores Wittgenstein's approach to the problem of radical skepticism.]

37

Wittgenstein on Causation and Induction

CONSTANTINE SANDIS AND CHON TEJEDOR

1 The Earlier Wittgenstein

Surprisingly little attention has been paid to the earlier Wittgenstein's approach to causation and induction. The main exceptions are Dilman (1973), Cook (1994), McGuinness (2002, chs 11 and 12), Glock (1996), and Tejedor (2015), out of which only the last revisits the material in the light of the New Wittgenstein debate. As we shall see, however, Wittgenstein's earlier treatment of causation and induction remains thought-provoking and relevant to contemporary debates in the philosophy of science.

Wittgenstein's approach to causation and induction in the *Tractatus* emerges in the context of two separate, but related discussions: a negative discussion that aims to expose a particular understanding of natural (or material) necessity as nonsensical, and a more positive discussion concerning the role played by laws in the natural sciences. These discussions emerge, respectively, in TLP 5.133–5.1362 and TLP 6.32–6.3611. We will examine them in turn.

2 The Negative Discussion (TLP 5.133–5.1362)

In order to understand Wittgenstein's critique of natural necessity, it is important to revisit his notion of an internal relation. In the *Tractatus*, Wittgenstein suggests that internal relations hold between propositions by virtue of the latter's truth-functional structures (TLP 5.2, 5.22). For instance, if q results from applying the logical operation of conjunction to p and r, q is internally related to both p and r. Indeed, q necessarily entails p (as well as r): if q is true, necessarily, p is true (TLP 5.131). This is made clear when one considers the truth functions that emerge for logical entailment, when p and q are internally related as above and when they are not: when p and q are *not* internally related to each other, the truth function for $q \rightarrow p$ is (TFTT)(p, q); contrast, when p and q *are* internally related as indicated above, the truth function for $q \rightarrow p$ is (TTTT)(p, q), hence tautologous (see TLP 5.101). The notion of an internal relation is therefore akin to that which, in other contexts, might be called a conceptual or an analytic relation.

A Companion to Wittgenstein, First Edition. Edited by Hans-Johann Glock and John Hyman.
© 2017 John Wiley & Sons, Ltd. Published 2017 by John Wiley & Sons, Ltd.

For Wittgenstein, the notions of internal relation and logical operation are closely associated; indeed, he presents logical operations as a mode of expressing internal relations (TLP 5.21).

The natural necessity view (NNV) criticized by Wittgenstein in the *Tractatus* suggests that some relations of necessary entailment arise between possible states, not by virtue of any internal relations between them, but by virtue of the obtaining of certain laws of nature. More specifically, the idea is that, if a particular law of nature (say *l*) obtains, then, necessarily, if *q* obtains, necessarily *p* obtains (where *l*, *q*, and *p* are not internally related to each other). Let us call these necessary relations of entailment between states not internally related to each other relations of natural entailment. The states in question are not internally related to each other since, *ex hypothesi*, the relation of natural entailment is not a merely analytic or conceptual relation.

Wittgenstein suggests that NNV gives rise to an understanding of causation and induction that is flawed. In this understanding, both causation and induction involve relations of natural entailment between possible states. Thus, causation amounts to the idea that, when *q* causes *p*, *q* necessarily entails *p* and does so in the absence of any internal relations between *p* and *q*, by virtue of the obtaining of a particular law of nature *l*. Similarly, this view, inductive inferences are possible in that a past possible state *q* necessitates a future possible state *p*, by virtue of the obtaining of some particular law of nature *l*. NNV therefore contends that both causation and induction involve statements of the form: "$l \Rightarrow [q \Rightarrow p]$," where "$\Rightarrow$" is intended to capture an operation of natural entailment between propositions not internally related to each other. It is worth noting that NNV incorporates a very particular understanding of the role of laws of nature. This view, laws of nature *ground* the relations of natural entailment between possible states and thereby *justify* inferences between them: causal laws justify inferences from causes to effects; inductive laws justify inferences from obtaining past possible states to future ones. There is an element of circularity here, since the relation obtaining between *q* and *p* is the same as the relation obtaining between *l* and $[p \Rightarrow q]$, viz., $l \Rightarrow [q \Rightarrow p]$.

For Wittgenstein, however, this approach to necessity, causation, and induction is flawed for a different reason. The problem, in a nutshell, is that it relies on a particular understanding of logical operations – one it simultaneously subverts. Thus, NNV is essentially confused: it is a self-stultifying hybrid that dissolves into nonsense when examined with care. Let us consider this idea in more detail.

For Wittgenstein, NNV, insofar as it turns crucially on the idea of a special relation of *entailment*, exploits one particular understanding of logical operations. For, when advocates of NNV advance that certain possible states (causally or inductively) necessitate others, their view is that this is indeed a form of necessity – on a par, in key respects, with logical necessity. Natural necessity is regarded as a *special* form of necessity: one that stems from a source other than internal relations, but a form of necessity nevertheless. More specifically, NNV assumes that the truth-value results derived from applying the operation of natural entailment to propositions should be treated like any other such results. Hence $l \Rightarrow [q \Rightarrow p]$ should be regarded as possessing a truth function and a truth table, and the truth-value combinations expressed in these should have a bearing on any other logical combinations into which *l*, *p*, and *q* may enter (see Chapter 17, LOGIC AND THE *TRACTATUS*). NNV does not purport to *replace* the logical understanding of entailment therefore, but rather to *restrict* its application. It suggests that, when certain circumstances (i.e., when the law of nature *l* does indeed), then, for *some* possible senses (i.e., only for those possible states that are the potential bearers of natural relations given the obtaining of *l*), the relevant entailment operation is ⇒, rather than →. At the same time, the ordinary operation of logical entailment → remains applicable to the propositions in question when the relevant law of nature does not obtain and to other propositions in all circumstances.

Wittgenstein suggests that this betrays a misconception. For the understanding of logical operation associated with the notions of compositionality of sense, of truth function, of truth table, and of necessary truth – i.e., with those very notions from which NNV itself derives its apparent force – turns crucially on treating logical operations as *applying in a uniform manner across propositions with different senses*. More precisely, it is central to the notion of logical operation that the processes involved in (and results drawn from) applying an operation to propositions should only depend on the truth-functional structures of these propositions – structures that are fully expressible from within logic alone, in purely symbolic notation. After all, this is precisely the notion of an operation that is behind the use of truth functions and truth tables: truth functions and truth tables express relations between propositional *forms* – forms to which many different propositions (with different senses, but bearing the same truth-functional relations to each other) belong (cf. TLP 5.24). (Cf. Glock, 1996, pp.368–71, who suggests that, for Wittgenstein, truth tables aim to capture specific senseful propositions.) Hence, when *l*, *p*, and *q* are *not* internally related to each other, the truth function for the logical operation $l \to [q \to p]$ should remain the same *irrespective of the senses of l, q, and p* (cf. TLP 5.4, 5.41). One of the central characteristics of this approach to logic is, therefore, that "there can *never* be surprises in logic" (TLP 6.1251), since "in logic process and result are equivalent." "Hence," again, Wittgenstein adds in parentheses, "the absence of surprise" (TLP 6.1261).

NNV attempts to gloss over what are in fact two very different approaches to logic: in the first, the processes involved in (and results drawn from) applying operations to propositions depend exclusively on the truth-functional structures of propositions; in the second, they do not. In the second approach, the application of operations also depends on the senses of propositions and on whether or not certain facts obtain in reality (i.e., whether or not the relevant law of nature obtains). The first approach does not allow for "surprises" in logic; the second does: I might be surprised to hear that ⇒ rather than → applies on a particular occasion – for instance, if I had been unaware that law *l* actually obtained. (To be sure, there are other respects in which there can be surprises in logic, for Wittgenstein. I may be surprised to find out that logical analysis reveals a complex proposition to be tautological, for instance. On Wittgenstein's approach to surprise in logic, see also Floyd, 2010.)

Thus, for Wittgenstein NNV is a self-stultifying position that dissolves into nonsense. One of the upshots of this is that the purported operation of natural entailment is in fact no operation whatsoever. Hence: "There is no possible way of making an inference from the existence of one situation to the existence of another, entirely different situation" (TLP 5.135). And again: "There is no causal nexus to justify such an inference" (TLP 5.136). Similarly, in connection to induction: "We *cannot* infer the events of the future from those of the present. Belief in the causal nexus is [nonsensical] *superstition*" (TLP 5.1361). And, in the midst of his more positive discussion of causation and the laws of the natural sciences: "There is no compulsion making one thing happen because another has happened. The only necessity that exists is *logical* necessity" (TLP 6.37).

On some readings of the *Tractatus*, Wittgenstein endorses the view that the only necessity is logical necessity (e.g., Anscombe, 1959, p.80; Boulter, 2002, p.70; see also Chapter 17, LOGIC AND THE *TRACTATUS*). In others – notably in some New Wittgensteinian readings (e.g., Diamond, 1988, p.24; and Read and Deans, 2011) – Wittgenstein does not endorse this view. In any case, NNV should be regarded as subverting itself and, in so doing, as subverting the notion of law of nature associated with it (Tejedor, 2011a, ch.3; 2013; and 2015). The rejection of NNV (and, *pari passu*, absolute control) has an ethical dimension, as exemplified in Islam's use of 'Inshallah'.

3 The Positive Discussion (TLP 6.32–6.3611)

Wittgenstein therefore proposes that we consider a different understanding of the role played by laws (including causal and inductive laws) in the natural sciences. In this alternative understanding, a law of nature is not a possible state represented by a senseful proposition and capable, when obtaining, of justifying certain inferences. Nor are laws of nature necessary and, *for this reason*, capable of justifying inferences. For the purpose of a law is simply not to justify inferences: not even the tautological laws of logic play such a role (TLP 5.132), since it is to misconceive the notion of a logical law to assume, as Frege and Russell did, that they justify deductive inferences (see Frege, 1979, p.175; Russell, [1905] 1994, p.517; cf. Glock, 1996, "logical inference"; and McGinn, 2006, chs 3 and 9).

Instead, for Wittgenstein, the notion of law associated with the natural sciences is that of an *instruction for the construction of senseful propositions within a particular natural science system*. Consider, for instance, the notion of a *causal* law of nature. Here a causal law is a set of instructions for the use of causal terms (e.g., "cause") – one that enables us to generate senseful propositions of the form stipulated by the causal system in question. For Wittgenstein, it is part of the remit of physics to come up with the instructions or causal laws that best serve its instrumental purposes *qua* natural science and, more generally, the instrumental purposes of human beings. In his view, the laws of the natural sciences (including physics) are optional, insofar as the systems to which they belong can be replaced by others; and they are a priori in that, being instructions for the use of signs, they are constitutive of the senseful propositions and thoughts (including beliefs and experiences) they generate. Hence:

> And just as in mechanics, for example, there are 'minimum-principles', such as the law of least action, so too in physics there are causal laws, laws of the causal form. (TLP 6.321)

> All such propositions, including the principle of sufficient reason, the laws of continuity in nature and of least effort in nature, etc. etc. – all these are *a priori* insights about the forms in which the propositions of science can be cast. (TLP 6.34)

> The form is optional. (TLP 6.341)

Causal laws are instructions that circumscribe what counts as a senseful proposition of the causal form (i.e., of the form "p causes q") within an optional system. In so doing, causal laws rule out certain uses of signs as irrelevant or purposeless within the system in question. For instance, a system that allows for action at a distance will allow for senseful propositions involving the notion of a causally efficacious magnet; contrast, a causal system that does not allow for action at a distance will not treat such propositions as senseful. For Wittgenstein, it is the role of the natural scientist, not that of the philosopher, to specify what these laws or principles are.

The laws (the instructions) of the natural sciences circumscribe our use of signs. This, Wittgenstein suggests, is the mark of a *law* being in play. And it is precisely for this reason that, in his view, the "law of induction" cannot be regarded as genuine law:

> The so-called law of induction cannot possibly be a law of logic, since it is obviously a proposition with sense. – Nor, therefore, can it be an *a priori* law. (TLP 6.31)

"Nature is uniform" not provide us with an instruction that circumscribes our use of signs: it does not rule in certain senses and rule others out in the way that causal laws do. When we observe our first black swan, having in the past only ever observed white ones, no law relating to the uniformity of nature *instructs us* to find a new name for this creature. Upon inspection of the animal, *we may or may not* end up calling it a *swan* – but that we *may* indeed end up opting for this term simply goes to show that there is *no instruction circumscribing our use of signs in place here*, no instruction relating to the uniformity of nature. Instead:

> The process of induction is the process of assuming the *simplest* law that can be made to harmonize with our experience. (TLP 6.363)

> This process, however, has no logical foundation but only a psychological one.
> It is clear that there are no grounds for believing that the simplest course of events will really happen. (TLP 6.3631)

It may be a psychologically sound procedure, when reflecting upon past observed facts, for a physicist to come up with the simplest system of instructions (of laws) that will satisfy our instrumental purposes. After all, such systems are optional and there may be several such systems, with different degrees of complexity, capable of fulfilling our purposes. Wittgenstein simply notes that, out of these systems, the simplest will be the most attractive to us, as a matter of human psychological fact. From the point of view of logic, however, there is nothing to require or justify the adoption of such a system over the others. Scholars disagree here on the extent to which Wittgenstein's view is similar to – or differs from – that of Hume (see Strawson, 1985, pp.11–16; Tejedor, 2011b; and Sandis, 2011, p.181; 2012, pp.199–200).

4   Transitions

Upon his return to philosophy in 1929, Wittgenstein re-examined the relation between hypotheses, probability calculations, and reality. In *Philosophical Remarks*, he maintains that statements of probability are not about the world because they can be neither verified nor falsified (PR §232) and notes the role our personal previous experiences play in determining what we are willing to accept as a natural law (PR §234). The latter emphasis on describing how we *actually* think and speak about causes, expectation, and grounds is further developed in "Remarks on Frazer's *Golden Bough*," Part I (see

Chapter 41, WITTGENSTEIN AND ANTHROPOLOGY), *Philosophical Grammar* (PG 109ff), and parts of the "Big Typescript" (pp. 32–3, 55, 84, 94ff, 179ff, 289ff).

This shift from insisting that causal and inductive statements *must* posses certain features to the descriptive exploration of how they actually work is further developed in his 1933–1935 Cambridge lectures (of which related dictations as the *Blue and Brown Books*), in which statements of one's reasons are distinguished from causal statements on the grounds that only the latter are hypotheses (see BB 15). Hyman (2015, p.118) argues that Wittgenstein here endorses "the Humean doctrine that a particular instance of causation counts as such only by conforming to a general pattern," a view that would later be attacked by Anscombe (1957, p.16; and 1971; cf. von Wright, 1974). A different interpretation that credits Wittgenstein with recognizing singular causation is given by Glock (2014).

In his Easter 1938 lectures on aesthetics, Wittgenstein has already moved toward a more liberal account of the different uses of the word "cause" (LC 13), only some of which may be systematically contrasted "reason." By this time, Russell's April 1936 paper for the *Aristotelian Society*, "The Limits of Empiricism," had inspired Wittgenstein to write down some thoughts under the heading "Cause and Effect: Intuitive Awareness" (see also van Gennip, 2011; and Chapter 5, WITTGENSTEIN AND RUSSELL). In this connection, Wittgenstein explicitly introduces the notion of the "cause-effect language game" (CE 373). And while he accepts Russell's claim that we do not always arrive at causal judgments by observing past regularities, he argues against him that this is not because we become "immediately aware" of the cause (e.g., CE 408). This is because our causal instincts precede any mastery of the notion of a cause that we might attain (e.g., in relation to necessary connection; see CE 374–5; cf. Z §§608–10; cf. the discussion in Klagge, 1999). Wittgenstein was fond of quoting, in this context, the opening scene of Goethe's *Faust*: "In the beginning was the deed" (CE 395); it is because we behave a certain way (e.g., in reaction to a burning flame) that we come to talk of inductive grounds or reasons, and not the other way around. As we shall see, this approach is championed in *Philosophical Investigations* (e.g., PI §§472–8) and taken to its natural conclusion in remarks published as *On Certainty*, via Part II of the "Remarks on Frazer's *Golden Bough*" cf. Chapter 1, WITTGENSTEIN'S PHILOSOPHICAL DEVELOPMENT).

5 Investigations

The general outlook noted above is inextricably tied up with Wittgenstein's thought that notions such as of "cause" and "necessity" refuse analysis in terms of necessary and sufficient conditions (cf. Chapter 21, NECESSITY AND APRIORITY). Accordingly, the claim that the *only* kind of necessity or possibility is logical necessity or possibility is to be replaced by a catalogue of different uses of the term "necessity" or "possibility," which in turn point to different yet interrelated meanings:

> Compare 'logically possible' with 'chemically possible'. One might perhaps call a combination chemically possible if a formula with the right valencies existed (e.g. H - O - O - O - H). Of course, such a combination need not exist; but even the formula HO_2 cannot have less than no combination corresponding to it in reality. (PI §521)

Whilst in the *Tractatus* the criterion for something's counting as a ground or reason (*Grund*) was bound up with logical considerations (TLP 5.1362, 5.1363, 6.363ff), in the *Investigations* the reader is requested to look at our practice(s) of calling something a reason and describe the conditions for the correct application of the concept. The earlier Wittgenstein urges that "there are no grounds for believing that the simplest eventuality will in fact be realized"; by contrast the later one reminds us that our reasons for calling something a "ground" cannot be based on still further grounds, for the chain of such reasons must have an end that cannot itself be in need of a justification (PI §§326, 482, 485; see also Dilman, 1973, pp.77–94). We don't need further reasons (i.e., justifications or inference rules) for viewing certain kinds of information as a reason (PI §§406–90). Rather, there is a causal explanation for why we came to adopt the concept of a reason in the first place, one that is grounded on nonverbal behavior that comes naturally to us in certain situations. The rules of grammar can only be justified pragmatically (PI §492). Language is not founded upon metaphysical or empirical *justification*. To think otherwise (e.g., by looking for further justifications) is to transgress the bounds of sense (PI §§491–570).

Why is it that if I burn my hand when I put my hand in a flame I am reluctant to do so again? Is it because I reason to myself "it burned me last time so it *must*, or is at any rate very *likely*, to burn me again"? Do I make a probability calculation here? What determines whether or not I have good reason to avoid fire in the future?

> "The certainty that I'll be able to go on after I've had this experience – seen this formula, for example – is simply based on induction." What does this mean? – "The certainty that the fire will burn me is based on induction." Does it mean that I reason to myself: "Fire has always burned me, so it will happen now too"? Or is the previous experience the *cause* of my certainty, not its reason? Whether the earlier experience is the cause of the certainty depends on the system of hypotheses, of natural laws, in terms of which we are considering the phenomenon of certainty.
>
> Is such confidence justified? – What people accept as justification shows how they think and live. (PI §325; see also PI §§466, 472–4)

Wittgenstein is not saying that there are no good "objective" reasons for inductive inference, only that we come to *count* things as good reasons because we are disposed to react a certain way. The character of the belief in the uniformity of nature can perhaps be seen most clearly in the case in which what is expected is something we fear. In such circumstances, nothing could induce me to put my hand into a flame – even though it is *only in the past* that I have burnt myself (PI §472); the belief that fire will burn me is here of the same kind as the instinctive fear (or in special situations wish or hope) that it will burn me (PI §473); I shall get burned if I put my hand in the fire – that is certainty. That is to say, here we see what certainty means – not just the meaning of the word "certainty" but also what the phenomenology of certainty amounts to (PI §474). This sort of statement about the past is simply what we call a reason for supposing that this will happen in the future. And if one is surprised at our playing such a game, I appeal to the *effect* of a past experience (to the fact that a burnt child fears the fire) (PI §480).

Past experiences do not justify our certainty by meeting some independent criterion of justification, such as that of logical necessity. Rather, determines what is to count as a justification or reason (PI §324). The criteria for when it is rational to believe something are tied not to logical proof but to paradigmatic cases of calling something a "reason" (PI §483). It is a mistake to think that things count as good reasons in virtue of either a logical property or empirical property, such as that of necessitating an event or rendering it probable:

> If anyone said that information about the past couldn't convince him that something would happen in the future, I wouldn't understand him. One might ask him: What do you expect to be told, then? What sort of information do you call a reason for believing this? What do you call "convincing"? In what kind of way do you expect to be convinced? – If *these* are not reasons, then what are reasons? – If you say that these are not reasons, then you must surely be able to state what must be the case for us to be warranted in saying that there are reasons for our supposition. For note: here reasons are not propositions which logically imply what is believed. (PI §481)

But it is not as if one can say: less is needed for belief than for knowledge. For this is not a matter of approximating to logical consequence (PI §481; cf. BT 397). The human disposition to think and act in certain ways is not the sort of thing that may be justified or unjustified (cf. the TLP remarks on the principles of the natural sciences and scientific representational systems, which were possible precursors to language-games (TLP 6.321, 6.34, 6.341, as cited above)). Rather, it is what provides us with a standard of justification, much as the Paris meter provides us with a metrical standard (PI §50; cf. Diamond, 2001; and Chapter 21, NECESSITY AND APRIORITY). These standards are arbitrary to the extent that it would be wrong to seek reasons for their existence that are of the same sort as the reasons they provide. But this is not to say that their existence is random or without explanation, or even without a pragmatic justification:

> Why does man [...] make boilers according to *calculations*, and not leave the thickness of their walls to chance? After all, it is only a fact of experience that boilers made according to these calculations do not explode so often. But, just as having once been burnt, he would do anything rather than put his hand into a fire, so too he would do anything rather than not calculate for a boiler [...]. Now, can't a boiler produced in this way explode? Oh, yes. (PI §466; see also PI §§467–85)

6 On Certainty

In work from 1946 onwards Wittgenstein develops an interest in what he calls the "tacit presuppositions" upon which our language-games rest (PPF §§31–3; cf. TLP 4.002; see also Chapter 26, LANGUAGES, LANGUAGE-GAMES, AND FORMS OF LIFE). In "Remarks on Frazer's *Golden Bough*," Part II, our presuppositions are claimed to be no more (or less) legitimate than those of allegedly superstitious people, "whereas they only possess a peculiar interpretation of the phenomena" (§10). This concern with the rational status of presuppositions culminates in some of the remarks that occur toward the end of *On Certainty*, by which time they have become the so-called "hinge-propositions" that are arguably not propositions at all but akin to heuristic maxims for interpreting phenomena (Moyal-Sharrock, 2005a; 2005b; cf. Hamilton, 2014, pp.104ff). Wittgenstein's view here is pluralistic: certainties may take the form of action (OC §204), dispositions (OC §337), expectations, laws, rules, propositions (OC §608), belief (in the sense of "faith," see OC §602), and even "unconditional truth" (OC §604). As Danièle Moyal-Sharrock has argued, these "hinge certainties" are *not* inferred from experience and do *not* function as grounds, but rather as the "scaffolding of our language games" (Moyal-Sharrock, 2005a, pp.80–2; see also Chapter 35, WITTGENSTEIN ON KNOWLEDGE AND CERTAINTY; for the view that talk of hinges here is metaphorical see Hamilton, 2014, p.97).

> Is it wrong for me to be guided in my actions by the propositions of physics? Am I to say that I have no good ground for doing so? Isn't precisely this what we call a 'good ground'? (OC §608).

> Supposing we met people who did not regard that as a telling reason. Now, how do we imagine this? Instead of the physicist, they consult an oracle. (And for that we consider them primitive). Is it wrong for them to consult an oracle and be guided by it? – If we call this "wrong" aren't we using our language-game as a base from which to *combat* theirs? (OC §609).

> I said I would 'combat' the other man, – but wouldn't I give him *reasons*? Certainly; but how far do they go? At the end of reason comes *persuasion*. (Think of what happens when missionaries convert natives). (OC §612)

We may have all sorts of pragmatic reasons for attempting such persuasions. These may but need not be progressive, but whatever progress they embody would not be a progress toward truth but only toward efficiency (OC §§610–12; cf. the choice of natural science systems in the *Tractatus*). The so-called "third" Wittgenstein of *On Certainty* is often accused of being a cultural relativist, but if there is any relativism there at all it is a *conceptual* one (OC §599; see Glock, 2007). This is all in keeping with the insights of the *Investigations*. Our certainty is not a kind of true belief or veridical perception but consists in our acting without further justification.

> Giving grounds, however, justifying the evidence, comes to an end; – but the end is not certain propositions striking us immediately as true, i.e. it is not a kind of seeing on our part; it is our acting, which lies at the bottom of the language-game. If the true is what is grounded, then the ground is not true, not yet false. (OC §§204–5)

The role played by regularities is a merely structural one:

> It would seem as if the language-game must '*show*' the facts that make it possible. (But that's not how it is). Then one can say that only a certain regularity in occurrences makes induction possible? The 'possible' would of course have to be '*logically possible*'. (OC §618)

Pace the *Tractatus*, then, the most fundamental laws and principles do not seem to be falsifiable empirical generalizations; surely this holds at best for very fundamental ones. Rather, in *On Certainty*, *they are* more akin to a "groundless" form of inference (OC §§135,166, 600) – one that in daily life renders us psychologically closed to doubt (OC §337; cf. TLP 6.3631). In this we are far closer to animals than rationalists take us to be:

> The squirrel does not infer by induction that it is going to need stores next week as well. And no more do we need a law of induction to justify our actions or our predictions. (OC §287; see also §619)

Here, as elsewhere, there are more commonalities between the later Wittgenstein and Hume than typically supposed. Accordingly, we must resist the temptation to move from talk of certainty to that of probability. For such a move would at best be rhetorical:

> Imagine people who were never quite certain of these things, but said that they were *very* probably so, and that it did not pay to doubt them. Such a person, then, would say in my situation: "It is extremely unlikely that I have ever been to the moon", etc. etc. *How* would the life of these people differ from ours? For there *are* people who say that it is merely extremely probable that water over a fire will boil and not freeze, and that therefore strictly speaking what we consider impossible is only improbable. What difference does this make in their lives? Isn't it just that they talk rather more about certain things than the rest of us? (OC §338)

In the *Investigations*, knowledge presupposes the possibility of doubt. Without abandoning this view, in the remarks of *On Certainty* Wittgenstein comes to highlight the ways in which new doubts and certainties lead to revisions of our language-games themselves, rather than the claims we make within them (OC §617), whilst also recognizing that there are some assumptions that we cannot abandon without our doubt seeming to "drag everything with it and plunge into chaos" (OC §613; see also §619). Such is our commitment to the laws of causation and induction.

References

Anscombe, G.E.M. (1957). *Intention*. Oxford: Blackwell.
Anscombe, G.E.M. (1959). *An Introduction to Wittgenstein's Tractatus*.
Anscombe, G.E.M. (1971). Causality and Determination. In G.E.M. Anscombe. *Metaphysics and the Philosophy of Mind: Collected Philosophical Papers* (Vol. II, pp. 33–47). Oxford: Blackwell.
Boulter, S. (2002). Hume on Induction: A Genuine Problem or Theology's Trojan Horse. *Philosophy*, 77, 67–86.
Cook, J. (1994). *Wittgenstein's Metaphysics*. Cambridge: Cambridge University Press.
Diamond, C. (1988) Throwing Away the Ladder. *Philosophy*, 63, 5–27.
Diamond, C. (2001). How Long is the Standard Meter in Paris?. In T.G. McCarthy and S.C. Stidd (Eds). *Wittgenstein in America* (pp.104–139). Oxford: Oxford University Press.
Dilman, I. (1973). *Induction and Causation: A Study in Wittgenstein*. Oxford: Blackwell.
Floyd, J. (2010). On Being Surprised: Wittgenstein on Aspect Perception, Logic and Mathematics. In W. Day and V. Krebs (Eds). *Seeing Wittgenstein Anew: New Essays on Aspect Seeing* (pp. 314–337). Cambridge: Cambridge University Press.
Frege, G. (1979). *Posthumous Writings*. Ed. H. Hermes, F. Kambartel, and F. Kaulbach (Eds). Trans. P. Long and R. White. Oxford: Blackwell.
Glock, H.-J. (1996). *A Wittgenstein Dictionary*. Oxford: Blackwell.
Glock, H.-J. (2007). Relativism, Commensurability and Translatability. *Ratio*, 20, 377–402.
Glock, H.-J. (2014). Reasons for Action: Wittgensteinian and Davidsonian Perspectives in Historical and Meta-Philosophical Context. *Nordic Wittgenstein Review*, 3, 7–46.
Hamilton, A. (2014). *The Routledge Guidebook to Wittgenstein and On Certainty*. London: Routledge.
Hyman, J. (2015). *Action, Knowledge, and Will*. Oxford: Oxford University Press.
Klagge, J. (1999). Wittgenstein on Non-Mediative Causality. *Journal of the History of Philosophy*, 37, 653–667.
McGinn, M. (2006). *Elucidating the Tractatus: Wittgenstein's Early Philosophy of Logic and Language*. Oxford: Clarendon Press.

McGuinness, B. (2002). *Approaches to Wittgenstein*. London: Routledge.
Moyal-Sharrock, D. (2005a). *Understanding Wittgenstein's On Certainty*. Basingstoke: Palgrave Macmillan.
Moyal-Sharrock, D. (2005b). Unravelling Certainty. In W.H. Brenner and D. Moyal-Sharrock (Eds). *Readings of Wittgenstein's On Certainty* (pp.76–99). Basingstoke: Palgrave Macmillan.
Read, R. and Deans, R. (2011). The Possibility of a Resolutely Resolute Reading of the *Tractatus*. In R. Read and M.A. Lavery (Eds). *Beyond the Tractatus Wars: The New Wittgenstein Debate* (pp.149–170). London: Routledge.
Russell, B. ([1905] 1994) Necessity and Possibility. In A. Urquhart (Ed.). (1994). *The Collected Papers of Bertrand Russell (Vol. 4): Foundations of Logic: 1903–13* (pp.507–520). London: Routledge.
Russell, B. (1936). The Limits of Empiricism. *Proceedings of the Aristotelian Society*, 36, 131–150.
Sandis, C. (2011). Pouring New Wine into Old Skin: The Meaning of Hume's Necessary Connexions. In K. Allen and T. Stoneham (Eds). *Causation and Modern Philosophy* (pp.166–187). London: Routledge.
Sandis, C. (2012). Action, Reason and the Passions. In A. Bailey and D. O'Brien (Eds). *The Continuum Companion to Hume* (pp.199–213). London: Bloomsbury.
Strawson, P.F. (1985). *Scepticism and Naturalism: Some Varieties*. London: Routledge.
Tejedor, C. (2011a). *Starting with Wittgenstein*. London: Bloomsbury.
Tejedor, C. (2011b). Normativity and Probable Reasoning: Hume on Induction. *Daimon*, 52, 15–33.
Tejedor, C. (2013). The Earlier Wittgenstein on the Notion of Religious Attitude. *Philosophy*, 88, 55–71.
Tejedor, C. (2015). *The Early Wittgenstein on Metaphysics, Natural Science, Language and Value*. London: Routledge.
van Gennip, K. (2011). Wittgenstein on Intuition, Rule-Following, and Certainty: Exchanges with Brouwer and Russell. In O. Kuusela and M. McGinn (Eds). *The Oxford Handbook of Wittgenstein* (pp.570–594). Oxford: Oxford University Press.
von Wright, G.H. (1974). *Causality and Determinism*. New York: Columbia University Press.

Further Reading

Hacker, P.M.S. (1996/2000). Inductive Reasoning. In P.M.S. Hacker. *Wittgenstein: Mind and Will. Volume 4 of an Analytical Commentary on the Philosophical Investigations. Part I. Essays* (pp.49–68). Oxford: Wiley-Blackwell.
Kremer, M. (2001). The Purpose of Tractarian Nonsense. *Noûs*, 35, 39–73.
McGinn, M. (2010). Wittgenstein and Internal Relations. *European Journal of Philosophy*, 18, 495–509.
Medina, J. (2003). Deflationism and the True Colours of Necessity in the *Tractatus*. *Dialectica*, 57, 357–385.
von Wright, G.H. (1941/65). *The Logical Problem of Induction*. Second edition. Oxford: Blackwell.
von Wright, G.H. (1960). *A Treatise on Induction and Probability*. Patterson: Littlefields, Adams and Co.
White, R. (1978). Wittgenstein on Identity. *Proceedings of the Aristotelian Society*, 78, 157–174.

38

Wittgenstein and Philosophy of Science

VASSO KINDI

The title of this chapter may refer to remarks by Wittgenstein that could be classified as philosophy of science – Wittgenstein wrote on logic, mathematics, psychology, the natural sciences, induction, causality, anthropology, psychoanalysis and Freud – but it may also refer to his relation to philosophy of science as a discipline. I will concentrate on this latter issue and discuss Wittgenstein's influence on how philosophy of science as a discipline developed.

Philosophy of science was formed as a distinct discipline in the early twentieth century around the work of the logical positivists, or logical empiricists, originally in Vienna in the mid-twenties and in other European cities such as Berlin and Prague. It further developed in the United States, where most logical positivists moved to escape persecution by the Nazis or World War II and met the American pragmatist philosophers of science. A major turn in the history of philosophy of science, which has been dubbed "historical," took place in the late 1950s and early 1960s with the work of philosophers such as N.R. Hanson, Stephen Toulmin, T.S. Kuhn, and Paul Feyerabend. In both the formative years and the historical turn in mid-twentieth century, Wittgenstein's philosophy had a major impact, which, in the former case, was initially acknowledged but eventually obliterated and in the latter initially ignored and eventually forgotten.

In this chapter I will concentrate on Wittgenstein's impact on historical philosophy of science. This relation has been very little discussed in the literature, in contrast to Wittgenstein's relation to the logical positivists. It will be useful, however, to first address this latter relation before turning toward the one with historical philosophy of science.

1 Wittgenstein and Logical Positivism

Logical positivism, or logical empiricism, is the school of thought that is most responsible for the shaping of philosophy of science as a contemporary, distinct academic discipline in the early twentieth century. Many philosophers of the past have addressed issues that pertain to science. But it was the logical positivists who identified philosophy with a particular way of doing philosophy of science, who devoted themselves to this

---

A Companion to Wittgenstein, First Edition. Edited by Hans-Johann Glock and John Hyman.
© 2017 John Wiley & Sons, Ltd. Published 2017 by John Wiley & Sons, Ltd.

activity alone – to the neglect of other areas of philosophy – and who defined the problems philosophy of science dealt with and bequeathed to later generations. Logical positivists are the "forebears" (Toulmin, 1969, p.51) of contemporary philosophers of science and their work forms "the core of our philosophical heritage" (Richardson and Hardcastle, 2003, p.x).

Logical positivism originated in a group of philosophers and scientists who had come together in the famous Vienna Circle in the 1920s. This group declared that it was indebted to Wittgenstein and in particular to his *Tractatus-Logico-Philosophicus*, first published in German in 1921. Wittgenstein is listed, along with Einstein and Russell, as a leading representative of the scientific world-conception in the Circle's manifesto of 1929. The members of the circle had read the *Tractatus*, line by line, in 1924–1925 and 1925–1926. Also, from November 1932 to March 1933 we have records of the Circle's protocols that show the development of the theses of the Vienna Circle in relation to the *Tractatus*. Rose Rand kept notes and from her edited transcripts we see what six prominent members of the group (viz., Schlick, Waismann, Carnap, Neurath, Hahn, and Kaufmann) thought about specific theses in relation to the *Tractatus*. They had six options (yes, no, meaningless, missing, indeterminate, no comment), which were marked in the transcripts by a different color or sign. In this way they expressed their views on 27 theses such as, "Language pictures reality," "The meaning [*Sinn*] of a sentence is the method of verification," "A definition is a convention" (see Stadler, 1997, pp.236–7; 323–7).

What the logical positivists found appealing in the *Tractatus*, as they read it, was the rejection of metaphysics as nonsensical, the identification of meaningful discourse with the propositions of natural science, the idea that philosophy is not a body of doctrines but the activity of analyzing language, the understanding of necessary propositions as tautologies, and the emphasis on logic and syntax (cf. Chapter 46, WITTGENSTEIN AND THE VIENNA CIRCLE; Chapter 12, METAPHYSICS: FROM INEFFABILITY TO NORMATIVITY; and Chapter 17, LOGIC AND THE *TRACTATUS*). They had anticipated some of these ideas in their own work, but found in the *Tractatus* a most appropriate expression of what they took to be a shared project. Herbert Feigl (1969, p.4), for instance, a founding member of the Vienna Circle, thought that Schlick attributed to Wittgenstein "profound philosophical insights which [Schlick] had formulated much more lucidly long before he succumbed to Wittgenstein's hypnotic spell." Schlick, on the other hand, considered Wittgenstein's work of inestimable significance (Schlick, [1928] 1979, p.136) and the decisive turning point in philosophy (Schlick, [1930] 1979). Carnap (1963, p.25) had a similar attitude – he thought that besides Russell and Frege, Wittgenstein had the greatest influence on his thinking. As Brian McGuinness (2002, p.185) notes, in general, the *Tractatus* "was greeted like Lohengrin in the opera: Ein Wunder! A miracle!"

The logical positivists, however, were far from a uniform group. The Vienna Circle was characterized by a variety of positions and attitudes. The relation of its members to Wittgenstein was also varied. Schlick and Waismann were very favorably disposed toward Wittgenstein. Waismann was called by Neurath Wittgenstein's "unhappy prophet," while Schlick was thought, again by Neurath, to be "totally Wittgensteinified" (McGuinness, 2002, pp.193, 194). Others were more skeptical or disapproving. Neurath "regarded as metaphysical the early Wittgenstein's ideas about the structure of propositional expressions mirroring the structure of the corresponding facts" and protested every time he thought they were "indulging in metaphysics" (Hempel, 2001, p.256). His protestations were so frequent that he originally proposed to just say "M!"

each time he thought the discussion was turning metaphysical. But later, to avoid constant interruptions, as Hempel recalls (2001, p.256), Neurath suggested to Schlick to let him call out "non-M" whenever they were *not* talking metaphysics. Menger (1982) had also expressed dissatisfaction with certain tenets of the group that were traced back to Wittgenstein.

Wittgenstein had agreed to regularly meet with some of the members of the Circle in the late 1920s. But after a while he preferred to limit his interactions with the group to Schlick and Waismann who undertook to put together an exposition of Wittgenstein's views. Carnap's preoccupation with Esperanto and his scientific (or, one might say, scientistic) orientation were alienating factors and drove Carnap and Wittgenstein apart. Carnap came to acknowledge a striking difference between his (and Schlick's) attitude on the one hand and Wittgenstein's on the other. Carnap (more than Schlick), Neurath, and other members of the Circle had the attitude of the intrepid, rational, unprejudiced, inquiring, enlightened scientist; Wittgenstein, according to Carnap, that of an artist.

Wittgenstein, however, had studied science and engineering and appreciated the rigor and sharpness of the scientific way of thinking. It was Wittgenstein who dismissed Carnap's scientific interest in parapsychological phenomena as not serious. Carnap thought that he would examine an important scientific problem with the impartiality and unprejudiced patience of a dissecting scientist. Wittgenstein "was shocked that any reasonable man could have any interest in such rubbish" (Carnap, 1963, p.26). On the other hand, Wittgenstein was critical of the ideological use of science, of the pretensions of scientists to offer authoritative judgments on all kinds of issues and of reducing any problem to a scientific one.

Wittgenstein's relation to Carnap was also marked by the accusation made by Wittgenstein that Carnap had plagiarized his ideas (cf. Letter to Carnap 20 August, 1932; Stadler, 2003, pp.429–34; Stern, 2007). The distance between them grew to such an extent that, as Carnap remembers in an unpublished portion of his autobiography cited by Stadler, Wittgenstein went to the extreme of not allowing his students at Cambridge to send Carnap the transcripts of his lectures.

> He asked to see the list of names [of friends and interested philosophers], and then approved all but my own. In my entire life, I have never experienced something remotely similar to this hatred directed against me. (Carnap; cited in Stadler, 2003, p.433)

The influence that Wittgenstein and his work exerted on the Vienna Circle is undeniable. It has been professed and acknowledged by the members of the group and has been documented in multiple ways. What has provoked controversy is what precisely this influence was. Wittgenstein himself "watched the development of logical positivism with growing distaste. [...] [B]y the mid-1930s he had disassociated himself entirely from ideas and doctrines which others continued to regard as *his* brain children" (Toulmin, 1969, p.36, emphasis in original). Although Wittgenstein had made several remarks on verification (for instance, in his Lectures of 1930–1933, recorded by G.E. Moore (M), in *Philosophical Remarks*, and in the conversations transcribed by Waismann (WVC)), he distanced himself from the logical positivists' "verification principle." He thought that it made philosophy look too much like mathematics (PPO 334). Anscombe remembers that "when someone mentioned the 'verification principle' at the Moral Sciences Club, Wittgenstein asked who invented it, and having it attributed to himself, exclaimed 'Who? *Me?*' in a tone of outrage" (Anscombe, 1995, p.405, emphasis in original). In PI §353 Wittgenstein explains:

> Asking whether and how a proposition can be verified is only a special form of the question "How do you mean?" The answer is a contribution to the grammar of the proposition. (PI §353)

What Wittgenstein's "verificationism" was and how it related to that of the Vienna Circle is a controversial issue in the literature (cf. Blank, 2011; Hymers, 2005; and Wrigley, 1989). But in philosophy of science, despite Wittgenstein's disapprobation of the logical positivist doctrine, it was initially thought that the *Tractatus* was a neopositivist book and that the logical positivists were just implementing Wittgenstein's ideas. Where he was thought to have hesitated, the logical positivists were thought to have marched on. Wittgenstein's intimation of ineffability and silence at the end of the *Tractatus*, his distinction of saying and showing, were brushed aside and in their place Carnap erected the logical syntax of science, which opened up space for new problems to be addressed by philosophers of science. Only later did it fully emerge that Wittgenstein's and the logical positivists' projects differed considerably (Hacker, 1996, pp.39–66; also 2001a).

Although Wittgenstein repudiated any association with a "verification principle," it seems clear that for a brief period of time, when he was conversing with the logical positivists in 1929 and later in his lectures until the mid-1930s, he upheld a form of verificationism. "If I can never verify the sense of a proposition completely, then I cannot have meant anything by the proposition either. [...] In order to determine the sense of a proposition, I should have to know a very specific procedure for when to count the proposition as verified" (WVC 47). "The meaning of a proposition is the mode of its verification" (LWL 66). "If you want to know the meaning of a sentence, ask for its verification" (AWL 29). Wittgenstein thought that meaning and verification are internally related in the case of propositions, which he distinguished from hypotheses. Propositions were taken to be judgments about sense-data (e.g., "This is red") and completely verified, while hypotheses were thought to be confirmed or disconfirmed by empirical evidence and not definitely verified (e.g., "This is a chair") (cf. Chapter 12, METAPHYSICS: FROM INEFFABILITY TO NORMATIVITY). He thought that the propositions of physics are hypotheses. Wittgenstein understood the verification of a proposition in the manner that an expectation is related to what is expected, i.e., that we cannot describe expecting p without using p (PR§§30–1). Verification becomes an a priori affair (LWL 66) that establishes connections between propositions and gives the proposition's grammar (AWL 19).

> How far is giving the verification of a proposition a grammatical statement about it? So far as it is, it can explain the meaning of its terms. Insofar as it is a matter of experience, as when one names a symptom, the meaning is not explained. (AWL 31)

Later Wittgenstein qualified his views about verification stating that it is a mere rule of thumb (M p.59); that it does not constitute the proposition's grammar but makes a contribution to it (PI §353); and that it is one of many ways to get clear about the use of a sentence (see in Hymers 2005, p. 220).

It seems that the logical positivists understood verification quite differently. They had epistemological concerns and treated propositions as experiential hypotheses.

Even Waismann, who was so close to Wittgenstein and made statements that echoed Wittgenstein's thought (for instance, that the proposition contains its method of verification and that you cannot look for a method of verification (WVC 247, 227)), contended that the statements $s_1, s_2, \ldots s_n$ connected to a proposition by a method of verification are "evidences that *speak for* or *against* the proposition p, that they *strengthen* or *weaken* it" (Waismann, 1978, p.125, emphasis in original). He thought that verification is always incomplete not only because we cannot exhaust the number of tests to verify a proposition but also because something unforeseen may always occur. This is the reason why Carnap preferred confirmation to verification.

> If by verification is meant a definitive and final establishment of truth, then no (synthetic) sentence is ever verifiable [...]. We can only confirm a sentence more and more. Therefore we speak of the problem of *confirmation* rather than of the problem of verification. (Carnap, 1936, p.420, emphasis in original)

Verification for Carnap was a matter of finding out whether "a given sentence is true or false" (1936, p.420). But this test presupposes that the sentence under consideration already has meaning. For Wittgenstein verification explains the sense of a proposition. "How a proposition is verified is what it says" (PR §166). The logical positivists used the principle of verification and the criterion of verifiability to police epistemologically meaningful discourse and develop a whole program of problems for philosophy of science – problems and paradoxes of confirmation, the confirmation of scientific theories, inductive probability, the logic of induction, etc. Wittgenstein, on the other hand, was interested in logical questions of meaning.

Recently, the Wittgenstein–Vienna Circle relation, more precisely the Wittgenstein–Carnap relation, has featured in controversies that surround the understanding of nonsense in the *Tractatus*. James Conant (2001) contends that the standard conception concerning the overcoming of metaphysics as nonsensical, advocated by Peter Hacker in his interpretation of the *Tractatus*, makes Wittgenstein and Carnap too similar since they are both taken to understand metaphysical nonsense as resulting from the violation of rules of logical syntax that govern linguistic usage (cf. Chapter 10, RESOLUTE READINGS OF THE *TRACTATUS* and chapter 12, METAPHYSICS: INEFFABILITY AND NONSENSE). Hacker (2003), on the other hand, criticizes Conant for misinterpreting and misrepresenting both Carnap and Wittgenstein. He insists on the deep differences that separate the two philosophers on multiple fronts, acknowledging at the same time that, in some respects, Carnap's argument regarding the elimination of metaphysics "does indeed converge on, although is not the same as, Wittgenstein's" (Hacker, 2001b, p.335). More recently, Oskari Kuusela (2012) has argued that it is wrong to think of Carnap's method of logical syntax as departing from Wittgenstein's approach. In Kuusela's view, it can rather be seen as an alternative, or a particular development of what Wittgenstein did. While Carnap's syntactical sentences are used to define syntactical concepts and principles, Wittgenstein's allegedly nonsensical elucidatory statements are seen by Kuusela as quasi-syntactical statements that are used to introduce the principles and the concepts of his logical notation. TLP 4.01, for instance, which says that a proposition is a picture of reality, may be taken to be similar to Carnap's example of a quasi-syntactical sentence, "Five is not a thing but a number." The latter, Carnap (1937/2001, p.285) says, is not a proper but a pseudo-object-sentence: it seems to be talking about the number five when in reality it talks about the word "five." Similarly, TLP 4.01, according to Kuusela, does not make a metaphysical statement about propositions but is meant to introduce a syntactical concept, the propositional variable.

These developments in the literature on early Wittgenstein have not reached philosophy of science, because here there is little interest in Wittgenstein and his relation to the logical positivists. After the exodus of the Vienna Circle members (mostly to the United States), references to Wittgenstein, who had originally such a visible influence on the school, ceased. Characteristically, the philosophy of science readers that were edited by the logical positivists in the United States, which were very instrumental in fixing the identity of the discipline and in forming a community of specialists, did not include any piece by Wittgenstein or any article discussing his work. For instance, the reader edited by Feigl and Brodbeck (1953) contains over 50 articles written by logical positivists, Einstein, Poincaré, Duhem, and Russell but there is no article on or by Wittgenstein. Ronald Giere (1996, pp.337–9) observes that, in general, the European origins of logical empiricism in North America "remained in relative obscurity [...]. It was something noticeably different from what had existed in Europe." Giere's hypothesis is that Carnap and Reichenbach thought their future lay in North America and that they had to choose projects that were appealing to their new cultural and philosophical milieu and audience. The relation to Wittgenstein was obscured and forgotten for other reasons as well. There was the estrangement from Carnap, the fact that Wittgenstein's most vehement advocates were not present in North America (Schlick had been assassinated in 1936 and Waismann, alienated from Wittgenstein, was settled in England), and most importantly, Wittgenstein's philosophy did not fit the orientation that philosophy of science was taking in the New World. Wittgenstein himself thought that philosophy in the United States had taken a radically different turn from his own work (cf. Letter to W.H. Watson, 8 April 1932). As Toulmin put it (1969, p.39), the logical empiricists chose Mach over Wittgenstein.

2 Wittgenstein and the Historical Turn in Philosophy of Science

The historical turn in philosophy of science in the late 1950s and early 1960s, that is, the turn away from the study of scientific theories as sets of statements and toward the study of scientific activity in different historical periods and in the course of time, has been associated mostly with the work of philosophers such as Toulmin, Hanson, Kuhn, and Feyerabend, who were active publishing books and papers at that time in the United States. All four had a relation to Wittgenstein. Two of them knew him personally (Toulmin and Feyerabend), and all of them were influenced by his work in ways that were consequential for the development of philosophy of science.

However, Wittgenstein's role in bringing about a major turn in philosophy of science has been largely overlooked and forgotten for various reasons. Wittgenstein's philosophy was not popular in the United States in the first place (Glock, 2008). Secondly, Wittgenstein was extensively perceived as being associated with the logical positivists, who were the target of the new developments in philosophy of science. Thirdly, Wittgenstein's later philosophy, which, as I will argue, has influenced the historical turn, became widely available to the academic community only after 1953 when *Philosophical Investigations* was published. This meant that it was difficult to appreciate and discuss the Wittgensteinian elements in the work of these groundbreaking philosophers of science. Consequently, this new philosophy of science was inevitably judged by the standards of the so-called received view, that is, the kind of philosophy of science that was dominant at that time in the United States and was formed and developed on the basis of the logical positivists' work.

Especially after the publication of Kuhn's *The Structure of Scientific Revolutions* in 1962 (second edition 1970), the discussion concentrated on whether Kuhn's, and Feyerabend's, work had breached the standards of rationality and good scientific practice. Indeed, Toulmin, Hanson, and even Feyerabend himself sided with Kuhn's critics, in certain respects disregarding the aspects of their own and Kuhn's work that could not be assimilated to the mainstream debate. Part of what was left out of consideration was precisely the Wittgensteinian elements in the work of the historical philosophers of science.

The neglect of the Wittgenstenian dimension was consequential in two respects. First, historical research was credited as the sole influence on the work of these philosophers (this is mostly the reason the turn was dubbed "historical"). Secondly, the innovative ideas that the historical philosophers of science had drawn from Wittgenstein's work were distorted and found inadequate when seen from the perspective of the received view. Historical philosophy of science was then vehemently criticized and eventually marginalized as a way of practicing philosophy of science. It has proven more influential in other fields such as science studies, where Wittgenstein's influence has also been strong (e.g., Bloor, 1983; Lynch, 1992).

In what follows, I will consider briefly in turn the connection between Wittgenstein and the four philosophers who were most responsible for bringing about the historical turn in philosophy of science in the late 1950s and early 1960s.

3 Toulmin

Stephen Toulmin, having studied physics and mathematics, attended Wittgenstein's lectures at Cambridge in 1941 and again in 1946–1947. In 1953 he published *Philosophy of Science. An Introduction*. In the preface he acknowledges his debt to Wittgenstein and W.H. Watson, whose book *On Understanding Physics* (1959), first published in 1938, he said, he had found to be a continual stimulus (Toulmin, 1953, p.vii). Watson, a physics professor at McGill University, was Wittgenstein's student and friend. He had attended Wittgenstein's lectures in 1929–1931 and had a copy, sent to him by Wittgenstein, of the manuscript of Wittgenstein's lectures of 1933–1934, which became later the "Blue Book." In his book, Watson aims at clarifying physics by doing philosophy in Wittgenstein's sense. To this end, instead of concentrating on knowledge taken to be "fixed and dead" (1959, p.xiv), he highlights, in the spirit of Wittgenstein's philosophy, the importance of scientific activity, of what scientists do, how they use knowledge, what purposes they have, what techniques they employ, and what training they get. He contends that theoretical invention in physics consists "in the erection of new logical structure, that is, in making a *system* of new ideas or devising a new method of representation" (Watson, 1959, p.18, emphasis in original). "Method of representation" is a Wittgensteinian term (see, for instance, PI §50) used also by Toulmin in *Philosophy of Science* (1953, p.34), where Toulmin repeats that "the heart of all major discoveries in the physical sciences is the discovery of novel methods of representation" and goes on to suggest that "the adoption of a new theory involves a *language-shift*" (Toulmin, 1953, p.13, emphasis in original).

Toulmin's *Foresight and Understanding* (1961) is even more clearly Wittgensteinian; although Wittgenstein's name is nowhere mentioned, Toulmin uses Wittgensteinian terminology ("paradigms," "objects of comparison"), and employs Wittgensteinian ideas. He compares, for instance, science to sports in order to claim that both terms cover a wide range of activities with similarities and dissimilarities between them that have multiple purposes. The analogy with Wittgenstein's discussion of games and his idea of family resemblance is quite obvious (PI §66). He also speaks of explanations reaching rock bottom (1961, p.42), which reminds us of Wittgenstein's justifications reaching bedrock (PI §217). In general, Toulmin rejects the attempts to capture what science is by giving what he calls "portmanteau definitions" (1961, p.15), and prefers to present science as a multifaceted activity instead. His account stresses the role of paradigms, that is, of models, ideals, and principles of regularity, to set patterns of expectation, to fix standards of rationality and intelligibility, to identify the anomalous and the accepted. These paradigms are not prejudices; they are, according to Toulmin, preconceived notions "both inevitable and proper" (1961, p.101). "We see the world through them to such an extent that we forget what it would look like without them: our very commitment to them tends to blind us to other possibilities" (1961, p.101). Toulmin's paradigms certainly foreshadow the more famous ones by Kuhn and clearly reflect Wittgenstein's discussion of paradigms and samples. Wittgenstein, who also spoke of preconceived ideas (e.g., Z §331), understood paradigms and samples as symbols that show and establish, by being followed, a particular way of conceiving the world.

4 Hanson

N.R. Hanson never met Wittgenstein but was at Oxford and Cambridge from 1949 to 1957. He was a graduate student at Oxford and held a lectureship at Cambridge from 1953 to 1957. While there he studied Wittgenstein's work and had copies of the manuscripts that were posthumously published as the *Blue and Brown Book* (Lund, 2010, p.26). Hanson's book *Patterns of Discovery* (1958) had a great impact on how philosophy of science developed. The book, especially its first chapter on "Observation," draws heavily on Wittgenstein's discussion of *seeing*. In the first chapter Hanson introduced the concept of theory-ladenness of observation, i.e., the thesis that we do not have pure, unvarnished perceptual data on which we may impose different interpretations, but rather that what we observe is already laden at the most basic level by the scientific theories that we have. According to Hanson, Brahe and Kepler may be aware of the same object when they watch the sun rise at dawn, but they actually *see* different things because of the two different astronomical theories they uphold. In Hanson's view, *seeing* is not a photochemical excitation. "People, not their eyes see. Cameras and eyeballs are blind" (1958, p.6; cf. PI §§281ff). People are the ones who have concepts, beliefs, and theories that permeate perception. This was a provocative thesis in philosophy of science since it undermined crucial tenets of the received view. According to the received view, observation statements, as distinct from theoretical statements, were taken to record pure perceptual experience. They were supposed to function as the terminus of justification, as the source of empirical meaning for the theoretical terms and sentences of scientific theories, as the tie of theories to the world, and as the theory-neutral basis for comparison and rational evaluation of theories. If observation is theory-laden, as

Hanson claimed, then there are no pure and neutral observation statements to perform all these roles. One is entrapped in theory, so to speak, and cannot test the theory against the world.

Hanson explicitly acknowledges his debt to Wittgenstein:

> It was his [Wittgenstein's] *analysis* of complex concepts such as *seeing*, *seeing as*, and *seeing that* which exposed the crude, bipartite philosophy of sense datum versus interpretation as being the technical legislation it really is. By means of philosophy he destroyed the dogma of immaculate perception. (Hanson, 1969, p.74, emphasis in original)

Hanson draws on Wittgenstein's discussion of *seeing* and *seeing as* in what is now labeled "Philosophy of Psychology – A Fragment" (PPF; cf. Chapter 33, WITTGENSTEIN ON SEEING ASPECTS), and uses *Gestalt* figures to show that even though the perceptual stimulus remains the same, what we see differs when we notice the two aspects of the drawings. Following Wittgenstein, he does not attribute the difference to two different interpretations imposed upon the same perceptual data. The concept of *seeing* "does not designate two diaphanous components, one optical, the other interpretative" (Hanson, 1958, p.9). For Hanson, one just sees something different each time, as one just hears that an oboe is out of tune without first interpreting the tones. Hanson, however, in his effort to combat the view that observation is "just opening one's eyes and looking" (1958, p.31), seems to equate *seeing* with *seeing as*, disregarding Wittgenstein's reservations. For Wittgenstein *seeing as* seems to involve an inferential process and, so, cannot be identified with *seeing* in general (see Glock, 1996, "aspect-perception"). Hanson, however, while he expressly denies that he means to identify the two notions, cites approvingly G.N.A. Vesey's statement that "all seeing is seeing as" (1958, p.182, n.5). And he says, *pace* Wittgenstein, that "the logic of 'seeing as' seems to illuminate the general perceptual case" (1958, p.19).

5   Kuhn

Thomas Kuhn was not acquainted with Wittgenstein personally. He came to his philosophy through his encounter with Stanley Cavell. They had regular meetings and conversations when they were both at Berkeley in the late 1950s, when Kuhn was finishing *Structure*. In that book, Wittgenstein makes "a cameo appearance" (Isaac, 2012, p.95) in chapter V, "The priority of paradigms." Wittgenstein is invoked there to account for the cohesion of a normal-scientific research tradition.

Kuhn realized from his historical research that scientists do not learn definitions in the abstract in order to apply them and do not adhere to a set of rules comprising "the scientific method." He couldn't, therefore, explain the practical agreement he found among scientists in scientific communities. He sought help in Wittgenstein's work. "What need we know, Wittgenstein asked, in order that we apply terms like 'chair', or 'leaf,' or 'game' unequivocally and without argument?" (Kuhn, 1970, pp.44–5). Kuhn refers to *Philosophical Investigations* and claims that Wittgenstein, instead of offering a set of characteristics that all games, for instance, share, suggests that the activities we call games bear a close "family resemblance" to each other. Instead of having a definition specifying necessary and sufficient conditions, we only need to have paradigms that resemble, in a crisscrossing way, their subsequent applications. Kuhn, however, interpreted Wittgenstein as saying that there are natural families, each constituted by a network of certain overlapping and crisscross resemblances. In his view, if there were no natural families, we would have to suppose common characteristics to account for the success in identifying and naming different items.

This is a misunderstanding on Kuhn's part of what Wittgenstein was saying. Kuhn seems to compare the families that Wittgenstein talks about to natural kinds, a thought that implies that the members of each family already have shared qualities that we read off. But Wittgenstein did not want to say that because family members are genetically related, they exhibit certain similarities. His point was exactly that members of a family, despite their genetic relation, do not all share the same phenotypical characteristics (PI §67). For that reason, Danto (1981, pp. 58–9), who recognized correctly that Wittgenstein's families are not species, was wrong to think that the concept of the family was "almost appallingly ill chosen" by Wittgenstein since it presupposes genetic affiliation. Danto was wrong because Wittgenstein introduced the idea of family resemblance to combat an essentialist understanding of concepts, i.e., to show that the unity of concepts is not secured by identifying a set of common characteristics, even if we can find them (see Chapter 25, VAGUENESS AND FAMILY RESEMBLANCE). The advantage of Wittgenstein's notion of family resemblance over definitions specifying common characteristics is not that it concerns similarities instead of essences; it is rather that agreement is secured not by appealing to definitions but by bringing together in practice varying applications that resemble each other in crisscrossing and overlapping ways. The similarities are not read off but rather established by the paradigm that is being followed.

Setting aside Kuhn's misinterpretation, following paradigms was the notion that helped Kuhn account for the cohesion exhibited in the practice of normal science. As Joel Isaac (2012, p.105) explains, the chapter on the priority of paradigms, with the reference to Wittgenstein, was not included in the penultimate draft of the book. Here is how Kuhn describes how it came to feature in the final draft:

> I wrote a chapter on revolutions, slowly but not with excessive difficulties [...]. Then I tried to write a chapter on normal science. And I kept finding that I had to – since I was taking a relatively classical, received view approach to what a scientific theory was – I had to attribute all sorts of agreement about this, that, and the other thing, which would have appeared in the axiomatization either as axioms or as definitions. And I was enough of a historian to know that that agreement did not exist among the people who were [concerned]. And that was the crucial point at which the idea of the paradigm as model entered. Once that was in place, and that was quite late in the year, the book sort of wrote itself. (Kuhn, 2000, p.296)

Kuhn denied in his last interview (2000, p.299) that he knew of Wittgenstein's use of the term "paradigm." As a matter of historical fact, it is not clear whether Kuhn took the term from Wittgenstein, or not. Cavell (2010, pp.354–5), for instance, remembers Kuhn telling him that he (Kuhn) knew of Wittgenstein's use of "paradigm." Philosophically, the connection to Wittgenstein was made by Cedarbaum (1983), while Janik and Toulmin (1973, p.284, n.12) thought that Wittgenstein's paradigms are significantly different from Kuhn's. In my view, however, the two concepts, the Kuhnian and the Wittgensteinian, are quite close (Kindi, 2012), despite Kuhn's misinterpretation. They both function as models and prototypes and they both induce and establish consensus by being followed. Learning from a paradigm (e.g., a scientific textbook or a color sample), involves learning concepts and the use of the corresponding words, learning the objects on which to apply them, learning what is allowed and what is not. Scientists, according to Kuhn, all learn how to solve puzzles (problems that closely resemble the original paradigm), thus developing the consensual practice of normal science.

Wittgenstein's influence on Kuhn, historically and philosophically speaking, has been very little discussed in the literature. There have been some sporadic references and very few more extensive treatments of the issue (Kindi, 1995a and 1995b; also Sharrock and Read, 2002). If, however, the Wittgensteinian elements in Kuhn's work were brought to bear on the debates that followed *Structure*, then issues that have been proven highly controversial (and "incriminating" for Kuhn), such as the issue of conceptual incommensurability, would have been dealt with rather differently. For instance, the problems commonly associated with incommensurability, such as the putative threat of irrationality, would not arise given Kuhn's (and Wittgenstein's) understanding of concepts. Kuhn's critics took concepts to be closed, well-circumscribed entities that subsist, fully or partially, through time. This is a requirement if we are to establish inferential relations between theories in order to explain one by the other, reduce one to the other, or reasonably substitute one for the other. So, when Kuhn spoke of radical differences between concepts of different theories, irrationality ensued since the transition from one paradigm to the next could not be mapped onto a logical inference. But if Kuhn's work is seen from a Wittgensteinian perspective, concepts will not be viewed as entities, but rather as uses of words in different circumstances. And if concepts are seen as uses of words, then the transition from one network to the next is a difference, big or small, in application and the threat of irrationality associated with incommensurability becomes less dramatic. The rationality of transition is not judged by considering reconstructed abstract arguments involving sharply defined, entity-like concepts, but by attending to the particular circumstances of word use in order to assess the actual considerations and options in the range of possibilities available to the scientists in question. Ironically, under this interpretation, the undesired consequences of incommensurability arise not for Kuhn, but for his opponents and their understanding of concepts.

6   Feyerabend

Paul Feyerabend also made use of Wittgenstein's understanding of concepts and of how words have a meaning. In his seminal paper "Explanation, Reduction and Empiricism," which was published in 1962 (the same year as *Structure*), Feyerabend explicitly invoked Wittgenstein (in a footnote) in connection with his (Feyerabend's) contextual theory of meaning (1962, p.68, n.83). In that article he criticizes the formal theories of reduction and explanation in the sciences, advanced most prominently by Ernest Nagel and the logical empiricist Carl Hempel. Feyerabend challenged both the deductive structure of explanation and reduction and the assumption it implies of meaning invariance. Meanings have to remain the same in order for the deductive inference to work. Feyerabend maintained that the meaning of a term is given contextually, i.e., it is "dependent upon the way in which the term has been incorporated into a theory" (1962, p.68) and claimed that elements of many pairs of theories (concepts, principles, laws, etc.) are "incommensurable and therefore incapable of mutual explanation and reduction" (p.75). The reason is that concepts of an earlier theory cannot be defined on the basis of primitive observational terms of the theory to which a reduction is attempted nor can there be found "correct empirical statements" to correlate corresponding terms and concepts (p.74). Feyerabend's criticism of the formal theories of reduction and explanation challenged a very central project of the logical empiricist philosophy of science that was dominant at the time in the United States.

Feyerabend had studied Wittgenstein's philosophy. He had written a critical review of *Philosophical Investigations* (Feyerabend, 1955), which was translated from German into English by G.E.M. Anscombe. Feyerabend was planning to study philosophy with Wittgenstein at Cambridge but his plans were thwarted by Wittgenstein's death in 1951. He went instead to study with Karl Popper in London. Feyerabend had met Wittgenstein in Vienna, in the context of the "Kraft Circle," which was named after Feyerabend's dissertation supervisor Viktor Kraft, a member of the original "Vienna Circle." Wittgenstein was invited to give a lecture there in 1949 and Feyerabend, who describes the visit as "brief and quite interesting," notes:

> Wittgenstein was very impressive in his way of presenting concrete cases, such as amoebas under a microscope (I cannot now recall the reason this example was used), but when he left we still did not know whether or not there was an external world, or, if there was one, what the arguments were in favor of it. 'You philosophers' said one of the participating engineers in despair, 'are all alike. There you tell us that Wittgenstein turned philosophy upside down. He talks just as much as everyone in this profession and can't give a straightforward answer to a straightforward question.' (Feyerabend, 1966, p.4)

Feyerabend endorsed these complaints later when, in reviewing Hanson's book (1958), he said that his pleasure reading it was

> sometimes a little diluted by the fact that in true Wittgensteinian fashion, many important points were buried beneath examples or aphorisms, or made in a rather indirect and qualified way. (Feyerabend, 1960, p.252)

Notably, the example of amoebas under the microscope mentioned in the quote above is the first example used by Hanson (1958, p.4) to illustrate the theory-ladenness of observation. Two microbiologists observing an amoeba, depending on the theories they have, see either a one-celled or a non-celled animal.

Feyerabend's ambivalent attitude toward Wittgenstein's philosophy is also shown in the comments he sent Kuhn in a letter of 1961. On the one hand he urges Kuhn to study Wittgenstein's remarks on *seeing*, as being original in comparison to Hanson's, and on the other he writes:

> People ask me to talk about Wittgenstein, because he is an influential contemporary philosopher [...]. I refuse to do this. And if they ask 'shall we read the *Philosophical Investigations?'* I reply 'If you want to waste your time, yes'. (Hoyningen-Huene, 1995, p.384)

Early in his career, Feyerabend was certainly influenced by Wittgenstein. His views on meaning bear affinities to Wittgenstein's, since a term's meaning is tied to use and is not dependent upon its connection to pure observation statements. But Feyerabend seems to understand "use" theoretically and not to appreciate the practical dimension of Wittgenstein's approach. In the same footnote where he mentions Wittgenstein in connection with his (Feyerabend's) contextual theory of meaning, he criticizes Wittgenstein for replacing a Platonism of concepts by a Platonism of games (1962, p. 68, n.83). Platonism implies for Feyerabend invariance of meaning; and what he seems to be saying is that Wittgenstein makes meaning invariant within each language-game or theory. This implies that, unlike Wittgenstein, he understands language-games as closed systems consisting of statements that fix completely the meaning of terms (cf. Chapter 26, LANGUAGES, LANGUAGE-GAMES, AND FORMS OF LIFE).

7 Conclusion

Harold Bloom, in his *Anxiety of Influence*, writes that strong poets make poetic history "by misreading one another, so as to clear imaginative space for themselves" (1973/97, p. 5). In the course of the twentieth century, Wittgenstein's work has influenced the development of philosophy of science as a discipline at decisive points: first in the beginning, when contemporary philosophy of science was founded, and then around mid-century, when it took a turn away (or even against) its previous practice. In both cases he was creatively read and misread. His philosophy (early and late) offered support for the aims and undertakings of the respective groups of philosophers, but it only functioned as a rung of a ladder. They used it and moved beyond it. In the case of logical positivism, it was relatively clear that Wittgenstein and the logical positivists were heading in different directions and had different priorities. They had a reverential attitude toward science; he was critical of the scientific world-conception. They had formed, originally at least, "a kind of International Liberation Front" (Toulmin, 1969, p. 51). Wittgenstein was dismissive of their militant language and perspective. In the case of the historical philosophers of science, Wittgenstein's philosophy helped to liberate them from the cast of the tradition, but it wasn't really studied in depth and hence not really appreciated either by them or their critics. If the Wittgensteinian elements in their work are brought to the fore, the innovative character of this major turn will be better comprehended. Old problems, for instance that of incommensurability, will be cast in a new light and new issues will emerge, for instance issues pertaining to the understanding of science as practice.

References

Anscombe, G.E.M. (1995). Ludwig Wittgenstein. *Philosophy*, 70, 395–407.
Blank, A. (2011). Wittgenstein on Verification and Seeing-As, 1930–1932. *Inquiry*, 54, 614–632.
Bloom, H. (1973/97). *The Anxiety of Influence*. Oxford: Oxford University Press.
Bloor, D. (1983). *Wittgenstein: A Social Theory of Knowledge*. New York: Columbia University Press.
Carnap, R. (1936). Testability and Meaning. *Philosophy of Science*, 3, 420–471.
Carnap, R. (1937/2001). *Logical Syntax of Language*. London: Routledge.
Carnap, R. (1963). Intellectual Autobiography. In P.A. Schlipp (Ed.). *The Library of Living Philosophers: The Philosophy of Rudolf Carnap* (pp. 3–84). La Salle: Open Court.
Cavell, S. (2010). *Little Did I Know: Excerpts from Memory*. Palo Alto: Stanford University Press.
Cedarbaum, D.G. (1983). Paradigms. *Studies in the History and Philosophy of Science*, 14, 173–213.

Conant, J. (2001). Two Conceptions of *die Überwindung der Metaphysik:* Carnap and Early Wittgenstein. In T.G. McCarthy and S.C. Stidd (Eds). *Wittgenstein in America* (pp.13–61). Oxford: Oxford University Press.

Danto, A. (1981). *The Transfiguration of the Commonplace*. Cambridge, MA: Harvard University Press.

Feigl, H. (1969). The Origin and Spirit of Logical Positivism. In P. Achinstein and S.F. Barker (Eds). *The Legacy of Logical Positivism* (pp.3–24). Baltimore: The Johns Hopkins Press.

Feigl, H. and Brodbeck, M. (1953). *Readings in the Philosophy of Science*. New York: Appleton-Century-Crofts.

Feyerabend, P. (1955). Wittgenstein's *Philosophical Investigations*. *Philosophical Review*, 64, 449–483.

Feyerabend, P. (1960). Review: Patterns of Discovery. *Philosophical Review*, 69, 247–252.

Feyerabend, P. (1962). Explanation, Reduction and Empiricism. *Minnesota Studies in the Philosophy of Science*, 3, 28–97.

Feyerabend, P. (1966). Herbert Feigl: A Biographical Sketch. In P. Feyerabend and G. Maxwell (Eds). *Mind, Matter, and Method: Essays in Philosophy and Science in Honor of Herbert Feigl* (pp.4–13). Minneapolis: University of Minnesota Press.

Giere, R. (1996). From *wissenschaftliche Philosophie* to Philosophy of Science. In R. Giere and A. Richardson (Eds). *The Origins of Logical Empiricism* (pp.335–354). Minneapolis: University of Minnesota Press.

Glock, H.-J. (1996). *A Wittgenstein Dictionary*. Oxford: Blackwell.

Glock, H.-J. (2008). The Influence of Wittgenstein on American Philosophy. In C.J. Misak (Ed.). *The Oxford Handbook of American Philosophy* (pp.375–402). Oxford: Oxford University Press.

Hacker, P.M.S. (1996). *Wittgenstein's Place in Twentieth-Century Analytic Philosophy*. Oxford: Blackwell.

Hacker, P.M.S. (2001a). Wittgenstein and the Vienna Circle: The Exaltation and Deposition of Ostensive Definition. In P.M.S. Hacker. *Wittgenstein: Connections and Controversies* (pp.242–267). Oxford: Blackwell.

Hacker, P.M.S. (2001b). On Carnap's Elimination of Metaphysics. In P.M.S. Hacker. *Wittgenstein: Connections and Controversies* (pp.324–344). Oxford: Blackwell.

Hacker, P.M.S. (2003). Wittgenstein, Carnap and the New American Wittgensteinians. *The Philosophical Quarterly*, 33, 1–23.

Hanson, N.R. (1958). *Patterns of Discovery*. Cambridge: Cambridge University Press.

Hanson, N.R. (1969). Logical Positivism and the Interpretation of Scientific Theories. In P. Achinstein and S.F. Barker (Eds). *The Legacy of Logical Positivism* (pp.57–84). Baltimore: The Johns Hopkins Press.

Hempel, C. (2001). Logical Positivism and the Social Sciences. In J.H. Fetzer (Ed.). *The Philosophy of Carl G. Hempel* (pp.253–275). Oxford: Oxford University Press.

Hoyningen-Huene, P. (1995). Two Letters of Paul Feyerabend to Thomas S. Kuhn on a Draft of *The Structure of Scientific Revolutions*. *Studies in History and Philosophy of Science*, 26, 353–387.

Hymers, M. (2005). Going around the Vienna Circle: Wittgenstein and Verification. *Philosophical Investigations*, 28, 205–234.

Isaac, J. (2012). Kuhn's Education: Wittgenstein, Pedagogy, and the Road to *Structure*. *Modern Intellectual History*, 9, 89–107.

Janik, A. and Toulmin, S. (1973). *Wittgenstein's Vienna*. New York: Simon and Schuster.

Kindi, V. (1995a). *Kuhn & Wittgenstein: Φιλοσοφική Έρευνα της Δομής των Επιστημονικών Επαναστάσεων* [Kuhn and Wittgenstein: Philosophical Investigation of *The Structure of Scientific Revolutions*.] Athens: Smili editions.

Kindi, V. (1995b). Kuhn's *The Structure of Scientific Revolutions* Revisited. *Journal for the General Philosophy of Science*, 26, 75–92.

Kindi, V. (2012). Kuhn's Paradigms. In V. Kindi and T. Arabatzis (Eds). *Kuhn's The Structure of Scientific Revolutions Revisited* (pp.91–111). London: Routledge.

Kuhn, T.S (1970). *The Structure of Scientific Revolutions*, second edition. Chicago: The University of Chicago Press. (Original publication 1962.)

Kuhn, T.S. (2000). A Discussion with Thomas Kuhn. In J. Conant and J. Haugeland (Eds). *The Road since Structure* (pp.255–323). Chicago: The University of Chicago Press.

Kuusela, O. (2012). Carnap and the *Tractatus*' Philosophy of Logic. *Journal for the History of Analytical Philosophy*, 1, 1–25.

Lund, M. (2010). *N.R. Hanson. Observation, Discovery and Scientific Change*. New York: Humanity Books.

Lynch, M. (1992). Extending Wittgenstein: The Pivotal Move from Epistemology to the Sociology of Science. In A. Pickering (Ed.). *Science as Practice and Culture* (pp.215–265). Chicago: The University of Chicago Press.

McGuinness, B. (2002). Relations with and within the Circle. In B. McGuinness. *Approaches to Wittgenstein* (pp.184–200). London: Routledge.

Menger, K. (1982). Memories of Moritz Schlick. In E.T. Gadol (Ed.). *Rationality and Science* (pp.83–103). Wien: Springer.

Richardson, A. and Hardcastle, G. L. (2003). Introduction. In A. Richardson and G. Hardcastle (Eds). *Minnesota Studies in the Philosophy of Science (Vol. 18): Logical Empiricism in North America* (pp.vii–xxix). Minneapolis: University of Minnesota Press.

Schlick, M. ([1928] 1979). Preface to: Friedrich Waismann, *Logik, Sprache, Philosophie: Kritik der Philosophie*. In H.L. Mulder and B.F.B. van de Velde-Schlick (Eds). *Philosophical Papers* (Vol. 2, pp.130–138). Dordrecht: Reidel.

Schlick, M. ([1930] 1979). The Turning Point in Philosophy. In H.L. Mulder and B.F.B. van de Velde-Schlick (Eds). *Philosophical Papers* (Vol. 2, pp.154–160). Dordrecht: Reidel.

Sharrock, W. and Read, R. (2002). *Kuhn: Philosopher of Scientific Revolution*. Cambridge: Polity Press.

Stadler, F. (1997). *The Vienna Circle: Studies in the Origins, Development, and Influence of Logical Empiricism*. New York: Springer.

Stadler, F. (2003). What is the Vienna Circle? Some Methodological and Historiographical Answers. *Vienna Circle Institute Yearbook (Vol. 10): The Vienna Circle and Logical Empiricism* (pp.xi–xxiii). New York: Kluwer.

Stern, D. (2007). Wittgenstein, the Vienna Circle, and Physicalism: A Reassessment. In A. Richardson and T. Uebel (Eds). *The Cambridge Companion to Logical Empiricism* (pp.305–331). Cambridge: Cambridge University Press.

Toulmin, S.E. (1953). *The Philosophy of Science: An Introduction*. New York: Hutchinson's University Library.

Toulmin, S.E. (1961). *Foresight and Understanding*. New York: Harper Torchbooks.

Toulmin, S.E. (1969). From Logical Analysis to Conceptual History. In P. Achinstein and S.F. Barker (Eds). *The Legacy of Logical Positivism* (pp.25–53). Baltimore: The Johns Hopkins Press.

Waismann, L. (1978). Verifiability. In A.G.N. Flew (Ed.). *Logic and Language* (pp.117–144). Oxford: Blackwell.

Watson, W.H. (1959). *On Understanding Physics*. New York: Harper Torchbooks. (Original publication 1938.)

Wrigley, M. (1989). The Origins of Wittgenstein's Verificationism. *Synthese*, 78, 265–290.

Further Reading

Coffa, A.J. (1991). *The Semantic Tradition from Kant to Carnap*. Cambridge: Cambridge University Press.

Giere, R.N. and Richardson, A.W. (Eds). (1996). *Origins of Logical Empiricism*. Minneapolis: University of Minnesota Press.

Hacker, P.M.S. (1972/86). *Insight and Illusion: Themes in the Philosophy of Wittgenstein.* Revised edition. Oxford: Clarendon Press.
McGuinness, B. (2002a). Philosophy of Science. In B. McGuinness. *Approaches to Wittgenstein* (pp.116–123). London: Routledge.
McGuinness, B. (2002b). The Value of Science. In B. McGuinness. *Approaches to Wittgenstein* (pp.124–130). London: Routledge.
McGuinness, B. (2002c). Wittgenstein and the Vienna Circle. In B. McGuinness. *Approaches to Wittgenstein* (pp.177–183). London: Routledge.
Wray, B.K. (2011). Kuhn and the Discovery of Paradigms. *Philosophy of the Social Sciences*, 41, 380–397.

Part IX

Ethics, Aesthetics, and Religion

39

Wittgenstein and Ethics

ROBERT L. ARRINGTON

Wittgenstein wrote very little about ethics. There is, to be sure, his early "A Lecture on Ethics," which consists of an application of the philosophy of language in his first masterpiece, *Tractatus Logico-Philosophicus*, to ethical concepts and judgments. Then there are occasional comments, such as some of those edited as *Culture and Value*, which appear to have ethical implications. Wittgenstein did not write at length about ethics in his later philosophy either, to be sure. Nevertheless, the later philosophy of *Philosophical Investigations* and other works exerted an enormous influence on ethical thinkers, resulting in a number of treatises that speak directly to ideas central to the later philosophy. This influence is especially felt in the emotivism and prescriptivism of mid-twentieth-century ethical theory, although at points the influence of Wittgenstein's earlier philosophizing and his philosophy of language is apparent as well in these "non-cognitivist" theories. Furthermore, there are ideas from *Philosophical Investigations* that have been used by some philosophers to develop distinctively "cognitivist" accounts of moral discourse.

We shall begin here by looking at the thought expressed in "A Lecture on Ethics," and then we shall consider the indirect applications of Wittgenstein's later philosophy to ethics.

By invitation from C.K. Ogden, Wittgenstein presented his lecture on ethics in 1929 to the Heretics Society in Cambridge. After attributing any difficulties in communicating his ideas to the fact that English is not his native tongue, Wittgenstein proceeds to communicate, in remarkably clear fashion and beautiful English, his thoughts on a subject of "general importance." He declines to give a "popular scientific" lecture on the subject because doing so would "make you believe that you understand a thing which actually you don't understand" (LE 4). Such a popular lecture, he says, would gratify "what I believe to be one of the lowest desires of modern people, namely the superficial curiosity about the latest discoveries of science" (LE 4).

"What is good?" G.E. Moore had asked in *Principia Ethica* (1903). Wittgenstein notes that we can get an idea of what Moore is asking about by inquiring "What is valuable?" or "What is important in life?" But these verbal equivalences get us no closer to

---

A Companion to Wittgenstein, First Edition. Edited by Hans-Johann Glock and John Hyman.
© 2017 John Wiley & Sons, Ltd. Published 2017 by John Wiley & Sons, Ltd.

understanding what good *is*. Wittgenstein begins his lecture by saying that each of these expressions can be used in two different senses, viz., what he calls the "trivial or relative" sense, on the one hand, and the "ethical or absolute sense" on the other (LE 4). The trivial question is easy to answer, because it merely asks the causal question about what action will cause or lead to the fulfillment of what some person wants or has as his purpose. Thus, for instance, if we want to know if a man is a good chess player, we simply want to know if he can move the chess pieces in situations of a certain degree of difficulty and with a certain level of dexterity; or, if we ask whether or not this is the *right* road we are merely asking if it is the right road relative to a certain destination. Such questions have a factual answer, depending on the relation between a man's chess moves and an agreed-upon standard of difficulty and dexterity. And the road is the right one if following it will lead the inquirer to his desired destination. A person could always respond "But I have no interest in playing chess well" or "But I don't want to go to Cambridge," in which case the discussion would cease. But if someone says to me that I am behaving like a beast, even though I might reply that I don't want to behave any better, my critic could reply "But you *ought* to behave better." This of course does not imply that it is all right for me to behave as I have. The question "Are you behaving well?" is not the trivial or relative sort of question. It has the ethical sense, asking about my conduct as measured against an *absolute* standard. Wittgenstein says that the difference between the two types of question comes to this:

> Every judgment of relative value is a mere statement of facts and can therefore be put in such a way that it loses all the appearance of a judgment of value. (LE 5–6)

With this distinction in mind, Wittgenstein is ready to state his conclusion:

> Now what I wish to contend is that, although all judgments of relative value can be shown to be mere statements of fact, no statement of fact can ever be, or imply, a judgment of absolute value. (LE 6)

What, he asks, if we had a book containing a complete description of the world, laying out in precise detail all of the facts contained in it (in the world, that is)? "What I want to say is, that this book would contain nothing that we would call an *ethical* judgment or anything that would logically imply such a judgment." He claims that all the facts contained in this book would "stand on the same level and in the same way all propositions stand on the same level." None of them would be propositions that are value judgments, and none of them would be sublime or important. In other words, none of them would be ethical propositions, and it would no longer make sense to draw the distinction between absolute and trivial ethical judgments. What he had called trivial judgments all make reference to someone's state of mind. But no state of mind "is in an ethical sense good or bad" (LE 6). If we describe someone as murdering another human being, this description may cause us pain or outrage. But this is just another fact – about our state of mind – and will have no ethical significance. "So far as facts and propositions are concerned, there is only relative value and relative good, right." His conclusion is dramatic and revolutionary: "Ethics [...] is supernatural" (LE 6). There is no such thing as "the absolutely right road" or the absolutely right act or mode of conduct. Such things are all "chimeras" (LE 7).

Wittgenstein thinks that when we use such expressions as "absolute value," "absolute good," and "absolute right" (as in fact we do), we are likely to have an experience something like the one we have when we wonder at the existence of the world. Or I may have the feeling that I am absolutely safe, which may prompt me to say something like "I am safe, nothing can injure me whatever happens." Admitting the reality of such experiences and expressions, it remains the case that "the verbal expression which we give to these experiences is nonsense!" (LE 8) I can wonder at the existence of something only if I *could* conceive it *not* to be the case. I can wonder at the size of a dog only if I can conceive of one smaller or larger. "But it is nonsense to say that I wonder at the existence of the world, because I cannot imagine it not existing." Hence the experience, which may be real, has no expression that is not nonsense. Similarly, the feeling I may have that some action is absolutely the right thing to do, while real enough, has no expression that makes sense.

Thus, there can be no science of ethics, just as there can be no science of miracles. It is not that science has *proved* that there can be no miracles, but just that the "scientific way of looking at a fact is not the way to look at it as a miracle." Similarly, although science has not proved that there are no ethical values, the ethical way of looking at people and events is not the scientific way. Since according to the *Tractatus* science incorporates the only meaningful way of talking, it follows that ethical propositions are not *false* but *meaningless*. This nonsensicality is their very essence. "Ethics in so far as it springs from the desire to say something about the ultimate meaning of life, the absolute good, the absolute valuable, can be no science"; and hence ethics gives us no knowledge (*ibid*). Nevertheless, Wittgenstein remorsefully states, "it is a document of a tendency in the *human* mind which I personally cannot help respecting deeply and I would not for my life ridicule it" (*ibid*). Making ethical judgments is a matter of trying to *go beyond the world* and beyond the limits of significant speech. This we cannot do.

As mentioned earlier, in this short lecture, Wittgenstein reiterates and slightly expands on what he had said about ethics in the *Tractatus*. For instance, section 6.421 of this book reads thus: "it is clear that ethics cannot be put into words. Ethics is transcendental." Ethics attempts to say what is *higher*, and this cannot be done. Moreover, no ethical implications can be drawn from descriptions of facts in the world: "How things are in the world is a matter of complete indifference for what is higher. God does not reveal himself *in* the world" (TLP §6.432). "What cannot be said can only be shown, not said." Thus, ethics can only be shown, perhaps through actions and the course of events. "And so it is impossible for there to be propositions of ethics" (TLP §6.42).

Although ignoring his statement of remorse cited above and other things he said about the "higher" and the "mystical," Wittgenstein's early thought was ardently accepted by members of the Vienna Circle, a group of philosophers and scientists meeting regularly in Vienna, led by Moritz Schlick. A.J. Ayer, a British visitor who attended some of these meetings, wrote a brief treatise attempting to summarize the thinking of this group. Its title was *Language, Truth and Logic* (1946). In this book, Ayer also devoted a chapter to ethical discourse, in which he related many of the ideas we have been discussing in this present chapter. Moral propositions, Ayer argued, are not empirical propositions, which can be known to be true or false by observations. Nor are they a priori propositions, which can be shown to be necessarily true or false by means of truth tables. Thus, he concluded, they are meaningless propositions, nonsense utterances used simply to express the speaker's feelings. This startling conclusion was adopted by many English-speaking thinkers, and dismissed with contempt by many others. Neither true nor false, ethical discourse, many began to think, falls outside the realm of meaningful speech.

It was Wittgenstein himself who overturned this new, positivistic, verificationist way of thinking. Soon after returning to Cambridge and philosophy in 1929, he began to rethink the views about the nature of language and its relation to the world that he had earlier propounded in the *Tractatus*. No longer identifying naming as the quintessential function of language or thinking of propositions as being essentially pictures of facts in the world, he began to stress the multiplicity of linguistic uses and to conceive of propositions as having radically different forms and logic. His authorized statement of his later-period thought has been posthumously edited as *Philosophical Investigations*. For later Wittgenstein, ostensive definition, as traditionally conceived, is no longer the only way in which *language* is tied to the world. Rather, language must be conceived as constituted by *language-games*, distinctive forms of rule-governed behavior with a variety of criteria for the appropriate or inappropriate, true or false, permissible or impermissible uses of language. These rules, in turn, are what constitute the *grammar* of language and specific kinds of language-game. Moreover, these language-games are incorporated into a multiplicity of linguistic practices, and it is only these practices that manifest the rules of grammar. The actual uses of words in specific language-games identify the conditions of appropriate or inappropriate application of these words, and of the sentences and utterances in the context of which they function. Language is a *human* activity, and its rules are human artifacts that no longer reflect the logical structure of the world, a relation that would be capable of verification or falsification by comparison to the logical structure of this world. On the contrary, grammar is *autonomous* (viz., just as much as human beings are).

This new conception of language immediately led many philosophers, who were uncomfortable with the idea that ethical, aesthetic, and religious discourse were just nonsense, to consider the possibility that judgments in these areas might not be used to state empirical facts about the ethical, aesthetic, or religious dimensions of the world. They might not have a fact-stating role at all, but rather a different use in distinctive human practices governed by *sui generis* grammatical rules. A.J. Ayer had already hinted at one such possibility when he identified ethical judgments as expressing personal feelings. Saying that lying is wrong, he wrote, might be tantamount to saying something like "Lying, boo!". Such an expression is not true or false, but *neither* is it nonsense.

Ayer's analysis was thought by some observers to be on the right track, but, as it stands, a bit primitive. The American philosopher Charles Stevenson developed a more sophisticated form of emotivism in his *Ethics and Language* (1944). Stevenson was intrigued by how much moral disagreement occurs in our moral discourse and why these disagreements so often go unresolved. If, as many naturalistic philosophers had maintained, moral terms refer to natural properties detectable by scientific methods, the moral judgments containing them should be open to empirical verification or falsification. But, in fact, this sort of confirmation does not often occur. Stevenson was also impressed by the fact that moral disagreements and arguments are highly dynamic affairs – the parties to the disputes are trying, it appears, not just to get their opponents to believe something different, but to *feel* and *act* differently. This suggested to Stevenson that feelings and attitudes are essentially involved in moral judgments and arguments. Feelings and attitudes, after all, are neither true nor false; and therefore, if they are being expressed and challenged in moral disagreements, there is little surprise in the fact that these disagreements are often not resolved. Stevenson shows how, to his mind, these attitudes and dynamic activities are built into the very meanings of moral terms and judgments. The latter, he maintains, have both emotive and descriptive meaning – they serve to express and evince or evoke attitudes as well as to make descriptive claims. The word "good," for instance, is often used by a person to describe himself as approving of some object or action, but at the same time it is used dynamically to *express* the speaker's "pro-attitude" toward the object. It is also used to urge someone else to approve of the subject matter as well. Hence, according to Stevenson, "*x* is good" often means something like "I approve of *x*, do so as well."

Stevenson's theory expresses both the influence of Wittgenstein's early thinking on ethics and his later idea that meaning is use and that meaning comes in a variety of forms. Moral judgments are not true or false, but meaning cannot be understood solely in terms of reference and description. The language-games in which we employ moral terms are integrated into our lives and our culture, in which we express and argue about "noncognitive" matters such as attitudes and have disagreements about cognitive matters, including the facts about the states of mind of one another. There are disagreements in attitude as well as disagreements in belief.

One of the implications of Stevenson's arguments was to cast doubt on the notion of validity in moral arguments. A moral argument is designed not so much to *prove* a moral judgment as to *persuade* and provoke agreement in belief and attitude in another person. By virtue of their emotive meaning, the judgments found in moral life are not such that one or more of them must necessarily be true if others are also true – thus the notion of validity does not apply to moral arguments.

This conclusion seemed implausible to the British moral philosopher R.M. Hare, who thought that the moral argumentation often found in moral discourse can be, and is frequently, evaluated and hence found to be good or bad and hence valid or invalid. Hare set out to show how this is possible in his *The Language of Morals* (1952).

Hare implicitly agreed with the later Wittgenstein (and Stevenson) that discourse is not necessarily descriptive. Rather, to say that something is good is to *commend* it, not simply to describe it. And to commend an object is to tell someone to choose it, or, in the case of actions, to *do* one or another of them. Moral judgments therefore serve as utterances akin to prescriptions, and prescriptions are neither true nor false. "You ought to close the door" does not describe some fact but is a way of commanding someone to close the door. Some facts are indeed implied by a moral judgment, facts such as "I want you to close the door" or "I have a pro-attitude toward your closing the door." It follows that these judgments have both an evaluative meaning, expressed by its imperatival nature, and a descriptive meaning that conveys some proposition about the speaker's state of mind (his attitudes, desires, and the like).

But if moral judgments are of this hybrid evaluative/descriptive nature, how can they be true or false and sustain relations of validity among themselves? Hare showed how prescriptions can be logically related. Moral judgments imply universal standards, which are also prescriptive. For instance, "You ought to close the door" might imply the universal principle "Everyone should close the door if requested to do so," which commands everyone to close the door under the specified condition. Hence, we are able to argue for our specific command by generating the following syllogism: (1) "Everyone ought to obey the order to close the door if requested to do so"; (2) "You have been requested to close the door"; (3) "Therefore you ought to close the door." Hare demonstrates how, to his mind, we can justify both premises of this argument and demonstrate its validity.

In this way, Hare can be seen to exemplify Wittgenstein's suggestion that various areas of discourse, such as the moral one, incorporate different uses of language (in Hare's case, the prescriptive use) and how specific forms of rationality are built into these language-games. In this sense, Hare's ethical theorizing, like Stevenson's, illustrates basic ideas of the later Wittgenstein's thought.

Stevenson and Hare, however, are noncognitivists. They do not believe in moral facts, and moral knowledge, if it can be said to exist at all, is of a very distinctive kind. But other philosophers have been influenced by the later Wittgenstein in such a way that they develop *cognitivist* ethical theories. For instance, D.Z. Phillips and H.O. Mounce, both distinguished Wittgenstein scholars, construct a theory in their book *Moral Practices* (1969) that emphasizes Wittgenstein's view that moral discourse is a kind of activity or *practice*, guided by rules that permit the use of moral terms under certain specifiable conditions, i.e., uses that accordingly can be considered true or false when these conditions do or do not hold. In this manner, moral knowledge and moral justification is possible *within* a practice. Phillips and Mounce allow that there may be alternative moral practices, differentiated by the different sets of rule that constitute them. Hence, they argue for a kind of moral relativism. What judgments are true or justified in one moral practice may be quite different from those found in another.

Still a different kind of cognitivism is found in the last chapter of the present author's *Rationalism, Realism, and Relativism* (1989) in which it is argued that the rules of what is often called *common morality* constitute the *only* rules of what is properly called morality. These rules are expressions of what Wittgenstein calls *grammatical statements*. For example, "Lying is wrong" is a grammatical statement defining in part what it means to be moral. Such statements are necessarily true, although they are also *defeasible*. They can be defeated under certain conditions, which can be built into the grammatical statement, e.g., "Lying is wrong unless doing so will save a person's life." These rules cannot be justified or criticized, given what Wittgenstein says about the autonomy of grammar (see Chapter 15, THE AUTONOMY OF GRAMMAR). Any people who do not follow them, who, for instance, frequently engage in lying and see nothing wrong in doing so, are simply not *moral* people (because, due to the grammar of "morality," "moral," etc., it would not be correct to call them "moral"); in other words, they do not participate in the moral language-game or practice of morality.

The ethical potential of Wittgenstein's views can also be made apparent, for instance, by comparing and contrasting them to the intuitionism of W.D. Ross. Obviously, there are substantial differences between the two. Ross believes that we cognize the truth of the principles of *prima facie* duty by an act of mind that he likens to the cognition of the a priori propositions of geometry and arithmetic. Relevant epistemological aspects of Wittgenstein's philosophy of mathematics are far removed from this conception of mathematical knowledge. However, interpreting Ross's principles of *prima facie* duty as grammatical statements may allow us to draw a connection between Ross and Wittgenstein. If, for instance, "one's *prima facie* duty is to tell the truth" is a grammatical statement, then it possesses a form of necessity – grammatical necessity, not logical in the sense specified by formal logic – that is not possessed by contingent, empirical moral propositions like "Mr X did something he ought not to do." Furthermore, in saying that the duty to tell the truth is a *prima facie* one, one is acknowledging that the duty to tell the truth can be overridden, such as in instances in which telling the truth would result in the death of a person. In vocabulary that has aptly been used to characterize Wittgenstein's idea of criteria, it is *defeasible*. As grammatical statements, the principles of *prima facie* duty *define* what it means to be moral. They tell us what it means to *speak* of someone being a moral person or a situation being of a moral kind. (See Arrington 2002 for further discussion.)

Finally, I shall comment briefly on the only passage in *Philosophical Investigations* in which Wittgenstein has something explicitly to say about ethical concepts. In PI §77, he discusses concepts that have no clear lines of distinction but rather "shade into one another." There can be no clear answer to the question whether a definition of such a concept is right or wrong: "anything and nothing – is right." He goes on in this section to say, "And this is the picture in which, for example, someone finds himself in ethics or aesthetics when he looks for definitions that correspond to our concepts." G.E. Moore began contemporary linguistic ethics when he asked what is good. He denied that the term "good" could be defined, on the grounds that it refers to a simple, indefinable, non-natural moral quality. Wittgenstein agrees that it cannot be defined, but not because of the unique, simple nature of what it supposedly refers to, but because the concept that it expresses has no sharp boundaries. Its various meanings may have a family resemblance to one another, but there is no one quality to which it refers or which would be its meaning. The concept of *right* has no clear meaning, but rather a multiplicity of uses that shade into one another. As he had said in his lecture on ethics, some of these uses indicate an *absolute* sense of "right," while others express a relative sense. And in both categories, there may be a variety of meanings that merely shade into one another. One right may be an absolute obligation, another an action justified only because it indicates the means to achieving a purpose or desire that someone else may not have. Ethics, as its twentieth- and twenty-first-century history clearly shows, is a murky business.

References

Arrington, R.L. (1989). *Rationalism, Realism, and Relativism*. Ithaca: Cornell University Press.
Arrington, R.L. (2002). A Wittgensteinian Approach to Ethical Intuitionism. In P. Stratton-Lake (Ed.). *Ethical Intuitionism: Re-Evaluations* (pp.271–289). Oxford: Oxford University Press.
Ayer, A.J. (1946). *Language, Truth and Logic*. New York: Dover.
Hare, R.M. (1952). *The Language of Morals*. Oxford: Clarendon Press.
Moore, G.E. (1903). *Principia Ethica*. Cambridge: Cambridge University Press.
Mounce, H.O. and Phillips, D.Z. (1969). *Moral Practices*. London: Routledge and Kegan Paul.
Stevenson, C.L. (1944). *Ethics and Language*. New Haven: Yale University Press.

Further Reading

Blackburn, S. (2010). *Practical Tortoise Raising and Other Essays*. Oxford: Oxford University Press.
De Mesel, B. and Thompson, J. (Eds). (2015). *Ethical Perspectives* (Vol. 22, Special Issue): *Wittgensteinian Approaches to Moral Philosophy*.
Glock, H.-J. (1996). *A Wittgenstein Dictionary*. Oxford: Blackwell.
Johnston, P. (1989/2014). *Wittgenstein and Moral Philosophy*. London: Routledge.
Lovibond, S. (1983). *Realism and Imagination in Ethics*. Oxford: Blackwell.
Oberdiek, H. (2009). Wittgenstein's Ethics: Boundaries and Boundary Crossings. In H.-J. Glock and J. Hyman (Eds). *Wittgenstein and Analytic Philosophy: Essays for P.M.S. Hacker* (pp.175–201). Oxford: Oxford University Press.

40

Wittgenstein and Aesthetics

SEVERIN SCHROEDER

Wittgenstein once remarked that while he took some interest in scientific questions, only conceptual and aesthetic questions could really grip him (CV 91). He was passionate about music and literature, and the sporadic aesthetic observations in his notebooks show a profound understanding of these art forms. He tried his hand at drawing and sculpture. For a couple of years he worked as an architect, together with Paul Engelmann, building a house in Vienna for his sister Margaret Stonborough, completed in 1928 (see Wijdeveld, 1993; and Hyman, 2016). In 1933 and again in 1938 he gave some lectures on aesthetics, students' notes of which have since been published. And yet, in Wittgenstein's philosophical writings aesthetics is only ever touched upon in passing.

One of the points that will, I hope, emerge from the following presentation is that the lack of sustained work on philosophical aesthetics in Wittgenstein's writings is not entirely accidental. For on his view, aesthetic issues are not susceptible of an abstract philosophical treatment. They belong to art criticism, rather than philosophy, and what is more, their discussion can only be addressed to an audience sharing a specific cultured taste.

1   Arts et Métiers

In the *Tractatus*, Wittgenstein stated that "Ethics and aesthetics are one and the same" (TLP 6.421), and hence equally ineffable. On this view, works of art can *make manifest* things that cannot be said. In a letter to his friend Paul Engelmann, he comments on the poem *Graf Eberhards Weißdorn* by Ludwig Uhland:

> The poem by Uhland is really magnificent. And this is how it is: if only you do not try to utter what is unutterable then *nothing* gets lost. But the unutterable will be – unutterably – *contained* in what has been uttered. (Letter to Engelmann 9 April 1917)

The claim that something important shows itself, but cannot be put into words, is generously employed in Wittgenstein's early philosophy, but absent from his later writings. He critically reverts to the idea of unutterable contents of works of art or other objects of aesthetic contemplation in the 1930s, in the "Brown Book," and more briefly in *Philosophical Investigations*, introducing a distinction between two kinds of cases in which we employ the terms "understanding," "expression," "meaning," or "says something."

> We speak of understanding a sentence in the sense in which it can be replaced by another which says the same; but also in the sense in which it cannot be replaced by any other. (Any more than one musical theme can be replaced by another.) (PI §531)

My understanding of the French sentence "*Il pleut*," its meaning, what it says, can be spelt out by a paraphrase in English: it means "It's raining." Not so in the case of understanding a theme in music. I may feel equally inclined to say that I know what it means, that I know what it's all about. But when asked "What is it all about?," I should not be able to say (PI §527). This is what Wittgenstein calls *intransitive* understanding (PG 79). We experience something as meaningful, we even seem to grasp the meaning, but we are unable to say what it is (BB 178–9).

Wittgenstein seems to have felt something like this about the poem by Uhland. It appears to have a distinctive meaning *beyond* the story it tells, significant contents that somehow one can grasp, but which cannot be put into words. But as Wittgenstein came to realize, this appearance is illusory. What gives one a peculiar and forceful impression need not for that matter be the bearer of a peculiar message (cf. BB 158).

> The same strange illusion which we are under when we seem to seek the something which a face expresses whereas, in reality, we are giving ourselves up to the features before us – that same illusion possesses us even more strongly if repeating a tune to ourselves and letting it make its full impression on us, we say 'This tune says *something*', and it is as though I had to find *what* it says. And yet I know that it doesn't say anything. (BB 166)

What in such a case we perceive is a specific configuration, something striking, a *Gestalt*. But one paradigm for what is recognizably specific in faces and sounds is what has a specific meaning. A distinctive facial expression is typically the expression of a particular feeling, attitude, or response. So we are naturally inclined to see a distinctive face as expressive *of something* even if as a matter of fact it does not express anything. Again, one paradigm of specific sounds are words that convey a particular message. Thus, musical sounds, being also distinctly organized as a recognizable *Gestalt*, can easily create the illusion of a quasi-linguistic utterance (cf. Z §161). And with verbal art, that effect is even more natural, but also more confusing. In the verbal sphere, a specific impression is normally created by the particular meaning words convey. Hence the specific aesthetic impression we get from a certain arrangement of words, the unique physiognomy of a period or a poem, is easily experienced as an additional poetic meaning, albeit one that we can't articulate.

Even if the ineffable aesthetic contents the young Wittgenstein thought he perceived in the poem by Uhland were an illusion, the phenomenon of intransitive understanding can be real enough. That is to say, it is not only that a striking musical or verbal physiognomy may give us a deceptive feeling of understanding; there can be some real understanding as to why notes or words are organized in some peculiar manner, even where their pattern doesn't represent anything. To understand music is to understand how it develops, how one thing leads to the next, how its parts, with their expressive qualities, relate to each other to make up a coherent whole. Wittgenstein once explained to John King how he didn't understand the ending of Beethoven's String Quartet in C sharp minor, op. 131, as in his perception it didn't seem to fit what went before (Rhees, 1981, pp.69–70). The perception of fit between musical passages that gives us a sense of intransitive understanding is based on familiarity with similar kinds of transition in music, but also on an ability to hear musical transitions as analogous to familiar non-musical movements or gestures, not least verbal ones.

> Why is just *this* the pattern of variation in loudness and tempo? [...] In order to 'explain' I could only compare it with something else which has the same rhythm (I mean the same pattern). (One says "Don't you see, this is as if a conclusion were being drawn" or "This is as it were a parenthesis", etc. [...] (PI §527)

Thus a repeat may be felt to be necessary. Why? "Well, sing it, then you will see that it is only the repeat that gives it its *tremendous* power." Yet this impression is informed by "the rhythm of our language, of our thinking & feeling" (CV 59). Or again, how to explain the apparent necessity with which in the Overture to *Figaro* the second idea succeeds the first? It seems the natural development. What more can one say?

> You could [...] compare the transition to a transition (the entry of a new character) in a story, e.g., or a poem. *That* is how this piece fits into the world of our thoughts & feelings. (CV 65)

What otherwise might appear to be an indescribable impression can be described, and thus made more familiar, by such a comparison. That is what in such a case understanding consists in (LC 37).

2 Belleville

Wittgenstein begins his 1938 "Lectures on Aesthetics" (according to Yorick Smythies's notes) with the remark that the subject of aesthetics is "very big and entirely misunderstood" (LC 1). What he means here by "aesthetics" is not the academic discipline of philosophical aesthetics (to which his lectures contribute), but its subject matter, namely: our aesthetic judgments and reactions, both *vis-à-vis* works of art and everyday objects. (It is clear from other passages and remarks too, that by "aesthetics" Wittgenstein tends to mean specific art and literary criticism, or considerations about other objects of aesthetic interest, rather than a branch of philosophy. For example, "What Aesthetics tries to do [...] is to give *reasons*, e.g. for having this word rather than that in a particular place in a poem, or for having this musical phrase rather than that in a particular place in a piece of music" (M 106). Cf. Johannessen, 2004.) It is probably the inclusion of aesthetic responses to everyday objects that makes the subject bigger than one may at first think it is. It comprises not only art criticism, but also the informed appreciation of clothes, furniture, and other artifacts. In his lectures Wittgenstein discusses the example of tailor-made suits (LC 5).

The fundamental misunderstanding Wittgenstein deplores is one of the nature and status of aesthetic judgments as envisaged by the philosophical tradition. One of the major concerns of modern philosophical aesthetics has been the justification of aesthetic judgments. Both Hume and Kant tried to explain how an aesthetic evaluation could be true or correct, and not just an expression of personal preference. More recently, in the same tradition, attempts have been made to ascertain the truth of some aesthetic judgments by means of scientific psychology, by testing whether the object in question causes pleasure in a suitable class of observers. Wittgenstein's lectures on aesthetics are characterized by his emphatic rejection of this traditional approach to the subject. He is scathing about the very idea of a science of aesthetics (LC 11), not just because its methods are problematic but because the whole project is irrelevant to aesthetics properly understood. From Wittgenstein's point of view, the very attempt to prove – be it by philosophical or psychological means – that aesthetic judgments can be objectively true is misguided.

At the center of Wittgenstein's account of aesthetics lies the notion of a "cultured taste" (LC 8). This need not be a taste in art. One of Wittgenstein's key examples is sartorial: "a person who knows a lot about suits" and is able to tell a tailor exactly which cut, length, and material he thinks right (LC 5–7). A *cultured taste*, or serious aesthetic appreciation, has three characteristics:

(i)   It is informed by an uncommonly detailed knowledge of its subject matter, a keen awareness of particulars and nuances that others might overlook (LC 7).
(ii) It is based on (though not fully determined by) a loose set of conventional rules (LC 5).
(iii) It manifests a certain consistency of judgment (LC 6).

The second characteristic reinforces the first. Knowledge of the conventional rules of prosody will sharpen one's awareness of the details of versification. One acquires the concepts to describe, and hence is far more likely to notice, small metric differences. Similarly, mastery of the rules of musical theory greatly enhances one's perception and understanding of the structural details of a piece of music. And familiarity with the iconographic and representational conventions of a period of painting will make one discern and appreciate more in a painting than is apparent to the untutored eye.

It is important to note that a cultured taste is built on mastery of certain conventional rules, but not exhaustively defined by it. Aesthetic appreciation requires more than knowledge of rules or the ability to apply them in straightforward cases. As a connoisseur, "I develop a feeling for the rules. I interpret the rules" (LC 5). That is to say, my familiarity with the rules – not only with their letter, but also with their spirit – informs my judgments in cases that cannot be adjudicated by mechanical application of rules. In some cases, Wittgenstein suggests, a rule may be more honored in the breach than the observance, for instance, when the perfect regularity of a meter would sound too wooden or monotonous, or when an extra-metrical stress serves to provide some special emphasis that is rhetorically apt.

Whereas Hume and Kant were anxious to free aesthetic judgments as much as possible from the contingencies of their cultural context, Wittgenstein, on the contrary, urges that these contingencies are of paramount importance. Social conventions, fashions, ideological background, and temperamental inclinations should not be regarded as distorting influences, but as the necessary underpinnings of any serious aesthetic appreciation. What gives substance and significance to our appreciation of art, what makes it more than a superficial liking, is the way it is anchored in a specific culture, a way of life defined by its customs and manners, its moral values, its religious and political beliefs. Hence the ideal of a timelessly valid aesthetic judgment, cut loose from all its cultural moorings, doesn't make any sense. Just as the proper appreciation of a bespoke suit is inseparable from the sensitivities of a culture in which suits are worn and seen as a manifestation of social respectability, and where small differences in material, color, and fit are noticed with approval or disapproval. To somebody from a different culture with very different sartorial customs a European three-piece suit may look exotically charming or beautiful, but such a person would be unable seriously to appreciate it (cf. LC 8–9).

Moreover, a cultured taste is hardly ever fully determined by a culture, but also to a large extent shaped by personal inclinations. Two equally knowledgeable connoisseurs of suits can have markedly different tastes: one, according to his temperament, likes an element of panache and daring in his dress, whereas the other prefers a suit to be as discreet as possible. Both their aesthetic judgments are equally respectable, being well informed (i), showing awareness of the relevant rules of fashion (ii), and displaying the consistency required for a taste (iii). Similarly, two people can be equally knowledgeable in their appreciation of Victorian poetry, yet have completely different lists of favorite poems, enjoying rather different aspects of Victorian poetry. And of course there are also much more radical differences among people's aesthetic orientation within the same culture. In our current society we find very different cultured tastes coexisting in each art form, sometimes overlapping, sometimes based on entirely different canons and quite different aesthetic conventions. Thus among serious music lovers you find tastes for classical opera, for contemporary dodecaphonic music, for jazz, or for progressive rock music, etc.

Wittgenstein has no interest whatsoever in adjudicating disagreements between different tastes: "Whenever we get to the point where the question is one of taste, it is no longer aesthetics" (AWL 38). Aesthetics is concerned with questions of right or wrong, correct or incorrect (LC 3) – but only relative to a given cultured taste. Only on the basis of some accepted rules and standards can there be what Wittgenstein calls aesthetics: a concern with art or other things that involves interesting aesthetic questions, explanations, and discussions. The attempt to adjudicate between different tastes, or to give aesthetic evaluations independently of a given cultured taste, is as pointless as the attempt to decide which is better, claret or Darjeeling.

3 Château Rouge

Wittgenstein rejects a psychological approach to aesthetics not only because he is not interested in finding an objective basis for our value judgments, but also because he is opposed to the idea that an object's aesthetic value lies in its positive psychological effects on an audience. The attraction of locating the value of something in its likely psychological effects, in the pleasure or enjoyment it is able to give us, is that it promises to make the most heterogeneous things commensurable. We *could* after all decide on a ranking of claret and Darjeeling (or even of claret and ice-skating), if only we could measure the pleasure they are able to afford us. And there would be nothing obscure or controversial about the value of a work of art once it was cashed out in terms of consumers' pleasure.

However, it is an illusion to think that just because we can use the same word "pleasure" with respect to claret, Darjeeling, and ice-skating, or indeed opera and motherhood, all these experiences involve the same kind of positive feeling, only in different quantities (AWL 37). In fact, the pleasure of claret is of a very different kind from the pleasure of Darjeeling, let alone ice-skating; just as different as claret is from Darjeeling or ice-skating.

Wittgenstein objects to the idea that works of art are instrumentally valuable because of their positive psychological effects. "The work of art does not seek to convey *something else*, just itself" (CV 67). Unlike a tin opener, a car, or an aspirin, a work of art is not to be regarded as a means to an end. Rather, it is appreciated for its own sake. That is not to deny that works of art *can* be, and often are, used as means to an end: as a source of information, as political propaganda, as a status symbol, or as an investment. But such uses are alien to art. Using a work of art in one of those ways is not to use it as a work of art.

There are other things that can be valued either as means to an end or for their own sake. A walk, for example, can serve the purpose of keeping in good health, or to familiarize oneself with the area, or as a convenient setting for a confidential conversation. But some people just enjoy walking with no such end in view. For them going for a walk is an end in itself. One might respond, however, that even such a person values a walk as a means to an end, namely as a means to certain agreeable experiences. And likewise, it might be objected that when we say that we value a work of art for its own sake, that is just a different way of saying that we value the aesthetic experiences that it can afford us.

Undeniably, when we appreciate a work of art we value it as a source of aesthetic experiences. But it would be rash therefore to regard works of art as means to an end. For that would suggest that one *uses* or *employs* a work of art in order to achieve an effect that is logically independent of that application. In that way, one applies a tin opener, thereby causing a tin to be open; and one uses, swallows, a tablet hoping thereby to cause one's headache to go away. Yet there is no such distinction between applying a means and achieving an end in the case of the appreciation of art. Looking at a picture or listening to music does not *cause* an aesthetic experience – it *is* an aesthetic experience. (It is arguable that in some cases, especially with longer narrative art forms, the aesthetic experience lasts much longer than the actual perception or perusal of the work of art (cf. Kivy, 2006), but even then the latter is clearly the core and most intensive part of that experience.)

Moreover, what is merely a means to an end is, at least in principle, replaceable without loss by other means to obtain the same end. Thus, if a work of art were regarded as a means to procuring enjoyable aesthetic experiences, it should be easily replaceable by other works of art of comparable efficacy; just as one good tin opener can without loss be replaced by another. But in fact, our attitude toward works of art is rarely that promiscuous (LC 29, 34). Somebody going to see an exhibition of Dutch still lifes will hardly be content to be shown a ballet instead, or a volume of sonnets, even if they have equally good claims to being enjoyable. That would be like asking for a tin opener and being given a waffle iron; both useful kitchen appliances, no doubt, but accommodating very different culinary interests. The concept of an enjoyable aesthetic experience is far less specific than most people's aesthetic interests most of the time. Hence, to say of a work of art that it is supposed *to afford us valuable aesthetic experiences* is rather like saying of a tin opener that it is *to be useful in the kitchen*. True, but not a specification of the object's value.

Furthermore, not only are the aesthetic experiences produced in us by a painting not equivalent to those produced by a play or a poem, they are also crucially different from those produced by other paintings. Works of art are essentially individual objects whose value lies in their individual characteristics (cf. Strawson, 1974). That is what distinguishes them from functionally defined objects, such as tin openers or cars. The aesthetic experience of listening to a performance of Mozart's *Requiem* is largely determined by the specific characteristics of (the performance of) the piece of music that is its intentional object. A description of my aesthetic experience would be a description of Mozart's *Requiem*, or a particular performance of it, as I perceived it. And this is obviously an experience that could not be produced by any other work (unless my perception was so careless and unschooled that I could not tell the two apart). Therefore, provided that an aesthetic experience of a work of art is appropriately discerning, it is impossible to separate it from the work of art, as if it were the work's aim and logically independent of it (cf. Budd, 1995, p.4). The link between work and experience is not just causal (like that between aspirin and the removal of a headache), but conceptual: one cannot take an interest in the latter without *ipso facto* being interested in the former. Therefore, the truism that our interest in works of art is due to an interest in the aesthetic experiences they promise to afford us is not an objection to the view that we are interested in works of art for their own sake. For the aesthetic experience is essentially an aesthetic experience of the work itself. So, the value of a work of art cannot usefully be explained as its function to produce certain effects.

4 Daumesnil

In his lectures, Wittgenstein speaks of aesthetic reactions and aesthetic explanations. *Aesthetic reactions* are specific criticisms, expressions of a directed discontent, e.g., "This door is too low. Make it higher" (LC 13). They have an intentional object: they are expressions of what one feels *about* an object of aesthetic contemplation; for example, that it is too low. Wittgenstein is concerned that such a directed feeling should not be misconstrued as an undirected feeling plus a causal hypothesis. It is not that I experience a feeling of discomfort, ask myself what produces that feeling, and then hit upon the hypothesis that it is caused by the lowness of the door. Unlike a causal hypothesis, my truthful report that the door looks too low to me is not subject to empirical confirmation or disconfirmation. In particular, it does not commit me to the claim that if the door were higher I would like it better. That may turn out not to be the case (perhaps once the proportions of the door have been rectified something else will bother me even more); and yet the fact remains that the door struck me as too low (cf. Schroeder, 1993).

Here is an example of an aesthetic reaction drawn from an essay by Dr Johnson in which he discourses on "the injury that grand imagery suffers from unsuitable language" (Johnson, 1751, p.88). He illustrates his view with the following passage from *Macbeth*:

> Come, thick night,
> And pall thee in the dunnest smoke of hell,
> That my keen knife see not the wound it makes,
> Nor heaven peep through the blanket of the dark,
> To cry "Hold, hold."
>
> (*Macbeth*, 1.5)

Johnson comments that the force of the poetry is greatly diminished by four inappropriately vulgar words, namely: "dun" ("now seldom heard but in the stable"), "knife" ("the name of an instrument used by butchers and cooks in the meanest employment"), "peep," and "blanket" ("who, without some relaxation of his gravity, can hear of the avengers of guilt *peeping through a blanket?*") (Johnson, 1751, pp. 86–7).

Frank Cioffi cites part of this example (Johnson's censure on the word "knife") in order to contradict Wittgenstein's claim that aesthetic reactions (which Cioffi subsumes under aesthetic explanations) should not be construed as causal explanations. Cioffi comments:

> Isn't it appropriate to protest that no one without an a priori notion of what constitutes permissible poetic diction could have suffered the 'Disturbance of his Attention from the Counteraction of the Words to the Ideas' of which Johnson complained and to support this claim by appealing to the fact that those without such preconceptions, though as familiar as Johnson with the domestic associations of the word knife, and just as capable of picking out the 'low' words, do not undergo such disturbances of the attention? And isn't this an inductive procedure? (Cioffi, 1998, p. 59)

In other words, Cioffi understands Johnson to put forward a causal hypothesis about the effect of "low" words upon readers of Shakespeare. And he submits that Johnson's hypothesis is false: that even readers who are aware of such words' domestic associations will not regard their occurrence in this passage as an aesthetic flaw; or, if they do, it will be due to some prejudice about permissible poetic diction.

It is true that judgments such as Johnson's are often *worded* very much like an empirical generalization about readers' responses; but is that indeed what they are? (In his first lecture on Aesthetics, Wittgenstein remarks that going by the form of words rather than by their use was "the main mistake made by philosophers of the present generation" (LC 2).) Suppose that Johnson was to realize that most readers of *Macbeth* did not mind the use of those household words, would he regard that as a falsification of his judgment? Probably not. He would rather deplore those readers' bad taste: their lack of poetic discrimination – which would show that his aesthetic judgment was not intended as an empirical generalization.

Of course Johnson has some preconceived ideas "of what constitutes permissible poetic diction." But far from being a deplorable prejudice, such preconceived ideas constitute what Wittgenstein calls a cultured taste. Needless to say, different centuries have different cultured tastes. So it is not at all surprising that Cioffi doesn't share Johnson's eighteenth-century reaction to "low" words in tragedy (cf. Schroeder, 1993, pp. 274–5).

5   Église d'Auteuil

Aesthetic explanations are answers to particular aesthetic puzzles, that is, puzzles about the effects a work of art has on us (LC 28). We are uneasy or unclear about a specific aesthetic impression and are looking for a satisfactory explanation or expression of it. In this case it seems harder to follow Wittgenstein in denying that there is room for causal investigations in aesthetics. Suppose looking at a façade, to begin with I just feel vaguely dissatisfied with it, before I realize that what is wrong with it is that the door is too low. In this context my complaint that the door was too low would not only be an aesthetic *reaction*, but also an aesthetic *explanation* of my previous impression that there was something wrong. And as such it would appear to be a causal hypothesis (cf. Budd, 2008, p. 269). But appearances here are somewhat misleading. It may well be true that it was the insufficient height of the door that caused my initial discontent, but when eventually I realize that the door is too low, this observation is not put forward as a hypothesis. For again, it will have the status of an aesthetic reaction, an avowal of my impression whose truth is guaranteed by my truthfulness. If we assume that my initial discontent was not in fact due to the lowness of the door (but, let us say, caused by a subconscious association with some personal memories), that will in no way invalidate my eventual observation that the door is too low. The point is that when I am looking for an explanation of my vague initial impression, that is because I am not satisfied with it. My explanatory aim is to clarify and sharpen it, that is, to replace an inchoate impression by a clear and precise one. The latter will in some cases also provide a causal explanation of the former, but that is only a side effect. My main concern is a better understanding, an enhanced appreciation of the object in question; not so much a better understanding of the early stages of my own imperfect understanding.

However, aesthetic explanations are not only concerned with sharpening inchoate first impressions by identifying crucial details to which we attribute the effect in question. Sometimes what we are unclear about is not so much *which* specific details of an object are responsible for its effect on us, but rather *why* those details should impress us in that way. Wittgenstein is particularly interested in the way aesthetic puzzlement can be cured by peculiar kinds of comparisons or by synoptic representations of relevant variations (LC 20, 29). The only criterion of correctness of such an aesthetic explanation is that it satisfies me; that it removes my puzzlement or disquiet about the impression in question (LC 18–19).

Another discussion of a passage in *Macbeth* provides a useful example of an *aesthetic puzzle* and its resolution by an *aesthetic explanation* (in Wittgenstein's sense of the term). It is from Thomas De Quincey's famous essay "On the Knocking at the Gate in *Macbeth*" (1823):

> From my boyish days I had always felt a great perplexity on one point in *Macbeth*. It was this: the knocking at the gate, which succeeds to the murder of Duncan, produced to my feelings an effect for which I never could account. The effect was, that it reflected back upon the murder a peculiar awfulness and a depth of solemnity; yet, however obstinately I endeavoured with my understanding to comprehend this, for many years I never could see *why* it should produce such an effect. (De Quincey, 1823, p.81)

Again, Wittgenstein would emphasize that no causal, psychological investigation can resolve this kind of puzzle. For one thing, psychological experiments trying to establish the psychological effects of certain kinds of experiences need to be made on a number of subjects (LC 21); but De Quincey is not concerned with the way people *generally* respond to this element in the play. For all he knows, he may be the only one on whom the knocking at the gate has such a powerful effect. Admittedly, that is unlikely. Those who share De Quincey's general aesthetic outlook will be likely to share many of his aesthetic responses, including those of perplexity; or at least it will be possible to communicate to them a sense of such a puzzlement and thus make them share it. Still, it is not unconceivable that some such aesthetic puzzlements may be idiosyncratic; and anyway, for resolving such a perplexity it is quite immaterial whether others share it or not.

Of course there are also causal explanations that concern only one person. For instance, I may want to know why a certain kind of food gives me a headache. A causal explanation of such an allergic reaction doesn't require that anybody else suffers from the same allergy. In such a case, a causal investigation would try to identify the ingredient that triggered my reaction and the general causal laws according to which it comes about. Both the causally active ingredient of the food and the physiological processes it triggers would originally be unknown to me. Thus research into this causal link would have to discover new facts underlying the explanandum and show them to be instances of general laws.

De Quincey's problem is rather different. He doesn't want to discover new, hidden, details of the play, but only arrange the known phenomena in a way that highlights certain aspects. Most importantly, a successful explanation in this case will not depend on general causal laws, which need to be objectively established, but merely on De Quincey's subjective satisfaction. He is looking for a redescription of the relevant phenomena that will make his reaction appear reasonable, or less puzzling, to him. (Cf. M 106: "Reasons [...] in Aesthetics, are 'of the nature of further descriptions.'") Thus, a crucial feature of this kind of explanation, that sets it apart from causal explanations, is that what seems right to the subject *is* right. The correct explanation is the one that satisfies me, that dissolves my sense of puzzlement (LC 18–19).

This is the explanation that satisfied De Quincey:

We were to be made to feel that [during the scenes of the murder] the human nature, i.e. the divine nature of love and mercy, spread through the hearts of all creatures, and seldom utterly withdrawn from man – was gone, vanished, extinct; and that the fiendish nature had taken its place. [...] The murderers and the murder must be insulated – cut off by an immeasurable gulf from the ordinary tide and succession of human affairs [...]. Hence it is, that when the deed is done, when the work of darkness is perfect, then the world of darkness passes away like a pageantry in the clouds: the knocking at the gate is heard; and it makes known audibly that the reaction has commenced; the human has made its reflux upon the fiendish; the pulses of life are beginning to beat again; and the re-establishment of the goings-on of the world in which we live first makes us profoundly sensible of the awful parenthesis that has suspended them. (De Quincey, 1823, pp.84–5)

Another feature of aesthetic puzzlement that Wittgenstein stresses is that it is often cured by *comparisons*: between the impression (or what makes the impression) in question and other, perhaps more familiar phenomena (LC 20). Again, De Quincey's discussion fits the bill. His solution of the puzzle of the aesthetic effect of the knocking at the gate is further elaborated by the following analogy:

if the reader has ever been present in a vast metropolis, on the day when some great national idol was carried in funeral pomp to his grave, and, chancing to walk near the course through which it passed, has felt powerfully in the silence and desertion of the streets, and in the stagnation of ordinary business, the deep interest which at that moment was possessing the heart of man – if all at once he should hear the death-like stillness broken up by the sound of wheels rattling away from the scene, and making known that the transitory vision was dissolved, he will be aware that at no moment was his sense of the complete suspension and pause in ordinary human concerns so full and affecting, as at that moment when the suspension ceases, and the goings-on of human life are suddenly resumed. (De Quincey, 1823, pp.84–5)

Being reminded of this experience from an entirely different area, we will, if we can see the similarity, find our impression of the knocking in *Macbeth* less odd, more familiar and understandable. The discovery of a persuasive comparison can remove from a phenomenon its disquieting appearance of uniqueness and anomaly (cf. RPP I §1000).

6 Faidherbe Chaligny

Wittgensteinian aesthetic explanations are not only employed to spot flaws or to resolve puzzles. Sometimes the *explanandum* may simply be a striking aesthetic experience that we strive to understand better, to bring into fuller consciousness: perhaps something not easily describable that we want to capture by words, thus to clarify our feelings.

Here is a simple example: in Anatole France's novel *Thais*, two characters, one virtuous, one sinful, live in different places, then meet, convert each other, and part again in opposite directions: the sinner goes into a monastery, while the originally virtuous man has become a sinner. E.M. Forster suggests a neat description of the experience of the book's symmetrical form:

> We just have a pleasure without knowing why, and when the pleasure is past, as it is now, and our minds are left free to explain it, a geometrical simile such as an hour glass will be found helpful. (Forster, 1928, p.138)

The book is the shape of an X, or hour glass: reflecting the way the two protagonists' paths converge, cross at the central moment, and diverge in opposite directions.

Other examples of such synoptic aesthetic explanations, that clarify one's experiences by giving them a poignant expression, are several remarks in which Wittgenstein tries to characterize the works of different composers, for instance:

> A Bruckner symphony can be said to have *two* beginnings: the beginning of the first idea & the beginning of the second idea. These two ideas stand to each other not as blood relations, but as man & woman. (CV 39)

7 Grands Boulevards

Sometimes an aesthetic explanation is not at all concerned with explaining or clarifying a *given* initial impression, but only with changing our perception, so as to achieve the right kind of impression. This is the type of aesthetic explanation we give to others in order to teach them how to look at a picture, how to play or hear a musical phrase, how to stress a line of poetry, or what to see as the key idea of a novel.

> What [aesthetics] does is to *draw one's attention* to certain features, to place things side by side so as to exhibit these features. To tell a person "This is the climax" is like saying "This is the man in the puzzle picture". (AWL 38–9)

A simple example of such an explanation is the metric instruction with which Friedrich Gottlieb Klopstock prefaced his odes to show the reader how his verses should be stressed. Wittgenstein describes how following this instruction made all the difference to his appreciation of those poems (LC 4–5).

Another example: one of the poems Boris Pasternak appended to his novel *Doctor Zhivago* is called "Hamlet" and may be taken to provide us with a hint as to how to read the novel: namely as a modern version of *Hamlet*, along the lines of Pasternak's own rather distinctive interpretation of the play (see Schroeder, 1992).

Or again: to somebody inclined to dismiss Bruckner's Ninth Symphony as a feeble imitation of Beethoven's Ninth, Wittgenstein suggests a different perspective:

> Bruckner's Ninth is a sort of *protest* against Beethoven's, and because of this becomes bearable, which as a sort of imitation it would not be. It stands to Beethoven's Ninth very much as Lenau's Faust stands to Goethe's, which means as the Catholic to the Enlightenment Faust. etc. etc. (CV 39)

"Look at it this way!" An aesthetic explanation of this kind is evidently not so much a hypothesis as a suggestion, or invitation, to change one's attitude toward a work of art in a way that is intended to enhance one's appreciation. Some such suggestions will be found almost universally persuasive, but others may appeal only to some people, with similar aesthetic inclinations. In some instances I may find myself unable to see a work as suggested by a critic (e.g., to see a character as more sinned against than sinning); or I may be able to look at it as suggested, but find this perspective rather unsatisfactory (say, contrived, or in conflict with certain other features of the work). To use Wittgenstein's analogy, I may not always be able to see the man in the puzzle picture, and even if I do I may find him clumsily drawn or not well integrated with the rest of the picture.

8   Hôtel de Ville

Finally, I'd like to illustrate one of the key points of Wittgenstein's account of aesthetic explanation by briefly considering a major debate in contemporary philosophical aesthetics, namely how to resolve the so-called Paradox of Tragedy, which was tellingly presented by Hume:

> It seems an unaccountable pleasure, which the spectators of a well-written tragedy receive from sorrow, terror, anxiety, and other passions, that are in themselves disagreeable and uneasy. The more they are touched and affected, the more are they delighted with the spectacle. (Hume, 1741/1985, p.216)

How are we to account for the fact that we *choose* to watch, for entertainment, theatrical or cinematographic representations of acts of violence and suffering, which should be rather painful to watch?

Various answers have been suggested. They can be grouped under three headings, as: (a) hedonic, (b) cognitivist, and (c) therapeutic answers, respectively.

(a) *Hedonic* answers to the Paradox of Tragedy agree with Hume that in spite of those apparently unpleasant elements, watching a tragedy is still a pleasurable experience.
  (i)   Some say that fictionality takes away the sting from otherwise painful scenes.
  (ii) Others have suggested that to the affluent theatregoer any kind of artificial excitement comes as a relief from the boredom of their dreary everyday life.

Related to this (or an extreme version of it), is the Faustian desire to live and feel with greater intensity: to share and undergo, if only imaginatively, *all* kinds of human experiences.

(iii) A common view is that the beauty of artistic representation (poetic language, skillful arrangement of scenes and dialogue, realistic representation of character, admirable performance of actors) can be strong enough to account for our enjoyment, in spite of some disagreeable contents one has to put up with.

(iv) Hume goes one step further: the delights of artistic representation do not only outweigh the unpleasant elements, but change the hedonic coloring of what would otherwise be negative experiences: "the whole impulse of those [negative] passions is converted into pleasure" (Hume, 1741/1985, p.220). Not only do the tragic contents not spoil our enjoyment of language and composition; they even enhance it.

(v) Nietzsche suggests that our pleasure in tragedy is to a large extent due to its displaying an unrealistic eloquence and intellectual brightness in people in extreme adversity, "where life approaches abysses and men in reality usually lose their heads and certainly linguistic felicity" (Nietzsche, [1882] 1991, §80). Hence, the representation of suffering even if not pleasant in itself is seen as a prerequisite of a greatly edifying rhetorical experience, which can help us to understand human suffering (see (b) below), and lends it the dignity it often lacks in real life.

(vi) More recently, Susan Feagin has identified a rather different source of our delight in tragedy. She observes that although our direct responses to the suffering represented are probably unpleasant, we can enjoy our meta-responses: it is pleasing to find that we are able to respond sympathetically to the hero's distress (Feagin, 1983).

(b) *Cognitivists*, by contrast, do not try to argue that watching violence and suffering on stage is an agreeable business. It may indeed be very painful and not at all pleasant, but aesthetic value is not always to be measured in the pleasure it promises. Art can be shocking, disturbing, even painful, and yet worthwhile when it is a source of insight and understanding. What we should expect from a good tragedy is not enjoyment, but insight in aspects of psychology or the human condition. (Nietzsche's view (see (a.v) above) combines a hedonic answer with cognitive elements.)

(c) Finally, there is of course the Aristotelian idea that tragedy has psycho-*therapeutic* value: "through pity and fear tragedy achieves the catharsis of such emotions" (*Poetics*, 6), that is, such disagreeable experiences can be beneficial in the long run by contributing to our mental equilibrium. On one reading of the notoriously problematic term "catharsis," they are beneficial by allowing us to let off a surplus of pent-up negative emotions; on another reading, by cleansing those emotions in us (whatever that is taken to mean).

So, who is right? Which is the correct solution to the Paradox of Tragedy? I think that what Wittgenstein's remarks about aesthetic puzzles and explanations can teach us is that the problem is misconceived and that any attempt to decide which is the correct answer is hopeless. If Wittgenstein is right, aesthetic puzzles are essentially concerned with individual responses to particular works of art. The right explanation is the one that you find resolves *your* puzzlement or satisfies *you*, even though it may not work for me (LC 18, 21). For I may never have experienced the same puzzlement, or even if I did ask the same question, I may not be satisfied by the same kind of answer. In short: aesthetic explanations don't have the generality that current debates in philosophical aesthetics, such as the debate about the Paradox of Tragedy, tend to assume. The question cannot be answered at the level of abstraction at which philosophical debates usually move.

Indeed, at such level of abstraction there is not even a paradox, but only a very common human inclination, namely to be fascinated by tragic accidents and acts of violence. The press coverage given to the details of gruesome murder cases and horrific disasters in tabloid newspapers (and, in some countries, also in broadsheets) is a clear indication that, in general, people relish to read or hear about others' misfortunes. To ask a reader of the *Daily Telegraph* or the *Guardian* why they don't feel distressed by the scenes of violence in *Hamlet* would be daft. If, however, you belong to the minority of people who don't care to read a minute account of how a 32-year-old accountant from Stevenage visited his parents in Slough and killed them both with an axe – then it is far from clear that you will enjoy watching the blinding of Gloucester (in *King Lear*) or the murder of Macduff's wife and children (in *Macbeth*), however much you appreciate the language and the acting. So, again, Hume's problem wouldn't be your problem, since you just don't experience this "unaccountable pleasure"; nor may you find any other aesthetic value in such scenes of extreme violence.

On the other hand, there is nothing wrong with any of those suggested explanations – as long as we understand them to be different people's solutions to *their* respective puzzlement. If Hume finds that scenes that would normally distress him become edifying and a pleasure to watch when skillfully expressed in iambic pentameters – that negative emotions are, so to speak, converted into positive ones by the beauty of language – who can gainsay this account of his aesthetic experiences? And some readers may indeed realize that they had similar experiences, which Hume's picture clarifies to them. Again, Nietzsche's keen enjoyment of occasions "to hear people in the most difficult situations speak well and at length" appeals to *me* as an explanation why I'm happy to watch people in such disagreeable situations, but it would hold little attraction for spectators that insist on naturalistic drama (like the lady described by James Thurber who complains that when Macduff finds Duncan's dead body he says things like: "Confusion has broke open the Lord's anointed temple," whereas, surely, as an innocent man he should rather have said something like "My God, there's a body in here!" (cited in Braunmuller, 1997, p.44)). Or again, if Susan Feagin can truthfully report that for her the distress of watching violent or tragic scenes on stage is outweighed by the self-conscious satisfaction she derives from finding herself able to sympathize with the victims, that is nothing we should quarrel with. At most we can say that that is not anything we have experienced ourselves.

So, in spite of the polemical tone in which these discussions are usually conducted, different authors' solutions to the so-called Paradox of Tragedy should not be seen as contradicting each other. Each presents – like De Quincey – a solution to his or her own aesthetic puzzle; an account of the values of tragedy (or the tragedies this person has in mind) that satisfies *him*, and perhaps people with similar tastes and sensitivities, but certainly not everybody. To expect that we should find a generally and objectively true solution to the Paradox of Tragedy is a misunderstanding of the nature of aesthetic problems. Frank Cioffi puts it nicely when he says about the kind of clarificatory, non-causal, remarks that Wittgenstein commends in his discussions of Freud and Frazer, but also in his lectures on aesthetics: "we must mentally prefix them with the salutation, 'To whom it may concern'" (Cioffi, 1998, p.18).

References

Braunmuller, A.R. (Ed.). (1997). *The New Cambridge Shakespeare: Macbeth*. Cambridge: Cambridge University Press.
Budd, M. (1995). *Values of Art*. London: Allen Lane.
Budd, M. (2008). Wittgenstein on Aesthetics. In M. Budd. *Aesthetic Essays* (pp.252–277). Oxford: Oxford University Press.
Cioffi, F. (1998). *Wittgenstein on Freud and Frazer*. Cambridge: Cambridge University Press.
De Quincey, Th. (1823). On the Knocking at the Gate in *Macbeth*. In Th. De Quincey (1985). *Confessions of an English Opium-Eater* (pp.81–86). Ed. G. Lindop. Oxford: Oxford University Press.
Feagin, F. (1983). The Pleasures of Tragedy. *American Philosophical Quarterly*, 20, 95–104.
Forster, E.M. (1928). *Aspects of the Novel*. London: Arnold.
Hume, D. (1741/1985). Of Tragedy. In E.F. Miller (Ed.). *Essays Moral, Political and Literary* (pp.216–225). Indianapolis: Liberty Fund.
Hyman, J. (2016). The Urn and the Chamber Pot. In S.S. Grève and J. Mácha (Eds). *Wittgenstein and the Creativity of Language* (pp.198–218). London: Palgrave Macmillan.
Johannessen, K.S. (2004). Wittgenstein and the Aesthetic Domain. In P. Lewis (Ed.). *Wittgenstein, Aesthetics and Philosophy* (pp.11–36). Aldershot: Ashgate.
Johnson, S. (1751). The Rambler. Reprinted in R.W. Desai (Ed.). (1997). *Johnson on Shakespeare* (pp.85–88). London: Sangam.
Kivy, P. (2006). *The Performance of Reading*. Oxford: Blackwell.
Nietzsche, F. ([1882] 1991). *The Gay Science*. Trans. W. Kaufmann. New York: Random House. (Original work published 1882.)
Rhees, R. (Ed.). (1981). *Recollections of Wittgenstein*. Oxford: Oxford University Press.
Schroeder, S. (1992). Hamlet als Messias: Eine Sinnlinie durch Pasternaks *Doktor Živago*. [Hamlet as Messiah: One Strand of Sense in Pasternak's *Doctor Zhivago*.] *Russian Literature*, 31, 71–98.
Schroeder, S. (1993). "Too Low!": Frank Cioffi on Wittgenstein's *Lectures on Aesthetics*. *Philosophical Investigations*, 16, 261–279.
Strawson, P.F. (1974). Aesthetic Appraisal and Works of Art. In P.F. Strwawson. *Freedom and Resentment and other Essays* (pp.178–188). London: Methuen.
Wijdeveld, P. (1993). *Ludwig Wittgenstein: Architect*. Amsterdam: Pepin Press.

Further Reading

Allen, R. and Turvey, M. (Eds). (2001). *Wittgenstein, Theory and the Arts*. London: Routledge. [A useful collection of articles on Wittgenstein, theory, and the arts.]
Rowe, M.R. (2004). Criticism without Theory. In P. Lewis (Ed.). *Wittgenstein, Aesthetics and Philosophy* (pp.73–93). Aldershot: Ashgate. [An illuminating further discussion of aesthetic explanations that try to change one's perception of a work of art.]
Sharpe, R.A. (2004). Wittgenstein's Music. In P. Lewis (Ed.). *Wittgenstein, Aesthetics and Philosophy* (pp.137–150). Aldershot: Ashgate. [An insightful discussion of Wittgenstein's thoughts about music.]

41

Wittgenstein and Anthropology

BRIAN R. CLACK

Wittgenstein's views concerning anthropology emerge predominantly from his notes on Sir James Frazer's *The Golden Bough*, and have as their focus the interpretation of ritual phenomena and the nature of anthropological explanation. His words on this subject are fragmentary and were not intended for publication – they were published posthumously as "Remarks on Frazer's *Golden Bough*." But the philosophical community has not ignored them. By contrast, they have had little impact on those working in the field of social anthropology. The anthropologist Rodney Needham, indeed, while lauding Wittgenstein's notes as one of the two "most radically instructive sources for the critical comprehension of ritual" (Needham, 1985, p.8), laments that Wittgenstein has had "scarcely any effect on the practice of the great majority of social anthropologists" (Needham, 1985, p.149). There are signs, however, that this may be changing (see James, 2005; Tambiah, 1990, pp.54–64). I shall begin by describing the theories and explanatory methods of Frazer before turning to Wittgenstein's critique of *The Golden Bough* and making an assessment of the significance of his contribution to anthropological discussions.

1 Intellectualism

The nominal purpose of *The Golden Bough* is to explain a peculiar ritual of classical antiquity, namely the rule regulating the succession to the priesthood at Nemi, Italy. But it extends well beyond this one task, and a complete theory of magic and religion is articulated within its copious pages. This theory is of the kind known as *intellectualism* and consists of two central contentions: that magic and religion emerged as explanatory theories of the natural world and its workings; and that these theoretical systems gave rise to rituals, conceived as instrumental actions, attempts to influence the course of natural events. According to the intellectualist approach, therefore, the foundation of religion (as well as of magic) is theoretical and speculative, with ritual actions being practical applications of that underlying intellectual theory.

A Companion to Wittgenstein, First Edition. Edited by Hans-Johann Glock and John Hyman.
© 2017 John Wiley & Sons, Ltd. Published 2017 by John Wiley & Sons, Ltd.

Magic (regarded by Frazer as the earliest of humanity's philosophies of life) arose when primitive human beings attempted to understand the world around them. The result of this primitive philosophizing was the production of what Frazer terms "theoretical magic," a system of belief based upon the positing of two laws: the law of homoeopathy and the law of contiguity, laws which can be manipulated to produce desired results. The first of these laws states that "like produces like," while the contention of the second is that "things which have once been in contact with each other continue to act on each other at a distance after the physical contact has been severed" (Frazer, 1922, p.11). When applied, these laws yield practical magic, a technique employed by primitives in their attempts to bend the will of nature to their own advantage. The practical form of the first law is homoeopathic magic, examples of which are numerous. To take the classic cases, the death of an enemy may be brought about by damaging or destroying a small likeness of the intended victim, while sprinkling a small amount of water on the ground is believed to produce rain. Such is the character of homoeopathic magic as Frazer presents it: desired events are to be produced by acts of imitation. Though such desires are perfectly reasonable, the methods used to achieve them suffer from one fatal flaw: they are completely futile. An imitation of a desired outcome cannot by itself produce that outcome. And it is important to emphasize this point: magic is, for Frazer, in essence an *error*.

Despite the presence of what John Skorupski (1976, p.5) calls "blocks to falsifiability" within the magical system (the inevitable appearance some day of the desired event, for instance), the flaws in magic are ultimately discovered, leading to its abandonment and the formulation in its place of a rival philosophy of life: religion. Instead of the impersonal manipulable laws hypothesized by magic, religion posits the existence of powerful supernatural beings – gods – who are responsible for the way the world operates, and to whom believers may appeal for assistance in their struggle with life's vicissitudes. The dawn of religion, therefore, brings not just a new theoretical structure (gods replacing impersonal laws) but also a new practical technique (supplications replacing spells). As with magic, however, flaws in the religious system are inevitably detected – prayer, for example, fails to yield concrete results – and it is replaced by a far more effective theory of life, namely, science. Frazer thus puts forward a vision of the progressive development of human beings in society, one in which the human mind moves from magic through religion to science, the history of civilization being a story of humankind's scientific liberation from superstitious ignorance.

2 Understanding Ceremonial Actions

There is much that Wittgenstein objects to in Frazer's presentation of the ritual life of humankind. A principal objection is that it is wrong to conceive of magical acts as being in the nature of errors. Frazer had contended that magic was something operating, as it were, *in lieu of science* and in the absence of adequate technology: it was "the bastard sister of science" (Frazer, 1922, p.50). Wittgenstein, contrariwise, warns us against presuming that primitives engage in magic because they lack adequate technological expertise: "The same savage, who stabs the picture of his enemy apparently in order to kill him, really builds his hut out of wood and carves his arrow skillfully and not in effigy" (GB 125). The remark is incisive, indicating the co-presence of magic and technology within a primitive society. Magic need not, then, be regarded as a (poor) substitute for technical proficiency, but rather as something that exists alongside it. Hence:

> One could begin a book on anthropology by saying: When one examines the life and behavior of mankind throughout the world, one sees that, except for what might be called animal activities, such as ingestion, etc., etc., etc., men also perform actions which bear a characteristic peculiar to themselves, and these could be called ritualistic actions. (GB 129)

Frazer, according to Wittgenstein, had not paid sufficient attention to this "peculiar characteristic," presenting all actions as being fundamentally *instrumental* in nature, and this failure to recognize the distinctive character of ceremonial actions is what Wittgenstein seeks to correct.

It is commonly thought that Wittgenstein wishes to replace Frazer's instrumental account of ritual with an *expressive* alternative, this expressive quality constituting precisely ritual's "peculiar characteristic." Many accounts of the "Remarks on Frazer" advance such a view (for representative examples, see Bell, 1984; Cook, 1983; Rudich and Stassen, 1971). An expressivist account of magic will deny that ceremonial actions are intended to effect some desired change in the natural world, and will instead envisage them as expressive of desires, feelings, and values. One of Wittgenstein's critical comments regarding Frazer's presentation of homeopathic magic seems to admit of just such an expressive interpretation:

> Burning in effigy. Kissing the picture of one's beloved. That is *obviously not* based on the belief that it will have some specific effect on the object which the picture represents. It aims at satisfaction and achieves it. Or rather: it *aims* at nothing at all; we just behave this way and then we feel satisfied. (GB 123)

It is easy enough to read this passage in an expressivist fashion. Destroying ceremonially the image of an enemy need no more be an attempt to influence the course of events than the analogous act of kissing a photograph of one's beloved. In this latter case, the action is best seen simply as an expression of love, and may thus provide the key to understanding the primitive ritual action, namely as an expression both of hatred and of the desire that the enemy really should pass away. Armed with this insight, an investigator may come to see the entirety of ceremonial behavior as expressive rather than instrumental: a rain dance is the expression of hope that rain may soon arrive; a planting ritual is the expression of the desire that the subsequent harvest be plentiful; and so on. In this light, ceremonial actions can be regarded as constituting a kind of language, a way of saying and expressing ideas and states of mind. Nowhere is this stated more succinctly than in Wittgenstein's declaration that "magic brings a wish to representation; it expresses a wish" (GB 125).

I have argued elsewhere (see Clack, 1996) that the expressivist interpretation flows from a view of the nature and function of language that is roundly rejected by Wittgenstein, and, accordingly, that he cannot straightforwardly be advancing such an account of ceremonial behavior and belief. The contention of that argument is that Wittgenstein's mature philosophy undermines the descriptive–nondescriptive, cognitive–noncognitive, and belief–attitude distinctions upon which expressivism rests. But even if we restrict ourselves to a consideration of his explicit engagement with Frazer, we find much that does not sit easily with expressivism. It is true that Wittgenstein often seems to seek to replace an instrumental reading of some ritual with one stressing expressive significance (for example, "toward morning, when the sun is about to rise, rites of daybreak are celebrated by the people, but not during the night, when they simply burn lamps" (GB 137)), but any neatly uniform expressivist view is compromised by comments such as the following:

> People at one time thought it useful to kill a man, sacrifice him to the god of fertility, in order to produce good crops. (AWL 33)

> There are dangers connected with eating and drinking, not only for savages, but also for us; nothing is more natural than the desire to protect oneself from these. (GB 127)

> When a man laughs too much in our company (or at least in mine), I half-involuntarily compress my lips, as if I believed I could thereby keep his closed. (GB 141)

In each of these cases, Wittgenstein lays an emphasis on goals sought, human sacrifice, for instance, being explained in terms of what people once thought regarding its usefulness in securing success at harvest time. But evidently an account of that kind does not run counter to the explanations advanced by Frazer, and we thus appear to be left with a puzzle: how can we resolve the apparent co-presence of expressivism and instrumentalism within Wittgenstein's critique of *The Golden Bough*?

There are several ways in which this tension might be removed. Firstly (and this, of course, would be entirely in keeping with the spirit of his philosophical enterprise), Wittgenstein may be eschewing *any* kind of generalized account of magic, either instrumental or expressive, in favor of focusing instead on the motley and varied character of ceremonial acts. Hence, the same judgment might be offered in respect of ritual actions as that given regarding language: "These phenomena have no one thing in common which makes us use the same word for all" (PI §65). Frazer's confusion, on this view, would not be that he explained *some particular rite* in instrumental terms, but rather that he supplied instrumental explanations in *all* cases. Frazer's fault, therefore, would lie in his essentialism, in the "craving for generality" (BB 17) leading him to seek to isolate the distinctively common element in all ceremonial actions. Wittgenstein would not then be replacing an instrumentalist account with an expressivist one, but simply recommending that an interpreter *look and see* what is going on in a specific rite, preserving the uniqueness and particularity of that instance. For, the field of ritual practices is *highly diverse*, some rites seeking changes in the natural world, others cementing social ties, still others evincing anxious hopes, and so on.

A second way of removing the aforementioned tension would be to stress that Wittgenstein is not setting out to correct an instrumental conception of ritual at all, but instead has his sights set on a rather different matter: the role of ratiocination in the production of rituals. According to the intellectualist tradition, ceremonial actions are practical applications of an earlier-established theory of the workings of nature, and hence are products of a process of reasoning. This is a contention consistently opposed by Wittgenstein:

> When, for example, [Frazer] explains to us that the king must be killed in his prime, because the savages believe that otherwise his soul would not be kept fresh, all one can say is: where that practice and these views occur together, the practice does not spring from the view, but they are both just there. (GB 119)

I believe that the characteristic feature of primitive man is that he does not act from *opinions* (contrary to Frazer). (GB 137)

It would be wrong to think that Wittgenstein in this latter remark is drawing a distinction between the "savage" and the "civilized" mind. Rather, he should, firstly, be thought of as making a judgment about the basis of ritual action (it does not spring from any opinion); and, secondly, his consideration of the non-opinionated nature of ritual should be seen in the context of his later desire to "regard man [...] as an animal; as a primitive being to which one grants instinct but not ratiocination" (OC §475). It is, of course, characteristic of Wittgenstein's later philosophy that he seeks to undermine an overly rationalistic conception of human agency and behavior (something seen clearly in his work both on "primitive reactions" (see Z §§540–5) and on our "intuitive awareness" of cause and effect (see CE)), and it may be that his consideration of the nature of ritual behavior helped to form this anti-rationalistic perspective.

Approached in such a manner, one begins to see each of Wittgenstein's reflections on specific rituals as doing something other than advancing either an expressive or an instrumental case. Hence, the remark considered earlier, comparing effigy-burning with picture-kissing, has as its purpose, not the substitution of an expressive rationale for an instrumental one, but rather an attack upon the intellectualist notion that such acts are rooted in a theory concerning causal connections. Kissing a picture, Wittgenstein claims, is "obviously *not based on a belief* that it will have a definite effect" (emphasis added), and it springs from no reasoning about the connection between the picture and the person pictured. Likewise, the emphasis of the lip-compressing example, as cited earlier, should fall on the "half-involuntary" nature of the act. These thoughts are evidently to the fore in one of Wittgenstein's most dramatic suggestions concerning ritual actions:

When I am furious about something, I sometimes beat the ground or a tree with my walking stick. But I certainly do not believe that the ground is to blame or that my beating can help anything. "I am venting my anger". And all rites are of this kind. Such actions may be called Instinct-actions. (GB 137)

Frank Cioffi is correct in regarding this remark as "dismally opinionated" and "profoundly un-Wittgensteinian" (Cioffi, 1990, p.43), for it appears to violate the nonessentialist requirements demanded both by Wittgenstein's philosophizing in general and by his thoughts about ritual in particular. Its exaggerated character does, however, have the virtue of bringing into clear light what remains somewhat shrouded in the "Remarks," namely that Wittgenstein wishes to emphasize, against the intellectualism of Frazer, the spontaneous, non-ratiocinated nature of (at least a great many) ceremonial actions. The suggestion that rituals are somehow spontaneous would seem to be refuted by the fact that their forms are meticulously prescribed, as well as by the fact that they have to be learned. Rather than denying this, Wittgenstein's claim would appear to be that, however rule-governed and carefully constructed a ritual may be, its form "would only be a later extension of instinct" (GB 151). The bedrock of ritual activity is held to be located in instinctual, spontaneous actions, rather than in ratiocination, as the intellectualist thinks.

A third tension-removing strategy would be controversial and might yet prove to be fruitful. Wittgenstein, recall, contends that magic "expresses a wish." Held captive by the pervasive instrumental–expressive dichotomy, a reader of that particular remark will tend to emphasize the word "expresses" and thereby arrive at the familiar judgment that Wittgenstein is advancing an expressivist conception of ritual. If, however, the word "wish" is emphasized, something rather different happens. Wittgenstein would now appear to be suggesting that the vital component of magical rites is that they are representations of wishes. This, interestingly, allows us to draw a connection between Wittgenstein's account of magic and that advanced by Freud in *Totem and Taboo*.

Freud's account of the nature of magic and religion is multifaceted, but at the heart of his analysis lies the *wish*: "It is easy to perceive the motives which lead men to practise magic: they are human wishes" (Freud, [1913] 1955, p.83). Ritual beliefs and practices, for Freud, give representation to wishes that have been left unsatisfied by reality. This, coupled with the primitive's sense of the omnipotence of his wishful thoughts, leads to the peculiar character of homoeopathic magic: the linking of an *imitation* of a desired state of affairs with the *attainment* of that state of affairs. Contrary to intellectualism, the Freudian view does not see magic as the product of ratiocination, but as the natural outpouring of "primary process" thought, governed by wishes and hallucinatory fulfillment (see Freud, [1911] 1958).

Much in Wittgenstein's account coheres with this Freudian view: the non-ratiocinative basis of ritual belief and practice; the claim that satisfaction ensues from merely imitative acts (such as kissing a photograph); the unearthing of the wishful basis of magic; and even the detection that the magician views his thoughts as having immense power: "With the magical healing of an illness, one *directs* the illness to leave the patient" (GB 129). The contribution this connection with Freud makes to the resolving of the instrumental–expressive tension is clear: an action can be expressive of a wish and yet *simultaneously* be felt to effect some change in the external world. Hence the expressive and the instrumental are here nonexclusive. Exploration of the connections between Wittgenstein and Freud on this matter would be worthwhile. It would further deepen our dawning realization of the influence on Wittgenstein of psychoanalytic thought (see Baker, 2004, pp.143–222; BT 644; and Chapter 43, WITTGENSTEIN AND PSYCHOANALYSIS), and help to clarify Wittgenstein's striking characterization of himself as "a disciple of Freud" (LC 41).

3 Anthropological Method

In addition to criticizing Frazer's interpretation of ritual phenomena, Wittgenstein also appears to make a number of corrective suggestions regarding the methodology appropriate for anthropological investigations. Curiously, he suggests that Frazer is wrong, not just regarding the particularities of the intellectualist explanations he offers for the existence of ritual practices, but in offering *any* explanation at all. What he seems to think preferable to explanation is an entirely descriptive approach, revolving around the notion of "perspicuous representation" (*übersichtliche Darstellung*), itself a key element of Wittgenstein's later philosophical methodology (see Chapter 16, SURVEYABILITY).

The eschewal of explanation and the corresponding recommendation of description can be seen in the following selection of remarks:

> The very idea of wanting to explain a practice – for example, the killing of the priest-king – seems wrong to me. (GB 119)

> I believe that the attempt to find an explanation is already therefore wrong, because one must only correctly piece together what one *knows*, without adding anything, and the satisfaction being sought through the explanation follows of itself. (GB 121)

> Here one can only *describe* and say: this is what human life is like. (GB 121)

> "And so the chorus points to a secret law" one feels like saying to Frazer's collection of facts. I *can* represent this law, this idea, by means of an evolutionary hypothesis, or also, analogously to the schema of a plant, by means of the schema of a religious ceremony, but also by means of the arrangement of its factual content alone, in a "*perspicuous*" representation. (GB 133)

> This perspicuous representation brings about the understanding which consists precisely in the fact that we "see the connections". (GB 133)

These ideas clearly foreshadow the sections of *Philosophical Investigations* in which Wittgenstein dismisses explanation from his enterprise ("We must do away with all *explanation*, and description alone must take its place" (PI §109)), and advances the notion of "perspicuous representation" as the means whereby one might "*command a clear view* of the use of our words" (PI §122), such a clear view of linguistic usage allowing one to avoid the bewitching "traps" and "false paths" that threaten to lead us into philosophical confusions (see BT 422–6).

Despite its importance for Wittgenstein's later philosophical project, the concept of perspicuous representation is itself contested and somewhat unclear. There are two competing interpretations, which we shall here briefly note. The commonly accepted view is that a perspicuous representation is something like a "bird's-eye view" of grammar (PR 52), meaning that the philosopher should aspire to a perspective in which she is, as Baker and Hacker once put it,

> able to 'take in at a glance' a segment of grammar, so that one will not be misled by surface grammar, false analogies, or pictures embedded in language which, considered independently of their application, mislead us. (Baker and Hacker, 1980/84, p. 306)

The construction of a perspicuous representation would here be the positive aim of philosophy, contrasting with the negative or therapeutic side of Wittgenstein's method, which highlights pieces of philosophical nonsense with the aim of removing them. These two sides are, however, intimately connected, since the removal of these problems is effected by the construction of an overview (*Übersicht*) of all uses of language.

Troubled in part by the ambitious aspects of such a global interpretation of perspicuity, Gordon Baker in his later work presented a more modest model, stressing that a representation is a perspicuous one simply if it introduces a degree of clarity into a confusing philosophical matter. He links the ideal of perspicuity to Wittgenstein's discussion of "seeing an aspect," suggesting that a perspicuous representation functions to remedy aspect blindness by bringing "hitherto unnoticed aspects of things to a person's awareness, i.e. to get him to *see* things differently" (Baker, 2004, p. 35). Hence, we are blind to certain aspects of the grammar of our language due to their familiarity and we need to *remind ourselves* of the ordinary uses to which such troubling segments are put. A representation is perspicuous when it succeeds in bringing us to such a clearer understanding. On Baker's view, therefore, the term "perspicuous representation" does not designate a systematic overview of our linguistic system, but rather the family of tools and methods employed so as to yield clarity and dissolve philosophical confusions.

Elements of these rival interpretations can be detected in the "Remarks on Frazer." There are certainly suggestions here that Wittgenstein wants, in the place of Frazer's explanatory schema, to construct a highly detailed description of religious practices, one in which similarities and differences between rituals could easily be seen. A "bird's-eye view" of ritual would appear to take the form of a comprehensive description of magical and religious phenomena, stripped of any explanatory or historical content. In such a fashion, one would be able "to see the data in their relation to one another and to embrace them in a general picture without putting it in the form of an hypothesis about temporal development" (GB 131).

Among those writers struck by the promise of such a technique is Avishai Margalit, who says that an account of ritual should take the form of "a sort of stamp album" (Margalit, 1992, p.308), in which the ceremonies of one's own tradition can be compared and contrasted with those of other cultures. Richard Eldridge (1987), likewise, proposes perspicuous representation as the proper way to bring out the expressive significance of ritual: arranged by likenesses, the material would provide a detailed picture of the attitudes and concerns expressed in religious ceremonies. One might, however, question both the justification for an exclusion of historical and explanatory considerations and the extent to which the project of perspicuous representation really does differ markedly from Frazer's approach. After all, once stripped of its theories, which Frazer (1936, p.xi) said he held only "very lightly," *The Golden Bough* is itself akin to a "stamp album" of rituals, grouping ceremonies thematically and enabling readers to survey similarities and differences.

The same concerns, moreover, which led Baker to reject the bird's-eye view model of perspicuity and to advance his smaller, more piecemeal interpretation, might also apply to these anthropological matters. Certain aspects of rituals are neglected in Frazer's accounts of them, and this leads to the confused judgment that magical and religious ceremonies are in the nature of erroneous proto-scientific actions. That confusion is dispelled by bringing a ritual phenomenon into connection with an act evidently not of such a mistaken character. The remark about effigy-burning can be read in this light. Once placed alongside the act of kissing a picture, the intellectualist picture begins to lose its hold on us and perspicuity is attained. Hence, the reminders Wittgenstein offers are not to be contrasted with the more systematic project of producing a complete description of ritual phenomena. Rather, each specific reminder employed, if successful in its clarification, may legitimately be termed a "perspicuous representation" of a segment of ritual life, the aim being to dismantle the misconceptions of a confused account of ceremonial life, allowing us thereby to see clearly the true nature of magical and religious actions.

The limitations of such a technique should not be ignored. Wittgenstein and his followers frequently deny the necessity for fieldwork and empirical inquiry when considering ritual. Witness Rush Rhees:

> We need not go in search of new facts, nor conjecture them, to understand how there came to be such forms of magic and of ritual. All that we need for this is with us [...] in our ways of thought and feeling. (Rhees, 1971, p.21)

But without such fieldwork the possibility of misunderstanding is surely great. For example, it may be that I do not expect any concrete result to follow from kissing a photograph of my beloved (I know she will not feel at a distance the touch of my lips), and my act does not express or even depend on any opinion about its likely effects. But this in itself tells me very little about the motivations and expectations of the primitive ritualist engaged in effigy-destruction. Linking magical rites with our own quasi-ceremonial acts may help to expand the range of possible motivations informing rituals, but the only way to establish what a ritualist actually expects or believes when he engages in ceremonial activity is through observation of *his* (and not *my*) behavior. The anthropological relevance of Wittgenstein's critique of Frazer seems therefore compromised by his stubborn rejection of the importance of empirical investigation. Although, of course, his primary interest in anthropological questions might well be said to have been one of a philosopher, not one of an anthropologist as such.

4 Wittgenstein and the Anthropological Study of Ritual

Wittgenstein's antipathy toward explanation has been noted above, but his reasons for denying the legitimacy of an explanatory project such as Frazer's are of a somewhat peculiar nature. Following his reflections on beating the ground as an exercise in anger-venting, he says that "an historical explanation, say, that I or my ancestors previously believed that beating the ground does help is shadow-boxing, for it is a superfluous assumption that explains *nothing*" (GB 137–9). This rather bald statement is subsequently tempered by a more measured one emphasizing only the *differences* between two kinds of inquiry: one which brings a ritual phenomenon "into connection with an instinct which I myself possess" and "a further investigation about the history of my instinct," which "moves on another track" (GB 139). This does not suggest that explanatory accounts of ritual are illicit, but simply that Wittgenstein has no interest in them.

Recognition of this point has led some writers to suggest that Wittgenstein's purpose in writing on ritual is very unlike Frazer's, for while Frazer is trying to understand *why* primitive peoples engage in magical practices, Wittgenstein's aims lie elsewhere. Thus, Cioffi argues that Wittgenstein's remarks on ritual should be read not for "their contribution to the explanatory tasks of anthropology or pre-history but for the light they shed on our relation to exotic practices" (Cioffi, 1990, p.69). The pattern that Cioffi discerns in the "Remarks" is as follows. We experience wonderment and perplexity when we read the tales of extraordinary customs chronicled within the pages of *The Golden Bough*; such perplexity leads us to reflect on those eccentric personal-ceremonial acts each of us performs; this reflection, however, does not – and nor is it intended to – illuminate the rationales of the exotic rites; rather, we reflect on our own ritualistic practices *for their own sake*.

This account of Wittgenstein's project certainly protects it from the charge that he is advancing a faulty method for reconstructing the motives of exotic ritualists, though in doing so it perhaps trivializes it, for as Cioffi notes, when one takes up Wittgenstein's methods (rather than those of, say, Frazer) it may legitimately be felt that "we have abandoned thinking for brooding" (Cioffi, 1984, p.172). A response to that criticism might be to suggest that with regard to certain phenomena – unhappy love, for example, or bereavement, or human wickedness – one requires, not an explanation, but something akin to *consolation*: "an hypothetical explanation will be of little help to someone, say, who is upset because of love. – It will not calm him," Wittgenstein writes (GB 123). The relevant question here, however, concerns why ritual behavior (the slaying of the priest at Nemi, for instance) should fall into that particular category, why such a practice does not call for empirical inquiry. And it is hard to see why Wittgenstein's rejection of empirical inquiry is not merely temperamental; harder still, perhaps, to detect, on this view, what value Wittgenstein's notes on *The Golden Bough* might have for anthropology as a scientific or at least academic discipline.

One must concede that Wittgenstein has not advanced the outlines of a coherent anthropological methodology. This is not, however, to say that he has nothing to offer researchers investigating the nature of ritual. First, a Wittgensteinian account of human agency, which, as seen earlier, de-emphasizes the role of ratiocination, may prove to be fruitful in an investigation into the wellsprings of ritual belief and practice. Secondly, one dramatically nonempirical feature of Wittgenstein's technique does in fact possess value for the project of understanding ritual. This concerns the consideration of merely *possible* ritual practices as a means of articulating general patterns of religious action:

> One sees how misleading Frazer's explanations are – I believe – by noting that one could very easily invent primitive practices oneself, and it would be pure luck if they were not actually found somewhere. That is, the principle according to which these practices are arranged is a much more general one than in Frazer's explanation and it is present in our own minds, so that we could think up all the possibilities. (GB 127)

Wittgenstein illustrates this insight by means of two examples: a king who must be kept *hidden* from everyone or must, contrariwise, be *shown* to everyone; and the case of Schubert's brother, cutting some of the composer's scores into pieces and distributing the pieces to his favorite pupils. As a sign of piety, the brother's act is perfectly understandable, as would alternative acts, such as burning the scores or leaving them untouched. Using the scores as scrap paper, on the other hand, would lack this mark of piety. Wittgenstein's conclusion: "The ceremonial (hot or cold) as opposed to the haphazard (lukewarm) characterizes piety" (GB 127). Such thoughts indicate, not simply our own "inwardness" with rituality, but also the principles according to which ritual is structured (the hot and the cold, for instance), principles that provide the researcher with some "conceptual evidence" regarding ritual, by which is meant here some broad understanding of general patterns of ritual activity (see Byrne, 1989, p.236). The conceptual evidence assembled by Wittgenstein may throw considerable light on the nature of ritual.

Finally, against Frazer's view that rituals serve a purely utilitarian function, Wittgenstein alerts our attention instead to conspicuous features of the world around which ceremonial activity revolves:

> It goes without saying that a man's shadow, which looks like him, or his mirror-image, the rain, thunderstorms, the phases of the moon, the changing of the seasons, the way in which animals are similar to and different from one another and in relation to man, the phenomena of death, birth, and sexual life, in short, everything we observe around us year in and year out, interconnected in so many different ways, will play a part in his thinking (his philosophy) and in his practices, or is precisely what we really know and find interesting. (GB 127–9)

Peter Winch (1967, p.38) refers to such features of the world and of human life as "limiting notions" (the principal ones would appear to be those isolated by T.S. Eliot as birth, copulation, and death), and we need only to think of examples of ritual in order to recognize how these notions form the backbone of such acts. In the ritual life of our own culture, for instance, it is possible that a person might attend a church ceremony for three types of events only – christenings, weddings, and funerals – each marking and dramatizing one such limit. The anthropological value of spelling out these limiting notions is that "they are inescapably involved in the life of all known human societies in a way which gives us a clue where to look, if we are puzzled about the point of an alien system of institutions" (Winch, 1967, p.38). This is a helpful recommendation. When confronted with a puzzling exotic ritual, one might try to make sense of it (as Frazer does) by thinking of it predominantly as a form of (attempted) technological activity. In this way the rite ceases to be mysterious, but the lifting of mystery is attained at the cost of turning the ritualists into simpletons (and of distorting the nature of ritual in the process). When, on the other hand, limiting notions are utilized to dispel mystery, a different outcome ensues. The idea of technological action will play no role in this elucidation (any more than it should play a role in the explication of a wedding or a funeral), but instead the rite would be contextualized and understood in terms of one or other perennial feature of the world impacting on the mind and activity of a being envisaged as "a ceremonial animal" (GB 129).

The characterization of the human animal as a ceremonial creature might indeed be regarded as the guiding principle of the "Remarks on Frazer." Whether he is reflecting on effigy-destruction, rain dances, or human sacrifice, Wittgenstein's concern is not to discern the motive (either "instrumental" or "expressive") informing a ritual act, but to emphasize the naturalness of ceremonial behavior. Rather than a peculiarity rendered redundant by the progress of scientific understanding, and as something to be understood in terms of the practical application of curious beliefs concerning supernatural realities, ritual is to be approached as "part of our natural history" (PI §25), and therefore as a manifestation of aspects of our shared being. This is presumably why his reflections on ritual action return to thoughts concerning "man and his past" and "all the strange things I see, and have seen and heard about, in myself and others" (GB 151). Though his thoughts on these matters remain tantalizingly undeveloped, the contents of the "Remarks on Frazer" probe deeply into the nature and bedrock of human ritual activity, and anthropological research might thus benefit markedly from Wittgenstein's pregnant insights into the ceremonial life of other cultures.

References

Baker, G.P. (2004). *Wittgenstein's Method: Neglected Aspects*. Ed. K. Morris. Oxford: Blackwell.
Baker, G.P. and Hacker, P.M.S. (1980/84). *Wittgenstein: Meaning and Understanding. Essays on the Philosophical Investigations*. Oxford: Blackwell.
Bell, R.H. (1984). Wittgenstein's Anthropology: Self-Understanding and Understanding other Cultures. *Philosophical Investigations*, 7, 295–312.
Byrne, P.A. (1989). *Natural Religion and the Nature of Religion*. London: Routledge.
Cioffi, F. (1984). When Do Empirical Methods Bypass "The Problems which Trouble Us"? In A.P. Griffiths (Ed.). *Philosophy and Literature* (pp.155–172). Cambridge: Cambridge University Press.
Cioffi, F. (1990). Wittgenstein on Making Homoeopathic Magic Clear. In R. Gaita (Ed.). *Value and Understanding* (pp. 42–71). London: Routledge and Kegan Paul.
Clack, B.R. (1996). Wittgenstein and Expressive Theories of Religion. *International Journal for Philosophy of Religion*, 40, 47–61.

Cook, J.W. (1983). Magic, Witchcraft, and Science. *Philosophical Investigations*, 6, 2–36.
Eldridge, R. (1987). Hypotheses, Criterial Claims, and Perspicuous Representations. *Philosophical Investigations*, 10, 226–245.
Frazer, J.G. (1922). *The Golden Bough*. London: Macmillan.
Frazer, J.G. (1936). *Balder the Beautiful* (Vol. 1). London: Macmillan.
Freud, S. ([1911] 1958). Formulations on the Two Principles of Mental Functioning. Translation in *The Standard Edition of the Complete Psychological Works of Sigmund Freud* (Vol. 12, pp.213–226). London: Hogarth Press. (Original work published 1911.)
Freud, S. ([1913] 1955). Totem and Taboo. Translation in *The Standard Edition of the Complete Psychological Works of Sigmund Freud* (Vol. 13, pp.1–162). London: Hogarth Press. (Original work published 1913.)
James, W. (2005). *The Ceremonial Animal: A New Portrait of Anthropology*. Oxford: Oxford University Press.
Margalit, A. (1992). Sense and Sensibility: Wittgenstein on *The Golden Bough*. *Iyyun*, 41, 301–318.
Needham, R. (1985). *Exemplars*. Berkeley: University of California Press.
Rhees, R. (1971). Introductory Note to Remarks on Frazer's *Golden Bough*. *The Human World*, 3, 18–28.
Rudich, N. and Stassen, M. (1971). Wittgenstein's Implied Anthropology. *History and Theory*, 10, 84–89.
Skorupski, J. (1976). *Symbol and Theory*. Cambridge: Cambridge University Press.
Tambiah, S.J. (1990). *Magic, Science, Religion, and the Scope of Rationality*. Cambridge: Cambridge University Press.
Winch, P. (1967). Understanding a Primitive Society. In D.Z. Phillips (Ed.). *Religion and Understanding* (pp.9–42). Oxford: Basil Blackwell.

Further Reading

Child, W. (2011). *Wittgenstein*. London: Routledge. Chapter 8.
Cioffi, F. (1998). *Wittgenstein on Freud and Frazer*. Cambridge: Cambridge University Press.
Clack, B.R. (1999). *Wittgenstein, Frazer and Religion*. London: Macmillan.
Clack, B.R. (2001). Wittgenstein and Magic. In R.L. Arrington and M. Addis (Eds). *Wittgenstein and Philosophy of Religion* (pp.12–28). London: Routledge.
Hacker, P.M.S. (1992). Developmental Hypotheses and Perspicuous Representations. *Iyyun*, 41, 277–299.

42

Wittgenstein and Philosophy of Religion

JOHN COTTINGHAM

1 Introduction

To speak of Wittgenstein having a "philosophy of religion" is in one way misleading, since he never produced any sustained piece of writing in this area. But religion was something about which Wittgenstein thought deeply, and his various scattered pronouncements on religious belief and commitment are rich and interesting enough to have exerted a strong influence on subsequent philosophical thinking about religion. Some have even seen him as the leading voice in a radical and controversial philosophical approach to religious language, the approach that has come to be known as noncognitivism or antirealism in the philosophy of religion. It is in fact doubtful that such an approach can be retrojected onto Wittgenstein himself, or that it represents a valid interpretation of his remarks about religious belief. But however that may be, Wittgenstein's diverse reflections on religion do succeed in uncovering a number of important features of the religious outlook that are easily overlooked, and which, when properly grasped, greatly enhance our understanding of what it is to subscribe to a religious worldview. These include (but are not exhausted by) a stress on religion as a form of life; a conception of religious claims as not competing with scientific explanations; the idea of religion as a framework of interpretation; and an emphasis on religious allegiance as passionate commitment. Wittgenstein's views may not amount to a systematic theory of religion, or of religious language, but taken together they amount to a distinctive and highly original contribution that no student of the subject can afford to ignore.

Religion, more specifically Christianity, was very important to Wittgenstein in his youth, and in certain ways it continued to exert its influence right up to the closing days of his life. He came from a wealthy Jewish family, long assimilated into Viennese high society; his millionaire father was nominally Lutheran, and his mother (whose father was Jewish though her mother was not) was a devout Catholic, and she had all her nine children, including Ludwig, baptized as Catholics (Kerr, 2008, p.28). Although Wittgenstein underwent a crisis of faith during his time at secondary school, we know that by his early twenties he was still intensely interested in Christianity. He was known during his World War I service as "the one with the Gospels": he had picked up a copy

---

A Companion to Wittgenstein, First Edition. Edited by Hans-Johann Glock and John Hyman.
© 2017 John Wiley & Sons, Ltd. Published 2017 by John Wiley & Sons, Ltd.

of Tolstoy's *The Gospel in Brief* in September 1914, which he "read and re-read, and always had with him under fire and at all times" (Malcolm, 1993, p.8). During his time as a prisoner of war, he decided to become a schoolmaster, and observed to a friend: "I'd most like to be a priest, but when I'm a teacher I can read the Gospel with the children" (McGuinness, 1990, p.274). Speaking later of this time, Wittgenstein remarked: "When I was a prisoner of war in Italy, I was compelled to attend Mass on Sundays. I was very glad of that compulsion" (RW 109). When he was dying, in 1951, Elizabeth Anscombe and other Catholics were at his bedside, and he was given a Catholic burial, though one of his friends, Maurice Drury, later agonized over whether this had been the right thing to do (Monk, 1990, pp.567–80). Wittgenstein could certainly not have been classified as a "believer" in any orthodox doctrinal sense; but it is significant that he considered that "Christianity is not a doctrine" (CV 28). Any possible turn back to the faith in which he was baptized would probably have had to have been on a very different basis – one he had vividly described over a decade before his final illness:

> Faith is faith in what my heart needs, not my speculative intelligence. For it is my soul, with its passions, as it were with its flesh and blood, that must be saved, not my abstract mind. (CV 33)

In similar vein, he observed on another occasion:

> The Christian religion is only for one who feels an infinite need [...]. To whom it is given in this anguish to open his heart instead of contracting it, accepts the means to salvation in his heart. (CV 46)

Yet despite his keen awareness of his own anguish, Wittgenstein himself never felt able to accept the offered "means of salvation." His lifelong wrestling with these problems went hand-in-hand with his evolving philosophical ideas on the status of religious language, belief, and allegiance; the main elements in his subtle and complex account will now be examined in turn.

2   Religious Language and the *Tractatus*

The famous last sentence of Wittgenstein's first published work, *Tractatus Logico-Philosophicus*, has clear implications for the credal claims of traditional religion: *wovon mann nicht sprechen kann, darüber muß man schweigen* ("what one cannot speak of, one must pass over in silence"). The aim of the *Tractatus*, Wittgenstein explains in his preface, is "to set a limit to thought, or rather not to thought, but to the expression of thoughts." He goes on to say that it is "only in language that the limit can be set, and what lies on the other side of the limit will simply be nonsense." The job of language is to represent facts in the world, as a picture represents its object; and it follows that all that can properly be *said* or asserted are the empirical propositions of natural science. Whenever someone wants to go beyond that, and say something metaphysical, then the correct method in philosophy would be to show the speaker "that he had failed to give a meaning to certain signs in his propositions" (TLP 6.53).

This might at first seem to prefigure the views of the logical positivists, who were to dismiss all religious language, along with ethical and aesthetic language, as incapable of verification and therefore nonsense; but Wittgenstein's position is more delicate and more interesting than this. In the closing sentences of the *Tractatus*, he talks about "the mystical" (*das Mystische*): it is not *how* things are in the world that is mystical, but *that* the world exists at all (6.44). And he goes on to mention some of the ideas that have traditionally been the concern of religion – God, death, the meaning of life. We are left with the thought that "there is that which cannot be put into words" (*es gibt Unaussprechliches*) but which can somehow *make itself manifest*, or "show itself" (*zeigt sich*, 6.522). Though Wittgenstein does not explicitly put it this way, his position seems to leave room for the idea that religious talk, though "nonsense" in the strict sense laid down by a correct theory of language, might nevertheless somehow be illuminating. For there are things that can be *shown*, even though they cannot strictly be *said* (see 4.1212; see also Chapter 11, INEFFABILITY AND NONSENSE IN THE *TRACTATUS*; cf. Chapter 10, RESOLUTE READINGS OF THE *TRACTATUS*).

The upshot is that there is an ambivalence in Wittgenstein's attitude in the *Tractatus* to the claims of religion, which (though he himself never draws any such parallel) is in some respects reminiscent of what one finds in Kantian philosophy. Kant in the *Critique of Pure Reason* had roundly condemned attempts to establish matters lying outside the limits of the phenomenal world described by science: if we leave the solid terrain of the "land of truth" (*das Land der Wahrheit*), and launch out into the "wide and stormy ocean," invoking "transcendent" ideas, relating to objects that "lie outside all possible experience," then, Kant argued, "we are cut off from any reasons that could establish the possibility of such objects" (Kant, [1781/87] 1965, A565, B593). And in a similar way, Wittgenstein's insistence that "the limits of language are the limits of my world" (TLP 5.6) seems on the face of it to close the door on any speculative metaphysics of the traditional kind that attempted to make assertions about God. But just as Kant, despite his views on the limits of knowledge, was able to "make room" for religious faith (1787, B, Introduction, p.xxx), so Wittgenstein evidently retained a respect, perhaps even a reverence, for the domain of the mystical, albeit that domain could never be captured in language. In this way, Wittgenstein's position puts one less in mind of the later verificationist steamroller of logical positivism than of the much earlier "apophatic" tradition in Jewish and Christian religious thought, which insists on the "breakdown of speech" that, in the face of the unknowability of God, "falls infinitely short of the mark" (Turner, 1995, p.19). In a lecture given some ten years after the publication of the *Tractatus*, Wittgenstein discusses the realm of ethics and value – a domain he had called "transcendental" in the closing part of the *Tractatus*, treating it, along with the aesthetic and the religious domains, as part of the "mystical" – and he uses a striking image to convey the inadequacy of language in this context:

> Our words used as we use them in science are vessels capable only of containing and conveying meaning and sense, *natural* meaning and sense. Ethics, if it is anything, is supernatural, and our words will only express facts; as a teacup will only hold a teacup full of water [even] if I were to pour out a gallon over it. (LE 7; see also Clack, 1999, p.35)

3 Later Developments

As many commentators have noted, Wittgenstein's view of the nature of language and meaning underwent significant changes between the publication of the *Tractatus* and the composition of his other great masterpiece, *Philosophical Investigations*; and these changes have important implications for his view of religious language. In the *Investigations*, we find a much less monolithic conception of the role of language: instead of having the single function of depicting states of affairs, language takes many diverse forms, just as the tools in a tool kit have many different purposes (PI §14). There is no general form of language; rather, if we are interested in meaning of linguistic utterances we should think about their *use* in a particular practice or activity – in a "language-game." "The term "language-game" is meant to bring into prominence "the fact that the *speaking* of a language is part of an activity, or of a form of life" (PI §23). One implication of this is that it is a mistake to try to assimilate all statements to the fact-depicting statements of natural science; and this in turn opens the way for construing religious language as having an entirely different function from the language of science.

4 Religion Not a Rival to Science

The view that religion is not to be construed as competing with science is a consistent theme in Wittgenstein's thinking about religion. In his "Remarks on Frazer's *Golden Bough*," Wittgenstein argues that the anthropologist James George Frazer committed a fundamental error in his account of ritual practices, by trying to understand them in quasi-scientific terms, as aimed at the production of certain effects (see Chapter 41, WITTGENSTEIN AND ANTHROPOLOGY; see also Bouveresse, 2007). Elsewhere, Wittgenstein makes an important distinction between *faith* and *superstition*. Superstition, unlike faith, "springs from fear and is a sort of false science" (CV 82). To take the baptism of a child as an example, if this is motivated by the belief that it will make the child's life more lucky or more successful, we have a case of mere superstition – a kind of primitive pseudo-technology. To promote the child's health and wellbeing one would do far better to have recourse to modern scientific medicine. But if the baptism is an act of joyful affirmation and thanksgiving for the new life – what Wittgenstein called a "trusting" (*ein Vertrauen*, CV 82) – then it is a genuine manifestation of religious faith.

Wittgenstein's point here provides the material for a possible riposte to a common attack mounted by atheist critics of religion such as Sigmund Freud, namely that religious behavior is an infantile response to our helplessness and the need for protection against natural threats – "the majestic, cruel and inexorable powers of nature" (Freud, [1929] 1985, p.195); David Hume similarly traced the origins of religion to the "incessant hopes and fears that actuate mankind" (Hume, 1757, ch.2). It is no doubt true that many religious adherents have had recourse to ritual practices in a desperate attempt to avert disaster; but assimilating all religious belief and activity to this model seems a massive oversimplification. The exclamation of Job in the Hebrew Bible, "though he slay me, yet will I trust in him" (Job 1:4), looks much more like an expression of *Vertrauen* than an attempt at superstitious manipulation; and many other similar scriptural texts could be cited. So seeing religion as a primitive, quasi-scientific attempt to control a hostile world, while it may fit the way some religious practitioners think, does not seem to match what is going on in large chunks of mainstream religious thought and practice.

Not only does Wittgenstein implicitly reject the hostile construal of religion as a primitive pseudo-technology, but he also makes it clear that he does not see religion as in any way assimilable to explanatory cosmology or science. He had little truck with the kind of theological metaphysics that attempts to present God's existence as something that can be demonstratively established, or even shown to be reasonably probable. A believer, he observed, would never come to believe as a result of the supposed "proofs" of God's existence (CV 85); and the whole project of "philosophical theology," he once remarked, struck him as "indecent" (RW 90). For those (including many prominent theologians and philosophers) who treat theism as a probable hypothesis for accounting for the existence or nature of the cosmos, Wittgenstein appears to have had something like bemused contempt: "Can you imagine St Augustine saying that the existence of God was highly probable!," he remarked to Drury (RW 90; contrast, for example, Swinburne, 2011). Consistently with his move away from the monolithic science-oriented view of language he had espoused in the *Tractatus*, Wittgenstein came to think that religious language should not be thought of as in any way competing with science: it had another function altogether.

5   Forms of Life, and the Importance of Context and Praxis

The lesson to be drawn from Wittgenstein's later philosophy is that if we wish to understand any type of language, including religious language, we have to look at the "form of life" in which it is embedded. Wittgenstein's interest in "forms of life" (*Lebensformen*), was in some respects a "holistic" reaction against the atomistic approach to meaning he had espoused in the *Tractatus* (where an individual proposition was taken to be a "picture of reality," TLP 4.01; see Chapter 8, THE PICTURE THEORY). Our language-games, he later came to see, are interwoven with a web of nonlinguistic activities, and cannot be understood apart from the context that gives them life. Wittgenstein insisted that "in a religious discourse we use such expressions as: 'I believe that so and so will happen' [...] differently to the way in which we use them in science." So to believe in the Last Judgment is not assimilable to an ordinary belief that a certain event will very probably happen at some time in the future (LC 57). As one commentator has aptly put it, Wittgenstein's aim is to show how concepts such as sin, redemption, judgment, grace, and atonement "can have an indispensable place in an individual's or a community's way of life, and to show how we can resist assimilating the use of these concepts to hypotheses, predictions and theoretical explanations" (Hyman, 2001, pp.6–7).

This leads us straight to a key feature of Wittgenstein's mature understanding of language: his emphasis on the role of activity or praxis in underpinning the way it works.

> It is characteristic of our language that the foundation out of which it grows consists in steady forms of life, regular activity. Its function is determined above all by the action which it accompanies. (CE 404)

This implies, in the case of religious language, that if we want to grasp the meaning of, for example, the priest's pronouncing the words "The Body of Christ" as he holds up the consecrated bread at the Eucharist, we cannot understand or evaluate the assertion in isolation (in the way we might, for example, understand and evaluate the assertion that the wafer of bread is of circular shape and 9 cm in diameter); rather, we need to place the utterance in the context of the entire liturgy of the Mass, the Gospel story of the Last Supper, the richly layered symbolism of communally shared bread and wine, and much else besides. This contrasts starkly with the stance taken by those critics of religion who proceed to evaluate religious claims on the basis of only a cursory grasp of their literal or surface meaning (compare the remarks on the Last Judgment offered in Dawkins, 2006, pp. 319ff). It does not of course follow that a richer contextual examination of the practices that give life to religion will end up *vindicating* those claims or justifying those practices; that question is one that Wittgenstein's remarks appear to leave open. But without a proper grasp of meaning, which in turn requires a preparedness to investigate context and praxis, the evaluation of truth cannot even get off the ground.

6 Wittgensteinian "Fideism," and his Alleged "Noncognitivism"

The term "fideism," which is often used to characterize Wittgenstein's position on religion (see Glock, 1996, p. 320), covers a spectrum of views that emphasize the role of faith, in contrast to (or as a supplement to) reason, for the formation of religious belief. In the middle ages, Anselm and Aquinas, along with other Christian philosophers, produced rational proofs of God's existence, but Aquinas asserted that in addition to the truths discoverable by natural reason there were revealed truths that had to be accepted on faith (see Aquinas [1259–65] 1975, bk. I, chs. 4–6); and Anselm described his whole philosophical enterprise in the *Proslogion* by giving it the subtitle "faith seeking understanding" (Anselm, [1077–8] 2008). For both these philosophers, faith and reason have complementary roles, so their position is very much not an exclusively or even mainly a "fideist" one. Nevertheless, in underlining the importance of faith (in Latin *fides*), they are stressing something over and above mere rational assent to a set of doctrines; for *fides*, like its Greek counterpart *pistis*, always connotes a stronger volitional component than simple assent – some further element of trust and commitment. As one moves toward extreme forms of fideism, such as that of Søren Kierkegaard, the volitional element becomes stronger. "Faith does not need proof," asserted Kierkegaard, "indeed it must regard proof as its enemy" (Kierkegaard, [1846] 1941, p. 31). And in a famous passage he observed: "Christianity is spirit, spirit is inwardness, inwardness is subjectivity, subjectivity is essential passion, and in its maximum an infinite, personal, passionate interest in one's eternal happiness" (p. 182). Wittgenstein shared with Kierkegaard the view that passionate commitment is central to what makes someone religious; and just as Kierkegaard had argued that true faith requires subjective commitment, not objective certainty or probability, so Wittgenstein thought there was something "ludicrous" in attempting to shore up the reasonableness of religious belief in the light of dispassionate scrutiny of the evidence (LC 58).

The Kierkegaardian or fideist influences on Wittgenstein's thought are particularly apparent in his often quoted remark in *Culture and Value*: "It appears to me as though a religious belief could only be (something like) passionately committing oneself to a system of reference" (CV 73). The implication here might be taken to be that belief, in the normal sense of the term, namely assent to a proposition with a certain cognitive content, drops out of the picture completely in Wittgenstein's conception of religious faith, leaving simply the volitional act of committing oneself. Extrapolating from this, those later writers who espoused a "noncognitivist" or antirealist approach to philosophy of religion maintained that religious language about God should not be understood as making factual claims, stating facts, or describing reality at all. Thus the well-known Welsh philosopher of religion D.Z. Phillips, explicitly invoking Wittgenstein's ideas about language-games, stressed that if we want to understand religious talk properly, we should not interpret it as referring to the "reality" of God. "Theological realism," observed Phillips, "often indulges in philosophy by italics. We are told that we could not worship unless we believed that God *exists*. We are told that we cannot talk to God unless he is *there* to talk to. And so on. But nothing is achieved by italicising these words. The task of clarifying their grammar when they are used remains" (Phillips, 1993, p.35).

There are two questions here. The first is whether rejecting a realist construal of religious language is tenable, and the second is whether this position can be laid at Wittgenstein's door. On the first question, many critics have insisted that the antirealist approach fails to match the actual beliefs and practices of ordinary religious adherents:

> When ordinary people pray it is because they think there is a God up there listening. But whether or not there is a God listening to their prayer isn't itself part of the language-game. The reason people play the language-game of religion is because they think there is something outside the language-game that gives it a point. (Searle, 1987, pp.344–5)

What is more, to say that a religious belief just *is* a commitment appears to sidestep the question of *justification* in a problematic way (cf. Hyman, 2001). Commitments, though it may be psychologically possible to make them in the absence of prior beliefs, seem to presuppose, for their validity, the objective truth of the beliefs logically required by the nature of the commitment. If I commit myself to a loved one, or to God, my commitment will lose its justification if the object of my commitment turns out not to exist, or to be wholly unworthy of my commitment.

On the second question, of whether Wittgenstein himself espoused this type of noncognitivist view, Severin Schroeder has argued that, contrary to the common reading of his remarks in *Culture and Value*, Wittgenstein is not proposing a *purely* expressivist construal of credal statements (Schroeder, 2007). In saying that religious belief "*can only be a passionate commitment*," Wittgenstein may simply be underlining the *inescapability* of a passionate, volitional element; he need not be saying that what is involved in the belief is *merely* the commitment – as if nothing else, no cognitive or doxastic (belief) elements, were entailed. On the matter of phrasing, Schroeder appears to have a strong case. To say, for example, "that remark *can only* have been a joke" does not imply that it was humorous *and nothing else*; it does not, for example rule out its being apt, or malicious, or referring to a true state of affairs. In any case, there are, as Schroeder points out, many passages where Wittgenstein makes it quite explicit that belief *is* involved in religious commitment. In the very next sentence following his remark about "passionate commitment," he goes on to say: "Hence, although it is *belief*, it is a way of living, or a way of judging life" (CV 73). What is more, we know from other remarks that Wittgenstein would have liked to commit himself to Christianity, but felt unable to make the commitment because he *could not bring himself to assent to the required beliefs* – for example a belief in the Last Judgment (CV 38).

A further text often cited in favor of a noncognitivist interpretation of Wittgenstein's view of religious belief is his remark that saying (as many philosophical theologians have done) that God's essence guarantees his existence "really means [...] that what is here at issue is not the existence of something [*daß es sich hier um eine Existenz nicht handelt]*" (CV 82). But it would be rash to read noncognitivism into this, given that it is actually quite close to standard mainstream Christian theology. On the standard conception found for example in Aquinas, God is not an individual being at all, not an "entity" alongside the other entities in the world, but is rather the source of all being (Davies, 2002, p.72); so it is not as if the theist's inventory of entities in the universe includes some extra item that is absent from the atheist's list. Hence, so far from being a heretical slide into a noncognitivist or antirealist view of God-talk, Wittgenstein's remark that in discussing God we are not dealing with *einer Existenz* is one that would seem quite in order to many orthodox theologians.

As noted above in our discussion of the *Tractatus*, Wittgenstein himself was attracted in his early writings to the idea of religion as related to the domain of the ineffable (TLP 6.522). In the light of this, it is plausible to interpret his later thinking about religion as preserving the core idea that our language about God cannot be construed as having straightforward propositional content (in the *Tractatus* sense), or as asserting the existence of an item in the world. But none of this entails a radically nonrealist conception of religious discourse; it is simply that we need to be careful to avoid assimilating the reality of God to the reality obtaining within the "world" – the reality possessed by contingent things, or, as the *Tractatus* put it, whatever happens to be "the case." Wittgenstein was clear that being religious is not a matter of proposing explanatory hypotheses about the world of a scientific or quasi-scientific kind, but rather of passionate commitment to a certain system of reference, a certain framework for interpreting the world. But this may be quite compatible with holding that to adopt the framework in question does indeed involve assent to certain theistic beliefs.

7 Religion as a Framework of Interpretation

A religious person passionately commits herself, according to Wittgenstein, "to a system of coordinates" (*zu einem Koordinatensystem*). A variant reading has the more general phrase "a system of reference" (*einem Bezugssystem*) (CV 73). These notions may seem at first to support the noncognitivist interpretation of Wittgenstein's views on religion; for a system of coordinates (for example, the points of the compass, or the metric system) is not itself a set of truth-claims: "a system of co-ordinates is [...] an intellectual apparatus we use to construct truths and falsehoods; it cannot itself be either true or false" (Hyman, 2001, p.5). One might draw a parallel here with the case of ethics, where Wittgenstein's mature view seems to be that "to make [ethical judgments] is to adopt a certain framework of action and justification, which itself cannot be justified" (Glock, 1996, p.110). The point here is that a system of reference or a system of measurement (for example the metric system) cannot itself be called true or false in the sense that a given measurement within the system ("this stick is two meters long") may be true or false. The metric system does not itself belong in the complete set of true propositions expressing metric measurements; rather it is a framework that generates the possibility of such measurements.

This point, correct though it is, does not however prevent one affirming the soundness of the metric system as a perfectly valid and rationally defensible framework for dealing with the world; and the same possibility still seems open in the case of a religious framework. Some systems might be rationally defended as more workable, more fitted for human life, more viable, than others. The amount of "passion" with which one commits oneself to the use of such a system does not in itself affect this question of rational evaluability: no doubt some people are passionately committed to the use of metric standards, but that does not put the matter of the appropriateness and viability of the metric system beyond rational evaluation, or shift it to the noncognitive domain of pure volitional or merely emotional preference. There is, moreover, one further suggestive point about the comparison of religious faith to a "reference system," which also pushes things in a more "cognitivist" direction. Although a system of coordinates cannot itself be true or false, the adoption of such a system does nevertheless itself *presuppose* certain truths – for example, the actual reality of the standard posited by the system (the paradigm "meter bar," or the properties of light in the more sophisticated standard now used). In the same way, a religious "system of reference" can be said to have cognitive implications (by presupposing that supreme creative reality without which the system would make no sense), as well as being, for those who adopt it, a valuable and rationally defensible way of making sense of human life (though "rationally defensible" here would not, as with the metrical case, be understood primarily in scientific and technological terms, but rather in moral and spiritual terms).

On this interpretation, Wittgenstein's central insight is that the primary function of a religious outlook is to provide a framework for understanding and interpreting the world in which we find ourselves. The religious adherent confronts, as we all do, a world full of pain and suffering, conditioned by the inescapable facts of human finitude and mortality; yet in the face of the resulting "anguish" and "infinite need" (CV 46) the believer passionately holds on to a "system of reference" that allows those potentially terrifying or depressing features to be viewed through the eyes of faith and hope. What is thereby generated, without in any way removing the dangers or the suffering, is a sense of the "peace that passeth all understanding" (Philippians 4:7); or, as Wittgenstein himself put it, "feeling absolutely *safe* – I mean the state of mind in which one is inclined to say 'I am safe, nothing can injure me whatever happens'" (LE 8).

8   The Question of Evidence

If the kind of interpretation just proposed is accepted, a crucial question remains about its implications for the defensibility or otherwise of adopting a religious outlook: does the Wittgensteinian talk of holding fast to a system of reference imply a view of religion that tries to insulate it from all contact with evidence or argument? Certainly Wittgenstein dismissed the idea that something like the Resurrection could be established or refuted by appeal to a "historical basis in the sense that the ordinary belief in historical facts could serve as a foundation" (LC 57). But this separation of a belief in the Resurrection from an "ordinary" historical belief does not in itself rule out the possibility of evidence of a different kind. Wittgenstein's point may be that the role of evidence in religious commitment is entirely different from that which it occupies on the "Humean" model – a dispassionate scrutiny of empirical probabilities based on past instances (the model that made Hume dryly observe that "the Christian religion not only was at first attended with miracles, but even at this day cannot be believed by any reasonable person without one" (Hume, 1748, sec.10)). The kind of evidence that, for the believer, supports faith is not evidence assessed from a detached standpoint, but experience that is available only as a result of certain inner transformations. This may partly be what Wittgenstein had in mind when he remarked: "Only love can believe the resurrection" (CV 33). Saying this need not imply some kind of subjectivism about religious truth; it merely makes the point that there may be some truths whose *accessibility conditions* include certain requirements as to the attitude of the subject (see Cottingham, 2005, ch.5). In other words, it may point to what one might call a "Pascalian" epistemology: the idea that opening the heart may have the result of disclosing evidence that was before occluded. It is not that there is no evidence of any kind, but rather that, as Pascal put it, there is "enough light for those who desire to see, and enough darkness for those of a contrary disposition" (Pascal, [1670] 1962, no.149).

Interpreting the Gospel accounts of the early disciples' belief in the Resurrection in Wittgensteinian terms, we may say that they seized passionately upon a new framework of interpretation: what had seemed total failure, marked by a horrible and humiliating execution, was subsequently perceived as the prelude to the triumphant proclamation of a message of hope. As noted earlier, we do not have to say that this interpretive shift implies no cognitive change – no change in belief contents. In adopting such a framework, the disciples surely *did* shift their beliefs: with the new framework went a return from despair to faith in God, and a belief that his power was manifested in the risen Christ. Nor, picking up the point just made about evidence, do we have to say that the new belief was held contra-rationally, or without any evidence whatever; what is suggested instead by the Gospel narrative (for example the report that "some doubted" even in the face of the post-Resurrection appearances of Christ, Matthew 28:17) is that the evidence was not "spectator evidence," readily accessible to any dispassionate observer, but was evidence of the kind that requires an inner transformation to enable the subject to apprehend it (see Coakley, 2002; Moser, 2008).

Attributing to Wittgenstein something like this view of the kind of evidence relevant to religious belief receives strong support from one of his most pregnant remarks about religion: "Life can educate one to a belief in God" (CV 86). It is clear that the "education" involved cannot, according to Wittgenstein, be the kind that one receives in the study or seminar room, through a dispassionate study of the evidence or arguments for God's existence. Rather, the "lessons of life" are ones that change one's emotional perspective, making one vulnerable, opening the heart, so that beliefs one was previously blocked from entertaining seriously now become live options (see Cottingham, 2009, pp.224ff). Conversion, in short, is a matter of breaking down the barriers to perception, or demolishing the defenses we all have against becoming open and receptive in this way. Wittgenstein himself confessed in 1946: "I cannot kneel to pray because it's as though my knees are stiff. I am afraid of disintegration (of my disintegration), if I become soft" (CV 56). And an enigmatic remark made in 1937 may also plausibly be taken as a comment on his own inability to become a believer: "The *edifice of your pride has* to be dismantled. And that means frightful work" (CV 30).

These considerations need not, of course, in any way imply that anyone who (like Wittgenstein himself) fails to take the road to conversion is therefore making a philosophical or personal mistake. On this point, as in all areas of his life, Wittgenstein himself was ready to be harshly self-critical; but on balance his views on religious belief seem in the end to be philosophically neutral on the question of whether adopting such a perspective is the right thing to do – albeit they often show a distinct sympathy for the religious worldview, and even a longing for the "safety" it seems to offer. What can be said, as we bring this discussion of Wittgenstein's views on religion to a close, is that his rich and fertile remarks have the merit of offering a far richer and more humane account of religion, and one that resonates much more closely with the actual struggles of believers, would-be believers, and those who cannot believe, than the great bulk of contemporary work in philosophy of religion. Here, as in so many other areas, Wittgenstein's ideas, though they may be temporarily eclipsed by the vicissitudes of academic fashion, seem sure to retain their compelling power for many generations to come.

References

Anselm ([1077–8] 2008). *Proslogion*. Translation in B. Davies and G.R. Evans (Eds). *Anselm: The Major Works*. Oxford: Oxford University Press.
Aquinas, T. ([1259–65] 1975). *Summa contra Gentiles*. Trans. A. Pegis. Notre Dame, IN: University of Notre Dame Press.
Bouveresse, J. (2007). Wittgenstein's Critique of Frazer. *Ratio*, 20, 357–376.
Clack, B.R. (1999). *An Introduction to Wittgenstein's Philosophy of Religion*. Edinburgh: Edinburgh University Press.
Coakley, S. (2002). The Resurrection and the "Spiritual Senses": On Wittgenstein, Epistemology and the Risen Christ. In S. Coakley. *Powers and Submissions: Spirituality, Philosophy and Gender* (pp. 130–152). Oxford: Blackwell.
Cottingham, J. (2005). *The Spiritual Dimension*. Cambridge: Cambridge University Press.
Cottingham, J. (2009). The Lessons of Life: Wittgenstein, Religion and Analytic Philosophy. In H.-J. Glock and J. Hyman (Eds). *Wittgenstein and Analytic Philosophy: Essays for P.M.S. Hacker* (pp. 203–227). Oxford: Oxford University Press.
Davies, B. (2002). *Aquinas*. London: Continuum.
Dawkins, R. (2006). *The God Delusion*. London: Bantam Press.
Freud, S. ([1929] 1985). *Civilization and its Discontents*. Translation in *The Penguin Freud Library* (Vol. 12). London: Penguin. (Original work published 1929.)
Glock, H.-J. (1996). *A Wittgenstein Dictionary*. Oxford: Blackwell.
Hume, D. (1748). *An Enquiry Concerning Human Understanding*. London: Millar.
Hume, D. (1757). *The Natural History of Religion*. London: Millar.
Hyman, J. (2001). The Gospel according to Wittgenstein. In R.L. Arrington (Ed.). *Wittgenstein and Religious Belief* (pp. 1–11). London: Routledge.
Kant, I. ([1781/87] 1965). *Critique of Pure Reason*. Trans. N. Kemp Smith. New York: St Martin's Press. (Original work published 1781/87.)
Kerr, F. (2008). *Work on Oneself: Wittgenstein's Philosophical Psychology*. Washington: Catholic University of America Press.
Kierkegaard, S. ([1846] 1941) *Concluding Unscientific Postscript*. Trans. D.F. Swenson. Princeton: Princeton University Press. (Original work published 1846.)
Malcolm, N. (1993). *Wittgenstein: A Religious Point of View?* London: Routledge.
McGuinness, B. (1990). *Wittgenstein: A Life*. Harmondsworth: Penguin.
Monk, R. (1990). *Ludwig Wittgenstein: The Duty of Genius*. London: Vintage.
Moser, P.K. (2008). *The Elusive God: Reorienting Religious Epistemology*. Cambridge: Cambridge University Press.
Pascal, B. ([1670] 1962). *Pensées*. Ed. L. Lafuma. Paris: Seuil. (Original work published 1670.)
Phillips, D.Z. (1993). *Wittgenstein and Religion*. London: Macmillan.
Schroeder, S. (2007). The Tightrope Walker. *Ratio*, 20, 442–463.
Searle, J. (1987). Wittgenstein. In B. Magee (Ed.). *The Great Philosophers* (pp. 320–347). London: BBC Books.
Swinburne, R. (2011). God as the Simplest Explanation of the Universe. In A. O'Hear (Ed.). *Philosophy and Religion* (pp. 3–24). Cambridge: Cambridge University Press.
Turner, D. (1995). *The Darkness of God*. Cambridge: Cambridge University Press.

Further Reading

Barrett, C. (1991). *Wittgenstein on Ethics and Religious Belief*. Oxford: Blackwell.
Kerr, F. (1996). *Theology after Wittgenstein*. Oxford: Blackwell.
Phillips, D.Z., Rhees, R., and von der Ruhr, M. (Eds). (2005). *Religion and Wittgenstein's Legacy*. London: Ashgate.
Schönbaumsfeld, G. (2007). *A Confusion of the Spheres*. Oxford: Oxford University Press.

43

Wittgenstein and Psychoanalysis

EDWARD HARCOURT

1 Introduction

Of the extraordinary roll call of Viennese cultural celebrities who were Wittgenstein's rough contemporaries, some were certainly far closer to Wittgenstein than Freud was. But though there is no evidence that Freud and Wittgenstein ever met, there were a number of indirect personal connections between them. And though psychoanalysis was not a major theme of Wittgenstein's work, it was a theme that Wittgenstein could not leave alone, and we find him going over much the same small set of questions about it for approximately the last 20 years of his life. After describing briefly some of the personal connections that relate Wittgenstein to psychoanalysis, I turn to psychoanalysis as it features in Wittgenstein's writing (which in practice means Freud). The subject can be divided into three main themes: the unconscious; dreams, jokes, and the nature of psychoanalytic explanation; and the relation between psychoanalysis and Wittgenstein's method in philosophy (on this latter theme see also Chapter 13, PHILOSOPHY AND PHILOSOPHICAL METHOD). All three themes have had, and continue to have, a considerable afterlife. Wittgenstein's continuing influence on philosophical thinking about the unconscious and about psychoanalytic explanation will be evident in my discussion of these themes in Wittgenstein's work itself. To capture some further echoes of Wittgenstein's writing about psychoanalysis, I also add two further sections, one on Wittgensteinian philosophy that has been self-consciously "psychoanalytical" in its method, the other on Wittgensteinian influences on post-Freudian psychoanalytic practice.

2 Wittgenstein's Connections to Freud

Though Freud continued to publish up to his death in 1939, the only works by him to which Wittgenstein refers in writing were written before World War I: *The Interpretation of Dreams* (1900), *The Psychopathology of Everyday Life* (1901), and *Jokes and their Relation to the Unconscious* (1905). (Wittgenstein also refers to Breuer, whose *Studies in Hysteria*, co-authored with Freud, appeared in 1895.) It is possible that Wittgenstein first read these works only around 1930, when he began to discuss psychoanalysis in his writing (MS 109, p.174), though the fact that these discussions are so short on detail and the early publication dates of the works themselves might be taken to suggest that Wittgenstein was relying on memories of his reading that go much further back. Wittgenstein would surely have been acquainted with psychoanalysis – whether through reading or not – well before his first written mention of it. The Breuer and Freud volume was in his family's library and it is reported that the Wittgenstein siblings took special pleasure in trading jokes with one another, under the influence of Freud's 1905 book (Prokop, 2003, p.104). Wittgenstein's sister Margarete took her adolescent son Thomas for analysis with Freud on account of his stammer (Prokop, 2003, pp.202, 222) which, since the boy was born in 1906, may be presumed to have occurred some time between 1916 and the early 1920s; "suppose you were analysed when you had a stammer" introduces some 1938 remarks of Wittgenstein's on the criteria for the truth of psychoanalytic interpretations (LC 25).

But even if Wittgenstein was acquainted with psychoanalysis well before 1930, indirect personal connections brought it closer to the forefront of his mind from the mid-1920s onwards. Wittgenstein's meetings with the Vienna Circle began in 1928; according to a junior member of the Circle, Heinrich Neider, "numerous members of the Vienna Circle were in analysis" (Bouveresse, [1991] 1995, p.7); certainly Schlick was (Money-Kyrle, 1979, p.266). More importantly, Frank Ramsey traveled to Austria in 1924 to have analysis with Freud's follower Theodor Reik (Forrester, 2004, p.11). Ramsey visited Wittgenstein in Lower Austria to ask him questions about the *Tractatus* and had an argument with him about Freud in England in 1925 (Forrester, 2004, p.17; see also Paul, 2012), before the two saw a great deal of each other after Wittgenstein's return to Cambridge in 1929. A third connection runs via Wittgenstein's sister Margarete, with whom he was in contact more or less throughout his life. She was already thinking about Freud's views of dream interpretation in 1918, complaining – as Wittgenstein himself did later – about Freud's determination to find sexual meaning in dreams ("pity he's so [...] one-track," Prokop, 2003, p.100). She also read Freud's *Civilization and Its Discontents* when it came out in 1930, finding it "dreadfully bad." As long as Freud stuck to "the bodily and the psychical" he got it "about 90% right," but "when he gets philosophical and deals with guilt, happiness and such, he comes out with unfortunate rubbish" (Prokop, 2003, p.202). She nonetheless entered an analysis with Freud in 1937, and in 1938 was instrumental in securing permission for him to leave Austria for England, receiving from Freud an inscribed copy of *The Future of an Illusion* on the day of his departure (Nedo and Ranchetti, 1983, p.301) and a letter from him from England (Subotincic, 2000, p.60). Margarete Wittgenstein also left an unpublished manuscript, apparently from the early 1940s, a "psychoanalytical investigation" of the success of the Nazis (Prokop, 2003, p.245, n.415). Even if Wittgenstein's interest in psychoanalysis was less long-standing than his sister's, it seems unlikely that his interest in it was not in part stimulated by hers (though perhaps also vice versa).

3   Freud in Wittgenstein's Writing: Introductory

There is an odd atmosphere to Wittgenstein's remarks about psychoanalysis. On the one hand he is on record as making some very enthusiastic remarks about it. He was "greatly impressed when he first read Freud" (WAM 39); on first reading *The Interpretation of Dreams*, he thought: "Here at last is a psychologist who has something to say" (RW 136). Nor was it just a matter of a good first impression: to Norman Malcolm in the 1940s he praised Freud's "extraordinary scientific achievement"; to M. O'C. Drury in 1948 he said "no one today can do psychoanalysis the way [Freud] did" (RR 154); and to Rush Rhees in the mid-1940s he described himself as "a disciple of Freud," "a follower of Freud" (LC 41), and as "one influenced by Freud" (PCR 12). On the other hand he can also be very negative about Freud: his "whole way of thinking wants combatting"; it requires "a very strong and keen and persistent criticism to see through the mythology" (LC 50); Freud offered "fanciful pseudo-explanations" (CV 62); "unless you think *very* clearly psychoanalysis is a dangerous and a foul practice" (WAM 39); Freud's followers had made "an abominable mess" (M 107).

One possibility, then, is that there is no settled judgment to be extracted from Wittgenstein's remarks about Freud, that is, nothing to be got by taking the balance of the positive and the negative: the only reality is his veering between the two. Another possibility is that, as Rhees says, Wittgenstein's remarks on psychoanalysis are a sustained attempt "to separate what is valuable in Freud" from what should be rejected (LC 41; cf. DB 16–17). The first possibility derives some support from the fact that Wittgenstein returns again and again to the same narrow set of psychoanalytic ideas: unless his interest in Freud had something of the character of an obsession, how could he have sustained himself for so long on such slender fare? But even if there is something to this, it is not a reason for *us* not to try to take the balance of the positive and the negative, and see what's left. The questions in relation to Wittgenstein's treatment of Freud that I shall address are therefore the following: where (in Wittgenstein's view) does the line fall between the objectionable and the unobjectionable in Freud? Are Wittgenstein's objections to Freud well founded? And, supposing they are, is the philosophically tidied-up version of psychoanalysis – which has been built upon Wittgenstein's remarks by more than one commentator – both coherent and more than mere common sense?

4 Freud in Wittgenstein's Writing I: The Unconscious

Sometimes Wittgenstein mentions the unconscious more or less *en passant*, to illustrate a more complex philosophical point; sometimes as a topic of interest in its own right. His most extensive remarks about it, which are of both kinds, occur in "The Blue Book" (BB 23, 57; cf. AWL 39 ff.). When "psychoanalysis talks of unconscious thoughts, acts of volition, etc.," no philosophical mistake is made, since all that has happened is that a "new notation" – that is, a new use of the words "thought" and so on – has been introduced. Indeed this usage *couldn't* involve a mistake, since notations on their own do not say anything, and can "at any time be retranslated into ordinary language" (BB 23). The notation is of philosophical interest, however, because it is so easy to think – falsely, thanks to the notation's "calling up new pictures and analogies" (BB 23) – that its use reports a new discovery. If we fall into that trap, we will "be misled into thinking that a stupendous discovery has been made" (like "the psychoanalysts [who] [...] were misled by their own way of expression into thinking that [...] they had, in a sense, discovered conscious thoughts which were unconscious" (BB 57; AWL 40; Freud, [1933] 1953–66a, p.159), but "the contribution [of psychoanalysis] to science lies precisely in having extended research to the mental field"); or else be "tempted to deny the possibility" of unconscious thoughts (BB 57, like those "revolted" by "the idea of there being" such things, ibid.), though these objectors to psychoanalysis were – if only they knew it – objecting only to a form of description.

Had the psychoanalysts then discovered nothing? The "unconscious toothache" example in the "Blue Book" suggests this view, since the phenomena dressed up as unconscious toothache by the new notation – a toothache in a particular tooth that comes and goes, perhaps – are boringly familiar (cf. PG 48, 106, 181; PI §149). But, according to the "Blue Book" account, the psychoanalysts *did* discover something: "new psychological reactions" (BB 57; M 102). Moreover Wittgenstein does not seem always to have regarded the language of unconscious states of mind as a terminological innovation (and so *a fortiori* not as an innovation misunderstood as a discovery). In a typescript from 1946–1947, he says that "we" – not just "the psychoanalysts" – would ("perhaps") say that a man who "suddenly climbs on a chair and then gets down again" without being able to say why, though "he reports having noticed this and that from the chair, and that it seems as if he climbed up in order to observe this," had "acted with *unconscious* intention" (RPP I §225; cf. LC 22–3; PPF 282). And in a 1931 manuscript, Wittgenstein speaks, without a trace of a scare-quote, about "unconscious contempt," and simply goes on to explain what that useful expression means (MS 155, pp.30v–31r).

5   Freud in Wittgenstein's Writing II: Dreams, Jokes, and the Nature of Psychoanalytic Explanation

On dreams, Wittgenstein agreed with Freud – though of course also with a great many others (Freud, [1900] 1953–66d, pp.1–5) – that

> dreams [...] seem to have something puzzling and in a special way interesting about them — so that we want an interpretation of them. (LC 45; cf. PCR 12; CV 75, 79; LW II §§195–6)

However, he thought Freud was wrong to claim that all dreams are wish-fulfillments (LC 42; CV 50; RR 154), or that they all have sexual meaning (LC 23–4, 47–8). He also said that "in Freudian analysis the dream is as it were dismantled. It loses its original sense *completely*," because it substitutes an interpretation for "the dream story [which] [...] has its own charm, like a painting that attracts & inspires us" (CV 78–9).

One might think from this last passage that Wittgenstein thought – in the spirit perhaps of "we must do away with all *explanation*, and description alone must take its place" (PI §109) – that dreams should simply be contemplated, and that *any* interpretation of them spoils them. But that suggestion is belied by the fact that Wittgenstein frequently interpreted his own dreams (DB *passim*), so the objection seems to be only to the straitjacket of wish-fulfillment or sexual interpretations. The guiding thought behind Wittgenstein's objections to the thematic monotony of Freudian dream-interpretation seems really to be "I will show you differences" (Monk, 1990, p.537).

Beyond this point, however, dreams are also an occasion – jokes are another – for Wittgenstein to charge Freud with confusion about the interrelation between, on the one hand, the criteria for the truth of psychoanalytic interpretations and, on the other, the standing of psychoanalysis as a would-be scientific enterprise. This objection extends beyond dreams to distinctively psychoanalytic claims to knowledge more generally. The objection may be introduced by Moore's summary of it from Wittgenstein's 1932 lectures:

> [Psychoanalysis] does not enable you to discover the *cause* but only the *reason* of, e.g., laughter. [...] [P]sychoanalysis is successful only if the patient agrees to the explanation offered by the analyst, and [...] since this is so, what is being agreed to isn't a hypothesis. (M 108)

That is, Freud claims that the criterion for the correctness of a psychoanalytic interpretation of a joke or dream is the patient's assent (cf. AWL 39–40). But assent, either the patient's or anybody else's, could not possibly be the criterion for the truth of a causal hypothesis, so it cannot be the case – as Freud also claims – that the interpretation is a hypothesis about the dream's or the laughter's unconscious causes. The link with the objections summarized in the previous section should be obvious: It's "the hypothetical part of his theory, the subconscious, [...] which is not satisfactory" (AWL 39; Cioffi, 1998, p.206). (Freud, incidentally, warns against the use of the word "subconscious" – as opposed to "unconscious" – "which has become so popular in the more recent literature of the psychoneuroses" ([1900] 1953–66d, p.615), a caution that evidently fell on deaf ears as far as Wittgenstein or at least his note-takers were concerned.)

Now there are many phenomena, dreams and laughter apparently included, for which in Wittgenstein's view the kind of explanation that depends on assent is entirely proper. One is having something on the tip of one's tongue (the speaker's saying "'that's it!' [...] certifies the word as having been found" (CV 68; cf. LC 18)); another is overruling another's claims about their feelings (MS 110, p.230). A third such type of explanation seems to be the wide class of what Wittgenstein calls "aesthetic explanations" which are not "causal" but do "what aesthetics does: puts two factors together"; and certainly Wittgenstein sees some of Freud's explanations as of this kind, e.g., of jokes (AWL 39), and Freud's connection between the fetal position and sleep (AWL 39; cf. LW II 86). Indeed it is even in order, in explanations where the patient's assent is the criterion for correctness, to say that the explanation gives the patient's unconscious state of mind (e.g., the unconscious reason for the joke), as long as we do not make the mistake of thinking that in so saying, we are saying something "as to what was happening at the moment when he laughed" (M 108). If that was all there was to it, the objection would be very mild: not to Freud's explanations themselves, nor to the *word* "unconscious," but only to Freud's self-understanding (a self-understanding that would be proper to a "psychologist," since "in psychology" we are "interested in causal connections" (AWL 38), though Freud himself – had he only been able to see it – wasn't one).

However, this is not quite all there is to it. For a start, Freud's scientistic self-misunderstanding has consequences: he doesn't stick to the limits of interpretation that the assent criterion imposes but corrects the patient if their explanation doesn't accord with his "hypothesis." This is a mistake he as it were would not have dared to make had he realized what he was doing. Secondly, the explanations Freud offers are, in Wittgenstein's view, unreliable in a way that saying what was on the tip of one's tongue is not: apropos Freud's explanation of a patient's "beautiful dream" Wittgenstein says "this ugly explanation makes you say you really had these thoughts, whereas in any ordinary sense you really didn't" (LC 20). People are "charmed" by the kind of interpretation Freud is prepared to recognize as correct, so they assent to it, but this complicating "charm" is no part of the operation of the assent criterion *per se*. Whereas in saying what's on the tip of one's tongue one is free to answer without undue influence from elsewhere, in Freud assent is contaminated by the "charm" of his various "mythologies" which attract us overwhelmingly to certain kinds of explanation. As to what this "charm" is, Wittgenstein makes various suggestions: the charm of any explanation of the form "this is only that," the charm of the ugly (LC 23), the charm of "origins" (LC 43) or the "secret cellar" (LC 25), the "new mythology." It's not clear which Wittgenstein loathes in Freud the more: the particular mythology that he is (in Wittgenstein's view) merely campaigning for, or the fact that he dresses up this campaign as a kind of science.

I would now like to offer two sets of remarks by way of commentary. First of all, Wittgenstein's assimilation of Freudian dream- or joke-interpretations to "aesthetic investigations" needs to be treated with great caution. In such investigations, various things are "laid alongside" the initial object of investigation, and whether anything is accomplished by so doing depends on somebody's assent. But whose? Wittgenstein's idea is that if dream-interpretations were not contaminated by Freudian suggestion, it's the *patient's* assent that would properly be decisive. But although you can (Wittgenstein says) "make a person see what Brahms was driving at by showing him lots of different pieces by Brahms, or by comparing him with a contemporary author" (M 106), it is one's interlocutor's assent, not Brahms's, that's relevant to the success of *this* exercise in "plac[ing] things side by side" (AWL 40). Moreover if this method fails to make your interlocutor "see what you see," this is not proof that you didn't, after all, see anything, but simply "an end of the discussion" (M 106; cf. LC 20–1). So if dream-interpretation were exactly like "aesthetic investigation," the (in Wittgenstein's view false) assumption that psychoanalytic interpretations are "hypotheses" would not be needed to show that Freud was not making any mistake in ignoring his patient's dissent and sticking to his own interpretation: it would just be a further case of one person not seeing what another sees. This wouldn't matter if all Wittgenstein's objections to Freud come to are that he thinks Freud regularly chooses objects of comparison that Wittgenstein would not (and that Wittgenstein finds distasteful, etc.). But if the objections are – as they seem to be – also in part methodological, the comparison of psychoanalytic interpretation with "aesthetic investigation" (which puzzled Moore (M 105)) is unhelpful.

Secondly, how plausible *is* it that patient assent is the criterion of correctness for explanations that refer to unconscious thoughts and feelings? Wittgenstein's discussion of unconscious motivation in the "Lectures on Aesthetics" is relevant here:

> Suppose Taylor and I are walking along the river and Taylor stretches out his hand and pushes me in the river. When I ask why he did this he says: "I was pointing out something to you," whereas the psycho-analyst says that Taylor subconsciously hated me. [...] When would we say that Taylor's explanation was correct? When he had never shown any unfriendly feelings, when a church-steeple and I were in his field of vision, and Taylor was known to be truthful. But, under the same circumstances, the psycho-analyst's explanation may also be correct. [...] The explanations could in a sense be contradictory and yet both be correct. (LC 22–3)

This is striking: The unconscious explanation "may [...] be correct," and yet there is no mention of its correctness depending on Taylor's assent. What *is* relevant to its correctness is a further fact, that "the person pushed in had a similarity with the father of the other person" (LC 22–3; cf. RPP I §225). The explanatory model Wittgenstein has in mind here seems closer to "aesthetic investigation" than to the patient's-assent-as-criterion model: even if it would be troubling to concede that, absent one's interlocutor's assent, reason-giving is simply at an end (because, for instance, further reasons might lie in general observations about the emotions to which human beings are subject), certainly the reasons in the Taylor case "are in the nature of further descriptions" (M 106). One might try to relieve the tension between Wittgenstein's treatment of "unconscious motive" in the Taylor case and his treatment of dream-interpretations by suggesting that further facts about the patient are relevant in the former case but not in the latter. This *might* be true of claims about what was on the tip of one's tongue, but it is surely not so for dreams: a psychoanalyst (or indeed anyone else) may be familiar with details of the dreamer's preoccupations, and with more general facts about what people in the patient's predicament think or feel, which suggest interpretations of the dream that the dreamer may well not acknowledge.

Indeed Wittgenstein's own remarks about the way in which patient assent may be contaminated – Wittgenstein dwells on the "charm" of certain kinds of explanation, but he might just as well have mentioned the prestige of the analyst, or the thrill of being of one mind with the analyst that assent can create (Caper, 1999, p.115) – gives us further reason to doubt whether patient assent can, *on its own*, be the criterion of correctness of the interpretation of a dream or joke. For it makes no sense to speak of contamination unless one can specify – as one surely can – what it would be for assent to be *un*contaminated. But if it can be either contaminated or uncontaminated then, though assent could still be *a* criterion, it won't be *the* criterion. Does Wittgenstein need to say that it is in order to push through his two chief objections to Freud? As to the first – that Freud contaminates patient assent by suggesting interpretations that are appealing but bad – clearly not. As to the second – that dream- or joke-interpretations, or ascriptions of unconscious motives, are not causal hypotheses – things are less clear. The patient's-assent criterion excludes the explanation-as-hypothesis view. But that criterion is not needed in order to exclude it, for it's also excluded by the idea that interpretation is a matter of "further description," *if* this is just another species of "aesthetic explanation" where failure to get the other to "see what you see" is just "an end" of the discussion (M 106), in the sense that there's no fact of the matter rather than that one has reached an epistemic impasse. If on the other hand exchanges of reasons in the psychological case are not to be thought of in this "no fact" way, why couldn't psychological explanations proceed by "further description" precisely because adding further descriptions is a way, if not of establishing a particular causal hypothesis, at least of ruling out inadmissible ones? The argument from the claim that various psychological explanations proceed by "further description" to the conclusion that they are not about causal hypotheses seems to need some extra premises.

6 Freud in Wittgenstein's Writing III: Psychoanalysis and the "Correct Method in Philosophy"

There is no doubt that in a certain phase of his philosophical development, Wittgenstein took the comparison between psychoanalysis and what he saw as the correct method in philosophy very seriously. This attitude on Wittgenstein's part may also have lasted long enough to explain some well-known methodological remarks in *Philosophical Investigations*. The chief question to which the comparison gives rise is whether it really casts light on Wittgenstein's method, or whether it is based to a greater or lesser extent on a misunderstanding of Freud's psychoanalysis.

Wittgenstein's explicit comparisons between Freud's method and his own occur between the time he began what became the so-called Big Typescript (around 1932) and the writing down of TS 220, in 1937 or 1938 (Baker, 1997/2004; 2003; Majetschak, 2008), and most saliently in the Big Typescript itself and in "Dictation for Schlick" and "Our Method," dictated to Waismann (VW 1–83; 277–311). The starting point for the comparison is the idea that philosophical problems stem from false "analogies" or "pictures" suggested to us by language – an idea that, as far as I know, has no echo in Freud. But once that point is granted, the comparison with psychoanalysis can take off. Philosophical puzzlement is a cause of mental disquiet or unease (M 114) – also presumably the condition of anyone who refers himself for psychoanalysis. Philosophy, like psychoanalysis, cures this unease by bringing what is unconscious to consciousness ("A simile at work in the unconscious is made harmless by being articulated" (VW 69; cf. MS 109, p.174; BT 409; PG 381–2)); and, though this comparison is more rarely drawn than the previous one, philosophy like psychoanalysis has to deal with resistances to giving up such analogies ("What has to be overcome is not a difficulty of the intellect but of the will," BT 407). Furthermore the success of this kind of philosophical cure depends – as, in Wittgenstein's view, the success of psychoanalytic treatment or interpretation (LC 25, 44, 52) – on the "patient's" assent to the "diagnosis" offered (BT 410; Baker, 1997/2004, p.159). Once assent is given, the effect is not only to remove the destructive power of the analogy but also to bring about "a new way of seeing things" (Baker, 1997/2004, p.158).

Some of these comparisons with Freud – that psychoanalysis proceeds by making the unconscious conscious, and that the difficulties in doing so are due to resistances on the patient's part – are comparisons Freud himself would have had no difficulty in recognizing (Majetschak, 2008, p.52). Others depend on Wittgenstein's own (counter-Freudian) understanding of what Freud was *really* doing. But even if all that is accepted, there is at least one point at which the comparison between their methods appears to falter. Baker has put it very clearly: while psychoanalysis addresses conflicts of "conative or affective states," philosophy seems to address only conflicts "in ways of seeing things," in people's "prejudices or dogmas [that] clash with each other and creat[e] fogs of confusion," or between different things that – thanks to these dogmas – we feel driven to say; in psychoanalysis we are concerned with "patterns of behaviour (e.g. manifestations of an Oedipus complex)," whereas in philosophy – seemingly – our concern is "with patterns in the uses of our words" (Baker, 1997/2004, pp.153, 159). The question is what we should make of this.

One response is exemplified by Alice Ambrose, Morris Lazerowitz, and their followers (Lazerowitz, 1985; Ambrose, 1966; 1972; Lazerowitz and Ambrose, 1984; Kennick, 1970). According to them, (non-Wittgensteinian) philosophers mistakenly believe their words are "being used to express a theory" when in fact they simply "herald a redefinition" (Lazerowitz, 1985, p.209). This is very close to Wittgenstein's own view of philosophical disagreements over solipsism, or over the existence of an unconscious mind, in the "Blue Book." (Ambrose of course was one of the students who transcribed the "Blue Book.") *Part* of the Wittgensteinian philosopher's task is therefore to "expose the verbal content behind the ontological façade" (Lazerowitz, 1985, p.209). However, Ambrose and Lazerowitz's conception of the proper Wittgensteinian method in philosophy has a further articulation. What makes it *difficult* for philosophers to acknowledge their theories as "mere linguistic contrivance[s]" (Lazerowitz, 1985, p.211) is that they are held in place by "unconscious ideas" of a kind that are the stuff of Freudian dream- or joke-interpretations, and that it is psychologically costly for the philosopher to renounce (1985, pp.236–7). Thus in Lazerowitz's view philosophers have been kept from seeing the claim that "one cannot think of what does not exist" as a mere "redefinition" because this would rob it of its psychological function of "fend[ing] off the invasion of anxiety," for the *unconscious* meaning of these words is that "there is something [sc., the penis] [...] not possessed by some and whose loss is feared by others" and "whose non-existence is too painful to be thought of," this latter point supplying the double meaning for "one cannot think" of it (1985, p.238).

Lazerowitz, Ambrose, and others have taken to heart Wittgenstein's idea that the method of philosophy is the method of psychoanalysis but, noting the apparent limits to the analogy claimed by Baker, have filled in the gap – the third layer of the "three-layer structure of a philosophical theory" (Ambrose, 1972, p.25) – on Wittgenstein's behalf, suggesting moreover that Wittgenstein only failed to do so himself because he couldn't bear to (1972, p.25). But their "completion" of Wittgenstein's method is unsatisfactory, and not just because the particular unconscious explanations they suggest would have attracted Wittgenstein's scorn. For one thing, solipsists and others usually offer arguments for their views and one will surely be the more inclined to look for an explanation in terms of unconscious defenses the weaker the argument offered, and in particular, the less satisfactorily the solipsist is able *by his own lights* to reply to objections. But Ambrose *et al.*'s diagnoses apply to philosophical positions *per se*, independently of the arguments anyone offers for them.

Secondly, philosophical problems are usually addressed in a way that bypasses the personal life of the "sufferer": we don't ask fellow philosophers about their dreams or their past or their current special others with a view to helping them to get clear on a philosophical issue, and it is not clear that doing so would help; but this sort of probing is essential in psychoanalysis. This is not to say that philosophical problem-solving isn't personalized (Baker, 1997/2004, p.210): different people may well need different approaches to help them get unstuck philosophically. But to say that is not to say that any particular person's way out of it need involve the examination of their personal lives. Of course it might be said that even if this investigation of the personal is usually missing from philosophy, it shouldn't be, and Ambrose *et al.* remedy that defect. But in fact it's precisely this kind of shaping of the investigation to the particular patient that is *missing* from their version of therapeutic philosophy: philosophical solipsism (for example) is at once a "symptom," but a symptom whose meaning we can ascertain without knowing anything in particular about the person whose symptom it is supposed to be (Brearley, 1984, p.183).

Eugen Fischer's view, which also takes the analogy between philosophy and psychological therapy very seriously, makes for an instructive contrast (2004; 2012). Fischer is impressed, like Baker, by the fact that the conflicts philosophy deals with *aren't* emotional ones – Wittgensteinian "drives to misunderstand" (Fischer, 2004, p.107) are precisely "diseases of the intellect" (CV 50); philosophical disquietude is sufficiently explained by the thought that mere platitudes get "distorted" "through inadvertent misinterpretation or mindless inference, in line with ideas [one] unreflectively rejects" (Fischer, 2004, p.112). So, though Wittgenstein's philosophy is indeed therapeutic in some sense, the correct object of comparison is not psychoanalysis but cognitive behavioral therapy (CBT):

> the problems Wittgenstein tries to cope with in sections 138–97 of the *Investigations* are in some pertinent ways similar [to those described by CBT and] [...] Wittgenstein attacks

[them] much in line with the 'cognitive approach', which proceeds by identifying and [...] breaking the relevant cognitive habits. (Fischer, 2004, p.91)

Were the analogy with CBT not available, then – supposing philosophical tangles are indeed cognitive and not emotional – the response to Ambrose and Lazerowitz might still be that a philosophical theory can be *like* "a kind of neurotic symptom" (Lazerowitz, 1985, pp.236–7) without actually being one. But once it *is* available, a necessarily incomplete analogy with psychoanalysis seems pointless, because it breaks down at just the point at which it might begin to be illuminating. Thus one would be forced to conclude that Wittgenstein made as much of the comparison with psychoanalysis as he did only because it was (unsurprisingly) the only form of psychological therapy he had ever encountered.

But are philosophical problems, as Wittgenstein saw them, merely cognitive tangles? The fact that Ambrose and Lazerowitz's psychoanalytical alternative is unsatisfactory doesn't show that they are, nor does the intellectualist view do justice to Wittgenstein's assertion that philosophical problems are "deep disquietudes" (PI §111), still less – though such remarks are rare in Wittgenstein – to the idea that in struggling with philosophical problems we need to overcome resistances of the will (BT 407). Wittgenstein's struggle with philosophical problems seemed to engulf his whole being, so it is not credible that he should have thought of them merely as intellectual problems, however troubling they too can be. The high color of the language in which he speaks of them and their solution surely betrays the presence of powerful emotions (Lazerowitz and Ambrose 1984, p.13). What's needed, then, is an account that captures the fact that for Wittgenstein philosophical problems were existential not merely intellectual, but without burdening his words with Freudian "conjectures" (Lazerowitz, 1985, p.211) about their unconscious meaning. I suggest that the more than merely intellectual significance that philosophical problems had for Wittgenstein stems not, indeed, from the fact that he saw them as symptoms of neurosis but from the fact that he saw ridding himself of them as a way of transforming himself into a "decent" person (which he constantly thought he wasn't (*Gesamtbriefwechsel* 25 June 1919; cf. ibid., 16 January 1918, 24 February 1925), of redeeming himself from the fallen state that philosophical puzzlement betokens. (I develop this suggestion further in Harcourt, 2012; cf. Forrester, 2004, p.17.)

7 Taking the Balance: "Bawdy," "Philosophical Froth" plus ...?

Wittgenstein has had a significant influence on philosophical commentary on psychoanalysis, and some influence on the development of psychoanalysis itself.

As to the former, one of the abiding criticisms of Freud has been that his work is not properly scientific, whether in the form of the claim that it is bad science, or that its claims are unfalsifiable and so not science at all. (The criterion of scientificity is Popper's, though Popper (1963, pp.37–8) was ready to forgive Freud a good deal: "Much of [Freud's work] is of considerable importance, [...] describ[ing] some facts, but in the manner of myths" and containing "most interesting psychological suggestions, but not in a testable form.") So the appeal of Wittgenstein's view to psychoanalysis is obvious: if Freud misunderstood the nature of his own enterprise, the criticism falls only on what Freud thought he was doing, not – at least as far as *this* line of criticism goes – on what he did. Wittgenstein's reconstruction has been developed, by applying his general approach to a wider range of Freudian concepts and writings than those Wittgenstein himself dealt with, to great effect by e.g., Alisdair MacIntyre (1958/2004) and Ilham Dilman (1983; 1984; 1988).

As to the latter, some Wittgensteinian versions of psychoanalysis (Dilman, MacIntyre) sound very like British "independent" psychoanalysis, and some British "independent" psychoanalysis – in its antitheoretical stance, its prizing of ordinariness of utterance, and its hostility to sexual reductionism or to reductionism about art and religion – sounds like Wittgenstein (Winnicott, 1985; Rycroft, 1991; Lomas, 1973). However, one must be cautious in claiming Wittgensteinian *influence* on "independent" psychoanalysis. Psychoanalysis had established itself in (and perhaps begun to be transformed by) Cambridge before Wittgenstein returned there in the late 1920s: analyst Susan Isaacs established the Malting House Lane school there in 1924; Isaacs, Ramsey, James Strachey, and others read papers to the Cambridge "1925 Group," a condition of membership of which was having been psychoanalyzed (Forrester, 2004, p.3); and many of the same people were also members of the Heretics, whose Secretary was John (A.J.T.D.) Wisdom and to whom Wittgenstein read his "A Lecture on Ethics" (PO 36–44) in 1929. So later British psychoanalysts and psychotherapists were able to discover a community of thought between Wittgenstein and their own immediate psychoanalytic ancestors (e.g., Michael Brearley who, like Dilman, studied philosophy with Wisdom; or John Heaton, Trinity undergraduate in the late 1940s: see Heaton, 2000; 2010, p.x). The history of these complex lineages is still to be written.

In any case, let's suppose that the Wittgensteinian rereadings succeed in showing that *all* the objectionable bits of Freud, his "bawdy" (LC 24) included, are "philosophical froth" (Dilman, 1983, p.3). They nonetheless give rise to an awkward question: is what's left over once the froth is gone more than mere common sense? It's often said by defenders of Freud that he didn't discover the unconscious, but only a *theory* of the unconscious. That is meant to block criticisms of Freud based on his sometimes exaggerated claims to originality, and the defense is worth making, since unconscious explanations of behavior by way of thoughts, emotions, intentions, and the like are a commonplace at least in imaginative literature way before Freud (and continue to be so now). But if what Freud *added* to such explanations is just a series of philosophical mistakes then, when – as Rhees puts it (LC 41) – we "separate what is valuable in Freud" from what should be rejected, we are left only with something we had plenty of already. That substantive challenge requires an answer, and unless it is answered, an interpretative challenge follows close on its heels: what on earth did *Wittgenstein* – after all, the originator of the substantive challenge – think was Freud's "extraordinary [...] achievement"?

The substantive question is a large one and I can only offer some indications here as to how it should be answered. First of all, if the Wittgensteinian reconstruction of psychoanalysis includes the thought that psychoanalysis is *simply* an exercise in "interpretation" or "giving reasons," it cannot be right. Psychoanalytic discourse is too various for any one simple theory about it to stand a chance of being correct (Farrell, 1981), not least because in between its (quite possibly bad) philosophical components and the interpretations of which "hermeneuticism" (Cioffi, 1998, p.130) makes so much lie a number of claims, both general and particular, about human beings and their behavior that are open to empirical confirmation or refutation. Many of those Freud made seem to be false (e.g., that "the mental apparatus endeavours to keep the quantity of excitation present in it as low as possible," Freud, [1920] 1953–66b, p.9), but his successors have made considerable efforts to repair the problem that "hermeneuticism" pretends to magic away.

Secondly – and focusing only on those aspects of the psychoanalytic enterprise that might be called interpretative – the worry that Wittgensteinian reconstruction narrows the gap between psychoanalysis and common sense almost to nothing rests, in part, on the thought that psychoanalytic explanations are all of one kind, and of a kind indeed that would be familiar even if Freud had never existed. Unfortunately Wittgenstein does little explicitly to discourage this thought with his insistent contrast between causal explanations and "giving reasons," which covers at least two sorts of reason, reasons for action and the "*reason* why [someone] laughed" (AWL 40). But there is in fact considerable variety to the explanations psychoanalysis offers.

In one very common kind of case, explanation appeals to an unconscious intention. This is so in Wittgenstein's case of the man who "suddenly climbs on a chair and then gets down again" (RPP I §225): he "noticed this and that from the chair," and in the circumstances, seeing those things would be a good enough reason for him to climb up, so we say he climbed up intentionally, though because he can't *say* why he did so, we say the intention was unconscious. If that were the only type of explanatory appeal to the unconscious to be found in Freud, there would be some substance to the worry that he added little to what we already knew. But this is not the only one, and I shall mention four further types (with no pretense that the list is exhaustive).

In the first type of case, we form an intention to say something, akratically fail to act on it (e.g., out of fear), but the thing "slips out" anyway (Freud, [1901] 2002, pp.87–8). Here it need not be the *intention* that's unconscious: the interesting feature of these cases is rather that the *phenomenology* of utterance has, for the agent, the character of the involuntary. But the action is so well explained by the agent's intentions – indeed by intentions he may be fully capable of avowing – that we say the "mistake" was an intentional action. A second kind of case of "symptomatic error" is exemplified by the following:

> Frau F. said, of her first lesson in a language course [...]: 'It's really interesting, the tutor is a nice young Englishman. In the very first lesson he indicated to me *durch die Bluse* [through my blouse]' – and corrects herself: '*durch die Blume* [lit., 'through the flower' but, colloquially, 'with veiled hints'] – that he would rather give me private tuition'. (Freud, [1901] 2002, p.78)

Here, unlike the last type of case, there is no unconscious communicative *intention* on Frau F.'s part: her attraction to the tutor simply betrays itself involuntarily in her utterance, much as emotions betray themselves in facial expressions.

Two further types of explanatory appeal to the unconscious may be illustrated by Freud's case of a girl's obsessive bedtime ritual, which involved arranging her bedding in a particular way (Freud, [1916/17] 1953–66c, pp.264–9). The arranging behavior consists of a series of (consciously) intentional actions. But these intentions – as it might be "I am making sure the pillow doesn't touch the headboard" – fail satisfactorily to explain the action, since the agent's *further* reasons for so acting give out immediately, and yet – unlike whistling or running one's fingers through one's hair – actions of this kind do not remotely make sense *without* a further reason. Now unconscious further reasons are – Freud says – ready to hand: the girl's ritual prevented her parents from going to bed, so it manifested her unconscious desire to prevent her parents from having sexual intercourse, thereby averting an outcome she (unconsciously) very much did not want, namely a sibling who would be her rival. But, as MacIntyre has recently emphasized, this is not – like the "chair" case – a matter of the girl's unconsciously acting for reasons, but rather of her "acting *as if* unconsciously guided by reasons." For here, "the motives that control [her] behaviour" "preclude [her] from acting as a practical reasoner does," since they preclude her from asking whether her reasons for action are *good* reasons (MacIntyre, 1958/2004, pp.25–6). (Compare also the way panic – which is of course conscious – both drives action and precludes one from evaluating reasons.) However, the girl could after all have prevented her parents from going to bed in any number of ways, so this last explanation doesn't reach to the details of the ritual, on which the girl was insistent. To focus on just one detail, the girl would fluff the eiderdown in such a way that it made a hump, then smooth it again. According to Freud, this was in some sense the girl's undoing of her mother's (imagined) pregnancy ([1916/17] 1953–66c, p.268). Though various accounts of what's going on are possible, it's attractive to say that the girl, in fluffing the eiderdown, is *intentionally undoing her mother's pregnancy*. The intention is of course unconscious (because she cannot say what she is doing). What's more she cannot evaluate her reasons for so doing. But even if the intention were conscious – as when a child strokes an injured parent to "make it better" – the intention alone wouldn't be a full explanation: the child's action might have no healing effect and it might know this. To see how undoing the pregnancy is what's intentionally being done, we must see that the relation between the action and the intention is mediated by the *symbolic* connection – yet another thing the girl cannot articulate – between the hump in the eiderdown and pregnancy (Gardner, 1993, p.116).

Of course it is a substantive historical question to what extent even explanations of these further kinds were already part of the cultural currency before Freud. Be that as it may, they all differ substantially from the explanatory pattern exemplified by Wittgenstein's "chair" case, and whose availability we did not need psychoanalysis to grasp. Moreover, all four patterns invoke ideas of meaning, symbol, what's of value to the patient and what's of value generally in order to supply a kind of intelligibility to the actions they explain, and so fall within a broad category of explanations that "give reasons." So even once psychoanalytic explanation is reconstructed along Wittgensteinian lines, there is a large gap between what psychoanalysis has presumptively taught us about the explanation of human behavior and mere common sense.

It's a further substantive question whether what occupies this gap deserves to be thought of as distinctively psychoanalytical, or rather as simply marking the overlap between psychoanalysis properly so called and non-psychoanalytical psychodynamic psychotherapies (Gardner, 1993). Be that as it may, I suggest that the gap is sufficient to explain why Wittgenstein said – and meant – that Freud's achievement was "extraordinary" (though I can still make nothing of his describing Freud's achievement as "scientific"). Moreover the particularistic character of what Freud, on this reconstruction, adds to common sense fits the fact that what Wittgenstein especially valued in Freud was finding "new psychological reactions," or "phenomena and connexions not previously known" (BB 57; M 102). There is further evidence that this is where Wittgenstein located the value of Freud's contribution in the use Wittgenstein makes of Freudian "phenomena and connexions" in his own nonphilosophical writing. In a 1930 diary entry, for example, commenting on his love of cinema, Wittgenstein compares films to dreams and says "Freudian thoughts/methods can be applied to them directly" (DB 28–31). Wittgenstein's diaries frequently record dreams, some of them with interpretations (DB *passim*; *Gesamtbriefwechsel* 14 March 1944). Though the interpretations are not narrowly Freudian in suggesting a fantasized wish-fulfillment or sexual meaning, they show that Wittgenstein expected his dreams to express matters of personal importance that were on his mind (e.g., racial identity, or his then intended wife Marguerite Respinger). And in a 1948 letter to one of his sisters, and not in the context of any philosophical discussion of psychoanalysis, he offers a psychoanalytical interpretation of the fact that he couldn't get a Mendelssohn passage out of his mind (*Gesamtbriefwechsel* 15.3.48 cf. RPP I §262; PPF 268). Passages such as these show how far Wittgenstein internalized some – as he saw it – psychoanalytical ways of thinking.

References

Ambrose, A. (1966). *Essays in Analysis*. London: George Allen and Unwin.
Ambrose, A. (1972). Ludwig Wittgenstein: A Portrait. In A. Ambrose and M. Lazerowitz (Eds). *Ludwig Wittgenstein: Philosophy and Language* (pp.13–25). London: George Allen and Unwin.
Baker, G.P. (1997/2004). "Our" Method of Thinking about "Thinking." In G.P. Baker. *Wittgenstein's Method: Neglected Aspects* (pp.144–178). Ed. K.J. Morris. Oxford: Blackwell.
Baker, G.P. (2003). Wittgenstein's Method and Psychoanalysis. Reprinted in G.P. Baker. (2004). *Wittgenstein's Method: Neglected Aspects* (pp.205–222). Ed. K.J. Morris. Oxford: Blackwell.
Bouveresse, J. ([1991] 1995). *Wittgenstein Reads Freud: The Myth of the Unconscious*. Trans. C. Cosman. Princeton: Princeton University Press. (Original work published 1991.)
Brearley, M. (1984). Psycho-Analysis and Philosophy. In I. Dilman (Ed.). *Philosophy and Life: Essays on John Wisdom* (pp.179–200). The Hague: Nijhoff.
Caper, R. (1999). *A Mind of One's Own*. London: Routledge.
Cioffi, F. (1998). Wittgenstein on Freud's "Abominable Mess." In F. Cioffi. *Wittgenstein on Freud and Frazer* (pp.206–234). Cambridge: Cambridge University Press.
Dilman, I. (1983). *Freud and Human Nature*. Oxford: Blackwell.
Dilman, I. (1984). *Freud and the Mind*. Oxford: Blackwell.
Dilman, I. (1988). *Freud: Insight and Change*. Oxford: Blackwell.
Farrell, B. A. (1981). *The Standing of Psychoanalysis*. Oxford: Oxford University Press.
Fischer, E. (2004). A Cognitive Self-Therapy: *Philosophical Investigations* 138–197. In E. Ammereller and E. Fischer (Eds). *Wittgenstein at Work. Method in the Philosophical Investigations* (pp.86–126). London: Routledge.
Fischer, E. (2012). Through Pictures to Problems: Cognitive Epistemology and Therapeutic Philosophy. In C. Jäger and W. Loeffler (Eds). *Epistemology: Contexts, Values, Disagreement* (pp.475–492). Frankfurt: Ontos.
Forrester, J. (2004). Freud in Cambridge. *Critical Quarterly*, 46, 1–26.
Freud, S. ([1900] 1953–66d). *The Standard Edition of the Complete Psychological Works of Sigmund Freud* (Vols 9–10): *The Interpretation of Dreams*. Trans. J. Strachey *et al.* London: Hogarth Press/Institute of Psychoanalysis. (Original work published 1900.)
Freud, S. ([1901] 2002). *The Psychopathology of Everyday Life*. Trans. A. Bell. London: Penguin. (Original work published 1901.)
Freud, S. ([1916/17] 1953–66c). *The Standard Edition of the Complete Psychological Works of Sigmund Freud* (Vols 15–16): *Introductory Lectures on Psycho-Analysis*. Trans. J. Strachey *et al.* London: Hogarth Press/Institute of Psychoanalysis. (Original work published 1916/17.)

Freud, S. ([1920] 1953–66b). Beyond the Pleasure Principle. In *The Standard Edition of the Complete Psychological Works of Sigmund Freud* (Vol. 18): *Beyond the Pleasure Principle and other Works* (pp. 3–66). Trans. J. Strachey *et al.* London: Hogarth Press/Institute of Psychoanalysis. (Original work published 1920.)

Freud, S. ([1933] 1953–66a). New Introductory Lectures on Psychoanalysis. In *The Standard Edition of the Complete Psychological Works of Sigmund Freud* (Vol. 22): *New Introductory Lectures on Psychoanalysis and other Works* (pp. 3–158). Trans. J. Strachey *et al.* London: Hogarth Press/Institute of Psychoanalysis. (Original work published 1933.)

Gardner, S. (1993). *Irrationality and the Philosophy of Psychoanalysis*. Cambridge: Cambridge University Press.

Harcourt, E. (2012). Wittgenstein, Ethics and Therapy. In C. Jäger and W. Loeffler (Eds). *Epistemology: Contexts, Values, Disagreement* (pp. 525–536). Frankfurt: Ontos.

Heaton, J. (2000). *Wittgenstein and Psychoanalysis*. Cambridge: Icon.

Heaton, J. (2010). *The Talking Cure: Wittgenstein's Therapeutic Method for Psychotherapy*. Basingstoke: Palgrave Macmillan.

Kennick, W.E. (1970). On Solipsism. In C. Hanly and M. Lazerowitz (Eds). *Psychoanalysis and Philosophy* (pp. 188–209). New York: International Universities Press.

Lazerowitz, M. (1985). The Passing of an Illusion. In M. Lazerowitz and A. Ambrose. *Necessity and Language* (pp. 200–240). Beckenham: Croom Helm.

Lazerowitz, M. and Ambrose, A. (1984). *Essays in the Unknown Wittgenstein*. Buffalo, NY: Prometheus Books.

Lomas, P. (1973). *True and False Experience*. London: Allen Lane.

MacIntyre, A. (1958/2004). *The Unconscious: A Conceptual Analysis*. Revised edition. London: Routledge.

Majetschak, S. (2008). Psychoanalyse der grammatischen Missdeutungen: Über die Beziehung Ludwig Wittgensteins zum Werk Sigmund Freuds. [Psychoanalysis of Grammatical Misinterpretations: On Ludwig Wittgenstein's Relationship with the Work of Sigmund Freud.] In A. Pichler and H. Hrachovec (Eds). *Wittgenstein and the Philosophy of Information* (pp. 37–59). Heusenstamm: Ontos.

Money-Kyrle, R. (1979). Looking Backwards – and Forwards. *International Review of Psycho-Analysis*, 6, 265–272.

Monk, R. (1990). *Wittgenstein: The Duty of Genius*. London: Cape.

Nedo, M. and Ranchetti, M. (1983). *Wittgenstein: Sein Leben in Bildern und Texten*. [Wittgenstein: His Life in Pictures and Texts.] Frankfurt: Suhrkamp.

Paul, M. (2012). *Frank Ramsey: A Sister's Memoir*. Huntingdon: Smith Gordon.

Popper, K. (1963). *Conjectures and Refutations*. London: Routledge and Kegan Paul.

Prokop, U. (2003). *Margaret Stonborough-Wittgenstein: Bauherrin, Intellektuelle, Mäzenin*. Vienna: Böhlau.

Rycroft, C. (1991). *Psychoanalysis and Beyond*. London: Hogarth Press.

Subotincic, N. (2000). Interpretation of Rooms: Sigmund Freud, his Collection, the Rooms and his Patients. In L. Wells-Bowie and E.S. Cathey (Eds). *Proceedings of the 88th Association of Collegiate Schools of Architecture (ACSA) Annual Meeting: Heterotopolis, Immigration, Ethnicity, and the American City* (pp. 55–61). Los Angeles: Association of Collegiate Schools of Architecture (ACSA) Press.

Winnicott, D.W. (1985). *Playing and Reality*. Harmondsworth: Penguin.

Further Reading

Allen, R. (1997). Psychoanalysis after Wittgenstein. *Psychoanalysis and Contemporary Thought*, 20, 299–322.

Farrell, B.A. (1946a). An Appraisal of Therapeutic Positivism I. *Mind*, 55, 25–48.

Farrell, B.A. (1946b). An Appraisal of Therapeutic Positivism II. *Mind*, 55, 133–150.
Gödde, G. (2010). Freud and Nineteenth-Century Philosophical Sources on the Unconscious. In A. Nichols and M. Liebscher (Eds). *Thinking the Unconscious* (pp.261–286). Cambridge: Cambridge University Press.
Kenny, A. (1984). Wittgenstein on the Nature of Philosophy. In A. Kenny. *The Legacy of Wittgenstein* (pp.24–38). Oxford: Blackwell.
Whyte, L.L. (1978). *The Unconscious Before Freud*. New York: St Martin's Press.
Wisdom, J. (A.J.T.D.). (1964). Philosophy and Psycho-Analysis. In J. Wisdom. *Philosophy and Psychoanalysis* (pp.169–181). Oxford: Blackwell.

Part X

Philosophical Schools and Traditions

44

Wittgenstein and the Aristotelian Tradition

ROGER POUIVET

1   The Legacy of Wittgenstein

The idea that Wittgenstein's thought could belong to *any* philosophical tradition might seem a total misinterpretation. After all, isn't philosophy for Wittgenstein a set of therapies that heals us of those "bumps the understanding has got by running its head up against the limits of language" (PI §119)? How then could his thinking belong to a philosophical tradition, except perhaps a tradition of anti-philosophy or a tradition of skepticism about metaphysical speculation?

The idea that Wittgenstein was part of the Aristotelian–Thomist tradition may seem even more far-fetched. Wittgenstein argued that we are suffering from a mythology about the nature of thought and meaning. He is often credited with the view that if the purpose of philosophy is curative, then we must give up the theoretical ambitions of the main philosophical traditions. Especially in the Aristotelian–Thomistic tradition, the philosophical project is metaphysical in purpose. It proposes to explain what reality is as such, independently of how it appears to us, what the nature of the mind is, what truth is, and so on. These ambitions can be illustrated either by Aristotle's *Metaphysics* or Thomas Aquinas's *Summa Theologiae*. Do these texts not exemplify the systematic conception of philosophy that Wittgenstein rejected, attacked, even mocked? Philosophy conceived as having mainly a negative, if not destructive role, does not seem compatible with the metaphysical confidence illustrated in Aristotle's thought, and even more in Thomistic scholasticism. If one would like to integrate Wittgenstein in a tradition, isn't Austrian philosophy historically the most plausible (Mulligan, 2012)? Or, thinking more broadly, isn't the skeptical tradition (Kripke, 1982), or even a "quietist" tradition, emphasizing the ordinary and the nontheoretical (Cavell, 1979), a more likely home than Aristotelian or Thomist metaphysics?

Perhaps. However, some philosophers close to Wittgenstein were also deeply affected by the Aristotelian–Thomist tradition, and were able to harmonize these influences on their ideas. This is the case with Elizabeth Anscombe, one of Wittgenstein's most trusted students, and by the time of his death in 1951 one of his closest friends. The same is true of Peter Geach. His thought is also under the dual influence of Aquinas and Wittgenstein.

A Companion to Wittgenstein, First Edition. Edited by Hans-Johann Glock and John Hyman.
© 2017 John Wiley & Sons, Ltd. Published 2017 by John Wiley & Sons, Ltd.

In this chapter, I shall attempt to show that it is not simply a coincidence that Anscombe, Geach, and other British philosophers were interested in Aristotle and Aquinas while also being influenced by Wittgenstein. Good reasons for this combination of sources can be found within Aristotle's, Aquinas's, and Wittgenstein's works. In Anscombe's and Geach's writings, as well as those of others during the twentieth century and since, this Aristotelian–Thomistic philosophical tradition is at work in a way that suggests that Wittgenstein can also be seen as belonging to it, even if this may sound historically bizarre.

According to Alasdair MacIntyre, "a tradition is an argument extended through time in which certain fundamental agreements are defined and redefined" (1988, p.12). But it is a mistake to believe that a tradition must always be understood by tracing the influence of ideas from the past to the present; sometimes it is in the reverse direction, from the present to the past, that a tradition is noticeable instead, e.g., when recent work leads to a reassessment of earlier thought (Pouivet, 2008). In this spirit, Anthony Kenny says:

> In the eyes of many people, Wittgenstein's importance in the history of philosophy, and in particular in the philosophy of mind, lies especially in his criticism of the Cartesian framework within which philosophy and psychology have been conducted throughout the modern era, well beyond the critique of Kant. One side-effect of Wittgenstein's liberation of philosophy from Cartesian prejudices is that it enables those who accept it to give a more sympathetic welcome to the writings of pre-Cartesian philosophers, and in particular to medieval scholastics. (Kenny, 1984b, p.xi)

Herbert McCabe, although his work is not widely known in the philosophical community, is a good example of the kind of philosopher Kenny has in mind. Kenny writes:

> [McCabe] was an admirer of Wittgenstein [...], he sought to graft the insights of the twentieth-century thinker on to those of the thirteenth-century thinker not out of a desire to appear up-to-date [...], but because he recognized a genuine affinity between the two masters. (Kenny, 2008, p.viii)

We can even speak of a "Wittgensteinian Thomism," as part of an "Analytical Thomism" (which can be non-Wittgensteinian). This label applies to philosophers, such as Anscombe, Geach, Kenny, and McCabe, even if the latter did not consider himself a Thomist, and also to David Braine (1993) and Fergus Kerr (1986). In the work of these authors, we can find a vindication of a remark of John Haldane's:

> Analytical Thomism is not concerned to appropriate St Thomas for the advancement of any particular set of doctrine. Equally, it is not a movement of pious exegesis. Instead, it seeks to deploy the methods and ideas of twentieth-century philosophy – of the sort dominant in the English-speaking world – in connection with the broad framework of ideas introduced and developed by Aquinas. (Haldane, 1997, p.486)

The label "Wittgensteinian Thomism" should therefore be understood as referring to a school of thought that does not rely on genealogical influences, but instead on "genuine affinities" between authors (Damonte, 2009), even if it does not in reality amount to a philosophical tradition (Glock, 2008, pp.220–1). It is this notion of "affinity" that helps us to understand Wittgenstein and Aquinas as being closer than might be expected. And surely, if this approach to Wittgenstein's philosophy offers a valid interpretation of his work, he cannot any longer be seen simply as an anti-philosopher, who merely destroys our illusions by displaying them as philosophical nonsense. At least in part, Wittgenstein carries on – in his own manner – an old (and allegedly obsolete) way of thinking, stemming from Aristotle and Aquinas. The motto of *Philosophical Investigations* is a quotation from Nestroy: "The trouble about progress is that it always looks much greater than it really is." This remark has an obvious bearing on this way of thinking about Wittgenstein's philosophical writings.

As a final introductory remark, we should acknowledge that the Aristotelian–Thomistic tradition certainly belongs to the history of Christian thought. However, Kenny is expressly agnostic and placing Wittgenstein within this tradition is certainly not for him to "christianize" Wittgenstein. What Kenny defends is the idea of a genuine affinity between Aquinas and Wittgenstein. Note also that some philosophers who defend the view that this affinity exists, are critical of what may be called the neo-Wittgensteinian positions in philosophy of religion, especially that of D.Z. Phillips (1994; cf. Hyman, 1999, and Davies, 2007). So, one should not confuse Wittgensteinian Thomism and a philosophy of religion that draws its inspiration, rightly or wrongly, from Wittgenstein.

2 Against Cartesian Privacy

Let us start out from the Wittgensteinian criticism of the Cartesian framework within which much of philosophy and psychology during the modern era have been conducted. Cartesian dualism asserts that it is not the body that defines our nature as human beings, but the mind, which is substantially distinct from the body. The essence of mind is consciousness: one's own awareness of one's own thoughts and feelings. Consequently, mind is better known than body. One of Wittgenstein's achievements was to challenge Descartes's conception of the mind. His private language argument (PI §§243–68; cf. Chapter 28, PRIVACY AND PRIVATE LANGUAGE) plays a crucial role here because it is directed against two fundamental mistakes: one concerning the nature of experience, and the other concerning the nature of language. The first is that experience is private, i.e., that no two people can be aware of the same experience. The second is that the meanings of psychological terms are established by internal ostensive definitions, and therefore require the existence of internal objects, mental objects, events, or states, corresponding to these terms. According to Kenny:

> Philosophers as different from each other as Descartes and Hume have thought it possible for an individual mind to classify and recognize its own thoughts and experiences while holding in suspense the question of the existence of the external world and other minds. Such a supposition seems to entail the possibility of a private language or of something very like one. If Wittgenstein is correct in thinking such a language is impossible then both the Cartesian and empiricist traditions in philosophy need radical overhaul. (Kenny, 1973, pp.13)

A private language would be a language that in principle cannot be understood by anyone except its unique user. The connection between on one hand sensations, internal states in general, and events in the mind in particular and, on the other, their outward expression would be contingent, and the meanings of the words in the language would be fixed by internal ostensive definitions. What Wittgenstein offers in *Philosophical Investigations* is an argument that makes a private language appear as a contradiction in terms. Wittgenstein writes:

> "Surely I can (inwardly) resolve to call this 'pain' in the future." – "But is it certain that you have resolved this? Are you sure that it was enough for this purpose to concentrate your attention on your feeling?" – An odd question. – (PI §263)

An internal ostensive definition, Wittgenstein argues, is incapable of establishing a rule and thereby a genuine meaning for a term. (See Chapter 28, PRIVACY AND PRIVATE LANGUAGE.)

Now, in Aristotle's philosophy, and in the medieval Aristotelian tradition that preceded Descartes, the mind is essentially the set of psychological faculties or powers that distinguishes human beings from other animals. Criticism of the "myth of interiority" (to borrow the title of a seminal book by Jacques Bouveresse, 1976) allowed philosophers to revive this Aristotelian conception of the mind. And since the distinctively human powers are defined by rationality as opposed to consciousness this is a completely different conception of the mind from the one formed by Descartes and inherited by the empiricists. The latter rapidly became orthodox in modern philosophy, and still seems to prevail in cognitive science. Hence, for readers of Aristotle's works, the private language argument was an invitation to reverse the direction of history. The modern account of mind had supplanted Aristotle's psychology and anthropology, and the Cartesian concept of the soul had replaced the idea Aquinas inherited from Aristotle, namely that "soul is the form of the body." But what was presented as the extraordinary discovery of subjectivity – the *ego*, the "I" – and of the decisive role of consciousness in the definition of the mind, appeared for a reader of *Philosophical Investigations* as the result of philosophical confusion.

Only human beings can say what they think and feel. But that is not because they alone have conscious experiences, to which they are granted privileged private access. It is because they have distinctive intellectual abilities and dispositions, including beliefs about themselves. These dispositions require a form of rationality that cannot be attributed to nonhuman animals, because they do not possess a language. And they are manifested in the use of psychological terms, when people say what they feel, believe, and think, as well as when they say what others feel, believe, and think. Wittgenstein not only makes room for the conception of mind as a kind of capacity, but also positively develops this conception through his elaboration of the distinctions between different human powers, abilities, and tendencies (for instance in the *Blue and Brown Books*; see also AWL 92; PG 47; and VW 356–9, 440–2, 464–5). As Geach explains, from both a Thomistic and Wittgensteinian perspective:

> What shows a man to have the concept *seeing* is not merely that he sees, but that he can take an intelligent part in our everyday use of the word 'seeing.' Our concept of sight has its life only in connection with a whole set of other concepts, some of them relating to the physical characteristics of visible objects, others relating to the behaviour of people who see things. (Geach, 1957, p.112)

Wittgenstein removes the phenomenon of meaning from the hidden inner workings of the psyche, and places it in the public sphere of language (cf. Chapter 29, THE INNER

AND THE OUTER). Aquinas thought that meaning is not in any material individual, that it transcends matter and individuality, and that this is what allows it to be sharable. He called it the *nature* or *form* of things. Aquinas's argument is certainly different from Wittgenstein's, and the way they argue is obviously not at all the same. But they reach a similar conclusion: meanings cannot be assimilated to subjective impressions or ideas in the mind, or in the brain. And this conclusion is not only inconsistent with Descartes's philosophy, but also with orthodox empiricist theories of meaning, since the latter are based on the claim, announced at the beginning of Hume's *Treatise of Human Nature*, that all the perceptions of the mind resolve themselves into interior impressions and ideas. In sum, it is the very notion of an internal representation as the ground of modern epistemology that Wittgenstein deconstructs.

Thus, according to Wittgenstein, we cannot explain our ability to reflect on and describe our thoughts and feelings merely by postulating a mind or self in which these impressions, emotions, thoughts, and so on, inhere. For the vocabulary that enables a person to identify her own sense-experience, thoughts, beliefs and feelings depends on the existence of a linguistic community, and therefore on a public world beyond the individual mind.

> "What would it be like if human beings did not manifest their pains (did not groan, grimace, etc.)? Then it would be impossible to teach a child the use of the word 'toothache'." – Well, let's assume that the child is a genius and invents a name for the sensation by himself! – But then, of course, he couldn't make himself understood when he used the word. – So does he understand the name, without being able to explain its meaning to anyone? – But what does it mean to say that he has 'named his pain'? – How has he managed this naming of pain? And whatever he did, what was its purpose? – When one says "He gave a name to his sensation", one forgets that much must be prepared in the language for mere naming to make sense. And if we speak of someone's giving a name to a pain, the grammar of the word "pain" is what has been prepared here; it indicates the post where the new word is stationed. (PI §257)

Wittgenstein's critique of the idea of a private language inevitably led some philosophers to pay closer attention to Aquinas's theory of the soul and intellect. They were not encouraged to engage in a critique of subjectivity, as French postmodern thinkers did. For, what Wittgenstein suggests, is something that could *not* surprise those who attentively read Aristotle's *De Anima* or Aquinas's elaborations of that text. However, it was perhaps difficult to understand, after Descartes, what a philosopher such as Aquinas said about the soul. Aquinas did not believe that a human being could survive as a self, as a pure consciousness. He claimed that the separated soul is not the self: "*Anima mea non est ego.*" Aquinas uses this phrase twice in his *Commentary on the First Epistle to the Corinthians*, in chapter 15. The text of *Philosophical Investigations* is therefore of great value in enabling us to understand Aquinas. This is why McCabe could say:

> In looking at Aquinas on the emotions it is clear how different his whole outlook is from that of pretty well all European philosophers from Descartes until Wittgenstein. The difference is that he did not hold a dualist view of human nature; he did not hold, that is, that to be human is to be two distinct substances, a material body and a non-material soul (*Summa Theologiae*, 1a2ae 22.1). The soul for him is the life of this body – what makes it a body instead of an inanimate mechanical lump of matter. When he speaks of the 'passions

of the soul' and in fact argues that the *passiones* are in the soul, Aquinas has no notion to deny that they are bodily (as, say, a Cartesian would have done had he said this); he means that in considering them we are considering the whole person and not just an abstraction from it that we might call "the body as such." (McCabe, 2008, p.71)

3 Causes and Reasons

In *Action, Emotion and Will* (1963) – under the influence of Aristotle, Aquinas, and Wittgenstein – Kenny presented an anti-causalist account of intentional action. It has a clear affinity with the theories of several philosophers influenced by Wittgenstein, including Anscombe (1957), Melden (1961), and Taylor (1964), although of course it also has distinctive characteristics of its own. The anti-causalists claimed that an explanation of the intentional action is not a causal explanation of the kind exemplified in the natural sciences, and that the agent's reasons for her action need to be distinguished from the physiological causes of the movements of her body, principally because there is a logical connection between words expressing intentional states and those describing the action explained by those states – for example, between the verbal expression of a desire to eat and the description of an activity as eating – that cannot exist between cause and effect. The opposing causalist view is that the reasons for an action are also its causes (Davidson, 1980). The debate between these opposing views was, in effect, a new example of the long-standing opposition between what Georg Henrik von Wright (1971) calls the Aristotelian tradition and the Galilean tradition:

> As to their views of scientific explanation, the contrast between the two traditions is usually characterized as causal *versus* teleological explanation. The first type of explanation is also called mechanistic, the second finalistic. The Galilean tradition in science runs parallel with the advance of the causal-mechanistic point of view in man's efforts to explain and predict phenomena, the Aristotelian tradition with his efforts to make effects teleologically or finalistically understandable. (von Wright, 1971, p.3)

About this Aristotelian tradition, Vincent Descombes writes:

> What is striking about von Wright's characterization of the intentionalist school is the surprising – some might say incongruous – alliance between Aristotle and Wittgenstein. Wittgenstein provides the idea that intention should be studied in its expressions, in the description of intentional action. Aristotle furnishes the ideas of practical rationality and finality. (Descombes, 2001, p.35)

As it happens, Davidson also claimed to be defending an Aristotelian position, with some justice, since Aristotle stated: "The origin of action – its efficient, not its final cause – is choice, and that of choice is desire and reasoning with a view to an end" (*Nicomachean Ethics*, 1139a). But the anti-causalist maintains that Davidson's Humean conception of efficient causes is so different from Aristotle's that he cannot in the end be plausibly regarded as a champion of Aristotle's doctrine.

The source of Kenny's, Anscombe's, Melden's, and Taylor's position can be found in the "Blue Book," where Wittgenstein argues that the grammar of "reason" differs from that of "cause." He points out that our knowledge of reasons is not inductive or hypothetical, as he assumes our knowledge of causes is. The mention of the reason, or the motive, can be another way of describing an action, but it is not the description of an event that would be independent (what can be called a "Humean cause"). In *Intention*, Anscombe shows that what we call the intention with which an agent performs an action is not a private mental event antecedent to action. Wittgenstein says:

> When I raise my arm 'voluntarily', I don't make use of any means to bring the movement about. My wish is not such a means either. (PI §614)

> "Willing, if it is not to be a sort of wishing, must be the action itself. It mustn't stop anywhere short of the action." If it is the action, then it is so in the ordinary sense of the word; so it is speaking, writing, walking, lifting a thing, imagining something. But it is also striving, trying, making an effort to speak, to write, to lift a thing, to imagine something, and so on. (PI §615)

Rightly or wrongly, Wittgenstein has been seen by many philosophers as renewing Aristotelian doctrines about mind and action in his own terms, especially as these doctrines are developed in some parts of Aquinas's works.

4 Intentionality

Kenny's article "Intentionality: Aquinas and Wittgenstein" was a milestone for Wittgensteinian Thomism. Kenny examines the question of what enables a thought to be *about* something. He attempts "to combine Aquinas's theory of intentional existence with the *prima facie* very different account of intentionality sketched by Wittgenstein" (1984a, p.76).

Aquinas's doctrine of the immaterial and intentional existence of the forms in the intellect might be seen as an example of medieval Scholastic philosophy that is completely devoid of interest in contemporary philosophy, to be studied only by historians. The doctrine is that what makes Fido what he is, namely a dog, is his "form." This form is *materially* realized in the material dog we see. In addition, it could be *intentionally* realized in our intellect. So the same form could be implemented in matter, thereby making Fido a dog, and realized intentionally in the intellect of someone thinking that Fido is a dog. However, Kenny claims,

> according to Aquinas, when I think of Socrates there is in my mind only the universal form of humanity; I can use this form to think of Socrates only by placing it within a context of sensory imagery (*phantasmata*). (Kenny, 1984a, p.68)

Forms existing in matter are only thinkable in the way that colors are visible in the dark, in other words, they are *potentially* thinkable.

All this seems very far from Wittgenstein! How could anyone imagine it is compatible with what Wittgenstein says, let alone that there is an affinity between the Thomist conception of thought and Wittgenstein's? But here is the decisive step in this interpretation: Kenny proposes to *identify* "intellectual" with "linguistic." It must be recognized that many historians of philosophy would refuse outright to follow this move (e.g., Putallaz, 2011). However, this is the kind of interpretative short circuit that connects Aquinas and Wittgenstein.

> If I say "I meant *him*", a picture might come to my mind, perhaps of how I looked at him, and so forth; but the picture is only like an illustration to a story. From it alone, it would mostly be impossible to infer anything at all; only when one knows the story, does one know what the picture is for. (PI §663)

What does "know the story" mean? In Thomist terms, it means that the intellect provides the text of the story and the mental images are its illustrations. And if "intellect" is now replaced by "language," Aquinas's doctrine is closer to Wittgenstein's remarks than any other theory proposed since the thirteenth century.

Kenny says that for Aquinas, "the actuality of the object of thought is the actuality of the power of thinking" (1984a, p.76). The object of thought is not to be assimilated to a material object; it is "actual" only in the sense that it can actually be thought about by an intellect. And that intellect in turn is a capacity: it is not a material object, it has no structure or matter. According to Kenny,

> if we want 'intellect' to mean a characteristically human capacity then it seems most helpful to regard the intellect as the capacity for thinking those thoughts that only a language-user can think. (1980, p.67)

Thus, Aquinas and Wittgenstein do not explain the intentionality of thought in terms of ideas that are present in or processes that occur in the mind, such as we find today in cognitive science. They do not believe that thinking about the world consists of internal operations supposedly accomplished by the thinking subject (a mind or brain). They both think that it consists in the exercise of intellectual or linguistic powers. Intentionality operates from within one's mastery of language and not independently of this mastery, as a non- or pre-linguistic precondition to our linguistic use.

Aquinas and Wittgenstein do not defend exactly the same doctrines about intentionality. But reading them in parallel enhances the understanding we can have of each of them, and assists us in understanding the issues they both raise.

5 Aquinas and Wittgenstein as Fellow Metaphysicians

In spite of the discussion above, the idea that Aquinas and Wittgenstein belong to the same philosophical tradition faces an insurmountable difficulty, for the role language plays in Wittgenstein's philosophy has no counterpart in Aquinas's thought. Kenny himself realized that the proximity Aquinas detects "between the operation of the intellect and the use of language" (1993, p.49) must not be overstated. But on the other hand, this identification (or near identification) of intellect and the possession of a language is a non-negotiable commitment of Wittgensteinian Thomism. But is it not also perhaps its fundamental weakness? In the view of some commentators, Aquinas explains language in terms of thought, and not the other way around, and he is also supposed to emphasize the importance of the *internal mental life* of the subject. Isn't Aquinas's own philosophy closer to Husserl's phenomenological treatment of intentionality in terms of a series of mental acts than to Wittgenstein's philosophy? And isn't it at odds with Wittgensteinian Thomism?

However, one can also wonder whether it is not because our interpretation of Aquinas is influenced by other trends in contemporary philosophy that we assume a strong dissociation between thought and language in Aquinas. After all, Aristotle and

Aquinas often examine our use of words. What is more, such an analysis seems to be central to their methods. In this respect Wittgenstein is closer to them than some twentieth-century philosophers, such as Bergson or Husserl, who wanted to explore the world of consciousness that Descartes had made central to modern philosophy.

But even if Aquinas and Wittgenstein share the view that philosophy requires a close study of the use of words, it remains difficult to claim that a metaphysician such as Aquinas and an antimetaphysician such as Wittgenstein have much in common (cf. Chapter 12, METAPHYSICS: FROM INEFFABILITY TO NORMATIVITY). However, let us consider a well-known passage in *Philosophical Investigations*, where Wittgenstein examines how we use the words "game" and "number." Wittgenstein asks himself what after all is common to all games: on what grounds do we call them games? The answer is that "if you look at them, you won't see something that is common to all, but similarities, affinities, and a whole series of them at that" (PI §66). McCabe claims that Wittgenstein's answer "has a great deal in common with that of Aristotle and St Thomas when they ask themselves what after all is being?" (1969, p.73, n.7). He adds that Aquinas's theory of the general use of the word "being" is "the well-known and often misinterpreted theory of analogy" (1969, p.73, n.7). This theory inquires into how we use "transcendental words." These are words that are so general and fundamental that their reference transcends not just ordinary kinds or species – such as dog or cat – but even general categories, such as event, relation, etc. And we use these words both within and outside metaphysics. According to McCabe, they can only be understood through a "theory of predication," i.e., a classification of statements according to the way they predicate properties of objects. What corresponds to the transcendental word "being" is not a peculiar entity, but a type of statement, namely "a is F."

The crucial point is that this account is not extralinguistic. It concerns reality, language, and thought at the same time, in a way that intertwines them just as firmly as Wittgenstein's remarks about games and numbers do. In *Summa Theologiae*, Aquinas claims that

> when we say God is good or wise we do not simply mean that he causes wisdom or goodness, but that he possesses these perfections transcendently. We conclude, therefore, that from the point of view of what the word means it is used primarily of God and derivatively of creatures. (*Summa Theologiae*, 1a 13.7)

It means that a term applied to God and things in the world is not applied univocally, for example when we say that God is good and that Peter or Jane is good. And yet the term "good" is not ambiguous, as if it had two completely different meanings. It is used *analogically*. As Brian Davies says:

> One should not push the parallel between Aquinas and Wittgenstein too far. But it is worth observing that they complement each other in at least this respect: both of them allow for literal talk using terms which differ in what Aquinas would call their *modus significandi*. Wittgenstein seems to be saying that knowing what is going on somewhere in being told that a tennis game is going on is knowing about something very different from what one would be knowing in knowing that, say, a game of patience is going on somewhere. But in each case one would know of a game taking place. In a similar way, Aquinas would argue, knowing what is true in knowing that I am good is knowing something very different from what one would know about in knowing that God is good. But we are not equivocating in speaking of me as good and of God as good. (Davies, 1992, pp.74–5)

This way of bringing together Wittgenstein's notions of "family resemblance" in the use of certain terms, such as game or number, and Aquinas's account of analogy might displease Wittgensteinians and Thomists alike. Wittgensteinian philosophers have commonly used the notion of "family resemblance" to attack the very idea of essence. By contrast, Thomists have regarded the so-called "theory of analogy" as a contribution to Scholastic philosophy that does define the forms or essences of things. According to them, it is to be included in the renaissance of Scholastic philosophy, as recommended in Pope's Leo XIII encyclical letter *Aeterni Patri* (1879). Thinking of Aquinas and Wittgenstein as belonging to the same tradition radically challenges the understanding we have of both the Austro-British philosopher and the *Doctor Communis*. Perhaps Wittgenstein is not the antiessentialist, let alone anti-philosopher, some have made him out to be. And perhaps Aquinas's account of being is less dependent on a "metaphysics of being" than has been claimed (even by Kenny, 2002).

McCabe takes the Aquinas–Wittgenstein connection much further. What, he asks, is being said when two things are said to be the same? For example, if Fido is a dog and Rover is a dog, why is Fido not Rover? The ostensible problem here does not arise between Fido and Clementina, a cat. They can both be in the garden, both be black, and both be the same size, without being the same thing – i.e., of the same species. Many philosophers thought that if X and Y are not identical, there must be something that can be predicated of X and not of Y. (This is the principle of the discernibility of nonidenticals.) By contrast, Aquinas's answer is to insist on the difference in the way words function in the subject part of a sentence and in the predicate part. "Words in the subject place are essentially to name, to pick out what it is you are talking about," writes McCabe (2008, p.37). But Aquinas detects one exception to this rule: *predicatio per identitatem* in an identity statement like "Cicero is Tully." It is not really a predication because the name in the predicate place – on the right-hand side of the identity – is not used to predicate something of Cicero, but to refer. Is this not exactly what Wittgenstein "rediscovered" (McCabe's expression, 2008, p.38) when he wrote that "a = b means then, that the sign 'a' is replaceable by the sign 'b'" (TLP 4.241)? Therefore, "whether Fido and Rover are identical or not, is not a matter of *what you say* about them but what it is you are talking *about*" (McCabe, 2008, p.39). Contrary to Leibniz and Russell, it is not a matter of whether what you say about Fido is the same as what you say about Rover, whether all and only the same predicates hold of them, but whether what you say about Fido is also about Rover. When we pick out Fido and Rover separately, we distinguish *two substances* possessing the *same nature*. Because of this last point, we are doing something different from when we are picking out Fido, a dog, and Clementina, a cat.

When we think, we have concepts of natures in mind. To have such a concept in mind is not to have an individual thing in mind, but the meaning of the word "dog," exactly what Aquinas called a nature. The same nature is common to countless individuals; it is a "universal." But it is not an entity; rather, it is a principle by means of which we classify entities, and understanding this enables us to understand that "x is *the same* as y with respect to being F, but, nonetheless, x and y are not identical." According to McCabe, "to have such concepts is to be able to handle words or other symbols" (2008, p.39), notably for the distinct purposes of, respectively, referring and classifying.

But how can we ignore Wittgenstein's emphasis on forms of life and his frequent use of the idea that human beings have a "natural history"? Is this not totally incompatible with Aquinas's metaphysical, albeit moderate, realism? Wittgenstein is sometimes understood as a conventionalist philosopher, suggesting that anything one says can be reduced to a move in a language-game played in *our* society. This sounds inimical to any metaphysics that purports to capture the nature of reality as it is independently of us. If I say "I see such-and-such," this is not justified by an independent reality; I am merely using words in a certain way and expecting reactions from others. Such a skeptical (or even postmodern) interpretation is apparently supported by a passage like the following:

> The rules of grammar may be called "arbitrary," if that is to mean that the purpose of grammar is nothing but that of language.
> If someone says, "If our language had not this grammar, it could not express these facts" – it should be asked what "could" means here. (PI §457)

And also at least by a possible interpretation of this famous passage:

> "So you are saying that human agreement decides what is true and what is false?" – What is true or false is what human beings say; and it is in their language that human beings agree. This is agreement not in opinions, but rather in form of life. (PI §241)

Do these passages not come into conflict with an Aristotelian–Thomistic understanding of Wittgenstein? Not necessarily, as has been shown by Paul O'Grady when he says:

> Endorsing an account of essence does not commit one to unrevisable conceptual schemes, it is closely connected to actual linguistic use, compatible with the relativity of cognition to the kind of cognizer, and best serves an account of the mind-world relation where coping serves as the master metaphor, rather than spectating. This is not far from Wittgenstein's late image of inquiry being akin to a river, with deeper structures changing much more slowly relative to the flow of the current. The flow of the river (descriptions) makes sense relative to the background context of river-bank, topography etc. (definitions). But even these may change over time. (O'Grady, 2012, p.641)

6 Was Wittgenstein a Metaphysician?

The way of reading Wittgenstein we encountered in the last section challenges the image of him as being opposed to any philosophical doctrine or claim. If it is correct, his place in the history of philosophy is quite different: he resurrected and renewed an Aristotelian account of the mind, which was either disparaged or neglected when the Cartesian paradigm held sway. A romantic image of Wittgenstein as a philosopher who cures us of all philosophy and metaphysics is incompatible with a reading of his work that places it in the context of the Aristotelian–Thomistic tradition in this way. So the question is whether we should preserve this fashionable image of Wittgenstein as an anti-philosopher (see Pouivet, 2014).

However, Wittgensteinian Thomism is certainly not all of a piece. Kenny finds agreement between Aquinas and Wittgenstein on the nature of the mind, but he is critical of the Thomist metaphysical project and preserves the antimetaphysical understanding of Wittgenstein's philosophy. In particular, he does not accept specific metaphysical doctrines of Thomism, such as Aquinas's distinction between essence and existence (in no case, except for God, does the essence of a thing indicate anything about whether that thing really is), or the thesis that God is a self-subsistent being (Kenny, 1980, p.60). By contrast, as we saw above, McCabe wants to reconcile Aquinas's metaphysics of being with Wittgenstein's philosophy:

> When Wittgenstein in the *Tractatus* says 'Not *how* the world is, is the mystical, but *that* it is' (TLP 6.44), it seems to me that he is engaged with the same question as St Thomas when he speaks of *esse*. As St Thomas distinguishes between the creative act of God (which we do not understand) and natural causality (which we do), between creation and transformation, Wittgenstein distinguishes the mystical from "what can be said" (TLP 6.53). (McCabe, 2002, pp.21)

For Aquinas it is the *esse* of things that leads us to speak of God, whereas for Wittgenstein in the *Tractatus*, it is their existence. But the sharp distinction between scientific language and silence was later replaced by the multiplicity of language-games (see Chapter 26, LANGUAGES, LANGUAGE-GAMES, AND FORMS OF LIFE), which has, as already noted, a counterpart in Aquinas's account of analogy.

Whatever the extent of overlap between Aquinas's and Wittgenstein's thought, and allowing for all the precautions that must be taken in detecting parallels between these two philosophers who belonged to different times and historical contexts, it seems to me that including Wittgenstein in the Aristotelian–Thomistic tradition bears considerable hermeneutic potential for understanding Wittgenstein (and Aquinas as well).

References

Anscombe, G.E.M. (1957). *Intention*. Oxford: Basil Blackwell.
Bouveresse, J. (1976). *Le mythe de l'intériorité*. [The Myth of Interiority.] Paris: Minuit.
Braine, D. (1993). *The Human Person: Animal and Spirit*. London: Duckworth.
Cavell, S. (1979). *The Claim of Reason: Wittgenstein, Skepticism, Morality, and Tragedy*. New York: Oxford University Press.
Damonte, M. (2009). *Wittgenstein, Tommaso e la cura dell'intenzionalita*. [Wittgenstein, Aquinas, and the Question of Intentionality.] Firenze: Athenaum.
Davidson, D. (1980). *Essays on Actions and Events*. Oxford: Oxford University Press.
Davies, B. (1992). *The Thought of Thomas Aquinas*. Oxford: Clarendon Press.
Davies, B. (2007). D.Z. Phillips on Belief in God. *Philosophical Investigations*, 30, 219–244.
Descombes, V. (2001). *The Mind's Provision: A Critique of Cognitivism*. Princeton: Princeton University Press.
Geach, P. (1957). *Mental Acts*. London: Routledge and Kegan Paul.
Glock, H.-J. (2008). *What is Analytical Philosophy?* Cambridge: Cambridge University Press.
Haldane, J.J. (1997). Analytical Thomism: A Brief Introduction. *The Monist*, 80, 485–486.
Hyman, J. (1999). Wittgensteinianism. In P.L. Quinn and C. Taliaferro (Eds). *A Companion to Philosophy of Religion* (pp.150–157). Oxford: Blackwell.
Kenny, A. (1963). *Action, Emotion and Will*. London: Routledge.
Kenny, A. (1973). *Wittgenstein*. Oxford: Blackwell.
Kenny, A. (1980). *Aquinas*. Oxford: Oxford University Press.
Kenny, A. (1984a). Intentionality: Aquinas and Wittgenstein. In A. Kenny. (1984). *The Legacy of Wittgenstein* (pp.61–76). Oxford: Blackwell.
Kenny, A. (1984b). *The Legacy of Wittgenstein*. Oxford: Blackwell.
Kenny, A. (1993). *Aquinas on Mind*. London: Routledge.
Kenny, A. (2002). *Aquinas on Being*. Oxford: Oxford University Press.

Kenny, A. (2008). Foreword. In H. McCabe. *On Aquinas* (pp.vii–ix). London: Continuum.
Kerr, F. (1986). *Theology after Wittgenstein*. Oxford: Blackwell.
Kripke, S.A. (1982). *Wittgenstein on Rules and Private Language: An Elementary Exposition*. Oxford: Blackwell.
MacIntyre, A. (1988). *Whose Justice? Which Rationality?* Notre Dame, IN: University of Notre Dame Press.
McCabe, H. (1969). Categories. In A. Kenny (Ed.). *Aquinas: A Collection of Critical Essays* (pp.54–92). London: Macmillan.
McCabe, H. (2002). *God Still Matters*. London: Continuum.
McCabe, H. (2008). *On Aquinas*. London: Continuum.
Melden, A.I. (1961). *Free Action*. London: Routledge and Kegan Paul.
Mulligan, K. (2012). *Wittgenstein et la philosophie austro-allemande*. [Wittgenstein and Austro-German Philosophy.] Paris: Vrin.
O'Grady, P. (2012). McCabe on Aquinas and Wittgenstein. *New Blackfriars*, 93, 631–644.
Phillips, D. Z. (1994). *Wittgenstein and Religion*. London: Macmillan.
Pouivet, R. (2008). *After Wittgenstein, St Thomas*. South Bend: St Augustine's Press.
Pouivet, R. (2014). Wittgenstein's Essentialism. In J. Dutant, D. Fassio, and A. Meylan (Eds). *Liber Amicorum Pascal Engel* (pp.449–464). Genève: Université de Genève.
Putatallaz, F.-X. (2011). Wittgenstein, saint Thomas et l'intériorité, une discutable lecture de Roger Pouivet. [Wittgenstein, St Thomas and Interiority: Roger Pouivet's Disputable Reading.] *Revue Thomiste*, 111, 35–65.
Taylor, C. (1964). *The Explanation of Behaviour*. London: Routledge and Kegan Paul.
von Wright, G.H. (1971). *Explanation and Understanding*. Ithaca: Cornell University Press.

Further Reading

Geach, P. (1969). *God and the Soul*. London: Routledge and Kegan Paul.
Haldane, J.J. (Ed.). (2002). *Mind, Metaphysics, and Value in the Thomistic and Analytical Traditions*. Notre Dame, IN: University of Notre Dame Press.
Kenny, A. (1973). *The Anatomy of the Soul: Historical Essays in the Philosophy of Mind*. Oxford: Blackwell.
Kenny, A. (2000). *Essays in the Aristotelian Tradition*. Oxford: Clarendon Press.
O'Grady, P. (2014). *Aquinas's Philosophy of Religion*. Basingstoke: Palgrave Macmillan.
Stout, J. and MacSwain, R. (Eds). (2004). *Grammar and Grace: Reformulations of Aquinas and Wittgenstein*. London: SCM Press.

45

Wittgenstein and Kantianism

ROBERT HANNA

> The limit of language is shown by its being impossible to describe the fact which corresponds to (is the translation of) a sentence, without simply repeating the sentence. (This has to do with the Kantian solution of the problem of philosophy.) (CV 10)
>
> May God grant the philosopher insight into what lies in front of everyone's eyes. (CV 63)

1 Introduction

In the 1970s, Peter Hacker and Bernard Williams argued that Wittgenstein was a Kantian transcendental idealist (Hacker, 1972; Williams, 1973). In the 1980s, Hacker officially rescinded this interpretation (Hacker, 1972/86, pp.ix and 206–14); and Williams in any case regarded Wittgenstein's transcendental idealism as a philosophical mistake. And ever since, there has been a lively debate about Wittgenstein's Kantianism, anti-Kantianism, or non-Kantianism. In my opinion, however, this particular line of Wittgenstein-interpretation and debate was a *dead letter* from the start: if I am correct, then Hacker and Williams adopted a false, or at least needlessly uncharitable, conception of Kant's transcendental idealism in particular and also of his Critical philosophy more generally, from the get-go – hence the gambit of interpreting Wittgenstein as a transcendental idealist or Critical philosopher in *that* sense was bound to lead to "obscurity and contradictions" (*Dunkelheit und Widersprüche*) (Kant, [1781/87] 1997, Aviii). But if we revolutionize the way we think about Kant, we can, correspondingly, revolutionize the way we think about Wittgenstein in the light of Kant's transcendental idealism and Critical philosophy.

No one doubts that throughout his philosophical writings, Wittgenstein saw a fundamental connection between language and human life. But if I am correct, then Wittgenstein's conception of human language is essentially the same as Kant's Critical conception of human rationality, and Wittgenstein and Kant are jointly engaged in the self-same project of what Jonathan Lear aptly dubs *transcendental anthropology*

A Companion to Wittgenstein, First Edition. Edited by Hans-Johann Glock and John Hyman.
© 2017 John Wiley & Sons, Ltd. Published 2017 by John Wiley & Sons, Ltd.

(Lear, 1982; Lear and Stroud, 1984; and Lear, 1986). What is transcendental anthropology? The short-and-sweet answer is that it is a way of doing philosophy that tells us

(i) how the apparent or manifest world *must be*, in order to conform to the innately specified forms and structures of the basic cognitive and practical capacities of rational human animals;
(ii) how rational human animals *must choose, act, and try to live*, in order to conform to the highest norms, rules, and standards they legislate for themselves, and also, tragically, almost inevitably fail to meet; and
(iii) how philosophy *must not be*, because otherwise it will inevitably, and tragically, fall into logical antinomy, radical skepticism, and cognitive/practical self-alienation.

In view of (ii) and (iii), we can clearly see how transcendental anthropology is also an intimate fellow-traveler with existentialism – as expressed, e.g., in Augustine's *Confessions* or Pascal's *Pensées* (which Kant would have known), and in Kierkegaard's *Fear and Trembling* or Dostoevsky's *Brothers Karamazov* (which Wittgenstein knew) – and shares with existentialism a radically metaphysically anthropocentric, meta-philosophically critical, morally-charged, and ultimately *tragic* sense of human life (see de Unamuno, [1912] 1921; Cavell, 1979, especially parts 1 and 4; and Bearn, 1997). Otherwise put, transcendental anthropology is *the philosophy of the rational human condition*.

Lear's critical judgment on the later Wittgenstein's transcendental anthropology is that it is ultimately a failure, due to an incoherence between the *prima-facie*-opposed "transcendental" (a.k.a. nonempirical) and "anthropological" (a.k.a empirical) levels of reflection (Lear, 1986, especially pp.283–93). As will become evident in the course of this chapter, however, my critical judgment is just the reverse. I think that Lear failed to understand Kant's transcendental idealism in the right way, and also failed to take into proper account the existential dimensions in Kant's and Wittgenstein's philosophical thinking.

If I am correct, then that is the "big picture" into which we can fit Wittgenstein, Kant, and the existentialists alike. But the specific purpose of this chapter is to explore two central themes in the philosophy of Wittgenstein, as deeply motivated by Kant and also importantly inflected by existential insights:

(i) how the apparent or manifest world necessarily conforms to human mind and life; and
(ii) the critique of self-alienated philosophy.

2   How the World Conforms 1: Kant, Transcendental Idealism, and Empirical Realism

According to Kant, a mental representation is *transcendental* when it is either part of, or derived from, our nonempirical (hence a priori) innately specified spontaneous cognitive capacities (Kant, [1781/87] 1997, A11/B25; Kant, [1783] 1977, 4: 373n.). Then Kant's transcendental idealism (TI) can be formulated as a two-part philosophical equation:

$$TI = (i) \text{Representational Transcendentalism} + (ii) \text{Cognitive Idealism}.$$

(i) Representational Transcendentalism: necessarily, all the forms or structures of rational human cognition are generated a priori by the empirically-triggered, yet stimulus-underdetermined, activities of our innately specified spontaneous cognitive capacities (i.e., cognitive competences, cognitive faculties, cognitive powers).

(ii) Cognitive Idealism: necessarily, all the proper objects of rational human cognition are nothing but sensory appearances or phenomena (i.e., mind-dependent, spatiotemporal, directly perceivable, apparent or manifest objects) and never things-in-themselves or noumena (i.e., mind-independent, non-sensible, non-spatiotemporal, real essences constituted by intrinsic non-relational properties) (see Kant, [1781/87] 1997, A369; Kant, [1783] 1977, 4: 293–4, 375).

Now (i) + (ii) also = Kant's "Copernican revolution" in metaphysics (Kant, [1781/87] 1997, Bxvi), which I will rationally reconstruct as

The Conformity Thesis: it is not the case that rational human minds passively conform to the objects they cognize, as in classical rationalism and classical empiricism. On the contrary, necessarily, all the proper objects of rational human cognition conform to – i.e., they have the same form or structure as, or are isomorphic to – the forms or structures that are nonempirically generated by our innately specified spontaneous cognitive capacities. So necessarily the essential forms or structures of the apparent or manifest world we cognize are mind-dependent.

In this way, all versions of Kant's TI hold that the apparent or manifest real world we cognize conforms to the nonempirical forms or structures of our innately specified cognitive capacities in some modally robust sense. Correspondingly, many Kantians are committed to what I call *strong transcendental idealism* (STI), which says:

(i) Things-in-themselves (a.k.a. *noumena*, or really-real things, i.e., things as they could exist in a "lonely" way, altogether independently of rational human minds or anything else, by virtue of their intrinsic non-relational properties) really exist and cause our perceptions, although rational human cognizers only ever perceive mere appearances or subjective phenomena.

(ii) Rational human cognizers actually impose the nonempirical forms or structures of their innate cognitive capacities onto the apparent or manifest world they cognize – i.e., necessarily, all the essential forms or structures of the proper objects of human cognition are literally type-identical to the a priori forms or structures that are nonempirically generated by our innately specified spontaneous cognitive capacities.

(iii) Necessarily, if all rational human cognizers went out of existence, then so would the apparent or manifest world they cognize.

But some other Kantians think that Kant's STI is objectively false and are committed instead only to the objective truth of what I call *weak or counterfactual transcendental idealism* (WCTI), which says:

(i) Things-in-themselves are logically possible, but at the same time it is knowably unknowable and unprovable whether things-in-themselves exist or not, hence for the purposes of an adequate anthropocentric or "human-faced" metaphysics, epistemology, and ethics, they can be ignored (*radical agnosticism and methodological eliminativism about things-in-themselves*).

(ii) Necessarily, all the proper objects of rational human cognition have the same forms or structures as – i.e., they are isomorphic to – the forms or structures that are nonempirically generated by our innately-specified spontaneous cognitive capacities, but at the same time those apparent or manifest worldly forms or structures are not literally type-identical to those a priori cognitive forms or structures (*the isomorphism-without-type-identity thesis*).

(iii) It is a necessary condition of the existence of the apparent or manifest world that if some rational human animals *were* to exist in that world, then they *would* veridically cognize that world, via either essentially nonconceptual (i.e., intuitional) content or conceptual content, at least to some extent (*the counterfactual cognizability thesis*).

(iv) The apparent or manifest world has at some earlier times existed without rational human animals to cognize it veridically, and could exist even if no rational human animals existed to cognize it veridically, even though some rational human animals now actually exist in that world – e.g., I (R.H.) now actually exist in the manifestly real world – who do in fact cognize it veridically, at least to some extent (*the existential thesis*).

Otherwise put, Kant's WCTI says that, necessarily, the manifestly real world we really cognize is pre-formatted for our cognition – but it exists outside our heads, not inside our heads.

Whether one accepts STI or WCTI, it remains importantly true that Kant's TI is sharply distinct from Berkeley's *subjective or phenomenal idealism* and also from Cartesian *skeptical idealism*. TI entails that necessarily some directly knowable material things actually exist outside my conscious states (i.e., inner sense) in space; in other words, it entails the falsity of both Berkeleyan subjective or phenomenal idealism and Cartesian skeptical idealism alike, and also the truth of empirical realism:

[The empirical realist] grants to matter, as appearance, a reality which need not be inferred, but is immediately perceived [*unmittelbar wahrgenommen*]. (Kant, [1781/87] 1997, A371)

Every outer perception [...] immediately proves [*beweiset unmittelbar*] something real in space, or rather is itself the real; to that extent, empirical realism is beyond doubt, i.e., to our outer intuitions there corresponds something real in space. (Kant, [1781/87] 1997, A375)

And this empirical realism is in fact the explicit two-part conclusion of Kant's "Refutation of Idealism":

The consciousness of my existence is at the same time [*zugleich*] an immediate consciousness of the existence of other things outside me. (Kant, [1781/87] 1997, B276)

3   How the World Conforms 2: Wittgenstein, Transcendental Solipsism, and Pure Realism

Wittgenstein's *Tractatus Logico-Philosophicus* offers a radically new conception of philosophical logic (cf. Chapter 17, LOGIC AND THE *TRACTATUS*), according to which:

(1) Not only mathematics but also metaphysics reduces to the propositions of logic (including both the truth-functional tautologies and the logico-philosophical truths of the *Tractatus* itself) together with factual propositions (see Chapter 12, METAPHYSICS: FROM INEFFABILITY TO NORMATIVITY).

(2) Factual propositions and facts alike reduce to logically-structured complexes of ontologically neutral "objects," which can variously play the structural roles of both particulars and universals (including both properties and relations).

(3) Factual propositions are nothing but linguistic facts that "picture" other facts according to one-to-one isomorphic correspondence relations (cf. Chapter 8, THE PICTURE THEORY and Chapter 32, WITTGENSTEIN ON INTENTIONALITY).

(4) All nonfactual propositions are either (a) "senseless" (*sinnlos*) truth-functional tautologies expressing nothing but the formal meanings and deductive implications of the logical constants, (b) the logico-philosophical propositions of the *Tractatus* itself, or (c) "nonsensical" (*unsinnig*) pseudo-propositions that violate logico-syntactic rules and logico-semantic categories, especially including all the synthetic a priori claims of traditional metaphysics.

(5) The logical constants do not represent facts or refer to objects of any sort (TLP 4.0312) but instead merely "display" (*darstellen*) the a priori logical "scaffolding of the world" (TLP 6.124), which is also "the limits of my language" (TLP 5.6), and can only be "shown" (*zeigen*) or non-propositionally indicated, *not* "said" (*sagen*) or propositionally described.

(6) The logical form of the world is therefore "transcendental": "Logic is not a theory but a reflexion of the world. Logic is transcendental" (TLP 6.13).

(7) The logical form of the world reduces to the language-using metaphysical subject or ego, who is not in any way part of the world but in fact solipsistically identical to the form of the world itself (cf. Chapter 9, WITTGENSTEIN ON SOLIPSISM):

> 5.63 I am my world. (The microcosm.) [...]
> 5.632 The subject does not belong to the world but it is a limit of the world.
> (TLP 5.63–5.632)

Looking at theses (5), (6), and (7), we can clearly see that Wittgenstein's radically new conception of philosophical logic is correspondingly radically ontologically ascetic, since everything logically reduces to one simple thing: the language-using metaphysical subject or ego. Indeed, it is by means of theses (5) and (6) that Wittgenstein directly expresses the surprising and often-overlooked but quite indisputable fact that the *Tractatus* is every bit as much a neo-Kantian idealistic metaphysical treatise inspired by Schopenhauer's neo-Kantian *World as Will and Representation* (see also Brockhaus, 1991) as it is a logico-philosophical treatise inspired by Frege's *Begriffsschrift*, Frege's attack on psychologism, Moore's and Russell's attacks on idealism, and Russell and Whitehead's *Principia Mathematica* (cf. Chapter 4, WITTGENSTEIN AND FREGE; Chapter 5, WITTGENSTEIN AND RUSSELL; Chapter 3, WITTGENSTEIN AND SCHOPENHAUER; Chapter 6, WITTGENSTEIN, HERTZ, AND BOLTZMANN).

Wittgenstein also carefully read *The Critique of Pure Reason* along with Ludwig Hänsel in 1918, three years before the publication of the *Tractatus*. I do not think that Wittgenstein's reading of the first *Critique* in 1918 directly or substantially influenced the *Tractatus* itself, since in fact virtually no changes were made to the manuscript of the *Tractatus* between 1918 and its publication in 1921 (see e.g., Potter, 2009; forthcoming). But I do think that Wittgenstein's early philosophy is essentially the result of his indirect engagement with Kant's Critical philosophy, via Schopenhauer, prior to 1918, and also that Wittgenstein's later philosophy is essentially, although mostly implicitly and without fanfare, the result of Wittgenstein's direct engagement with Kant's Critical philosophy after 1918 (but cf. Chapter 1, WITTGENSTEIN'S PHILOSOPHICAL DEVELOPMENT). So whereas Moore and Russell explicitly abandoned and rejected Kant's Critical epistemology and metaphysics, Wittgenstein, both early and late, creatively absorbed and sublimated them.

From this standpoint, we can see that the *Tractatus* is basically an essay in transcendental logic in the Kantian sense. As Wittgenstein stresses in the preface of the *Tractatus*, he "makes no claim to novelty in points of detail" and does not care whether he is borrowing ideas from other philosophers, especially Frege and Russell. It is also very clear from the *Notebooks 1914–16* that Wittgenstein was heavily influenced by Schopenhauer. Indeed Wittgenstein told von Wright that "he had read Schopenhauer's *Die Welt als Wille und Vorstellung* in his youth and that his first philosophy was a Schopenhauerian epistemological idealism" (WAM 6). And in 1931, Wittgenstein wrote that "Boltzmann, Hertz, Schopenhauer, Frege, Russell, Kraus, Loos, Weininger, Spengler, [and] Sraffa have influenced me" (CV 19). It is notable that Kant's name does not appear on this list. But as the first epigraph of this chapter shows, in 1931 Wittgenstein also saw a fundamental parallel between his own work and "the Kantian solution to the problem of philosophy."

More precisely, if I am correct, then:

(i) In the *Tractatus* Wittgenstein accepts the basic framework of Kant's transcendental idealism/empirical realism and theory of cognition, and in particular Wittgenstein accepts a version of strong transcendental idealism or STI, but rejects Kant's "modal dualism" of analytic and synthetic a priori necessary truths and opts for a "modal monism" of logically necessary truths.

(ii) In the *Tractatus* Wittgenstein accepts Schopenhauer's reduction of both the metaphysical subject and the metaphysical object (or "thing-in-itself") of Kant's transcendental idealism, to the will.

(iii) In the *Tractatus* Wittgenstein accepts the Frege–Russell idea that logic is first philosophy, but rejects both of their conceptions of logic: for Wittgenstein, logic is neither the science of laws of truth nor the absolutely general science of deduction; instead, for Wittgenstein, logic is transcendental in the Kantian sense.

One of the initially most puzzling features of the *Tractatus* is its background metaphysics of *solipsism* and *pure realism* (cf. Chapter 9, WITTGENSTEIN ON SOLIPSISM):

> 5.64 Here we see that solipsism strictly carried out coincides with pure realism. The I in solipsism shrinks to an extensionless point and there remains the reality co-ordinated with it.

> 5.641 There is therefore really a sense in which in philosophy we can talk of a non-psychological I.
> The I occurs in philosophy through the fact that "the world is my world".
> The philosophical I is not the man, not the human body or the human soul of which psychology treats, but the metaphysical subject, the limit – not a part of the world.

These propositions compactly express Wittgenstein's creative absorption and sublimation of Kant's transcendental idealism, in the specific sense of strong transcendental idealism or STI, and also Kant's empirical realism, in the first *Critique*. In the *Notebooks 1914–16*, Wittgenstein even more explicitly presents this line of thinking:

> This is the way I have travelled: Idealism singles men out from the world as unique, solipsism singles me alone out, and at last I see that I too belong with the rest of the world, and so on the one side *nothing* is left over, and on the other side, as unique, *the world*. In this way idealism leads to realism if it is strictly thought out. (NB 15.10.16)

What plays the specific ontological and epistemic roles of things-in-themselves or noumena in STI are Wittgenstein's *objects* (TLP 2.014–2.0232). Correspondingly, what plays the specific ontological and epistemic roles of empirically real appearances, objective real phenomena, or objects of experience in STI are Wittgenstein's atomic facts (TLP 1–2.11; see Chapter 7, LOGICAL ATOMISM). So in these ways, according to Wittgenstein, *I* am my world (TLP 5.63) and the world is *my* world (TLP 5.641), the subject does not belong to the world but is a limit of the world (TLP 5.631–5.632), and the metaphysical subject is a nonpsychological ego (TLP 5.633, 5.641).

What basic reasons does Wittgenstein have for holding this specifically Schopenhauerian and solipsistic version of Kant's STI? The answer is that they follow directly from

(i) the Tractarian thesis that the world of facts is constructed by the language-using subject; together with
(ii) the Tractarian thesis that the objects, or Wittgensteinian things-in-themselves, are given as an independent constraint on language and thought; together with
(iii) the Tractarian thesis that language is fundamentally a language of thought.

In short, Wittgenstein's specifically Schopenhauerian and solipsistic version of Kant's STI in the *Tractatus* is *linguistic* STI (LSTI):

5.6 *The limits of my language* mean the limits of my world. (TLP 5.6)

Strikingly, Wittgenstein's transcendental solipsism, i.e., his LSTI, has two importantly distinct although fully complementary dimensions:

(1) a transcendental solipsism/LSTI of the representing subject; and
(2) a transcendental solipsism/LSTI of the willing subject.

Or, as he puts it:

6.373 The world is independent of my will.
[...]
6.43 If good or bad willing changes the world, it can only change the limits of the world, not the facts; not the things that can be expressed in language.
In brief, the world must thereby become quite another. It must wax or wane as a whole.
The world of the happy man is a different one from that of the unhappy man. (TLP 6.373–6.43)

Wittgenstein's transcendental solipsism/LSTI of the representing subject says that all worldly facts are metaphysically dependent on my mind in the double sense that linguistic form (and its a priori essence, logical form) enters directly into the constitution of every fact, and that language itself is constructed by the individual subject. But Wittgenstein's solipsism/LSTI of the willi*ng* subject, by sharp contrast, says that the specific internal nature of the objects is metaphysically dependent on my attitudes, desires, and volitions – on my willing. The world of facts is independent of my will, but the form and limits of the world, i.e., the global a priori structure of the world, which is partially constituted by the specific internal nature of the objects, is dependent on my will. Now the world and my life are the same thing (TLP 5.621–5.63). Thus the world can "wax or wane" as a whole, depending on my acts of willing, just as all the events of my life depend on my will. They do not however depend on my will in the sense that I can actually change any facts – I cannot—but in the sense that I can control the personal meaning or *value* of those facts, which is bound up essentially with the world's global structure. So my will determines how I value the world and my life, which in turn partially determines the "substance" of the world by partially determining the nature of the objects, and thereby partially determining the global a priori structure of the world. In this way, the world of the happy person, say, is metaphysically distinct from the world of the unhappy person. Here we can see that although the constitution of the facts is dual (with language on the one side, and the objects on the other) the metaphysical subject ultimately grounds both of the dual inputs by acting both as the language-user and also as the partial determiner of the specific character of the objects and of the world's global a priori structure, i.e., of its transcendental structure. In that sense, whether I live in "the world of the happy," or not, is solely up to me, and something for which I am alone fully responsible, no matter what the natural facts may be. This is obviously a doctrine that Wittgenstein shares with the existentialists, and this elective affinity shows up again in his later reflections on Christianity and Kierkegaard (CV 53).

This existential up-to-me-ness of world-structuring, in turn, is directly reflected in the dependence of the world on the individual representing subject. Wittgenstein wants to argue that his transcendental solipsism/LSTI, when properly understood, is in fact a "pure realism." In order to make sense of this, we must remember that the classical philosophical thesis of realism comes in two very different versions:

(i) Noumenal Realism: things in the world have an essentially mind-independent existence and nature – i.e., they are things-in-themselves.
(ii) Empirical Realism: things in the apparent or manifest world are directly knowable by means of veridical human cognition, at least to some extent.

Classical rationalists and classical empiricists hold (i) – with sharply different degrees of epistemic confidence about the knowability of things-in-themselves, to be sure – and reject (ii). By sharp contrast, both Kant and Wittgenstein hold (ii) and firmly reject any version of (i), and also hold that in order to be an empirical realist/pure realist, one must also be a transcendental idealist/transcendental solipsist.

More precisely, Wittgenstein's pure realism is that nothing mediates between our correct use of language and the facts we thereby know: we cognize facts directly through the correct use of complete propositional symbols, and we cognize objects directly through the correct use of names. Then, provided that our judgments are true, we know the facts directly. This does not, however, in and of itself tell us how transcendental solipsism/LSTI leads to pure realism. Here Wittgenstein wants to say that his transcendental solipsism/LSTI is not a solipsism/LSTI of the psychologically individual subject, who is individuated by her body and her own personal history, but rather a solipsism/LSTI of the individual subject considered as an anonymous or generic representer and language-user. This anonymous or generic subject is an "extensionless point" precisely because she functions only as the means of representing the world.

Here Wittgenstein uses the striking analogy of the visual field and the eye: the seeing eye is the necessary vehicle or means of vision, but it is not itself part of the visual field or its contents; rather the seeing eye is presupposed by the visual field and its contents. Similarly, the world contains all the facts, including the facts about my psychologically individual subject. But when all of these facts have been recorded, there is still something left over, namely, the anonymous or generic representing language-using subject as such, which is contentless, yet presupposed by all the facts. Then when we consider the world of facts from the standpoint of that anonymous or generic representing language-using subject as such, we recognize that this entire world (my world, my life, the totality of facts) is directly presented to me and also fully knowable by me just insofar as I linguistically represent it.

4 How the World Conforms 3: To Forms of Life

For Wittgenstein in *Philosophical Investigations*, and also throughout his later philosophy, including for instance the writings published as *On Certainty*, language is ultimately a kind of rational human action, indeed the fundamental kind of rational human action. To twist Goethe's famous line from *Faust* ("In the beginning was the Deed"; Wittgenstein quotes this, see e.g., OC §402), we can say that for the later Wittgenstein meaningful utterances just *are* human deeds, and the language-practices made up of meaningful words, a.k.a. "language-games," just *are* living collections of human deeds:

> Words are deeds [*Taten*]. (CV §46)

> In this way, I should like to say the words "Oh, *let* him come!" are charged with my desire. And words can be wrung from us, – like a cry. Words can be *hard* to say: such, for example, as are used to effect a renunciation, or to confess a weakness. (Words are also deeds [*Taten*].) (PI §546)

Rational human animals are essentially linguistic agents, and our use of language is essentially the mastery of a skill (PI §20). In turn, this opens up the very idea of meaning to every conceivable role that language can play in rational human activity (PI §23). What I want to propose now is that although in the *Investigations*, via the private language argument (PI §§ 243–315; see Chapter 28, PRIVACY AND PRIVATE LANGUAGE), the later Wittgenstein clearly, explicitly, and specifically rejects the solipsism of LSTI in the *Tractatus*, he never rejects and in fact permanently continues to hold onto the transcendental idealism of LSTI – only in later writings he does so in a communitarian or social-practical version that is essentially equivalent to Kant's weak or counterfactual transcendental idealism, WCTI (see also Lear, 1982).

The basic connection here relies on the notion of rational human life, i.e., the individual and social biological, conscious, and cognitive life of language-using creatures like us. Now Kant essentially identifies rational human mind and rational human life:

> Life is the subjective condition of all our possible experience. (Kant, [1783] 1977, 4: 335)

> The mind for itself is entirely life (the principle of life itself). (Kant, [1790] 2000, 5: 278)

In the *Tractatus*, exactly the same essential identification is made, in two explicit steps and an implicit conclusion: (1) the world is life, and (2) I am my world, therefore (3) I am life:

> 5.621 The world and life are one.
> 5.63 I am my world. (The microcosm.) (TLP 5.621–5.63)

In the *Investigations*, this two-part essential identification between rational human mind and life is extended to a four-part essential identification that includes the intentional activity of judging and also the social language-using practices – language-games – in which rational human mind, life, and judging are ineluctably embedded:

> The term "language-game" is meant to bring into prominence the fact that the *speaking* of a language is part of an activity [*Tätigkeit*], or a form of life [*Lebensform*]. (PI §23)

> So you are saying that human agreement decides what is true and what is false? – It is what human beings *say* that is true and false; and they agree in the *language* they use. That is not agreement in opinions but in form of life. (PI §241)

> If language is to be a means of communication there must be agreement not only in definitions but also (queer as this may sound) in judgments. This seems to abolish logic, but does not do so. (PI §242)

And in *On Certainty*, the fourfold essential identification of rational human mind, life, judging, and language-games is extended to an explicit acknowledgment of the cognitive-practical apriority and certainty that naturally flow from our membership in language-games:

> We just *can't* investigate everything, and for that reason we are forced to rest content with assumption. If I want the door to turn, the hinges must stay put. My *life* consists in my being content to accept many things. (OC §§343–4)

> You must bear in mind that the language-game is so to say something unpredictable. I mean: it is not based on grounds [...]. It is there – like our life. (OC §559; cf. Chapter 35, WITTGENSTEIN ON KNOWLEDGE AND CERTAINTY and Chapter 36, WITTGENSTEIN ON SKEPTICISM)

If rational human mind, life, judging, and language-games are all essentially the same, and if these naturally yield cognitive-practical apriority and certainty for the members of language-games, then it follows that the a priori forms and structures of rational human mind are essentially the same as the a priori forms and structures of life, judging, and language-using. And if the manifestly real world necessarily conforms to the former, as The Conformity Thesis requires, then it necessarily conforms to the latter too. So the manifestly real world in which we live, move, and have our being necessarily conforms to our *forms of life*: "what has to be accepted, the given, is – so one could say, *forms of life*" (PPF §345).

5 The Critique of Self-Alienated Philosophy 1: Kant's Critical Meta-Philosophy

The 1781 edition (A) of the *Critique of Pure Reason* does not include a motto. But the 1787 edition (B) includes a Latin quotation from the preface of Francis Bacon's *Great Instauration* of 1620. Now, given that "instauration" means "restoration" or "renewal," the point of the Motto, then, is just to establish the following analogy:

> As *The Great Instauration* is to scholastic metaphysics, so the *Critique of Pure Reason* is to classical rationalist metaphysics.

Both are proposing a restorative, renewing, and indeed revolutionary anthropocentric turn in philosophy. But Kant's revolutionary turn goes well beyond Bacon's, and has three sources:

(i) the self-annihilating character of classical rationalist metaphysics, demonstrated by the antinomy of pure reason, evident in the fact that contradictory claims seem to be equally supported by metaphysical reasoning; this demonstrated the need for a critique of pure reason, discovered by Kant in 1766, and beautifully captured by the first few sentences of the A edition preface:

> Human reason has this peculiar fate in one species of its cognitions which it cannot dismiss, since they are given to it as problems by the very nature of reason itself, but which it also cannot answer, since they transcend every capacity of human reason [...]. The battlefield of these endless controversies is called *metaphysics*. (Kant, [1781/87] 1997, Avii–viii)

(ii) Hume's skeptical empiricism about the content, truth, and justification of human cognition, especially as applied to the classical rationalist metaphysical concepts of causation and causal necessity, remembered by Kant in 1771 or 1772; and

(iii) Kant's own revolutionary idealistic thesis about the necessary conformity of the ontic structure of space and time to the mentalistic structure of rational human sensible cognition, discovered and formulated by him between "the year of great light," 1769, and 1772.

These three philosophical sources combined to produce the three-part critical meta-philosophy of the *Critique of Pure Reason*, which is

(i) the rejection of classical rationalist metaphysics,
(ii) the rejection of the equal and opposite destructive and self-alienating radical skepticism that follows from the self-annihilating character of classical rationalist metaphysical reasoning, and
(iii) the revolutionary replacement of classical rationalist metaphysics by a new, inherently anthropocentric, and *mitigated* kind of rationalist metaphysics: transcendental idealism.

6   The Critique of Self-Alienated Philosophy 2: Wittgensteinian Analysis as Critique

According to what I call *the logico-decompositional theory of philosophical analysis*, dominant in the writings of Frege, Moore, Russell, and early Wittgenstein, from the late 1870s to the mid-1920s, philosophical analysis is the process of logically decomposing propositions into conceptual or metaphysical simples that are mind-independently real yet immediately and infallibly apprehended with self-evidence, and then rigorously logically reconstructing those propositions by formal deduction from general logical laws and premises that express logical definitional knowledge in terms of the simple constituents (Hanna, 2007). But in the *Investigations*, the later Wittgenstein's devastating critique of the semantic and logical doctrines of his own earlier philosophical self in the *Tractatus* motivates a radically wider and more open-textured conception of philosophical analysis. At the same time, his self-critique of Tractarian solipsism – the private language argument – further radicalizes his conception of philosophical analysis by rejecting several of the fundamental assumptions of classical rationalist Cartesian epistemology and metaphysics that had been explicitly or implicitly retained by Frege, Moore, Russell, and "the author of the *Tractatus Logico-Philosophicus*" (PI §23). Indeed, Wittgenstein's radical transformation of philosophical analysis goes significantly and seriously beyond the analytic tradition, and also returns us full-circle to Kantian transcendental Critical meta-philosophy.

In the *Tractatus*, Wittgenstein extends the Frege–Moore–Russell conception of logical-decompositional analysis. According to the Tractarian account, the proper targets of this analysis are propositions. Logical analysis consists in completely and uniquely decomposing propositional symbols into their constituent simple symbols, whether names of objects or logical constants (TLP 3.23–3.261). Objects are known by direct cognitive acquaintance (TLP 2.0123–2.01231), and logical constants are known "transcendentally," or by means of a priori showing (TLP 4.12–4.1213). Every proposition has a unique and complete decomposition (TLP 3.25). The way in which those names are configured into a propositional structure is made manifest through the process of analysis itself. Logical analysis is thus essentially a series of logical "elucidations" (*Erläuterungen*). Indeed, logical analysis is essentially the *activity* (*Tätigkeit*) but not the *theory* (*Lehre*) of decomposing a proposition into its simple constituent symbols (TLP 4.112).

More precisely, the Tractarian activist conception of logical analysis has two basic parts, and correspondingly two basic aims.

First, the activity of analysis is a "critique of language" (TLP 4.0031) in that it displays the fact that most propositions and questions that have been written about philosophical matters are not false but nonsensical (*unsinnig*) (TLP 4.003), recognizes that truths of logic are tautologous and non-pictorial, hence "say nothing" (*sagen nichts*) (TLP 6.11), then asserts as fully significant only the propositions of natural science (TLP 6.53), then recognizes its own propositions as nonsensical, and finally ends in mystical silence (TLP 6.54). (On this latter point see especially Chapter 12, META-PHYSICS: FROM INEFFABILITY TO NORMATIVITY and Chapter 10, RESOLUTE READINGS OF THE *TRACTATUS*.) Thus the first basic aim of Tractarian logical analysis is to articulate the difference between sense (factual meaningfulness) and nonsense. Here we must remember that "nonsense" for early Wittgenstein is literally *what is other than sense*, i.e., everything of a cognitive or semantic nature that is other than what is described or pictured or "said" by atomic propositions. Thus it can be either sheer absurdity, or *meaninglessness*, e.g., Lewis Carroll's *Jabberwocky*, or else it can be *illuminatingly what is other than sense* in some other nonatomic-fact-representing, but still logically, semantically, aesthetically, or ethically important way.

Second, the activity of logical analysis is the process of logically clarifying thoughts, consisting in a series of propositional elucidations that "make clear and delimit sharply the thoughts which otherwise are [...] opaque and blurred" (TLP 4.112). Thus the second basic aim of Tractarian logical analysis is to reveal the deep or *logico*-grammatical structure of natural language and thought, as opposed to its merely surface or *psychologico*-grammatical structure. In order to reveal the deep structure of language, Tractarian philosophers must construct and study symbolic logical systems, such as those developed in Frege's *Begriffsschrift* and Whitehead and Russell's *Principia Mathematica*. Such symbolic systems are "ideal" in the sense that the syntax of a *Begriffsschrift*-type notational system itself displays, encodes, or mirrors the deep structure of natural language and thought, and thereby also the deep structure of the world of facts that language and thought represent. Even so, Tractarian analysis does not aim at the *prescriptive reform* of natural language or thought. On the contrary, everything in natural language and thought is perfectly in order, just as it is (TLP 5.5563).

In the *Investigations* there is a radical turn in Wittgenstein's conception of philosophy from logical analysis or the "logical clarification of thoughts" (TLP 4.112), to what I will call *the critique of pure logic*, or CPL, which says that logic is not anything "sublime" but instead is really nothing but grammar. Here is a rational reconstruction of CPL:

(1) Frege, Moore, Russell, the author of the *Tractatus*, Carnap, the members of the Vienna Circle, and others, all explicitly or implicitly hold the thesis that logic is something "sublime": universal, a priori, necessary, and noumenally essential (PI §89).
(2) Furthermore, logic is required to carry out any complete or partial decompositional analysis of our forms of language, propositions, and thoughts, which reveals their "hidden" "simple" structures and constituents, that is, their decomposable essences (PI §§91–6).
(3) But in fact,
    (3i) every sentence in our language is in order just as it is;
    (3ii) vagueness is a constitutive feature of meaning;
    (3iii) language is essentially a spatiotemporal phenomenon, not something abstract; and
    (3iv) the essence of language, proposition, thought, and the world is something that "already lies open to view and that becomes surveyable by a rearrangement" (PI §92; see §§98–100, 108–9).
(4) So neither language, nor propositions, nor thought, nor the world have hidden decomposable noumenal essences, and therefore the thesis that logic is sublime is false.
(5) Furthermore the thesis that logic is sublime turns out to be only a methodological assumption we have unintentionally imposed upon the phenomena, indeed nothing but an artifact of an idealized metaphysical "picture" that lay hidden in our language and held us captive (PI §§101–8, 110–15).

(6) Now,

> the philosophy of logic speaks of sentences and words in exactly the sense in which we speak of them in ordinary life when we say, e.g., "Here is a Chinese sentence," or "No, that only looks like writing; it is actually an ornament" and so on. (PI §108)

> That is: we can regard logic as purely descriptive, not noumenally essential; and "what *we* do is to bring words back from their metaphysical use to their everyday use" by asking "is the word ever actually used in this way in the language which is its original home" (PI §116).

(7) Therefore we should adopt the thesis that logic is really nothing but "grammar," the latter

> shedding light on our problem by clearing misunderstandings away [...]. [...] misunderstandings concerning the use of words, caused, among other things by certain analogies between the forms of expression in different regions of language [...]. [...] [And] some of them can be removed by substituting one form of expression for another; this may be called an "analysis" of our forms of expression, for the process is sometimes like one of taking things apart. (PI §90)

(8) Furthermore, the goal of logic-as-grammar is to produce a "perspicuous representation" of language, propositions, thought, and the world, which produces "that understanding which consists in 'seeing connections'" (PI §122).

(9) So logic is not sublime, and logical-decompositional analysis is impossible, but logic-as-grammar is possible, and grammar in this sense is the descriptive logic of our language-games, i.e., what represents a priori forms of life, which are transcendentally embedded in our communal practices.

(10) Therefore to the extent that logic as a theory of valid reasoning still exists in the form of logic-as-grammar, this logic is fully transcendental in the Kantian and also Tractarian sense.

Now let us suppose that CPL is sound. What does philosophy become after the collapse of logical analysis? Here are the three essential texts:

> The work of the philosopher consists in assembling reminders for a particular purpose. (PI §127)

> If one tried to advance *theses* in philosophy, it would never be possible to question them, because everyone would agree to them. (PI §128)

> It is not our aim to refine or complete the system of rules for the use of words in unheard-of ways. For the clarity that we are aiming at is indeed *complete* clarity. But that simply means that the philosophical problems should *completely* disappear. The real discovery is one that makes me capable of stopping doing philosophy when I want to. – The one that gives philosophy peace, so that it is no longer tormented by questions which bring *itself* into question [...]. There is not *a* philosophical method, though there are indeed methods, like different therapies. (PI §133)

And here is the two-part answer to that question – "what does philosophy become after the collapse of logical analysis?"

First, the later Wittgenstein's conception of philosophy in fact shares some fundamental features in common with his activist conception of logical analysis in the

Tractatus (cf. Chapter 13, PHILOSOPHY AND PHILOSOPHICAL METHOD). But this activist conception of logical analysis is now minus the "sublimity" or "noumenal essentialism" of logic, that is to say, minus the comprehensive noumenal essentialist metaphysical picture of logic, language, thought, and the world that would justify the logical-decompositional theory of analysis, but still accepting the transcendental character of logic, now understood to be logic-as-grammar. Logic is *not* sublime, but logic *is* transcendental, even in the *Investigations*. In short, the later Wittgenstein's radical turn in philosophy towards logic-as-grammar is simply a radical return to Kant's Critical meta-philosophy, that is, a radical return to transcendental logic understood as transcendental dialectic, which is the meta-philosophical critique of metaphysical illusion in philosophy, as a form of rational self-knowledge (Kant, [1781/87] 1997, A61–2/B85–6, A293–8/B349–54). The main idea is that, as a logical grammarian, one

(i) displays and diagnoses the dialectical structure of philosophical problems, i.e., displays and diagnoses "the civil status of a contradiction, or its status in civil life" (PI §125);
(ii) describes, unpacks, compares, and contrasts the concepts implicit in our various ordinary uses of language and states a priori truisms about them (PI §§123–6); and then
(iii) stops doing philosophy when one wants to, in order to change one's life, or the direction of one's life, and in order to achieve "insight into what lies in front of everyone's eyes" (PI §133).

Second, and as a direct consequence of this, the other crucial thing about the later Wittgenstein's conception of philosophy is that it is fundamentally noncognitive, that is, fundamentally desire-based, emotive, normative, and practical. On this view, philosophy is neither a natural science nor a mere source of factual knowledge but rather essentially a self-conscious and deliberative activity – that of "doing philosophy." In turn, doing philosophy means achieving perspicuous insight into what already is completely there in front of us: rational human animals and their language, fully embedded in their apparent or manifest world, intentionally acting according to the normatively guiding a priori structures of their living, shared social practices, i.e., according to the forms of rational human life (PI §241). In the light of this, we can now also say that the aim of philosophy for the later Wittgenstein is precisely to achieve a Kant-style Critical insight into what lies before everyone's eyes, i.e., into the cognitive and practical capacities of creatures like us, and into the nature of our apparent or manifest world.

7 Conclusion

As Quine (see, e.g., Hylton, 2007, especially chs 9 and 12), Reichenbach (1951), and Sellars so clearly saw in the 1950s, after the successive downfalls of logicism and logical empiricism/positivism during the first half of the twentieth century, analytic philosophy became, essentially, a series of minor variations on the theme of *scientific philosophy*:

> In the dimension of describing and explaining the world, science is the measure of all things, of what is that it is, and of what is not that it is not. (Sellars, 1963, p.173)

This is philosophy in Sellars's scientific image. But the later Wittgenstein, following Kant's lead, radically challenges and rejects this essentially *scientistic* conception of philosophy:

> I had to deny *scientific knowledge* [*Wissen*] in order to make room for *faith* [*Glauben*]. (Kant, [1781/87] 1997, Bxxix–xxx)

> It was true to say that our considerations could not be scientific ones [*wissenschaftlich*]. It was not of any possible interest to us to find out empirically 'that, contrary to our preconceived ideas, it is possible think such-and-such' – whatever that may mean [...]. And we may not advance any kind of theory [...]. We must do away with all *explanation*, and description alone must take its place. These are, of course, not empirical problems; they are solved, rather, by looking into the workings of our language, and that in such a way as to make us recognize those workings: *in spite of* an urge to misunderstand them. The problems are solved, not by giving new information, but by arranging what we have always known. (PI §109)

In this way, transcendental anthropology as practiced by Kant and Wittgenstein does not *either* seek a humanly impossible, absolutely justifying, pure rational insight into things-in-themselves, *or* draw Pyrrhonian skeptical conclusions from our inevitable and tragic failure to achieve a godlike "intellectual intuition" of ourselves and the world (Kant, [1781/87] 1997, B72), *or* fall into scientism. For all three of these philosophical projects, whether dogmatically rationalistic, destructively skeptical, or reductively naturalistic, are equally inherently self-alienating and "inauthentic" in the existentialists' sense. Indeed, it is significant that even when, in 1986, Hacker officially rescinds his earlier Kant-oriented interpretation of Wittgenstein from 1972, he still admits that

> more than any other philosophers, Kant and Wittgenstein were concerned with the nature of philosophy itself and sought to curb its metaphysical pretensions by clarifying its status and circumscribing what one may rationally hope for in philosophical investigation. Both saw philosophical and metaphysical *pretensions of reason* as at least a large part of the subject, and the eradication of such illusions as a major goal of their work. (Hacker, 1972/86, p.207)

Otherwise put, with a tragic sense of life, Kant and Wittgenstein both fully recognize that we must renounce every variety of *the bad faith of reason* in order to make room for an authentic, autonomous, rational human life, and in turn, in order to make room for an anthropocentric rationalist version of Kierkegaard's "knighthood of faith," as it were, *the knighthood of rational faith*, whereby you can radically change your life, or change the direction of your life – and this is the deepest lesson of transcendental anthropology.

References

Bearn, G.C.F. (1997). *Waking to Wonder: Wittgenstein's Existential Investigations*. Albany: SUNY Press.
Brockhaus, R. (1991). *Pulling Up the Ladder: The Metaphysical Roots of Wittgenstein's Tractatus Logico-Philosophicus*. Chicago: Open Court.
Cavell, S. (1979). *The Claim of Reason: Wittgenstein, Skepticism, Morality, and Tragedy*. Oxford: Oxford University Press.

de Unamuno, M. ([1912] 1921). *Tragic Sense of Life*. Trans. J.E. Crawford Flitch. London: Macmillan. (Original work published 1912.)

Hacker, P.M.S. (1972). *Insight and Illusion: Wittgenstein on Philosophy and the Metaphysics of Experience*. Oxford: Clarendon Press.

Hacker, P.M.S. (1972/86). *Insight and Illusion: Themes in the Philosophy of Wittgenstein*. Revised edition. Oxford: Clarendon Press.

Hanna, R. (2007). Kant, Wittgenstein, and the Fate of Analysis. In M. Beaney (Ed.). *The Analytic Turn* (pp.145–167). London: Routledge.

Hylton, P. (2007). *Quine*. London: Routledge.

Kant, I. ([1781/87] 1997). *Critique of Pure Reason*. Trans. P. Guyer and A. Wood. Cambridge: Cambridge University Press. (Original work published 1781/87.)

Kant, I. ([1783] 1977). *Prolegomena to Any Future Metaphysics*. Trans. J. Ellington. Indianapolis: Hackett. (Original work published 1783.)

Kant, I. ([1790] 2000). *Critique of the Power of Judgment*. Trans. P. Guyer and E. Matthews. Cambridge: Cambridge University Press. (Original work published 1790.)

Lear, J. (1982). Leaving the World Alone. *Journal of Philosophy*, 79, 382–403.

Lear, J. (1986). Transcendental Anthropology. In J. McDowell and P. Pettit (Eds). *Subject, Context, and Thought* (pp.267–298). Oxford: Oxford University Press.

Lear, J. and Stroud, B. (1984). The Disappearing "We." *Proceedings of the Aristotelian Society* (Supplementary Volume), 58, 219–258.

Potter, M. (2009). *Wittgenstein's Notes on Logic*. Oxford: Oxford University Press.

Potter, M. (forthcoming). *Wittgenstein 1916*. Oxford: Oxford University Press.

Reichenbach, H. (1951). *The Rise of Scientific Philosophy*. Berkeley: University of California Press.

Sellars, W. (1963). Empiricism and the Philosophy of Mind. In W. Sellars. *Science, Perception, and Reality* (pp.127–196). New York: Humanities Press.

Williams, B. (1973). Wittgenstein and Idealism. Reprinted in B. Williams. (1981). *Moral Luck: Philosophical Papers 1973–1980* (pp.144–163). Cambridge: Cambridge University Press.

Further Reading

Cavell, S. (1962). The Availability of Wittgenstein's Later Philosophy. *Philosophical Review*, 71, 67–93.

Dostoyevsky, F. ([1880] 1958). *The Brothers Karamazov*. Trans. D. Magarshack. Harmondsworth: Penguin. (Original work published 1880.)

Glock, H.-J. (1997). Kant and Wittgenstein: Philosophy, Necessity and Representation. *International Journal of Philosophical Studies*, 5, 285–305.

Hacker, P.M.S. (1996). *Wittgenstein's Place in Twentieth-Century Analytic Philosophy*. Oxford: Blackwell.

Hanna, R. (2008). Kant in the Twentieth Century. In D. Moran (Ed.). *The Routledge Companion to Twentieth-Century Philosophy* (pp.149–203). London: Routledge.

Kierkegaard, S. (2000). *The Essential Kierkegaard*. Trans. H.V. Hong and E.H. Hong. Princeton: Princeton University Press.

Lear, J. (1989). On Reflection: The Legacy of Wittgenstein's Later Philosophy. *Ratio*, 2, 19–45.

Monk, R. (1990). *Wittgenstein: The Duty of Genius*. London: Jonathan Cape.

Sellars, W. (1963). Philosophy and the Scientific Image of Man. In W. Sellars. *Science, Perception, and Reality* (pp.1–40). New York: Humanities Press.

Sullivan, P. (2004). What is the *Tractatus* About? In M. Kölbel and B. Weiss (Eds). *Wittgenstein's Lasting Significance* (pp.32–45). London: Routledge.

46

Wittgenstein and the Vienna Circle

THOMAS UEBEL

The topic of the philosophical relationship between Wittgenstein and the Vienna Circle is of considerable interest both to interpreters of the work of Wittgenstein and of the Circle. Answers to questions concerning the nature and extent of the influences between them have long been thought to inform the systematic understanding of the philosophies involved. Importantly, our knowledge of the relation between Wittgenstein and the Vienna Circle has an interesting history of its own, reflecting in part the perceived relative standing of the two parties; each of whom, after all, prescribed a radical reorientation of philosophy as traditionally practiced.

To begin with we may note that even though the members of the Vienna Circle were not the first readers of *Tractatus Logico-Philosophicus*, they certainly helped to make the book more widely known through their own writings of the late 1920s and early 1930s. In this they were aided, no doubt, by the notoriety of their own doctrines, which they advertised as partly derived from what they read in the *Tractatus*. One issue of great sensitivity, therefore, has been the extent to which Wittgenstein himself was implicated, rightly or wrongly, by the uncompromisingly antimetaphysical stance of the type adopted by the Circle. For followers of Wittgenstein in his Cambridge period and post-World War II interpreters of his work, its reception by the Circle long served as a cautionary warning against predictable pitfalls of any *Tractatus* interpretation. For more recent historians of the Vienna Circle, by contrast, the rendition of relations to Wittgenstein has become a test case for gauging the sophistication of the Circle interpretation offered: long but falsely thought of as monolithic, the Circle's pluralism demands recognition.

Matters are further complicated by the fact that neither Wittgenstein's nor the Vienna Circle's various philosophical views remained static during the years in question. From this follow not only obvious demands on the interpretation of the views of Wittgenstein and of the members of the Vienna Circle but also of their mutual relation. So the question must also be raised whether, at the time, either party understood the other correctly. (For overviews of the development of Wittgenstein's philosophy and the interpretations it has received, see Glock, 2001; 2007; as well as Chapter 1, WITTGENSTEIN'S PHILOSOPHICAL DEVELOPMENT; for an overview of the philosophies of the Vienna Circle, see Uebel, 2011.)

A Companion to Wittgenstein, First Edition. Edited by Hans-Johann Glock and John Hyman.
© 2017 John Wiley & Sons, Ltd. Published 2017 by John Wiley & Sons, Ltd.

Quite apart from these interpretative questions, it must be noted that there has been unclarity about the facts of their association. Given the prominence that was accorded to Wittgenstein's *Tractatus* in important writings issuing from the Vienna Circle, it was perhaps excusable that in the past the popular imagination sometimes turned Wittgenstein into a member of that Circle. The collectively authored manifesto *The Scientific World-Conception: The Vienna Circle* of 1929 sought to stress Wittgenstein's independence by designating him, alongside Einstein and Russell, not as a "member" or even "associate" but a "leading representative of the scientific world-conception" (Hahn, Carnap, and Neurath, [1929] 2012, p.108). More carelessly Feigl and Blumberg introduced Wittgenstein as one of the "foremost philosophical exponents" of the movement of logical positivism (1931, p.281). The early critic Weinberg spoke of "Wittgenstein's logical positivism" (1935, p.398; cf. 1936, p.26) and Ayer began his positivist *Language, Truth and Logic* by stating that its views "derive from the doctrines of Bertrand Russell and Wittgenstein" (1936/46, p.31).

Given the critical distance that Wittgenstein himself was reported to have kept from most of the members of the Circle after some initial contact, it was likewise excusable that particularly among students of Wittgenstein's posthumously published *Philosophical Investigations* the view gained currency that whatever association there may have been early on, it was deeply misguided from the start. The aim of this chapter is, first, to present the historical facts against which the philosophical relations between Wittgenstein and the Vienna Circle have to be assessed and, second, to give an overview of the Circle's reception of Wittgenstein's philosophy. Numerous topics are barely raised, yet others – notably the priority dispute over physicalism between Wittgenstein and Carnap (see Stern, 2007) – must remain unmentioned.

1 Facts about the Association

The first contact with Wittgenstein by any of the members of the future "Vienna Circle" – at the time they were known, if at all, simply as the "Schlick-Kreis" – was via Wittgenstein's first publication, either as the "*Logisch-philosophische Abhandlung*" published in Ostwald's *Annalen der Natur-und Kulturphilosophie* (1921) or in its bilingual book form as *Tractatus Logico-Philosophicus* (1922). That this work was read in meetings of the Vienna Circle line-by-line is well known; less well established are the precise circumstances. Personal meetings only followed later; when and how they ended also has remained somewhat unclear.

2 Readings of the *Tractatus*

In 1922, Moritz Schlick was appointed to a chair in philosophy at the University of Vienna with the support of the mathematician Hans Hahn. Hahn himself had returned to Vienna as a professor only in 1921 and had been a member, together with the physicist Philipp Frank, the political economist Otto Neurath, and others, of a group that met 1907 and 1912 for discussions mainly of philosophy of science. (On this so-called "first Vienna Circle," see, e.g., Frank, 1949, pp.1–3; Haller, [1985] 1991; Uebel, 2003.) Schlick, a trained physicist turned philosopher, was known as the author of a critical-realist *General Theory of Knowledge* ([1918] 1974) and valued – amongst others by

Einstein himself – for his analyses of the epistemological foundations of the special and general theories of relativity. From 1924 onwards, Schlick convened regular meetings attended by Hahn, Neurath, and (when in Vienna by the then Prague-based) Frank, as well as by the Viennese philosophers Viktor Kraft and Felix Kaufmann, the mathematician Kurt Reidemeister, and Schlick's students Herbert Feigl and Friedrich Waismann. In later years other current and former students of Schlick and Hahn, such as Karl Menger and Kurt Gödel, and interested younger colleagues, such as Rudolf Carnap, were invited to join. It was this group of philosophers of science and scientists interested in foundational questions of their disciplines that soon after its formation encountered Wittgenstein's *Tractatus*.

Schlick's first letter to Wittgenstein in December 1924 (WVC, p.13) recalls how the Circle became acquainted with his book:

> In the Institute of Philosophy during every winter semester I customarily hold regular meetings with colleagues and gifted students who are interested in the foundations of logic and mathematics, and in this circle your name has often been mentioned, especially since my colleague, the mathematician Prof. Reidemeister gave a report on your work which impressed all of us greatly.

Intense discussions followed the initial presentation by Reidemeister. In November 1925 Schlick wrote to Carnap that "in our Thursday circle this semester we are reading the treatise by Wittgenstein page by page," and in March 1926 that they had not reached the end and so would continue in the summer semester. Carnap, who joined the Circle's discussions in that summer semester and who was appointed *Privatdozent* at the start of the following academic year, noted his attendance of the "sentence by sentence" reading in his autobiography (1963, p.24). While Carnap gave no dates there, his diary indicates that the Thursday evening meetings devoted to the *Tractatus* finished in the course of the winter semester 1926/1927. We can conclude – albeit tentatively – that the Circle's *Tractatus*-focused discussions spread (but not continuously) across three academic years from late 1924 to early 1927.

From 1927/1928, when Menger joined the Circle, "the *Tractatus* as such was no longer on the agenda," as he remembered: "But it loomed over the discussions and especially over all that Schlick said and thought" (1982, p.88). By then the main focus of Schlick's interests had shifted away from the philosophy of physics toward philosophy of logic and language. But these readings had also nourished a certain *corps d'esprit* among the participants, expressed in a common terminology that Menger, having joined only afterwards, claimed never to have been able to share (1982, p.86).

3 Personal Interactions with Wittgenstein

Schlick's letter to Wittgenstein of December 1924 expressed the wish to meet him personally. Despite further pleasantries in messages no meeting between them took place until Wittgenstein invited him in February 1927 to see whether a discussion of logical problems would be "of use" (WVC, pp.13–14). Their initial encounter left Schlick spellbound. After additional meetings Wittgenstein agreed to let Schlick be accompanied at first by Waismann, then also by Carnap and Feigl (and his fiancée) at various times that summer and then had further meetings with them – but without Carnap – throughout 1928. No notes were taken on those occasions, but reports indicate that while sometimes questions concerning the foundations of mathematics and Ramsey's work were being discussed, at other times Wittgenstein preferred to read poetry to his guests. It would seem that Wittgenstein still largely felt that, as he had written to Keynes in July 1924, "everything that I really had to say, I have said, and so the spring has run dry" (WVC, p.12).

Wittgenstein nevertheless revealed a philosophical temperament in sharp contrast to what his book had led some of his visitors to expect. Carnap wrote:

> Our attitude toward philosophical problems was not very different from that which scientists have towards their problems. [...] I sometimes had the impression that the deliberately rational and unemotional attitude of the scientists and likewise any ideas which had the flavor of "enlightenment" were repugnant to Wittgenstein. (Carnap, 1963, p.26)

Feigl also spoke of "diametrically opposed personalities" and reported Wittgenstein's "exasperation" with Carnap's probing for further explanations: "If he can't smell it, I can't help him. He just has got no nose!" (Feigl, 1969/81, p.64).

Schlick, by contrast, had no such difficulties with Wittgenstein and with them a true meeting of minds appears to have taken place. Their correspondence reveals deep mutual respect and their friendship was only severed by Schlick's murder in June 1936. More than philosophy was involved. It is helpful here to remember Waismann's account of "two personalities" in Schlick – an "analytical talent" and "acute thinker" known to most of his colleagues and a "poet" for whom "listening to a concert or gazing at a landscape it could happen, in his own words, that the doors to the infinite suddenly opened to him" (Waismann, [1938] 1979, pp.xv–xvi). Schlick was able to feel attuned to Wittgenstein's personality in a way Carnap or Feigl were incapable of. And while Waismann was about as faithful an *amanuensis* as could be wished for, it was only Schlick whom Wittgenstein treated as an equal.

Even though Schlick once invited him, Wittgenstein never attended a meeting of his discussion group. Most members of the Vienna Circle are likely therefore to have seen Wittgenstein only once, if at all. That occasion was L.E.J. Brouwer's lecture "Mathematics, Science and Language" in Vienna in March 1928. (Hahn, who chaired the meeting, walked into the auditorium to welcome Wittgenstein personally.) Menger, who had suggested to Waismann that he should persuade Wittgenstein to attend, observed: "Motionless from beginning to end, Wittgenstein looked at the speaker with a slightly startled expression, at first, which later gave way to a faint smile of enjoyment" (Menger, 1994, p.131). Schlick, Waismann and Feigl were able to accompany Wittgenstein to a café afterwards. Later Feigl reported: "suddenly and very volubly Wittgenstein began talking philosophy – at great length. Perhaps this was the turning point" for it "marked the return of Wittgenstein to strong philosophical interests and activities" (Feigl, 1969/81, p.64; cf. Pitcher, 1964, p.8).

From 1929 on, after he had relocated to Cambridge, Wittgenstein only met with Schlick and Waismann when back in Vienna during vacations (see also LUDWIG WITTGENSTEIN: A SKETCH OF HIS LIFE). Already in 1928 it had been decided that Waismann should write a readily accessible exposition of Wittgenstein's philosophy, called *Logik, Sprache, Philosophie*, to be published as the first volume of Schlick's and Frank's series "Writings on the Scientific World-Conception." At first it was to be a "logical ordering and structuring" of the ideas of the *Tractatus* alone, then also of the latest modifications that Wittgenstein applied to the *Tractatus*, still later a representation of Wittgenstein's new philosophy. This project has been characterized as having had three phases (see VW xix, xxx; and Stern, 2007, pp.316–17). During the first, Waismann not only worked on the manuscript for the book (and took notes of the discussions with Wittgenstein from December 1929 until July 1932), but also interrupted work on the book to prepare a paper on Wittgenstein's conception of mathematics for the Second Conference on the Epistemology of the Exact Sciences, organized in Königsberg in September 1930 by Reidemeister. (For the notes see WVC 33–211; for the lecture Waismann, [1982] 1986.) By autumn 1931, however, Wittgenstein had become deeply dissatisfied with Waismann's rendition of his Tractarian philosophy as updated with regard to his new ideas about hypotheses and the definition of sense in terms of verification. Finding "*many, many* formulations in that book that I am no longer in agreement with" (as he wrote to Schlick in November; see WVC, p. 24, original emphasis), at their next meeting in December (see WVC 182–6) Wittgenstein also objected strongly to the "dogmatism" of Waismann's "Theses" (composed to characterize Wittgenstein's new position and serving as the basis for numerous discussions in the Circle; see WVC 233–61). It would appear that Wittgenstein realized that his new ideas could no longer be shoehorned into an emendation of the *Tractatus*. The plan for Waismann's exposition was abandoned, ending phase one.

Since apart from a brief discussion of claims by Carnap in July 1932 (which set off the priority dispute neglected here) Waismann's published notes of the meetings with Wittgenstein end with those of 9 December 1931, it is sometimes thought that their contact ended thereabouts, especially since in light of his dispute with Carnap Wittgenstein no longer cared to communicate his ideas to the Circle as a whole. However, it was resolved with Schlick that Wittgenstein should become the co-author with Waismann of a different book giving an exposition of his *new* ideas by dictating passages from manuscripts he had been working on. To this end Wittgenstein met Waismann numerous times during December 1931 and January 1932, and during March and April 1932; by the end of May 1932, to judge from a letter by Schlick, a two-volume work was envisaged to emerge (see LSP 652; and Manninen, 2011, pp.248–9). The dictations that Wittgenstein gave in the Christmas vacation 1931/1932 – and which Wittgenstein wanted transmitted to Schlick who was still visiting at Stanford: "Have you received Waismann's notes of what I dictated at Christmas?" (WVC 24) – clearly record the fresh start he had reported to Schlick in the fall. (These dictations are not identical with the "Diktat für Schlick," D 302; see Manninen, 2011, pp.251–4.) It appeared that work was advancing well, yet when Wittgenstein returned to Vienna at Easter 1934 and inspected the rewritten large but still unfinished manuscript produced by Waismann he rejected it again. Waismann bravely reported to Schlick in August 1934:

> [Wittgenstein] has the marvellous gift of always seeing everything as if for the first time. But I think it's obvious how difficult any collaboration is, since he follows the inspiration of the moment and demolishes what he has previously planned. (WVC 26; also VW xxvii)

This time Waismann was unable to follow Wittgenstein's suggestion for a radical rewrite – especially as Wittgenstein never delivered the new plan that he promised. Thus ended phase two.

Wittgenstein may at this point have resolved to write the book on his new philosophy on his own. A third phase began in which, it has been claimed, Wittgenstein withdrew from the joint project, and left Waismann and Schlick to proceed as they wished. Yet Wittgenstein's meetings with Waismann did not cease this time either, for they met still five more times in December 1934 and January 1935 and once at Easter 1935. What precisely the purpose of these meetings was has not been established as yet, but Waismann was kept informed about Wittgenstein's developing ideas and he also retained access to his dictations to Schlick and a copy of the "Blue Book" which Wittgenstein had dictated in Cambridge in 1933/1934 (see Manninen 2011, pp.261–5; and LSP 653). Even so, their association did not end happily.

In January 1936 – notably still over two years before the *Anschluss* – Waismann lost his university position as librarian, officially for economic reasons but mostly likely due to anti-Semitism on the part of the authorities. Surviving precariously from giving private tuition he published a paper on the concept of identity ([1936] 1977), which prompted Wittgenstein to complain about having been insufficiently acknowledged as the source of its main idea. Still Waismann felt he had to plough on with the book project, feeling that otherwise Wittgenstein's new conception of philosophy might be forever lost (Waismann in a letter to Carnap; see Baker, 1979, p.257). When Waismann arrived in Cambridge in October 1937, in effect as a fugitive, Wittgenstein was not there but on his return reportedly avoided all contact. The extent of their alienation has been disputed (see Baker, 1979, p.245; VW xxi; and McGuinness, 2011, p.13), but Waismann was well advised to take up a position in Oxford in 1939. That year he also completed both German and English versions of his book but both, *Logik, Sprache, Philosophie* (LSP) and *Principles of Linguistic Philosophy* (PLP) were published only posthumously. His later work shows anti-Wittgensteinian tendencies and he expressed deep personal disappointment. Thus Heinrich Neider reported:

> When I visited Waismann after the war in Oxford once, he said: "Yes, I have broken totally with Wittgenstein. Wittgenstein is the great disappointment of my life. He wholly entered the camp of obscurantists." (See the recollection of Neider, 1977, p.33, trans. TU; see also Hacker, 1995)

As noted, Wittgenstein's relations with Schlick were of a happier nature. Wittgenstein shared highly significant typescripts with him and gave dictations to him when they met. (Von Wright's inventory of Wittgenstein's papers lists eight dictations for Schlick, numbered 302–8 and a typescript version of "*Grosses Format*," numbered 140; see PO 492, 500–11; see also Iven, 2009, pp.78–80.) The dating of some of these dictations has been difficult, but progress has been made. One hypothesis: in September 1933 Wittgenstein and Schlick spent ten days together at the Adriatic coast in Istria and it was their intense work there that resulted in the "Dictation for Schlick" echoes of which can be found in Schlick's lectures during the following year (see Iven, 2009; for discussion see Schulte, 2011, pp.237–41; Manninen, 2011, p.251; and Oakes and Pichler, 2013). Schlick also had access to a significant portion of Wittgenstein's "Big Typescript" (TS 213), a compilation of remarks from his notebooks of the years 1929–1932 which probably was first assembled with new additions in 1933 and subsequently formed the basis for various revisions including "*Grosses Format*" (a version of which Schlick was holding). Also in Schlick's possession was the dictation called "Mulder V," now dated to 1934, the text of which largely overlaps with sections I–III of Part I of what was published posthumously as *Philosophical Grammar* that was drawn from the "Big Typescript" material. So we can take Schlick to have been well informed about the changes that Wittgenstein's philosophy underwent in the early 1930s – even independently of the reports from Waismann. (Whether he correctly understood every turn of Wittgenstein's thought is another matter.)

4   The Influence of Wittgenstein on the Vienna Circle

What did the Vienna Circle learn from Wittgenstein? Here we must note right away three basic points. First, that when the *Tractatus* was read by the Circle in the years 1924–1927, it was read not for its own sake but largely for the contribution its general theory of symbolism might make to their ongoing inquiries into the foundations of the empirical and formal sciences. When they decided that it did make a very significant contribution indeed, they saw it do so as regards the nature of logic, language, and philosophy. Second, we must note that their longer-term reception of the *Tractatus* was influenced, from around 1928 onwards, by what they gathered about its author's own views about what he had written. Third, we must note that different readers drew different lessons from Wittgenstein's book and the conversations with him or reports thereof.

Important corollaries follow for the assessment of the Circle's *Tractatus* reception. First, that their views of Wittgenstein's broadly speaking "Tractarian" philosophy were never intended to be faithful copies of the *Tractatus* itself. Second, that by no means all members of the Circle intended to be faithful even to what they perceived of the Tractarian philosophy. To speak of the Vienna Circle as simply having misunderstood Wittgenstein is wide of the mark. There were, to be sure, misunderstandings (some understandable once we consider the context), but there were also clear agreements and equally clear – and intended – disagreements with Wittgenstein. The misunderstandings also were not limited to Wittgenstein's critics: that Schlick and Waismann had extensive access to Wittgenstein's manuscripts does not mean that they comprehended correctly the drift and nuance of every remark made therein (see Uebel, 2007, pp. 356–70). Moreover – and this point holds for the Circle as a whole – there is no evidence to suggest that prior to the fall of 1931 they were given any indication that Wittgenstein's new conceptions (e.g., on verification and so-called hypotheses) were meant as more than modifications of the *Tractatus*. (It is likely that Wittgenstein himself did not realize this fully until then.) To criticize Waismann's "Theses," for instance, for "fundamental distortions of Wittgenstein's ideas" (see Baker and Hacker, 1986, p.246) is rather anachronistic, given that their point was precisely to present that fusion of old and new, and that Wittgenstein's views were far from stable.

Schlick's and Waismann's extensive access to Wittgenstein-in-transition also highlights that there is considerable substance to the distinction (first drawn by Neurath and later publicized by Carnap) between the "left wing" (Carnap mentioned Neurath, Hahn, and himself) and the "more conservative right wing" (Schlick and Waismann) of the Circle. Despite its political overtones, the distinction refers to philosophical orientations: while the former broke away from what they took to be Wittgenstein's positions on a variety of issues, the latter "remained in personal contact with Wittgenstein and were inclined to maintain his views and formulations" (Carnap, 1963, pp.57–8). To be sure, news of Wittgenstein's ideas were transmitted across the boundary still after 1929. But especially after the summer of 1932, such information was harder to come by, and Carnap and Neurath were reduced to anticipate, like everybody else, the publication of Waismann's ill-fated book.

Before tracing some elements of Wittgenstein's influence and reactions to it in greater detail, let's fix the starting point. Consider how the *Tractatus* was characterized in the annotated bibliography of the collaborative manifesto "The Scientific World-Conception" (see Uebel, 2008).

> This book discusses the logical foundations of our language, the foundations of any symbolic system capable of expressing thoughts. There exists a fundamental relation between the states of affairs of the world and the sentences of language. It is this: our statements are logical pictures of states of affairs. All thought, speech and communication is nothing but such a logical picturing. What cannot be pictured cannot be expressed by language and cannot be represented, formulated, communicated in any way whatsoever. This book wants to draw a limit to thinking or rather – not to thinking but to the expression of thought. To be sure, there exists what cannot be expressed, but this 'shows itself' in language (in the logical construction of the symbols). The clear separation of what can be spoken of and what cannot constitutes the most important result of this book. This insight is applied to a number of issues in logic and epistemology which are solved in a surprisingly simple way once one has understood the nature of symbolic representation. In this fashion the nature of logic is elucidated and it is proved that there is only one logic, the inner nature of probability is uncovered, etc. This perspective leads to a new conception of the nature of philosophy. There is no philosophical knowledge that could be expressed and formulated. [... Here follows a quotation of 4.112 and first part of 4.114.] The correct solution of philosophical questions consists in correcting the language such that in the corrected language the question can no longer be posed. In this sense this book does not offer a theory but gives the way for a reader to go beyond the stage where philosophical questions are still being asked. Whoever understands these sentences correctly will see that in the end they are nonsensical. They must be overcome, then the world is viewed aright. (Hahn, Carnap, and Neurath, [1929] 2012, p.111)

While not everyone agreed to the truth of the propositions asserted by the book, all agreed to this being a correct description of its content.

5 Logic

In 1927 Hahn characterized Wittgenstein's book as "probably [...] the most important contribution to philosophy since the publication of Russell's basic writings": "To me [...] the *Tractatus* has explained the role of logic" (quoted in Menger, 1980, p.xii). For Wittgenstein, "the propositions of logic are tautologies" (TLP 6.1). Now, already Schlick had asserted something similar about syllogistic logic in his *General Theory of Knowledge* ([1918] 1974, p.115) – namely that all strict deductive inference is of an analytic nature – but only Wittgenstein established this conclusion for the new logic of Frege and Russell. This fundamental debt to Wittgenstein was agreed upon and often stressed by all members of the Vienna Circle.

Wittgenstein illustrated the truths of logic by his examples of the truth tables and he used "tautologous" to indicate the purely formal nature of their truth. Tautologies "lack sense" and "do not represent any possible situations" for they "admit *all* possible situations" (TLP 4.461, 4.462, original emphasis). Necessary truths were propositions that held in every possible case and were true in virtue of their logical form alone (TLP 6.113), irrespective of their content. Wittgenstein's conception of the tautologous nature of logic constituted the first of two significant breaks with the logicist tradition.

For Frege and Russell, logic still spoke of reality, albeit at the greatest level of generality (see Ricketts, 1996, pp. 59–64). Against this universalist conception Wittgenstein held that "all theories that make a proposition of logic appear to have content are false" (TLP 6.111). Second, unlike Frege and Russell, Wittgenstein did not hold that arithmetic was analytical or tautologous because three of the axioms of *Principia Mathematica* used to derive arithmetic (the axioms of choice, infinity, and reducibility) "are not logical propositions," i.e., are not true in virtue of their form alone (TLP 6.1232).

Hahn's summary of Wittgenstein's advance brings out clearly its attraction to empiricists:

> If logic were to be conceived – as it has actually been conceived – as a theory of the most general propositions of objects, as a theory of objects as such, then empiricism would in fact be confronted with an insuperable difficulty. But in reality logic does not say anything at all about objects; logic is not something to be found in the world; rather, logic first comes into being when – using symbolism – people *talk about the world*. (Hahn, [1929] 1980, p. 40, orig. emphasis)

Unlike Wittgenstein, however, Hahn was not ready to give up on logicism. Under pressure to explain away the nonlogical nature of the axioms of choice, infinity, and reducibility with their existential commitments, he noted at the First Conference on the Epistemology of the Exact Sciences in Prague in September 1929 that "the task of developing mathematics as a pure logic has not yet been completed – if only because the task of giving a satisfactory account of logic itself still awaits completion" ([1930] 1980a, p. 25). Since Hahn was happy to stick with Wittgenstein's characterization of logic, this remark suggests that the task at hand was that of determining in what sense the concept of tautology might be amended so as to cover (not only predicate logic but also) arithmetic. However advanced, Wittgenstein's *Tractatus* conception was not deemed by Hahn – or Carnap – to be the final word on the matter.

As regards moves in the Vienna Circle toward a conventionalist conception of logic, one may consider them wrong-headed from the start or as less than fully satisfactorily stated. But it is at best misleading to call the resultant view a "caricature of the *Tractatus*," for instance, on account of it being "in head-on collision" with "the transcendental dimension of logic which the *Tractatus* stressed" (see Baker, 1988, pp. 250 and 255; Hacker, 2001, 14). Although the criticism is justified from the perspective of the later Wittgenstein and deserves more attention than can be given here, Hahn's and Carnap's intentions were not to provide a faithful interpretation of the *Tractatus*, but to develop an *alternative*. To bring this out, consider Hahn's early steps in this direction. (Carnap's own conventionalist disagreements with Wittgenstein on the matter are well documented in his own *Logical Syntax of Language*; see Carnap, [1934] 2002, §§18, 43, 52, especially 73 and 82.)

In lectures of 1932, Hahn characterized tautologous propositions as "merely express[ing] a dependence in the assignment of designations to objects" ([1933] 1987, p. 32). A footnote signals that he meant this to be a wider sense of "tautological" than Wittgenstein's "narrower sense" (pp. 280–1). Having repeatedly stressed that logic arises from how people talk about the world, Hahn brought epistemic considerations to bear by contrasting the class of logical propositions with propositions that are "in principle accessible to verification by experience" ([1930] 1980a, p. 25). While Wittgenstein's invocation of the distinction between factual and logical propositions turned on his conception of logical form, Hahn's turned on "the way in which the symbolism used is supposed to *designate*" ([1929] 1980, p.41, original emphasis). Hahn did not simply revert to the conception of analytic truths as truths in virtue of meaning, however: rather, he disagreed with what he took to be Wittgenstein's view of *what made meaning possible*.

Wittgenstein's transcendentalism about logic – "Logic is not a body of doctrine, but a mirror-image of the world. Logic is transcendental" (TLP 2.18) – showed that his advance over the universalist conception was only partial: his logic still reflected the "formal – logical – properties of [...] the world" (TLP 6.12). It was this transcendentalism that was to be replaced with a form of conventionalism. For Hahn, logic concerned "the way we *want* to talk about objects, or how we *want* to assign designations to them" ([1933] 1987, p.31, emphasis added). Moreover, if we regard logical truths as "flowing from agreements about the use of words" and logical inference as "flow[ing] from the way we talk about objects" (pp. 34 and 33), who is to say that we are bound to use words and talk about objects in just one way? Along with a move toward conventionalism, Hahn here signaled also yet another disagreement, the challenge to the *Tractatus* conception of the one universal logic that Wittgenstein still shared with Frege and Russell. This challenge was realized fully only in Carnap's *Logical Syntax of Language*. But Hahn can be counted as an early supporter of Carnap's logical pluralist opposition to Wittgenstein's conception of logic, preferring the development of a calculus conception of logic to the latter's adherence to the conception of logic as a universal language. (For a comprehensive account of Carnap's road from the Tractarian conception of logic to the logical tolerance of *Logical Syntax*, see Awodey and Carus, 2007; for a discussion of Hahn's role, see Uebel, 2005; for the universal language/calculus distinction see van Heijenoort, 1967.)

6   Language

It is widely noted that it was Wittgenstein who effected the linguistic turn of philosophical attention from the nature of judgment to the nature of the proposition, and that the Vienna Circle followed him in this. It is also often noted that while the Vienna Circle was notorious for a verificationist theory of meaning, wielded widely in its campaign to eradicate metaphysics, such a theory is not to be found in the *Tractatus*, which reads instead: "To understand a proposition means to know what is the case if it is true" (TLP 4.024; cf. 4.431). Yet the Circle's verificationism was (partly) indebted to Wittgenstein after all: Waismann recorded him on 22 December 1929 coining the slogan "the sense of a proposition is its verification." Wittgenstein's verificationism was strict, demanding conclusive verification (albeit only in principle, not on every occasion of use): "If I can never verify the sense of a proposition completely, then I cannot have meant anything by the proposition either. Then the proposition signifies nothing whatsoever" (WVC 47). It would lead too far here to explore what prompted Wittgenstein's embrace of strict verificationism. For the Circle it amounted to an attempt to operationalize the claim that "a proposition is a truth-function of elementary propositions" (TLP 5). This conception demanded simples and elementary propositions the nature of which the *Tractatus* never specified. In the Circle's understanding these simples were psychologized and Wittgenstein's contemporaneous concern with the description of immediate experience ("phenomenology") seemed to confirm their interpretation. (Compare McGuinness, [1967] 1979, p.45, who specifies Wittgenstein's fluctuating view on the "primary language" in *Philosophical Remarks*; see also Hacker, 1972/86, pp.141–2; and Pears, 1992, p.34.)

What Carnap called "Wittgenstein's principle of verifiability" (1963, p.57) was quickly and widely accepted in the Circle – at least for a short while (and with the possible exception of Neurath). The consequence that flows from both the demand that all meaningful propositions are truth functions of elementary propositions and strict verificationism was readily embraced by Wittgenstein and then Waismann and Schlick: laws of nature were not to be regarded as meaningful propositions in their own right but as "hypotheses" which were understood in turn as directions – i.e., rules – for constructing propositions whose own status was left rather unclear (see WVC 99, 159 and 255; and Schlick, [1931] 1979, p.188). By contrast, Carnap wrote, "some of us, especially Neurath, Hahn and I, came to the conclusion that we had to look for a more liberal criterion of significance than verifiability" (1963, p.57). Elsewhere he dated the beginning of this liberalization to "about 1931," which agrees with his characterization of meaningfulness in "The Elimination of Metaphysics" and its date of composition. There he stated that only those statements were meaningful that were syntactically well formed and whose nonlogical terms were reducible to terms occurring in the basic observational evidence statements of science ([1932] 1959, §2). Whatever its shortcomings, this characterization allowed universally quantified statements to be meaningful, provided they were syntactically and terminologically correct. Hahn took a similar position in his lectures from 1932 when he endorsed the hypothetico-deductive method ([1933] 1987, §§4–5), while Neurath simply hand-waved in this direction, claiming that "a statement which cannot be controlled is a thesis devoid of sense" ([1931] 1983a, p.48). For his part, Schlick did not give up strict verificationism until his "Meaning and Verification" ([1936] 1979).

These moves on the part of Carnap, Hahn, and Neurath were not so much capitulations in the face of overwhelming difficulties, but constituted a return to a position already held before their acceptance of Wittgenstein's principle. Carnap's "Pseudoproblems in Philosophy" of 1928, for instance, had required empirically significant statements to be such that they possessed "factual content," which in turn meant that experiential support for them or their negation was at least conceivable ([1928] 2003, §7), where the support via deductive or inductive reasoning was not required to be conclusive. This criterion stood in the tradition of Mach's dictum that "where neither confirmation nor refutation is possible, science is not concerned" ([1883] 1960, p.587). It is important to note, therefore, that the Circle's concern with criteria of empirical significance clearly predates the enunciation of Wittgenstein's verificationist principle.

What must also be taken account of is the opposition by some members of the Vienna Circle to correspondence theories of truth. For instance, Hahn's claim that "it is a big mistake to infer the structure of the world from the structure of language" ([1930] 1980b, p.8) expressed his opposition – shared with Carnap, Frank, and Neurath – to the correspondence conception they perceived to be inherent in Wittgenstein's picture theory of meaning. By contrast, Schlick had no such worries. His conception of truth as the unique coordination of statement and fact, already advertised in his *General Theory of Knowledge*, was readily adapted to Wittgenstein's picture theory (see Schlick [1918] 1974, §10; and [1926] 1979). Here again a gulf was opening between the two wings of the Circle that was not even bridged by Carnap's acceptance of Tarski's semantic conception of truth in 1935.

One more significant disagreement concerning language has to be noted. It is well known that in discussions of Tarski's lecture to the Circle in 1930 and on a later occasion Schlick and Waismann rejected the idea of metalinguistic discourse by means of metalanguages (see Carnap, 1963, p.30; Menger, 1980, pp.xii–xiii; and 1982, pp.94–5). In doing so they followed Wittgenstein's lead. What McGuinness designated the "*Grundgedanke*" of the *Tractatus* was "that the 'logical constants' are not representatives; that there can be no representatives of the logic of facts" (TLP 4.0312). This *Grundgedanke* is closely related to Wittgenstein's rejection of the conception of logical truths as maximally general ones – "there are no 'logical objects' or 'logical constants' (in Frege's and Russell's sense)" (TLP 5.4) – and to his distinction between what can be said and what can only be shown. If all "saying" is affirming facts and this involves representing them (as it does in the picture theory; see Chapter 8, THE PICTURE THEORY), then "saying" requires objects; if there are no logical objects of which logical constants are representatives, then the latter cannot name the former – and logical facts or "the logic of facts" can only be shown.

> Propositions can represent the whole of reality, but they cannot represent what they must have in common with reality in order to be able to represent it – logical form. In order to represent logical form we should have to be able to station ourselves with propositions somewhere outside of logic, that is to say outside the world. (TLP 4.12)

Since we cannot do so and since "what *can* be shown, *cannot* be said" (TLP 4.1212), it follows that the idea of speaking about the logical form of an object language in a metalanguage that contains the object language as its proper part is deeply flawed. Unlike Schlick and Waismann, however, Carnap, Hahn, and Neurath sided with Tarski (as did Menger and Gödel). This disagreement followed from their emerging difference with the *Tractatus* conception of the transcendental nature of logic, but it also reflects differences about the nature of philosophy. For Carnap and Neurath, *metalinguistic discourse* was not only legitimate but essential to philosophy as they understood it.

7 Philosophy

The *Tractatus* remarks on philosophy were seized upon by all in the Circle but understood differently by different members. "Philosophy," Wittgenstein wrote, "aims at the logical clarification of thoughts. Philosophy is not a body of doctrine but an activity." Accordingly it "does not result in 'philosophical propositions', but rather in the clarification of propositions." Consequently, "a philosophical work consists essentially of elucidations" (TLP 4.112). The interpretive difficulties here are immense: to this day readers are divided over how the characterization of philosophy as elucidatory is to be reconciled with the seemingly paradoxical penultimate proposition of the *Tractatus* according to which the elucidations provided in the book itself are "nonsensical" and should be "thrown away like a ladder after [one] has climbed up on it" (TLP 6.54). The puzzle turns on the already mentioned application of the saying/showing distinction to talk of language and so, given the linguistic turn, to philosophical talk, especially to elucidations. Did Wittgenstein really mean to delegitimize all his attempts to logically clarify thoughts and propositions or did he allow for a special kind of important or illuminating nonsense? (See Chapter 11, INEFFABILITY AND NONSENSE IN THE *TRACTATUS* and Chapter 10, RESOLUTE READINGS OF THE *TRACTATUS*.)

Among his Vienna Circle readers two interpretations can be distinguished. Importantly, both of them tried to *take Wittgenstein at his word*, one following him wherever he seemed to lead, the other expressing disagreement. Schlick and Waismann adopted the view that Wittgenstein's doctrine about meaning and the relation between language and the world as mediated by a shared logical form was deeply insightful. Neurath and, later, Carnap rejected the very idea that there could be strictly speaking ineffable truths, never mind important ones.

Schlick wrote in his preface to the Waismann book that never appeared in their lifetime:

> The inestimable significance of Wittgenstein's work lies precisely in this, that in it this nature of the logical is completely elucidated and established for all time to come. This happens in that, for the first time, an entirely clear and rigorous concept of 'form' is provided [...]. The new insights are absolutely crucial to the destiny of philosophy [...]. [...] [N]ow for the first time their foundations have been so deeply laid that philosophy has arrived at its turning-point. (Schlick, [1976] 1979, p.136; see also PLP)

Schlick followed Wittgenstein, who claimed that philosophy must be "something whose place is above or below the natural sciences, not beside them" (TLP 4.111; see also Chapter 13, PHILOSOPHY AND PHILOSOPHICAL METHOD). For Schlick, "philosophy elucidates propositions, science verifies them" and "the philosophical activity of giving significance is thus the alpha and omega of all scientific knowledge" ([1930] 1979, p.157).

Neurath disagreed: "*We do not need a metaphysical ladder of elucidation*. On this point we cannot follow Wittgenstein, whose great significance for logic does not therefore diminish in merit" ([1932] 1983b, p.60, original emphasis). To begin with, this presented a different conception of the metaphysics inveighed against from Schlick, for whom metaphysics now consisted in trying to say what can only be shown. But Neurath's rejection of elucidations – which Carnap seconded in a footnote ([1932] 1934, p.74) that much annoyed Wittgenstein – also presented a different conception of the activity that is philosophy: "it is impossible to separate the 'clarification of concepts' from the 'pursuit of science' to which it belongs. Both are inseparably bound up together" (Neurath, 1983b, p.59). Neurath rejected elucidations "not only because they are meaningless, but also because they are not necessary" (p.60). It was possible after all, he insisted, to use language to speak about language. In due course, philosophy became what Carnap called the "logic of science," a metalinguistic inquiry, the formal concern of which was in turn complemented by the empirical studies of science: philosophy became part of "unified science" as scientific metatheory.

Taking this path away from Wittgenstein was not unproblematic. Neurath's and Carnap's dismissal of Tractarian views did not keep up with Wittgenstein's own development. From the time of the "Big Typescript" on, Wittgenstein no longer subscribed to the idea of one universal logic showing basic features of reality in an ineffable fashion (see Hacker, 2001, p.152). To be sure, for Carnap and Neurath this remained hearsay at best and they missed out on the radically new approach toward thinking about the mind and language that Wittgenstein was in the process of developing by transforming his earlier strictures against trying to say what can only be shown into prescriptions for the perspicuous representation of autonomous grammars of natural languages. Whether Carnap's and Neurath's naturalistic approach would have allowed them to appreciate this new philosophy is yet another matter, of course. Carnap resolutely pursued a calculus conception of logic and language that was radically at odds also with Wittgenstein's new view. This again underscores that many members of the Vienna Circle, for all their debt to Wittgenstein, came to his philosophy book with their agendas largely set and that of the older members only Schlick changed course.

8   The Viennese *Tractatus* Interpretations Compared

Neurath's opposition to the metaphysics of the *Tractatus* already during the Circle's readings of the book is well captured in an often-repeated anecdote. Neurath proposed: "In order to minimize my interruptions, let me rather call out "*non*-M!" whenever you are *not* talking metaphysics" (see Hempel, 1969, p.168, emphasis added). Years later he commented about the ending of the *Tractatus* that

> it is at least misleading in its wording: it sounds as if there were "a something" of which one cannot speak. We should say: if one really wants to abstain fully from a metaphysical mood, "we must pass over in silence," but not "about something." (Neurath, [1932] 1983b, p.60)

Carnap took longer but came to agree:

> Earlier, when we were reading Wittgenstein's book in the Circle, I had erroneously believed that his attitude towards metaphysics was similar to ours. I had not paid sufficient attention to the statements in his book about the mystical [...]. Only personal contact with him helped me to see more clearly his attitude at this point. (Carnap, 1963, p.27)

As noted, Carnap had the impression that "any ideas which had the flavor of 'enlightenment' were repugnant to Wittgenstein" (1963, p.26).

Carnap's impression seems confirmed by Wittgenstein's remarks on 17 December 1930 about Schlick's *Problems of Ethics* (see Schlick, [1930] 1939, p.11).

> Schlick says that in theological ethics there used to be two conceptions of the essence of the good: according to the shallower interpretation the good is good because it is what God wants; according to the profounder interpretation God wants the good because it is good. I think that the first interpretation is the profounder one: what God commands, that is good. For it cuts off the way to any explanation 'why' it is good, while the second interpretation is the shallow, rationalist one, which proceeds 'as if' you could give reasons for what is good. (WVC 115)

Since this passage has been used to illustrate a version of the recent "resolute" readings of the *Tractatus* (Kremer, 2013) we may employ it as a point of reference for a concluding comparison of the Circle's readings of it.

Neurath's and Schlick's readings of the *Tractatus* are representative of what here shall be called the "positivist" and the "metaphysical" readings, respectively. All versions of the metaphysical reading agree that with his elucidations Wittgenstein meant to assert propositions that are strictly speaking ineffable but nonetheless true. The positivist reading also does not dispute the attribution of this intention to Wittgenstein – in that respect it agrees with the metaphysical reading – but its evaluative stance is quite the opposite. The positivist reading rejects the apparatus of elucidations as objectionably metaphysical and far from true but cognitively meaningless. By contrast, the metaphysical readings, agreeing that elucidations convey deep truths, differ among themselves in how they deal with the resultant paradox: by either accepting the metaphysical nature of elucidations under some guise or other or by quibbling with the assessment as metaphysical. In addition, different "postpositivist" readings (not adopted in the Circle) can be distinguished that agree with the positivist diagnosis that elucidations be rejected – not because they are meaningless for essentially verificationist reasons that would rule out any metaphysics but because they make for incoherent metaphysics (e.g., Hacker, 2001; see also Chapter 12, METAPHYSICS: FROM INEFFABILITY TO NORMATIVITY) or because they misrepresent what Wittgenstein later would call "grammatical propositions" (Glock, 2010).

With its negative evaluation of the metaphysics of elucidations the positivist and the postpositivist readings agree with the so-called resolute reading. However, the resolute reading also disputes the intention all the other readings attribute to Wittgenstein. Instead, it holds that Wittgenstein himself sought to bring his readers to dismiss his propositions as nonsensical. To "see the world aright" (6.54) meant to see that logic and language, like ethics, had to do without an explanation of their ground and simply had to be accepted. It is perhaps not altogether clear whether resolute readings of the *Tractatus* always come with an endorsement of the perspective they outline. But Carnap and Neurath certainly would have considered such an endorsement to express antienlightenment sentiments to which they were deeply opposed – especially so since they no longer subscribed to the idea of the one universal logic that was fundamental to the *Tractatus*. Schlick, by contrast, was not disturbed by Wittgenstein's post-Tractarian acquiescence in the ways of natural language. On how the *Tractatus* was meant to be understood, however, both wings of the Circle agreed.

9   Conclusion

The repeated and close readings of the *Tractatus* in the Circle between 1924 and 1927 and the discussions of the "Theses" based on it and (some of) Wittgenstein's new ideas from 1928 to 1930 allowed, with considerable reflection and differential access to the subsequent development of his ideas, both for deep appreciation and critical distance. Schlick and Waismann became advocates of Wittgenstein's evolving philosophy while Neurath, Hahn, and Carnap represented the opposition – with Neurath formulating its antimetaphysical and Hahn and Carnap its metalogical objections.

It may be added that none of the surviving members of the Vienna Circle took much notice of Wittgenstein's *Philosophical Investigations* in the 1950s – except the one who had started the Circle on its Tractarian adventure. The mathematician Reidemeister returned to philosophy only after World War II and then was much concerned to contain the irrationalism of Heideggerian existential philosophy while conceding the shortcomings of positivism. In a plenary address at the Second International Union for the Philosophy of Science in Zurich in 1954 Reidemeister therefore sought to illuminate the important relations that obtain between exact thinking and hermeneutic understanding (1955, pp.55–6) – and in doing so he pointed to Wittgenstein's then just published *Philosophical Investigations* as providing much-needed and very apposite help.

References

Awodey, S. and Carus, A. (2007). The Turning Point and the Revolution: Philosophy of Mathematics in Logical Empiricism from *Tractatus* to *Logical Syntax*. In A. Richardson and T. Uebel (Eds). *The Cambridge Companion to Logical Empiricism* (pp.165–192). Cambridge: Cambridge University Press.

Ayer, A. J. (1936/46). *Language, Truth and Logic*. Second revised edition. London: Gollancz.

Baker, G.P. (1979). *Verehrung und Verkehrung*: Waismann and Wittgenstein. In C.G. Luckhardt (Ed.). *Wittgenstein: Sources and Perspectives* (pp.243–285). Hassocks: Harvester.

Baker, G.P. (1988). *Wittgenstein, Frege and the Vienna Circle*. Oxford: Basil Blackwell.

Baker, G.P. and Hacker, P.M.S. (1986). Wittgenstein and the Vienna Circle: The Exaltation and Deposition of Ostensive Definition. In S. Shanker (Ed.). *Ludwig Wittgenstein: Critical Assessments* (Vol.1, pp.241–262). London: Routledge.

Carnap, R. ([1928] 2003). Pseudoproblems in Philosophy. Translation in R. Carnap. (2003). *The Logical Structure of the World/Pseudoproblems in Philosophy*. Chicago: Open Court. (Original work published 1928.)

Carnap, R. ([1932] 1934). *The Unity of Science*. Trans. M. Black. London: Kegan, Paul, Trench Teubner and Company. (Original work published 1932.)

Carnap, R. ([1932] 1959). The Elimination of Metaphysics through Logical Analysis of Language. Translation in A.J. Ayer (Ed.). *Logical Positivism* (pp.60–81). New York: Free Press. (Original work published 1932.)

Carnap, R. ([1934] 2002). *The Logical Syntax of Language*. Trans. A. Smeaton. Chicago: Open Court. (Original work published 1934.)

Carnap, R. (1963). Intellectual Autobiography. In P.A. Schilpp (Ed.). *The Philosophy of Rudolf Carnap* (pp.3–84). Lasalle: Open Court.

Feigl, H. (1969/81). The *Wiener Kreis* in America. Reprinted in H. Feigl. *Inquiries and Provocations* (pp.57–93). Ed. R.S. Cohen. Dordrecht: Reidel.

Feigl, H. and Blumberg, A.E. (1931). Logical Positivism. *Journal of Philosophy*, 28, 281–296.

Frank, P. (1949). Historical Introduction. In P. Frank. *Modern Science and its Philosophy* (pp.1–51). Cambridge, MA: Harvard University Press.

Glock, H.-J. (2001). The Development of Wittgenstein's Philosophy. In H.-J. Glock (Ed.). *Wittgenstein: A Critical Reader* (pp.1–25). Oxford: Blackwell.

Glock, H.-J. (2007). Perspectives on Wittgenstein: An Intermittently Opinionated Survey. In G. Kahane, E. Kanterian, and O. Kuusela (Eds). *Wittgenstein and his Interpreters: Essays in Memory of Gordon Baker* (pp.37–65). Oxford: Blackwell.

Glock, H.-J. (2010). All Kinds of Nonsense. In E. Ammereller and E. Fischer (Eds). *Wittgenstein at Work: Method in the Philosophical Investigations* (pp.221–245). London: Routledge.

Hacker, P.M.S. (1972/86). *Insight and Illusion: Themes in the Philosophy of Wittgenstein*. Revised edition. Oxford: Clarendon Press.

Hacker, P.M.S. (1995). Wittgenstein and Post-War Philosophy at Oxford. In J. Hintikka and K. Puhl (Eds). *The British Tradition in Twentieth-Century Philosophy* (pp.100–121). Vienna: Hölder-Pichler-Tempsky.

Hacker, P.M.S. (2001). When the Whistling had to Stop. In P.M.S. Hacker. *Wittgenstein: Connections and Controversies* (pp.141–169). Oxford: Clarendon Press.

Hahn, H. ([1929] 1980). Empiricism, Mathematics and Logic. Translation in H. Hahn. (1980). *Empiricism, Logic, Mathematics* (pp.39–42). Ed. B. McGuinness. Dordrecht: Reidel. (Original work published 1929.)

Hahn, H. ([1930] 1980a). The Significance of the Scientific World View, especially for Mathematics and Physics. Translation in H. Hahn. (1980). *Empiricism, Logic, Mathematics* (pp.20–30). Ed. B. McGuinness. Dordrecht: Reidel. (Original work published 1930.)

Hahn, H. ([1930] 1980b). Superfluous Entities, or Occam's Razor. Translation in H. Hahn. (1980). *Empiricism, Logic, Mathematics* (pp.1–19). Ed. B. McGuinness. Dordrecht: Reidel. (Original work published 1930.)

Hahn, H. ([1933] 1987). Logic, Mathematics, and Knowledge of Nature. Translation in B. McGuinness (Ed.). (1987). *Unified Science* (pp.24–45). Dordrecht: Kluwer. (Original work published 1933.)

Hahn, H., Carnap, R., and Neurath, O. ([1929] 2012). The Scientific World-Conception: The Vienna Circle. Translation in F. Stadler and T. Uebel (Eds). (2012). *Wissenschaftliche Weltauffassung: Der Wiener Kreis* (pp.75–116). New York: Springer. (Original work published 1929.)

Haller, R. ([1985] 1991). The First Vienna Circle. Translation in T. Uebel (Ed.). *Rediscovering the Forgotten Vienna Circle* (pp.95–108). Dordrecht: Kluwer. (Original work published 1985.)

Hempel, C.G. (1969). Logical Positivism and the Social Sciences. In P. Achinstein and S.F. Barker (Eds). *The Legacy of Logical Positivism* (pp.163–194). Baltimore: Johns Hopkins Press.

Iven, M. (2009). Wittgenstein und Schlick: Zur Geschichte eines Diktats. [Wittgenstein and Schlick: On the History of a Dictation.] In F. Stadler, H.J. Wendel, and E. Glassner (Eds). *Stationen: Moritz Schlick Studien* (Vol. 1, pp.63–80). Vienna: Springer.

Kremer, M. (2013). The Whole Meaning of a Book of Nonsense: Reading Wittgenstein's *Tractatus*. In M. Beaney (Ed.). *The Oxford Handbook of the History of Analytical Philosophy* (pp.451–485). Oxford: Oxford University Press.

Mach, E. ([1883] 1960). *The Science of Mechanics*. Trans. T.J. McCormack. Chicago: Open Court. (Original work published 1883.)

Manninen, J. (2011). Waismann's Testimony of Wittgenstein's Fresh Starts in 1931–35. In B. McGuinness (Ed.). *Friedrich Waismann: Causality and Logical Positivism* (pp.243–265). Dordrecht: Kluwer.

McGuinness, B. ([1967] 1979). Preface of the Editor. In B. McGuinness (Ed.). *Wittgenstein and the Vienna Circle: Conversations recorded by Friedrich Waismann*. Oxford: Blackwell. (Original work published 1967.)

McGuinness, B. (2011). Waismann: The Wandering Scholar. In B. McGuinness (Ed.). *Friedrich Waismann: Causality and Logical Positivism* (pp.9–16). Dordrecht: Kluwer.

Menger, K. (1980). Introduction. In H. Hahn. *Empiricism, Logic and Mathematics* (pp.ix–xvii). Ed. B. McGuinness. Dordrecht: Reidel.

Menger, K. (1982). Memories of Moritz Schlick. In E.T. Gadol (Ed.). *Rationality and Science* (pp.83–103). Vienna: Springer.

Menger, K. (1994). *Reminiscences of the Vienna Circle and the Mathematical Colloquium*. Ed. L. Golland, B. McGuinness, and A. Sklar. Dordrecht: Kluwer.

Neider, H., (1977). Gespräch mit Heinrich Neider, led by R. Haller and R. Rutte. *Conceptus*, 28, 21–42.

Neurath, O. (([1931] 1983a). Physicalism: The Philosophy of the Vienna Circle. In O. Neurath. *Philosophical Papers 1913–1946* (pp.48–51). Ed. by R.S. Cohen and M. Neurath. Dordrecht: Reidel.

Neurath, O. ([1932] 1983b). Sociology in the Framework of Physicalism. In O. Neurath. *Philosophical Papers 1913–1946* (pp.58–90). Ed. by R.S. Cohen and M. Neurath. Dordrecht: Reidel.

Oakes, M. and Pichler, A. (2013). Computational Stylometry of Wittgenstein's "Diktat für Schlick." *Bergen Language and Linguistics Studies*, 3, 221–238.

Pears, D. (1992). Wittgenstein and the Vienna Circle. *Acta Philosophica Fennica*, 52, 33–42.

Pitcher, G. (1964). *The Philosophy of Wittgenstein*. Englewood Cliffs: Prentice-Hall.

Reidemeister, K. (1955). Prolegomena einer kritischen Philosophie. [Prolegomena of a Critical Philosophy.] In *Proceedings of the Second International Union for the Philosophy of Science (Vol. 1): Plenary Sessions* (pp.46–56). Neuchatel: Editions du Griffon.

Ricketts, T. (1996). Pictures, Logic, and the Limits of Sense in Wittgenstein's *Tractatus*. In H. Sluga and D. Stern (Eds). *The Cambridge Companion to Wittgenstein* (pp.59–99). Cambridge: Cambridge University Press.

Schlick, M. ([1918] 1974). *General Theory of Knowledge*. Lasalle: Open Court. (Original work published 1918.)

Schlick, M. ([1926] 1979). Experience, Cognition, Metaphysics. Translation in M. Schlick. *Philosophical Papers* (Vol. 2, pp.99–111). Ed. H.L. Mulder and B. van de Velde-Schlick. Dordrecht: Reidel. (Original work published 1926.)

Schlick, M. ([1930] 1939). *Problems of Ethics*. New York: Prentice-Hall. (Original work published 1930.)

Schlick, M. ([1930] 1979). The Turning Point in Philosophy. Translation in M. Schlick. *Philosophical Papers* (Vol. 2, pp.154–160). Ed. H.L. Mulder and B. van de Velde-Schlick. Dordrecht: Reidel. (Original work published 1930.)

Schlick, M. ([1931] 1979). Causality in Contemporary Physics. Translation in M. Schlick. *Philosophical Papers* (Vol. 2, pp.176–209). Ed. H.L. Mulder and B. van de Velde-Schlick. Dordrecht: Reidel. (Original work published 1931.)

Schlick, M. ([1936] 1979). Meaning and Verification. Translation in M. Schlick. *Philosophical Papers* (Vol. 2, pp.456–481). Ed. H.L. Mulder and B. van de Velde-Schlick. Dordrecht: Reidel. (Original work published 1936.)

Schlick, M. ([1976] 1979). Preface to Friedrich Waismann, *Logik, Sprache, Philosophie*. Translation in M. Schlick. *Philosophical Papers* (Vol. 2, pp.130–138). Ed. H.L. Mulder and B. van de Velde-Schlick. Dordrecht: Reidel. (Original work published 1976.)

Schulte, J. (2011). Waismann as Spokesman for Wittgenstein. In B. McGuinness (Ed.). *Friedrich Waismann: Causality and Logical Positivism* (pp.225–242). Dordrecht: Springer.

Stern, D. (2007). Wittgenstein, the Vienna Circle, and Physicalism. In A. Richardson and T. Uebel (Eds). *The Cambridge Companion to Logical Empiricism* (pp.305–331). Cambridge: Cambridge University Press.

Uebel, T. (2003). On the Austrian Roots Logical Empiricism: The First Vienna Circle. In P. Parrini, M. Salmon, and W. Salmon (Eds). *Logical Empiricism: Historical and Contemporary Perspectives* (pp.67–93). Pittsburgh: University of Pittsburgh Press.

Uebel, T. (2005). Learning Logical Tolerance: Hans Hahn on the Foundations of Mathematics. *History and Philosophy of Logic*, 26, 175–209.

Uebel, T. (2007). *Empiricism at the Crossroads: The Vienna Circle's Protocol-Sentence Debate*. Chicago: Open Court.

Uebel, T. (2008). Writing a Revolution: On the Production and Early Reception of the Vienna Circle's Manifesto. *Perspectives on Science*, 16, 70–102.

Uebel, T. (2011). Vienna Circle. In E. Zalta (Ed.). *Stanford Encyclopedia of Philosophy*. http://plato.stanford.edu/entries/vienna-circle/ (last accessed 15 June 2016).

van Heijenoort, J. (1967). Logic as Language and Logic as Calculus. *Synthese*, 17, 324–330.

Waismann, F. ([1936] 1977). The Concept of Identity. Translation in F. Waismann. *Philosophical Papers* (pp.22–29). Ed. B. McGuinness. Dordrecht: Reidel. (Original work published 1936.)

Waismann, F. ([1938] 1979). Foreword. Translation in M. Schlick. *Philosophical Papers* (Vol. 2, pp.xiii–xxiii). Ed. H.L. Mulder and B. van de Velde-Schlick. Dordrecht: Reidel. (Original work published 1938.)

Waismann, F. ([1982] 1986). The Nature of Mathematics. Translation in S. Shanker (Ed.). *Ludwig Wittgenstein: Critical Assessments* (Vol. 3, pp.60–78). London: Croom Helm. (Original work published 1982.)

Weinberg, J. (1935). Are there ultimate Simples?. *Philosophy of Science*, 2, 387–399.

Weinberg, J. (1936). *An Examination of Logical Positivism*. London: Kegan Paul, Trench, Trubner and Co.

Further Reading

Important information beyond *Wittgenstein and the Vienna Circle* (WVC) is given in:

Manninen, J. (2011). Waismann's Testimony of Wittgenstein's Fresh Starts in 1931–35. In B. McGuinness (Ed.). *Friedrich Waismann: Causality and Logical Positivism* (pp. 243–265). Dordrecht: Kluwer.

McGuinness, B. (2011). Waismann: The Wandering Scholar. In B. McGuinness (Ed.). *Friedrich Waismann: Causality and Logical Positivism* (pp. 9–16). Dordrecht: Kluwer.

Schulte, J. (2011). Waismann as Spokesman for Wittgenstein. In B. McGuinness (Ed.). *Friedrich Waismann: Causality and Logical Positivism* (pp. 225–242). Dordrecht: Springer.

For a compact characterization of the Circle as misinterpreters of Wittgenstein see:

Hacker, P.M.S. (1996). *Wittgenstein's Place in Twentieth-Century Analytic Philosophy*. Oxford: Blackwell. Chapter 3.

More even-handed interpretations are pursued in:

Haller, R. (1988). *Questions on Wittgenstein*. London: Routledge. Chapter 2.

McGuinness, B. (2002). *Approaches to Wittgenstein: Collected Papers*. London: Routledge. Chapters 16 and 17.

The so-called plagiarism dispute between Wittgenstein and Carnap is discussed in:

Stern, D. (2007). Wittgenstein, the Vienna Circle, and Physicalism. In A. Richardson and T. Uebel (Eds). *The Cambridge Companion to Logical Empiricism* (pp. 305–331). Cambridge: Cambridge University Press.

Uebel, T. (1995). Physicalism in Wittgenstein and the Vienna Circle. In K. Gavroglu, J. Stachel, and M. Wartofsky (Eds). *Physics, Philosophy and the Scientific Community* (pp. 327–356). Dordrecht: Kluwer.

47

Wittgenstein and Ordinary Language Philosophy

ANITA AVRAMIDES

Here are three characterizations of ordinary language philosophy:

> A loosely structured philosophical movement holding that the significance of concepts, including those central to traditional philosophy [...] is fixed by linguistic practice. (Heil, 1995, p.551)

> A method of doing philosophy rather than a set of doctrines. It is diverse in its methods and attitudes. It belongs to the general category of analytic philosophy ... (Martinich, 1998, p.143)

> The label 'ordinary language philosophy' was more often used by the enemies than by the alleged practitioners of what it was intended to designate. It was supposed to designate a certain kind of philosophy that flourished, mainly in Britain and therein mainly in Oxford, for twenty years or so, roughly after 1945. (Warnock, 1998, p.147)

I shall take it that it is as much a question how we understand "ordinary language philosophy" as it is a question how we are to understand Wittgenstein's relationship to it. Had this chapter been written some time before the turn of the twenty-first century, and so closer to the time when many of the philosophers under discussion here still roamed the philosophical landscape, it would very likely have had a rather simpler structure. The question how we understand the work of at least *some* of those who are often characterized as ordinary language philosophers has taken an interesting turn in recent years. And while there have always been interesting questions to be addressed when considering Wittgenstein's relationship to this school (or, movement) in philosophy, work in more recent times has opened up important and interesting new avenues of exploration in this connection.

All three characterizations of ordinary language philosophy (OLP) given above bring out an important aspect of it: the first identifies language – or linguistic practice – as of central concern. The second reminds us that we should see those labeled as "ordinary language philosophers" as proposing a method and as adopting an attitude, as opposed to setting out a doctrine or set of doctrines. It also informs us that OLP belongs to that

---

A Companion to Wittgenstein, First Edition. Edited by Hans-Johann Glock and John Hyman.
© 2017 John Wiley & Sons, Ltd. Published 2017 by John Wiley & Sons, Ltd.

larger movement referred to as "analytic philosophy." The third explains that this style of philosophy flourished largely in Oxford during the period from, roughly, 1945 until the mid-1960s (and, thus, is sometimes referred to as "Oxford Philosophy"). It also suggests that the very name of this movement was the work of those hostile to it, indicating that this way of proceeding in philosophy while attractive to some was vigorously rejected by others. At the heart of the very business of philosophy lies the question how we are to understand the business of philosophy: what is its method and how should it proceed? These questions received a very particular definition around the early-to-mid twentieth century.

When one looks back on the history of philosophy, there are periods – some of them relatively prolonged – where there appears to be general agreement about the business of philosophy. But from around the mid-to-late nineteenth century one sees certain upheavals and partings of the way. From common roots in Kant's writings one sees philosophy on the Continent proceed in one direction (the phenomenological movement) while in Britain proceed in quite another (the analytic movement). The origin of analytic philosophy is itself a controversial matter. Michael Dummett has argued that the sources of analytic philosophy were the writings of philosophers who wrote, principally or exclusively, in the German language, namely in the work of such philosophers as Husserl, Bolzano, Brentano, Meinong, and Frege (see Dummett, 1993, p.ix). Dummett has largely concentrated his efforts on explaining Frege's contribution to the origins of analytic philosophy, and to that moment which many take to characterize this origin: the linguistic turn. Dummett claims that the linguistic turn occurs in Frege's *Die Grundlagen der Arithmetik* of 1884, when Frege raises the Kantian question, "How are numbers given to us, granted that we have no idea or intuition of them?" Frege's answer to this question relies on his celebrated context principle, which is formulated in terms of an inquiry into language rather than into modes of thought: it is only in the context of a sentence (*Satz*) that a word has meaning. With this principle Dummett takes Frege to have turned an epistemological inquiry into a linguistic one – sweeping aside a tradition initiated by Descartes and ushering in a new era in philosophy. The analytic era takes from the work of Frege its most fundamental tenet: that a philosophical account of thought can be attained through a philosophical account of language. Dummett gives Frege the title of "grandfather of analytic philosophy," while identifying Bertrand Russell and G.E. Moore as "uncles" (Dummett, 1993, p.171). Russell and Moore pursued their analytic philosophy in Cambridge, where they were joined by Wittgenstein. Wittgenstein's *Tractatus Logico-Philosophicus* has been characterized by Peter Hacker as a form of critical philosophy that accepts the Kantian task of circumscribing the bounds of thought while taking a most unKantian – linguistic – point of departure. (Cf. TLP 4.0031: "All philosophy is a 'critique of language' [...].") Somewhat at odds with Dummett's interpretation, Hacker suggests that it was Wittgenstein's *Tractatus* that engendered the linguistic turn characteristic of twentieth-century analytic philosophy (see Hacker, 1997, p.3).

Early analytic philosophy was associated with logical positivism. According to von Wright (1982, p.108), the *Tractatus* made Wittgenstein one of the "spiritual fathers" of logical positivism. This may be because many read that work as, in the words of Hacker, "the swan-song of metaphysics" and the rejection of metaphysics was a major tenet of logical positivism (Hacker, 2001, p.330). The logical positivists agreed with Hume that philosophy that contains neither abstract reasoning concerning quantity or number nor experimental reasoning concerning matters of fact and existence should be committed to the flames because it must contain "nothing but sophistry and illusion" (Hume, [1748/51] 1975, p.165). "Sophistry and illusion" also summed up the positivist attitude toward the metaphysics that they saw as being practiced largely in Continental Europe in the nineteenth and early twentieth centuries. Many early analytic philosophers – for example, Bertrand Russell, and others who took themselves to be following in Frege's footsteps – joined forces with these logical positivists in their combat against metaphysics, and they also embraced the logical positivist enthusiasm for science and logic. However, while these analytic philosophers turned their attention to language, the turn was not yet to ordinary language. In fact these analytic philosophers are often found denouncing ordinary language, expressing their frustration with its vagaries and imprecision. In the place of ordinary language, they promoted the development and study of ideal or formal languages, languages that answer to the rigors of logic and science – language abstracted from its daily use.

Thus one finds a divide developing within early analytical philosophy. While *all* analytic philosophers can be taken to be united in their rejection of the "the deep paradoxes and mystery mongering of their continental contemporaries" and while all were hostile "to the lofty, loose rhetoric of old-fashioned idealism" (Warnock, 1998, p.147), they were divided in their approach to the study of language. Just as some early analytic philosophers turned away from metaphysics and toward ideal language, others can be seen to turn away from metaphysics *and* the ideal language of logic and science. These analytic philosophers argued that imprecision and ambiguity are of the essence of the expressive power of language and they insisted that language cannot be studied in abstraction from its daily use. They emphasized a more humanistic attitude, central to which was a deep respect for language as it is used in its everyday context. These are the so-called "ordinary language philosophers."

Among the philosophers associated with OLP, J.L. Austin holds a particular place. Oswald Hanfling suggests that, more than anyone else, it is Austin who has come to be regarded as "the archetypical ordinary language philosopher" (Hanfling, 2000, p.26). Hanfling also suggests that Austin was fascinated by words and their meanings – quite apart from their relevance to problems in philosophy. Indeed, Austin writes that his work may be seen in times to come as the beginning of "a true and comprehensive *science of language*" (1956b, p.232). Once this science has been established, Austin believes that "we shall have rid ourselves of one more part of philosophy" (ibid). What Austin has in mind here can, perhaps, be made clearer if we consider a metaphor that he offers. Austin suggests that when we look over the history of human inquiry we can consider philosophy to have a place akin to the sun's place in the solar system: just as the sun throws off parts of itself that cool and progress in a well-regulated manner toward being a planet, so philosophy throws off parts of itself (e.g., mathematics, and physics) that come in time to "take up station as a science" (ibid). Insofar as Austin is to be regarded as an ordinary language philosopher, these remarks suggest that he is willing to think of such a philosophy as an early moment in the birth of a new science.

Other ordinary language philosophers may be considered more strictly philosophical in their interests in language. The list here most certainly includes Gilbert Ryle and John Wisdom. Some would also include P.F. Strawson, while others add H.P. Grice (although there is good reason to doubt that this is correct). According to Warnock, the presence of Wittgenstein "broods, so to speak, over the group" (1998, p.149). The question of Wittgenstein's relationship to this group is complex. Firstly, it should be clear that insofar as Wittgenstein's work is associated with this movement in philosophy, it is the work he produced in the 1930s and 1940s. After a lengthy break from philosophy, Wittgenstein returned to philosophy and to Cambridge in 1929 and began to develop a new approach to his thinking in philosophy (how new is not an issue I shall engage with here, although I shall come back to the question at the end of this chapter). Central to this new approach is the attitude taken toward language. While in his earlier work Wittgenstein sought to discover a rigid logical structure within language, he sought in his later work to let language off that leash. Wittgenstein's later attitude is that we must not constrain language but simply observe it. David Pears describes Wittgenstein's later work as "full of perfectly detailed descriptions of language, which are presented dialectically in a way that invites the reader to take part in the dialogue" (Pears, 1971, p.14). Observing language in use while using it, one might say. This may be the work of an analytic philosopher, but it is no longer work that can be closely aligned with that of Frege, Russell, and Moore. Russell himself firmly rejected Wittgenstein's later work as "a trivial investigation of language" (Pears 1971, p.19).

This rejection by some of Wittgenstein's later work has been taken to mark an important moment in the divide between analytic philosophers. While many Cambridge philosophers were distancing themselves from Wittgenstein's new work, many Oxford philosophers were embracing it. These Oxford philosophers saw Wittgenstein's new work as at one with what they were practicing. Austin, for example, writes that language is a long-evolved, complex, and subtle instrument and advises that philosophers should afford it careful scrutiny. He points out that language has evolved over many generations and that the distinctions made within it and the connections marked by it "have stood up to the long test of time of the survival of the fittest" and are "more subtle [...] than any you or I are likely to think up in our armchairs of an afternoon" (Austin, 1956a, p.182). Austin acknowledges that ordinary language has no claim to be the last word in philosophy, but he insists that it would be prudent to at least allow it the *first* word (ibid, p.185). Referring to ordinary language, Austin remarks in his characteristically lively manner: "too evidently, there is gold in them thar hills" (ibid, p.181). This attitude, which can be identified in Austin's work, is sometimes taken to be the central credo of the ordinary language movement. We can compare what Austin writes here with Wittgenstein's suggestion that we turn our attention to the employment of words (cf. Z §463).

It is clear that certain ideas are in the air, and the air is breathed in by many in Oxford and some in Cambridge. I leave it to the scholars to identify the details of influence. What I can record is that Wittgenstein, while living and working in Cambridge, is said to have regarded Oxford as a "philosophical desert" (Warnock, 1998, p.148). Warnock also tells us that, while the substance of Wittgenstein's later work was akin to that going on in Oxford, "the characteristic cool, ironic urbanity of manner was odious to him." Warnock concludes that Wittgenstein would have "furiously disclaimed any kinship" with the ordinary language philosophers of his day (ibid). Marie McGinn and Oskari Kuusela remind us that Wittgenstein rejected the idea of parties and taking sides in philosophy, but explain that they can see why those identified as ordinary language philosophers "would have wanted to claim a powerful mind such as the later Wittgenstein to be on their side" (2011, p.6). Dummett goes so far as to write (admittedly in a rather bad-tempered review of Ernest Gellner's *Words and Things*) that "Wittgenstein's later philosophy is totally distinct both from logical positivism and from the ordinary-language movement" (Dummett, 1978, p.433). In another place Dummett writes in a more even-tempered manner that "the doctrines of 'ordinary language philosophy' were a caricature, but not a gross caricature, of the views of the later Wittgenstein" (1978, p.445).

From all this we may conclude that one needs to separate out the question of whether Wittgenstein would himself have identified his work with OLP from the question whether those who are identified as ordinary language philosophers would claim Wittgenstein as an ally. Separate from both of these is the question whether there is a tendency on the part of many to amalgamate the work of these philosophers. This is clearly the case. This tendency can be attributed as much to those who champion this work as to those who are hostile to it, but I am inclined to believe that it is largely the work of the latter group. According to those who rejected the work being done both by the likes of Austin and Ryle *and* by Wittgenstein there was a tendency to cast Wittgenstein as a heresiarch and Austin as a pedant (see Warnock 1998, p.149).

Perhaps it would be best simply to agree that the impact of the later Wittgenstein's philosophy was coincident with the influence of ordinary language philosophy and that this can in part be attributed to certain overarching ideas shared by both. While there are important differences amongst those classified as ordinary language philosophers, for those who are hostile they do not matter. As indicated earlier, there is a rejection by all those classified as ordinary language philosophers of the idea that philosophy is in the business of constructing grand metaphysical systems. According to OLP – and here one need not hesitate to include Wittgenstein's name – there is a tendency to be misled by language into metaphysical pseudo-profundities. Pears explains that what Wittgenstein tries to do is to teach us to resist the enchantment of language, which tempts us to accept the pictures associated with metaphysics and other philosophical errors (Pears, 1971, p.16). For instance, the ready availability of nominalizations in our language can lead us to reify meanings, minds, or possibilities. Austin, too, advises that we need to be careful about our use of words – we must "examine what we should say when" and thereby "forearm ourselves against the traps that language sets us" (Austin, 1956a, pp.181–2). Thus we find that in as much as we are to pay attention to the uses of language, we should not accept everything we ordinarily say blindly or without careful consideration. One area where Wittgenstein believes we are led astray by language is when thinking about the mind. There is, for example, a certain asymmetry recorded in our language concerning what we feel in our own case and what we observe in the case of another when we say, "I know what I mean by 'toothache' but the other person can't *know* it" (LPE 276). Wittgenstein notes that we observe this asymmetry and we "look on this as a mirror image of the nature of things" (LPE 277). There is no doubt that this is how some philosophers reason. Wittgenstein comments: "But if you look closer you will see that this is an entire misrepresentation of the use of the word 'toothache'" (LPE 281). We have allowed ourselves to be bewitched by language. McGinn observes that, for Wittgenstein, language is "both the source of philosophical problems and the means to overcome them" (1997, p.12).

In PI §114 Wittgenstein refers explicitly to the *Tractatus*, and writes, as though speaking to his earlier self: "One thinks that one is tracing the outline of the thing's nature over and over again, and one is merely tracing round the frame through which we look at it." The frame to which he refers is the frame of language, and what our language does is frame a picture that holds us captive (cf. PI §115). So language can be the source of the problem but, if we are careful, language can also be the means to overcome our problems. What we will find is that: "The confusions which occupy us arise when language is like an engine idling, not when it is doing work" (PI §132). In PI §116 Wittgenstein writes the lines that some have pointed to as evidence of his standing as an ordinary language philosopher: "What *we* do is try to bring words back from their metaphysical to their everyday use" (*auf ihre alltägliche Verwendung*). These words are clearly designed to turn us away from metaphysics. Whether they are words designed to turn us in the direction of ordinary language is disputed by some, as we shall see below.

The turn away from metaphysics that one finds in the work of Wittgenstein and OLP is connected with the idea – expressed particularly well by Wittgenstein – that the study of language should content itself with surveying what lies *on the surface*. Philosophers run into problems and difficulties when they do not rest content with this surface, but insist on trying to reach beyond our words to something that "lies *beneath* the surface" (PI §92). We insist on trying to understand what we take to be "the essence of language," and we take it that such understanding will tell us something about the essence of the world (whether, for example, it is to be understood as the realist thinks or the idealist); we are led back to metaphysics. Where philosophers tend to strive to understand by amassing generalities that lead ultimately to pronouncements about the nature of the things, Wittgenstein advises that we simply observe what we do (cf. BB 19–20). Rather than start with the question "*What is* language?" – anticipating a reply that can settle the question once and for all and independently of any future experience – Wittgenstein asks us to "simply look and see" how we use language (cf. PI §93). From time to time we find Wittgenstein commenting on his own earlier views of language, of his own tendency to turn away from natural and toward ideal languages. In PI §107 he explains that we want to understand what we take to be the hidden essence of language, and we find that the examination of "actual language" (*die tatsächliche Sprache*) does not yield this. In reaction, we decide to move in the direction of logic and an ideal language in order to achieve the understanding we seek. He comments:

> We have got onto slippery ice where there is no friction and so in a certain sense the conditions are ideal, but also, just because of that, we are unable to walk. We want to walk: so we need friction. Back to the rough ground! (PI §107)

The rough ground is provided by the *tatsächliche Sprache*, in other words, the *Sprache des Alltags*.

At the point at which Wittgenstein asks us to observe what we do with language he insists that we rest content with descriptions and eschew explanations: "Philosophy may in no way interfere with the actual use of language; it can in the end only describe it" (PI §124). Here we find Wittgenstein introducing a certain attitude toward the business of philosophy, and it appears to be different from the business of science. In PI §126 he writes, "One might also give the name 'philosophy' to what is possible *before* all the new discoveries and inventions." And in PI §128 Wittgenstein tells us that it is not the business of philosophy to advance theses. Pears writes of the "new philosophy" – which he attributes to both Wittgenstein and OLP – that its "method is always to bring us back to the linguistic phenomenon" (Pears, 1971, p.16). This method has been characterized as "piecemeal" (Bernard Williams) or "plodding if necessary" (G.E. Moore) (Warnock, 1998, p.149). Austin also warns philosophers not to bite off more than they can chew. An adherence to this piecemeal method sometimes – but not always – manifested itself in a hostility to philosophical theories, systematic examinations, and general conclusions. However, a notable exception here is Austin. While

Austin acknowledged that philosophers should pay close attention to the use of words ("our tools"), he was not hostile to systematic theory (see Austin 1956a, pp.185ff).

In a paper devoted to exploring the question of whether analytic philosophy can – or ought to be – systematic, Dummett tells us that,

> in those English philosophical circles dominated by the later Wittgenstein or by Austin [...] the answer given to this question is a resounding "No"; for them, the attempt to be systematic in philosophy was the primal error, founded upon a total misconception of the character of the subject. (1978, p.438)

This attitude manifested itself somewhat differently in the work of Austin and that of the later Wittgenstein. As Dummett reads Wittgenstein, the resistance to systematization in philosophy is connected to a particular view about the nature of philosophy. Dummett understands Wittgenstein to advocate a fundamental difference between the business of philosophy and the business of science – and Dummett tells us that we are here to understand "science" in the most general sense, as embracing "any discipline (art history, for example) whose aim is to arrive at and establish *truths*" (ibid). In the place of establishing truths what Wittgenstein urges is that philosophy should be thought of as aiming "to substitute a clear vision for a distorted one," a vision that will reveal "very familiar facts known to everybody" (ibid, p.439). Not all philosophers would agree that Wittgenstein opposes systematization in philosophy, as I explain below.

Dummett also claims to find a resistance to systematization, especially of language, in Austin's work. And he sees a connection between this and the fact that Austin repeatedly urges philosophers to collect particular facts about our language use (Dummett, 1978, pp.439–40). But it is not clear that Dummett is right to see a connection here. As noted earlier, Austin is not resistant to systematization, nor does he contrast the business of science and that of philosophy as sharply as Dummett implies. For example, Austin acknowledges that psychology produces novel cases and that it also produces new methods for bringing the phenomenon under study, and he tells us that such work may require that we revise the classifications of ordinary life – the classifications embodied in ordinary language and studied by philosophy (Austin, 1956a, p.186). We must here recall that Austin does not take attention to ordinary language to be the *last* word in understanding.

Dummett also notes a connection between the fact that ordinary language philosophers turn their attention to the particular use of particular sentences and a tendency on their part to disregard any distinction between semantics and pragmatics, between the literal meaning of our words and what someone may choose to convey by uttering them (cf. Dummett, 1978, pp.445–7; cf. also Grice, 1989). The idea of literal meaning was sometimes rejected by these philosophers as yet another attempt at generalization and theory-building in philosophy. Attention to the use we make of words in our ordinary speech thus came to be seen as deeply threatening to much work in philosophy. But Dummett also believes that Wittgenstein should not be taken to have agreed with OLP here. What Dummett takes Wittgenstein to be drawing attention to is the way in which our, human, linguistic practice is interwoven with our nonlinguistic activities (ibid; for an interesting discussion of this issue see Glock, 1996).

According to Hacker, Wittgenstein "thought of himself in 1931 as the destroyer of the great tradition of Western philosophy" (2007, p.102), and as developing a "new subject" (2001, p.332). This new philosophy "is above all an activity, not a body of doctrine" (ibid, pp. 332–3). Hacker writes that for the later Wittgenstein philosophy can be taken to have "a double aspect" (2001, p. 324). We can think of philosophy as a kind of therapy for diseases of the understanding, for the conceptual entanglements to which we are prone. According to Hacker, this aspect of philosophy has a "negative tenor," which he takes to be "counterbalanced by the more positive notion of attaining a survey of philosophically problematic domains of grammar" (ibid, p. 333). Hacker takes Wittgenstein – along with many of the ordinary language philosophers – to be interested in what sometimes gets called "conceptual geography." Hacker writes:

> It is the business of philosophy [...] to make it possible for us to get a clear view of the conceptual structure that troubles us: the state of affairs *before* the contradiction is resolved. (Hacker, 2001, p. 334)

Hacker reads Wittgenstein as taking the business of philosophy to be the assembling of rules for the uses of words, and the exploration of the ways in which our concepts hang together. The important point, as he sees it, is that these rules and mappings are such that everyone would acknowledge them. Hacker sees nothing either dogmatic, or intrinsically conservative, in this exercise (cf. Hacker, 2007, p. 105).

This positive aspect of philosophical investigation introduces a certain systematization into philosophy that Hacker is careful to distinguish from the systematization to be found in science. This positive aspect is not to be confused with the construction of theories – whether scientific *or* philosophical. Rather, philosophers should aim to provide thorough surveys of the sources of error and confusion; they should give methodical descriptions of segments of grammar (cf. 2001, p. 342; and also 1972/86, ch.vi, sec. 6). Hacker takes this to count as being systematic in philosophy – but this is not the systematization of theory-building and it should not be taken to be knowledge accumulation (1972/86, p. 178). Hacker reads Wittgenstein as distinguishing between the amassing of knowledge in science and the achievement of understanding in philosophy (2001, p. 324). Thus, Hacker allows that Wittgenstein aims to solve problems in his work (ibid, p. 336), and he believes he is following Wittgenstein when he writes: "Philosophy is neither the queen of the sciences nor their under-labourer, but is rather the tribunal of sense" (ibid, p. 343). Philosophy plays this important role through careful attention to the use of language. In one place Hacker writes: "This may appear to trivialize a profound subject to a matter of mere words. But [...] there is nothing trivial about language. We are *essentially* language-using creatures." Language, he reminds us, moulds our nature, informs our thought, and infuses our lives (1997, pp. 11–12).

The idea that Wittgenstein's work should be read as containing a negative and a positive "aspect" is something fiercely contested by Gordon Baker. Baker was a one-time collaborator with Hacker, and together they published several important volumes devoted to the interpretation of Wittgenstein's work. But Baker, in his mid-to-late career, found himself in deep disagreement with Hacker's (and his own earlier) interpretation of Wittgenstein. Much of this disagreement can be focused on Baker's rejection of what Hacker identifies as a positive and a negative aspect in Wittgenstein's later work. It should be noted that if Wittgenstein is indeed as hostile to a positive project as Baker suggests, he is also arguably more remote from those ordinary language philosophers that regard such a project as legitimate, notably from Austin and Strawson.

In PI §122 Wittgenstein writes: "A main source of our failure to understand is that we do not *command a clear view of [übersehen]* the use of our words." Baker teases out different understandings of what Wittgenstein might mean here. One understanding he labels the "Birds Eye View Model," and he claims this represents what Hacker identifies in his positive, systematic, aspect of the business of philosophy. Baker rejects this view precisely because of its aim of systematization, of providing a "logical geography" of concepts. Baker understands the avowed aim of this view as to obtain "a kind of synoptic view without getting lost in the details" and to obtain this by delineating "the salient logical articulations forged by grammar, the central structure of the net of language, not the local refinements" (Baker and Hacker, 1980/2009, p.543). Baker came to see this project as a mistaken understanding of PI §122, one that turns its back on the very thing it should be embracing – that is, drawing attention to differences in our use of words understood as drawing attention to "hidden *aspects*" or unnoticed patterns in the use of our words (Baker, 1991, p.41).

Baker's understanding of the *way* in which philosophy draws attention to neglected aspects of the uses of our words also brings him into conflict with Hacker. According to Baker, the philosophical method has much in common with therapies such as psychoanalysis. There are references dotted throughout Wittgenstein's later writing to the idea of philosophy as a form of therapy (cf. PI §255 and PI §133). Hacker acknowledges references to therapy and to psychoanalysis in Wittgenstein's writings, but he insists that Wittgenstein only intended us to understand an analogy here and that this analogy does not play an important part in the understanding of method in philosophy. Hacker insists that the confusions that Wittgenstein is concerned to head off with his method are not targeted at individual patients (as is the case in psychoanalysis) so much as at schools of thought or ways of thinking that one finds in philosophy. Baker, on the other hand, understands these references to therapy as crucial to understanding Wittgenstein's method in philosophy. The centrality and importance of therapy in Wittgenstein's work, he argues, goes hand-in-hand with Wittgenstein's method of drawing attention to the neglected aspects of the uses of our words. Baker writes at one point: "Accepting Wittgenstein's methods of therapy as a form of *philosophical* investigation presupposes reconceptualising the boundary between logic and psychology" (Baker, 2003, p.219). What Baker takes Wittgenstein to be concerned with, when looking at the uses of sentences, is what the speaker of those sentences has in mind when uttering them (Baker, 2003, p.208). We look at what the speaker is trying to say, we observe the puzzling things she does say, and we direct her attention to how those words are used in everyday life. We do this by offering to change her aspect on her use of her words, and we do this with the use of analogies, comparisons, pictures, and the like. As Baker reads him, Wittgenstein sees philosophical problems as "deep disquiets" on the part of individuals (ibid, p.213). It follows that the role of philosophy is a therapeutic one, and this does not stand in contrast to any other role.

The stark contrast between these two interpretations of Wittgenstein's later work can be seen if we look at what they have to say about psychological concepts. While Baker takes Hacker to understand Wittgenstein as urging that philosophers discern "the genealogical tree of psychological concepts," Baker himself understands Wittgenstein to urge that philosophers discern the variety of language-games to which these psychological concepts belong and to which "new joints" are added (Baker, 1991, p.47). Baker understands the "clear view" of which Wittgenstein writes in PI §122 as "a view from nowhere," which should not be confused with any particular way of seeing things (ibid). Baker writes: "Wittgenstein advocated nothing more (and nothing less!) than different possible ways of looking at things" (ibid, p.45). Baker does not read

Wittgenstein as advocating *another* way of doing philosophy, but rather as simply pointing out the many different ways in which our words are "integrated into human activity" (ibid, p.78).

Baker's understanding of Wittgenstein's method in his later philosophy extends to an understanding of PI §116, quoted above: "What *we* do is to bring words back from their metaphysical to their everyday use." Baker notes, not unreasonably, that this passage has often been cited as "decisive textual evidence" for the assimilation of Wittgenstein's later work with that of OLP (Baker, 2002, p.94), and Baker suggests that this assimilation partly explains why Wittgenstein's work has "been relegated to the sidelines in contemporary analytic philosophy" (ibid, p.105). Baker takes this assimilation to be in error and believes that appreciation of this might help to bring Wittgenstein's work in from the sidelines. Baker reminds us of the traditional conception of metaphysics as a science of essences, and he agrees that there is a clear emphasis in Wittgenstein's later work on the idea that philosophy should turn its back on this business. What Baker thinks is less clear is whether we should understand reference to "everyday use" in PI §122 as a reference to ordinary language. In particular, Baker questions whether we really do find in Wittgenstein's later work an idea that philosophy should concern itself with the surveying and mapping of ordinary language. As Baker reads PI §122, "everyday" is to be read as simply equivalent to "non-metaphysical" (ibid, p.92). And as Wittgenstein draws our attention away from the metaphysical use of language he draws it to the myriad of possibilities that exist in our language – possibilities that cut against the metaphysical search for essence. We should resist the idea that language *must* be a certain way. Baker writes, "No claim is made that this [non-metaphysical] use is sacrosanct, or that we have no right to depart from it" (ibid, p.103). Baker takes it to be a mistake to put any emphasis on *the* everyday or ordinary use of language.

Baker's work on the later Wittgenstein has opened up new avenues of exploration and debate, and at the heart of this debate we can identify the issue of Wittgenstein's standing as an ordinary language philosopher. Of course, whether Baker is right to distinguish between Wittgenstein and the other so-called ordinary language philosophers will depend not just on his interpretation of Wittgenstein's later work but also on an examination of the work of these other philosophers. Avner Baz (2012) and Alice Crary (2010) advocate that we read Wittgenstein's work in a new light, arguably akin to that in which Baker reads it, but they *also* urge us to read Austin's work in this light.

Thus we see that Baker is not the only philosopher in recent times to have opened up fresh avenues for debate. Within the world of Wittgenstein scholarship there is a group that has come to be known as "the new Wittgensteinians." Just as the label "ordinary language philosophy" can be thought to bring together a range of different ideas, so the work here referred to also brings together a variety of new ideas in Wittgenstein scholarship. As well as those mentioned above, the names associated with this movement include James Conant, Juliet Floyd, Warren Goldfarb, Oskari Kuusela, Marie McGinn, and Rupert Read. Inspiration for this work comes from such philosophers as Stanley Cavell, Cora Diamond, and John McDowell.

One strand in this new work in Wittgenstein interpretation relates directly to our discussion of Wittgenstein's relationship to ordinary language philosophy. McGinn and Kuusela accept the thought, prevalent in this "new" literature, that there is less of a discontinuity between Wittgenstein's early and later work than earlier commentators generally supposed. They argue that Wittgenstein, in his later work, comes to reject only the idea that there is *a* logic of language. What they take Wittgenstein to have come later to appreciate is that formal logical methods can also be "complemented with other methods of conceptual, grammatical, or logical clarification that take into account other aspects of language besides its rule-governedness" (2011, p.6). McGinn and Kuusela suggest that, if they are correct in their interpretation, then not only is there an underlying unity to Wittgenstein's work, but one can point to this in an attempt to uncover an underlying unity within analytical philosophy itself. In particular, they suggest that there need not be a perceived conflict between "the scientific aspirations of analytic philosophy and [a commitment to] common sense" (ibid). Some, following this line of thought, have suggested that science should be thought of as one way in which we ordinarily use language (see, for example, Read, 2010).

The question of the business of philosophy, and its relationship to the business of science are matters of deep importance to the academic and intellectual life of the community. One issue that these questions touch on is this: is our study of use confined to what we do at present, or can it be expanded to incorporate new and creative extensions of use? Baz suggests that the important contrast is between use that serves the purposes of the speaker and use that undermines these purposes – the former is genuine, while the latter is only apparent use (Baz, 2012, p.3). If we look back to the writing of Cavell, someone to whom Baz is indebted, we find an interesting observation. Cavell claims that when we read in the work of Wittgenstein and Austin references to "what we ordinarily say" the emphasis is not so much on the "ordinariness" of our words but on the "we" who use them (1979). Human beings share, not just a language, but a nature. While we might agree that language evolves through use, we must also acknowledge that this evolution is ultimately answerable to the agreement of those who use it – and that agreement will ultimately be determined by the nature of those language-users. Wittgenstein writes, for example:

> The teacher will sometimes say "That's right". If the pupil should ask, "Why?" – he will answer nothing, or at any rate nothing relevant, not even: "Well, because we all do it like that"; that will not be the reason. (Z §319)

While there has been a tendency in philosophy as it is practiced today to confine the work of both Wittgenstein and the "ordinary language philosophers" to a particular moment in the history of philosophy, I have tried to demonstrate the continued relevance and importance of this work to philosophy. The question of what is the business of philosophy is itself an important philosophical question.

References

Austin, J.L. (1956a). A Plea for Excuses. Reprinted in J.L. Austin (1961/79). *Philosophical Papers* (pp.175–205). Ed. J.O. Urmson and G.J. Warnock. Third edition. Oxford: Oxford University Press.

Austin, J.L. (1956b). Ifs and cans. Reprinted in J.L. Austin (1961/79). *Philosophical Papers* (pp.205–233). Ed. J.O. Urmson and G.J. Warnock. Third edition. Oxford: Oxford University Press.

Baker, G.P. (1991). *Philosophical Investigations* §122: Neglected Aspects. Reprinted in G.P. Baker. (2004). *Wittgenstein's Method: Neglected Aspects* (pp.22–52). Ed. K.J. Morris. Oxford: Blackwell.

Baker, G.P. (2002). Wittgenstein on Metaphysical/Everyday Use. In G.P. Baker. (2004). *Wittgenstein's Method: Neglected Aspects* (pp.92–108). Ed. K.J. Morris. Oxford: Blackwell.

Baker, G.P. (2003). Wittgenstein's Method and Psychoanalysis. Reprinted in G.P. Baker. (2004). *Wittgenstein's Method: Neglected Aspects* (pp.205–222). Ed. K.J. Morris. Oxford: Blackwell.

Baker, G.P. and Hacker, P.M.S. (1980/2009). Wittgenstein: Understanding and Meaning. Volume 1 of an Analytical Commentary on the Philosophical Investigations. Part 1. Essays. Second edition. Extensively revised by P.M.S. Hacker. Oxford: Wiley-Blackwell.

Baz, A. (2012). *When Words Are Called For*. Cambridge, MA: Harvard University Press.

Cavell, S. (1979). Excursus in Wittgenstein's Vision of Language. In S. Cavell. *The Claim of Reason* (pp.168–191). Oxford: Oxford University Press.

Crary, A. (2010). The Happy Truth: J.L. Austin's *How To Do Things With Words*. *Inquiry*, 45, 59–80.

Dummett, M. (1978). *Truth and Other Enigmas*. Cambridge, MA: Harvard University Press.

Dummett, M. (1993). *Origins of Analytical Philosophy*. Cambridge, MA: Harvard University Press.

Glock, H.-J. (1996). Abusing Use. *Dialectica*, 50, 205–224.

Grice, H.P. (1989). Logic and Conversation. In H.P. Grice. *Studies in the Way of Words* (pp.22–41). Cambridge, MA: Harvard University Press.

Hacker, P.M.S. (1972/86). *Insight and Illusion: Themes in the Philosophy of Wittgenstein*. Revised edition. Oxford: Clarendon Press.

Hacker, P.M.S. (1997). *Wittgenstein on Human Nature*. London: Weidenfeld and Nicolson.

Hacker, P.M.S. (2001). Philosophy. In H.-J. Glock (Ed.). *Wittgenstein: A Critical Reader* (pp.322–348). Oxford: Blackwell.

Hacker, P.M.S. (2007). Gordon Baker's Late Interpretation of Wittgenstein. In G. Kahane, E. Kanterian, and O. Kuusela (Eds). *Wittgenstein and his Interpreters* (pp.88–123). Oxford: Blackwell.

Hanfling, O. (2000). *Philosophy and Ordinary Language*. London: Routledge.

Heil, J. (1995). Ordinary Language Philosophy. In R. Audi (Ed.). *The Cambridge Dictionary of Philosophy* (p.551). Cambridge: Cambridge University Press.

Hume, D. ([1748/51] 1975). *Enquiries Concerning Human Understanding and Concerning the Principles of Morals*. Ed. L.A. Selby-Bigge. Third edition. Revised by P.H. Nidditch. Oxford: Oxford University Press. (Original work published in 1748 and 1751.)

Kuusela, O. and McGinn, M. (Eds). (2011). *The Oxford Handbook of Wittgenstein*. Oxford: Oxford University Press.

Martinich, A.P. (1998). Ordinary Language Philosophy. In E. Craig (Ed.). *The Concise Routledge Encyclopedia of Philosophy* (pp.143–147). London: Routledge.

McGinn, M. (1997). *Wittgenstein and the Philosophical Investigations*. London: Routledge.

Pears, D. (1971). *Wittgenstein*. London: Fontana.

Read, R. (2010). Ordinary/Everyday Language. In K.D. Jolley (Ed). *Wittgenstein: Key Concepts*. Durham: Acumen.

von Wright, G.H. (1982). Wittgenstein in Relation to his Times. In B. McGuinness (Ed.). *Wittgenstein and his Times* (pp.108–121). Oxford: Blackwell.

Warnock, G. (1998). Ordinary Language Philosophy. In E. Craig (Ed.). *The Concise Routledge Encyclopedia of Philosophy* (pp.147–153). London: Routledge.

Further Reading

Austin, J.L. (1961/79). *Philosophical Papers*. Ed. J.O. Urmson and G.J. Warnock. Third edition. Oxford: Oxford University Press.

Baker, G.P. (2001). Wittgenstein's "Depth Grammar." Reprinted in G.P. Baker. (2004). *Wittgenstein's Method: Neglected Aspects* (pp.73–92). Ed. K.J. Morris. Oxford: Blackwell.

Beaney, M. (Ed.). (2013). *The Oxford Handbook of the History of Analytic Philosophy*. Oxford: Oxford University Press.

Conant, J. (2005). Stanley Cavell's Wittgenstein. *The Harvard Review of Philosophy*, 13, 50–64.

Dummett, M. (1973). *The Seas of Language*. Oxford: Clarendon Press.

Fann, K.T. (Ed.). (1969a). *Symposium on J.L. Austin*. New York: Humanitas Press Inc.

Fann, K.T. (Ed.). (1969b). *Wittgenstein: The Man and his Philosophy*. California: University of California Press.

Grève, S.S. and Mácha, J. (Eds). (2016). *Wittgenstein and the Creativity of Language*. Basingstoke: Palgrave Macmillan.

Gustafsson, M. and Sörli, R. (Eds). (2011). *The Philosophy of J.L. Austin*. Oxford: Oxford University Press.

Hacker, P.M.S. (1996). *Wittgenstein's Place in Twentieth-Century Analytic Philosophy*. Oxford: Blackwell.

48

Wittgenstein and Pragmatism

DAVID BAKHURST AND CHERYL MISAK

The question of the affinity between Wittgenstein's philosophy and pragmatism is one that has been often discussed, usually by philosophers sympathetic to a broadly affirmative answer (e.g., Haack, 1982; Goodman, 1998). Hilary Putnam (1995) asks "Was Wittgenstein a pragmatist?" and *almost* answers yes. And Robert Brandom (1994, p.23) makes so bold as to represent Wittgenstein as advancing a pragmatist theory of norms. But the question is a delicate one, if only because characterizing the core elements of pragmatism is almost as contestable as interpreting Wittgenstein's thought. Moreover, while Wittgenstein was undoubtedly influenced by pragmatist thinkers, the nature of that influence is by no means straightforward. It is well known that Wittgenstein was impressed by William James (one of the few philosophers he would admit to having read), despite his mostly critical comments about James's views. Less often noted, however, is the affinity between Wittgenstein's thought and the philosophy of Charles Sanders Peirce. Though there are important differences of philosophical style and substance between the two thinkers, they share a number of profound insights about meaning, knowledge, and philosophical method. Or so we shall suggest.

1 The Historical Context

Pragmatism came into being in 1867 in a reading group in Cambridge Massachusetts, the members of which included Peirce and James. Although Peirce was acknowledged as the founder of the movement, he was a difficult person and he could not secure an academic post. It was therefore James – America's most famous academic and one of the fathers of modern psychology – who became the public face of pragmatism. James's views were well known across the Atlantic. In 1901 he delivered the Gifford Lectures in Edinburgh and in 1909 the Hibbert Lectures in Oxford. Both Bertrand Russell and G.E. Moore reviewed James's book *Pragmatism* (1907), and were outspoken in rejecting his account of truth (see Russell 1909, 1910; Moore 1907). Wittgenstein would have been aware of the hostile reception to James's pragmatism, but this did not prevent him from finding things of interest in his writings. He read James's *Varieties of Religious Experience* (the published Gifford Lectures, 1902) in 1912 and wrote to Russell that "This book does me a *lot* of good" (Letter to Russell, 22 June 1912). Many years later he commended the volume to his friend Maurice Drury. As has sometimes been noted (e.g., Hallett, 1977, p.40), Wittgenstein's notion of family resemblance (PI §67) may have been inspired by James's antiessentialist treatment of the concept of religion (1902, ch.2). Wittgenstein also studied James's *Principles of Psychology* (1890) in the 1930s and 1940s (for a time it was the only philosophical work on his book case (Passmore, 1957/68, p.592, n.4)) and he discusses various Jamesian positions in his later writings. It is sometimes thought that Wittgenstein was interested in James merely as an exemplification of error, but as Russell Goodman has argued (2002, pp.62–3, citing Z §456), this fails to appreciate how much Wittgenstein admired James as a deep thinker not afflicted by the "loss of problems" syndrome that diminishes so many philosophers. Goodman stresses that Wittgenstein mentions Russell and Frege in the *Investigations*, but he *addresses* James (p.96).

No less than Russell and Moore, Wittgenstein explicitly rejected what he and other philosophers took to be the heart of Jamesian pragmatism: the identification of the true with the useful. Wittgenstein is clear: "But aren't you a pragmatist? No. For I am not saying that a proposition is true if it is useful" (RPP I §266); "If I want to carve a block of wood into a particular shape any cut that gives it the right shape is a good one. But I don't call an argument a good argument just because it has the consequences I want (Pragmatism)" (PG 185; cf. OC §474). Wittgenstein was also dismissive of the Jamesian ideas of the Oxford pragmatist F.C.S. Schiller, describing his "The Value of Formal Logic" (1932) as "philosophical nonsense" (and not in a good way!). There is no reason to think that Wittgenstein ever warmed to such views. O.K. Bouwsma relates that Wittgenstein was also very rude about John Dewey (see WC 28–9). In 1949, upon learning that Dewey was still living, Wittgenstein commented, "Ought not to be."

For all that, however, there are parallels between Wittgenstein's thought and aspects of James's philosophy that we would now unhesitatingly associate with pragmatism, such as James's interest in philosophy as "method only" (1907, p.31), his respect for "common sense," and his concern to describe the complex detail of human life. Moreover, it is likely that Wittgenstein was influenced, albeit circuitously, by Peirce. Haack (1982) and Sahlin (1997) argue that Wittgenstein learnt about Peirce's thought from his discussions with Frank Ramsey. Ramsey was one of the few scholars in England to have read Peirce attentively, and in the 1920s he explicitly advanced pragmatist views bearing Peirce's influence (1926/90; [1927–29] 1991). So while it may be that Wittgenstein arrived independently at the themes of his philosophy that most resemble Peirce's – the reflections posthumously published as *On Certainty* – it is probable that he was exposed to Peircean ideas through Ramsey.

Yet even where Wittgenstein is at his most pragmatist, he is not entirely comfortable with the idea. In *On Certainty* (§422), he writes, "So I am trying to say something that sounds like pragmatism. Here I am being thwarted by a kind of *Weltanschauung*." What Wittgenstein meant by that last sentence is disputable. How exactly did a "worldview" get in the way of his embracing pragmatism? We shall return to this question after we have explored in detail a number of points of contact between Wittgenstein's thought and the pragmatist tradition.

2 The Primacy of Practice: Meaning and Use

Putnam (1995, p. 52) observes that though the later Wittgenstein may not have been a pragmatist "in the strict sense," he "shares a central – perhaps *the* central – emphasis with pragmatism: the emphasis on the primacy of practice." Though Wittgenstein might have resisted the idea that he gave "primacy" to any concept, there is clearly a sense in which Putnam is right. A lesson of Wittgenstein's later philosophy is that to understand mind and meaning, we must see them in their relation to human activity, as aspects of our natural history. Accordingly, explanation of mind and meaning finds its terminus in an appeal to practice – to customs, traditions, and forms of life. Wittgenstein was fond of quoting Goethe's *Faust*, "*Im Anfang war die Tat*" ("In the beginning was the deed") (OC §402; CV p. 36). It would be hard to find a pragmatist, classical or contemporary, who would not concur. Wittgenstein and the pragmatists are united in their rejection of the contemplative (or, in Dewey's words "spectator") model of mind familiar from the Cartesian tradition. We should think of ideas, concepts, beliefs, and theories, not on the model of pictorial representations of reality, but as tools or instruments we deploy in our engagement with the world.

The devil is, of course, in the details. In "How to Make our Ideas Clear" [1878], Peirce advances a principle he later called "the pragmatic maxim." To attain clarity we must:

> Consider what effects, which might conceivably have practical bearings, we conceive the object of our conception to have. Then, our conception of these effects is the whole of our conception of the object. (Peirce, 1982–99, vol. 3, p. 266)

As Peirce explains, to have a conception of, say, wine is to have a view about the consequences for experience of something's being wine, and to believe that a substance is wine is to have certain dispositions to act (or habits of action) in accord with these consequences. In this way our concepts are essentially related to practice. In short: "we must look to the upshot of our concepts in order rightly to apprehend them" (1931–58, vol. 5, §3).

Thus, from its inception, the pragmatic maxim was advanced broadly in the spirit of positivism and verificationism. Peirce reformulated the maxim many times over the course of his life (for example, replacing the indicative mood with the subjunctive: a diamond that lies on the ocean floor, never to be scratched, is still hard, for "it is a real fact that it *would* resist pressure" (1931–58, vol. 8, §208)). As James portrays the maxim:

> [T]he tangible fact at the root of all our thought-distinctions, however subtle, is that there is no one of them so fine as to consist in anything but a possible difference of practice. (James, 1907, p. 29)

And: "there can *be* no difference anywhere that doesn't *make* a difference elsewhere" (p. 30). If a belief has no consequences for practice, it is empty, useless for inquiry. In Peirce's words, the pragmatic maxim thus determines "the admissibility of hypotheses to rank as hypotheses" (1963, ms. 318, p. 8). On such grounds, Peirce attacks the Catholic doctrine of transubstantiation:

> We can consequently mean nothing by wine but what has certain effects, direct or indirect, upon our senses; and to talk of something as having all the sensible characters of wine, yet being in reality blood, is senseless jargon. (Peirce, 1982–99, vol. 3, p. 266)

And James too looks to the maxim to resolve philosophical disputes, maintaining that "in every genuine metaphysical debate some practical issue, however conjectural and remote, is involved" (1982–99, vol.1, p.52). The meaning of any philosophical proposition must ultimately reside in "some particular consequence, in our future practical experience, whether active or passive"; so where a philosophical controversy turns on matters of "no conceivable practical consequence to anybody at any time or place," the issue "is only a specious and verbal difference, unworthy of further contention" (1982–99, vol.1, pp.259–60).

In all this, parallels with Wittgenstein are evident. As Glock (1996, p.382) has argued, even in the *Tractatus*, with its picture theory of propositions, Wittgenstein is committed to a verificationist criterion of meaning*less*ness (a proposition is meaningless if it cannot be verified or falsified), and he later (at least for a short period of time) embraced verificationism full-blown in his interactions with the Vienna Circle. He then moved to the more relaxed view of meaning and use expressed in the *Investigations* where: "For a *large* class of cases of the employment of the word 'meaning' – though not for *all* – this word can be explained in this way: the meaning of a word is its use in the language" (PI §43; cf. BB 4). Wittgenstein famously illuminates the relation of meaning and use with the notion of "language-games," invoked (a) to model "ways of using signs," real and fictional, that are simpler than everyday language, and (b) to refer to human language as a whole, "the human language-game" (OC §554) embracing "language and the activities into which it is woven" (PI §7). By reflecting on language-games we appreciate the myriad ways that words can have or lack meaning. Thus although Wittgenstein often argues in a way that accords with the pragmatist dictum that a real difference must make a difference (such as in the famous case of the "beetle in the box" (PI §293)), his insights about the diversity of language led him away from any one-dimensional verificationism toward the view that "Asking whether and how a proposition can be verified is only a special form of the question 'What do you mean?'" (PI §353; translation modified DB/CM), and he came to disavow the very idea of a *theory* of meaning based on verification or any other notion.

This last point is important, because for all the parallels between Peirce and Wittgenstein, there is little doubt that the former's approach to meaning would have struck the later Wittgenstein as too theoretical. For example, in his account of signs (well known to Ogden and Richards), Peirce argues that meaning resides in the sign's effects on interpreters. The highest kind of meaning, he thinks, lies in the effects of the acceptance of a proposition on the interpreter's train of thought and action. This distinguishes Peirce's pragmatism from crude forms of behaviorism, where meaning and mental states are reducible to overt behavior, but this would not redeem the position for Wittgenstein, who (perhaps with Ramsey in mind) explicitly denies we can equate meaning with the effects of utterances (see, e.g., PI §§493–8). To understand the meaning of an expression we must look to its use; but Wittgenstein insisted this is not to *theorize* meaning as use.

It is important, however, that Peirce did not think that a sign's effects are all there is to its meaning, or that there is a single way to elucidate meaning. The pragmatic maxim captures only one way, albeit the most efficacious for inquiry (Misak, 1991, pp.12ff). Moreover, Peirce is not the kind of pragmatist (think of Quine or Rorty) who holds that normative notions such as a meaning or intentionality can be reduced to, or eliminated in favor of, talk about practices or behavior. Indeed, Peirce's enemy is the nominalist who refuses to admit law, intentions, and norms into his picture of reality. Expounding his (admittedly obscure) category of *thirdness*, Peirce asserts:

> Brute action is secondness, any mentality involves thirdness. Analyze for instance the relation involved in 'A gives B to C.' Now what is giving? It does not consist [in] A's putting B away from him and C's subsequently taking B up. It is not necessary that any material transfer should take place. It consists in A's making C the possessor according to *Law*. There must be some kind of law before there can be any kind of giving, – be it but the law of the strongest. (Peirce, 1931–58, vol.8, §331)

Thus, Peirce would likely have concurred with the wholeheartedly "normativist" view of the relation of meaning and practice attributed to Wittgenstein by Glock (Glock, 2005; for similar readings see, e.g., Baker and Hacker, 1985/2014; McDowell, 1998, chs 11–14). On such a reading, the meaning of an expression is linked to the rules for its use. Such rules are exemplified by the practices that are constitutive of them, and understanding them cannot (on pain of a regress) be a matter of grasping an interpretation; it is rather acquiring a technique, entering a custom, learning a practice. But there is no suggestion that such techniques, customs, and practices can be characterized without reference to normative notions. This is at least one of the senses in which language-games are autonomous according to Wittgenstein (PG §§68, 133, 184–5; Z §320). They may be embedded in "the stream of life," in our nonlinguistic practices and our natural reactions and activities, but they cannot be reduced to such behaviors or explained in terms of ends and purposes that are external to them. All this Peirce could have accepted, save Wittgenstein's conclusion that such insights put paid to systematic philosophical theorizing about meaning.

3 Knowledge

If the most obvious affinity between Wittgenstein and the pragmatists resides in their mutual emphasis on practice, the most explicit coincidence of views is found in the comparison of Wittgenstein's *On Certainty* and pragmatist conceptions of knowledge, especially Peirce's. Peirce maintains that no attempt to revise human knowledge can start from scratch, aspiring, as Descartes did, to establish knowledge on an indubitable foundation of certain belief. Rather, we must start from where we find ourselves, already possessed of beliefs. Any inquirer has a body of settled belief, on which to act and against which to assess new evidence and hypotheses. It is doubt that leads us to inquire into the cogency of our beliefs, but we can evaluate some belief only if we hold others steady. Peirce maintains that only genuine, properly motivated doubts can stimulate inquiry. He gives no credence to what he calls "paper" or "tin" doubts of the kind marshaled by Descartes. The mere possibility of being mistaken does not engender a living doubt:

> But in truth, there is but one state of mind from which you can 'set out', namely, the very state of mind in which you actually find yourself at the time you do 'set out' – a state in which you are laden with an immense mass of cognition already formed, of which you cannot divest yourself if you would [...]. Do you call it *doubting* to write down on a piece of paper that you doubt? If so, doubt has nothing to do with any serious business. (Peirce, 1931–58, vol.5, p.416)

Our body of belief is an interconnected whole, any part of which is fallible, and which we revise as and when the force of experience throws particular beliefs into genuine doubt.

Wittgenstein seems entirely in step with this holistic account of knowledge. Many remarks in *On Certainty* describe knowledge as "an enormous system" in which alone any "particular bit" has "the value we give it" (§410). Like Peirce, Wittgenstein holds that the revision of belief makes sense only against a background that is not called into question ("A doubt that doubted everything would not be a doubt" (§450)) and that doubt must be properly motivated and purposeful ("A doubt without an end is not even a doubt" (§625)).

Both Wittgenstein and Peirce have interesting things to say about propositions that are "exempt from doubt." Wittgenstein writes that,

> 341. [...] the *questions* that we raise and our *doubts* depend upon the fact that some propositions are exempt from doubt, are as it were like hinges on which those turn.
> 342. That is to say, it belongs to the logic of our scientific investigations that certain things are *in deed* not doubted. (OC §§341–2)

Wittgenstein describes these "propositions" (often referred to as "hinge" or "framework" propositions) as lying apart "from the route travelled by enquiry" (§88), "removed from the traffic" or "shunted onto an unused siding" (§210). They include "The earth has existed for many years past" (§411) and "This is my hand" (§§412–14), together with very particular claims, such as "I have never been in Asia Minor" (§419) and "I am in England" (§§420–1). Propositions of this kind are part of the scaffolding of our thoughts (§211) or our "frame of reference" (§83). There is no logical guarantee that any such proposition will not legitimately be called into question in future – even the "river bed" of thought can shift. But if knowledge is to be possible at all, a large number of such beliefs must simply stand fast.

Wittgenstein also admits a class of propositions he calls "grammatical propositions" or "norms of description." Such propositions express the rules by which language-games are to be played. They include definitions (verbal and ostensive); exemplifications; mathematical propositions; and such truths about color as "nothing can be red and green all over" (see Glock, 1996, p.152). The truth of such propositions is guaranteed not by their form but by their role in constituting language rules. Though Wittgenstein admits these roles can change and hence that the relation between grammatical and empirical propositions is fluid (OC §§309, 321), his philosophy distinguishes between (a) propositions that are necessarily true because their negation is rendered nonsensical by a grammatical rule and (b) those that we cannot give up without undermining our entire system of beliefs. Thus there is an – admittedly nonstandard – sense in which a distinction between conceptual and empirical truth is preserved in Wittgenstein's thought.

Peirce would have no complaint about Wittgenstein's hinge propositions, acknowledging them as part of the body of background belief that must be accepted if inquiry is to be possible. Peirce is skeptical about the idea of conceptual or analytic truth, like many of his successors in the pragmatist tradition, and nothing in his philosophy plays quite the role of Wittgenstein's grammatical propositions. He does, however, admit certain "regulative assumptions" that provide the framework within which inquiry is possible and as such are placed beyond doubt. We have to accept, for instance, that on the whole our observations can be explained; that there are answers to the questions into which we are inquiring; and that there are real things independent of our beliefs that can be explored by empirical investigation. Though their acceptance may be a necessary condition of inquiry, such regulative assumptions have no logical guarantee. If inquiry demands that we accept the principle of bivalence, we do so by a "saltus" – an unjustified leap (Peirce, 1976, p.xiii). The necessity that compels the assumption is practical. "[H]owever destitute of evidentiary support it may be," we adopt it:

> For the same reason that a general who has to capture a position, or see his country ruined, must go on the hypothesis that there is some way in which he can and shall capture it. (Peirce, 1931–58, vol.7, p.219)

Where such assumptions enable practices at the heart of our humanity – seeking answers to questions, for instance – they will be deeply entrenched. Nonetheless, they remain hypotheses or "hopes," rather than transcendental truths or constitutive principles.

For all they share, Wittgenstein's and Peirce's respective treatments of knowledge betray an important difference of philosophical temperament. For Peirce, as for many pragmatists, the central notion in his account of knowledge is *inquiry* and the guiding picture is one of the knower constructing and sustaining a conception of the world, under the impetus of experience and in the course of his practical engagement with reality. His style of thinking is systematic and scientific, and he casts the knower in the role of the inquirer concerned to order and categorize, theorize and explain, in order to solve problems and thereby, so far as possible, to master and control. Wittgenstein, in contrast, does not embrace this rather monolithic view of inquiry. All pragmatists would agree with him on the following:

> I did not get my picture of the world by satisfying myself of its correctness; nor do I have it because I am satisfied of its correctness. No: it is the inherited background against which I distinguish between true and false. (OC §94)

But where James, for example, casts the background as comprising "discoveries of our remote ancestors," Wittgenstein does not portray it as emerging out of any kind of inquiry. For him, we inherit a world-picture as we acquire language, and language "did not emerge from some kind of ratiocination" (§475). The language-game "is not based on grounds [...]. It is there – like our life" (§559).

Similarly, Wittgenstein writes:

> But it isn't that the situation is like this: We just *can't* investigate everything, and for that reason we are forced to rest content with assumption. If I want the door to turn, the hinges must stay put. (OC §343)

Hinge propositions are not assumptions in the sense that, though they are amenable to confirmation or proof, we are forced for reasons of expediency to accept them (like the General in Peirce's example). Rather, such propositions stand beyond or (better) beneath proof (more like Peirce's example of the principle of bivalence and other regulative assumptions). Not that the term assumption is entirely out of place. At §411, Wittgenstein writes:

> If I say '*we assume* that the earth has existed for many years past' (or something similar), then of course it sounds strange that we should *assume* such a thing. But in the entire system of our language-games it belongs to the foundations. The assumption, one might say, forms the basis of action, and therefore, naturally, of thought. (OC §411)

But if hinge propositions are assumptions, they are not assumptions we make on pragmatic grounds. (I do not assume that the earth existed before my birth in the way I might assume that my children are at school, or that my car will start.) Such beliefs, if so we may call them, are too deeply entrenched for that. Indeed, if there is awkwardness about our being said to "believe" or "know" hinge propositions, as Wittgenstein suggests, it is not because such propositions could only warrant cognitive attitudes *less than* belief and knowledge. It is not that, bereft of grounds, our only recourse is to adopt such propositions for practical purposes, as if our reason for thinking that objects exist is that we should never get anything done on the basis of a contrary hypothesis. When it comes to hinge propositions, we are beyond giving reasons for their acceptance, whether it be reasons supporting them directly or reasons deriving from the calamitous consequences of abandoning them. The same is true of grammatical propositions – if we ask "What is the reason why the King in chess may move only one square in any direction?," we cannot expect anything but the answer "That's how the game is played," together perhaps with some historical facts about the evolution of chess. And this is also true of norms of reasoning: Wittgenstein rejects the view that we engage in inductive reasoning because it pays, arguing that principles of induction are not justified by the success of inductive reasoning; rather they define what it is to make rational predictions (see, e.g., OC §§128–31; PI §§466–85).

The thought that Wittgenstein and Peirce share is that what is exempt from doubt is so because otherwise we lose our bearings. But it is a question whether they characterize this loss differently or not. Does Peirce think that without such assumptions, we could not go on with inquiry? Or, does he maintain, with Wittgenstein, that without them the fabric of our language-games, of our very form of life, would begin to unravel?

4   Truth

Peirce thought it a small step from his conception of inquiry to a compelling view of truth. Like James, Peirce links the truth of a hypothesis to the consequences of believing it. But he takes a different view of what the relevant consequences are. As J.B. Pratt (1909, pp.186–7) put it:

> [A] distinction must be made; namely between the 'good', harmonious, and logically confirmatory consequences of religious concepts as such, and the good and pleasant consequences which come from believing these concepts. It is one thing to say a belief is true because the logical consequences that flow from it fit in harmoniously with our otherwise grounded knowledge; and quite another to call it true because it is pleasant to believe.

James takes the latter view; Peirce the former. (Indeed, Peirce mocked James's view: "Oh, I could not believe so-and-so, because I should be wretched if I did" (1931–58, vol.5, §377).) Peirce takes the truth of a hypothesis to rest on its empirical confirmation, its fit with our otherwise well-established knowledge, and so on. The relevant consequence, then, resides in the durability of the beliefs in question. They are true insofar as they will stand up to anything inquiry can throw at them, now and in the future. True belief is "indefeasible" belief. This leads Peirce to his less-than-ideal formulation: "The opinion which is fated to be ultimately agreed to by all who investigate, is what we mean by the truth, and the object represented in this opinion is the real" (1982–99, vol.3, p.273).

When Wittgenstein distances himself from the pragmatist view of truth, he has James in mind. What, then, would he say about Peirce's account? In his later philosophy, Wittgenstein abandoned the broadly correspondence account of truth he had assumed in his early work and, like Ramsey, embraced a deflationary account of truth with pragmatist overtones, observing that the proposition "'p' is true" is equivalent to "p" (see PI §136). This approach might be thought too austere to be aligned with Peirce's. Yet both Peirce and Wittgenstein are concerned to link truth to assertion. Moreover, the Peircean could be seen as correcting Wittgenstein in this respect: to assert that p is true is not just to assert that p, but to warrant that p is and will remain assertible come what may. It might be countered that Peirce links truth to agreement in a problematic way and that at *Investigations* §241 Wittgenstein takes pains to distance himself from such a position:

> "So you are saying that human agreement decides what is true and what is false?" – What is true or false is what human beings *say*; and it is in their *language* that human beings agree. This is agreement not in opinions, but rather in form of life.

But it is by no means obvious that Peirce is cornered into a form of linguistic idealism: the idea that true beliefs are those on which there is agreement at the end of inquiry is internally related to the thought that the agreement is warranted by how things are. It is not the idea that truth depends on what some finite collection of finite beings happen to agree is the case at some finite time (see Misak, 1991, ch.1; note that even James in "The Will to Believe" writes that "throughout the breadth of physical nature facts are what they are quite independently of us" (1896, p.26)). Thus though there are differences of substance and style between Peirce and Wittgenstein, they may be less dramatic than might first appear.

5 James and Wittgenstein on Religious Belief

James is well known (and was so during Wittgenstein's time) for a strong claim he made in "The Will to Believe." He argues there that it is sometimes reasonable to believe a hypothesis before one has conclusive evidence in its favor. If a hypothesis is underdetermined by the data, it can nevertheless be reasonable to accept it if there is something to gain by so doing. This is true, he argues, especially of religious beliefs. In this, James rejects William Clifford's evidentialism – the view that it is only rational to believe that p in proportion to the evidence for p. For Clifford, where evidence underdetermines the matter, one must suspend judgment: "it is wrong always, everywhere, and for anyone, to believe anything upon insufficient evidence" (1879, p.186). James responds that in religious matters, agnosticism is also a decision, and one based as much on an act of will as the theist's commitment. Where religious hypotheses are live options for us, the issues they raise are so "momentous" that we are "forced" to take a side: the agnostic, it might be said, is therefore in bad faith.

For James, then, religious beliefs may be adopted for the role they play in our lives and it is from that role that religious terms derive their significance. In *Varieties of Religious Experience*, James explores in careful detail the significance of religious ideas in personal life (he is not concerned with issues theological or ecclesiastical). In his postscript to that work, James takes a bolder position than in "The Will to Believe," confessing his willingness to entertain a form of supernaturalism. With regard to the evidence for God's existence, James cites "the phenomenon of 'prayerful communion'" in which it appears that "something ideal, which in one sense is part of ourselves and in another sense is not ourselves, actually exerts an influence, raises our centre of personal energy, and produces regenerative effects unattainable in other ways," and attests that he is so "impressed by the importance of these phenomena" that he adopts "the hypothesis which they so naturally suggest" (1902, pp.411–12).

As we have noted, Wittgenstein greatly admired James's *Varieties of Religious Experience*. In the *Tractatus*, Wittgenstein regards religion, together with ethics, aesthetics, and all matters of value, as entirely transcendental: "The sense of the world," he writes, "must lie outside the world" (TLP 6.41) and hence religious belief does not pertain to the facts of the world, but is more like a way of seeing those facts under a certain aspect, so that "the world of the happy is quite another than that of the unhappy" (6.43). But he later modified this view, stressing that the meaning of religious expressions, and the significance of religious practices, resides in their role in our lives. Contrary to appearances, religious statements are not descriptions of reality, natural or supernatural; religious terms do not refer to entities; religious explanations of events are not causal; and religious stories are not historical narratives. Religious beliefs are "pictures" that we can make use of in our lives and "*practice* gives the words their sense" (CV p.97). Thus to embrace religious belief is "(something like) passionately committing oneself to a system of coordinates. Hence although it's belief, it's really a way of living, or a way of judging life" (CV p.73).

All of this shows James's influence. There is nonetheless an important difference between them. While James sometimes sounds much like Wittgenstein in arguing that religious experience lies beyond the realm of evidence, he more often than not takes religion to be a part of inquiry. Contrast the following quotation from Wittgenstein:

> Life can educate you to 'believing in God'. And *experiences* too are what do this but not visions, or other sense experiences, which show us the 'existence of this being', but, e.g. sufferings of various sorts. And they do not show us God as sense experience does an object, nor do they give rise to *conjectures* about him. Experiences, thoughts, – life can force this concept on us. (CV p.97)

Although there is much here with which James would have agreed, the crucial difference is that Wittgenstein does not think of God's existence as a hypothesis. Hence it is wrongheaded to ask, as James does, into the merits of the evidence that supports it and to consider grounds on which it is reasonable to adopt it. Accepting God's existence is a matter of "shaping" one's life a certain way (CV p.97), but the decision to do so is not based on reasons, practical or evidential. James's position is too epistemological for Wittgenstein's tastes.

In this sense Wittgenstein's position is more radical than James's. It is also less obviously coherent. For how can a believer understand the true character of her own religious beliefs, if that requires acknowledging that such beliefs do not assert what they purport to? If the picture of God's grace is to uplift me, I cannot believe that it is *merely* a picture; that there is in fact nothing for my redemption to consist in, except perhaps for my engendering a mood by the use of a metaphor. But a metaphor for what? Of course, advocates of Wittgensteinian fideism might complain that such questions only reveal a missing of the point and a hollowness of spirit. But here James seems on a surer footing, even if his case for the reasonableness of religious belief is some way short of compelling.

6 Philosophy of Psychology

James's most significant influence over Wittgenstein lies in the philosophy of psychology. Wittgenstein was fascinated by James's masterpiece *The Principles of Psychology*, especially the chapter "The Stream of Thought," and in his later writing on mind and meaning he engages repeatedly with James's ideas.

James's method in psychology is empiricist and introspectionist, and he is a master of the description of mental life. Even when those descriptions are misleading, as Wittgenstein often thought they were, they reveal something interesting about the way we understand ourselves. But, as we observed above, Wittgenstein did not turn to James only as a source of illuminating error. He agreed, for instance, with James's perceptive rejection of the idea that all action is initiated by an act of volition, and in making this point Wittgenstein deployed an example taken straight from James: that of simply finding oneself getting out of bed (BB 151; 1890, pp. 1132–3). In general, however, James's empiricism inclines him to believe there are subjective psychological events accompanying all manifestations of mind and meaning, and it is the various expressions of this inclination (including James's ideo-motor theory of action), that Wittgenstein subjects to criticism in the *Investigations* and other writings on psychology. For example, Wittgenstein thinks James guilty of confusing meanings with experiences and feelings. In the "Blue Book" (pp. 78–9), Wittgenstein criticizes James's view that the meaning of such terms as "and," "if," "or" is bound up with feelings associated with them. But even though Wittgenstein concludes that "[t]he meaning of a word is not the experience one has in hearing or uttering it, and the sense of a sentence is not a complex of these experiences" (PPF §37), he does not pour scorn on James's interest in the phenomenology of meaning and understanding. In the *Investigations*, he discusses mental imagery associated with the names of the days of the week and how such imagery can contribute to the "secondary meaning" of expressions (PPF §§275–8); James's view (1890, p. 726) that words have a soul as well as a body (evinced by the fact that in some contexts words cannot be replaced without violence to what is said, just as one musical phrase cannot just be substituted for another (PI §§530–1; cf. p. 215)); and the feeling of words being on the tip of one's tongue (PPF §§298–300). In all this, Wittgenstein takes James tremendously seriously. There *is* such a thing as the "*field* of a word" (§297), but, as Goodman observes (2002, p. 145), the context needed to elucidate it is not experience, but grammar and culture, practices and forms of life. For James, in contrast, everything returns to experience, to how "every definite image in the mind is steeped and dyed in the free water that flows around it" (1890, p.246). James's views on intention, emotion, the self, and personal identity all inform Wittgenstein's treatment of these and cognate issues, and though Wittgenstein is consistently preoccupied with how little such concepts are illuminated by appeal to experiences that supposedly accompany their deployment or constitute their objects, he always "proceeds with the assistance, and not just on the wreckage of the theories of William James," as Goodman nicely puts it (2002, p.120). He admired the depth and sensitivity of James's powers of description and the humanity of his vision. In all this, of course, it is James's distinctive style of empiricism that engages Wittgenstein's imagination. Indeed, had Wittgenstein not, with Russell and Moore, taken pragmatism to amount to Jamesian views of truth, he might have concluded that the principal problem with James's psychology is that it does not go far enough down the pragmatist path. Though James is attentive, especially in his account of the emotions, to the bodily manifestations of mind, his preoccupation with experience means that he fails to do precisely what an all-out pragmatist must; namely, to understand mind and meaning in the context of the "stream of life" (LW I §913; PR 81) rather than the stream of thought.

7   Conclusion: Philosophy as Method

Let us return to *On Certainty* §422 and consider what Wittgenstein meant when he wrote: "So I am trying to say something that sounds like pragmatism. Here I am being thwarted by a kind of *Weltanschauung*." One possible explanation is that Wittgenstein rejects pragmatism because it is itself a *Weltanschauung*, a substantive philosophical theory (an "ism"). To embrace it would thus be at odds with his therapeutic approach to philosophy, on which the philosopher advances no theses (PI §128) but marshals "recollections for a particular purpose" (§127); namely, to attain a "surveyable representation," "*an overview* of the use of our words" (§122). In this way, we "struggle against the bewitchment of our intelligence by the resources of our language" (§109), so that we should be able "to break off philosophizing" when we want to (§133). For Wittgenstein, both early and later, philosophy is not doctrine but method (TLP 4.112, 6.53; M 113–14; BT 406–35; PI §§118–33).

If this was behind Wittgenstein's rejection of pragmatism it is too bad that he did not know Peirce better. For Peirce himself advanced the view that pragmatism should be seen exclusively as a method for the clarification of concepts and writes, almost as if in answer to Wittgenstein: "It will be seen that pragmatism is not a *Weltanschauung* but is a method of reflexion having for its purpose to render ideas clear" (from Peirce's personal interleaved copy of the *Century Dictionary*, 1931–58, vol.5, p.13, n.1). And, as we have already noted, James also asserts that pragmatism "is method only." Peirce expresses his view as a matter of getting clear about our *ideas* rather than the meaning of words, but he is sufficiently attentive to questions of meaning that this emphasis does not strike a significant discord with Wittgenstein. One bone of contention is that Peirce, at least, did not think philosophy could or should wither away. Another is whether we may speak of a *single* method (which Wittgenstein denies: "There is not a single philosophical method, though there are indeed methods, different therapies, as it were" (PI §133d)).

It is not obvious, however, that the suggested interpretation is correct. Wittgenstein did not identify a *Weltanschauung* with a substantive doctrine. Indeed, he was not averse to using the term to describe his own stance. In the so-called *Big Typescript*, he writes:

> The concept of a surveyable representation is of fundamental significance for us. It designates our form of representation, the way we look at things. (A kind of "*Weltanschauung*", as is apparently typical of our time. Spengler.) (BT 417)

In the *Investigations* (§122), the parenthetical remark transforms into "(Is this a "*Weltanschauung*"?)" but this does not suggest Wittgenstein is unfriendly to the notion. Of course even if Wittgenstein meant, not that he was uncomfortable by pragmatism's being a *Weltanschauung*, but that his own *Weltanschauung* was an obstacle to accepting it, his reason may yet have been that he wanted nothing to do with an "ism."

We feel, however, that there is more to Wittgenstein's reticence than this. It may issue from his perception that pragmatism is too scientific in style, too epistemological in orientation. In the passages leading up to OC §422, Wittgenstein discusses empirical propositions that are the "foundation of all my action" (§414). The reference to action suggests "something like" pragmatism, but, as we argued above, Wittgenstein does not see such background beliefs as adopted or accepted out of a kind of practical necessity as preconditions of inquiry. For Wittgenstein, there is no reason, rational or pragmatic, why we embrace such propositions (§359). Their certainty lies "beyond being justified or unjustified"; it is "something animal." (Here, though, the resonances with Santayana's version of pragmatism as "animal faith" are striking.) They are accepted, not as preconditions of inquiry, but because: "My *life* consists in my being content to accept many things" (§344), including the character of that life itself: "What has to be accepted, the given, is – one might say – *forms of life*" (PPF §345). One might say that, while for the pragmatists the fundamental concept is *inquiry*, for Wittgenstein it is *life*. This marks a crucial difference of perspective, awareness of which may have underlain OC §422.

There are other, related, differences of intellectual temperament that deserve note. Much as Wittgenstein found uplifting James's exploration of "the feelings, acts, and experiences of individual men in their solitude" (1902, p.34), it is hard to believe he had sympathy with the optimism and meliorism pervading James's pragmatism. James writes that,

> if you follow the pragmatist method, you cannot look on any such word [God, Matter, Reason, the Absolute, Energy] as closing your quest. You must bring out of each word its practical cash-value [...]. *Theories thus become instruments, not answers to enigmas, in which we can rest*. (James, 1907, pp.31–2)

And that cash-value, James thinks, ought to be positive:

> Design, free-will, the absolute mind, spirit instead of matter, have for their sole meaning a better promise as to this world's outcome. Be they false or be they true the meaning of them is this meliorism. (p.63)

Dewey, of course, takes this melioristic strain of pragmatism even further. This is all very unlike Wittgenstein, whose outlook "was typically one of gloom" (von Wright, 1967, p.27).

He would have deplored the idea of philosophy as a social project devoted to the betterment of humanity, and double-deplored the idea that this required an alliance between philosophy and natural science (see Goodman, 2002, p.166). Wittgenstein never departed from the *Tractarian* view that "the word 'philosophy' must mean something that stands above or below, but not beside the natural sciences" (TLP 4.111), and he was adamant that philosophy, done properly, "just puts everything before us, and neither explains nor deduces anything" (PI §126). While philosophical illumination may result in the betterment of the individual, the proper end of philosophy is not social improvement. Even when it comes to language, philosophy "leaves everything as it is" (PI §124). Such differences of philosophical temper may also lie behind OC §422.

It is one thing, however, to understand the differences between Wittgenstein's philosophy and the spirit of pragmatism, another to take a view about how significant those differences are, whether, in view of all the affinities, they might be surmounted, and if so, where the path to reconciliation may lie. Those are issues over which reasonable people, including the authors of this chapter, may fail to see eye-to-eye.

References

Baker, G.P. and Hacker, P.M.S. (1985/2014). *Wittgenstein: Rules, Grammar and Necessity. Volume 2 of an Analytical Commentary on the Philosophical Investigations. Essays and Exegesis of §§185–242*. Second edition. Extensively revised by P.M.S. Hacker. Oxford: Wiley-Blackwell.

Brandom, R. (1994). *Making it Explicit*. Cambridge, MA: Harvard University Press.

Clifford, W.K. (1879). The Ethics of Belief. In W.K. Clifford. *Lectures and Essays* (Vol. 2, pp.177–211). Ed. L.S. Pollock and F. Pollock. London: Macmillan.

Glock, H.-J. (1996). *A Wittgenstein Dictionary*. Oxford: Blackwell.

Glock, H.-J. (2005). Ramsey and Wittgenstein: Mutual Influences. In M.J. Frápolli (Ed.). *F.P. Ramsey: Critical Assessments* (pp.41–68). London: Continuum.

Goodman, R. (1998). Wittgenstein and Pragmatism. *Parallex*, 4, 91–105.

Goodman, R. (2002). *Wittgenstein and William James*. Cambridge: Cambridge University Press.

Haack, R. (1982). Wittgenstein's Pragmatism. *American Philosophical Quarterly*, 19, 163–171.

Hallett, G. (1977). *A Companion to Wittgenstein's Philosophical Investigations*. Ithaca: Cornell University Press.

James, W. (1890). *The Principles of Psychology*. Reprinted in W. James. (1975–1988). *The Works of William James* (Vols 8 and 9). Ed. F.H. Burkhard, F. Bowers, and I.K. Skrupskelis. Cambridge, MA: Harvard University Press.

James, W. (1896). The Will to Believe. Reprinted in W. James. (1975–1988). *The Works of William James* (Vol. 6). Ed. F.H. Burkhard, F. Bowers, and I.K. Skrupskelis. Cambridge, MA: Harvard University Press.

James, W. (1902). *Varieties of Religious Experience*. Reprinted in W. James. (1975–1988). *The Works of William James* (Vol. 15). Ed. F.H. Burkhard, F. Bowers, and I.K. Skrupskelis. Cambridge, MA: Harvard University Press.

James, W. (1907). *Pragmatism*. Reprinted in W. James. (1975–1988). *The Works of William James* (Vol. 1). Ed. F.H. Burkhard, F. Bowers, and I.K. Skrupskelis. Cambridge, MA: Harvard University Press.

McDowell, J. (1998). *Mind, Value, and Reality*. Cambridge, MA: Harvard University Press.

Misak, C. (1991). *Truth and the End of Inquiry: A Peircean Account of Truth*. Oxford: Oxford University Press.

Moore, G.E. (1907). Professor James's *Pragmatism*. *Proceedings of the Aristotelian Society*, 8, 33–77.

Passmore, J. (1957/68). *A Hundred Years of Philosophy*. Second edition. Harmondsworth: Penguin.

Peirce, C.S. (1931–58). *Collected Papers of Charles Sanders Peirce. 8 Vols*. Vols 1–6 ed. C. Hartshorne and P. Weiss. Vols 7–8 ed. A. Burks. Cambridge, MA: Belknap Press.
Peirce, C.S. (1963). *Charles S. Peirce Papers*. Cambridge, MA: Houghton Library, Harvard University.
Peirce, C.S. (1976). *Mathematical Philosophy: New Elements of Mathematics* (Vol. 4). Ed. C. Eisele. The Hague: Mouton.
Peirce, C.S. (1982–99). *The Writings of Charles S. Peirce: A Chronological Edition. 6 Vols*. Ed. N. Hauser, M. Fisch, and E. Moore. Bloomington: Indiana University Press.
Pratt, J.B. (1909). *What is Pragmatism?*. New York: Macmillan.
Putnam, H. (1995). *Pragmatism*. Oxford: Blackwell.
Ramsey, F.P. (1926/90). Truth and Probability. Reprinted in F.P. Ramsey. *Philosophical Papers* (pp. 52–94). Ed. D.H. Mellor. Cambridge: Cambridge University Press.
Ramsey, F.P. ([1927–29] 1991). *On Truth: Original Manuscript Materials (1927–1929) from the Ramsey Collection at the University of Pittsburgh*. Ed. N. Rescher and U. Majer. Dordrecht: Kluwer.
Russell, B. (1909). Pragmatism. Reprinted in B. Russell. (1993). *Logical and Philosophical Papers, 1909–13* (pp. 257–284). Ed. J.G. Slater. London: Routledge.
Russell, B. (1910). William James's Conception of Truth. Reprinted in B. Russell. (1966/2009). *Philosophical Essays* (pp. 104–122). London: Routledge.
Sahlin, N.-E. (1997). "He is no good for my Work": On the Philosophical Relations between Ramsey and Wittgenstein. In M. Sintonen (Ed.). *Knowledge and Inquiry: Essays on Jaakko Hintikka's Epistemology and Philosophy of Science* (pp. 61–84). New York: Rodopi.
Schiller, F.C.S. (1932). The Value of Formal Logic. *Mind*, 41, 53–71.
von Wright, G.H. (1967). A Biographical Sketch. In K.T. Fann (Ed.). *Ludwig Wittgenstein: The Man and his Philosophy* (pp. 13–29). New York: Dell.

Further Reading

Diamond, C. (1988). Throwing Away the Ladder: How to Read the *Tractatus*. *Philosophy*, 63, 5–27.
Methven, S.J. (2014). Whistling in 1929: Ramsey and Wittgenstein on the Infinite. *European Journal of Philosophy*. doi: 10.1111/ejop.12089.
Misak, C. (2011). American Pragmatism and Indispensability Arguments. *Transactions of the Charles S. Peirce Society*, 47, 261–273.
Misak, C. (2016). *Cambridge Pragmatism: From Peirce and James to Ramsey and Wittgenstein*. Oxford: Oxford University Press.
Moyal-Sharrock, D. (2004). Introduction: The Idea of a Third Wittgenstein. In D. Moyal-Sharrock (Ed.). *The Third Wittgenstein* (pp. 1–12). Aldershot: Ashgate.

49

Wittgenstein and Naturalism

CHRISTOPHER HOOKWAY

"Naturalism" is a controversial label in philosophy. It can express the rejection of all things "supernatural" and the refusal to embrace a priori rationalism. And it can also be presented as a manifestation of scientism, the refusal to draw any distinctions between philosophy and the sciences. If we ask "Is Wittgenstein's philosophy naturalistic?," different answers can be given, depending upon how we understand "nature" and which applications and uses of "nature" we are concerned with. In this introduction we shall describe three ways in which the debate may be held.

One origin of contemporary debates about naturalism goes back to century-old debates about psychologism in logic. John Stuart Mill, among others, claimed that psychology could provide theoretical foundations for research in logic (1843). This stance could be adopted because, it was held, logic was concerned with belief and inference, and psychology was our best source of information about the character of belief and reasoning. Logicians such as Frege, Husserl, Peirce, and others emphasized that logic was concerned with normative issues about how we *should* reason and about the validity of arguments. When Christof Sigwart provided grounds for logic in "feelings of logicality," he was charged with ignoring the objectivity of logicality. And when it was noted that logic had a role in the regulation of psychological reasoning, it was argued this would lead to circularity. Thus Peirce argued that there could be no role for the natural sciences in "normative logic" (Hookway, 2012, ch.5; Hanna, 2006).

Similar debates have emerged from Quine's endorsement of naturalized epistemology (1969, pp.69–90). Quine argued that the relations between experience and our beliefs were a causal matter that could be best studied in psychology. This led to the conclusion that logic should depend upon the natural sciences and, indeed – according to the holist Quine – that disciplines such as logic and probability theory could count as natural sciences.

Traditionally, naturalists seek to bring together philosophy and the natural sciences; physicalism, i.e., the view that only the phenomena reckoned with by physics exist, is a philosophical outlook characteristic of naturalism. But there are other forms of naturalism too. Naturalism has implications for metaphysics and epistemology as well as other areas of philosophy. In metaphysics, naturalists are likely to see their subject

---

A Companion to Wittgenstein, First Edition. Edited by Hans-Johann Glock and John Hyman.
© 2017 John Wiley & Sons, Ltd. Published 2017 by John Wiley & Sons, Ltd.

matter as composed of things that can be described in the natural sciences. A naturalist will deny that anything exists beyond the "natural world"; there is nothing supernatural. But some naturalists, notably Quine, countenance abstract entities (in Quine's case of an extensional kind) insofar as assuming their existence plays a useful or indispensable role in the theories of natural science.

The vagueness of "naturalism" means that the question of whether Wittgenstein was a naturalist, or was sympathetic to naturalism to some degree, is not easy to answer. We shall begin by identifying a form of naturalism that Wittgenstein would definitely have rejected; we shall show how Wittgenstein's positions in *Tractatus Logico-Philosophicus*, *Philosophical Investigations*, and some of his later writings are not compatible with naturalism so understood. Then we shall examine some views from all of these writings that might be described as having a naturalistic character. In the process of doing this, we will obtain a better understanding of what naturalism can involve.

The debate over naturalism, as we shall understand it, involves adopting distinctive kinds of methods to be employed in philosophy. Let us begin with a distinctive explanation of naturalism that would be employed both by some philosophers who endorse it and by others who reject it. This explanation involves the following three elements:

(a) Philosophy seeks the correct answers to philosophical questions or problems.
(b) As with scientific problems, we seek a body of philosophical theory that can be used to find answers to these questions, to provide philosophical explanations.
(c) Philosophical theory does not differ from other kinds of scientific theory: we test our theories empirically using the method of science; and we are ready for our theories to exploit results from natural sciences such as psychology, evolutionary biology, and neuroscience.

The philosophical problems that we face include epistemological questions about how we can answer skepticism, logical questions about the normative standards we should adopt in our reasoning and inquiry, and metaphysical issues concerning the nature of necessity and questions about universals and laws. The most important feature of this kind of naturalism is that it holds that philosophy is concerned with finding *explanations* and it expects to provide these explanations by providing *theories* that resemble causal scientific ones (on the question of what type of explanation Wittgenstein inveighed against see Chapter 37, WITTGENSTEIN ON CAUSATION AND INDUCTION).

In its most extreme form, naturalism treats philosophy as part of natural science, and we must keep this position in mind when we study Wittgenstein's views about naturalism. Wittgenstein would reject this sort of view, in particular because he rejects the ideas that philosophy should seek explanations and theories. We shall explore both some of Wittgenstein's reasons for rejecting this picture of the role for philosophy and also consider some ideas that have affinities to naturalism in some of his writings.

We will not discuss all of the writings in which Wittgenstein discussed naturalistic issues, instead focusing on passages where he explicitly used words like "natural." First, we address themes in the *Tractatus*, focusing on Wittgenstein's remarks about "natural science." Then we shall examine the views that emerge in Wittgenstein's later work, beginning with his remarks about the importance for philosophy of studying the "natural history of mankind."

CHRISTOPHER HOOKWAY

1 Tractatus Logico-Philosophicus

At a first reading, Wittgenstein's *Tractatus Logico-Philosophicus* provides a substantive philosophical theory that gives a systematic account of the nature of reality and of representation, and explains the foundations of logic and mathematics (see Chapter 17, LOGIC AND THE *TRACTATUS*; and Chapter 18, WITTGENSTEIN'S EARLY PHILOSOPHY OF MATHEMATICS). It appears that he seeks theoretical explanations in philosophy. In that case, we expect to ask whether our knowledge of this philosophical vision is grounded naturalistically, making use of experience, or of scientific knowledge or whether this knowledge is a priori and grounded in a rationalist manner or through Kantian transcendental reasoning. His philosophical outlook would be naturalistic only if he articulated a philosophical theory that was intended to form part of natural science.

In fact, Wittgenstein refused to formulate the issue in this way and his relations to naturalism are more complex and indirect than may be expected. We shall argue that he rejected naturalism when it is formulated as above, but that he might be described as endorsing a more sophisticated form of naturalism. He seems to hold the following relevant views:

(1) All knowledge is naturalistic.
(2) All the assertions that can be legitimately endorsed by philosophers are not naturalistic.
(3) There can be no philosophical knowledge.

The option of denying the possibility of philosophical knowledge was adopted not just by the *Tractatus* but also by Schlick. It means that one needs to distinguish between *epistemic* naturalism, the claim that all knowledge is of a scientific kind, and *metaphilosophical* naturalism, the idea that philosophy is part of or continuous with science. The *Tractatus* and Schlick were committed to the former while rejecting the latter (see Glock, 2008, pp.138–9).

We shall defend this understanding of the place of naturalism in the *Tractatus* and evaluate his position. The most important sources are found in the passage beginning at 4.11.

First, he tells us that "philosophy is not one of the natural sciences," adding that "the word 'philosophy' must mean something whose place is above or below the natural sciences" (4.111). He also distances himself from naturalism by denying the relevance to philosophy of two disciplines that philosophers sympathetic to naturalism are most likely to use in developing their philosophical theories: "Psychology is no more closely related to philosophy than any other natural science"; "Darwin's theory has no more to do with philosophy than any other hypothesis in natural science" (4.1121).

What Wittgenstein means by "natural science" here is not easy to clarify. He gives no explanation of the term, and he gives few examples of natural sciences. To be a meaningful proposition and to be a hypothesis of a natural science may be the same thing. At any rate, Wittgenstein contrasts them not just with the nonsensical pronouncements of metaphysics and ethics, but also with tautologies and contradictions, which are limiting cases of propositions with a sense, senseless yet not nonsensical. He says nothing about the methods that are employed in natural sciences, and it is left open whether all natural sciences employ the same methods. Indeed, his introduction of the term "natural science" (4.11) says no more than this: "The totality of true propositions is the whole of natural science." Thus he does not follow many natural scientists in claiming that their inquiries depend upon induction. At 6.31, Wittgenstein observes that induction cannot be a law of logic, "because it is obviously a proposition with sense." He continues, "the procedure of induction consists in accepting as true the *simplest* law that can be reconciled with our experience" and concludes that adoption of this procedure "has no logical justification" (6.363–6.3631). So long as a discipline seeks truths that conform to the picture theory of meaning, there may be room for methodological pluralism within the natural sciences.

According to Wittgenstein, philosophy "is not a doctrine but an activity." The activity in question aims at "the logical clarification of thought" (4.112) and thereby of propositions. It is needed because "without philosophy thoughts are, as it were, cloudy and indistinct: its task is to make them clear and to give them sharp boundaries" (4.112). He also says that philosophy "must set limits to what cannot be thought" (4.114). In that case, we face two questions. First: just how does this sort of clarification work? And, second: why is it not possible for philosophy to be a natural science?

Wittgenstein tells us that "propositions can represent the whole of reality" (4.12). But propositions cannot represent "what they have in common with reality in order to be able to represent it – logical form" (4.12). Philosophy is concerned with structural properties or internal properties. A property is internal when "it is unthinkable that its object should not possess it" (4.123). And, according to Wittgenstein, "it is impossible to assert by means of propositions that such internal properties and relations exist" (4.1252). The idea here seems to be that these internal properties and relations are presuppositions of meaning and reference; they have to be taken for granted when we formulate a proposition. We cannot formulate or assert propositions about things that are, in effect, the presuppositions of all thought and meaning. Propositions can represent reality, but they cannot represent logical form: "In order to be able to represent logical form, we should be able to station ourselves with propositions somewhere outside logic, that is to say outside the world" (4.12).

It is at this point that Wittgenstein introduces the idea that things like logical form can only be *shown*: such forms manifest themselves to us, but we cannot express them in thought clearly or indeed meaningfully. The dichotomy between what can be said and what can be shown replaces the dichotomy between the empirical and the a priori or transcendental. We have a dichotomy between natural science and the non-propositional necessary conditions for the possibility of natural science with the aforementioned exceptions of tautologies and contradictions (see also Chapter 11, INEFFABILITY AND NONSENSE IN THE *TRACTATUS*).

How does Wittgenstein make philosophy a respectable discipline? What things are there for philosophy to do? We shall consider three passages. First, "philosophy sets limits to what can be thought; and in doing so, to what cannot be thought." In doing this it sets limits to "the much disputed sphere of natural science" (4.113). It does this by "presenting clearly what can be said" (4.115). This seems to say that our philosophical clarifications consist in uttering many clear propositions, providing many statements of natural science. So we become aware of the limits of thought by saying lots of things that can be said. This rests on the assumption that if we *do* assert a proposition clearly, then it is a meaningful proposition. And our asserting, or uttering, a proposition clearly shows or manifests that it is meaningful. Presumably we can't clearly *say* of some proposition that it is meaningful.

At the end of the book, Wittgenstein describes "the correct method in philosophy":

> to say nothing except what can be said, i.e. propositions of natural science – i.e. something that has nothing to do with philosophy – and then, whenever someone else wanted to say something metaphysical, to demonstrate to him that he had failed to give a meaning to certain signs in his propositions. Although it would not be satisfying to the other person – he would not have the feeling that we were teaching him philosophy – *this* method would be the only strictly correct one. (TLP 6.53)

David Pears describes this as a sort of conversation, and, if it works, it will enable participants to behave rationally, asserting propositions only if they are meaningful propositions of natural science. And they will be free of the tendency to make philosophical assertions. Moreover, as is well known, participation in such a conversation will enable us to see that many of the propositions that occur in the *Tractatus* were not meaningful propositions of natural science and, thus, were "meaningless" (6.54). The value of these "propositions" is a means/end value: reflecting on them enables us to reach a position where we no longer need them. In particular, they provide the guidelines for the process of critical analysis to which proper philosophy reduces, in particular guidelines for devising an ideal notation capable of capturing the logical syntax or grammar of language. (Cf. Chapter 10, RESOLUTE READINGS OF THE *TRACTATUS*, and Chapter 13, PHILOSOPHY AND PHILOSOPHICAL METHOD.)

So where does Wittgenstein stand on naturalism here? Wittgenstein recognizes no need for philosophical theory, naturalistic or otherwise. Thus he rejects the philosophical outlook described in the introduction. Philosophy is not engaging in a search for theory, and it is not seeking philosophical explanations. Thus far, his approach to philosophy is not naturalistic. However, he *does* hold that the correct method for philosophy is to utter nothing but naturalistic propositions: serious philosophy avoids anything that is not naturalistic. Psychological propositions can be used in the process of philosophical clarification, just as any other kind of proposition can. But their role does not consist in providing answers to questions and, it seems, their subject matter is philosophically irrelevant. The usage of these naturalistic propositions is a therapeutic one, but that does not undermine the general point that philosophers should only make naturalistic claims.

Exactly how this process of clarification works is not always easy to understand: Wittgenstein does not give concrete examples of how we are to clarify propositions, and neither does he provide illuminating accounts of how we should go about explaining that particular propositions are meaningless in carrying out his method (save, perhaps, the, admittedly gnomic, hints concerning the application of logic in 5.556ff).

The important point is that there is no respectable discourse that is not part of natural science. It is also important that Wittgenstein saw a need to write *Tractatus Logico-Philosophicus*, and Wittgenstein's readers have to study it in order to grasp what is most important in his philosophical activities. What is most fundamental to this understanding is something that cannot be said and can only be shown. Perhaps we cannot give a naturalistic account of what is most important to understanding. Philosophy does not provide theory and explanation, but the only propositions we can use are ones that could also be used by those who do seek scientific theories.

2 Philosophical Investigations

Most readers would probably have to acknowledge that the Wittgenstein of the *Tractatus* is not a naturalistic philosopher, even if his philosophical investigations involved researches in natural science. The philosophical use of natural science is too indirect, confined e.g., to references to the propositions of psychology (5.541) and to a very brief account of causality and physics (6.32–6.372). Does the same hold of *Philosophical Investigations?* Many philosophers would answer "No," and agree with Marie McGinn's claim that "the outlook of Wittgenstein's later philosophy, is thoroughgoing naturalism" (1989, p.147). She explains this as follows:

> The philosophical enterprise is conceived as the interrogation of a particular natural phenomenon – the phenomenon of a human practice – in the attempt to understand its workings in such a way that philosophical puzzlement and perplexity no longer arises. (McGinn, 1989, p.147)

However, there are some clues that lead us in the other direction: Wittgenstein continues to hold that there is no role for *theory* in philosophy; and philosophy is not interested in explanation. We shall examine a number of passages from Wittgenstein's later writings that support this reading. And, just as we started our examination of the *Tractatus* by considering passages in which Wittgenstein gave a central role to "natural science," we shall now begin with passages in which he gives a central role to "natural history." Unsurprisingly, Wittgenstein sees no role for the investigation of natural laws in philosophy. This is evident in *On Certainty*: he allows that we may follow natural laws in carrying out inferences, but this "is not an item in our considerations" (OC §135). Our philosophical needs are not fully met by appeal to a natural law; presumably we need to be able to understand the rationality of these inferences, and natural laws will not provide this.

We can now trace several themes in Wittgenstein's work that support the idea that his philosophy is naturalistic. The first is a Humean one, which is, as Pears puts it, "not to theorize about things but to describe them as we find them in daily life" (Pears, 1995, p.411). The strategy is naturalistic because it depends upon empirical observations of particular events and practices. We are not trying to identify rules and principles. It is naturalistic because we aim to describe natural objects, and because we employ natural, empirical methods in pursuing philosophical clarifications. And its most distinctive feature is that it abjures theory and transcendental arguments to the effect that language must possess certain features. On the other hand, as in the *Tractatus*, the philosophical goal is one of clarification.

Second, describing this practice, Wittgenstein wrote: "What we are supplying are really remarks in the natural history of human beings" (PI §415; RFM I §142). It is natural to think of natural history as a "naturalistic" discipline, one that relies on observation. However, Wittgenstein tells us that investigations into natural history do not involve discovering "curiosities" but, rather, it relies upon "observations that no one has doubted, but which have escaped remark only because they are always before our eyes" (PI §415; RFM I §142). The inquiry is observational, but it makes no observations of anything in particular.

This introduces a restricted kind of naturalism: philosophy involves observation, and Wittgenstein rejects Platonist rationalism; there is nothing supernatural in the world of

Philosophical Investigations. As in *Tractatus Logico-Philosophicus*, philosophy has no positive interest in philosophical theory. Philosophical observation is focused on particular cases, rather than on formulating generalizations. Moreover, the role of observation is largely therapeutic or critical; the observations enable us to escape from philosophical puzzles. Philosophy doesn't provide solutions to philosophical problems; it shows us how to reach a position where we can leave the problems behind.

Philosophers such as C.I. Lewis and Rudolf Carnap employed a distinction between analytic and synthetic propositions. Analytic propositions are true by definition, or they are a presupposition of the meanings of terms that they contain. Synthetic propositions are empirically testable using the method of science, and can be thought of as unproblematically naturalistic. If someone wants to inquire into whether bachelors can be married or whether red things are colored, we could remind them that we are already committed to their truth by our readiness to use the words "bachelor" and "red." Or we can urge them to observe just how we use these words. Even thinkers who reject the analytic/synthetic distinction could proceed in this way. A philosopher such as Quine would hold that the apparently special status of "red things are colored" is due to the fact that this proposition is deeply embedded in our web of beliefs and concepts. Although it is not "analytic," the proposition is one whose truth we are committed to because of its embedded position in our system of beliefs and concepts. This has similarities to what occurs when philosophers use everyday observations in order to disarm philosophical problems.

Wittgenstein doesn't use the analytic/synthetic distinction, but he does make the related claim that some propositions have a "grammatical" or conventional status. In *On Certainty*, he explains how some propositions form the "scaffolding" of our inquiries (OC §211). He explains this by writing that the "questions that we *raise and doubts* depend on the fact that some propositions are exempt from doubt; are as it were hinges on which those turn" (OC §§341–2). They are apparently empirical claims that also seem to function rather like rules; their special status "belongs to the logic of our scientific investigations" (OC §§341–2; for the debate on whether hinge propositions are part of grammar as Wittgenstein understood it see Glock, 2015). So the philosophers' everyday observations remind the speaker of the logical statuses that these ordinary propositions have: we are reminded of their rule-like character (see also Chapter 14, GRAMMAR AND GRAMMATICAL STATEMENTS and Chapter 15, THE AUTONOMY OF GRAMMAR).

What can we infer from this about Wittgenstein's attitude toward naturalism?

First, Wittgenstein tells us that "our considerations cannot be scientific ones" (PI §109). Indeed, he holds that "we may not advance any kind of theory" (PI §109).

Second, we learn that "we must do away with anything hypothetical in our considerations" (PI §109), i.e., no empirical conjectures of the kind featuring in natural science.

Third: "We must do away with all explanation, and description must take its place" (PI §109). He explains, very carefully, that these clarifications have a different role. This suggests that he is not seeking a philosophical theory. This means that he has common cause with his younger self: Wittgenstein continues to reject the possibility of naturalistic theories or explanations (see also Chapter 13, PHILOSOPHY AND PHILOSOPHICAL METHOD).

But in this case, room seems to be left open for positive philosophical activities that are not indirect. Philosophical insight can come from noticing important facts, even if they are facts that should not be surprising. As Wittgenstein puts it, we should not be making discoveries that conflict with preconceived ideas (PI §109).

Having dismissed any role for explanation in philosophy, Wittgenstein does identify a positive aspect for the descriptions that philosophers offer. First, the description that a philosopher uses "gets its light, that is to say its purpose, from the philosophical problems." These problems are not empirical ones and "they are solved rather, by looking into the workings of our language, and that in such a way as to make us recognize those workings – despite an urge to misunderstand them. The problems are solved, not by giving new information, but by arranging what we have already known" (PI §109). It provides us with "a clear view of our use of words" (PI §122). In an interesting passage, we are told that philosophical understanding consists in "seeing connexions" (PI §122). Moreover, it is in line with the anti-theory aspect of *Philosophical Investigations* that Wittgenstein advises that, when we face mathematical or logical problems, we should not expect to obtain help from a mathematical or logical discovery; we should seek a clear view of the troubling mathematical issues that will lead the contradiction to be resolved (PI §125).

> A perspicuous representation produces just that understanding which consists in 'seeing connexions'. [...] The concept of a perspicuous representation is of fundamental significance for us. (PI §122)

Hence:

> It is the business of philosophy, not to resolve a contradiction by means of a mathematical or logico-mathematical discovery, but to make it possible to get a clear view of the state of mathematics that troubles us: the state of contradiction is resolved. (PI §125)

3 Natural History

In a passage that is suggestive of naturalism, Wittgenstein began to describe the methods he employed in his philosophical writings as supplying "remarks in the natural history of human beings" (PI §415, RFM I §142; on Wittgenstein's conception of natural history see Schulte, 2004). Once again, he insisted that these observations did not provide surprising observations or "curiosities." Rather, as he had observed before, they provided observations that no one has doubted, but which have escaped remark because they are always before our ideas. We shall identify three aspects of Wittgenstein's thought that are relevant to finding a more sophisticated aspect to naturalism and nature.

First, Wittgenstein raises a question about how we should describe what happens when someone masters a language-game. He suggests that it would be wrong to say that "a child that has mastered a language-game must *know* certain things." At best, we can say that the child "must be able to do certain things," or the child "learns to act in such a way; and in so reacting it doesn't so far know anything" (OC §538). This kind of automatic capacity to act is one component of natural history. The connection with natural history is clarified when we are told that when a child acquires knowledge of natural history, this presupposes that she can ask "What is that plant called?" and can reply correctly to the question (OC §§534–5).

The emphasis here is on the automatic character of these verbal responses, and this feature is an important element in "natural history." The immediacy of our judgments or reactions appears to be one thing that he regards as an effect of human nature.

The second aspect of Wittgenstein's remarks about natural history involves the recognition of the contingent nature of our concepts. Once we allow that our concepts may have been different if facts of nature were different, then we could react in different ways to these questions.

And, thirdly, we might then consider how far our concepts are adequate to our needs in the circumstances in which we find ourselves. We could ask questions about what concepts we could adopt if we find ourselves in very different circumstances, or about how far our concepts would still meet our interests given such changes. These questions concern what Wittgenstein describes as the "basis of our grammar" (PI II 230), the psychological or biological processes whereby conceptual change might occur in these circumstances. Interesting as they are, these questions belong to natural science and are not relevant to philosophy.

Wittgenstein's remarks about natural history are likely to remind the reader of John McDowell's use of Aristotelian ideas in *Mind and World* (1994, 84ff). Our character is largely composed of dispositions and capacities that it is second nature for us to trust. Our trust in them is automatic, much of the time, and their use is a manifestation of our rationality and good sense. It is likely that such capacities are realized when we make our philosophical judgments, seeing how philosophical conundrums are resolved once we have a clear perception of our thought. This can be seen as part of our nature, the product of our teaching and experience, and the form taken by our reasoning and understanding. McDowell sees this as a distinctive kind of naturalism, one that relies on the importance of our natures, but without depending upon our possession of scientific knowledge of the laws that govern nature.

Wittgenstein recognized the philosophical importance of the fact that differences in facts of nature can lead to changes concerning which concepts we properly employ. We have to be careful in identifying the role of natural laws in all areas of philosophy. Wittgenstein points to different philosophical morals here: it leads us to resist the tendency to believe that certain concepts are "absolutely the right ones," and helps us to see that our concepts do not capture fundamental essences.

They are not of value to us solely because we need reliable predictions about in just what way our concepts would change in distinctive purposes. Our interest is in logical matters, not in natural science. Our interests are in "how human beings modify their concepts in response to experience" (Z §352).

> I am not saying: if such-and-such facts of nature were different people would have different concepts (in the sense of a hypothesis). But: if anyone believes that certain concepts are absolutely the correct ones, and that having different ones would mean not realizing something that we realize – then let him imagine certain very general facts of nature to be different from what we are used to, and the formation of concepts different from the usual ones will become intelligible to him. (PI II 230)

Wittgenstein appears to be arguing that the character of our concepts depends upon natural facts, and that our concepts could have been different if those natural facts had been different: "It is as if our concepts involved a scaffolding of facts" (Z §350). But the details of the naturalistic grounding of our concepts have no relevance to philosophy.

> That would presumably mean: If you imagine certain facts otherwise, describe them otherwise, than the way they are, then you can no longer imagine the application of

certain concepts, because the rules for their application have no analogue in the new circumstances. – So what I am saying comes to *this*: A law is given for human beings, and a jurisprudent may well be capable of drawing consequences for any case that ordinarily comes his way; thus the law evidently has its use, makes sense. Nevertheless its validity presupposes all sorts of things, and if the being that he is to judge is quite deviant from ordinary human beings, then e.g. the decision whether he has done a deed with evil intent will become not difficult but (simply) impossible. (Z §350)

"If human beings were not in general agreed about the colours of things, if undetermined cases were not exceptional, then our concept of colour could not exist." No: – our concept *would* not exist. (Z §351)

Indeed, he asks whether "certain facts are favourable to the formation of certain concepts":

And does experience teach us this? It is a fact of experience that human beings alter their concepts, exchange them for others when they learn new facts; when in this way, what was formerly important to them becomes unimportant, and *vice versa*. (Z §352)

4   Conclusions: Perspicuous Representations

In *Philosophical Investigations*, Wittgenstein observed that "the concept of a perspicuous representation is of fundamental significance for us" (PI §122). This need arises because "we do not command a clear view of the use of our words." This is particularly important if we agree that philosophical problems take the form: "I don't know my way around." Our ordinary grammar lacks this kind of perspicuity, and it is the role for philosophy to help us to obtain it. (See also Chapter 16, SUVERYABILITY.)

We have to deploy different vocabularies and different methods depending upon our intellectual goals. If our aim is to arrive at new predictions and a better scientific understanding of our surroundings, our cognitive goals will be well served by the natural sciences: we need to be able to apply adequate scientific theories. One form of naturalism holds that the results of scientific theorizing provide us with the results required by philosophy. Once we can explain the events and processes that inhabit the natural world, many of our cognitive needs can be met. But according to Wittgenstein, the challenges that give rise to philosophical problems cannot be answered by scientific explanations. We need to guide reasoning effectively and to grasp how we can avoid the emergence of contradictions. In that case, we are not simply looking for an answer to a question.

As Wittgenstein put it, philosophy needs to make observations, but the observations we make are of things that are obvious, that surprise us only because of their familiarity. We also have to use observation to learn how to identify the connections between experiences that enable us to resolve philosophical problems. Whether that is enough to make philosophy naturalistic is unclear. There is one further reason to suggest that Wittgenstein does endorse a distinctive kind of naturalism: our ability to make these observations and resolve these problems depends upon our nature, including the traits that ensure that it is second nature for us to deal with our experience in these ways.

References

Glock, H.-J. (2008). *What is Analytic Philosophy?* Cambridge: Cambridge University Press.
Glock, H.-J. (2015). Philosophy Rehinged? In A. Coliva and D. Moyal-Sharrock (Eds). *The International Journal for the Study of Scepticism* (Special Issue): *Hinge Epistemology: Basic Beliefs after Moore and Wittgenstein*, 274–308.
Hanna, R. (2006). *Rationality and Logic*. Cambridge, MA: MIT Press.
Hookway, C.J. (2012). *The Pragmatic Maxim: Essays on Peirce and Pragmatism*. Oxford: Oxford University Press.
McDowell, J.H. (1994). *Mind and World*. Cambridge, MA: Harvard University Press.
McGinn, M. (1989). *Sense and Certainty: A Dissolution of Scepticism*. Oxford: Basil Blackwell.
Mill, J.S. (1843). *A System of Logic, Ratiocinative and Inductive*. London: Routledge and Kegan Paul.
Pears, D. (1995). Wittgenstein's Naturalism. *The Monist*, 78, 411–424.
Quine, W.V. (1969). *Ontological Relativity and Other Essays*. New York: Columbia University Press.
Schulte, J. (2004). Readings of "Natural History" and Ways of Making Sense of Other People. In T. Demeter (Ed.). *Essays on Wittgenstein and Austrian Philosophy* (pp.179–195). Amsterdam: Rodopi.

Further Reading

Hookway, C.J. (1996). Perspicuous Representations. In R.L. Arrington and H.-J. Glock (Eds). *Wittgenstein and Quine* (pp.62–79). London and New York: Routledge.
Keil, G. (2008). Naturalism. In D. Moran (Ed.). *The Routledge Companion to Twentieth-Century Philosophy* (pp.254–307). London: Routledge.
McGinn, M. (2010). Wittgenstein and Naturalism. In D. Macarthur and M. de Caro (Eds). *Naturalism and Normativity* (pp.322–351). New York: Columbia University Press.
Philström, S. (2003). *Naturalizing the Transcendental: A Pragmatic View*. New York: Humanity Books.

50

Wittgenstein and Continental Philosophy

STEPHEN MULHALL

Before attempting to relate Wittgenstein's work to that of continental philosophy, we need to acknowledge just how contentious the term "continental philosophy" actually is.

For most of the twentieth century, academic philosophy in the English-speaking world was conducted in ways that made no such acknowledgment. On the contrary, it presupposed that there was a clearly-understood and clear-cut choice to be made between two fundamentally different traditions or approaches to the subject, the analytic and the continental, with most philosophy departments in that world choosing to identify themselves as analytic. And since Wittgenstein's work, both early and late, is deeply woven into the origins and development of what was referred to as analytic philosophy, this presupposition in turn made it seem self-evident that his writings should be characterized as essentially analytic, so that his relation to continental philosophy could be simply characterized in wholly negative terms – as essentially uncontinental, and most likely anti-continental, that is, not only having nothing in common with that other tradition, but also providing distinctive terms for its criticism.

However, even the labels used to articulate this supposedly fundamental division raise suspicions about its intelligibility, let alone its usefulness. For they define one side in terms of allegiance to a certain method – that of the analysis of language or concepts – and the other in terms of a geographical location. Bernard Williams once compared it to an attempt to divide cars into front-wheel drive and Japanese. This peculiar cross-categorization also obscures the fact that many of the most influential members of the analytic tradition, including Wittgenstein himself, came from continental Europe, and that some philosophy departments in both North America and the United Kingdom stubbornly retained an allegiance to continental ways of doing things. It seems unwise to place much initial trust in such a patently misbegotten dichotomy.

Nevertheless, good sense can be made of the idea that there is or was such a thing as the analytic tradition in philosophy, and that Wittgenstein was central to its development. Simplifying ruthlessly, we might distinguish three main evolutionary phases (see Glock, 2008). It began at the end of the nineteenth century in Cambridge, when Frege's and Russell's revolutionary developments in logical theory were then applied (with the help of G.E. Moore and the early Wittgenstein) to the field of philosophy, and purported to demonstrate that a clear understanding of the logical structure of language and thought revealed that many of the perennial problems of philosophy (to which its metaphysical theorizing was a response) were based on a misunderstanding of our means of representation. Its second phase was inaugurated when the Vienna Circle transformed the ideas contained in Wittgenstein's *Tractatus* into the tenets of logical positivism. Their verification principle condemned as meaningless not only all evaluative propositions, but also the metaphysical propositions and projects of the Western philosophical tradition; philosophy could therefore justify its own continued existence only by restricting itself to winnowing out the meaningless from the meaningful, and analyzing in further detail the logical structure of scientific propositions.

Political developments in Europe during the 1930s led many of the leading logical positivists to flee to America, thereby embedding their version of analytic philosophy into this new cultural context, just as Wittgenstein began to criticize the presuppositions of the *Tractatus* and develop a wholly new way of philosophizing (thereby inaugurating the third phase of analytic philosophy). On this later view, the confusions characteristic of philosophy could be clarified by means of a careful description of the overt grammatical structures of our ordinary practices of employing words, an approach that seemed to dovetail with that of J.L. Austin in Oxford, and brought about the brief hegemony of what became known as ordinary language philosophy. Its dominance was ultimately ended by the importation from America (in the 1960s and 1970s) of arguments and ideas associated with Quine and Davidson, which were themselves both developments of and critical reactions to the earlier American importation of logical positivism, and put in question any attempt sharply to distinguish the normative structure of language from its empirical content – a distinction without which it appeared that neither logical positivism nor ordinary language philosophy could continue to defend its methods. At this point, analytic philosophy began to fragment into an increasingly heterogeneous array of projects.

The story of analytic philosophy is relatively easily narrated at this level of generality, because it makes sense to regard it as a distinctive school or movement – a collective enterprise held together by shared (or at least overlapping) commitments to certain methods and doctrines that developed over time, but only within recognizable limits. Of course, any such narrative risks characterizing the contributions of individual members of the tradition in a way that underplays their individuality, and thereby underestimates the range and depth of disagreement between them. This is particularly important in Wittgenstein's case, since it is arguable that his early work was as radically critical of Frege's and Russell's philosophical orientation as it was supportive of it; that it was profoundly misunderstood by the Vienna Circle; and that his later work is less happily described as a final evolution in the development of analytic philosophy than as a fundamental internal critique of it.

However that may be, an analogous story cannot be told of continental philosophy, because that label was used to denote all the major philosophical schools or movements that held sway on the continent of Europe (primarily in Germany and France) from the death of Kant to the present day. It thus includes German idealism (especially Hegel), Marxism, Nietzschean genealogy (including Foucault), existentialism (from Kierkegaard to Sartre and Camus), phenomenology (from Husserl to Heidegger, Sartre, and Merleau-Ponty), critical theory (especially the work of Adorno, Horkheimer, and Habermas), deconstruction (Derrida), and so on. Analytic philosophy could usefully be compared with any one of these schools or movements, each of which *is* held together by certain shared commitments; but it makes no sense at all to compare it with all of them – as if there were some set of commitments that every one of them shared, or some particular continental philosopher who could go proxy for all.

So it is unsurprising that these continental philosophers never identified themselves as such (even if their stubborn Anglophone defenders were sometimes forced to do so). Rather like the idea of a continental breakfast, that of continental philosophy is one used primarily by those outside the cultures to which it primarily applies. It is, in short, essentially an invention of analytic philosophers, and applies to anything and everything in the post-Kantian philosophical scene that is not analytic philosophy. And it's true that many continental philosophers did (although each in different ways) reject commitments central to the analytic tradition – whether by questioning the priority of logical analysis, by pursuing avowedly metaphysical (and so purportedly meaningless) projects or at least taking them seriously enough to engage in critical dialogue with them (and so presenting the history of the subject as an essential context for its current work), or by aligning philosophy more with the humanities and social theory than with the natural sciences.

In that sense, there is a minimal (although essentially negative) descriptive content to the idea of continental philosophy. But it was never really a purely descriptive category; anyone who grew up within the philosophical culture that deployed it knew that it was a term of disapprobation, and at the limit a term of abuse. For it tended to be assumed (not entirely without justification, or at least provocation, in some cases) that continental philosophers not only did not do philosophy the right way, they did it in such a way as to threaten the very integrity of the subject: their querying of the philosophical value of formal logic was taken as a rejection of rational standards, and their willingness to construct metaphysical systems was taken as a willing embrace of obfuscation and nonsense. Continental philosophy was thus a kind of anti-philosophy, what Plato would have called sophistry (see Glendinning, 2006). Such an assumption is hardly likely to encourage rigorous or charitable engagements with the texts and traditions indiscriminately denoted by this label.

Clearly, then, we will have to make some preliminary assumptions about these textual fields if we are to have two sufficiently precisely defined phenomena of appropriately comparable scale to relate to one another with any prospect of illuminating either. So I propose to focus exclusively on the relationship between Wittgenstein's later philosophy and three philosophers who are commonly described as "continental": Heidegger, Derrida, and Nietzsche (without presupposing that the label is attached to tokens of a single general philosophical type, and with primary attention paid to Heidegger). This approach leaves open what form or forms the relation between Wittgenstein and continental philosophy might take. In the present context, the most pertinent possible modes of that relation would include: presenting Wittgenstein as a critic of the continental philosophers under consideration; presenting these continental philosophers as critical of Wittgenstein; identifying points at which Wittgenstein and these "continental" philosophers criticize similar philosophical targets, for similar reasons; and identifying methodological analogies between them – in particular, similarities between their conceptions of philosophy's nature and point.

Because the idea of a division between analytic and continental philosophy, and the related idea of Wittgenstein as an exemplary instance of the former approach, have gone so deep in Anglophone philosophical life, most of those willing to take an interest in the topic of this chapter have tended to assume that Wittgenstein's work is primarily a resource for criticizing continental philosophy (e.g., Stone, 2000; Rogers Horn, 2005). Of the rather smaller number of continental philosophers who have taken a similar interest, whilst some have been content to view Wittgenstein as one more suitable object of a given continental line of criticism, others have been more interested in identifying and elaborating analogies between his approach and that of some continental counterparts (e.g., Staten, 1984). And as the unquestionable status of the analytic/continental opposition has crumbled, along with the obviousness of Wittgenstein's analytic allegiances, as Anglophone philosophers became ever more aware of the historical specificity and internal complexity of the analytic tradition in the aftermath of its fragmentation, so more American and British philosophers have begun to explore those putative analogies (e.g., Glendinning, 1998 and 2007).

My treatment will primarily aim to identify overlapping targets and terms of criticism and methodological analogies, primarily by exploring relations between Wittgenstein and Heidegger, although I will also touch on themes in Derrida and Nietzsche. In so doing, I must assume the legitimacy of a particular reading of each; and I must likewise take for granted certain ways of reading Wittgenstein as a critic of analytic philosophy. Leaving myself unguarded in these ways is unavoidable; whether there are compensating benefits is for the reader to judge.

1 Heidegger and Wittgenstein: Beginning, Being, and Context

Heidegger's *Being and Time* begins with a quotation from Plato's *Sophist* (244a):

> 'For manifestly you have long been aware of what you mean when you use the expression "*being*". We, however, who used to think we understood it, have now become perplexed.'
> Do we in our time have an answer to the question of what we really mean by the word 'being'? Not at all. So it is fitting that we should raise anew *the question of the meaning of Being*. But are we nowadays even perplexed at our inability to understand the expression 'Being'? Not at all. So first of all we must reawaken an understanding for the meaning of this question. Our aim in the following treatise is to work out the question of the meaning of *Being*, and to do so concretely. Our provisional aim is the interpretation of *time* as the possible horizon for any understanding whatsoever of Being. (Heidegger, [1927] 1962, foreword)

Wittgenstein's *Philosophical Investigations* begins again in section 89, orienting its sustained discussion of its methods with a second quotation from Augustine, whose words also inaugurate the book's first section:

> [Logical investigation] arises neither from an interest in the facts of nature, nor from a need to grasp causal connections, but from an urge to understand the foundations, or essence, of everything empirical. Not, however, as if to this end we had to hunt out new facts; it is, rather, essential to our investigation that we do not seek to learn anything *new* by it. We want to *understand* something that is already in plain view. For *this* is what we seem in some sense not to understand.
> Augustine says in *Confessions* XI. 14, 'quid est ergo tempus? Si nemo ex me quaerat scio; si quaerenti explicare velim, nescio'. [What, then, is time? I know well enough what it is, provided that nobody asks me; but if I am asked what it is and try to explain, I am baffled.] –

This could not be said about a question of natural science ('What is the specific gravity of hydrogen?', for instance). Something that one knows when nobody asks one, but no longer knows when one is asked to explain it, is something that has to be *called to mind*. (And it is obviously something which, for some reason, it is difficult to call to mind.) (PI §89)

The network of specific differences between these two passages is difficult to evaluate, but the general similarity is hard to deny. For Heidegger sees in the words of Plato's Stranger from Elea exactly what Wittgenstein finds in those of Augustine: the onset of a prototypically philosophical mood or moment, in which a taken-for-granted understanding of something utterly everyday reveals itself to be unreliable, and thereby induces a tormenting bewilderment. Both thereby characterize a distinctively philosophical question as one expressive of disorientation rather than ignorance – a loss of one's bearings with respect to one's ordinary practical comprehension of things (centrally manifest in our ordinary capacity to talk about them); recovery from such bewilderment will therefore amount to an achievement of reorientation, to be brought about by re-collecting or re-membering the everyday, pre-theoretical understanding with which we have somehow lost touch. And both suspect us of overlooking the significance of questions of this kind – of failing to be struck by the distinctiveness of such questions, and so by the sheer strangeness of the fact that we can find ourselves gripped by them; this is implicit in Heidegger's talk of our needing to "reawaken an understanding for the meaning of [such] questions," and in Wittgenstein's concluding registration of the sheer "difficulty" of responding to them in the way their distinctiveness requires.

Both certainly agree that the natural sciences (or indeed any ontic science, as Heidegger would call it – any body of systematic knowledge) could not help in this kind of task. They further agree that recovering the relevant understanding is in the first instance a matter of calling to mind what we mean by the relevant words or expressions. To be sure, Augustine expresses bewilderment about a phenomenon, whereas the Eleatic Stranger is perplexed by an expression; but Wittgenstein quickly interprets Augustine's condition as one to be addressed by reminding him of the various kinds of statement we make about that phenomenon, just as Heidegger moves happily between talk of inquiring into the meaning of "Being" and talk of inquiring into the meaning of Being. Each therefore presupposes that recovering our understanding of an expression and recovering our understanding of that to which it refers are internally related.

Admittedly, where Heidegger presents grasping the meaning of one particular expression as the fundamental philosophical project, Augustine is specifically baffled by a different expression, and Wittgenstein anyway appears less concerned with which expression that is than with the exemplary nature of the bafflement it induces and the means for its alleviation – as if the moral to be drawn concerns the capacity of any and every expression at once to induce such bafflement and to provide the grammatical means for its overcoming. On the other hand, Heidegger no sooner identifies "Being" as his privileged term than he claims that the perplexity it induces can be addressed only by relating it to the very term about which Augustine expresses bewilderment – that of "time"; and it soon turns out that the privilege granted to "Being" is granted precisely because a grasp of its meaning is internal to grasping the meaning of pretty much anything:

> Whenever one cognises anything or makes an assertion, whenever one comports oneself towards entities, even towards oneself, some use is made of 'Being' [...]. 'The sky *is* blue', 'I *am* merry' and the like. (Heidegger, [1927] 1962, 1.23)

Heidegger quickly emphasizes the breadth of this range of reference. For his key introductory elucidation of the term "Being" runs as follows:

> In the question which we are to work out, *what is asked about* is Being – that which determines entities as entities, that on the basis of which entities are already understood [...]. The Being of entities 'is' not itself an entity [...]. Being is always the Being of an entity. (Heidegger, [1927] 1962, 1.25–6, 2.29)

"Being" is not an entity, not an object or a property of an object, but that which determines any and every object as an object, which means determining it as an object of a particular kind or nature (hence necessarily equipped with properties of a particular kind or nature), and as really existing as opposed to not being there; to be a particular kind of thing, that thing must be, and nothing can be without being something in particular (possessed of an underlying or essential nature). Hence, Being is met with always and only as the Being of an entity; but by the same token it is necessarily encountered whenever one encounters anything.

Heidegger's careful alignment of an understanding of Being as "that which determines entities as entities" with an understanding of it as "that on the basis of which entities are understood" makes it hard to overlook the analogy with Wittgenstein's conception of grammar as revelatory of the underlying nature of things – as articulated in his claim that "Essence is expressed in grammar" (PI §371). Wittgenstein's formulation is also simultaneously turned toward reality and toward our means and modes of understanding it (thereby presenting them as internally related); and it is equally general in its implications – it is the essential nature of anything whatever that finds expression in the grammar of our expressions for it.

Since Wittgenstein's methodological assumptions are in this respect far closer to Heidegger's than one might have expected, it's worth considering the possibility that other aspects of Heidegger's conception of Being might bring out dimensions of Wittgenstein's conception of grammar that would otherwise escape our notice. The dimension I want to highlight here is Heidegger's sense that the various different ways in which entities disclose themselves to us are simultaneously interwoven with one another – that they display what Aristotle called a unity of analogy, or a categorical interconnectedness.

Heidegger thinks of ontic sciences such as biology, history, and physics as what results from our making an issue of our implicit everyday understanding of a given range of the world we inhabit; we rigorously thematize it with a view to systematically interrogating it, and develop thereby a body of knowledge that may surpass or even subvert our initial understanding, but that is made possible by it and that is no less open to further questioning. In particular, everything we thereby come to know takes for granted certain basic ways in which the ontic science demarcates and structures its own area of study – conceptual and methodological resources that can themselves be thematized and interrogated (when, for example, a philosopher of science inquires into the validity of inductive reasoning). Such inquiries concern the conditions for the possibility of such scientific theorizing, what Heidegger calls the ontological presuppositions of ontic inquiry; and whether one inquires into them as a practitioner of the discipline or as a philosopher, the subject matter could not be within the purview of a purely intra-disciplinary inquiry (which would necessarily presuppose what is here being put in question). It is, in short, the business of philosophy.

The object of investigation here is a regional ontology; every region of ontic knowledge presupposes one, and thus invites this kind of questioning. And the results of that questioning themselves provoke further inquiry: given that each ontic region discloses an ontology, the relations between the various regional ontologies inevitably become a matter for philosophical inquiry. For on the one hand, each ontology will differ from others, as each ontic region has its own distinctive nature. But on the other, each region may open up onto cognate regions (as chemistry might shed light on biology, or as Heidegger thinks theology has deformed anthropology, psychology, and biology ([1927] 1962, p.10)), thus revealing that its ontology bears upon those others; and of course each regional ontology is an ontology – each performs the same determinative function with respect to its region, each determines the Being of a certain range or domain of beings, even if differently in each case. How, then, is this synthesis – this plaiting or interweaving – of categorial diversity and categorial unity to be understood? What is it for beings to be? This is the question of the meaning of Being – what Heidegger calls the enterprise of fundamental ontology.

Note that Heidegger does not and could not think of fundamental ontology as an inquiry into some domain that is essentially distinct from (say, foundational in relation to) regional ontological inquiry – as if Being as such had a domain of its own in addition to the domains of regional ontology, as if we could directly contemplate Being as opposed to one of its regions. On the contrary, since Being is always the Being of some entity or other, the question of fundamental ontology must always take regional ontologies and their interrelations as its concern; and anyone who pursues a given regional ontological inquiry without reflecting upon how, if at all, its deliverances and presuppositions relate to those of other such inquiries is simply failing to pursue that inquiry in a properly rigorous manner. Fundamental ontology is regional ontology radicalized, or fully realized; it is not an alternative or supplement to regional ontological inquiry, but a manner of relating oneself to it.

The relevant relation is one that acknowledges (as opposed to either repressing or prematurely fixing) the inherently and multiply situated or contextual nature of regional ontological inquiry: the way in which it relates to other regional ontological inquiries (or might do so otherwise, or utterly fails to do so), which involves acknowledging the way in which the ontic science from which it arises relates to other ontic sciences (or might so relate or fails to), which in turn involves acknowledging the way in which the aspect of our pre-theoretical understanding of things from which that science arises relates to other aspects of that understanding (or fails to). Every one of these nodes or elements – be it a branch of philosophy, a means of acquiring knowledge, or a mode of practical activity – is what it is by virtue of its actual and possible relations to all of the others; so a proper grasp of any requires acknowledging that relatedness as an undismissable issue, something about which questions can always be posed and inquiries pursued.

Call this Heidegger's context principle: its implications are widely ramifying, but for present purposes, one is most pertinent. Since philosophy is parasitic upon the ontic sciences, then insofar as its constituent regional ontological inquiries hang together with one another, so must the ontic sciences from which those inquiries take their bearing. Their results hang together internally (making it possible to form coherent bodies of knowledge, as opposed to accumulations of purely local data) and externally (insofar as the understanding they systematize has a possible bearing upon other such forms of understanding – whether by complementing, qualifying, challenging, or otherwise putting it in question). And for Heidegger, if the ontic sciences (and the pre-theoretical understanding that engenders them) did not manifest this kind of unity-in-diversity, then to precisely that extent the idea that they are ways of disclosing a reality that holds (and holds together) independently of our ways of grasping it would lack any genuine substance.

It is the multiple bearings of each such mode of inquiry on other such modes that gives substance to the thought that each mode gets a purchase on some aspect of things as they really are. For they make manifest that and how the purchase that each offers hangs together with the purchase offered by other such modes. Hence, to show that and how these inquiries relate to one another just *is* to show that genuine comprehension is attainable by their means – that each can claim to articulate a way of distinguishing reality from illusion, a way of getting at the truth of things; and to show that each really is a way of getting to grips with reality just *is* to show that there is a multifaceted reality with which we might intelligibly get to grips.

In short: to think of the question of the meaning of Being as a genuine question is to think of our ontic sciences and their pre-theoretical antecedents as genuine modes of understanding – as ways of disclosing how things really are; it is to think of them as discursive articulations that are also articulations of reality.

What bearing do these matters have on Wittgenstein? The short answer is: they might lead us to reconsider the significance of Wittgenstein's own context principle: "To imagine a language means to imagine a form of life" (PI §19). A longer answer would take us back to the first appearance of Augustine in Wittgenstein's text, at the very beginning of *Philosophical Investigations*, which Wittgenstein's most recent translators render into English as follows:

> When grown-ups named some object and at the same time turned towards it, I perceived this, and I grasped that the thing was signified by the sound they uttered, since they meant to point it out. This, however, I gathered from their gestures, the natural language of all peoples, the language that by means of facial expression and the play of eyes, the movements of the limbs and the tone of voice, indicates the affections of the soul when it desires, or clings to, or rejects, or recoils from, something. In this way, little by little, I learnt to understand what things the words, which I heard uttered in their respective places in various sentences, signified. And once I got my tongue around these signs, I used them to express my wishes. (PI §1 [Augustine, *Confessions*, I.8])

Wittgenstein detects in this passage a particular picture of the essence of human language ("the words in language name objects – sentences are combinations of such names"), notes that Augustine "does not mention any difference between kinds of word," and then asks us to think of the following use of language:

> I send someone shopping. I give him a slip of paper marked 'five red apples'. He takes the slip to the shopkeeper, who opens the drawer marked apples; then he looks up the word 'red' in a chart and finds a colour sample next to it; then he says the series of elementary number-words – I assume that he knows them by heart – up to the word 'five', and for each number-word he takes an apple of the same colour as the sample out of the drawer. – It is in this and similar ways that one operates with words. (PI §1)

And in the very next section, he invites us to imagine a language for which the description given by Augustine is right:

> The language is meant to serve for communication between a builder A and an assistant B. A is building with building stones: there are blocks, pillars, slabs and beams. B has to pass him the stones and to do so in the order in which A needs them. For this purpose they make use of a language consisting of the words 'block', 'pillar', 'slab', 'beam'. A calls them out; B brings the stone which he has learnt to bring at such-and-such a call. – Conceive of this as a complete primitive language. (PI §2)

If we assume that the shopping trip exemplifies an ordinary operation with words for which the description given by Augustine is *not* right (Mulhall, 2001, queries this assumption), then what is it about that tale that resists Augustine's description? The most obvious such feature is the diversity of the kinds of words at work in the tale: although "apple" is a word of the kind that Wittgenstein claims Augustine was primarily thinking of (nouns and proper names), "red" and "five" are not. The contrast here with the builders seems clear, since all of their words are nouns, and indeed names for the same kind of object. Then we will take away from Wittgenstein's tale the moral that philosophers need to recall and display differences – that language-games are astonishingly various, and that this variety is itself subject to variation over time (as new games come into existence and others suffer obsolescence) (PI §23).

But an equally striking feature of the tale is the extent to which the three different words used by the list-writer, the shopper, and the shopkeeper interact with one another as smoothly as do the three people involved in this transaction – each word as if made to work in the company of the others. How the shopkeeper responds to the word "apple" certainly differs from his modes of response to the words "red" and "five," but those responses are coordinated: each relates him differently to a single line on the list, to the items inside one particular drawer, and to the contents of a single bag he finally hands over to the shopper – the five red apples on which all three words have an equal and integrated purchase, and without which this particular purchase could not have been planned or made. At the same time, part of the significance of the shopping list is that it asks for five red apples, and not five red tomatoes, or five green apples, or one red apple; it therefore involves grasping the way in which each of those three words operates within a more general linguistic field (those of number, color, and fruit) whose ranges of application connect the words on the shopping list to an indefinite variety of other contexts in which number words, color words, and words for fruit might be put to work. The grocer's counting aloud as he extracts apples from his drawer might equally well have accompanied a bird-watcher's annotation of her observations; the color chart he uses to discriminate between the items in his apple drawer might equally well have been used to pick out the right fabric with which to upholster his sofa; and the label on his apple drawer might equally well have been used beside an illustration in a child's alphabet book.

In short, each way of using these words in this context is what it is because it could also be employed elsewhere; the collective capacity of these words to effect an economic transaction at the grocer's is inseparable from their individual ability to effect a widely-ramifying range of equally but differently collaborative operations elsewhere, each differently dependent on the availability of other words with which to achieve something in a variety of other environments or work-worlds. Their individual significance is thus constituted by their distinctive place in an interlocking, overlapping, and crosscutting network of forms of human practical activity. By contrast, the builders' "language" consists of individual words that shun collaboration with each other – even, apparently, that of conjunction – and that conjure up no other obvious contexts of human practical activity into which they might fit, except perhaps other building sites, as long as they require no other kinds of building stone. It is precisely the perfection of their fit with the four kinds of object they name that reduces their capacity to transcend their current context toward a bare minimum, and raises the self-sufficiency of their mode of operation toward an airless maximum. Such a conjunction of the primitive and the complete risks depriving us of grounds for regarding what we have before us as a language at all; and what secures that conjunction is precisely the difficulty of regarding this tale, unlike that of the shopping trip, as a depiction of one amongst a variety of related ways in which one operates with words – as a situated part of a form of life with language.

So it is vitally important accurately to depict this variety and interrelatedness – call it the way in which words worthy of the name generalize, project themselves from context to context. This becomes clearer when, a few sections after introducing the builders, Wittgenstein restates his critique of Augustine's picture:

> If we say 'Every word in the language signifies something', we have so far said nothing *whatever*; unless we explain exactly *what* distinction we wish to make. [...]
>   Suppose someone said '*All* tools serve to modify something. So, a hammer modifies the position of a nail, a saw the shape of a board, and so on.' – and what is modified by a rule, a glue-pot and nails? – 'Our knowledge of thing's length, the temperature of the glue, and the solidity of a box.' – Would anything be gained by this assimilation of expressions? – (PI §§13–14)

This comparison of words to pieces of equipment naturally calls to mind Heidegger's attempt to clarify the distinctive nature of human modes of existence by means of a phenomenology of tools, objects understood as ready-to-hand, handy for the performance of certain tasks. His example is a hammer; and his complex analysis results in the claim that our ability to grasp a hammer as a hammer is ultimately conditioned by a socially-constituted web of assignments of significance or meaning. But he insists that these meaning-relations must not be understood in an overly formal or formalized way:

> The phenomenal content of these 'Relations' and 'Relata' [...] is such that they resist any sort of mathematical functionalization [: that is, having] their 'properties' defined mathematically in 'functional concepts'. They are rather relationships in which concernful circumspection as such already dwells. ([1927] 1962, pp.18, 121–2)

Heidegger's point is not just that the capacity to grasp a hammer as a hammer involves grasping its role in a complex web of interrelated carpentry equipment; for a hammer is not just something with one particular functional role in one precisely definable kind of practical activity. A hammer is certainly something we use to drive nails into surfaces: but anyone who understands its nature as a tool for this particular purpose must also possess an indefinite range of related know-how – when to use nails as opposed to screws and which kinds of nail in different cases, the variety of materials from which a usable hammer can be made (and when one material is more appropriate than another), and so on. Moreover, anyone who grasps a hammer as a hammer will also grasp the indefinite number of other tasks that a hammer can be used to perform (securing wedges, loosening joints, propping open windows, repelling intruders, playing "toss-the-hammer," and so on); and he will also grasp the ways in which an indefinite range of other objects might be used instead of a hammer – as a hammer – to perform any of these tasks. Knowing what a hammer is involves knowing all of this: it is an inherently open-ended capacity, one that cannot be captured by a finite list of precise rules. For our practical activities always engage with and are developed in specific situations, but there is no way of specifying a closed set of all the possible ways and contexts in which our knowledge of a hammer and its capacities might be pertinently deployed. This kind of (circumspective) understanding is more like a capacity to improvise in the face of unforeseen demands and opportunities – to find new ways of marrying tool to circumstance, of seeing how this object can be used to achieve this goal in these conditions, and thereby to deepen our understanding of just what it means for it to be a tool of this kind.

In the light of this understanding of tools, the critical force of Wittgenstein's analogy between the claim that all words signify something and the claim that all tools modify something takes on a new aspect. To be sure, he wants us to question whether anything is achieved by assimilating words and tools in the envisaged manner. If we stretch our initial everyday notion of "modification" so that it applies not only to those tools that we do normally say modify things (such as hammers) but also to tools about which that thought never crosses our mind (such as a glue-pot), we have to jettison more and more of its initial grammatical substance, to the point at which it becomes an empty form, which can be applied to any and every tool only because its applicability tells us nothing of substance about how any of them actually works. So advanced, the claim that "all tools modify something" does not even tell us something true about hammers, since it doesn't tell us anything at all.

But Wittgenstein doesn't ever say that the notion of "modification" cannot – with sufficient ingenuity and commitment – be extended far beyond its original sphere of reference; on the contrary, he offers us a short series of examples of exactly how that extension might be grounded (ones strangely reminiscent of his later willingness to allow that, and to show how, sense might be made of the idea that "roses have teeth" (PPF §314)). In short, he acknowledges that the term "modification" is itself inherently modifiable: it is precisely capable of being projected beyond its initial contexts of use in ways that were not always already encoded within it, but that are facilitated by our grasp of the shape or point of its uses within that context, and with respect to which we can elicit agreement from others.

So we cannot coherently respond to the Augustinian tool-characterizer by flatly denying that the term "modifier" can be applied to anything outside its initial context of use; that would be to deprive the term of the very open-endedness or projectibility – the modifiability – that is implicitly at work in the shopping trip tale, and that is fatefully reduced to a minimum in the builders' language-game (the "use" of "language" for which Augustine's description is right). Doing so would mean countering the Augustinian in a way that aligns us with his most fundamental confusion; and it would obscure the fact that what leads us into the distinctively philosophical condition of failing to mean anything by our words just when we take ourselves to be conveying a metaphysical revelation is the very projective capacity without which words simply would not be words. In this sense, Wittgenstein's vision of language locates the root of philosophical bewilderment in the nature of language itself, and not merely in some essentially accidental misapprehension of it.

So one might say that the analogy Wittgenstein draws between a claim about words and a claim about tools invites us to see that the former would be closer to the truth if it made use of the concept invoked in the latter. For the capacity of words to signify is in truth a matter of their being inherently modifiable, essentially open to new contexts of use in ways that illuminate further reaches of significance in both word and context. And one might further say that, so modified, the concept of modification is not far from the truth about tools either: characterizing a hammer's essence in terms of its ability to modify the position of a nail is both a profoundly misleading claim about its equipmental nature (insofar as it identifies that nature with one specific task, as the builders' language tethers each of its terms to one kind of object), and a profoundly illuminating way of conceiving it (insofar as it invites us to consider hammers, and by extension all tools, as inherently modifiable, adaptable in ranges of ways to ranges of equipmental and non-equipmental contexts). In short, the way to make both claims at once substantial and illuminating is to modify each in the light of the other.

2 Derrida and Nietzsche: Iterability and Asceticism

In conclusion, I shall gesture toward ways in which Wittgenstein's citations of Augustine might also facilitate a conversation with two other continental philosophers – Derrida and Nietzsche (the former inheriting Heidegger, the latter inherited by him).

Derridean concerns are at work in various ways when Wittgenstein responds to Augustine by telling the tale of a shopping trip. Anyone familiar with Derrida's writings about writing in relation to speech could hardly avoid being struck by the fact that, whereas Augustine's child is grappling with words as spoken by his elders as they go about their own business, Wittgenstein's shopper is operating with a written text, which functions in the absence of any oral contribution from its bearer. Furthermore, whereas the words in Augustine's tale coexist with those uttering and hearing them, never quite detaching themselves from (as if reinforced or substantiated by) their presence (and in particular by the child's presence to himself in his own consciousness), the shopping list achieves the satisfaction of the desires of its composer in his absence – quite as if unobtrusively endorsing Derrida's view that the meaningfulness of words is such as to make it necessarily possible that they can function in the absence of their author. Indeed, the implicit presence in Wittgenstein's tale of an indefinite range of interrelated contexts in which each word on that shopping list might find or resist finding a home, and in the absence of which they would not be the words they are, would for Derrida be another aspect of the iterability that the list-maker's absent presence already indicates.

When Derrida offered his first and (I believe only) reading of Wittgenstein (in Glendinning, 2001), it was a response to just this tale, and in particular to the shopkeeper's peculiarly externalized ways with words whose meaning he has patently internalized:

> To me what this description highlights is the installation of a certain 'technology', *through iterability*, within our mental operations [...]. [T]he technology which is implied in arithmetic, in calculation, in grammar, in semantics, and so on [...]. [This] would imply that a certain '*techne*' is already at work within the so-called 'private' or 'inner' sphere of mental operations [...]. But in the 'running' supposed by iterability, '*techne*' is not simply opposed to the possibility of a non-mechanical decision. Indeed it is its very chance [...]. Otherwise, that of which it is the chance would be [...] just a programmed effect implying a predictability or a pure know-how, which would be the annihilation of every responsibility. (p.117)

This reading positively demands further dialogue between Wittgenstein and Derrida – in the first instance, concerning the costs and benefits of aligning arithmetic and calculation with grammar and semantics in a list of "technologies" or "*techne*" (an alignment that Wittgenstein famously questions in questioning the analogy between language and calculi, despite the fact that his own rule-following remarks appear to treat the technique of expanding an arithmetical series as if it could be exemplary of the normativity of language use more generally). But of course, to claim that a technology is implicit in all the items on that list is not to say that it is involved in each in exactly the same way; and one should not overlook Derrida's resistance to any implication of a pure know-how – call it a philosophically purified conception of know-how: one that would make such understanding a matter of programming or the algorithmic, rather a matter of taking personal responsibility for the particular ways in which we find ourselves unpredictably willing to project the grammar of a word. His claim is not that iterability is either the mechanical aspect of a *techne*, or a composite of its mechanical and nonmechanical aspects; it is rather that iterability puts in question the idea that any kind of *techne* can be properly grasped except as involving both dimensions or aspects – each enabling and enabled by the other.

As for Nietzsche: dialogue might begin from Wittgenstein's response to his second citation of Augustine in reflecting on his philosophical methods, which he presents as counters to philosophy's drive to sublime the logic of our language. I've argued elsewhere that this notion of subliming has at least three facets: that of the subliminal, of sublimation, and of sublimity; Wittgenstein thereby attributes to traditional philosophy a sense of the essence it seeks as hidden behind or within the empirical, hence as needing to be distilled from its impurities, with a view to liberating it and us from our own confinement in the everyday (Mulhall, 2001, pp.87–93). But the truth as Wittgenstein sees it is otherwise:

> We have got onto slippery ice where there is no friction, and so, in a certain sense, the conditions are ideal; but also, just because of that, we are unable to walk. We want to walk; so we need *friction*. Back to the rough ground! (PI §107)

It is difficult to think of a more concisely elegant expression of the signature Nietzschean thought that philosophy is constitutionally and lethally inclined to privilege Being over Becoming – investing in the construction of an ideal realm of essence, rather than facing the messiness of spatiotemporal reality, and in particular the humiliating reality of our ambulatory animal need for the friction it makes possible. Now recall that Wittgenstein's primary way of characterizing that rough ground is his invocation of family-resemblance concepts – the unity of which consists of overlapping strands of resemblance. Given that such resemblances hold not just within a generation but between them, and so presuppose not only the passage of time but also a reiterated generative mechanism of grafting external elements onto the family tree (by marriage), thereby identifying its continuing vitality with an ability to renew its inner logic by means of external contingency, it's hard to avoid the implicitly genealogical dimension of Wittgenstein's analogical figure. Might he then intend a distinctively evaluative – an ethico-spiritual – critique of philosophy, as implicitly committed to an ascetic ideal that denigrates the distinctive vitality of the human animal? Perhaps this is why he once compared philosophical uneasiness and its resolution to "the suffering of an ascetic who stood raising a heavy ball, amid groans, and whom someone released by telling him 'Drop it'" (PO 175).

References

Glendinning, S. (1998). *On Being with Others*. London: Routledge.
Glendinning, S. (2006). *The Idea of Continental Philosophy*. Edinburgh: University of Edinburgh Press.
Glendinning, S. (2007). *In the Name of Phenomenology*. London: Routledge.
Glendinning, S. (Ed.). (2001). *Arguing with Derrida*. Oxford: Blackwell.
Glock, H.-J. (2008). *What is Analytic Philosophy?* Cambridge: Cambridge University Press.
Heidegger, M. ([1927] 1962). *Being and Time*. Trans. J. Macquarrie and E. Robinson. New York: Harper and Row. (Original work published 1927.)
Mulhall, S. (2001). *Inheritance and Originality*. Oxford: Oxford University Press.
Rogers Horn, P. (2005). *Gadamer and Wittgenstein on the Unity of Language*. London: Ashgate.
Staten, H. (1984). *Wittgenstein and Derrida*. Oxford: Blackwell.
Stone, M. (2000). Wittgenstein and Deconstruction. In A. Crary and R. Read (Eds). *The New Wittgenstein* (pp.83–117). London: Routledge.

Further Reading

Conant, J. (1996). Putting Two and Two Together: Kierkegaard, Wittgenstein and the Point of View for their Work as Authors. In D.Z. Phillips (Ed.). *The Grammar of Religious Belief* (pp.248–331). New York: St Martin's Press.
Egan, D., Reynolds, S., and Wendland, A. (Eds). (2013). *Wittgenstein and Heidegger*. London: Routledge.
Janik, A.S. and Toulmin, S. (1973). *Wittgenstein's Vienna*. New York: Simon and Schuster.
Kuusela, O., Ometita, M., and Ucan, T. (Eds). (forthcoming). *Wittgenstein and Phenomenology*. New York: Routledge.
Morris, K. (2007). Wittgenstein's Method: Ridding People of Philosophical Prejudices. In G. Kahane, E. Kanterian, and O. Kuusela (Eds). *Wittgenstein and His Interpreters: Essays in Memory of Gordon Baker* (pp.66–87). Oxford: Blackwell. [Discussion of Wittgenstein and Nietzsche.]
Mulhall, S. (1990). *On Being in the World: Wittgenstein and Heidegger on Seeing Aspects*. London: Routledge.
Stekeler, P. (2004). A Second Wave of Enlightenment: Kant, Wittgenstein and the Continental Tradition. In M. Kölbel and B. Weiss (Eds). *Wittgenstein's Lasting Significance* (pp.285–304). London: Routledge.

Index

ability *see* disposition
acquaintance 161, 467, 523, 534, 693
action 165, 261, 352, 384, 387, 388, 399, 418, 491–500, 509, 510, 547, 549, 552, 558, 559, 579, 580, 583, 606–611, 629, 631, 632, 636, 637, 643, 646, 662, 663, 674, 675, 690, 733–735, 738, 741, 743
Adorno, T. 758
aesthetics 71, 533, 581, 612–626, 655, 656
  and ethics 4, 28, 63, 65, 66, 71, 72, 211, 216, 221, 307, 611, 740
agreement/disagreement 266, 267, 366, 400, 437, 438, 448, 514, 595, 596, 608, 609, 616, 658, 670, 679, 691, 708, 728, 739, 767
ambiguity/synonymy 62, 104, 228, 234, 263, 298, 362, 371, 372, 410, 412, 417, 480, 484, 492, 520, 677, 720
Ambrose, A. 17, 37, 658–660
analysis *see* logical analysis
analytic/synthetic 35, 209, 238, 242, 262, 263, 270, 271, 346, 417, 576, 577, 687, 702, 706–708, 736, 752; *see also* analytic *under* definition
"and so on" 375, 509
Anscombe, G.E.M. 9, 19, 23, 45. 111, 159, 161, 196, 197, 202, 203, 217, 302, 385, 491, 492, 497–500, 579, 581, 589, 590, 598, 640, 669, 670, 674, 675
anthropology 35, 284, 356, 357, 587, 627–637, 642, 672, 682, 683, 697, 736; *see also* human being
antirealism 305, 310, 332–343; *see also* realism/antirealism
a priori *see* analytic/synthetic, philosophy
Aquinas, T. 502, 644, 646, 669–680

arbitrariness of grammar/autonomy of language 51, 52, 168, 169, 248, 254–256, 269–277, 350, 351, 554, 610
architecture 13, 16, 29, 66, 612
argument
  private language 85, 116, 168, 189, 334, 445, 530, 671, 672, 690, 693
  skeptical 377, 387, 388; *see also* Kripke
  substance 128, 132–138
  transcendental 35, 751; *see also* transcendental/transcendentalism
Aristotle 407–409, 669–677, 762
arithmetic 26, 63, 78, 221, 256, 261, 262, 265, 267, 270, 274, 275, 297, 305–312, 324, 336, 375, 376, 387, 543, 610, 707, 768, 769
aspect
  perception, continuous 520
  blindness 633
  dawning/-lighting up 520, 521, 530, 531
  duck-rabbit figure 519–521
  perception/seeing 309, 517–531, 595
assertability 305, 307, 310, 311, 314, 340
  condition 333, 336, 340, 342, 343
assertion 10, 77, 83, 85, 104, 214, 264, 265, 309–314, 324, 325, 342, 376, 402, 427, 428, 435, 447, 573, 739, 748, 750, 761
assumption 50, 60, 63, 67, 85, 86, 114, 165, 247, 352, 387, 404, 503, 525, 552, 565, 585, 691, 693, 694, 736–738, 762
atomism, logical *see* logical atomism
Augustine 32, 35, 37, 237, 361, 492, 643, 683, 760–769
Augustinian picture of language 361, 362, 420, 421

A Companion to Wittgenstein, First Edition. Edited by Hans-Johann Glock and John Hyman.
© 2017 John Wiley & Sons, Ltd. Published 2017 by John Wiley & Sons, Ltd.

INDEX

Austin, J.L. 74, 78, 238, 566, 720–728, 759
avowal (*Äußerung/Ausdruck*) 165, 172, 173, 185, 188, 189, 224, 339, 340, 354–357, 365, 370, 372, 620, 662, 726, 734, 759
axiom 79, 81, 212, 303, 325, 335, 539, 596; *see also* set theory
   of choice 707
   of infinity 202, 707
   of reducibility 293, 294, 707
Ayer, A.J. 60, 61, 607, 608, 700

Bacon, F. 692
Bedeutung (meaning/reference) 74, 83, 84, 87, 199, 280, 286, 309, 437, 505–507, 515; *see also* Frege, reference, *Sinn* (sense/meaning)
Beethoven, L. van 614, 623
beetle in the box 116, 462, 734
Begriffsschrift 63, 181, 190, 205, 234, 694; *see also* notation, *Begriffsschrift under* Frege
behavior/behaviorism 66, 204, 240, 244, 261, 262, 270, 281, 310, 312, 332, 391, 404, 425, 465–476, 484, 485, 497, 498, 527, 529, 551, 582, 608, 629, 631, 635, 637, 642, 658–663, 672, 734, 735
   pain 488, 449, 458, 459, 471, 474
belief
   basic 548, 549, 552–554, 556, 559, 560
   forming of 553, 560, 567, 569, 570, 574
   justified true 548, 550, 570, 584, 739
   propositional 549, 553, 560
   religious 639, 642, 644, 645, 648, 740, 741; *see also* faith
Berkeley, G. 71, 224, 402, 526, 528, 530, 685
bipolarity 27, 214, 217, 221, 236, 307, 483; *see also* negation
bivalence 333, 641, 737, 738; *see also* bipolarity
Black, M. 77, 167, 198, 437
Boltzmann, L. 8, 110–121. 687
Bolzano, B. 64, 719
bounds of sense *see* language/sense/thought *under* limit
Bouwsma, O.K. 43, 75, 732
Bradley, F.H. 212
Brahe, T. de 594
Brahms, J. von 5, 6, 656

brain 164, 224, 227, 380, 385, 409, 560, 589, 673, 676
Brentano, F. 719
broom 70, 130, 131
Brouwer, L.E.J. 315, 324, 334, 702
Burge, T. 384

calculus 164, 171, 215, 216, 219–221, 242, 244, 252, 253, 258, 260, 265, 274, 320–330, 342, 349–352, 511, 708, 712; *see also* logical analysis
Camus, A. 758
Cantor, G. 327
Carnap, R. 217, 234–236, 240, 351, 370, 588–592, 694, 700–713, 752
Carroll, L. 81, 694
Cartesianism 225, 264, 550, 564, 670–674, 679, 685, 693, 733; *see also* inner/outer
category 63, 65, 94, 199, 213, 313, 416, 456, 486, 525, 635, 663, 718, 735, 759; *see also* logical form
catharsis 624
causation/cause 420, 576–585, 692, 747; *see also* explanation, induction
   cause vs. reason/motive/ground 116, 262, 553, 554, 581, 655, 674
   law/principle of 113, 579
Cavell, S. 42–46, 270, 338, 424, 595, 596, 669, 683, 727, 728
certainty 19, 85, 111, 226, 248, 264, 239, 246, 447, 467–469, 493, 541, 547–561, 564, 565, 573, 582–585, 691, 734; *see also* On Certainty *under* works of Ludwig Wittgenstein
chess 70, 222, 226, 244, 246, 257, 263, 324, 423, 427, 476, 539, 606, 738
Christianity 226, 639–641, 644–647, 671, 689; *see also* faith; religion
   Catholic 6, 10, 623, 639, 640, 733
   Protestant 5, 6
Church, A. 302, 303, 308; *see also* Church's *under* theorem
clarity/clarification 24, 74, 75, 112, 120, 183, 184, 236, 245, 246, 385, 391, 431, 484, 633, 634, 695, 700, 711, 733, 742, 749
   logical 3, 74, 179, 181, 233, 694, 710, 728, 749
   philosophical 181, 190, 204, 205, 214, 327, 329, 710, 749–751
Coffey, P. 10

cognitive science *see* cognitive *under* science
Collingwood, R.G. 222
color 533–544
    blindness 424, 539, 541, 543
    exclusion/incompatibility problem 34, 67, 70, 72, 220, 348–351, 535, 536
    octahedron/geometry 536, 540
    primary vs. secondary 255, 348, 539
    sample 378, 597
common sense 165, 243, 282, 338, 402, 465, 469, 563, 653, 661–663, 728, 732
complex *see* simple/complex *under* object, Russell's theory *under* judgment
compositionalism 220, 237, 578, 693–696
computer 246
concept *passim*
    color 412, 424, 539, 541, 543; *see also* color
    family resemblance 246, 259, 412–415, 518, 520, 527, 581, 769; *see also* family resemblance
    formal 82, 84, 216, 217, 234, 308, 315, 347; *see also* propositional *under* variable
    formation/conceptual change 242, 245, 288, 324, 409, 754
    "horse" *see* concept "horse" *under* paradox
    psychological 3, 24, 246, 527, 530, 726; *see also* psychology, philosophical
conjecture 111, 262, 283, 284, 314, 446, 455, 525, 526, 660, 740, 752
    Epsilon 317
    Goldbach's 316, 322, 323
    mathematical 316
    Taniyama-Shimura 317
consciousness 159, 166, 171, 173, 232, 282, 380, 384, 385, 394, 542, 622, 658, 671–673, 677, 685, 768
consistency/inconsistency 67, 179, 204, 219, 243, 247, 249, 272, 311, 319, 325, 356, 522, 556, 615, 616; *see also* contradiction
constant *see* logical constant
constructivism 334, 335
contextualism 420, 425–432, 550, 559
contradiction 8, 26, 28, 34, 35, 62, 63, 67–70, 78, 79, 94, 116–119, 162, 163, 165, 215–217, 223, 235, 270, 295, 325, 326, 332, 347–351, 402, 434, 435, 498, 534–536, 540, 672, 682, 696, 725, 748, 749, 753, 755

convention/conventionalism 44, 61–64, 115, 169–171, 225, 239, 254–257, 335–337, 342, 352, 355, 356, 370, 401, 402, 423, 588, 615, 616, 678, 707, 708, 752; *see also* arbitrariness of grammar/autonomy of language
Cooper, T. 326
correctness 83, 112, 198, 203, 308–310, 398–400, 403, 548, 553, 656, 737
    constitution of 396
    criteria of 448, 460, 620, 655–657
    phenomenology of 397–404
    standard of 375, 396, 460–462
criteria
    applicability 66, 254, 256, 364–368, 373
    of identity *see* criteria *under* identity
    of correctness *see* criteria *under* correctness
    outer/public 270, 496, 497, 527, 528, 530; *see also* inner/outer
culture 3, 7, 13, 15, 17, 227, 258, 274–276, 282, 424, 609, 612, 615, 616, 619, 634, 637, 741, 759; *see also* aesthetics

Dallago, C. 12
Darwin, C. 32, 119, 120, 748
Davidson, D. 234, 499, 674, 758
De Quincey, T. 620–625
decidability 314
decision 227, 238, 257, 273, 297, 335, 337, 402, 414, 447, 455, 456, 449, 740, 755, 768; *see also* intentionality
    procedure 216, 219, 295, 302, 314
deconstruction 173, 671, 758
deed (*Tat*) 552, 559, 560, 565, 581, 621, 690, 733, 736, 755
definition
    analytic 240, 246, 247, 459
    ostensive 51, 220, 223, 270, 334, 361–374, 448, 459–462, 471, 472, 608, 671, 672
    private 223, 334, 445, 458–462, 530
    piecemeal 297, 298
    verbal 361, 369, 539
deflationism 340, 341
depiction *see* representation
Derrida, J. 758–760, 768, 769
Descartes, R. 167, 171, 225, 231, 502, 551, 671–673, 677, 716, 735
description
    bundle of 366, 367
    complete 132, 606, 634
    definite 94, 170, 171, 301

designation *see* name, naming
desire *see* intentionality
determinacy of sense 220, 253, 411–418
Dewey, J. 732. 733, 743
dialogue 4, 50, 392, 407, 530, 624, 721, 759, 769
  Socratic/Platonic 408, 415
  with Frege 78, 83
disposition 350, 380, 381, 387, 388, 391, 403–408, 475, 560, 583, 648, 672, 733, 754
dog 243, 362, 363, 409, 423, 607, 675–678
dogmatism 32–34, 216, 242, 243, 279, 468, 555, 697, 703, 725
Dostoevsky, F. 683
doubt 51, 93, 226, 238, 282, 321, 324, 335, 338, 414, 440, 447, 454–460, 493–496, 547–560, 564–566, 584, 585, 648, 657, 685, 735–738, 751–753
dream/dreaming 327, 651–664
Drury, M.O'C. 18, 19, 71, 93, 223, 280, 281, 640, 643, 653, 732
Duhem, P. 592
Dummett, M. 236, 274, 276, 319, 332–343, 401–404, 531, 719, 721, 724

Einstein. A. 110, 588, 592, 700, 701
Eliot, T.S. 636
elucidation 3, 28, 43, 74, 76, 176, 177, 191, 195, 199, 204–206, 217, 231, 253, 241, 242, 361, 401, 557, 637, 693, 694, 710–713, 762
emotivism 605, 608
empiricism 233, 237, 305, 521, 530, 543, 684, 692, 707, 741, 742
  logical 587, 592, 696
Engelmann, P. 13, 16, 25, 29, 35, 48, 52, 77, 612
enlightenment 623, 702, 712, 713
entailment 252, 354, 557, 573, 576; *see also* inference
  natural 577, 578
epistemology *see* certainty, induction, skepticism
equation 29, 120, 256, 264–266, 305–310, 315, 531, 683
essentialism 31, 240, 596, 630, 631, 678, 696, 732
ethics 1, 4, 7, 13, 14, 28, 29, 60, 65, 66, 71, 72, 93, 179, 211, 216, 221, 307, 332, 339, 605–611, 612, 641, 646, 661, 684, 712, 713, 740, 748; *see also* and ethics *under* aesthetics, value

Evans, G. 472
exclusion, logical 244, 307, 535, 536, 544; see also exclusion/incompatibility problem *under* color
existence 2, 29, 34, 76, 104, 132–134, 143–146, 209, 212, 220, 275, 307, 332, 347, 361, 374, 435–440, 447, 503, 578, 583, 607, 671, 679, 680, 684, 685, 689, 719, 747, 766
  five minutes ago 557, 567–570, 573
  God's 642–648, 740
existentialism 683, 758
expectation *see* intentionality
explanation *passim*; *see also* elucidation, justification, ostensive *under* definition
  aesthetic 618–625, 655, 657
  causal 239–242, 582, 619–621, 662, 674
  must come to an end 118, 552, 553, 556, 566, 572, 584
  of meaning 61, 63, 67, 69, 72, 167, 220, 407, 408, 415
  super 369
externalism 41–44, 568–570

fact *see also* state of affairs
  atomic 61, 70, 127, 143–149, 155, 438, 688
  superlative 404, 405
  very general facts of nature 212, 424, 474, 657, 754
faith 5, 417, 583, 639–644, 647, 647, 697, 740, 743; *see also* Christianity
falsehood 94, 146, 147, 226, 270, 425
family resemblance 31, 35, 221, 242, 246, 259, 407–418, 518, 520, 527, 530, 581, 594–596, 611, 678, 732, 769
Feagin, S. 624, 625
fear 274, 582, 624, 642, 659, 662
Feigl, H. 588, 592, 700–702
Fermat, P. de 317–322; *see also* Fermat's *under* theorem
Feyerabend, P. 47, 117, 587, 592, 593, 597–599
Ficker, L. von 12. 14
fideism 644, 741
finitism, strict 336, 337
first person authority *see* first/third person asymmetry
first/third person asymmetry 170, 173, 386, 466, 471, 527

fly-bottle 75, 86, 224, 245
form of life 69–72, 87, 267, 336, 353, 356, 357, 424, 425, 639, 642, 643, 679, 691, 738, 739, 764, 766
form of representation (*Form der Darstellung*) 71, 114, 115, 120, 224, 239, 278, 743
formalism 87, 305, 310, 312; *see also* nominalism
Foucault, M. 758
France, A. 622
Frazer, J.G. 32, 280–284, 580–583, 626–637, 642
Frege, G. 4, 9, 10, 24, 26, 27, 32, 42, 60, 71, 74–87, 94, 106–108, 141–149, 155–157, 160, 163, 199, 209, 212–215, 219, 225–227, 232–234, 263, 297–300, 309–312, 334, 337, 351, 365, 410, 412, 413, 416, 434, 446–449, 452, 462, 504, 507, 518, 579, 588, 687, 693, 694, 707–710, 719–721, 732, 746, 758, 758
  Begriffsschrift 63, 77, 82, 86, 686, 694
  Grundgesetze der Arithmetik 8, 76, 77
Freud, S. 6, 163, 587, 626, 632, 642, 651–664; *see also* psychoanalysis
Frey, G. 317
function
  descriptive 311–314, 339–342
  propositional 94, 100–105, 296, 298, 374
  truth- *see* function *under* truth

game *see* calculus; language-game
Geach, P. 81, 129, 669–672
Gellner, E. 721
genealogical tree (*Stammbaum*) 246, 726
general propositional form (*allgemeine Satzform*) 62–65, 70, 204, 206, 211, 221, 297–303, 313
generality 83, 132, 212, 219, 223, 300, 307, 625, 707, 757
  craving for 16, 243, 630
genuine duration 529
geometry 114, 117, 171, 221, 222, 283, 311, 521, 540, 543, 610, 622
Gestalt see gestalt *under* psychology
God 10, 12, 13, 16, 19, 209, 226, 267, 336, 553, 607, 630, 641–648, 677–680, 682, 712, 740, 743; *see also* religion
Gödel, K. 100, 319, 320, 323, 324, 342, 701, 710

Goethe, J.W. von 280, 281, 287, 288, 540–543, 581, 623, 690, 733
Goldbach, C. 316, 322, 323
Gorgias 407–409
grammar
  depth vs. surface 220, 242, 307, 339, 421, 433, 633
  logical 177, 205, 234, 253, 536, 696
  philosophical 31, 48, 59, 69, 70
Grice, H.P. 417, 418, 493, 494, 558, 720, 724
ground *see* cause vs. reason/motive/ground *under* causation/cause

Hahn, H. 588, 700–702, 705–710, 713
Hanson, R. 587, 592–595, 598
Hardy, G.H. 321–323
harmony between language and reality 221, 514, 515
Hegel, G.W.F. 118, 758
Heidegger, M. 25, 713, 758–768
Heretics Society 605, 661
hermeneuticism 661, 662
hermeneutics 218
Hertz, H.R. 4, 8, 25, 32, 110–121, 232, 687
Hilbert, D. 77, 305, 327
Hintikka, J. 33, 42, 46, 47
Hitler, A. 7, 18
Hobbes, T. 297
holism 31, 170, 521, 522, 643, 736, 746; *see also* contextualism
Horkheimer, M. 758
Horwich, P. 333, 334, 340, 341, 352, 403, 423
human being 11, 50, 51, 85, 233, 238, 271, 362, 362, 370, 424, 448, 458, 471, 474, 482, 518, 547, 554, 556, 579, 606, 608, 628, 657, 661, 671–673, 678, 679, 691, 728, 739, 751–755
Hume, D. 1, 35, 224, 225, 446, 486, 550, 552, 580, 581, 585, 615, 623–626, 642, 647, 671–675, 692, 719, 751
Husserl, E. 676, 677, 719, 746, 758
hypothesis 72, 110, 113, 115, 118–120, 144, 163, 164, 171, 209, 226, 239, 241, 246, 270, 274, 280–285, 382, 422, 448–450, 457, 462, 524, 567, 573, 580–582, 590, 592, 623, 628, 633, 634, 643, 646, 655–656, 703, 705, 709, 733, 735–740, 748, 754
  causal 618–620, 655, 657
  continuum 325

775

INDEX

I/ego/self 34, 64, 65, 68, 71, 72, 160–173, 225, 370, 446, 478–490, 672, 673, 686–689, 693, 742
idea *see* mental image/picture, mental phenomenon, representation
idealism 72, 77, 78, 84, 85, 160, 166, 167, 191, 216, 247, 502, 685, 686, 720, 739, 758
  epistemological 60, 85, 687
  transcendental 59, 68, 72, 682–684, 687, 690, 692
identity 28, 64, 94, 95, 113, 142, 143, 153–156, 199, 301, 306–311, 341, 354, 364, 364, 365, 369, 370, 437, 453, 507, 524, 592, 678, 685, 704, 742
  criteria of 168, 239, 246, 362, 439, 440, 446, 450, 452, 489, 742
  numerical vs. qualitative 450, 451
  of Indiscernibles 453
  sign of 201, 234, 309, 310
illusion 119, 167, 170, 172, 180, 181, 204, 223, 224, 227, 249, 379, 400, 452, 552, 613, 617, 671, 696, 697, 720, 764
imagery 285, 378, 382, 384, 618, 675, 741
imagination 204, 322, 382, 457, 489, 518, 538, 700, 742
indexical 425, 427, 429
induction 115, 553, 554, 576–585, 587, 591, 749
  law of 580, 738
  mathematical 308
ineffable 13, 65, 173, 179, 181, 185, 195–227, 235, 236, 241, 437, 549, 558, 560, 588, 590, 612, 613, 646, 711, 712
inference 61, 147, 180, 218, 222, 225, 265, 335, 445, 448, 456, 473, 497, 531, 541, 558, 567, 577–579, 582, 584, 746, 751
  deductive 113, 247, 579, 597, 686, 706, 709
  logical 68, 80–83, 133, 152, 215, 219, 301, 329, 350, 351, 579, 597, 708
inner/outer 445, 447, 455, 465–477, 523, 672; *see also* avowal, psychology, philosophical, privacy
instinct 285, 322, 554, 559, 560, 581, 582, 631, 635
instruction 6, 71, 203–205, 260–262, 375, 378, 384, 388, 393, 394, 403, 431, 579, 580, 622

intentionality 114, 118, 211, 213, 214, 219, 221, 386, 447, 476, 477, 491–500, 502–516, 558, 618, 662, 663, 674–676, 691, 696, 734; *see also* harmony between language and reality, isomorphism
interlocutor 50–52, 86, 168, 243, 326, 375–388, 392, 396–400, 407, 408, 430, 488–490, 656; *see also* voice
  vs. narrator 50–52
intermediate link 281–287
internal property *see* internal *under* relation
introspection 225, 445, 500, 527, 741
intuition 50, 64, 264, 276, 297, 299, 302, 310, 312, 355, 361, 402, 493, 507–509, 531, 564, 568, 631, 685, 697, 719
intuitionism 315, 333–336, 339, 610; *see also* intuition
irrationalism *see* rationality/rationalism
isomorphism 70, 221, 434, 438, 439, 502, 503, 515, 685

James, W. 497, 731–734, 738–744
Johnson, S. 618, 619
Jourdain, P. 8, 76, 78, 92
judgment
  aesthetic 614–616, 619
  agreement in 448, 615, 691
  ethical/moral 65, 341, 606–609, 646
  Last Judgment 643–645
  maxim of (Kant) 172
  Russell's theory of 92–105, 143–145, 439
justification 68, 70, 76, 77, 95, 98–103, 169, 171, 189, 243, 256, 271–277, 307, 334, 350–352, 384–388, 396, 457, 469, 470, 498, 500, 548–553, 561, 582–584, 594, 610, 615, 634, 645, 646, 692, 749, 759; *see also* explanation
must come to an end *see* must come to an end *under* explanation

Kant, I. 1, 4, 35, 60–71, 112–119, 160, 164, 167, 171–173, 209, 222, 232–236, 241, 245–247, 265, 270, 297, 446, 458, 486, 531, 615, 641, 670, 682–697, 719, 748, 758
Kenny, A. 23, 42, 46, 47, 131, 247, 354, 453, 458, 459, 670–680
Kepler, J. 594
Keynes, J.M. 14, 16, 18, 218, 702
Kierkegaard, S. 29, 218, 664, 683, 689, 697, 758

776

kinaesthesis 497
Kirchhoff, G. 110, 120
Klimt, G. 6
Klopstock, F.G. 622
Köhler, W. 517, 521–523
Kokoschka, O. 6
Kraus, K. 6–8, 13–14, 687
Kripke, S. 32, 366, 342, 354–357, 369, 370, 376, 377, 386–388, 402–405, 449, 458, 510, 527, 669
Kuhn, T.S. 587, 592–598

Labor, J. 6
ladder 14, 43, 66, 161, 176, 180, 195, 197, 235, 236, 287, 599, 710, 711
language
  critique of 233, 693, 719
  essence of 31, 34, 210, 235, 252, 694, 723
  ideal 63, 64, 234, 245, 720, 723; *see also* *Begriffsschrift*
  natural/ordinary 29, 33, 181, 196, 203, 234, 243, 244, 246, 253, 258, 265–267, 334, 338, 422, 488, 505, 522, 653, 694, 713, 764; *see also* ordinary language philosophy
  of thought 163–165, 171, 434, 688
  primary vs. secondary 33, 709; *see also* phenomenology
  primitive 391, 409, 420, 765
  sign 200
language-game 3, 31, 33, 35, 37, 38, 59, 68–71, 87, 157, 169, 172, 242, 243, 246, 253, 254, 258–261, 339–342, 353–357, 369, 393, 409, 411, 418, 420–432, 454, 457, 462, 468–470, 474, 499, 510, 513, 523, 533–539, 543, 549, 551, 554, 556, 558, 560, 572, 581–585, 599, 608–610, 642–645, 679, 680, 690, 691, 695, 726, 734–738, 753, 765, 767
  fictional 420, 734
law 112–120 and *passim*
  natural 115, 241, 577–582, 751, 754
  of causation *see* law/principle *under* causation/cause
  of excluded middle 315, 324, 332–339
  of induction *see* law *under* induction
  of logic 79, 80, 151, 209, 215, 222, 270, 315, 324, 350, 579, 580, 693, 749
  of thought 112, 118, 120, 233
learning *see* teaching
Leibniz, G.W. 162, 678

Lenau, N. 623
length 273, 355–357, 367–373, 538, 541, 558, 615, 766; *see also* length *under* sample, standard meter
Lewis, C.I. 752
Lichtenberg, G.C. 541
limit 267, 274, 636
  of experience/knowledge 64, 209, 446, 641
  of language/sense/thought 78, 85, 119, 160, 163, 166, 167, 180, 211, 216, 217, 233, 234, 236, 248, 275, 295, 308, 311, 348, 351, 414, 479, 480, 505, 515, 549, 582, 603, 640, 641, 669, 682, 686, 688, 706, 719, 748, 749; *see also* nonsense
  of the subject 162, 173, 687
  of the world 34, 119, 165–167, 171, 215, 479–483, 641, 686, 688
linguistics 1, 340, 415
lion 235, 560
Locke, J. 1, 225, 232, 446, 449, 462
logic 293–303 and *passim*
  formal 246, 269, 273, 610, 728, 732, 759
  Fregean 86, 146, 299, 300
  predicate 295, 298–302, 707
  propositional 94, 293, 298–302
  transcendental 64, 687, 696
logical analysis 3, 28, 31, 127–129, 163, 171, 204–206, 210, 217, 236, 242, 243, 483, 578, 693–696, 759
logical atomism 31, 63, 70, 127–139, 437, 503, 688
logical constant 11, 26, 79, 129, 216, 294–300, 303, 434, 435, 505, 507, 517, 686, 693, 710
logical form 16, 33, 35, 60, 65, 68, 86, 96, 97, 107, 108, 135, 136, 200, 212, 234, 536, 688, 708
  of facts/propositions 2, 3, 135, 205, 221, 232, 234, 236, 297, 301, 347, 434, 504, 505, 706, 710, 749
  of language/reality/the world 31, 135, 434, 686, 711
  of names/objects 35, 64, 127, 128, 213, 503–507, 513, 515
logical grammar *see* logical *under* grammar
logical inference *see* logical *under* inference
logical necessity *see* logical *under* necessity
logical positivism 16, 231, 236, 239, 333, 335, 336, 587–593, 599, 640, 641, 700, 719–721, 758

777

INDEX

logical relation *see* logical *under* relation
logical space 64, 117, 307, 347, 437, 536
logical syntax 2, 29, 33, 34, 151, 196–206,
    212, 216, 221, 234, 236, 243, 253,
    306, 347, 348, 590, 591, 750
logicism 26, 93, 100, 293, 312, 696, 707
Loos, A. 29, 687
lying/lie 101, 456, 500, 608, 610

Mach, E. 110, 120, 521, 592, 709
magic 224, 227, 281, 285, 627–635, 662
Mahler, G. 6
Malcolm, N. 19, 42, 46, 163, 164, 434, 458,
    640, 653
Marx, K. 758
mathematics 305–321; *see also* arithmetic,
    geometry, set theory
  and logic 8, 71, 238, 247, 269, 273, 333,
    334, 337, 346, 530, 587, 701, 748
  applied 288, 298, 308, 310
  pure 269, 273, 309–311, 315, 329, 330
Maxwell, J.C. 110, 111, 118
meaning of life (*Sinn des Lebens*) 13, 118,
    607, 641
meaning *see* Augustinian picture of language,
    Bedeutung (meaning/reference), *Sinn*
    (sense/meaning)
  is use 236, 249, 274, 462, 609
meaningless 32, 59, 60, 63, 69, 78, 82, 119,
    167, 168, 173, 206, 257, 273, 364,
    455, 549, 559, 573, 588, 607, 594,
    711, 713, 734, 750, 758, 759; *see also*
    nonsense, senseless
measure/measuring 130, 239, 267, 273,
    275, 313, 329, 349, 350, 354–357,
    369, 370, 422, 424, 606, 616, 646,
    696; *see also* standard meter
mechanism 68, 105, 362, 363, 367, 368,
    404, 462, 769
  mental 377, 379–386, 468, 469, 506, 508
Meinong, A. 719
memory 1, 368, 459–461, 526
Mendelssohn, F. 6, 664
Menger, K. 589, 701, 702, 706, 710
mental image/picture 118, 371, 372, 378,
    379, 382, 384, 391, 399, 430, 431,
    459, 676, 741
mental phenomenon (act/event/process/
    state) 226, 233, 253, 372, 381–284,
    399, 401, 404, 447, 448, 450, 466–476,
    496, 500, 504–512, 528, 537, 627, 675,
    676, 734

mentalism 163, 372, 692; *see also*
    Cartesianism, psychologism
Merleau-Ponty, M. 758
metalogic 215–221, 307, 713
metaphilosophy 249, 279, 341, 692
metaphor 25, 64, 80, 116, 117, 160, 163,
    184, 188, 287, 339, 584, 679, 720, 741
metaphysics 1–3, 11, 64, 94, 95, 118, 127,
    128, 162, 164, 196, 205, 209–227,
    232–245, 437, 475, 478, 483, 487, 533,
    537, 588–591, 641, 642, 669, 677–680,
    684–687, 692, 693, 708–713, 719–723,
    727, 746, 748
  of symbolism 212, 215, 216, 219, 220
meter stick *see* standard meter
method
  of projection 213, 220, 393, 434, 505,
    511, 512; *see also* pictorial/picturing
    under relation
  of verification 588, 591; *see also*
    verification/verificationism, verification/
    verifiability *under* principle
  philosophical 1, 3, 42–44, 47, 52, 82,
    117, 167, 231–249, 341, 390, 632,
    695, 718, 726, 731, 742, 769
  scientific 1, 15, 236, 238, 239, 540, 542,
    595, 608, 747, 752
  myth of mere method 231, 248, 249
Mill, J.S. 223, 410, 746
mind and machine *see* human being
mind vs. body 160, 166, 170, 172, 223,
    238, 445, 446, 451, 452, 474, 478,
    482, 489, 492, 671–674, 687, 689,
    741; *see also* I/ego/self, inner/outer
minima sensibilia of the *Tractatus* 212, 534
minimalism 340, 341
model 3, 33, 68, 72, 107, 110, 112, 113,
    117, 118, 187, 188, 191, 213, 218,
    244, 287, 288, 307, 312, 314, 380,
    404, 405, 433, 434, 457, 458, 462,
    467, 471, 503, 523, 533, 594, 596,
    633, 634, 642, 647, 656, 727, 733,
    734; *see also* paradigm
  or picture 2, 28, 112, 118, 433; *see also*
    picture
  replacement 448, 449
Moore, G.E. 9, 11–13, 17, 18, 27, 28, 45, 81,
    83, 95, 210, 232, 243, 247, 439, 467,
    483, 547–551, 555, 556, 559–561,
    563–566, 589, 605, 611, 655, 656, 686,
    693, 694, 719, 721, 723, 731, 732, 742,
    758; *see also* Moore's *under* paradox

778

Morell, O. 9
motive *see* cause vs. reason/motive/ground *under* causation/cause
Mozart, W.A. 6, 7, 618
mystical/mysticism 13, 14, 60, 68, 159, 162, 334, 534, 607, 641, 680, 693, 712
mythology 241, 242, 653, 656, 669

name
  color 213, 367, 368, 371, 373, 448
  combination/concatenation of 2, 129, 134, 151, 220, 252, 347, 434, 505, 537
  proper 81–83, 98, 103, 149, 212, 234, 362–374, 421, 765
  simple 2, 61, 62, 64, 150, 155, 212–215, 220, 505, 506
naming 51, 87, 254, 285, 362, 372, 373, 409, 426, 436, 460, 537, 596, 608, 673; *see also* name
natural history 51, 410, 637, 678, 733, 747, 751, 753, 754
naturalism 119, 237, 238, 288, 385, 608, 625, 697, 712, 740, 746–755
necessity 51, 52, 67, 69, 81, 211, 212, 215, 219, 221, 222, 235, 238–240, 248, 262, 264, 269, 270, 276, 288, 312, 335, 336, 346–357, 401, 435, 455, 457, 540, 576–582, 610, 614, 634, 692, 737, 743; *see also* necessary *under* proposition
  logical 211, 215, 237, 249, 335, 348, 349, 401, 535, 577–582
Necker cube 517, 519
negation 26, 27, 62, 84, 211, 213, 214, 224, 256, 264–266, 273, 276, 298, 299, 341, 347, 435, 455, 456, 507, 709, 736; *see also* bipolarity
  double 80, 256, 264, 265, 273
  joint 63, 215, 299, 517
Neider, H. 652, 704
Nestroy, J.N. 26, 671
Neurath, O. 235, 588, 589, 700, 701, 705, 706, 709–713
Newton, I. 8, 111–115, 222, 540, 541
Nietzsche, F. 71, 72, 159, 624, 625, 758–760, 768–770
nominalism 247, 734
nonsense 2, 63, 65, 70, 82, 97, 98, 102, 103, 107, 179, 180–188, 195–206, 213–219, 222, 223, 227, 233, 235, 236, 242, 256, 266, 267, 275, 295, 312, 316, 348, 350, 427, 428, 445, 457, 499, 558, 577, 578, 591, 607, 608, 633, 640, 641, 693, 711, 732, 759; *see also* meaningless, resolute reading
  mere/plain/sheer/austere conception of 196–201, 206, 213, 223, 235
  substantial/illuminating 180, 181, 196–201, 206, 218, 235, 711
N-operator 181, 296, 299–303, 347–349
norm of description/representation 86, 115, 217, 222, 241, 262, 264, 266, 336, 736
normativity 209–227, 375, 461, 735
  linguistic 259–262, 769
  of meaning 375–377, 387
notation 80, 82, 133, 164, 169, 190, 212, 216, 219, 234, 236, 244, 249, 300, 302, 303, 311, 315, 393, 438, 534, 578, 653, 654, 694, 750
  logical 63, 181, 183, 204–206, 299, 309, 591
number
  cardinal 308, 395
  natural 78, 246, 297, 305, 308, 317, 328, 337, 376, 393–395, 412
  prime 315, 316

object (*Gegenstand*)
  inner 264, 523, 530
  logical 11, 26, 79, 83, 213, 226, 233, 435, 710, 713
  material 222–226, 233, 332, 446, 451, 452, 676
  of comparison 253, 420–422, 594, 656, 659
  private 445, 462, 530
  simple/complex 35, 61–64, 127, 128, 132–139, 143, 212–215, 220, 301, 361, 503, 505, 506, 508, 512, 513, 515, 518, 522, 534, 535, 537, 540
Ogden, C.K. 9, 15, 29, 148, 151, 234, 435, 480, 605, 734
open texture 414–416, 693
operation 28, 62, 63, 129, 154, 216, 219, 233, 235, 296–303, 305, 308, 312, 347, 383, 440, 469, 511, 517, 526, 576–578, 655, 676, 708, 765–768
ordinary language philosophy 4, 718–728, 758
Ostwald, W. 700
other minds 446, 458, 671
overview *see* perspicuous/surveyable (re)presentation/overview (*übersichtliche Darstellung*)

INDEX

paradigm 34, 74, 242, 417, 454, 582, 594–596, 613, 647, 679; *see also* sample
paradox 8, 29, 100, 106, 211, 235, 341, 415, 591, 720
  liar's 100
  Moore's 467
  of aspect perception 520–530
  of inference 81
  of the concept "horse" 79–82
  of the *Tractatus* 179, 217, 710, 713
  of Tragedy 623–625
  rule-following 399–401, 510
  Russell's 8, 75–79, 92, 100, 105, 108, 293
  skeptical 386–388
  Sorites 412, 413
Pascal, B. 648, 683
Pasternak, B. 623
patterns in the tapestry of life (*Lebensteppich*) 469
Peirce, C.S. 731–742, 746
Penrose, R. 321
personal identity *see* criteria of *under* identity
perspicuous/surveyable (re)presentation/overview (*übersichtliche Darstellung*) 35, 120, 245, 279–286, 340, 354, 632–634, 695, 711, 753, 755; *see also* surveyability
phenomenalism 332; *see also* sense-data
phenomenology 237, 249, 397–404, 483, 537, 541, 582, 662, 708, 741, 758, 766
philosophy
  analytic 1, 87, 346, 478, 696, 718–721, 724, 727, 728, 757–760
  as critical activity 3, 217, 232
  continental 4, 757–769
  elenctic rather than deductive 247, 248
  leaves everything as it is 245, 320, 744
  of mathematics 4, 8, 9, 38, 264, 305–330, 335, 336, 338, 342, 401, 610
  of mind 1, 4, 159, 237, 383, 384, 445, 465, 478, 670
  of religion 639–649, 671
  of science 114, 120, 576, 587–599, 700, 713
  political *see* politics/political philosophy
  problems of 14, 16, 96, 231, 758
  systematic 50, 161, 735
physics 8, 110–121, 209, 222, 224, 246, 294, 321, 340, 537, 539, 579, 584, 590, 593, 701, 720, 746, 751, 762
pictorial form (*Form der Abbildung*) 107, 130, 503–505

picture *see also* picture theory, pictorial/picturing *under* relation, mental image/picture
  logical 2, 3, 28, 35, 107, 128, 130, 213, 221, 307, 503–505, 508, 706
picture theory 35, 62, 63, 65, 69, 70, 83, 107, 113, 114, 128, 130–136, 141–157, 165, 206, 211, 214, 220, 221, 235, 243, 305–307, 310–312, 433, 434, 440, 503, 507, 508, 643, 709, 710
Pinsent, D. 9–13, 92
Plato 32, 68, 95, 107, 232, 233, 247, 276, 305, 307, 312, 332, 407–411, 415–417, 599, 751, 759–761
Platonism 247, 276, 305, 307, 332, 599; *see also* Plato
pleasure 274, 326, 598, 615–617, 622–625, 652
Poincaré, H. 592
politics/political philosophy 1, 93, 407, 408, 450, 451, 616, 617, 700, 705, 758
Popper, K. 598, 660
possibility
  combinatorial 127, 128, 130, 212, 213, 222, 434, 503
  inference- *see* possibility *under* inference
  possible world *see* possible *under* world
  truth *see* possibility *under* truth
practice
  linguistic 237, 239, 243, 315, 381, 510, 511, 608, 708, 724, 735
  mathematical 321, 322, 324, 328
  primitive 284, 285, 636
pragmatics 376, 724
pragmatism 4, 68, 69, 343, 553, 731–744
  pragmatic maxim 733, 734
predicate 83, 86, 100, 104, 105, 150–152, 172, 209, 226, 234, 293, 306, 311, 312, 315, 316, 336, 340–342, 367, 370, 518, 535, 677, 678
  psychological 169, 170, 354
  truth 340, 342, 437, 440, 441
prescriptivism 605
principle *see also* axiom, law
  closure 556, 558, 567–574
  context 87, 170, 400, 719, 763, 764
  of excluded middle *see* excluded middle *under* law
  of indiscernibility of identicals 309
  verification/verifiability 591, 709
  vicious circle 100, 101
Prior, A. 351, 436, 441

privacy 445–463, 671
　epistemic 446–450, 454–457
private language argument *see* private language *under* argument
probability 29, 85, 519, 580, 582, 585, 591, 644, 647, 706, 746
proof 10, 24, 81, 237, 263, 288, 333–338, 342, 388, 493, 582, 656, 737, 738
　mathematical 120, 223, 273, 276, 288, 305, 306, 309–317, 321–327, 332, 531
　of God's existence 643, 644
　Sheffer's 301
property, internal/external *see* internal/external *under* relation
proposition (*Satz*) *passim*
　complex/molecular 252, 295, 296, 433–435, 578
　elementary/atomic 2, 28, 33, 34, 61–63, 67, 68, 70, 107, 127–135, 142–145, 151, 155–157, 163, 164, 212–215, 220, 235, 252, 279, 295, 296, 298, 301, 302, 307–309, 346–348, 433–437, 505–508, 534–536, 694, 708, 709; *see also* logical atomism
　genuine 62, 63, 235, 316, 341, 453, 735
　grammatical 217, 221–223, 237, 239, 265, 369, 457, 514, 539, 713, 736, 738
　hinge 339, 553, 556, 557, 567–573, 583, 763–738, 752
　mathematical 264–267, 306–315, 321, 323–326, 336, 339, 340, 342, 736
　necessary 2, 52, 233, 234, 238, 239, 588
　pseudo 197, 234, 235, 306, 307, 339, 436, 437, 686; *see also* nonsense
propositional function *see* propositional *under* function
propositional sign (*Satzzeichen*) 105, 128–133, 137, 139, 434, 438–441, 504, 505
propositional variable *see* propositional *under* variable
pseudo-proposition *see* pseudo *under* proposition
psychoanalysis 163, 168, 248, 249, 587, 632, 651–664, 726; *see also* Freud
psychologism 79, 80, 87, 163, 233, 334, 686, 746
psychology, philosophical 9, 38, 45, 741; *see also Remarks on the Philosophy of Psychology under* works of Ludwig Wittgenstein
　gestalt 281, 521, 522, 530, 595, 613
Putnam, H. 240, 333, 336, 338–340, 354, 358, 731–733

Pyrrhonism 31, 246–248, 697; *see also* skepticism
Pythagoras 441

quantifying 82, 100, 212, 214, 234, 295–303, 347, 348, 367, 436, 441, 709
quietism 191, 245, 337
Quine, W.V. 1, 103, 224, 238, 417, 696, 634, 646, 647, 652, 658

Ramsey, F.P. 15–17, 29, 32, 41, 42, 67, 68, 77, 100, 144, 195, 196, 203, 217, 235, 247, 294, 307, 348, 435, 436, 652, 661, 702, 732, 734, 739
rationality/rationalism 238, 239, 246, 247, 351, 383–388, 553, 572, 593, 594, 597, 610, 672, 674, 682, 684, 713, 746, 751, 754
realism/antirealism 147, 157, 160, 165–167, 214, 305, 310, 332–343, 502, 508, 610, 645, 678
　empirical 167, 212, 216, 683, 685, 687, 689
　pure 166, 167, 481, 482, 685–689
　vs. idealism 247, 687
reason *see* cause vs. reason/motive/ground *under* causation/cause
recognition *see* memory
reference 3, 34, 42, 83, 87, 84, 107, 143, 145, 149, 154, 155, 162, 221, 225, 271, 272, 275, 281, 282, 306, 309–316, 328, 332, 351, 335, 361–366, 370–374, 427, 437, 448, 458, 459, 462, 466, 473, 475, 483, 606, 609, 677, 712, 727, 735, 736, 743, 749; *see also Bedeutung*
　co-reference 364–366, 371
　system of (*Bezugssystem*) 644, 646, 647
regularity 274–277, 554, 555, 581, 584, 594, 615
Reichenbach, H. 370, 592, 696
Reik, T. 652
relation
　internal/external 42, 112, 129, 131, 151, 157, 162, 219, 222, 280, 507, 531, 558, 576–578, 590, 739, 749, 761–763
　logical 117, 164, 220, 221, 247, 348, 466, 535, 540, 548, 558
　pictorial/picturing 60, 62, 69, 130, 131, 160, 161, 165, 199, 504–515
　theory of judgment in Russell 95–99, 102, 103, 144, 145, 150

INDEX

relativism 543, 584, 610
religion 1, 4, 9, 211, 216, 221, 242, 307,
    627, 628, 632, 639–649, 661, 671,
    732, 740; *see also* God,
reminders 237, 242–244
representation (*Vorstellung*) 447; *see also*
    projection *under* method, perspicuous/
    surveyable (re)presentation/overview
  internal 676
  linguistic/symbolic 167, 234, 307, 505,
    508, 706
  mode of 94, 416, 423, 425
  nature of 211, 217, 706
  norm of 86, 217, 222, 241, 264, 266
  norm of *see* norm of description/
    representation
  theory of *see* representation *under* theory
resolute reading 47, 48, 59, 175–192,
    195–206, 235, 712, 713 *see also*
    nonsense
  Jacobin vs. Girondin 190, 191, 205
  strong vs. weak 205, 206
Respinger, M. 664
Rhees, R. 9, 19, 23, 40, 45, 160, 319, 614,
    634, 653, 661
Ribet, K. 317
Richards, I.A. 734
Rilke, R.M. 12
ritual 281, 284, 459, 627–637, 642, 647,
    662, 663
river-bed 679, 736
Robinson, A. 320
Robinson, A. 320
Rorty, R. 246, 247, 734
Rosh, E. 416
Ross, W.D. 610
rule *see also* grammar; logical syntax
  application of 317, 335, 390, 394, 397,
    400–404, 615
  following 87, 260, 261, 285, 288, 317,
    335, 337, 338, 342, 343, 390–405,
    563, 769
  grammatical 71, 221, 237, 239, 241,
    244–246, 253, 256, 257, 262–267,
    311, 315, 350–353, 457, 536, 557–
    559, 608, 736
  grasping in a flash 261, 392, 394, 399,
    404su
  of inference *see* logical *under* inference
  of language 256, 260, 262, 293
  skepticism *see* rule-following *under*
    skepticism

ruler *see* measure/measuring, standard meter
rule-skepticism *see* rule-following *under*
    skepticism
Russell, B. 1–4, 8–19, 23, 26–29, 32, 33,
    60, 63, 73–83, 92–108, 111, 127,
    135, 136, 142–147, 150, 160–164,
    167, 195, 210–219, 232–239, 293,
    294, 296, 299–303, 312, 337, 342,
    433, 435, 438, 439, 446, 506, 508,
    531, 579, 581, 588, 592, 678, 686,
    687, 693, 694, 700, 706–708, 710,
    719–721, 731, 742, 757, 758
  paradox *see* Russell's *under* paradox
  Principia Mathematica 26, 94, 100, 108,
    293, 298, 342, 531, 686, 694, 707
Ryle, G. 236, 243–245, 217, 491, 720, 722

sample 220, 223, 254, 368–374, 378, 412,
    423, 448, 459–461, 512, 538, 539,
    594, 597, 764; *see also* paradigm
  color 378, 597, 764
  length 370; *see also* standard meter
Sartre, J.P. 758
saying/showing 13, 27, 81–83, 106, 137,
    139, 163, 176, 181, 198, 199, 202,
    203, 206, 303, 348, 590, 693, 710, 711
scaffolding 209, 223, 348, 583, 686, 736,
    752, 754
Schiele, E. 6
Schiller, F.C.S. 732
Schlick, M. 16, 236, 278, 279, 408, 588,
    589, 592, 607, 652, 658, 700–706,
    709–713, 748
Schopenhauer, A. 4, 6–8, 59–72, 111, 118,
    159–167, 171, 232, 491, 492, 496,
    686–688
Schubert, F. 636
science
  cognitive 1, 383, 384, 672, 676
  natural 1–3, 119, 120, 203, 209, 210,
    307, 506, 576, 578–584, 587, 588,
    640, 642, 674, 693, 696, 711, 744,
    746–755, 759, 761; *see also* naturalism
  ontic 761–764
Searle, J. 244, 366, 367, 645
seeing *passim*
  aspect- *see* perception/seeing *under* aspect
  concept of 530, 595
  connections 245, 283, 286, 288, 695
self-consciousness *see* consciousness
Sellars, W. 502, 503, 507, 508, 515, 516,
    696, 697

782

semantics 60, 62–67, 71, 94, 242, 244, 307, 333, 335, 338–340, 350, 356, 376, 416, 425, 724, 768, 769
sensation 50, 51, 262, 264, 382, 404, 465–477, 478, 489, 497, 521, 522, 526, 540, 671, 673; *see also* kinaesthesis
   private 445–462; *see also* private *under* object, private language *under* argument
sense *see* Sinn (sense/meaning)
   indeterminacy of 413–415, 418
sense/meaning distinction *see* Sinn (sense/meaning), *Bedeutung* (meaning/reference)
sense-data 159, 225, 226, 590
senseless (*sinnlos*) 28, 62, 63, 78, 168, 196, 197, 199, 201, 206, 215, 217, 235, 295, 308, 348, 370, 457, 686, 733, 748; *see also* meaningless, nonsense
sentence *see* proposition, propositional sign
series, arithmetical/numerical 87, 260–262, 308, 376, 393–395, 421, 509, 510, 764, 769
set theory 324–330
Shakespeare, W. 619
   King Lear 625
   Macbeth 618–622, 625
Sheffer, H. 300, 301
Shimura, G. 317
sign
   and symbol 62, 71, 200
   identity sign *see* sign *under* identity
   language *see* sign *under* language
   primitive/nonprimitive 129–133, 298, 299, 505
   propositional *see* propositional sign
   simple 127–129, 132, 133, 137, 410, 433, 434, 516; *see also* simple *under* name
Sigwart, C. 746
simple *see* simple/complex *under* object
Sinn (sense/meaning) 62, 74, 83, 87, 309, 437, 507, 588; *see also* Bedeutung (meaning/reference), Frege
situation (*Sachlage*) 2, 62, 128, 130, 131, 134, 137, 148, 152–154, 437, 438, 505–507, 578, 706; *see also* state of affairs
skepticism 167, 320, 460, 502, 525, 561, 563–574, 669, 747
   radical/universal 165, 550, 563, 566, 567, 574, 683, 692
   rule-following 32, 388, 563; *see also* other minds

Skinner, F. 17, 18, 45
Socrates 187, 240, 241, 247, 407–409, 415, 675
solipsism 85, 159–173, 216, 224–225, 242, 479–482, 489, 533, 563, 658, 659, 685–690, 693; *see also* I/ego/self
   transcendental 167, 212, 216, 685, 688, 689
sortal 362, 363, 367, 372
soul 483, 630, 640, 672–674, 687, 741, 764; *see also* I/self, solipsism
speech act 306, 513
Spengler, O. 32, 35, 280–282, 286–288, 687, 743
Spinoza, B. 409
Sraffa, P. 16–18, 32, 35, 687
standard meter 254, 355–357, 368–372, 538; *see also* measure/measuring
standard of correctness 375, 396, 460–462
state of affairs (*Sachverhalt*) 2, 28, 62, 84, 127, 135, 213, 215, 295, 296, 301, 307, 311, 347, 349, 434–439, 503–508, 512–515, 632, 645, 725; *see also* fact, situation
Stonborough Wittgenstein, M. 6, 7, 16, 18
Strawson, P.F. 42, 44, 223, 241–245, 417, 452, 458, 580, 618, 720, 725
style 4, 5, 16, 17, 25, 26, 32, 41–53, 61, 74, 75, 162, 246–248, 274, 284–287, 297, 390, 391, 470, 491, 531, 696, 719, 731, 737, 739, 742, 743
substance argument *see* substance *under* argument
suicide 7–9, 12, 14, 92, 111, 534
superstition 281–283, 578, 642
surveyability 120, 231, 245, 278–288, 303, 336, 337, 422, 694, 723, 725, 727, 742, 743; *see also* perspicuous/surveyable (re)presentation/overview
symbol 10, 60–64, 71, 80, 106, 107, 128, 130, 150, 151, 154–156, 200, 201, 265, 302, 437, 536, 617, 663
symptom 168, 239, 352–354, 362, 462, 527, 528, 590, 659, 660
syntacticism 337–339
syntax *see* logical syntax
synthetic a priori 35, 61, 206, 222, 232, 270, 302, 686, 687; *see also* analytic/synthetic

Taniyama, Y. 317
Tarski, A. 217, 324, 330, 709, 710

INDEX

tautology 2, 62, 63, 144, 163, 204, 215, 216, 293–296, 301, 302, 310, 347, 348, 369, 534, 535, 707; *see also* logic
teaching/learning 66, 238, 244, 254, 256, 258, 391, 400, 421, 470–472, 476, 497, 500, 596, 549, 735, 750, 754
theorem
  Church's 302, 303
  Fermat's last 317, 321, 322
  Gödel's 319, 320, 323–324, 342
  Pythagoras's 441
  Tarski's 324
theory
  picture *see* picture theory
  of descriptions 94, 301, 433
  of symbolism 10, 83, 106, 235, 705
  set *see* set theory
  of types 10, 12, 79, 83, 98–108, 235, 293
  of meaning 14, 59, 61, 63, 65, 67, 70–72, 113, 180, 181, 197, 201, 206, 221, 234, 333, 338, 391, 401, 434, 440, 597, 599, 708, 734, 749
therapy 42, 69, 165–168, 182, 191, 195, 205, 231, 235, 236, 246, 248, 249, 337–341, 409, 420, 623, 624, 633, 659–663, 669, 695, 725, 726, 742, 750, 752; *see also* resolute reading, psychoanalysis
third Wittgenstein 47, 584
Thurber, J. 625
Tolstoy, L.N. 12, 640
toothache 50, 243, 353, 354, 453, 459, 468, 470, 472, 477, 484–486, 654, 673, 722; *see also* pain *under* behavior
Toulmin, S. 61, 117, 587–599
training (*Abrichten*) 258, 262, 335, 391, 397, 554
Trakl, G. 12
transcendental/transcendentalism 13, 25, 59–72, 167, 212, 216, 232, 233, 247, 486, 607, 641, 677, 682–697, 707, 708, 710, 737, 740, 748, 749; *see also* transcendental *under* idealism, transcendental *under* argument
truth 433–442 and *passim*; *see also* falsehood
  condition 61, 142–150, 155, 156, 295, 333–343, 425
  function 2, 62, 70, 127–132, 211, 215, 219, 220, 235, 293, 296–303, 308, 309, 324, 342, 347, 348, 361, 433, 435, 505, 534, 536, 540, 541, 576–578, 685, 686, 708, 709; *see also* analytic/synthetic, logical *under* inference
  possibility 215, 302, 308, 347
  table 181, 216, 219, 252, 299, 348, 535, 577, 578, 607, 706; *see also* notation
  value 27, 34, 84, 107, 133–135, 215, 294, 295, 303, 306, 313, 332, 333, 336, 577

Uhland, L. 612, 613
unconscious/unconsciousness 163, 415, 458, 474, 560, 651–664
understanding
  first-order vs. second-order 378, 379
  in a flash 392, 394, 399, 404
  pre-theoretical 32, 761, 763, 764
  transitive vs. intransitive 613, 614
undogmatic procedure 243

vagueness 86, 226, 407–418, 694, 747
value 3, 11, 28, 29, 65, 66, 79, 94, 104, 115, 118, 144, 212, 226, 245, 300, 303, 312, 327, 347, 349, 403, 404, 424, 451, 571, 606, 607, 616–618, 624, 625, 629, 636, 637, 641, 663, 673, 689, 736, 740, 743, 750, 754, 759; *see also* ethics
  aesthetic 60, 65, 68, 69, 616, 624, 625
  truth- *see* value *under* truth
variable 34, 93, 94, 100, 104, 212, 213, 216, 217, 272, 276, 294, 300, 301, 309, 315, 523
  propositional 300, 347–441, 518, 592
verification/verificationism 170, 305, 306, 310, 313–316, 333, 340, 343, 390, 549, 588–591, 608, 641, 703, 705, 707–709, 733, 734, 758
Victoria, Queen 475
Vienna Circle 1, 4, 29, 33, 588–592, 598, 607, 652, 694, 699–713, 734, 758
visual field 13, 165, 168, 235, 370, 481, 521, 522, 533–535, 542, 543, 690
voice 31, 43, 48–53, 376, 556; *see also* interlocutor
von Wright, G.H. 9, 10, 19, 60, 111, 581, 674, 687, 704, 719, 743

Waismann, F. 32, 45, 114, 236, 253, 278, 279, 362, 414, 415, 440, 588–592, 658, 701–713
Walter, B. 6
Weininger, O. 6–8, 687
Weyl, H. 77, 315
Whitehead, A.N. 100–104, 293, 298, 531, 686, 694
Wiles, A. 317

will/willing 60, 64, 66, 71, 72, 164–166, 491–497, 675, 688; *see also* intentionality, Schopenhauer
Winch, P. 23, 434, 504, 544, 636, 637
Wisdom, J. 236, 319, 661, 720
Wittgenstein, H(ermine) 8, 9, 16, 18
Wittgenstein, K(arl) 5, 6
Wittgenstein, L(eopoldine) 6
Wittgenstein's self-critique of the *Tractatus* 29–38, 160, 177
works of Ludwig Wittgenstein
  Big Typescript 29, 30, 32, 34, 37, 38, 48, 52, 116, 253, 254, 279, 286, 409, 412, 519, 581, 658, 704, 711, 743
  Blue and Brown Books 17, 29, 36, 37, 71, 116, 160, 167–172, 216, 260, 306, 352, 353, 380, 48, 452, 479, 486–488, 519, 581, 593, 594, 613, 653, 654, 658, 672, 674, 704, 741
  Culture and Value 74, 163, 605, 644, 645
  Nachlass, Wittgenstein's 19, 25, 45–49, 159, 460
  On Certainty 30, 33, 38, 47, 48, 270, 287, 547–561, 563, 564, 574, 581–584, 690, 691, 732, 735, 736, 742, 751, 752
  Philosophical Grammar 24, 30, 31, 37, 48, 49, 52, 270, 274, 335, 363, 381, 383, 438, 515, 581, 704
  Philosophical Investigations 1, 4, 17, 18, 23, 41–53, 286, 488–490, 537, 671–673, 700, 713, 751–755 and *passim*
  Philosophical Remarks 24, 30, 36, 86, 116, 216, 306, 453, 479, 483–485, 536, 536, 580, 589, 709
  Remarks on Colour 30, 38, 533, 535, 537, 540, 541, 543
  Remarks on the Foundations of Mathematics 87, 274, 275, 319, 323, 334, 342, 519
  Remarks on the Philosophy of Psychology 30, 491, 519, 525, 539, 540
  Tractatus Logico-Philosophicus 1, 11, 13, 15, 28, 41, 59, 92, 113, 252, 361, 479, 503, 534, 588, 605, 640, 685, 693, 699, 700, 719, 747–752; *see also* Wittgenstein's self-critique of the *Tractatus*
  Zettel 38, 75, 274, 519
world
  external 85, 446, 472, 473, 564, 598, 632, 671
  language and 157, 160, 162, 167, 480, 711
  my/microcosm 166, 478–482, 641, 686–691; *see also* I/ego/self, solipsism
  possible 133, 134, 356
world-picture (*Weltbild*)/world-view (*Weltanschauung*) 280–282, 287, 549, 559, 732, 737, 742, 743; *see also* hinge- *under* proposition, Spengler

Zen 218